S0-BYU-354

See inside back cover for chapters 23–35

economics

economics

Paul Krugman

Princeton University

Robin Wells

Princeton University

WORTH PUBLISHERS

Publishers: Catherine Woods and Craig Bleyer
Senior Acquisitions Editor: Charlie Van Wagner
Executive Development Editor: Sharon Balbos
Development Editor: Marilyn Freedman
Associate Editor: Marie McHale
Consultant: Andreas Bentz
Director of Market Development: Steven Rigolosi
Marketing Manager: Scott Guile
Associate Managing Editor: Tracey Kuehn
Project Editor: Anthony Calcara
Art Director, Cover Designer: Babs Reingold
Interior Designer: Babs Reingold
Layout Designer: Lee Ann Mahler
Illustrations: TSI Graphics and Lyndall Culbertson
Photo Research Manager: Patricia Marx
Photo Researcher: Elyse Rieder
Production Manager: Barbara Anne Seixas
Composition: TSI Graphics
Printing and Binding: R. R. Donnelley and Sons

ISBN: 1-57259-150-1 (EAN: 9781572591509)

Library of Congress Control Number: 2005936310

Worth Publishers
41 Madison Avenue
New York, NY 10010

www.worthpublishers.com

To beginning students everywhere, which we all were at one time.

About the Authors

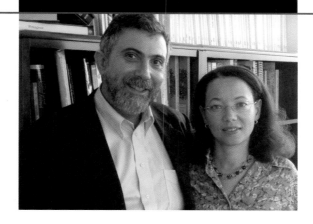

Paul Krugman is Professor of Economics at Princeton University, where he regularly teaches the principles course. He received his BA from Yale and his PhD from MIT. Prior to his current position, he taught at Yale, Stanford, and MIT. He also spent a year on the staff of the Council of Economic Advisers in 1982–1983. His research is mainly in the area of international trade, where he is one of the founders of the "new trade theory," which focuses on increasing returns and imperfect competition. He also works in international finance, with a concentration in currency crises. In 1991, Krugman received the American Economic Association's John Bates Clark medal. In addition to his teaching and academic research, Krugman writes extensively for nontechnical audiences. Krugman is a regular op-ed columnist for the *New York Times.* His latest trade book is a best-selling collection of his *Times* articles entitled *The Great Unraveling: Losing Our Way in the New Century.* His earlier books, *Peddling Prosperity* and *The Age of Diminished Expectations,* have become modern classics.

Robin Wells is Researcher in Economics at Princeton University, where she regularly teaches undergraduate courses. She received her BA from the University of Chicago and her PhD from the University of California at Berkeley; she then did postdoctoral work at MIT. She has taught at the University of Michigan, the University of Southampton (United Kingdom), Stanford, and MIT. Her teaching and research focus on the theory of organizations and incentives. She writes regularly for academic journals.

Preface

FROM PAUL

Robin and I like to think that we wrote this book with Orwell's injunction in mind. We wanted to write a different sort of book, one that gives as much attention to the task of making sure the student understands how economic models apply to the real world as it gives to the models themselves. We wanted to adapt Orwell's principle to the writing of an economics textbook: to let the purpose of economics—to achieve a deeper understanding of the world—rather than the mechanics of economics dictate the writing.

We believe that writing in this style reflects a commitment to the reader—a commitment to approach the material from a beginner's point of view, to make the material entertaining and accessible, to make discovery a joy. That's the fun part. But we also believe that there is another, equally compelling obligation on the part of an author of a principles of economics text. Economics is an extremely powerful tool. Many of us who are economists originally started in other disciplines (I started in history, Robin in chemistry). And we fell in love with economics because we believed it offers a coherent worldview that offers real guidelines to making the world a better place. (Yes, most economists are idealists at heart.) But like any powerful tool, economics should be treated with great care. For us, this obligation became a commitment that students would learn the appropriate use of the models—understand their assumptions and know their limitations as well as their positive uses. Why do we care about this? Because we don't live in a "one model of the economy fits all" world. To achieve deeper levels of understanding of the real world through economics, students must learn to appreciate the kinds of trade-offs and ambiguities that economists and policy makers face when applying their models to real-world problems. We hope this approach will make students more insightful and more effective participants in our common economic, social, and political lives.

To those familiar with my academic work, this perspective will probably look familiar. There I tried to make the problem to be solved the focus and to avoid unnecessary technique. I tried to simplify. And I tried to choose topics that had important real-world implications. Writing for a large, nontechnical audience has only reinforced and expanded these tendencies. I had to begin with the working assumption that readers initially have no reason to care about what I am writing about—that it is my responsibility to show them why they should care. So the beginning of each chapter of this book is written according to the dictum: "If you haven't hooked them by the third sentence, then you've lost them." I've also learned that about all you can take for granted in writing for a lay audience is basic numeracy—addition and subtraction, but no more than that. Concepts must be fully explained; likely confusions must be anticipated and headed off. And most of all, you must be judicious in choosing the content and pacing of the writing—don't overwhelm your reader.

FROM ROBIN

Like Paul, I wanted to write a book that appeals to students without unduly sacrificing an instructor's obligation to teach economics well. I arrived at a similar perspective on how this book should be written, but by a different path. It came from my experiences teaching economics in a business school for a few years. Facing students who were typically impatient with abstraction and often altogether unhappy to be taking economics (and who would often exact bloody revenge in teaching evaluations), I learned how important it is to hook the students into the subject matter. Teaching with case studies, I found that concepts had been truly learned only when students could successfully apply them. And one of the most important lessons I learned was not to patronize. We—economists, that is—often assume that people who aren't familiar with conceptual thinking aren't smart and capable. Teaching in a business school showed me otherwise. The majority of my students were smart and capable, and many had shouldered a lot of responsibility in their working lives. Although adept at solving practical problems, they weren't trained to think conceptually. I had to learn to acknowledge the practical skills that they did have, but also show them the importance of the conceptual skills they didn't have. Although I eventually returned to an economics department, the lessons I learned about teaching economics in a business school stayed with me and, I believe, have been crucial ingredients in writing this textbook.

Advantages of This Book

Despite our fine words, why should any instructor use our text? We believe our book distinguishes itself in several ways that will make your introductory economics course an easier and more successful undertaking for the following reasons:

> **Chapters build intuition through real examples.** In every chapter, we use real-world examples, stories, applications, and case studies to teach concepts and motivate student learning. We believe that the best way to introduce concepts and reinforce them is through real-world examples; students simply relate more easily to them.

> **Pedagogical features reinforce learning.** We've worked hard to craft a set of features that will be genuinely helpful to students. We describe these features in the next section, "Tools for Learning."

> **Chapters have been written to be accessible and entertaining.** We have used a fluid and friendly writing style that makes the concepts accessible. And we have tried whenever possible to use examples that matter directly to students; for example, choosing what course to take or considering why decisions made by economic policy makers have important implications for what the job market will look like when they graduate.

> **Real-world data illustrate concepts.** Examples are often accompanied by real-world data so that students can see what real economic numbers look like and how they relate to the models.

> **Although easy to understand, the book also prepares students for further coursework.** Too often, instructors find that selecting a textbook means choosing between two unappealing alternatives: a textbook that is "easy to teach" but leaves major gaps in students' understanding, or a textbook that is "hard to teach" but adequately prepares students for future coursework. We have worked very hard to create an easy-to-understand textbook that offers the best of both worlds.

> **The book permits flexible yet conceptually structured use of chapters.** We recognize that instructors of the microeconomics course may prefer to teach our micro chapters in a sequence different from the one found in the book. Chapters 1 through 22 were written with that in mind—instructors can use the chapters in any order they wish.

We also recognize that instructors of the macroeconomics course will have different preferences about which topics to emphasize and how much detail to give tools of analysis. For this reason, our macroeconomics chapters are flexible, allowing instructors to craft a course that fits their needs.

For a detailed look at the organization of our chapters and ways to use them, see pages xii through xxi of this preface.

Tools for Learning

We have structured each of the chapters around a common set of features. The following features are intended to help students learn better while also keeping them engaged.

"What You Will Learn in This Chapter"

To help readers get oriented, the first page of each chapter contains a preview of the chapter's contents, in an easy-to-review bulleted list format, that alerts students to the critical concepts and details the objectives of the chapter.

Opening Story

In contrast to other books in which each chapter begins with a recitation of some aspect of economics, we've adopted a unique approach: we open each chapter with a compelling story that often extends through the entire chapter. Stories were chosen to accomplish two things: to illustrate important concepts in the chapter and then to encourage students to want to read on to learn more.

As we've mentioned, one of our main goals is to build intuition with realistic examples. Because each chapter is introduced with a real-world story, students will relate more easily to the material. For example, Chapter 3 teaches supply and demand in the context of a market for scalped tickets to a sports event (our opening story on page 56 is "Gretzky's Last Game"). We introduce Chapter 24, on macroeconomic data—usually one of the driest subjects in macroeconomics—with the story of how an accurate estimate of real GDP growth steadied nervous Portuguese officials and helped the country make the transition from dictatorship to democracy (see "After the Revolution" on page 559.). For a complete list of our opening stories, see the inside front and back covers.

"Economics in Action" Case Studies

In addition to introducing chapters with vivid stories, we conclude virtually every major text section with still more examples: a real-world case study called "Economics in Action." This feature provides a short but compelling application of the major concept just covered in that section. Students will experience an immediate payoff from being able to apply the concepts they've just read about. For example, in Chapter 6 we use the case of eBay, the online auctioneer, to communicate the concept of efficiency (see "eBay and Efficiency" on page 151). Our discussion of long-run fiscal issues (Chapter 29, "Fiscal Policy), which includes the question of solvency, is followed by an account of Argentina's debt default (see "Argentina's Creditors Take a Haircut" on page 713). For a complete list of all the "Economics in Action" cases in the text, see the inside front and back covers and our table of contents.

Unique End-of-Section Review: "Quick Review" and "Check Your Understanding" Questions

Economics contains a lot of jargon and abstract concepts that can quickly overwhelm the principles student. So we provide **"Quick Reviews,"** short bulleted summaries of concepts at the end of each major section. This review helps ensure that students understand what they have just read.

The **"Check Your Understanding"** feature, which appears along with every "Quick Review," consists of a short set of review questions; solutions to these questions appear at the back of the book in the section set off with a burgundy tab at the edge of each page. These questions and solutions allow students to immediately test their understanding of the section just read. If they're not getting the questions right, it's a clear signal for them to go back and reread before moving on.

The "Economics in Action" cases, followed by the "Quick Reviews" and "Check Your Understanding" questions comprise our unique end-of-section pedagogical set that encourages students to apply what they've learned (via the "Economics in Action") and then review it (with the "Quick Reviews" and "Check Your Understanding" questions). Our hope is that students will be more successful in the course if they use this carefully constructed set of study aids.

"For Inquiring Minds" Boxes

To further our goal of helping students build intuition with real-world examples, almost every chapter contains one or more "For Inquiring Minds" boxes, in which concepts are applied to real-world events in unexpected and sometimes surprising ways, generating a sense of the power and breadth of economics. These boxes help impress on students that economics can be fun despite being labeled "the dismal science."

In a Chapter 10 box, for example, students learn how prices in a budget line serve the same function as the number of points assigned to a particular food in a Weight Watchers' diet plan (see "Food for Thought on Budget Constraints" on page 240.) In Chapter 30, "Money, Banking, and the Federal Reserve System," we point out the puzzling fact that there's $2,500 worth of currency in circulation for every man, woman, and child in the United States (how many people do you know who keep $2,500 in their wallets?). We then explain how currency in domestic cash registers and in the hands of foreigners resolves the puzzle (see "What's with All the Currency?" on page 725.) For a list of all "For Inquiring Minds" boxes, see the inside front and back covers and our table of contents.

"Pitfalls" Boxes

Certain concepts are prone to be misunderstood when students begin their study of economics. We try to alert students to these mistakes in "Pitfalls" boxes, where common misunderstandings are spelled out and corrected. For example, the difference between increasing total cost and increasing marginal cost (see "Pitfalls" on page 167) and the tricky business of how to read an exchange rate (see "Which Way Is Up?" on page 846). For a list of all the "Pitfalls" boxes, see the table of contents.

Student-Friendly Graphs

Comprehending graphs is often one of the biggest hurdles for principles students. To help alleviate that problem, this book has been designed so that figures are large, clear, and easy for students to follow. Many contain helpful annotations—in an easy-to-see balloon label format—that link to concepts within the text. Figure captions have been written to complement the text discussion of figures and to help students more readily grasp what they're seeing.

We've worked hard to make these graphs student-friendly. For example, to help students navigate one of the stickier thickets—the distinction between a shifting curve and movement along a curve—we encourage students to see this difference by using two types of arrows: a shift arrow (⟶) and what we call a "movement-along" arrow (⟶⟶). You can see these arrows in Figures 3-12 and 3-13 on pages 73 and 74.

In addition, several graphs in each chapter are accompanied by the icon *>web...* , which indicates that these graphs are available online as simulations (the graphs are animated in a Flash format and can be manipulated). Every interactive graph is accompanied by a quiz on key concepts to further help students in their work with graphs.

Instructing students in the use of graphs is also enhanced by our use of real-world data (especially in the macroeconomics chapters), often presented in charts that can be compared directly to the analytical figures. For example, the aggregate supply curve can seem like a highly abstract concept, but in Chapter 27, "Aggregate Supply and Aggregate Demand," we make it less abstract by illustrating the concept with the actual behavior of aggregate output and the aggregate price level during the 1930s (see Figure 27-6 on page 645).

Helpful Graphing Appendix For students who would benefit from an explanation of how graphs are constructed, interpreted, and used in economics, we've included a detailed graphing appendix after Chapter 2 on page 41. This appendix is more comprehensive than most because we know that some students need this helpful background, and we didn't want to breeze through the material. Our hope is that this comprehensive graphing appendix will better prepare students to use and interpret the graphs in this textbook and then out in the real world (in newspapers, magazines, and elsewhere).

Definitions of Key Terms

Every key term, in addition to being defined in the text, is also placed and defined in the margin to make it easier for students to study and review.

"A Look Ahead"

The text of each chapter ends with "A Look Ahead," a short overview of what lies ahead in upcoming chapters. This concluding section provides students with a sense of continuity among chapters.

End-of-Chapter Review

In addition to the "Quick Review" at the end of each major section, each chapter ends with a complete but brief **Summary** of the key terms and concepts. In addition, a list of the **Key Terms** is placed at the end of each chapter along with page references.

For each chapter we have a comprehensive set of **End-of-Chapter Problems** that test intuition and the ability to calculate important variables. Much care has been devoted to the creation of these problems. Instructors can be assured that they provide a true test of students' learning.

Macroeconomic Data

To supplement our in-chapter use of real-world data to illustrate macroeconomic concepts, we've included a broad selection of macroeconomic data at the back of the book in a section set off with blue tabs at the edge of each page. These data series include most of the important macroeconomic variables for the United States. Selected early years illustrate the behavior of the economy during the Great Depression and the post–World War II boom. The series also include data for each year from 1970 to 2004 for full coverage of recent years.

The Organization of This Book and How to Use It

This book is organized as a series of building blocks in which conceptual material learned at one stage is clearly built upon and then integrated into the conceptual material covered in the next stage. These building blocks correspond to the sixteen parts into which the chapters are divided. We'll now walk through those building blocks, giving a brief overview of each part and chapter, followed by a look at the ways an instructor can tailor this book to meet his or her needs.

Part 1: What Is Economics?

In the **Introduction, "The Ordinary Business of Life,"** students are initiated into the study of economics in the context of a shopping trip on any given Sunday in everyday America. It provides students with basic definitions of terms such as *economics,* the *invisible hand,* and *market structure.* In addition it serves as a "tour d'horizon" of economics, explaining the difference between microeconomics and macroeconomics.

In **Chapter 1, "First Principles,"** nine principles are presented and explained: four principles of individual choice, covering concepts such as opportunity cost, marginal analysis, and incentives; and five principles of interaction between individuals, covering concepts such as gains from trade, market efficiency, and market failure. In later chapters, we build intuition by frequently referring to these principles in the explanation of specific models. Students learn that these nine principles form a cohesive conceptual foundation for all of economics.

Chapter 2, "Economic Models: Trade-offs and Trade," shows students how to think like economists by using three models—the production possibility frontier, comparative advantage and trade, and the circular-flow diagram—to analyze the world around them. It gives students an early introduction to gains from trade and to international comparisons. The **Chapter 2 appendix** contains a comprehensive math and graphing review.

Part 2: Supply and Demand

In this part we provide students with the basic analytical tools they need to understand how markets work, tools that are common to microeconomics and macroeconomics.

Chapter 3, "Supply and Demand," covers the standard material in a fresh and compelling way: supply and demand, market equilibrium, and surplus and shortage are all illustrated using an example of the market for scalped tickets to a sports event. Students learn how the demand and supply curves of scalped tickets shift in response to the announcement of a star player's impending retirement.

Chapter 4, "The Market Strikes Back," covers various types of market interventions and their consequences: price and quantity controls, inefficiency and deadweight loss, and excise taxes. Through tangible examples such as New York City rent control regulations and New York City taxi licenses, the costs generated by attempts to control markets are made real to students.

In **Chapter 5, "Elasticity,"** the actions of OPEC and their consequences for the world market for oil taken together are the real-world motivating example in our discussion of the price elasticity of demand. In this chapter, we introduce the various elasticity measures and show how elasticities are used to evaluate the incidence of an excise tax.

Part 3: Individuals and Markets

Through examples such as a market for used textbooks and eBay, students learn how markets increase welfare in **Chapter 6, "Consumer and Producer Surplus."** Although the concepts of market efficiency and deadweight loss are strongly emphasized, we also preview the ways in which a market can fail.

Chapter 7, "Making Decisions," is a unique chapter. Microeconomics is fundamentally a science of how to make decisions. Therefore, to emphasize how decisions should be made and to distinguish between what is and isn't a marginal decision, we have included an entire section on "either–or" versus "how much" decisions—a distinction that is particularly useful in later chapters where we compare a firm's output decision to its entry/exit decision. In addition, in Chapter 7 we reprise the concept of opportunity cost; present a thorough treatment of marginal analysis; explain the concept of sunk cost; and, for instructors who wish to teach it, cover present discounted value. Full coverage of sunk cost at this point will help students later in understanding the irrelevance of fixed cost in the firm's short-run output decision. We think this chapter will be an important teaching aid because it helps students develop a deeper intuition about the common conceptual foundations of microeconomic models.

What Comes Next: The Firm or the Consumer? You may have noticed that we have placed the chapters covering the producer before the chapters covering the consumer. Why have we done this? Because we believe that it is a more natural conceptual progression to cover the producer after Chapter 7, "Making Decisions," than it is to cover the consumer. Since students have just studied opportunity cost, economic profit versus accounting profit, marginal benefit and marginal cost, and sunk cost, we think examining the firm's cost curves, its output decision, and its entry/exit decision is an easier next step for them to undertake.

We are aware that some instructors are likely to be skeptical of this approach. We have often heard instructors say that the consumer should be studied before the producer because students can relate to being a consumer but not to being the owner of a firm. We hope, however, to change that viewpoint because what we really want students to do is not just relate to being a consumer but *think like a rational consumer—a consumer who maximizes utility subject to scarce resources.* And we believe that it is easier for students to understand utility maximization (utility being an inherently slippery concept) after they have come to understand profit maximization.

Nonetheless, we want to strongly emphasize that it is very easy for instructors who wish to follow a traditional chapter sequence—with the consumer before the firm—to do just that. We wrote the chapters so that there is no loss whatsoever if an instructor follows Chapter 7 with Chapter 10, "The Rational Consumer," and Chapter 11, "Consumer Preferences and Consumer Choice" (an optional chapter).

Part 4: The Producer

In **Chapter 8, "Behind the Supply Curve: Inputs and Costs,"** we develop the production function and the various cost measures of the firm. There is an extensive discus-

sion of the difference between average cost and marginal cost, illustrated by examples such as a student's grade point average. **Chapter 9, "Perfect Competition and the Supply Curve,"** explains the output decision of the perfectly competitive firm, its entry/exit decision, the industry supply curve, and the equilibrium of a perfectly competitive market. We draw on examples such as generic pharmaceuticals and the California energy crisis of 2000–2001 to contrast the behavior of oligopolists and monopolists.

Part 5: The Consumer

Chapter 10, "The Rational Consumer," provides a complete treatment of consumer behavior for instructors who don't cover indifference curves. There is a simple, intuitive exposition of the budget line, the optimal consumption choice, diminishing marginal utility, and income and substitution effects and their relationship to market demand. Students learn, for example, that a budget line constructed using prices is much like a Weight Watchers' diet plan constructed using a "point" system. **Chapter 11, "Consumer Preferences and Consumer Choice,"** offers a more detailed treatment for those who wish to cover indifference curves. It contains an analysis of the optimal consumption choice using the marginal rate of substitution as well as income and substitution effects.

What Comes Next: Markets and Efficiency or Market Structure? Many instructors are likely to consider the next two chapters—Chapter 12, "Factor Markets and the Distribution of Income," and Chapter 13 "Efficiency and Equity"—optional. For those who wish to skip them, the next topic area will be market structure beyond perfect competition: monopoly, oligopoly, and monopolistic competition. Chapters 12 and 13 are likely to be used by instructors who want more in-depth coverage of microeconomics, as well as those who wish to emphasize labor markets, welfare, and public policy issues. Instructors who prefer a traditional sequence of topics may wish to go from Part 5 ("The Consumer") to Part 4 ("The Producer") to Part 7 ("Market Structure: Beyond Perfect Competition"), bypassing Part 6 ("Markets and Efficiency") altogether or covering it later. This is a good choice for those who wish to contrast the difference between the perfectly competitive firm's output decision and the monopolist's output decision. But those who follow the existing chapter sequence—"The Producer" followed by "The Consumer" followed by "Market Structure: Beyond Perfect Competition"—will be able to draw a tighter connection among consumer behavior, monopoly pricing, price discrimination, product differentiation, and monopolistic competition. We have written the chapters so that either sequence works equally well.

Part 6: Markets and Efficiency

Chapter 12, "Factor Markets and the Distribution of Income," covers the competitive factor market model and the factor distribution of income. In addition, the efficiency-wage model of the labor market is discussed, and the influences of education, discrimination, and market power are also addressed. It presents, we hope, a balanced and well-rounded view of the strengths and limitations of the competitive market model of labor markets and leads to a greater appreciation of the issues of efficiency and equity discussed in the next chapter. For instructors who covered indifference curves in Chapter 11, the **Chapter 12 appendix** offers a detailed examination of the labor–leisure trade-off and the backward-bending labor supply curve.

In **Chapter 13, "Efficiency and Equity,"** after recapping efficiency in a single market, we compare and contrast this to what it means to have efficiency in a market economy as a whole. Why draw the distinction between partial equilibrium and general equilibrium in a principles course? Doing so gives students a deeper understanding of the often-conflicting objectives of efficiency and equity—something that really can't be fully explored in a partial equilibrium setting. As a real-world example, we discuss the reunification of West and East Germany in terms of the trade-offs faced by German policy makers, who sacrificed some efficiency-enhancing measures in order to reduce the income differences between East and West Germans.

Part 7: Market Structure: Beyond Perfect Competition

Chapter 14, "Monopoly," is a full treatment of monopoly, including topics such as price discrimination and the welfare effects of monopoly. We provide an array of compelling examples, such as De Beers Diamonds, price manipulation by California power companies, and airline ticket-pricing. In **Chapter 15, "Oligopoly,"** we present basic game theory in both a one-shot and repeated-game context, as well as an integrated treatment of the kinked demand curve model. The models are applied to a wide set of actual examples, such as Archer Daniels Midland, a European vitamin cartel, OPEC, and airline ticket-pricing wars. In **Chapter 16, "Monopolistic Competition and Product Differentiation,"** students are brought face to face early on with an example of monopolistic competition that is a familiar feature of their lives: the food court at the local mall. We go on to cover entry and exit, efficiency considerations, and advertising in monopolistic competition.

What Comes Next: Extending Market Boundaries or Microeconomics and Public Policy? The next section of the book, "Extending Market Boundaries," is devoted to applications and extensions of the competitive market model: Chapter 17, "International Trade," and Chapter 18, "Uncertainty, Risk, and Private Information." Both of these chapters are entirely optional. Instructors who prefer to skip one or both of these chapters can proceed to the following section, "Microeconomics and Public Policy."

Part 8: Extending Market Boundaries

In Chapter 2, we presented a full exposition of gains from trade and the difference between comparative and absolute advantage, illustrated with an international example (trade between high-wage and low-wage countries). **Chapter 17, "International Trade,"** builds on that material. It contains a recap of comparative advantage, traces the sources of comparative advantage, considers tariffs and quotas, and explores the politics of trade protection. In response to current events, we give in-depth coverage to the controversy over imports from low-wage countries.

The inclusion in a principles text of **Chapter 18, "Uncertainty, Risk, and Private Information,"** may come as a surprise to some—a common reaction being "Isn't this material too hard for principles students?" We believe that, with our treatment, the answer is "no" for many more students than is typically expected. In this chapter we explain attitudes toward risk, grounded in the basic concept of diminishing marginal utility. This allows us to analyze a simple competitive insurance market and to examine the benefits and limits of diversification. Next comes an easily comprehensible and intuitive presentation of private information in the context of adverse selection and moral hazard, with illustrations drawn from the market for lemons (used cars) and franchising. We believe that instructors will be surprised by how easy it is to teach this material and how much it will enlighten students about the relevance of economics to their everyday lives.

Part 9: Microeconomics and Public Policy

Chapter 19, "Externalities," covers negative externalities and solutions such as Coasian private trades, emissions taxes, and a system of tradable permits. We also examine positive externalities, technological spillovers, and the resulting arguments for industrial policy. **Chapter 20, "Public Goods and Common Resources,"** makes an immediate impression by opening with the story of how "The Great Stink of 1858" compelled Londoners to build a public sewer system. Students learn how to classify goods into four categories (private goods, common resources, public goods, and artificially scarce goods) based on two dimensions: excludability and rivalry in consumption.

Chapter 21, "Taxes, Social Insurance, and Income Distribution," begins with a review of the burden of taxation and considerations of equity versus efficiency. Next, it examines the structure of taxes, current tax policy, and public spending in the United States. This is followed by an investigation into the sources of poverty and their implications for government tax and transfer policies. From this chapter, students can gain an appreciation of the difficult questions policy makers face in addressing issues of economic efficiency and welfare.

Part 10: New Directions for Markets

This section of the book contains one chapter, **Chapter 22, "Technology, Information Goods, and Network Externalities."** Starting with the example of sharing music files over the Internet, this chapter introduces the concept of information goods and network externalities and analyzes the problems they cause for efficient pricing. We discuss the implications for standard-setting and the ambiguities that network externalities present for regulatory policy. Students will see how these issues affect their daily lives through references to Kazaa, Apple Computers, and Microsoft.

Teaching Macroeconomics: Short Run or Long Run First?

The history of macroeconomic theory is one in which short-run and long-run issues vie for priority. The long-run focus of classical economists gave way to the short-run focus of Keynesian economics, then the pendulum swung back to the long run, and lately it seems to be swinging back to the short run. This struggle over priority is reproduced every time an instructor must decide how to teach the subject. Two issues are particularly tricky. First, should long-run economic growth be covered early or later, after the business cycle has been discussed? Second, should classical, full-employment analysis of the price level come before or after business-cycle analysis?

We cover long-run growth early (Part 12, Chapters 25 and 26) because we feel that an early discussion of the long-run growth of real GDP helps students understand why the business cycle involves fluctuations around an upward trend. We have, however, structured the subsequent short-run analysis (Part 13, Chapters 27–31) in a way that allows instructors to reverse this order, deferring our chapter on long-run growth (Chapter 25) until later in the course. However, we've taken a firmer stand when it comes to the second question. We believe that the fundamental approach of this book—to tie macroeconomics to real-world concerns—requires that a discussion of the short-run effects of demand and supply shocks come before a discussion of the classical model.

Although some macroeconomics textbooks treat the classical model first, and some even devote more space to long-run analysis than to the short run, we believe—based on our own teaching experience—that this is a formula for losing the interest of beginning students. We are, after all, living in a time of activist monetary and fiscal policy. Students are likely to read newspaper accounts of the Federal Reserve's attempts to stabilize the economy or of debates over the impact of tax cuts on job creation. If students begin their study of macroeconomics with models in which monetary policy has no effect on aggregate output, they will get the impression that what they are learning in the classroom is irrelevant to the real world. In this book we explain early why demand shocks have no effect on output in the long run, but we don't emphasize the long-run neutrality of money before describing how monetary and fiscal policy work in the short run.

We also believe that students could lose their sense that macroeconomics is relevant if the book starts with a model best used to explain inflation. We're living in a time when sustained high inflation is a distant memory in wealthy nations—and even in many developing countries. The great majority of students likely to use this book hadn't been born the last time the U.S. core inflation rate was above 6%. In contrast, the effects of short-run demand and supply shocks—such as the 2001 recession and the subsequent jobless recovery, or the surge in energy prices from 2003 to 2005—are fresh in our memories. We believe that a book aimed at showing students how economics applies to the real world must emphasize early on, rather than later, how macroeconomic models help us understand such events.

We believe that the diffidence with which some textbooks approach the short run is partly driven by reluctance to enter an area that was marked by fierce debates in the 1970s and 1980s. But the ferocity of those debates, like double-digit inflation, has receded into the past. Yes, there are still serious disputes about macroeconomic theory and policy. But as we explain in Chapter 34, "The Making of Modern Macroeconomics," there is also far more consensus than in the past. Students are best served by a book that emphasizes the macroeconomic issues that matter most to public debate rather than downplays these issues out of fear of stepping into contentious areas. That's why we have chosen to provide an extended early discussion of the short-run effects of demand and supply shocks and the role of fiscal and monetary policy in responding to these shocks.

Finally, one last issue involves the order in which the short run should be taught. Some instructors prefer to begin their coverage with a traditional Keynesian discussion of the determinants of aggregate expenditure. Some prefer to place that discussion after a basic introduction to aggregate supply and aggregate demand. And a third group prefers to skip that analysis altogether. We've used a structural innovation to make all three approaches work, by including an intuitive discussion of the multiplier in Chapter 27, "Aggregate Supply and Aggregate Demand," followed by a more detailed, algebraic discussion in Chapter 28, "Income and Expenditure." Instructors who follow the table of contents, teaching Chapter 28 after Chapter 27, can treat the famous 45-degree diagram and its associated algebra as a more in-depth discussion of the multiplier principle students have already learned. Instructors who choose to teach Chapter 28 first can treat Chapter 27's discussion as a reinforcement of the graphical and algebraic analysis. And instructors who skip Chapter 28 will find that the intuitive discussion of the multiplier in Chapter 27 is sufficient for the analysis of fiscal and monetary policy.

Part 11: Introduction to Macroeconomics

Chapter 23, "Macroeconomics: The Big Picture," introduces the big ideas in macroeconomics. Starting with an example close to students' hearts—how the business cycle affects the job prospects of graduates—this chapter provides a quick overview of recessions and expansions, employment and unemployment, long-run growth, inflation versus deflation, and the open economy.

Chapter 24, "Tracking the Macroeconomy," explains how the numbers macroeconomists use are calculated, and why. We start with a real-world example of how an estimate of real GDP helped save a country from policy mistakes, then turn to the basics of national income accounting, unemployment statistics, and price indexes.

Long-Run Growth We begin our discussion of macroeconomic models with long-run economic growth. We believe that students are best prepared to understand the significance of fluctuations around long-run trends if they first acquire an understanding of where long-run trends come from. Instructors can, however, defer Chapter 25 until later in the course if they choose.

Part 12: The Economy in the Long Run

Chapter 25, "Long-Run Economic Growth," starts with a reality TV show—a BBC series about a family that spent three months living life as it was in 1900—to illustrate the human significance of economic growth. When we turn to economic data, we emphasize an international perspective—economic growth is a story about the world as a whole, not just the United States. The chapter uses a streamlined approach to the aggregate production function to present an analysis of the sources of economic growth and the reasons some countries have been more successful than others.

Chapter 26, "Savings, Investment Spending, and the Financial System," introduces students to financial markets and institutions. We group it with Chapter 25 in this part because it highlights the role of these markets and institutions in economic growth. Chapter 26 is also, however, integral to short-run analysis, for two reasons. First, its analysis of the market for loanable funds and the determination of interest rates provides an analytical tool that will be helpful for understanding monetary policy, international capital flows, and other topics covered later in the book. Second, its discussion of financial institutions provides background when we turn to the role of banks in creating money.

The Short Run Macroeconomics as we know it emerged during the Great Depression, and the effort to understand short-run fluctuations and the effects of monetary and fiscal policy remains as important as ever. So we devote a large block of chapters (Chapters 27–31) to short-run fluctuations. These chapters are, however, structured to allow instructors to choose their preferred level of detail. In particular, we know that some instructors want to place more emphasis than others on the consumption function and the multiplier. So we provide a basic, intuitive explanation of the multiplier in Chapter 27 but reserve a detailed discussion of consumer behavior and how it relates to the 45-degree diagram for Chapter 28, which is designed to be optional (but can be taught before Chapter 27 if instructors choose to do so).

There is also an ongoing debate among economics instructors about whether the traditional presentation of aggregate supply and aggregate demand, which treats the aggregate quantities of goods and services demanded and supplied as functions of the price *level,* should be replaced with a framework that treats them as functions of the *inflation rate.* In this alternative framework, the "aggregate supply curve" is really the short-run Phillips curve, and the "aggregate demand curve" is really a representation of the effects of monetary policy that leans against inflation. We understand the appeal of such a presentation, which makes for an easier transition to the discussion of inflation. But we believe that this approach blurs the important distinction between the private sector's behavior and the effects of policy responses on that behavior. Furthermore, a crucial insight from the traditional aggregate supply–aggregate demand approach is the economy's ability to correct itself in the long run. This insight is lost in the alternative approach. So we introduce short-run macroeconomics with a traditional focus on the aggregate price level, and we treat ongoing inflation as a "medium run" issue, reserved for Part 14.

Part 13: Short-Run Economic Fluctuations

Part 13 begins with **Chapter 27, "Aggregate Supply and Aggregate Demand."** This chapter's opening story covers the economic slump of 1979–1982, which startled Americans with its combination of recession and inflation. This leads into an analysis of how both demand shocks and supply shocks affect the economy. In analyzing demand shocks, we offer a simple, intuitive explanation of the concept of the multiplier, using the idea of successive increases in spending after an initial shock to explain how the aggregate demand curve shifts. In analyzing supply shocks, we emphasize positive shocks, such as the productivity surge of the late 1990s, as well as negative shocks. The chapter concludes with the key insight that demand shocks affect only output in the short run.

Chapter 28, "Income and Expenditure," is an optional chapter for instructors who want to go into some detail about the sources of changes in aggregate demand. We use real-world data to delve more deeply into the determinants of consumer and investment spending, introduce the famous 45-degree diagram, and present a fully fleshed-out explanation of the logic of the multiplier. For instructors who would like more algebraic detail, the **Chapter 28 appendix** shows how to derive the multiplier algebraically.

Chapter 29, "Fiscal Policy," starts in Japan, where discretionary fiscal policy has taken the form of huge public works projects, often of doubtful value. This leads into an analysis of the role of discretionary fiscal policy in shifting the aggregate demand curve, which makes use of the intuitive explanation of the multiplier from Chapter 27. We also cover automatic stabilizers—using the woes of Europe's "stability pact" to illustrate their importance—and long-run issues of debt and solvency. The **Chapter 29 appendix** shows how to introduce taxes into the analysis. It shows more specifically than the main text how the size of the multiplier depends on the tax rate, and it provides an intuitive explanation, in terms of successive rounds of spending, of how taxes reduce the multiplier.

Part 13 concludes with two chapters on monetary policy. **Chapter 30, "Money, Banking, and the Federal Reserve System,"** covers the roles of money, the ways in which banks create money, and the structure and role of the Federal Reserve and other central banks. We use episodes from U.S. history together with the story of the creation of the euro to illustrate how money and monetary institutions have evolved.

Chapter 31, "Monetary Policy," covers the role of Federal Reserve policy in driving interest rates and aggregate demand. In the real-world examples, we took full advantage of the dramatic developments in monetary policy since 2000, which make it easier than ever before to illustrate what the Federal Reserve does. We also made a special effort to build a bridge between the short run and the long run. For example, we carefully explain how the Federal Reserve can set the interest rate in the short run, even though that rate reflects the supply and demand for savings in the long run.

The Medium Run An important set of questions in macroeconomics revolves around unemployment and inflation: can monetary and fiscal policy be used to reduce unemployment, does the attempt to reduce unemployment cause inflation, is there a trade-off between inflation and unemployment? These questions fall into the category of "medium-run" issues, which apply to periods long enough that wages and prices can't be taken as given, but short enough that productivity and population growth don't dominate the story.

Part 14: The Supply Side and the Medium Run

Chapter 32, "Labor Markets, Unemployment, and Inflation," begins with stories of how real people move into and out of unemployment. It explains why there is always some frictional and structural unemployment, illustrated by the problem of "Eurosclerosis." It then turns to the relationship between unemployment and the output gap. It concludes with the Phillips curve, the role of inflation expectations, and how this relates to the natural rate hypothesis.

Chapter 33, "Inflation, Disinflation, and Deflation," covers the causes and consequences of inflation, as well as the reasons disinflation imposes large costs in lost output and employment. A unique final section analyzes the effects of deflation and the problems that a "zero bound" poses for monetary policy. As we explain, these issues, dormant for more than half a century after the Great Depression, surfaced in Japan in the 1990s and have had a major impact on policy thinking.

If There's Time We recognize that many instructors will find that there's only enough time to cover core chapters up through Chapter 33, on inflation. For those with enough time, however, Parts 15 and 16 (and Chapter 25, on long-run growth, for instructors who choose to cover it later) broaden the analysis. Part 15 offers a brief history of macroeconomic thought. Part 16 takes the analysis into international economics.

Part 15: Events and Ideas

Macroeconomics has always been a field in flux, with new policy issues constantly arising and traditional views often challenged. **Chapter 34, "The Making of Modern Macroeconomics,"** provides a unique overview of the history of macroeconomic thought, set in the context of changing policy concerns, then turns to a description of the current state of macroeconomic debates (there's more agreement than people think.)

Part 16: The Open Economy

Chapter 35, "Open-Economy Macroeconomics," analyzes the special issues raised for macroeconomics by the open economy. We frame the discussion with real-world concerns: Britain's debate over whether to adopt the euro, America's current account deficit, China's accumulation of dollar reserves.

For instructors and students who want to delve more deeply into international macroeconomics, we provide a supplemental chapter—available on the Web, at www.worthpublishers.com/krugmanwells, and in booklet form. This chapter, **"Currencies and Crises,"** takes students into the world of currency speculation and international financial crises, with an emphasis on the dramatic events that have unfolded in developing countries over the past decade.

Core and Optional Chapters Plus Possible Outlines

For an overview of what chapters are considered core and optional, see pages xviii-xix of this preface. For ideas on using this book to meet specific course goals, see pages xx-xxi.

WHAT'S CORE, WHAT'S OPTIONAL: MICROECONOMICS

As noted earlier, we realize that some of our chapters will be considered optional. Below and on the facing page is a list of what we view as core chapters and those that could be considered optional. We've annotated the list of optional chapters to indicate what they cover should you wish to consider incorporating them into your course.

Core

1. First Principles
2. Economic Models: Trade-offs and Trade

3. Supply and Demand
4. The Market Strikes Back
5. Elasticity
6. Consumer and Producer Surplus

8. Behind the Supply Curve: Inputs and Costs
9. Perfect Competition and the Supply Curve
10. The Rational Consumer

14. Monopoly
15. Oligopoly
16. Monopolistic Competition and Product Differentiation

19. Externalities
20. Public Goods and Common Resources
21. Taxes, Social Insurance, and Income Distribution

Optional

Introduction: The Ordinary Business of Life

Appendix: Graphs in Economics
A comprehensive review of graphing and math for students who would find such a refresher helpful.

7. Making Decisions
A unique chapter aimed at helping students understand how decisions should be made in any context. Includes coverage of marginal analysis and cost-benefit analysis. Pairs well with Chapter 6. Prepares students for coverage of models in upcoming chapters.

11. Consumer Preferences and Consumer Choice
This chapter offers a more detailed treatment of consumer behavior for instructors who wish to cover indifference curves.

12. Factor Markets and the Distribution of Income plus Appendix: Indifference Curve Analysis of Labor Supply
For instructors who want to go more in depth, this chapter covers the efficiency-wage model of the labor market as well as the influences of education, discrimination, and market power. The appendix examines the labor–leisure trade-off and the backward-bending labor supply curve.

13. Efficiency and Equity
A unique chapter that explores what it means to have efficiency in a market economy as a whole. Gives students a deeper understanding of the often-conflicting objectives of efficiency and equity. Intended for instructors who emphasize welfare and public policy issues.

17. International Trade
This chapter recaps comparative advantage, considers tariffs and quotas, and explores the politics of trade protection. Coverage here links back to the international coverage in Chapter 2.

18. Uncertainty, Risk, and Private Information
A unique, applied chapter that explains attitudes toward risk, examines the benefits and limits of diversification, and considers private information in the context of adverse selection and moral hazard.

22. Technology, Information Goods, and Network Externalities
A unique chapter that shows students how to use economic models to analyze information goods. A nice treat for students and instructors!

WHAT'S CORE, WHAT'S OPTIONAL: MACROECONOMICS

Core

Optional

A chapter for instructors who want to provide full details on the determinants of aggregate demand: the consumption function, the determinants of investment spending, and the determination of equilibrium by the requirement that planned spending equal GDP. The appendix offers an algebraic treatment of the multiplier for instructors who want to supplement the graphical analysis

A more rigorous derivation of the role of taxes in reducing the multiplier and acting as an automatic stabilizer

A chapter for instructors who like to cover the history of economic ideas and the current state of policy debate. It offers a unique survey of changing macroeconomic thought, leading up to current debates about monetary policy.

A chapter for instructors who want to take a more international approach. It covers the ways in which capital flows affect financial markets, the importance of exchange rates and exchange rate regimes, and the effects of monetary policy changes under fixed and floating rates.

Supplemental chapter: Currencies and Crises
Available on the Web, at www.worthpublishers.com/krugmanwells, and in booklet form for instructors and students who want to cover currency speculation and international financial problems.

THREE MICRO OUTLINES

To illustrate how instructors can use this book to meet their specific goals, we offer the following possible outlines that are alternatives to simply covering the chapters in order. By no means exclusive, these outlines reflect a likely range of different ways in which this book could be used.

Traditional

Part 1
1. First Principles
2. Economic Models: Trade-offs and Trade
   Appendix: Graphs in Economics

Part 2
3. Supply and Demand
4. The Market Strikes Back
5. Elasticity

Part 3
6. Consumer and Producer Surplus
7. Making Decisions

Part 5*
10. The Rational Consumer
11. Consumer Preferences and Consumer Choice

Part 4*
8. Behind the Supply Curve: Inputs and Costs
9. Perfect Competition and the Supply Curve

Part 7
14. Monopoly
15. Oligopoly
16. Monopolistic Competition and Product Differentiation

Part 9
19. Externalities
20. Public Goods and Common Resources
21. Taxes, Social Insurance, and Income Distribution

Public Policy and Welfare

Part 1
1. First Principles
2. Economic Models: Trade-offs and Trade
   Appendix: Graphs in Economics

Part 2
3. Supply and Demand
4. The Market Strikes Back
5. Elasticity

Part 3
6. Consumer and Producer Surplus
7. Making Decisions

Either **Part 4, then 5** Or,
Part 5, then Part 4

Part 6
12. Factor Markets and the Distribution of Income
    Appendix: Indifference Curve Analysis of Labor Supply
13. Efficiency and Equity

Part 7
14. Monopoly
15. Oligopoly
16. Monopolistic Competition and Product Differentiation

Part 8
17. International Trade
18. Uncertainty, Risk, and Private Information

Part 9
19. Externalities
20. Public Goods and Common Resources
21. Taxes, Social Insurance, and Income Distribution

Part 10
22. Technology, Information Goods, and Network Externalities

Applied Microeconomics

Part 1
1. First Principles
2. Economic Models: Trade-offs and Trade
   Appendix: Graphs in Economics

Part 2
3. Supply and Demand
4. The Market Strikes Back
5. Elasticity

Part 3
6. Consumer and Producer Surplus
7. Making Decisions

Either **Part 4, then 5** Or,
Part 5, then Part 4

Part 6
12. Factor Markets and the Distribution of Income
    Appendix: Indifference Curve Analysis of Labor Supply
13. Efficiency and Equity

Part 7
14. Monopoly
15. Oligopoly
16. Monopolistic Competition and Product Differentiation

Part 8
17. International Trade
18. Uncertainty, Risk, and Private Information

Part 9
19. Externalities
20. Public Goods and Common Resources
21. Taxes, Social Insurance, and Income Distribution

*Instructors who wish to follow a decision-based sequence should use the parts of this text as we've ordered them: Part 4, "The Producer," followed by Part 5, "The Consumer."

THREE MACRO OUTLINES

Supplements and Media

Worth Publishers is pleased to offer an exciting and useful supplements and media package to accompany this textbook. The package has been crafted to help instructors teach their principles course and to help students grasp concepts more readily.

The entire package has been coordinated by Martha Olney, University of California-Berkeley, to provide consistency in level and quality. Rosemary Cunningham, Agnes Scott College, has coordinated all of the quizzing materials in the Study Guide, Test Bank, and all the online materials to guarantee uniformity.

Since accuracy is so critically important, all the supplements have been scrutinized and double-checked by members of the supplements team, reviewers, and a team of additional accuracy checkers. The time and care that have been put into the supplements and media ensure a seamless package.

Companion Website for Students and Instructors

econ X change

(www.worthpublishers.com/krugmanwells)

The companion website for the Krugman/Wells text offers valuable tools for both the instructor and students.

For instructors, this completely customized website offers many opportunities for quizzing and, most important, powerful grading tools. The site gives you the ability to track students' interaction with the Practice Quizzing Center and the Graphing Center by accessing an online gradebook. Instructors have the option to have student results emailed directly to them.

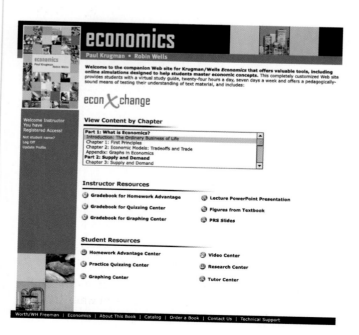

For students, the site offers many opportunities to practice, practice, practice. On the site, students can find animated graphs, practice quizzes, videos, graphing tutorials, and links to many other resources designed to help them master economic concepts. In essence, this site provides students with a virtual study guide, twenty-four hours a day, seven days a week by offering a pedagogically sound means of testing their understanding of text material.

This helpful, powerful site contains the following:

Homework Advantage Center Worth's secure, interactive, online homework system is accessible through the Krugman/Wells website. Using the Homework Advantage Center, instructors can easily create automatically graded homework assignments, quizzes, and tests. This online quizzing engine, which includes algorithmically generated questions, allows for repeatable, varied assignments for students. Students get immediate, individualized results after submitting their work. All student responses are stored in an electronic gradebook so that instructors can easily grade exams and generate reports.

The gradebook has the following features that allow for flexibility in assessing students' abilities.

- Grades can be organized into as many as 25 related categories (tests, papers, homework, etc.).
- Assignments can be independently weighted.
- Letter grade cutoffs can be adjusted, and custom grading created ("Fair," "Good," "Excellent," and so on).
- Assignment scores and category averages can be entered or displayed as percentages, points, letter grades, or according to your own customized grading scheme.
- Gradebooks can be set up to report final averages as points earned across all categories.
- Student properties can include ID number, password (for online testing), e-mail address, and status (active, withdraw, incomplete).
- Grades can be dropped manually or automatically.
- Assignment, category, and final scores can be curved.
- Numerous reports can be customized and printed with an interactive print preview.
- Results can be merged from TheTestingCenter.Com.
- Student rosters can be imported and exported.

Practice Quizzing Center Developed by Debbie Mullin, University of Colorado-Colorado Springs, this quizzing engine provides 20 multiple-choice questions per chapter with appropriate feedback and page references to the textbook. The questions as well as the answer choices are randomized to give students a different quiz with every refresh of the screen. All student answers are saved in an online database that can be accessed by instructors.

Graphing Center Developed by Cadre LLC in conjunction with Debbie Mullin, University of Colorado-Colorado Springs, the Graphing Center includes selected graphs from the textbook that have been animated in a Flash format. Approximately five graphs from each chapter have been animated and are identified in the textbook by a web icon **>web...** within the appropriate figure. Working with these animated figures enhances student understanding of the effects of the shifts and movements of the curves. Every interactive graph is accompanied by questions that quiz students on key concepts from the textbook and provide instructors with feedback on student progress. Student responses and interactions are tracked and stored in an online database that can be accessed by the instructor.

Research Center Created and continually updated by Jules Kaplan, University of Colorado-Boulder, the Research Center allows students to easily and effectively locate outside resources and readings that relate to topics covered in the textbook. It lists web addresses that hotlink to relevant websites; each URL is accompanied by a detailed description of the site and its relevance to each chapter, allowing students to conduct research and explore related readings on specific topics with ease. Also hotlinked are relevant articles by Paul Krugman and other leading economists.

Video Center In video interviews, the text's authors, Paul Krugman and Robin Wells, comment on specific aspects of each chapter and their relevance to students' lives. Each video is embedded in a Flash format with other pedagogical features and a running transcript of the authors' remarks. Videos can be presented in class to generate discussion or assigned as homework to give students a deeper understanding of key topics in the textbook.

Student PowerPoint Created by Can Erbil, Brandeis University, this PowerPoint presentation is ideal for students who need extra help in understanding the concepts in each chapter. The PowerPoint presentations for each chapter come complete with animations, notes, summaries, and graphics. This tool enables students to review and practice and helps them to more readily grasp economic concepts.

➤ Aplia

Aplia, founded by Paul Romer, Stanford University, is the first web-based company to integrate pedagogical features from a textbook with interactive media. Specifically designed for use with the Krugman/Wells text, the figures, end-of-chapter problems, boxes, text, and other pedagogical resources have been combined with Aplia's interactive media to save time for professors and encourage students to exert more effort in their learning.

The integrated online version of the Aplia media and the Krugman/Wells text includes:

➤ Extra problem sets suitable for homework and keyed to specific topics from each chapter

➤ Regularly updated news analyses

➤ Real-time online simulations of market interactions

➤ Interactive tutorials to assist with math

➤ Graphs and statistics

➤ Instant online reports that allow instructors to target student trouble areas more efficiently

With Aplia, you retain complete control and flexibility for your course. You choose the topics you want students to cover, and you decide how to organize it. You decide whether online activities are practice (ungraded or graded). You can even edit the Aplia content—making cuts or addtions as you see fit for your course.

For a preview of Aplia materials and to learn more, visit http://www.aplia.com.

Additional Student Supplements

Student CD-ROM This CD-ROM contains all of the multimedia content found on the Krugman/Wells Companion website, including the practice quizzes, interactive graphs, Krugman/Wells videos, and the student PowerPoint slides. This CD-ROM is ideal for students with limited web access or for use in a lab setting. Available upon request, this CD can be packaged with the textbook at no additional cost to the student.

Micro and Macro Study Guides Prepared by Rosemary Cunningham, Agnes Scott College, and Elizabeth Sawyer-Kelly, University of Wisconsin-Madison, and coordinated by Martha Olney, University of California-Berkeley, the Study Guides reinforce the topics and key concepts covered in the text. For each chapter, the Study Guides provide:

- An introduction
- A fill-in-the-blank chapter review
- Learning tips with graphical analysis
- Four or five comprehensive problems and exercises
- Twenty multiple-choice questions
- Solutions to all fill-in-the-blank reviews, problems, exercises, and quizzes found in the Study Guides.

Additional Instructor Supplements

Micro and Macro Instructor's Resource Manuals The Instructor's Resource Manuals written by Diane Keenan, Cerritos Community College and David Findlay, Colby College, are an ideal resource for instructors teaching principles of economics. The manuals include:

- Chapter-by-chapter learning objectives
- Chapter outlines
- Teaching tips and ideas
- Hints on how to create student interest
- Common misunderstandings that are typical among students
- Activities that can be conducted in or out of the classroom
- Detailed solutions to every end-of-chapter problem from the textbook

Printed Test Banks The Test Banks for Micro and Macro, coordinated by Rosemary Cunningham, Agnes Scott College, with contributing authors Jack Chambless, Valencia Community College; Ardeshir Dalal, Northern Illinois University; Mark Funk, University of Arkansas-Little Rock; Lynn Gillette, University of Kentucky; Gus W. Herring, Brookhaven College; Ranita Wyatt, Dallas Community College District, Doris Bennett, Jacksonville State University; Diego Mendez-Carbajo, Illinois Wesleyan University; Richard Gosselin, Houston Community College; Gus W. Herring, Brookhaven College; James Swofford, University of South Alabama; and James Wetzel, Virginia Commonwealth University, provide a wide range of creative and versatile questions ranging in levels of difficulty. Selected questions are paired with original graphs and graphs from the textbook to reinforce comprehension. Totaling over 5,000 questions, the Test Banks offers 150 multiple-choice questions and 20 true/false questions per chapter assessing comprehension, interpretation, analysis, and synthesis. Each question is conveniently cross referenced to the page number in the text where the appropriate topic is discussed. Questions have been checked for continuity with the text content, reviewed extensively, and checked again for accuracy.

Diploma 6 Computerized Test Bank The Krugman/Wells printed Test Banks are also available in CD-ROM format, powered by Brownstone, for both Windows and Macintosh users. With Diploma, you can easily create tests, write and edit questions, and create study sessions for students. You can add an unlimited number of questions; scramble questions; and include pictures, equations, and multimedia links. Tests can be printed in a wide range of formats or administered to students with Brownstone's network or Internet testing software. The software's unique synthesis of flexible word-processing and database features creates a program that is extremely intuitive and capable. With Diploma you can:

- Work with complete word-processing functions (including creating tables).
- Work with myriad question formats, including multiple choice, true/false, short answer, matching, fill in the blank, and essay.
- Attach feedback (rationales) to questions (or answers).
- Create, install, and use an unlimited number of question banks.
- Incorporate references (including tables, figures, and case studies).
- Attach customized instructions.

- Use multiple graphic formats (BMP, DIB, RLE, DXF, EPS, FPX, GIF, IMG, JPG, PCD, PCX, DCX, PNG, TGA, TIF, WMF, and WPG).
- Take advantage of a powerful algorithm engine for complex, dynamic question types and dynamic equations.
- Export self-grading tests (in HTML formats) for use with web browsers.
- Export test files in Rich Text File format for use with any word-processing program.
- Export test files to EDU, WebCT, and Blackboard course management systems.
- Preview and re-format tests before printing them.
- Include custom splash screens that feature graphics or images.
- Post tests to Diploma's online testing site, TheTestingCenter.com.

This computerized Test Bank is accompanied by a gradebook that enables you to record students' grades throughout a course; it also includes the capacity to track student records and view detailed analyses of test items, curve tests, generate reports, add weights to grades, and allows you to:

- Organize grades into as many as 25 related categories.
- Adjust letter grade cutoffs and create customized grading.
- Enter/display assignment scores and category averages as percentages, points, letter grades, or according to your own customized grading scheme.
- Report final averages as points earned across all categories.
- Customize student properties (including ID number, password, e-mail address, and status).
- Drop grades either manually or automatically.
- Import and export student rosters.

Diploma Online Testing at www.brownstone.net is another useful tool within the Brownstone software that allows instructors to provide online exams for students using Test Bank questions. With Diploma, you can easily create and administer secure exams over a network and over the Internet, with questions that incorporate multimedia and interactive exercises. The program allows you to restrict tests to specific computers or time blocks, and it includes an impressive suite of gradebook and result-analysis features.

Lecture PowerPoint Presentation Created by Can Erbil, Brandeis University, the enhanced PowerPoint presentation slides are designed to assist you with lecture preparation and presentation by providing original animations, graphs from the textbook, data tables, and bulleted lists of key concepts suitable for large lecture presentation. Although the slides are organized by topic from the text's table of contents, you can customize these slides to suit your individual needs by adding your own data, questions, and lecture notes. You can access these files on the instructor's side of the website or on the Instructor's Resource CD-ROM.

Instructor's Resource CD-ROM Using the Instructor's Resource CD-ROM, you can easily build classroom presentations or enchance your online courses. This CD-ROM contains all text figures (in JPEG and GIF formats), video clips of interviews with Paul Krugman and Robin Wells, animated graphs, and enhanced PowerPoint slides. You can choose from the various resources, edit, and save for use in your classroom.

Overhead Transparencies Worth is also happy to provide you with more than 200 vivid color acetates of text figures designed for superior projection quality.

Web-CT E-pack The Krugman/Wells WebCT E-Packs enable you to create a thorough, interactive, and pedagogically sound online course or course website. The Krugman/Wells E-Pack provides you with cutting-edge online materials that facilitate critical thinking and learning, including course outlines, preprogrammed quizzes, links, activities, threaded discussion topics, animated graphs, and a whole array of other materials. Best of all, this material is pre-programmed and fully functional in the WebCT environment. Prebuilt materials eliminate hours of course-preparation work and offer significant support as you develop your online course. You can also obtain a WebCT-formatted version of the text's test bank.

Blackboard The Krugman/Wells Blackboard Course Cartridge allows you to combine Blackboard's popular tools and easy-to-use interface with the Krugman/Wells' text-specific, rich web content, including course outlines, preprogrammed quizzes, links, activities, interactive graphs, and a whole array of other materials. The result: an interactive, comprehensive online course that allow for effortless implementation, management, and use. The Worth electronic files are organized and prebuilt to work within the Blackboard software and can be easily downloaded from the Blackboard content showcases directly onto your department server. You can also obtain a Blackboard-formatted version of the book's test bank.

Dallas TeleLearning videos The Krugman/Wells text was chosen to accompany the economics telecourse developed by the Dallas Community College District (DCCCD). For use in class, instructors have access to videos produced by the DCCCD, the nation's leading developer of distance-learning materials. These videos dramatize key economic concepts and can be used in a classroom setting.

EduCue Personal Response System (PRS)—"Clickers"

Instructors can create a dynamic, interactive classroom environment with a personal response system, powered by EduCue. This wireless remote system allows you to ask your students questions, record their responses, and calculate grades instantly during lectures. Students use a hand-held wireless device (about the size of a television remote control) to transmit immediate feedback to a lecture hall receiver.

Wall Street Journal **Edition** For adopters of the Krugman/Wells text, Worth Publishers and the *Wall Street Journal* are offering a 10-week subscription to students at a tremendous savings. Professors also receive their own free *Wall Street Journal* subscription plus additional instructor supplements created exclusively by the *Wall Street Journal*. Please contact your local sales rep for more information or go to the *Wall Street Journal* online at www.wsj.com.

Financial Times **Edition** For adopters of the Krugman/Wells text, Worth Publishers and the *Financial Times* are offering a 15-week subscription to students at a tremendous savings. Professors also receive their own free *Financial Times* subscription for one year. Students and professors may access research and archived information at www.ft.com.

Acknowledgments

Writing a textbook is a team effort and we could never have reached this point without all of the talented and thoughtful consultants, reviewers, focus-group participants, class testers, and others who have been so generous with their insights on our work.

We are indebted to the following reviewers and other consultants for their suggestions and advice on our chapters:

Ashley Abramson, *Barstow College*
Ljubisa Adamovich, *Florida State University*
Lee Adkins, *Oklahoma State University*
Elena Alvarez, *State University of New York, Albany*
David A. Anderson, *Centre College*
Fahima Aziz, *Hamline University*
Sheryl Ball, *Virginia Polytechnic Institute and State University*
Charles L. Ballard, *Michigan State University*
Cynthia Bansak, *San Diego State University*
Richard Barrett, *University of Montana*
Daniel Barszcz, *College of DuPage*
Charles A. Bennett, *Gannon University*
Andreas Bentz, *Dartmouth College*
Ruben Berrios, *Clarion University*
Joydeep Bhattacharya, *Iowa State University*
Harmanna Bloemen, *Houston Community College*
Michael Bordo, *Rutgers University, NBER*
James Bradley, Jr., *University of South Carolina*

William Branch, *University of Oregon*
Michael Brandl, *University of Texas, Austin*
Greg Brock, *Georgia Southern University*
Raymonda L. Burgman, *DePauw University*
Charles Callahan III, *State University of New York, Brockport*
James Carden, *University of Mississippi*
Bill Carlisle, *University of Utah*
Leonard A. Carlson, *Emory University*
Andrew Cassey, *University of Minnesota*
Shirley Cassing, *University of Pittsburgh*
Yuna Chen, *South Georgia College*
Jim Cobbe, *Florida State University*
Eleanor D. Craig, *University of Delaware*
Rosemary Thomas Cunningham, *Agnes Scott College*
James Cypher, *California State University, Fresno*
Susan Dadres, *Southern Methodist University*
Ardeshir Dalal, *Northern Illinois University*
A. Edward Day, *University of Texas, Dallas*
Dennis Debrecht, *Carroll College*
Stephen J. DeCanio, *University of California, Santa Barbara*
J. Bradford DeLong, *University of California, Berkeley*
Julie Derrick, *Brevard Community College*
Carolyn Dimitri, *Montgomery College, Rockville*
Patrick Dolenc, *Keene State College*
Amitava Dutt, *University of Notre Dame*
Jim Eaton, *Bridgewater College*
Jim Eden, *Portland Community College*
Rex Edwards, *Moorpark College*
Can Erbil, *Brandeis University*
Sharon J. Erenburg, *Eastern Michigan University*
Joe Essuman, *University of Wisconsin, Waukesha*
David N. Figlio, *University of Florida*
David W. Findlay, *Colby College*
Eric Fisher, *Ohio State University/University of California, Santa Barbara*
Oliver Franke, *Athabasca University*
Rhona Free, *Eastern Connecticut State University*
K. C. Fung, *University of California, Santa Cruz*
Susan Gale, *New York University*
Neil Garston, *California State University, Los Angeles*
E. B. Gendel, *Woodbury University*
J. Robert Gillette, *University of Kentucky*
Lynn G. Gillette, *University of Kentucky*
James N. Giordano, *Villanova University*
Robert Godby, *University of Wyoming*
David Goodwin, *University of New Brunswick*
Lisa Grobar, *California State University, Long Beach*
Philip Grossman, *St. Cloud State University*
Wayne Grove, *Syracuse University*
Alan Gummerson, *Florida International University*
Jang-Ting Guo, *University of California, Riverside*

Jonathan Hamilton, *University of Florida*

Mehdi Haririan, *Bloomsburg University of Pennsylvania*

Hadley Hartman, *Santa Fe Community College*

Julie Heath, *University of Memphis*

John Heim, *Rensselaer Polytechnic Institute*

Jill M. Hendrickson, *University of the South*

Rob Holm, *Franklin University*

David Horlacher, *Middlebury College*

Robert Horn, *James Madison University*

Scott Houser, *California State University, Fresno*

Patrik T. Hultberg, *University of Wyoming*

Aaron Jackson, *Bentley College*

Nancy Jianakoplos, *Colorado State University*

Donn Johnson, *Quinnipiac University*

Bruce Johnson, *Centre College*

Philipp Jonas, *Western Michigan University*

Michael Jones, *Bridgewater State College*

James Jozefowicz, *Indiana University of Pennsylvania*

Kamran M. Kadkhah, *Northeastern University*

Matthew Kahn, *Columbia University*

Barry Keating, *University of Notre Dame*

Diane Keenan, *Cerritos College*

Bill Kerby, *California State University, Sacramento*

Kyoo Kim, *Bowling Green University*

Philip King, *San Francisco State University*

Sharmila King, *University of the Pacific*

Kala Krishna, *Penn State University, NBER*

Jean Kujawa, *Lourdes College*

Maria Kula, *Roger Williams University*

Michael Kuryla, *Broome Community College*

Tom Larson, *California State University, Los Angeles*

Susan K. Laury, *Georgia State University*

Jim Lee, *Texas A&M University, Corpus Christi*

Tony Lima, *California State University, Hayward*

Solina Lindahl, *California State Polytechnic University, Pomona*

Malte Loos, *Christian-Albrechts Universität Kiel*

Marty Ludlum, *Oklahoma City Community College*

Mark Maier, *Glendale Community College*

Rachel McCulloch, *Brandeis University*

Doug Meador, *William Jewell College*

Diego Mendez-Carbajo, *Illinois Wesleyan University*

Juan Mendoza, *State University of New York at Buffalo*

Jeffrey Michael, *Towson University*

Jenny Minier, *University of Miami*

Ida A. Mirzaie, *John Carroll University*

Kristen Monaco, *California State University, Long Beach*

Marie Mora, *University of Texas, Pan American*

W. Douglas Morgan, *University of California, Santa Barbara*

Peter B. Morgan, *University of Michigan*

Tony Myatt, *University of New Brunswick, Fredericton*

Kathryn Nantz, *Fairfield University*

John A. Neri, *University of Maryland*

Charles Newton, *Houston Community College*

Joe Nowakowski, *Muskingum College*

Seamus O'Cleireacain, *Columbia University/State University of New York, Purchase*

Martha Olney, *University of California, Berkeley*

Kerry Pannell, *DePauw University*

Chris Papageorgiou, *Louisiana State University*

Brian Peterson, *Central College*

John Pharr, *Dallas County Community College*

Clifford Poirot, *Shawnee State University*

Raymond E. Polchow, *Zane State College*

Adnan Qamar, *University of Texas, Dallas*

Jeffrey Racine, *University of South Florida*

Matthew Rafferty, *Quinnipiac University*

Dixie Watts Reaves, *Virginia Polytechnic Institute and State University*

Siobhán Reilly, *Mills College*

Thomas Rhoads, *Towson University*

Libby Rittenberg, *Colorado College*

Malcom Robinson, *Thomas More College*

Michael Rolleigh, *Williams College*

Christina Romer, *University of California, Berkeley*

Brian P. Rosario, *University of California, Davis*

Bernard Rose, *Rocky Mountain College*

Patricia Rottschaefer, *California State University, Fullerton*

Jeff Rubin, *Rutgers University*

Henry D. Ryder, *Gloucester Community College*

Allen Sanderson, *University of Chicago*

Rolando Santos, *Lakeland Community College*

Christine Sauer, *University of New Mexico*

Elizabeth Sawyer-Kelly, *University of Wisconsin, Madison*

Edward Sayre, *Agnes Scott College*

Robert Schwab, *University of Maryland*

Adina Schwartz, *Lakeland College*

Gerald Scott, *Florida Atlantic University*

Stanley Sedo, *University of Maryland*

William Shambora, *Ohio University*

Gail Shields, *Central Michigan University*

Amy Shrout, *West High School*

Eugene Silberberg, *University of Washington*

Bill Smith, *University of Memphis*

Ray Smith, *College of St. Scholastica*

Judy Smrha, *Baker University*

Marcia S. Snyder, *College of Charleston*

John Solow, *University of Iowa*

David E. Spencer, *Brigham Young University*

Denise Stanley, *California State University, Fullerton*

Martha A. Starr, *American University*

Richard Startz, *University of Washington*

Carol Ogden Stivender, *University of North Carolina, Charlotte*

Jill Stowe, *Texas A&M University, Austin*

William Stronge, *Florida Atlantic University*

Rodney Swanson, *University of California, Los Angeles*

Sarinda Taengnoi, *Western New England College*

Lazina Tarin, *Central Michigan University*

Jason Taylor, *University of Virginia*

Mark Thoma, *University of California, San Diego*

Mehmet Tosun, *West Virginia University*

Karen Travis, *Pacific Lutheran University*

Sandra Trejos, *Clarion University*

Arienne Turner, *Fullerton College*

Neven Valev, *Georgia State University*

Kristin Van Gaasbeck, *California State University*

Abu Wahid, *Tennessee State University*

Stephan Weiler, *Colorado State University*

James N. Wetzel, *Virginia Commonwealth University*

Robert Whaples, *Wake Forest University*

Roger White, *University of Georgia*

Jonathan B. Wight, *University of Richmond*

Mark Wohar, *University of Nebraska, Omaha*

William C. Wood, *James Madison University*

Ken Woodward, *Saddleback College*

Bill Yang, *Georgia Southern University*

Cemile Yavas, *Pennsylvania State University*

Andrea Zanter, *Hillsborough Community College*

We must also thank the following graduate student reviewers for their assistance: Kristy Piccinini, University of California, Berkeley; Lanwei Yang, University of California, Berkeley; Casey Rothschild, Massachusetts Institute of Technology; and Naomi E. Feldman, University of Michigan, Ann Arbor.

During the course of drafting our manuscript, we met with instructors of principles courses for face-to-face focus-group sessions that afforded us invaluable input. We appreciate the forthright advice and suggestions from these colleagues:

Michael Bordo, *Rutgers University*

Jim Cobbe, *Florida State University*

Tom Creahan, *Morehead State University*

Stephen DeCanio, *University of California, Santa Barbara*

Jim Eden, *Portland Community College, Sylvania*

David Flath, *North Carolina State University*

Rhona Free, *Eastern Connecticut State University*

Rick Godby, *University of Wyoming*

Wayne Grove, *Syracuse University*

Jonathan Hamilton, *University of Florida*

Robert Horn, *James Madison University*

Patrik Hultberg, *University of Wyoming*

Bruce Johnson, *Centre College*

Jim Jozefowicz, *Indiana University of Pennsylvania*

Jim Lee, *Texas A&M University, Corpus Christi*

Rachel McCulloch, *Brandeis University*

Ida Mirzaie, *John Carroll University*

Henry D. Ryder, *Gloucester Community College*

Marcia Snyder, *College of Charleston*

Brian Trinque, *University of Texas, Austin*

William C. Wood, *James Madison University*

Many thanks to the class testers who took the time to use early drafts of our chapters in their classrooms. The following instructors should know that we made use of their helpful suggestions. We also extend special thanks to so many of your students who filled out user surveys about our chapters. This student input inspired us.

Ashley Abramson, *Barstow College*

Terry Alexander, *Iowa State University*

Fahima Aziz, *Hamline University*

Benjamin Balak, *Rollins College*

Leon Battista, *Bronx Community College*

Richard Beil, *Auburn University*

Charles Bennett, *Gannon University*

Scott Benson, *Idaho State University*

Andreas Bentz, *Dartmouth College*

John Bockino, *Suffolk County Community College*

Ellen Bowen, *Fisher College, New Bedford*

Anne Bresnock, *University of California, Los Angeles*

Bruce Brown, *California State Polytechnic University, Pomona*

John Buck, *Jacksonville University*

Raymonda Burgman, *University of Southern Florida*

William Carlisle, *University of Utah*

Kevin Carlson, *University of Massachusetts, Boston*

Fred Carstensen, *University of Connecticut*

Shirley Cassing, *University of Pittsburgh*

Ramon Castillo-Ponce, *California State University, Los Angeles*

Emily Chamlee-Wright, *Beloit College*

Anthony Chan, *Santa Monica College*

Mitch Charkiewiecz, *Central Connecticut State University*

Yuna Chen, *South Georgia College*

Maryanne Clifford, *Eastern Connecticut State University*

Julia Chismar, *St. Joseph's High School*

Gregory Colman, *Pace University*

Sarah Culver, *University of Alabama*

Rosa Lea Danielson, *College of DuPage*

Lew Dars, *University of Massachusetts/Dartmouth*

Stephen Davis, *Southwest Minnesota State University*

Tom DelGiudice, *Hofstra University*

Arna Desser, *United States Naval Academy*

Nikolay Dobrinov, *University of Colorado*

Patrick Dolenc, *Keene State College*

Stratford Douglas, *West Virginia University*

Julie Dvorak, *Warren Township High School*

Dorsey Dyer, *Davidson County Community College*

Mary Edwards, *St. Cloud State University*

Fritz Efaw, *University of Tennessee, Chattanooga*

Herb Elliot, *Alan Hancock College*

Can Erbil, *Brandeis University*

Yee Tien Fu, *Stanford University*

Yoram Gelman, *Lehman College, The City University of New York*

E.B. Gendel, *Woodbury College*

Doug Gentry, *St. Mary's College*

Tommy Georgiades, *DeVry University*

Satyajit Ghosh, *University of Scranton*

Richard Glendening, *Central College*

Patrick Gormely, *Kansas State University*

Richard Gosselin, *Houston Community College, Central*

Patricia Graham, *University of Northern Colorado*

Kathleen Greer Rossman, *Birmingham Southern College*

Wayne Grove, *Syracuse University*

Eleanor Gubins, *Rosemont College*

Alan Haight, *State University of New York, Cortland*

Gautam Hazarika, *University of Texas, Brownsville*

Tom Head, *George Fox University*

Susan Helper, *Case Western Reserve University*

Paul Hettler, *Duquesne University*

Roger Hewett, *Drake University*

Michael Hilmer, *San Diego State University*

Jill Holman, *University of Wisconsin, Milwaukee*

Scott Houser, *California State University, Fresno*

Ray Hubbard, *Central Georgia Technical College*

Murat Iyigun, *University of Colorado*

Habib Jam, *Rowan University*

Louis Johnston, *College of St. Benedict/St. John's University*

Jack Julian, *Indiana University of Pennsylvania*

Soheila Kahkashan, *Towson University*

Charles Kaplan, *St. Joseph's College*

Jay Kaplan, *University of Colorado, Boulder*

Bentzil Kasper, *Broome Community College*

Kurt Keiser, *Adams State College*

Ara Khanjian, *Ventura College*

Sinan Koont, *Dickinson College*

Emil Kreider, *Beloit College*

Kenneth Kriz, *University of Nebraska, Omaha*

Tom Larson, *California State University, Los Angeles*

Delores Linton, *Tarrant County College, Northwest*

Rolf Lokke, *Albuquerque Academy*

Ellen Magenheim, *Swarthmore College*

Diana McCoy, *Truckee Meadows Community College*

Garrett Milam, *Ryerson University*

Robert Miller, *Fisher College, New Bedford Campus*

Michael Milligan, *Front Range Community College*

Cathy Miners, *Fairfield University*

Larry Miners, *Fairfield University*

Kristen Monaco, *California State University, Long Beach*

Marie Mora, *University of Texas, Pan American*

James Mueller, *Alma College*

Ranganath Murthy, *Bucknell University*

Sylvia Nasar, *Columbia University*

Gerardo Nebbia, *Glendale Community College*

Anthony Negbenebor, *Gardner-Webb University*

Joseph Nowakowski, *Muskingum College*

Charles Okeke, *Community College of Southern Nevada*

Kimberley Ott, *Kent State University, Salem Campus*

Philip Packard, *St. Mary's College*

Jamie Pelley, *Mary Baldwin College*

Michael Perelman, *California State University*

Mary K. Perkins, *Howard University*

John Pharr, *Dallas Community College, Cedar Valley*

Jerome Picard, *Mount Saint Mary College*

Ray Polchow, *Muskingum Area Technical College*

Ernest Poole, *Fashion Institute of Technology*

Reza Ramazani, *St. Michael's College*

Charles Reichheld, *Cuyahoga Community College*

Siobhan Reilly, *Mills College*

Michael Righi, *Bellevue Community College*

Carl Riskin, *Queens College, The City University of New York*

Malcolm Robinson, *Thomas More College*

Charles Rock, *Rollins College*

Richard Romano, *Broome Community College*

Jeff Romine, *University of Colorado, Denver*

Bernie Rose, *Rocky Mountain College*

Dan Rubenson, *Southern Oregon University*

Jeff Rubin, *Rutgers University*

Lynda Rush, *California State Polytechnic University, Pomona*

Martin Sabo, *Community College of Denver*

Sara Saderion, *Houston Community College, Southwest*

George Sawdy, *Providence College*

Ted Scheinman, *Mt. Hood Community College*

Russell Settle, *University of Delaware*

Anna Shostya, *Pace University*

Amy Shrout, *West High School*

Millicent Sites, *Carson-Newman College*

Judy Smrha, *Baker University*

John Somers, *Portland Community College*

Jim Spellicy, *Lowell High School*

Tesa Stegner, *Idaho State University*

Kurt Stephenson, *Virginia Tech*

Charles Stull, *Kalamazoo College*

Laddie Sula, *Loras College*

David Switzer, *University of Northern Michigan*

Deborah Thorsen, *Palm Beach Community College*

Andrew Toole, *Cook College/Rutgers University*

Arienne Turner, *Fullerton College*

Anthony Uremovic, *Joliet Junior College*

Jane Wallace, *University of Pittsburgh*

Tom Watkins, *Eastern Kentucky University*
James Wetzel, *Virginia Commonwealth University*
Mark Witte, *Northwestern University*
Larry Wolfenbarger, *Macon State College*
James Woods, *Portland State University*
Mickey Wu, *Coe College*
David Yerger, *Indiana University of Pennsylvania*
Eric Young, *Bishop Amat Memorial High School*
Lou Zaera, *Fashion Institute of Technology*
Andrea Zanter, *Hillsborough Community College, Dale Mabry Campus*
Stephen Zill, *De Anza College*

We also appreciate the contributions of our Two-Year/Community College Advisory Panel:

Kathleen Bromley, *Monroe Community College*
Barbara Connolly, *Westchester Community College*
Will Cummings, *Grossmont College*
Richard Gosselin, *Houston Community College, Central*
Gus Herring, *Brookhaven College*
Charles Okeke, *Community College of Southern Nevada*
Charles Reichheld, *Cuyahoga Community College*
Sara Saderion, *Houston Community College, Southwest*
Ted Scheinman, *Mt. Hood Community College*
J. Ross Thomas, *Albuquerque Technical Vocational Institute*
Deborah Thorsen, *Palm Beach Community College*
Ranita Wyatt, *Dallas Community College*

We must thank the following instructors for their creativity and contributions to the *Microeconomics* and *Macroeconomics* card decks:

Charles Antholt, *Western Washington University*
Richard Ball, *Haverford University*
Edward Blomdahl, *Bridgewater State College*
Michael Brace, *Jamestown Community College*
Gregory Brock, *Georgia Southern University*
Joseph Cavanaugh, *Wright State University*
Tom Cooper, *Georgetown College*
James Craven, *Clark College*
Ardeshir Dalal, *Northern Illinois University*
Asif Dowla, *St. Mary's College of Maryland*
James Dulgeroff, *San Bernardino Valley Community College*
Tom Duston, *Keene State College*
Tomas Dvorak, *Union College*
Debra Dwyer, *State University of New York, Stony Brook*
Michael Ellis, *New Mexico State University*
Can Erbil, *Brandeis University*
John Erkkila, *Lake Superior State University*
Chuck Fischer, *Pittsburg State University*
Eric Fisher, *Ohio State University*
John Fitzgerald, *Bowdoin College*
Rajeev Goel, *Illinois State University*

Pat Graham, *University of Northern Colorado*
Hart Hodges, *Western Washington University*
Naphtali Hoffman, *Elmira College*
Yu Hsing, *Southeastern Louisiana University*
Miren Ivankovic, *Southern Wesleyan University*
Allan Jenkins, *University of Nebraska, Kearney*
Elia Kacapyr, *Ithaca College*
Farida Khan, *University of Wisconsin, Parkside*
Maureen Kilkenny, *Iowa State University*
Kent Klitgaard, *Wells College*
Janet Koscianski, *Shippensburg University*
Charles Kroncke, *College of Mount Saint Joseph*
Margaret Landman, *Bridgewater State College*
Bill Lee, *St. Mary's College*
Diego Mendez-Carbajo, *Illinois Wesleyan University*
Nelson Nagai, *San Joaquin Delta College*
William O'Dea, *State University of New York, Oneonta*
Douglas Orr, *Eastern Washington University*
Phil Packard, *Saint Mary's College of California*
Brian Peterson, *Central College*
Joe Pomykala, *Towson University*
Kevin Quinn, *Bowling Green State University*
Lynda Rush, *California State Polytechnic University, Pomona*
Richard Schatz, *Whitworth College*
Peter Schwartz, *University of North Carolina, Charlotte*
Kathleen Segerson, *University of Connecticut*
Esther-Mirjam Sent, *University of Nijmegen*
Millicent Sites, *Carson-Newman College*
Herrick Smith, *Nease High School*
M. N. Srinivas, *Center for Computer-Assisted Legal Instruction (CALI)*
Jean-Philippe Stijns, *Northeastern University*
Chuck Stull, *Kalamazoo College*
Michael Szenberg, *Pace University*
Ross Thomas, *Albuquerque Technical Vocational Institute*
Maurice Weinrobe, *Clark University*
James N. Wetzel, *Virginia Commonwealth University*
Gary Wolfram, *Hillsdale College*
William C. Wood, *James Madison University*
Paul Zak, *Claremont Graduate University*
Alina Zapalska, *U.S. Coast Guard Academy*

We would also like to thank the hundreds of instructors who took the time to offer their useful feedback to online marketing surveys about our project. There are nearly 800 of you out there. We only wish we had enough room in this small space to thank each of you.

The following key people critically read every page in virtually every chapter from many of our drafts and offered us so much: Andreas Bentz, Dartmouth College, oversaw accuracy checking, but his role turned into much more than that—a constant, tireless adviser who clarified our work at every step. It is extremely rare to find someone as faithful as Andreas has been to this project, and we are immensely grateful to him. Martha Olney, University of California, Berkeley, provided insightful input throughout—we had a number of moments when we realized that her advice saved us from a serious pedagogical misstep. Our deepest thanks also go to Martha. Development editor Marilyn Freedman helped us in shaping a book that instructors can really use and injected much-needed doses of common sense at crucial moments. We've even relied on her to sort out pedagogical differences between the two of us. Several other people have played an invaluable role as close readers of our chapters: Elizabeth Sawyer-Kelly, University of Wisconsin, Madison; David Findlay, Colby College; Sharon J. Ehrenburg, Eastern Michigan University; Malte Loos, Christian-Albrechts Universität Kiel; and Kristy Piccinni and Lanwei Yang, both graduate students at the University of California, Berkeley. The detailed and wise input from all of you has been enormously helpful to us! (Thanks, too, Kristy for your work on our glossary.) Special thanks go to Dave Figlio, University of Florida, for his invaluable help as a reviewer and for his contributions to the labor and inflation chapters.

Thanks to Rhona Free for her contributions, particularly for the essential role she played in the development of our graphing appendix. We must also extend special thanks to Rosemary Cunningham, Agnes Scott College, for her assistance with end-of-chapter problems.

We'd like to thank the current and former Worth people who made this project possible. Paul Shensa and Bob Worth suggested that we write this book. Craig Bleyer, publisher, kept the writing process moving, with just the right mix of patience and whip-cracking. Craig's able leadership and patience helped us realize our vision for this book and get all versions of it finished and out to the market.

Elizabeth Widdicombe, president of Freeman and Worth, and Catherine Woods, publisher at Worth, urged us on and kept faith with what must have been a very exasperating project at times.

We have had an incredible production and design team on this book. Tracey Kuehn, our associate managing editor, has worked tirelessly and with great skill to turn our rough manuscript into this beautiful textbook—and on a very tight schedule. And, thank you, Anthony Calcara, our project editor. Karen Osborne, our copyeditor, did a fine job helping us streamline and refine our writing. Babs Reingold created the spectacular cover for this book and came up with a book design that awed us each time we saw a new chapter in page proof. All we can say is "wow" and thanks. And we would not have been so awed with the look of each and every spread without the page-layout magic that Lee Mahler worked for us. Thanks, too, to Barbara Seixas for her work on the manufacturing end. We've heard about some of the miracles you've worked for us, Barbara, and we appreciate all you've done. The lovely photos you see in this book come to us courtesy of Elyse Rieder and Julie Tesser, our photo researchers. Thanks, too, to Patricia Marx and Ted Szczepanski for their assistance with photos. And for all of her help, thanks to Liz Saxon, editorial assistant.

Many thanks to Charlie Van Wagner, senior acquisitions editor, for devising and coordinating the impressive collection of media and supplements that accompany our *Microeconomics* textbook. Thanks are also extended to Marie McHale, associate editor, for doing the same on our *Macroeconomics* supplements. And many thanks to the incredible team of supplements writers and coordinators who worked with Charlie and Marie to make the supplements and media package so strong.

Thanks to Steve Rigolosi, director of market development, and Scott Guile, marketing manager, for their energetic and creative work in marketing this book. Thanks to Tom Kling, national economics consultant, for his critical role in helping to seed business for this text. And thank you, Bruce Kaplan, for all of your behind-the-scenes work supporting sales and marketing efforts. Thank you, Barbara Monteiro of Monteiro and Company as well as John Murphy and Dori Weintraub of St. Martin's Press, for your help with publicity for the book.

And most of all, special thanks to Sharon Balbos, executive development editor on this project, who must have been as stressed out as we were—but kept her cool throughout many years of tough slogging. We hope that this book lives up to the level of dedication and professionalism that she put into this project.

Paul Krugman   Robin Wells

BRIEF CONTENTS

CONTENTS

Credits

Photo Credits

Grateful acknowledgment is given for permission to reprint the following cover photos:

Front Cover

Row 1 (left to right): Empty shopping cart, Photodisc; Hip kids sharing headphones, ©image100 Ltd./Veer; Freight yard, Brand X Pictures; **Row 2 (left to right):** Indian woman on cell phone and computer, Photodisc; Happy graduates, © image 100 Ltd.; Meeting with laptop Photodisc/Getty Images; Tractor hauling haybales, Stockbyte; **Row 3 (left to right):** Gas pump, Trish Marx; Figures from Tokyo Stock Exchange, Media Bakery; Man checking classified ads, Photodisc; Nuclear plant cooling tower with steam, EyeWire; **Row 4:** Oil pumping rig, EyeWire; **Row 5:** Bar-B-Q Sign, Photodisc; **Row 6 (left to right):** Big Ben and Commonwealth of Flags, Photodisc; Business man on cell phone in front of Petronas Towers, Kuala Lumpur, Malaysia, ©image100 Ltd.; Food stand, The Image Bank/Getty Images; Depression-era man with sign asking for work, The Image Bank/Getty Images; **Row 7 (left to right):** New York Stock Exchange interior, Image Source; Close-up of Euro/dollar, Corbis; Postal worker dropping letter in mail slot, Photodisc; Electronic components assembly, Thinkstock; **Row 8 (left to right):** Satellite dish, Stockbyte; Couple crossing street with sales signs in background, Image Source; Wood frame building under construction, EyeWire; Businesspeople paying taxi fare, Photodisc; **Row 9 (left to right):** Portrait of a young woman, Photodisc; Fresh vegetables, Photodisc; Busy Hong Kong intersection, Photodisc; Used car lot, Photodisc

Back Cover

Row 1 (left to right): Wood frame building under construction, EyeWire; Market fruit stand, Photodisc; Vancouver skyline, Photodisc; International money, Lyndall Culbertson/Photodisc; **Row 2 (left to right):** Barge with freight, Image State; Man making pizza at a pizza stand, Photodisc; Shoe repair window, Photodisc; **Row 3 (left to right):** Fresh fish, Photodisc; Plumber working, Photodisc; St. Louis Arch at sunset, Photodisc; **Row 4:** Refinery, EyeWire; **Row 5:** Manhattan, Photodisc; **Row 6 (left to right):** Making cappuccino, Photodisc; Depression-era woman, Dorothea Lange/Corbis; Dark meeting with laptop and videoconference, Photodisc; **Row 7 (left to right):** European hotel, Photodisc; Sign for drive-up bank, Photodisc; Woman holding bicycle on assembly line, EyeWire; **Row 8 (left to right):** Window display in men's shop, Photodisc; Logging truck, EyeWire; Chemical plant, EyeWire; **Row 9 (left to right):** Antique store, Photodisc; Trishaw, Phnom Penh, Cambodia, Photodisc

Author photo

Page v: Ted Szczepanski

Text Credits

Chapter 5

Source information for Table 5-1, page 113:

Eggs, beef: Kuo S. Huang and Biing-Hwan Lin, Estimation of Food Demand and Nutrient Elasticities from Household Survey Data, United States Department of Agriculture Economic Research Service Technical Bulletin, No. 1887 (Washington, DC: U.S. Department of Agriculture, 2000);

Stationery, gasoline, airline travel, foreign travel: H. S. Houthakker and Lester D. Taylor, *Consumer Demand in the United States, 1929–1970: Analyses and Projections* (Cambridge, MA: Harvard University Press, 1966);

Housing, restaurant meals: H. S. Houthakker and Lester D. Taylor, *Consumer Demand in the United States: Analyses and Projections,* 2nd ed. (Cambridge, MA: Harvard University Press, 1970).

Chapter 12

Source article of "For Inquiring Minds" box on page 300:

C. Camerer et al., Labor Supply of New York City Cab Drivers: One Day at a Time. *Quarterly Journal of Economics, 112,* 407–471.

Chapter 19

Source article of "Economics in Action" on page 461:
M. Gross, J.L. Sindelar, J. Mullahy, and R. Anderson, Policy Watch: Alcohol and Cigarette Taxes, *Journal of Economic Perspectives, 7,* 211–222, 1993.

Introduction: The Ordinary Business of Life

ANY GIVEN SUNDAY

I<span></span>T'S SUNDAY AFTERNOON IN THE SUMMER of 2003, and Route 1 in central New Jersey is a busy place. Thousands of people crowd the shopping malls that line the road for 20 miles, all the way from Trenton to New Brunswick. Most of the shoppers are cheerful—and why not? The stores in those malls offer an extraordinary range of choice; you can buy everything from sophisticated electronic equipment to fashionable clothes to organic carrots. There are probably 100,000 distinct items available

The scene along Route 1 that summer day was, of course, perfectly ordinary—very much like the scene along hundreds of other stretches of road, all across America, that same afternoon. But the discipline of economics is mainly concerned with ordinary things. As the great nineteenth-century economist Alfred Marshall put it, economics is "a study of mankind in the ordinary business of life."

What can economics say about this "ordinary business"? Quite a lot, it turns

Delivering the goods: the market economy in action

Robert Landau/Corbis

along that stretch of road. And most of these items are not luxury goods that only the rich can afford; they are products that millions of Americans can and do purchase every day.

out. What we'll see in this book is that even familiar scenes of economic life pose some very important questions—questions that economics can help answer. Among these questions are:

- How does our economic system work? That is, how does it manage to deliver the goods?

- When and why does our economic system go astray, leading people into counterproductive behavior?

- Why are there ups and downs in the economy? That is, why does the economy sometimes have a "bad year"?

- Finally, why is the long run mainly a story of ups rather than downs? That is, why has America, along with other advanced nations, become so much richer over time?

Let's take a look at these questions and offer a brief preview of what you will learn in this book.

The Invisible Hand

That ordinary scene in central New Jersey would not have looked at all ordinary to an American from colonial times—say, one of the patriots who helped George Washington win the battle of Trenton in 1776. (At the time, Trenton was a small village with not a shopping mall in sight, and farms lined the unpaved road that would eventually become Route 1.)

Imagine that you could transport an American from the colonial period forward in time to our own era. (Isn't that the plot of a movie? Several, actually.) What would this time-traveler find amazing?

Surely the most amazing thing would be the sheer prosperity of modern America—the range of goods and services that ordinary families can afford. Looking at all that wealth, our transplanted colonial would wonder, "How can I get some of that?" Or perhaps he would ask himself, "How can my society get some of that?"

The answer is that to get this kind of prosperity, you need a well-functioning system for coordinating productive activities—the activities that create the goods and services people want and get them to the people who want them. That kind of system is what we mean when we talk about the **economy**. And **economics** is the study of economies, at the level both of individuals and of society as a whole.

An economy succeeds to the extent that it, literally, delivers the goods. A time-traveler from the eighteenth century—or even from 1950—would be amazed at how many goods and services the modern American economy delivers and at how many people can afford them. Compared with any past economy and with all but a few other countries today, America has an incredibly high standard of living.

So our economy must be doing something right, and the time-traveler might want to compliment the person in charge. But guess what? There isn't anyone in charge. The United States has a **market economy**, in which production and consumption are the result of decentralized decisions by many firms and individuals. There is no central authority telling people what to produce or where to ship it. Each individual producer makes what he or she thinks will be most profitable; each consumer buys what he or she chooses.

The alternative to a market economy is a *command economy,* in which there *is* a central authority making decisions about production and consumption. Command economies have been tried, most notably in the Soviet Union between 1917 and 1991. But they didn't work very well. Producers in the Soviet Union routinely found themselves unable to produce because they did not have crucial raw materials, or they succeeded in producing but then found that nobody wanted their products. Consumers were often unable to find necessary items—command economies are famous for long lines at shops.

Market economies, however, are able to coordinate even highly complex activities and to reliably provide consumers with the goods and services they want. Indeed, people quite casually trust their lives to the market system: residents of any major city

An **economy** is a system for coordinating society's productive activities.

Economics is the study of economies, at the level both of individuals and of society as a whole.

A **market economy** is an economy in which decisions about production and consumption are made by individual producers and consumers.

would starve in days if the unplanned yet somehow orderly actions of thousands of businesses did not deliver a steady supply of food. Surprisingly, the unplanned "chaos" of a market economy turns out to be far more orderly than the "planning" of a command economy.

In 1776, in a famous passage in his book *The Wealth of Nations*, the pioneering Scottish economist Adam Smith wrote about how individuals, in pursuing their own interests, often end up serving the interests of society as a whole. Of a businessman whose pursuit of profit makes the nation wealthier, Smith wrote: "[H]e intends only his own gain, and he is in this, as in many other cases, led by an invisible hand to promote an end which was no part of his intention." Ever since, economists have used the term **invisible hand** to refer to the way a market economy manages to harness the power of self-interest for the good of society.

ECONOMICS THROUGH THE AGES

BARTER — I'LL SPLIT MY NEXT MAMMOTH WITH YOU IF I CAN CRASH IN YOUR CAVE. / ARE YOU **NUTS**? I'M STUPID BUT I'M NOT DUMB!

CASH — LET ME TELL YOU AGAIN: I GIVE YOU A PIECE OF PAPER PRINTED BY A GROUP OF PEOPLE WHO PROMISE TO GIVE YOU STUFF, AND YOU GIVE ME STUFF IN EXCHANGE. / I DUNNO.

CREDIT — I KNOW IT'S WEIRD, BUT THE TINT OF THE PLASTIC DETERMINES WHETHER OR NOT I'M TREATED WITH RESPECT. / AND THEY TRUST YOU TO PAY "WHENEVER"?

NEW ECONOMY — I'LL GIVE YOU A BANNER AD IF I CAN CO-BRAND YOUR E-COMMERCE SEGMENT. / SOUNDS TASTY TO ME!

8-3-00-C

The study of how individuals make decisions and how these decisions interact is called **microeconomics**. One of the key themes in microeconomics is the validity of Adam Smith's insight: Individuals pursuing their own interests often do promote the interests of society as a whole.

So part of the answer to our time-traveler's question—"How can my society achieve the kind of prosperity you take for granted?"—is that his society should learn to appreciate the virtues of a market economy and the power of the invisible hand.

But the invisible hand isn't always our friend. It's also important to understand when and why the individual pursuit of self-interest can lead to counterproductive behavior.

The **invisible hand** refers to the way in which the individual pursuit of self-interest can lead to good results for society as a whole.

Microeconomics is the branch of economics that studies how people make decisions and how these decisions interact.

My Benefit, Your Cost

One thing that our time-traveler would not admire about modern Route 1 is the traffic. In fact, although most things have gotten better in America over time, traffic congestion has gotten a lot worse.

When traffic is congested, each driver is imposing a cost on all the other drivers on the road—he is literally getting in their way (and they are getting in his way). This cost can be substantial: in major metropolitan areas, each time someone drives to work, as opposed to taking public transportation or working at home, he can easily impose $15 or more in hidden costs on other drivers. Yet when deciding whether or not to drive, commuters have no incentive to take the costs they impose on others into account.

Traffic congestion is a familiar example of a much broader problem: sometimes the individual pursuit of one's own interest, instead of promoting the interests of society as a whole, can actually make society worse off. When this happens, it is known as **market failure**. Other important examples of market failure involve air and water pollution as well as the overexploitation of natural resources such as fish and forests.

The good news, as you will learn as you use this book to study microeconomics, is that economic analysis can be used to diagnose cases of market failure. And often, economic analysis can also be used to devise solutions for the problem.

When the individual pursuit of self-interest leads to bad results for society as a whole, there is **market failure**.

Good Times, Bad Times

Route 1 was bustling on that summer day in 2003—but it wasn't bustling quite as much as merchants would have liked, because in mid-2003 the U.S. economy wasn't doing all that well. The main problem was jobs: in early 2001, businesses began laying off workers in large numbers, and as of June 2003, employment had not yet started to recover.

Such troubled periods are a regular feature of modern economies. The fact is that the economy does not always run smoothly: it experiences *fluctuations,* a series of ups and downs. By middle age, a typical American will have experienced three or four downs, known as **recessions**. (The U.S. economy experienced serious recessions beginning in 1973, 1980, 1981, 1990, and 2001.) During a severe recession, millions of workers may be laid off.

Like market failure, recessions are a fact of life; but also like market failure, they are a problem to which economic analysis offers some solutions. Recessions are one of the main concerns of the branch of economics known as **macroeconomics**, which is concerned with the overall ups and downs of the economy. If you study macroeconomics, you will learn how economists explain recessions and how government policies can be used to minimize the damage from economic fluctuations.

Despite the occasional recession, however, over the long run the story of the U.S. economy contains many more ups than downs. And that long-run ascent is the subject of our final question.

> A **recession** is a downturn in the economy.

> **Macroeconomics** is the branch of economics that is concerned with overall ups and downs in the economy.

Onward and Upward

At the beginning of the twentieth century, most Americans lived under conditions that we would now think of as extreme poverty. Only 10 percent of homes had flush toilets, only 8 percent had central heating, only 2 percent had electricity, and almost nobody had a car, let alone a washing machine or air conditioning.

Such comparisons are a stark reminder of how much our lives have been changed by **economic growth**, the growing ability of the economy to produce goods and services.

Why does the economy grow over time? And why does economic growth occur faster in some times and places than in others? These are key questions for economics because economic growth is a good thing, as those shoppers on Route 1 can attest, and most of us want more of it.

> **Economic growth** is the growing ability of the economy to produce goods and services.

An Engine for Discovery

We hope we have convinced you that the "ordinary business of life" is really quite extraordinary, if you stop to think about it, and that it can lead us to ask some very interesting and important questions.

In this book, we will describe the answers economists have given to these questions. But this book, like economics as a whole, isn't a list of answers: it's an introduction to a discipline, a way to address questions like those we have just asked. Or as Alfred Marshall, who described economics as a study of the "ordinary business of life," put it: "Economics . . . is not a body of concrete truth, but an engine for the discovery of concrete truth."

So let's turn the key in the ignition.

KEY TERMS

>First Principles

COMMON GROUND

THE ANNUAL MEETING OF THE AMERICAN Economic Association draws thousands of economists, young and old, famous and obscure. There are booksellers, business meetings, and quite a few job interviews. But mainly the economists gather to talk and listen. During the busiest times, 60 or more presentations may be taking place simultaneously, on questions that range from the future of the stock market to who does the cooking in two-earner families.

What do these people have in common? An expert on the stock market probably knows very little about the economics of housework, and vice versa. Yet an economist who wanders into the wrong seminar and ends up listening to presentations on some unfamiliar topic is nonetheless likely to hear much that is familiar. The reason is that all economic analysis is based on a set of common principles that apply to many different issues.

Some of these principles involve *individual choice*—for economics is, first of all, about the choices that individuals make. Do you choose to work over the summer or take a backpacking trip? Do you buy a new CD or go to a movie? These decisions involve *making a choice* among a limited number of alternatives—limited because no one can have everything that he or she wants. Every question in economics at its most basic level involves individuals making choices.

But to understand how an economy works, you need to understand more than how individuals make choices. None of us are Robinson Crusoe, alone on an island—we must make decisions in an environment that is shaped by the decisions of others. Indeed, in a modern economy even the simplest decisions you make—say, what to have for breakfast—are shaped by the decisions of thousands of other people, from the banana grower in Costa Rica who decided to grow the fruit you eat to the farmer in Iowa who provided the corn in your cornflakes. And because each of us in a market economy depends on

One must choose.

Richard Hamilton Smith/Corbis

What you will learn in this chapter:

➤ A set of principles for understanding the economics of how individuals make choices

➤ A set of principles for understanding how individual choices interact so many others—and they, in turn, depend on us—our choices interact. So although all economics at a basic level is about individual choice, in order to understand how market economies behave we must also understand economy-wide *interaction*— how my choices affect your choices, and vice versa.

In this chapter, we will look at nine basic principles of economics—four principles involving individual choice and five involving the way individual choices interact.

Individual Choice: The Core of Economics

Every economic issue involves, at its most basic level, **individual choice**—decisions by an individual about what to do and what *not* to do. In fact, you might say that it isn't economics if it isn't about choice.

Step into a big store like a Wal-Mart or Home Depot. There are thousands of different products available, and it is extremely unlikely that you—or anyone else—could afford to buy everything you might want to have. And anyway, there's only so much space in your dorm room or apartment. So will you buy another bookcase or a mini-refrigerator? Given limitations on your budget and your living space, you must choose which products to buy and which to leave on the shelf.

The fact that those products are on the shelf in the first place involves choice—the store manager chose to put them there, and the manufacturers of the products chose to produce them. All economic activities involve individual choice.

Four economic principles underlie the economics of individual choice, as shown in Table 1-1. We'll now examine each of these principles in more detail.

Resources Are Scarce

You can't always get what you want. Everyone would like to have a beautiful house in a great location (and help with the housecleaning), two or three luxury cars, and frequent vacations in fancy hotels. But even in a rich country like the United States, not many families can afford all that. So they must make choices—whether to go to Disney World this year or buy a better car, whether to make do with a small backyard or accept a longer commute in order to live where land is cheaper.

Limited income isn't the only thing that keeps people from having everything they want. Time is also in limited supply: there are only 24 hours in a day. And because the time we have is limited, choosing to spend time on one activity also means choosing not to spend time on a different activity—spending time studying for an exam means forgoing a night at the movies. Indeed, many people are so limited by the number of hours in the day that they are willing to trade money for time. For example, convenience stores normally charge higher prices than a regular supermarket. But they fulfill a valuable role by catering to time-pressured customers who would rather pay more than travel farther to the supermarket.

Why do individuals have to make choices? The ultimate reason is that *resources are scarce*. A **resource** is anything that can be used to produce something else. Lists of the economy's resources usually begin with land, labor (the available time of workers), capital (machinery, buildings, and other man-made productive assets), and human capital (the educational achievements and skills of workers). A resource is **scarce** when the quantity of the resource available isn't large enough to satisfy all productive uses. There are many scarce resources. These include natural resources—resources that come from the physical environment, such as minerals, lumber, and petroleum. There is also a limited quantity of human resources—labor, skill, and intelligence. And in a growing world economy with a rapidly increasing human population, even clean air and water have become scarce resources.

Individual choice is the decision by an individual of what to do, which necessarily involves a decision of what not to do.

TABLE 1-1

Principles That Underlie the Economics of Individual Choice

1. Resources are scarce.

2. The real cost of something is what you must give up to get it.

3. "How much?" is a decision at the margin.

4. People usually exploit opportunities to make themselves better off.

A **resource** is anything that can be used to produce something else.

Resources are **scarce**—the quantity available isn't large enough to satisfy all productive uses.

Just as individuals must make choices, the scarcity of resources means that society as a whole must make choices. One way for a society to make choices is simply to allow them to emerge as the result of many individual choices, which is what usually happens in a market economy. For example, Americans as a group have only so many hours in a week: how many of those hours will they spend going to supermarkets to get lower prices, rather than saving time by shopping at convenience stores? The answer is the sum of individual decisions: each of the millions of individuals in the economy makes his or her own choice about where to shop, and the overall choice is simply the sum of those individual decisions.

But for various reasons, there are some decisions that a society decides are best not left to individual choice. For example, the authors live in an area that until recently was mainly farmland but is now being rapidly built up. Most local residents feel that the community would be a more pleasant place to live if some of the land were left undeveloped. But no individual has an incentive to keep his or her land as open space, rather than selling it to a developer. So a trend has emerged in many communities across the United States of local governments purchasing undeveloped land and preserving it as open space. We'll see in later chapters why decisions about how to use scarce resources are often best left to individuals but sometimes should be made at a higher, community-wide, level.

Opportunity Cost: The Real Cost of Something Is What You Must Give Up to Get It

It is the last term before you graduate, and your class schedule allows you to take only one elective. There are two, however, that you would really like to take: History of Jazz and Beginning Tennis.

Suppose you decide to take the History of Jazz course. What's the cost of that decision? It is the fact that you can't take Beginning Tennis. Economists call that kind of cost—what you must forgo in order to get something you want—the **opportunity cost** of that item. So the opportunity cost of the History of Jazz class is the enjoyment you would have derived from the Beginning Tennis class.

The concept of opportunity cost is crucial to understanding individual choice because, in the end, all costs are opportunity costs. Sometimes critics claim that economists are concerned only with costs and benefits that can be measured in dollars and cents. But that is not true. Much economic analysis involves cases like our elective course example, where it costs no extra tuition to take one elective course—that is, there is no direct monetary cost. Nonetheless, the elective you choose has an opportunity cost—the other desirable elective course that you must forgo because your limited time permits taking only one.

You might think that opportunity cost is an add-on—that is, something *additional* to the monetary cost of an item. Suppose that an elective class costs additional tuition of $750; now there is a monetary cost to taking History of Jazz. Is the opportunity cost of taking that course something separate from that monetary cost?

Well, consider two cases. First, suppose that taking Beginning Tennis also costs $750. In this case, you would have to spend that $750 no matter which class you take. So what you give up to take the History of Jazz class is still the Beginning Tennis class, period—you would have to spend that $750 either way. But suppose there isn't any fee for the tennis class. In that case, what you give up to take the jazz class is the tennis class *plus* whatever you would have bought with the $750.

Either way, the cost of taking your preferred class is what you must give up to get it. *All* costs are ultimately opportunity costs.

Sometimes the money you have to pay for something is a good indication of its opportunity cost. But many times it is not. One very important example of how poorly monetary cost can indicate opportunity cost is the cost of attending college.

> The real cost of an item is its **opportunity cost**: what you must give up in order to get it.

At many cash registers—for example, the one in our college cafeteria—there is a little basket full of pennies. People are encouraged to use the basket to round their purchases up or down: if it costs $5.02, you give the cashier $5 and take two pennies from the basket; if it costs $4.99, you pay $5 and the cashier throws in a penny. It makes everyone's life a bit easier. Of course, it would be easier still if we just abolished the penny, a step that some economists have urged.

But then why do we have pennies in the first place? If it's too small a sum to worry about, why calculate prices that exactly?

The answer is that a penny wasn't always such a negligible sum: the purchasing power of a penny has been greatly reduced by inflation. Forty years ago, a penny had more purchasing power than a nickel does today.

Why does this matter? Well, remember the saying: "A penny saved is a penny earned." But there are other ways to earn money, so you must decide whether saving a penny is a productive use of your time. Could you earn more by devoting that time to other uses?

Forty years ago, the average wage was about $2 an hour. A penny was equivalent to 18 seconds' worth of work—it was worth saving a penny if doing so took less than 18 seconds. But wages have risen along with overall prices, so that the average worker is now paid more than $17 per hour. A penny is therefore equivalent to just over 2 seconds of work—and so it's not worth the opportunity cost of the time it takes to worry about a penny more or less.

In short, the rising opportunity cost of time in terms of money has turned a penny from a useful coin into a nuisance.

Tiger Woods understood the concept of opportunity cost. The rest is history.

Tuition and housing are major monetary expenses for most students; but even if these things were free, attending college would still be an expensive proposition because most college students, if they were not in college, would have a job. That is, by going to college, students *forgo* the income they could have made if they had worked instead. This means that the opportunity cost of attending college is what you pay for tuition and housing *plus* the forgone income you would have earned in a job.

It's easy to see that the opportunity cost of going to college is especially high for people who could be earning a lot during what would otherwise have been their college years. That is why star athletes often skip college or, like Tiger Woods, leave before graduating.

"How Much?" Is a Decision at the Margin

Some important decisions involve an "either-or" choice—for example, you decide either to go to college or to begin working; you decide either to take economics or to take something else. But other important decisions involve "how much" choices—for example, if you are taking both economics and chemistry this semester, you must decide how much time to spend studying for each. When it comes to understanding "how much" decisions, economics has an important insight to offer: "how much" is a decision made *at the margin*.

Suppose you are taking both economics and chemistry. And suppose you are a pre-med student, so that your grade in chemistry matters more to you than your grade in economics. Does that therefore imply that you should spend *all* your study time on chemistry and wing it on the economics exam? Probably not; even if you think your chemistry grade is more important, you should put some effort into studying for economics.

Spending more time studying for economics involves a benefit (a higher expected grade in that course) and a cost (you could have spent that time doing something else, such as studying to get a higher grade in chemistry). That is, your decision involves a **trade-off**—a comparison of costs and benefits.

How do you decide this kind of "how much" question? The typical answer is that you make the decision a bit at a time, by asking how you should spend the next hour.

You make a **trade-off** when you compare the costs with the benefits of doing something.

Say both exams are on the same day, and the night before you spend time reviewing your notes for both courses. At 6:00 P.M., you decide that it's a good idea to spend at least an hour on each course. At 8:00 P.M., you decide you'd better spend another hour on each course. At 10:00 P.M., you are getting tired and figure you have one more hour to study before bed—chemistry or economics? If you are pre-med, it's likely to be chemistry; if you are pre-MBA, it's likely to be economics.

Note how you've made the decision to allocate your time: at each point the question is whether or not to spend *one more hour* on either course. And in deciding whether to spend another hour studying for chemistry, you weigh the costs (an hour forgone of studying for economics or an hour forgone of sleeping) versus the benefits (a likely increase in your chemistry grade). As long as the benefit of studying one more hour for chemistry outweighs the cost, you should choose to study for that additional hour.

Decisions of this type—what to do with your next hour, what to do with your next dollar, and so on—are **marginal decisions**. They involve making trade-offs *at the margin*: comparing the costs and benefits of doing a little bit more of an activity versus doing a little bit less. The study of such decisions is known as **marginal analysis**.

Many of the questions that we face in economics—as well as in real life—involve marginal analysis: How many workers should I hire in my shop? At what mileage should I change the oil in my car? What is an acceptable rate of negative side effects from a new medicine? Marginal analysis plays a central role in economics because it is the key to deciding "how much" of an activity to do.

> Decisions about whether to do a bit more or a bit less of an activity are **marginal decisions**. The study of such decisions is known as **marginal analysis**.

People Usually Exploit Opportunities to Make Themselves Better Off

One day, while listening to the morning financial news, the authors heard a great tip about how to park cheaply in Manhattan. Garages in the Wall Street area charge as much as $30 per day. But according to the newscaster, some people had found a better way: instead of parking in a garage, they had their oil changed at the Manhattan Jiffy Lube, where it costs $19.95 to change your oil—and they keep your car all day!

It's a great story, but unfortunately it turned out not to be true—in fact, there is no Jiffy Lube in Manhattan. But if there were, you can be sure there would be a lot of oil changes there. Why? Because when people are offered opportunities to make themselves better off, they normally take them—and if they could find a way to park their car all day for $19.95 rather than $30, they would.

When you try to predict how individuals will behave in an economic situation, it is a very good bet that they will exploit opportunities to make themselves better off. Furthermore, individuals will *continue* to exploit these opportunities until they have been fully exhausted—that is, people will exploit opportunities until those opportunities have been fully taken.

If there really were a Manhattan Jiffy Lube and an oil change really were a cheap way to park your car, we could safely predict that before long the waiting list for oil changes would be weeks, if not months.

In fact, the principle that people will exploit opportunities to make themselves better off is the basis of *all* predictions by economists about individual behavior. If the earnings of those who get MBAs soar while the earnings of those who get law degrees decline, we can expect more students to go to business school and fewer to go to law school. If the price of gasoline rises and stays high for an extended period of time, we can expect people to buy smaller cars with higher gas mileage—making themselves better off in the presence of higher gas prices by driving more fuel-efficient cars.

When changes in the available opportunities offer rewards to those who change their behavior, we say that people face new **incentives**. If the price of parking in Manhattan rises, those who can find alternative ways to get to their Wall Street jobs

> An **incentive** is anything that offers rewards to people who change their behavior.

The true reward for learning is, of course, the learning itself. But teachers and schools often feel that it's worth throwing in a few extras. Elementary school students who do well get gold stars; at higher levels, students who score well on tests may receive trophies, plaques, or even gift certificates.

But what about cash?

A few years ago, some Florida schools stirred widespread debate by offering actual cash bonuses to students who scored high on the state's standardized exams. At Parrott Middle School, which offered the highest amounts, an eighth-grader with a top score on an exam received a $50 savings bond.

Many people questioned the monetary awards. In fact, the great majority of teachers feel that cash rewards for learning are a bad idea—the dollar amounts can't be made large enough to give students a real sense of how important their education is, and they make learning seem like work-for-pay. So why did the schools engage in the practice?

The answer, it turns out, is that the previous year the state government had introduced a pay-for-performance scheme for schools: schools whose students earned high marks on the state exams received extra state funds. The problem arose of how to motivate the students to take the exams as seriously as the school administrators

did. Parrott's principal defended the pay-for-grades practice by pointing out that good students would often "Christmas tree" their exams—ignore the questions and fill out the bubble sheets in the shape of Christmas trees. With large sums of money for the school at stake, he decided to set aside his misgivings and pay students to do well on the exams.

Does paying students for grades lead to higher grades? Interviews with students suggest that it does spur at least some students to try harder on state exams. And some Florida schools that have introduced rewards for good grades on state exams report substantial improvements in student performance.

will save money by doing so—and so we can expect fewer people to drive to work.

One last point: economists tend to be skeptical of any attempt to change people's behavior that *doesn't* change their incentives. For example, a plan that calls on manufacturers to reduce pollution voluntarily probably won't be effective; a plan that gives them a financial incentive to reduce pollution is a lot more likely to work.

Individual Choice: Summing It Up

We have just seen that there are four basic principles of individual choice:

- *Resources are scarce.* It is always necessary to make choices.
- *The real cost of something is what you must give up to get it.* All costs are opportunity costs.
- *"How much?" is a decision at the margin.* Usually the question is not "whether," but "how much." And that is a question whose answer hinges on the costs and benefits of doing a bit more.
- *People usually exploit opportunities to make themselves better off.* As a result, people will respond to incentives.

So are we ready to do economics? Not yet—because most of the interesting things that happen in the economy are the result not merely of individual choices but of the way in which individual choices *interact*.

economics in action

A Woman's Work

One of the great social transformations of the twentieth century was the change in the nature of women's work. In 1900, only 6 percent of married women worked for pay outside the home. By the early twenty-first century, the number was about 60 percent.

What caused this transformation? Changing attitudes toward work outside the home certainly played a role: in the first half of the twentieth century, it was often considered improper for a married woman to work outside the home if she could afford not to, whereas today it is considered normal. But an important driving force was the invention and growing availability of home appliances, especially washing machines. Before these appliances became available, housework was an extremely laborious task—much more so than a full-time job. In 1945, government researchers clocked a farm wife as she did the weekly wash by hand; she spent 4 hours washing clothes and 4½ hours ironing, and she walked more than a mile. Then she was equipped with a washing machine; the same wash took 41 minutes, ironing was reduced to 1¾ hours, and the distance walked was reduced by 90 percent.

The point is that in pre-appliance days, the opportunity cost of working outside the home was very high: it was something women typically did only in the face of dire financial necessity. With modern appliances, the opportunities available to women changed—and the rest is history. ∎

> > > > > > > > > > > > > > > > > > >

▶▶CHECK YOUR UNDERSTANDING 1-1

1. Explain how each of the following situations illustrates one of the four principles of individual choice.
   a. You are on your third trip to a restaurant's all-you-can-eat dessert buffet and are feeling very full. Although it would cost you no additional money, you forgo another slice of coconut cream pie but have a slice of chocolate cake.
   b. Even if there were more resources in the world, there would still be scarcity.
   c. Different teaching assistants teach several Economics 101 tutorials. Those taught by the teaching assistants with the best reputations fill up quickly, with spaces left unfilled in the ones taught by assistants with poor reputations.
   d. To decide how many hours per week to exercise, you compare the health benefits of one more hour of exercise to the effect on your grades of one less hour spent studying.

2. You make $45,000 per year at your current job with Whiz Kids Consultants. You are considering a job offer from Brainiacs, Inc., which will pay you $50,000 per year. Which of the following are elements of the opportunity cost of accepting the new job at Brainiacs, Inc.?
   a. The increased time spent commuting to your new job
   b. The $45,000 salary from your old job
   c. The more spacious office at your new job

Solutions appear at back of book.

Interaction: How Economies Work

As we learned in the Introduction, an economy is a system for coordinating the productive activities of many people. In a market economy, such as the one we live in, that coordination takes place without any coordinator: each individual makes his or her own choices. Yet those choices are by no means independent of each other: each individual's opportunities, and hence choices, depend to a large extent on the choices made by other people. So to understand how a market economy behaves, we have to examine this **interaction** in which my choices affect your choices, and vice versa.

When studying economic interaction, we quickly learn that the end result of individual choices may be quite different from what any one individual intends.

For example, over the past century farmers in the United States have eagerly adopted new farming techniques and crop strains that have reduced their costs and increased their yields. Clearly, it's in the interest of each farmer to keep up with the latest farming techniques. But the end result of each farmer trying to increase his or her own income has actually been to drive many farmers out of business. Because American farmers have been so successful at producing larger yields, agricultural

Interaction of choices—my choices affect your choices, and vice versa—is a feature of most economic situations. The results of this interaction are often quite different from what the individuals intend.

TABLE 1-2

Principles That Underlie the Interaction of Individual Choices

1. There are gains from trade.

2. Markets move toward equilibrium.

3. Resources should be used as efficiently as possible to achieve society's goals.

4. Markets usually lead to efficiency.

5. When markets don't achieve efficiency, government intervention can improve society's welfare.

In a market economy, individuals engage in **trade**: They provide goods and services to others and receive goods and services in return.

There are **gains from trade**: people can get more of what they want through trade than they could if they tried to be self-sufficient. This increase in output is due to **specialization**: each person specializes in the task that he or she is good at performing.

---

prices have steadily fallen. These falling prices have reduced the incomes of many farmers, and as a result fewer and fewer people find farming worth doing. That is, an individual farmer who plants a better variety of corn is better off; but when many farmers plant a better variety of corn, the result may be to make farmers as a group worse off.

A farmer who plants a new, more productive corn variety doesn't just grow more corn. Such a farmer also affects the market for corn through the increased yields attained, with consequences that will be felt by other farmers, consumers, and beyond.

Just as there are four economic principles that fall under the theme of choice, there are five principles that fall under the theme of interaction. These five principles are summarized in Table 1-2. We will now examine each of these principles more closely.

There Are Gains from Trade

Why do the choices I make interact with the choices you make? A family could try to take care of all its own needs—growing its own food, sewing its own clothing, providing itself with entertainment, writing its own economics textbooks. But trying to live that way would be very hard. The key to a much better standard of living for everyone is **trade**, in which people divide tasks among themselves and each person provides a good or service that other people want in return for different goods and services that he or she wants.

The reason we have an economy, not many self-sufficient individuals, is that there are **gains from trade**: by dividing tasks and trading, two people (or 6 billion people) can each get more of what they each want than they could get by being self-sufficient. Gains from trade arise, in particular, from this division of tasks, which economists call **specialization**—a situation in which different people each engage in a different task.

The advantages of specialization, and the resulting gains from trade, were the starting point for Adam Smith's 1776 book *The Wealth of Nations*, which many regard as the beginning of economics as a discipline. Smith's book begins with a description of an eighteenth-century pin factory where, rather than each of the 10 workers making a pin from start to finish, each worker specialized in one of the many steps in pin-making:

> One man draws out the wire, another straights it, a third cuts it, a fourth points it, a fifth grinds it at the top for receiving the head; to make the head requires two or three distinct operations; to put it on, is a particular business, to whiten the pins is another; it is even a trade by itself to put them into the paper; and the important business of making a pin is, in this manner, divided into about eighteen distinct operations . . . Those ten persons, therefore, could make among them upwards of forty-eight thousand pins in a day. But if they had all wrought separately and independently, and without any of them having been educated to this particular business, they certainly could not each of them have made twenty, perhaps not one pin a day. . . .

The same principle applies when we look at how people divide tasks among themselves and trade in an economy. *The economy, as a whole, can produce more when each person specializes in a task and trades with others.*

The benefits of specialization are the reason a person typically chooses only one career. It takes many years of study and experience to become a doctor; it also takes many years of study and experience to become a commercial airline pilot. Many doctors might well have had the potential to become excellent pilots, and vice versa;

"I hunt and she gathers—otherwise we couldn't make ends meet."

but it is very unlikely that anyone who decided to pursue both careers would be as good a pilot or as good a doctor as someone who decided at the beginning to specialize in that field. So it is to everyone's advantage that individuals specialize in their career choices.

Markets are what allow a doctor and a pilot to specialize in their own fields. Because markets for commercial flights and for doctors' services exist, a doctor is assured that she can find a flight and a pilot is assured that he can find a doctor. As long as individuals know that they can find the goods and services that they want in the market, they are willing to forgo self-sufficiency and are willing to specialize. But what assures people that markets will deliver what they want? The answer to that question leads us to our second principle of economy-wide interaction.

Markets Move Toward Equilibrium

It's a busy afternoon at the supermarket; there are long lines at the checkout counters. Then one of the previously closed cash registers opens. What happens?

The first thing that happens, of course, is a rush to that register. After a couple of minutes, however, things will have settled down; shoppers will have rearranged themselves so that the line at the newly opened register is about the same length as the lines at all the other registers.

How do we know that? We know from our fourth principle of individual choice that people will exploit opportunities to make themselves better off. This means that people will rush to the newly opened register in order to save time standing in line. And things will settle down when shoppers can no longer improve their position by switching lines—that is, when the opportunities to make themselves better off have all been exploited.

A story about supermarket checkout lines may seem to have little to do with economy-wide interactions, but in fact it illustrates an important principle. A situation in which individuals cannot make themselves better off by doing something different—the situation in which all the checkout lines are the same length—is what economists call an **equilibrium**. An economic situation is in equilibrium when no individual would be better off doing something different.

Recall the story about the mythical Jiffy Lube, where it was supposedly cheaper to leave your car for an oil change than to pay for parking. If that opportunity had

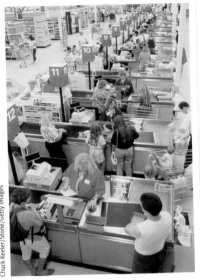

Witness equilibrium in action at the checkout lines in your neighborhood supermarket.

Chuck Keeler/Stone/Getty Images

An economic situation is in **equilibrium** when no individual would be better off doing something different.

---

really existed and people were still paying $30 to park in garages, the situation would *not* have been an equilibrium.

And that should have been a giveaway that the story couldn't be true. In reality, people would have seized an opportunity to park cheaply, just as they seize opportunities to save time at the checkout line. And in so doing they would have eliminated the opportunity! Either it would have become very hard to get an appointment for an oil change or the price of a lube job would have increased to the point that it was no longer an attractive option (unless you really needed a lube job).

As we will see, markets usually reach equilibrium via changes in prices, which rise or fall until no opportunities for individuals to make themselves better off remain.

The concept of equilibrium is extremely helpful in understanding economic interactions because it provides a way of cutting through the sometimes complex details of those interactions. To understand what happens when a new line is opened at a supermarket, you don't need to worry about exactly how shoppers rearrange themselves, who moves ahead of whom, which register just opened, and so on. What you need to know is that any time there is a change, the situation will move to an equilibrium.

The fact that markets move toward equilibrium is why we can depend on them to work in a predictable way. In fact, we can trust markets to supply us with the essentials of life. For example, people who live in big cities can be sure that the supermarket shelves will always be fully stocked. Why? Because if some merchants who distribute food *didn't* make deliveries, a big profit opportunity would be created for any merchant who did—and there would be a rush to supply food, just like the rush to a newly opened cash register. So the market ensures that food will always be available for city dwellers. And, returning to our previous principle, this allows city dwellers to be city dwellers—to specialize in doing city jobs rather than living on farms and growing their own food.

A market economy also allows people to achieve gains from trade. But how do we know how well such an economy is doing? The next principle gives us a standard to use in evaluating an economy's performance.

Resources Should Be Used as Efficiently as Possible to Achieve Society's Goals

Suppose you are taking a course in which the classroom is too small for the number of students—many people are forced to stand or sit on the floor—despite the fact that large, empty classrooms are available nearby. You would say, correctly, that this is no way to run a college. Economists would call this an *inefficient* use of resources.

But if an inefficient use of resources is undesirable, just what does it mean to use resources *efficiently*? You might imagine that the efficient use of resources has something to do with money, maybe that it is measured in dollars-and-cents terms. But in economics, as in life, money is only a means to other ends. The measure that economists really care about is not money but people's happiness or welfare. Economists say that *an economy's resources are used efficiently when they are used in a way that has fully exploited all opportunities to make everyone better off.* To put it another way, an economy is **efficient** if it takes all opportunities to make some people better off without making other people worse off.

In our classroom example, there clearly was a way to make everyone better off—moving the class to a larger room would make people in the class better off without hurting anyone else in the college. Assigning the course to the smaller classroom was an inefficient use of the college's resources, while assigning the course to the larger classroom would have been an efficient use of the college's resources.

When an economy is efficient, it is producing the maximum gains from trade possible given the resources available. Why? Because there is no way to rearrange how resources are used in a way that can make everyone better off. When an economy is efficient, one person can be made better off by rearranging how resources are used *only*

An economy is **efficient** if it takes all opportunities to make some people better off without making other people worse off.

by making someone else worse off. In our classroom example, if all larger classrooms were already occupied, the college would have been run in an efficient way: your class could be made better off by moving to a larger classroom only by making people in the larger classroom worse off by making them move to a smaller classroom.

Should economic policy makers always strive to achieve economic efficiency? Well, not quite, because efficiency is not the only criterion by which to evaluate an economy. People also care about issues of fairness or **equity**. And there is typically a trade-off between equity and efficiency: policies that promote equity often come at a cost of decreased efficiency in the economy, and vice versa.

To see this, consider the case of disabled-designated parking spaces in public parking lots. Many people have great difficulty walking due to age or disability, so it seems only fair to assign closer parking spaces specifically for their use. You may have noticed, however, that a certain amount of inefficiency is involved. To make sure that there is always an appropriate space available should a disabled person want one, there are typically quite a number of disabled-designated spaces. So at any one time there are typically more such spaces available than there are disabled people who want one. As a result, desirable parking spaces are unused. (And the temptation for non-disabled people to use them is so great that we must be dissuaded by fear of getting a ticket.) So, short of hiring parking valets to allocate spaces, there is a conflict between *equity*, making life "fairer" for disabled people, and *efficiency*, making sure that all opportunities to make people better off have been fully exploited by never letting close-in parking spaces go unused.

Exactly how far policy makers should go in promoting equity over efficiency is a very difficult question that goes to the heart of the political process. As such, it is not a question that economists can answer. What is important for economists, however, is to always seek to use the economy's resources as efficiently as possible in the pursuit of society's goals, whatever those goals may be.

> **Equity** means that everyone gets his or her fair share. Since people can disagree about what's "fair," equity isn't as well-defined a concept as efficiency.

Markets Usually Lead to Efficiency

No branch of the U.S. government is entrusted with ensuring the general economic efficiency of our market economy—we don't have agents who go around making sure that brain surgeons aren't plowing fields, that Minnesota farmers aren't trying to grow oranges, that prime beachfront property isn't taken up by used-car dealerships, that colleges aren't wasting valuable classroom space. The government doesn't need to enforce efficiency because in most cases the invisible hand does the job.

In other words, the incentives built into a market economy already ensure that resources are usually put to good use, that opportunities to make people better off are not wasted. If a college were known for its habit of crowding students into small classrooms while large classrooms go unused, it would soon find its enrollment dropping, putting the jobs of its administrators at risk. The "market" for college students would respond in a way that induces administrators to run the college efficiently.

A detailed explanation of why markets are usually very good at making sure that resources are used well will have to wait until we have studied how markets actually work. But the most basic reason is that in a market economy, in which individuals are free to choose what to consume and what to produce, opportunities for mutual gain are normally taken. If there is a way in which some people can be made better off, people will usually be able to take advantage of that opportunity. And that is exactly what defines efficiency: all the opportunities to make everyone better off have been exploited.

As we learned in the Introduction, however, there are exceptions to this principle that markets are generally efficient. In cases of *market failure*, the individual pursuit of self-interest found in markets makes society worse off—that is, the market outcome is inefficient. And, as we will see in examining the next principle, when markets fail, government intervention can help. But short of instances of market failure, the general rule is that markets are a remarkably good way of organizing an economy.

When Markets Don't Achieve Efficiency, Government Intervention Can Improve Society's Welfare

Let's recall from the Introduction the nature of the market failure caused by traffic congestion—a commuter driving to work has no incentive to take into account the cost that his or her action inflicts on other drivers in the form of increased traffic congestion. There are several possible remedies to this situation; examples include charging road tolls, subsidizing the cost of public transportation, or taxing sales of gasoline to individual drivers. All these remedies work by changing the incentives of would-be drivers—motivating them to drive less and use alternative transportation. But they also share another feature: each relies on government intervention in the market.

This brings us to our fifth and last principle of interaction: *When markets don't achieve efficiency, government intervention can improve society's welfare.* That is, when markets go wrong, an appropriately designed government policy can sometimes move society closer to an efficient outcome by changing how society's resources are used.

A very important branch of economics is devoted to studying why markets fail and what policies should be adopted to improve social welfare. We will study these problems and their remedies in depth in later chapters, but here we give a brief overview of why markets fail. They fail for three principal reasons:

- Individual actions have *side effects* that are not properly taken into account by the market.
- One party prevents mutually beneficial trades from occurring in the attempt to capture a greater share of resources for itself.
- Some goods, by their very nature, are unsuited for efficient management by markets.

An important part of your education in economics is learning to identify not just when markets work but also when they don't work—and to judge what government policies are appropriate in each situation.

economics in action

Restoring Equilibrium on the Freeways

In 1994 a powerful earthquake struck the Los Angeles area, causing several freeway bridges to collapse and thereby disrupting the normal commuting routes of hundreds of thousands of drivers. The events that followed offer a particularly clear example of interdependent decision making—in this case, the decisions of commuters about how to get to work.

In the immediate aftermath of the earthquake, there was great concern about the impact on traffic, since motorists would now have to crowd onto alternative routes or detour around the blockages by using city streets. Public officials and news programs warned commuters to expect massive delays and urged them to avoid unnecessary travel, reschedule their work to commute before or after the rush, or use mass transit. These warnings were unexpectedly effective. In fact, so many people heeded them that in the first few days following the quake, those who maintained their regular commuting routine actually found the drive to and from work faster than before.

Of course, this situation could not last. As word spread that traffic was actually not bad at all, people abandoned their less convenient new commuting methods and reverted to their cars—and traffic got steadily worse. Within a few weeks after the quake, serious traffic jams had appeared. After a few more weeks, however, the situation stabilized: the reality of worse-than-usual congestion discouraged enough drivers to prevent the nightmare of citywide gridlock from materializing. Los Angeles traffic, in short, had settled into a new equilibrium, in which each commuter was making the best choice he or she could, given what everyone else was doing.

This was not, by the way, the end of the story: fears that the city would strangle on traffic led local authorities to repair the roads with record speed. Within only 18 months after the quake, all the freeways were back to normal, ready for the next one. ■

> > > > > > > > > > > > > > > > > > > >

>>CHECK YOUR UNDERSTANDING 1-2

1. Explain how each of the following situations illustrates one of the five principles of interaction.
   a. Using the college website, any student who wants to sell a used textbook for at least $X is able to sell it to another who is willing to pay $X.
   b. At a college tutoring co-op, students can arrange to provide tutoring in subjects they are good in (like economics) in return for receiving tutoring in subjects they are poor in (like philosophy).
   c. The local municipality imposes a law that requires bars and nightclubs near residential areas to keep their noise levels below a certain threshold.
   d. To provide better care for low-income patients, the city of Tampa has decided to close some underutilized neighborhood clinics and shift funds to the main hospital.
   e. On the college website, books of a given title with approximately the same level of wear and tear sell for about the same price.

2. Which of the following describes an equilibrium situation? Which does not? Explain your answer.
   a. The restaurants across the street from the university dining hall serve better-tasting and cheaper meals than those served at the university dining hall. The vast majority of students continue to eat at the dining hall.
   b. You currently take the subway to work. Although taking the bus is cheaper, the ride takes longer. So you are willing to pay the higher subway fare in order to save time.

Solutions appear at back of book.

>>QUICK REVIEW

- A feature of most economic situations is the *interaction* of choices made by individuals, the end result of which may be quite different than what was intended. In a market economy, this takes the form of *trade* between individuals.
- Individuals interact because there are *gains from trade*. Gains from trade arise from *specialization*.
- Economic situations normally move toward *equilibrium*.
- As far as possible, there should be an *efficient* use of resources to achieve society's goals. But efficiency is not the only way to evaluate an economy; *equity* may also be desirable, and there is often a trade-off between equity and efficiency.
- Markets normally *are* efficient, except for certain well-defined exceptions.
- When markets fail to achieve efficiency, government intervention can improve society's welfare.

• A LOOK AHEAD •

The nine basic principles we have described lie behind almost all economic analysis. Although they can be immediately helpful in understanding many situations, they are usually not enough. Applying the principles to real economic issues takes one more step.

That step is the creation of *models*—simplified representations of economic situations. Models must be realistic enough to provide real-world guidance but simple enough that they allow us to see clearly the implications of the principles described in this chapter. So our next step is to show how models are used to actually do economic analysis.

SUMMARY

1. All economic analysis is based on a short list of basic principles. These principles apply to two levels of economic understanding. First, we must understand how individuals make choices; second, we must understand how these choices interact.

2. Everyone has to make choices about what to do and what *not* to do. **Individual choice** is the basis of economics—if it doesn't involve choice, it isn't economics.

3. The reason choices must be made is that **resources**—anything that can be used to produce something else—are **scarce.** Individuals are limited in their choices by money and time; economies are limited by their supplies of human and natural resources.

4. Because you must choose among limited alternatives, the true cost of anything is what you must give up to get it—all costs are **opportunity costs.**

5. Many economic decisions involve questions not of "whether" but of "how much"—how much to spend on some good, how much to produce, and so on. Such decisions must be taken by performing a **trade-off** *at the margin*—by comparing the costs and benefits of doing a bit more or a bit less. Decisions of this type are called **marginal decisions,** and the study of them, **marginal analysis,** plays a central role in economics.

6. The study of how people *should* make decisions is also a good way to understand actual behavior. Individuals usually exploit opportunities to make themselves better off. If opportunities change, so does behavior: people respond to **incentives.**

7. **Interaction**—my choices depend on your choices, and vice versa—adds another level to economic understanding.

When individuals interact, the end result may be different from what anyone intends.

8. The reason for interaction is that there are **gains from trade:** by engaging in the **trade** of goods and services with one another, the members of an economy can all be made better off. Underlying gains from trade are the advantages of **specialization,** of having individuals specialize in the tasks they are good at.

9. Economies normally move toward **equilibrium**—a situation in which no individual can make himself or herself better off by taking a different action.

10. An economy is **efficient** if all opportunities to make someone better off without making others worse off are taken. Resources should be used as efficiently as possible to achieve society's goals. But efficiency is not the sole way to evaluate an economy: **equity,** or fairness, is also desirable, and there is often a trade-off between equity and efficiency.

11. Markets usually lead to efficiency, with some well-defined exceptions.

12. When markets fail and do not achieve efficiency, government intervention can improve society's welfare.

KEY TERMS

Individual choice, p. 6
Resource, p. 6
Scarce, p. 6
Opportunity cost, p. 7
Trade-off, p. 8

Marginal decisions, p. 9
Marginal analysis, p. 9
Incentive, p. 9
Interaction, p. 11
Trade, p. 12

Gains from trade, p. 12
Specialization, p. 12
Equilibrium, p. 13
Efficient, p. 14
Equity, p. 15

PROBLEMS

1. In each of the following situations, identify which of the nine principles is at work.

   a. You choose to shop at the local discount store rather than paying a higher price for the same merchandise at the local department store.

   b. On your spring vacation trip, your budget is limited to $35 a day.

   c. The student union provides a website on which departing students can sell items such as used books, appliances, and furniture rather than giving them away to their roommates as they formerly did.

   d. You decide how many cups of coffee to have when studying the night before an exam by considering how much more work you can do by having another cup versus how jittery it will make you feel.

   e. There is limited lab space available to do the project required in Chemistry 101. The lab supervisor assigns lab time to each student based on when that student is able to come.

   f. You realize that you can graduate a semester early by forgoing a semester of study abroad.

   g. At the student union, there is a bulletin board on which people advertise used items for sale, such as bicycles. Once you have adjusted for differences in quality, all the bikes sell for about the same price.

   h. You are better at performing lab experiments, and your lab partner is better at writing lab reports. So the two of you agree that you will do all the experiments, and she will write up all the reports.

   i. State governments mandate that it is illegal to drive without passing a driving exam.

2. Describe some of the opportunity costs when you decide to do the following.

   a. Attend college instead of taking a job

   b. Watch a movie instead of studying for an exam

   c. Ride the bus instead of driving your car

3. Liza needs to buy a textbook for the next economics class. The price at the college bookstore is $65. One online site offers it for $55 and another site for $57. All prices include sales tax. The accompanying table indicates the typical shipping and handling charges for the textbook ordered online.

   a. What is the opportunity cost of buying online?

   b. Show the relevant choices for this student. What determines which of these options the student will choose?

Shipping method	Delivery time	Charge
Standard shipping	3–7 days	$3.99
Second-day air	2 business days	$8.98
Next-day air	1 business day	$13.98

4. Use the concept of opportunity cost to explain the following.

   a. More people choose to get graduate degrees when the job market is poor.

   b. More people choose to do their own home repairs when the economy is slow.

   c. There are more parks in suburban areas than in urban areas.

d. Convenience stores, which have higher prices than super-markets, cater to busy people.

e. Fewer students enroll in classes that meet before 10:00 A.M.

5. In the following examples, state how you would use the principle of marginal analysis to make a decision.

a. Deciding how many days to wait before doing your laundry

b. Deciding how much library research to do before writing your term paper

c. Deciding how many bags of chips to eat

d. Deciding how many lectures of a class to skip

6. This morning you made the following individual choices: you bought a bagel and coffee at the local café, you drove to school in your car during rush hour, and you typed your roommate's term paper because you are a fast typist—in return for which she will do your laundry for a month. In each of these actions, describe how your individual choices interacted with the individual choices made by others. Were other people left better off or worse off by your choices in each case?

7. On the east side of the Hatatoochie River lives the Hatfield family, while the McCoy family lives on the west side. Each family's diet consists of fried chicken and corn-on-the-cob, and each is self-sufficient, raising their own chickens and growing their own corn. Explain the conditions under which each of the following would be true.

a. The two families are made better off when the Hatfields specialize in raising chickens, the McCoys specialize in raising corn, and the two families trade.

b. The two families are made better off when the McCoys specialize in raising chickens, the Hatfields specialize in raising corn, and the two families trade.

8. Which of the following situations describes an equilibrium? Which does not? If the situation does not describe an equilibrium, what would an equilibrium look like?

a. Many people regularly commute from the suburbs to downtown Pleasantville. Due to traffic congestion, the trip takes 30 minutes when you travel by highway, but only 15 minutes when you go by side streets.

b. At the intersection of Main and Broadway are two gas stations. One station charges $3.00 per gallon for regular gas and the other charges $2.85 per gallon. Customers can get service immediately at the first station, but must wait in a long line at the second.

c. Every student enrolled in Economics 101 must also attend a weekly tutorial. This year there are two sections offered: section A and section B, which meet at the same time in adjoining classrooms and are taught by equally competent instructors. Section A is overcrowded, with people sitting on the floor and often unable to see the chalkboard. Section B has many empty seats.

9. In each of the following cases, explain whether you think the situation is efficient or not. If it is not efficient, why not? What actions would make the situation efficient?

a. Electricity is included in the rent at your dorm. Some residents in your dorm leave lights, computers, and appliances on when they are not in their rooms.

b. Although they cost the same amount to prepare, the cafeteria in your dorm consistently provides too many dishes that diners don't like, such as tofu casserole, and too few dishes that diners do like, such as roast turkey with dressing.

c. The enrollment for a particular course exceeds the spaces available. Some students who need to take this course to complete their major are unable to get a space while others who are taking it as an elective do get a space.

10. Discuss the efficiency and equity implications of each of the following policies. How would you go about balancing the concerns of equity and efficiency in these areas?

a. The government pays the full tuition for every college student to study whatever subject he or she wishes.

b. When people lose their jobs, the government provides unemployment benefits until they find new ones.

11. Governments often adopt certain policies in order to promote desired behavior among their citizens. For each of the following policies, determine what the incentive is and what behavior the government wishes to promote. In each case, why do you think that the government might wish to change people's behavior, rather than allow their actions to be solely determined by individual choice?

a. A tax of $5 per pack is imposed on cigarettes.

b. The government pays parents $100 when their child is vaccinated for measles.

c. The government pays college students to tutor children from low-income families.

d. The government imposes a tax on the amount of air pollution that a company discharges.

12. In each of the following situations, explain how government intervention could improve society's welfare by changing people's incentives. In what sense is the market going wrong?

a. Pollution from auto emissions has reached unhealthy levels.

b. Everyone in Woodville would be better off if streetlights were installed in the town. But no individual resident is willing to pay for installation of a streetlight in front of his or her house because it is impossible to recoup the cost by charging other residents for the benefit they receive from it.

>web... To continue your study and review of concepts in this chapter, please visit the Krugman/Wells website for quizzes, animated graph tutorials, web links to helpful resources, and more.

www.worthpublishers.com/krugmanwells

>>Economic Models: Trade-offs and Trade

TUNNEL VISION

IN 1901 WILBUR AND ORVILLE WRIGHT built something that would change the world. No, not the airplane—their successful flight at Kitty Hawk would come two years later. What made the Wright brothers true visionaries was their wind tunnel, an apparatus that let them experiment with many different designs for wings and control surfaces. These experiments gave them the knowledge that would make heavier-than-air flight possible.

A miniature airplane sitting motionless in a wind tunnel isn't the same thing as an actual aircraft in flight. But it is a very useful model of a flying plane—a simplified representation of the real thing that can be used to answer crucial questions, such as how much lift a given wing shape will generate at a given airspeed.

Needless to say, testing an airplane design in a wind tunnel is cheaper and safer than building a full-scale version and hoping it will fly. More generally, models play a crucial role in almost all scientific research—economics very much included.

In fact, you could say that economic theory consists mainly of a collection of models, a series of simplified representations of economic reality that allow us to understand a variety of economic issues.

Clearly, the Wright brothers believed in their model.

In this chapter, we will look at three economic models that are crucially important in their own right and also illustrate why such models are so useful. We'll conclude with a look at how economists actually use models in their work.

What you will learn in this chapter:

➤ Why **models**—simplified representations of reality—play a crucial role in economics

➤ Three simple but important models: the **production possibility frontier, comparative advantage,** and the **circular-flow diagram**

➤ The difference between **positive economics,** which tries to describe the economy and predict its behavior, and **normative economics,** which tries to prescribe economic policy

➤ When economists agree and why they sometimes disagree

Landov Photos

Models in Economics: Some Important Examples

A **model** is any simplified representation of reality that is used to better understand real-life situations. But how do we create a simplified representation of an economic situation?

One possibility—an economist's equivalent of a wind tunnel—is to find or create a real but simplified economy. For example, economists interested in the economic role of money have studied the system of exchange that developed in World War II prison camps, in which cigarettes became a universally accepted form of payment even among prisoners who didn't smoke.

Another possibility is to simulate the workings of the economy on a computer. For example, when changes in tax law are proposed, government officials use *tax models*—large computer programs—to assess how the proposed changes would affect different types of people.

The importance of models is that they allow economists to focus on the effects of only one change at a time. That is, they allow us to hold everything else constant and study how one change affects the overall economic outcome. So the **other things equal assumption**, which means that all other relevant factors remain unchanged, is an important assumption when building economic models.

> A **model** is a simplified representation of a real situation that is used to better understand real-life situations.

> The **other things equal assumption** means that all other relevant factors remain unchanged.

FOR INQUIRING MINDS

MODELS FOR MONEY

What's an economic model worth, anyway? In some cases, quite a lot of money.

Although many economic models are developed for purely scientific purposes, others are developed to help governments make economic policies. And there is a growing business in developing economic models to help corporations make decisions.

Who models for money? There are dozens of consulting firms that use models to predict future trends, offer advice based on their models, or develop custom models for business and government clients. A notable example is Global Insight, the world's biggest economic consulting firm. It was created by a merger between Data Resources, Inc., founded by professors from Harvard and MIT, and Wharton Economic Forecasting Associates, founded by professors at the University of Pennsylvania.

One particularly lucrative branch of economics is finance theory, which helps investors figure out what assets, such as shares in a company, are worth. Finance theorists often become highly paid "rocket scientists" at big Wall Street firms because financial models demand a high level of technical expertise.

Unfortunately, the most famous business application of finance theory came spectacularly to grief. In 1994 a group of Wall Street traders teamed up with famous finance theorists—including two Nobel Prize winners—to form Long-Term Capital Management (LTCM), a fund that used sophisticated financial models to invest the money of wealthy clients. At first, the fund did very well. But in 1998 bad news from all over the world—with countries as disparate as Russia, Japan, and Brazil in trouble at the same time—inflicted huge losses on LTCM's investments. For a few anxious days, many people feared not only that the fund would collapse but also that it would bring many other companies down with it. Thanks in part to a rescue operation organized by government officials, this did not happen; but LTCM was closed a few months later, with some of its investors losing most of the money they had put in.

What went wrong? Partly it was bad luck. But experienced hands also faulted the economists at LTCM for taking too many risks. Their models said that a run of bad news like the one that actually happened was extremely unlikely—but a sensible economist knows that sometimes even the best model misses important possibilities.

But you can't always find or create a small-scale version of the whole economy, and a computer program is only as good as the data it uses. (Programmers have a saying: garbage in, garbage out.) For many purposes, the most effective form of economic modeling is the construction of "thought experiments": simplified, hypothetical versions of real-life situations.

In Chapter 1 we illustrated the concept of equilibrium with the example of how customers at a supermarket would rearrange themselves when a new cash register opens. Though we didn't say it, this was an example of a simple model—an imaginary supermarket, in which many details were ignored (what are the customers buying? never mind), that could be used to answer a "what if" question: what if another cash register were opened?

As the cash register story showed, it is often possible to describe and analyze a useful economic model in plain English. However, because much of economics involves changes in quantities—in the price of a product, the number of units produced, or the number of workers employed in its production—economists often find that using some mathematics helps clarify an issue. In particular, a numerical example, a simple equation, or—especially—a graph can be key to understanding an economic concept.

Whatever form it takes, a good economic model can be a tremendous aid to understanding. The best way to make this point is to consider some simple but important economic models and what they tell us. First, we will look at the *production possibility frontier*, a model that helps economists think about the trade-offs every economy faces. Then we will turn to *comparative advantage*, a model that clarifies the principle of gains from trade—trade both between individuals and between countries. Finally, we'll examine the *circular-flow model*, which helps economists analyze the monetary transactions taking place in the economy as a whole.

In discussing these models, we make considerable use of graphs to represent mathematical relationships. Such graphs will play an important role throughout this book. If you are already familiar with the use of graphs, the material that follows should not present any problem. If you are not, this would be a good time to turn to the appendix of this chapter, which provides a brief introduction to the use of graphs in economics.

Trade-offs: The Production Possibility Frontier

The hit movie *Cast Away*, starring Tom Hanks, was an update of the classic story of Robinson Crusoe, the hero of Daniel Defoe's eighteenth-century novel. Hanks played the sole survivor of a plane crash, stranded on a remote island. As in the original story of Robinson Crusoe, the character played by Hanks had limited resources: the natural resources of the island, a few items he managed to salvage from the plane, and, of course, his own time and effort. With only these resources, he had to make a life. In effect, he became a one-man economy.

The first principle of economics we introduced in Chapter 1 was that resources are scarce and that, as a result, any economy—whether it contains one person or millions of people—faces trade-offs. For example, if a castaway devotes resources to catching fish, he cannot use those same resources to gather coconuts.

To think about the trade-offs that face any economy, economists often use the model known as the **production possibility frontier**. The idea behind this model is to improve our understanding of trade-offs by considering a simplified economy that produces only two goods. This simplification enables us to show the trade-off graphically.

What to do? Even a castaway faces trade-offs.

Figure 2-1 shows a hypothetical production possibility frontier for Tom, a castaway alone on an island, who must make a trade-off between production of fish and production of coconuts. The frontier—the curve in the diagram—shows the maximum number of fish Tom can catch during a week *given* the quantity of coconuts he gathers, and vice versa. That is, it answers questions of the form, "What is the maximum number of fish Tom can catch if he also gathers 20 (or 25, or 30) coconuts?" (We'll explain the bowed-out shape of the curve in Figure 2-1 shortly, after we've seen how to interpret the production possibility frontier.)

There is a crucial distinction between points *inside* or *on* the curve (the shaded area) and *outside* the curve. If a production point lies inside or on the frontier—like the point labeled *C*, at which Tom catches 20 fish and gathers 20 coconuts—it is feasible. After all, the frontier tells us that if Tom catches 20 fish, he could also gather a maximum of 25 coconuts, so he could certainly gather 20 coconuts. On the other hand, a production point that lies outside the frontier—such as the hypothetical production point shown in the figure as point *D*, where Tom catches 40 fish and gathers 30 coconuts—isn't feasible. (In this case, Tom could catch 40 fish and gather no coconuts *or* he could gather 30 coconuts and catch no fish, but he can't do both.)

In Figure 2-1 the production possibility frontier intersects the horizontal axis at 40 fish. This means that if Tom devoted all his resources to catching fish, he would catch 40 fish per week but would have no resources left over to gather coconuts. The production possibility frontier intersects the vertical axis at 30 coconuts; this means that if Tom devoted all his resources to gathering coconuts, he could gather 30 coconuts per week but would have no resources left over to catch fish.

The figure also shows less extreme trade-offs. For example, if Tom decides to catch 20 fish, he is able to gather 25 coconuts; this production choice is illustrated by point *A*. If Tom decides to catch 30 fish, he can gather at most only 20 coconuts, as shown by point *B*.

Thinking in terms of a production possibility frontier simplifies the complexities of reality. The real-world economy produces millions of different goods. Even a castaway on an island would produce more than two different items (for example, he would need clothing and housing as well as food). But in this model we imagine an economy that produces only two goods.

If we simplify reality, however, the production possibility frontier helps us understand some aspects of the real economy better than we could without the model.

The **production possibility frontier** illustrates the trade-offs facing an economy that produces only two goods. It shows the maximum quantity of one good that can be produced for any given quantity produced of the other.

Figure 2-1

The Production Possibility Frontier

The production possibility frontier illustrates the trade-offs facing an economy that produces two goods. It shows the maximum quantity of one good that can be produced given the quantity of the other good produced. Here, the maximum number of coconuts that Tom can gather depends on the number of fish he catches, and vice versa. His feasible production is shown by the area *inside* or *on* the curve. Production at point *C* is feasible but not efficient. Points *A* and *B* are feasible and efficient, but point *D* is not feasible. **>web...**

>web... Throughout our book, this icon will be used to indicate which graphs are available in an interactive format on our text's website. You can work with these interactive graph tutorials and find additional learning resources if you go to www.worthpublishers.com/krugmanwells.

First of all, the production possibility frontier is a good way to illustrate the general economic concept of *efficiency*. Recall from Chapter 1 that an economy is efficient if there are no missed opportunities—there is no way to make some people better off without making other people worse off. A key element of efficiency is that there are no missed opportunities in production—there is no way to produce more of one good without producing less of other goods.

As long as Tom is on the production possibility frontier, his production is efficient. At point *A*, the 25 coconuts he gathers are the maximum number he can get *given* that he has chosen to catch 20 fish; at point *B*, the 20 coconuts he gathers are the maximum he can get *given* his choice to catch 30 fish; and so on.

But suppose that for some reason Tom was at point *C*, producing 20 fish and 20 coconuts. Then this one-person economy would definitely be *inefficient*: it could be producing more of both goods.

The production possibility frontier is also useful as a reminder of the fundamental point that the true cost of any good is not just the amount of money it costs to buy, but everything else in addition to money that must be given up in order to get that good—the *opportunity cost*. If Tom were to catch 30 fish instead of 20, he would be able to gather only 20 coconuts instead of 25. So the opportunity cost of those 10 extra fish is the 5 coconuts not gathered. And if 10 extra fish have an opportunity cost of 5 coconuts, each 1 fish has an opportunity cost of $^5/_{10} = 0.5$ coconuts.

We can now explain the bowed-out shape of the production possibility frontier we saw in Figure 2-1: it reflects an assumption about how opportunity costs change as the mix of output changes. Figure 2-2 shows the same production possibility frontier as Figure 2-1. The arrows in Figure 2-2 illustrate the fact that with this bowed-out production possibility frontier, Tom faces *increasing opportunity cost*: the more fish he catches, the more coconuts he has to give up to catch an additional fish, and vice versa. For example, to go from producing zero fish to producing 20 fish, he has to give up 5 coconuts. That is, the opportunity cost of those 20 fish is 5 coconuts. But to increase his fish production to 40—that is, to produce an additional 20 fish—he must give up 25 more coconuts, a much higher opportunity cost.

Economists believe that opportunity costs are usually increasing. The reason is that when only a small amount of a good is produced, the economy can use

Figure 2-2

Increasing Opportunity Cost

The bowed-out shape of the production possibility frontier reflects increasing opportunity cost. In this example, to produce the first 20 fish, Tom must give up 5 coconuts. But to produce an additional 20 fish, he must give up 25 more coconuts. **>web...**

resources that are especially well suited for that production. For example, if an economy grows only a small amount of corn, that corn can be grown in places where the soil and climate are perfect for corn-growing but less suitable for growing anything else, like wheat. So growing that corn involves giving up only a small amount of potential wheat production. If the economy grows a lot of corn, however, land that isn't so great for corn and would have been well suited for wheat must be pressed into service, so the additional corn production will involve sacrificing considerably more wheat production.

Finally, the production possibility frontier helps us understand what it means to talk about *economic growth*. We introduced the concept of economic growth in the Introduction, defining it as *the growing ability of the economy to produce goods and services*. As we saw, economic growth is one of the fundamental features of the real economy. But are we really justified in saying that the economy has grown? After all, although the U.S. economy produces more of many things than it did a century ago, it produces less of other things—for example, horse-drawn carriages. Production of many goods, in other words, is actually down. So how can we say for sure that the economy as a whole has grown?

The answer, illustrated in Figure 2-3, is that economic growth means an *expansion of the economy's production possibilities*: the economy *can* produce more of everything. For example, if Tom's production is initially at point *A* (20 fish and 25 coconuts), economic growth means that he could move to point *E* (25 fish and 30 coconuts). *E* lies outside the original frontier; so in the production possibility frontier model, growth is shown as an outward shift of the frontier.

What the economy actually produces depends on the choices people make. After his production possibilities expand, Tom might not actually choose to produce both more fish and more coconuts—he might choose to increase production of only one good, or he might even choose to produce less of one good. But even if, for some reason, he chooses to produce either fewer coconuts or fewer fish than before, we would still say that his economy has grown—because he *could* have produced more of everything.

The production possibility frontier is a very simplified model of an economy. Yet it teaches us important lessons about real-life economies. It gives us our first clear sense of a key element of economic efficiency, it illustrates the concept of opportunity cost, and it makes clear what economic growth is all about.

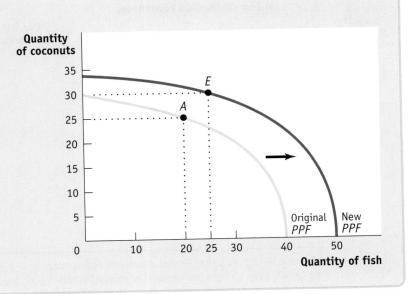

Figure 2-3

Economic Growth

Economic growth results in an *outward shift* of the production possibility frontier because production possibilities are expanded. The economy can now produce more of everything. For example, if production is initially at point *A* (20 fish and 25 coconuts), it could move to point *E* (25 fish and 30 coconuts).

Comparative Advantage and Gains from Trade

Among the nine principles of economics described in Chapter 1 was that of *gains from trade*—the mutual gains that individuals can achieve by specializing in doing different things and trading with one another. Our second illustration of an economic model is a particularly useful model of gains from trade—trade based on *comparative advantage*.

Let's stick with Tom stranded on his island, but now let's suppose that a second castaway, who just happens to be named Hank, is washed ashore. Can they benefit from trading with each other?

It's obvious that there will be potential gains from trade if the two castaways do different things particularly well. For example, if Tom is a skilled fisherman and Hank is very good at climbing trees, clearly it makes sense for Tom to catch fish and Hank to gather coconuts—and for the two men to trade the products of their efforts.

But one of the most important insights in all of economics is that there are gains from trade even if one of the trading parties isn't especially good at anything. Suppose, for example, that Hank is less well suited to primitive life than Tom; he's not nearly as good at catching fish, and compared to Tom even his coconut-gathering leaves something to be desired. Nonetheless, what we'll see is that both Tom and Hank can live better by trading with each other than either could alone.

For the purposes of this example, let's slightly redraw Tom's production possibilities represented by the production possibility frontier in panel (a) of Figure 2-4. According to this diagram, Tom could catch at most 40 fish, but only if he gathered no coconuts, and could gather 30 coconuts, but only if he caught no fish, as before.

In Figure 2-4, we have replaced the curved production possibility frontier of Figure 2-1 with a straight line. Why do this, when we've already seen that economists regard a bowed-out production possibility frontier as normal? The answer is that it simplifies our discussion—and as we have explained, modeling is all about simplification. The principle of comparative advantage doesn't depend on the assumption of straight-line production possibility frontiers, but it is easier to explain with that assumption.

The straight-line production possibility frontier in panel (a) of Figure 2-4 has a *constant slope* of $-\frac{3}{4}$. (The appendix to this chapter explains how to calculate the slope of a line.) That is, for every 4 additional fish that Tom chooses to catch, he

Figure 2-4 **Production Possibilities for Two Castaways**

(a) Tom's Production Possibilities

Quantity of coconuts

Tom's consumption without trade

Tom's PPF

Quantity of fish

(b) Hank's Production Possibilities

Quantity of coconuts

Hank's consumption without trade

Hank's PPF

Quantity of fish

Here, each of the two castaways has a constant opportunity cost of fish and a straight-line production possibility frontier: In Tom's case, each fish always has an opportunity cost of $\frac{3}{4}$ of a coconut. In Hank's case, each fish always has an opportunity cost of 2 coconuts. **>web...**

gathers 3 fewer coconuts. So Tom's opportunity cost of a fish is ¾ of a coconut regardless of how many or how few fish he catches. In contrast, a production possibility frontier is curved when the opportunity cost of a good changes according to how much of the good has already been produced. For example, you can see from Figure 2-2 that if Tom starts at the point of having caught zero fish and gathers 30 coconuts, his opportunity cost of catching 20 fish is 5 coconuts. But once he has already caught 20 fish, the opportunity cost of an additional 20 fish increases to 25 coconuts.

Panel (b) of Figure 2-4 shows Hank's production possibilities. Like Tom's, Hank's production possibility frontier is a straight line, implying a constant opportunity cost of fish in terms of coconuts. His production possibility frontier has a constant slope of −2. Hank is less productive all around: at most he can produce 10 fish or 20 coconuts. But he is particularly bad at fishing; whereas Tom sacrifices ¾ of a coconut per fish caught, for Hank the opportunity cost of a fish is 2 whole coconuts. Table 2-1 summarizes the two castaways' opportunity costs for fish and coconuts.

Now Tom and Hank could go their separate ways, each living on his own side of the island, catching his own fish and gathering his own coconuts. Let's suppose that they start out that way and make the consumption choices shown in Figure 2-4: in the absence of trade, Tom consumes 28 fish and 9 coconuts per week, while Hank consumes 6 fish and 8 coconuts.

But is this the best they can do? No, it isn't. Given that the two castaways have different opportunity costs, they can strike a deal that makes both of them better off.

Table 2-2 shows how such a deal works: Tom specializes in the production of fish, catching 40 per week, and gives 10 to Hank. Meanwhile, Hank specializes in the production of coconuts, gathering 20 per week, and gives 10 to Tom. The result is shown in Figure 2-5 on page 28. Tom now consumes more of both goods than before: instead of 28 fish and 9 coconuts, he consumes 30 fish and 10 coconuts. And Hank also consumes more, going from 6 fish and 8 coconuts to 10 fish and 10 coconuts. As Table 2-2 also shows, both Tom and Hank experience gains from trade: Tom's consumption of fish increases by two, and his consumption of coconuts increases by one. Hank's consumption of fish increases by four, and his consumption of coconuts by two.

So both castaways are better off when they each specialize in what they are good at and trade. It's a good idea for Tom to catch the fish for both of them because his opportunity cost of a fish is only ¾ of a coconut not gathered versus 2 coconuts for Hank. Correspondingly, it's a good idea for Hank to gather coconuts for the both of them.

Or we could put it the other way around: Because Tom is so good at catching fish, his opportunity cost of gathering coconuts is high: ⁴⁄₃ fish not caught for every coconut gathered. Because Hank is a pretty poor fisherman, his opportunity cost of gathering coconuts is much less, only ½ a fish per coconut.

TABLE 2-1

Tom's and Hank's Opportunity Costs of Fish and Coconuts

	Tom's Opportunity Cost	Hank's Opportunity Cost
One fish	3/4 coconut	2 coconuts
One coconut	4/3 fish	1/2 fish

TABLE 2-2

How the Castaways Gain from Trade

		Without Trade		With Trade		Gains from Trade
		Production	Consumption	Production	Consumption	
Tom	Fish	28	28	40	30	+2
	Coconuts	9	9	0	10	+1
Hank	Fish	6	6	0	10	+4
	Coconuts	8	8	20	10	+2

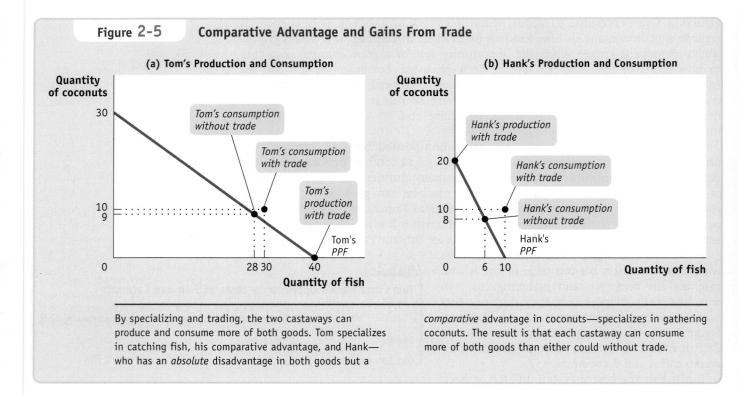

Figure 2-5   **Comparative Advantage and Gains From Trade**

(a) Tom's Production and Consumption

Tom's consumption without trade

Tom's consumption with trade

Tom's production with trade

Tom's PPF

(b) Hank's Production and Consumption

Hank's production with trade

Hank's consumption with trade

Hank's consumption without trade

Hank's PPF

By specializing and trading, the two castaways can produce and consume more of both goods. Tom specializes in catching fish, his comparative advantage, and Hank—who has an *absolute* disadvantage in both goods but a *comparative* advantage in coconuts—specializes in gathering coconuts. The result is that each castaway can consume more of both goods than either could without trade.

An individual has a **comparative advantage** in producing a good or service if the opportunity cost of producing the good is lower for that individual than for other people.

An individual has an **absolute advantage** in an activity if he or she can do it better than other people. Having an absolute advantage is not the same thing as having a comparative advantage.

What we would say in this case is that Tom has a **comparative advantage** in catching fish and Hank has a comparative advantage in gathering coconuts. An individual has a comparative advantage in producing something if the opportunity cost of that production is lower for that individual than for other people. In other words, Hank has a comparative advantage over Tom in producing a particular good or service if Hank's opportunity cost of producing that good or service is lower than Tom's.

The story of Tom and Hank clearly simplifies reality. Yet it teaches us some very important lessons that apply to the real economy, too.

First, the model provides a clear illustration of the gains from trade: by agreeing to specialize and provide goods to each other, Tom and Hank can produce more and therefore both be better off than if they tried to be self-sufficient.

Second, the model demonstrates a very important point that is often overlooked in real-world arguments: as long as people have different opportunity costs, *everyone has a comparative advantage in something, and everyone has a comparative disadvantage in something.*

Notice that in our example Tom is actually better than Hank at producing both goods: Tom can catch more fish in a week, and he can also gather more coconuts. That is, Tom has an **absolute advantage** in both activities: he can produce more output with a given amount of input (in this case, his time) than Hank. You might therefore be tempted to think that Tom has nothing to gain from trading with the less competent Hank.

But we've just seen that Tom can indeed benefit from a deal with Hank because *comparative*, not *absolute*, advantage is the basis for mutual gain. It doesn't matter that it takes Hank more time to gather a coconut; what matters is that for him the opportunity cost of that coconut in terms of fish is lower. So Hank, despite his absolute disadvantage, even in coconuts, has a comparative advantage in coconut-gathering. Meanwhile Tom, who can use his time better by catching fish, has a comparative *disadvantage* in coconut-gathering.

If comparative advantage were relevant only to castaways, it might not be that interesting. In fact, however, the idea of comparative advantage applies to many activities in the economy. Perhaps its most important application is to trade—not between individuals, but between countries. So let's look briefly at how the model of comparative advantage helps in understanding both the causes and the effects of international trade.

Comparative Advantage and International Trade

Look at the label on a manufactured good sold in the United States, and there's a good chance you will find that it was produced in some other country—in China, or Japan, or even in Canada, eh? On the other side, many U.S. industries sell a large fraction of their output overseas (this is particularly true of agriculture, high technology, and entertainment).

Should all this international exchange of goods and services be celebrated, or is it cause for concern? Politicians and the public often question the desirability of international trade, arguing that the nation should produce goods for itself rather than buying them from foreigners. Industries around the world demand protection from foreign competition: Japanese farmers want to keep out American rice, American steelworkers want to keep out European steel. And these demands are often supported by public opinion. Economists, however, have a very positive view of international trade. Why? Because they view it in terms of comparative advantage.

Figure 2-6 shows, with a simple example, how international trade can be interpreted in terms of comparative advantage. Although the example as constructed is hypothetical, it is based on an actual pattern of international trade: American exports of pork to Canada and Canadian exports of aircraft to the United States. Panels (a) and (b) of Figure 2-6 illustrate hypothetical production possibility frontiers for the United States and

Figure 2-6   Comparative Advantage and International Trade

In this hypothetical example, Canada and the United States produce only two goods: pork and aircraft. Aircraft are measured on the vertical axis and pork on the horizontal axis. Panel (a) shows the U.S. production possibility frontier. It is relatively flat, implying that the United States has a comparative advantage in pork production. Panel (b) shows the Canadian production possibility frontier. It is relatively steep, implying that Canada has a comparative advantage in aircraft production. Just like two individuals, both countries gain from specialization and trade. **>web...**

Canada, with pork measured on the horizontal axis and aircraft measured on the vertical axis. The U.S. production possibility frontier is flatter than the Canadian frontier, implying that the United States has a comparative advantage in pork and Canada has a comparative advantage in aircraft.

Although the consumption points in Figure 2-6 are hypothetical, they illustrate a general principle: just like the example of Tom and Hank, the United States and Canada can both achieve mutual gains from trade. If the United States concentrates on producing pork and ships some of its output to Canada, while Canada concentrates on aircraft and ships some of its output to the United States, both countries can consume more than if they insisted on being self-sufficient.

Moreover, these mutual gains don't depend on each country being better at producing one kind of good. Even if one country has, say, higher output per person-hour in both industries—that is, even if one country has an absolute advantage in both industries—there are still mutual gains from trade.

But how does trade actually take place in market interactions? This brings us to our final model, the circular-flow diagram, which helps economists analyze the transactions that take place in a market economy.

Transactions: The Circular-Flow Diagram

The little economy created by Tom and Hank on their island lacks many features of the economy modern Americans live in. For one thing, though millions of Americans are self-employed, most workers are employed by someone else, usually a company with hundreds or thousands of employees. Also, Tom and Hank engage only in the simplest of economic transactions, **barter**, in which an individual directly trades a good or service he or she has for a good or service he or she wants. In the modern economy, simple barter is rare: usually people trade goods or services for money—pieces of colored paper with no inherent value—and then trade those pieces of colored paper for the goods or services they want. That is, they sell goods or services and buy other goods or services.

And they both sell and buy a lot of different things. The U.S. economy is a vastly complex entity, with more than a hundred million workers employed by hundreds of thousands of companies, producing millions of different goods and services. Yet you can learn some very important things about the economy by considering the simple model shown in Figure 2-7, the **circular-flow diagram.** This diagram represents the transactions that take place in an economy by two kinds of flows around a circle: flows of physical things such as goods, services, labor, or raw materials in one direction, and flows of money that pay for these physical things in the opposite direction. In this case the physical flows are shown in yellow, the money flows in green.

The simplest circular-flow diagram models an economy that contains only two kinds of "inhabitants": **households** and **firms**. A household consists of either an individual or a group of people (usually, but not necessarily, a family) that share their income. A firm is an organization (usually, but not necessarily, a corporation) that produces goods and services for sale—and that employs members of households.

As you can see in Figure 2-7, there are two kinds of markets in this model economy. On one side (here the left side) there are **markets for goods and services** in which households buy the goods and services they want from firms. This produces a flow of goods and services to households and a return flow of money to firms.

On the other side, there are **factor markets**. A **factor of production** is a resource used to produce goods and services. Economists usually use the term *factor of production* to refer to a resource that is not used up in production. For example, workers use sewing machines to convert cloth into shirts; the workers and the sewing machines are factors of production, but the cloth is not. Broadly speaking, the main factors of

Trade takes the form of **barter** when people directly exchange goods or services that they have for goods or services that they want.

The **circular-flow diagram** is a model that represents the transactions in an economy by flows around a circle.

A **household** is a person or a group of people that share their income.

A **firm** is an organization that produces goods and services for sale.

Firms sell goods and services that they produce to households in **markets for goods and services**.

Firms buy the resources they need to produce—**factors of production**—in **factor markets**.

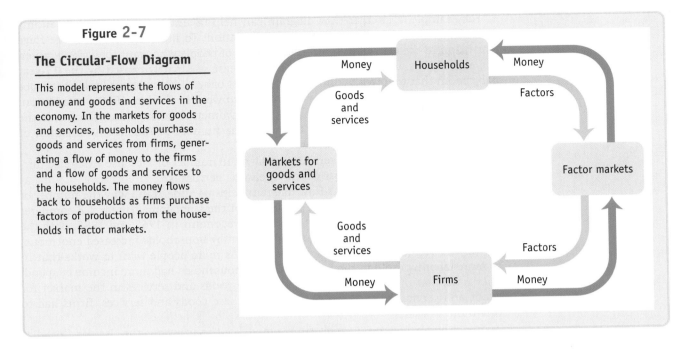

Figure 2-7

The Circular-Flow Diagram

This model represents the flows of money and goods and services in the economy. In the markets for goods and services, households purchase goods and services from firms, generating a flow of money to the firms and a flow of goods and services to the households. The money flows back to households as firms purchase factors of production from the households in factor markets.

production are labor, land, capital, and human capital. Labor is the work of human beings; land is a resource supplied by nature; capital refers to "created" resources such as machines and buildings; and human capital refers to the educational achievements and skills of the labor force, which enhance its productivity. Of course, each of these is really a category rather than a single factor: land in North Dakota is quite different from land in Florida.

The factor market most of us know best is the *labor market*, in which workers are paid for their time. Besides labor, we can think of households as owning and selling the other factors of production to firms. For example, when a corporation pays dividends to its stockholders, who are members of households, it is in effect paying them for the use of the machines and buildings that ultimately belong to those investors.

In what sense is Figure 2-7 a model? That is, in what sense is it a *simplified* representation of reality? The answer is that this picture ignores a number of real-world complications. A few examples:

■ In the real world, the distinction between firms and households isn't always that clear-cut. Consider a small, family-run business—a farm, a shop, a small hotel. Is this a firm or a household? A more complete picture would include a separate box for family businesses.

■ Many of the sales firms make are not to households but to other firms; for example, steel companies sell mainly to other companies such as auto manufacturers, not to households. A more complete picture would include these flows of goods and money within the business sector.

■ The figure doesn't show the government, which in the real world diverts quite a lot of money out of the circular flow in the form of taxes but also injects a lot of money back into the flow in the form of spending.

Figure 2-7, in other words, is by no means a complete picture either of all the types of "inhabitants" of the real economy or of all the flows of money and physical items that take place among these inhabitants.

Despite its simplicity, the circular-flow diagram, like any good economic model, is a very useful aid to thinking about the economy.

For example, a circular-flow diagram can help us understand how the economy manages to provide jobs for a growing population. To illustrate, consider the huge expansion in the U.S. labor force—the number of people who want to work—between the early 1960s and the late 1980s. This increase was partly caused by the 15-year baby boom that followed World War II; the first baby boomers began looking for jobs in the early 1960s and the last of them went to work in the late 1980s. In addition, social changes led a much higher fraction of women to seek paid work outside the home. As a result, between 1962 and 1988 the number of Americans employed or seeking jobs increased by 71 percent.

That's a lot of new job seekers. But luckily, the number of jobs also expanded during the same period, by almost exactly the same percentage.

Or was it luck? The circular-flow diagram helps us understand why the number of jobs available grew along with the expansion of the labor force. Figure 2-8 compares the money flows around the circle for the U.S. economy in 1962 and 1988. Both the money paid to households and the money spent by households increased enormously over the period—and that was no accident. As more people went to work—that is, as more labor was sold in the factor markets—households had more income to spend. They used that increased income to buy more goods and services in the market for goods and services. And in order to produce these goods and services, firms had to hire more workers!

So, despite being an extremely simple model of the economy, the circular-flow diagram helps us to understand some important facts about the real U.S. economy. The number of jobs isn't fixed, the model tells us, because it depends on how much households spend; and the amount households spend depends on how many people are working. It is, in other words, no accident that the economy somehow creates enough jobs even when the working population grows rapidly.

Figure 2-8 **Growth in the U.S. Economy from 1962 to 1988**

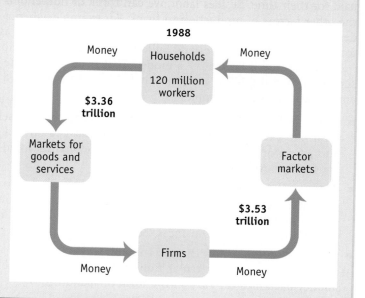

These two circular-flow diagrams—one corresponding to 1962, the other corresponding to 1988—help us understand how the U.S. economy was able to produce enough jobs for its rapidly growing labor force. A roughly twofold increase in the number of workers from 1962 to 1988 was accompanied by a ninefold increase in money flows between households and firms. As the labor force grew, money going to households increased and their spending on goods and services increased. This led firms to hire more workers to meet the increased desire for goods and services and generated more jobs for households.

economics in action

Rich Nation, Poor Nation

Try taking off your clothes—at a suitable time and in a suitable place, of course—and take a look at the labels inside that say where they were made. It's a very good bet that much, if not most, of your clothing was manufactured overseas, in a country that is much poorer than the United States—say, in El Salvador, Sri Lanka, or Bangladesh.

Why are these countries so much poorer than we are? The immediate reason is that their economies are much less *productive*—firms in these countries are just not able to produce as much from a given quantity of resources as comparable firms in the United States or other wealthy countries. Why countries differ so much in productivity is a deep question—indeed, one of the main questions that preoccupy economists. But in any case, the difference in productivity is a fact.

But if the economies of these countries are so much less productive than ours, how is it that they make so much of our clothing? Why don't we do it for ourselves?

The answer is "comparative advantage." Just about every industry in Bangladesh is much less productive than the corresponding industry in the United States. But the productivity difference between rich and poor countries varies across goods; it is very large in the production of sophisticated goods like aircraft but not that large in the production of simpler goods like clothing. So Bangladesh's position with regard to clothing production is like Hank's position with respect to coconut gathering: he's not as good at it as his fellow castaway, but it's the thing he does comparatively well.

The point is that Bangladesh, though it is at an absolute disadvantage compared with the United States in almost everything, has a comparative advantage in clothing production. This means that both the United States and Bangladesh are able to consume more because they specialize in producing different things, with Bangladesh supplying our clothing and the United States supplying Bangladesh with more sophisticated goods. ∎

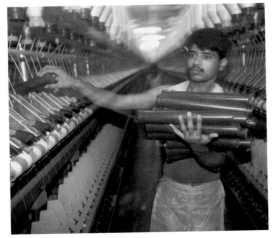

Although less productive than American workers, Bengali workers have a comparative advantage in clothing production.

> > > > > > > > > > > > > > > > > > >

>>CHECK YOUR UNDERSTANDING 2-1

1. True or false? Explain your answer.
   a. An increase in the amount of resources available to Tom for use in producing coconuts and fish does not change his production possibility frontier.
   b. A technological change that allows Tom to catch more fish for any amount of coconuts gathered results in a change in his production possibility frontier.
   c. The production possibility frontier is useful because it illustrates how much of one good an economy must give up to get more of another good regardless of whether resources are being used efficiently.

2. In Italy, an automobile can be produced by 8 workers in one day and a washing machine by 3 workers in one day. In the United States, an automobile can be produced by 6 workers in one day, and a washing machine by 2 workers in one day.
   a. Which country has an absolute advantage in the production of automobiles? In washing machines?
   b. Which country has a comparative advantage in the production of washing machines? In automobiles?
   c. What pattern of specialization results in the greatest gains from trade between the two countries?

3. Use the circular-flow diagram to explain how an increase in the amount of money spent by households results in an increase in the number of jobs in the economy. Describe in words what the circular-flow model predicts.

Solutions appear at back of book.

Using Models

Economics, we have now learned, is mainly a matter of creating models that draw on a set of basic principles but add some more specific assumptions that allow the modeler to apply those principles to a particular situation. But what do economists actually *do* with their models?

Positive versus Normative Economics

Imagine that you are an economic adviser to the governor of your state. What kinds of questions might the governor ask you to answer?

Well, here are three possible questions:

1. How much revenue will the tolls on the state turnpike yield next year?

2. How much would that revenue increase if the toll were raised from $1 to $1.50?

3. Should the toll be raised, bearing in mind that a toll increase will reduce traffic and air pollution near the road but will impose some financial hardship on frequent commuters?

There is a big difference between the first two questions and the third one. The first two are questions about facts. Your forecast of next year's toll collection will be proved right or wrong when the numbers actually come in. Your estimate of the impact of a change in the toll is a little harder to check—revenue depends on other factors besides the toll, and it may be hard to disentangle the causes of any change in revenue. Still, in principle there is only one right answer.

But the question of whether tolls should be raised may not have a "right" answer—two people who agree on the effects of a higher toll could still disagree about whether raising the toll is a good idea. For example, someone who lives near the turnpike but doesn't commute on it will care a lot about noise and air pollution but not so much about commuting costs. A regular commuter who doesn't live near the turnpike will have the opposite priorities.

This example highlights a key distinction between two roles of economic analysis. Analysis that tries to answer questions about the way the world works, which have definite right and wrong answers, is known as **positive economics**. In contrast, analysis that involves saying how the world *should* work is known as **normative economics**. To put it another way, positive economics is about description, normative economics is about prescription.

Positive economics occupies most of the time and effort of the economics profession. And models play a crucial role in almost all positive economics. As we mentioned earlier, the U.S. government uses a computer model to assess proposed changes in national tax policy, and many state governments have similar models to assess the effects of their own tax policy.

It's worth noting that there is a subtle but important difference between the first and second questions we imagined the governor asking. Question 1 asked for a simple prediction about next year's revenue—a **forecast**. Question 2 was a "what if" question, asking how revenue would change if the tax law were to change. Economists are often called upon to answer both types of questions, but models are especially useful for answering "what if" questions.

The answers to such questions often serve as a guide to policy, but they are still predictions, not prescriptions. That is, they tell you what will happen if a policy is changed; they don't tell you whether that result is good or not. Suppose that your economic model tells you that the governor's proposed increase in highway tolls will raise property values in communities near the road but will hurt those people who must use the turnpike to get to work. Does that make this proposed toll increase a good idea or a bad one? It depends on whom you ask. As we've just seen, someone who is very concerned with the communities near the road will support the increase, but someone who is very concerned with the welfare of drivers will feel differently. That's a value judgment—it's not a question of economic analysis.

Positive economics is the branch of economic analysis that describes the way the economy actually works.
Normative economics makes prescriptions about the way the economy *should* work.

A **forecast** is a simple prediction of the future.

Still, economists often do end up giving policy advice. That is, they do engage in normative economics. How can they do this when there may be no "right" answer?

One answer is that economists are also citizens, and we all have our opinions. But economic analysis can often be used to show that some policies are clearly better than others, regardless of anyone's opinions.

Suppose that policy A makes everyone better off than policy B—or at least makes some people better off without making other people worse off. Then A is clearly more efficient than B. That's not a value judgment: we're talking about how best to achieve a goal, not about the goal itself.

For example, two different policies have been used to help low-income families obtain housing: rent control, which limits the rents landlords are allowed to charge, and rent subsidies, which provide families with additional money to pay rent. Almost all economists agree that subsidies are the more efficient policy. (In Chapter 4 we'll see why this is so.) And so the great majority of economists, whatever their personal politics, favor subsidies over rent control.

When policies can be clearly ranked in this way, then economists generally agree. But it is no secret that economists sometimes disagree. Why does this happen?

When and Why Economists Disagree

Economists have a reputation for arguing with each other. Where does this reputation come from?

One important answer is that media coverage tends to exaggerate the real differences in views among economists. If nearly all economists agree on an issue—for example, the proposition that rent controls lead to housing shortages—reporters and editors are likely to conclude that there is no story worth covering, and so the professional consensus tends to go unreported. But when there is some issue on which prominent economists take opposing sides—for example, whether cutting taxes right now would help the economy—that does make a good news story. So you hear much more about the areas of disagreement within economics than you do about the large areas of agreement.

It is also worth remembering that economics is, unavoidably, often tied up in politics. On a number of issues powerful interest groups know what opinions they want to hear; they therefore have an incentive to find and promote economists who profess those opinions, giving these economists a prominence and visibility out of proportion to their support among their colleagues.

But although the appearance of disagreement among economists exceeds the reality, it remains true that economists often *do* disagree about important things. For example, some very respected economists argue vehemently that the U.S. government should replace the income tax with a *value-added tax* (a national sales tax, which is the main source of government revenue in many European countries). Other equally respected economists disagree. Why this difference of opinion?

One important source of differences is in values: as in any diverse group of individuals, reasonable people can differ. In comparison to an income tax, a value-added tax typically falls more heavily on people of modest means. So an economist who values a society with more social and income equality for its own sake will tend to oppose a value-added tax. An economist with different values will be less likely to oppose it.

A second important source of differences arises from economic modeling. Because economists base their conclusions on models, which are simplified representations of reality, two economists can legitimately disagree about which simplifications are appropriate—and therefore arrive at different conclusions.

THE GLASS IS HALF FULL.

HALF EMPTY.

ECONOMISTS

TOLES   UNIVERSAL PRESS SYND.
8 ©2001 THE BUFFALO NEWS

THE CONSUMER IS HALF ALIVE.

FOR INQUIRING MINDS

WHEN ECONOMISTS AGREE

"If all the economists in the world were laid end to end, they still couldn't reach a conclusion." So goes one popular economist joke. But do economists really disagree that much?

Not according to a classic survey of members of the American Economic Association, reported in the May 1992 issue of the *American Economic Review*. The authors asked respondents to agree or disagree with a number of statements about the economy; what they found was a high level of agreement among professional economists on many of the statements. At the top, with more than 90 percent of the economists agreeing, were "Tariffs and import quotas usually reduce gen-

eral economic welfare" and "A ceiling on rents reduces the quantity and quality of housing available." What's striking about these two statements is that many non-economists disagree: tariffs and import quotas to keep out foreign-produced goods are favored by many voters, and proposals to do away with rent control in cities like New York and San Francisco have met fierce political opposition.

So is the stereotype of quarreling economists a myth? Not entirely: economists do disagree quite a lot on some issues, especially in macroeconomics. But there is a large area of common ground.

Suppose that the U.S. government were considering introducing a value-added tax. Economist A may rely on a model that focuses on the administrative costs of tax systems—that is, the costs of monitoring, processing papers, collecting the tax, and so on. This economist might then point to the well-known high costs of administering a value-added tax and argue against the change. But Economist B may think that the right way to approach the question is to ignore the administrative costs and focus on how the proposed law would change savings behavior. This economist might point to studies suggesting that value-added taxes promote higher consumer saving, a desirable result.

Because the economists have used different models—that is, made different simplifying assumptions—they arrive at different conclusions. And so the two economists may find themselves on different sides of the issue.

Most such disputes are eventually resolved by the accumulation of evidence showing which of the various models proposed by economists does a better job of fitting the facts. However, in economics as in any science, it can take a long time before research settles important disputes—decades, in some cases. And since the economy is always changing, in ways that make old models invalid or raise new policy questions, there are always new issues on which economists disagree. The policy maker must then decide which economist to believe.

The important point is that economic analysis is a method, not a set of conclusions.

economics in action

Economists in Government

Many economists are mainly engaged in teaching and research. But quite a few economists have a more direct hand in events.

As described in For Inquiring Minds on page 21, economists play a significant role in the business world, especially in the financial industry. But the most striking involvement of economists in the "real" world is their extensive participation in government.

This shouldn't be surprising: One of the most important functions of government is to make economic policy, and almost every government policy decision must take economic effects into consideration. So governments around the world employ economists in a variety of roles.

In the U.S. government, a key role is played by the Council of Economic Advisers, a branch of the Executive Office (that is, the staff of the president) whose sole purpose is to advise the White House on economic matters and to prepare the annual *Economic Report of the President*. Unusually for a government agency, most of the economists at the Council are not long-term civil servants; instead, they are mainly professors on leave for one or two years from their universities. Many of the nation's best-known economists have served on the Council of Economic Advisers at some point during their careers.

Economists also play an important role in many other parts of the U.S. government. Indeed, as the Bureau of Labor Statistics *Occupational Outlook Handbook* says, "Some economists work in almost every area of government." Needless to say, the Bureau of Labor Statistics is itself a major employer of economists.

It's also worth noting that economists play an especially important role in two international organizations headquartered in Washington, D.C.: the International Monetary Fund, which provides advice and loans to countries experiencing economic difficulties, and the World Bank, which provides advice and loans to promote long-term economic development.

Do all these economists in government disagree with each other all the time? Are their positions largely dictated by political affiliation? The answer to both questions is no. Although there are important disputes over economic issues in government, and politics inevitably plays some role, there is broad agreement among economists on many issues, and most economists in government try very hard to assess issues as objectively as possible. ■

> > > > > > > > > > > > > > > > > > >

>>CHECK YOUR UNDERSTANDING 2-2

1. Which of the following statements is a positive statement? Which is a normative statement?
   a. Society should take measures to prevent people from engaging in dangerous personal behavior.
   b. People who engage in dangerous personal behavior impose higher costs on society through higher medical costs.

2. True or false? Explain your answer.
   a. Policy choice A and policy choice B attempt to achieve the same social goal. Policy choice A, however, results in a much less efficient use of resources than policy choice B. Therefore economists are more likely to agree on choosing policy choice B.
   b. When two economists disagree on the desirability of a policy, it's typically because one of them has made a mistake.
   c. Policy makers can always use economics to figure out which goals a society should try to achieve.

Solutions appear at back of book.

• A LOOK AHEAD •

This chapter has given you a first view of what it means to do economics, starting with the general idea of models as a way to make sense of a complicated world and then moving on to three simple introductory models.

To get a real sense of how economic analysis works, however, and to show just how useful such analysis can be, we need to move on to a more powerful model. In the next two chapters we will study the quintessential economic model, one that has an amazing ability to make sense of many policy issues, predict the effects of many forces, and change the way you look at the world. That model is known as "supply and demand."

SUMMARY

1. Almost all economics is based on **models,** "thought experiments" or simplified versions of reality, many of which use mathematical tools such as graphs. An important assumption in economic models is the **other things equal assumption,** which allows analysis of the effect of a change in one factor by holding all other relevant factors unchanged.

2. One important economic model is the **production possibility frontier.** It illustrates: opportunity cost (showing how much less of one good can be produced if more of the other good is produced); efficiency (an economy is efficient if it produces on the production possibility frontier); and economic growth (an expansion of the production possibility frontier).

3. Another important model is **comparative advantage,** which explains the source of gains from trade between individuals and countries. Everyone has a comparative advantage in something—some good or service in which that person has a lower opportunity cost than everyone else. But it is often confused with **absolute advantage,** an ability to produce a particular good or service better than anyone else. This confusion leads some to erroneously conclude that there are no gains from trade between people or countries.

4. In the simplest economies people **barter**—trade goods and services for one another—rather than trade them for money, as in a modern economy. The **circular-flow diagram** is a model representing transactions within the economy as flows of goods, services, and income between **households** and **firms.** These transactions occur in **markets for goods and services** and **factor markets,** markets for **factors of production** such as labor. It is useful in understanding how spending, production, employment, income, and growth are related in the economy.

5. Economists use economic models for both **positive economics,** which describes how the economy works, and for **normative economics,** which prescribes how the economy should work. Positive economics often involves making **forecasts.** Economists can determine correct answers for positive questions, but typically not for normative questions, which involve value judgments. The exceptions are when policies designed to achieve a certain prescription can be clearly ranked in terms of efficiency.

6. There are two main reasons economists disagree. One, they may disagree about which simplifications to make in a model. Two, economists may disagree—like everyone else—about values.

KEY TERMS

Model, p. 21
Other things equal assumption, p. 21
Production possibility frontier, p. 22
Comparative advantage, p. 28
Absolute advantage, p. 28

Barter, p. 30
Circular-flow diagram, p. 30
Household, p. 30
Firm, p. 30
Markets for goods and services, p. 30

Factor markets, p. 30
Factors of production, p. 30
Positive economics, p. 34
Normative economics, p. 34
Forecast, p. 34

PROBLEMS

1. Atlantis is a small, isolated island in the South Atlantic. The inhabitants grow potatoes and catch fresh fish. The accompanying table shows the maximum annual output combinations of potatoes and fish that can be produced. Obviously, given their limited resources and available technology, as they use more of their resources for potato production, there are fewer resources available for catching fish.

Maximum annual output options	Quantity of potatoes (pounds)	Quantity of fish (pounds)
A	1,000	0
B	800	300
C	600	500
D	400	600
E	200	650
F	0	675

a. Draw a production possibility frontier with potatoes on the horizontal axis and fish on the vertical axis illustrating these options, showing points A–F.

b. Can Atlantis produce 500 pounds of fish and 800 pounds of potatoes? Explain. Where would this point lie relative to the production possibility frontier?

c. What is the opportunity cost of increasing the annual output of potatoes from 600 to 800 pounds?

d. What is the opportunity cost of increasing the annual output of potatoes from 200 to 400 pounds?

e. Can you explain why the answers to parts c and d are not the same? What does this imply about the slope of the production possibility frontier?

2. In the ancient country of Roma, only two goods, spaghetti and meatballs, are produced. There are two tribes in Roma, the Tivoli and the Frivoli. By themselves, the Tivoli each month can produce either 30 pounds of spaghetti and no meatballs,

or 50 pounds of meatballs and no spaghetti, or any combination in between. The Frivoli, by themselves, each month can produce 40 pounds of spaghetti and no meatballs, or 30 pounds of meatballs and no spaghetti, or any combination in between.

a. Assume that all production possibility frontiers are straight lines. Draw one diagram showing the monthly production possibility frontier for the Tivoli and another showing the monthly production possibility frontier for the Frivoli. Show how you calculated them.

b. Which tribe has the comparative advantage in spaghetti production? In meatball production?

In A.D. 100 the Frivoli discover a new technique for making meatballs that doubles the quantity of meatballs they can produce each month.

c. Draw the new monthly production possibility frontier for the Frivoli.

d. After the innovation, which tribe now has the absolute advantage in producing meatballs? In producing spaghetti? Which has the comparative advantage in meatball production? In spaghetti production?

3. Peter Pundit, an economics reporter, states that the European Union (EU) is increasing its productivity very rapidly in all industries. He claims that this productivity advance is so rapid that output from the EU in these industries will soon exceed that of the United States and, as a result, the United States will no longer benefit from trade with the EU.

a. Do you think Peter Pundit is correct or not? If not, what do you think is the source of his mistake?

b. If the EU and the United States continue to trade, what do you think will characterize the goods that the EU exports to the United States and the goods that the United States exports to the EU?

4. You are in charge of allocating residents to your dormitory's baseball and basketball teams. You are down to the last four people, two of whom must be allocated to baseball and two to basketball. The accompanying table gives each person's batting average and free-throw average. Explain how you would use the concept of comparative advantage to allocate the players. Begin by establishing each player's opportunity cost of free throws in terms of batting average.

Name	Batting average	Free-throw average
Kelley	70%	60%
Jackie	50%	50%
Curt	10%	30%
Gerry	80%	70%

Why is it likely that the other basketball players will be unhappy about this arrangement but the other baseball players will be satisfied? Nonetheless, why would an economist say that this is an efficient way to allocate players for your dormitory's sports teams?

5. The economy of Atlantis has developed, and the inhabitants now use money in the form of cowry shells. Draw a circular-flow diagram showing households and firms. Firms produce potatoes and fish, and households buy potatoes and fish. Households also provide the land and labor to firms. Identify where in the flows of cowry shells or physical things (goods and services, or resources) each of the following impacts would occur. Describe how this impact spreads around the circle.

a. A devastating hurricane floods many of the potato fields.

b. A very productive fishing season yields a very large number of fish caught.

c. The inhabitants of Atlantis discover the Macarena and spend several days a month at dancing festivals.

6. An economist might say that colleges and universities "produce" education, using faculty members and students as inputs. According to this line of reasoning, education is then "consumed" by households. Construct a circular-flow diagram like the one found in this chapter to represent the sector of the economy devoted to college education: colleges and universities represent firms, and households both consume education and provide faculty and students to universities. What are the relevant markets in this model? What is being bought and sold in each direction? What would happen in the model if the government decided to subsidize 50 percent of all college students' tuition?

7. Your dormitory roommate plays loud music most of the time; you, however, would prefer more peace and quiet. You suggest that she buy some earphones. She responds that although she would be happy to use earphones, she has many other things that she would prefer to spend her money on right now. You discuss this situation with a friend who is an economics major. The following exchange takes place:

He: How much would it cost to buy earphones?
You: $15.
He: How much do you value having some peace and quiet for the rest of the semester?
You: $30.
He: It is efficient for you to buy the earphones and give them to your roommate. You gain more than you lose; the benefit exceeds the cost. You should do that.
You: It just isn't fair that I have to pay for the earphones when I'm not the one making the noise.

a. Which parts of this conversation contain positive statements and which parts contain normative statements?

b. Compose an argument supporting your viewpoint that your roommate should be the one to change her behavior. Similarly, compose an argument from the viewpoint of your roommate that you should be the one to buy the earphones. If your dormitory has a policy that gives residents the unlimited right to play music, whose argument is likely to win? If your dormitory has a rule that a person must stop playing music whenever a roommate complains, whose argument is likely to win?

8. A representative of the American clothing industry recently made the following statement: "Workers in Asia often work in sweatshop conditions earning only pennies an hour. American workers are more productive and as a result earn higher wages. In order to preserve the dignity of the American workplace, the government should enact legislation banning imports of low-wage Asian clothing."

   a. Which parts of this quote are positive statements? Which parts are normative statements?

   b. Is the policy that is being advocated consistent with the preceding statements about the wages and productivities of American and Asian workers?

   c. Would such a policy make some Americans better off without making any other Americans worse off? That is, would this policy be efficient from the viewpoint of all Americans?

   d. Would low-wage Asian workers benefit from or be hurt by such a policy?

9. Are the following statements true or false? Explain your answers.

   a. "When people must pay higher taxes on their wage earnings, it reduces their incentive to work" is a positive statement.

   b. "We should lower taxes to encourage more work" is a positive statement.

   c. Economics cannot always be used to completely decide what society ought to do.

   d. "The system of public education in this country generates greater benefits to society than the cost of running the system" is a normative statement.

   e. All disagreements among economists are generated by the media.

10. Evaluate the following statement: "It is easier to build an economic model that accurately reflects events that have already occurred than to build an economic model to forecast future events." Do you think that this is true or not? Why? What does this imply about the difficulties of building good economic models?

11. Economists who work for the government are often called on to make policy recommendations. Why do you think it is important for the public to be able to differentiate normative statements from positive statements in these recommendations?

12. The mayor of Gotham City, worried about a potential epidemic of deadly influenza this winter, asks an economic adviser the following series of questions. Does each question require the economic adviser to make a positive assessment or a normative assessment?

   a. How much vaccine will be in stock in the city by the end of November?

   b. If we offer to pay 10 percent more per dose to the pharmaceutical companies providing the vaccines, will they provide additional doses?

   c. If there is a shortage of vaccine in the city, whom should we vaccinate first—the elderly or the very young? (Assume that a person from one group has an equal likelihood of dying from influenza as a person from the other group.)

   d. If the city charges $25 per shot, how many people will pay?

   e. If the city charges $25 per shot, it will make a profit of $10 per shot, money that can go to pay for inoculating poor people. Should the city engage in such a scheme?

13. Assess the following statement: "If economists just had enough data, they could solve all policy questions in a way that maximizes the social good. There would be no need for divisive political debates, such as whether the government should provide free medical care for all."

>web... To continue your study and review of concepts in this chapter, please visit the Krugman/Wells website for quizzes, animated graph tutorials, web links to helpful resources, and more.

www.worthpublishers.com/krugmanwells

Chapter 2 Appendix:
Graphs in Economics

Getting the Picture

Whether you're reading about economics in the *Wall Street Journal* or in your economics textbook, you will see many graphs. Visual images can make it much easier to understand verbal descriptions, numerical information, or ideas. In economics, graphs are the type of visual image used to facilitate understanding. To fully understand the ideas and information being discussed, you need to be familiar with how to interpret these visual aids. This appendix explains how graphs are constructed and interpreted and how they are used in economics.

Graphs, Variables, and Economic Models

One reason to attend college is that a bachelor's degree provides access to higher-paying jobs. Additional degrees, such as MBAs or law degrees, increase earnings even more. If you were to read an article about the relationship between educational attainment and income, you would probably see a graph showing the income levels for workers with different amounts of education. And this graph would depict the idea that, in general, more education increases income. This graph, like most of those in economics, would depict the relationship between two economic variables. A **variable** is a quantity that can take on more than one value, such as the number of years of education a person has, the price of a can of soda, or a household's income.

A quantity that can take on more than one value is called a **variable**.

As you learned in this chapter, economic analysis relies heavily on *models*, simplified descriptions of real situations. Most economic models describe the relationship between two variables, simplified by holding constant other variables that may affect the relationship. For example, an economic model might describe the relationship between the price of a can of soda and the number of cans of soda that consumers will buy, assuming that everything else that affects consumers' purchases of soda stays constant. This type of model can be described mathematically or verbally, but illustrating the relationship in a graph makes it easier to understand. Next we show how graphs that depict economic models are constructed and interpreted.

How Graphs Work

Most graphs in economics are based on a grid built around two perpendicular lines that show the values of two variables, helping you visualize the relationship between them. So a first step in understanding the use of such graphs is to see how this system works.

Two-Variable Graphs

Figure 2A-1 on page 42 shows a typical two-variable graph. It illustrates the data in the accompanying table on outside temperature and the number of sodas a typical vendor can expect to sell at a baseball stadium during one game. The first column shows the values of outside temperature (the first variable) and the second column shows the values of the number of sodas sold (the second variable). Five combinations or pairs of the two variables are shown, each denoted by *A* through *E* in the third column.

Now let's turn to graphing the data in this table. In any two-variable graph, one variable is called the *x*-variable and the other is called the *y*-variable. Here we have made outside temperature the *x*-variable and number of sodas sold the *y*-variable. The solid

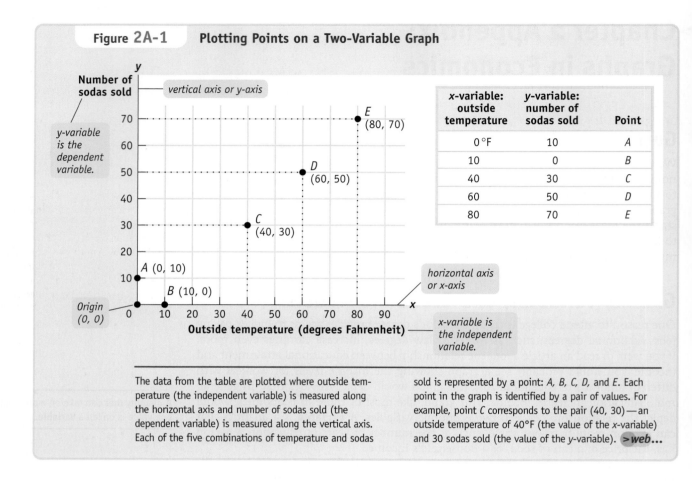

Figure 2A-1	Plotting Points on a Two-Variable Graph

x-variable: outside temperature	y-variable: number of sodas sold	Point
0 °F	10	A
10	0	B
40	30	C
60	50	D
80	70	E

The data from the table are plotted where outside temperature (the independent variable) is measured along the horizontal axis and number of sodas sold (the dependent variable) is measured along the vertical axis. Each of the five combinations of temperature and sodas sold is represented by a point: *A, B, C, D,* and *E.* Each point in the graph is identified by a pair of values. For example, point *C* corresponds to the pair (40, 30)—an outside temperature of 40°F (the value of the *x*-variable) and 30 sodas sold (the value of the *y*-variable). **>web...**

The line along which values of the *x*-variable are measured is called the **horizontal axis** or **x-axis.** The line along which values of the *y*-variable are measured is called the **vertical axis** or **y-axis.** The point where the axes of a two-variable graph meet is the **origin.**

horizontal line in the graph is called the **horizontal axis** or **x-axis,** and values of the *x*-variable—outside temperature—are measured along it. Similarly, the solid vertical line in the graph is called the **vertical axis** or **y-axis,** and values of the *y*-variable—number of sodas sold—are measured along it. At the **origin,** the point where the two axes meet, each variable is equal to zero. As you move rightward from the origin along the *x*-axis, values of the *x*-variable are positive and increasing. As you move up from the origin along the *y*-axis, values of the *y*-variable are positive and increasing.

You can plot each of the five points *A* through *E* on this graph by using a pair of numbers—the values that the *x*-variable and the *y*-variable take on for a given point. In Figure 2A-1, at point *C*, the *x*-variable takes on the value 40 and the *y*-variable takes on the value 30. You plot point *C* by drawing a line straight up from 40 on the *x*-axis and a horizontal line across from 30 on the *y*-axis. We write point *C* as (40, 30). We write the origin as (0, 0).

Looking at point *A* and point *B* in Figure 2A-1, you can see that when one of the variables for a point has a value of zero, it will lie on one of the axes. If the value of *x* is zero, the point will lie on the vertical axis, like point *A*. If the value of *y* is zero, the point will lie on the horizontal axis, like point *B*.

A **causal relationship** exists between two variables when the value taken by one variable directly influences or determines the value taken by the other variable. In a causal relationship, the determining variable is called the **independent variable;** the variable it determines is called the **dependent variable.**

Most graphs that depict relationships between two economic variables represent a **causal relationship,** a relationship in which the value taken by one variable directly influences or determines the value taken by the other variable. In a causal relationship, the determining variable is called the **independent variable;** the variable it determines is called the **dependent variable.** In our example of soda sales, the outside temperature is the independent variable. It directly influences the number of sodas that are sold, the dependent variable in this case.

By convention, we put the independent variable on the horizontal axis and the dependent variable on the vertical axis. Figure 2A-1 is constructed consistent with this convention; the independent variable (outside temperature) is on the horizontal axis and the dependent variable (number of sodas sold) is on the vertical axis. An important exception to this convention is in graphs showing the economic relationship between the price of a product and quantity of the product: although price is generally the independent variable that determines quantity, it is always measured on the vertical axis.

Curves on a Graph

Panel (a) of Figure 2A-2 contains some of the same information as Figure 2A-1, with a line drawn through the points B, C, D, and E. Such a line on a graph is called a **curve,** regardless of whether it is a straight line or a curved line. If the curve that shows the relationship between two variables is a straight line, or linear, the variables have a **linear relationship.** When the curve is not a straight line, or nonlinear, the variables have a **nonlinear relationship.**

A point on a curve indicates the value of the y-variable for a specific value of the x-variable. For example, point D indicates that at a temperature of 60°F, a vendor can expect to sell 50 sodas. The shape and orientation of a curve reveal the general nature of the relationship between the two variables. The upward tilt of the curve in panel (a) of Figure 2A-2 suggests that vendors can expect to sell more sodas at higher outside temperatures.

> A **curve** is a line on a graph that depicts a relationship between two variables. It may be either a straight line or a curved line. If the curve is a straight line, the variables have a **linear relationship.** If the curve is not a straight line, the variables have a **nonlinear relationship.**

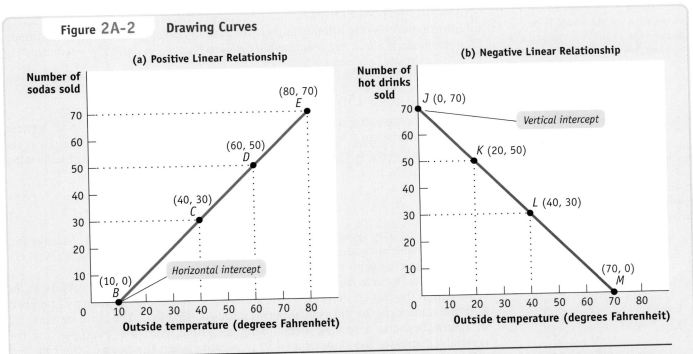

Figure 2A-2   Drawing Curves

(a) Positive Linear Relationship

(b) Negative Linear Relationship

The curve in panel (a) illustrates the relationship between the two variables, outside temperature and number of sodas sold. The two variables have a positive linear relationship: positive because the curve has an upward tilt, and linear because it is a straight line. It implies that an increase in x (outside temperature) leads to an increase in y (number of sodas sold). The curve in panel (b) is also a straight line, but it tilts downward. The two variables

here, outside temperature and number of hot drinks sold, have a negative linear relationship: an increase in x (outside temperature) leads to a decrease in y (number of hot drinks sold). The curve in panel (a) has a horizontal intercept at point B, where it hits the horizontal axis. The curve in panel (b) has a vertical intercept at point J, where it hits the vertical axis and a horizontal intercept at point M, where it hits the horizontal axis. **>web...**

Two variables have a **positive relationship** when an increase in the value of one variable is associated with an increase in the value of the other variable. It is illustrated by a curve that slopes upward from left to right.

Two variables have a **negative relationship** when an increase in the value of one variable is associated with a decrease in the value of the other variable. It is illustrated by a curve that slopes downward from left to right.

The **horizontal intercept** of a curve is the point at which it hits the horizontal axis; it indicates the value of the x-variable when the value of the y-variable is zero.

The **vertical intercept** of a curve is the point at which it hits the vertical axis; it shows the value of the y-variable when the value of the x-variable is zero.

The **slope** of a line or curve is a measure of how steep it is. The slope of a line is measured by "rise over run"— the change in the y-variable between two points on the line divided by the change in the x-variable between those same two points.

When variables are related this way—that is, when an increase in one variable is associated with an increase in the other variable—the variables are said to have a **positive relationship.** It is illustrated by a curve that slopes upward from left to right. Because this curve is also linear, the relationship between outside temperature and number of sodas sold illustrated by the curve in panel (a) of Figure 2A-2 is a positive linear relationship.

When an increase in one variable is associated with a decrease in the other variable, the two variables are said to have a **negative relationship.** It is illustrated by a curve that slopes downward from left to right, like the curve in panel (b) of Figure 2A-2. Because this curve is also linear, the relationship it depicts is a negative linear relationship. Two variables that might have such a relationship are the outside temperature and the number of hot drinks a vendor can expect to sell at a baseball stadium.

Return for a moment to the curve in panel (a) of Figure 2A-2 and you can see that it hits the horizontal axis at point B. This point, known as the **horizontal intercept,** shows the value of the x-variable when the value of the y-variable is zero. In panel (b) of Figure 2A-2 the curve hits the vertical axis at point J. This point, called the **vertical intercept,** indicates the value of the y-variable when the value of the x-variable is zero.

A Key Concept: The Slope of a Curve

The **slope** of a line or curve is a measure of how steep it is and indicates how sensitive the y-variable is to a change in the x-variable. In our example of outside temperature and the number of cans of soda a vendor can expect to sell, the slope of the curve would indicate how many more cans of soda the vendor could expect to sell with each 1° increase in temperature. Interpreted this way, the slope gives meaningful information. Even without numbers for x and y, it is possible to arrive at important conclusions about the relationship between the two variables by examining the slope of a curve at various points.

The Slope of a Linear Curve

Along a linear curve the slope, or steepness, is measured by dividing the "rise" between two points on the curve by the "run" between those same two points. The rise is the amount that y changes, and the run is the amount that x changes. Here is the formula:

$$\frac{\text{Change in } y}{\text{Change in } x} = \frac{\Delta y}{\Delta x} = \text{Slope}$$

In the formula, the symbol Δ (the Greek uppercase delta) stands for "change in." When a variable increases, the change in that variable is positive; when a variable decreases, the change in that variable is negative.

The slope of a curve is positive when the rise (the change in the y-variable) has the same sign as the run (the change in the x-variable). That's because when two numbers have the same sign, the ratio of those two numbers is positive. The curve in panel (a) of Figure 2A-2 has a positive slope: along the curve, both the y-variable and the x-variable increase. The slope of a curve is negative when the rise and the run have different signs. That's because when two numbers have different signs, the ratio of those two numbers is negative. The curve in panel (b) of Figure 2A-2 has a negative slope: along the curve, an increase in the x-variable is associated with a decrease in the y-variable.

Figure 2A-3 illustrates how to calculate the slope of a linear curve. Let's focus first on panel (a). From point A to point B the value of y changes from 25 to 20 and the value of x changes from 10 to 20. So the slope of the line between these two points is:

$$\frac{\text{Change in } y}{\text{Change in } x} = \frac{\Delta y}{\Delta x} = \frac{-5}{10} = -\frac{1}{2} = -0.5$$

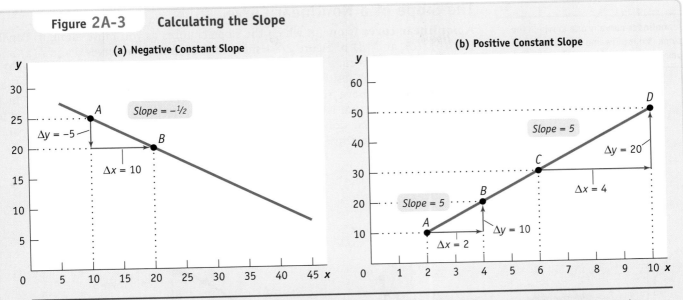

Figure 2A-3   Calculating the Slope

(a) Negative Constant Slope

(b) Positive Constant Slope

Panels (a) and (b) show two linear curves. Between points *A* and *B* on the curve in panel (a), the change in *y* (the rise) is −5 and the change in *x* (the run) is 10. So the slope from *A* to *B* is $\Delta y/\Delta x$ = −5/10 = −½ = −0.5, where the negative sign indicates that the curve is downward sloping. In panel (b), the curve has a slope from *A* to *B* of $\Delta y/\Delta x$ = 10/2 = 5. The slope from *C* to *D* is $\Delta y/\Delta x$ =

20/4 = 5. The slope is positive, indicating that the curve is upward sloping. Furthermore, the slope between *A* and *B* is the same as the slope between *C* and *D*, making this a linear curve. The slope of a linear curve is constant: it is the same regardless of where it is calculated along the curve. **>web...**

Because a straight line is equally steep at all points, the slope of a straight line is the same at all points. In other words, a straight line has a constant slope. You can check this by calculating the slope of the linear curve between points *A* and *B* and between points *C* and *D* in panel (b) of Figure 2A-3.

Between *A* and *B*: $\dfrac{\Delta y}{\Delta x} = \dfrac{10}{2} = 5$

Between *C* and *D*: $\dfrac{\Delta y}{\Delta x} = \dfrac{20}{4} = 5$

Horizontal and Vertical Curves and Their Slopes

When a curve is horizontal, the value of *y* along that curve never changes—it is constant. Everywhere along the curve, the change in *y* is zero. Now, zero divided by any number is zero. So, regardless of the value of the change in *x*, the slope of a horizontal curve is always zero.

If a curve is vertical, the value of *x* along the curve never changes—it is constant. Everywhere along the curve, the change in *x* is zero. This means that the slope of a vertical line is a ratio with zero in the denominator. A ratio with zero in the denominator is equal to infinity—that is, an infinitely large number. So the slope of a vertical line is equal to infinity.

A vertical or a horizontal curve has a special implication: it means that the *x*-variable and the *y*-variable are unrelated. Two variables are unrelated when a change in one of the variables (the independent variable) has no effect on the other variable (the dependent variable). Or to put it a slightly different way, two variables are unrelated when the dependent variable is constant regardless of the value of the independent variable. If, as is usual, the *y*-variable is the dependent variable, the curve is horizontal. If the dependent variable is the *x*-variable, the curve is vertical.

The Slope of a Nonlinear Curve

A **nonlinear curve** is one in which the slope is not the same between every pair of points.

A **nonlinear curve** is one in which the slope changes as you move along it. Panels (a), (b), (c), and (d) of Figure 2A-4 show various nonlinear curves. Panels (a) and (b) show nonlinear curves whose slopes change as you move along them, but the slopes always remain positive. Although both curves tilt upward, the curve in panel (a) gets steeper as you move from left to right in contrast to the curve in panel (b), which gets flatter. A curve that is upward sloping and gets steeper, as in panel (a), is said to have *positive increasing* slope. A curve that is upward sloping but gets flatter, as in panel (b), is said to have *positive decreasing* slope.

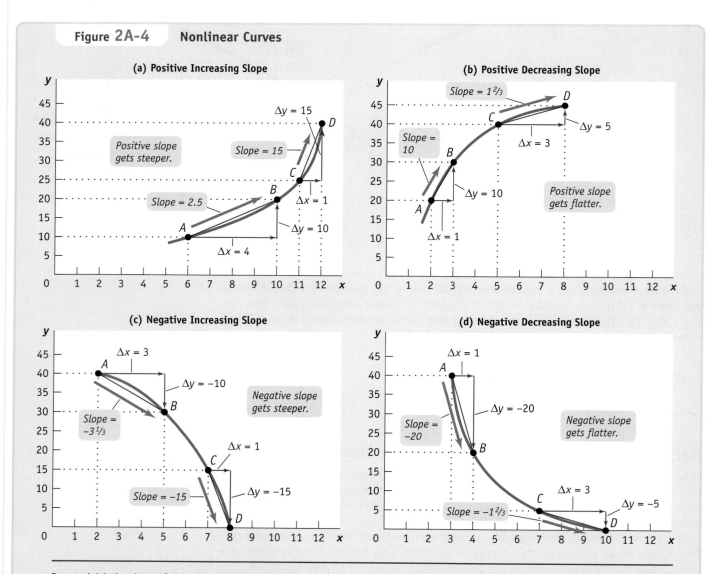

Figure 2A-4   Nonlinear Curves

(a) Positive Increasing Slope

(b) Positive Decreasing Slope

(c) Negative Increasing Slope

(d) Negative Decreasing Slope

In panel (a) the slope of the curve from A to B is $\Delta y/\Delta x = 10/4 = 2.5$, and from C to D it is $\Delta y/\Delta x = 15/1 = 15$. The slope is positive and increasing; it gets steeper as you move to the right. In panel (b) the slope of the curve slope from A to B is $\Delta y/\Delta x = 10/1 = 10$, and from C to D it is $\Delta y/\Delta x = 5/3 = 1\frac{2}{3}$. The slope is positive and decreasing; it gets flatter as you move to the right. In panel (c) the slope from A to B is $\Delta y/\Delta x = -10/3 = -3\frac{1}{3}$, and from C to D it is $\Delta y/\Delta x = -15/1 = -15$. The slope is negative and increasing; it gets steeper as you move to the

right. And in panel (d) the slope from A to B is $\Delta y/\Delta x = -20/1 = -20$, and from C to D it is $\Delta y/\Delta x = -5/3 = -1\frac{2}{3}$. The slope is negative and decreasing; it gets flatter as you move to the right. The slope in each case has been calculated by using the arc method—that is, by drawing a straight line connecting two points along a curve. The average slope between those two points is equal to the slope of the straight line between those two points. **>web...**

When we calculate the slope along these nonlinear curves, we obtain different values for the slope at different points. How the slope changes along the curve determines the curve's shape. For example, in panel (a) of Figure 2A-4, the slope of the curve is a positive number that steadily increases as you move from left to right, whereas in panel (b), the slope is a positive number that steadily decreases.

The slopes of the curves in panels (c) and (d) are negative numbers. Economists often prefer to express a negative number as its **absolute value,** which is the value of the negative number without the minus sign. In general, we denote the absolute value of a number by two parallel bars around the number; for example, the absolute value of −4 is written as $|-4| = 4$. In panel (c), the absolute value of the slope steadily increases as you move from left to right. The curve therefore has *negative increasing* slope. And in panel (d), the absolute value of the slope of the curve steadily decreases along the curve. This curve therefore has *negative decreasing* slope.

> The **absolute value** of a negative number is the value of the negative number without the minus sign.

Calculating the Slope Along a Nonlinear Curve

We've just seen that along a nonlinear curve, the value of the slope depends on where you are on that curve. So how do you calculate the slope of a nonlinear curve? We will focus on two methods: the *arc method* and the *point method*.

The Arc Method of Calculating the Slope An arc of a curve is some piece or segment of that curve. For example, panel (a) of Figure 2A-4 shows an arc consisting of the segment of the curve between points *A* and *B*. To calculate the slope along a nonlinear curve using the arc method, you draw a straight line between the two end-points of the arc. The slope of that straight line is a measure of the average slope of the curve between those two end-points. You can see from panel (a) of Figure 2A-4 that the straight line drawn between points *A* and *B* increases along the *x*-axis from 6 to 10 (so that $\Delta x = 4$) as it increases along the *y*-axis from 10 to 20 (so that $\Delta y = 10$). Therefore the slope of the straight line connecting points *A* and *B* is:

$$\frac{\Delta y}{\Delta x} = \frac{10}{4} = 2.5$$

This means that the average slope of the curve between points *A* and *B* is 2.5.

Now consider the arc on the same curve between points *C* and *D*. A straight line drawn through these two points increases along the *x*-axis from 11 to 12 ($\Delta x = 1$) as it increases along the *y*-axis from 25 to 40 ($\Delta y = 15$). So the average slope between points *C* and *D* is:

$$\frac{\Delta y}{\Delta x} = \frac{15}{1} = 15$$

Therefore the average slope between points *C* and *D* is larger than the average slope between points *A* and *B*. These calculations verify what we have already observed—that this upward-tilted curve gets steeper as you move from left to right and therefore has positive increasing slope.

The Point Method of Calculating the Slope The point method calculates the slope of a nonlinear curve at a specific point on that curve. Figure 2A-5 on page 48 illustrates how to calculate the slope at point *B* on the curve. First, we draw a straight line that just touches the curve at point *B*. Such a line is called a **tangent line:** the fact that it just touches the curve at point *B* and does not touch the curve at any other point on the curve means that the straight line is *tangent* to the curve at point *B*. The slope of this tangent line is equal to the slope of the nonlinear curve at point *B*.

> A **tangent line** is a straight line that just touches, or is tangent to, a nonlinear curve at a particular point. The slope of the tangent line is equal to the slope of the nonlinear curve at that point.

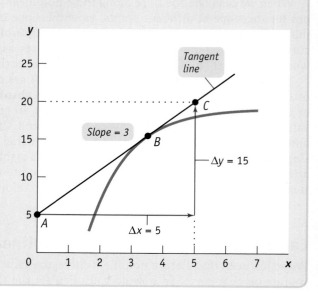

Figure 2A-5

Calculating the Slope Using the Point Method

Here a tangent line has been drawn, a line that just touches the curve at point *B*. The slope of this line is equal to the slope of the curve at point *B*. The slope of the tangent line, measuring from *A* to *C*, is $\Delta y / \Delta x = {}^{15}\!/_5 = 3$. **>web...**

You can see from Figure 2A-5 how the slope of the tangent line is calculated: from point *A* to point *C*, the change in *y* is 15 units and the change in *x* is 5 units, generating a slope of:

$$\frac{\Delta y}{\Delta x} = \frac{15}{5} = 3$$

By the point method, the slope of the curve at point *B* is equal to 3.

A natural question to ask at this point is how to determine which method to use—the arc method or the point method—in calculating the slope of a nonlinear curve. The answer depends on the curve itself and the data used to construct it. You use the arc method when you don't have enough information to be able to draw a smooth curve. For example, suppose that in panel (a) of Figure 2A-4 you have only the data represented by points *A*, *C*, and *D* and don't have the data represented by point *B* or any of the rest of the curve. Clearly, then, you can't use the point method to calculate the slope at point *B*; you would have to use the arc method to approximate the slope of the curve in this area by drawing a straight line between points *A* and *C*. But if you have sufficient data to draw the smooth curve shown in panel (a) of Figure 2A-4, then you could use the point method to calculate the slope at point *B*—and at every other point along the curve as well.

Maximum and Minimum Points

The slope of a nonlinear curve can change from positive to negative or vice versa. When the slope of a curve changes from positive to negative, it creates what is called a *maximum* point of the curve. When the slope of a curve changes from negative to positive, it creates a *minimum* point.

Panel (a) of Figure 2A-6 illustrates a curve in which the slope changes from positive to negative as you move from left to right. When *x* is between 0 and 50, the slope of the curve is positive. At *x* equal to 50, the curve attains its highest point—the largest value of *y* along the curve. This point is called the **maximum** of the curve. When *x* exceeds 50, the slope becomes negative as the curve turns downward. Many important curves in economics, such as the curve that represents how the profit of a firm changes as it produces more output, are hill-shaped like this.

In contrast, the curve shown in panel (b) of Figure 2A-6 is U-shaped: it has a slope that changes from negative to positive. At *x* equal to 50, the curve reaches its lowest

A nonlinear curve may have a **maximum** point, the highest point along the curve. At the maximum, the slope of the curve changes from positive to negative.

Figure 2A-6 **Maximum and Minimum Points**

(a) Maximum

Maximum point

y increases as x increases.

y decreases as x increases.

(b) Minimum

Minimum point

y decreases as x increases.

y increases as x increases.

Panel (a) shows a curve with a maximum point, the point at which the slope changes from positive to negative. Panel (b) shows a curve with a minimum point, the point at which the slope changes from negative to positive.

point—the smallest value of *y* along the curve. This point is called the **minimum** of the curve. Various important curves in economics, such as the curve that represents how the costs of some firms change as output increases, are U-shaped like this.

> A nonlinear curve may have a **minimum** point, the lowest point along the curve. At the minimum, the slope of the curve changes from negative to positive.

Graphs That Depict Numerical Information

Graphs can also be used as a convenient way to summarize and display data without assuming some underlying causal relationship. Graphs that simply display numerical information are called *numerical graphs*. Here we will consider four types of numerical graphs: *time-series graphs, scatter diagrams, pie charts,* and *bar graphs*. These are widely used to display real, empirical data about different economic variables because they often help economists and policy makers identify patterns or trends in the economy. But as we will also see, you must be careful not to misinterpret or draw unwarranted conclusions from numerical graphs. That is, you must be aware of both the usefulness and the limitations of numerical graphs.

Types of Numerical Graphs

You have probably seen graphs in newspapers that show what has happened over time to economic variables such as the unemployment rate or stock prices. A **time-series graph** has successive dates on the horizontal axis and the values of a variable that occurred on those dates on the vertical axis. For example, Figure 2A-7 on page 50 shows the unemployment rate in the United States from 1989 to mid-2004. A line connecting the points that correspond to the unemployment rate for each year gives a clear idea of the overall trend in unemployment over these years.

Figure 2A-8 on page 50 is an example of a different kind of numerical graph. It represents information from a sample of 158 countries on average life expectancy and gross national product (GNP) per capita—a rough measure of a country's standard of living. Each point here indicates an average resident's life expectancy and the log of GNP per capita for a given country. (Economists have found that the log of GNP rather than the simple level of GNP is more closely tied to average life expectancy.) The points

> A **time-series graph** has dates on the horizontal axis and values of a variable that occurred on those dates on the vertical axis.

Figure 2A-7

Time-Series Graph

Time-series graphs show successive dates on the *x*-axis and values for a variable on the *y*-axis. This time-series graph shows the seasonally adjusted unemployment rate in the United States from 1989 to mid-2004.

Source: Bureau of Labor Statistics.

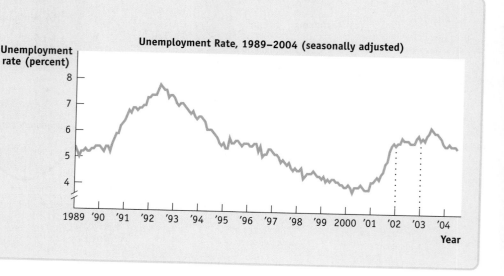

lying in the upper right of the graph, which show combinations of high life expectancy and high log GNP per capita, represent economically advanced countries such as the United States. Points lying in the bottom left of the graph, which show combinations of low life expectancy and low log GNP per capita, represent economically less advanced countries such as Afghanistan and Sierra Leone. The pattern of points indicates that there is a positive relationship between life expectancy and log GNP per capita: on the whole, people live longer in countries with a higher standard of living. This type of graph is called a **scatter diagram,** a diagram in which each point corresponds to an actual observation of the *x*-variable and the *y*-variable. In scatter diagrams, a curve is typically fitted to the scatter of points; that is, a curve is drawn that approximates as closely as possible the general relationship between the variables. As you can see, the fitted curve in Figure 2A-8 is upward sloping, indicating the underlying positive relationship between the two variables. Scatter diagrams are often used to show how a general relationship can be inferred from a set of data.

A **scatter diagram** shows points that correspond to actual observations of the *x*- and *y*-variables. A curve is usually fitted to the scatter of points.

Figure 2A-8

Scatter Diagram

In a scatter diagram, each point represents the corresponding values of the *x*- and *y*-variables for a given observation. Here, each point indicates the observed average life expectancy and the log of GNP per capita of a given country for a sample of 158 countries. The upward-sloping fitted line here is the best approximation of the general relationship between the two variables.

Source: Eduard Bos et al., *Health, Nutrition, and Population Indicators: A Statistical Handbook* (Washington, DC: World Bank, 1999).

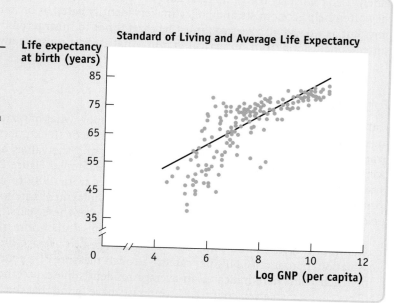

Figure 2A-9

Pie Chart

A pie chart shows the percentages of a total amount that can be attributed to various components. This pie chart shows the percentages of total federal revenues that come from each source.

Source: Executive Office of the President, Office of Management and Budget.

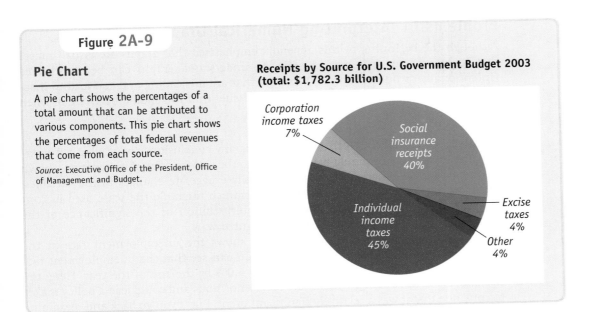

Receipts by Source for U.S. Government Budget 2003 (total: $1,782.3 billion)

A **pie chart** shows the share of a total amount that is accounted for by various components, usually expressed in percentages. For example, Figure 2A-9 is a pie chart that depicts the various sources of revenue for the U.S. government budget in 2003, expressed in percentages of the total revenue amount, $1,782.3 billion. As you can see, social insurance receipts (the revenues collected to fund Social Security, Medicare, and unemployment insurance) accounted for 40% of total government revenue and individual income tax receipts accounted for 45%.

Bar graphs use bars of various heights or lengths to indicate values of a variable. In the bar graph in Figure 2A-10, the bars show the percent change in the number of unemployed workers in the United States from 2001 to 2002, separately for White, Black or African-American, and Asian workers. Exact values of the variable that is being measured may be written at the end of the bar as in this figure. For instance, the number of unemployed Asian workers in the United States increased by 35% between 2001 and 2002. But even without the precise values, comparing the heights or lengths of the bars can give useful insight into the relative magnitudes of the different values of the variable.

A **pie chart** shows how some total is divided among its components, usually expressed in percentages.

A **bar graph** uses bars of varying height or length to show the comparative sizes of different observations of a variable.

Figure 2A-10

Bar Graph

A bar graph measures a variable by using bars of various heights or lengths. This bar graph shows the percent increase in the number of unemployed between 2001 and 2002, separately for White, Black or African-American, and Asian workers.

Source: Bureau of Labor Statistics.

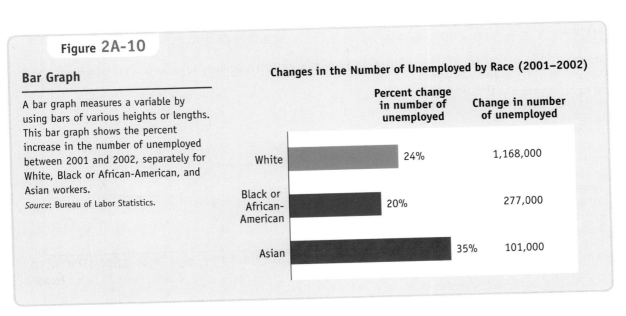

Changes in the Number of Unemployed by Race (2001–2002)

Problems in Interpreting Numerical Graphs

Although the beginning of this appendix emphasized that graphs are visual images that make ideas or information easier to understand, graphs can be constructed (intentionally or unintentionally) in ways that are misleading and can lead to inaccurate conclusions. This section raises some issues that you should be aware of when you interpret graphs.

Features of Construction Before drawing any conclusions about what a numerical graph implies, you should pay attention to the scale, or size of increments, shown on the axes. Small increments tend to visually exaggerate changes in the variables, whereas large increments tend to visually diminish them. So the scale used in construction of a graph can influence your interpretation of the significance of the changes it illustrates—perhaps in an unwarranted way.

Take, for example, Figure 2A-11, which shows the unemployment rate in the United States in 2002 using a 0.1% scale. You can see that the unemployment rate rose from 5.6% at the beginning of 2002 to 6.0% by the end of the year. Here, the rise of 0.4% in the unemployment rate looks enormous and could lead a policy maker to conclude that it was a relatively significant event. But if you go back and reexamine Figure 2A-7, which shows the unemployment rate in the United States from 1989 to 2004, you can see that this would be a misguided conclusion. Figure 2A-7 includes the same data shown in Figure 2A-11, but it is constructed with a 1% scale rather than a 0.1% scale. From it you can see that the rise of 0.4% in the unemployment rate during 2002 was, in fact, a relatively insignificant event, at least compared to the rise in unemployment during 1990 or during 2001. This comparison shows that if you are not careful to factor in the choice of scale in interpreting a graph, you can arrive at very different, and possibly misguided, conclusions.

Related to the choice of scale is the use of *truncation* in constructing a graph. An axis is **truncated** when part of the range is omitted. This is indicated by two slashes (//) in the axis near the origin. You can see that the vertical axis of Figure 2A-11 has been truncated—the range of values from 0 to 5.6 has been omitted and a // appears in the axis. Truncation saves space in the presentation of a graph and allows larger increments to be used in constructing it. As a result, changes in the variable depicted on a graph that has been truncated appear larger compared to a graph that has not been truncated and that uses smaller increments.

An axis is **truncated** when some of the values on the axis are omitted, usually to save space.

Figure 2A-11

Interpreting Graphs: The Effect of Scale

Some of the same data for 2002 used for Figure 2A-7 are represented here, except that here they are shown using 0.1% increments rather than 1% increments. As a result of this change in scale, the rise in the unemployment rate during 2002 looks much larger in this figure compared to Figure 2A-7.

Source: Bureau of Labor Statistics.

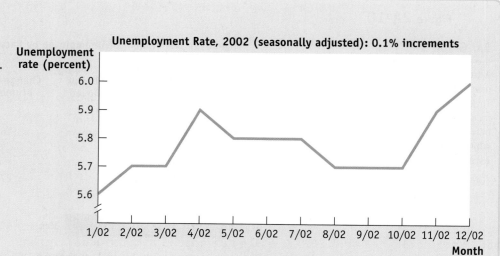

You must also pay close attention to exactly what a graph is illustrating. For example, in Figure 2A-10, you should recognize that what is being shown here are percentage changes in the number of unemployed, not numerical changes. The unemployment rate for Asian workers increased by the highest percentage, 35% in this example. If you confused numerical changes with percentage changes, you would erroneously conclude that the greatest number of newly unemployed workers were Asian. But, in fact, a correct interpretation of Figure 2A-10 shows that the greatest number of newly unemployed workers were white: the total number of unemployed white workers grew by 1,168,000 workers, which is greater than the increase in the number of unemployed Asian workers, which is 101,000 in this example. Although there was a higher percentage increase in the number of unemployed Asian workers, the number of unemployed Asian workers in the United States in 2001 was much smaller than the number of unemployed white workers, leading to a smaller number of newly unemployed Asian workers than white workers.

Omitted Variables   From a scatter diagram that shows two variables moving either positively or negatively in relation to each other, it is easy to conclude that there is a causal relationship. But relationships between two variables are not always due to direct cause and effect. Quite possibly an observed relationship between two variables is due to the *unobserved* effect of a third variable on each of the other two variables. An unobserved variable that, through its influence on other variables, creates the erroneous appearance of a direct causal relationship among those variables is called an **omitted variable.** For example, in New England, a greater amount of snowfall during a given week will typically cause people to buy more snow shovels. It will also cause people to buy more de-icer fluid. But if you omitted the influence of the snowfall and simply plotted the number of snow shovels sold versus the number of bottles of de-icer fluid, you would produce a scatter diagram that showed an upward tilt in the pattern of points, indicating a positive relationship between snow shovels sold and de-icer fluid sold. To attribute a causal relationship between these two variables, however, is misguided; more snow shovels sold do not cause more de-icer fluid to be sold, or vice versa. They move together because they are both influenced by a third, determining, variable—the weekly snowfall—which is the omitted variable in this case. So before assuming that a pattern in a scatter diagram implies a cause-and-effect relationship, it is important to consider whether the pattern is instead the result of an omitted variable. Or to put it succinctly: Correlation is not causation.

> An **omitted variable** is an unobserved variable that, through its influence on other variables, creates the erroneous appearance of a direct causal relationship among those variables.

Reverse Causality   Even when you are confident that there is no omitted variable and that there is a causal relationship between two variables shown in a numerical graph, you must also be careful that you don't make the mistake of **reverse causality**—coming to an erroneous conclusion about which is the dependent and which is the independent variable by reversing the true direction of causality between the two variables. For example, imagine a scatter diagram that depicts the grade point averages (GPAs) of 20 of your classmates on one axis and the number of hours that each of them spends studying on the other. A line fitted between the points will probably have a positive slope, showing a positive relationship between GPA and hours of studying. We could reasonably infer that hours spent studying is the independent variable and that GPA is the dependent variable. But you could make the error of reverse causality: you could infer that a high GPA causes a student to study more whereas a low GPA causes a student to study less.

> The error of **reverse causality** is committed when the true direction of causality between two variables is reversed.

The significance of understanding how graphs can mislead or be incorrectly interpreted is not purely academic. Policy decisions, business decisions, and political arguments are often based on interpretation of the types of numerical graphs that we've just discussed. Problems of misleading features of construction, omitted variables, and reverse causality can lead to very important and undesirable consequences.

PROBLEMS

1. Study the four accompanying diagrams. Consider the following statements and indicate which diagram matches each statement. Which variable would appear on the horizontal and which on the vertical axis? In each of these statements, is the slope positive, negative, zero, or infinity?

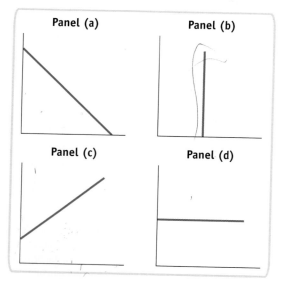

a. If the price of movies increases, fewer consumers go to see movies.

b. More experienced workers typically have higher incomes than less experienced workers.

c. Whatever the temperature outside, Americans consume the same number of hot dogs per day.

d. Consumers buy more frozen yogurt when the price of ice cream goes up.

e. Research finds no relationship between the number of diet books purchased and the number of pounds lost by the average dieter.

f. Regardless of its price, Americans buy the same quantity of salt.

2. During the Reagan administration, economist Arthur Laffer argued in favor of lowering income tax rates in order to increase tax revenues. Like most economists, he believed that at tax rates above a certain level, tax revenue would fall because high taxes would discourage some people from working and that people would refuse to work at all if they received no income after paying taxes. This relationship between tax rates and tax revenue is graphically summarized in what is widely known as the Laffer curve. Plot the Laffer curve relationship assuming that it has the shape of a nonlinear curve. The following questions will help you construct the graph.

a. Which is the independent variable? Which is the dependent variable? On which axis do you therefore measure the income tax rate? On which axis do you measure income tax revenue?

b. What would tax revenue be at a 0% income tax rate?

c. The maximum possible income tax rate is 100%. What would tax revenue be at a 100% income tax rate?

d. Estimates now show that the maximum point on the Laffer curve is (approximately) at a tax rate of 80%. For tax rates less than 80%, how would you describe the relationship between the tax rate and tax revenue, and how is this relationship reflected in the slope? For tax rates higher than 80%, how would you describe the relationship between the tax rate and tax revenue, and how is this relationship reflected in the slope?

3. In the accompanying figures, the numbers on the axes have been lost. All you know is that the units shown on the vertical axis are the same as the units on the horizontal axis.

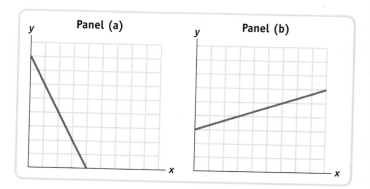

a. In panel (a), what is the slope of the line? Show that the slope is constant along the line.

b. In panel (b), what is the slope of the line? Show that the slope is constant along the line.

4. Answer each of the following questions by drawing a schematic diagram.

a. Taking measurements of the slope of a curve at three points farther and farther to the right along the horizontal axis, the slope of the curve changes from −0.3, to −0.8, to −2.5, measured by the point method. Draw a schematic diagram of this curve. How would you describe the relationship illustrated in your diagram?

b. Taking measurements of the slope of a curve at five points farther and farther to the right along the horizontal axis, the slope of the curve changes from 1.5, to 0.5, to 0, to −0.5, to −1.5, measured by the point method. Draw a schematic diagram of this curve. Does it have a maximum or a minimum?

5. The accompanying table shows the relationship between workers' hours of work per week and their hourly wage rate. Apart from the fact that they receive a different hourly wage rate and work different hours, these five workers are otherwise identical.

Name	Quantity of labor (hours per week)	Wage rate (per hour)
Athena	30	$15
Boris	35	30
Curt	37	45
Diego	36	60
Emily	32	75

a. Which variable is the independent variable? Which is the dependent variable?

b. Draw a scatter diagram illustrating this relationship. Draw a (nonlinear) curve that connects the points. Put the hourly wage rate on the vertical axis.

c. As the wage rate increases from $15 to $30, how does the number of hours worked respond according to the relationship depicted here? What is the average slope of the curve between Athena's and Boris's data points?

d. As the wage rate increases from $60 to $75, how does the number of hours worked respond according to the relationship depicted here? What is the average slope of the curve between Diego's and Emily's data points?

6. Studies have found a relationship between a country's yearly rate of economic growth and the yearly rate of increase in airborne pollutants. It is believed that a higher rate of economic growth allows a country's residents to have more cars and travel more, thereby releasing more airborne pollutants.

a. Which variable is the independent variable? Which is the dependent variable?

b. Suppose that in the country of Sudland, when the yearly rate of economic growth fell from 3.0% to 1.5%, the yearly rate of increase in airborne pollutants fell from 6% to 5%. What is the average slope of a nonlinear curve between these points using the arc method?

c. Now suppose that when the yearly rate of economic growth rose from 3.5% to 4.5%, the yearly rate of increase in airborne pollutants rose from 5.5% to 7.5%. What is the average slope of a nonlinear curve between these two points using the arc method?

d. How would you describe the relationship between the two variables here?

7. An insurance company has found that the severity of property damage in a fire is positively related to the number of firefighters arriving at the scene.

a. Draw a diagram that depicts this finding with number of firefighters on the horizontal axis and amount of property damage on the vertical axis. What is the argument made by this diagram? Suppose you reverse what is measured on the two axes. What is the argument made then?

b. In order to reduce its payouts to policyholders, should the insurance company therefore ask the city to send fewer firefighters to any fire?

8. The accompanying table illustrates annual salaries and income tax owed by five individuals. Apart from the fact that they receive different salaries and owe different amounts of income tax, these five individuals are otherwise identical.

Name	Annual salary	Annual income tax owed
Susan	$22,000	$3,304
Bill	63,000	14,317
John	3,000	454
Mary	94,000	23,927
Peter	37,000	7,020

a. If you were to plot these points on a graph, what would be the average slope of the curve between the points for Bill's and Mary's salaries and taxes using the arc method? How would you interpret this value for slope?

b. What is the average slope of the curve between the points for John's and Susan's salaries and taxes using the arc method? How would you interpret that value for slope?

c. What happens to the slope as salary increases? What does this relationship imply about how the level of income taxes affects a person's incentive to earn a higher salary?

>web... To continue your study and review of concepts in this chapter, please visit the Krugman/Wells website for quizzes, animated graph tutorials, web links to helpful resources, and more.

www.worthpublishers.com/krugmanwells

>> Supply and Demand

GRETZKY'S LAST GAME

THERE ARE SEVERAL WAYS YOU CAN GET tickets for a sporting event. You might have a season pass that gives you a seat at every home game, you could buy a ticket for a single game from the box office, or you could buy a ticket from a *scalper*. Scalpers buy tickets in advance—either from the box office or from season ticket-holders who decide to forgo the game—and then resell them shortly before the event.

Scalping is not always legal, but it is often profitable. A scalper might buy tickets at the box office and then, after the box office has sold out, resell them at a higher price to fans who have decided at the last minute to attend the event. Of course, the profits are not guaranteed. Sometimes an event is unexpectedly "hot" and scalped tickets can be sold for high prices, but sometimes an event is unexpectedly "cold" and scalpers end up selling at a loss.

Over time, however, even with some unlucky nights, scalpers can make money from eager fans.

Ticket scalpers in the Canadian city of Ottawa had a good few days in April 1999. Why? Because Wayne Gretzky, the Canadian hockey star, unexpectedly announced that he would retire from the sport and that the April 15 match between the Ottawa Senators and his team, the New York Rangers, would be his last game on Canadian soil. Many Canadian fans wanted to see the great Gretzky play one last time—and would not give up just because the box office had long since sold out.

Clearly, scalpers who had already stocked up on tickets—or who could acquire more tickets—were in for a bonanza. After the announcement, scalped tickets began selling for four or five times their face value. It was just a matter of supply and demand.

What you will learn in this chapter:

➤ What a **competitive market** is and how it is described by the **supply and demand model**

➤ What the **demand curve** is and what the **supply curve** is

➤ The difference between **movements along a curve** and **shifts of a curve**

➤ How the supply and demand curves determine a market's **equilibrium price** and **equilibrium quantity**

➤ In the case of a **shortage** or **surplus,** how price moves the market back to equilibrium

Shelly/Castellanos/Zuma

AFB/Corbis

Ronal Siemoneit/Corbis

Fans paid hundreds, even thousands, of dollars to see Wayne Gretzky and Michael Jordan play their last games. How much would you pay to see a music star, such as Jennifer Lopez, one last time? What about your favorite athlete?

But what do we mean by that? Many people use *supply and demand* as a sort of catchphrase to mean "the laws of the marketplace at work." To economists, however, the concept of supply and demand has a precise meaning: it is a *model of how a market behaves* that is extremely useful for understanding many—but not all—markets.

In this chapter, we lay out the pieces that make up the supply and demand model, put them together, and show how this model can be used to understand how many—but not all—markets behave.

Supply and Demand: A Model of a Competitive Market

Ticket scalpers and their customers constitute a market—a group of sellers and buyers. More than that, they constitute a particular type of market, known as a competitive market. Roughly, a **competitive market** is a market in which there are many buyers and sellers of the same good or service. More precisely, the key feature of a competitive market is that no individual's actions have a noticeable effect on the price at which the good or service is sold.

It's a little hard to explain why competitive markets are different from other markets until we've seen how a competitive market works. So let's take a rain check—we'll return to that issue at the end of this chapter. For now, let's just say that it's easier to model competitive markets than other markets. When taking an exam, it's always a good strategy to begin by answering the easier questions. In this book, we're going to do the same thing. So we will start with competitive markets.

When a market is competitive, its behavior is well described by a model known as the **supply and demand model**. And because many markets *are* competitive, the supply and demand model is a very useful one indeed.

There are five key elements in this model:

- The *demand curve*
- The *supply curve*
- The set of factors that cause the demand curve to shift, and the set of factors that cause the supply curve to shift
- The *equilibrium price*
- The way the equilibrium price changes when the supply or demand curves shift

To understand the supply and demand model, we will examine each of these elements.

A **competitive market** is a market in which there are many buyers and sellers of the same good or service.

The **supply and demand model** is a model of how a competitive market works.

The Demand Curve

How many people wanted to buy scalped tickets to see the New York Rangers and the Ottawa Senators play that April night? You might at first think the answer was: every hockey fan in Ontario who didn't already have a ticket. But although every hockey fan wanted to see Wayne Gretzky play one last time, most fans weren't willing to pay four or five times the normal ticket price. In general, the number of people who want to buy a hockey ticket, or any other good, depends on the price. The higher the price, the fewer people who want to buy the good; the lower the price, the more people who want to buy the good.

So the answer to the question "How many people will want to buy a ticket to Gretzky's last game?" depends on the price of a ticket. If you don't yet know what the price will be, you can start by making a table of how many tickets people would want to buy at a number of different prices. Such a table is known as a *demand schedule*. This, in turn, can be used to draw a *demand curve*, which is one of the key elements of the supply and demand model.

The Demand Schedule and the Demand Curve

A **demand schedule** shows how much of a good or service consumers will want to buy at different prices.

A **demand schedule** is a table showing how much of a good or service consumers will want to buy at different prices. At the right of Figure 3-1, we show a hypothetical demand schedule for tickets to a hockey game.

According to the table, if scalped tickets are available at $100 each (roughly their face value), 20,000 people are willing to buy them; at $150, some fans will decide this price is too high, and only 15,000 are willing to buy. At $200, even fewer people want tickets, and so on. So the higher the price, the fewer the tickets people want to purchase. In other words, as the price rises, the quantity of tickets demanded falls.

A **demand curve** is a graphical representation of the demand schedule. It shows how much of a good or service consumers want to buy at any given price.

The graph in Figure 3-1 is a visual representation of the information in the table. (You might want to review the discussion of graphs in economics in the appendix to Chapter 2.) The vertical axis shows the price of a ticket, and the horizontal axis shows the quantity of tickets. Each point on the graph corresponds to one of the entries in the table. The curve that connects these points is a **demand curve**. A demand curve is a graphical representation of the demand schedule, another way of showing how much of a good or service consumers want to buy at any given price.

The **quantity demanded** is the actual amount consumers are willing to buy at some specific price.

Suppose scalpers are charging $250 per ticket. We can see from Figure 3-1 that 8,000 fans are willing to pay that price; that is, 8,000 is the **quantity demanded** at a price of $250.

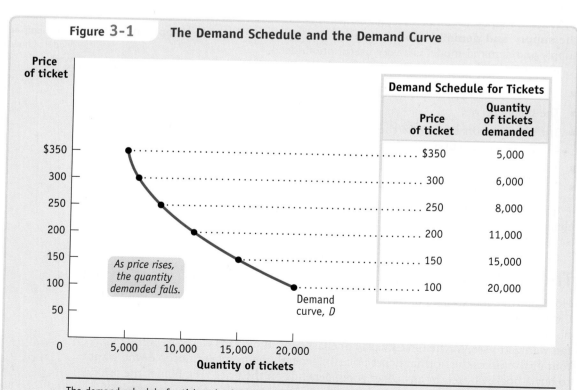

Figure 3-1   The Demand Schedule and the Demand Curve

As price rises, the quantity demanded falls.

Demand curve, *D*

Demand Schedule for Tickets

Price of ticket	Quantity of tickets demanded
$350	5,000
300	6,000
250	8,000
200	11,000
150	15,000
100	20,000

The demand schedule for tickets is plotted to yield the corresponding demand curve, which shows how much of a good consumers want to buy at any given price. The demand curve and the demand schedule reflect the law of demand: As price rises, the quantity demanded falls. Similarly, a decrease in price raises the quantity demanded. As a result, the demand curve is downward sloping.

Note that the demand curve shown in Figure 3-1 slopes downward. This reflects the general proposition that a higher price reduces the number of people willing to buy a good. In this case, many people who would lay out $100 to see the great Gretzky aren't willing to pay $350. In the real world, demand curves almost always, with some very specific exceptions, *do* slope downward. The exceptions are goods called "Giffen goods," but economists think these are so rare that for practical purposes we can ignore them. Generally, the proposition that a higher price for a good, *other things equal*, leads people to demand a smaller quantity of that good is so reliable that econ-omists are willing to call it a "law"—the **law of demand.**

The **law of demand** says that a higher price for a good, other things equal, leads people to demand a smaller quantity of the good.

Shifts of the Demand Curve

When Gretzky's retirement was announced, the immediate effect was that more peo-ple were willing to buy tickets for that April 15 game at any given price. That is, at every price the quantity demanded rose as a consequence of the announcement. Figure 3-2 illustrates this phenomenon in terms of the demand schedule and the demand curve for scalped tickets.

The table in Figure 3-2 shows two demand schedules. The second one shows the demand schedule after the announcement, the same one shown in Figure 3-1. But the first demand schedule shows the demand for scalped tickets *before* Gretzky announced his retirement. As you can see, after the announcement the number of people willing to pay $350 for a ticket increased, the number willing to pay $300 increased, and so on. So at each price, the second schedule—the schedule after the announcement—shows a larger quantity demanded. For example, at $200, the quan-tity of tickets fans were willing to buy increased from 5,500 to 11,000.

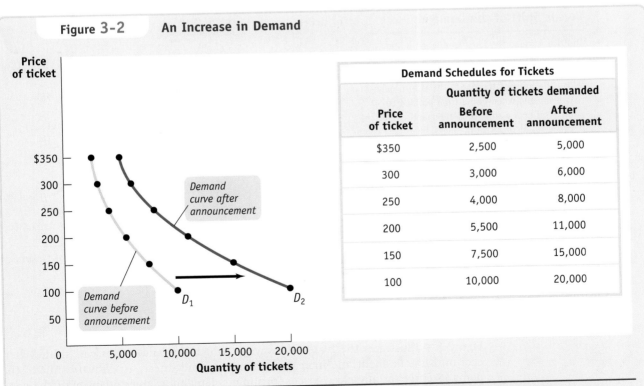

Figure 3-2   An Increase in Demand

Demand Schedules for Tickets		
	Quantity of tickets demanded	
Price of ticket	Before announcement	After announcement
$350	2,500	5,000
300	3,000	6,000
250	4,000	8,000
200	5,500	11,000
150	7,500	15,000
100	10,000	20,000

Announcement of Gretzky's retirement generates an increase in demand—a rise in the quantity demanded at any given price. This event is represented by the two demand schedules—one showing demand before the announcement, the other showing demand after the announcement—and their corresponding demand curves. The increase in demand shifts the demand curve to the right. **>web...**

The announcement of Gretzky's retirement generated a *new* demand schedule, one in which the quantity demanded is greater at any given price than in the original demand schedule. The two curves in Figure 3-2 show the same information graphically. As you can see, the new demand schedule after the announcement corresponds to a new demand curve, D_2, that is to the right of the demand curve before the announcement, D_1. This **shift of the demand curve** shows the change in the quantity demanded at any given price, represented by the change in position of the original demand curve D_1 to its new location at D_2.

It's crucial to make the distinction between such shifts of the demand curve and **movements along the demand curve**, changes in the quantity demanded of a good that result from a change in that good's price. Figure 3-3 illustrates the difference.

The movement from point A to point B is a movement along the demand curve: the quantity demanded rises due to a fall in price as you move down D_1. Here, a fall in price from $350 to $215 generates a rise in the quantity demanded from 2,500 to 5,000 tickets. But the quantity demanded can also rise when the price is unchanged if there is an increase in demand—a rightward shift of the demand curve. This is illustrated in Figure 3-3 by the shift of the demand curve from D_1 to D_2. Holding price constant at $350, the quantity demanded rises from 2,500 tickets at point A on D_1 to 5,000 tickets at point C on D_2.

When economists say "the demand for X increased" or "the demand for Y decreased," they mean that the demand curve for X or Y shifted—*not* that the quantity demanded rose or fell because of a change in the price.

> A **shift of the demand curve** is a change in the quantity demanded at any given price, represented by the change of the original demand curve to a new position, denoted by a new demand curve.
>
> A **movement along the demand curve** is a change in the quantity demanded of a good that is the result of a change in that good's price.

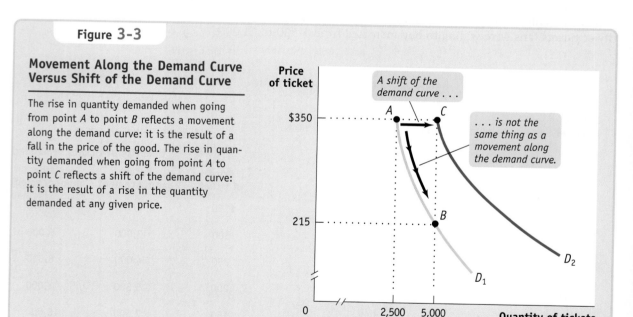

Figure 3-3

Movement Along the Demand Curve Versus Shift of the Demand Curve

The rise in quantity demanded when going from point A to point B reflects a movement along the demand curve: it is the result of a fall in the price of the good. The rise in quantity demanded when going from point A to point C reflects a shift of the demand curve: it is the result of a rise in the quantity demanded at any given price.

Understanding Shifts of the Demand Curve

Figure 3-4 illustrates the two basic ways in which demand curves can shift. When economists talk about an "increase in demand," they mean a *rightward* shift of the demand curve: at any given price, consumers demand a larger quantity of the good than before. This is shown in Figure 3-4 by the rightward shift of the original demand curve D_1 to D_2. And when economists talk about a "decrease in demand," they mean a *leftward* shift of the demand curve: at any given price, consumers demand a smaller quantity of the good than before. This is shown in Figure 3-4 by the leftward shift of the original demand curve D_1 to D_3.

Figure 3-4

Shifts of the Demand Curve

Any event that increases demand shifts the demand curve to the right, reflecting a rise in the quantity demanded at any given price. Any event that decreases demand shifts the demand curve to the left, reflecting a fall in the quantity demanded at any given price.

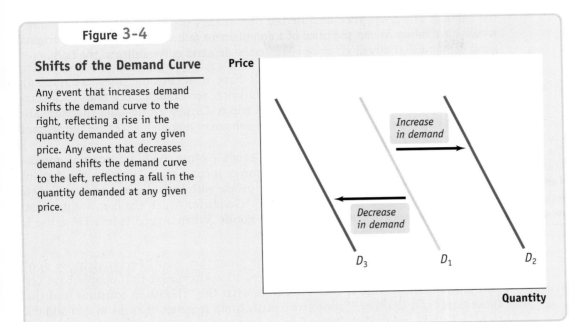

But what causes a demand curve to shift? In our example, the event that shifts the demand curve for tickets is the announcement of Gretzky's imminent retirement. But if you think about it, you can come up with other things that would be likely to shift the demand curve for those tickets. For example, suppose there is a music concert the same evening as the hockey game, and the band announces that it will sell tickets at half-price. This is likely to cause a decrease in demand for hockey tickets: hockey fans who also like music will prefer to purchase half-price concert tickets rather than hockey game tickets.

Economists believe that there are four principal factors that shift the demand curve for a good:

- Changes in the prices of related goods
- Changes in income
- Changes in tastes
- Changes in expectations

Although this is not an exhaustive list, it contains the four most important factors that can shift demand curves. When we said before that the quantity of a good demanded falls as its price rises, *other things equal*, we were referring to the factors that shift demand as remaining unchanged.

Changes in the Prices of Related Goods If you want to have a good night out but aren't too particular about what you do, a music concert is an alternative to the hockey game—it is what economists call a *substitute* for the hockey game. A pair of goods are **substitutes** if a fall in the price of one good (music concerts) makes consumers less willing to buy the other good (hockey games). Substitutes are usually goods that in some way serve a similar function: concerts and hockey games, muffins and doughnuts, trains and buses. A fall in the price of the alternative good induces some consumers to purchase it *instead of* the original good, shifting the demand for the original good to the left.

But sometimes a fall in the price of one good makes consumers *more* willing to buy another good. Such pairs of goods are known as **complements**. Complements are usually goods that in some sense are consumed together: sports tickets and parking at the stadium garage, hamburgers and buns, cars and gasoline. If the garage next to the hockey arena offered free parking, more people would be willing to buy tickets to see

Two goods are **substitutes** if a fall in the price of one of the goods makes consumers less willing to buy the other good.

Two goods are **complements** if a fall in the price of one good makes people more willing to buy the other good.

the game at any given price because the cost of the "package"—game plus parking— would have fallen. When the price of a complement falls, the quantity of the original good demanded at any given price rises; so the demand curve shifts to the right.

Changes in Income   When individuals have more income, they are normally more likely to purchase a good at any given price. For example, if a family's income rises, it is more likely to take that summer trip to Disney World—and therefore also more likely to buy plane tickets. So a rise in consumer incomes will cause the demand curves for most goods to shift to the right.

Why do we say "most goods," not "all goods"? Most goods are **normal goods**— the demand for them increases when consumer income rises. However, the demand for some products falls when income rises—people with high incomes are less likely to take buses than people with lower incomes. Goods for which the demand decreases when income rises are known as **inferior goods**. When a good is inferior, a rise in income shifts the demand curve to the left.

> When a rise in income increases the demand for a good—the normal case— we say that the good is a **normal good**.
>
> When a rise in income decreases the demand for a good, it is an **inferior good**.

Changes in Tastes   Why do people want what they want? Fortunately, we don't need to answer that question—we just need to acknowledge that people have certain preferences, or tastes, that determine what they choose to consume and that these tastes can change. Economists usually lump together changes in demand due to fads, beliefs, cultural shifts, and so on under the heading of changes in *tastes* or *preferences*.

For example, once upon a time men wore hats. Up until around World War II, a respectable man wasn't fully dressed unless he wore a dignified hat along with his suit. But the returning GIs adopted a more informal style, perhaps due to the rigors of the war. And, President Eisenhower, who had been supreme commander of Allied Forces, often went hatless. The demand curve for hats had shifted leftward, reflecting a decline in the demand for hats.

The main distinguishing feature of changes in tastes is that economists have little to say about them and usually take them as given. When tastes change in favor of a good, more people want to buy it at any given price, so the demand curve shifts to the right. When tastes change against a good, fewer people want to buy it at any given price, so the demand curve shifts to the left.

Changes in Expectations   You could say that the increase in demand for tickets to the April 15 hockey game was the result of a change in expectations: fans no longer expected to have future opportunities to see Gretzky in action, so they became more eager to see him while they could.

Depending on the specifics of the case, changes in expectations can either decrease or increase the demand for a good. For example, savvy shoppers often wait for seasonal sales—say, buying holiday gifts during the post-holiday markdowns. In this case, expectations of a future drop in price lead to a decrease in demand today. Alternatively, expectations of a future rise in price are likely to cause an increase in demand today.

Expected changes in future income can also lead to changes in demand: if you expect your income to rise in the future, you will typically borrow today and increase your demand for certain goods; and if you expect your income to fall in the future, you are likely to save today and reduce your demand for some goods.

economics in action

Beating the Traffic

All big cities have traffic problems, and many local authorities try to discourage driving in the crowded city center. If we think of an auto trip to the city center as a good that people consume, we can use the economics of demand to analyze anti-traffic policies.

One common strategy of local governments is to reduce the demand for auto trips by lowering the prices of substitutes. Many metropolitan areas subsidize bus and rail service, hoping to lure commuters out of their cars.

An alternative strategy is raising the price of complements: several major U.S. cities impose high taxes on commercial parking garages, both to raise revenue and to discourage people from driving into the city. (Short time limits on parking meters, combined with vigilant parking enforcement, is a related tactic.)

However, few cities have been willing to adopt the politically controversial direct approach: reducing congestion by raising the price of driving. So it was a shock when, in 2003, London imposed a "congestion charge" of £5 (about $9) on all cars entering the city center during business hours.

Compliance is monitored with automatic cameras that photograph license plates. People can either pay the charge in advance or pay it by midnight of the day they have driven. If they don't pay and are caught, a fine of £100 (about $180) is imposed for each transgression. (A full description of the rules can be found at www.cclondon.com.)

Not surprisingly, the result of the new policy confirms the law of demand: according to an August 2003 news report, traffic into central London had fallen 32 percent and cars were traveling more than a third faster as a result of the congestion charge. ■

>> CHECK YOUR UNDERSTANDING 3-1

1. Explain whether each of the following events represents (i) a *shift of* the demand curve or (ii) a *movement along* the demand curve.
   a. A store owner finds that customers are willing to pay more for umbrellas on rainy days.
   b. When XYZ Telecom, a long-distance telephone service provider, offered reduced rates on weekends, the volume of weekend calling increased sharply.
   c. People buy more long-stem roses the week of Valentine's Day, even though the prices are higher than at other times during the year.
   d. The sharp rise in the price of gasoline leads many commuters to join carpools in order to reduce their gasoline purchases.

Solutions appear at back of book.

The Supply Curve

Ticket scalpers have to acquire the tickets they sell, and many of them do so from ticket-holders who decide to sell. The decision of whether to sell your own ticket to a scalper depends in part on the price offered: the higher the price offered, the more likely that you will be willing to sell.

So just as the quantity of tickets that people are willing to buy depends on the price they have to pay, the quantity that people are willing to sell—the **quantity supplied**—depends on the price they are offered. (Notice that this is the supply of tickets *to the market in scalped tickets*. The number of seats in the stadium is whatever it is, regardless of the price—but that's not the quantity we're concerned with here.)

The **quantity supplied** is the actual amount of a good or service people are willing to sell at some specific price.

The Supply Schedule and the Supply Curve

The table in Figure 3-5 on page 64 shows how the quantity of tickets made available varies with the price—that is, it shows a hypothetical **supply schedule** for tickets to Gretzky's last game.

A supply schedule works the same way as the demand schedule shown in Figure 3-1: in this case, the table shows the quantity of tickets season subscribers are willing to sell at different prices. At a price of $100, only 2,000 people are willing to part with their tickets. At $150, some more people decide that it is worth passing up the game in order to have more money for something else, increasing the quantity of tickets available to 5,000. At $200, the quantity of tickets supplied rises to 7,000, and so on.

A **supply schedule** shows how much of a good or service would be supplied at different prices.

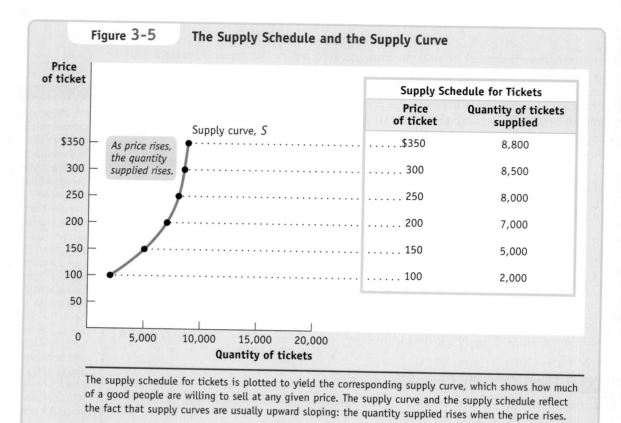

Figure 3-5   The Supply Schedule and the Supply Curve

As price rises, the quantity supplied rises.

Supply curve, *S*

Supply Schedule for Tickets	
Price of ticket	Quantity of tickets supplied
$350	8,800
300	8,500
250	8,000
200	7,000
150	5,000
100	2,000

The supply schedule for tickets is plotted to yield the corresponding supply curve, which shows how much of a good people are willing to sell at any given price. The supply curve and the supply schedule reflect the fact that supply curves are usually upward sloping: the quantity supplied rises when the price rises.

> A **supply curve** shows graphically how much of a good or service people are willing to sell at any given price.

In the same way that a demand schedule can be represented graphically by a demand curve, a supply schedule can be represented by a **supply curve,** as shown in Figure 3-5. Each point on the curve represents an entry from the table.

Suppose that the price scalpers offer rises from $200 to $250; we can see from Figure 3-5 that the quantity of tickets sold to them rises from 7,000 to 8,000. This is the normal situation for a supply curve, reflecting the general proposition that a higher price leads to a higher quantity supplied. So just as demand curves normally slope downward, supply curves normally slope upward: the higher the price being offered, the more hockey tickets people will be willing to part with—the more of any good they will be willing to sell.

Shifts of the Supply Curve

When Gretzky's retirement was announced, the immediate effect was that people who already had tickets for the April 15 game became less willing to sell those tickets to scalpers at any given price. So the quantity of tickets supplied at any given price fell: the number of tickets people were willing to sell at $350 fell, the number they were willing to sell at $300 fell, and so on. Figure 3-6 shows us how to illustrate this event in terms of the supply schedule and the supply curve for tickets.

> A **shift of the supply curve** is a change in the quantity supplied of a good or service at any given price. It is represented by the change of the original supply curve to a new position, denoted by a new supply curve.

The table in Figure 3-6 shows two supply schedules; the schedule after the announcement is the same one as in Figure 3-5. The first supply schedule shows the supply of scalped tickets *before* Gretzky announced his retirement. And just as a change in demand schedules leads to a shift of the demand curve, a change in supply schedules leads to a **shift of the supply curve**—a change in the quantity supplied at any given price. This is shown in Figure 3-6 by the shift of the supply curve before the announcement, S_1, to its new position after the announcement, S_2. Notice that S_2 lies to the left of S_1, a reflection of the fact that quantity supplied decreased at any given price in the aftermath of Gretzky's announcement.

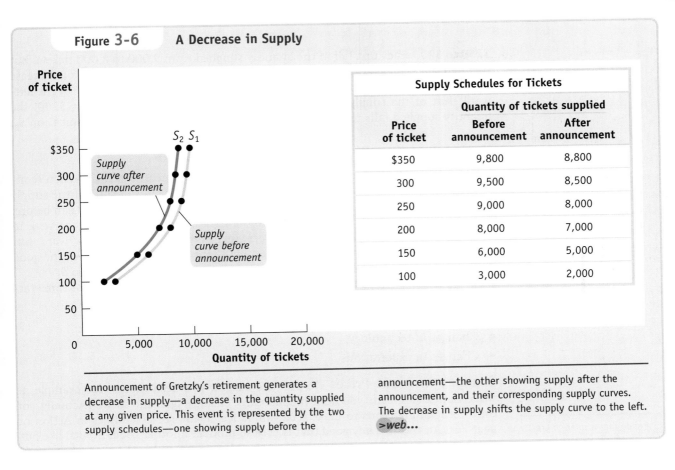

Figure 3-6   **A Decrease in Supply**

	Supply Schedules for Tickets		
		Quantity of tickets supplied	
Price of ticket	Before announcement	After announcement
$350	9,800	8,800
300	9,500	8,500
250	9,000	8,000
200	8,000	7,000
150	6,000	5,000
100	3,000	2,000

Announcement of Gretzky's retirement generates a decrease in supply—a decrease in the quantity supplied at any given price. This event is represented by the two supply schedules—one showing supply before the announcement—the other showing supply after the announcement, and their corresponding supply curves. The decrease in supply shifts the supply curve to the left.

>*web*...

As in the analysis of demand, it's crucial to draw a distinction between such shifts of the supply curve and **movements along the supply curve**—changes in the quantity supplied that result from a change in price. We can see this difference in Figure 3-7. The movement from point *A* to point *B* is a movement along the supply curve: the quantity supplied falls along S_1 due to a fall in price. Here, a fall in price from

A **movement along the supply curve** is a change in the quantity supplied of a good that is the result of a change in that good's price.

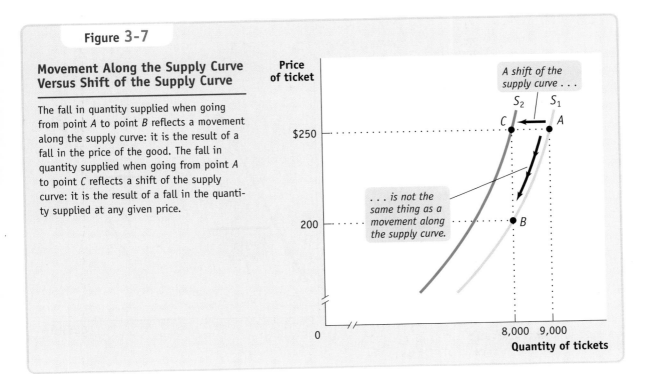

Figure 3-7

Movement Along the Supply Curve Versus Shift of the Supply Curve

The fall in quantity supplied when going from point *A* to point *B* reflects a movement along the supply curve: it is the result of a fall in the price of the good. The fall in quantity supplied when going from point *A* to point *C* reflects a shift of the supply curve: it is the result of a fall in the quantity supplied at any given price.

$250 to $200 leads to a fall in the quantity supplied from 9,000 to 8,000 tickets. But the quantity supplied can also fall when the price is unchanged if there is a decrease in supply—a leftward shift of the supply curve. This is shown in Figure 3-7 by the leftward shift of the supply curve from S_1 to S_2. Holding price constant at $250, the quantity supplied falls from 9,000 tickets at point A on S_1 to 8,000 at point C on S_2.

Understanding Shifts of the Supply Curve

Figure 3-8 illustrates the two basic ways in which supply curves can shift. When economists talk about an "increase in supply," they mean a *rightward* shift of the supply curve: at any given price, people will supply a larger quantity of the good than before. This is shown in Figure 3-8 by the shift to the right of the original supply curve S_1 to S_2. And when economists talk about a "decrease in supply," they mean a *leftward* shift of the supply curve: at any given price, people supply a smaller quantity of the good than before. This is represented in Figure 3-8 by the leftward shift of S_1 to S_3.

Economists believe that shifts of supply curves are mainly the result of three factors (though, as in the case of demand, there are other possible causes):

- Changes in input prices
- Changes in technology
- Changes in expectations

Changes in Input Prices To produce output, you need inputs—for example, to make vanilla ice cream, you need vanilla beans, cream, sugar, and so on. (Actually, you only need vanilla beans to make *good* vanilla ice cream; see Economics in Action on page 76.) An **input** is any good that is used to produce another good. Inputs, like output, have prices. And an increase in the price of an input makes the production of the final good more costly for those who produce and sell the good. So sellers are less willing to supply the good at any given price, and the supply curve shifts to the left. For example, newspaper publishers buy large quantities of newsprint (the paper on which newspapers are printed). When newsprint prices rose sharply in 1994–1995, the supply of newspapers fell: several newspapers went out of business and a number of new publishing ventures were canceled. Similarly, a fall in the price of an input makes the production of the final good less costly for sellers. They are more willing to supply the good at any given price, and the supply curve shifts to the right.

An **input** is a good that is used to produce another good.

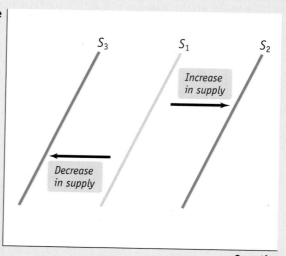

Figure 3-8

Shifts of the Supply Curve

Any event that increases supply shifts the supply curve to the right, reflecting a rise in the quantity supplied at any given price. Any event that decreases supply shifts the supply curve to the left, reflecting a fall in the quantity supplied at any given price.

Price

S_3 S_1 S_2

Increase in supply

Decrease in supply

Quantity

Changes in Technology When economists talk about "technology," they don't necessarily mean high technology—they mean all the ways in which people can turn inputs into useful goods. The whole complex set of activities that turn corn from an Iowa farm into cornflakes on your breakfast table is technology in this sense. And when a better technology becomes available, reducing the cost of production—that is, letting a producer spend less on inputs yet produce the same output—supply increases, and the supply curve shifts to the right. For example, an improved strain of corn that is more resistant to disease makes farmers willing to supply more corn at any given price.

Changes in Expectations Imagine that you had a ticket for the April 15 game but couldn't go. You'd want to sell the ticket to a scalper. But if you heard a credible rumor about Gretzky's imminent retirement, you would know that the ticket would soon sky-rocket in value. So you'd hold off on selling the ticket until his decision to retire was made public. This illustrates how expectations can alter supply: an expectation that the price of a good will be higher in the future causes supply to decrease today, but an expectation that the price of a good will be lower in the future causes supply to increase today.

economics in action

Down (and Up) on the Farm

Many countries have designed farm policies based on the belief—or maybe the hope—that producers *won't* respond much to changes in the price of their product. But they have found out, to their dismay, that the price does indeed matter.

Advanced countries (including the United States) have historically tried to legislate farm prices *up*. (Chapter 4 describes how such price floors work in practice.) The point was to raise farmers' incomes, not to increase production—but production nonetheless did go up. Until the nations of the European Union began guaranteeing farmers high prices in the 1960s, they had limited agricultural production and imported much of their food. Once price supports were in place, production expanded rapidly, and European farmers began growing more grains and producing more dairy products than consumers wanted to buy.

In poorer countries, especially in Africa, governments have often sought to keep farm prices *down*. The typical strategy was to require farmers to sell their produce to a "marketing board," which then resold it to urban consumers or overseas buyers. A famous example is Ghana, once the world's main supplier of cocoa, the principal ingredient in chocolate. From 1965 until the 1980s, farmers were required to sell their cocoa beans to the government at prices that lagged steadily behind those chocolate manufacturers were paying elsewhere. The Ghanaian government hoped that cocoa production would be little affected by this policy and that it could profit by buying low and selling high. In fact, production fell sharply. By 1980, Ghana's share of the world market was down to 12 percent, while other cocoa-exporting countries that did not follow the same policy—including its African neighbors—were steadily increasing their sales.

Today Europe is trying to reform its agricultural policy, and most developing countries have abandoned their efforts to hold farm prices down. Governments seem finally to have learned that supply curves really do slope upward after all. ∎

> > > > > > > > > > > > > > > > > > >

>>**CHECK YOUR UNDERSTANDING 3-2**

1. Explain whether each of the following events represents (i) a *shift of* the supply curve or (ii) a *movement along* the supply curve.
   a. More homeowners put their houses up for sale during a real estate boom that causes house prices to rise.
   b. Many strawberry farmers open temporary roadside stands during harvest season, even though prices are usually low at that time.

continued

continued

c. Immediately after the school year begins, fast-food chains must raise wages to attract workers.
d. Many construction workers temporarily move to areas that have suffered hurricane damage, lured by higher wages which represent the price of labor.
e. Since new technologies have made it possible to build larger cruise ships (which are cheaper to run per passenger), Caribbean cruise lines have offered more cabins, at lower prices, than before.

Solutions appear at back of book.

Supply, Demand, and Equilibrium

We have now covered the first three key elements in the supply and demand model: the supply curve, the demand curve, and the set of factors that shift each curve. The next step is to put these elements together to show how they can be used to predict the actual price at which a good will be bought and sold.

What determines the price at which a good is bought and sold? In Chapter 1 we learned the general principle that *markets move toward equilibrium*, a situation in which no individual would be better off taking a different action. In the case of a competitive market, we can be more specific: a competitive market is in equilibrium when the price has moved to a level at which the quantity demanded of a good equals the quantity supplied of that good. At that price, no individual seller could make herself better off by offering to sell either more or less of the good and no individual buyer could make himself better off by offering to buy more or less of the good.

The price that matches the quantity supplied and the quantity demanded is the **equilibrium price;** the quantity bought and sold at that price is the **equilibrium quantity.** The equilibrium price is also known as the **market-clearing price:** it is the price that "clears the market" by ensuring that every buyer willing to pay that price finds a seller willing to sell at that price, and vice versa.

You may notice from this point on that we will no longer focus on middlemen such as scalpers but focus directly on the market price and quantity. Why? Because the function of a middleman is to bring buyers and sellers together to trade. But what makes buyers and sellers willing to trade is in reality not the middleman, but the price they agree upon—the equilibrium price. By going deeper and examining how price functions within a market, we can safely assume that the middlemen are doing their job and leave them in the background.

So, how do we find the equilibrium price and quantity?

Finding the Equilibrium Price and Quantity

The easiest way to determine the equilibrium price and quantity in a market is by putting the supply curve and the demand curve on the same diagram. Since the supply curve shows the quantity supplied at any given price and the demand curve shows the quantity demanded at any given price, the price at which the two curves cross is the equilibrium price: the price at which quantity supplied equals quantity demanded.

Figure 3-9 combines the demand curve from Figure 3-1 and the supply curve from Figure 3-5. They *intersect* at point *E*, which is the equilibrium of this market; that is, $250 is the equilibrium price and 8,000 tickets is the equilibrium quantity.

Let's confirm that point *E* fits our definition of equilibrium. At a price of $250 per ticket, 8,000 ticket-holders are willing to resell their tickets and 8,000 people who do not have tickets are willing to buy. So at the price of $250 the quantity of tickets supplied equals the quantity demanded. Notice that at any other price the market would not clear: every willing buyer would not be able to find a willing seller, or vice versa. In other words, if the price were more than $250, the quantity supplied would exceed the quantity demanded; if the price were less than $250, the quantity demanded would exceed the quantity supplied.

A competitive market is in equilibrium when price has moved to a level at which the quantity demanded of a good equals the quantity supplied of that good. The price at which this takes place is the **equilibrium price**, also referred to as the **market-clearing price**. The quantity of the good bought and sold at that price is the **equilibrium quantity**.

PITFALLS

BOUGHT *AND* SOLD?
We have been talking about the price at which a good is bought *and* sold, as if the two were the same. But shouldn't we make a distinction between the price received by sellers and that paid by buyers? In principle, yes; but it is helpful at this point to sacrifice a bit of realism in the interests of simplicity—by assuming away the difference between the prices received by sellers and those paid by buyers. In reality, people who sell hockey tickets to scalpers, although they sometimes receive high prices, generally receive less than those who eventually buy these tickets pay. No mystery there: that difference is how a scalper or any other "middleman"—someone who brings buyers and sellers together—makes a living. In many markets, however, the difference between the buying and selling price is quite small. It is therefore not a bad approximation to think of the price paid by buyers as being the *same* as the price received by sellers. And that is what we will assume in the remainder of this chapter.

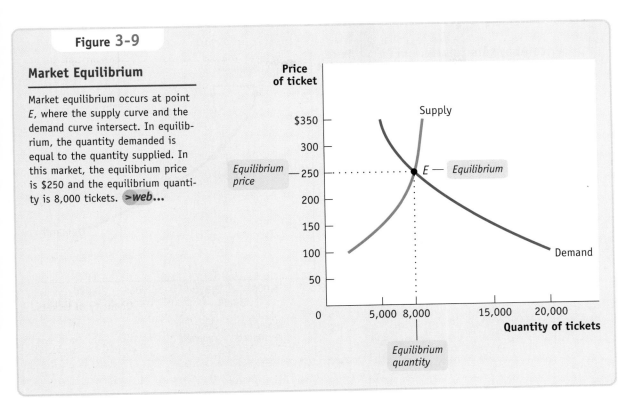

Figure 3-9

Market Equilibrium

Market equilibrium occurs at point *E*, where the supply curve and the demand curve intersect. In equilibrium, the quantity demanded is equal to the quantity supplied. In this market, the equilibrium price is $250 and the equilibrium quantity is 8,000 tickets. **>web...**

The model of supply and demand, then, predicts that given the demand and supply curves shown in Figure 3-9, 8,000 tickets would change hands at a price of $250 each.

But how can we be sure that the market will arrive at the equilibrium price? We begin by answering three simpler questions:

1. Why do all sales and purchases in a market take place at the same price?
2. Why does the market price fall if it is above the equilibrium price?
3. Why does the market price rise if it is below the equilibrium price?

Why Do All Sales and Purchases in a Market Take Place at the Same Price?

There are some markets where the same good can sell for many different prices, depending on who is selling or who is buying. For example, have you ever bought a souvenir in a "tourist trap" and then seen the same item on sale somewhere else (perhaps even in the next store) for a lower price? Because tourists don't know which shops offer the best deals and don't have time for comparison shopping, sellers in tourist areas can charge different prices for the same good.

But in any market where the buyers and sellers have both been around for some time, sales and purchases tend to converge at a generally uniform price, so that we can safely talk about *the* market price. It's easy to see why. Suppose a seller offered a potential buyer a price noticeably above what the buyer knew other people to be paying. The buyer would clearly be better off shopping elsewhere—unless the seller was prepared to offer a better deal. Conversely, a seller would not be willing to sell for significantly less than the amount he knew most buyers were paying; he would be better off waiting to get a more reasonable customer. So in any well-established, ongoing market, all sellers receive and all buyers pay approximately the same price. This is what we call the *market price*.

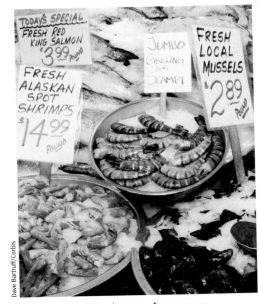

The market price is the same for everyone.

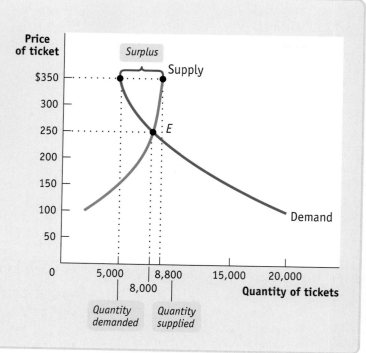

Figure 3-10

Price Above Its Equilibrium Level Creates a Surplus

The market price of $350 is above the equilibrium price of $250. This creates a surplus: at $350 per ticket, suppliers would like to sell 8,800 tickets but fans are willing to purchase only 5,000, so there is a surplus of 3,800 tickets. This surplus will push the price down until it reaches the equilibrium price of $250. **>web...**

Why Does the Market Price Fall If It Is Above the Equilibrium Price?

Suppose the supply and demand curves are as shown in Figure 3-9, but the market price is above the equilibrium level of $250—say, $350. This situation is illustrated in Figure 3-10. Why can't the price stay there?

As the figure shows, at a price of $350 there would be more tickets available than hockey fans wanted to buy: 8,800 versus 5,000. The difference of 3,800 is the **surplus**—also known as the *excess supply*—of tickets at $350.

This surplus means that some would-be sellers are being frustrated: they cannot find anyone to buy what they want to sell. So the surplus offers an incentive for those 3,800 would-be sellers to offer a lower price in order to poach business from other sellers. It also offers an incentive for would-be buyers to seek a bargain by offering a lower price. Sellers who reject the lower price will fail to find buyers, and the result of this price cutting will be to push the prevailing price down until it reaches the equilibrium price. So, the price of a good will fall whenever there is a surplus—that is, whenever the price is above its equilibrium level.

Why Does the Market Price Rise If It Is Below the Equilibrium Price?

Now suppose the price is below its equilibrium level—say, at $150 per ticket, as shown in Figure 3-11. In this case, the quantity demanded (15,000 tickets) exceeds the quantity supplied (5,000 tickets), implying that there are 10,000 would-be buyers who cannot find tickets: there is a **shortage**, also known as an *excess demand*, of 10,000 tickets.

When there is a shortage, there are frustrated would-be buyers—people who want to purchase tickets but cannot find willing sellers at the current price. In this situation, either buyers will offer more than the prevailing price or sellers will realize that they can charge higher prices. Either way, the result is to drive up the prevailing price. This bidding up of prices happens whenever there are shortages—and there will be shortages whenever the price is below its equilibrium level. So the price will always rise if it is below the equilibrium level.

There is a **surplus** of a good when the quantity supplied exceeds the quantity demanded. Surpluses occur when the price is above its equilibrium level.

There is a **shortage** of a good when the quantity demanded exceeds the quantity supplied. Shortages occur when the price is below its equilibrium level.

SHIRVANIAN USA

BIG TIPPER

TAXI

© 1998 Cartoonists & Writers Syndicate http://CartoonWeb.com

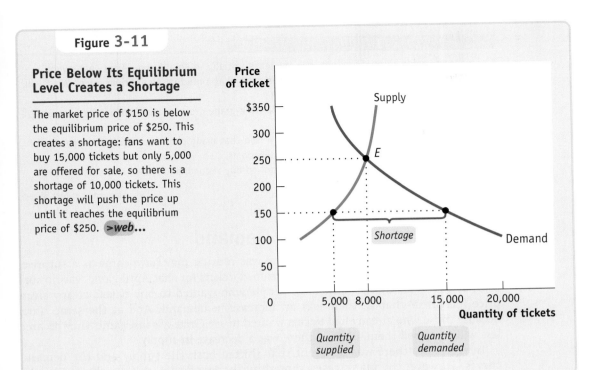

Figure 3-11

Price Below Its Equilibrium Level Creates a Shortage

The market price of $150 is below the equilibrium price of $250. This creates a shortage: fans want to buy 15,000 tickets but only 5,000 are offered for sale, so there is a shortage of 10,000 tickets. This shortage will push the price up until it reaches the equilibrium price of $250. **>web...**

Using Equilibrium to Describe Markets

We have now seen that a market tends to have a single price; that the market price falls if it is above the equilibrium level but rises if it is below that level. So the market price always *moves toward* the equilibrium price, the price at which there is neither surplus nor shortage.

economics in action

A Fish Story

In market equilibrium, something remarkable supposedly happens: everyone who wants to sell a good finds a willing buyer, and everyone who wants to buy that good finds a willing seller. It's a beautiful theory—but is it realistic?

In New York City the answer can be seen every day, just before dawn, at the famous Fulton Fish Market, which has operated since 1835 (though it has moved from its original Fulton Street location). There, every morning, fishermen bring their catch and haggle over prices with restaurant owners, shopkeepers, and a variety of middlemen and brokers.

The stakes are high. Restaurant owners who can't provide their customers with the fresh fish they expect stand to lose a lot of business, so it's important that would-be buyers find willing sellers. It's even more important for fishermen to make a sale: unsold fish loses much, if not all, of its value. But the market does reach equilibrium: just about every would-be buyer finds a willing seller, and vice versa. The reason is that every day the price of each type of fish quickly converges to a level that matches the quantity supplied and the quantity demanded.

So the tendency of markets to reach equilibrium isn't just theoretical speculation. You can see (and smell) it happening, early every morning. ■

> > > > > > > > > > > > > > > > > >

1. In the following three situations, the market is initially in equilibrium. After each event described below, does a surplus or shortage exist at the original equilibrium price? What will happen to the equilibrium price as a result?
   a. 1997 was a very good year for California wine-grape growers, who produced a bumper-size crop.
   b. After a hurricane, Florida hoteliers often find that many people cancel their upcoming vacations, leaving them with empty hotel rooms.
   c. After a heavy snowfall, many people want to buy secondhand snowblowers at the local tool shop.

Solutions appear at back of book.

Changes in Supply and Demand

Wayne Gretzky's announcement that he was retiring may have come as a surprise, but the subsequent rise in the price of scalped tickets for that April game was no surprise at all. Suddenly the number of people who wanted to buy tickets at any given price increased—that is, there was an increase in demand. And at the same time, because those who already had tickets wanted to see Gretzky's last game, they became less willing to sell them—that is, there was a decrease in supply.

In this case, there was an event that shifted both the supply and the demand curves. However, in many cases something happens that shifts only one of the curves. For example, a freeze in Florida reduces the supply of oranges but doesn't change the demand. A medical report that eggs are bad for your health reduces the demand for eggs but does not affect the supply. That is, events often shift either the supply curve or the demand curve, but not both; it is therefore useful to ask what happens in each case.

We have seen that when a curve shifts, the equilibrium price and quantity change. We will now concentrate on exactly how the shift of a curve alters the equilibrium price and quantity.

What Happens When the Demand Curve Shifts

Coffee and tea are substitutes: if the price of tea rises, the demand for coffee will increase, and if the price of tea falls, the demand for coffee will decrease. But how does the price of tea affect the *market* for coffee?

Figure 3-12 shows the effect of a rise in the price of tea on the market for coffee. The rise in the price of tea increases the demand for coffee. Point E_1 shows the equilibrium corresponding to the original demand curve, with P_1 the equilibrium price and Q_1 the equilibrium quantity bought and sold.

An increase in demand is indicated by a *rightward* shift of the demand curve from D_1 to D_2. At the original market price P_1, this market is no longer in equilibrium: a shortage occurs because the quantity demanded exceeds the quantity supplied. So the price of coffee rises and generates an increase in the quantity supplied, an upward *movement along the supply curve*. A new equilibrium is established at point E_2, with a higher equilibrium price P_2 and higher equilibrium quantity Q_2. This sequence of events reflects a general principle: *When demand for a good increases, the equilibrium price and the equilibrium quantity of the good both rise.*

And what would happen in the reverse case, a fall in the price of tea? A fall in the price of tea decreases the demand for coffee, shifting the demand curve to the *left*. At the original price, a surplus occurs as quantity supplied exceeds quantity demanded. The price falls and leads to a decrease in the quantity supplied, with a lower equilibrium price and a lower equilibrium quantity. This illustrates another general principle: *When demand for a good decreases, the equilibrium price of the good and the equilibrium quantity of the good both fall.*

Figure 3-12

Equilibrium and Shifts of the Demand Curve

The original equilibrium in the market for coffee is at E_1, at the intersection of the supply curve and the original demand curve D_1. A rise in the price of tea, a substitute, shifts the demand curve rightward to D_2. A shortage exists at the original price P_1, so both price and the quantity supplied rise, a movement along the supply curve. A new equilibrium is reached at E_2, with a higher equilibrium price P_2 and a higher equilibrium quantity Q_2. When demand for a good increases, the equilibrium price and the equilibrium quantity of the good both rise. **>web...**

To summarize how a market responds to a change in demand: *An increase in demand leads to a rise in both the equilibrium price and the equilibrium quantity. A decrease in demand leads to a fall in both the equilibrium price and the equilibrium quantity.*

What Happens When the Supply Curve Shifts

In the real world, it is a bit easier to predict changes in supply than changes in demand. Physical factors that affect supply, like the availability of inputs, are easier to get a handle on than the fickle tastes that affect demand. Still, with supply as with demand, what we really know are the *effects* of shifts of the supply curve.

A spectacular example of a change in technology increasing supply occurred in the manufacture of semiconductors—the silicon chips that are the core of computers, video games, and many other devices. In the early 1970s, engineers learned how to use a process known as photolithography to put microscopic electronic components onto a silicon chip; subsequent progress in the technique has allowed ever more components to be put on each chip. Figure 3-13 (page 74) shows the effect of such an innovation on the market for silicon chips. The demand curve does not change. The original equilibrium is at E_1, the point of intersection of the original supply curve S_1 and the demand curve, with equilibrium price P_1 and equilibrium quantity Q_1. As a result of the technological change, supply increases and S_1 shifts *rightward* to S_2. At the original price P_1, a surplus of chips now exists and the market is no longer in equilibrium. The surplus causes a fall in price and a rise in quantity demanded, a downward movement along the demand curve. The new equilibrium is at E_2, with an equilibrium price P_2 and an equilibrium quantity Q_2. In the new equilibrium E_2, the price is lower and the equilibrium quantity higher than before. This may be stated as a general principle: *An increase in supply leads to a fall in the equilibrium price and a rise in the equilibrium quantity.*

What happens to the market when supply decreases? A decrease in supply leads to a *leftward* shift of the supply curve. At the original price, a shortage now exists; as a result, the equilibrium price rises and the quantity demanded falls. This describes the sequence of events in the newspaper market in 1994–1995, which we

Figure 3-13

Equilibrium and Shifts of the Supply Curve

The original equilibrium in the market for silicon chips is at E_1, at the intersection of the demand curve and the original supply curve S_1. After a technological change increases the supply of silicon chips, the supply curve shifts rightward to S_2. A surplus exists at the original price P_1, so price falls and the quantity demanded rises, a movement along the demand curve. A new equilibrium is reached at E_2, with a lower equilibrium price P_2 and a higher equilibrium quantity Q_2. When supply of a good increases, the equilibrium price of the good falls and the equilibrium quantity rises. **>web...**

Price of chip

An increase in supply . . . S_1

S_2

Price falls P_1

E_1

. . . leads to a movement along the demand curve to a lower equilibrium price and higher equilibrium quantity.

P_2 E_2

Demand

$Q_1 \longrightarrow Q_2$ **Quantity of chips**

Quantity rises

discussed earlier: a decrease in the supply of newsprint led to a rise in the price and the closure of many newspapers. We can formulate a general principle: *A decrease in supply leads to a rise in the equilibrium price and a fall in the equilibrium quantity.*

To summarize how a market responds to a change in supply: *An increase in supply leads to a fall in the equilibrium price and a rise in the equilibrium quantity. A decrease in supply leads to a rise in the equilibrium price and a fall in the equilibrium quantity.*

Simultaneous Shifts in Supply and Demand

Finally, it sometimes happens that events shift *both* the demand and supply curves. In fact, this chapter began with an example of such a simultaneous shift. Wayne Gretzky's announcement that he was retiring increased the demand for scalped tickets because more people wanted to see him play one last time; but it also decreased the supply because those who already had tickets became less willing to part with them.

Figure 3-14 illustrates what happened. In both panels we show an increase in demand—that is, a rightward shift of the demand curve, from D_1 to D_2. Notice that the rightward shift in panel (a) is relatively larger than the one in panel (b). Both panels also show a decrease in supply—that is, a leftward shift of the supply curve, from S_1 to S_2. Notice that the leftward shift in panel (b) is relatively larger than the one in panel (a).

In both cases, the equilibrium price rises, from P_1 to P_2, as the equilibrium moves from E_1 to E_2. But what happens to the equilibrium quantity, the quantity of scalped tickets bought and sold? In panel (a) the increase in demand is large relative to the decrease in supply, and the equilibrium quantity rises as a result. In panel (b) the decrease in supply is large relative to the increase in demand, and the equilibrium quantity falls as a result. That is, when demand increases and

PITFALLS

WHICH CURVE IS IT, ANYWAY?
When the price of some good changes, in general we can say that this reflects a change in either supply or demand. But it is easy to get confused about which one. A helpful clue is the direction of change in the quantity. If the quantity sold changes in the *same* direction as the price—for example, if both the price and the quantity rise—this suggests that the demand curve has shifted. If the price and the quantity move in *opposite* directions, the likely cause is a shift in the supply curve.

Figure 3-14   **Simultaneous Shifts of the Demand and Supply Curves**

(a) One Possible Outcome:
Price Rises, Quantity Rises

(b) Another Possible Outcome:
Price Rises, Quantity Falls

In panel (a) there is a simultaneous rightward shift of the demand curve and leftward shift of the supply curve. Here the increase in demand is relatively larger than the decrease in supply, so the equilibrium price and equilibrium quantity both rise.

In panel (b) there is also a simultaneous rightward shift of the demand curve and leftward shift of the supply curve. Here the decrease in supply is relatively larger than the increase in demand, so the equilibrium price rises and the equilibrium quantity falls.

supply decreases, the actual quantity bought and sold can go either way, depending on *how much* the demand and supply curves have shifted.

In general, when supply and demand shift in opposite directions, we can't predict what the ultimate effect will be on the quantity bought and sold. What we can say is that a curve that shifts a disproportionately greater distance than the other curve will have a disproportionately greater effect on the quantity bought and sold. That said, we can make the following prediction about the outcome when the supply and demand curves shift in opposite directions:

■ When demand increases and supply decreases, the price rises but the change in the quantity is ambiguous.

■ When demand decreases and supply increases, the price falls but the change in the quantity is ambiguous.

But suppose that the demand and supply curves shift in the same direction. Can we safely make any predictions about the changes in price and quantity? In this situation, the change in quantity bought and sold can be predicted but the change in price is ambiguous. The two possible outcomes when the supply and demand curves shift in the same direction (which you should check for yourself) are as follows:

■ When both demand and supply increase, the quantity increases but the change in price is ambiguous.

■ When both demand and supply decrease, the quantity decreases but the change in price is ambiguous.

SUPPLY, DEMAND, AND CONTROLLED SUBSTANCES

The big "issue" movie of the year 2000 was *Traffic*, a panoramic treatment of the drug trade. The movie was loosely based on the 1989 British TV miniseries *Traffik*. Despite the lapse of 11 years, the basic outlines of the situation—in which the drug trade flourishes despite laws that are supposed to prevent it—had not changed. Not only has the so-called war on drugs by law enforcement officials not succeeded in eliminating the trade in illegal drugs; according to most assessments, it has not even done much to reduce consumption.

The failure of the war on drugs has a historical precedent: during Prohibition, from 1920 to 1933, the sale and consumption of alcohol was illegal in the United States. But liquor, produced and distributed by "bootleggers," nonetheless remained widely available. In fact, by 1929 per capita consumption of alcohol was higher than it had been a decade earlier. As with illegal drugs today, the production and distribution of the banned substance became a large enterprise that flourished despite its illegality.

Why is it so hard to choke off markets in alcohol and drugs? Think of the war on drugs as a policy that shifts the supply curve but has not done much to shift the demand curve.

Although it is illegal to use drugs such as cocaine, just as it was once illegal to drink alcohol, in practice the war on drugs focuses mainly on the suppliers. As a result, the cost of supplying drugs includes the risk of being caught and sent to jail, perhaps even of being executed. This undoubtedly reduces the quantity of drugs supplied *at any given price*, in effect shifting the supply curve for drugs to the left. In Figure 3-15, this is shown as a shift in the supply curve from S_1

to S_2. If the war on drugs had no effect on the price of drugs, and the price remained at P_1, this leftward shift would reflect a reduction in the quantity of drugs supplied equal in magnitude to the leftward shift of supply.

But as we have seen, when the supply curve for a good shifts to the left, the effect is to raise the market price of that good. In Figure 3-15 the effect of the war on drugs would be to move the equilibrium from E_1 to E_2, and to raise the price of drugs from P_1 to P_2, a movement along the demand curve. Because the market price rises, the actual decline in the quantity of drugs supplied is less than the decline in the quantity that would have been supplied at the original price.

The crucial reason Prohibition was so ineffective was that as the market price of alcohol rose, consumers trimmed back only

slightly on their consumption—yet the higher prices were enough to induce many potential suppliers to take the risk of jail time. So while Prohibition raised the price of alcohol, it did not do much to reduce consumption. Unfortunately, the same seems to be true of current drug policy. The policy raises the price of drugs to those who use them, but this does not do much to discourage consumption. Meanwhile, the higher prices are enough to induce suppliers to provide drugs despite the penalties.

What is the answer? Some argue that the policy should be refocused on the demand side—more antidrug education, more counseling, and so on. If these policies worked, they would shift demand to the left. Others argue that drugs, like alcohol, should be made legal but heavily taxed. While the debate goes on, so does the war on drugs.

Figure 3-15

Effects of the War on Drugs

The war on drugs shifts the supply curve to the left. However, we can see by comparing the original equilibrium E_1 with the new equilibrium E_2 that the actual reduction in the quantity of drugs supplied is much smaller than the shift of the supply curve. The equilibrium price rises from P_1 to P_2—a movement along the demand curve. This leads suppliers to provide drugs despite the risks.

economics in action

Plain Vanilla Gets Fancy

Vanilla doesn't get any respect. It's such a common flavoring that "plain vanilla" has become a generic term for ordinary, unembellished products. But between 2000 and 2003, plain vanilla got quite fancy—at least if you looked at the price. At the supermarket, the price of a small bottle of vanilla extract rose from about $5 to about $15. The wholesale price of vanilla beans rose 400 percent.

The cause of the price spike was bad weather—not here, but in the Indian Ocean. Most of the world's vanilla comes from Madagascar, an island nation off Africa's southeast coast. A huge cyclone struck there in 2000, and a combination of colder-than-normal weather and excessive rain impeded recovery.

The higher price of vanilla led to a fall in the quantity demanded: worldwide consumption of vanilla fell about 35 percent from 2000 to 2003. Consumers didn't stop eating vanilla-flavored products; instead, they switched (often without realizing it) to ice cream and other products flavored with synthetic vanillin, which is a by-product of wood pulp and petroleum production.

Notice that there was never a shortage of vanilla: you could always find it in the store if you were willing to pay the price. That is, the vanilla market remained in equilibrium. ∎

> > > > > > > > > > > > > > > > > > >

>> CHECK YOUR UNDERSTANDING 3-4

1. In each of the following examples, determine (i) the market in question; (ii) whether a shift in demand or supply occurred, the direction of the shift, and what induced the shift; and (iii) the effect of the shift on the equilibrium price and the equilibrium quantity.
   a. As the price of gasoline fell in the United States during the 1990s, more people bought large cars.
   b. As technological innovation has lowered the cost of recycling used paper, fresh paper made from recycled stock is used more frequently.
   c. As a local cable company offers cheaper pay-per-view films, local movie theaters have more unfilled seats.

2. Periodically, a computer chip maker like Intel introduces a new chip that is faster than the previous one. In response, demand for computers using the earlier chip decreases as customers put off purchases in anticipation of machines containing the new chip. Simultaneously, computer makers increase their production of computers containing the earlier chip in order to clear out their stocks of those chips.

   Draw two diagrams of the market for computers containing the earlier chip: (a) one in which the equilibrium quantity falls in response to these events and (b) one in which the equilibrium quantity rises. What happens to the equilibrium price in each diagram?

   Solutions appear at back of book.

Competitive Markets—And Others

Early in this chapter, we defined a competitive market and explained that the supply and demand framework is a model of competitive markets. But we took a rain check on the question of why it matters whether or not a market is competitive. Now that we've seen how the supply and demand model works, we can offer some explanation.

To understand why competitive markets are different from other markets, compare the problems facing two individuals: a wheat farmer who must decide whether to grow more wheat, and the president of a giant aluminum company—say, Alcoa—who must decide whether to produce more aluminum.

For the wheat farmer, the question is simply whether the extra wheat can be sold at a price high enough to justify the extra production cost. The farmer need not worry about whether producing more wheat will affect the price of the wheat he or she was already planning to grow. That's because the wheat market is competitive. There are thousands of wheat farmers, and no one farmer's decision will have much impact on the market price.

For the Alcoa executive, things are not that simple because the aluminum market is *not* competitive. There are only a few big players, including Alcoa, and each of them is well aware that its actions *do* have a noticeable impact on the market price. This adds a whole new level of complexity to the decisions producers have to make. Alcoa can't decide whether or not to produce more aluminum just by asking whether the additional product will sell for more than it costs to make. The company also has to ask whether producing more aluminum will drive down the market price and reduce its profit.

When a market is competitive, individuals can base decisions on less complicated analyses than those used in a noncompetitive market. This in turn means that it's easier for economists to build a model of a competitive market than of a noncompetitive market.

Don't take this to mean that economic analysis has nothing to say about noncompetitive markets. On the contrary, economists can offer some very important insights into how other kinds of markets work. But those insights require other models. In the next chapter, we will focus on what we can learn about competitive markets from the very useful model we have just developed: supply and demand.

• A LOOK AHEAD •

We've now developed a model that explains how markets arrive at prices and why markets "work" in the sense that buyers can almost always find sellers, and vice versa. But this model could use a little more clarification.

But, nothing demonstrates a principle quite as well as what happens when people try to defy it. And governments do, fairly often, try to defy the principles of supply and demand. In the next chapter we consider what happens when they do—the revenge of the market.

SUMMARY

1. The **supply and demand model** illustrates how a **competitive market**, one with many buyers and sellers, works.

2. The **demand schedule** shows the **quantity demanded** at each price and is represented graphically by a **demand curve**. The **law of demand** says that demand curves slope downward.

3. A **movement along the demand curve** occurs when the price changes and causes a change in the quantity demanded. When economists talk of increasing or decreasing demand, they mean **shifts of the demand curve**—a change in the quantity demanded at any given price. An increase in demand causes a rightward shift of the demand curve. A decrease in demand causes a leftward shift.

4. There are four main factors that shift the demand curve:
   - A change in the prices of related goods, such as **substitutes** or **complements**
   - A change in income: when income rises, the demand for **normal goods** increases and the demand for **inferior goods** decreases.
   - A change in tastes
   - A change in expectations

5. The **supply schedule** shows the **quantity supplied** at each price and is represented graphically by a **supply curve**. Supply curves usually slope upward.

6. A **movement along the supply curve** occurs when the price changes and causes a change in the quantity supplied. When economists talk of increasing or decreasing supply, they mean **shifts of the supply curve**—a change in the quantity supplied at any given price. An increase in supply causes a rightward shift of the supply curve. A decrease in supply causes a leftward shift.

7. There are three main factors that shift the supply curve:
   - A change in **input** prices
   - A change in technology
   - A change in expectations

8. The supply and demand model is based on the principle that the price in a market moves to its **equilibrium price, or market-clearing price,** the price at which the quantity demanded is equal to the quantity supplied. This quantity is the **equilibrium quantity**. When the price is above its market-clearing level, there is a **surplus** that pushes the price down. When the price is below its market-clearing level, there is a **shortage** that pushes the price up.

9. An increase in demand increases both the equilibrium price and the equilibrium quantity; a decrease in demand has the opposite effect. An increase in supply reduces the equilibrium price and increases the equilibrium quantity; a decrease in supply has the opposite effect.

10. Shifts of the demand curve and the supply curve can happen simultaneously. When they shift in opposite directions, the change in price is predictable but the change in quantity is not. When they shift in the same direction, the change in quantity is predictable but the change in price is not. In general, the curve that shifts the greater distance has a greater effect on the changes in price and quantity.

KEY TERMS

Competitive market, p. 57
Supply and demand model, p. 57
Demand schedule, p. 58
Demand curve, p. 58
Quantity demanded, p. 58
Law of demand, p. 59
Shift of the demand curve, p. 60
Movement along the demand curve, p. 60

Substitutes, p. 61
Complements, p. 61
Normal good, p. 62
Inferior good, p. 62
Quantity supplied, p. 63
Supply schedule, p. 63
Supply curve, p. 64
Shift of the supply curve, p. 64

Movement along the supply curve, p. 65
Input, p. 66
Equilibrium price, p. 68
Equilibrium quantity, p. 68
Market-clearing price, p. 68
Surplus, p. 70
Shortage, p. 70

PROBLEMS

1. A survey indicated that chocolate ice cream is America's favorite ice-cream flavor. For each of the following, indicate the possible effects on demand and/or supply and equilibrium price and quantity of chocolate ice cream.

a. A severe drought in the Midwest causes dairy farmers to reduce the number of milk-producing cattle in their herds by a third. These dairy farmers supply cream that is used to manufacture chocolate ice cream.

b. A new report by the American Medical Association reveals that chocolate does, in fact, have significant health benefits.

c. The discovery of cheaper synthetic vanilla flavoring lowers the price of vanilla ice cream.

d. New technology for mixing and freezing ice cream lowers manufacturers' costs of producing chocolate ice cream.

2. In a supply and demand diagram, draw the shift in demand for hamburgers in your hometown due to the following events. In each case show the effect on equilibrium price and quantity.

a. The price of tacos increases.

b. All hamburger sellers raise the price of their french fries.

c. Income falls in town. Assume that hamburgers are a normal good for most people.

d. Income falls in town. Assume that hamburgers are an inferior good for most people.

e. Hot dog stands cut the price of hot dogs.

3. The market for many goods changes in predictable ways according to the time of year, in response to events such as holidays, vacation times, seasonal changes in production, and so on. Using supply and demand, explain the change in price in each of the following cases. Note that supply and demand may shift simultaneously.

a. Lobster prices usually fall during the summer peak harvest season, despite the fact that people like to eat lobster during the summer months more than during any other time of year.

b. The price of a Christmas tree is lower after Christmas than before and fewer trees are sold.

c. The price of a round-trip ticket to Paris on Air France falls by more than $200 after the end of school vacation in September. This happens despite the fact that generally worsening weather increases the cost of operating flights to Paris, and Air France therefore reduces the number of flights to Paris at any given price.

4. Show in a diagram the effect on the demand curve, the supply curve, the equilibrium price, and the equilibrium quantity of each of the following events.

a. The market for newspapers in your town.

Case 1: The salaries of journalists go up.
Case 2: There is a big news event in your town, which is reported in the newspapers.

b. The market for St. Louis Rams cotton T-shirts.

Case 1: The Rams win the national championship.
Case 2: The price of cotton increases.

c. The market for bagels.

Case 1: People realize how fattening bagels are.
Case 2: People have less time to make themselves a cooked breakfast.

d. The market for the Krugman and Wells economics textbook.

Case 1: Your professor makes it required reading for all of his or her students.
Case 2: Printing costs for textbooks are lowered by the use of synthetic paper.

5. Suppose that the supply schedule of Maine lobsters is as follows:

Price of lobster (per pound)	Quantity of lobster supplied (pounds)
$25	800
20	700
15	600
10	500
5	400

Suppose that Maine lobsters can be sold only in the United States. The U.S. demand schedule for Maine lobsters is as follows:

Price of lobster (per pound)	Quantity of lobster demanded (pounds)
$25	200
20	400
15	600
10	800
5	1,000

a. Draw the demand curve and the supply curve for Maine lobsters. What is the equilibrium price and quantity of lobsters?

Now suppose that Maine lobsters can be sold in France. The French demand schedule for Maine lobsters is as follows:

Price of lobster (per pound)	Quantity of lobster demanded (pounds)
$25	100
20	300
15	500
10	700
5	900

b. What is the demand schedule for Maine lobsters now that French consumers can also buy them? Draw a supply and demand diagram that illustrates the new equilibrium price and quantity of lobsters. What will happen to the price at which fishermen can sell lobster? What will happen to the price paid by U.S. consumers? What will happen to the quantity consumed by U.S. consumers?

6. Find the flaws in reasoning in the following statements, paying particular attention to the distinction between shifts of and movements along the supply and demand curves. Draw a diagram to illustrate what actually happens in each situation.

a. "A technological innovation that lowers the cost of producing a good might seem at first to result in a reduction in the price of the good to consumers. But a fall in price will increase demand for the good, and higher demand will send the price up again. It is not certain, therefore, that an innovation will really reduce price in the end."

b. "A study shows that eating a clove of garlic a day can help prevent heart disease, causing many consumers to demand more garlic. This increase in demand results in a rise in the price of garlic. Consumers, seeing that the price of garlic has gone up, reduce their demand for garlic. This causes the demand for garlic to decrease and the price of garlic to fall. Therefore, the ultimate effect of the study on the price of garlic is uncertain."

7. Some points on a demand curve for a normal good are given here:

Price	Quantity demanded
$23	70
21	90
19	110
17	130

Do you think that the increase in quantity demanded (from 90 to 110 in the table) when price decreases (from 21 to 19) is due to a rise in consumers' income? Explain clearly (and briefly) why or why not.

8. Aaron Hank is a star hitter for the Bay City baseball team. He is close to breaking the major league record for home runs hit during one season, and it is widely anticipated that in the next game he will break that record. As a result, tickets for the team's next game have been a hot commodity. But today it is announced that, due to a knee injury, he will not in fact play in the team's next game. Assume that season ticket-holders are able to resell their tickets if they wish. Use supply and demand diagrams to explain the following.

a. Show the case in which this announcement results in a lower equilibrium price and a lower equilibrium quantity than before the announcement.

b. Show the case in which this announcement results in a lower equilibrium price and a higher equilibrium quantity than before the announcement.

c. What accounts for whether case a or case b occurs?

d. Suppose that a scalper had secretly learned before the announcement that Aaron Hank would not play in the next game. What actions do you think he would take?

9. In *Rolling Stone* magazine, several fans and rock stars, including Pearl Jam, were bemoaning the high price of concert tickets. One superstar argued, "It just isn't worth $75 to see me play. No one should have to pay that much to go to a concert." Assume this star sold out arenas around the country at an average ticket price of $75.

a. How would you evaluate the arguments that ticket prices are too high?

b. Suppose that due to this star's protests, ticket prices were lowered to $50. In what sense is this price too low? Draw a diagram using supply and demand curves to support your argument.

c. Suppose Pearl Jam really wanted to bring down ticket prices. Since the band controls the supply of its services, what do you recommend they do? Explain using a supply and demand diagram.

d. Suppose the band's next CD was a total dud. Do you think they would still have to worry about ticket prices being too high? Why or why not? Draw a supply and demand diagram to support your argument.

e. Suppose the group announced their next tour was going to be their last. What effect would this likely have on the demand for and price of tickets? Illustrate with a supply and demand diagram.

10. The accompanying table gives the annual U.S. demand and supply schedules for pickup trucks.

Price of truck	Quantity of trucks demanded (millions)	Quantity of trucks supplied (millions)
$20,000	20	14
25,000	18	15
30,000	16	16
35,000	14	17
40,000	12	18

a. Plot the demand and supply curves using these schedules. Indicate the equilibrium price and quantity on your diagram.

b. Suppose the tires used on pickup trucks are found to be defective. What would you expect to happen in the market for pickup trucks? Show this on your diagram.

c. Suppose that the U.S. Department of Transportation imposes costly regulations on manufacturers that cause them to reduce supply by one-third at any given price. Calculate and plot the new supply schedule and indicate the new equilibrium price and quantity on your diagram.

11. After several years of decline, the market for handmade acoustic guitars is making a comeback. These guitars are usually made in small workshops employing relatively few highly skilled luthiers. Assess the impact on the equilibrium price and quantity of handmade acoustic guitars as a result of each of the following events. In your answers indicate which curve(s) shift(s) and in which direction.

a. Environmentalists succeed in having the use of Brazilian rosewood banned in the United States, forcing luthiers to seek out alternative, more costly woods.

b. A foreign producer reengineers the guitar-making process and floods the market with identical guitars.

c. Music featuring handmade acoustic guitars makes a comeback as audiences tire of heavy metal and grunge music.

d. The country goes into a deep recession and the income of the average American falls sharply.

12. *Demand twisters*: Sketch and explain the demand relationship in each of the following statements.

a. I would never buy a Britney Spears CD! You couldn't even give me one for nothing.

b. I generally buy a bit more coffee as the price falls. But once the price falls to $2 per pound, I'll buy out the entire stock of the supermarket.

c. I spend more on orange juice even as the price rises. (Does this mean that I must be violating the law of demand?)

d. Due to a tuition rise, most students at a college find themselves with lower disposable income. Almost all of them eat more frequently at the school cafeteria and less often at restaurants, even though prices at the cafeteria have risen too. (This one requires that you draw both the demand and the supply curves for dormitory cafeteria meals.)

13. Will Shakespeare is a struggling playwright in sixteenth-century London. As the price he receives for writing a play increases, he is willing to write more plays. For the following situations, use a diagram to illustrate how each event affects the equilibrium price and quantity in the market for Shakespeare's plays.

a. The playwright Christopher Marlowe, Shakespeare's chief rival, is killed in a bar brawl.

b. The bubonic plague, a deadly infectious disease, breaks out in London.

c. To celebrate the defeat of the Spanish Armada, Queen Elizabeth declares several weeks of festivities, which involves commissioning new plays.

14. The small town of Middling experiences a sudden doubling of the birth rate. After three years, the birth rate returns to normal. Use a diagram to illustrate the effect of these events on the following.

a. The market for an hour of babysitting services in Middling today

b. The market for an hour of babysitting services 14 years into the future, after the birth rate has returned to normal, by which time children born today are old enough to work as babysitters

c. The market for an hour of babysitting services 30 years into the future, when children born today are likely to be having children of their own

15. Use a diagram to illustrate how each of the following events affects the equilibrium price and quantity of pizza.

a. The price of mozzarella cheese rises.

b. The health hazards of hamburgers are widely publicized.

c. The price of tomato sauce falls.

d. The incomes of consumers rise and pizza is an inferior good.

e. Consumers expect the price of pizza to fall next week.

16. Although he was a prolific artist, Pablo Picasso painted only 1,000 canvases during his "Blue Period." Picasso is now dead, and all of his Blue Period works are currently on display in museums and private galleries throughout Europe and the United States.

a. Draw a supply curve for Picasso Blue Period works. Why is this supply curve different from ones you have seen?

b. Given the supply curve from part a, the price of a Picasso Blue Period work will be entirely dependent on what factor(s)? Draw a diagram showing how the equilibrium price of such a work is determined.

c. Suppose that rich art collectors decide that it is essential to acquire Picasso Blue Period art for their collections. Show the impact of this on the market for these paintings.

17. Draw the appropriate curve in each of the following cases. Is it like or unlike the curves you have seen so far? Explain.

a. The demand for cardiac bypass surgery, given that the government pays the full cost for any patient

b. The demand for elective cosmetic plastic surgery, given that the patient pays the full cost

c. The supply of Rembrandt paintings

d. The supply of reproductions of Rembrandt paintings

>web... To continue your study and review of concepts in this chapter, please visit the Krugman/Wells website for quizzes, animated graph tutorials, web links to helpful resources, and more.

www.worthpublishers.com/krugmanwells

>The Market Strikes Back

BIG CITY, NOT-SO-BRIGHT IDEAS

NEW YORK CITY IS A PLACE WHERE YOU can find almost anything—that is, almost anything, except a taxicab when you need one or a decent apartment at a rent you can afford. You might think that New York's notorious shortages of cabs and apartments are the inevitable price of big-city living. However, they are largely the product of government policies—specifically, of government policies that have, one way or another, tried to prevail over the market forces of supply and demand.

In the previous chapter, we learned the principle that a market moves to equilibrium—that the market price rises or falls to the level at which the quantity of a good that people are willing to supply is equal to the quantity that other people want to demand. But sometimes governments try to defy that principle. When they do, the market strikes back in predictable ways. And our ability to predict what will happen when governments try to defy supply and demand shows the power and usefulness of supply and demand analysis itself.

The shortages of apartments and taxicabs in New York are particular examples that illuminate what happens when the logic of the market is defied. New York's housing shortage is the result of *rent control,* a law that prevents landlords from raising rents except when specifically given permission. Rent control was introduced during World War II to protect the interests of tenants, and it still remains in force. Many other American cities have had rent control at one time or another, but with the notable exceptions of New York and San Francisco, these controls have largely been done away with. Similarly, New York's limited supply of taxis is the result of a licensing system introduced in the 1930s. New York taxi licenses are known as "medallions," and only taxis with medallions are allowed to pick up passengers. And although this

New York City: An empty taxi is hard to find.

system was originally intended to protect the interests of both drivers and customers, it has generated a shortage of taxis in the city. The number of medallions remained fixed from 1937 until 1995, and only a handful of additional licenses have been issued since then.

4

What you will learn in this chapter:

➤ The meaning of **price controls** and **quantity controls,** two kinds of government intervention in markets

➤ How price and quantity controls create problems and make a market **inefficient**

➤ Why economists are often deeply skeptical of attempts to intervene in markets

➤ Who benefits and who loses from market interventions, and why they are used despite their well-known problems

➤ What an **excise tax** is and why its effect is similar to a quantity control

➤ Why the **deadweight loss** of a tax means that its true cost is more than the amount of tax revenue collected

In this chapter, we begin by examining what happens when governments try to control prices in a competitive market, keeping the price in a market either below its equilibrium level—a *price ceiling* such as rent control—or above it—a *price floor*. We then turn to schemes such as taxi medallions that attempt to dictate the quantity of a good bought and sold. Finally, we consider the effects of taxes on sales or purchases.

Why Governments Control Prices

You learned in Chapter 3 that a market moves to equilibrium—that is, the market price moves to the level at which the quantity supplied equals the quantity demanded. But this equilibrium price does not necessarily please either buyers or sellers.

After all, buyers would always like to pay less if they could, and sometimes they can make a strong moral or political case that they should pay lower prices. For example, what if the equilibrium between supply and demand for apartments in a major city leads to rental rates that an average working person can't afford? In that case, a government might well be under pressure to impose limits on the rents landlords can charge.

Sellers, however, would always like to get more money for what they sell, and sometimes they can make a strong moral or political case that they should receive higher prices. For example, consider the labor market: the price for an hour of a worker's time is the wage rate. What if the equilibrium between supply and demand for less-skilled workers leads to wage rates that are below the poverty level? In that case, a government might well find itself pressured to require employers to pay a rate no lower than some specified minimum wage.

In other words, there is often a strong political demand for governments to intervene in markets. When a government intervenes to regulate prices, we say that it imposes **price controls**. These controls typically take the form either of an upper limit, a **price ceiling**, or a lower limit, a **price floor**.

> **Price controls** are legal restrictions on how high or low a market price may go. They can take two forms: a **price ceiling,** a maximum price sellers are allowed to charge for a good, or a **price floor,** a minimum price buyers are required to pay for a good.

Unfortunately, it's not that easy to tell a market what to do. As we will now see, when a government tries to legislate prices—whether it legislates them *down* by imposing a price ceiling or *up* by imposing a price floor—there are certain predictable and unpleasant side effects.

We should note an important caveat here: our analysis in this chapter considers only what happens when price controls are imposed on *competitive markets*, which, as you should recall from Chapter 3, are markets with many buyers and sellers in which no buyer or seller can have any influence on the price. When markets are *not* competitive—as in a monopoly, where there is only one seller—price controls don't necessarily cause the same problems. In practice, however, price controls often *are* imposed on competitive markets—like the New York apartment market. And so the analysis in this chapter applies to many important real-world situations.

Price Ceilings

Aside from rent control, there are not many price ceilings in the United States today. But at times they have been widespread. Price ceilings are typically imposed during crises—wars, harvest failures, natural disasters—because these events often lead to sudden price increases that hurt many people but produce big gains for a lucky few. The U.S. government imposed ceilings on many prices during World War II: the war sharply increased demand for raw materials, such as aluminum and steel, and price controls prevented those with access to these raw materials from earning huge profits. Price controls on oil were imposed in 1973, when an embargo by Arab oil-exporting countries seemed likely to generate huge profits for U.S. oil companies. (See

Economics in Action on page 89.) Price controls were imposed on California's whole-sale electricity market in 2001, when a shortage was creating big profits for a few power-generating companies but leading to higher bills for consumers.

Rent control in New York is, believe it or not, a legacy of World War II: it was imposed because the war produced an economic boom, which increased demand for apartments at a time when the labor and raw materials that might have been used to build them were being used to win the war instead. Although most price controls were removed soon after the war ended, New York's rent limits were retained and gradually extended to buildings not previously covered, leading to some very strange situations.

You can rent a one-bedroom apartment in Manhattan on fairly short notice—if you are able and willing to pay about $1,700 a month and live in a less-than-desirable area. Yet some people pay only a small fraction of this for comparable apartments and others pay hardly more for bigger apartments in better locations.

Aside from producing great deals for some renters, however, what are the broader consequences of New York's rent control system? To answer this question, we turn to the model we developed in Chapter 3: the supply and demand model.

Modeling a Price Ceiling

To see what can go wrong when a government imposes a price ceiling on a competitive market, consider Figure 4-1, which shows a simplified model of the market for apartments in New York. For the sake of simplicity, we imagine that all apartments are exactly the same and would therefore rent for the same price in an uncontrolled market. The table in the figure shows the demand and supply schedules; the implied demand and supply curves are shown on the left of the figure. We show the quantity of apartments on the horizontal axis and the monthly rent per apartment on the vertical axis. You can see that in an unregulated market the equilibrium would be at point E: 2 million apartments would be rented for $1,000 each per month.

Figure 4-1   The Market for Apartments in the Absence of Government Controls

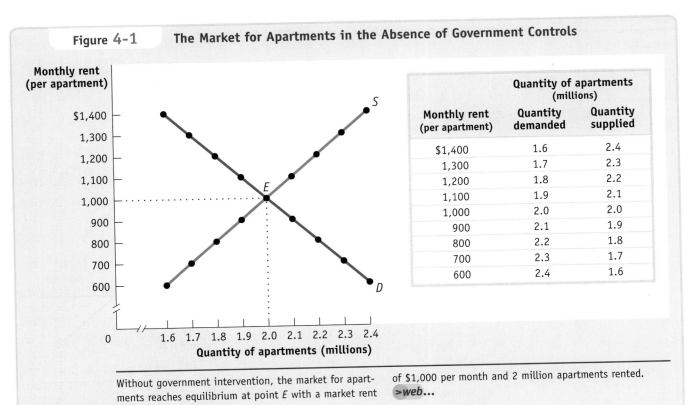

Monthly rent (per apartment)	Quantity of apartments (millions)	
	Quantity demanded	Quantity supplied
$1,400	1.6	2.4
1,300	1.7	2.3
1,200	1.8	2.2
1,100	1.9	2.1
1,000	2.0	2.0
900	2.1	1.9
800	2.2	1.8
700	2.3	1.7
600	2.4	1.6

Without government intervention, the market for apartments reaches equilibrium at point E with a market rent of $1,000 per month and 2 million apartments rented. **>web...**

Now suppose that the government imposes a price ceiling, limiting rents to a price below the equilibrium price—say no more than $800.

Figure 4-2 shows the effect of the price ceiling, represented by the line at $800. At the enforced rental rate of $800, landlords will have less incentive to offer apartments, so they won't be willing to supply as many as they would at the equilibrium rate of $1,000. So they will choose point A on the supply curve, offering only 1.8 million apartments for rent, 200,000 fewer than in the free-market situation. At the same time, more people will want to rent apartments at a price of $800 than at the equilibrium price of $1,000; as shown at point B on the demand curve, at a monthly rent of $800 the quantity of apartments demanded rises to 2.2 million, 200,000 more than in the free-market situation and 400,000 more than are actually available at the price of $800. So there is now a persistent shortage of rental housing: at that price, 400,000 more people want to rent than are able to find apartments.

Do price ceilings always cause shortages? No. If a price ceiling is set above the equilibrium price, it won't have any effect. Suppose that the equilibrium rental rate on apartments is $1,000 per month and the city government sets a ceiling of $1,200. Who cares? In this case, the price ceiling won't be binding—it won't actually constrain market behavior—and it will have no effect.

Why a Price Ceiling Causes Inefficiency

The housing shortage shown in Figure 4-2 is not merely annoying: like any shortage induced by price controls, it can be seriously harmful because it leads to *inefficiency*. We introduced the concept of *efficiency* back in Chapter 1, where we learned that an economy is efficient if there is no way to make some people better off without making others worse off. We also learned the basic principle that a market economy, left to itself, is usually efficient.

A market or an economy becomes **inefficient** when there are missed opportunities—ways in which production or consumption could be rearranged that would make some people better off without making other people worse off.

> A market or an economy is **inefficient** if there are missed opportunities: some people could be made better off without making other people worse off.

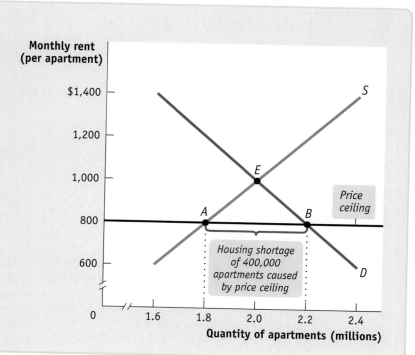

Figure 4-2

The Effects of a Price Ceiling

The dark horizontal line represents the government-imposed price ceiling on rents of $800 per month. This price ceiling reduces the quantity of apartments supplied to 1.8 million, point A, and increases the quantity demanded to 2.2 million, point B. This creates a persistent shortage of 400,000 units: 400,000 people who want apartments at the legal rent of $800 but cannot get them.

Rent control, like all price ceilings, creates inefficiency in at least three distinct ways: in the allocation of apartments to renters, in the time wasted searching for apartments, and in the inefficiently low quality or condition in which landlords maintain apartments. In addition to inefficiency, price ceilings give rise to illegal behavior as people try to circumvent them.

Inefficient Allocation to Consumers In the case shown in Figure 4-2, 2.2 million people would like to rent an apartment at $800 per month, but only 1.8 million apartments are available. Of those 2.2 million who are seeking an apartment, some want an apartment badly and are willing to pay a high price to get one. Others have a less urgent need and are only willing to pay a low price, perhaps because they have alternative housing. An efficient allocation of apartments would reflect these differences: people who really want an apartment will get one and people who aren't all that anxious to find an apartment won't. In an inefficient distribution of apartments, the opposite will happen: some people who are not especially anxious to find an apartment will get one but others who are very anxious to find an apartment won't. And because under rent control people usually get apartments through luck or personal connections, rent control generally results in an **inefficient allocation to consumers** of the few apartments available.

To see the inefficiency involved, consider the plight of the Lees, a family with young children who have no alternative housing and would be willing to pay up to $1,500 for an apartment—but are unable to find one. Also consider George, a retiree who lives most of the year in Florida but still has a lease on the New York apartment he moved into 40 years ago. George pays $800 per month for this apartment, but if the rent were even slightly more—say, $850—he would give it up and stay with his children when he is in New York.

This allocation of apartments—George has one and the Lees do not—is a missed opportunity: there is a way to make the Lees and George both better off at no additional cost. The Lees would be happy to pay George, say, $1,200 a month to sublet his apartment, which he would happily accept since the apartment is worth no more than $850 a month to him. George would prefer the money he gets from the Lees to keeping his apartment; the Lees would prefer to have the apartment rather than the money. So both would be made better off by this transaction—and nobody else would be hurt.

Generally, if people who really want apartments could sublet them from people who are less eager to stay in them, both those who gain apartments and those who trade their leases for more money would be better off. However, subletting is illegal under rent control because it would occur at prices above the price ceiling. But just because subletting is illegal doesn't mean it never happens; in fact, it does occur in New York, although not on a scale that would undo the effects of rent control. This illegal subletting is a kind of *black market activity*, which we will discuss shortly.

Wasted Resources A second reason a price ceiling causes inefficiency is that it leads to **wasted resources**. The Economics in Action on page 89 describes the gasoline shortages of 1979, when millions of Americans spent hours each week waiting in lines at gas stations. The *opportunity cost* of the time spent in gas lines—the wages not earned, the leisure time not enjoyed—constituted wasted resources from the point of view of consumers and of the economy as a whole. Because of rent control, the Lees will spend all their spare time for several months searching for an apartment, time they would rather have spent working or in family activities. That is, there is an opportunity cost to the Lees' prolonged search for an apartment—the leisure or income they had to forgo. If the market for apartments worked freely, the Lees would quickly find an apartment at the equilibrium rent of $1,000 and have time to earn more or to enjoy themselves—an outcome that would make them better off without making anyone else worse off. Again, rent control creates missed opportunities.

Inefficiently Low Quality A third way a price ceiling causes inefficiency is by causing goods to be of **inefficiently low quality**.

Price ceilings often lead to inefficiency in the form of **inefficient allocation to consumers**: people who want the good badly and are willing to pay a high price don't get it, and those who care relatively little about the good and are only willing to pay a low price do get it.

Price ceilings typically lead to inefficiency in the form of **wasted resources**: people spend money and expend effort in order to deal with the shortages caused by the price ceiling.

Price ceilings often lead to inefficiency in that the goods being offered are of **inefficiently low quality**: sellers offer low-quality goods at a low price even though buyers would prefer a higher quality at a higher price.

Again, consider rent control. Landlords have no incentive to provide better conditions because they cannot raise rents to cover their repair costs but are still able to find tenants easily. In many cases tenants would be willing to pay much more for improved conditions than it would cost for the landlord to provide them—for example, the upgrade of an antiquated electrical system that cannot safely run air conditioners or computers. But any additional payment for such improvements would be legally considered a rent increase, which is prohibited. Indeed, rent-controlled apartments are notoriously badly maintained, rarely painted, subject to frequent electrical and plumbing problems, sometimes even hazardous to inhabit. As one former manager of Manhattan buildings described his job: "At unregulated apartments we'd do most things that the tenants requested. But on the rent-regulated units, we did absolutely only what the law required. . . . We had a perverse incentive to make those tenants unhappy. With regulated apartments, the ultimate objective is to get people out of the building."

This whole situation is a missed opportunity—some tenants would be happy to pay for better conditions, and landlords would be happy to provide them for payment. But such an exchange would occur only if the market were allowed to operate freely.

Black Markets And that leads us to a last aspect of price ceilings: the incentive they provide for *illegal activities*, specifically the emergence of **black markets**. We have already described one kind of black market activity—illegal subletting by tenants. But it does not stop there. Clearly, there is a temptation for a landlord to say to a potential tenant, "Look, you can have the place if you slip me an extra few hundred in cash each month"—and for the tenant to agree, if he or she is one of those people who would be willing to pay much more than the maximum legal rent.

> A **black market** is a market in which goods or services are bought and sold illegally—either because it is illegal to sell them at all or because the prices charged are legally prohibited by a price ceiling.

What's wrong with black markets? In general, it's a bad thing if people break *any* law, because it encourages disrespect for the law in general. Worse yet, in this case illegal activity worsens the position of those who try to be honest. If the Lees are scrupulous about not breaking the rent control law but others—who may need an apartment less than the Lees do—are willing to bribe landlords, the Lees may *never* find an apartment.

So Why Are There Price Ceilings?

We have seen three common results of price ceilings:

- A persistent shortage of the good
- Inefficiency arising from this persistent shortage in the form of inefficient allocation of the good to consumers, resources wasted in searching for the good, and the inefficiently low quality of the good offered for sale
- The emergence of illegal, black market activity

Given these unpleasant consequences, why do governments still sometimes impose price ceilings—and why does rent control, in particular, persist in New York?

One answer is that although price ceilings may have adverse effects, they do benefit some people. In practice, New York's rent control rules—which are more complex than our simple model—hurt most residents but give a small minority of renters much cheaper housing than they would get in an unregulated market. And those who benefit from the controls are typically better organized and more vocal than those who are harmed by them.

Also, when price ceilings have been in effect for a long time, buyers may not have a realistic idea of what would happen without them. In our previous example, the rental rate in an uncontrolled market (Figure 4-1) would be only 25 percent higher than in the controlled market (Figure 4-2)—$1,000 instead of $800. But how would renters know that? Indeed, they might have heard about black market transactions at much higher prices—the Lees or some other family paying George $1,200 or more—and would not realize that these black market prices are much higher than the price that would prevail in a fully free market.

A last answer is that government officials often do not understand supply and demand analysis! It is a great mistake to suppose that economic policies in the real world are always sensible or well informed.

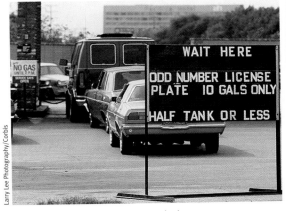

Hurry up and wait: filling your tank circa 1979.

economics in action

Oil Shortages in the 1970s

In 1979 a revolution overthrew the government of Iran, one of the world's major petroleum-exporting countries. The political chaos in Iran disrupted oil production there, and the sudden fall in world supply caused the price of crude oil to shoot up by 300 percent.

In most of the world this price increase made gasoline more expensive at the pump but did not lead to shortages. In the United States, however, gasoline was subject to a price ceiling, imposed six years earlier during an oil crisis sparked by the Arab–Israeli war of 1973. The main purpose of those price controls was to prevent U.S. oil producers from reaping large profits as a result of temporary disruptions of supply.

As we learned in Chapter 3, a fall in supply generally raises prices. But here, because the price of gasoline at the pump couldn't rise, the reduction in supply showed up as shortages. As it turned out, these shortages became much worse because of panic: drivers who weren't sure when they would next be able to get gas rushed to fill up even if they still had plenty in their tanks. This produced a temporary surge in demand and long lines at gas stations.

For a few months the gasoline shortage dominated the national scene. Hours were wasted sitting in gasoline lines; families canceled vacations for fear of being stranded. Eventually, higher production began to work its way through the refineries, increasing supply. And the end of the summer driving season reduced demand. Both together led to a fall in price.

In 1981 price controls on gasoline, now discredited as a policy, were abolished. But the uncontrolled gasoline market faced a major test in the spring of 2000. Oil-producing nations restricted their output in order to drive up prices and achieved unexpected success, more than doubling world prices over a period of a few months. Prices at the pump rose sharply—many people altered their driving plans and some felt distinctly poorer as a result of the higher prices. But there were no shortages and life continued in the United States without nearly as much disruption as price controls had generated in the 1970s.

Interestingly, however, the oil price shock of 2000 *did* cause serious disruptions in some European countries—because truck drivers and farmers, protesting the high price of fuel, blocked deliveries. This protest was an extreme illustration of the reasons why governments sometimes try to control prices despite the known problems with price controls! ■

> > > > > > > > > > > > > > > > > >

Larry Lee Photography/Corbis

►► QUICK REVIEW

➤ *Price controls* take the form of either legal maximum prices—*price ceilings*—or legal minimum prices—*price floors*.

➤ A price ceiling below the equilibrium price benefits successful buyers but causes predictable adverse effects such as persistent *shortages*, which lead to three types of *inefficiencies*: *inefficient allocation to consumers*, *wasted resources*, and *inefficiently low quality*.

➤ Price ceilings also produce *black markets*, as buyers and sellers attempt to evade the price restriction.

>>CHECK YOUR UNDERSTANDING 4-1

1. Homeowners near Middletown University's stadium used to rent parking spaces in their driveways to fans at a going rate of $11. A new town ordinance now sets a maximum parking fee of $7. Use the accompanying supply and demand diagram to explain how each of the following corresponds to a price-ceiling concept.

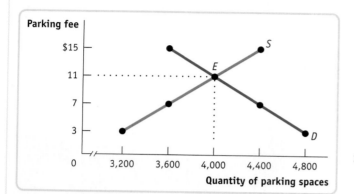

a. Some homeowners now think it's not worth the hassle to rent out spaces.
b. Some fans who used to carpool to the game now drive alone.
c. Some fans can't find parking and leave without seeing the game.

Explain how each of the following arises from the price ceiling.

d. Some fans now arrive several hours early to find parking.
e. Friends of homeowners near the stadium regularly attend games, even if they aren't big fans. But some serious fans have given up because of the parking situation.
f. Some homeowners rent spaces for more than $7 but pretend that the buyers are non-paying friends or family.

2. True or false? Explain your answer. Compared to a free market, price ceilings at a price below the equilibrium price do the following:
a. Increase quantity supplied
b. Make some people who want to consume the good worse off
c. Make all producers worse off

Solutions appear at back of book.

Price Floors

Sometimes governments intervene to push market prices up instead of down. *Price floors* have been widely legislated for agricultural products, such as wheat and milk, as a way to support the incomes of farmers. Historically, there were also price floors on such services as trucking and air travel, although these were phased out by the United States in the 1970s. If you have ever worked in a fast-food restaurant, you are likely to have encountered a price floor: the United States and many other countries maintain a lower limit on the hourly wage rate of a worker's labor—that is, a floor on the price of labor, called the **minimum wage**.

The **minimum wage** is a legal floor on the wage rate, which is the market price of labor.

Just like price ceilings, price floors are intended to help some people but generate predictable and undesirable side effects. Figure 4-3 shows hypothetical supply and demand curves for butter. Left to itself, the market would move to equilibrium at point *E*, with 10 million pounds of butter bought and sold at a price of $1 per pound.

But now suppose that the government, in order to help dairy farmers, imposes a price floor on butter of $1.20 per pound. Its effects are shown in Figure 4-4, where the line at $1.20 represents the price floor. At a price of $1.20 per pound, producers would want to supply 12 million pounds (point *B* on the supply curve) but consumers would want to buy only 9 million pounds (point *A* on the demand curve). There would therefore be a persistent surplus of 3 million pounds of butter.

Does a price floor always lead to an unwanted surplus? No. Just as in the case of a price ceiling, the floor may not be binding—that is, it may be irrelevant. If the equilibrium price of butter is $1 per pound but the floor is set at only $0.80, the floor has no effect.

But suppose that a price floor is binding: what happens to the unwanted surplus? The answer depends on government policy. In the case of agricultural price floors, governments buy up unwanted surplus. Therefore the U.S. government has at times found itself warehousing thousands of tons of butter, cheese, and other farm products. (The European Commission, which administers price floors for a number of European countries, once found itself the owner of a so-called butter mountain, equal in weight to the entire population of Austria.) The government then has to find a way to dispose of these unwanted goods.

Some countries pay exporters to sell products at a loss overseas; this is standard procedure for the European Union. (See For Inquiring Minds on page 92.) At one point the United States tried giving away surplus cheese to the poor. In some cases, governments have actually destroyed the surplus production. To avoid the problem of

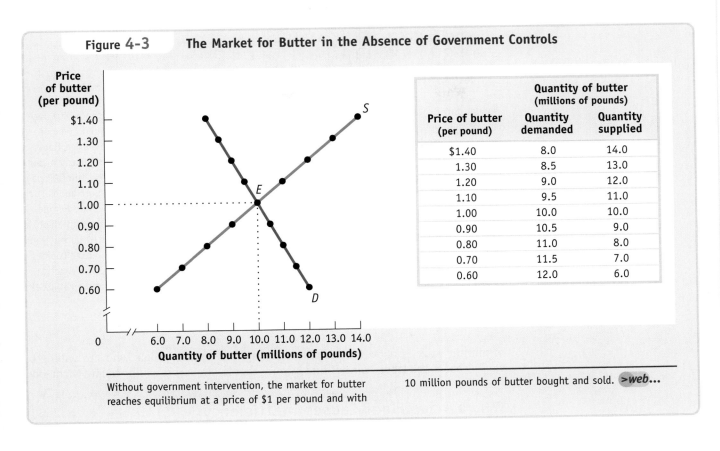

Figure 4-3   The Market for Butter in the Absence of Government Controls

Price of butter (per pound)	Quantity of butter (millions of pounds)	
Price of butter (per pound)	Quantity demanded	Quantity supplied
$1.40	8.0	14.0
1.30	8.5	13.0
1.20	9.0	12.0
1.10	9.5	11.0
1.00	10.0	10.0
0.90	10.5	9.0
0.80	11.0	8.0
0.70	11.5	7.0
0.60	12.0	6.0

Without government intervention, the market for butter reaches equilibrium at a price of $1 per pound and with 10 million pounds of butter bought and sold. **>web...**

dealing with the unwanted supplies, the U.S. government typically pays farmers not to produce the products at all.

When the government is not prepared to purchase the unwanted surplus, a price floor means that would-be sellers cannot find buyers. This is what happens when there is a price floor on the wage rate paid for an hour of labor, the *minimum wage*: when the

Figure 4-4

The Effects of a Price Floor

The dark horizontal line represents the government-imposed price floor of $1.20 per pound of butter. The quantity of butter demanded falls to 9 million pounds while the quantity supplied rises to 12 million pounds, generating a persistent surplus of 3 million pounds of butter. **>web...**

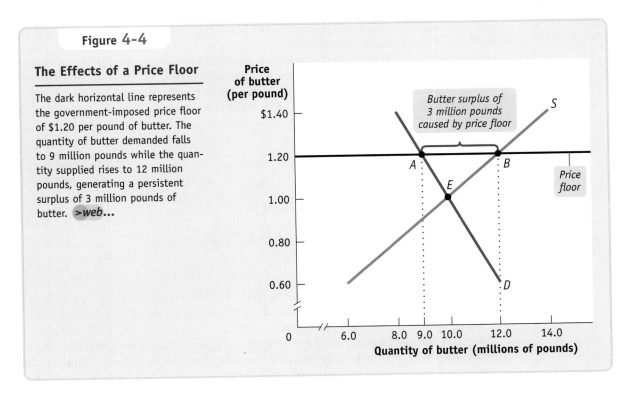

minimum wage is above the equilibrium wage rate, some people who are willing to work—that is, sell labor—cannot find buyers—that is, employers willing to give them jobs.

Why a Price Floor Causes Inefficiency

The persistent surplus that results from a price floor creates missed opportunities—inefficiencies—that resemble those created by the shortage that results from a price ceiling. These include inefficient allocation of sales among sellers, wasted resources, inefficiently high quality, and the temptation to break the law by selling below the legal price.

Inefficient Allocation of Sales Among Sellers
Like a price ceiling, a price floor can lead to *inefficient allocation*—but in this case **inefficient allocation of sales among sellers** rather than inefficient allocation to consumers.

> Price floors lead to **inefficient allocation of sales among sellers**: those who would be willing to sell the good at the lowest price are not always those who actually manage to sell it.

An episode from the Belgian movie *Rosetta*, a realistic fictional story, illustrates the problem of inefficient allocation of selling opportunities quite well. Like many European countries, Belgium has a high minimum wage, and jobs for young people are scarce. At one point Rosetta, a young woman who is very anxious to work, loses her job at a fast-food stand because the owner of the stand replaces her with his son—a very reluctant worker. Rosetta would be willing to work for less money, and with the money he would save, the owner could give his son an allowance and let him do something else. But to hire Rosetta for less than the minimum wage would be illegal.

Wasted Resources
Also like a price ceiling, a price floor generates inefficiency by *wasting resources*. The most graphic examples involve agricultural products with price floors when the government buys up the unwanted surplus. The surplus production is sometimes destroyed, which is a pure waste; in other cases the stored produce goes, as officials euphemistically put it, "out of condition" and must be thrown away.

Price floors also lead to wasted time and effort. Consider the minimum wage. Would-be workers who spend many hours searching for jobs, or waiting in line in the hope of getting jobs, play the same role in the case of price floors as hapless families searching for apartments in the case of price ceilings.

Inefficiently High Quality
Again like price ceilings, price floors lead to inefficiency in the quality of goods produced.

We saw that when there is a price ceiling, suppliers produce products that are of inefficiently low quality: buyers prefer higher-quality products and are willing to pay for them, but sellers refuse to improve the quality of their products because the price ceiling prevents their being compensated for doing so. This same logic applies to price floors, but in reverse: suppliers offer goods of **inefficiently high quality**.

How can this be? Isn't high quality a good thing? Yes, but only if it is worth the cost. Suppose that suppliers spend a lot to make goods of very high quality but that this quality is not worth all that much to consumers, who would rather receive the money spent on that quality in the form of a lower price. This represents a missed opportunity: suppliers and buyers could make a mutually beneficial deal in which buyers got goods of somewhat lower quality for a much lower price.

A good example of the inefficiency of excessive quality comes from the days when transatlantic airfares were set artificially high by international treaty. Forbidden to compete for customers by offering lower ticket prices, airlines instead offered expensive services, like lavish in-flight meals that went largely uneaten. At one point the regulators tried to restrict this practice by defining maximum service standards—for example, that snack service should consist of no more than a sandwich. One airline then introduced what it called a "Scandinavian Sandwich," a towering affair that forced the convening of another conference to define *sandwich*. All of this was wasteful, especially considering that what passengers really wanted was less food and lower airfares.

Since the deregulation of U.S. airlines in the 1970s, American passengers have experienced a large decrease in ticket prices accompanied by a decrease in the quality of in-flight service—smaller seats, lower-quality food, and so on. Everyone complains about the service—but thanks to lower fares, the number of people flying on U.S. carriers has grown several hundred percent since airline deregulation.

Illegal Activity Finally, like price ceilings, price floors can provide an incentive for *illegal activity*. For example, in countries where the minimum wage is far above the equilibrium wage rate, workers desperate for jobs sometimes agree to work off the books for employers who conceal their employment from the government—or bribe the government inspectors. This practice, known in Europe as "black labor," is especially common in Southern European countries such as Italy and Spain (see Economics in Action below).

> Price floors often lead to inefficiency in that goods of **inefficiently high quality** are offered: sellers offer high-quality goods at a high price, even though buyers would prefer a lower quality at a lower price.

So Why Are There Price Floors?

To sum up, a price floor creates various negative side effects:

- A persistent surplus of the good
- Inefficiency arising from the persistent surplus in the form of inefficient allocation of sales among sellers, wasted resources, and an inefficiently high level of quality offered by suppliers
- The temptation to engage in illegal activity, particularly bribery and corruption of government officials

So why do governments impose price floors when they have so many negative side effects? The reasons are similar to those for imposing price ceilings. Government officials often disregard warnings about the consequences of price floors either because they believe that the relevant market is poorly described by the supply and demand model or, more often, because they do not understand the model. Above all, just as price ceilings are often imposed because they benefit some influential buyers of a good, price floors are often imposed because they benefit some influential *sellers*.

economics in action

"Black Labor" in Southern Europe

The best-known example of a price floor is the minimum wage. Most economists believe, however, that the minimum wage has relatively little effect on the job market in the United States, mainly because the floor is set so low. (This effectively makes the U.S. minimum wage a *nonbinding* price floor—a political symbol more than a substantive policy.) In 1968, the U.S. minimum wage was 53 percent of the average wage of blue-collar workers; by 2003, it had fallen to about 34 percent.

The situation is different, however, in many European countries, where minimum wages have been set much higher than in the United States. This has happened despite the fact that European workers are somewhat less productive than their American counterparts, which means that the equilibrium wage in Europe—the wage that would clear the labor market—is probably lower in Europe than in the United States. Moreover, European countries often require employers to pay for health and retirement benefits, which are more extensive and therefore more costly than comparable American benefits. These mandated benefits make the actual cost of hiring a European worker considerably more than the worker's paycheck.

The result is that in Europe the price floor on labor is definitely binding: the minimum wage is well above the wage rate that would make the quantity of labor supplied by workers equal to the quantity of labor demanded by employers.

The persistent surplus that results from this price floor appears in the form of high unemployment—millions of workers, especially young workers, seek jobs but cannot find them. In countries where the enforcement of labor laws is lax, however, there is a second, entirely predictable result: widespread evasion of the law. In both Italy and Spain, officials believe there are hundreds of thousands, if not millions, of workers who are employed by companies that pay them less than the legal minimum, fail to provide the required health and retirement benefits, or both. In many cases the jobs are simply unreported: Spanish economists estimate that about a third of the country's reported unemployed are in the black labor market—working at unreported jobs. In fact, Spaniards waiting to collect checks from the unemployment office have been known to complain about the long lines that keep them from getting back to work!

Employers in these countries have also found legal ways to evade the wage floor. For example, Italy's labor regulations apply only to companies with 15 or more workers. This gives a big cost advantage to small Italian firms, many of which remain small in order to avoid having to pay higher wages and benefits. And sure enough, in some Italian industries there is an astonishing proliferation of tiny companies. For example, one of Italy's most successful industries is the manufacture of fine woolen cloth, centered in the Prato region. The average textile firm in that region employs only four workers! ∎

< < < < < < < < < < < < < < < < < < <

>>QUICK REVIEW

➤ The most familiar price floor is the *minimum wage*. Price floors are also commonly imposed on agricultural goods.

➤ A price floor above the equilibrium price benefits successful sellers but causes predictable adverse effects such as a persistent *surplus*, which leads to three kinds of inefficiencies: *inefficient allocation of sales among sellers*, *wasted resources*, and *inefficiently high quality*.

➤ Price floors encourage illegal activity, such as workers who work off the books, often leading to official corruption.

>>CHECK YOUR UNDERSTANDING 4-2

1. The state legislature mandates a price floor for gasoline of $4 per gallon. Assess the following statements and illustrate your answer using the figure provided:

a. Proponents of the law claim it will increase the income of gas station owners. Opponents claim it will hurt gas station owners because they will lose customers.

b. Proponents claim consumers will be better off because gas stations will provide better service. Opponents claim consumers will be generally worse off because they prefer to buy gas at cheaper prices.

c. Proponents claim that they are helping gas station owners without hurting anyone else. Opponents claim that consumers are hurt and will end up doing things like buying gas in a nearby state or on the black market.

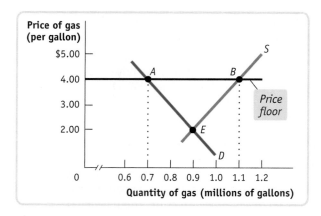

Controlling Quantities

In the 1930s, New York City instituted a system of licensing for taxicabs: only taxis with a "medallion" were allowed to pick up passengers. Because this system was intended to assure quality, medallion owners were supposed to maintain certain standards, including safety and cleanliness. A total of 11,787 medallions were issued, with taxi owners paying $10 for each medallion.

In 1995, there were still only 11,787 licensed taxicabs in New York, even though the city had meanwhile become the financial capital of the world, a place where hundreds of thousands of people in a hurry tried to hail a cab every day. (An additional 400 medallions were issued in 1995, and in 2003 plans were announced to issue 900 more over a period of three years.)

The result of this restriction on the number of taxis was that those medallions became very valuable: if you wanted to operate a New York taxi, you had to lease a medallion from someone else or buy one for a going price of about $250,000.

It turns out that the New York story is not unique; other cities introduced similar medallion systems in the 1930s and, like New York, have issued few new medallions since. In San Francisco and Boston, as in New York, taxi medallions trade for six-figure prices.

A taxi medallion system is a form of **quantity control**, or **quota**, by which the government regulates the quantity of a good that can be bought and sold rather than the price at which it is transacted. The total amount of the good that can be transacted under the quantity control is called the **quota limit**. Typically, the government limits quantity in a market by issuing **licenses;** only people with a license can legally supply the good. A taxi medallion is just such a license. The government of New York City limits the number of taxi rides that can be sold by limiting the number of taxis to only those who hold medallions. There are many other cases of quantity controls, ranging from limits on how much foreign currency (for instance, British pounds or Mexican pesos) people are allowed to buy to the quantity of clams New Jersey fishing boats are allowed to catch. Notice, by the way, that although there are price controls on both sides of the equilibrium price—price ceilings and price floors—in the real world, quantity controls always set an upper, not a lower, limit on quantities. After all, nobody can be forced to buy or sell more than they want to!

Some of these attempts to control quantities are undertaken for good economic reasons, some for bad ones. In many cases, as we will see, quantity controls introduced to address a temporary problem become politically hard to remove later because the beneficiaries don't want them abolished, even after the original reason for their existence is long gone. But whatever the reasons for such controls, they have certain predictable—and usually undesirable—economic consequences.

The Anatomy of Quantity Controls

To understand why a New York taxi medallion is worth so much money, we consider a simplified version of the market for taxi rides, shown in Figure 4-5 on page 96. Just as we assumed in the analysis of rent controls that all apartments are the same, we now suppose that all taxi rides are the same—ignoring the real-world complication that some taxi rides are longer, and thus more expensive, than others. The table in the figure shows supply and demand schedules. The equilibrium—indicated by point E in the figure and by the shaded entries in the table—is a fare of $5 per ride, with 10 million rides taken per year. (You'll see in a minute why we present the equilibrium this way.)

The New York medallion system limits the number of taxis, but each taxi driver can offer as many rides as he or she can manage. (Now you know why New York taxi drivers are so aggressive!) To simplify our analysis, however, we will assume that a medallion system limits the number of taxi rides that can legally be given to 8 million per year.

Until now, we have derived the demand curve by answering questions of the form: "How many taxi rides will passengers want to take if the price is $5 per ride?" But it is possible to reverse the question and ask instead: "At what price will consumers want to buy 10 million rides per year?" The price at which consumers want to buy a given quantity—in this case, 10 million rides at $5 per ride—is the **demand price** of that

A **quantity control**, or **quota**, is an upper limit on the quantity of some good that can be bought or sold. The total amount of the good that can be legally transacted is the **quota limit**.

A **license** gives its owner the right to supply a good.

The **demand price** of a given quantity is the price at which consumers will demand that quantity.

Figure 4-5 **The Market for Taxi Rides in the Absence of Government Controls**

Fare (per ride)	Quantity of rides (millions per year)	
	Quantity demanded	Quantity supplied
$7.00	6	14
6.50	7	13
6.00	8	12
5.50	9	11
5.00	10	10
4.50	11	9
4.00	12	8
3.50	13	7
3.00	14	6

Without government intervention, the market reaches equilibrium with 10 million rides taken per year at a fare of $5 per ride.

quantity. You can see from the demand schedule in Figure 4-5 that the demand price of 6 million rides is $7, the demand price of 7 million rides is $6.50, and so on.

Similarly, the supply curve represents the answer to questions of the form: "How many taxi rides would taxi drivers supply at a price of $5 each?" But we can also reverse this question to ask: "At what price will suppliers be willing to supply 10 million rides per year?" The price at which suppliers will supply a given quantity—in this case, 10 million rides at $5 per ride—is the **supply price** of that quantity. We can see from the supply schedule in Figure 4-5 that the supply price of 6 million rides is $3, the supply price of 7 million rides is $3.50, and so on.

> The **supply price** of a given quantity is the price at which producers will supply that quantity.

Now we are ready to analyze a quota. We have assumed that the city government limits the quantity of taxi rides to 8 million per year. Medallions, each of which carries the right to provide a certain number of taxi rides per year, are made available to selected people in such a way that a total of 8 million rides will be provided. Medallion holders may then either drive their own taxis or rent their medallions to others for a fee.

Figure 4-6 shows the resulting market for taxi rides, with the line at 8 million rides per year representing the quota limit. Because the quantity of rides is limited to 8 million, consumers must be at point A on the demand curve, corresponding to the shaded entry in the demand schedule: the demand price of 8 million rides is $6. Meanwhile, taxi drivers must be at point B on the supply curve, corresponding to the shaded entry in the supply schedule: the supply price of 8 million rides is $4.

But how can the price received by taxi drivers be $4 when the price paid by taxi riders is $6? The answer is that in addition to the market in taxi rides, there will also be a market in medallions. Medallion-holders may not always want to drive their taxis: they may be ill or on vacation. So those who do not want to drive their own taxis will sell the right to use the medallion to someone else. So we need to consider two sets of transactions here, and hence two prices: (1) the transactions in taxi rides and the price at which these will occur, and (2) the transactions in medallions and the price at which these will occur. It turns out that since we are looking at two markets, the $4 and $6 prices will both be right.

To see how this all works, consider two imaginary New York taxi drivers, Sunil and Harriet. Sunil has a medallion but can't use it because he's recovering from a severely sprained wrist. So he's looking to rent his medallion out to someone else. Harriet

Figure 4-6   Effect of a Quota on the Market for Taxi Rides

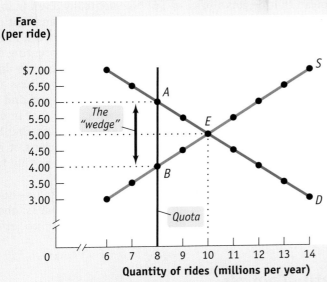

Fare (per ride)	Quantity of rides (millions per year)	
	Quantity demanded	Quantity supplied
$7.00	6	14
6.50	7	13
6.00	8	12
5.50	9	11
5.00	10	10
4.50	11	9
4.00	12	8
3.50	13	7
3.00	14	6

The table shows the demand price and the supply price corresponding to each quantity: the price at which that quantity would be demanded and supplied, respectively. The city government imposes a quota of 8 million rides by selling licenses for only 8 million rides, represented by the dark vertical line. The price paid by consumers rises to $6 per ride, the demand price of 8 million rides, shown by point *A*. The supply price of 8 million rides is only $4 per ride, shown by point *B*. The difference between these two prices is the quota rent per ride, the earnings that accrue to the owner of a license. The quota rent drives a wedge between the demand price and the supply price. **>web...**

oesn't have a medallion but would like to rent one. Furthermore, at any point in time here are many other people like Harriet who would like to rent a medallion as well as any others like Sunil who have a medallion to rent. Suppose Sunil agrees to rent his edallion to Harriet. To make things simple, assume that any driver can give only one e per day and that Sunil is renting his medallion to Harriet for one day. What rental e will they agree on?

o answer this question, we need to look at the transactions from the viewpoints of drivers. Once she has the medallion, Harriet knows she can make $6 per day—emand price of a ride under the quota. And she is willing to rent the medallion f she makes at least $4 per day—the supply price of a ride under the quota. So cannot demand a rent of more than $2—the difference between $6 and $4. And riet offered Sunil less than $2—say, $1.50—there would be other eager drivers to offer him more, up to $2. Hence, in order to get the medallion, Harriet must nil at least $2. Therefore, since the rent can be no more than $2 and no less it must be exactly $2.

o coincidence that $2 is exactly the difference between $6, the demand price of rides, and $4, the supply price of 8 million rides. In every case in which the sup-od is legally restricted, there is a **wedge** between the demand price of the quan-cted and the supply price of the quantity transacted. This wedge, illustrated by -headed arrow in Figure 4-6, has a special name: the **quota rent**. It is the earn-ccrue to the license-holder from ownership of a valuable commodity, the he case of Sunil and Harriet, the quota rent of $2 goes to Sunil because he ense, and the remaining $4 from the total fare of $6 goes to Harriet.

4-6 also illustrates the quota rent in the market for New York taxi rides. mits the quantity of rides to 8 million per year, a quantity at which the e of $6 exceeds the supply price of $4. The wedge between these two the quota rent that results from the restrictions placed on the quantity ⌐ this market.

A quantity control, or quota, drives a **wedge** between the demand price and the supply price of a good; that is, the price paid by buyers ends up being higher than that received by sellers. The difference between the demand and supply price at the quota limit is the **quota rent,** the earnings that accrue to the license-holder from own-ership of the right to sell the good. It is equal to the market price of the license when the licenses are traded.

But wait a second. What if Sunil doesn't rent out his medallion? What if he uses it himself? Doesn't this mean that he gets a price of $6? No, not really. Even if Sunil doesn't rent out his medallion, he could have rented it out, which means that the medallion has an *opportunity cost* of $2: if Sunil decides to drive his own taxi rather than renting it to Harriet, the $2 represents his opportunity cost of not renting out his medallion. That is, the $2 quota rent is now the rental income he forgoes by driving his own taxi. In effect, Sunil is in two businesses—the taxi-driving business and the medallion-renting business. He makes $4 per ride from driving his taxi and $2 per ride from renting out his medallion. It doesn't make any difference that in this particular case he has rented his medallion to himself! So regardless of whether the medallion owner uses the medallion himself or herself, or rents it to others, it is a valuable asset. And this is represented in the going price for a New York City taxi medallion: in 2004, it was around $250,000.

Notice, by the way, that quotas—like price ceilings and price floors—don't always have a real effect. If the quota were set at 12 million rides—that is, above the equilibrium quantity in an unregulated market—it would have no effect because it would not be binding.

The Costs of Quantity Controls

Like price controls, quantity controls can have some undesirable side effects. The first is the by-now-familiar problem of *inefficiency* due to missed opportunities: quantity controls prevent mutually beneficial transactions from occurring, transactions that would benefit both buyers and sellers. Looking back at Figure 4-6, you can see that starting at the quota limit of 8 million rides, New Yorkers would be willing to pay at least $5.50 per ride for an additional 1 million rides and that taxi drivers would be willing to provide those rides as long as they got at least $4.50 per ride. These are rides that would have taken place if there were no quota limit. The same is true for the next 1 million rides: New Yorkers would be willing to pay at least $5 per ride when the quantity of rides is increased from 9 to 10 million, and taxi drivers would be willing to provide those rides as long as they got at least $5 per ride. Again, these rides would have occurred without the quota limit. Only when the market has reached the free-market equilibrium quantity of 10 million rides are there no "missed-opportunity rides"—the quota limit of 8 million rides has caused 2 million "missed-opportunity rides." Generally, *as long as the demand price of a given quantity exceeds the supply price, there is a missed opportunity.* A buyer would be willing to buy the good at a price that the seller would be willing to accept, but such a transaction does not occur because it is forbidden by the quota.

And because there are transactions that people would like to make but are not allowed to, quantity controls generate an incentive to evade them or even to break the law. New York's taxi industry again provides clear examples. Taxi regulation applies only to those drivers who are hailed by passengers on the street. A car service that makes prearranged pickups does not need a medallion. As a result, such hired cars provide much of the service that might otherwise be provided by taxis, as in other cities. In addition, there are substantial numbers of unlicensed cabs that simply defy the law by picking up passengers without a medallion. Because these cabs are illegal, their drivers are completely unregulated, and they generate a disproportionately large share of traffic accidents in New York.

In fact, in 2004 the hardships caused by the limited number of New York taxis led city leaders to authorize an increase in the number of licensed taxis from 12,187 to a little over 13,000 by 2007—a move that certainly cheered New York riders. But those who already owned medallions were less happy with the increase; they understood that the nearly 900 new taxis would reduce or eliminate the shortage of taxis. As a result, taxi drivers might find their revenues decline as they would no longer always be assured of finding willing customers. And, in turn, the value of a medallion would fall. So, to placate the medallion owners, city officials also agreed in 2004 to raise fares by 25 percent, a move that slightly diminished the newfound cheer of New York riders.

In sum, quantity controls typically create the following undesirable side effects:

- Inefficiencies, or missed opportunities, in the form of mutually beneficial transactions that don't occur
- Incentives for illegal activities

economics in action

The Clams of New Jersey

Forget the refineries along the Jersey Turnpike; one industry that New Jersey *really* dominates is clam fishing. The Garden State supplies 80 percent of the world's surf clams, whose tongues are used in fried-clam dinners, and 40 percent of the quahogs, which are used to make clam chowder.

In the 1980s, however, excessive fishing threatened to wipe out New Jersey's clam beds. To save the resource, the U.S. government introduced a clam quota, which sets an overall limit on the number of bushels of clams that may be caught and allocates licenses to owners of fishing boats based on their historical catches.

Notice, by the way, that this is an example of a quota that is probably justified by broader economic and environmental considerations—unlike the New York taxicab quota, which has long since lost any economic rationale. Still, whatever its rationale, the New Jersey clam quota works the same way as any other quota.

Once the quota system was established, many boat owners stopped fishing for clams. They realized that rather than operate a boat part time, it was more profitable to sell or rent their licenses to someone else, who could then assemble enough licenses to operate a boat full time. Today, there are about 50 boats fishing for clams; the license required to operate one is worth more than the boat itself. ■

>>> > > > > > > > > > > > > > > > >

>> CHECK YOUR UNDERSTANDING 4-3

1. Suppose that the supply and demand for taxi rides is given by Figure 4-5 but the quota is set at 6 million rides instead of 8 million. Find the following and indicate them on Figure 4-5.
   a. The price of a ride
   b. The quota rent
   c. Suppose the quota limit on taxi rides is increased to 9 million. What happens to the quota rent?
2. Assume that the quota limit is 8 million rides. Suppose demand decreases due to a decline in tourism. What is the smallest parallel leftward shift in demand that would result in the quota no longer having an effect on the market? Illustrate your answer using Figure 4-5.

Solutions appear at back of book.

A Surprise Parallel: Taxes

To provide the services we want, from national defense to public parks, governments must collect taxes. But taxes impose costs on the economy. Among the most important roles of economics is tax analysis: figuring out the economic costs of taxation, determining who bears those costs, and suggesting ways to change the tax system that will reduce the costs it imposes. It turns out that the same analysis we have just used to understand quotas can be used, with hardly any modification, to make a preliminary analysis of taxes, too.

Why Is a Tax Like a Quota?

Suppose that the supply and demand curves for New York taxis were exactly as shown in Figure 4-5. This means that in the absence of government action, the equilibrium price of a taxi ride will be $5 and 10 million rides will be bought and sold.

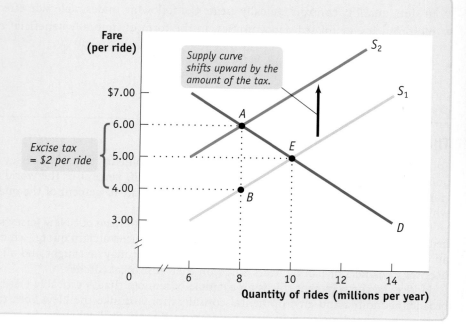

Figure 4-7

Effect of an Excise Tax Levied on Sales of Taxi Rides

S_1 is the supply curve before the tax. After the city requires drivers to pay a tax of \$2 for every ride they give, the supply curve shifts upward by \$2, to the new supply curve S_2. This means that the price drivers receive net of tax is \$4, represented by point B on the old supply curve S_1. And the price paid by riders is \$6, represented by point A on the new supply curve S_2. The tax drives a wedge between the demand price, \$6, and the original supply price, \$4.

An **excise tax** is a tax on sales of a good or service.

Now suppose that instead of imposing a quota on the quantity of rides, the city imposes an **excise tax**—a tax on sales. Specifically, it charges taxi drivers \$2 for each ride they provide. What is the effect of the tax?

From the point of view of a taxi driver, the tax means that he or she doesn't get to keep all of the fare: if a passenger pays \$5, \$2 is collected as a tax, so the driver gets only \$3. For any given quantity of rides supplied, the *post-tax supply price* is higher than the pre-tax supply price. For example, drivers will now require a price of \$6 to supply as many rides as they would have been willing to supply at a price of \$4 in the absence of the \$2 tax.

So the tax on sales shifts the supply curve upward, by the amount of the tax. This is shown in Figure 4-7, where S_1 is the supply curve before the tax is imposed and S_2 is the supply curve after the tax is imposed. The market equilibrium moves from E, where the price is \$5 per ride and 10 million rides are bought and sold, to A, where the price is \$6 per ride and 8 million rides are bought and sold. A is, of course, on both the demand curve D and the new supply curve S_2.

But how do we know that 8 million rides will be supplied at a price of \$6? Because the price *net of the tax* is \$4 and the pre-tax supply price of 8 million rides is \$4, as shown by point B in Figure 4-7.

Does all this look familiar? It should. The equilibrium with a \$2 tax on rides, which reduces the quantity bought and sold to 8 million rides, looks just like the equilibrium with a quota of 8 million rides, which leads to a quota rent of \$2 per ride. Just like a quota, the tax *drives a wedge* between the demand price and the original, pre-tax supply price.

The only difference is that instead of paying a \$2 rent to the owner of a license, drivers pay a \$2 tax to the city. In fact, there is a way to make an excise tax and a quota completely equivalent. Imagine that instead of issuing a limited number of licenses, the city simply sold licenses at \$2 each. This \$2 license fee would, for all practical purposes, be a \$2 excise tax.

Finally, imagine that instead of selling licenses at a fixed price, the city were to issue 8 million licenses and auction them off—that is, sell them for whatever price the, um, traffic will bear. What would be the price of a license? Surely it would be \$2—the quota rent. And so in this case the quota rent would act just like an excise tax.

Who Pays an Excise Tax?

We have just imagined a tax that must be paid by the *sellers* of a good. But what would happen if the tax were instead paid by the *buyers*—say, if you had to pay a special \$2 tax to ride in a taxicab?

Figure 4-8

Effect of an Excise Tax Levied on Purchases of Taxi Rides

D_1 is the demand curve before the tax. After the city requires riders to pay the $2 tax per ride, the demand curve shifts down by $2 to the new demand curve D_2. Drivers again receive, net of tax, $4, represented by point B, while riders again pay a total price of $6, represented by point A. The incidence of the tax is exactly the same as in Figure 4-7. This shows that who officially pays a tax is irrelevant when answering the question of who bears the burden of the tax.

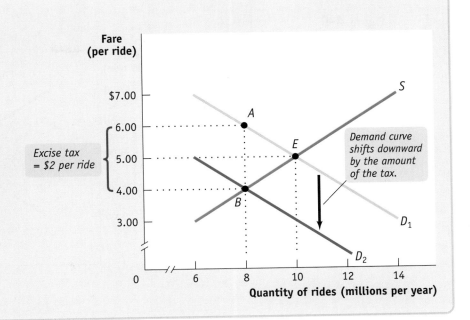

The answer is shown in Figure 4-8. If a taxi rider must pay a $2 tax on each ride, then the price riders pay must be $2 less in order for the quantity of taxi rides demanded post-tax to be the same quantity as that demanded pre-tax. So the demand curve shifts *downward*, from D_1 to D_2, by the amount of the tax. This shifts the equilibrium from E to B, where the market price is $4 per ride and 8 million rides are bought and sold. In this case, $4 is the supply price of 8 million rides and $6 is the demand price—but in effect riders do pay $6, when you include the tax. So it is just as if riders were on their original demand curve at point A.

If you compare Figures 4-7 and 4-8, you will immediately notice that they show the same price effect. In each case, buyers pay an effective price of $6, sellers receive an effective price of $4, and 8 million rides are bought and sold. *It doesn't seem to make any difference who officially pays the tax.*

This insight is a general one in analyzing taxes: the **incidence** of a tax—who really bears the burden of the tax—is often not a question you can answer by asking who actually writes the check to the government. In this particular case, a $2 tax on taxi rides is reflected in a $1 increase in the price paid by buyers and a $1 decrease in the price received by sellers; so the incidence of the tax is actually evenly split between buyers and sellers. This incidence is the same regardless of whether the check to the city government is made out by buyers or by sellers.

The incidence of an excise tax isn't always split evenly between buyers and sellers as in this example. Depending on the shapes of supply and demand curves, the incidence of an excise tax may be divided differently.

> The **incidence** of a tax is a measure of who really pays it.

The Revenue from an Excise Tax

Although both buyers and sellers lose from an excise tax, the government does collect revenue—which is the whole point of the tax. How much revenue does the government collect? The revenue is equal to the area of the shaded rectangle in Figure 4-9 on the next page.

To see why this is the revenue collected by a $2 tax on taxi rides, notice that the *height* of the rectangle is $2. This is the amount of the tax per ride; it is also, as we have seen, the size of the wedge that the tax drives between the supply price and the demand price. Meanwhile, the *width* of the rectangle is 8 million rides, which is the equilibrium quantity of rides given that $2 tax.

Figure 4-9

The Revenue from an Excise Tax

The government revenue collected by this excise tax is equal to the area of the shaded rectangle. In this case it is $2 per ride × 8 million rides = $16 million.

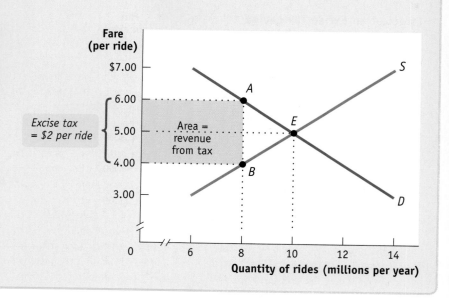

The revenue collected by the tax is

Revenue = $2 per ride × 8 million rides = $16 million

But the area of the rectangle is

Area = height × width = $2 per ride × 8 million rides = $16 million

This is a general principle: *The revenue collected by an excise tax is equal to the area of the rectangle whose height is the wedge that the tax drives between the supply and demand curves, and whose width is the quantity bought and sold under the tax.*

The Costs of Taxation

What is the cost of a tax? You might be inclined to answer that it is the money taxpayers pay to the government. But suppose the government used that money to provide services everyone wants or simply handed the money back to taxpayers. Would we then say that the tax didn't cost anything?

No—because a tax, like a quota, prevents mutually beneficial transactions from occurring. Consider Figure 4-9 once more. With a $2 tax on taxi rides, riders pay $6 per ride but drivers receive only $4. There are therefore some potential riders who would be willing to pay only, say, $5.50 per ride; and there are some drivers who would be willing to charge them, say, $4.50. If those drivers and riders could be brought together, this would be a mutually beneficial transaction. But such a deal would be illegal, because the $2 tax would not have been paid.

More broadly, we know that there are 2 million potential taxi rides that would have been taken in the absence of the tax, to the mutual benefit of riders and drivers, that do not take place because of that tax.

So an excise tax imposes additional costs, over and above the money actually paid in taxes, in the form of inefficiency, which occurs because the tax discourages mutually beneficial transactions. This is the **excess burden**, or **deadweight loss**, from a tax. And all real-world taxes do impose some excess burden, although badly designed taxes impose bigger excess burdens than well-thought-out ones.

Economists sometimes say that the real cost of a tax is not the taxes that people pay but the taxes that they *don't* pay. What they mean is that people change their

The **excess burden**, or **deadweight loss**, from a tax is the extra cost in the form of inefficiency that results because the tax discourages mutually beneficial transactions.

IF SELLING CIGARETTES IS A CRIME, ONLY CRIMINALS WILL SELL CIGARETTES

Cigarettes have long been subject to state excise taxes. As the antismoking movement has gained political power, many states and local governments have increased those taxes. Officials see high taxes on cigarettes as a way of doing well by doing good—raising more revenue while discouraging a bad habit. In 2002, increases at both the state and local levels raised the tax on a pack of cigarettes sold in New York City from $1.19 to $3.

But tobacco-growing states have not followed the trend. In Virginia, for example, the cigarette tax is only 2.5 cents per pack. And this divergence has created an opportunity for those who don't mind breaking the law: there is large-scale smuggling of cigarettes from low-tax tobacco-growing states to high-tax locations like New York.

Authorities believe that interstate cigarette smuggling, like alcohol smuggling during Prohibition, has largely been taken over by organized crime. But there is still room for smaller players: in July 2000, the FBI broke up a group, based in Charlotte, North Carolina, that had been funneling its profits to a foreign group that the U.S. government classifies as a terrorist organization.

behavior in order to avoid taxes—for example, by walking instead of taking a taxi—and in so doing miss opportunities for mutual benefit.

One final point: like all of the other government policies analyzed in this chapter, taxes create incentives for illegal activity. For Inquiring Minds above explains how excise taxes on cigarettes have given rise to a substantial smuggling business. And, of course, even seemingly respectable people have been known to be a bit creative with their income taxes.

economics in action

Who Pays the FICA?

Anyone who works for an employer receives a paycheck that itemizes not only the money received but also the money deducted for various taxes. One of the big items for most people is *FICA*, which stands for Federal Insurance Contributions Act. This is the money taken out of your paycheck for the Social Security and Medicare systems, which provide income and medical care to retired and disabled Americans.

As of the time of writing, most American workers paid 7.65 percent of their earnings in FICA. But this is literally only the half of it: employers are required to pay an equal amount.

So how should we think about FICA? Well, it's like an excise tax—a tax on the sale and purchase of labor. Half of it is a tax on the sellers—that is, workers. The other half is a tax on the buyers—that is, employers.

But we already know that the incidence of a tax does not really depend on who actually makes out the check. So the fact that employers nominally pay half the FICA tells us nothing about who really bears the burden.

In fact, most economists believe that the real effect of the FICA is, to a very good approximation, to reduce wages by the full amount of the combined employee and employer payments. That is, you not only pay your own share; your employer's share is reflected in a lower wage, so that you really pay that share, too. Your employer, though she pays the tax, is fully compensated by the lower wage rate. So workers, not employers, bear the burden of both halves of the tax.

>> QUICK REVIEW

➤ Like a quota, an *excise tax* drives a wedge between the demand price and the supply price.

➤ The *incidence* of an excise tax does not depend on who officially pays it, the buyer or the seller.

➤ Like a quota, an excise tax creates inefficiency, by preventing mutually beneficial transactions between buyers and sellers. This *excess burden*, or *deadweight loss*, means that the true cost is always larger than the amount paid in taxes.

➤ Like quotas, taxes create an incentive for illegal activity.

The reason economists think that workers, not employers, really pay the FICA is that the supply of labor (the number of workers willing to take jobs) is much less responsive to the wage rate than is the demand for labor (the number of jobs employers are willing to offer). According to this reasoning, since workers are relatively unresponsive to decreases in the wage rate, employers can easily pass the burden of the tax on to them through lower wages. ∎

< < < < < < < < < < < < < < < < < <

>>CHECK YOUR UNDERSTANDING 4-4

1. Use Figure 4-3 to answer the following questions.
   a. What amount of excise tax generates the same level of inefficiency as a quota of 9 million pounds of butter?
   b. What quota level generates the same level of inefficiency as an excise tax of $0.60 per pound of butter?
   c. In part a, find how the burden of an excise tax is split between buyers and sellers. That is, explain how much of the tax is paid by buyers and how much by sellers in each case.

Solutions appear at back of book.

• A LOOK AHEAD •

In the last two chapters we have gotten a first taste of how economic models help us understand the real world. As we've seen, supply and demand—a simple model of how competitive markets work—can be used to understand and predict the effects of everything from bad weather to misconceived government policies.

In the chapters to come, we'll see how models—including supply and demand, but also going beyond it—can shed light on a wide variety of economic phenomena and issues.

SUMMARY

1. Governments often intervene in markets in attempts to "defy" supply and demand. Interventions can take the form of **price controls** or **quantity controls**. But they generate predictable and undesirable side effects, consisting of various forms of inefficiency and illegal activity.

2. A **price ceiling**, a maximum market price below the equilibrium price, benefits successful buyers but creates persistent shortages: Because the price is maintained below the equilibrium price, the quantity demanded is increased and the quantity supplied is decreased compared to the equilibrium quantity. This leads to predictable problems: **inefficiencies** in the form of **inefficient allocation to consumers**, **wasted resources**, and **inefficiently low quality**. It also encourages illegal activity as people turn to **black markets** to get the good. Because of these problems, price ceilings have generally lost favor as an economic policy tool. But some governments continue to impose them either because they don't understand the effects or because the price ceilings benefit some influential group.

3. A **price floor**, a minimum market price above the equilibrium price, benefits successful sellers but creates persistent surplus: because the price is maintained above the equilibrium price, the quantity demanded is decreased and the quantity supplied is increased compared to the equilibrium quantity. This leads to predictable problems: inefficiencies in the form of **inefficient allocation of sales among sellers**, **wasted resources**, and **inefficiently high quality**. It also encourages illegal activity and black markets. The most well known kind of price floor is the **minimum wage**, but price floors are also commonly applied to agricultural products.

4. **Quantity controls**, or **quotas**, limit the quantity of a good that can be bought or sold. The amount allowed for sale is the **quota limit**. The government issues **licenses** to individuals, the right to sell a given quantity of the good. The owner of a license earns a **quota rent**, earnings that accrue from ownership of the right to sell the good. It is equal to the difference between the **demand price** at the quota limit, what consumers are willing to pay for that amount, and the **supply price** at the quota limit, what suppliers are willing to accept for that amount. Economists say that a quota drives a **wedge** between the demand price and the supply price; this wedge is equal to the quota rent. Quantity controls generate inefficiency in the form of mutually beneficial transactions that don't occur in addition to encouraging illegal activity.

5. **Excise taxes**—taxes on the purchase or sale of a good—have effects similar to quotas. They raise the price paid by buyers and reduce the price received by sellers, driving a wedge between the two. The **incidence** of the tax—the division of higher prices to consumers and lower prices to sellers—does not depend on who officially pays the tax. Excise taxes cause inefficiency—called **excess burden** or **deadweight loss**—because they prevent some mutually beneficial transactions. They also encourage illegal activity in attempts to avoid the tax.

PROBLEMS

1. Suppose it is decided that rent control in New York City will be abolished and that market rents will now prevail. Assume that all rental units are identical and are therefore offered at the same rent. To address the plight of residents who may be unable to pay the market rent, an income supplement will be paid to all low-income households equal to the difference between the old controlled rent and the new market rent.

   a. Use a diagram to show the effect on the rental market of the elimination of rent control. What will happen to the quality and quantity of rental housing supplied?

   b. Now use a second diagram to show the additional effect of the income-supplement policy on the market. What effect does it have on the market rent and quantity of rental housing supplied in comparison to your answers to part a?

   c. Are tenants better or worse off as a result of these policies? Are landlords better or worse off?

   d. From a political standpoint, why do you think cities have been more likely to resort to rent control rather than a policy of income supplements to help low-income people pay for housing?

2. In order to ingratiate himself with voters, the mayor of Gotham City decides to lower the price of taxi rides. Assume, for simplicity, that all taxi rides are the same distance and therefore cost the same. The accompanying table shows the demand and supply schedules for taxi rides.

Fare (per ride)	Quantity of rides (millions per year)	
	Quantity demanded	Quantity supplied
$7.00	10	12
6.50	11	11
6.00	12	10
5.50	13	9
5.00	14	8
4.50	15	7

   a. Assume that there are no restrictions on the number of taxi rides that can be supplied in the city (i.e., there is no medallion system). Find the equilibrium price and quantity.

   b. Suppose that the mayor sets a price ceiling at $5.50. How large is the shortage of rides? Illustrate with a diagram. Who loses and who benefits from this policy?

   c. Suppose that the stock market crashes and, as a result, people in Gotham City are poorer. This reduces the quantity of taxi rides demanded by 6 million rides per year at any given price. What effect will the mayor's new policy have now? Illustrate with a diagram.

   d. Suppose that the stock market rises and the demand for taxi rides returns to normal (that is, returns to the demand schedule given in the table). The mayor now decides to ingratiate himself with taxi drivers. He announces a policy in which operating licenses are given to existing taxi drivers; the number of licenses is restricted such that only 10 million rides per year can be given. Illustrate the effect of this policy on the market, and indicate the resulting price and quantity transacted. What is the quota rent per ride?

3. In the late eighteenth century, the price of bread in New York City was controlled, set at a predetermined price above the market price.

   a. Draw a diagram showing the effect of the policy. Did the policy act as a price ceiling or a price floor?

   b. What kinds of inefficiencies were likely to have arisen when the controlled price of bread was above the market price? Explain in detail.

   One year during this period, a poor wheat harvest caused a leftward shift in the supply of bread and therefore an increase in its market price. New York bakers found that the controlled price of bread in New York was below the market price.

   c. Draw a diagram showing the effect of the price control on the market for bread during this one-year period. Did the policy act as a price ceiling or a price floor?

   d. What kinds of inefficiencies do you think occurred during this period? Explain in detail.

4. The accompanying table shows the demand and supply schedules for milk per year. The U.S. government decides that the incomes of dairy farmers should be maintained at a level that allows the traditional family dairy farm to survive. It therefore implements a price floor of $1 per pint by buying surplus milk until the market price is $1 per pint.

Price of milk (per pint)	Quantity of milk (millions of pints per year)	
	Quantity demanded	Quantity supplied
$1.20	550	850
1.10	600	800
1.00	650	750
0.90	700	700
0.80	750	650

   a. How much surplus milk will be produced as a result of this policy?

   b. What will be the cost to the government of this policy?

   c. Since milk is an important source of protein and calcium, the government decides to provide the surplus milk it purchases to elementary schools at a price of only $0.60 per pint. Assume that schools will buy any amount of milk available at this low price. But parents now reduce their purchases of milk at any price by 50 million pints per year because they know their children are getting milk at school. How much will the dairy program now cost the government?

   d. Give two examples of inefficiencies arising from wasted resources that are likely to result from this policy. What is the missed opportunity in each case?

5. As noted in the text, European governments tend to make greater use of price controls than does the American government. For example, the French government sets minimum starting yearly wages for new hires who have completed *le bac*, certification roughly equivalent to a high school diploma. The demand schedule for new hires with *le bac* and the supply schedule for similarly credentialed new job seekers are given in the accompanying table. The price here—given in euros, the currency used in France—is the same as the yearly wage.

Wage (per year)	Quantity demanded (new job offers per year)	Quantity supplied (new job seekers per year)
€45,000	200,000	325,000
40,000	220,000	320,000
35,000	250,000	310,000
30,000	290,000	290,000
25,000	370,000	200,000

   a. In the absence of government interference, what is the equilibrium wage and number of graduates hired per year? Illustrate with a diagram. Will there be anyone seeking a job at the equilibrium wage who is unable to find one— that is, will there be anyone who is involuntarily unemployed?

   b. Suppose the French government sets a minimum yearly wage of €35,000. Is there any involuntary unemployment at this wage? If so, how much? Illustrate with a diagram. What if the minimum wage is set at €40,000? Also illustrate with a diagram.

   c. Given your answer to part b and the information in the table, what do you think is the relationship between the level of involuntary unemployment and the level of the minimum wage? Who benefits from such a policy? Who loses? What is the missed opportunity here?

6. Until recently, the standard number of hours worked per week for a full-time job in France was 39 hours, just as in the United States. But in response to social unrest over high levels of involuntary unemployment, the French government instituted a 35-hour workweek—a worker could not work more than 35 hours per week even if both the worker and employer wanted it. The motivation behind this policy was that if current employees worked fewer hours, employers would be forced to hire more new workers. Assume that it is costly for employers to train new workers. French employers were greatly opposed to this policy and threatened to move their operations to neighboring countries that did not have such employment restrictions. Can you explain their attitude? Give an example of both an inefficiency and an illegal activity that are likely to arise from this policy.

7. For the last 70 years the U.S. government has used price supports to provide income assistance to American farmers. At times the government has used price floors, which it maintains by buying up the surplus farm products. At other times, it has used target prices, a policy by which the government gives the farmer an amount equal to the difference between the market price and the target price for each unit sold. Consider the market for corn depicted in the accompanying figure.

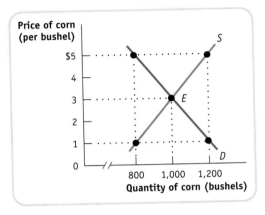

a. If the government sets a price floor of $5 per bushel, how many bushels of corn are produced? How many are purchased by consumers? By the government? How much does the program cost the government? How much revenue do corn farmers receive?

b. Suppose the government sets a target price of $5 per bushel for any quantity supplied up to 1,000 bushels. How many bushels of corn are purchased by consumers and at what price? By the government? How much does the program cost the government? How much revenue do corn farmers receive?

c. Which of these programs (in parts a and b) costs corn consumers more? Which program costs the government more? Explain.

d. What are the inefficiencies that arise in each of these cases (parts a and b)?

8. The waters off the North Atlantic coast were once teeming with fish. Now, due to overfishing by the commercial fishing industry, the stocks of fish are seriously depleted. In 1991, the National Marine Fishery Service of the U.S. government implemented a quota to allow fish stocks to recover. The quota limited the amount of swordfish caught per year by all U.S.-licensed fishing boats to 7 million pounds. As soon as the U.S. fishing fleet had met the quota limit, the swordfish catch was closed down for the rest of the year. The accompanying table gives the hypothetical demand and supply schedules for swordfish caught in the United States per year.

Price of swordfish (per pound)	Quantity of swordfish (millions of pounds per year)	
	Quantity demanded	Quantity supplied
$20	6	15
18	7	13
16	8	11
14	9	9
12	10	7

a. Use a diagram to show the effect of the quota on the market for swordfish in 1991.

b. How do you think fishermen will change how they fish in response to this policy?

c. Use your diagram from part a to show an excise tax that achieves the same reduction in the amount of pounds of swordfish caught as the quota. What is the amount of the tax per pound?

d. What kinds of activities do you think an excise tax will tempt people to engage in?

e. The excise tax is collected from the fishermen, who protest that they alone are bearing the burden of this policy. Why might this protest be misguided?

9. The U.S. government would like to help the American auto industry compete against foreign automakers that sell trucks in the United States. It can do this either by imposing a quota on the number of foreign trucks imported or by imposing an excise tax on each foreign truck sold in the United States. The hypothetical demand and supply schedules for imported trucks are given in the accompanying table.

Price of imported truck	Quantity of imported trucks (thousands)	
	Quantity demanded	Quantity supplied
$32,000	100	400
31,000	200	350
30,000	300	300
29,000	400	250
28,000	500	200
27,000	600	150

a. In the absence of government interference, what is the price of an imported truck? How many are sold in the United States? Illustrate with a diagram.

b. Suppose the government adopts a quota, allowing no more than 200,000 foreign trucks to be imported. What is the effect on the market for these trucks? Illustrate using your diagram from part a and explain.

c. Now suppose that, instead of a quota, the government imposes an excise tax of $3,000 per truck. Illustrate the effect of this excise tax in your diagram from part a. How many trucks will now be purchased and at what price? What will the foreign automaker receive per truck?

d. Calculate the government revenue raised by the excise tax in part c. Then illustrate it on your diagram from that part. Do you think the government, from a revenue standpoint, prefers an excise tax or a quota?

e. Explain how the government policy, whether it be a quota or an excise tax, benefits American automakers. Whom does it hurt? What is the missed opportunity here and how does it reflect inefficiency?

10. In Maine, you must have a license to harvest lobster commercially; these licenses are issued yearly. The state of Maine is concerned about the dwindling supplies of lobsters found off its coast. The state fishery department has decided to place a yearly quota of 80,000 pounds of lobsters harvested in all Maine waters. It has also decided to give licenses this year only to those fishermen who had licenses last year. The accompanying figure shows the demand and supply curves for Maine lobsters.

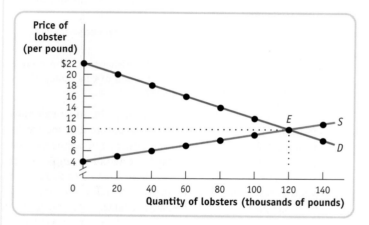

a. In the absence of government restrictions, what are the equilibrium price and quantity?

b. What is the *demand price* at which consumers wish to purchase 80,000 pounds of lobsters?

c. What is the *supply price* at which suppliers are willing to supply 80,000 pounds of lobsters?

d. What is the *quota rent* per pound of lobster when 80,000 pounds are sold?

e. Find an excise tax that achieves the same reduction in the harvest of lobsters. Show it on the figure. What is the government revenue collected from this tax?

f. Explain a transaction that benefits both buyer and seller but is prevented by the quota restriction. Explain a transaction that benefits both buyer and seller but is prevented by the excise tax.

11. In each of the following cases involving taxes, explain: (i) whether the incidence of the tax falls more heavily on consumers or producers, (ii) why government revenue raised from the tax is not a good indicator of the true cost of the tax, and (iii) what missed opportunity, or inefficiency, arises.

a. The government imposes an excise tax on the sale of all college textbooks. Before the tax was imposed, 1 million textbooks were sold every year at a price of $50. After the tax is imposed, 600,000 books are sold yearly; students pay $55 per book, $30 of which publishers receive.

b. The government imposes an excise tax on the sale of all airplane tickets. Before the tax was imposed, 3 million airline tickets were sold every year at a price of $500. After the tax is imposed, 1.5 million tickets are sold yearly; travelers pay $550 per ticket, $450 of which the airlines receive.

c. The government imposes an excise tax on the sale of all toothbrushes. Before the tax, 2 million toothbrushes were sold every year at a price of $1.50. After the tax is imposed, 800,000 toothbrushes are sold every year; consumers pay $2 per toothbrush, $1.25 of which producers receive.

>web... To continue your study and review of concepts in this chapter, please visit the Krugman/Wells website for quizzes, animated graph tutorials, web links to helpful resources, and more.

www.worthpublishers.com/krugmanwells

> Elasticity

DRIVE WE MUST

IN EARLY 1998, LUIS TELLEZ HELD A secret meeting with his Saudi Arabian counterpart. Tellez was Mexico's oil minister, the government official who decided how many barrels of oil Mexico would produce and sell to other countries. The purpose of the secret meeting? To increase their earnings, or revenues, from selling oil by raising the world price of oil, which had fallen 50 percent over the previous two years. This low world price was creating serious problems for both governments, which depended on revenue from oil sales. But a plan to raise oil prices would not succeed unless other oil-exporting countries were also willing to commit to reductions in oil production.

Why was it necessary to reduce production? Why not just raise prices? Because by the *law of demand*, a price increase leads to a fall in the quantity demanded. So if output didn't also fall, there would soon be a surplus of oil on the market, pushing the price right back down again. To make the plan work, Tellez had to persuade his fellow oil ministers to produce less. But how much less?

If consumers responded to the price increase by using a lot less oil, output would have to fall by a large amount. And

if output fell by a large enough amount in response to the price increase, revenue would decline, not increase. The crucial question for Tellez, then, was how responsive the quantity of oil demanded was to changes in the price of oil.

But how do we define *responsiveness?* The answer, and what Tellez needed to know in this case, is a particular number: the *price elasticity of demand*. In this chapter, we will show how the price elasticity of demand is measured and why it is the best measure of how the quantity demanded

Gassing up: A hard habit to break.

responds to changes in price. We will then see that the price elasticity of demand is only one of a family of related concepts, including the *income elasticity of demand* and the *price elasticity of supply*. Finally, we will see how elasticities are used to determine who bears the greater share of the burden of a tax—producers or consumers.

What you will learn in this chapter:

➤ The definition of **elasticity,** a measure of responsiveness to changes in prices or incomes

➤ The importance of the **price elasticity of demand,** which measures the responsiveness of the quantity demanded to price

➤ The meaning and importance of the **income elasticity of demand,** a measure of the responsiveness of demand to income

➤ The significance of the **price elasticity of supply,** which measures the responsiveness of the quantity supplied to price

➤ What factors influence the size of these various elasticities

➤ How elasticity affects the incidence of a tax, the measure of who bears its burden

Defining and Measuring Elasticity

Luis Tellez, who is a trained economist, knew that to calculate the cut in oil output needed to achieve his price target, he would have to know the *price elasticity of demand* for oil.

The Price Elasticity of Demand

Figure 5-1 shows a hypothetical world demand curve for oil. At a price of $20 per barrel, world consumers would demand 10 million barrels of oil per day (point *A*); at a price of $21 per barrel, the quantity demanded would fall to 9.9 million barrels (point *B*).

Figure 5-1, then, tells us the response of the quantity demanded to a particular change in the price. But how can we turn this into a measure of price responsiveness? The answer is to calculate the *price elasticity of demand*.

The price elasticity of demand compares the *percent change in quantity demanded* to the *percent change in price* as we move along the demand curve. As we'll see later in this chapter, the reason economists use percent changes is to get a measure that doesn't depend on the units in which a good is measured (say, gallons versus barrels of oil). But before we get to that, let's look at how elasticity is calculated.

To calculate the price elasticity of demand, we first calculate the *percent change in the quantity demanded* and the corresponding *percent change in the price* as we move along the demand curve. These are defined as follows:

$$\textbf{(5-1)} \quad \%\text{ change in quantity demanded} = \frac{\text{Change in quantity demanded}}{\text{Initial quantity demanded}} \times 100$$

and

$$\textbf{(5-2)} \quad \%\text{ change in price} = \frac{\text{Change in price}}{\text{Initial price}} \times 100$$

In Figure 5-1, we see that when the price rises from $20 to $21, the quantity demanded falls from 10 million to 9.9 million barrels, yielding a change in the

---

Figure 5-1

The World Demand for Oil

At a price of $20 per barrel, the world quantity of oil demanded is 10 million barrels per day (point *A*). When price rises to $21 per barrel, world demand falls to 9.9 million barrels per day (point *B*).

quantity demanded of 0.1 million barrels. So the percent change in the quantity demanded is

$$\% \text{ change in quantity demanded} = \frac{0.1 \text{ million barrels}}{10 \text{ million barrels}} \times 100 = 1\%$$

The initial price is $20 and the change in the price is $1, so the percent change in price is

$$\% \text{ change in price} = \frac{\$1}{\$20} \times 100 = 5\%$$

To calculate the price elasticity of demand, we find the ratio of the percent change in the quantity demanded to the percent change in the price:

(5-3) Price elasticity of demand $= \dfrac{\% \text{ change in quantity demanded}}{\% \text{ change in price}}$

In Figure 5-1, the price elasticity of demand is therefore

$$\frac{1\%}{5\%} = 0.2$$

> The **price elasticity of demand** is the ratio of the percent change in the quantity demanded to the percent change in the price as we move along the demand curve.

The *law of demand* says that demand curves slope downward. This means that the price elasticity of demand is, in strictly mathematical terms, a negative number (if the price rises, which is a positive percent change, the quantity demanded falls, which is strictly speaking a *negative* percent change). However, it is a nuisance to keep writing that minus sign. So when economists talk about the price elasticity of demand, they usually drop the minus sign and report the absolute value of the elasticity. In this case, for example, economists would usually say "the price elasticity of demand is 0.2," taking it for granted that you understand they mean *minus* 0.2. As we have just done, we follow this convention and drop the minus sign when referring to the price elasticity of demand.

The larger the price elasticity of demand, the more responsive the quantity demanded is to the price. When the price elasticity of demand is large—when consumers change their quantity demanded by a large percentage compared with the percent change in the price—economists say that demand is highly elastic.

As we'll see shortly, a price elasticity of 0.2 indicates a small response of quantity demanded to price. That is, the quantity demanded will fall by a relatively small amount when price rises. This is what economists call *inelastic* demand. And inelastic demand was exactly what Tellez needed for his strategy to increase revenue by raising oil prices.

Using the Midpoint Method to Calculate Elasticities

Price elasticity of demand compares the *percent change in quantity demanded* with the *percent change in price*. When we look at some other elasticities, which we will do shortly, we'll see why it is important to focus on percent changes. But at this point we need to discuss a technical issue that arises when you calculate percent changes in variables and how economists deal with it.

The best way to understand the issue is with a real example. Suppose you were trying to estimate the price elasticity of demand for gasoline by comparing gasoline prices and consumption in different countries. Because of high taxes, gasoline usually costs about three times as much per gallon in Europe as it does in the United States. So what is the percent difference between American and European gas prices?

Well, it depends on which way you measure it. The price of gasoline in Europe is three times higher than in the United States, so it is 200 percent higher. The price of gasoline in the United States is one-third as high as in Europe, so it is 66.7 percent lower.

This is a nuisance: we'd like to have a percent measure of the difference in prices that doesn't depend on which way you measure it. A good way to avoid computing different elasticities for rising and falling prices is to use the *midpoint method*.

The **midpoint method** replaces the usual definition of the percent change in a variable, X, with a slightly different definition:

The **midpoint method** is a technique for calculating the percent change. In this approach, we calculate changes in a variable compared with the average, or midpoint, of the starting and final values.

$$\textbf{(5-4)} \quad \% \text{ change in } X = \frac{\text{Change in } X}{\text{Average value of } X} \times 100$$

where the average value of X is defined as

$$\text{Average value of } X = \frac{\text{Starting value of } X + \text{final value of } X}{2}$$

When calculating the price elasticity of demand using the midpoint method, both the percent change in the price and the percent change in the quantity demanded are found using this method.

To see how this method works, suppose you have the following data for some good:

	Price	**Quantity demanded**
Situation A	$0.90	1,100
Situation B	$1.10	900

To calculate the percent change in quantity going from situation A to situation B, we compare the change in the quantity demanded—200 units—with the *average* of the quantity demanded in the two situations. So we calculate

$$\% \text{ change in quantity demanded} = \frac{200}{(1,100 + 900)/2} \times 100 = \frac{200}{1,000} \times 100$$

$$= 20\%$$

In the same way, we calculate

$$\% \text{ change in price} = \frac{\$0.20}{(\$0.90 + \$1.10)/2} \times 100 = \frac{\$0.20}{\$1.00} \times 100$$

$$= 20\%$$

So in this case we would calculate the price elasticity of demand to be

$$\text{Price elasticity of demand} = \frac{\% \text{ change in quantity demanded}}{\% \text{ change in price}} = \frac{20\%}{20\%} = 1$$

The important point is that we would get the same result, a price elasticity of demand of 1, whether we go up the demand curve from situation A to situation B or down from situation B to situation A.

To arrive at a more general formula for price elasticity of demand, suppose that we have data for two points on a demand curve. At point 1 the quantity demanded and price are (Q_1, P_1); at point 2 they are (Q_2, P_2). Then the formula for calculating the price elasticity of demand is:

$$\text{(5-5)} \quad \text{Price elasticity of demand} = \dfrac{\dfrac{Q_2 - Q_1}{(Q_1 + Q_2)/2}}{\dfrac{P_2 - P_1}{(P_1 + P_2)/2}}$$

As before, when reporting a price elasticity of demand calculated by the midpoint method, we usually drop the negative sign and report the absolute value.

economics in action

Estimating Elasticities

You might think it's easy to estimate price elasticities of demand from real-world data: just compare percent changes in prices with percent changes in quantities demanded. Unfortunately, it's rarely that simple because changes in price aren't the only thing affecting changes in the quantity demanded: other factors—such as changes in income, changes in population, and changes in the prices of other goods—shift the demand curve, thereby changing the quantity demanded for any given price. To estimate price elasticities of demand, economists must use careful statistical analysis to separate the influence of these different factors, holding other things equal.

The most comprehensive effort to estimate price elasticities of demand was a mammoth study by the economists Hendrik S. Houthakker and Lester D. Taylor. Some of their results are summarized in Table 5-1. These estimates show a wide range of price elasticities. There are some goods, like eggs, for which demand hardly responds at all to changes in the price; there are other goods, most notably foreign travel, where the quantity demanded is very sensitive to the price.

Notice that Table 5-1 is divided into two parts: inelastic and elastic demand. We'll explain in the next section the significance of that division. ∎

> > > > > > > > > > > > > > > > > > > >

TABLE 5-1

Some Estimated Price Elasticities of Demand

Good	Price elasticity of demand
Inelastic demand	
Eggs	0.1
Beef	0.4
Stationery	0.5
Gasoline	0.5
Elastic demand	
Housing	1.2
Restaurant meals	2.3
Airline travel	2.4
Foreign travel	4.1

Please find source information on the copyright page.

> **>> QUICK REVIEW**
> ➤ The *price elasticity of demand* is equal to the percent change in the quantity demanded divided by the percent change in the price as you move along the demand curve.
> ➤ Percent changes are best measured using the *midpoint method*, in which the percent change in each variable is calculated using the average of starting and final values.

>> CHECK YOUR UNDERSTANDING 5-1

1. The price of strawberries falls from $1.50 to $1.00 per carton and the quantity demanded goes from 100,000 to 200,000 cartons. Use the midpoint method to find the price elasticity of demand.

2. At the present level of consumption, 4,000 movie tickets, and at the current price, $5 per ticket, the price elasticity of demand for movie tickets is 1. Using the midpoint method, calculate the percentage by which the owners of movie theaters must reduce price in order to sell 5,000 tickets.

3. The price elasticity of demand for ice-cream sandwiches is 1.2 at the current price of $0.50 per sandwich and the current consumption level of 100,000 sandwiches. Calculate the change in the quantity demanded when price rises by $0.05. Use Equations 5-1 and 5-2 to calculate percent changes, and Equation 5-3 to relate price elasticity of demand to the percent changes.

Solutions appear at back of book.

Interpreting the Price Elasticity of Demand

Mexico and other oil-producing countries believed they could succeed in driving up oil prices with only a small decrease in the quantity sold because the price elasticity of oil demand was low. But what does that mean? How low does a price elasticity have to be for us to classify it as low? How high does it have to be for us to consider it high? And what determines whether the price elasticity of demand is high or low, anyway?

To answer these questions, we need to look more deeply at the price elasticity of demand.

How Elastic Is Elastic?

As a first step toward classifying price elasticities of demand, let's look at the extreme cases.

First, consider the demand for a good when people pay no attention to the price—say, shoelaces. Suppose that U.S. consumers will buy 1 billion pairs of shoelaces per year regardless of the price. In this case, the demand curve for shoelaces would look like the curve shown in panel (a) of Figure 5-2: it would be a vertical line at 1 billion pairs of shoelaces. Since the percent change in the quantity demanded is zero for *any* change in the price, the price elasticity of demand in this case is zero. The case of a zero price elasticity of demand is known as **perfectly inelastic demand**.

The opposite extreme occurs when even a tiny rise in the price will cause the quantity demanded to drop to zero or even a tiny fall in the price will cause the quantity demanded to get extremely large. Panel (b) of Figure 5-2 shows the case of pink tennis balls; we suppose that tennis players really don't care what color their balls are and that other colors, such as neon green and vivid yellow, are available at $5 per dozen balls. In this case, consumers will buy no pink balls if they cost more than $5 per dozen but will buy only pink balls if they cost less than $5. The demand curve will therefore be a horizontal line at a price of $5 per dozen balls. As you move back and forth along this line, there is a change in the quantity demanded but no change in the price. Roughly speaking, when you divide a number by zero, you get infinity, so a horizontal demand curve implies an infinite price elasticity of demand. When the price elasticity of demand is infinite, economists say that demand is **perfectly elastic**.

The price elasticity of demand for the vast majority of goods is somewhere between these two extreme cases. Economists use one main criterion for classifying these intermediate cases: they ask whether the price elasticity of demand is higher or lower than 1. When the price elasticity of demand is greater than 1, economists say that demand is **elastic**. When the price elasticity of demand is less than 1, they say that demand is **inelastic**. The borderline case is **unit-elastic demand**, where the price elasticity of demand is—surprise—exactly 1.

> Demand is **perfectly inelastic** when the quantity demanded does not respond at all to changes in the price. When demand is perfectly inelastic, the demand curve is a vertical line.

> Demand is **perfectly elastic** when any price increase will cause the quantity demanded to drop to zero. When demand is perfectly elastic, the demand curve is a horizontal line.

> Demand is **elastic** if the price elasticity of demand is greater than 1, **inelastic** if the price elasticity of demand is less than 1, and **unit-elastic** if the price elasticity of demand is exactly 1.

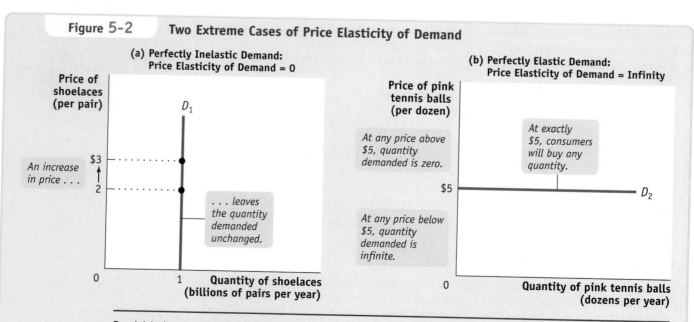

Figure 5-2   Two Extreme Cases of Price Elasticity of Demand

(a) Perfectly Inelastic Demand:
Price Elasticity of Demand = 0

Price of shoelaces (per pair)

D_1

An increase in price . . .

$3

2

. . . leaves the quantity demanded unchanged.

0   1   **Quantity of shoelaces**
(billions of pairs per year)

(b) Perfectly Elastic Demand:
Price Elasticity of Demand = Infinity

Price of pink tennis balls (per dozen)

At any price above $5, quantity demanded is zero.

At exactly $5, consumers will buy any quantity.

$5 D_2

At any price below $5, quantity demanded is infinite.

0   **Quantity of pink tennis balls**
(dozens per year)

Panel (a) shows a perfectly inelastic demand curve, which is a vertical line. The quantity of shoelaces demanded is always 1 billion pairs, regardless of price. As a result, the price elasticity of demand is zero—the quantity demanded is unaffected by the price. Panel (b) shows a perfectly elastic demand curve, which is a horizontal line. At a price of $5, consumers will buy any quantity of pink tennis balls, but will buy none at a price above $5. If price falls below $5, they will buy an extremely large number of pink tennis balls and none of any other color.

To see why a price elasticity of demand equal to 1 is a useful dividing line, let's consider a hypothetical example: a toll bridge operated by the state highway department. Other things equal, the number of drivers who use the bridge depends on the toll, the price the highway department charges for crossing the bridge: the higher the toll, the fewer the drivers who use the bridge.

Figure 5-3 shows three hypothetical demand curves—one in which demand is unit-elastic, one in which it is inelastic, and one in which it is elastic. In each case, point *A* shows the quantity demanded if the toll is $0.90 and point *B* shows the quantity demanded if the toll is $1.10. An increase in the toll from $0.90 to $1.10 is an increase of 20% if we use the midpoint method to calculate percent changes.

Panel (a) shows what happens when the toll is raised from $0.90 to $1.10 and the demand curve is unit-elastic. Here the 20% price rise leads to a fall in the quantity of cars using the bridge each day from 1,100 to 900, which is a 20% decline (again using the midpoint method). So the price elasticity of demand is 20%/20% = 1.

Panel (b) shows a case of inelastic demand when the toll is raised from $0.90 to $1.10. The same 20% price rise reduces the quantity demanded from 1,050 to 950. That's only a 10% decline, so in this case the price elasticity of demand is 10%/20% = 0.5.

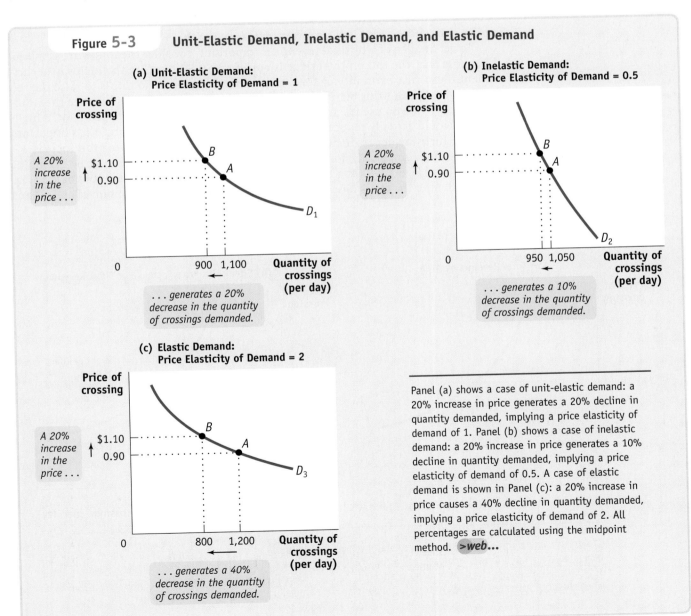

Figure 5-3   **Unit-Elastic Demand, Inelastic Demand, and Elastic Demand**

(a) Unit-Elastic Demand:
Price Elasticity of Demand = 1

A 20% increase in the price . . .

. . . *generates a 20% decrease in the quantity of crossings demanded.*

(b) Inelastic Demand:
Price Elasticity of Demand = 0.5

A 20% increase in the price . . .

. . . *generates a 10% decrease in the quantity of crossings demanded.*

(c) Elastic Demand:
Price Elasticity of Demand = 2

A 20% increase in the price . . .

. . . *generates a 40% decrease in the quantity of crossings demanded.*

Panel (a) shows a case of unit-elastic demand: a 20% increase in price generates a 20% decline in quantity demanded, implying a price elasticity of demand of 1. Panel (b) shows a case of inelastic demand: a 20% increase in price generates a 10% decline in quantity demanded, implying a price elasticity of demand of 0.5. A case of elastic demand is shown in Panel (c): a 20% increase in price causes a 40% decline in quantity demanded, implying a price elasticity of demand of 2. All percentages are calculated using the midpoint method. **>web...**

Panel (c) shows a case of elastic demand when the toll is raised from $0.90 to $1.10. The 20% price increase causes the quantity demanded to fall from 1,200 to 800—a 40% decline, so the price elasticity of demand is 40%/20% = 2.

Why does it matter whether demand is unit-elastic, inelastic, or elastic? Because this classification predicts how changes in the price of a good will affect the *total revenue* earned by producers from the sale of that good. In many real-life situations, such as the one faced by Luis Tellez, it is crucial to know how price changes affect total revenue. **Total revenue** is defined as the total value of sales of a good or service: the price multiplied by the quantity sold.

> The **total revenue** is the total value of sales of a good or service. It is equal to the price multiplied by the quantity sold.

(5-6)   Total revenue = Price × quantity sold

Total revenue has a useful graphical representation that can help us understand why knowing the price elasticity of demand is crucial when we ask whether a price rise will increase or reduce total revenue. Panel (a) of Figure 5-4 shows the same demand curve as panel (a) of Figure 5-3. We see that 1,100 drivers will use the bridge if the toll is $0.90. The total revenue at a price of $0.90 is therefore $0.90 × 1,100 = $990. This value is equal to the area of the green rectangle, which is drawn with the bottom left corner at the point (0, 0) and the top right corner at (1,100, 0.90). In general, the total revenue at any given price is equal to the area of a rectangle whose height is the price and whose width is the quantity demanded at that price.

To get an idea of why total revenue is important, consider the following scenario. Suppose that the toll on the bridge is currently $0.90 but that the highway department must raise extra money for road repairs. One way to do this is to raise the toll on the bridge. But this plan might backfire, since a higher toll will reduce the number of drivers who use the bridge. And if traffic on the bridge dropped a lot, a higher toll would actually reduce total revenue instead of increasing it. So it's important for the highway department to know how drivers will respond to a toll increase.

We can see graphically how the toll increase affects total bridge revenue by examining panel (b) of Figure 5-4. At a toll of $0.90, total revenue is given by the sum of the areas A and B. After the toll is raised to $1.10, total revenue is given by the sum of areas B and

Figure 5-4   Total Revenue

(a) Total Revenue by Area

Price of crossing

$0.90

Total revenue = price x quantity = $990

0   1,100

Quantity of crossings (per day)

(b) Effect of a Price Increase on Total Revenue

Price of crossing

Price effect of price increase: higher price for each unit sold

$1.10

0.90

C

Quantity effect of price increase: fewer units are sold

B   A   D

0   900 1,100

Quantity of crossings (per day)

The green rectangle in panel (a) represents total revenue generated from 1,100 drivers who each pay a toll of $0.90. Panel (b) shows how total revenue is affected when the price increases from $0.90 to $1.10. Due to the quantity effect, total revenue falls by area A. Due to the price effect, total revenue increases by the area C. The overall effect can go either way, depending upon the price elasticity of demand. **>web...**

C. So when the toll is raised, revenue represented by area *A* is lost but revenue represented by area *C* is gained. These two areas have important interpretations. Area *C* represents the revenue gain that comes from the additional $0.20 paid by drivers who continue to use the bridge. That is, the 900 who continue to use the bridge contribute an additional $0.20 × 900 = $180 per day to total revenue, represented by area *C*. On the other hand, 200 drivers who would have used the bridge at a price of $0.90 no longer do so, generating a loss to total revenue of $0.90 × 200 = $180 per day, represented by area *A*.

Except in the rare case of a good with perfectly elastic or perfectly inelastic demand, when a seller raises the price of a good, two countervailing effects are present:

■ *A price effect.* After a price increase, each unit sold sells at a higher price, which tends to raise revenue.

■ *A quantity effect.* After a price increase, fewer units are sold, which tends to lower revenue.

But then, you may ask, what is the ultimate effect on total revenue: does it go up or down? The answer is that, in general, the effect on total revenue can go either way—a price rise may increase total revenue or may lower it. If the price effect, which tends to raise total revenue, is the stronger of the two effects, then total revenue goes up. If the quantity effect, which tends to reduce total revenue, is the stronger, then total revenue goes down. And if the strengths of the two effects are exactly equal—as in our toll bridge example, where a $180 gain offsets a $180 loss—total revenue is unchanged by the price increase.

The price elasticity of demand tells us what happens to total revenue when price changes: its size determines which effect—the price effect or the quantity effect—is stronger. Specifically:

■ If demand for a good is *elastic* (the price elasticity of demand is greater than 1), an increase in price reduces total revenue. In this case, the quantity effect is stronger than the price effect.

■ If demand for a good is *inelastic* (the price elasticity of demand is less than 1), a higher price increases total revenue. In this case, the price effect is stronger than the quantity effect.

■ If demand for a good is *unit-elastic* (the price elasticity of demand is 1), an increase in price does not change total revenue. In this case, the quantity effect and the price effect exactly offset each other.

Table 5-2 shows how the effect of a price increase on total revenue depends on the price elasticity of demand, using the same data as in Figure 5-3. An increase in the price from $0.90 to $1.10 leaves total revenue unchanged at $990 when demand is unit-elastic. When demand is inelastic, the price effect dominates the quantity effect; the same price increase leads to an increase in total revenue from $945 to $1,045. And when demand is elastic, the quantity effect dominates the price effect; the price increase leads to a decline in total revenue from $1,080 to $880.

TABLE 5-2

Price Elasticity of Demand and Total Revenue

	Price of crossing = $0.90	Price of crossing = $1.10
Unit-elastic demand (price elasticity of demand = 1)		
Quantity demanded	1,100	900
Total revenue	$990	$990
Inelastic demand (price elasticity of demand = 0.5)		
Quantity demanded	1,050	950
Total revenue	$945	$1,045
Elastic demand (price elasticity of demand = 2)		
Quantity demanded	1,200	800
Total revenue	$1,080	$880

The price elasticity of demand also predicts the effect of a *fall* in price on total revenue. When the price falls, the same two countervailing effects are present, but they work in the opposite directions as in the case of a price rise. There is the price effect of a lower price per unit sold, which tends to lower revenue. This is countered by the quantity effect of more units sold, which tends to raise revenue. Which effect dominates depends on the price elasticity. Here is a quick summary:

- When demand is *elastic*, the quantity effect dominates the price effect; so a fall in price increases total revenue.
- When demand is *inelastic*, the price effect dominates the quantity effect; so a fall in price reduces total revenue.
- When demand is *unit-elastic*, the two effects exactly balance; so a fall in price has no effect on total revenue.

Price Elasticity Along the Demand Curve

Suppose that an economist says that "the price elasticity of demand for coffee is 0.25." What he or she means is that *at the current price* the elasticity is 0.25. In the previous discussion of the toll bridge, what we were really describing was the elasticity *at the price* of $0.90. Why this qualification? Because for the vast majority of demand curves, the price elasticity of demand at one point along the curve is different from the price elasticity of demand at other points along the same curve.

To see this, consider the table in Figure 5-5, which shows a hypothetical demand schedule. It also shows in the last column the total revenue generated at each price and quantity combination in the demand schedule. The upper panel of the graph in Figure 5-5 shows the corresponding demand curve. The lower panel illustrates the same data on total revenue: the height of a bar at each quantity demanded—which corresponds to a particular price—measures the total revenue generated at that price.

In Figure 5-5, you can see that when the price is low, raising the price increases total revenue: starting at a price of $1, raising the price to $2 increases total revenue from $9 to $16. This means that when the price is low, demand is inelastic. Moreover, you can see that demand is inelastic on the entire section of the demand curve from a price of $0 to a price of $5.

When the price is high, however, raising it further reduces total revenue: starting at a price of $8, raising the price to $9 reduces total revenue, from $16 to $9. This means that when the price is high, demand is elastic. Furthermore, you can see that demand is elastic over the section of the demand curve from a price of $5 to $10.

For the vast majority of goods, the price elasticity of demand changes along the demand curve. So whenever you measure the elasticity, you are really measuring it at a particular point or section of the demand curve.

What Factors Determine the Price Elasticity of Demand?

1998 was not the first time Americans had been subject to an attempt by oil-exporting countries to increase revenue by raising oil prices. In the 1970s, gasoline prices in the United States jumped significantly after oil exporters reduced output and raised oil prices. Americans initially reacted by changing their consumption of gasoline very little. Over time, however, they gradually adapted to the higher prices. After a few years, drivers had cut their consumption of gasoline in various ways: increased carpooling, greater use of public transportation, and, most importantly, replacement of large, gas-guzzling cars with smaller, more fuel-efficient models.

The experience of the 1970s illustrates the three main factors that determine elasticity: whether close substitutes are available, whether the good is a necessity or a luxury, and how much time has elapsed since the price change. We'll briefly examine each of these three factors.

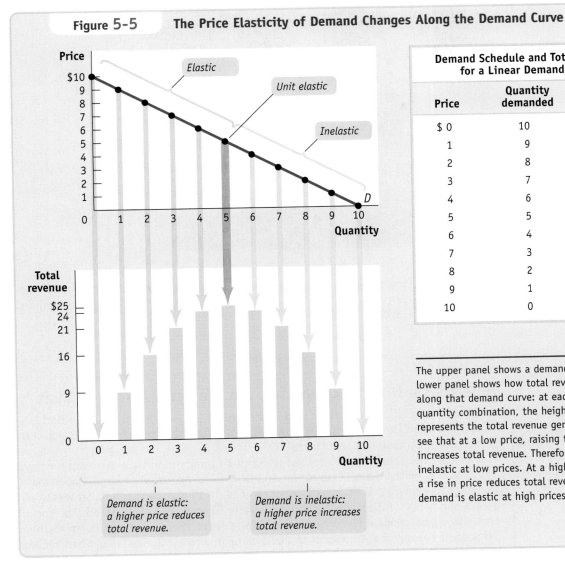

Figure 5-5   **The Price Elasticity of Demand Changes Along the Demand Curve**

Demand Schedule and Total Revenue for a Linear Demand Curve		
Price	Quantity demanded	Total revenue
$ 0	10	$ 0
1	9	9
2	8	16
3	7	21
4	6	24
5	5	25
6	4	24
7	3	21
8	2	16
9	1	9
10	0	0

Demand is elastic: a higher price reduces total revenue.

Demand is inelastic: a higher price increases total revenue.

The upper panel shows a demand curve. The lower panel shows how total revenue changes along that demand curve: at each price and quantity combination, the height of the bar represents the total revenue generated. You can see that at a low price, raising the price increases total revenue. Therefore demand is inelastic at low prices. At a high price, however, a rise in price reduces total revenue. Therefore demand is elastic at high prices.

Whether Close Substitutes Are Available The price elasticity of demand tends to be high if there are other goods that consumers regard as similar and would be willing to consume instead. The price elasticity of demand tends to be low if there are no close substitutes.

Whether the Good Is a Necessity or a Luxury The price elasticity of demand tends to be low if a good is something you must have, like a life-saving medicine. The price elasticity of demand tends to be high if the good is a luxury—something you can easily live without.

Time In general, the price elasticity of demand tends to increase as consumers have more time to adjust to a price change. This means that the long-run price elasticity of demand is often higher than the short-run elasticity.

So when gasoline prices first increased dramatically in the United States at the end of the 1970s, consumption fell very little because there were no close substitutes for gasoline and because driving their cars was necessary for people to carry out the ordinary tasks of life. Over time, however, Americans changed their habits in ways that enabled them to gradually reduce their gasoline consumption. The result was a steady

Mike Thompson, Detroit Free Press. Reprinted by permission.

decline in gasoline consumption over the next decade, even though the price of gasoline did not continue to rise, confirming that the long-run price elasticity of demand for gasoline was indeed much larger than the short-run elasticity.

economics in action

America's a Nice Place to Live, but We Can't Afford to Visit

In 1992, 18.6 million Canadians visited the United States, but only 11.8 million U.S. residents visited Canada. By 2002, however, roles had been reversed: more U.S. residents visited Canada than vice versa.

Why did the tourist traffic reverse direction? Canada didn't get any warmer from 1992 to 2002—but it did get cheaper for Americans. The reason was a large change in the exchange rate between the two nations' currencies: in 1992 a Canadian dollar was worth $0.80, but by 2002 it had fallen in value by nearly 20 percent to about $0.65. This meant that Canadian goods and services, particularly hotel rooms and meals, were about 20 percent cheaper for Americans in 2002 compared to 1992. So Canada had become a cheap vacation destination for Americans by 2002. Things were not so rosy, however, when viewed from the other side of the border: American vacations had become 20 percent more expensive for Canadians. Canadians responded by vacationing in their own country or in other parts of the world besides the United States.

Foreign travel is an example of a good that has a high price elasticity of demand: as we saw in Table 5-1, it has been estimated at about 4.1. One reason is that foreign travel is a luxury good for most people—you may regret not going to Paris this year, but you can live without it. A second reason is that a good substitute for foreign travel typically exists—domestic travel. A Canadian who finds it too expensive to vacation in San Francisco this year is likely to find that Vancouver is a pretty good alternative. ■

< < < < < < < < < < < < < < < < < <

>>**CHECK YOUR UNDERSTANDING 5-2**

1. For each case, choose the condition that characterizes demand: elastic demand, inelastic demand, or unit-elastic demand.
   a. Total revenue decreases when price increases.
   b. The additional revenue generated by an increase in quantity sold is exactly offset by revenue lost from the fall in price received per unit.
   c. Total revenue falls when output increases.
   d. Producers in an industry find they can increase their total revenues by working together to reduce industry output.

continued

2. For the following goods, what is the elasticity of demand? Explain. What is the shape of the demand curve?
   a. Demand by a snake-bite victim for an antidote
   b. Demand by students for green erasers

Solutions appear at back of book.

Other Demand Elasticities

The quantity of a good demanded depends not only on the price of that good but on other variables. In particular, demand curves shift because of changes in the prices of related goods and changes in consumers' incomes. It is often important to have a measure of these other effects, and the best measures are—you guessed it—elasticities. Specifically, we can best measure how the demand for a good is affected by prices of other goods using a measure called the *cross-price elasticity of demand*, and we can best measure how demand is affected by changes in income using the *income elasticity of demand*.

The Cross-Price Elasticity of Demand

In Chapter 3 you learned that the demand for a good is often affected by the prices of other, related goods—goods that are substitutes or complements. There you saw that a change in the price of a related good shifts the demand curve of the original good, reflecting a change in the quantity demanded at any given price. The strength of such a "cross" effect on demand can be measured by the **cross-price elasticity of demand**, defined as the ratio of the percent change in the quantity demanded of one good to the percent change in the price of the other.

> The **cross-price elasticity of demand** between two goods measures the effect of the change in one good's price on the quantity demanded of the other good. It is equal to the percent change in the quantity demanded of one good divided by the percent change in the other good's price.

(5-7)   Cross-price elasticity of demand between goods A and B

$$= \frac{\text{\% change in quantity of A demanded}}{\text{\% change in price of B}}$$

When two goods are substitutes, like hot dogs and hamburgers, the cross-price elasticity of demand is positive: a rise in the price of hot dogs increases the demand for hamburgers—that is, it causes a rightward shift of the demand curve for hamburgers. If the goods are close substitutes, the cross-price elasticity will be positive and large; if they are not close substitutes, the cross-price elasticity will be positive and small. So when the cross-price elasticity of demand is positive, it is a measure of how closely substitutable for each other two goods are.

When two goods are complements, like hot dogs and hot dog buns, the cross-price elasticity is negative: a rise in the price of hot dogs decreases the demand for hot dog buns—that is, it causes a leftward shift of the demand curve for hot dog buns. As with substitutes, the size of the cross-price elasticity of demand between two complements tells us how strongly complementary they are: if the cross-price elasticity is only slightly below zero, they are weak complements; if it is very negative, they are strong complements.

Note that in the case of the cross-price elasticity of demand, the sign (plus or minus) is very important: it tells us whether the two goods are complements or substitutes. So we cannot drop the minus sign as we did for the price elasticity of demand.

Our discussion of the cross-price elasticity of demand is a useful place to return to a point we made earlier: elasticity is a *unit-free* measure—that is, it doesn't depend on the units in which goods are measured.

To see the potential problem, suppose someone told you that "if the price of hot dog buns rises by $0.30, Americans will buy 10 million fewer hot dogs this year." If you've ever bought hot dog buns, you'll immediately wonder: is that a $0.30 increase in the price *per bun*, or is it a $0.30 increase in the price *per package* (buns are usually sold by the dozen)? It makes a big difference what units we are talking about! However, if someone says that the cross-price elasticity of demand between buns and hot dogs is –0.3, it doesn't matter whether buns are sold individually or by the package. So elasticity is defined as a ratio of percent changes, as a way of making sure that confusion over units doesn't arise.

The Income Elasticity of Demand

The **income elasticity of demand** is a measure of how much the demand for a good is affected by changes in consumers' incomes. It allows us to determine whether a good is a normal or inferior good as well as measure how intensely the demand for the good responds to changes in income.

> The **income elasticity of demand** is the percent change in the quantity of a good demanded when a consumer's income changes divided by the percent change in the consumer's income.

$$(5\text{-}8) \quad \text{Income elasticity of demand} = \frac{\%\ \text{change in quantity demanded}}{\%\ \text{change in income}}$$

Just as the cross-price elasticity of demand between two goods can be either positive or negative, depending on whether the goods are substitutes or complements, the income elasticity of demand for a good can also be either positive or negative. Recall from Chapter 3 that goods can be either *normal goods*, for which demand increases when income rises, or *inferior goods*, for which demand decreases when income rises. These definitions relate directly to the sign of the income elasticity of demand:

- When the income elasticity of demand is positive, the good is a normal good—that is, the quantity demanded at any given price increases as income increases.

- When the income elasticity of demand is negative, the good is an inferior good—that is, the quantity demanded at any given price decreases as income increases.

Economists often use estimates of the income elasticity of demand to predict which industries will grow most rapidly as the incomes of consumers grow over time. In doing this, they often find it useful to make a further distinction among normal goods, identifying which are *income-elastic* and which are *income-inelastic*.

> The demand for a good is **income-elastic** if the income elasticity of demand for that good is greater than 1.
>
> The demand for a good is **income-inelastic** if the income elasticity of demand for that good is positive but less than 1.

The demand for a good is **income-elastic** if the income elasticity of demand for that good is greater than 1. When income rises, the demand for income-elastic goods rises *faster* than income. Luxury goods such as second homes and international travel tend to be income-elastic. The demand for a good is **income-inelastic** if the income elasticity of demand for that good is positive but less than 1. When income rises, the demand for income-inelastic goods rises, but more slowly than income. Necessities such as food and clothing tend to be income-inelastic.

FOR INQUIRING MINDS

WHERE HAVE ALL THE FARMERS GONE?

What percentage of Americans live on farms? Sad to say, the U.S. government no longer publishes that number. In 1991 the official percentage was 1.9, but in that year the government decided it was no longer a meaningful indicator of the size of the agricultural sector because a large proportion of those who live on farms actually make their living doing something else. But in the days of the Founding Fathers, the great majority of Americans lived on farms. As recently as the 1940s, one American in six—or approximately 17%—still did.

Why do so few people now live and work on farms in the United States? There are two main reasons, both involving elasticities.

First, the income elasticity of demand for food is much less than 1—it is income-

inelastic. As consumers grow richer, other things equal, spending on food rises less than income. As a result, as the U.S. economy has grown, the share of income it spends on food—and therefore the share of total income earned by farmers—has fallen.

Second, agriculture has been a technologically progressive sector for approximately 150 years in the United States, with steadily increasing yields over time. You might think that technological progress would be good for farmers. But competition among farmers means that technological progress leads to lower food prices. Meanwhile, the demand for food is price-inelastic, so falling prices of agricultural goods, other things equal, reduce the total revenue of farmers. That's right: progress in

farming is good for consumers but bad for farmers.

The combination of these effects explains the relative decline of farming. Even if farming weren't such a technologically progressive sector, the low income elasticity of demand for food would ensure that the income of farmers grows more slowly than the economy as a whole. The combination of rapid technological progress in farming with price-inelastic demand for farm products reinforces this effect, further reducing the growth of farm income. In short, the U.S. farm sector has been a victim of success—the U.S. economy's success as a whole (which reduces the importance of spending on food) and its own success in increasing yields.

economics in action

Spending It

The U.S. Bureau of Labor Statistics carries out extensive surveys of how families spend their incomes. This is not just a matter of intellectual curiosity. Quite a few government programs involve some adjustment for changes in the cost of living; to estimate those changes, the government must know how people spend their money. But an additional payoff to these surveys is evidence on the income elasticity of demand for various goods.

What stands out from these studies? The classic result is that the income elasticity of demand for "food eaten at home" is considerably less than 1: as a family's income rises, the share of its income spent on food consumed at home falls. Correspondingly, the lower a family's income, the higher the share of income spent on food consumed at home. In poor countries, many families spend more than half their income on food consumed at home. While the income elasticity of "food eaten at home" is estimated at less than 0.5 in the United States, "food eaten away from home" (restaurant meals) is estimated to be much higher—close to 1. Families with higher incomes eat out more often and at fancier places. In 1950,

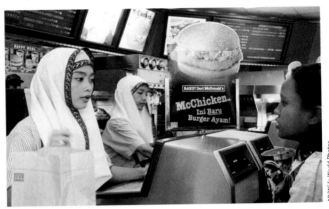

Judging from the activity at this busy McDonald's, incomes are rising in Jakarta, Indonesia.

about 19 percent of U.S. income was spent on food consumed at home, a number which has dropped to 7 percent today. But over the same time period, the share of U.S. income spent on food away from home has stayed constant at 5 percent. In fact, a sure sign of rising income levels in developing countries is the arrival of fast-food restaurants that cater to newly affluent customers. For example, McDonald's can now be found in Jakarta, Shanghai, and Bombay.

There is one clear example of an inferior good found in the surveys: rental housing. Families with higher income actually spend less on rent than families with lower income, because they are much more likely to own their own homes. And the category identified as "other housing"—which basically means second homes—is highly income-elastic. Only higher-income families can afford a vacation home at all, so "other housing" has an income elasticity of demand greater than 1. ∎

> > > > > > > > > > > > > > > > > > > >

>>QUICK REVIEW

- Goods are substitutes when the *cross-price elasticity of demand* is positive. Goods are complements when the cross-price elasticity of demand is negative.
- Inferior goods have a negative *income elasticity of demand*. Most goods are normal goods, which have a positive income elasticity of demand.
- Normal goods may be either *income-elastic*, with an income elasticity of demand greater than 1, or *income-inelastic*, with an income elasticity of demand that is positive but less than 1.

>>CHECK YOUR UNDERSTANDING 5-3

1. After Chelsea's income increased from $12,000 to $18,000 a year, her purchases of CDs increased from 10 to 40 CDs a year. Calculate Chelsea's income elasticity of demand for CDs using the midpoint method.

2. Expensive restaurant meals are income-elastic goods for most people, including Sanjay. Suppose his income falls by 10% this year. What can you predict about the change in Sanjay's consumption of expensive restaurant meals?

3. As the price of margarine rises by 20%, a manufacturer of baked goods increases its quantity of butter demanded by 5%. Calculate the cross-price elasticity of demand between butter and margarine. Are butter and margarine substitutes or complements for this manufacturer?

Solutions appear at back of book.

The Price Elasticity of Supply

The Tellez plan to drive up the price of oil would have been much less effective if a higher price had induced large increases in output by countries that were not party to the agreement. For example, if American oil producers had responded to the higher price by significantly increasing their production, they could have pushed the price of oil back down. But they didn't—in fact, producers of oil who were not members of OPEC (Organization of Petroleum Exporting Countries) did not respond much to the higher price. This was another critical element in the success of the Tellez plan: a low responsiveness in output to a higher price of oil from other oil producers. To measure the response of producers to price changes, we need a measure parallel to the price elasticity of demand—the *price elasticity of supply*.

Measuring the Price Elasticity of Supply

> The **price elasticity of supply** is a measure of the responsiveness of the quantity of a good supplied to the price of that good. It is the ratio of the percent change in the quantity supplied to the percent change in the price as we move along the supply curve.

The **price elasticity of supply** is defined the same way as the price elasticity of demand:

(5-9) $\text{Price elasticity of supply} = \dfrac{\% \text{ change in quantity supplied}}{\% \text{ change in price}}$

The only difference is that this time we consider movements along the supply curve rather than movements along the demand curve.

Suppose that the price of tomatoes rises by 10%. If the quantity of tomatoes supplied also increases by 10% in response, the price elasticity of supply of tomatoes is 1 (10%/10%), and supply is unit-elastic. If the quantity supplied increases by 5%, the price elasticity of supply is 0.5 and supply is inelastic; if the quantity increases by 20%, the price elasticity of supply is 2 and supply is elastic.

As in the case of demand, the extreme values of the price elasticity of supply have a simple graphical representation.

Panel (a) of Figure 5-6 shows the supply of cell phone frequencies, the portion of the radio spectrum which is suitable for sending and receiving cell phone signals. Governments own the right to sell the use of this part of the radio spectrum to cell phone operators inside their borders. In Chapter 7, we will discuss how governments

Figure 5-6 **Two Extreme Cases of Price Elasticity of Supply**

Panel (a) shows a perfectly inelastic supply curve, which is a vertical line. The price elasticity of supply is zero: the quantity supplied is always the same, regardless of price. Panel (b) shows a perfectly elastic supply curve, which is a horizontal line. At a price of $12, producers will supply any quantity, but will supply none at a price below $12. If price rises above $12, they will supply an extremely large quantity.

recently sold off their cell phone frequencies to the highest bidder in an auction. But governments can't increase or decrease the number of cell phone frequencies that they have to offer—for technical reasons, the quantity of frequencies suitable for cell phone operation is a fixed quantity. So the supply curve for cell phone frequencies is a vertical line, which we have assumed is set at the quantity of 100 frequencies. As you move up and down that curve, the change in the quantity supplied by the government is zero, whatever the change in price. So panel (a) illustrates a case in which the price elasticity of supply is zero. This is a case of **perfectly inelastic supply.**

Panel (b) shows the supply curve for pizza. We suppose that it costs $12 to produce a pizza, including all opportunity costs such as the implicit cost of capital invested in pizza parlors. At any price below $12, it would be unprofitable to produce pizza and all the pizza parlors in America would go out of business. Alternatively, there are many producers who could operate pizza parlors if they were profitable. The ingredients—dough, tomatoes, cheese—are plentiful. And if necessary, more tomatoes could be grown, more milk could be produced to make mozzarella, and so on. So any price above $12 would elicit an extremely large quantity of pizzas supplied. The implied supply curve is therefore a horizontal line at $12. Since even a tiny increase in the price would lead to a huge increase in the quantity supplied, the price elasticity of supply would be more or less infinite. This is a case of **perfectly elastic supply**.

As our cell phone frequencies and pizza examples suggest, real-world instances of both perfectly inelastic and perfectly elastic supply are easy to find—much easier than their counterparts in demand.

There is **perfectly inelastic supply** when the price elasticity of supply is zero, so that changes in the price of the good have no effect on the quantity supplied. A perfectly inelastic supply curve is a vertical line.

There is **perfectly elastic supply** when even a tiny increase or reduction in the price will lead to very large changes in the quantity supplied, so that the price elasticity of supply is infinite. A perfectly elastic supply curve is a horizontal line.

What Factors Determine the Price Elasticity of Supply?

Our examples tell us the main determinant of the price elasticity of supply: the availability of inputs. In addition, as with the price elasticity of demand, time may also play a role in the price elasticity of supply. Here we briefly summarize the two factors.

The Availability of Inputs The price elasticity of supply tends to be large when inputs are easily available. It tends to be small when inputs are difficult to obtain.

Time The price elasticity of supply tends to become larger as producers have more time to respond to a price change. This means that the long-run price elasticity of supply is often higher than the short-run elasticity.

The price elasticity of pizza supply is very high because the inputs needed to expand the industry are readily available. The price elasticity of cell phone frequencies is zero because an essential input—the radio spectrum—cannot be increased at all.

Many industries are like pizza and have large price elasticities of supply: they can be readily expanded because they don't require any special or unique resources. On the other hand, the price elasticity of supply is usually substantially less than perfectly elastic for goods that involve limited natural resources: minerals like gold or copper, agricultural products like coffee that flourish only on certain types of land, renewable resources like ocean fish that can only be exploited up to a point without destroying the resource.

But given enough time, producers are often able to significantly change the amount they produce in response to a price change, even when production involves a limited natural resource. For example, consider again the effects of a surge in oil prices, but this time focus on the supply response. If oil prices were to rise to $50 per barrel and stay there for a number of years, there would almost certainly be a substantial increase in oil production. Oil companies would search for and exploit oil in inaccessible places, such as deep-sea waters; costly equipment would be put in place to squeeze still more oil out of already-exploited reservoirs; and so on. But Rome wasn't built in a day, and all these oil-production efforts can't take place in a month or even a year.

For this reason, economists often make a distinction between the short-run elasticity of supply, usually referring to a few weeks or months, and the long-run elasticity of supply, usually referring to several years. In most industries, the long-run elasticity of supply is larger than the short-run elasticity.

economics in action

European Farm Surpluses

One of the policies we analyzed in Chapter 4 was the imposition of a *price floor*, a lower limit on the price of a good. We saw that price floors are often used by governments to support the incomes of farmers but create large unwanted surpluses of farm produce. The most dramatic example of this is found in the European Union, where price floors have created a "butter mountain," a "wine lake," and so on.

Were European politicians unaware that their price floors would create huge surpluses? They probably knew that surpluses would arise, but underestimated the price elasticity of agricultural supply. In fact, when the agricultural price supports were put in place, many analysts thought they were unlikely to lead to big increases in production. After all, European countries are densely populated and there was little new land available for cultivation.

What the analysts failed to realize, however, was how much farm production could expand by adding other resources, especially fertilizer and pesticides. So although farm acreage didn't increase much, farm production did! ∎

< < < < < < < < < < < < < < < < < < <

>>CHECK YOUR UNDERSTANDING 5-4

1. Using the midpoint method, calculate the price elasticity of supply for web-design services when the price per hour rises from $100 to $150 and the number of hours transacted increases from 300,000 hours to 500,000. Is supply elastic, inelastic, or unit-elastic?

2. True or false? If the demand for milk were to rise, then, in the long run, milk-drinkers would be better off if supply were elastic rather than inelastic.

3. True or false? Long-run price elasticities of supply are generally larger than short-run price elasticities of supply. Therefore the short-run supply curves are generally flatter than the long-run supply curves.

4. True or false? When supply is perfectly elastic, changes in demand have no effect on price.

Solutions appear at back of book.

An Elasticity Menagerie

We've just run through quite a few different elasticities. Keeping them all straight can be a problem. So in Table 5-3 we provide a summary of all the elasticities we have discussed and their implications.

Using Elasticity: The Incidence of an Excise Tax

In Chapter 4 we introduced the concept of the *incidence* of a tax—the measure of who really bears the burden of the tax. We saw in the case of an excise tax—a tax on sales or purchases of a product—that the incidence does not depend on who literally pays the money to the government. It doesn't matter, in other words, whether the tax is assessed on the sellers or the buyers. But we also noted that to determine who really pays the tax, we need the concept of elasticity.

We are now ready to see how the price elasticity of demand and the price elasticity of supply determine the incidence of an excise tax.

TABLE 5-3

An Elasticity Menagerie

Name	Possible values	Significance
Price elasticity of demand = $\dfrac{\text{\% change in quantity demanded}}{\text{\% change in price}}$ (use absolute value)		
Perfectly inelastic demand	0	Price has no effect on quantity demanded (vertical demand curve).
Inelastic demand	Between 0 and 1	A rise in price increases total revenue.
Unit-elastic demand	Exactly 1	Changes in price have no effect on total revenue.
Elastic demand	Greater than 1, less than ∞	A rise in price reduces total revenue.
Perfectly elastic demand	∞	A rise in price causes quantity demanded to fall to 0. A fall in price leads to an infinite quantity demanded (horizontal demand curve).
Cross-price elasticity of demand = $\dfrac{\text{\% change in quantity \textit{of one good} demanded}}{\text{\% change in price \textit{of another good}}}$		
Complements	Negative	Quantity demanded of one good falls when the price of another rises.
Substitutes	Positive	Quantity demanded of one good rises when the price of another rises.
Income elasticity of demand = $\dfrac{\text{\% change in quantity demanded}}{\text{\% change in income}}$		
Inferior good	Negative	Quantity demanded falls when income rises.
Normal good, income-inelastic	Positive, less than 1	Quantity demanded rises when income rises, but not as rapidly as income.
Normal good, income-elastic	Greater than 1	Quantity demanded rises when income rises, and more rapidly than income.
Price elasticity of supply = $\dfrac{\text{\% change in quantity supplied}}{\text{\% change in price}}$		
Perfectly inelastic supply	0	Price has no effect on quantity supplied (vertical supply curve).
●	Greater than 0, less than ∞	Ordinary upward-sloping supply curve.
Perfectly elastic supply	∞	Any fall in price causes quantity supplied to fall to 0. Any rise in price elicits an infinite quantity supplied (horizontal supply curve).

When an Excise Tax Is Paid Mainly by Consumers

Figure 5-7 on page 128 shows an excise tax that falls mainly on consumers: an excise tax on gasoline, which we set at $1 per gallon. (There really is a federal excise tax on gasoline, though it is actually only about $0.18 per gallon in the United States. In addition, states impose excise taxes between $0.08 and $0.30 per gallon.) According to Figure 5-7, in the absence of the tax, gasoline would sell for $1 per gallon.

Two key assumptions are reflected in the supply and demand curves. First, the price elasticity of demand for gasoline is very low, so the demand curve is relatively steep. Second, the price elasticity of supply is very high, so the supply curve is relatively flat.

We know from Chapter 4 that an excise tax drives a wedge, equal to the size of the tax, between the price paid by consumers and the price received by producers. This

Figure 5-7

An Excise Tax Paid Mainly by Consumers

The relatively steep demand curve here reflects a low price elasticity of demand for gasoline. The relatively flat supply curve reflects a high price elasticity of supply. The pre-tax price of a gallon of gas is $1.00, and a tax of $1.00 per gallon is imposed. The cost to consumers rises by $0.95 to $1.95, reflecting the fact that most of the burden of the tax falls on consumers. Only a small portion of the tax is borne by producers: the price they receive falls by only $0.05 to $0.95.

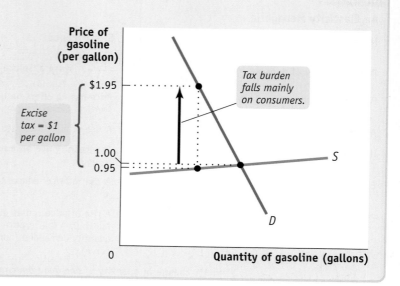

wedge drives the price paid by consumers up, and the price received by producers down. But as we can see from the figure, in this case those two effects are very unequal in size. The price received by producers falls only slightly, from $1.00 to $0.95, while the price paid by consumers rises by a lot, from $1.00 to $1.95.

This example illustrates a general principle: When the price elasticity of demand is low and the price elasticity of supply is high, the burden of an excise tax falls mainly on consumers. This is probably a good description of the main excise taxes actually collected in the United States today, such as taxes on cigarettes and alcoholic beverages.

When an Excise Tax Is Paid Mainly by Producers

Figure 5-8 shows an excise tax paid mainly by producers. In this case, we consider a $5.00 per day tax on downtown parking in a small city. In the market equilibrium, parking would cost $6.00 per day in the absence of the tax.

The price elasticity of supply is assumed to be very low because the lots used for parking have very few alternative uses. So the supply curve is relatively steep. The price elasticity of demand, however, is high: consumers can easily switch to other parking spaces a few minutes' walk from downtown. So the demand curve is relatively flat.

The tax drives a wedge between the price paid by consumers and the price received by producers. This time, however, the price to consumers rises only slightly, from $6.00 to $6.50, but the price received by producers falls a lot, from $6.00 to $1.50. So a consumer bears only $0.50 of the $5 tax, with a producer bearing the remaining $4.50.

Again, this example illustrates a general principle: When the price elasticity of demand is high and the price elasticity of supply is low, the burden of an excise tax falls mainly on producers. A real-world example is the tax on purchases of existing houses. Over the past few years, house prices in many towns in desirable locations have gone up as well-off outsiders move in, a process called gentrification. Some of these towns have imposed taxes on house sales in an effort to extract money from the new arrivals. But this ignores the fact that the elasticity of demand for houses in a particular town is often high, because buyers can choose to move to other towns. Furthermore, the elasticity of supply is probably low, because most sellers must sell their houses due to things like job transfers to other locations. So taxes on home purchases are actually paid mainly by the sellers—not, as town officials imagine, by wealthy buyers.

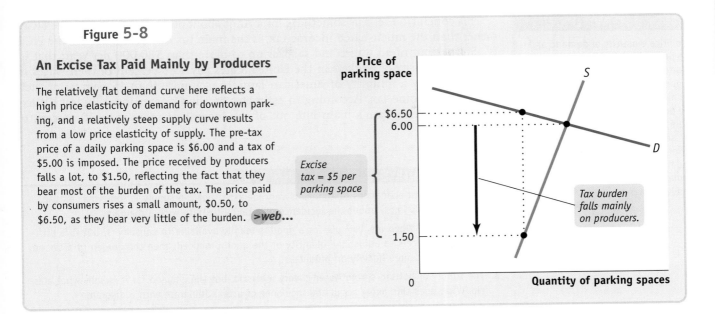

Figure 5-8

An Excise Tax Paid Mainly by Producers

The relatively flat demand curve here reflects a high price elasticity of demand for downtown parking, and a relatively steep supply curve results from a low price elasticity of supply. The pre-tax price of a daily parking space is $6.00 and a tax of $5.00 is imposed. The price received by producers falls a lot, to $1.50, reflecting the fact that they bear most of the burden of the tax. The price paid by consumers rises a small amount, $0.50, to $6.50, as they bear very little of the burden. *>web...*

Putting It All Together

We've just seen that when the price elasticity of supply is high and the price elasticity of demand is low, an excise tax falls mainly on consumers; when the price elasticity of supply is low and the price elasticity of demand is high, an excise tax falls mainly on producers. This leads us to the general rule: When the price elasticity of demand is higher than the price elasticity of supply, an excise tax falls mainly on the producers. When the price elasticity of supply is higher than the price elasticity of demand, an excise tax falls mainly on consumers. So elasticity—not who literally pays the tax—determines the incidence of an excise tax.

economics in action

So Who Does Pay the FICA?

As we explained in Chapter 4, one of the main taxes levied by the federal government is the FICA, or payroll tax. Half of this tax is paid by workers, half by their employers. But we have learned that this tells us nothing about who *really* pays the tax, that is, about the incidence of the FICA.

So who does pay the FICA? Almost all economists who have studied the issue agree that the answer is that the FICA is a tax on workers, not on their employers.

The reason for this conclusion lies in a comparison of the price elasticities of the supply of labor by households and the demand for labor by firms. The evidence suggests that the price elasticity of demand for labor is quite high, at least 3. That is, an increase in average wages of 1 percent would lead to at least a 3 percent decline in the number of hours of work demanded. The price elasticity of supply of labor, however, is generally believed to be very low. The reason is that although a rise in the wage rate increases the incentive to work, it also makes people richer and more able to afford leisure. So the number of hours people are willing to work increases very little—if at all—when the wage per hour goes up.

Our analysis already tells us that when the price elasticity of demand is much higher than the price elasticity of supply, the burden of an excise tax falls mainly on the suppliers. So the FICA falls mainly on the suppliers of labor, that is, workers—even though on paper half the tax is paid by employers.

This conclusion tells us something important about our tax system: that the FICA, rather than the much-hated income tax, is the main tax on most families. The FICA is 15.3 percent of all wages and salaries up to more than $80,000 per year; that is, the great majority of workers in the United States pay 15.3 percent of their wages in FICA. But only a minority of American families pay more than 15 percent of their income in income tax. According to estimates by the Congressional Budget Office, the FICA is Uncle Sam's main bite out of the income of more than 70 percent of families. ■

< < < < < < < < < < < < < < < < < < <

>> CHECK YOUR UNDERSTANDING 5-5

1. The demand for economics textbooks is very inelastic, but the supply is somewhat elastic. What does this imply about the incidence of a tax? Illustrate with a diagram.

2. True or false? When a substitute for a good is readily available to consumers, but it is difficult for producers to adjust the quantity of the good produced, then the burden of a tax on the good falls more heavily on producers.

3. The supply of bottled spring water is very inelastic, but the demand for it is somewhat elastic. What does this imply about the incidence of a tax? Illustrate with a diagram.

4. True or false? Other things equal, consumers would prefer to face a less elastic supply curve when a tax is imposed.

Solutions appear at back of book.

• A LOOK AHEAD •

The concept of elasticity deepens our understanding of supply and demand, among other things helping us predict not only in which direction prices will move but also by how much. For example, we now know that supply and demand elasticities determine how the burden of a tax will be divided between producers and consumers. And, to come back to an example from very early on in this chapter, the concept of elasticity was just what Luis Tellez needed to be able to engineer a reduction in output by oil-exporting countries that led to an increase in oil prices and an increase in their total oil revenues.

But we don't yet have a way to translate the changes in prices that result from a tax, or from any other change in the situation, into a measure of gains or losses to individuals. In the next chapter, we show how to make that translation—how to use the supply and demand curves to calculate gains and losses to producers and consumers.

SUMMARY

1. Many economic questions depend on the size of consumer or producer response to changes in prices or other variables. *Elasticity* is a general measure of responsiveness that can be used to answer such questions.

2. The **price elasticity of demand**—the percent change in the quantity demanded divided by the percent change in the price (dropping the minus sign)—is a measure of the responsiveness of the quantity demanded to changes in the price. In practical calculations, it is usually best to use the **midpoint method**, which calculates percent changes in prices and quantities based on the average of starting and final values.

3. The responsiveness of the quantity demanded to price can range from **perfectly inelastic demand**, where the quantity demanded is unaffected by the price, to **perfectly elastic demand**, where there is a unique price at which consumers will buy as much or as little as they are offered. When demand is perfectly inelastic, the demand curve is a vertical line; when it is perfectly elastic, the demand curve is a horizontal line.

4. The price elasticity of demand is classified according to whether it is more or less than 1. If it is greater than 1, demand is **elastic**; if it is less than 1, demand is **inelastic**; if it is exactly 1, demand is **unit-elastic**. This classification

determines how **total revenue**, the total value of sales, changes when the price changes. If demand is elastic, total revenue falls when the price increases and rises when the price decreases. If demand is inelastic, total revenue rises when the price increases and falls when the price decreases.

5. The price elasticity of demand depends on whether there are close substitutes for the good in question, whether the good is a necessity or a luxury, and the length of time that has elapsed since the price change.

6. The **cross-price elasticity of demand** measures the effect of a change in one good's price on the quantity of another good demanded. The cross-price elasticity of demand can be positive, in which case the goods are substitutes, or negative, in which case they are complements.

7. The **income elasticity of demand** is the percent change in the quantity of a good demanded when a consumer's income changes divided by the percent change in income. The income elasticity of demand indicates how intensely the demand for a good responds to changes in income. It can be negative; in that case the good is an inferior good. Goods with positive income elasticities of

demand are normal goods. If the income elasticity is greater than 1, a good is **income-elastic**; if it is positive and less than 1, the good is **income-inelastic**.

8. The **price elasticity of supply** is the percent change in the quantity of a good supplied divided by the percent change in the price. If the quantity supplied does not change at all, we have an instance of **perfectly inelastic supply**; the supply curve is a vertical line. If the quantity supplied is zero below some price but infinite above that price, we have an instance of **perfectly elastic supply**; the supply curve is a horizontal line.

9. The price elasticity of supply depends on the availability of resources to expand production and on time. It is higher when inputs are easily available and the longer the time elapsed since the price change.

10. The incidence of an excise tax depends on the price elasticities of supply and demand. If the price elasticity of demand is higher than the price elasticity of supply, the tax falls mainly on producers; if the price elasticity of supply is higher than the price elasticity of demand, the tax falls mainly on consumers.

KEY TERMS

Price elasticity of demand, p. 111
Midpoint method, p. 112
Perfectly inelastic demand, p. 114
Perfectly elastic demand, p. 114
Elastic demand, p. 114

Inelastic demand, p. 114
Unit-elastic demand, p. 114
Total revenue, p. 116
Cross-price elasticity of demand, p. 121
Income elasticity of demand, p. 122

Income-elastic demand, p. 122
Income-inelastic demand, p. 122
Price elasticity of supply, p. 124
Perfectly inelastic supply, p. 125
Perfectly elastic supply, p. 125

PROBLEMS

1. TheNile.com, the online bookseller, wants to increase its total revenue. Currently, every book it sells is priced at $10.50. One suggested strategy is to offer a discount that lowers the price of a book to $9.50, a 10% reduction in price using the midpoint method. TheNile.com knows that its customers can be divided into two distinct groups according to their likely responses to the discount. The accompanying table shows how the two groups respond to the discount.

	Group A (sales per week)	Group B (sales per week)
Volume of sales before the 10% discount	1.55 million	1.50 million
Volume of sales after the 10% discount	1.65 million	1.70 million

a. Using the midpoint method, calculate the price elasticities of demand for Group A and Group B.

b. Explain how the discount will affect total revenue from each group.

c. Suppose TheNile.com knows which group each customer belongs to when he or she logs on and can choose whether or not to offer the 10% discount. If TheNile.com wants to increase its total revenue, should discounts be offered to Group A or to Group B, to neither group, or to both groups?

2. Do you think the price elasticity of demand for Ford sport-utility vehicles (SUVs) will increase, decrease, or remain the same when each of the following events occurs? Explain your answer.

a. Other car manufacturers, such as General Motors, decide to make and sell SUVs.

b. SUVs produced in foreign countries are banned from the American market.

c. Due to ad campaigns, Americans believe that SUVs are much safer than ordinary passenger cars.

d. The time period over which you measure the elasticity lengthens. During that longer time, new models such as four-wheel-drive cargo vans appear.

3. U.S. winter wheat production increased dramatically in 1999 after a bumper harvest. The supply curve shifted rightward; as a result, the price decreased and the quantity demanded increased (a movement along the demand curve). The accompanying table describes what happened to prices and the quantity demanded of wheat.

	1998	1999
Quantity demanded (bushels)	1.74 billion	1.9 billion
Average price (per bushel)	$3.70	$2.72

a. Using the midpoint method, calculate the price elasticity of demand for winter wheat.

b. What is the total revenue for U.S. wheat farmers in 1998 and 1999?

c. Did the bumper harvest increase or decrease the total revenue of American wheat farmers? How could you have predicted this from your answer to part a?

4. The accompanying table gives part of the supply schedule for personal computers in the United States.

Price of computer	Quantity of computers supplied
$1,100	12,000
900	8,000

a. Calculate the price elasticity of supply when the price increases from $900 to $1,100 using the midpoint method.

b. Suppose firms produce 1,000 more computers at any given price due to improved technology. As price increases from $900 to $1,100, is the price elasticity of supply now greater than, less than, or the same as it was in part a?

c. Suppose a longer time period under consideration means that the quantity supplied at any given price is 20% higher than the figures given in the table. As price increases from $900 to $1,100, is the price elasticity of supply now greater than, less than, or the same as it was in part a?

5. The accompanying table lists the cross-price elasticities of demand for several goods, where the percent price change is measured for the first good of the pair, and the percent quantity change is measured for the second good.

Good	Cross-price elasticities of demand
Air-conditioning units and kilowatts of electricity	−0.34
Coke and Pepsi	+0.63
High-fuel-consuming sport-utility vehicles (SUVs) and gasoline	−0.28
McDonald's burgers and Burger King burgers	+0.82
Butter and margarine	+1.54

a. Explain the sign of each of the cross-price elasticities. What does it imply about the relationship between the two goods in question?

b. Compare the absolute values of the cross-price elasticities and explain their magnitudes. For example, why is the cross-price elasticity of McDonald's and Burger King less than the cross-elasticity of butter and margarine?

c. Use the information in the table to calculate how a 5% increase in the price of Pepsi affects the quantity of Coke demanded.

d. Use the information in the table to calculate how a 10% decrease in the price of gasoline affects the quantity of SUVs demanded.

6. What can you conclude about the price elasticity of demand in each of the following statements?

a. "The pizza delivery business in this town is very competitive. I'd lose half my customers if I raised the price by as little as 10%."

b. "I owned both of the two Jerry Garcia autographed lithographs in existence. I sold one on eBay for a high price. But when I sold the second one, the price dropped a lot."

c. "My economics professor has chosen to use the Krugman/Wells textbook for this class. I have no choice but to buy this book."

d. "I always spend a total of exactly $10 per week on coffee."

7. Take a linear demand curve like that shown in Figure 5-5, where the range of prices for which demand is elastic and inelastic is labeled. In each of the following scenarios, the supply curve shifts. Show along which portion of the demand curve (that is, the elastic or the inelastic portion) the supply curve must have shifted in order to generate the event described. In each case, show on the diagram the quantity effect and the price effect.

a. Recent attempts by the Colombian army to stop the flow of illegal drugs into the United States have actually benefited drug dealers.

b. New construction increased the number of seats in the football stadium and resulted in greater total revenue from box-office ticket sales.

c. A fall in input prices has led to higher output of Porsches. But total revenue for the Porsche Company has declined as a result.

8. The accompanying table shows the price and yearly quantity sold of souvenir T-shirts in the town of Crystal Lake according to the average income of the tourists visiting.

Price of T-shirt	Quantity of T-shirts demanded when average tourist income is $20,000	Quantity of T-shirts demanded when average tourist income is $30,000
$4	3,000	5,000
5	2,400	4,200
6	1,600	3,000
7	800	1,800

a. Using the midpoint method, calculate the price elasticity of demand when the price of a T-shirt rises from $5 to $6 when the average tourist income is $20,000. Also calculate it when the average tourist income is $30,000.

b. Using the midpoint method, calculate the income elasticity of demand when the average tourist income increases from $20,000 to $30,000 when the price of a T-shirt is $4. Also calculate it when the price is $7.

9. A recent study determined the following elasticities for Volkswagen Beetles:

$$\text{Price elasticity of demand} = 2$$
$$\text{Income elasticity of demand} = 1.5$$

The supply of Beetles is elastic. Based on this information, are the following statements true or false? Explain your reasoning.

a. A 10% increase in the price of a Beetle will reduce the quantity demanded by 20%.

b. An increase in consumer income will increase the price and quantity sold of Beetles. Since price elasticity of demand is greater than 1, total revenue will go down.

10. In each of the following cases, do you think the price elasticity of supply is (i) perfectly elastic; (ii) perfectly inelastic; (iii) elastic, but not perfectly elastic; or (iv) inelastic, but not perfectly inelastic? Explain using a diagram.

a. An increase in demand this summer for luxury cruises leads to a huge jump in the sales price of a cabin on the Queen Mary.

b. The price of a kilowatt of electricity is the same during periods of high electricity demand as during periods of low electricity demand.

c. Fewer people want to fly during February than during any other month. The airlines cancel about 10% of their flights as ticket prices fall about 20% during this month.

d. Owners of vacation homes in Maine rent them out during the summer. Due to the soft economy this year, a 30% decline in the price of a vacation rental leads more than half of homeowners to occupy their vacation homes themselves during the summer.

11. Use an elasticity concept to explain each of the following observations.

a. During economic boom times, the number of new personal care businesses, such as gyms and tanning salons, is proportionately greater than the number of other new businesses, such as grocery stores.

b. Cement is the primary building material in Mexico. After new technology makes cement cheaper to produce, the supply curve for the Mexican cement industry becomes relatively flatter.

c. Some goods that were once considered luxuries, like a telephone, are now considered virtual necessities. As a result, the demand curve for telephone services has become steeper over time.

d. Consumers in a less developed country like Guatemala spend proportionately more of their income on equipment for producing things at home, like sewing machines, than consumers in a more developed country like Canada.

12. Taiwan is a major world supplier of semiconductor chips. A recent earthquake severely damaged the production facilities of Taiwanese chip-producing companies, sharply reducing the amount of chips they could produce.

a. Assume that the total revenue of a typical non-Taiwanese chip manufacturer rises due to these events. In terms of an elasticity, what must be true for this to happen? Illustrate the change in total revenue with a diagram, indicating the price effect and the quantity effect of the Taiwan earthquake on this company's total revenue.

b. Now assume that the total revenue of a typical non-Taiwanese chip manufacturer falls due to these events. In terms of an elasticity, what must be true for this to happen? Illustrate the change in total revenue with a diagram, indicating the price effect and the quantity effect of the Taiwan earthquake on this company's total revenue.

13. There is a debate about whether sterile hypodermic needles should be passed out free of charge in cities with high drug use. Proponents argue that doing so will reduce the incidence of diseases, such as HIV/AIDS, that are often spread by needle sharing among drug users. Opponents believe that doing so will encourage more drug use by reducing the risks of this behavior. As an economist asked to assess the policy, you must know the following: (i) how responsive the spread of diseases like HIV/AIDS is to the price of sterile needles; and (ii) how responsive drug use is to the price of sterile needles. Assuming that you know these two things, use the concepts of price elasticity of demand for sterile needles and the cross-price elasticity between drugs and sterile needles to answer the following questions.

a. In what circumstances do you believe this is a beneficial policy?

b. In what circumstances do you believe this is a bad policy?

14. Suppose the government imposes an excise tax of $1 for every gallon of gas sold. Before the tax, the price of a gallon of gas is $2. Consider the following four after-tax scenarios. In each case, (i) use an elasticity concept to explain what must be true for this scenario to arise; (ii) determine who bears relatively more of the burden of the tax, producers or consumers; and (iii) illustrate your answer with a diagram.

a. The price of gasoline paid by consumers rises to $3 per gallon. Assume that the demand curve is downward sloping.

b. The price paid by consumers remains at $2 per gallon after the tax is imposed. Assume that the supply curve is upward sloping.

c. The price of gasoline paid by consumers rises to $2.75.

d. The price of gasoline paid by consumers rises to $2.25.

15. Describe how the following events will affect the incidence of taxation—that is, after the event, will the tax fall more heavily on consumers or producers in comparison to before the event? Use the concept of elasticity to explain your answer.

a. Sales of gasoline are taxed. Ethanol, a substitute for gasoline, becomes widely available.

b. Sales of electricity to California residents are taxed. Regulations are introduced that make it much more difficult for California utility companies to divert supplies of electricity from the California market to markets in neighboring states like Nevada.

c. Sales of electricity to California residents are taxed. Regulations are introduced that make it much easier for California utility companies to divert supplies of electricity from the California market to markets in neighboring states like Nevada.

d. The sale of municipally provided water is taxed. Legislation is introduced that forbids the use of private sources of water such as wells and the diversion of rivers.

16. In devising taxes, there is often a debate about (i) who bears the burden of the tax and (ii) whether the tax achieves some desirable social goal, such as discouraging undesirable behavior by making it more expensive. In the case of cigarettes, smokers tend to be highly addicted and have lower income than the average nonsmoker. Taxes on cigarettes have historically had the effect of raising the price to consumers almost one for one with the size of the tax.

a. Why might such a tax be undesirable when considering issues of tax equity—that is, whether or not the tax burden falls more heavily on lower-income people? How do the price elasticities of supply and demand for cigarettes affect the equity of cigarette taxation?

b. How do the price elasticities of supply and demand for cigarettes affect the effectiveness of the tax in discouraging smoking?

c. In light of your answers to parts a and b and the historical response of price to the tax, what trade-offs must policy makers make when considering a cigarette tax?

17. Worldwide, the average coffee grower has increased the amount of acreage under cultivation over the past few years. The result has been that the average coffee plantation produces significantly more coffee than it did 10 to 20 years ago. Unfortunately for the growers, however, this has also been a period in which their total revenues have plunged. In terms of an elasticity, what must be true for these events to have occurred? Illustrate these events with a diagram, indicating the quantity effect and the price effect that gave rise to these events.

>*web*... To continue your study and review of concepts in this chapter, please visit the Krugman/Wells website for quizzes, animated graph tutorials, web links to helpful resources, and more.

www.worthpublishers.com/krugmanwells

Consumer and Producer Surplus

MAKING GAINS BY THE BOOK

THERE IS A LIVELY MARKET IN SECOND-hand college textbooks. At the end of each term, some students who took a course decide that the money they can get by selling their used books is worth more to them than keeping the books. And some students who are taking the course next term prefer to buy a somewhat battered but inexpensive used textbook rather than pay the full price for a new one.

Textbook publishers and authors are not happy about these transactions, because they cut into sales of new books. But both the students who sell used books and those who buy them clearly benefit from the existence of the market. That is why many college bookstores facilitate their trade, buying used textbooks and selling them alongside the new books.

But can we put a number on what used textbook buyers and sellers gain from these transactions? Can we answer the question, "*How much* do the buyers and sellers of textbooks gain from the existence of the used-book market?"

Yes, we can. In this chapter we will see how to measure benefits, such as those to buyers of used textbooks, from being able to purchase a good—known as *consumer surplus*. And we will see that there is a corresponding measure, *producer surplus*, of the benefits sellers receive from being able to sell a good.

The concepts of consumer surplus and producer surplus are extremely useful for analyzing a wide variety of economic issues.

How much am I willing to pay for that used textbook?

They let us calculate how much benefit producers and consumers receive from the existence of a market. They also allow us to calculate how the welfare of consumers and producers is affected by changes in market

What you will learn in this chapter:

➤ The meaning of **consumer surplus** and its relationship to the demand curve

➤ The meaning of **producer surplus** and its relationship to the supply curve

➤ The meaning and importance of **total surplus** and how it can be used both to measure the gains from trade and to evaluate the efficiency of a market

➤ How to use changes in total surplus to measure the deadweight loss of taxes prices. Such calculations play a crucial role in evaluating many economic policies.

What information do we need to calculate consumer and producer surplus? The answer, surprisingly, is that all we need are the demand and supply curves for a good. That is, the supply and demand model isn't just a model of how a competitive market works—it's also a model of how much consumers and producers gain from participating in that market. So our first step will be to learn how consumer and producer surplus can be derived from the demand and supply curves. We will then see how these concepts can be applied to actual economic issues.

Consumer Surplus and the Demand Curve

The market in used textbooks is not a big business in terms of dollars and cents. But it is a convenient starting point for developing the concepts of consumer and producer surplus.

So let's look at the market for used textbooks, starting with the buyers. The key point, as we'll see in a minute, is that the demand curve is derived from their tastes or preferences—and that those same preferences also determine how much they gain from the opportunity to buy used books.

Willingness to Pay and the Demand Curve

A used book is not as good as a new book—it will be battered and coffee-stained, may include someone else's highlighting, and may not be completely up to date. How much this bothers you depends on your own preferences. Some potential buyers would prefer to buy the used book if it is only slightly cheaper than a new book, while others would buy the used book only if it is considerably cheaper. Let's define a potential buyer's **willingness to pay** as the maximum price at which he or she would buy a good, in this case a used textbook. An individual won't buy the book if it costs more than this amount but is eager to do so if it costs less. If the price is just equal to an individual's willingness to pay, he or she is indifferent between buying and not buying.

The table in Figure 6-1 shows five potential buyers of a used book that costs $100 new, listed in order of their willingness to pay. At one extreme is Aleisha, who will buy a second-hand book even if the price is as high as $59. Brad is less willing to have a used book and will buy one only if the price is $45 or less. Claudia is willing to pay only $35, Darren only $25. And Edwina, who really doesn't like the idea of a used book, will buy one only if it costs no more than $10.

How many of these five students will actually buy a used book? It depends on the price. If the price of a used book is $55, only Aleisha buys one; if the price is $40, Aleisha and Brad both buy used books, and so on. So the information in the table on willingness to pay also defines the *demand schedule* for used textbooks.

As we saw in Chapter 3, we can use this demand schedule to derive the market demand curve shown in Figure 6-1. Because we are considering only a small number of consumers, this curve doesn't look like the smooth demand curves of earlier chapters, where markets contained hundreds or thousands of consumers. This demand curve is step-shaped, with alternating horizontal and vertical segments. Each horizontal segment—each step—corresponds to one potential buyer's willingness to pay. However, we'll see shortly that for the analysis of consumer surplus it doesn't matter whether the demand curve is stepped, as in this figure, or whether there are many consumers, making the curve smooth.

A consumer's **willingness to pay** for a good is the maximum price at which he or she would buy that good.

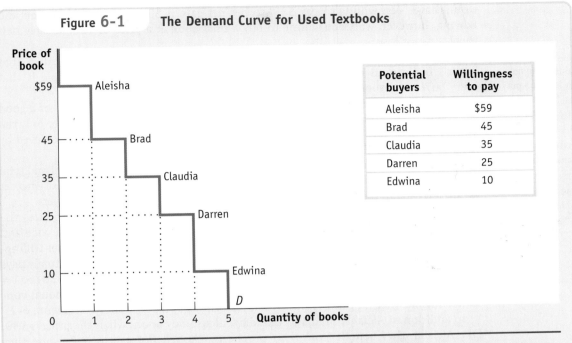

> ### Figure 6-1   The Demand Curve for Used Textbooks
>
> | Potential buyers | Willingness to pay |
> |---|---|
> | Aleisha | $59 |
> | Brad | 45 |
> | Claudia | 35 |
> | Darren | 25 |
> | Edwina | 10 |
>
> With only five potential consumers in this market, the demand curve is step-shaped. Each step represents one consumer, and its height indicates that consumer's willingness to pay, the maximum price at which each student will buy a used textbook, as indicated in the table. Aleisha has the highest willingness to pay at $59, Brad has the next highest at $45, and so on down to Edwina with the lowest at $10. At a price of $59 the quantity demanded is one (Aleisha); at a price of $45 the quantity demanded is two (Aleisha and Brad), and so on until you reach a price of $10 at which all five students are willing to purchase a book.

Willingness to Pay and Consumer Surplus

Suppose that the campus bookstore makes used textbooks available at a price of $30. In that case Aleisha, Brad, and Claudia will buy books. Do they gain from their purchases, and if so, how much?

The answer, shown in Table 6-1, is that each student who purchases a book does achieve a net gain but that the amount of the gain differs among students.

Aleisha would have been willing to pay $59, so her net gain is $59 − $30 = $29. Brad would have been willing to pay $45, so his net gain is $45 − $30 = $15. Claudia

TABLE 6-1

Consumer Surplus When the Price of a Used Textbook Is $30

Potential buyer	Willingness to pay	Price paid	Individual consumer surplus = willingness to pay − price paid
Aleisha	$59	$30	$29
Brad	45	30	15
Claudia	35	30	5
Darren	25	—	—
Edwina	10	—	—
		Total consumer surplus: $49	

would have been willing to pay $35, so her net gain is $35 − $30 = $5. Darren and Edwina, however, won't be willing to buy a used book at a price of $30, so they neither gain nor lose.

The net gain that a buyer achieves from the purchase of a good is called that buyer's **individual consumer surplus**. What we learn from this example is that every buyer of a good achieves some individual consumer surplus.

The sum of the individual consumer surpluses achieved by all the buyers of a good is known as the **total consumer surplus** achieved in the market. In Table 6-1, the total consumer surplus is the sum of the individual consumer surpluses achieved by Aleisha, Brad, and Claudia: $29 + $15 + $5 = $49.

Economists often use the term **consumer surplus** to refer to both individual and total consumer surplus. We will follow this practice; it will always be clear in context whether we are referring to the consumer surplus achieved by an individual or by all buyers.

Total consumer surplus can be represented graphically. Figure 6-2 reproduces the demand curve from Figure 6-1. Each step in that demand curve is one book wide and represents one consumer. For example, the height of Aleisha's step is $59, her willingness to pay. This step forms the top of a rectangle, with $30—the price she actually pays for a book—forming the bottom. The area of Aleisha's rectangle, ($59 − $30) × 1 = $29, is her consumer surplus from purchasing a book at $30. So the individual consumer surplus Aleisha gains is the *area of the dark blue rectangle* shown in Figure 6-2.

In addition to Aleisha, Brad and Claudia will also buy books when the price is $30. Like Aleisha, they benefit from their purchases, though not as much, because they each have a lower willingness to pay. Figure 6-2 also shows the consumer surplus gained by Brad and Claudia; again, this can be measured by the areas of the appropriate rectangles. Darren and Edwina, because they do not buy books at a price of $30, receive no consumer surplus.

The total consumer surplus achieved in this market is just the sum of the individual consumer surpluses received by Aleisha, Brad, and Claudia. So total consumer surplus is equal to the combined area of the three rectangles—the entire shaded area in Figure 6-2. Another way to say this is that total consumer surplus is equal to the area that is under the demand curve but above the price.

Figure 6-2

Consumer Surplus in the Used-Textbook Market

At a price of $30, Aleisha, Brad, and Claudia each buy a book but Darren and Edwina do not. Aleisha, Brad, and Claudia get individual consumer surpluses equal to the difference between their willingness to pay and the price, illustrated by the areas of the shaded rectangles. Both Darren and Edwina have a willingness to pay less than $30, so they are unwilling to buy a book in this market; they receive zero consumer surplus. The total consumer surplus is given by the entire shaded area—the sum of the individual consumer surpluses of Aleisha, Brad, and Claudia—equal to $29 + $15 + $5 = $49.

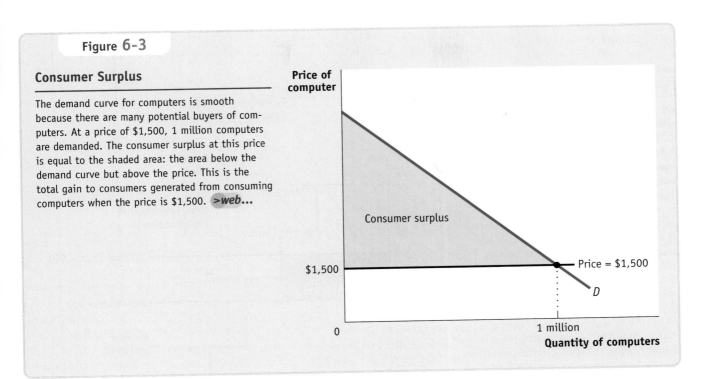

Figure 6-3

Consumer Surplus

The demand curve for computers is smooth because there are many potential buyers of computers. At a price of $1,500, 1 million computers are demanded. The consumer surplus at this price is equal to the shaded area: the area below the demand curve but above the price. This is the total gain to consumers generated from consuming computers when the price is $1,500. **>web...**

This illustrates the following general principle: *The total consumer surplus generated by purchases of a good at a given price is equal to the area below the demand curve but above that price.* The same principle applies regardless of the number of consumers.

When we consider large markets, this graphical representation becomes extremely helpful. Consider, for example, the sales of personal computers to millions of potential buyers. Each potential buyer has a maximum price that he or she is willing to pay. With so many potential buyers, the demand curve will be smooth, like the one shown in Figure 6-3.

Suppose that at a price of $1,500, a total of 1 million computers are purchased. How much do consumers gain from being able to buy those 1 million computers? We could answer that question by calculating the consumer surplus of each individual buyer and then adding these numbers up to arrive at a total. But it is much easier just to look at Figure 6-3 and use the fact that the total consumer surplus is equal to the shaded area. As in our original example, consumer surplus is equal to the area below the demand curve but above the price.

How Changing Prices Affect Consumer Surplus

It is often important to know how much consumer surplus *changes* when the price changes. For example, we may want to know how much consumers are hurt if a frost in Florida drives up orange prices or how much consumers gain if the introduction of fish farming makes salmon less expensive. The same approach we have used to derive consumer surplus can be used to answer questions about how changes in prices affect consumers.

Let's return to the example of the market for used textbooks. Suppose that the bookstore decided to sell used textbooks for $20 instead of $30. How much would this increase consumer surplus?

The answer is illustrated in Figure 6-4 on page 140. As shown in the figure, there are two parts to the increase in consumer surplus. The first part, shaded dark blue, is the gain of those who would have bought books even at the higher price. Each of the students who would have bought books at $30—Aleisha, Brad, and Claudia—pays $10 less, and therefore each gains $10 in consumer surplus from the fall in price to

Figure 6-4

Consumer Surplus and a Fall in the Price of Used Textbooks

There are two parts to the increase in consumer surplus generated by a fall in price from $30 to $20. The first is given by the dark blue rectangle: each person who would have bought at the original price of $30—Aleisha, Brad, and Claudia—receives an increase in consumer surplus equal to the total fall in price, $10. So the area of the dark blue rectangle corresponds to an amount equal to 3 × $10 = $30. The second part is given by the light blue rectangle: the increase in consumer surplus for those who would *not* have bought at the original price of $30 but who buy at the new price of $20—namely, Darren. Darren's willingness to pay is $25, so he now receives consumer surplus of $5. The total increase in consumer surplus is 3 × $10 + $5 = $35, represented by the sum of the shaded areas. Likewise, a rise in price from $20 to $30 would decrease consumer surplus by an amount equal to the sum of the shaded areas.

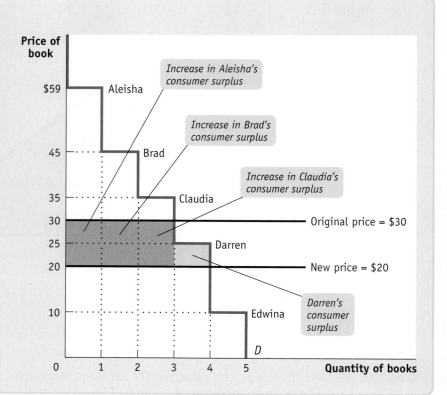

$20. So the dark blue area represents the $30 increase in consumer surplus to those three buyers. The second part, shaded light blue, is the gain to those who would not have bought a book at $30 but are willing to pay more than $20. In this case that means Darren, who would not have bought a book at $30 but does buy one at $20. He gains $5—the difference between his willingness to pay $25 and the new price of $20. So the light blue area represents a further $5 gain in consumer surplus. The total increase in consumer surplus is the sum of the shaded areas, $35. Likewise, a rise in price from $20 to $30 would decrease consumer surplus by an amount equal to the sum of the shaded areas.

Figure 6-4 illustrates that when the price of a good falls, the area under the demand curve but above the price—which we have seen is equal to the total consumer surplus—increases. Figure 6-5 shows the same result for the case of a smooth demand curve, the demand for personal computers. Here we assume that the price of computers falls from $5,000 to $1,500, leading to an increase in the quantity demanded from 200,000 to 1 million units. As in the used-textbook example, we divide the gain in consumer surplus into two parts. The dark blue rectangle in Figure 6-5 corresponds to the dark blue area in Figure 6-4: it is the gain to the 200,000 people who would have bought computers even at the higher price of $5,000. As a result of the price fall, each receives additional surplus of $3,500. The light blue triangle in Figure 6-5 corresponds to the light blue area in Figure 6-4: it is the gain to people who would not have bought the good at the higher price but are willing to do so at a price of $1,500. For example, the light blue triangle includes the gain to someone who would have been willing to pay $2,000 for a computer and therefore gains $500 in consumer surplus when he or she is able to buy a computer for only $1,500. As before, the total gain in consumer surplus is the sum of the shaded areas, the increase in the area under the demand curve but above the price.

What would happen if the price of a good were to rise instead of fall? We would do the same analysis in reverse. Suppose, for example, that for some reason the price

Figure 6-5

A Fall in the Price Increases Consumer Surplus

A fall in the price of a computer from $5,000 to $1,500 leads to an increase in the quantity demanded and an increase in consumer surplus. The change in total consumer surplus is given by the sum of the shaded areas: the total area below the demand curve but between the old and new prices. Here, the dark blue area represents the increase in consumer surplus for the 200,000 consumers who would have bought a computer at the original price of $5,000; they each receive an increase in consumer surplus of $3,500. The light blue area represents the increase in consumer surplus for those willing to buy at a price equal to or greater than $1,500 but less than $5,000. Similarly, a rise in the price of a computer from $1,500 to $5,000 generates a decrease in consumer surplus equal to the sum of the two shaded areas. **>web...**

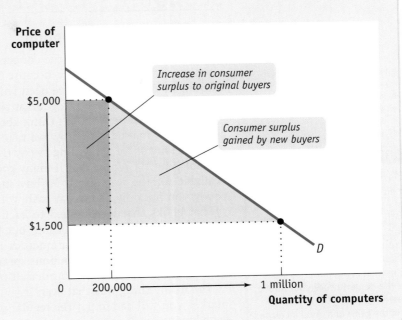

of computers rises from $1,500 to $5,000. This would lead to a fall in consumer surplus, equal to the shaded area in Figure 6-5. This loss consists of two parts. The dark blue rectangle represents the loss to consumers who would still buy a computer, even at a price of $5,000. The light blue triangle represents the loss to consumers who decide not to buy a computer at the higher price.

FOR INQUIRING MINDS

I WANT A NEW DRUG . . .

The pharmaceutical industry is constantly introducing new prescription drugs. Some of these drugs do the same thing as other, existing drugs, but a bit better—for example, pretty good allergy medicines have been around for years, but newer versions that are somewhat more effective or have fewer side effects keep emerging. Other drugs do something that was previously considered impossible—a famous example from the late 1990s was Propecia, the pill that slows and in some cases reverses hair loss.

Such innovations raise a difficult question for the people who are supposed to measure economic growth: how do you calculate the contribution of a new product to the economy?

You might at first say that it's just a matter of dollars and cents. But that could be wrong, in either direction. A new painkiller that is just slightly better than aspirin might have huge sales, because it would take over the painkiller market—but it wouldn't really add much to

consumer welfare. On the other hand, the benefits of a drug that cures the previously incurable might be much larger than the money actually spent on it—after all, people *would have been willing* to pay much more.

Consider, for example, the benefits of antibiotics. When penicillin was introduced in 1941, it transformed the treatment of infectious disease; illnesses that had previously crippled or killed millions of people were suddenly easy to treat. Presumably most people would be willing to pay a lot not to go back to the days before penicillin. Yet the average American spends only a few dollars per year on antibiotics.

The right way to measure the gains from a new drug—or any new product—is therefore to try to figure out what people would have been willing to pay for the good, and subtract what they actually pay. In other words, the gains from a new drug should be measured by calculating consumer surplus!

economics in action

When Money Isn't Enough

The key insight we get from the concept of consumer surplus is that purchases yield a net benefit to the consumer, because the consumer pays a price that is less than the amount he or she would have been willing to pay for the good. Another way to say this is that the right to buy a good at the going price is a valuable thing in itself.

Most of the time we don't think about the value associated with the right to buy a good. In a market economy, we take it for granted that we can buy whatever we want, as long as we are willing to pay the price. But that hasn't always been true. For example, during World War II many goods were rationed in order to make resources available for the war effort. To buy sugar, meat, coffee, gasoline, and many other goods, you not only had to pay cash; you also had to present stamps or coupons from special books that were issued to each family by the government. These pieces of paper, which represented nothing but the right to buy goods at the market price, quickly became valuable commodities in themselves. As a result, black markets in meat stamps and gasoline coupons sprang into existence. Moreover, criminals began stealing coupons and even counterfeiting stamps.

The funny thing was that even if you had bought a gasoline coupon on the black market, you still had to pay the regular price of gasoline to fill your tank. So what you were buying on the black market was not the good but *the right to buy the good*—that is, people who bought ration coupons on the black market were paying for the right to get some consumer surplus. ∎

< < < < < < < < < < < < < < < < < <

>> CHECK YOUR UNDERSTANDING 6-1

1. Consider the market for cheese-stuffed jalapeno peppers. There are two consumers, Casey and Josie, and their willingness to pay for each pepper is given in the accompanying table. Use the table (i) to construct the demand schedule for peppers for prices of $0.00, $0.10, and so on, up to $0.90; and (ii) to calculate the total consumer surplus when the price of a pepper is $0.40.

Quantity of peppers	Casey's willingness to pay	Josie's willingness to pay
1st pepper	$0.90	$0.80
2nd pepper	0.70	0.60
3rd pepper	0.50	0.40
4th pepper	0.30	0.30

Solutions appear at back of book.

Producer Surplus and the Supply Curve

Just as buyers of a good would have been willing to pay more for their purchase than the price they actually pay, sellers of a good would have been willing to sell it for less than the price they actually receive. We can therefore carry out an analysis of producer surplus and the supply curve that is almost exactly parallel to that of consumer surplus and the demand curve.

Cost and Producer Surplus

Consider a group of students who are potential sellers of used textbooks. Because they have different preferences, the various potential sellers differ in the price at which they are willing to sell their books. The table in Figure 6-6 shows the prices at which several different students would be willing to sell. Andrew is willing to sell the book as long as he can get anything more than $5; Betty won't sell unless she can get at least $15; Carlos, unless he can get $25; Donna, unless she can get $35; Engelbert, unless he can get $45.

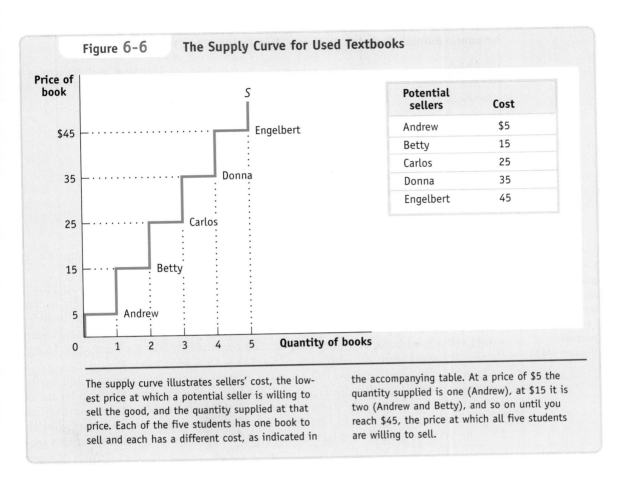

Figure 6-6   **The Supply Curve for Used Textbooks**

Potential sellers	Cost
Andrew	$5
Betty	15
Carlos	25
Donna	35
Engelbert	45

The supply curve illustrates sellers' cost, the lowest price at which a potential seller is willing to sell the good, and the quantity supplied at that price. Each of the five students has one book to sell and each has a different cost, as indicated in the accompanying table. At a price of $5 the quantity supplied is one (Andrew), at $15 it is two (Andrew and Betty), and so on until you reach $45, the price at which all five students are willing to sell.

The lowest price at which a potential seller is willing to sell has a special name in economics: it is called the seller's **cost**. So Andrew's cost is $5, Betty's is $15, and so on.

Using the term *cost*, which people normally associate with the monetary cost of producing a good, may sound a little strange when applied to sellers of used textbooks. The students don't have to manufacture the books, so it doesn't cost the student who sells a book anything to make that book available for sale, does it?

Yes, it does. A student who sells a book won't have it later, as part of a personal collection. So there is an *opportunity cost* to selling a textbook, even if the owner has completed the course for which it was required. And remember that one of the basic principles of economics is that the true measure of the cost of doing anything is always its opportunity cost—the real cost of something is what you must give up to get it.

So it is good economics to talk of the minimum price at which someone will sell a good as the "cost" of selling that good, even if he or she doesn't spend any money to make the good available for sale. Of course, in most real-world markets the sellers are also those who produce the good—and therefore *do* spend money to make the good available for sale. In this case the cost of making the good available for sale *includes* monetary costs—but it may also include other opportunity costs.

Getting back to the example, suppose that Andrew sells his book for $30. Clearly he has gained from the transaction: he would have been willing to sell for only $5, so he has gained $25. This gain, the difference between the price he actually gets and his cost—the minimum price at which he would have been willing to sell—is known as his **individual producer surplus.**

Just as we derived the demand curve from the willingness to pay of different consumers, we can derive the supply curve from the cost of different producers. The step-shaped curve in Figure 6-6 shows the supply curve implied by the costs shown in the

A potential seller's **cost** is the lowest price at which he or she is willing to sell a good.

Individual producer surplus is the net gain to a seller from selling a good. It is equal to the difference between the price received and the seller's cost.

TABLE 6-2

Producer Surplus When the Price of a Used Textbook Is $30

Potential seller	Cost	Price received	Individual producer surplus = price received − cost
Andrew	$5	$30	$25
Betty	15	30	15
Carlos	25	30	5
Donna	35	—	—
Engelbert	45	—	—
			Total producer surplus: $45

Total producer surplus in a market is the sum of the individual producer surpluses of all the sellers of a good. Economists use the term **producer surplus** to refer both to individual and to total producer surplus.

accompanying table. At a price less than $5, none of the students are willing to sell; at a price between $5 and $15, only Andrew is willing to sell, and so on.

As in the case of consumer surplus, we can add the individual producer surpluses of sellers to calculate the **total producer surplus**, the total gains to sellers in the market. Economists use the term **producer surplus** to refer to either total or individual producer surplus. Table 6-2 shows the net gain to each of the students who would sell a used book at a price of $30: $25 for Andrew, $15 for Betty, and $5 for Carlos. The total producer surplus is $25 + $15 + $5 = $45.

As with consumer surplus, the producer surplus gained by those who sell books can be represented graphically. Figure 6-7 reproduces the supply curve from Figure 6-6. Each step in that supply curve is one book wide and represents one seller. The height of Andrew's step is $5, his cost. This forms the bottom of a rectangle, with $30, the price he actually receives for his book, forming the top. The area of this rectangle, ($30 − $5) × 1 = $25, is his producer surplus. So the producer surplus Andrew gains from selling his book is the *area of the dark red rectangle* shown in the figure.

Let's assume that the campus bookstore is willing to buy all the used copies of this book that students are willing to sell at a price of $30. Then, in addition to Andrew, Betty and Carlos will also sell their books. They will also benefit from their sales, though not as much as Andrew, because they have higher costs. Andrew, as we have

Figure 6-7

Producer Surplus in the Used-Textbook Market

At a price of $30, Andrew, Betty, and Carlos each sell a book but Donna and Engelbert do not. Andrew, Betty, and Carlos get individual producer surpluses equal to the difference between the price and their cost, illustrated here by the shaded rectangles. Donna and Engelbert each have a cost that is greater than the price of $30, so they are unwilling to sell a book and therefore receive zero producer surplus. The total producer surplus is given by the entire shaded area, the sum of the individual producer surpluses of Andrew, Betty, and Carlos, equal to $25 + $15 + $5 = $45.

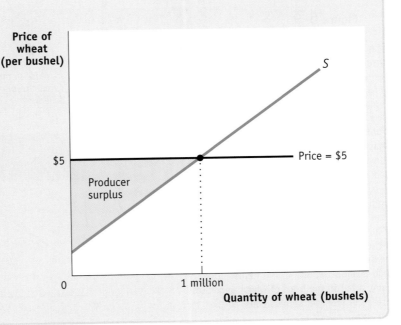

Figure 6-8

Producer Surplus

Here is the supply curve for wheat. At a price of $5 per bushel, farmers supply 1 million bushels. The producer surplus at this price is equal to the shaded area: the area above the supply curve but below the price. This is the total gain to producers—farmers in this case—from supplying their product when the price is $5. >*web*...

seen, gains $25. Betty gains a smaller amount: since her cost is $15, she gains only $15. Carlos gains even less, only $5.

Again, as with consumer surplus, we have a general rule for determining the total producer surplus from sales of a good: *The total producer surplus from sales of a good at a given price is the area above the supply curve but below that price.*

This rule applies both to examples like the one shown in Figure 6-7, where there are a small number of producers and a step-shaped supply curve, and to more realistic examples where there are many producers and the supply curve is more or less smooth.

Consider, for example, the supply of wheat. Figure 6-8 shows how producer surplus depends on the price per bushel. Suppose that, as shown in the figure, the price is $5 per bushel and farmers supply 1 million bushels. What is the benefit to the farmers from selling their wheat at a price of $5? Their producer surplus is equal to the shaded area in the figure—the area above the supply curve but below the price of $5 per bushel.

Changes in Producer Surplus

If the price of a good rises, producers of the good will experience an increase in producer surplus, though not all producers gain the same amount. Some producers would have produced the good even at the original price; they will gain the entire price increase on every unit they produce. Other producers will enter the market because of the higher price; they will gain only the difference between the new price and their cost.

Figure 6-9 on page 146 is the supply counterpart of Figure 6-5. It shows the effect on producer surplus of a rise in the price of wheat from $5 to $7 per bushel. The increase in producer surplus is the entire shaded area, which consists of two parts. First, there is a red rectangle corresponding to the gains to those farmers who would have supplied wheat even at the original $5 price. Second, there is an additional pink triangle that corresponds to the gains to those farmers who would not have supplied wheat at the original price but are drawn into the market by the higher price.

If the price were to fall from $7 to $5 per bushel, the story would run in reverse. The whole shaded area would now be the decline in producer surplus, the fall in the area above the supply curve but below the price. The loss would consist of two parts, the loss to farmers who would still grow wheat at a price of $5 (the red rectangle) and the loss to farmers who decide not to grow wheat because of the lower price (the pink triangle).

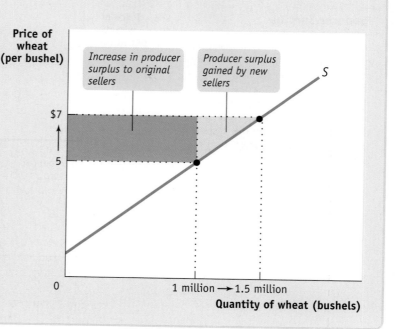

Figure 6-9

A Rise in the Price Increases Producer Surplus

A rise in the price of wheat from $5 to $7 leads to an increase in the quantity supplied and an increase in producer surplus. The change in total producer surplus is given by the sum of the shaded areas: the total area above the supply curve but between the old and new prices. The red area represents the gain to the farmers who would have supplied 1 million bushels at the original price of $5; they each receive an increase in producer surplus of $2 for each of those bushels. The triangular pink area represents the increase in producer surplus achieved by the farmers who supply the additional 500,000 bushels because of the higher price. Similarly, a fall in the price of wheat generates a decrease in producer surplus equal to the shaded areas. **>web...**

economics in action

Gaining from Disaster

In 1992 Hurricane Andrew swept through Florida, destroying thousands of homes and businesses. The state quickly began rebuilding, with the help of thousands of construction workers who moved temporarily to Florida to help out.

These construction workers were not motivated mainly by sympathy for Florida residents. They were lured by the high wages available there—and took home billions of dollars.

But how much did the temporary workers actually gain? Certainly we should not count all the money they earned in Florida as a net benefit. For one thing, most of these workers would have earned something—though not as much—if they had stayed home. In addition to this opportunity cost, the temporary move to Florida had other costs: the expense of motel rooms and of transportation, the wear and tear of being away from families and friends.

Clearly the workers viewed the benefits as being larger than the costs—otherwise they wouldn't have gone down to Florida in the first place. But the producer surplus earned by those temporary workers was much less than the money they earned. ∎

< < < < < < < < < < < < < < < < < < < <

>>**CHECK YOUR UNDERSTANDING 6-2**

1. Consider the market for cheese-stuffed jalapeno peppers. There are two producers, Cara and Jamie, and their costs of producing each pepper are given in the accompanying table. Use the table (i) to construct the supply schedule for peppers for prices of $0.00, $0.10, and so on, up to $0.90; and (ii) to calculate the total producer surplus when the price of a pepper is $0.70.

Quantity of peppers	Cara's cost	Jamie's cost
1st pepper	$0.10	$0.30
2nd pepper	0.10	0.50
3rd pepper	0.40	0.70
4th pepper	0.60	0.90

Solutions appear at back of book.

Consumer Surplus, Producer Surplus, and the Gains from Trade

One of the nine core principles of economics we introduced in Chapter 1 is that markets are a remarkably effective way to organize economic activity: they generally make society as well off as possible given the available resources. The concepts of consumer surplus and producer surplus can help us deepen our understanding of why this is so.

The Gains from Trade

Let's go back to the market in used textbooks but now consider a much bigger market—say, one at a large state university—where there are many potential buyers and sellers. Let's line up incoming students—who are potential buyers of the book—in order of their willingness to pay, so that the entering student with the highest willingness to pay is potential buyer number 1, the student with the next highest willingness to pay is number 2, and so on. Then we can use their willingness to pay to derive a demand curve like the one in Figure 6-10. Similarly, we can line up outgoing students, who are potential sellers of the book, in order of their cost, starting with the student with the lowest cost, then the student with the next lowest cost, and so on, to derive a supply curve like the one shown in the same figure.

As we have drawn the curves, the market reaches equilibrium at a price of $30 per book, and 1,000 books are bought and sold at that price. The two shaded triangles show the consumer surplus (blue) and the producer surplus (red) generated by this market. The sum of consumer and producer surplus is known as the **total surplus** generated in a market.

The striking thing about this picture is that both consumers and producers gain—that is, both consumers and producers are better off because there is a market in this good. But this should come as no surprise—it illustrates another core principle of economics: there are *gains from trade*. These gains from trade are the reason everyone is better off participating in a market economy than they would be if each individual tried to be self-sufficient.

But are we as well off as we could be? This brings us to the question of the efficiency of markets.

> The **total surplus** generated in a market is the total net gain to consumers and producers from trading in the market. It is the sum of the producer and the consumer surplus.

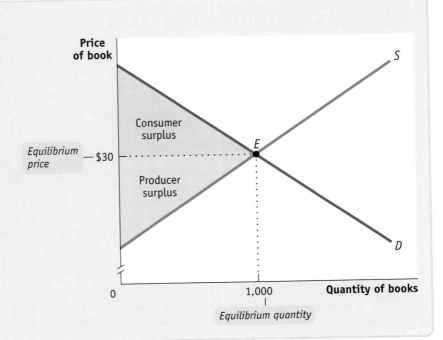

Figure 6-10

Total Surplus

In the market for used textbooks, the equilibrium price is $30 and the equilibrium quantity is 1,000 books. Consumer surplus is given by the blue area, the area below the demand curve but above the price. Producer surplus is given by the red area, the area above the supply curve but below the price. The sum of the blue and the red areas is total surplus, the total benefit to society from the production and consumption of the good. **>web**...

The Efficiency of Markets: A Preliminary View

Markets produce gains from trade, but in Chapter 1 we made a bigger claim: that markets are usually *efficient*. That is, we claimed that once the market has produced its gains from trade, there is usually no way to make some people better off without making others worse off (with some well-defined exceptions).

We're not yet ready to carry out a full discussion of the efficiency of markets—that will have to wait until we've looked in more detail at the behavior of producers and consumers. However, we can get an intuitive sense of the efficiency of markets by noticing a key feature of the market equilibrium shown in Figure 6-10: the maximum possible total surplus is achieved at market equilibrium. That is, the market equilibrium allocates the consumption of the good among potential consumers and sales of the good among potential sellers in a way that achieves the highest possible gain to society.

How do we know this? By comparing the total surplus generated by the consumption and production choices in the market equilibrium to the surplus generated by a different set of production and consumption choices. We can show that any change from the market equilibrium reduces total surplus.

Let's consider three ways in which you might try to increase the total surplus:

1. *Reallocate consumption among consumers*—take the good away from buyers who would have purchased the good in the market equilibrium, and instead give it to potential consumers who would not have bought it in equilibrium.

2. *Reallocate sales among sellers*—take sales away from sellers who would have sold the good in the market equilibrium, and instead compel potential sellers who would not have sold the good in equilibrium to sell it.

3. *Change the quantity traded*—compel consumers and producers to transact either more or less than the equilibrium quantity.

It turns out that each of these actions will not only fail to increase the total surplus; in fact, each will reduce the total surplus.

Figure 6-11 shows why reallocating consumption of the good among consumers will reduce the total surplus. Points *A* and *B* show the positions on the demand curve of two potential buyers of a used book, Ana and Bob. As we can see from the figure,

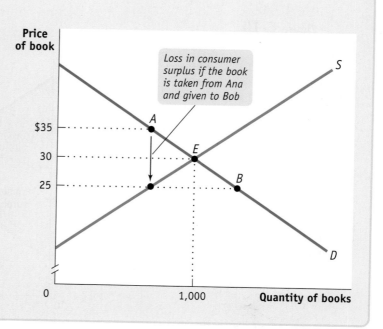

Figure 6-11

Reallocating Consumption Lowers Consumer Surplus

Ana (point *A*) has a willingness to pay of $35. Bob (point *B*) has a willingness to pay of only $25. At the market equilibrium price of $30, Ana purchases a book but Bob does not. If we rearrange consumption by taking a book from Ana and giving it to Bob, consumer surplus declines by $10 and, as a result, total surplus declines by $10. The market equilibrium generates the highest possible consumer surplus by ensuring that those who consume the good are those who value it the most. **>web**...

Ana is willing to pay $35 for a book, but Bob is willing to pay only $25. Since the equilibrium price is $30, Ana buys a book and Bob does not.

Now suppose that we try to reallocate consumption. This would mean taking a book away from somebody who *would* have bought one at the equilibrium price of $30, like Ana, and giving that book to someone who would *not* have bought at that price, like Bob. But since the book is worth $35 to Ana, but only $25 to Bob, this would *reduce total consumer surplus* by $35 − $25 = $10.

This result doesn't depend on which two students we pick. Every student who buys a book in equilibrium has a willingness to pay that is *more* than $30, and every student who doesn't buy a book has a willingness to pay that is *less* than $30. So reallocating the good among consumers always means taking a book away from a student who values it more and giving it to a student who values it less, which necessarily reduces consumer surplus.

A similar argument, illustrated by Figure 6-12, holds for producer surplus. Here points *X* and *Y* show the positions on the supply curve of Xavier, who has a cost of $25, and Yvonne, who has a cost of $35. At the equilibrium price of $30, Xavier would sell his book but Yvonne would not. If we reallocated sales, forcing Xavier to keep his book and forcing Yvonne to give up hers, total producer surplus would be reduced by $35 − $25 = $10. Again, it doesn't matter which two students we choose. Any student who sells a book in equilibrium has a lower cost than any student who does not, so reallocating sales among sellers necessarily increases total cost and reduces producer surplus. In this way the market equilibrium generates the highest possible producer surplus: it ensures that those who sell their books are those who most value the right to sell them.

Finally, changing the quantity bought and sold reduces the sum of producer and consumer surplus. Figure 6-13 on page 150 shows all four students: potential buyers Ana and Bob, and potential sellers Xavier and Yvonne. To reduce sales, we would have to prevent someone like Xavier, who would have sold the book in equilibrium, from making the sale; and the book would then not be made available to someone like Ana who would have bought it in equilibrium. As we've seen, however, Ana would be willing to pay $35, but Xavier's cost is only $25. So preventing this sale would reduce total surplus by $35 − $25 = $10. Once again, this result doesn't depend on which two students we pick: any student who would have sold the book in equilibrium has

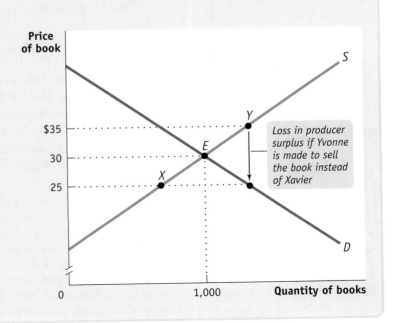

Figure 6-12

Reallocating Sales Lowers Producer Surplus

Yvonne (point *Y*) has a cost of $35, $10 more than Xavier (point *X*) who has a cost of $25. At the market equilibrium price of $30, Xavier sells a book, but Yvonne does not. If we rearrange sales by preventing Xavier from selling his book and compelling Yvonne to sell hers, producer surplus declines by $10 and, as a result, total surplus declines by $10. The market equilibrium generates the highest possible producer surplus by assuring that those who sell the good are those who value the right to sell it the most. **>web...**

Figure 6-13

Changing the Quantity Lowers Total Surplus

If Xavier (point *X*) were prevented from selling his book to someone like Ana (point *A*), total surplus would fall by $10, the difference between Ana's willingness to pay ($35) and Xavier's cost ($25). This means that total surplus falls whenever fewer than 1,000 books—the equilibrium quantity—are transacted. Likewise, if Yvonne (point *Y*) were compelled to sell her book to someone like Bob (point *B*), total surplus would also fall by $10, the difference between Yvonne's cost ($35) and Bob's willingness to pay ($25). This means that total surplus falls whenever more than 1,000 books are transacted. These two examples show that at market equilibrium, all beneficial transactions—and only beneficial transactions—occur.

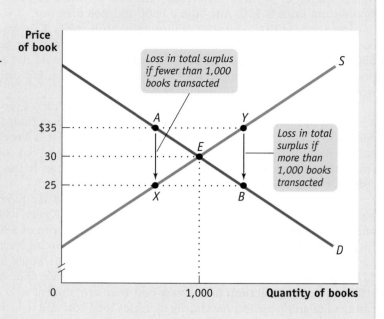

a cost of *less* than $30, and any student who would have purchased the book in equilibrium would be willing to pay *more* than $30, so preventing any sale that would have taken place in equilibrium reduces total surplus.

Finally, to increase sales would mean forcing someone like Yvonne, who would not have sold her book in equilibrium, to sell it, and giving it to someone like Bob, who would not have bought a book in equilibrium. Because Yvonne's cost is $35 but Bob is only willing to pay $25, this reduces total surplus by $10. And once again it doesn't matter which two students we pick—anyone who wouldn't have bought the book is willing to pay less than $30, and anyone who wouldn't have sold has a cost of more than $30.

What we have shown is that the market equilibrium maximizes total surplus—the sum of producer and consumer surplus. It does this because the market performs four important functions:

1. It allocates consumption of the good to the potential buyers who value it the most, as indicated by the fact that they have the highest willingness to pay.

2. It allocates sales to the potential sellers who most value the right to sell the good, as indicated by the fact that they have the lowest cost.

3. It ensures that every consumer who makes a purchase values the good more than every seller who makes a sale, so that all transactions are mutually beneficial.

4. It ensures that every potential buyer who doesn't make a purchase values the good less than every potential seller who doesn't make a sale, so that no mutually beneficial transactions are missed.

A caveat: it's important to realize that although the market equilibrium maximizes the total surplus, this does not mean that it is the best outcome for every individual consumer and producer. Other things being equal, each buyer would like to pay less and each seller would like to receive more. So some people would benefit from the price controls discussed in Chapter 4. A price ceiling that held down the market price would leave some consumers—those who managed to make a purchase—better off than they would be at equilibrium. A price floor that kept the price up would benefit some sellers—those who managed to make a sale.

But in the market equilibrium there is no way to make some people better off without making others worse off—and that's the definition of efficiency.

Maximizing total surplus at your local hardware store.

Photodisc/Getty Images

A Few Words of Caution

Markets are an amazingly effective way to organize economic activity; we've just demonstrated that, under certain conditions, a market is actually efficient—there is literally no way to make some people better off without making others worse off.

But how secure is this result? Are markets really that good?

The answer is "not always." As we discussed briefly in Chapter 1 in our ninth and final principle of economics (*when markets don't achieve efficiency, government intervention can improve society's welfare*), markets can fail to be efficient for a number of reasons. When a market is not efficient, we have what is known as a case of **market failure**. We will examine various causes of *market failure* in depth in later chapters; for now, let's review the three main reasons why markets sometimes fall short of efficiency in reality.

Market failure occurs when a market fails to be efficient.

First, markets can fail when, in an attempt to capture more resources, one party prevents mutually beneficial trades from occurring. This situation arises, for instance, when a market contains only a single seller of a good, known as a *monopolist*. In this case, the assumption we have relied on in supply and demand analysis—that no individual buyer and seller can have a noticeable effect on the market price—is no longer valid; the monopolist can determine the market price. As we'll see in Chapter 14, this gives rise to inefficiency as a monopolist manipulates the market price in order to increase profits, thereby preventing mutually beneficial trades from occurring.

Second, actions of individuals sometimes have *side effects* on the welfare of other individuals that markets don't take into account. The best-known example of such an *externality* is pollution. We'll see in Chapter 19 that pollution and other externalities also give rise to inefficiency.

Third, markets for some goods can fail because these goods, by their very nature, are unsuited for efficient management by markets. In Chapter 18 we will analyze goods that fall into this category because of problems of *private information*—information about a good that some people possess but others don't. In Chapter 20, we will encounter other types of goods that fall into this category—*public goods, common resources*, and *artificially scarce goods*. These are goods for which markets fail because of problems in limiting people's access to and consumption of the good. And in Chapter 22 we will learn about *information goods:* goods like a downloaded tune, that are costly to create but, once created, cost nothing to consume.

But even with these caveats, it's remarkable how well markets work at maximizing the gains from trade.

economics in action

eBay and Efficiency

Garage sales are an old American tradition: they are a way for families to sell items they don't want to other families that have some use for them, to the benefit of both parties. But many potentially beneficial trades were missed. For all Mr. Smith knew, there was someone 1,000 miles away who would really have loved that 1930s gramophone he had in the basement; for all Ms. Jones knew, there was someone 1,000 miles away who had that 1930s gramophone she had always wanted. But there was no way for Mr. Smith and Ms. Jones to find each other.

Enter eBay, the online auction service. eBay was founded in 1995 by Pierre Omidyar, a programmer whose fiancée was a collector of Pez candy dispensers and wanted a way to find potential sellers. The company, which says that its mission is "to help practically anyone trade practically anything on earth," provides a way for would-be buyers and would-be sellers of unique or used items to find each other, even if they don't live in the same neighborhood or even the same city.

"I got it from eBay"

The potential gains from trade were evidently large: in 2004, 135 million people were registered by eBay, and in the same year $34 billion in goods were bought and sold using the service. The Omidyars now possess a large collection of Pez dispensers. They are also billionaires. ■

< < < < < < < < < < < < < < < < <

>> CHECK YOUR UNDERSTANDING 6-3

1. Using the tables in Check Your Understanding 6-1 and 6-2, find the equilibrium price and quantity in the market for cheese-stuffed jalapeno peppers. What is total surplus in the equilibrium in this market, and who receives it?

2. Show how each of the following three actions reduces total surplus:
   a. Having Josie consume one less pepper, and Casey one more pepper, than in the market equilibrium
   b. Having Cara produce one less pepper, and Jamie one more pepper, than in the market equilibrium
   c. Having Josie consume one less pepper, and Cara produce one less pepper, than in the market equilibrium

Solutions appear at back of book.

Applying Consumer and Producer Surplus: The Efficiency Costs of a Tax

The concepts of consumer and producer surplus are extremely useful in many economic applications. Among the most important of these is assessing the efficiency cost of taxation.

In Chapter 4 we introduced the concept of an *excise tax*, a tax on the purchase or sale of a good. We saw that such a tax drives a *wedge* between the price paid by consumers and that received by producers: the price paid by consumers rises, and the price received by producers falls, with the difference equal to the tax per unit. The *incidence* of the tax—how much of the burden falls on consumers, how much on producers—does not depend on who actually writes the check to the government. Instead, as we saw in Chapter 5, the burden of the tax depends on the price elasticities of supply and demand: the higher the price elasticity of demand, the greater the burden on producers; the higher the price elasticity of supply, the greater the burden on consumers.

We also learned that there is an additional cost of a tax, over and above the money actually paid to the government. A tax causes a *deadweight loss* to society, because less of the good is produced and consumed than in the absence of the tax. As a result, some mutually beneficial trades between producers and consumers do not take place.

Now we can complete the picture, because the concepts of consumer and producer surplus are what we need to pin down precisely the deadweight loss that an excise tax imposes.

Figure 6-14 shows the effects of an excise tax on consumer and producer surplus. In the absence of the tax, the equilibrium is at E, and the equilibrium price and quantity are P_E and Q_E, respectively. An excise tax drives a wedge equal to the amount of the tax between the price received by producers and the price paid by consumers, reducing the quantity bought and sold. In this case, where the tax is T dollars per unit, the quantity bought and sold falls to Q_T. The price paid by consumers rises to P_C, the demand price of the reduced quantity, Q_T, and the price received by producers falls to P_P, the supply price of that quantity. The difference between these prices, $P_C - P_P$, is equal to the excise tax, T.

What we can now do, using the concepts of producer and consumer surplus, is show exactly how much surplus producers and consumers lose as a result of the tax.

We saw earlier, in Figure 6-5, that a fall in the price of a good generates a gain in consumer surplus that is equal to the sum of the areas of a rectangle and a triangle. A price increase causes a loss to consumers that looks exactly the same. In the case of an excise tax, the rise in the price paid by consumers causes a loss equal to the sum

Figure 6-14

A Tax Reduces Consumer and Producer Surplus

Before the tax, the equilibrium price and quantity are P_E and Q_E, respectively. After an excise tax of T per unit is imposed, the price to consumers rises to P_C and consumer surplus falls by the sum of the dark blue rectangle, labeled A, and the light blue triangle, labeled B. The tax also causes the price to producers to fall to P_P; producer surplus falls by the sum of the red rectangle, labeled C, and the pink triangle, labeled F. The government receives revenue from the tax, $Q_T \times T$, which is given by the sum of the areas A and C. Areas B and F represent the losses to consumer and producer surplus that are not collected by the government as revenue; they are the deadweight loss to society of the tax. **>web...**

of the area of the dark blue rectangle labeled A and the area of the light blue triangle labeled B in Figure 6-14.

Meanwhile, the fall in the price received by producers causes a fall in producer surplus. This, too, is the sum of the areas of a rectangle and a triangle. The loss in producer surplus is the sum of the areas of the red rectangle labeled C and the pink triangle labeled F in Figure 6-14.

Of course, although consumers and producers are hurt by the tax, the government gains revenue. The revenue the government collects is equal to the tax per unit sold, T, multiplied by the quantity sold, Q_T. This revenue is equal to the area of a rectangle Q_T wide and T high. And we already have that rectangle in the figure: it is the sum of rectangles A and C. So the government gains part of what consumers and producers lose from an excise tax.

But there is a part of the loss to producers and consumers from the tax that is not offset by a gain to the government—specifically, the two triangles B and F. The deadweight loss caused by the tax is equal to the combined area of these triangles. It represents the total surplus that would have been generated by transactions that do not take place because of the tax.

Figure 6-15 on page 154 is a version of the same picture, leaving out the shaded rectangles—which represent money shifted from consumers and producers to the government—and showing only the deadweight loss, this time as a triangle shaded yellow. The base of that triangle is the tax wedge, T; the height of the triangle is the reduction the tax causes in the quantity sold, $Q_E - Q_T$. Notice that if the excise tax *didn't* reduce the quantity bought and sold in this market—if Q_T weren't less than Q_E—the deadweight loss represented by the yellow triangle would disappear. This observation ties in with the explanation given in Chapter 4 of why an excise tax generates a deadweight loss to society: the tax causes inefficiency because it discourages mutually beneficial transactions between buyers and sellers.

The idea that deadweight loss can be measured by the area of a triangle recurs in many economic applications. Deadweight-loss triangles are produced not only by excise taxes but also by other types of taxation. They are also produced by other kinds of distortions of markets, such as monopoly. And triangles are often used to evaluate other public policies besides taxation—for example, decisions about whether to build new highways.

Figure 6-15

The Deadweight Loss of a Tax

A tax leads to a deadweight loss because it creates inefficiency: some mutually beneficial transactions never take place because of the tax, namely the transactions $Q_E - Q_T$. The yellow area here represents the value of the deadweight loss: it is the total surplus that would have been gained from the $Q_E - Q_T$ transactions. If the tax had not discouraged transactions—had the number of transactions remained at Q_E—no deadweight loss would have been incurred.

>web...

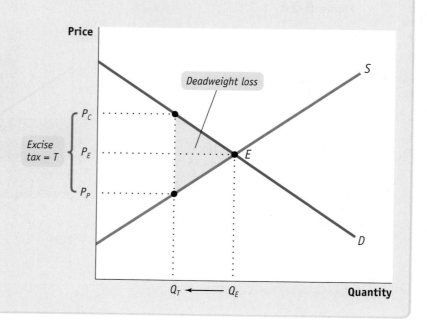

The general rule for economic policy is that other things equal, you want to choose the policy that produces the smallest deadweight loss. This principle gives valuable guidance on everything from the design of the tax system to environmental policy. But how can we predict the size of the deadweight loss associated with a given policy? For the answer to that question, we return to a familiar concept: elasticity.

Deadweight Loss and Elasticities

The deadweight loss from an excise tax arises because it prevents some mutually beneficial transactions from occurring. In particular, the producer and consumer surplus that is forgone from these missing transactions is equal to the size of the deadweight loss itself. This means that the larger the number of transactions that are impeded by the tax, the larger the deadweight loss.

This gives us an important clue in understanding the relationship between elasticity and the size of the deadweight loss from a tax. Recall that when demand or supply is elastic, it means that the quantity demanded or the quantity supplied is relatively responsive to price. So a tax imposed on a good for which either demand or supply, or both, is elastic will cause a relatively large decrease in the quantity bought and sold and a large deadweight loss. And when we say that demand or supply is inelastic, we mean that the quantity demanded or the quantity supplied is relatively unresponsive to price. As a result, a tax imposed when demand or supply, or both, is inelastic will cause a relatively small decrease in the quantity bought and sold and a small deadweight loss.

The four panels of Figure 6-16 illustrate the positive relationship between price elasticity of either demand or supply and the deadweight loss of taxation. In each panel, the size of the deadweight loss is given by the area of the shaded triangle. In panel (a), the deadweight-loss triangle is large because demand is relatively elastic—a large number of transactions fail to occur because of the tax. In panel (b), the same supply curve is drawn as in panel (a), but demand is now relatively inelastic; as a result, the triangle is small because only a small number of transactions are forgone. Likewise, panels (c) and (d) contain the same demand curve but different supply curves. In panel (c), an elastic supply curve gives rise to a large deadweight-loss triangle, but in panel (d) an inelastic supply curve gives rise to a small deadweight-loss triangle.

Figure 6-16 Deadweight Loss and Elasticities

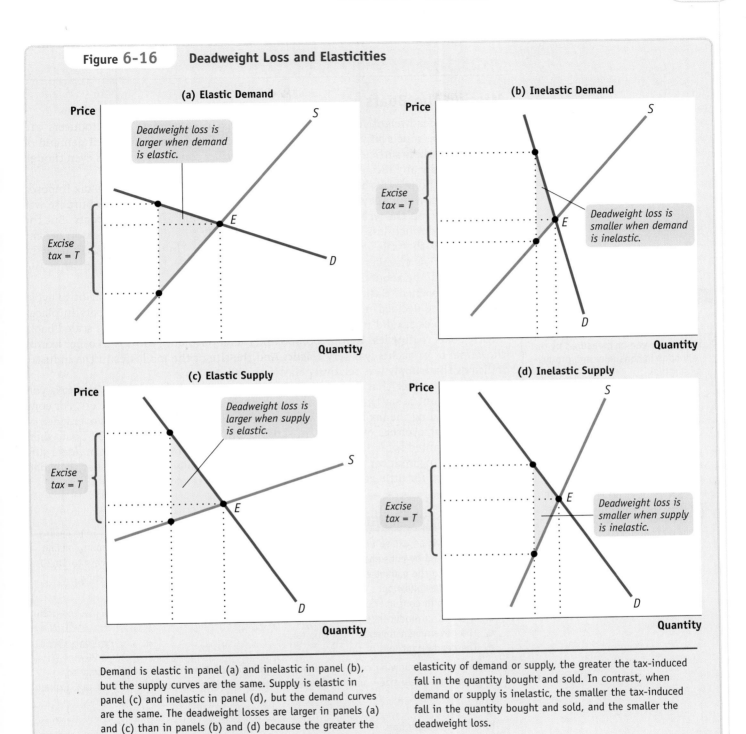

(a) Elastic Demand

Deadweight loss is larger when demand is elastic.

Excise tax = T

(b) Inelastic Demand

Excise tax = T

Deadweight loss is smaller when demand is inelastic.

(c) Elastic Supply

Deadweight loss is larger when supply is elastic.

Excise tax = T

(d) Inelastic Supply

Excise tax = T

Deadweight loss is smaller when supply is inelastic.

Demand is elastic in panel (a) and inelastic in panel (b), but the supply curves are the same. Supply is elastic in panel (c) and inelastic in panel (d), but the demand curves are the same. The deadweight losses are larger in panels (a) and (c) than in panels (b) and (d) because the greater the elasticity of demand or supply, the greater the tax-induced fall in the quantity bought and sold. In contrast, when demand or supply is inelastic, the smaller the tax-induced fall in the quantity bought and sold, and the smaller the deadweight loss.

As the following story illustrates, the implication of this result is clear: if you want to lessen the efficiency costs of taxation, you should devise taxes to fall on goods for which either demand or supply, or both, is relatively inelastic. And this lesson carries a flip-side: using a tax to purposely decrease the amount of a harmful activity, such as underage drinking, will have the most impact when that activity is elastically demanded or supplied. In the extreme case in which demand is perfectly inelastic (a vertical demand curve), the quantity demanded is unchanged by the imposition of the tax. As a result, the tax imposes no deadweight loss. Similarly, if supply is perfectly inelastic (a vertical supply curve), the quantity supplied is unchanged by the tax and there is also no deadweight loss.

economics in action

Missing the Boats

Because of deadweight losses, the costs of a tax to consumers and producers can sometimes be much larger than the actual value of taxes paid. In fact, if demand or supply, or both, is sufficiently elastic, a tax can inflict considerable losses even though it raises hardly any revenue.

A case in point was the infamous "yacht tax" of 1990, a special sales tax imposed by the U.S. government on yachts whose price exceeded $100,000. The purpose was to raise taxes on the wealthy, the only people who could afford such boats. But the tax generated much less revenue than expected, only $7 million. The reason for the low yield was that sales of $100,000-plus yachts in the United States fell sharply, by 71 percent. The number of jobs in the yacht industry, in both manufacturing and sales, also fell, by about 25 percent.

What happened? Basically, potential yacht buyers changed their behavior to avoid the tax. Some decided not to buy yachts at all; others bought their boats in places where the sales tax did not apply, such as the Bahamas; and still others scaled back, buying boats costing less than $100,000 and thereby avoiding the tax. In other words, the demand for yachts was very elastic. And the size of the job losses in the industry indicates that supply was relatively elastic as well.

Despite the fact that few potential yacht buyers ended up paying the tax, you would not want to say that it imposed no costs on consumers and producers. For consumers, avoiding the tax had its own costs, such as the expense and inconvenience of buying a boat overseas or the loss in satisfaction from buying a $99,000 boat when you really wanted something fancier. Moreover, the sales force and boat builders suffered a loss in producer surplus. Policy makers eventually concluded that pain had been inflicted for little gain in tax revenue, and the tax was repealed in 1993. ∎

< < < < < < < < < < < < < < < < < <

>> **CHECK YOUR UNDERSTANDING 6-4**

1. Suppose that an excise tax of $0.40 is imposed on cheese-stuffed jalapeno peppers, raising the price paid by consumers to $0.70 and lowering the price received by producers to $0.30. Compared to the market equilibrium without the tax from Check Your Understanding 6-3, calculate the following:
   a. The loss in consumer surplus and who loses consumer surplus
   b. The loss in producer surplus and who loses producer surplus
   c. The government revenue from this tax
   d. The deadweight loss of the tax

2. In each of the following cases, focus on the elasticity of demand and use a diagram to illustrate the likely size—small or large—of the deadweight loss resulting from a tax. Explain your reasoning.
   a. Gasoline
   b. Milk chocolate bars

Solutions appear at back of book.

● **A LOOK AHEAD** ●

We have now almost completed our tour of the supply and demand model. But there is one more topic we need to address: how do producers and consumers make decisions? Up to now we have looked at simple situations where it is immediately clear what an individual should do. For example, a consumer should buy if the price is less than his or her willingness to pay. But not all situations are that simple. In the next chapter, we take a deeper look at how producers and consumers make decisions.

SUMMARY

1. The **willingness to pay** of each individual consumer determines the demand curve. When price is less than or equal to the willingness to pay, the potential consumer purchases the good. The difference between price and willingness to pay is the net gain to the consumer, the **individual consumer surplus.**

2. The **total consumer surplus** in a market, the sum of all individual consumer surpluses in a market, is equal to the area below the demand curve but above the price. A rise in the price of a good reduces consumer surplus; a fall in the price increases consumer surplus. The term **consumer surplus** is often used to refer both to individual and to total consumer surplus.

3. The **cost** of each potential producer, the lowest price at which he or she is willing to supply a unit of that good, determines the supply curve. If the price of a good is above a producer's cost, a sale generates a net gain to the producer, known as the **individual producer surplus.**

4. The **total producer surplus,** the sum of the individual producer surpluses, is equal to the area above the supply curve but below the price. A rise in the price of a good increases producer surplus; a fall in the price reduces producer surplus. The term **producer surplus** is often used to refer both to the individual and to the total producer surplus.

5. **Total surplus,** the total gain to society from the production and consumption of a good, is the sum of consumer and producer surplus.

6. Usually, markets are efficient and achieve the maximum total surplus. Any possible rearrangement of consumption or sales, or change in the quantity bought and sold, reduces total surplus.

7. Under certain conditions, **market failure** occurs and markets fail to be efficient. This situation arises from three principal sources: attempts to capture more resources that create inefficiencies, side effects of some transactions, and problems in the nature of the good.

8. Economic policies can be evaluated by their effect on total surplus. For example, an excise tax generates revenue for the government but lowers total surplus. The loss in total surplus exceeds the tax revenue, resulting in a deadweight loss to society. The value of this deadweight loss is shown by the triangle that represents the value of the transactions discouraged by the tax. The greater the elasticity of demand or supply, or both, the larger the deadweight loss of a tax.

KEY TERMS

Willingness to pay, p. 136
Individual consumer surplus, p. 138
Total consumer surplus, p. 138
Consumer surplus, p. 138

Cost, p. 143
Individual producer surplus, p. 143
Total producer surplus, p. 144

Producer surplus, p. 144
Total surplus, p. 147
Market failure, p. 151

PROBLEMS

1. Determine the amount of consumer surplus generated in each of the following situations.

   a. Paul goes to the clothing store to buy a new T-shirt, for which he is willing to pay up to $10. He picks out one he likes with a price tag of exactly $10. At the cash register, he is told that his T-shirt is on sale for half the posted price.

   b. Robin goes to the CD store hoping to find a used copy of the *Eagles Greatest Hits* for up to $10. The store has one copy selling for $10.

   c. After soccer practice, Phil is willing to pay $2 for a bottle of mineral water. The 7-Eleven sells mineral water for $2.25 per bottle.

2. Determine the amount of producer surplus generated in each of the following situations.

   a. Bob lists his old Lionel electric trains on eBay. He sets a minimum acceptable price, known as his *reserve price*, of $75. After five days of bidding, the final high bid is exactly $75.

   b. Jenny advertises her car for sale in the used-car section of the student newspaper for $2,000, but she is willing to sell the car for any price higher than $1,500. The best offer she gets is $1,200.

   c. Sanjay likes his job so much that he would be willing to do it for free. However, his annual salary is $80,000.

3. Hollywood writers negotiate a new agreement with movie producers that they will receive 10 percent of the revenue from every video rental of a movie they worked on. They have no such agreement for movies shown on pay-per-view television.

   a. When the new writers' agreement comes into effect, what will happen in the market for video rentals—that is, will supply or demand shift, and how? As a result, how will consumer surplus in the market for video rentals change? Illustrate with a diagram. Do you think the writers' agreement will be popular with consumers who rent videos?

   b. Consumers consider video rentals and pay-per-view movies substitutable to some extent. When the new writers' agreement comes into effect, what will happen in the market for pay-per-view movies—that is, will supply or demand shift, and how? As a result, how will producer surplus in the market for pay-per-view movies change? Illustrate with a diagram. Do you think the writers' agreement will be popular with cable television companies that show pay-per-view movies?

4. There are six potential consumers of computer games, each willing to buy only one game. Consumer 1 is willing to pay $40 for a computer game, consumer 2 is willing to pay $35, consumer 3 is willing to pay $30, consumer 4 is willing pay $25, consumer 5 is willing to pay $20, and consumer 6 is willing to pay $15.

a. Suppose the market price is $29. What is the total consumer surplus?

b. Now the market price decreases to $19. What is the total consumer surplus now?

c. When the price fell from $29 to $19, how much did each consumer's individual consumer surplus change?

5. In an effort to provide more affordable rental housing for low-income families, the city council of Collegetown decides to impose a rent ceiling well below the current market equilibrium rent.

a. Illustrate the effect of this policy in a diagram. Indicate consumer and producer surplus before and after the introduction of the rent ceiling.

b. Will this policy be popular with renters? With landlords?

c. An economist explains to the city council that this policy is creating a deadweight loss. Illustrate the deadweight loss in your diagram.

6. On Thursday nights, a local restaurant has a pasta special. Ari likes the restaurant's pasta, and his willingness to pay for each serving is shown in the accompanying table.

Quantity of pasta (servings)	Willingness to pay for pasta (per serving)
1	$10
2	8
3	6
4	4
5	2
6	0

a. If the price of a serving of pasta is $4, how many servings will Ari buy? How much consumer surplus does he receive?

b. The following week, Ari is back at the restaurant again, but now the price of a serving of pasta is $6. By how much does his consumer surplus decrease compared to the previous week?

c. One week later, he goes to the restaurant again. He discovers that the restaurant is offering an "all you can eat"

special for $25. How much pasta will Ari eat, and how much consumer surplus does he receive now?

d. Suppose you own the restaurant and Ari is a "typical" customer. What is the highest price you can charge for the "all you can eat" special and still attract customers?

7. The accompanying diagram shows the market for cigarettes. The current equilibrium price per pack is $4, and every day 40 million packs of cigarettes are sold. In order to recover some of the health care costs associated with smoking, the government imposes a tax of $2 per pack. This will raise the equilibrium price to $5 per pack and reduce the equilibrium quantity to 30 million packs.

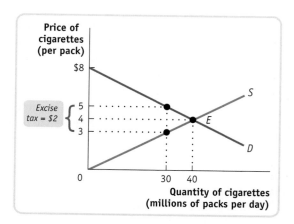

The economist working for the tobacco lobby claims that this tax will reduce consumer surplus for smokers by $40 million per day, since 40 million packs now cost $1 more per pack. The economist working for the lobby for sufferers of second-hand smoke argues that this is an enormous overestimate and that the reduction in consumer surplus will be only $30 million per day, since after the imposition of the tax only 30 million packs of cigarettes will be bought and each of these packs will now cost $1 more. They are both wrong. Why?

8. Consider the original market for pizza in Collegetown, illustrated in the accompanying table. Collegetown officials decide to impose an excise tax on pizza of $4 per pizza.

Price of pizza	Quantity of pizza demanded	Quantity of pizza supplied
$10	0	6
9	1	5
8	2	4
7	3	3
6	4	2
5	5	1
4	6	0
3	7	0
2	8	0
1	9	0

a. What is the quantity of pizza bought and sold after the imposition of the tax? What is the price paid by consumers? What is the price received by producers?

b. Calculate the consumer surplus and the producer surplus after the imposition of the tax. By how much has the imposition of the tax reduced consumer surplus? By how much has it reduced producer surplus?

c. How much tax revenue does Collegetown earn from this tax?

d. Calculate the deadweight loss from this tax.

9. Consider once more the original market for pizza in Collegetown, illustrated in the table in Problem 8. Now Collegetown officials impose a price floor on pizza of $8.

a. What is the quantity of pizza bought and sold after the imposition of the price floor?

b. Calculate the consumer surplus and the producer surplus after the imposition of the price floor.

10. You are the manager of Fun World, a small amusement park. The accompanying diagram shows the demand curve of a typical customer at Fun World.

a. Suppose that the price of each ride is $5. At that price, how much consumer surplus does an individual consumer get? (Recall that the area of a triangle is ½ × the base of the triangle × the height of the triangle.)

b. Suppose that Fun World considers charging an admission fee, even though it maintains the price of each ride at $5. What is the maximum admission fee it could charge? (Assume that all potential customers have enough money to pay the fee.)

c. Suppose that Fun World lowered the price of each ride to zero. How much consumer surplus does an individual consumer get? What is the maximum admission fee Fun World could therefore charge?

11. The accompanying diagram illustrates a taxi driver's individual supply curve (assume that each taxi ride is the same distance).

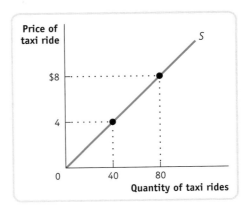

a. Suppose the city sets the price of taxi rides at $4 per ride. What is this taxi driver's producer surplus? (Recall that the area of a triangle is ½ × the base of the triangle × the height of the triangle.)

b. Suppose now that the city keeps the price of a taxi ride set at $4, but it decides to charge taxi drivers a "licensing fee." What is the maximum licensing fee the city could extract from this taxi driver?

c. Suppose that the city allowed the price of taxi rides to increase to $8 per ride. How much producer surplus does an individual taxi driver now get? What is the maximum licensing fee the city could charge this taxi driver?

12. The state needs to raise money, and the governor has a choice of imposing an excise tax of the same amount on one of two previously untaxed goods: the state can tax either sales of restaurant meals or sales of gasoline. Both the demand for and the supply of restaurant meals are more elastic than the demand for and the supply of gasoline. If the governor wants to minimize the deadweight loss caused by the tax, which good should be taxed? For each good, draw a diagram that illustrates the deadweight loss from taxation.

>web... To continue your study and review of concepts in this chapter, please visit the Krugman/Wells website for quizzes, animated graph tutorials, web links to helpful resources, and more.

www.worthpublishers.com/krugmanwells

>> Making Decisions

A TALE OF TWO INVASIONS

What you will learn in this chapter:

➤ How economists model decision making by individuals and firms

➤ The importance of **implicit** as well as **explicit costs** in decision making

➤ The difference between **accounting profit** and **economic profit**, and why economic profit is the correct basis for decisions

➤ The difference between "either–or" and "how much" decisions

➤ The **principle of marginal analysis**

➤ What **sunk costs** are and why they should be ignored

➤ How to make decisions in cases where time is a factor

ON JUNE 6, 1944, ALLIED SOLDIERS stormed the beaches of Normandy, beginning the liberation of France from German rule. Long before the assault, however, Allied generals had to make a crucial decision: *where* would the soldiers land?

They had to make what we call an "either–or" decision. *Either* the invasion force could cross the English Channel at its narrowest point, Calais—which was what the Germans expected—*or* it could try to surprise the Germans by landing farther west, in Normandy. Since men and landing craft were in limited supply, the Allies could not do both. In fact they chose to rely on surprise. The German defenses in Normandy were too weak to stop the landings, and the Allies went on to liberate France and win the war.

Thirty years earlier, at the beginning of World War I, German generals had to make a different kind of decision. They, too, planned to invade France, in this case via land, and had decided to mount that invasion through Belgium. The decision they had to make was not an "either–or" but a "how much" decision: *how much* of their army should be allocated to the invasion force, and

how much should be used to defend Germany's border with France? The original plan, devised by General Alfred von Schlieffen, allocated most of the German army to the invasion force; on his deathbed, Schlieffen is supposed to have pleaded, "Keep the right wing [the invasion force] strong!" But his successor, General Helmuth von Moltke, weakened the plan: he reallocated some of the divisions that were supposed to race through Belgium to the defense. The weakened invasion force wasn't strong

Decision: Attack here? Or there?

enough: the defending French army stopped it 30 miles from Paris. Most military historians believe that by allocating too few men to the attack, von Moltke cost Germany the war.

So Allied generals made the right decision in 1944; German generals made the wrong decision in 1914. The important point for this chapter is that in both cases the generals had to apply the same logic that applies to economic decisions, like production decisions by businesses and consumption decisions by households.

In this chapter we will survey the principles involved in making economic decisions. These principles will help us understand how any individual—whether a consumer or a producer—makes an economic decision. We begin by taking a deeper look at the significance of opportunity cost for economic decisions and the role it plays in "either–or" decisions. Next we turn to the problem of making "how much" decisions and the usefulness of *marginal analysis*. We then examine what kind of costs should be ignored in making a decision—costs which economists call *sunk costs*. We end by considering the concept of *present value* and its importance for making decisions when costs and benefits arrive at different times.

Opportunity Cost and Decisions

In Chapter 1 we introduced some core principles underlying economic decisions. We've just seen two of those principles at work in our tale of two invasions. The first is that *resources are scarce*—the invading Allies had a limited number of landing craft, and the invading Germans had a limited number of divisions. Because resources are scarce, the true cost of anything is its *opportunity cost*—that is, the real cost of something is what you must give up to get it. When it comes to making decisions, it is crucial to think in terms of opportunity cost, because the opportunity cost of an action is often considerably more than the simple monetary cost.

Explicit versus Implicit Costs

Suppose that, after graduating from college, you have two options: to go to school for an additional year to get an advanced degree or to take a job immediately. You would like to take the extra year in school but are concerned about the cost.

But what exactly is the cost of that additional year of school? Here is where it is important to remember the concept of opportunity cost: the cost of that year spent getting an advanced degree is what you forgo by not taking a job for that year.

This cost, like any cost, can be broken into two parts: the *explicit cost* of the year's schooling and the *implicit cost*.

An **explicit cost** is a cost that requires an outlay of money. For example, the explicit cost of the additional year of schooling includes tuition. An **implicit cost,** on the other hand, does not involve an outlay of money; instead, it is measured by the value, in dollar terms, of all the benefits that are forgone. For example, the implicit cost of the year spent in school includes the income you would have earned if you had taken that job instead.

> An **explicit cost** is a cost that involves actually laying out money. An **implicit cost** does not require an outlay of money; it is measured by the value, in dollar terms, of the benefits that are forgone.

A common mistake, both in economic analysis and in real business situations, is to ignore implicit costs and focus exclusively on explicit costs. But often the implicit cost of an activity is quite substantial—indeed, sometimes it is much larger than the explicit cost.

Table 7-1 on page 162 gives a breakdown of hypothetical explicit and implicit costs associated with spending an additional year in school instead of taking a job. The explicit cost consists of tuition, books, supplies, and a home computer for doing assignments—all of which require you to spend money. The implicit cost is the salary you would have earned if you had taken a job instead. As you can see, the forgone salary is $35,000 and the explicit cost is $9,500, making the implicit cost more than three times as much as the explicit cost. So ignoring the implicit cost of an action can lead to a seriously misguided decision.

TABLE 7-1

Opportunity Cost of an Additional Year of School

Explicit cost		Implicit cost	
Tuition	$7,000	Forgone salary	$35,000
Books and supplies	1,000		
Home computer	1,500		
Total explicit cost	9,500	Total implicit cost	35,000
Total opportunity cost = Total explicit cost + Total implicit cost = $44,500			

There is another, slightly different way of looking at the implicit cost in this example that can deepen our understanding of opportunity cost. The forgone salary is the cost of using your own resources—your time—in going to school rather than working. The use of your *time* for more schooling, despite the fact that you don't have to spend any money, is nonetheless costly to you. This illustrates an important aspect of opportunity cost: in considering the cost of an activity, you should include the cost of using any of your own resources for that activity. You can calculate the cost of using your own resources by determining what they would have earned in their next best use.

FOR INQUIRING MINDS

FAMOUS COLLEGE DROPOUTS

What do Bill Gates, Tiger Woods, and Sarah Michelle Gellar (a.k.a. Buffy the Vampire Slayer) have in common? None of them have a college degree.

Nobody doubts that all three are easily smart enough to have gotten their diplomas. However, they all made the rational decision that the implicit cost of getting a degree would have been too high—by their late teens, each had a very promising career that would have had to be put on hold to get a college degree. Gellar would have had to postpone her acting career; Woods would have had to put off

winning one major tournament after another and becoming the world's best golfer; Gates would have had to delay developing the most successful and most lucrative software ever sold, Microsoft's computer operating system.

In fact, extremely successful people—especially those in careers like acting or athletics, where starting early in life is especially crucial—are often college dropouts. It's a simple matter of economics: the opportunity cost of their time at that stage in their lives is just too high to postpone their careers for a college degree.

Accounting Profit versus Economic Profit

As the example of going to school suggests, taking account of implicit as well as explicit costs can be very important for individuals making decisions. The same is true of businesses.

Consider the case of Kathy's Kopy Shoppe, a small business operating in a local shopping center. Kathy makes copies for customers, who pay for her services. Out of that revenue, she has to pay her expenses: the cost of supplies and the rent for her store space. We suppose that Kathy owns the copy machines themselves. This year Kathy has $100,000 in revenue and $60,000 in expenses. Is her business profitable?

At first it might seem that the answer is obviously yes: she receives $100,000 from her customers and has expenses of only $60,000. Doesn't this mean that she has a profit of $40,000? Not according to her accountant, who reduces the number by $5,000 for the yearly *depreciation* (reduction in value) of the copy machines.

Depreciation occurs because machines wear out over time. The yearly depreciation amount reflects what an accountant estimates to be the reduction in the value of the machines due to wear and tear that year. This leaves $35,000, which is the business's **accounting profit.** Basically, the accounting profit of a company is its revenue minus its explicit cost and depreciation. The accounting profit is the number that Kathy has to report on her income tax forms and that she would be obliged to report to anyone thinking of investing in her business.

> The **accounting profit** of a business is the business's revenue minus the explicit cost and depreciation.

Accounting profit is a very useful number, but suppose that Kathy wants to decide whether to keep her business going or to do something else. To make this decision, she will need to calculate her **economic profit**—the revenue she receives minus her opportunity cost, which may include implicit as well as explicit costs. In general, when economists use the simple term *profit*, they are referring to economic profit. (We will adopt this simplification in later chapters of this book.)

> The **economic profit** of a business is the business's revenue minus the opportunity cost of its resources. It is usually less than the accounting profit.

Why does Kathy's economic profit differ from her accounting profit? Because she may have implicit costs over and above the explicit cost her accountant has calculated. Businesses can face implicit costs for two reasons. First, a business's **capital**—its equipment, buildings, tools, inventory, and financial assets—could have been put to use in some other way. If the business owns its capital, it does not pay any money for its use, but it pays an implicit cost because it does not use the capital in some other way. Second, the owner devotes time and energy to the business that could have been used elsewhere—a particularly important factor in small businesses, whose owners tend to put in many long hours.

> The **capital** of a business is the value of its assets—equipment, buildings, tools, inventory, and financial assets.

If Kathy had rented her copy machines from the manufacturer, their rent would have been an explicit cost. But because Kathy owns her own machines, she does not pay rent on them and her accountant deducts an estimate of their depreciation in the profit statement. However, this does not account for the opportunity cost of the machines—what Kathy forgoes by owning them. Suppose that instead of using the machines for her own business, the best alternative Kathy has is to sell them for $50,000 and put the money into a bank account where it would earn yearly interest of $3,000. This $3,000 is an implicit cost of running the business.

It is generally known as the **implicit cost of capital,** the opportunity cost of the capital used by a business; it reflects the income that could have been realized if the capital had been used in its next best alternative way. It is just as much a true cost as if Kathy had rented the machines instead of owning them.

> The **implicit cost of capital** is the opportunity cost of the capital used by a business—the income the owner could have realized from that capital if it had been used in its next best alternative way.

Finally, Kathy should take into account the opportunity cost of her own time. Suppose that instead of running her own shop, she could earn $34,000 as an office manager. That $34,000 is also an implicit cost of her business.

Table 7-2 summarizes the accounting for Kathy's Kopy Shoppe, taking both explicit and implicit costs into account. It turns out, unfortunately, that although the business makes an accounting profit of $35,000, its economic profit is actually negative.

TABLE 7-2

Profit at Kathy's Kopy Shoppe	
Revenue	$100,000
Explicit cost	− 60,000
Depreciation	− 5,000
Accounting profit	**35,000**
Implicit cost of business	
Income Kathy could have earned on capital in the next best way	− 3,000
Income Kathy could have earned as manager	− 34,000
Economic profit	**−2,000**

"I've done the numbers, and I will marry you."

This means that Kathy would be better off financially if she closed the business and devoted her time and capital to something else.

In real life, discrepancies between accounting profits and economic profits are extremely common. As the following Economics in Action explains, this is a message that has found a receptive audience among real-world businesses.

economics in action

Farming in the Shadow of Suburbia

Beyond the sprawling suburbs, most of New England is covered by dense forest. But this is not the forest primeval: if you hike through the woods, you encounter many stone walls, relics of the region's agricultural past when stone walls enclosed fields and pastures. In 1880, more than half of New England's land was farmed; by 2003, the amount was down to 10 percent.

The remaining farms of New England are mainly located close to large metropolitan areas. There farmers get high prices for their produce from city dwellers who are willing to pay a premium for locally grown, extremely fresh fruit and vegetables.

But now even these farms are under economic pressure caused by a rise in the implicit cost of farming close to a metropolitan area. As metropolitan areas have expanded during the last two decades, farmers increasingly ask themselves whether they could do better by selling their land to property developers.

In 2003, the average value of an acre of farmland in the United States as a whole was $1,270; in Rhode Island, the most densely populated of the New England states, the average was $9,300. The Federal Reserve Bank of Boston has noted that "high land prices put intense pressure on the region's farms to generate incomes that are substantial enough to justify keeping the land in agriculture." The important point is that the pressure is intense even if the farmer owns the land because the land is a form of capital used to run the business. So maintaining the land as a farm instead of selling it to a developer constitutes a large implicit cost of capital. A fact provided by the U.S. Department of Agriculture (USDA) helps us put a dollar figure on the portion of the implicit cost of capital due to development pressure for some Rhode Island farms. In 2003, a USDA program designed to prevent development of Rhode Island farmland by paying owners for the "development rights" to their land paid an average of $4,145 per acre for those rights alone.

About two-thirds of New England's farms remaining in business earn very little money. They are maintained as "rural residences" by people with other sources of income—not so much because they are commercially viable, but more out of a personal commitment and the satisfaction these people derive from farm life. Although many businesses have important implicit costs, they can also have important benefits to their owners that go beyond the revenue earned. ■

< < < < < < < < < < < < < < < < <

>> CHECK YOUR UNDERSTANDING 7-1

1. Karma and Don run a furniture-refinishing business from their home. Which of the following represent an explicit cost of the business and which represent an implicit cost?
   a. Supplies such as paint stripper, varnish, polish, sandpaper, and so on
   b. Basement space that has been converted into a workroom
   c. Wages paid to a part-time helper
   d. A van that they inherited and use only for transporting furniture
   e. The job at a larger furniture restorer that Karma gave up in order to run the business

Making "How Much" Decisions: The Role of Marginal Analysis

As the story of the two wars at the beginning of this chapter demonstrated, there are two types of decisions: "either–or" decisions and "how much" decisions. To help you get a better sense of that distinction, Table 7-3 offers some examples of each kind of decision.

Although many decisions in economics are "either–or," many others are "how much." Not many people will stop driving if the price of gasoline goes up, but many people will drive less. How much less? A rise in wheat prices won't necessarily persuade a lot of people to take up farming for the first time, but it will persuade farmers who were already growing wheat to plant more. How much more?

TABLE 7-3

"How Much" versus "Either–Or" Decisions

"How much" decisions	"Either–or" decisions
How many days before you do your laundry?	Tide or Cheer?
How many miles do you go before an oil change in your car?	Buy a car or not?
How many jalapenos on your nachos?	An order of nachos or a sandwich?
How many workers should you hire in your company?	Run your own business or work for someone else?
How much should a patient take of a drug that generates side effects?	Prescribe drug A or drug B for your patients?
How many troops do you allocate to your invasion force?	Invade at Calais or in Normandy?

To understand "how much" decisions, we use an approach known as *marginal analysis*. Marginal analysis involves comparing the benefit of doing a little bit more of some activity with the cost of doing a little bit more of that activity. The benefit of doing a little bit more of something is what economists call its *marginal benefit*, and the cost of doing a little bit more of something is what they call its *marginal cost*.

Why is this called "marginal" analysis? A margin is an edge; what you do in marginal analysis is push out the edge a bit and see whether that is a good move.

We will begin our study of marginal analysis by focusing on marginal cost, and we'll do that by considering a hypothetical company called Felix's Lawn-Mowing Service, operated by Felix himself with his tractor-mower.

Marginal Cost

Felix is a very hard-working individual; if he works continuously, he can mow 7 lawns in a day. It takes him an hour to mow each lawn. The opportunity cost of an hour of Felix's time is $10 because he could make that much at his next best job.

His one and only mower, however, presents a problem when Felix works this hard. Running his mower for longer and longer periods on a given day takes an increasing toll on the engine and ultimately necessitates more—and more costly—maintenance and repairs.

The second column of Table 7-4 on page 166 shows how the total daily cost of Felix's business depends on the quantity of lawns he mows in a day. For simplicity, we assume that Felix's only costs are the opportunity cost of his time and the cost of upkeep for his mower.

At only 1 lawn per day, Felix's daily cost is $10.50: $10.00 for an hour of his time plus $0.50 for some oil. At 2 lawns per day, his daily cost is $21.75: $20.00 for 2 hours of his time and $1.75 for mower repair and maintenance. At 3 lawns per day, the daily cost has risen to $35.00: $30.00 for 3 hours of his time and $5.00 for mower repair and maintenance.

TABLE **7-4**

Felix's Marginal Cost of Mowing Lawns

Quantity of lawns mowed	Felix's total cost	Felix's marginal cost of lawn mowed
0	$0	
		$10.50
1	10.50	
		11.25
2	21.75	
		13.25
3	35.00	
		15.50
4	50.50	
		18.00
5	68.50	
		20.75
6	89.25	
		23.75
7	$113.00	

The third column of Table 7-4 contains the cost incurred by Felix for each *additional* lawn he mows, calculated from information in the second column. The 1st lawn he mows costs him $10.50; this number appears in the third column between the lines representing 0 lawn and 1 lawn because $10.50 is Felix's cost of going from 0 to 1 lawn mowed. The next lawn, going from 1 to 2, costs him an additional $11.25. So $11.25 appears in the third column between the lines representing the 1st and 2nd lawn, and so on.

The increase in Felix's cost when he mows one more lawn is his **marginal cost** of lawn-mowing. In general, the marginal cost of any activity is the additional cost incurred by doing one more unit of that activity.

The marginal costs shown in Table 7-4 have a clear pattern: Felix's marginal cost is greater the more lawns he has already mowed. That is, each time he mows a lawn, the additional cost of doing yet another lawn goes up. Felix's lawn-mowing business has what economists call **increasing marginal cost:** each additional lawn costs more to mow than the previous one. Or, to put it slightly differently, with increasing marginal cost, the marginal cost of an activity rises as the quantity already done rises.

Figure 7-1 is a graphical representation of the third column in Table 7-4. The horizontal axis measures the quantity of lawns mowed, and the vertical axis measures the

The **marginal cost** of an activity is the additional cost incurred by doing one more unit of that activity.

There is **increasing marginal cost** from an activity when each additional unit of the activity costs more than the previous unit.

Figure 7-1

The Marginal Cost Curve

The height of each bar is equal to the marginal cost of mowing the corresponding lawn. For example, the 1st lawn mowed has a marginal cost of $10.50, equal to the height of the bar extending from 0 to 1 lawn. The bars ascend in height, reflecting increasing marginal cost: each additional lawn is more costly to mow than the previous one. As a result, the marginal cost curve (drawn by plotting points in the top center of each bar) is upward sloping. >*web...*

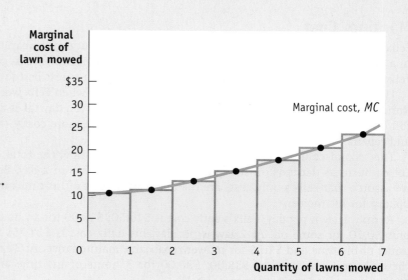

marginal cost of a mowed lawn. The height of each shaded bar indicates the marginal cost incurred by mowing a given lawn. For example, the bar stretching from 4 to 5 lawns is at a height of $18.00, equal to the cost of mowing the 5th lawn. Notice that the bars form a series of ascending steps, a reflection of the increasing marginal cost of lawn-mowing. The **marginal cost curve,** the red curve in Figure 7-1, shows the relationship between marginal cost and the quantity of the activity already done. We draw it by plotting a point in the center at the top of each bar and connecting the points.

The marginal cost curve is upward sloping, due to increasing marginal cost. Not all activities have increasing marginal cost; for example, it is possible for marginal cost to be the same regardless of the number of lawns already mowed. Economists call this case *constant* marginal cost. It is also possible for some activities to have a marginal cost that initially falls as we do more of the activity and then eventually rises. These sorts of activities involve gains from specialization: as more output is produced, more workers are hired, allowing each one to specialize in the task that he or she performs best. The gains from specialization yield a lower marginal cost of production.

Now that we have established the concept of marginal cost, we move to the parallel concept of marginal benefit.

Marginal Benefit

Felix's business is in a town where some of the residents are very busy but others are not so busy. For people who are very busy, the opportunity cost of an hour of their time spent mowing the lawn is very high. So they are willing to pay Felix a fairly high sum to do it for them. People with lots of free time, however, have a lower opportunity cost of an hour of their time spent mowing the lawn. So they are willing to pay Felix only a relatively small sum. And between these two extremes lie other residents who are moderately busy and so are willing to pay a moderate price to have their lawns mowed.

We'll assume that on any given day, Felix has one potential customer who will pay him $35 to mow her lawn, another who will pay $30, a third who will pay $26, a fourth who will pay $23, and so on. Table 7-5 lists what he can receive from each of his seven potential customers per day, in descending order according to price. So if Felix goes from 0 to 1 lawn mowed, he can earn $35; if he goes from 1 to 2 lawns mowed, he can earn an additional $30; and so on. The third column of Table 7-5 shows the **marginal benefit** to Felix of each additional lawn mowed. In general, marginal benefit is the additional benefit derived from undertaking one more unit of an activity. Because it arises from doing one more lawn, each marginal benefit value appears between the lines associated with successive quantities of lawns.

It's clear from Table 7-5 that the more lawns Felix has already mowed, the smaller his marginal benefit from mowing one more. So Felix's lawn-mowing business has what

> The **marginal cost curve** shows how the cost of undertaking one more unit of an activity depends on the quantity of that activity that has already been done.

PITFALLS

INCREASING TOTAL COST VERSUS INCREASING MARGINAL COST

The concept of *increasing marginal cost* plays an important role in economic analysis, but students sometimes get confused about what it means. That's because it is easy to wrongly conclude that whenever total cost is increasing, marginal cost must also be increasing. But the following example shows that this conclusion is misguided.

Suppose that we change the numbers of our example: the marginal cost of mowing the 6th lawn is now $20, and the marginal cost of mowing the 7th lawn is now $15. In both instances total cost increases as Felix does an additional lawn: it increases by $20 for the 6th lawn and by $15 for the 7th lawn. But in this example marginal cost is *decreasing*: the marginal cost of the 7th lawn is less than the marginal cost of the 6th lawn. So we have a case of increasing total cost and decreasing marginal cost. What this shows us is that, in fact, totals and marginals can sometimes move in opposite directions.

> The **marginal benefit** from an activity is the additional benefit derived from undertaking one more unit of that activity.

TABLE 7-5

Felix's Marginal Benefit of Mowing Lawns

Quantity of lawns mowed	Felix's total benefit	Felix's marginal benefit of lawn mowed
0	$0	
		$35.00
1	35.00	
		30.00
2	65.00	
		26.00
3	91.00	
		23.00
4	114.00	
		21.00
5	135.00	
		19.00
6	154.00	
		18.00
7	$172.00	

Figure 7-2

The Marginal Benefit Curve

The height of each bar is equal to the marginal benefit of mowing the corresponding lawn. For example, the 1st lawn mowed has a marginal benefit of $35, equal to the height of the bar extending from 0 to 1 lawn. The bars descend in height, reflecting decreasing marginal benefit each additional lawn produces a smaller benefit than the previous one. As a result, the marginal benefit curve (drawn by plotting points in the top center of each bar) is downward sloping. *>web…*

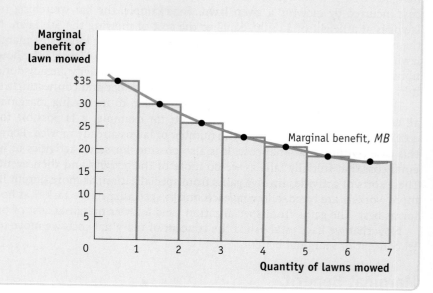

There is **decreasing marginal benefit** from an activity when each additional unit of the activity produces less benefit than the previous unit.

The **marginal benefit curve** shows how the benefit from undertaking one more unit of an activity depends on the quantity of that activity that has already been done.

economists call **decreasing marginal benefit:** each additional lawn mowed produces less benefit than the previous lawn. Or, to put it slightly differently, with decreasing marginal benefit, the marginal benefit of an activity falls as the quantity already done rises.

Just as marginal cost could be represented with a marginal cost curve, marginal benefit can be represented with a **marginal benefit curve,** shown in blue in Figure 7-2. The height of each bar shows the marginal benefit of each additional lawn mowed; the curve through the middle of each bar's top shows how the benefit of each additional unit of the activity depends on the number of units that have already been undertaken.

Felix's marginal benefit curve is downward sloping because he faces decreasing marginal benefit from lawn-mowing. Not all activities have decreasing marginal benefit; in fact, there are many activities for which marginal benefit is constant—that is, it is the same regardless of the number of units already undertaken. In later chapters where we study firms, we will see that the shape of a firm's marginal benefit curve from producing output has important implications for how it behaves within its industry. We'll also see in Chapters 10 and 11 why economists assume that declining marginal benefit is the norm when considering choices made by consumers. Like increasing marginal cost, decreasing marginal benefit is so common that for now we can take it as the norm.

Now we are ready to see how the concepts of marginal benefit and marginal cost can be brought together to answer the question of "how much" of an activity an individual should undertake.

Marginal Analysis

Table 7-6 shows the marginal cost and marginal benefit numbers from Tables 7-4 and 7-5. It also adds an additional column: the net gain to Felix from one more lawn mowed, equal to the difference between the marginal benefit and the marginal cost.

We can use Table 7-6 to determine how many lawns Felix should mow. To see this, imagine for a moment that Felix planned to mow only 3 lawns today. We can immediately see that this is too small a quantity. If Felix mows an additional lawn, increasing the quantity from 3 to 4, he realizes a marginal benefit of $23 and incurs a marginal cost of only $15.50—so his net gain would be $23.00 − $15.50 = $7.50. But even 4 lawns is still too few: if Felix increases the quantity from 4 to 5, his marginal benefit is $21.00 and his marginal cost is only $18.00, for a net gain of $21.00 − $18.00 = $3.00 (as indicated by the highlighting in the table).

TABLE 7-6

Felix's Net Gain from Mowing Lawns

Quantity of lawns mowed	Felix's marginal benefit of lawn mowed	Felix's marginal cost of lawn mowed	Felix's net gain of lawn mowed
0			
	$35.00	$10.50	$24.50
1			
	30.00	11.25	18.75
2			
	26.00	13.25	12.75
3			
	23.00	15.50	7.50
4			
	21.00	18.00	3.00
5			
	19.00	20.75	−1.75
6			
	18.00	23.75	−5.75
7			

But if Felix goes ahead and mows 7 lawns, that is too many. We can see this by looking at the net gain from mowing that 7th lawn: Felix's marginal benefit is $18.00, but his marginal cost is $23.75. So mowing that 7th lawn would produce a net gain of $18.00 − $23.75 = −$5.75; that is, a net *loss* for his business. Even 6 lawns is too many: by increasing the quantity of lawns mowed from 5 to 6, Felix incurs a marginal cost of $20.75 compared with a marginal benefit of only $19.00. He is best off at mowing 5 lawns, the largest quantity of lawns for which marginal benefit is at least as great as marginal cost.

The upshot is that Felix should mow 5 lawns—no more and no less. If he mows fewer than 5 lawns, his marginal benefit from one more is greater than his marginal cost; he would be passing up a net gain by not mowing more lawns. If he mows more than 5 lawns, his marginal benefit from the last lawn mowed is less than his marginal cost, resulting in a loss for that lawn. So 5 lawns is the quantity that generates Felix's maximum possible total net gain; it is what economists call the **optimal quantity** of lawns mowed.

Figure 7-3 on page 170 shows graphically how the optimal quantity can be determined. Felix's marginal benefit and marginal cost curves are both shown. If Felix mows fewer than 5 lawns, the marginal benefit curve is *above* the marginal cost curve, so he can make himself better off by mowing more lawns; if he mows more than 5 lawns, the marginal benefit curve is *below* the marginal cost curve, so he would be better off mowing fewer lawns.

The table in Figure 7-3 confirms our result. The second column repeats information from Table 7-6, showing marginal benefit minus marginal cost—or the net gain—for each lawn. The third column shows total net gain according to the quantity of lawns mowed. The total net gain after doing a given lawn is simply the sum of numbers in the second column up to and including that lawn. For example, the net gain is $24.50 for the first lawn and $18.75 for the second. So the total net gain after doing the first lawn is $24.50, and the total net gain after doing the second lawn is $24.50 + $18.75 = $43.25. Our conclusion that 5 is the optimal quantity is confirmed by the fact that the greatest total net gain, $66.50, occurs when the 5th lawn is mowed.

The example of Felix's lawn-mowing business shows how you go about finding the optimal quantity: increase the quantity as long as the marginal benefit from one more unit is greater than the marginal cost, but stop before the marginal benefit becomes less than the marginal cost.

In many cases, however, it is possible to state this rule more simply. When a "how much" decision involves relatively large quantities, the rule simplifies to this: the optimal quantity is the quantity at which marginal benefit is equal to marginal cost.

The **optimal quantity** of an activity is the quantity that generates the maximum possible total net gain.

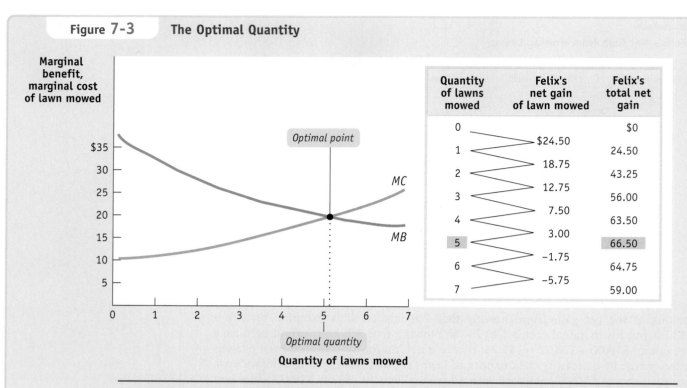

Figure 7-3 **The Optimal Quantity**

The optimal quantity of an activity is the quantity that generates the highest possible total net gain. It is the quantity at which marginal benefit is equal to marginal cost. Equivalently, it is the quantity at which the marginal benefit curve and the marginal cost curve intersect.

Here they intersect at approximately 5 lawns. The table beside the graph confirms that 5 is indeed the optimal quantity: the total net gain is maximized at 5 lawns, generating $66.50 in total net gain for Felix.

The **principle of marginal analysis** says that the optimal quantity of an activity is the quantity at which marginal benefit is equal to marginal cost.

PITFALLS

MUDDLED AT THE MARGIN

The idea of setting marginal benefit *equal* to marginal cost sometimes confuses people. Aren't we trying to maximize the *difference* between benefits and costs? And don't we wipe out our gains by setting benefits and costs equal to each other? But what we are doing is setting *marginal,* not *total,* benefit and cost equal to each other.

Once again, the point is to maximize the total net gain from an activity. If the marginal benefit from the activity is greater than the marginal cost, doing a bit more will increase that gain. If the marginal benefit is less than the marginal cost, doing a bit less will increase the total net gain. So only when the *marginal* benefit and cost are equal is the difference between *total* benefit and cost at a maximum.

To see why this is so, consider the example of a farmer who finds that her optimal quantity of wheat produced is 5,000 bushels. Typically, she will find that in going from 4,999 to 5,000 bushels, her marginal benefit is only very slightly greater than her marginal cost—that is, the difference between marginal benefit and marginal cost is close to zero. Similarly, in going from 5,000 to 5,001 bushels, her marginal cost is only very slightly greater than her marginal benefit—again, the difference between marginal cost and marginal benefit is very close to zero. So a simple rule for her in choosing the optimal quantity of wheat is to produce the quantity at which the difference between marginal benefit and marginal cost is approximately zero—that is, the quantity at which marginal benefit equals marginal cost.

Economists call this rule the **principle of marginal analysis.** It says that the optimal quantity of an activity is the quantity at which marginal benefit equals marginal cost. Graphically, the optimal quantity is the quantity of an activity at which the marginal benefit curve *intersects* the marginal cost curve. In fact, this graphical method works quite well even when the numbers involved aren't that large. For example, in Figure 7-3 the marginal benefit and marginal cost curves cross each other at about 5 lawns mowed—that is, marginal benefit equals marginal cost at about 5 lawns mowed, which we have already seen is Felix's optimal quantity.

A Principle with Many Uses

The principle of marginal analysis can be applied to just about any "how much" decision—including those decisions where the benefits and costs are not necessarily expressed in dollars and cents. Here are a few examples:

- The number of traffic deaths can be reduced by spending more on highways, requiring better protection in cars, and so on. But these measures are expensive. So we can talk about the marginal cost to society of eliminating one more traffic fatality. And we can then ask whether the marginal benefit of that life saved is large enough to warrant doing this. (If you think no price is too high to save a life, see the following Economics in Action.)

- Many useful drugs have side effects that depend on the dosage. So we can talk about the marginal cost, in terms of these side effects, of increasing the dosage of a drug. The drug also has a marginal benefit in helping fight the disease. So the optimal quantity of the drug is the quantity that makes the best of this trade-off.

- Studying for an exam has costs because you could have done something else with the time, such as studying for another exam or sleeping. So we can talk about the marginal cost of devoting another hour to studying for your chemistry final. The optimal quantity of studying is the level at which the marginal benefit in terms of a higher grade is just equal to the marginal cost.

economics in action

The Cost of a Life

What's the marginal benefit to society of saving a human life? You might be tempted to answer that human life is infinitely precious. But in the real world, resources are scarce, so we must decide how much to spend on saving lives since we cannot spend infinite amounts. After all, we could surely reduce highway deaths by dropping the speed limit on interstates to 40 miles per hour, but the cost of such a lower speed limit—in time and money—is more than anyone is willing to pay.

Generally, people are reluctant to talk in a straightforward way about comparing the marginal cost of a life saved with the marginal benefit—it sounds too callous. Sometimes, however, the question becomes unavoidable.

For example, the cost of saving a life became an object of intense discussion in the United Kingdom in 1999, after a horrifying train crash near London's Paddington Station killed 31 people. There were accusations that the British government was spending too little on rail safety. However, the government estimated that improving rail safety would cost an additional $4.5 million per life saved. But if that amount was worth spending—that is, if the estimated marginal benefit of saving a life exceeded $4.5 million—then the implication was that the British government was spending way too little on *traffic safety*. The estimated marginal cost per life saved through highway improvements was only $1.5 million, making it a much better deal than saving lives through greater rail safety. ∎

> > > > > > > > > > > > > > > > > > >

>> CHECK YOUR UNDERSTANDING 7-2

1. For each of the "how much" decisions listed in Table 7-3, describe the nature of the marginal cost and of the marginal benefit.

2. Suppose that Felix's marginal cost, instead of increasing, is the same for every lawn he mows.
   a. Assume Felix's marginal cost is $18.50. Using Table 7-6, find the optimal quantity of mowed lawns. What is his total net gain?
   b. How high would marginal cost have to be such that Felix's optimal quantity of lawns mowed is 0? Can you specify a marginal cost for which the optimal quantity is 3?

Solutions appear at back of book.

This vet left law school to pursue his dream career. The cost for a year of law school was lost—a sunk cost. But he and his patients are now happy.

A **sunk cost** is a cost that has already been incurred and is nonrecoverable. A sunk cost should be ignored in decisions about future actions.

Sunk Costs

When making decisions, knowing what to ignore is important. Although we have devoted much attention in this chapter to costs that are important to take into account when making a decision, some costs should be ignored when doing so. In this section we will focus on the kinds of costs that people should ignore—what economists call *sunk costs*—and why they should be ignored.

To gain some intuition, consider the following scenario. You own a car that is a few years old, and you have just replaced the brake pads at a cost of $250. But then you find out that the entire brake system is defective and must be replaced—including the newly installed brake pads. This will cost you an additional $1,500. Alternatively, you could sell the car and buy another of comparable quality, but with no brake defects, by spending an additional $1,600. What should you do: fix your old car, or sell it and buy another?

Some might say that you should take the latter option. After all, this line of reasoning goes, if you repair your car, you will end up having spent $1,750: $1,500 for the brake system and $250 for the brake pads you replaced. If you were instead to sell your old car and buy another, you would spend only $1,600.

But this reasoning, although it sounds plausible, is wrong. It is wrong because it ignores the fact that you have *already* spent $250 on brake pads, and that $250 is *non-recoverable*. That is, having been spent already, the $250 cannot be recouped. Therefore, it should be ignored and should have no effect on your decision whether to repair your car and keep it or not. From an economist's viewpoint, the real cost at this time of repairing and keeping your car is $1,500, not $1,750. Therefore, the correct decision is to repair your car and keep it rather than spend $1,600 on a new car.

In this example, the $250 that has already been spent and cannot be recovered is what economists call a **sunk cost.** Sunk costs should be ignored in making decisions about future actions because they have no influence on their costs and benefits. It's like the old saying, "There's no use crying over spilled milk": once something is gone and can't be recovered, it is irrelevant in making decisions about what to do in the future.

It is often psychologically hard to ignore sunk costs. And if, in fact, the costs haven't yet been incurred, then they should be taken into consideration. That is, if you had known at the beginning that it would cost $1,750 to repair your car, then the right choice *at that time* would have been to buy a new car for $1,600. But once the $250 has already been paid for brake pads, it is no longer something that should be included in your decision making about your next actions. It may be hard to accept that "bygones are bygones," but it is the right thing to do.

economics in action

The Next Generation

Recently, several European countries held "spectrum auctions," auctions in which telephone companies bid for portions of a country's airwave space. The telephone companies planned to use this airwave space to offer new mobile phone services to consumers. Companies believed they could earn large profits by providing these new services, so-called third-generation, or 3G, mobile phone services, which include features such as videocalling and mobile Internet access. Eager to capture what they expected to be large future profits, telephone companies paid billions of dollars for portions of the European airwave space.

But some technology experts were worried. They believed that the companies had exaggerated expectations of future profits and, as a result, had paid too much for the airwave space. These experts feared that once the companies realized that the airwave space was worth much less than what they had paid, the companies would be unwilling to put up the additional money needed for physical infrastructure, such as the towers used to transmit the signals that are necessary to the 3G services.

It turned out that the technology experts were right about the exaggerated expectations: within a few months of the spectrum auctions, telephone companies realized that they had paid far more for the portions of airwave space than they were really worth.

But was the experts' second conjecture correct: would the overpayment for the airwaves really prevent the future investment needed to provide 3G services? The answer at this point is no. Several companies, including Vodaphone, the British company that owns a substantial part of the American company Verizon, have pushed ahead in building the required infrastructure. As of 2004, 3G was available in over 30 countries worldwide.

Technology experts were wrong about the effect of overpayment because they didn't understand the concept of sunk costs. That is, they didn't understand that once made, those payments for airwave space couldn't be recovered; therefore, they wouldn't affect the telephone companies' willingness to spend additional money to complete the project. After the companies came to the painful—and quite embarrassing—realization of their overpayment, it didn't change the fact that it was still profitable to build the infrastructure needed to provide the new services. In the end, they appear to have made the right economic calculation—and in the process admitted to themselves that "there's no use crying over a lost billion or two." ■

> > > > > > > > > > > > > > > > > > > >

>>**CHECK YOUR UNDERSTANDING 7-3**

1. You have decided to go into the ice-cream business and have bought a used ice-cream truck for $8,000. Now you are reconsidering. What is your sunk cost in the following scenarios?
   a. The truck cannot be resold.
   b. It can be resold, but only at a 50 percent discount.

2. You have gone through two years of medical school but are suddenly wondering whether you wouldn't be happier as a musician. Which of the following statements are potentially valid arguments and which are not?
   a. "I can't give up now, after all the time and money I've put in."
   b. "If I had thought about it from the beginning, I never would have gone to med school, so I should give it up now."
   c. "I wasted two years, but never mind—let's start from here."
   d. "My parents would kill me if I stopped now." (*Hint:* we're discussing *your* decision-making ability, not your parents'.)

Solutions appear at back of book.

The Concept of Present Value

In many cases, individuals must make decisions whose consequences extend some ways into the future. For example, when you decide to attend college, you are committing yourself to years of study, which you expect will pay off for the rest of your life. So the decision to attend college is the decision to embark on a long-term project.

As we have already seen, the basic rule in deciding whether or not to undertake a project is that you should compare the benefits of that project with its costs, implicit as well as explicit. But sometimes there can be a problem in making these comparisons: the benefits and costs of a project may not arrive at the same time.

Sometimes the costs of a project come at an earlier date than the benefits. For example, going to college involves large immediate costs: tuition, income forgone because you are in school, and so on. The benefits, such as a higher salary in your future career, come later, often much later.

In other cases, the benefits of a project come at an earlier date than the costs. If you take out a loan to pay for a vacation cruise, the satisfaction of the vacation will come immediately, but the burden of making payments will come later.

But why is time an issue?

Borrowing, Lending, and Interest

In general, having a dollar today is worth more than having a dollar a year from now. To see why, let's consider two examples.

First, suppose that you get a new job that comes with a $1,000 bonus, which will be paid at the end of the first year. But you would like to spend the extra money now—say, on new clothes for work. Can you do that?

The answer is yes—you can borrow money today and use the bonus to repay the debt a year from now. But if that is your plan, you cannot borrow the full $1,000 today. You must borrow less than that, because a year from now you will have to repay the amount borrowed *plus interest*.

Now consider a different scenario. Suppose that you are paid a bonus of $1,000 today, and you decide that you don't want to spend the money right now. What do you do with it? You put it in the bank; in effect, you are lending the $1,000 to the bank, which in turn lends it out to its customers who wish to borrow. At the end of a year, you will get more than $1,000 back—you will have the $1,000 plus the interest earned.

What all of this means is that $1,000 today is worth more than $1,000 a year from now. The reason is that if you want to have the money today, you must borrow it and pay interest. That is, you must pay a price for using the money today. And, correspondingly, if you forgo using the money today and lend it to someone else, you earn interest on the money. That is, you earn something by letting someone else use your money. When someone borrows money for a year, the **interest rate** is the price, calculated as a percentage of the amount borrowed, charged by the lender.

Because of the interest paid on borrowing, you can't evaluate a project just by adding up all the costs and benefits when those costs and benefits arrive at different times. You must take time into account when evaluating the project because a $1 benefit that comes today is worth more than a $1 benefit that comes a year from now; and a $1 cost that comes today is more burdensome to you than a $1 cost that comes next year. Fortunately, there is a simple way to adjust for these complications.

What we will now see is that the interest rate can be used to convert future benefits and costs into what economists call their *present values*. By using present values in evaluating a project, you can evaluate a project *as if* all its costs and benefits were occurring today rather than at different times. This allows people to "factor out" the complications created by time. We'll start by defining exactly what the concept of present value is.

> When someone borrows money for a year, the **interest rate** is the price, calculated as a percentage of the amount borrowed, charged by the lender.

Defining Present Value

The key to the concept of present value is to understand that you can use the interest rate to compare the value of a dollar realized today with the value of a dollar realized later. Why the interest rate? Because the interest rate correctly measures the cost of delaying a dollar of benefit and, correspondingly, the benefit of delaying a dollar of cost. Let's illustrate this with some examples.

Suppose, first, that you are evaluating whether or not to take a job in which your employer promises to pay you a bonus at the end of the first year. What is the value to you today of $1 of bonus money to be paid to you one year in the future? A slightly different way of asking the same question: what would you be willing to accept today in place of receiving $1 one year in the future?

The way to answer this question is to observe that you need *less* than $1 today in order to be assured of having $1 one year from now. Why? Because any money that you have today can be lent out at interest, turning it into a greater sum at the end of the year.

The symbol r is used to represent the rate of interest, expressed as a fraction—that is, if the interest rate is 10%, then $r = 0.10$. If you lend out X, at the end of a year you will receive your X back, plus the interest on your X, which is $X \times r$. Thus, at the end of the year you will receive $\$X + \$X \times r$, which is $\$X \times (1 + r)$. What we want to know is how much you would have to lend out today to have $1 a year from now. If the amount you lend out is $\$X$, it must be true that

(7-1) $\$X \times (1 + r) = \$1$

Rearranging, we can solve for $\$X$, the amount you need today in order to generate $1 one year from now.

(7-2) $\$X = \$1/(1 + r)$

This means that you would be willing to accept $\$X$ today for every $1 to be paid one year from now. The reason is that by lending out $\$X$ today, you can be assured of having $1 one year from now. If we plug into the equation the value of the yearly interest rate—say it is 10%, which means that $r = 0.10$—then we can solve for $\$X$: $\$X$ is equal to $1/1.10, which is approximately $0.91. So you would be willing to accept $0.91 today in exchange for every $1 to be paid to you one year from now. Economists have a special name for $\$X$—it's called the **present value** of $1.

To see that this technique works for future costs as well as future benefits, consider the following example. Suppose you enter into an agreement that obliges you to pay $1 one year from now—say, to pay off your student loan when you graduate in a year. How much money would you need today to ensure that you have $1 in a year? The answer is $\$X$, the present value of $1, which in our example is $0.91. The reason $0.91 is the right answer is that if you lend it out for one year at an interest rate of 10%, you will receive $1 in return at the end.

> The **present value** of $1 realized one year from now is equal to $\$1/(1 + r)$: the amount of money you must lend out today in order to have $1 in one year. It is the value to you today of $1 realized one year from now.

What these two examples show us is that the present value concept provides a way to calculate the value today of $1 that is realized in the future—regardless of whether that $1 is realized as a benefit (the bonus) or a cost (the student loan payback). This means that to evaluate a project today that has benefits and/or costs to be realized in the future, we just use the relevant interest rate to convert those future dollars into their present values. In that way we have "factored out" the complication that time creates for decision making.

In the next section we will work out an example of using the present value concept to evaluate a project. But before we do that, it is worthwhile to note that the present value method can be used for projects in which the $1 is realized more than a year later—say, two, three, or even more years.

Suppose you are considering a project that will pay you $1 *two* years from today. What is the value to you today of $1 received two years into the future? We can find the answer to that question by expanding our formula for present value.

Let's call $\$V$ the amount of money you need to lend today at an interest rate of r in order to have $1 in two years. So if you lend $\$V$ today, you will receive $\$V \times (1 + r)$ in one year. And if you *re-lend* that sum for yet another year, you will receive $\$V \times (1 + r) \times (1 + r) = \$V \times (1 + r)^2$ at the end of the second year. At the end of two years, $\$V$ will be worth $\$V \times (1 + r)^2$; if $r = 0.10$, then this becomes $\$V \times (1.10)^2 = \$V \times (1.21)$.

Now we are ready to answer the question of what $1 realized two years in the future is worth today. In order for the amount lent today, $\$V$, to be worth $1 two years from now, it must satisfy this formula:

(7-3) $\$V \times (1 + r)^2 = \$1$

Rearranging, we can solve for $\$V$:

(7-4) $\$V = \$1/(1 + r)^2$

Given $r = 0.10$, this means that $V = \$1/1.21 = \$0.83$. So when the interest rate is 10%, $1 realized two years from today is worth $0.83 today because by lending out $0.83 today you can be assured of having $1 in two years. And that means that the present value of $1 realized two years into the future is $0.83.

From this example we can see how the present value concept can be expanded to a number of years even greater than two. If we ask what value of $1 realized N number of years into the future is, the answer is given by a generalization of the present value formula: it is equal to $\$1/(1 + r)^N$.

Using Present Value

Suppose you have to choose one of three projects to undertake. Project A has an immediate payoff to you of $100, while project B requires that you put up $10 of your own money today in order to receive $115 a year from now. Project C gives you an immediate payoff of $119 but requires that you pay $20 a year from now. We'll assume that the annual interest rate is 10%—that is, $r = 0.10$.

The problem in evaluating these three projects is that they have costs and benefits that are realized at different times. That is, of course, where the concept of present value becomes extremely helpful: by using present value to convert any dollars realized in the future into today's value, you factor out the issue of time. This allows you to calculate the **net present value** of a project—the present value of current and future benefits minus the present value of current and future costs. And the best project is the one with the highest net present value.

Table 7-7 shows how this is done for each of the three projects. The second and third columns show how many dollars are realized and when they are realized; costs are indicated by a minus sign. The fourth column shows the equations used to convert the flows of dollars into their present value, and the fifth column shows the actual amounts of the total net present value for each of the three projects.

For instance, to calculate the net present value of project B, we need to calculate the present value of $115 received in one year. The present value of $1 received in one year would be $\$1/(1 + r)$. So the present value of $115 is 115 times $\$1/(1 + r)$; that is, $\$115/(1 + r)$. The net present value of project B is the present value of today's and future benefits minus the present value of today's and future costs: $-\$10 + \$115/(1 + r)$.

From the fifth column, we can immediately see which is the preferred project—it is project C. That's because it has the highest net present value, $100.82, which is higher than the net present value of project A ($100) and much higher than the net present value of project B ($94.55).

This example shows how important the concept of present value is. If we had failed to use the present value calculations and instead had simply added up the dollars generated by each of the three projects, we could have easily been misled into believing that project B was the best project and project C was the worst one.

> The **net present value** of a project is the present value of current and future benefits minus the present value of current and future costs.

TABLE 7-7

The Net Present Value of Three Projects

Project	Dollars realized today	Dollars realized one year from today	Present value formula	Net present value given $r = 0.10$
A	$100	—	$100	$100.00
B	-$10	$115	$-\$10 + \$115/(1 + r)$	$94.55
C	$119	-$20	$\$119 - \$20/(1 + r)$	$100.82

economics in action

How Big Is That Jackpot, Anyway?

For a clear example of present value at work, consider the case of lottery jackpots.

Recently, the Pennsylvania State Lottery's "Super 6" offered the lucky winner $4 million. Well, sort of. That $4 million was available only if you chose to take your winnings in the form of an "annuity," consisting of $200,000 per year for the next 20 years. If you wanted cash up front, the jackpot was only $2 million.

Why was Pennsylvania so stingy about quick payoffs? It was all a matter of present value.

In fact, the lottery budgeted only $2 million for the jackpot. If the winner had been willing to take the annuity, the lottery would have invested that money, buying U.S. government bonds (in effect lending the money to the federal government). The money would have been invested in such a way that the investments would pay $200,000 each year, just enough to pay the annuity. This worked, of course, because at the interest rates prevailing at the time, the present value of a $4 million annuity spread over 20 years was just about $2 million. Or to put it another way, the opportunity cost to the lottery of that annuity was $2 million.

So why didn't they just call it a $2 million jackpot? Hey, $4 million sounds more impressive! But it was really the same thing. ∎

> > > > > > > > > > > > > > > > > >

>> **QUICK REVIEW**

> ➤ When costs or benefits arrive at different times, you must take the complication created by time into account. This is done by transforming any dollars realized in the future into their *present value*.

> ➤ $1 in benefit realized a year from now is worth $1/(1 + r)$ today, where r is the *interest rate*. Similarly, $1 in cost realized a year from now is valued at a cost of $1/(1 + r)$ today.

> ➤ When comparing several projects in which costs and benefits arrive at different times, you should choose the project that generates the highest *net present value*.

>>CHECK YOUR UNDERSTANDING 7-4

1. Consider the three alternative projects shown in Table 7-7. This time, however, suppose that the interest rate is only 2%.
   a. Calculate the net present values of the three projects. Which one is now preferred?
   b. Explain why the preferred choice is different with a 2% interest rate than with a 10% rate.

Solutions appear at back of book.

• A LOOK AHEAD •

This chapter laid out the basic concepts that we need to understand economic decisions. These concepts, as we will soon see, provide the necessary tools for understanding not only the behavior behind the supply and demand curves but also the implications of markets for consumer and producer welfare.

But to get there we need a bit more context—we need to know something more about the kinds of decisions that producers and consumers must make. We start with producers: in the next two chapters we will see how marginal analysis determines how much a profit-maximizing producer chooses to produce.

SUMMARY

1. All economic decisions involve the allocation of scarce resources. Some decisions are "either–or" decisions, in which the question is whether or not to do something. Other decisions are "how much" decisions, in which the question is how many resources to put into some use.

2. The cost of using a resource for a particular activity is the opportunity cost of that resource. Some opportunity costs are **explicit costs;** they involve a direct payment of cash. Other opportunity costs, however, are **implicit**

costs; they involve no outlay of money but represent the inflows of cash that are forgone. Both explicit and implicit costs should be taken into account in making decisions. Companies use **capital** and their owners' time. So companies should base decisions on **economic profit,** which takes into account implicit costs such as the opportunity cost of the owners' time and **the implicit cost of capital.** The **accounting profit,** which companies calculate for the purposes of taxes and public reporting, is often considerably larger than the economic profit because it includes only explicit costs and depreciation, not implicit costs.

3. A "how much" decision is made using marginal analysis, which involves comparing the benefit to the cost of doing an additional unit of an activity. The **marginal cost** of an activity is the additional cost incurred by doing one more unit of the activity, and the **marginal benefit** of an activity is the additional benefit gained by doing one more unit. The **marginal cost curve** is the graphical illustration of marginal cost, and the **marginal benefit curve** is the graphical illustration of marginal benefit.

4. Marginal cost and marginal benefit typically depend on how much of the activity has already been done. In the case of **increasing marginal cost,** each additional unit costs more than the unit before; this is represented by an upward-sloping marginal cost curve. In the case of **decreasing marginal benefit,** each additional unit produces a smaller benefit than the unit before; this is represented by a downward-sloping marginal benefit curve.

5. The **optimal quantity** of an activity is the quantity that generates the maximum possible total net gain. According to the **principle of marginal analysis,** the optimal quantity is the quantity at which marginal benefit is equal to marginal cost. It is the quantity at which the marginal cost curve and the marginal benefit curve intersect.

6. A cost that has already been incurred and that is nonrecoverable is a **sunk cost.** Sunk costs should be ignored in decisions about future actions because they have no effect on future benefits and costs.

7. In order to evaluate a project in which costs or benefits are realized in the future, you must first transform them into their **present values** using the **interest rate,** r. The present value of \$1 realized one year from now is $\$1/(1 + r)$, the amount of money you must lend out today to have \$1 one year from now. Once this transformation is done, you should choose the project with the highest **net present value.**

KEY TERMS

Explicit cost, p. 161
Implicit cost, p. 161
Accounting profit, p. 163
Economic profit, p. 163
Capital, p. 163
Implicit cost of capital, p. 163

Marginal cost, p. 166
Increasing marginal cost, p. 166
Marginal cost curve, p. 167
Marginal benefit, p. 167
Decreasing marginal benefit, p. 168
Marginal benefit curve, p. 168

Optimal quantity, p. 169
Principle of marginal analysis, p. 170
Sunk cost, p. 172
Interest rate, p. 174
Present value, p. 175
Net present value, p. 176

PROBLEMS

1. Hiro owns and operates a small business that provides economic consulting services. During the year he spends \$55,000 on travel to clients and other expenses, and the computer that he owns depreciates by \$2,000. If he didn't use the computer, he could sell it and earn yearly interest of \$100 on the money created through this sale. Hiro's total revenue for the year is \$100,000. Instead of working as a consultant for the year, he could teach economics at a small local college and make a salary of \$50,000.

   a. What is Hiro's accounting profit?

   b. What is Hiro's economic profit?

   c. Should Hiro continue working as a consultant, or should he teach economics instead?

2. Jackie owns and operates a web-design business. Her computing equipment depreciates by \$5,000 per year. She runs the business out of a room in her home. If she didn't use the room as her business office, she could rent it out for \$2,000 per year. Jackie knows that if she didn't run her own business, she could return to her previous job at a large software company that would pay her a salary of \$60,000 per year. Jackie has no other expenses.

   a. How much total revenue does Jackie need to make in order to break even in the eyes of her accountant? That is, how much total revenue would give Jackie just zero accounting profit?

   b. How much total revenue does Jackie need to make in order for her to want to remain self-employed? That is, how much total revenue would give Jackie just zero economic profit?

3. You own and operate a bike store. Each year, you receive revenue of \$200,000 from your bike sales, and it costs you \$100,000 to obtain the bikes. In addition, you pay \$20,000 for electricity, taxes, and other expenses per year. Instead of running the bike store, you could become an accountant and receive a yearly salary of \$40,000. A large clothing retail chain wants to expand and offers to rent the store from you for \$50,000 per year. How do you explain to your friends that despite making a profit, it is too costly for you to continue running your store?

4. Suppose you have just paid your nonrefundable fee of $1,000 for your meal plan for this academic term. This allows you to eat dinner in the cafeteria every evening.

   a. You are offered a part-time job in a restaurant where you can eat for free each evening. Your parents say that you should eat dinner in the cafeteria anyway, since you have already paid for those meals. Are your parents right? Explain why or why not.

   b. Now suppose that you are offered a part-time job in a restaurant, but rather than being able to eat there for free, the restaurant only gives you a large discount on your meals there. Each meal at the restaurant will cost you $2, and if you eat there each evening this semester it will add up to $200. Your roommate says that you should eat in the restaurant since it costs less than the $1,000 that you paid for the meal plan. Is your roommate right? Explain why or why not.

5. You have already bought a $10 ticket for the college soccer game in advance. The ticket cannot be resold. You know that going to the soccer game will give you a benefit equal to $20. After you have bought the ticket, you hear that there will be a professional baseball post-season game at the same time. Tickets to the baseball game cost $20, and you know that going to the baseball game will give you a benefit equal to $35. You tell your friends the following: "If I had known about the baseball game before buying the ticket to the soccer game, I would have gone to the baseball game instead. But now that I already have the ticket to the soccer game, it's better for me to just go to the soccer game." Are you making the correct decision? Justify your answer by calculating the benefits and costs of your decision.

6. Amy, Bill, and Carla all mow lawns for money. Each of them operates a different lawn mower. The accompanying table shows the total cost to Amy, Bill, and Carla of mowing lawns.

Quantity of lawns mowed	Amy's total cost	Bill's total cost	Carla's total cost
0	$0	$0	$0
1	20	10	2
2	35	20	7
3	45	30	17
4	50	40	32
5	52	50	52
6	53	60	82

   a. Calculate Amy's, Bill's, and Carla's marginal costs, and draw each of their marginal cost curves.

   b. Who has increasing marginal cost, who has decreasing marginal cost, and who has constant marginal cost?

7. You are the manager of a gym, and you have to decide how many customers to admit each hour. Assume that each customer stays exactly one hour. Customers are costly to admit because they inflict wear and tear on the exercise equipment. Moreover, each additional customer generates more wear and tear than the customer before. As a result, the gym faces increasing marginal cost. The accompanying table shows the marginal costs associated with each number of customers per hour.

Quantity of customers per hour	Marginal cost of customer
0	
	$14.00
1	
	14.50
2	
	15.00
3	
	15.50
4	
	16.00
5	
	16.50
6	
	17.00
7	

   a. Suppose that each customer pays $15.25 for a one-hour workout. Use the principle of marginal analysis to find the optimal number of customers that you should admit per hour.

   b. You increase the price of a one-hour workout to $16.25. What is the optimal number of customers per hour that you should admit now?

8. Georgia and Lauren are economics students who go to a karate class together. Both have to choose how many classes to go to per week. Each class costs $20. The accompanying table shows Georgia's and Lauren's estimates of the marginal benefit that each of them gets from each class per week.

Quantity of classes	Lauren's marginal benefit of each class	Georgia's marginal benefit of each class
0		
	$23	$28
1		
	19	22
2		
	14	15
3		
	8	7
4		

   a. Use marginal analysis to find Lauren's optimal number of karate classes per week

   b. Will Georgia be willing to go to the same number of classes per week that are optimal for Lauren?

9. The Centers for Disease Control and Prevention (CDC) recommended against vaccinating the whole population against the smallpox virus because the vaccination has undesirable, and sometimes fatal, side effects. Suppose the accompanying

table gives the data that are available about the effects of a smallpox vaccination program.

Percent of population vaccinated	Deaths due to smallpox	Deaths due to vaccination side effects
0	200	0
10	180	4
20	160	10
30	140	18
40	120	33
50	100	50
60	80	74

a. Calculate the marginal benefit (in terms of lives saved) and the marginal cost (in terms of lives lost) of each 10% increment of smallpox vaccination. Calculate the net gain of a 10% increment in population vaccinated.

b. Using marginal analysis, decide what percentage of the population should optimally be vaccinated.

10. Patty delivers pizza using her own car, and she is paid according to how many pizzas she delivers. The accompanying table shows Patty's total benefit and total cost when she works a specific number of hours.

Quantity of hours worked	Total benefit	Total cost
0	$0	$0
1	30	10
2	55	21
3	75	34
4	90	50
5	100	70

a. Use marginal analysis to decide how many hours Patty should work. In other words, what is the optimal number of hours Patty should work?

b. Calculate the total net gain to Patty from working 0 hours, 1 hour, 2 hours, and so on. Now suppose Patty chooses to work for 1 hour. Compare her total net gain from working for 1 hour with her total net gain from working the optimal number of hours. How much would she lose by working for only 1 hour?

11. Assume De Beers is the sole producer of diamonds. When it wants to sell more diamonds, it must lower its price in order to induce consumers to buy more. Furthermore, each additional diamond that is produced costs more than the previous one due to the difficulty of mining for diamonds. De Beers's total benefit schedule is given in the accompanying table, along with its total cost schedule.

Quantity of diamonds	Total benefit	Total cost
0	$0	$0
1	1,000	50
2	1,900	100
3	2,700	200
4	3,400	400
5	4,000	800
6	4,500	1,500
7	4,900	2,500
8	5,200	3,800

a. Draw the marginal cost curve and the marginal benefit curve and, from your diagram, graphically derive the optimal quantity of diamonds to produce.

b. Calculate the total net gain to De Beers from producing each quantity of diamonds. Which quantity gives De Beers the highest total net gain?

12. You have won the state lottery. There are two ways in which you can receive your prize. You can either have $1 million in cash now, or you can have $1.2 million that is paid out as follows: $300,000 now, $300,000 in one year's time, $300,000 in two years' time, and $300,000 in three years' time. The interest rate is 20%. How would you prefer to receive your prize?

13. The drug company Pfizer is considering whether to invest in the development of a new cancer drug. Development will require an initial investment of $10 million now; beginning one year from now, the drug will generate annual profits of $4 million for three years.

a. If the interest rate is 12%, should Pfizer invest in the development of the new drug? Why or why not?

b. If the interest rate is 8%, should Pfizer invest in the development of the new drug? Why or why not?

>web... To continue your study and review of concepts in this chapter, please visit the Krugman/Wells website for quizzes, animated graph tutorials, web links to helpful resources, and more.

www.worthpublishers.com/krugmanwells

Behind the Supply Curve: Inputs and Costs

THE FARMER'S MARGIN

OBEAUTIFUL FOR SPACIOUS SKIES, FOR amber waves of grain." So begins the song "America the Beautiful." And those amber waves of grain are for real: though farmers are now only a small minority of America's population, our agricultural industry is immensely productive and feeds much of the world.

If you look at agricultural statistics, however, something may seem a bit surprising: when it comes to yield per acre, U.S. farmers are often nowhere near the top. For example, farmers in western European countries grow about three times as much wheat per acre as their U.S. counterparts. Are the Europeans better at growing wheat than we are?

No: European farmers are very skillful, but no more so than Americans. They produce more wheat per acre because they employ more inputs—more fertilizer and, especially, more labor—per acre. Of course, this means that European farmers have higher costs than their American counterparts. But because of government policies, European farmers receive a much higher price for their wheat than American farmers. This gives them an incentive to use more inputs and to expend more effort at the margin to increase the crop yield per acre.

Notice our use of the phrase "at the margin." Like most decisions that involve a comparison of benefits and costs, decisions about inputs and production involve a comparison of marginal quantities—the marginal cost versus the marginal benefit of producing a bit more from each acre.

In Chapter 7 we used the example of Felix's Lawn-Mowing Service to illustrate the *principle of marginal analysis*, showing

What you will learn in this chapter:

➤ The importance of the firm's **production function,** the relationship between quantity of inputs and quantity of output

➤ Why production is often subject to **diminishing returns to inputs**

➤ What the various forms of a firm's costs are and how they generate the firm's **marginal** and **average cost curves**

➤ Why a firm's costs may differ in the **short run** versus the **long run**

➤ How the firm's technology of production can generate **economies of scale**

American farming practices (at left) or European farming practices (at right)? How intensively an acre of land is worked—a decision at the margin—depends on the price of wheat a farmer faces.

how Felix could use marginal analysis to determine the optimal number of lawns to mow daily—that is, the number that generates the maximum total net gain or profit. In this chapter and in Chapter 9, we will show how marginal analysis can be used to understand the output decisions that lie behind the supply curve. The first step in this analysis is to show how the relationship between a firm's inputs and its output—its *production function*—determines its *cost curves*, the relationship between cost and quantity of output produced. That is what we do in this chapter. In Chapter 9, we will see how to go from the firm's cost curves to the supply curve.

The Production Function

A *firm* is an organization that produces goods or services for sale. To do this, it must transform inputs into output. The quantity of output a firm produces depends on the quantity of inputs; this relationship is known as the firm's **production function**. As we'll see, a firm's production function underlies its *cost curves*. But as a first step, let's look at the characteristics of a hypothetical production function.

Inputs and Output

To understand the concept of a production function, let's consider a farm that we assume, for the sake of simplicity, produces only one output, wheat, and uses only two inputs, land and labor. This particular farm is owned by a couple named George and Martha. They hire workers to do the actual physical labor on the farm. Moreover, we will assume that all potential workers are of the same quality—they are all equally knowledgeable and capable of performing farmwork.

George and Martha's farm sits on 10 acres of land; no more acres are available to them, and they are currently unable to either increase or decrease the size of their farm by selling, buying, or leasing acreage. Land here is what economists call a **fixed input**—an input whose quantity is fixed and cannot be varied. On the other hand, George and Martha are free to decide how many workers to hire. The labor provided by these workers is called a **variable input**—an input whose quantity the firm can vary. (In Chapter 7, when we considered the example of Felix's Lawn-Mowing Service, Felix's fixed input was his lawn mower and his variable input was his own labor.)

In reality, whether or not the quantity of an input is really fixed depends on the time horizon. In the **long run**—that is, given that a long enough period of time has elapsed—firms can adjust the quantity of any input. So there are no fixed inputs in the long run, only in the **short run**. Later in this chapter we'll look more carefully at the distinction between the short run and the long run. But for now, we will restrict our attention to the short run and assume that at least one input is fixed.

George and Martha know that the quantity of wheat they produce depends on the number of workers they hire. Given modern farming techniques, one worker can cultivate the 10-acre farm, albeit not very intensively. When an additional worker is added, the land is divided equally among all the workers: each worker has 5 acres to cultivate when 2 workers are employed, each cultivates 3⅓ acres when 3 are employed, and so on. So as additional workers are employed, the 10 acres of land are cultivated more intensively and more bushels of wheat are produced. The relationship between the quantity of labor and the quantity of output, for a given amount of the fixed input, constitutes the farm's production function. The production function for George and Martha's farm is given in the first two columns of the table in Figure 8-1; the diagram there shows the same information graphically. The curve in Figure 8-1 shows how the quantity of output depends on the quantity of the variable input, for a given quantity of the fixed input; it is called the farm's **total product curve**. The physical quantity of output, bushels of wheat, is measured on the vertical axis, while the quantity of the

A **production function** is the relationship between the quantity of inputs a firm uses and the quantity of output it produces.

A **fixed input** is an input whose quantity is fixed and cannot be varied.

A **variable input** is an input whose quantity the firm can vary.

The **long run** is the time period in which all inputs can be varied.

The **short run** is the time period in which at least one input is fixed.

The **total product curve** shows how the quantity of output depends on the quantity of the variable input, for a given quantity of the fixed input.

Figure 8-1   Production Function and Total Product Curve for George and Martha's Farm

Quantity of labor L (workers)	Quantity of wheat Q (bushels)	Marginal product of labor $MPL = \Delta Q / \Delta L$ (bushels per worker)
0	0	
		19
1	19	
		17
2	36	
		15
3	51	
		13
4	64	
		11
5	75	
		9
6	84	
		7
7	91	
		5
8	96	

The table shows the production function, the relationship between the quantity of the variable input (labor, measured in number of workers) and the quantity of output (bushels of wheat) for a given quantity of the fixed input. It also calculates the marginal product of labor on George and Martha's farm. The total product curve shows the production function graphically. It slopes upward because more wheat is produced as more workers are employed. It also becomes flatter because the marginal product of labor declines as more and more workers are employed.

variable input, labor, that is, the number of workers employed, is measured on the horizontal axis. The total product curve here is upward sloping, reflecting the fact that more bushels of wheat are produced as more workers are employed.

Although the total product curve in Figure 8-1 slopes upward along its entire length, the slope isn't constant: as you move up the curve to the right, it flattens out. To understand this changing slope, look at the third column of the table in Figure 8-1, which shows the *change in the quantity of output* that is generated by adding one more worker. That is, it shows the **marginal product** of labor: the additional quantity of output from using one more unit of labor (that is, one more worker).

In this case, we have data at intervals of 1 worker—that is, we have information on the quantity of output when there are 3 workers, 4 workers, and so on. Sometimes data aren't available in increments of 1 unit—for example, you might have information only on the quantity of output when there are 40 workers and when there are 50 workers. In this case, you can use the following equation to figure out the marginal product of labor:

> The **marginal product** of an input is the additional quantity of output that is produced by using one more unit of that input.

$$\textbf{(8-1)} \quad \begin{array}{c}\text{Marginal} \\ \text{product} \\ \text{of labor}\end{array} = \frac{\text{Change in quantity of output}}{\text{Change in quantity of labor}} = \begin{array}{c}\text{Change in quantity of} \\ \text{output generated by one} \\ \text{additional unit of labor}\end{array}$$

or

$$MPL = \Delta Q / \Delta L$$

In this equation, Δ, the Greek uppercase delta, represents the change in a variable.

Now we can explain the significance of the slope of the total product curve: it is equal to the marginal product of labor. Remember from the Chapter 2 Appendix that the slope of a line is equal to "rise" over "run" (see page 44). This implies that the slope of the total product curve is the change in the quantity of output (the "rise") divided by the change in the quantity of labor (the "run"). And this, as we can see from Equation 8-1, is simply the marginal product of labor. So the fact that the marginal product of the first worker is 19 also means that the slope of the total product curve in going from 0 to 1 worker is 19. Similarly, the slope of the total product curve in going from 1 to 2 workers is the same as the marginal product of the second worker, 17, and so on.

In this example, the marginal product of labor steadily declines as more workers are hired—that is, each successive worker adds less to output than the previous worker. So as employment increases, the total product curve gets flatter.

Figure 8-2 shows how the marginal product of labor depends on the number of workers employed on the farm. The marginal product of labor, *MPL*, is measured on the vertical axis in units of physical output—bushels of wheat—produced per additional worker, and the number of workers employed is measured on the horizontal axis. You can see from the table in Figure 8-1 that if 5 workers are employed instead of 4, output rises from 64 to 75 bushels; so in this case the marginal product of labor is 11 bushels—the same number found in Figure 8-2. To indicate that 11 bushels is the marginal product when employment rises from 4 to 5, we place the point corresponding to that information halfway between 4 and 5 workers.

In this example the marginal product of labor falls as the number of workers increases. That is, there are *diminishing returns to labor* on George and Martha's farm. In general, there are **diminishing returns to an input** when an increase in the quantity of that input, holding the quantity of all other inputs fixed, reduces that input's marginal product.

There are **diminishing returns to an input** when an increase in the quantity of that input, holding the levels of all other inputs fixed, leads to a decline in the marginal product of that input.

To grasp why diminishing returns can occur, think about what happens as George and Martha add more and more workers, without increasing the number of acres. As the number of workers increases, the land is farmed more intensively and the number of bushels increases. But each additional worker is working with a smaller share of the 10 acres—the fixed input—than the previous worker. As a result, the additional

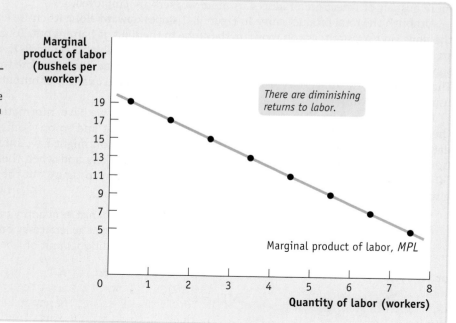

Figure 8-2

Marginal Product of Labor Curve for George and Martha's Farm

The marginal product of labor curve plots each worker's marginal product, the increase in the quantity of output generated by each additional worker. The change in the quantity of output is measured on the vertical axis and the number of workers employed on the horizontal axis. The first worker employed generates an increase in output of 19 bushels, the second worker generates an increase of 17 bushels, and so on. The curve slopes downward due to diminishing returns. **>web...**

Marginal product of labor (bushels per worker)

There are diminishing returns to labor.

Marginal product of labor, *MPL*

Quantity of labor (workers)

Figure 8-3   Total Product, Marginal Product, and the Fixed Input

This figure shows how the quantity of output—illustrated by the total product curve—and marginal product depend on the level of the fixed input. Panel (a) shows two total product curves for George and Martha's farm, TP_{10} when their farm is 10 acres and TP_{20} when it is 20 acres. With more land, each worker can produce more wheat. So an increase in the fixed input shifts the total product curve up from TP_{10} to TP_{20}. This

also implies that the marginal product of each worker is higher when the farm is 20 acres than when it is 10 acres. As a result, an increase in acreage also shifts the marginal product of labor curve up from MPL_{10} to MPL_{20}. Panel (b) shows the marginal product of labor curves. Note that both marginal product of labor curves still slope downward due to diminishing returns.

worker cannot produce as much output as the previous worker. So it's not surprising that the marginal product of the additional worker falls.

The crucial thing to emphasize about diminishing returns is that, like many propositions in economics, it is an "other things equal" proposition: each successive unit of an input will raise production by less than the last *if the quantity of all other inputs is held fixed.*

What would happen if the levels of other inputs were allowed to change? You can see the answer in Figure 8-3. Panel (a) shows two total product curves, TP_{10} and TP_{20}. TP_{10} is the farm's total product curve when its total area is 10 acres (the same curve as in Figure 8-1). TP_{20} is the total product curve when the farm has increased to 20 acres. Except when 0 workers are employed, TP_{20} lies everywhere above TP_{10} because with more acres available, any given number of workers produces more output. Panel (b) shows the corresponding marginal product of labor curves. MPL_{10} is the marginal product of labor curve given 10 acres to cultivate (the same curve as in Figure 8-2) and MPL_{20} is the marginal product of labor curve given 20 acres. Both curves slope downward because, in each case, the amount of land is fixed, albeit at different levels. But MPL_{20} lies everywhere above MPL_{10}, reflecting the fact that the marginal product of the same worker is higher when he or she has more of the fixed input to work with.

Figure 8-3 demonstrates a general result: the position of the total product curve depends on the quantities of other inputs. If you change the quantity of the other inputs, both the total product curve and the marginal product curve of the remaining input will shift. The importance of the "other things equal" assumption in discussing diminishing returns is illustrated in the following For Inquiring Minds.

PITFALLS

WHAT'S A UNIT?

The marginal product of labor (or any other input) is defined as the increase in the quantity of output when you increase the quantity of that input by one unit. But what do we mean by a "unit" of labor? Is it an additional hour of labor, an additional week, or a person-year?

The answer is that it doesn't matter, *as long as you are consistent.* One common source of error in economics is getting units confused—say, comparing the output added by an additional *hour* of labor with the cost of employing a worker for a *week.* Whatever units you use, always be careful that you use the same units throughout your analysis of any problem.

WAS MALTHUS RIGHT?

The idea of diminishing returns first became influential with the writings of Thomas Malthus, an English pastor whose 1798 book *An Essay on the Principle of Population* was deeply influential in its own time and continues to provoke heated argument to this day.

Malthus argued that as its population grew (while its land area remained fixed), a country would find it increasingly difficult to grow enough food. Though more intensive cultivation of the land could increase yields, each successive farmer would add less to the total than the last as the marginal product of labor declined. Eventually, food production per capita (the average output of an existing worker) would decline as the population exceeded some level.

He drew a powerful conclusion from this argument—namely, that misery was the normal condition of humankind. Imagine a country in which land was abundant and population low, so that everyone had plenty

to eat. Then families would, he argued, be large (as they were at the time in the United States, where land was abundant), and the population would grow rapidly—until the pressure of population on the land had reduced the condition of most people to a level where starvation and disease held the population in check. (It was arguments like these that led the historian Thomas Carlyle to dub economics the "dismal science").

Happily, Malthus's prediction has turned out to be quite wrong. The world's population has increased from about 1 billion people when Malthus wrote to more than 6 billion today, but in most of the world people eat better now than ever before. In England, in particular, a fivefold increase in population was accompanied by a dramatic rise in the standard of living.

So was Malthus completely wrong? And does the wrongness of his prediction refute the whole idea of diminishing returns? No, on both counts.

First of all, the Malthusian story actually works pretty well as a description of 57 out of the last 59 centuries: peasants in eighteenth-century France probably did not live much better than Egyptian peasants in the age of the pyramids. It just so happens that scientific and technological progress since the eighteenth century has been so rapid that it has far outpaced any problems caused by diminishing returns.

The concept of diminishing returns does not mean that using more labor to grow food, even on a given amount of land, will lead to a decline in the marginal product of labor—*if* there is also a radical improvement in farming technology. It does mean that the marginal product declines when *all* other things—land, farming technology, and a host of other factors—remain the same. And so the happy fact that Malthus's predictions were wrong does not invalidate the concept of diminishing returns.

From the Production Function to Cost Curves

Once George and Martha know their production function, they know the relationship between inputs of labor and land and output of wheat. But if they want to maximize their profits, they need to translate this knowledge into information about the relationship between the quantity of output and cost. Let's see how they can do this.

To translate information about a firm's production function into information about its cost, we need to know how much the firm must pay for its inputs. We will assume that George and Martha face either an explicit or an implicit cost of $400 for the use of the land. As we learned in Chapter 7, it is irrelevant whether George and Martha must rent the land for $400 from someone else, or they own the land themselves and forgo earning $400 by renting it to someone else. Either way, they pay an opportunity cost of $400 by using the land to grow wheat. Moreover, since the land is a fixed input, the $400 George and Martha pay for it is a **fixed cost**, denoted by *FC*—a cost that does not depend on the quantity of output produced. In business, fixed cost is often referred to as "overhead cost."

We also assume that George and Martha must pay each worker $200. Using their production function, George and Martha know that the number of workers they must hire depends on the amount of wheat they intend to produce. So the cost of labor, which is equal to the number of workers multiplied by $200, is a **variable cost**, denoted by *VC*—a cost that depends on the quantity of output produced. Adding the fixed cost and the variable cost of a given quantity of output gives the **total cost**, or *TC*, of that quantity of output. We can express the relationship among fixed cost, variable cost, and total cost as an equation:

A **fixed cost** is a cost that does not depend on the quantity of output produced. It is the cost of the fixed input.

A **variable cost** is a cost that depends on the quantity of output produced. It is the cost of the variable input.

The **total cost** of producing a given quantity of output is the sum of the fixed cost and the variable cost of producing that quantity of output.

(8-2)   Total cost = Fixed cost + Variable cost

or

$$TC = FC + VC$$

The table in Figure 8-4 shows how total cost is calculated for George and Martha's farm. The second column shows the number of workers employed. The third column shows the corresponding level of output, taken from the table in Figure 8-1. The fourth column shows the variable cost, equal to the number of workers multiplied by $200. The fifth column shows the fixed cost, which is $400 regardless of how many workers are employed. The sixth column shows the total cost of output, which is the variable cost plus the fixed cost.

The first column labels each row of the table with a letter, from *A* to *I*. These labels will be helpful in understanding our next step: drawing the **total cost curve**, a curve that shows how total cost depends on the quantity of output.

George and Martha's total cost curve is shown in the diagram in Figure 8-4, where the horizontal axis measures the quantity of output in bushels of wheat and the vertical

> The **total cost curve** shows how total cost depends on the quantity of output.

Figure 8-4

Total Cost Curve for George and Martha's Farm

The table shows the variable cost, fixed cost, and total cost for various output quantities on George and Martha's 10-acre farm. The total cost curve shows how total cost (measured on the vertical axis) depends on the quantity of output (measured on the horizontal axis). The labeled points on the curve correspond to the rows of the table. The total cost curve slopes upward because the number of workers employed, and hence total cost, increases as the quantity of output increases. The curve gets steeper as output increases due to diminishing returns to labor.

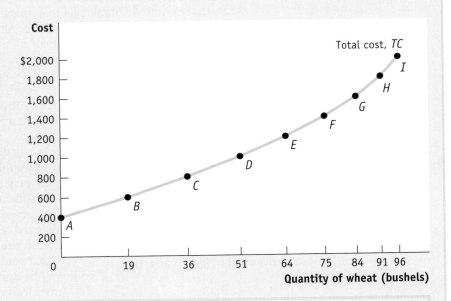

Point on graph	Quantity of labor L (workers)	Quantity of wheat Q (bushels)	Variable cost VC	Fixed cost FC	Total cost TC = FC + VC
A	0	0	$0	$400	$400
B	1	19	200	400	600
C	2	36	400	400	800
D	3	51	600	400	1,000
E	4	64	800	400	1,200
F	5	75	1,000	400	1,400
G	6	84	1,200	400	1,600
H	7	91	1,400	400	1,800
I	8	96	1,600	400	2,000

axis measures total cost in dollars. Each point on the curve corresponds to one row of the table in Figure 8-4. For example, point *A* shows the situation when 0 workers are employed: output is zero, and total cost is equal to fixed cost, $400. Similarly, point *B* shows the situation when 1 worker is employed: output is 19 bushels, and total cost is $600, equal to the sum of $400 in fixed cost and $200 in variable cost.

Like the total product curve, the total cost curve is upward sloping: due to the variable cost, the more output produced, the higher the farm's total cost. But unlike the total product curve, which gets flatter as employment rises, the total cost curve gets *steeper*. That is, the slope of the total cost curve is greater as the amount of output produced increases. And as we will soon see, the steepening of the total cost curve is also due to diminishing returns to the variable input. Before we can understand this, we must first look at the relationships among several useful measures of cost.

economics in action

The Mythical Man-Month

The concept of diminishing returns to an input was first formulated by economists during the late eighteenth century. These economists, notably including Thomas Malthus, drew their inspiration from agricultural examples; they noticed, in particular, that as an individual tried to employ more workers in agriculture, he or she was forced to cultivate poorer quality land. Although still valid, such examples can seem somewhat musty and old-fashioned in our modern information economy.

However, the idea of diminishing returns to an input applies with equal force to the most modern of economic activities—such as, say, the design of software. In 1975 Frederick P. Brooks Jr., a project manager at IBM during the days when it dominated the computer business, published a book titled *The Mythical Man-Month* that soon became a classic—so much so that a special anniversary edition was published 20 years later.

The chapter that gave its title to the book is basically about diminishing returns in the writing of software. Brooks observed that multiplying the number of programmers assigned to a project did not produce a proportionate reduction in the time it took to get the program written. A project that could be done by 1 programmer in 12 months could *not* be done by 12 programmers in 1 month—hence the "mythical man-month," the false notion that the number of lines of programming code produced was proportional to the number of code writers employed. In fact, above a certain number, adding another programmer on a project actually *increased* the time to completion.

The argument of *The Mythical Man-Month* is summarized in Figure 8-5. The upper part of the figure shows how the quantity of the project's output, as measured by the number of lines of code produced per month, varies with the number of programmers. Each additional programmer accomplishes less than the previous one, and beyond a certain point an additional programmer is actually counterproductive. The lower part of the figure shows the marginal product of each successive programmer, which falls as more programmers are employed and eventually becomes negative. In other words, programming is subject to diminishing returns so severe that at some point more programmers

Figure 8-5 **The Mythical Man-Month**

Beyond a certain point, an additional programmer is counterproductive.

TP

MPL

Beyond a certain point, adding an additional programmer is counterproductive—output falls and the slope of the total product curve becomes negative. At this point the marginal product of labor curve crosses the horizontal axis—and the marginal product of labor becomes negative.

actually have negative marginal product. The source of the diminishing returns lies in the nature of the production function for a programming project: each programmer must coordinate his or her work with that of all the other programmers on the project, leading to each person spending more and more time communicating with others as the number of programmers increases. In other words, other things equal, there are diminishing returns to labor. It is likely, however, that if fixed inputs devoted to programming projects are increased—say, installing a faster e-mail system—the problem of diminishing returns for additional programmers can be mitigated.

A reviewer of the reissued edition of *The Mythical Man-Month* summarized the reasons for these diminishing returns: "There is an inescapable overhead to yoking up programmers in parallel. The members of the team must 'waste time' attending meetings, drafting project plans, exchanging e-mail, negotiating interfaces, enduring performance reviews, and so on . . . At Microsoft, there will be at least one team member that just designs T-shirts for the rest of the team to wear." (from www.ercb.com, Dr. Dobb's Electronic Review of Computer Books.) ■

> > > > > > > > > > > > > > > > > > >

>>QUICK REVIEW

➤ The firm's *production function* is the relationship between quantity of inputs and output. The *total product curve* shows how the quantity of output depends upon the quantity of the *variable input* for a given quantity of the *fixed input*, and its slope is equal to the *marginal product* of the variable input. In the *short run*, the fixed input cannot be varied; in the *long run* all inputs are variable.

➤ When the levels of all other inputs are fixed, *diminishing returns to an input* may arise, yielding a downward sloping marginal product curve and a total product curve that becomes flatter as more output is produced.

➤ The *total cost* of a given quantity of output equals the *fixed cost* plus the *variable cost* of that output. The *total cost curve* becomes steeper as more output is produced due to diminishing returns.

>>CHECK YOUR UNDERSTANDING 8-1

1. Bernie's ice-making company produces ice cubes using a 10-ton machine and electricity. The quantity of output, measured in terms of pounds of ice, is given in this table:

Quantity of electricity (kilowatts)	Quantity of ice (pounds)
0	0
1	1,000
2	1,800
3	2,400
4	2,800

a. What is the fixed input? What is the variable input?
b. Construct a table showing the marginal product of the variable input. Does it show diminishing returns?
c. Suppose a 50 percent increase in the size of the fixed input increases output by 100 percent for any given amount of the variable input. What is the fixed input now? Construct a table showing the quantity of output and marginal product in this case.

Solutions appear at back of book.

Two Key Concepts: Marginal Cost and Average Cost

We've just seen how to derive a firm's total cost curve from its production function. Our next step is to take a deeper look at total cost by deriving two extremely useful measures: *marginal cost* and *average cost*. As we'll see, these two measures of the cost of production have a somewhat surprising relationship to each other. Moreover, they will prove to be vitally important in Chapter 9, where we will use them to analyze the firm's output decision and the market supply curve.

Marginal Cost

We defined marginal cost in Chapter 7: it is the change in total cost generated by producing one more unit of output. We've already seen that marginal product is easiest to calculate if data on output are available in increments of one unit of input. Similarly, marginal cost is easiest to calculate if data on total cost are available in increments of one unit of output. When the data come in less convenient increments, it's still possible to calculate marginal cost over each interval. But for the sake of simplicity, let's work with an example in which the data come in convenient increments.

Ben's Boots produces leather footwear; Table 8-1 shows how its costs per day depend on the number of boots it produces per day. The firm has fixed cost of $108 per day, shown in the second column, which represents the daily cost of its boot-making machine. The third column shows the variable cost, and the fourth column shows the total cost. Panel (a) of Figure 8-6 plots the total cost curve. Like the total cost curve for George and Martha's farm in Figure 8-4, this curve is upward sloping, getting steeper as you move up it to the right.

The significance of the slope of the total cost curve is shown by the fifth column of Table 8-1, which calculates *marginal cost*: the cost of each additional unit. The general formula for marginal cost is

(8-3) $\text{Marginal cost} = \dfrac{\text{Change in total cost}}{\text{Change in quantity of output}} = \begin{array}{c}\text{Change in total cost}\\ \text{generated by one}\\ \text{additional unit of}\\ \text{output}\end{array}$

or

$$MC = \Delta TC/\Delta Q$$

As in the case of marginal product, marginal cost is equal to "rise" (the increase in total cost) divided by "run" (the increase in the quantity of output). So just as marginal product is equal to the slope of the total product curve, marginal cost is equal to the slope of the total cost curve.

Now we can understand why the total cost curve gets steeper as we move up it to the right: as you can see in Table 8-1, the marginal cost at Ben's Boots rises as output increases. Panel (b) of Figure 8-6 shows the *marginal cost curve* corresponding to the data in Table 8-1. Notice that, as in Figure 8-2, we plot the marginal cost for increasing output from 0 to 1 pair of boots halfway between 0 and 1, the marginal cost for increasing output from 1 to 2 pairs of boots halfway between 1 and 2, and so on.

Why is the marginal cost curve upward sloping? Because there are diminishing returns to inputs in this example. As output increases, the marginal product of the

TABLE 8-1

Costs at Ben's Boots

Quantity of boots Q (pairs)	Fixed cost FC	Variable cost VC	Total cost TC = FC + VC	Marginal cost of pair MC = ΔTC/ΔQ
0	$108	$0	$108	
				$12
1	108	12	120	
				36
2	108	48	156	
				60
3	108	108	216	
				84
4	108	192	300	
				108
5	108	300	408	
				132
6	108	432	540	
				156
7	108	588	696	
				180
8	108	768	876	
				204
9	108	972	1,080	
				228
10	108	1,200	1,308	

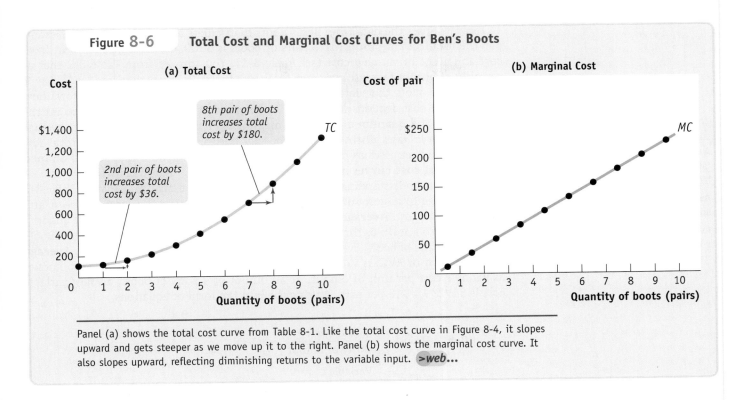

Figure 8-6   Total Cost and Marginal Cost Curves for Ben's Boots

(a) Total Cost

8th pair of boots increases total cost by $180.

2nd pair of boots increases total cost by $36.

TC

(b) Marginal Cost

MC

Panel (a) shows the total cost curve from Table 8-1. Like the total cost curve in Figure 8-4, it slopes upward and gets steeper as we move up it to the right. Panel (b) shows the marginal cost curve. It also slopes upward, reflecting diminishing returns to the variable input. **>web...**

variable input declines. This implies that more and more of the variable input must be used to produce each additional unit of output as the amount of output already produced rises. And since each unit of the variable input must be paid for, the cost per additional unit of output also rises.

In addition, recall that the flattening of the total product curve is also due to diminishing returns to inputs in production: the marginal product of an input falls as more of that input is used if the quantities of other inputs are fixed. The flattening of the total product curve as output increases and the steepening of the total cost curve as output increases are just flip-sides of the same phenomenon. That is, as output increases, the marginal cost of output also increases because the marginal product of the variable input is falling.

We will return to marginal cost in Chapter 9, when we consider the firm's profit-maximizing output decision. But our next step is to introduce another measure of cost: *average cost*.

Average Cost

In addition to total cost and marginal cost, it's useful to calculate one more measure, **average total cost**, often simply called **average cost**. The average total cost is total cost divided by the quantity of output produced; that is, it is equal to total cost per unit of output. If we let *ATC* denote average total cost, the equation looks like this:

Average total cost, often referred to simply as **average cost**, is total cost divided by quantity of output produced.

$$\textbf{(8-4)} \quad ATC = \frac{\text{Total cost}}{\text{Quantity of output}} = TC/Q$$

Average total cost is important because it tells the producer how much the *average* or *typical* unit of output costs to produce. Marginal cost, meanwhile, tells the producer how much *one more* unit of output costs to produce. Although they may look very similar, these two measures of cost typically differ. And confusion between them is a major source of error in economics, both in the classroom and in real life, as illustrated by Economics in Action on page 196.

Table 8-2 uses the data from Ben's Boots to calculate average total cost. For example, the total cost of producing 4 pairs of boots is $300, consisting of $108 in fixed cost and $192 in variable cost (see Table 8-1). You can see from Table 8-2 that as quantity of output increases, average total cost first falls, then rises.

Figure 8-7 plots that data to yield the *average total cost curve*, which shows how average total cost depends on output. As before, cost in dollars is measured on the vertical axis and quantity of output is measured on the horizontal axis. The average total cost curve has a distinctive U shape that corresponds to how average total cost first falls and then rises as output increases. Economists believe that such **U-shaped average total cost curves** are the norm for producers in many industries.

To help our understanding of why the average total cost curve is U-shaped, Table 8-2 breaks average total cost into its two underlying components, *average fixed cost* and *average variable cost*. **Average fixed cost**, or AFC, is fixed cost divided by the quantity of output, also known as the fixed cost per unit of output. For example, if Ben's Boots produces 4 pairs of boots, average fixed cost is $108/4 = $27 per pair of boots. **Average variable cost**, or AVC, is variable cost divided by the quantity of output, also known as variable cost per unit of output. At an output of 4 pairs of boots, average variable cost is $192/4 = $48 per pair. Writing these in the form of equations,

> A **U-shaped average total cost curve** falls at low levels of output, then rises at higher levels.
>
> **Average fixed cost** is the fixed cost per unit of output.
>
> **Average variable cost** is the variable cost per unit of output.

$$(8\text{-}5) \quad AFC = \frac{\text{Fixed cost}}{\text{Quantity of output}} = FC/Q$$

$$AVC = \frac{\text{Variable cost}}{\text{Quantity of output}} = VC/Q$$

Average total cost is the sum of average fixed cost and average variable cost; it has a U shape because these components move in opposite directions as output rises.

Average fixed cost falls as more output is produced because the numerator (the fixed cost) is a fixed number but the denominator (the quantity of output) increases as more is produced. Another way to think about this relationship is that, as more output is produced, the fixed cost is spread over more units of output; the end result is that the fixed cost *per unit of output*—the average fixed cost—falls. You can see this effect in the fourth column of Table 8-2: average fixed cost drops continuously as output increases.

TABLE 8-2

Average Costs for Ben's Boots

Quantity of boots Q (pairs)	Total cost TC	Average total cost of pair $ATC = TC/Q$	Average fixed cost of pair $AFC = FC/Q$	Average variable cost of pair $AVC = VC/Q$
1	$120	$120.00	$108.00	$12.00
2	156	78.00	54.00	24.00
3	216	72.00	36.00	36.00
4	300	75.00	27.00	48.00
5	408	81.60	21.60	60.00
6	540	90.00	18.00	72.00
7	696	99.43	15.43	84.00
8	876	109.50	13.50	96.00
9	1,080	120.00	12.00	108.00
10	1,308	130.80	10.80	120.00

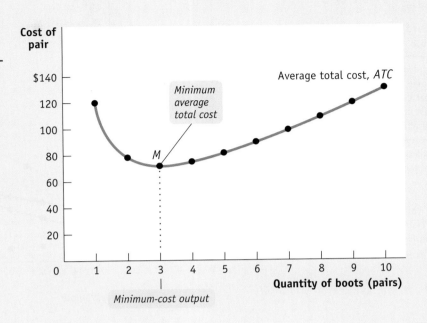

Figure 8-7

Average Total Cost Curve for Ben's Boots

The average total cost curve at Ben's Boots is U-shaped. At low levels of output, average total cost falls because the "spreading effect" of falling average fixed cost dominates the "diminishing returns effect" of rising average variable cost. At higher levels of output, the opposite is true and average total cost rises. At point *M*, corresponding to an output of three pairs of boots per day, average total cost is at its minimum level, the minimum average total cost. **>web...**

Cost of pair

Average total cost, *ATC*

Minimum average total cost

M

Minimum-cost output

Quantity of boots (pairs)

Average variable cost, however, rises as output increases. As we've seen, this reflects diminishing returns to the variable input: each additional unit of output incurs more variable cost to produce than the previous unit. So variable cost rises at a faster rate than the quantity of output increases.

Increasing output, therefore, has two opposing effects on average total cost—the "spreading effect" and the "diminishing returns effect":

- The spreading effect: the larger the output, the more production that can "share" the fixed cost, and therefore the lower the average fixed cost.

- The diminishing returns effect: the more output produced, the more variable input it requires to produce additional units, and therefore the higher the average variable cost.

At low levels of output, the spreading effect is very powerful because even small increases in output cause large reductions in average fixed cost. So at low levels of output, the spreading effect dominates the diminishing returns effect and causes the average total cost curve to slope downward. But when output is large, average fixed cost is already quite small, so increasing output further has only a very small spreading effect. Diminishing returns, on the other hand, usually grow increasingly important as output rises. As a result, when output is large, the diminishing returns effect dominates the spreading effect, causing the average total cost curve to slope upward. At the bottom of the U-shaped average total cost curve, point *M* in Figure 8-7, the two effects exactly balance each other. At this point average total cost is at its minimum level, the minimum average total cost.

Figure 8-8 on page 194 brings together in a single picture four members of the family of cost curves that we have derived from the total cost curve: the marginal cost curve (*MC*), the average total cost curve (*ATC*), the average variable cost curve (*AVC*), and the average fixed cost curve (*AFC*). All are based on the information in Tables 8-1 and 8-2. As before, cost is measured on the vertical axis and the quantity of output is measured on the horizontal axis.

Let's take a moment to note some features of the various cost curves. First of all, marginal cost is upward sloping—the result of diminishing returns that make an additional unit of output more costly to produce than the one before. Average variable cost

Figure 8-8

Marginal Cost and Average Cost Curves for Ben's Boots

Here we have the family of cost curves for Ben's Boots: the marginal cost curve (*MC*), the average total cost curve (*ATC*), the average variable cost curve (*AVC*), and the average fixed cost curve (*AFC*). Note that the average total cost curve is U-shaped and the marginal cost curve crosses the average total cost curve at the bottom of the U, point *M*, corresponding to the minimum average total cost from Table 8-2 and Figure 8-7. **>web...**

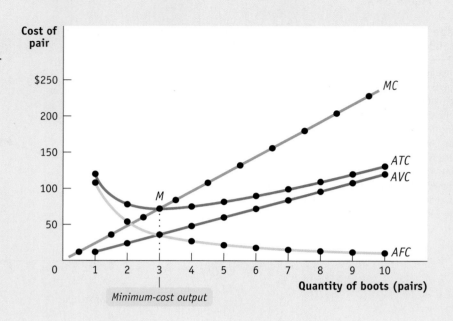

also is upward sloping—again, due to diminishing returns—but is flatter than the marginal cost curve. This is because the higher cost of an additional unit of output is averaged across all units, not just the additional units, in the average variable cost measure. Meanwhile, average fixed cost is downward sloping because of the spreading effect.

Finally, notice that the marginal cost curve intersects the average total cost curve from below, crossing it at its lowest point, point *M* in Figure 8-8. This last feature is our next subject of study.

Minimum Average Total Cost

For a U-shaped average total cost curve, average total cost is at its minimum level at the bottom of the U. Economists call the quantity that corresponds to the minimum average total cost the **minimum-cost output.** In the case of Ben's Boots, the minimum-cost output is three pairs of boots per day.

In Figure 8-8, the bottom of the U is at the level of output at which the marginal cost curve crosses the average total cost curve from below. Is this an accident? No—it reflects general principles that are always true about a firm's marginal cost and average total cost curves:

The **minimum-cost output** is the quantity of output at which average total cost is lowest—the bottom of the U-shaped average total cost curve.

- At the minimum-cost output, average total cost *is equal to* marginal cost.
- At output less than the minimum-cost output, marginal cost *is less than* average total cost and average total cost is falling.
- And at output greater than the minimum-cost output, marginal cost *is greater than* average total cost and average total cost is rising.

To understand this principle, think about how your grade in one course—say, a 3.0 in physics—affects your overall grade point average. If your GPA before receiving that grade was more than 3.0, the new grade lowers your average.

Similarly, if marginal cost—the cost of producing one more unit—is less than average total cost, producing that extra unit lowers average total cost. This is shown in Figure 8-9 by the movement from A_1 to A_2. In this case, the marginal cost of producing an additional unit of output is low, as indicated by the point MC_L on the marginal cost curve. And when the cost of producing the next unit of output is less

Figure 8-9

The Relationship Between the Average Total Cost and the Marginal Cost Curves

To see why the marginal cost curve (*MC*) must cut through the average total cost curve at the minimum average total cost (point *M*), corresponding to the minimum-cost output, we look at what happens if marginal cost is different from average total cost. If marginal cost is *less* than average total cost, an increase in output must reduce average total cost, as in the movement from A_1 to A_2. If marginal cost is *greater* than average total cost, an increase in output must increase average total cost, as in the movement from B_1 to B_2.

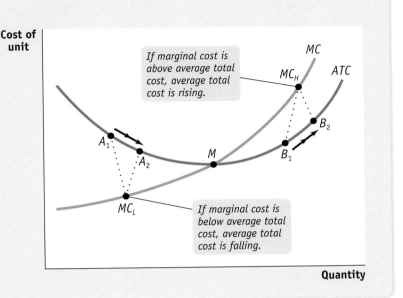

than average total cost, increasing production reduces average total cost. So any quantity of output at which marginal cost is less than average total cost must be on the downward-sloping segment of the U.

But if your grade in physics is more than the average of your previous grades, this new grade raises your GPA. Similarly, if marginal cost is greater than average total cost, producing that extra unit raises average total cost. This is illustrated by the move from B_1 to B_2 in Figure 8-9, where the marginal cost, MC_H, is higher than average total cost. So any quantity of output at which marginal cost is greater than average total cost must be on the upward-sloping segment of the U.

Finally, if a new grade is exactly equal to your previous GPA, the additional grade neither raises nor lowers that average—it stays the same. This corresponds to point *M* in Figure 8-9: when marginal cost equals average total cost, we must be at the bottom of the U, because only at that point is average total cost neither falling nor rising.

Does the Marginal Cost Curve Always Slope Upward?

Up to this point, we have emphasized the importance of diminishing returns, which lead to a marginal product curve that is always downward sloping and a marginal cost curve that is always upward sloping. In practice, however, economists believe that marginal cost curves often slope *downward* as a firm increases its production from zero up to some low level, sloping upward only at higher levels of production: they look like the curve *MC* in Figure 8-10 on page 196.

This initial downward slope occurs because a firm that employs only a few workers often cannot reap the benefits of specialization of labor. For example, one individual producing boots would have to perform all the tasks involved: making soles, shaping the upper part, sewing the pieces together, and so on. As more workers are employed, they can divide the tasks, with each worker specializing in one or a few aspects of boot-making. This specialization can lead to *increasing* returns at first, and so to a downward-sloping marginal cost curve. Once there are enough workers to permit specialization, however, diminishing returns set in. So typical marginal cost curves actually have the "swoosh" shape shown by *MC* in Figure 8-10. For the same reason, average variable cost curves typically look like *AVC* in Figure 8-10: they are U-shaped rather than strictly upward sloping.

Figure 8-10

More Realistic Cost Curves

In practice, the marginal cost curve often begins with a section that slopes downward. As output rises from a low level, a firm is capable of engaging in specialization and division of labor, which leads to increasing returns. At higher levels of output, however, diminishing returns lead to upward-sloping marginal cost. When marginal cost has a downward-sloping section, average variable cost is U-shaped. However, the basic results—U-shaped average total cost, and marginal cost that cuts through the minimum average total cost—remain the same. **>web...**

However, as Figure 8-10 also shows, the key features we saw from the example of Ben's Boots remain true: the average total cost curve is U-shaped, and the marginal cost curve passes through the point of minimum average total cost as well as through the point of minimum average variable cost.

economics in action

The Cost of Power

One of the great resources of the western United States is the availability of suitable sites for producing hydroelectric power: electricity generated by the force of water penned up behind a dam. When conditions are right—basically, when a large river runs through a deep but narrow valley—hydroelectric power can be much cheaper than electricity generated using fossil fuels, such as coal, or nuclear power. The western states, although they contain less than one-sixth of America's population, have more than half of the country's hydroelectric generating capacity. This advantage in cheap power has helped them attract industries, such as aluminum smelting, that are heavy users of electricity.

Is it a good idea for the governments of these western states to encourage more industries that make heavy use of electricity to move into their jurisdictions? Until the 1980s, most politicians and business leaders thought so, and many energy-intensive industries did in fact move into the region. But then, to the surprise and anger of consumers, western power companies began demanding higher prices, saying that they were no longer able to cover their costs at the old rates. What went wrong?

The answer is that officials had confused the *average total cost* of producing electricity with its *marginal cost*. Because of this confusion, they underestimated the cost of providing electricity to the new industries moving into their states.

The average total cost of producing power using existing facilities in the West is low, because much of it comes from hydroelectric power. But the marginal cost of providing additional power capacity is high, because it has become increasingly difficult to add new dams—most of the good sites have already been taken, and environmental considerations rule out many of the remaining sites. So when new energy-using businesses move to the West, to satisfy the new demand power

Confusing marginal cost and average total cost proved a very costly mistake for the company that built this dam and its customers.

companies must build expensive new power plants that run on fossil fuels or nuclear energy. So the marginal cost of electricity is much higher than the average total cost.

But electricity is a regulated industry (something we'll discuss in Chapter 14), and the rates electricity companies charge consumers are generally set to reflect average total cost. This gives rise to a seemingly paradoxical effect: when a factory moves into a western state, it pays less for the electricity it consumes than the extra, or marginal, cost incurred by the utility company to provide that electricity—so to cover its higher average total cost, the power company must raise the rates it charges all consumers.

If public officials had understood the difference between average total cost and marginal cost, they might have avoided this trap—either by charging new electricity users higher rates or by discouraging new electricity-using businesses from moving to their states. ■

> > > > > > > > > > > > > > > > > > > >

>> CHECK YOUR UNDERSTANDING 8-2

1. Alicia's Apple Pies is a roadside business. Alicia must pay $9.00 in rent each day. In addition, it costs her $1.00 to produce the first pie of the day, and each subsequent pie costs 50% more to produce than the one before. For example, the second pie costs $1.00 × 1.5 = $1.50 to produce, and so on.
   a. Calculate Alicia's marginal cost, variable cost, average total cost, average variable cost, and average fixed cost as her daily pie output rises from 0 to 6. (*Hint:* The variable cost of two pies is just the marginal cost of the first, plus the marginal cost of the second pie, and so on.)
   b. Indicate the range of pies for which the spreading effect dominates and the range for which the diminishing returns effect dominates.
   c. What is Alicia's minimum-cost output? Explain why making one more pie lowers Alicia's average total cost when output is lower than the minimum-cost output. Similarly, explain why making one more pie raises Alicia's average total cost when output is greater than the minimum-cost output.

Solutions appear at back of book.

Short-Run versus Long-Run Costs

Up to this point, we have treated fixed cost as completely outside the control of a firm because we have focused on the short run. But as we noted earlier, all inputs are variable in the long run: this means that in the long run fixed cost may also be varied. In the long run, in other words, a firm's fixed cost becomes a variable it can choose. For example, given time, Ben's Boots can acquire additional boot-making machinery or dispose of some of its existing machinery. In this section, we will examine how a firm's costs behave in the short run and in the long run. We will also see that the firm will choose its fixed cost in the long run based on the level of output it expects to produce.

Let's begin by supposing that Ben's Boots is considering whether to acquire additional boot-making machines. Acquiring additional machinery will affect its total cost in two ways. First, the firm will have to either rent or buy the additional machinery; either way, that will mean higher fixed cost in the short run. Second, if the workers have more equipment, they will be more productive: fewer workers will be needed to produce any given output, so variable cost for any given output level will be reduced.

The table in Figure 8-11 on page 198 shows how acquiring an additional machine affects costs. In our original example, we assumed that Ben's Boots had a fixed cost of $108. The left half of the table shows variable cost as well as total cost and average total cost assuming a fixed cost of $108. The average total cost curve for this level of fixed cost is given by ATC_1 in Figure 8-11. Let's compare that to a situation in which the firm buys an additional boot-making machine, doubling its fixed cost to $216 but reducing its variable cost at any given level of output. The right half of the table shows the firm's variable cost, total cost, and average total cost with this higher level of fixed cost. The average total cost curve corresponding to $216 in fixed cost is given by ATC_2 in Figure 8-11.

Figure 8-11

Choosing the Level of Fixed Cost for Ben's Boots

There is a trade-off between higher fixed cost and lower variable cost for any given output level, and vice versa. ATC_1 is the average total cost curve corresponding to a fixed cost of $108; it leads to high variable cost. ATC_2 is the average total cost curve corresponding to a higher fixed cost of $216 but lower variable cost. At low output levels, fewer than 4 pairs of boots per day, ATC_1 lies below ATC_2: average total cost is lower with only $108 in fixed cost. But as output goes up, average total cost is lower with the higher amount of fixed cost, $216: at more than 4 pairs of boots per day, ATC_2 lies below ATC_1.

	Low fixed cost (FC = $108)			High fixed cost (FC = $216)		
Quantity of boots (pairs)	High variable cost	Total cost	Average total cost of pair ATC_1	Low variable cost	Total cost	Average total cost of pair ATC_2
1	$12	$120	$120.00	$6	$222	$222.00
2	48	156	78.00	24	240	120.00
3	108	216	72.00	54	270	90.00
4	192	300	75.00	96	312	78.00
5	300	408	81.60	150	366	73.20
6	432	540	90.00	216	432	72.00
7	588	696	99.40	294	510	72.90
8	768	876	109.50	384	600	75.00
9	972	1,080	120.00	486	702	78.00
10	1,200	1,308	130.80	600	816	81.60

From the figure you can see that when output is small, 4 pairs of boots per day or fewer, average total cost is smaller when Ben's Boots forgoes the additional machinery and maintains the lower fixed cost of $108: ATC_1 lies below ATC_2. For example, at 3 pairs of boots per day, average total cost is $72 without the additional machinery and $90 with the additional machinery. But as output increases beyond 4 pairs per day, the firm's average total cost is lower if it acquires the additional machinery, raising its fixed cost to $216. For example, at 9 pairs of boots per day, average total cost is $120 when fixed cost is $108, but only $78 when fixed cost is $216.

Why does average total cost change like this when fixed cost increases? When output is low, the increase in fixed cost from the additional machinery outweighs the reduction in variable cost from higher worker productivity—that is, there are too few units of output over which to spread the additional fixed cost. So if Ben's Boots plans to produce fewer than 4 pairs of boots per day, it would be better off to choose the lower level of fixed cost, $108, to achieve a lower average total cost of production. When planned output is high, however, it should acquire the additional machinery.

In general, for each output level there is some choice of fixed cost that minimizes the firm's average total cost for that output level. So when the firm has a desired output level that it expects to maintain over time, it should choose the level of fixed cost appropriate to that level—that is, the level of fixed cost that minimizes its average total cost.

Now that we are studying a situation in which fixed cost can change, we need to take time into account when discussing average total cost. All of the average cost curves we have considered until now are defined for a given level of fixed cost—that is, they are defined for the short run, the period of time over which fixed cost doesn't vary. To reinforce that distinction, for the rest of this chapter we will refer to these average total cost curves as "short-run average total cost curves."

For most firms, it is realistic to assume that there are many possible choices of fixed cost, not just two. This implies that for such a firm, many possible short-run average total cost curves will exist, each corresponding to a different choice of fixed cost and so giving rise to what is called a firm's "family" of short-run average total cost curves.

At any given time, a firm will find itself on one of its short-run cost curves, the one corresponding to its current level of fixed cost; a change in output will cause it to move along that curve. If the firm expects that change in output level to be long-standing, then it is likely that the firm's current level of fixed cost is no longer appropriate. Given sufficient time, it will want to adjust its fixed cost to a new level that minimizes average total cost for its new output level. For example, if Ben's Boots had been producing 2 pairs of boots per day with a fixed cost of $108 but found itself increasing its output to 8 pairs per day for the foreseeable future, then in the long run it should increase its fixed cost to a level that minimizes average total cost at the 8-pairs-per-day output level.

Suppose we do a thought experiment and calculate the lowest possible average total cost that can be achieved for each output level if the firm were to choose its fixed cost for each output level. Economists have given this thought experiment a name: the *long-run average total cost curve*. Specifically, the **long-run average total cost curve**, or *LRATC*, is the relationship between output and average total cost when fixed cost has been chosen to minimize average total cost *for each level of output*. If there are many possible choices of fixed cost, the long-run average total cost curve will have the familiar, smooth U shape, as shown by *LRATC* in Figure 8-12.

The **long-run average total cost curve** shows the relationship between output and average total cost when fixed cost has been chosen to minimize average total cost for each level of output.

Figure 8-12

Short-Run and Long-Run Average Total Cost Curves

If Ben's Boots has chosen the level of fixed cost that minimizes short-run average total cost at an output of six pairs of boots per day and actually ends up producing six pairs per day, it will be on *LRATC* at point *C*. But if it produces more or less, in the short run it will be on the short-run average total cost curve *ATC*$_6$ and not on *LRATC*. So if it produces only three pairs per day, its average total cost is shown by point *B*, not point *A*. If it produces nine pairs per day, its average total cost is shown by point *Y*, not point *X*. There are economies of scale when long-run average total cost declines as output increases, and there are diseconomies of scale when long-run average total cost increases as output increases.

We can now draw the distinction between the short run and the long run more fully. In the long run, when a producer has had time to choose the fixed cost appropriate for its desired level of output, that producer will be on some point on the long-run average total cost curve. But if the output level is altered, the firm will no longer be on its long-run average total cost curve and will instead be moving along its current short-run average total cost curve. It will not be on its long-run average total cost curve again until it readjusts its fixed cost for its new output level.

Figure 8-12 illustrates this point. The curve ATC_3 shows short-run average total cost if a boot producer has chosen the level of fixed cost that minimizes average total cost at an output of 3 pairs of boots per day. This is confirmed by the fact that at 3 pairs per day, ATC_3 touches $LRATC$, the long-run average total cost curve. Similarly, ATC_6 shows short-run average total cost if a boot producer has chosen the level of fixed cost that would minimize average total cost if its output is 6 pairs of boots per day. It touches $LRATC$ at 6 pairs per day. And ATC_9 shows short-run average total cost if a boot producer has chosen the level of fixed cost that would minimize average total cost if its output is 9 pairs of boots per day. It touches $LRATC$ at 9 pairs per day.

Suppose that the firm has initially chosen to be on ATC_6. If the firm actually produces 6 pairs of boots per day, it will be at point C on both its short-run and long-run average total cost curves. Suppose, however, that the firm ends up producing only 3 pairs of boots per day. In the short run, its average total cost is indicated by point B on ATC_6; it is no longer on $LRATC$. If the firm had known that it would be producing only 3 pairs per day, it would have been better off to reduce its fixed cost and achieve lower average total cost. That is, it would have been better off to choose the level of fixed cost corresponding to ATC_3. Then it would have found itself at point A on the long-run average total cost curve, which lies below point B.

Suppose, on the other hand, that the firm ends up producing 9 pairs of boots per day. In the short run its average total cost is indicated by point Y on ATC_6. But it would be better off to incur a higher fixed cost in order to reduce its variable cost and move to ATC_9. This would allow it to reach point X on the long-run average total cost curve, which lies below Y.

The distinction between short-run and long-run average total costs is extremely important in making sense of how real firms operate over time. A company that has to increase output suddenly to meet a surge in demand will typically find that in the short run its average total cost rises sharply because it is hard to get extra production out of the existing facilities. But given time to build new factories or add machinery, short-run average total cost falls.

Economies and Diseconomies of Scale

There are **economies of scale** when long-run average total cost declines as output increases.

There are **diseconomies of scale** when long-run average total cost increases as output increases.

There are **constant returns to scale** when long-run average total cost is constant as output increases.

Finally, what determines the shape of the long-run average total cost curve? The answer is that *scale*, the size of a firm's operations, is often an important determinant of its long-run average total cost of production. Firms that experience scale effects in production find that their long-run average total cost changes substantially depending on the quantity of output they produce. There are **economies of scale** when long-run average total cost declines as output increases. As you can see in Figure 8-12, Ben's Boots experiences economies of scale over output levels ranging from 0 to 6 pairs of boots—the output levels over which the long-run average total cost curve is declining. There are **diseconomies of scale** when long-run average total cost increases as output increases. For Ben's Boots, diseconomies of scale occur at output levels of 6 pairs of boots or more, the output levels over which its long-run average total cost curve is rising.

Although it is not shown in Figure 8-12, there is a third possible relationship between long-run average total cost and scale: firms experience **constant returns to scale** when long-run average total cost is constant as output increases. In this case, the firm's long-run average total cost curve is horizontal over the output levels for which there are constant returns to scale.

What explains these scale effects in production? The answer ultimately lies in the firm's technology of production. Economies of scale often arise from the increased *specialization* that larger output levels allow—a larger scale of operation means that individual workers can limit themselves to more specialized tasks, becoming more skilled and efficient at doing them. Another source of economies of scale is very large initial set-up cost; in some industries—such as auto manufacturing, electricity generating, or petroleum refining—a very large initial cost in the form of plant and equipment is necessary to produce any output. As we'll see in Chapter 14, where we study monopoly, economies of scale have very important implications for how firms and industries interact and behave.

Diseconomies of scale, on the other hand, typically arise in large firms due to problems of coordination and communication: as the firm grows in size, it becomes ever more difficult and therefore costly to communicate and organize its activities. While economies of scale induce firms to get larger, diseconomies of scale tend to limit their size. And when constant returns to scale exist, scale has no effect on a firm's long-run average total cost: it is the same regardless of whether the firm produces 1 unit or 100,000 units.

Summing Up Costs: The Short and Long of It

If a firm is to make the best decisions about how much to produce, it has to understand how its costs relate to the quantity of output it chooses to produce. Table 8-3 provides a quick summary of the concepts and measures of cost you have learned about.

TABLE 8-3

Concepts and Measures of Cost

	Measurement	Definition	Mathematical term
Short run	Fixed cost	Cost that does not depend on the quantity of output produced	FC
	Average fixed cost	Fixed cost per unit of output	$AFC = FC/Q$
Short run and long run	Variable cost	Cost that depends on the quantity of output produced	VC
	Average variable cost	Variable cost per unit of output	$AVC = VC/Q$
	Total cost	The sum of fixed cost (short-run) and variable cost	$TC = FC$ (short-run) $+ VC$
	Average total cost (average cost)	Total cost per unit of output	$ATC = TC/Q$
	Marginal cost	The change in total cost generated by producing one more unit of output	$MC = \Delta TC/\Delta Q$
Long run	Long-run average total cost	Average cost when fixed cost has been chosen to minimize total cost for each level of output	$LRATC$

economics in action

There's No Business Like Snow Business

Anyone who has lived both in a snowy city, like Chicago, and in a city that only occasionally experiences significant snowfall, like Washington, D.C., is aware of the differences in total cost that arise from making different choices about fixed cost.

In Washington, even a minor snowfall—say, an inch or two overnight—is enough to create chaos during the next morning's commute. The same snowfall in Chicago

A lesson in economies of scale: cities with higher average annual snowfall maintain larger snowplow fleets.

has hardly any effect at all. The reason is not that Washingtonians are wimps and Chicagoans are made of sterner stuff; it is that Washington, where it rarely snows, has only a fraction as many snowplows and other snow-clearing equipment as cities where heavy snow is a fact of life.

In this sense Washington and Chicago are like two producers who expect to produce different levels of output, where the "output" is snow removal. Washington, which rarely has significant snow, has chosen a low level of fixed cost in the form of snow-clearing equipment. This makes sense under normal circumstances but leaves the city unprepared when major snow does fall. Chicago, which knows that it will face lots of snow, chooses to accept the higher fixed cost that leaves it in a position to respond effectively. ■

< < < < < < < < < < < < < < < < < <

>>CHECK YOUR UNDERSTANDING 8-3

1. The accompanying table shows three possible combinations of fixed cost and average variable cost.
    a. For each of the three choices, calculate the average total cost of producing 12,000, 22,000, and 30,000 units. For each of these quantities, which choice results in the lowest average total cost?
    b. Suppose that the firm, which has historically produced 12,000 units, experiences a sharp, permanent increase in demand that leads it to produce 22,000 units. Explain how its average total cost will change in the short run and in the long run.

Choice	Fixed cost	Average variable cost
1	$8,000	$1.00
2	12,000	0.75
3	24,000	0.25

    c. Explain what the firm should do instead if it believes the change in demand is temporary.

2. In each of the following cases, explain what kind of scale effects you think the firm will experience and why.
    a. A telemarketing firm in which employees make sales calls using computers and telephones
    b. An interior design firm in which design projects are based on the expertise of the firm's owner
    c. A diamond-mining company

Solutions appear at back of book.

● A LOOK AHEAD ●

We've now seen how to use information about how a firm produces to analyze that firm's costs. Our next step is to go from our analysis of costs to an analysis of the supply curve. To understand the supply curve for a particular good, we will need to look both at how a profit-maximizing firm chooses its quantity of output and at how it decides whether to enter or exit the industry producing that good.

SUMMARY

1. The relationship between inputs and output is a producer's **production function.** In the **short run,** the quantity of a **fixed input** cannot be varied but the quantity of a **variable input** can. In the **long run,** the quantities of all inputs can be varied. For a given amount of fixed input, the **total product curve** shows how the quantity of output changes as the quantity of the variable input changes. We may also calculate the **marginal product** of an input, the increase in output from using one more unit of that input.

2. There are **diminishing returns to an input** when its marginal product declines as more of the input is used, holding the quantity of all other inputs fixed.

3. **Total cost,** represented by the **total cost curve,** is equal to the sum of **fixed cost,** which does not depend on output, and **variable cost**, which does depend on output. Due to diminishing returns, marginal cost, the increase in total cost generated by producing one more unit of output, normally increases as output increases.

4. **Average total cost** (also known as **average cost**), total cost divided by quantity of output, is the cost of the average unit of output while marginal cost is the cost of one more unit produced. Economists believe that **U-shaped average total cost curves** are typical, because average total cost consists of two parts: **average fixed cost,** which falls when output increases (the spreading effect) and **average variable cost,** which rises with output (the diminishing returns effect).

5. When average total cost is U-shaped, the bottom of the U is the level of output at which average total cost is minimized, the point of **minimum-cost output.** This is also the point at which the marginal cost curve crosses the average total cost curve from below. Due to gains from specialization, the marginal cost curve may slope downward initially before sloping upward, giving it a "swoosh" shape.

6. In the long run, a producer can change its fixed input and its level of fixed cost. By accepting higher fixed cost, a firm can lower its variable cost for any given output level, and vice versa. The **long-run average total cost curve** shows the relationship between output and average total cost when fixed cost has been chosen to minimize average total cost at each level of output. A firm moves along its short-run average total cost curve as it increases output, and returns to a point on both its short-run and long-run average total cost curves once it has adjusted fixed cost to its new output level.

7. As output increases, there are **economies of scale** if long-run average total cost declines; **diseconomies of scale** if it increases; and **constant returns to scale** if it remains constant. Scale effects depend on the technology of production.

KEY TERMS

Production function, p. 182
Fixed input, p. 182
Variable input, p. 182
Long run, p. 182
Short run, p. 182
Total product curve, p. 182
Marginal product, p. 183
Diminishing returns to an input, p. 184

Fixed cost, p. 186
Variable cost, p. 186
Total cost, p. 186
Total cost curve, p. 187
Average total cost, p. 191
Average cost, p. 191
U-shaped average total cost curve, p. 192

Average fixed cost, p. 192
Average variable cost, p. 192
Minimum-cost output, p. 194
Long-run average total cost curve, p. 199
Economies of scale, p. 200
Diseconomies of scale, p. 200
Constant returns to scale, p. 200

PROBLEMS

1. Marty's Frozen Yogurt is a small shop that sells cups of frozen yogurt in a university town. Marty owns three frozen-yogurt machines. His other inputs are refrigerators, frozen-yogurt mix, cups, sprinkle toppings, and, of course, workers. He estimates that his daily production function when he varies the number of workers employed (and at the same time, of course, yogurt mix, cups, and so on) is as shown in the accompanying table.

Quantity of labor (workers)	Quantity of frozen yogurt (cups)
0	0
1	110
2	200
3	270
4	300
5	320
6	330

   a. What are the fixed inputs and variable inputs in the production of cups of frozen yogurt?

   b. Draw the total product curve. Put the quantity of labor on the horizontal axis and the quantity of frozen yogurt on the vertical axis.

   c. What is the marginal product of the first worker? The second worker? The third worker? Why does marginal product decline as the number of workers increases?

2. The production function for Marty's Frozen Yogurt is given in Problem 1. Marty pays each of his workers $80 per day. The cost of his other variable inputs is $0.50 per cup of yogurt. His fixed cost is $100 per day.

   a. What is Marty's variable cost and total cost when he produces 110 cups of yogurt? 200 cups? Calculate variable and total cost for every level of output given in Problem 1.

   b. Draw Marty's variable cost curve. On the same diagram, draw his total cost curve.

   c. What is the marginal cost per cup for the first 110 cups of yogurt? For the next 90 cups? Calculate the marginal cost for all remaining levels of output.

3. The production function for Marty's Frozen Yogurt is given in Problem 1. The costs are given in Problem 2.

   a. For each of the given levels of output, calculate the average fixed cost (AFC), average variable cost (AVC), and average total cost (ATC) per cup of frozen yogurt.

b. On one diagram, draw the *AFC*, *AVC*, and *ATC* curves.

c. What principle explains why the *AFC* declines as output increases? What principle explains why the *AVC* increases as output increases? Explain your answers.

d. How many cups of frozen yogurt are produced when average total cost is minimized?

4. The accompanying table shows a car manufacturer's total cost of producing cars.

Quantity of cars	TC
0	$500,000
1	540,000
2	560,000
3	570,000
4	590,000
5	620,000
6	660,000
7	720,000
8	800,000
9	920,000
10	1,100,000

a. What is this manufacturer's fixed cost?

b. For each level of output, calculate the variable cost (*VC*). For each level of output except zero output, calculate the average variable cost (*AVC*), average total cost (*ATC*), and average fixed cost (*AFC*). What is the minimum-cost output?

c. For each level of output, calculate this manufacturer's marginal cost (*MC*).

d. On one diagram, draw the manufacturer's *AVC*, *ATC*, and *MC* curves.

5. Magnificent Blooms is a florist specializing in floral arrangements for weddings, graduations, and other events. Magnificent Blooms has a fixed cost associated with space and equipment of $100 per day. Each worker is paid $50 per day. The daily production function for Magnificent Blooms is shown in the accompanying table.

Quantity of labor (workers)	Quantity of floral arrangements
0	0
1	5
2	9
3	12
4	14
5	15

a. What is the marginal product, *MPL*, of the first, second, third, fourth, and fifth workers? What principle explains why the marginal product per worker declines as the number of workers employed increases?

b. What is the marginal cost (*MC*) of producing each of the first 5 floral arrangements? The sixth through ninth floral arrangements? The remaining levels of output? What principle explains why the marginal cost per floral arrangement increases as the number of arrangements increases?

6. You have the information shown in the accompanying table about a firm's costs. Complete the missing data.

Quantity	TC	MC	ATC	AVC
0	$20			
		$20		
1	?		?	?
		10		
2	?		?	?
		16		
3	?		?	?
		20		
4	?		?	?
		24		
5	?		?	?

7. Evaluate each of the following statements: If a statement is true, explain why; if it is false, identify the mistake and try to correct it.

a. A decreasing marginal product tells us that marginal cost must be rising.

b. An increase in fixed cost increases the minimum-cost output.

c. An increase in fixed cost increases marginal cost.

d. When marginal cost is above average total cost, average total cost must be falling.

8. Mark and Jeff operate a small company that produces souvenir footballs. Their fixed cost is $2,000 per month. They can hire workers for $1,000 per worker per month. Their monthly production function for footballs is as given in the accompanying table.

Quantity of labor (workers)	Quantity of footballs
0	0
1	300
2	800
3	1,200
4	1,400
5	1,500

a. For each quantity of labor, calculate average variable cost (*AVC*), average fixed cost (*AFC*), average total cost (*ATC*), and marginal cost (MC).

b. On one diagram, draw in the *AVC*, *ATC*, and *MC* curves.

c. At what level of output is Mark and Jeff's average total cost minimized?

9. You produce widgets. Currently you produce 4 widgets at a total cost of $40.

   a. What is your average total cost?

   b. Suppose you could produce one more (the fifth) widget at a marginal cost of $5. If you do produce that fifth widget, what will your average total cost be? Has your average total cost increased or decreased? Why?

   c. Suppose instead that you could produce one more (the fifth) widget at a marginal cost of $20. If you do produce that fifth widget, what will your average total cost be? Has your average total cost increased or decreased? Why?

10. In your economics class, each homework problem set is graded on the basis of a maximum score of 100. You have completed 9 out of 10 of the problem sets for the term, and your current average grade is 88. What range of grades for your 10th problem set will raise your overall average? What range will lower your overall average? Explain.

11. Don owns a small concrete-mixing company. His fixed cost is the cost of the concrete-batching machinery and his mixer trucks. His variable cost is the cost of the sand, gravel, and other inputs for producing concrete; the gas and maintenance for the machinery and trucks; and his workers. He is trying to decide how many mixer trucks to purchase. He has estimated the costs shown in the accompanying table based on estimates of the number of orders his company will receive per week.

Quantity of trucks	FC	VC 20 orders	VC 40 orders	VC 60 orders
2	$6,000	$2,000	$5,000	$12,000
3	7,000	1,800	3,800	10,800
4	8,000	1,200	3,600	8,400

   a. For each level of fixed cost, calculate Don's total cost for producing 20, 40, and 60 orders per week.

   b. If Don is producing 20 orders per week, how many trucks should he purchase and what will his average total cost be? Answer the same questions for 40 and 60 orders per week.

12. Consider Don's concrete-mixing business described in Problem 11. Suppose Don purchased 3 trucks, expecting to produce 40 orders per week.

   a. Suppose that, in the short run, business declines to 20 orders per week. What is Don's average total cost per order in the short run? What will his average total cost per order in the short run be if his business booms to 60 orders per week?

   b. What is Don's long-run average total cost for 20 orders per week? Explain why his short-run average total cost of producing 20 orders per week when the number of trucks is fixed at 3 is greater than his long-run average total cost of producing 20 orders per week.

   c. Sketch Don's long-run average total cost curve. Sketch his short-run average total cost curve if he owns 3 trucks.

13. True or False? Explain your reasoning.

   a. The short-run average total cost can never be less than the long-run average total cost.

   b. The short-run average variable cost can never be less than the long-run average total cost.

   c. In the long run, choosing a higher level of fixed cost shifts the long-run average total cost curve upward.

14. Wolfsburg Wagon (WW) is a small automaker. The accompanying table shows WW's long-run average total cost.

Quantity of cars	LRATC of car
1	$30,000
2	20,000
3	15,000
4	12,000
5	12,000
6	12,000
7	14,000
8	18,000

   a. For which levels of output does WW experience economies of scale?

   b. For which levels of output does WW experience diseconomies of scale?

   c. For which levels of output does WW experience constant returns to scale?

>**web**... To continue your study and review of concepts in this chapter, please visit the Krugman/Wells website for quizzes, animated graph tutorials, web links to helpful resources, and more.

www.worthpublishers.com/krugmanwells

>> Perfect Competition and the Supply Curve

DOING WHAT COMES NATURALLY

FOOD CONSUMERS IN THE UNITED States are concerned about health issues. Demand for "natural" foods and beverages, such as bottled water and organically grown fruits and vegetables, increased rapidly over the past decade. The small group of farmers who had pioneered organic farming techniques prospered thanks to higher prices.

But everyone knew that the high prices of organic produce were unlikely to persist even if the new, higher demand for naturally grown food continued: the supply of organic food, while not that price-elastic in the short run, was surely much more price-elastic in the long run. Over time, farms already producing organically would increase their capacity, and conventional farmers would enter the organic food business. So the increase in the quantity supplied in response to the increase in price would be much larger in the long run than in the short run.

Where does the supply curve come from? Why is there a difference between the short-run and the long-run supply curve? In this chapter we will use our understanding of costs, developed in Chapter 8, as the basis for an analysis of the supply curve. As we'll see, this will require that we understand the behavior both of individual firms and of an entire industry, composed of these many individual firms.

Our analysis in this chapter assumes that the industry in question is characterized by *perfect competition*. We begin by explaining the concept of perfect competition, providing a brief introduction to the conditions that give rise to a perfectly competitive industry. We then show how a producer under perfect competition decides how much to produce. Finally, we use the cost curves of the individual producers to derive the *industry supply curve* under perfect competition. By analyzing the way a competitive industry evolves over time, we will come to understand the distinction between the short-run and long-run effects of changes in demand on a competitive industry—such as, for example, the effect of America's new taste for organic food on the organic farming industry. We will conclude with a deeper discussion of the conditions necessary for perfect competition.

Whether it's organic strawberries or satellites, how a good is produced determines its cost of production.

Perfect Competition

Suppose that Yves and Zoe are neighboring farmers, both of whom grow organic tomatoes. Both sell their output to the same grocery store chains that carry organic foods; so, in a real sense, Yves and Zoe compete with each other.

Does this mean that Yves should try to stop Zoe from growing tomatoes or that Yves and Zoe should form an agreement to grow less? Almost certainly not: there are hundreds or thousands of organic tomato farmers, and Yves and Zoe are competing with all those other growers as well as with each other. Because so many farmers sell organic tomatoes, if any one of them produced more or less, there would be no measureable effect on market prices.

When people talk about business competition, the image they often have in mind is a situation in which two or three rival firms are intensely struggling for advantage. But economists know that when a business focuses on a few main competitors, it's actually a sign that competition is fairly limited. As the example of organic tomatoes suggests, when there is enough competition it doesn't even make sense to identify your opponents: there are so many competitors that you cannot single out any one of them as a rival.

We can put it another way: Yves and Zoe are **price-taking producers.** A producer is a price-taker when its actions cannot affect the market price of the good it sells. As a result, a price-taking producer considers the market price as given. When there is enough competition—when competition is what economists call "perfect"—then every producer is a price-taker. And there is a similar definition for consumers: a **price-taking consumer** is a consumer who cannot influence the market price of the good by his or her actions. That is, the market price is unaffected by how much or how little of the good the consumer buys.

> A **price-taking producer** is a producer whose actions have no effect on the market price of the good it sells.
>
> A **price-taking consumer** is a consumer whose actions have no effect on the market price of the good he or she buys.

Defining Perfect Competition

In a **perfectly competitive market**, all market participants, both consumers and producers, are price-takers. That is, neither consumption decisions by individual consumers nor production decisions by individual producers affect the market price of the good.

The supply and demand model, which we introduced in Chapter 3 and have used repeatedly since then, is a model of a perfectly competitive market. It depends fundamentally on the assumption that no individual buyer or seller of a good, such as scalped tickets to a hockey game or organic tomatoes, believes that he or she can affect the price at which he or she can sell or buy the good.

> A **perfectly competitive market** is a market in which all market participants are price-takers.

As a general rule, consumers are indeed price-takers. Instances in which consumers are able to affect the prices they pay are rare. It is, however, quite common for producers to have a significant ability to affect the prices they receive, a phenomenon we'll address in Chapter 14. So the model of perfect competition is appropriate for some but not all markets. An industry in which producers are price-takers is called a **perfectly competitive industry.** Clearly, some industries aren't perfectly competitive; in later chapters we'll see how to analyze industries that don't fit the perfectly competitive model.

> A **perfectly competitive industry** is an industry in which producers are price-takers.

Under what circumstances will all producers be price-takers? In the next section we will see that there are two necessary conditions for a perfectly competitive industry and that a third condition is often present as well.

Two Necessary Conditions for Perfect Competition

The markets for major grains, like wheat and corn, are perfectly competitive: individual wheat and corn farmers, as well as individual buyers of wheat and corn, take market prices as given. In contrast, the markets for some of the food items made from these grains—in particular, breakfast cereals—are by no means perfectly competitive. There is intense competition among cereal brands, but not *perfect* competition. To understand the difference between the market for wheat and the market for shredded wheat cereal is to understand the two necessary conditions for perfect competition.

First, for an industry to be perfectly competitive, it must contain many producers, none of whom have a large **market share**. A producer's market share is the fraction of the total industry output represented by that producer's output. The distribution of market share constitutes a major difference between the grain industry and the breakfast cereal industry. There are thousands of wheat farmers, none of whom account for more than a small fraction of 1 percent of total wheat sales. The breakfast cereal industry, however, is dominated by four producers: Kellogg's, General Mills, Post, and Quaker Foods. Kellogg's alone accounts for about one-third of all cereal sales. Kellogg's executives know that if they try to sell more corn flakes, they are likely to drive down the market price of corn flakes. That is, they know that their actions influence market prices, simply because they are so large a part of the market that changes in their production will significantly affect the overall quantity supplied. It makes sense to assume that producers are price-takers only when an industry does *not* contain any large players like Kellogg's.

Second, an industry can be perfectly competitive only if consumers regard the products of all producers as equivalent. This clearly isn't true in the breakfast cereal market: consumers don't consider Cap'n Crunch to be a good substitute for Wheaties. As a result, the maker of Wheaties has some ability to increase its price without fear that it will lose all its customers to the maker of Cap'n Crunch. Contrast this with the case of a **standardized product,** sometimes known as a **commodity.** Consumers regard the output of one wheat producer as a perfect substitute for that of another producer. Consequently, one farmer cannot increase the price for his or her wheat without losing all his or her sales to other wheat farmers. So the second necessary condition for a competitive industry is that the industry output is a standardized product.

> A producer's **market share** is the fraction of the total industry output represented by that producer's output.

> A good is a **standardized product**, also known as a **commodity**, when consumers regard the products of different producers as the same good.

FOR INQUIRING MINDS

WHAT'S A STANDARDIZED PRODUCT?

A perfectly competitive industry must produce a standardized product. But is it enough for the products of different firms actually to be the same? No: people must also *think* that they are the same. And producers often go to great lengths to convince consumers that they have a distinctive, or *differentiated*, product, even when they don't.

Consider, for example, champagne—not the superexpensive premium champagnes but the more ordinary stuff. Most people cannot tell the difference between champagne actually produced in the Champagne region of France, where the product originated, and similar products from Spain or California. But the French government has sought and obtained legal protection for the firms of Champagne, ensuring that around the world only bubbly wine from that region

In the end, only kimchi eaters can tell you if there is truly a difference between Korean-produced kimchi and the Japanese-produced variety.

AP/Wide World Photos

can be called champagne. If it's from someplace else, all the seller can do is say that it was produced by the *méthode Champenoise*. This creates a differentiation in the minds of consumers and lets the champagne producers of Champagne charge higher prices.

In a less Eurocentric example, Korean producers of *kimchi*, the spicy fermented cabbage that is the national side dish, are doing their best to convince consumers that the same product packaged by Japanese firms is just not the real thing. The purpose is, of course, to ensure higher prices for Korean *kimchi*.

So is an industry perfectly competitive if it sells products that are indistinguishable except in name but that consumers, for whatever reason, don't think are standardized? No. When it comes to defining the nature of competition, the consumer is always right.

Free Entry and Exit

All perfectly competitive industries have many producers with small market shares, producing a standardized product. Most perfectly competitive industries are also characterized by one more feature: it is easy for new firms to enter the industry or for firms that are currently in the industry to leave. That is, no obstacles in the form of government regulations or limited access to key resources prevent new producers from entering the market. And no additional costs are associated with shutting down a company and leaving the industry. Economists refer to the arrival of new firms into an industry as *entry*; they refer to the departure of firms from an industry as *exit*. When there are no obstacles to entry into or exit from an industry, we say that the industry has **free entry and exit.**

Free entry and exit is not strictly necessary for perfect competition. In Chapter 4 we described the case of New Jersey clam fishing, where regulations have the effect of limiting the number of fishing boats. Despite this, there are enough boats operating that the fishermen are price-takers. But free entry and exit is a key factor in most competitive industries. It ensures that the number of producers in an industry can adjust to changing market conditions. And, in particular, it ensures that producers in an industry cannot artificially keep other firms out.

There is **free entry and exit** into and from an industry when new producers can easily enter into or leave that industry.

To sum up, then, perfect competition depends on two necessary conditions. First, the industry must contain many producers, each having a small market share. Second, the industry must produce a standardized product. In addition, perfectly competitive industries are normally characterized by free entry and exit.

How does an industry that meets these three criteria behave? As a first step toward answering that question, let's look at how an individual producer in a perfectly competitive industry maximizes profit.

economics in action

The Pain of Competition

Sometimes it is possible to see an industry become perfectly competitive. In fact, it happens on a regular basis in the case of pharmaceuticals: the conditions for perfect competition are often met as soon as the patent on a popular drug expires.

When a company develops a new drug, it is usually able to receive a patent—a legal monopoly that gives it the exclusive right to sell that drug for 20 years from the date of filing. When the patent expires, the field is open for other companies to sell their own versions of the drug—marketed as "generics" and sold under the medical name of the drug rather than the brand name used by the original producer. Generics are standardized products, much like aspirin, and are often sold by many producers.

A good example came in 1984, when Upjohn's patent on ibuprofen—a painkiller that the company still markets under the brand name Motrin—expired. Most people who use ibuprofen, like most people who use aspirin, now purchase a generic version made by one of many producers.

The shift to perfect competition, not coincidentally, is accompanied by a sharp fall in market price. When its patent expired, Upjohn immediately cut the price of Motrin by 35 percent, but as more companies started selling the generic drug, the price of ibuprofen eventually fell by another two-thirds.

Ten years later the patent on the painkiller naproxen—sold under the brand name Naprosyn—expired. The generic version of naproxen was soon selling at only one-tenth of the original price of Naprosyn. ∎

> > > > > > > > > > > > > > > > > > >

▸▸ QUICK REVIEW

➤ Neither the actions of a *price-taking producer* nor those of a *price-taking consumer* can influence the market price of a good.

➤ In a *perfectly competitive market* all producers and consumers are price-takers. Consumers are almost always price-takers, but this is often not true of producers. An industry in which producers are price-takers is a *perfectly competitive industry*.

➤ A perfectly competitive industry contains many producers, each of which produces a *standardized product* (also known as a *commodity*) but none of which has a large *market share*.

➤ Most perfectly competitive industries are also characterized by *free entry and exit*.

>>CHECK YOUR UNDERSTANDING 9-1

1. In each of the following situations, do you think the industry described will be perfectly competitive or not? Explain your answer.
   a. There are two producers of aluminum in the world, a good sold in many places.
   b. Only a handful of companies produce natural gas from the North Sea. The price of natural gas is determined by global supply and demand, of which North Sea production represents a small share.
   c. Dozens of designers sell high-fashion clothes. Each designer has a distinctive style and a loyal clientele.
   d. There are many baseball teams in the United States, one or two in each major city, and each selling tickets to its events.

   Solutions appear at back of book.

Production and Profits

Consider Jennifer and Jason, who run an organic tomato farm. Suppose that the market price of organic tomatoes is $18 per bushel and that Jennifer and Jason are price-takers—they can sell as much as they like at that price. Then we can use the data in Table 9-1 to find their profit-maximizing level of output by direct calculation.

TABLE 9-1

Profit for Jennifer and Jason's Farm When Market Price Is $18

Quantity of tomatoes Q (bushels)	Total revenue TR	Total cost TC	Profit TR − TC
0	$0	$14	$−14
1	18	30	−12
2	36	36	0
3	54	44	10
4	72	56	16
5	90	72	18
6	108	92	16
7	126	116	10

The first column shows the quantity of output in bushels, and the second column shows Jennifer and Jason's total revenue from their output: the market value of their output. Total revenue, *TR*, is equal to the market price multiplied by the quantity of output:

(9-1) $TR = P \times Q$

In this example, total revenue is equal to $18 per bushel times the quantity of output in bushels.

The third column of Table 9-1 shows Jennifer and Jason's total cost. The fourth column of Table 9-1 shows their profit, equal to total revenue minus total cost:

(9-2) $\text{Profit} = TR - TC$

As indicated by the numbers in the table, profit is maximized at an output of 5 bushels, where profit is equal to $18. But we can gain more insight into the profit-maximizing choice of output by viewing it as a problem of marginal analysis, a task we'll do next.

Using Marginal Analysis to Choose the Profit-Maximizing Quantity of Output

Recall from Chapter 7 the *principle of marginal analysis:* the optimal amount of an activity is the level at which marginal benefit is equal to marginal cost. To apply this principle, consider the effect on a producer's profit of increasing output by 1 unit. The marginal benefit of that unit is the additional revenue generated by selling it; this measure has a name—it is called the **marginal revenue** of that output. The general formula for marginal revenue is:

Marginal revenue is the change in total revenue generated by an additional unit of output.

$$(9\text{-}3) \quad \text{Marginal revenue} = \frac{\text{Change in total revenue}}{\text{Change in output}} = \begin{array}{c}\text{Change in total revenue}\\\text{generated by one}\\\text{additional unit of output}\end{array}$$

or

$$MR = \Delta TR / \Delta Q$$

So Jennifer and Jason would maximize their profit by producing bushels up to the point at which the marginal revenue is equal to marginal cost. We can summarize this as the producer's **optimal output rule:** profit is maximized by producing the quantity at which the marginal revenue of the last unit produced is equal to its marginal cost. That is, $MR = MC$ at the optimal quantity of output.

We can learn how to apply the optimal output rule with the help of Table 9-2, which provides various short-run cost measures for Jennifer and Jason's farm. The second column contains the farm's variable cost, and the third column shows its total cost of output based on the assumption that the farm incurs a fixed cost of $14. The fourth column shows their marginal cost. Notice that, in this example, the marginal cost falls as output increases from a low level before rising, so that the marginal cost curve has the "swoosh" shape described in Chapter 8. (Shortly it will become clear that this shape has important implications for short-run production decisions.)

The **optimal output rule** says that profit is maximized by producing the quantity of output at which the marginal revenue of the last unit produced is equal to its marginal cost.

TABLE 9-2

Short-Run Costs for Jennifer and Jason's Farm

Quantity of tomatoes Q (bushels)	Variable cost VC	Total cost TC	Marginal cost of bushel $MC = \Delta TC/\Delta Q$	Marginal revenue of bushel	Net gain of bushel = $MR - MC$
0	$0	$14			
			$16	$18	$2
1	16	30			
			6	18	12
2	22	36			
			8	18	10
3	30	44			
			12	18	6
4	42	56			
			16	18	2
5	58	72			
			20	18	−2
6	78	92			
			24	18	−6
7	102	116			

The fifth column contains the farm's marginal revenue, which has an important feature: Jennifer and Jason's marginal revenue is constant at $18 for every output level. The sixth and final column of Table 9-2 shows the calculation of the net gain per bushel of tomatoes, which is equal to marginal revenue minus marginal cost— or, equivalently, market price minus marginal cost. As you can see, it is positive for the 1st through 5th bushels; producing each of these bushels raises Jennifer and Jason's profit. For the 6th and 7th bushels, however, net gain is negative: producing

WHAT IF MARGINAL REVENUE AND MARGINAL COST AREN'T EXACTLY EQUAL?

The optimal output rule says that to maximize profit, you should produce the quantity at which marginal revenue is equal to marginal cost. But what do you do if there is no output level at which marginal revenue equals marginal cost? In that case, you produce the largest quantity for which marginal revenue exceeds marginal cost. This is the case in Table 9-2 at an output of 5 bushels. The simpler version of the optimal output rule applies when production involves large numbers, such as hundreds or thousands of units. In such cases marginal cost comes in small increments, and there is always a level of output at which marginal cost almost exactly equals marginal revenue.

The **price-taking firm's optimal output rule** says that a price-taking firm's profit is maximized by producing the quantity of output at which the market price is equal to the marginal cost of the last unit produced.

The **marginal revenue curve** shows how marginal revenue varies as output varies.

them would decrease, not increase, profit. (You can verify this by examining Table 9-1.) So 5 bushels are Jennifer and Jason's profit-maximizing output; it is the level of output at which marginal cost is equal to the market price, $18.

This example, in fact, illustrates another general rule derived from marginal analysis—the **price-taking firm's optimal output rule,** which says that a price-taking firm's profit is maximized by producing the quantity of output at which the market price is equal to the marginal cost of the last unit produced. That is, $P = MC$ at the *price-taking firm's* optimal quantity of output. In fact, the price-taking firm's optimal output rule is just an application of the optimal output rule to the particular case of a price-taking firm. Why? Because in the case of a price-taking firm, *marginal revenue is equal to price.* A price-taking firm cannot influence the market price by its actions. It always takes the market price as given because it cannot lower the market price by selling more or raise the market price by selling less. So, for a price-taking firm, the additional revenue generated by producing one more unit is always the market price. We will need to keep this fact in mind in future chapters, where we will learn that marginal revenue is not equal to the market price if the industry is not perfectly competitive and, as a result, firms are not price-takers.

For the remainder of this chapter, we will assume that the firms in question are, like Jennifer and Jason's farm, perfectly competitive. Figure 9-1 shows that Jennifer and Jason's profit-maximizing quantity of output is, indeed, the number of bushels at which the marginal cost of production is equal to price. The figure shows the marginal cost curve, *MC*, drawn from the data in the last column of Table 9-1. As in Chapter 8, we plot the marginal cost of increasing output from 1 to 2 bushels halfway between 1 and 2, and so on. The horizontal line at $18 is Jennifer and Jason's **marginal revenue curve, MR.** Note that whenever a firm is a price-taker, its marginal revenue curve is a horizontal line at the market price: it can sell as much as it likes at the market price. Regardless of whether it sells more or less, the market price is unaffected. In effect, the individual firm faces a horizontal, perfectly elastic demand curve for its output—an individual demand curve for its output that is equivalent to

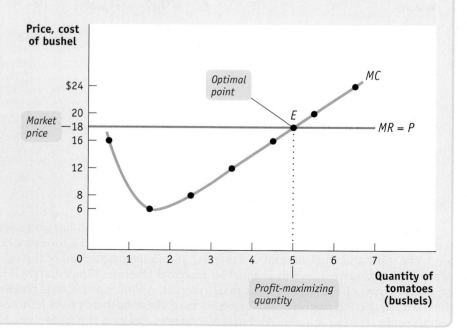

Figure 9-1

The Price-Taking Firm's Profit-Maximizing Quantity of Output

At the profit-maximizing quantity of output, the market price is equal to marginal cost. It is located at the point where the marginal cost curve crosses the marginal revenue curve, which is a horizontal line at the market price. Here, the profit-maximizing point is at an output of 5 bushels of tomatoes, the output quantity at point *E*.

its marginal revenue curve. The marginal cost curve crosses the marginal revenue curve at point E. Sure enough, the quantity of output at E is 5 bushels.

Does this mean that the firm's production decision can be entirely summed up as "produce up to the point where the marginal cost of production is equal to the price"? No, not quite. Before applying the principle of marginal analysis to determine how much to produce, a potential producer must as a first step answer an "either–or" question: should it produce at all? If the answer to that question is yes, it then proceeds to the second step—a "how much" decision: maximizing profit by choosing the quantity of output at which marginal cost is equal to price.

To understand why the first step in the production decision involves an "either–or" question, we need to ask how we determine whether it is profitable or unprofitable to produce at all.

When Is Production Profitable?

Recall from Chapter 7 that a firm's decision whether or not to stay in a given business depends on its *economic profit*—a measure based on the opportunity cost of resources used in the business. To put it a slightly different way: in the calculation of profit, a firm's total cost incorporates the implicit cost—the benefits forgone in the next best use of the firm's resources—as well as the explicit cost in the form of actual cash outlays.

We will assume that all costs, implicit as well as explicit, are included in the cost numbers given in Table 9-1; as a result, the profit numbers in Table 9-2 are economic profit. So what determines whether Jennifer and Jason's farm earns a profit or generates a loss? The answer is that, given the farm's cost curves, whether or not it is profitable depends on the market price of tomatoes—specifically, *whether the market price is more or less than the farm's minimum average total cost.*

Table 9-3 calculates short-run average variable cost and short-run average total cost for Jennifer and Jason's farm. These are short-run values, because we take fixed cost as given. (We'll turn to the effects of changing fixed cost shortly.) The short-run average total cost curve, ATC, is shown in Figure 9-2 on page 214, along with the marginal cost curve, MC, from Figure 9-1. As you can see, average total cost is minimized at point C, corresponding to an output of 4 bushels—the *minimum-cost output*—and an average total cost of $14 per bushel.

To see how these curves can be used to decide whether production is profitable or unprofitable, recall that profit is equal to total revenue minus total cost, $TR - TC$. This means:

■ If $TR > TC$, the firm is profitable.

■ If $TR = TC$, the firm breaks even.

■ If $TR < TC$, the firm incurs a loss.

TABLE 9-3

Average Costs for Jennifer and Jason's Farm

Quantity of tomatoes Q (bushels)	Variable cost VC	Total cost TC	Average variable cost of bushel $AVC = VC/Q$	Average total cost of bushel $ATC = TC/Q$
1	$16.00	$30.00	$16.00	$30.00
2	22.00	36.00	11.00	18.00
3	30.00	44.00	10.00	14.67
4	42.00	56.00	10.50	14.00
5	58.00	72.00	11.60	14.40
6	78.00	92.00	13.00	15.33
7	102.00	116.00	14.57	16.57

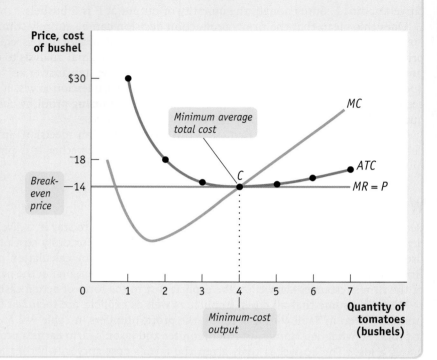

Figure 9-2

Costs and Production in the Short Run

This figure shows the marginal cost curve, *MC*, and the short-run average total cost curve, *ATC*. When the market price is $14, output will be 4 bushels of tomatoes (the minimum-cost output), represented by point *C*. The price of $14, equal to the firm's minimum average total cost, is the firm's *break-even price*. **>web...**

We can also express this idea in terms of revenue and cost per unit of output. If we divide profit by the number of units of output, *Q*, we obtain the following expression for profit per unit of output:

(9-4) $\text{Profit}/Q = TR/Q - TC/Q$

TR/Q is average revenue—that is, the market price. *TC/Q* is average total cost. So a firm is profitable if the market price for its product exceeds the average total cost of the quantity the firm produces; a firm loses money if the market price is less than average total cost of the quantity the firm produces. This means:

- If *P* > *ATC*, the firm is profitable.
- If *P* = *ATC*, the firm breaks even.
- If *P* < *ATC*, the firm incurs a loss.

Figure 9-3 illustrates this result, showing how the market price determines whether a firm is profitable. It also shows how profits are depicted graphically. Each panel shows the marginal cost curve, *MC*, and the short-run average total cost curve, *ATC*. Average total cost is minimized at point *C*. Panel (a) shows the case we have already analyzed, in which the market price of tomatoes is $18 per bushel. Panel (b) shows the case in which the market price of tomatoes is lower, $10 per bushel.

In panel (a), we see that at a price of $18 per bushel the profit-maximizing quantity of output is 5 bushels, indicated by point *E* where the marginal cost curve, *MC*, intersects the marginal revenue curve—which for a price-taking firm is a horizontal line at the market price. At that quantity of output, average total cost is $14.40 per bushel, indicated by point *Z*. Since the price per bushel exceeds average total cost per bushel, Jennifer and Jason's farm is profitable.

Jennifer and Jason's total profits when the market price is $18 are represented by the area of the shaded rectangle in panel (a). To see why, notice that total profit can be expressed in terms of profit per unit:

(9-5)   Profit = $TR - TC = (TR/Q - TC/Q) \times Q$

or, equivalently,

Profit = $(P - ATC) \times Q$

since P is equal to TR/Q and ATC is equal to TC/Q. The height of the shaded rectangle in panel (a) corresponds to the vertical distance between points E and Z. It is equal to $P - ATC = \$18.00 - \$14.40 = \$3.60$ per bushel. The shaded rectangle has a width equal to the output: $Q = 5$ bushels. So the area of that rectangle is equal to

Figure 9-3

Profitability and the Market Price

In panel (a) the market price is $18. The farm is profitable because price exceeds minimum average total cost, the break-even price, $14. The farm's optimal output choice is indicated by point E, corresponding to an output of 5 bushels. The average total cost of producing 5 bushels is indicated by point Z on the ATC curve, corresponding to an amount of $14.40. The vertical distance between E and Z corresponds to the farm's per-unit profit, $18.00 - $14.40 = $3.60. Total profit is given by the area of the shaded rectangle, 5 × $3.60 = $18.00.

In panel (b) the market price is $10; the farm is unprofitable because the price falls below the minimum average total cost, $14. The farm's optimal output choice when producing is indicated by point A, corresponding to an output of three bushels. The farm's per-unit loss, $14.67 − $10.00 = $4.67, is represented by the vertical distance between A and Y. The farm's total loss is represented by the shaded rectangle, 3 × $4.67 = $14.00 (adjusted for rounding error). **>web...**

(a) Market Price = $18

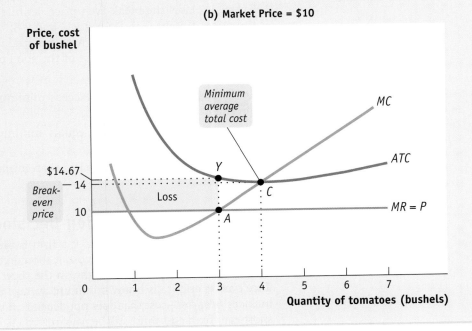

(b) Market Price = $10

Jennifer and Jason's profit: 5 bushels × $3.60 profit per bushel = $18—the same number we calculated in Table 9-2.

What about the situation illustrated in panel (b)? Here the market price of tomatoes is $10 per bushel. Setting price equal to marginal cost leads to a profit-maximizing output of 3 bushels, indicated by point A. At this output, Jennifer and Jason have an average total cost of $14.67 per bushel, indicated by point Y. At their profit-maximizing output quantity—3 bushels—average total cost exceeds the market price. This means that Jennifer and Jason's farm generates losses, not profits.

How much do they lose by producing when the market price is $10? On each bushel they lose $ATC - P = \$14.67 - \$10.00 = \$4.67$, an amount corresponding to the vertical distance between points A and Y. And, they would produce 3 bushels, which corresponds to the width of the shaded rectangle. So, the total value of the losses is $\$4.67 \times 3 = \$14.00$ (adjusted for rounding error), an amount that corresponds to the area of the shaded rectangle in panel (b).

But how does a producer know, in general, whether or not its business will be profitable? It turns out that the crucial test lies in a comparison of the market price to the producer's *minimum average total cost*. On Jennifer and Jason's farm, minimum average total cost, which is equal to $14, occurs at an output quantity of 4 bushels. Whenever the market price exceeds minimum average total cost, the producer can find some output level for which the average total cost is less than the market price. That means that the producer can find a level of output at which the firm makes a profit. Jennifer and Jason's farm will be profitable whenever the market price exceeds $14. And they will achieve the highest profit by producing the quantity at which marginal cost equals the market price.

On the other hand, if the market price is less than minimum average total cost, there is no output level at which price exceeds average total cost. As a result, the firm will be unprofitable at any quantity of output. As we saw, at a price of $10—an amount less than minimum average total cost—Jennifer and Jason did indeed lose money. By producing the quantity at which marginal cost equals the market price, Jennifer and Jason did the best they could, but the best that they could do was a loss of $14. Any other quantity would have increased the size of their loss.

The **break-even price** of a price-taking firm is the market price at which it earns zero profits.

The minimum average total cost of a price-taking firm is called its **break-even price,** the price at which it earns zero profits. A firm will earn positive profits when the market price is above the break-even price, and it will suffer losses when the market price is below the break-even price. Jennifer and Jason's break-even price of $14 is the price at point C in Figures 9-2 and 9-3.

So the rule for determining whether a producer of a good is profitable depends on a comparison of the market price of the good to the producer's break-even price—its minimum average total cost:

- Whenever the market price exceeds minimum average total cost, the producer is profitable.

- Whenever the market price equals minimum average total cost, the producer breaks even.

- Whenever the market price is less than minimum average total cost, the producer is unprofitable.

The Short-Run Production Decision

You might be tempted to say that if a firm is unprofitable because the market price is below its minimum average total cost, it shouldn't produce any output. In the short run, however, this conclusion isn't right. In the short run, sometimes the firm should produce even if price falls below minimum average total cost. The reason is that total cost includes *fixed cost*—cost that does not depend on the amount of output produced. In the short run, fixed cost must still be paid, regardless of whether or not a firm produces. For example, if Jennifer and Jason have rented a tractor for the year, they have to pay that rent regardless of whether they produce any tomatoes. Since it cannot be changed in the short run, their fixed cost is irrelevant to their decision about whether to produce or shut down in the short run. Although fixed cost should play no role in the decision about whether to produce at all in the short run, other costs—variable costs—do matter. An example of variable costs is the wages of workers who must be hired to help with planting and harvesting. Variable costs can be saved by *not* producing; so they should play a role in determining whether or not to produce in the short run.

Let's turn to Figure 9-4: it shows both the short-run average total cost curve, ATC, and the short-run average *variable* cost curve, AVC, drawn from the information in Table 9-3. Recall that the difference between the two curves—the vertical distance between them—represents average fixed cost, the fixed cost per unit of output, FC/Q. Because the marginal cost curve has a "swoosh" shape—falling at first before rising—the short-run average variable cost curve is U-shaped: the initial fall in marginal cost causes average variable cost to fall as well, before rising marginal cost eventually pulls it up again. The short-run average variable cost curve reaches its minimum value of $10 at point A, at an output of 3 bushels.

We are now prepared to fully analyze the optimal production decision in the short run. We need to consider two cases:

- When the market price is below minimum average *variable* cost
- When the market price is greater than or equal to minimum average *variable* cost

When the market price is below minimum average variable cost, the price the firm receives is not covering its variable cost per unit. A firm in this situation should cease production immediately. Why? Because there is no level of output at which the firm's total revenue covers its variable costs—the costs it can avoid by not operating. In this case the firm maximizes its profits by not producing at all—by, in effect, minimizing its losses. It will still incur a fixed cost in the short run, but it will no longer incur any variable cost. This means that the minimum average variable cost is equal to the **shut-down price,** the price at which the firm ceases production in the short run.

A firm will cease production in the short run if the market price falls below the **shut-down price**, which is equal to minimum average variable cost.

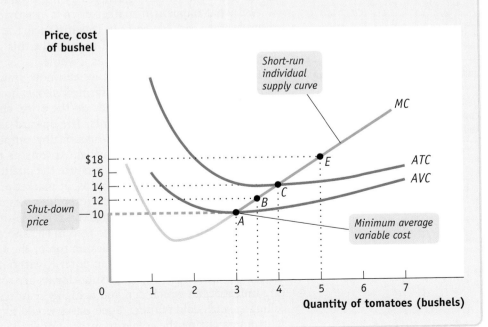

Figure 9-4

The Short-Run Individual Supply Curve

When the market price exceeds Jennifer and Jason's *shut-down price* of $10, the minimum average variable cost indicated by point A, they will produce the output quantity at which marginal cost is equal to price. So at any price above minimum average *variable* cost, the short-run individual supply curve is the firm's marginal cost curve; this corresponds to the upward-sloping segment of the individual supply curve. When market price falls below minimum average variable cost, the firm ceases operation in the short run. This corresponds to the vertical segment of the individual supply curve along the vertical axis.

When price is greater than minimum average variable cost, however, the firm should produce in the short run. In this case, the firm maximizes profit—or minimizes its loss—by choosing the output quantity at which its marginal cost is equal to the market price. For example, if the market price of tomatoes is $18 per bushel, Jennifer and Jason should produce at point E in Figure 9-4, corresponding to an output of 5 bushels. Note that point C in Figure 9-4 corresponds to the farm's break-even price of $14 per bushel. Since E lies above C, Jennifer and Jason's farm will be profitable; they will generate a per-bushel profit of $18.00 − $14.40 = $3.60 when the market price is $18.

But what if the market price lies between the shut-down price and the break-even price—that is, between minimum average *variable* cost and minimum average *total* cost? In the case of Jennifer and Jason's farm, this corresponds to prices anywhere between $10 and $14—say, a market price of $12. At $12, Jennifer and Jason's farm is not profitable; since the market price is below minimum average total cost, the farm is losing the difference between price and average total cost per unit produced. Yet, even if it isn't covering its total cost per unit, it is covering its variable cost per unit and some—but not all—of the fixed cost per unit. If a firm in this situation shuts down, it would incur no variable cost but would incur the *full* fixed cost. As a result, shutting down generates an even greater loss than continuing to operate.

This means that whenever price falls between minimum average total cost and minimum average variable cost, the firm is better off producing some output in the short run. The reason is that by producing, it can cover its variable cost per unit and at least some of its fixed cost, even though it is incurring a loss. In this case, the firm maximizes profit—that is, minimizes its loss—by choosing the quantity of output at which its marginal cost is equal to the market price. So if Jennifer and Jason face a market price of $12 per bushel, their profit-maximizing output is given by point B in Figure 9-4, corresponding to an output of 3.5 bushels.

It's worth noting that the decision to produce when the firm is covering its variable costs but not all of its fixed cost is similar to the decision to ignore *sunk costs,* a concept we studied in Chapter 7. You may recall that a sunk cost is a cost that has already been incurred and cannot be recouped; and because it cannot be changed, it should have no effect on any current decision. In the short-run production decision, fixed cost is, in effect, like a sunk cost—it has been spent, and it can't be recovered in the short run. This comparison also illustrates why variable cost does indeed matter in the short run: it can be avoided by not producing.

And what happens if market price is exactly equal to the shut-down price, minimum average variable cost? In this instance, the firm is indifferent between producing 3 units or 0 units. As we'll see shortly, this is an important point when looking at the behavior of an industry as a whole.

Putting everything together, we can now draw the **short-run individual supply curve** of Jennifer and Jason's farm; it shows how the profit-maximizing quantity of output in the short run depends on the price, the red line in Figure 9-4. As you can see, the curve is in two segments. The upward-sloping red segment starting at point A shows the short-run profit-maximizing output when market price is above the shut-down price of $10 per bushel. As long as the market price is above the shut-down price, Jennifer and Jason produce the quantity of output at which marginal cost is equal to the market price. That is, at market prices above the shut-down price, the firm's short-run supply curve corresponds to its marginal cost curve. But at any market price below minimum average variable cost—in this case, $10 per bushel—the firm shuts down and output drops to zero in the short run. This corresponds to the vertical segment of the curve that lies on top of the vertical axis.

Do firms really shut down temporarily without going out of business? Yes. In fact, in some businesses temporary shut-downs are routine. The most common examples are industries in which demand is highly seasonal, like outdoor amusement parks in climates with cold winters. Such parks would have to offer very low prices to entice customers during the colder months—prices so low that the owners would not cover

The **short-run individual supply curve** shows how an individual producer's profit-maximizing output quantity depends on the market price, taking fixed cost as given.

their variable costs (principally wages and electricity). The wiser choice economically is to shut down until warm weather brings enough customers who are willing to pay a higher price.

Changing Fixed Cost

Although fixed cost cannot be altered in the short run, in the long run firms can acquire or get rid of machines, buildings, and so on. As we learned in Chapter 8, in the long run the level of fixed cost is a matter of choice. We saw that a firm will choose the level of fixed cost that minimizes the average total cost for its desired output quantity. Now we will focus on an even bigger question facing a firm when choosing its fixed cost: whether to incur *any* fixed cost at all by remaining in its current business.

In the long run, a producer can always eliminate fixed cost by selling off its plant and equipment. If it does so, of course, it can't ever produce—it has exited the industry. In contrast, a potential producer can take on some fixed cost by acquiring machines and other resources, which puts it in a position to produce—it can enter the industry. In most perfectly competitive industries the set of producers, although fixed in the short run, changes in the long run as firms enter or leave the industry.

Consider Jennifer and Jason's farm once again. In order to simplify our analysis, we will sidestep the problem of choosing among several possible levels of fixed cost. Instead, we will assume from now on that Jennifer and Jason have only one possible choice of fixed cost if they operate, the amount of $14 that was the basis for the calculations in Tables 9-1, 9-2, and 9-3. Alternatively, they can choose a fixed cost of zero if they exit the industry. (With this assumption, Jennifer and Jason's short-run average total cost curve and long-run average total cost curve are one and the same.)

Suppose that the market price of organic tomatoes is consistently less than $14 over an extended period of time. In that case, Jennifer and Jason never fully cover their fixed cost: their business runs at a loss. In the long run, then, they can do better by closing their business and leaving the industry. In other words, *in the long run* firms will exit an industry if the market price is consistently less than their break-even price—their minimum average total cost.

On the other hand, suppose, that the price of organic tomatoes is consistently above the break-even price, $14, for an extended period of time. Because their farm is profitable, Jennifer and Jason will remain in the industry and continue producing. But things won't stop there. The organic tomato industry meets the criterion of *free entry*: there are many potential organic tomato producers because the necessary inputs are easy to obtain. And the cost curves of those potential producers are likely to be similar to those of Jennifer and Jason, since the technology used by other producers is likely to be very similar to that used by Jennifer and Jason. If the price is high enough to generate profits for existing producers, it will also attract some of these potential producers into the industry. So *in the long run* a price in excess of $14 should lead to entry: new producers will come into the organic tomato industry.

As we will see in the next section, exit and entry lead to an important distinction between the *short-run industry supply curve* and the *long-run industry supply curve*.

Summing Up: The Perfectly Competitive Firm's Profitability and Production Conditions

In this chapter, we've studied where the supply curve for a perfectly competitive firm comes from. Every perfectly competitive firm makes its production decisions by maximizing profit, and these decisions determine the supply curve. Table 9-4 on page 220 summarizes the competitive firm's profitability and production conditions. It also relates them to entry and exit from the industry.

TABLE 9-4

Summary of the Perfectly Competitive Firm's Profitability and Production Conditions

Profitability Condition (minimum *ATC* = break-even price)	Result
P > minimum *ATC*	Firm profitable. Entry into industry in the long run.
P = minimum *ATC*	Firm breaks even. No entry into or exit from industry in the long run.
P < minimum *ATC*	Firm unprofitable. Exit from industry in the long run.

Production Condition (minimum *AVC* = shut-down price)	Result
P > minimum *AVC*	Firm produces in the short run. If *P* < minimum *ATC*, firm covers variable cost and some but not all of fixed cost. If *P* > minimum *ATC*, firm covers all variable cost and fixed cost.
P = minimum *AVC*	Firm indifferent between producing in the short run or not. Just covers variable cost.
P < minimum *AVC*	Firm shuts down in the short run. Does not cover variable cost.

economics in action

California Screaming

Between November 2000 and May 2001, the state of California went through an electricity crisis. Supplies of power were limited, and the wholesale price of electricity—the price at which generators sell power to the local utilities, which then provide it to customers—ran consistently at more than 10 times its normal level.

During the crisis, some economists accused the power generators of deliberately withholding electricity from the market in order to drive up prices. That is, they argued that competition wasn't perfect, that producers weren't taking prices as given. We'll discuss why it might have been in the interests of producers to withhold power in Chapter 14.

The interesting point for now is to ask how you could tell whether or not producers were acting as price-takers. And the answer was that economists used data on electricity generating costs to estimate marginal cost curves for producers. They could then ask whether the producers were actually generating as much power as they should have if they were setting price equal to marginal cost. The conclusion of several influential studies, including a federal investigation by the Justice Department, was that they were not.

Eventually, power companies were caught red-handed: tape recordings revealed they purposely shut down plants in order to drive up prices. Economists applying marginal analysis had gotten it right. ∎

< < < < < < < < < < < < < < < < <

>>CHECK YOUR UNDERSTANDING 9-2

1. Draw a short-run diagram showing a U-shaped average total cost curve, a U-shaped average variable cost curve, and a "swoosh"-shaped marginal cost curve. On it, indicate the range of output and the range of price for which the following actions are optimal.
   a. The firm shuts down immediately.
   b. The firm operates in the short run despite sustaining a loss.
   c. The firm operates while making a profit.

2. The state of Maine has a very active lobster industry, which harvests lobsters during the summer months. During the rest of the year, lobsters can be obtained from other parts of the world but at a much higher price. Maine is also full of "lobster shacks," roadside restaurants serving lobster dishes that are open only during the summer. Explain why it is optimal for lobster shacks to operate only during the summer.

Solutions appear at back of book.

The Industry Supply Curve

Why will an increase in the demand for organic tomatoes lead to a large price increase at first but a much smaller increase in the long run? The answer lies in the behavior of the **industry supply curve**—the relationship between the price and the total output of an industry as a whole. The industry supply curve is what we referred to in earlier chapters as *the* supply curve or the market supply curve. But here we take some extra care to distinguish between the *individual supply curve* of a single firm and the supply curve of the industry as a whole.

As you might guess from the previous section, the industry supply curve must be analyzed in somewhat different ways for the short run and the long run. Let's start with the short run.

> The **industry supply curve** shows the relationship between the price of a good and the total output of the industry as a whole.

The Short-Run Industry Supply Curve

Recall that in the short run the number of producers in an industry is fixed—there is no entry or exit. We can best understand how the industry supply curve emerges from individual producer supply curves by imagining that all the producers are alike. So let's assume that there are 100 organic tomato farms, each with the same costs as Jennifer and Jason's farm.

Each of these 100 farms will have an individual short-run supply curve like the one in Figure 9-4. At a price below $10, no farms will produce. At a price of more than $10, each farm will produce the quantity of output at which its marginal cost is equal to the market price. As you can see from Figure 9-4, this will lead them to produce 4 bushels if the price is $14 per bushel, 5 bushels if the price is $18, and so on. So if there are 100 organic tomato farmers and the price of organic tomatoes is $18 per bushel, the industry as a whole will produce 500 bushels, corresponding to 100 farmers × 5 bushels per farmer, and so on. The result is the **short-run industry supply curve**, shown as S in Figure 9-5. This curve shows the quantity that producers will supply at each price, *taking the number of producers as given*.

The demand curve D in Figure 9-5 crosses the short-run industry supply curve at E_{MKT}, corresponding to a price of $18 and a quantity of 500 bushels. Point E_{MKT} is a **short-run market equilibrium:** the quantity supplied equals the quantity demanded, taking the number of producers as given. But the long run may look quite different, because in the long run farms may enter or exit the industry.

> The **short-run industry supply curve** shows how the quantity supplied by an industry depends on the market price given a fixed number of producers.
>
> There is a **short-run market equilibrium** when the quantity supplied equals the quantity demanded, taking the number of producers as given.

Figure 9-5

The Short-Run Market Equilibrium

The short-run industry supply curve, S, is the industry supply curve taking the number of producers—here, 100—as given. It is generated by adding together the individual supply curves of the 100 producers. Below the shut-down price of $10, no producer wants to produce in the short run. Above $10, the short-run industry supply curve slopes upward, as each producer increases output as price increases. It intersects the demand curve, D, at point E_{MKT}, the point of short-run market equilibrium, corresponding to a market price of $18 and a quantity of 500 bushels. **>web...**

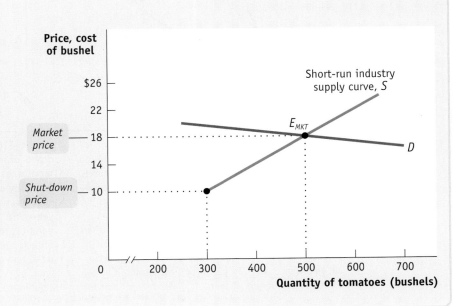

The Long-Run Industry Supply Curve

Suppose that in addition to the 100 farmers currently in the organic tomato business, there are many other potential producers. Suppose also that each of these potential producers would have the same cost curves as existing producers like Jennifer and Jason if it entered the industry

When will additional producers enter the industry? Whenever existing producers are making a profit—that is, whenever the market price is above the break-even price of $14 per bushel, the minimum average total cost of production. For example, at a price of $18 per bushel, new firms will enter the industry.

What will happen as additional producers enter the industry? Clearly, the quantity supplied at any given price will increase. The short-run industry supply curve will shift to the right. This will, in turn, alter the market equilibrium and result in a lower market price. Existing firms will respond to the lower market price by reducing their output, but the total industry output will increase because of the larger number of firms in the industry.

Figure 9-6 illustrates the effects of this chain of events on an existing firm and on the market; panel (a) shows how an individual existing firm responds to entry, and panel (b) shows how the market responds to entry. (Note that these two graphs have been rescaled in comparison to Figure 9-4 to better illustrate how profit changes in response to price.) In panel (b), S_1 is the initial short-run industry supply curve, based on the existence of 100 producers. The initial short-run market equilibrium is at E_{MKT}, with an equilibrium market price of $18 and a quantity of 500 bushels. At this price existing producers are profitable, which is reflected in panel (a): an existing firm makes a total profit represented by the shaded rectangle labeled A when market price is $18.

Figure 9-6   The Long-Run Market Equilibrium

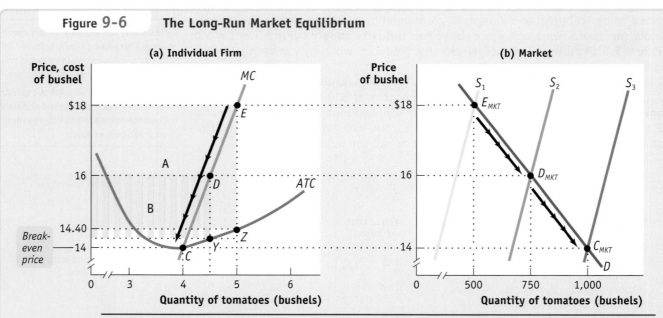

Point E_{MKT} of panel (b) shows the initial short-run market equilibrium, at the intersection of the demand curve, D, and the initial short-run industry supply curve, S_1. Because the market price ($18) is above the break-even price ($14), each of the 100 existing producers makes an economic profit; this is illustrated in panel (a), where the rectangle labeled A shows the profit of an existing firm. These profits induce entry by additional producers, shifting the short-run industry supply curve outward from S_1 to S_2 in panel (b). This results in a new short-run equilibrium at point D_{MKT} with a lower market

price of $16 and higher industry output. The output and profits of existing firms are reduced; but some profit remains, as shown by the rectangle labeled B in panel (a). Entry continues shifting out the short-run industry supply curve, as price falls and industry output increases yet again. Entry finally ceases once an equilibrium, at point C_{MKT} on supply curve S_3, is reached. Here market price is equal to the break-even price; existing producers make zero economic profits and there is no incentive for entry or exit. Therefore C_{MKT} is also a long-run market equilibrium.

These profits will induce new producers to enter the industry, shifting the short-run industry supply curve to the right. For example, the short-run industry supply curve when the number of producers has increased to 167 is S_2. Corresponding to this supply curve is a new short-run market equilibrium labeled D_{MKT}, with a market price of $16 and a quantity of 750 bushels. At $16, each firm produces 4.5 bushels, so that industry output is $167 \times 4.5 = 750$ bushels (rounded). From panel (a) you can see the effect of the entry of 67 new producers on an existing firm: the fall in price causes it to reduce its output, and its profit falls to the area represented by the shaded rectangle labeled B.

Although diminished, the profit of existing firms at D_{MKT} means that entry will continue and the number of firms will continue to rise. If the number of producers rises to 250, the short-run industry supply curve shifts out again to S_3, and the market equilibrium is at C_{MKT}, with a quantity supplied and demanded of 1,000 bushels and a market price of $14 per bushel.

Like E_{MKT} and D_{MKT}, C_{MKT} is a short-run equilibrium. But it is also something more. Because the price of $14 is each firm's break-even price, an existing producer makes zero economic profits—neither a profit nor a loss—when producing its profit-maximizing output of 4 bushels. At this price there is no incentive either for potential producers to enter or for existing producers to exit the industry. So C_{MKT} corresponds to a **long-run market equilibrium**—a situation in which quantity supplied equals the quantity demanded given that sufficient time has elapsed for producers to either enter or exit the industry. In a long-run market equilibrium, all existing and potential producers have fully adjusted to their optimal long-run choices; as a result, no producer has an incentive to either enter or exit the industry.

To explore further the significance of the difference between short-run and long-run equilibrium, consider the effect of an increase in demand on an industry with free entry that is initially in long-run equilibrium. Panel (b) in Figure 9-7 on page 224 shows the market adjustment; panels (a) and (c) show how an existing individual firm behaves during the process.

In panel (b) of Figure 9-7, D_1 is the initial demand curve and S_1 is the initial short-run industry supply curve. Their intersection at point X_{MKT} is both a short-run and a long-run market equilibrium, because the equilibrium price of $14 leads to zero economic profits—and therefore neither entry nor exit. It corresponds to point X in panel (a), where an individual existing firm is operating at the minimum of its average total cost curve.

Now suppose that the demand curve shifts out for some reason to D_2. As shown in panel (b), in the short run, industry output moves along the short-run industry supply curve S_1 to the new short-run market equilibrium at Y_{MKT}, the intersection of S_1 and D_2. The market price rises to $18 per bushel and industry output increases from Q_X to Q_Y. This corresponds to the movement from X to Y in panel (a), as an existing firm increases its output in response to the rise in the market price.

But we know that Y_{MKT} is not a long-run equilibrium, because $18 is higher than minimum average total cost, so existing producers are making economic profits. This will lead additional firms to enter the industry. Over time entry will cause the short-run industry supply curve to shift to the right. In the long run, the short-run industry supply curve will have shifted out to S_2, and the equilibrium will be at Z_{MKT}—with the price falling back to $14 per bushel and industry output increasing yet again, from Q_Y to Q_Z. Like X_{MKT} before the increase in demand, Z_{MKT} is both a short-run and a long-run market equilibrium.

The effect of entry on an existing firm is illustrated in panel (c), in the movement from Y to Z along the firm's individual supply curve. The firm reduces its output in response to the fall in price, ultimately arriving back at its original output quantity, corresponding to the minimum of its average total cost curve. In fact, every firm that is now in the industry—the initial set of firms and the new entrants—will operate at the minimum of its average total cost curves, at point Z. This means that the entire increase in industry output, from Q_X to Q_Z, comes from production by new entrants.

A market is in **long-run market equilibrium** when the quantity supplied equals the quantity demanded, given that sufficient time has elapsed for entry into and exit from the industry to occur.

| Figure 9-7 | The Effect of an Increase in Demand in the Short Run and the Long Run |

Panel (b) shows how an industry adjusts in the short and long run to an increase in demand; panels (a) and (c) show the corresponding adjustments by an existing firm. Initially the market is at point X_{MKT} in panel (b), a short-run and long-run equilibrium at a price of $14 and industry output of Q_X. An existing firm makes zero profit, operating at point X in panel (a) at minimum average total cost. Demand increases as D_1 shifts rightward to D_2, and raises the market price to $18. Existing firms increase their output and industry output moves along the short-run industry supply curve S_1 to a short-run equilibrium at Y_{MKT}. Correspondingly, the existing firm in panel (a) moves from point X to point Y. But at a price of $18 existing firms are profitable. As shown in panel (b), in the long run

new entrants arrive and the short-run industry supply curve shifts rightward, from S_1 to S_2. There is a new equilibrium at point Z_{MKT}, at a lower price of $14 and higher industry output of Q_Z. An existing firm responds by moving from Y to Z in panel (c), returning to its initial output level and zero profit. Production by new entrants accounts for the total increase in industry output, $Q_Z - Q_X$. Like X_{MKT}, Z_{MKT} is also a short-run and long-run equilibrium: with existing firms earning zero economic profits, there is no incentive for any firms to enter or exit the industry. The horizontal line passing through X_{MKT} and Z_{MKT}, LRS, is the *long-run industry supply curve*: at the break-even price of $14, producers will produce any amount that consumers demand in the long run.

The long-run industry supply curve shows how the quantity supplied responds to the price once producers have had time to enter or exit the industry.

The line *LRS* that passes through X_{MKT} and Z_{MKT} in panel (b) is the **long-run industry supply curve.** It shows how the quantity supplied by an industry responds to the price given that producers have had time to enter or exit the industry.

In this particular case, the long-run industry supply curve is horizontal at $14. In other words, in this industry supply is *perfectly elastic* in the long run—given time to enter or exit, producers will supply any quantity consumers demand at a price of $14. Perfectly elastic long-run supply is actually a good assumption for many industries. However, in other industries even the long-run industry supply curve is upward sloping. The usual reason even the long-run industry supply curve is upward sloping is that producers must use some input that is in limited supply and as the industry expands, the price of that input is driven up. For example, beach-resort hotels must compete for a limited quantity of prime beachfront property.

Whether the long-run industry supply curve is horizontal or upward sloping, however, the long-run price elasticity of supply is *higher* than the short-run price elasticity whenever there is free entry and exit. As shown in Figure 9-8, the long-run industry supply curve is always flatter than the short-run industry supply curve. The reason is entry and exit: a high price attracts entry by new producers, resulting in a

Figure 9-8

Comparing the Short-Run and Long-Run Industry Supply Curves

The long-run industry supply curve may slope upward, but it is always flatter—more elastic—than the short-run industry supply curve. This is because of entry and exit: a higher price attracts new entrants in the long run, resulting in a rise in industry output and a fall in price; a fall in price induces existing producers to exit in the long run, generating a fall in industry output and a rise in price. **>web...**

Short-run industry supply curve, S

Long-run industry supply curve, LRS

The long-run industry supply curve is always flatter—more elastic—than the short-run industry supply curve.

rise in industry output and a fall in price; a low price induces existing firms to exit, leading to a fall in industry output and an increase in price.

The distinction between the short-run industry supply curve and the long-run industry supply curve is very important in practice. We often see a sequence of events like that shown in Figure 9-7: an increase in demand initially leads to a large price increase, but prices return to their initial level once new firms have entered the industry. Or we see the sequence in reverse: a fall in demand reduces prices in the short run, but they return to their initial level as producers exit the industry.

The Cost of Production and Efficiency in Long-run Equilibrium

Our analysis leads us to three conclusions about the cost of production and efficiency in the long-run equilibrium of a perfectly competitive industry. These results will be important in our discussion in Chapter 14 of how monopoly gives rise to inefficiency.

First, in a perfectly competitive industry in equilibrium, the value of marginal cost is the same for all firms. That's because all firms produce the quantity of output at which marginal cost equals the market price, and as price-takers they all face the same market price.

Second, in a perfectly competitive industry with free entry and exit, each firm will have zero economic profit in long-run equilibrium. Each firm produces the quantity of output that minimizes its average total cost—corresponding to point Z in panel (c) of Figure 9-7. So the total cost of production of the industry's output is minimized in a perfectly competitive industry.

The third and final conclusion is that the long-run market equilibrium of a perfectly competitive industry is efficient: no mutually beneficial transactions go unexploited. To understand this we need to recall a fundamental requirement for efficiency from Chapter 6: all consumers who have a willingness to pay greater than or equal to sellers' costs actually get the good. And we also learned that a market is efficient (except under certain, well-defined conditions)—the market price matches all consumers with a willingness to pay greater than or equal to the market price to all sellers who have a cost of producing the good less than or equal to the market price.

How do we know that the long-run equilibrium of a perfectly competitive industry is efficient? Because each firm produces the output level at which price is equal to marginal cost. And marginal cost is in fact the same as seller's cost—the lowest price the firm is willing to accept for the good. So the long-run equilibrium of a market with a perfectly competitive industry is indeed efficient.

economics in action

A Crushing Reversal

For some reason, starting in the mid-1990s, Americans began drinking a lot more wine. Part of this increase in demand may have reflected a booming economy, but the surge in wine consumption continued even after the economy stumbled in 2001. By 2002, Americans were consuming 35 percent more wine than they did in 1993.

At first, the increase in wine demand led to sharply higher prices; between 1993 and 2000, the price of red wine grapes rose approximately 50 percent, and California grape growers earned high profits. As a result, there was a rapid expansion of the industry, both because existing grape growers expanded their capacity and because new growers entered the market. Between 1994 and 2002, production of red wine grapes almost doubled.

The result was predictable: the price of grapes fell as the supply curve shifted out. As demand growth slowed in 2002, prices plunged by 17 percent. The effect was to end the California wine industry's expansion. In fact, some grape producers began to exit the industry. ■

As production expanded and prices fell, profits in the California wine industry shriveled.

Kate Kline/Foodpix/Getty Images

>**CHECK YOUR UNDERSTANDING 9-3**

1. Which of the following events will induce firms to enter an industry? Which will induce firms to exit? When will entry or exit cease? Explain your answer.
   a. A technological advance lowers the fixed cost of production of every firm in the industry.
   b. The wages paid to workers in the industry go up.
   c. A change in consumer tastes increases demand for the good.
   d. The price of a key input rises due to a shortage of that input.

2. Assume that the egg industry is perfectly competitive and is in long-run equilibrium with a perfectly elastic long-run industry supply curve. Health concerns about cholesterol then lead to a decrease in demand. Construct a figure similar to Figure 9-7, showing the short-run behavior of the industry and how long-run equilibrium is reestablished.

Solutions appear at back of book.

• A LOOK AHEAD •

In this chapter, we have seen how the rational decisions of producers in a perfectly competitive industry give rise to that industry's supply curve. But this is, of course, only half the story. To complete the picture we must turn next to the decisions made by rational consumers and how these decisions give rise to the demand curve.

SUMMARY

1. In a **perfectly competitive market** all producers are **price-taking producers** and all consumers are **price-taking consumers**—no one's actions can influence the market price. Consumers are normally price-takers, but producers often are not. In a **perfectly competitive industry,** all producers are price-takers.

2. There are two necessary conditions for a perfectly competitive industry: there are many producers, none of whom have a large **market share,** and the industry produces a **standardized product** or **commodity**—goods that consumers regard as equivalent. A third condition is often satisfied as well: **free entry and exit** into and from the industry.

3. A producer chooses output according to the **optimal output rule:** produce the quantity at which **marginal revenue** equals marginal cost. For a price-taking firm, marginal revenue is equal to price and its **marginal revenue curve** is a horizontal line at the market price. It chooses output according to the **price-taking firm's optimal output rule:** produce the quantity at which price equals marginal cost. However, a firm that produces the optimal quantity may not be profitable.

4. A firm is profitable if total revenue exceeds total cost or, equivalently, if the market price exceeds its **break-even price**—minimum average total cost. If market price exceeds the break-even price, the firm is profitable; if it is less, the firm is unprofitable; if it is equal, the firm breaks even. When profitable, the firm's per-unit profit is $P - ATC$; when unprofitable, its per-unit loss is $ATC - P$.

5. Fixed cost is irrelevant to the firm's optimal short-run production decision, which depends on its **shut-down price**—its minimum average variable cost—and the market price. When the market price exceeds the shut-down price, the firm produces the output quantity where marginal cost equals the market price. When the market price falls below the shut-down price, the firm ceases production in the short run. This generates the firm's **short-run individual supply curve**.

6. Fixed cost matters in the long run. If the market price is below minimum average total cost for an extended period of time, firms will exit the industry. If above, existing firms are profitable and new firms will enter the industry.

7. The **industry supply curve** depends on the time period. The **short-run industry supply curve** is the industry supply curve given that the number of firms is fixed. The **short-run market equilibrium** is given by the intersection of the short-run industry supply curve and the demand curve.

8. The **long-run industry supply curve** is the industry supply curve given sufficient time for entry into and exit from the industry. In the **long-run market equilibrium**—given by the intersection of the long-run industry supply curve and the demand curve—no producer has an incentive to enter or exit. The long-run industry supply curve is often horizontal. It may slope upward if there is limited supply of an input; but it is always flatter than the short-run industry supply curve.

9. In the long-run market equilibrium of a competitive industry, profit maximization leads each firm to produce at the same marginal cost, which is equal to market price. Free entry and exit means that each firm earns zero economic profit—producing the output corresponding to its minimum average total cost. So the total cost of production of an industry's output is minimized. The outcome is efficient because every consumer with a willingness to pay greater or equal to marginal cost gets the good.

KEY TERMS

Price-taking producer, p. 207
Price-taking consumer, p. 207
Perfectly competitive market, p. 207
Perfectly competitive industry, p. 207
Market share, p. 208
Standardized product, p. 208
Commodity, p. 208

Free entry and exit, p. 209
Marginal revenue, p. 211
Optimal output rule, p. 211
Price-taking firm's optimal output rule, p. 212
Marginal revenue curve, p. 212
Break-even price, p. 216

Shut-down price, p. 217
Short-run individual supply curve, p. 218
Industry supply curve, p. 221
Short-run industry supply curve, p. 221
Short-run market equilibrium, p. 221
Long-run market equilibrium, p. 223
Long-run industry supply curve, p. 224

PROBLEMS

1. For each of the following, is the business a price-taking producer? Explain your answers.

   a. A cappuccino café in a university town where there are dozens of very similar cappuccino cafés

   b. The makers of Pepsi-Cola

   c. One of many sellers of zucchini at a local farmers' market

2. For each of the following, is the industry perfectly competitive? Referring to market share, standardization of the product, and/or free entry and exit, explain your answers.

   a. Aspirin

   b. Shania Twain concerts

   c. SUVs

3. Kate's Katering provides catered meals, and the catered meals industry is perfectly competitive. Kate's machinery costs $100 per day and is the only fixed input. Her variable cost is comprised of the wages paid to the cooks and the food ingredients. The variable cost associated with each level of output is given in the accompanying table.

Quantity of meals	VC
0	$0
10	200
20	300
30	480
40	700
50	1,000

a. Calculate the total cost, the average variable cost, the average total cost, and the marginal cost for each quantity of output.

b. What is the break-even price? What is the shut-down price?

c. Suppose that the price at which Kate can sell catered meals is $21 per meal. In the short run, will Kate earn a profit? In the short run, should she produce or shut down?

d. Suppose that the price at which Kate can sell catered meals is $17 per meal. In the short run, will Kate earn a profit? In the short run, should she produce or shut down?

e. Suppose that the price at which Kate can sell catered meals is $13 per meal. In the short run, will Kate earn a profit? In the short run, should she produce or shut down?

4. Bob produces DVD movies for sale, which requires only a building and a machine that copies the original movie onto a DVD. Bob rents a building for $30,000 per month and rents a machine for $20,000 a month. Those are his fixed costs. His variable cost is given in the accompanying table.

Quantity of DVDs	VC
0	$0
1,000	5,000
2,000	8,000
3,000	9,000
4,000	14,000
5,000	20,000
6,000	33,000
7,000	49,000
8,000	72,000
9,000	99,000
10,000	150,000

a. Calculate Bob's average variable cost, average total cost, and marginal cost for each quantity of output.

b. There is free entry into the industry: anyone who enters will face the same costs as Bob. Suppose that currently the price of a DVD is $23. What will Bob's profit be? Is this a long-run equilibrium? If not, what will the price of DVD movies be in the long run?

5. Consider Bob's DVD company described in Problem 4. Assume that DVD production is a perfectly competitive industry. In each case, explain your answers.

a. What is Bob's break-even price? What is his shut-down price?

b. Suppose the price of a DVD is $2. What should Bob do in the short run?

c. Suppose the price of a DVD is $7. What is the profit-maximizing quantity of DVDs that Bob should produce? What will his total profit be? Will he produce or shut down in the short run? Will he stay in the industry or exit in the long run?

d. Suppose instead that the price of DVDs is $20. Now what is the profit-maximizing quantity of DVDs that Bob should produce? What will his total profit be now? Will he produce or shut down in the short run? Will he stay in the industry or exit in the long run?

6. Consider again Bob's DVD company described in Problem 4.

a. Draw Bob's marginal cost curve.

b. Over what range of prices will Bob produce no DVDs in the short run?

c. Draw Bob's individual supply curve.

7. a. A profit-maximizing business incurs an economic loss of $10,000 per year. Its fixed cost is $15,000 per year. Should it produce or shut down in the short run? Should it stay in the industry or exit in the long run?

b. Suppose instead this business has a fixed cost of $6,000 per year. Should it produce or shut down in the short run? Should it stay in the industry or exit in the long run?

8. Four students have each started companies selling late-night snack deliveries to dorms and student apartment complexes. Each student has estimated her or his individual supply schedule as given in the accompanying table.

Delivery charge	Quantity supplied by:			
	Aleesha	Brent	Christine	Dominic
$1	1	5	3	7
2	3	8	6	12
3	5	11	9	17
4	7	15	12	21
5	9	21	15	23

a. Draw the four individual supply curves.

b. Determine the short-run industry supply schedule. Draw the short-run industry supply curve.

9. The first sushi restaurant opens in town. Initially people are very cautious about eating tiny portions of raw fish, as this is a town where large portions of grilled meat have always been popular. Soon, however, an influential health report warns consumers against grilled meat and suggests that they increase their consumption of fish, especially raw fish. The sushi restaurant becomes very popular and its profit increases.

a. What will happen to the short-run profit of the sushi restaurant? What will happen to the number of sushi restaurants in town in the long run? Will the first sushi restaurant be able to sustain its short-run profit over the long run? Explain your answers.

b. Local steakhouses suffer from the popularity of sushi and start incurring losses. What will happen to the number of steakhouses in town in the long run? Explain your answer.

10. A perfectly competitive firm has the following short-run total cost:

Quantity	TC
0	$5
1	10
2	13
3	18
4	25
5	34
6	45

Market demand for the firm's product is given by the following market demand schedule:

Price	Quantity demanded
$12	300
10	500
8	800
6	1,200
4	1,800

a. Calculate this firm's marginal cost and, for all output levels except zero, the firm's average variable cost and average total cost.

b. There are 100 firms in this industry that all have identical costs to those of this firm. Draw the short-run industry supply curve. In the same diagram, draw the market demand curve.

c. What is the market price, and how much profit will each firm make?

11. A new vaccine against a deadly disease has just been discovered. Presently, 55 people die from the disease each year. The new vaccine will save lives, but it is not completely safe. Some recipients of the shots will die from adverse reactions. The projected effects of the inoculation are given in the accompanying table:

Percent of population inoculated	Total deaths due to disease	Total deaths due to inoculation	Marginal benefit of inoculation	Marginal cost of inoculation	"Profit" of inoculation
0	55	0	—	—	—
10	45	0	—	—	—
20	36	1	—	—	—
30	28	3	—	—	—
40	21	6	—	—	—
50	15	10	—	—	—
60	10	15	—	—	—
70	6	20	—	—	—
80	3	25	—	—	—
90	1	30	—	—	—
100	0	35	—	—	—

a. What are the interpretations of "marginal benefit" and "marginal cost" here? Calculate marginal benefit and marginal cost per each 10 percent increase in the rate of inoculation. Write your answers in the table.

b. What proportion of the population should optimally be inoculated?

c. What is the interpretation of "profit" here? Calculate the profit for all levels of inoculation.

12. Evaluate each of the following statements. If a statement is true, explain why; if it is false, identify the mistake and try to correct it.

a. A profit-maximizing firm should select the output level at which the difference between the market price and marginal cost is greatest.

b. An increase in fixed cost lowers the profit-maximizing quantity of output produced in the short run.

>> The Rational Consumer

A CLAM TOO FAR

To ENTICE CUSTOMERS, RESTAURANTS sometimes offer "all-you-can-eat" specials: all-you-can-eat salad bars, all-you-can-eat breakfast buffets, and all-you-can-eat fried-clam dinners.

But how can a restaurant owner who offers such a special be sure she won't be eaten out of business? If she charges $12.99 for an all-you-can-eat clam dinner, what prevents her average customer from wolfing down $30 worth of clams?

The answer is that even though every once in a while you see someone really take advantage of the offer—heaping a plate high with 30 or 40 fried clams—it's a rare occurrence. And even those of us who like fried clams shudder a bit at the sight. Five or even 10 fried clams can be a treat, but 30 clams is ridiculous. Anyone who pays for an all-you-can-eat meal wants to make the most of it, but a sensible person knows when one more clam would be one clam too many.

Notice what we just did in that last sentence. We said that customers in a restaurant want to "make the most" of their meal; that sounds as if they are trying to maximize something. And we also said that they will stop when consuming one more clam would be a mistake; that sounds as if they are making a marginal decision.

When we analyze the behavior of *producers*, it makes sense to assume that they maximize profits. But what do consumers maximize? Isn't it all a matter of taste?

The answer is yes, it is a matter of taste—and economists can't say much about where tastes come from. But economists *can* say a lot about how a rational individual goes about satisfying his or her tastes. And that is in fact the way that economists think about consumer choice. They work with a model of a *rational consumer*—a consumer who knows what he or she wants and makes the most of the available opportunities.

In this chapter we will show how to analyze the decisions of a rational consumer and how this analysis can be used to derive the market demand curve.

When is more of a good thing too much?

What you will learn in this chapter:

➤ How consumers choose to spend their income on goods and services

➤ Why consumers make choices by maximizing **utility,** a measure of satisfaction from consumption

➤ Why the **principle of diminishing marginal utility** applies to the consumption of most goods and services

➤ How to use marginal analysis to find the **optimal consumption bundle**

➤ How choices by individual consumers give rise to the market demand curve

➤ What **income** and **substitution effects** are

We will begin by showing how the concept of *utility*—a measure of consumer satisfaction—allows us to begin thinking about rational consumer choice. We will then look at how *budget constraints* determine what a consumer can buy and how marginal analysis can be used to determine the consumption choice that maximizes utility. Finally, we will see how to use marginal analysis to derive the demand curve.

Utility: Getting Satisfaction

When analyzing consumer behavior, we're talking about people trying to get what they want—that is, about subjective feelings. Yet there is no simple way to measure subjective feelings. How much satisfaction do I get from my third fried clam? Is it less or more than yours? Does it even make sense to ask the question?

Luckily, it turns out that we don't need to make comparisons between your feelings and mine. All that is required to analyze consumer behavior is to suppose that each individual is trying to maximize some personal measure of the satisfaction gained from consumption of goods and services. That measure is known as the consumer's **utility,** a concept we use to understand behavior but don't expect to measure in practice. Nonetheless, we'll see that the assumption that consumers maximize utility helps us think clearly about consumer choice.

The **utility** of a consumer is a measure of the satisfaction the consumer derives from consumption of goods and services.

Utility and Consumption

An individual's utility depends on everything that individual consumes, from apples to Ziploc bags. The set of all the goods and services an individual consumes is known as the individual's **consumption bundle.** The relationship between an individual's consumption bundle and the total amount of utility it generates is known as the **utility function.** The utility function is a personal matter; two people with different tastes will have different utility functions. Someone who actually likes to consume 40 fried clams at a sitting must have a utility function that looks different from that of someone who would rather stop at 5 clams.

An individual's **consumption bundle** is the collection of all the goods and services consumed by that individual.

An individual's **utility function** gives the total utility generated by his or her consumption bundle.

This terminology is closely parallel to the terminology we used to describe producer decisions in Chapters 8 and 9. A producer uses inputs to produce output according to a production function; a consumer uses consumption to "produce" utility according to a utility function.

Obviously, people do not have a little computer in their heads that calculates the utility generated by their consumption choices. Nonetheless, people must make choices, and they usually base them on at least a rough attempt to decide which choice will give them greater satisfaction. I can have either soup or salad with my dinner. Which will I enjoy more? I can go to Disney World this year or save the money toward buying a new car. Which will make me happier?

The concept of a utility function is just a way of representing the fact that people must make such choices and that they make those choices in a more or less rational way.

How do we measure utility? For the sake of simplicity, it is useful to suppose that we can measure utility in hypothetical units called—what else?—**utils.**

A **util** is a unit of utility.

Figure 10-1, on page 232, illustrates a utility function. It shows the total utility that Cassie, who likes fried clams, gets from an all-you-can-eat clam dinner. We suppose that her consumption bundle consists of a side of cole slaw, which comes with the meal, plus a number of clams to be determined. The table that accompanies the figure shows how Cassie's total utility depends on the number of clams; the curve in panel (a) of the figure shows that same information graphically.

Cassie's utility function is upward sloping over most of the range shown, but it gets flatter as the number of clams consumed increases. And in this example it eventually

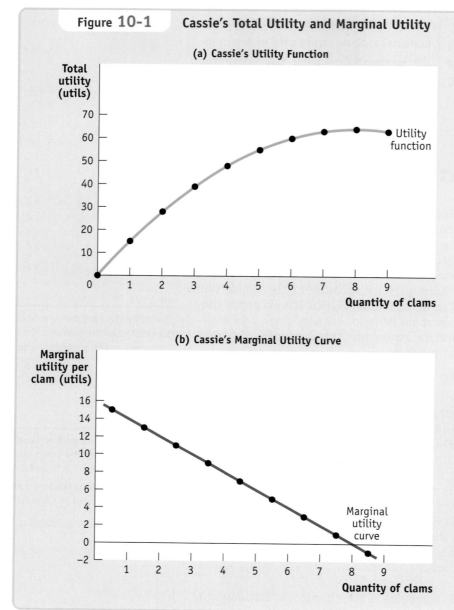

Figure 10-1 Cassie's Total Utility and Marginal Utility

(a) Cassie's Utility Function

Total utility (utils) — Utility function

(b) Cassie's Marginal Utility Curve

Marginal utility per clam (utils) — Marginal utility curve

Quantity of clams	Total utility (utils)	Marginal utility per clam (utils)
0	0	
		15
1	15	
		13
2	28	
		11
3	39	
		9
4	48	
		7
5	55	
		5
6	60	
		3
7	63	
		1
8	64	
		−1
9	63	

Panel (a) shows how Cassie's total utility depends on her consumption of fried clams. It increases until it reaches its maximum utility level of 64 utils at 8 clams consumed and decreases after that. Marginal utility is calculated in the table. Panel (b) shows the marginal utility curve, which slopes downward due to diminishing marginal utility. That is, each additional clam gives Cassie less utility than the previous clam.

turns downward. According to the information in the table in Figure 10-1, nine clams is a clam too far: adding that additional clam actually makes Cassie worse off. If she's rational, of course, Cassie will realize that and not consume the ninth clam.

So when Cassie chooses how many clams to consume, she will make this decision by considering the *change* in her total utility from consuming one more clam. This illustrates the general point: to maximize *total* utility, consumers must focus on *marginal* utility.

The Principle of Diminishing Marginal Utility

The **marginal utility** of a good or service is the change in total utility generated by consuming one additional unit of that good or service. The **marginal utility curve** shows how marginal utility depends on the quantity of a good or service consumed.

In addition to showing how Cassie's total utility depends on the number of clams she consumes, the table in Figure 10-1 also shows the **marginal utility** generated by consuming each additional clam—that is, the *change* in total utility from consuming one additional clam. Panel (b) shows the implied **marginal utility curve.** Following our practice in Chapters 7, 8, and 9 with the marginal cost curve, the marginal utility curve is constructed by plotting points at the midpoint of the unit intervals.

FOR INQUIRING MINDS

IS MARGINAL UTILITY REALLY DIMINISHING?

Are all goods really subject to diminishing marginal utility? Of course not; there are a number of goods for which, at least over some range, marginal utility is surely *increasing*.

For example, there are goods that require some experience to enjoy. The first time you do it, downhill skiing involves a lot more fear than enjoyment—or so they say: the authors have never tried it! It only becomes a pleasurable activity if you do it enough to become reasonably competent. And even some less strenuous forms of consumption

take practice; people who are not accustomed to drinking coffee say it has a bitter taste and can't understand its appeal. (The authors, on the other hand, regard coffee as one of the basic food groups.)

Another example would be goods that only deliver if you buy enough; the great Victorian economist Alfred Marshall, who more or less invented the supply and demand model, gave the example of wallpaper: buying only enough to do half a room is worse than useless. If you need two rolls of wallpaper to finish a room, the marginal

utility of the second roll is larger than the marginal utility of the first roll.

So why does it make sense to assume diminishing marginal utility? For one thing, most goods don't suffer from these qualifications: nobody needs to learn to like ice cream. Also, although most people don't ski and some people don't drink coffee, those who do ski or drink coffee do enough of it that the marginal utility of one more ski run or one more cup is less than that of the last. So *in the relevant range*, marginal utility is still diminishing.

The marginal utility curve is downward sloping: each successive clam adds less to total utility than the previous clam. This is reflected in the table: marginal utility falls from a high of 15 utils for the first clam consumed to −1 for the ninth clam consumed. The fact that the ninth clam has negative marginal utility means that consuming it actually reduces total utility. (Restaurants that offer all-you-can-eat meals depend on the proposition that you can have too much of a good thing.) Not all marginal utility curves eventually become negative. But it is a generally accepted proposition that marginal utility curves do slope downward—that consumption of most goods and services is subject to *diminishing marginal utility*.

The basic idea behind the **principle of diminishing marginal utility** is that the additional satisfaction a consumer gets from one more unit of a good or service declines as the amount of that good or service consumed rises. Or, to put it slightly differently, the more of a good or service you consume, the closer you are to being satiated—reaching a point at which an additional unit of the good adds nothing to your satisfaction. For someone who almost never gets to eat a banana, the occasional banana is a marvelous treat (as it was in Eastern Europe before the fall of communism, when bananas were very hard to find). For someone who eats them all the time, a banana is just, well, a banana.

The principle of diminishing marginal utility plays the same role in the analysis of consumer behavior that the principle of diminishing returns to an input plays in the analysis of producer behavior. Like the principle of diminishing returns to an input, the principle of diminishing marginal utility isn't always true. But it is true in the great majority of cases, enough to serve as a foundation for our analysis of consumer behavior.

The **principle of diminishing marginal utility** says that each successive unit of a good or service consumed adds less to total utility than the previous unit.

economics in action

Oysters versus Chicken

Is a particular food a special treat, something you consume on special occasions? Or is it an ordinary, take-it-or-leave-it dish? The answer depends a lot on how much of that food people normally consume, which determines how much utility they get *at the margin* from having a bit more.

Consider chicken. Modern Americans eat a lot of chicken, so much that they regard it as nothing special. Yet this was not always the case. Traditionally chicken was a luxury dish because chickens were expensive to raise. Restaurant menus from two centuries ago show chicken dishes as the most expensive items listed. Even as recently as 1928, Herbert Hoover ran for president on the slogan "A chicken in every pot," a promise of great prosperity.

What changed the status of chicken was the emergence of new, technologically advanced methods for raising and processing the birds. (You don't want to know.) These methods made chicken abundant, cheap, and also—thanks to the principle of diminishing marginal utility—nothing to get excited about.

The reverse evolution took place for oysters. Not everyone likes oysters, or for that matter has ever tried them—they are definitely not ordinary food. But they are regarded as a delicacy by some; at restaurants that serve them, an oyster appetizer often costs more than the main course.

Yet oysters were once very cheap and abundant—and were regarded as poverty food. In *The Pickwick Papers* by Charles Dickens, published in the 1830s, the author remarks that "poverty and oysters always seem to go together."

What changed? Pollution, which destroyed many oyster beds, greatly reduced the supply, but human population growth greatly increased the demand. As a result, thanks to the principle of diminishing marginal utility, oysters went from being a common food, regarded as nothing special, to being a highly prized luxury good. ■

< < < < < < < < < < < < < < < < < < <

>> QUICK REVIEW

- *Utility* is a measure of a consumer's satisfaction from consumption, expressed in units of *utils*. Consumers try to maximize their utility. A consumer's *utility function* shows the relationship between the *consumption bundle* and the total utility it generates.
- To maximize utility, a consumer considers the *marginal utility* from consuming one more unit of a good or service, illustrated by the *marginal utility curve*.
- In the consumption of most goods and services, and for most people, the *principle of diminishing marginal utility* holds: each successive unit consumed adds less to total utility than the previous unit.

>> CHECK YOUR UNDERSTANDING 10-1

1. Explain why a rational consumer who has diminishing marginal utility for a good would not consume an additional unit when it generates negative marginal utility, even when that unit is free.

2. Marta drinks three cups of coffee a day, for which she has diminishing marginal utility. Which of her three cups generates the greatest increase in total utility? Which generates the least?

3. In each of the following cases, does the consumer have diminishing, constant, or increasing marginal utility? Explain your answers.
   a. The more Mabel exercises, the more she enjoys each additional visit to the gym.
   b. Although Mei's classical CD collection is huge, her enjoyment from buying another CD has not changed as her collection has grown.
   c. When Dexter was a struggling student, his enjoyment from a good restaurant meal was greater than now, when he has them more frequently.

Solutions appear at back of book.

Budgets and Optimal Consumption

The principle of diminishing marginal utility explains why most people eventually reach a limit, even at an all-you-can-eat buffet where the cost of another clam is measured only in future indigestion. Under ordinary circumstances, however, it costs some additional resources to consume more of a good, and consumers must take that cost into account when making choices.

What do we mean by cost? As always, the fundamental measure of cost is *opportunity cost*. Because the amount of money a consumer can spend is limited, a decision to consume more of one good is also a decision to consume less of some other good.

Budget Constraints and Budget Lines

Consider Sammy, whose appetite is exclusively for clams and potatoes (there's no accounting for tastes). He has a weekly income of $20 and since, given his appetite, more of either good is better than less, he spends all of it on clams and potatoes. We will assume that clams cost $4 per pound and potatoes cost $2 per pound. What are his possible choices?

Whatever Sammy chooses, we know that the cost of his consumption bundle cannot exceed the amount of money he has to spend. That is,

(10-1) Expenditure on clams + expenditure on potatoes ≤ total income

Consumers always have limited income, which constrains how much they can consume. So the requirement illustrated by Equation 10-1—that a consumer must choose a consumption bundle that costs no more than his or her total income—is known as the consumer's **budget constraint.** It's a simple way of saying that consumers can't spend more than the total amount of income available to them. In other words, consumption bundles are affordable when they obey the budget constraint. We call the set of all of Sammy's affordable consumption bundles his **consumption possibilities.** As we will see, which consumption bundles are in this set depends on the consumer's income and the prices of goods and services.

Figure 10-2 shows Sammy's consumption possibilities. The quantity of clams in his consumption bundle is measured on the horizontal axis and the quantity of potatoes on the vertical axis. The downward-sloping line connecting points A through F shows which consumption bundles are affordable and which are not. Every bundle on or inside this line (the shaded area) is affordable; every bundle outside this line is unaffordable. As an example of one of the points, let's look at point C, representing 2 pounds of clams and 6 pounds of potatoes, and check whether it satisfies Sammy's budget constraint. The cost of bundle C is 2 pounds of clams × $4 per pound + 6 pounds of potatoes × $2 per pound = $8 + $12 = $20. So bundle C does indeed satisfy Sammy's budget constraint: it costs no more than his weekly income of $20. In

> A **budget constraint** requires that the cost of a consumer's consumption bundle be no more than the consumer's total income.
>
> A consumer's **consumption possibilities** is the set of all consumption bundles that can be consumed given the consumer's income and prevailing prices.

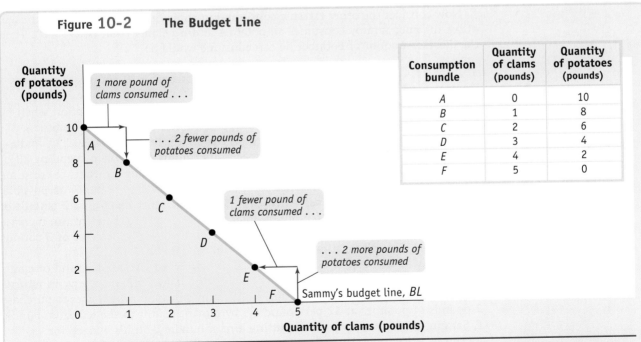

Figure 10-2   The Budget Line

Consumption bundle	Quantity of clams (pounds)	Quantity of potatoes (pounds)
A	0	10
B	1	8
C	2	6
D	3	4
E	4	2
F	5	0

The *budget line* represents all the possible combinations of quantities of potatoes and clams that Sammy can purchase if he spends all of his income. Also, it is the boundary between the set of affordable consumption bundles (the *consumption possibilities*) and unaffordable ones. Given that clams cost $4 per pound and potatoes cost $2 per pound, if Sammy spends all of his income on clams (bundle F), he can purchase 5 pounds of clams; if he spends all of his income on potatoes (bundle A), he can purchase 10 pounds of potatoes. The slope of the budget line here is −2: 2 pounds of potatoes must be forgone for 1 more pound of clams, reflecting the opportunity cost of clams in terms of potatoes. So the location and slope of the budget line depend on the consumer's income and the prices of the goods.

A consumer's **budget line** shows the consumption bundles available to a consumer who spends all of his or her income.

fact, bundle C costs exactly as much as Sammy's income. By doing the arithmetic, you can check that all the other points lying on the downward-sloping line are also bundles at which Sammy spends all of his income.

The downward-sloping line has a special name, the **budget line**. It shows all the consumption bundles available to Sammy when he spends all of his income. Let's use Figure 10-2 to gain an intuitive understanding of Sammy's budget line. For brevity's sake, we will denote the quantity of clams (in pounds) by Q_C and the quantity of potatoes (in pounds) by Q_P. We will also define P_C to be the price of one pound of clams, P_P to be the price of one pound of potatoes, and N to be Sammy's income. So if we restate Sammy's budget constraint of Equation 10-1 in terms of this new notation, it becomes

(10-2) $(Q_C \times P_C) + (Q_P \times P_P) \leq N$

Whenever Sammy consumes a bundle on his *budget line,* he spends all of his income, so that his expenditure on clams and potatoes is exactly equal to his income. The equation for Sammy's budget line is therefore

(10-3) $(Q_C \times P_C) + (Q_P \times P_P) = N$

Now consider what happens when Sammy spends all $20 of his income on clams (that is, $Q_P = 0$). In that case the greatest amount of clams he can consume is

$$Q_C = N/P_C = \$20/\$4 \text{ per pound of clams} = 5 \text{ pounds of clams}$$

So the horizontal intercept of the budget line—Sammy's clam consumption when he consumes zero potatoes—is at point F, where he consumes 5 pounds of clams.

Now consider the other extreme consumption choice given that Sammy spends all of his income: Sammy consumes all potatoes and no clams (that is, $Q_C = 0$). Then the greatest amount of potatoes he can consume would be

$$Q_P = N/P_P = \$20/\$2 \text{ per pound of potatoes} = 10 \text{ pounds of potatoes}$$

So the vertical intercept of the budget line—Sammy's potato consumption when he consumes zero clams—is at point A, where he consumes 10 pounds of potatoes.

The remaining four bundles indicated on the budget line—points B, C, D, and E—can be understood by considering the trade-offs Sammy faces when spending all of his income. Starting at bundle A, consider what happens if Sammy wants to consume 1 pound of clams while still consuming as many pounds of potatoes as possible. Consuming 1 pound of clams, which costs $4, requires that he give up 2 pounds of potatoes, which cost $2 per pound. In order to move 1 unit to the right (an increase of 1 pound of clams), Sammy must also move 2 units down (a decrease of 2 pounds of potatoes). This places him at bundle B on his budget line.

Similarly, if we start at bundle F and allow Sammy to give up 1 pound of clams (moving 1 unit to the left), how many pounds of potatoes will he receive in return? Giving up 1 pound of clams frees up $4 of Sammy's income, which goes to purchase 2 pounds of potatoes at $2 per pound. So by moving 1 unit to the left from bundle F, Sammy also moves up 2 units, putting him at bundle E on his budget line.

This exercise shows that when Sammy spends all of his income, he trades off more clams for fewer potatoes, or vice versa, by "sliding" along his budget line. In particular, if we assume that Sammy can consume fractions of pounds of clams and potatoes as well as whole pounds, his budget line is indeed the line connecting the points A through F in Figure 10-2.

Do we need to consider the other bundles in Sammy's consumption possibilities, the ones that lie *within* the shaded region in Figure 10-2 bounded by the budget line? The answer is, for all practical situations, no: as long as Sammy doesn't get satiated— that is, as long as his marginal utility from consuming either good is always positive—

and he doesn't get any utility from saving income rather than spending it, then he will always choose to consume a bundle that lies on his budget line.

Because changing a consumption bundle involves sliding up or down the budget line, the *slope* of the budget line tells us the opportunity cost of each good in terms of the other. Recall from Chapter 2 that we used the slope of the production possibility frontier to illustrate the opportunity cost to the economy of an additional unit of one good in terms of how much of the other good must be forgone, a cost that arose from the economy's limited productive resources. In this case, the slope of the budget line illustrates the opportunity cost to an individual of consuming one more unit of one good in terms of how much of the other good in his or her consumption bundle must be forgone. The scarce "resource" here is money—the consumer has a limited budget.

The slope of Sammy's budget line—the rise over run—is −2; 2 pounds of potatoes must be forgone to obtain another pound of clams. Economists call the number of pounds of potatoes that must be forgone in order to obtain one more pound of clams the *relative price* of one pound of clams in terms of potatoes. The relative price of the good on the horizontal axis in terms of the good on the vertical axis is equal to minus the slope of the budget line.

One important point about the budget line may be obvious but nonetheless needs emphasizing: the position of a consumer's budget line—how far *out* it is from the origin—depends on that consumer's income. Suppose that Sammy's income were to rise to $32 per week. Then he could afford to buy 8 pounds of clams, or 16 pounds of potatoes, or any consumption bundle in between; as shown in Figure 10-3, his budget line would move *outward*. However, if his income were to shrink to $12 per week, his budget line would shift *inward*: he would be able to consume at most 3 pounds of clams or 6 pounds of potatoes. In all these cases, the slope of the budget line would not change because the relative price of clams in terms of potatoes does not change: for 1 more pound of clams, Sammy still has to give up 2 pounds of potatoes.

Clearly, a larger income would increase Sammy's consumption possibilities; and utility analysis can tell us how he would take advantage of those possibilities to increase his total utility by consuming more of one or both goods. Conversely, a smaller income would reduce Sammy's consumption possibilities. He would be forced to consume less, and his utility would be lower. But for now let's continue to assume that Sammy's income is fixed at $20 per week.

Given that $20 per week budget, what point on his budget line will Sammy choose?

Figure 10-3

Changes in Income Shift the Budget Line

If Sammy's income increases from $20 to $32 per week, he is clearly better off: his consumption possibilities have increased, and his budget line shifts, from BL_1, outward to its new position at BL_2. If Sammy's income decreases from $20 to $12, he is clearly worse off: his consumption possibilities have decreased and his budget line shifts inward toward the origin, from BL_1 to BL_3. >*web*...

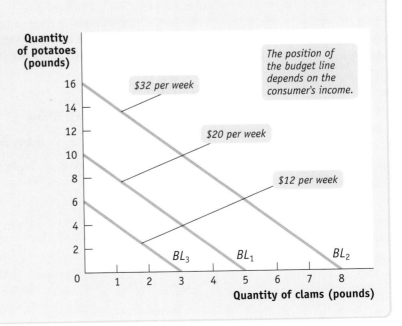

Optimal Consumption Choice

Because Sammy has a budget constraint, which means that he will consume a consumption bundle on the budget line, a choice to consume a given quantity of clams also determines his potato consumption, and vice versa. We want to find the consumption bundle—the point on the budget line—that maximizes Sammy's total utility. This bundle is Sammy's **optimal consumption bundle,** the consumption bundle that maximizes total utility given the budget constraint.

The **optimal consumption bundle** is the consumption bundle that maximizes a consumer's total utility given his or her budget constraint.

TABLE 10-1

Sammy's Utility from Clam and Potato Consumption

Utility from clam consumption		Utility from potato consumption	
Quantity of clams (pounds)	Utility from clams (utils)	Quantity of potatoes (pounds)	Utility from potatoes (utils)
0	0	0	0
1	15	1	11.5
2	25	2	21.4
3	31	3	29.8
4	34	4	36.8
5	36	5	42.5
		6	47.0
		7	50.5
		8	53.2
		9	55.2
		10	56.7

Table 10-1 shows how much utility Sammy gets from different levels of consumption of clams and potatoes, respectively. According to the table, Sammy has a healthy appetite; the more of either good he consumes, the higher his utility.

But because he has a limited budget, he must make a trade-off: the more pounds of clams he consumes, the fewer pounds of potatoes, and vice versa. That is, he must choose a point on his budget line.

Table 10-2 shows how his total utility varies as he slides down his budget line. Each of six possible consumption bundles, *A* through *F* from Figure 10-2, is given in the first column. The second column shows the level of clam consumption corresponding to each

TABLE 10-2

Sammy's Budget and Total Utility

Consumption Bundle	Quantity of clams (pounds)	Utility from clams (utils)	Quantity of potatoes (pounds)	Utility from potatoes (utils)	Total utility (utils)
A	0	0	10	56.7	56.7
B	1	15	8	53.2	68.2
C	2	25	6	47.0	72.0
D	3	31	4	36.8	67.8
E	4	34	2	21.4	55.4
F	5	36	0	0	36.0

choice. The third column shows the utility Sammy gets from consuming those clams. The fourth column shows the quantity of potatoes Sammy can afford *given* the level of clam consumption; this quantity goes down as his clam consumption goes up, because he is sliding down the budget line. The fifth column shows the utility he gets from consuming those potatoes. And the final column shows his *total utility*. In this example, Sammy's total utility is the sum of the utility he gets from clams and the utility he gets from potatoes.

Figure 10-4 illustrates the result graphically. Panel (a) shows Sammy's budget line, to remind us that when he decides to consume more clams he is also deciding to consume fewer potatoes. Panel (b) then shows how his total utility depends on that choice. The horizontal axis in panel (b) has two sets of labels: it shows both the quantity of clams, increasing from left to right, and the quantity of potatoes, increasing from right to left. The reason we can use the same axis to represent consumption of both goods is, of course, the budget line: the more pounds of clams Sammy consumes, the fewer pounds of potatoes he can afford, and vice versa.

Figure 10-4

Optimal Consumption Bundle

Panel (a) shows Sammy's budget line and his six possible consumption bundles. Panel (b) shows how his total utility is affected by his consumption bundle, which must lie on his budget line. The quantity of clams is measured from left to right on the horizontal axis, and the quantity of potatoes is measured from right to left. His total utility is maximized at bundle *C*, where he consumes 2 pounds of clams and 6 pounds of potatoes. This is Sammy's *optimal consumption bundle.*

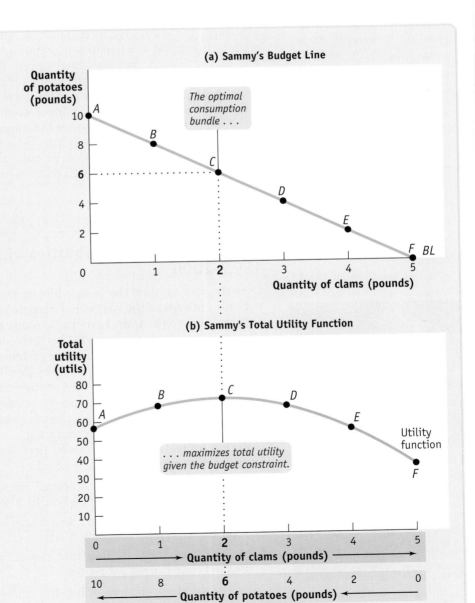

Clearly, the consumption bundle that makes the best of the trade-off between clam consumption and potato consumption, the optimal consumption bundle, is the one that maximizes Sammy's total utility. That is, Sammy's optimal consumption bundle puts him at the top of the utility function.

As always, we can find the top of the curve by direct observation. We can see from Figure 10-4 that Sammy's total utility is maximized at point C—that his optimal consumption bundle contains 2 pounds of clams and 6 pounds of potatoes. But we know that we usually gain more insight into "how much" problems when we use marginal analysis. So in the next section we turn to representing and solving the optimal consumption choice problem with marginal analysis.

economics in action

The Consumption Possibilities of American Workers, 1895–2000

Over the past century, the budget line of the average American worker has shifted radically outward as the nation has become vastly richer. A good illustration of this outward shift comes from a comparison made by the economist J. Bradford DeLong (find the article at http://econ161.berkeley.edu/TCEH/Slouch_wealth2.html).

He compared the cost of a number of items in the 1895 Montgomery Ward catalog to the cost of similar items today by calculating the number of hours an average worker would need to work to earn enough money to buy them. If we assume that a worker puts in 2,000 hours per year—40 hours per week, with two weeks of vacation—we can calculate how many units of each good a worker could purchase by spending an entire year's income only on that good.

According to DeLong's estimates, here are the amounts of various goods that workers then and now could have bought:

- In 1895, an average worker's annual income would have bought 7.7 one-speed bicycles; in 2000, it would have bought 278 bicycles.

- In 1895, the worker's income would have bought 45 full sets of dinner plates; in 2000, it would have bought 556 sets.

- In 1895, a worker's income would have bought 0.83 of a Steinway piano; in 2000, it would have bought 1.8 pianos.

By any standard, the budget line has shifted out enormously. DeLong estimates that the shift for the average good is approximately sevenfold. That is, today's workers can on average purchase seven times as much of a randomly chosen good

Today, the average American worker's annual income buys a lot more bicycle than it did in 1895.

as their predecessors could have in 1895. Of course, in a way this understates the rise in purchasing power: there are many goods, like computers, that were not available in 1895 at any price. ∎

> —

➤ The *budget constraint* requires that a consumer's total expenditure be no more than his or her income. The set of consumption bundles that satisfy the budget constraint is the consumer's *consumption possibilities*.

➤ A consumer who spends all of his or her income chooses a point on his or her *budget line*. Its slope is equal to the opportunity cost of the good on the horizontal axis in terms of the good on the vertical axis.

➤ The consumption choice that maximizes total utility given the consumer's budget constraint is the *optimal consumption bundle*. It must lie on the consumer's budget line.

>>CHECK YOUR UNDERSTANDING 10-2

1. In the following two examples, draw the budget line. Make sure that you calculate the following: (i) the vertical intercept of the budget line; (ii) the horizontal intercept of the budget line; (iii) the slope of the budget line; (iv) the opportunity cost of the good on the horizontal axis in terms of the good on the vertical axis.

   a. A consumption bundle consisting of movie tickets and buckets of popcorn. Each ticket costs $5.00, each bucket of popcorn costs $2.50, and the consumer's income is $10.00. Movie tickets are on the vertical axis and buckets of popcorn are on the horizontal axis.

   b. A consumption bundle consisting of underwear and socks. Each pair of socks costs $1.50, each pair of underwear costs $4.00, and the consumer's income is $12.00. Pairs of socks are on the vertical axis and pairs of underwear are on the horizontal axis.

Solutions appear at back of book.

Spending the Marginal Dollar

Marginal analysis is often the best way to think about "how much" decisions. In this case, Sammy is making a decision about the quantity of clams to consume, taking into account the fact that the more clams he consumes, the fewer potatoes he can afford. As we've seen, we can find his optimal consumption choice by finding the total utility he receives from each consumption bundle on his budget line and then choosing the bundle at which total utility is maximized. But is there a way to use marginal analysis instead?

The answer is yes: we can think about the problem of choosing an optimal consumption bundle in terms of the decision a consumer must make about how much to spend on each good. The marginal decision then becomes one of how to *spend the marginal dollar*—how to allocate an additional dollar between clams and potatoes. As we'll see in a moment, looking at Sammy's decision in terms of how he allocates his income gives us an important insight into the relationship between prices and consumer decisions.

Our first step is to ask how much additional utility Sammy gets from spending an additional dollar on either good—the **marginal utility per dollar** spent on either clams or potatoes.

Marginal Utility per Dollar

We've already introduced the concept of marginal utility, the additional utility a consumer gets from consuming one more unit of a good or service; now let's see how this concept can be used to derive the related measure of marginal utility per dollar.

Table 10-3, on page 242, shows how to calculate the marginal utility per dollar spent on clams and potatoes, respectively.

In panel (a) of the table, the first column shows different possible levels of clam consumption. The second column shows the utility Sammy derives from each level of clam consumption; the third column then shows the marginal utility, the increase in utility Sammy gets from consuming an additional pound of clams. Panel (b) does the same thing for potatoes. The next step is to derive marginal utility *per dollar* for each good. To do this, we must divide the marginal utility of the good by its price in dollars.

To see why we must divide by the price, compare the third and fourth columns of panel (a). Consider what happens if Sammy increases his clam consumption from 2 pounds to 3 pounds. As we can see, this increase in clam consumption raises his total utility by 6 utils. But he must spend $4 for that additional pound, so the increase in his utility per additional dollar spent on clams is 6 utils/$4 = 1.50 utils per dollar.

The **marginal utility per dollar** spent on a good or service is the additional utility from spending one more dollar on that good or service.

PITFALLS

THE RIGHT MARGINAL COMPARISON

Marginal analysis helps us understand "how-much" decisions by showing that they involve setting the marginal *benefit* of some activity equal to its marginal *cost*. But to get this right, it's important to be careful what "marginals" you compare. In the case of consumption, it's tempting but wrong to say that the marginal utility of consumption of any two goods must be the same.

The right answer is that the marginal utility *per dollar* must be the same. This takes prices into account. If a milkshake costs four times as much as an order of french fries, the optimal consumption choice isn't where you gain the same amount of utility from an extra milkshake as from an extra order of french fries; it's where the milkshake adds four times as much to utility. With the money that buys one milkshake you could have bought four orders of french fries, so the one milkshake has to add four times as much to your utility as one order of french fries. In other words, the marginal utility per dollar has to be the same for milkshakes and french fries.

TABLE 10-3

Marginal Utility per Dollar

(a) Clams (price of clams = $4 per pound)				(b) Potatoes (price of potatoes = $2 per pound)			
Quantity of clams (pounds)	Utility from clams (utils)	Marginal utility per pound of clams (utils)	Marginal utility per dollar (utils)	Quantity of potatoes (pounds)	Utility from potatoes (utils)	Marginal utility per pound of potatoes (utils)	Marginal utility per dollar (utils)
0	0			0	0		
		15	3.75			11.5	5.75
1	15			1	11.5		
		10	2.50			9.9	4.95
2	25			2	21.4		
		6	1.50			8.4	4.20
3	31			3	29.8		
		3	0.75			7.0	3.50
4	34			4	36.8		
		2	0.50			5.7	2.85
5	36			5	42.5		
						4.5	2.25
				6	47.0		
						3.5	1.75
				7	50.5		
						2.7	1.35
				8	53.2		
						2.0	1.00
				9	55.2		
						1.5	0.75
				10	56.7		

Similarly, if he increases his clam consumption from 3 pounds to 4 pounds, his marginal utility is 3 utils per clam but his marginal utility per dollar is 3 utils/$4 = 0.75 utils per dollar. Notice that because of diminishing marginal utility per pound of clams, Sammy's marginal utility per pound of clams falls as the quantity of clams he consumes rises. As a result, his marginal utility per dollar spent on clams also falls as the quantity of clams he consumes rises.

So the last column of panel (a) shows how Sammy's marginal utility per dollar spent on clams depends on the quantity of clams he consumes. Similarly, the last column of panel (b) shows how his marginal utility per dollar spent on potatoes depends on the quantity of potatoes he consumes. Again, marginal utility per dollar spent on each good falls as the quantity of that good consumed rises, because of diminishing marginal utility.

We will use the symbols MU_C and MU_P to represent the marginal utility per pound of clams and potatoes, respectively. Then the marginal utility per dollar spent on clams is MU_C/P_C and the marginal utility per dollar spent on potatoes is MU_P/P_P. In general, the additional utility generated from an additional dollar spent on a good is equal to:

(10-4) Marginal utility per dollar spent on a good
= Marginal utility of one unit of the good / Price of one unit of the good
= MU_{good}/P_{good}

Now let's see how this concept helps us derive a consumer's optimal consumption using marginal analysis.

Optimal Consumption

The curve in panel (a) of Figure 10-5 shows Sammy's marginal utility per dollar spent on clams, MU_C/P_C, as derived in Table 10-3. The curve in panel (b) shows his marginal utility per dollar spent on potatoes, MU_P/P_P. We already know from Figure

Figure 10-5 Marginal Utility per Dollar

(a) Clams

Marginal utility per dollar (utils)

At the optimal consumption bundle, marginal utility per dollar spent on clams . . .

B_C

C_C

MU_C/P_C

Quantity of clams (pounds)

(b) Potatoes

Marginal utility per dollar (utils)

. . . is equal to the marginal utility per dollar spent on potatoes.

C_P

B_P

MU_P/P_P

Quantity of potatoes (pounds)

Panel (a) shows Sammy's marginal utility per dollar spent on clams; panel (b) shows his marginal utility per dollar spent on potatoes. Points C_c in panel (a) and C_p in panel (b) correspond to bundle C in Figure 10-4, Sammy's optimal consumption bundle of 2 pounds of clams and 6 pounds of potatoes. At these points his marginal utility per dollar spent on each good is 2. This illustrates the *optimal* consumption rule: at the optimal consumption bundle, the marginal utility per dollar spent on each good and service is the same. At any other consumption bundle along Sammy's budget line, such as bundle B in Figure 10-4, which is represented here by points B_c and B_p, consumption is not optimal: he can increase his utility at no additional cost by reallocating his spending.

10-4 that Sammy's optimal consumption bundle, C, consists of 2 pounds of clams and 6 pounds of potatoes. From Figure 10-5 we can read off the marginal utility per dollar spent on clams and potatoes, respectively, at that optimal consumption bundle, which corresponds to points C_C and C_P. And we see something interesting: when Sammy consumes 2 pounds of clams and 6 pounds of potatoes, his marginal utility per dollar spent is the same, 2, for both goods. That is, at the optimal consumption bundle $MU_C/P_C = MU_P/P_P = 2$.

This isn't an accident. Consider another one of Sammy's possible consumption bundles, say B in Figure 10-4, at which he consumes 1 pound of clams and 8 pounds of potatoes. The marginal utility per dollar spent on each good is shown by points B_C and B_P in Figure 10-5. At that consumption bundle, Sammy's marginal utility per dollar spent on clams would be approximately 3, but his marginal utility per dollar spent on potatoes would be only approximately 1. This shows that he has made a mistake: he is consuming too many potatoes and not enough clams.

How do we know this? If Sammy's marginal utility per dollar spent on clams is higher than his marginal utility per dollar spent on potatoes, he has a simple way to make himself better off while staying within his budget: spend $1 less on potatoes and $1 more on clams. By spending an additional dollar on clams, he adds about 3 utils to his total utility; meanwhile, by spending $1 less on potatoes, he subtracts only about 1 util from his total utility. Because his marginal utility per dollar spent is higher for clams than for potatoes, reallocating his spending toward clams and away from potatoes would increase his total utility. On the other hand, if his marginal utility per dollar spent on potatoes is higher, he can increase his utility by spending less on clams and more on potatoes. So if Sammy has in fact chosen his optimal consumption bundle, his marginal utility per dollar spent on clams and potatoes must be equal.

BUT ARE CONSUMERS REALLY RATIONAL?

Many companies offer retirement plans that allow their employees to put aside part of their salaries tax-free. These plans, called 401(k)s, can save a worker thousands of dollars in taxes each year. But the plans sometimes have disadvantages: some companies invest their employees' savings mainly in their own stock, which can be disastrous if the company gets in trouble, leaving the employee with no savings *and* no job. (That's what happened to the employees of Enron.)

Clearly, then, people should carefully decide how much of their money to put in an employer-administered retirement plan. They should compare the marginal utility of a dollar spent on current consumption with the marginal utility of a dollar saved for retirement. They should weigh the tax advantages of saving through the employer plan against the risks of letting the employer decide where their savings are invested.

But recent economic research suggests that most people aren't careful at all. For example, some companies have an "opt-in" system for 401(k)s—that is, in some companies employees must ask to be enrolled. Other companies have an "opt-out" system— employees are automatically enrolled unless they request otherwise. This shouldn't make a difference—if the plan is managed well, people should opt in; if it's managed poorly (that is, investing mainly in company's own stock), they should opt out. Yet when companies switch to automatic enrollment, the number of employees in their 401(k) plans

rises dramatically. As the National Bureau of Economic Research put it, workers seem to follow the path of least resistance, instead of comparing their options and maximizing their utility.

Studies of saving behavior are one example of a growing field known as "behavioral economics." Behavioral economists question the whole concept of the rational consumer. Their research focuses on situations in which people don't seem to be rational—that is, when they behave in ways that can't easily be explained by utility maximization.

One key insight in behavioral economics comes from the work of Herbert Simon, who won the Nobel prize in economics in 1978. Simon argued that sometimes individuals find that it isn't actually rational to go to great lengths to maximize utility, since searching for the perfect answer is itself a costly activity. Instead, he argued, they engage in *bounded rationality*: individuals save time and effort by making decisions that are "good enough," rather than perfect. In the case of savings plans, this might involve following the path of least resistance: not bothering to participate in a well-managed

opt-in plan, and not bothering to opt out of a poorly managed automatic plan.

Today's behavioral economists use insights from psychology to understand behavior seemingly at odds with rationality. The 2002 Nobel prize went to Daniel Kahneman, a psychologist who, with his late co-author Amos Tversky, laid out a theory of how people make choices in the face of uncertainty. This work and other insights into nonrational behavior are having an important influence on analysis of financial markets, labor markets, and other economic concerns.

But it's hard to find a behavioral economist who thinks that the insights of this field should replace the analysis of utility maximization. The theory of the rational consumer remains the main way in which economists analyze consumer behavior.

Great new car, but are you saving enough for retirement?

Mark Richards/Photo Edit

The **optimal consumption rule** says that when a consumer maximizes utility, the marginal utility per dollar spent must be the same for all goods and services in the consumption bundle.

This is a general principle, known as the **optimal consumption rule**: when a consumer maximizes utility in the face of a budget constraint, the marginal utility per dollar spent on each good or service in the consumption bundle is the same. That is, for any two goods C and P the optimal consumption rule says that at the optimal consumption bundle

(10-5) $\dfrac{MU_C}{P_C} = \dfrac{MU_P}{P_P}$

It's easiest to understand this rule using examples in which the consumption bundle contains only two goods, but it applies no matter how many goods or services a consumer buys: in the optimal consumption bundle, the marginal utilities per dollar spent for each and every good or service in that bundle are equal.

economics in action

Self-Service Gasoline

At the end of the 1970s the price of gasoline in the United States shot up because of a combination of world oil shortages and deregulation. At the same time, many gas stations began offering drivers a discount if they pumped their own gas.

Many people argued that the rise of self-service gas was a response to higher gas prices and that if gas prices ever went down again, people would once again be willing to pay the price of full service.

But economists in general were skeptical of this conclusion. Consumers, they argued, were making a calculation: the extra utility gained from spending on other goods was worth the extra effort. And gas stations offered a price break on self-service gas because it saved them labor; so the price break would remain even if gas prices went down. So economists argued that people would continue to use self-service pumps even if gas prices fell back to traditional levels.

In the event, gas prices did fall; by the late 1990s they were actually lower, adjusted for inflation, than they had been for generations. But most drivers continued to use self-service gas. ■

> > > > > > > > > > > > > > > > > >

>> CHECK YOUR UNDERSTANDING 10-3

1. In Figure 10-5 you can see that marginal utility per dollar spent on clams and marginal utility per dollar spent on potatoes are approximately equal at a consumption bundle consisting of 3 pounds of clams and 8 pounds of potatoes. Explain why this is not Sammy's optimal consumption bundle. Illustrate your answer using the budget line in Figure 10-4.

2. Explain what is faulty about the following statement, using data from Table 10-3: "In order to maximize utility, Sammy should consume the bundle that gives him the maximum marginal utility per dollar for each good."

Solutions appear at back of book.

From Utility to the Demand Curve

We have now analyzed the optimal consumption choice of a consumer whose income we take as given and who faces one particular set of prices—in our Sammy example, $20 of income per week, $4 per pound of clams, and $2 per pound of potatoes.

But the main reason we want to understand consumer behavior is to go behind the market demand curve—to understand how the market demand curve is explained by the utility-maximizing behavior of individual consumers.

Individual Demand and Market Demand

Let's begin by reviewing the relationship between prices and quantity demanded, both at the individual level and at the level of the market as a whole.

The **individual demand curve** for a good shows the relationship between the quantity of a good demanded by an individual consumer and the market price of that good. For example, suppose that Bert is a consumer of fried clams and that panel (a) of Figure 10-6 on page 246 shows how many pounds of clams he will buy at any given market price per pound. Then D_{Bert} is Bert's individual demand curve.

The *market demand curve* shows how the quantity of a good demanded by all consumers depends on the market price of that good. The market demand curve is the *horizontal sum* of the individual demand curves of all consumers. To see what we mean by the term *horizontal sum*, assume for a moment that there are only two consumers of fried clams, Bert and Ernie. Ernie's individual demand curve is shown in panel (b). Panel (c) shows the market demand curve. At any given price, the quantity demanded

The **individual demand curve** for a good shows the relationship between quantity demanded and price for an individual consumer.

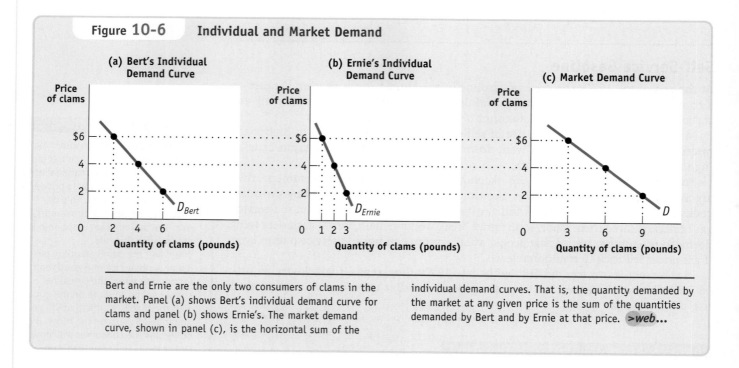

Figure 10-6 **Individual and Market Demand**

(a) Bert's Individual Demand Curve

Price of clams

$6
4
2

D_{Bert}

0 2 4 6

Quantity of clams (pounds)

(b) Ernie's Individual Demand Curve

Price of clams

$6
4
2

D_{Ernie}

0 1 2 3

Quantity of clams (pounds)

(c) Market Demand Curve

Price of clams

$6
4
2

D

0 3 6 9

Quantity of clams (pounds)

Bert and Ernie are the only two consumers of clams in the market. Panel (a) shows Bert's individual demand curve for clams and panel (b) shows Ernie's. The market demand curve, shown in panel (c), is the horizontal sum of the individual demand curves. That is, the quantity demanded by the market at any given price is the sum of the quantities demanded by Bert and by Ernie at that price. **>web...**

by the market is the sum of the quantities demanded by Bert and Ernie. For example, at a price of $6 per pound, Bert demands 2 pounds of clams and Ernie demands 1 pound; so the quantity demanded by the market is 3 pounds. At a price of $4 per pound, Bert demands 4 pounds and Ernie demands 2 pounds; so the quantity demanded by the market is 6 pounds—and so on.

But what lies behind the individual demand curves? The *law of demand* tells us that if the price of a good increases, the quantity demanded of that good decreases. But let's now use our analysis of consumer choice to get a deeper understanding of the law of demand.

Marginal Utility, the Substitution Effect, and the Law of Demand

Suppose that the price of fried clams, P_C, rises. This doesn't change the marginal utility a consumer gets from an additional pound of clams, MU_C, at any given level of clam consumption. However, it reduces the marginal utility *per dollar spent* on fried clams, MU_C/P_C. And the decrease in marginal utility per dollar spent on clams gives the consumer an incentive to consume fewer clams.

To see why, recall the optimal consumption rule: a utility-maximizing consumer chooses a consumption bundle for which the marginal utility per dollar spent on all goods is the same. If the marginal utility per dollar spent on clams falls because the price of clams rises, the consumer can increase his or her utility by purchasing fewer clams and more of other goods.

The opposite happens if the price of clams falls. In that case the marginal utility per dollar spent on clams, MU_C/P_C, increases at any given level of clam consumption. A consumer can increase his or her utility by purchasing more clams and less of other goods.

So when the price of a good increases, an individual will normally consume less of that good and more of other goods. Correspondingly, when the price of a good decreases, an individual will normally consume more of that good and less of other goods. This means that the individual demand curve, which relates an individual's consumption of a good to the price of that good, is normally downward sloping—that is, it obeys the law of demand.

An alternative way to think about why individual demand curves slope downward is to focus on opportunity costs. When the price of clams—or any other good—decreases, an individual doesn't have to give up as many units of other goods in order to buy one more unit of clams. So consuming clams becomes more attractive. Conversely, when the price of a good increases, consuming that good becomes a less attractive use of resources, and the consumer buys less.

This effect of a price change on the quantity consumed by a consumer is always present. It is known as the **substitution effect**—the change in the quantity consumed as the consumer substitutes the good that has become relatively cheaper in place of the good that has become relatively more expensive. When a good absorbs only a small share of the consumer's spending, the substitution effect is essentially the whole story about why the individual demand curve of that consumer slopes downward. And, by implication, when a good absorbs only a small share of the typical consumer's spending, the substitution effect is essentially the sole explanation of why the market demand curve slopes downward. However, some goods, such as housing, absorb a large share of a typical consumer's spending. For such goods, the story behind the individual demand curve and the market demand curve becomes slightly more complicated.

> The **substitution effect** of a change in the price of a good is the change in the quantity consumed of that good as the consumer substitutes the good that has become relatively cheaper in place of the good that has become relatively more expensive.

The Income Effect

For the vast majority of goods, the substitution effect is pretty much the whole story behind the slopes of the individual and market demand curves. There are, however, some goods, like food or housing, that account for a substantial share of many consumers' spending. In such cases another effect, called the income effect, also comes into play.

Consider the case of a family that spends half its income on rental housing. Now suppose that the price of housing increases. This will have a substitution effect on the family's demand: other things equal, the family will have an incentive to consume less housing—say, by moving to a smaller apartment—and more of other goods. But the family will also, in a real sense, be made poorer by that higher housing price—its income will buy less housing than before. And this reduction in its purchasing power will have an additional effect, beyond the substitution effect, on the family's consumption bundle, including its consumption of housing.

The change in the quantity consumed of a good that results from a change in the overall purchasing power of the consumer due to the change in the price of a good is known as the **income effect** of the price change. Here we find that a change in the price of a good in effect changes a consumer's income, because such a price change alters the consumer's purchasing power. This is part of the effect of prices on consumption choices.

> The **income effect** of a change in the price of a good is the change in the quantity consumed of that good that results from a change in the consumer's purchasing power due to the change in the price of the good.

It's possible to give more precise definitions of the substitution effect and the income effect of a price change, and we do this in Chapter 11. For most purposes, however, there are only two things you need to know about the distinction between these two effects.

First, for the great majority of goods and services, the income effect is not important and has no significant effect on individual consumption. So most market demand curves slope downward solely because of the substitution effect—end of story.

Second, when it matters at all, the income effect usually reinforces the substitution effect. That is, when the price of a good that absorbs a substantial share of income rises, consumers of that good become a bit poorer because their purchasing power falls. And the vast majority of goods are *normal* goods, goods for which demand decreases when income falls. So this effective reduction in income leads to a reduction in the quantity demanded and reinforces the substitution effect.

However, in the case of an *inferior* good, a good for which demand increases when income falls, the income and substitution effects work in opposite directions. Although the substitution effect tends to produce a decrease in the quantity of any good demanded as its price increases, in the case of an inferior good the income effect of a price increase tends to produce an *increase* in the quantity demanded.

GIFFEN GOODS

Back when Ireland was a desperately poor country—not the prosperous "Celtic Tiger" it has lately become—it was claimed that the Irish would eat *more* potatoes when the price of potatoes went up. That is, some observers claimed that Ireland's demand curve for potatoes sloped upward, not downward.

Can this happen? In theory, yes. If Irish demand for potatoes actually sloped upward, it would have been a real-life case of a "Giffen good," named after a nine-teenth-century statistician who thought (probably wrongly) that he saw an upward-sloping demand curve in some data he was studying.

Here's the story. Suppose that there is some good that absorbs a large share of consumers' budgets and that this good is also *inferior*—people demand less of it when their income rises. The classic supposed example was, as you might guess, potatoes in Ireland, back when potatoes were an inferior good—they were what poor people ate—and when the Irish were very poor.

Now suppose that the price of potatoes increases. This would, *other things equal*, cause people to substitute other goods in

place of potatoes. But other things are not equal: given the higher price of potatoes, people are poorer. And this *increases* the demand for potatoes, because potatoes are an inferior good.

If this income effect outweighs the sub-stitution effect, a rise in the price of pota-toes would increase the quantity demanded; the law of demand would not hold.

In a way the point of this story—which has never been validated in any real situa-tion, nineteenth-century Ireland included—is how unlikely such an event is. The law of demand really is a law, with few exceptions.

As a result, there are hypothetical cases involving inferior goods in which the dis-tinction between income and substitution effects are important (see For Inquiring Minds). As a practical matter, however, it's not a subject we need to worry about when discussing the demand for most goods. Typically, income effects are important only for a very limited number of goods and when discussing *factor markets,* as we'll see in Chapter 12.

economics in action

Mortgage Rates and Consumer Demand

Most people buy houses with mortgages—loans backed by the value of the house. The interest rates on such mortgages change over time; for example, they fell quite a lot over the period from 2000 to 2003. When that happens, the cost of housing falls for millions of people—even people who have mortgages at high interest rates are often able to "refinance" them at lower rates.

It's not surprising that the demand for housing goes up when mortgage rates go down. Economists have noticed, however, that the demand for many other goods also rises when mortgage rates fall. Some of these goods are items connected with new or bigger houses, such as furniture. But people also buy new cars, eat more meals in restaurants, and take more vacations. Why?

The answer illustrates the distinction between substitution and income effects. When housing becomes cheaper, there is a *substitution effect:* people have an incen-tive to substitute housing in place of other goods in their consumption bundle. But housing also happens to be a good that absorbs a large part of consumer spending, with many families spending a quarter or more of their income on mortgage pay-ments. So when the price of housing falls, people are in effect richer—there is a noticeable *income effect*.

The increase in the quantity of housing demanded when mortgage rates fall is the result of both effects: housing becomes a better buy compared with other consumer goods, and people also buy more and bigger houses because they feel richer. And because they feel richer, they also buy more of all other normal goods, such as cars, restaurant meals, and vacations. ■

< < < < < < < < < < < < < < < < < < <

In each of the following cases, state whether the income effect, the substitution effect, or both are significant. In which cases do they move in the same direction? In opposite directions? Why?

1. Orange juice represents a small share of Clare's spending. She buys more lemonade and less orange juice when the price of orange juice goes up. She does not change her spending on other goods.

2. Apartment rents have risen dramatically this year. Since rent absorbs a major part of her income, Delia moves to a smaller apartment. Assume that rental housing is a normal good.

3. The cost of a semester-long meal ticket at the student cafeteria rises, representing a significant increase in living costs. As a result, many students have less money to spend on weekend meals at restaurants so eat in the cafeteria instead. Assume that cafeteria meals are an inferior good.

Solutions appear at back of book.

• A LOOK AHEAD •

At this point we have the basic tools to understand consumer behavior; taken together with our analysis of producer behavior (which is in Chapters 8 and 9), we have the background behind both the supply and the demand curves.

There is more to say about consumer choice; those who want to pursue the subject further should proceed to Chapter 11. Those eager to move on can, however, skip to Chapter 12 and the next subject: how the same tools that we have used to analyze the markets for *goods and services* can also be used to analyze the markets for *factors of production*.

SUMMARY

1. Consumers maximize a measure of satisfaction called **utility.** Each consumer has a **utility function** that determines the level of total utility from his or her **consumption bundle,** the goods and services that are consumed. We measure utility in hypothetical units called **utils.**

2. A good's or service's **marginal utility** is the additional utility generated by consuming one more unit of the good or service. We usually assume that the **principle of diminishing marginal utility** holds: consumption of another unit of a good or service yields less additional utility than the previous unit. As a result, the **marginal utility curve** is downward sloping.

3. A **budget constraint** limits a consumer's spending to no more than his or her income. It defines the consumer's **consumption possibilities,** the set of all affordable consumption bundles. A consumer who spends all of his or her income will choose a consumption bundle on the **budget line,** the slope of which is equal to the opportunity cost of the good on the horizontal axis in terms of the good on the vertical axis. An individual chooses the consumption bundle that maximizes total utility, the **optimal consumption bundle.**

4. We use marginal analysis to find the optimal consumption bundle by analyzing how to allocate the marginal dollar. The **optimal consumption rule** says that at the optimal consumption bundle the **marginal utility per dollar** spent on each good and service—the marginal utility of a good or service divided by its price—is the same.

5. An **individual demand curve** for a good shows how an individual consumer's quantity demanded depends on price. Individual demand curves are summed horizontally to yield the market demand curve. Changes in the price of a good affect the quantity consumed in two possible ways: the **substitution effect** and the **income effect.** Most goods absorb only a small share of a consumer's spending; for these goods, only the substitution effect—buying less of the good that has become relatively more expensive and more of the good that has become relatively cheaper—is significant. It causes the individual and the market demand curves to slope downward. When a good absorbs a large fraction of spending, the income effect is also significant: an increase in a good's price makes a consumer poorer, but a decrease in price makes a consumer richer. This change in purchasing power makes consumers demand more or less of a good, depending on whether the good is normal or inferior. For normal goods, the substitution and income effects reinforce each other. For inferior goods, however, they work in opposite directions.

KEY TERMS

Utility, p. 231
Consumption bundle, p. 231
Utility function, p. 231
Util, p. 231
Marginal utility, p. 232
Marginal utility curve, p. 232

Principle of diminishing marginal utility, p. 233
Budget constraint, p. 235
Consumption possibilities, p. 235
Budget line, p. 236
Optimal consumption bundle, p. 238

Marginal utility per dollar, p. 241
Optimal consumption rule, p. 244
Individual demand curve, p. 245
Substitution effect, p. 247
Income effect, p. 247

PROBLEMS

1. For each of the following situations, decide whether Al has increasing, constant, or diminishing marginal utility.

   a. The more economics classes Al takes, the more he enjoys the subject. And the more classes he takes, the easier each one gets, making him enjoy each additional class even more than the one before.

   b. Al likes loud music. In fact, according to him, "the louder, the better." Each time he turns the volume up a notch, he adds 5 utils to his total utility.

   c. Al enjoys watching old episodes of the sitcom *Friends*. He claims that old episodes are always funny, but he does admit that the more he sees an episode, the less funny it gets.

   d. Al loves toasted marshmallows. The more he eats, however, the fuller he gets and the less he enjoys each additional marshmallow. And there is a point at which he becomes satiated: beyond that point, more marshmallows actually make him feel worse rather than better.

2. Use the concept of marginal utility to explain the following: Newspaper vending machines are designed so that once you have paid for one paper, you could take more than one paper at a time. But soda vending machines, once you have paid for one soda, dispense only one soda at a time.

3. Brenda likes to have bagels and coffee for breakfast. The accompanying table shows Brenda's total utility from various consumption bundles of bagels and coffee.

Consumption bundle		Total utility (utils)
Quantity of bagels	Quantity of coffee (cups)	
0	0	0
0	2	28
0	4	40
1	2	48
1	3	54
2	0	28
2	2	56
3	1	54
3	2	62
4	0	40
4	2	66

Suppose Brenda knows she will consume 2 cups of coffee for sure. However, she can choose to consume different quantities of bagels: she can choose either 0, 1, 2, 3, or 4 bagels.

   a. Calculate Brenda's marginal utility from bagels as she goes from consuming 0 bagel to 1 bagel, from 1 bagel to 2 bagels, from 2 bagels to 3 bagels, and from 3 bagels to 4 bagels.

   b. Draw Brenda's marginal utility curve of bagels. Does Brenda have increasing, diminishing, or constant marginal utility of bagels?

4. Brenda from Problem 3 now has to make a decision about how many bagels and how much coffee to have for breakfast. She has $8 of income to spend on bagels and coffee. Use the information on her utility given in the table in Problem 3.

   a. Bagels cost $2 each, and coffee costs $2 per cup. Which bundles are on Brenda's budget line? For each of these bundles, what is the level of utility (in utils) that Brenda experiences? Which bundle is therefore her optimal bundle?

   b. The price of bagels increases to $4, but the price of coffee remains at $2 per cup. Which bundles are now on Brenda's budget line? For each of these bundles, what is the level of utility (in utils) that Brenda experiences? Which bundle is therefore her optimal bundle?

   c. Compare your answers from parts a and b. As the price of bagels increased from $2 to $4, what happened to the quantity of bagels that Brenda chose to consume? What does this imply about the slope of Brenda's demand curve for bagels? In words, describe the substitution effect and the income effect of this increase in the price of bagels. (Bagels are a normal good.)

5. Bruno can spend his income on two different goods: Britney Spears CDs and notebooks for his class notes. He is thinking about the following three bundles: bundle *A* contains 5 CDs and 5 notebooks; bundle *B* contains 10 CDs and 2 notebooks; and bundle *C* contains 3 CDs and 6 notebooks. For each of the following situations, draw the budget line and decide which of these bundles are possible consumption bundles. That is, determine which of these bundles he can consume given his income and prices. Place CDs on the horizontal axis and notebooks on the vertical axis.

   a. CDs cost $10 each, and notebooks cost $2 each. Bruno has income of $60.

   b. CDs cost $10 each, and notebooks cost $5 each. Bruno has income of $110.

c. Bruno's income and the prices for CDs and notebooks are such that he can just buy bundle *C* (that is, bundle *C* is on his budget line). The opportunity cost of 1 CD is 1 notebook.

6. Bruno from Problem 5 is best friends with Bernie, who shares his love for notebooks and Britney Spears CDs. The accompanying table shows Bernie's utilities from notebooks and Britney Spears CDs.

Quantity of notebooks	Utility from notebooks (utils)	Quantity of CDs	Utility from CDs (utils)
0	0	0	0
2	70	1	80
4	130	2	150
6	180	3	210
8	220	4	260
10	250	5	300

The price of a notebook is $5, the price of a CD is $10, and Bernie has $50 of income to spend.

a. Which consumption bundles of notebooks and CDs can Bernie consume if he spends all his income? Draw Bernie's budget line with CDs on the horizontal axis and notebooks on the vertical axis.

b. Calculate the marginal utility of each notebook and the marginal utility of each CD. Then calculate the marginal utility per dollar spent on notebooks and the marginal utility per dollar spent on CDs.

c. Draw a diagram like Figure 10-5 in which the marginal utility per dollar spent on notebooks is shown in one panel and the marginal utility per dollar spent on CDs in the other panel. Using this diagram and the optimal consumption rule, predict which bundle—from all the bundles on his budget line—Bernie will choose.

7. For each of the following situations, decide whether the bundle Lakshani is thinking about consuming is optimal or not. If it is not optimal, how could Lakshani improve her overall level of utility? That is, determine which good she should spend more on and which good should she spend less on.

a. Lakshani has $200 to spend on sneakers and sweaters. Sneakers cost $50 per pair, and sweaters cost $20 each. She is thinking about buying 2 pairs of sneakers and 5 sweaters. She tells her friend that the additional utility she would get from the second pair of sneakers is the same as the additional utility she would get from the fifth sweater.

b. Lakshani has $5 to spend on pens and pencils. Each pen costs $0.50 and each pencil costs $0.10. She is thinking about buying 6 pens and 20 pencils. The last pen would add five times as much to her total utility as the last pencil.

c. Lakshani has $50 per season to spend on tickets to football games and tickets to soccer games. Each football ticket costs $10 and each soccer ticket costs $5. She is thinking about buying 3 football tickets and 2 soccer tick-

ets. Her marginal utility from the third football ticket is twice as much as her marginal utility from the second soccer ticket.

8. Cal "Cool" Cooper has $200 to spend on cell phones and sunglasses.

a. Each cell phone costs $100 and each pair of sunglasses costs $50. Which bundles lie on Cal's budget line? Draw a diagram like Figure 10-5 in which the marginal utility per dollar spent on cell phones is shown in one panel and the marginal utility per dollar spent on sunglasses is shown in the other panel. Using this diagram and the optimal consumption rule, decide how Cal should allocate his money. That is, from all the bundles on his budget line, which bundle will Cal choose? The accompanying table gives his utility of cell phones and sunglasses.

Quantity of cell phones	Utility from cell phones (utils)	Quantity of sunglasses	Utility from sunglasses (utils)
0	0	0	0
1	400	2	600
2	700	4	700

b. The price of cell phones falls to $50 each, but the price of sunglasses remains at $50 per pair. Which bundles lie on Cal's budget line? Draw a diagram like Figure 10-5 in which the marginal utility per dollar spent on cell phones is shown in one panel and the marginal utility per dollar spent on sunglasses is shown in the other panel. Using this diagram and the optimal spending rule, decide how Cal should allocate his money. That is, from all the bundles on his budget line, which bundle will Cal choose? The accompanying table gives his utility of cell phones and sunglasses.

Quantity of cell phones	Utility from cell phones (utils)	Quantity of sunglasses	Utility from sunglasses (utils)
0	0	0	0
1	400	1	325
2	700	2	600
3	900	3	825
4	1,000	4	700

c. How does Cal's consumption of cell phones change as the price of cell phones falls? In words, describe the income effect and the substitution effect of this fall in the price of cell phones. (Cell phones are a normal good.)

9. Damien Matthews is a busy actor. He allocates his free time to watching movies and working out at the gym. The accompanying table shows his utility from the number of times per week he watches a movie or goes to the gym.

Quantity of gym visits per week	Utility from gym visits (utils)	Quantity of movies per week	Utility from movies (utils)
1	100	1	60
2	180	2	110
3	240	3	150
4	280	4	180
5	310	5	190
6	330	6	195
9	340	7	197

Damien has 14 hours per week to spend on watching movies and going to the gym. Each movie takes 2 hours and each gym visit takes 2 hours. (*Hint:* Damien's free time is analogous to income he can spend. The hours needed for each activity are analogous to the price of that activity.)

a. Which bundles of gym visits and movies can Damien consume per week if he spends all his time either going to the gym or watching movies? Draw Damien's budget line in a diagram with gym visits on the horizontal axis and movies on the vertical axis.

b. Calculate the marginal utility of each gym visit and the marginal utility of each movie. Then calculate the marginal utility per hour spent at the gym and the marginal utility per hour spent watching movies.

c. Draw a diagram like Figure 10-5 in which the marginal utility per hour spent at the gym is shown in one panel and the marginal utility per hour spent watching movies is shown in the other panel. Using this diagram and the optimal consumption rule, decide how Damien should allocate his time.

10. Anna Jenniferson is an actress, and on the set of a new movie she meets Damien from Problem 9. She tells him that she likes watching movies much more than going to the gym. In fact, she says that if she had to give up seeing 1 movie, she would need to go to the gym twice to make up for the loss in utility from not seeing the movie. A movie takes 2 hours, and a gym visit also lasts 2 hours. Damien tells Anna that she is not watching enough movies. Is he right?

11. Sven is a poor student who covers most of his dietary needs by eating cheap breakfast cereal, since it contains most of the important vitamins. As the price of cereal increases, he decides to buy even less of other foods and even more breakfast cereal to maintain his intake of important nutrients. This makes breakfast cereal a Giffen good for Sven. Describe in words the substitution effect and the income effect from this increase in the price of cereal. In which direction does each effect move, and why? What does this imply for the slope of Sven's demand curve for cereal?

12. In each of the following situations, describe the substitution effect and (if it is significant) the income effect. In which direction does each of these effects move? Why?

a. Ed spends a large portion of his income on his children's education. Because tuition fees rise, one of his children has to withdraw from college.

b. Homer spends much of his monthly income on home mortgage payments. The interest on his adjustable-rate mortgage falls, lowering his mortgage payments, and Homer decides to move to a larger house.

c. Pam thinks that Spam is an inferior good. Yet as the price of Spam rises, she decides to buy less of it.

13. Restaurant meals and housing (measured in the number of rooms) are the only two goods that Neha can buy. She has income of $1,000 and the price of each room is $100. The relative price of one room in terms of restaurant meals is 5. How many restaurant meals can she buy if she spends all her money on them?

14. Inflation increases the prices of all goods by 20%. At the same time, Ina's income increases from $50,000 to $55,000. Compare the situation after both of these changes have happened with the situation before any of these changes have happened.

a. After these changes, has Ina's budget line become steeper, less steep, or equally as steep compared to before?

b. After these changes, has Ina's budget line shifted outward, inward, or not at all, compared to before?

15. Margo's marginal utility of one visit to the hair salon is 100 utils per visit. Her marginal utility of a new pair of high-heeled shoes is 300 utils per pair. The price of a visit to the hair salon is $50 per visit. She currently spends all her income, and she buys her optimal consumption bundle. What is the price of a pair of high-heeled shoes?

>web... To continue your study and review of concepts in this chapter, please visit the Krugman/Wells website for quizzes, animated graph tutorials, web links to helpful resources, and more.

www.worthpublishers.com/krugmanwells

Consumer Preferences and Consumer Choice

11

A TALE OF TWO CITIES

DO YOU WANT TO EARN A HIGH SALARY? Maybe you should consider moving to San Jose, California, the metropolitan area that contains much of Silicon Valley, America's leading cluster of high-tech industries. The average family in San Jose has an income far higher than that of the average American family. According to bestplaces.net, a website that compares living conditions in different cities, average household income in San Jose is more than twice as high as that in Cincinnati.

But before you rush to San Jose, there's something else you should know: housing is very expensive there—about four times as expensive per square foot of living space as in Cincinnati. Understandably, the average apartment or house in San Jose is small by American standards.

So is life better or worse in San Jose than in Cincinnati? It depends a lot on what you want. For young people without children, the high wage they can earn in San Jose probably outweighs the high price of housing. They are willing to accept more cramped living quarters in return for the ability to consume greater quantities of other goods such as restaurant meals or clothing. People with large families, however, might prefer midwestern locations like Cincinnati, where the average wage is lower than in San Jose but a dollar buys many more square feet of living space. That is, they would choose to eat fewer restaurant meals but live in more spacious housing.

For individuals whose preferences lie somewhere between those of childless yuppies and those of proud parents, the choice between San Jose and Cincinnati may not be easy. In fact, some people would be *indifferent* between living in the two locations. That's not to say that they would live the same way in San Jose and in Cincinnati; in San Jose they would live in small apartments and eat out a lot, but in Cincinnati they would be homebodies.

What you will learn in this chapter:

➤ Why economists use **indifference curves** to illustrate a person's preferences

➤ The importance of the **marginal rate of substitution,** the rate at which a consumer is just willing to substitute one good for another

➤ An alternative way of finding a consumer's optimal consumption bundle using indifference curves and the budget line

➤ How the shape of indifference curves helps determine whether goods are substitutes or complements

➤ An in-depth understanding of income and substitution effects

Spacious house in the suburbs or cozy apartment in the city—how would you choose?

And they would find both lifestyles equally good.

Our comparison of San Jose and Cincinnati has several morals. One is that different people have different preferences. But we also see that even given an individual's preferences, there may be different consumption bundles that yield the same total utility. This insight leads to the concept of *indifference curves,* a useful way to represent individual preferences.

The example also shows that an individual's total utility depends not only on income but also on prices—and that both income and prices affect consumer choices. We will apply this more complete analysis of consumer choice to the important distinction between *complements* and *substitutes.* Finally, we will use this insight to examine further the *income* and *substitution effects* we covered briefly in Chapter 10.

But, let's begin with indifference curves.

Mapping the Utility Function

In Chapter 10 we introduced the concept of a utility function, which determines a consumer's total utility given his or her consumption bundle. In Figure 10-1 we saw how Cassie's total utility changed as we changed the quantity of fried clams consumed, holding fixed the quantities of other items in her bundle. That is, in Figure 10-1 we showed how total utility changed as consumption of only *one* good changed. But we also learned in Chapter 10, from our example of Sammy, that finding the optimal consumption bundle involves the problem of how to allocate the last dollar spent between *two* goods, clams and potatoes. In this chapter we will extend the analysis by learning how to express total utility as a function of consumption of two goods. In this way we will deepen our understanding of the trade-off involved when choosing the optimal consumption bundle and of how the optimal consumption bundle itself changes in response to changes in the prices of goods. In order to do that, we now turn to a different way of representing a consumer's utility function, based on the concept of *indifference curves.*

Indifference Curves

Ingrid is a consumer who buys only two goods: housing, measured in the number of rooms, and restaurant meals. How can we represent her utility function in a way that takes account of her consumption of both goods?

One way is to draw a three-dimensional picture. Figure 11-1 shows a three-dimensional "utility hill." The distance along the horizontal axis measures the quantity of housing Ingrid consumes in terms of numbers of rooms; the distance along the vertical axis measures the number of restaurant meals she consumes. The altitude or height of the hill at each point is indicated by a contour line, along which the height of the hill is constant. For example, point *A,* which corresponds to a consumption bundle of 3 rooms and 30 restaurant meals, lies on the contour line labeled 450. So the total utility Ingrid receives from consuming 3 rooms and 30 restaurant meals is 450 utils.

A three-dimensional picture like Figure 11-1 helps us think about the relationship between consumption bundles and total utility. But anyone who has ever used a topographical map to plan a hiking trip knows that it is possible to represent a three-dimensional surface in only two dimensions. A topographical map doesn't offer a three-dimensional view of the terrain; instead, it conveys information about altitude solely through the use of contour lines.

The same principle can be applied to representing the utility function. In Figure 11-2 Ingrid's consumption of rooms is measured on the horizontal axis and her consumption of restaurant meals on the vertical axis. The curve here corresponds to the contour line in Figure 11-1, drawn at a total utility of 450 utils. This curve shows all

Figure 11-1

Ingrid's Utility Function

The three-dimensional hill shows how Ingrid's total utility depends on her consumption of housing and restaurant meals. Point A corresponds to consumption of 3 rooms and 30 restaurant meals. That consumption bundle yields Ingrid 450 utils, corresponding to the height of the hill at point A. The lines running around the hill are contour lines, along which the height is constant. So every point on a given contour line generates the same level of utility.

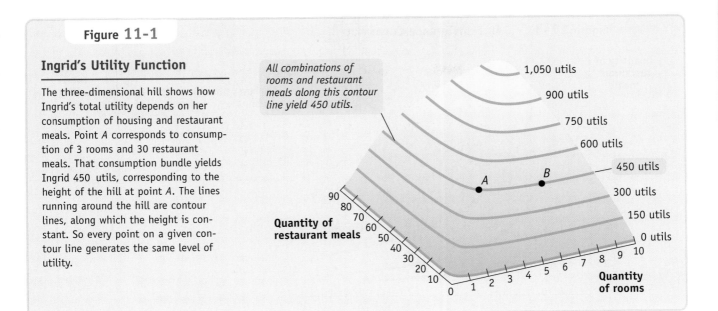

All combinations of rooms and restaurant meals along this contour line yield 450 utils.

the consumption bundles that yield a total utility of 450 utils. One point on that contour line is A, a consumption bundle consisting of 3 rooms and 30 restaurant meals. Another point on that contour line is B, a consumption bundle consisting of 6 rooms but only 15 restaurant meals. Because B also lies on the contour line, it yields Ingrid the same total utility—450 utils—as A. We say that Ingrid is *indifferent* between A and B: because A and B yield the same total utility level, Ingrid is equally well off with either bundle.

A contour line that maps consumption bundles yielding the same amount of total utility is known as an **indifference curve.** An individual is always indifferent between any two bundles that lie on the same indifference curve. Given a consumer's tastes, there is an indifference curve corresponding to each possible level of total utility. The indifference curve in Figure 11-2 shows consumption bundles that yield Ingrid 450 utils; different indifference curves would show consumption bundles that yield Ingrid 400 utils, 500 utils, and so on.

An **indifference curve** is a line that shows all the consumption bundles that yield the same amount of total utility for an individual.

Figure 11-2

An Indifference Curve

An indifference curve is a contour line along which total utility is constant. In this case we show all the consumption bundles that yield Ingrid 450 utils. Consumption bundle A, consisting of 3 rooms and 30 restaurant meals, yields the same total utility as bundle B, consisting of 6 rooms and 15 restaurant meals. That is, Ingrid is indifferent between bundle A and bundle B.

web...

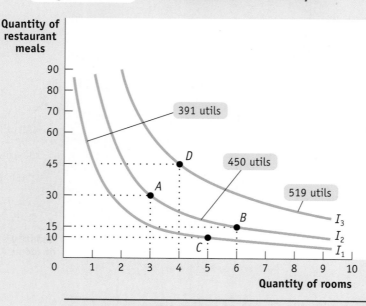

Figure 11-3   An Indifference Curve Map

Consumption bundle	Quantity of rooms	Quantity of meals	Total utility (utils)
A	3	30	450
B	6	15	450
C	5	10	391
D	4	45	519

The utility function can be represented in as much detail as we want by showing a number of indifference curves, each corresponding to a different level of total utility. In this figure bundle *C* lies on an indifference curve corresponding to a total utility of 391 utils. As in Figure 11-2, bundles *A* and *B* lie on an indifference curve corresponding to a total utility of 450 utils. Bundle *D* lies on an indifference curve corresponding to a total utility of 519 utils. Ingrid prefers any bundle on I_2 to any bundle on I_1, and she prefers any bundle on I_3 to any bundle on I_2. **>web...**

The entire utility function of an individual can be represented by an **indifference curve map**, a collection of indifference curves in which each curve corresponds to a different level of total utility.

A collection of indifference curves that represents a consumer's entire utility function, with each indifference curve corresponding to a different level of total utility, is known as an **indifference curve map**. Figure 11-3 shows three indifference curves, I_1, I_2, and I_3, from Ingrid's indifference curve map, as well as several consumption bundles, *A*, *B*, *C*, and *D*. The accompanying table lists each bundle, its composition of rooms and restaurant meals, and the total utility it yields. Because bundles *A* and *B* generate the same number of utils, 450, they lie on the same indifference curve, I_2. Although Ingrid is indifferent between *A* and *B*, she is certainly not indifferent between *A* and *C*: as you can see from the table, *C* generates only 391 utils, a lower total utility than *A* or *B*. So Ingrid prefers consumption bundles *A* and *B* to bundle *C*. This is represented by the fact that *C* is on indifference curve I_1, and I_1 lies below I_2. Bundle *D*, though, generates 519 utils, a higher total utility than *A* and *B*. It is on I_3, an indifference curve that lies above I_2. Clearly, Ingrid prefers *D* to either *A* or *B*. And, even more strongly, she prefers *D* to *C*.

FOR INQUIRING MINDS

ARE UTILS USEFUL?

In the table that accompanies Figure 11-3 we give the number of utils achieved at each of the indifference curves shown in the figure. But is this information actually needed?

The answer is no. As you will see shortly, the indifference curve map tells us all we need to know in order to find a consumer's optimal consumption bundle. That is, it's important that Ingrid has higher total utility along indifference curve I_2 than she does along I_1, but it doesn't matter *how much* higher her total utility is. In other words, we don't have to measure utils in order to understand how consumers make choices.

Economists say that consumer theory requires an "ordinal" measure of utility—one that ranks consumption bundles in terms of desirability—so that we can say that bundle *X* is better than bundle *Y*. The theory does not, however, require "cardinal" utility, which actually assigns a specific number to the total utility yielded by each bundle.

So why introduce the concept of utils at all? The answer is that it is much easier to understand the basis of rational choice by using the concept of measurable utility.

Properties of Indifference Curves

No two individuals have the same indifference curve map because no two individuals have the same preferences. But economists believe that every indifference curve map has two general properties, illustrated in panel (a) of Figure 11-4:

- *Indifference curves never cross.* Suppose that we tried to draw an indifference curve map like the one depicted in the left diagram in panel (a), in which two indifference curves cross at *A*. What is the total utility at *A*? Is it 100 utils or 200 utils? Indifference curves cannot cross because each consumption bundle must correspond to a unique total utility level—not, as shown at *A*, two different total utility levels.

Figure 11-4   Properties of Indifference Curves

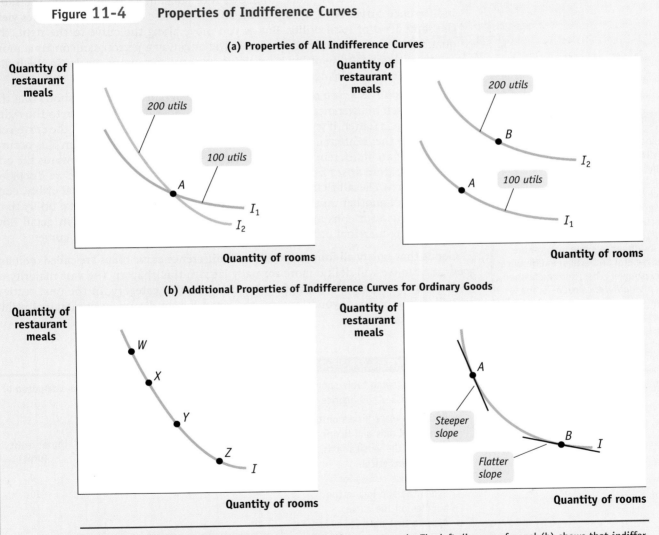

(a) Properties of All Indifference Curves

(b) Additional Properties of Indifference Curves for Ordinary Goods

Panel (a) represents two general properties that all indifference curve maps share. The left diagram shows why indifference curves cannot cross: if they did, a consumption bundle such as *A* would yield both 100 and 200 utils, a contradiction. The right diagram of panel (a) shows that indifference curves that are farther out yield higher total utility: bundle *B*, which contains more of both goods than bundle *A*, yields higher total utility. Panel (b) depicts two additional properties of indifference curves for ordinary goods. The left diagram of panel (b) shows that indifference curves slope downward: as you move down the curve from bundle *W* to bundle *Z*, consumption of rooms increases. To keep total utility constant, this must be offset by a reduction in quantity of restaurant meals. The right diagram of panel (b) shows a convex-shaped indifference curve. The slope of the indifference curve gets flatter as you move down the curve to the right, a feature arising from diminishing marginal utility.

■ *The farther out an indifference curve lies—the farther it is from the origin—the higher the level of total utility it indicates.* The reason, illustrated in the right diagram in panel (a), is that we assume that more is better—over the set of consumption bundles we are considering, the consumer is not satiated. Bundle *B*, on the outer indifference curve, contains more of both goods than bundle *A* on the inner indifference curve. So *B* generates a higher total utility level (200 utils) and therefore lies on a higher indifference curve than *A*.

Furthermore, economists believe that, for most goods, consumers' indifference curve maps also have two additional properties. They are illustrated in panel (b) of Figure 11-4:

■ *Indifference curves are downward sloping.* Here, too, the reason is that more is better. The left diagram in panel (b) shows four consumption bundles on the same indifference curve: *W, X, Y,* and *Z*. By definition these consumption bundles yield the same level of total utility. But as you move along the curve to the right, the quantity of rooms consumed increases. The only way a person can consume more rooms without gaining utility is by giving up some restaurant meals. So the indifference curve must be downward sloping.

■ *Indifference curves have a convex shape.* The right diagram in panel (b) shows that the slope of each indifference curve changes as you move down the curve to the right: the curve gets flatter. If you move up an indifference curve to the left, the curve gets steeper. So the indifference curve is steeper at *A* than it is at *B*. When this occurs, we say that an indifference curve has a *convex* shape—it is bowed-in towards the origin. This feature arises from diminishing marginal utility, a principle we discussed in Chapter 10. Recall that when a consumer has diminishing marginal utility, consumption of another unit of a good generates a smaller increase in total utility than the previous unit consumed. In the next section, we will examine in detail how diminishing marginal utility gives rise to convex-shaped indifference curves.

Goods that satisfy all four properties of indifference curve maps are called *ordinary goods*, a term we will define more formally later in this chapter. The vast majority of goods in any consumer's utility function fall into this category. In the next section we will define ordinary goods and see the key role that diminishing marginal utility plays for them. ■

< < < < < < < < < < < < < < < < < < < <

>> CHECK YOUR UNDERSTANDING 11-1

1. The accompanying table shows Samantha's preferences for consumption bundles composed of chocolate kisses and licorice drops.

    a. With chocolate kisses on the horizontal axis and licorice drops on the vertical axis, draw hypothetical indifference curves for Samantha and locate the bundles on the curves. Assume that both items are ordinary goods.

Consumption bundle	Quantity of chocolate kisses	Quantity of licorice drops	Total utility (utils)
A	1	3	6
B	2	3	10
C	3	1	6
D	2	1	4

    b. Suppose you don't know the number of utils provided by each bundle. Assuming that more is better, predict Samantha's ranking of each of the four bundles to the extent possible.

2. On the left diagram in panel (a) of Figure 11-4, draw a point *B* anywhere on the 200 utils indifference curve and a point *C* anywhere on the 100 utils indifference curve (but *not* at the same location as point *A*). By comparing the utils generated by bundles *A* and *B* and those generated by bundles *A* and *C*, explain why indifference curves cannot cross.

Solutions appear at back of book.

Indifference Curves and Consumer Choice

At the beginning of the last section we used indifference curves to represent the preferences of Ingrid, whose consumption bundles consist of rooms and restaurant meals. Our next step is to show how to use Ingrid's indifference curve map to find her utility-maximizing consumption bundle given her budget constraint.

It's important to understand how our analysis here relates to what we did in Chapter 10. We are not offering a new theory of consumer behavior in this chapter—just as in Chapter 10, consumers are assumed to maximize total utility. In particular, we know that consumers will follow the *optimal consumption rule* from Chapter 10: the optimal consumption bundle lies on the budget line, and the marginal utility per dollar is the same for every good in the bundle.

But as we'll see shortly, we can derive this optimal consumer behavior in a somewhat different way—a way that yields deeper insights into consumer choice.

The Marginal Rate of Substitution

The first component of our approach is a new concept, the *marginal rate of substitution*. The essence of this concept is illustrated in Figure 11-5.

Recall from the last section that for most goods, consumers' indifference curves are downward sloping and convex. Figure 11-5 shows such an indifference curve. The points labeled V, W, X, Y, and Z all lie on this indifference curve—that is, they represent consumption bundles that yield Ingrid the same level of total utility. The table accompanying the figure shows the components of each of the bundles. As we move along the indifference curve from V to Z, Ingrid's consumption of housing steadily increases from 2 rooms to 6 rooms, but her total utility is kept constant. As we move

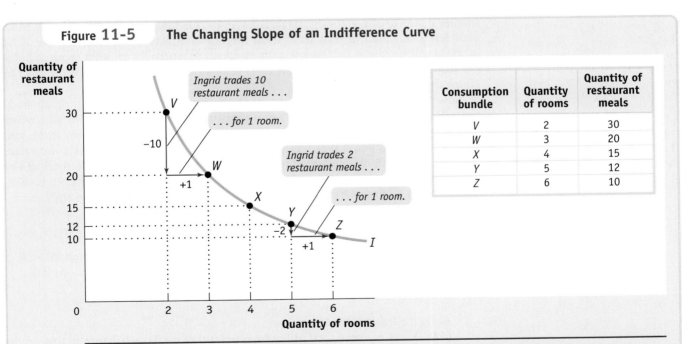

Figure 11-5 **The Changing Slope of an Indifference Curve**

Consumption bundle	Quantity of rooms	Quantity of restaurant meals
V	2	30
W	3	20
X	4	15
Y	5	12
Z	6	10

This indifference curve is downward sloping and convex, implying that restaurant meals and rooms are ordinary goods for Ingrid. As Ingrid moves down her indifference curve from V to Z, she trades off reduced consumption of restaurant meals for increased consumption of housing. However, the terms of that trade-off change. As she moves from V to W, she is willing to give up 10 restaurant meals in return for 1 more room. As her consumption of rooms rises and her consumption of restaurant meals falls, she is willing to give up fewer restaurant meals in return for each additional room. The flattening of the slope as you move from left to right arises from diminishing marginal utility. ▸*web*...

down the indifference curve, then, Ingrid is trading more of one good for less of the other, with the *terms* of that trade-off—the ratio of additional rooms consumed to restaurant meals sacrificed—chosen to keep her total utility constant.

Notice that the quantity of restaurant meals that Ingrid is willing to give up in return for an additional room changes along the indifference curve. As we move from *V* to *W*, housing consumption rises from 2 to 3 rooms and restaurant meal consumption falls from 30 to 20—a trade-off of 10 restaurant meals for 1 additional room. But as we move from *Y* to *Z*, housing consumption rises from 5 to 6 rooms and restaurant meal consumption falls from 12 to 10, a trade-off of only 2 restaurant meals for an additional room.

To put it in terms of slopes, the slope of the indifference curve between *V* and *W* is −10: the change in restaurant meal consumption, −10, divided by the change in housing consumption, 1. Similarly, the slope of the indifference curve between *Y* and *Z* is −2. So the indifference curve gets flatter as we move down it to the right—that is, it has a convex shape, one of the four properties of an indifference curve for ordinary goods.

Why does the trade-off change in this way? Let's think about it intuitively, then work through it more carefully. When Ingrid moves down her indifference curve, whether from *V* to *W* or from *Y* to *Z*, she gains utility from her additional consumption of housing but loses an equal amount of utility from her reduced consumption of restaurant meals. But at each step, the initial position from which Ingrid begins is different. At *V*, Ingrid consumes only a small quantity of rooms, so because of diminishing marginal utility her marginal utility per room at that point is high. At *V*, then, an additional room adds a lot to Ingrid's total utility. But at *V* she already consumes a large quantity of restaurant meals, so her marginal utility of restaurant meals is low at that point. This means that it takes a large reduction in her quantity of restaurant meals consumed to offset the increased utility she gets from the extra room of housing.

At *Y*, in contrast, Ingrid consumes a much larger quantity of rooms and a much smaller quantity of restaurant meals than at *V*. This means that an additional room adds fewer utils, and a restaurant meal forgone subtracts more utils, than at *V*. So Ingrid is willing to give up fewer restaurant meals in return for another room of housing at *Y* (where she gives up 2 meals for 1 room) than she is at *V* (where she gives up 10 meals for 1 room).

Now let's express the same idea—that the trade-off Ingrid is willing to make depends on where she is starting from—by using a little math. We do this by examining how the slope of the indifference curve changes as we move down it. Moving down the indifference curve—reducing restaurant meal consumption and increasing housing consumption—will produce two opposing effects on Ingrid's total utility: lower restaurant meal consumption will reduce her total utility, but higher housing consumption will raise her total utility. And since we are moving down the indifference curve, these two effects must exactly cancel out:

> *Along the indifference curve:*
> **(11-1)** (Change in total utility because of lower restaurant consumption) +
> (Change in total utility because of higher housing consumption) = 0

or, rearranging terms,

> *Along the indifference curve:*
> **(11-2)** −(Change in total utility from restaurant meals) = (Change in total utility from housing)

Let's now focus on what happens as we move only a short distance down the indifference curve, trading off a small increase in housing consumption for a small decrease in restaurant meal consumption. Following our notation from Chapter 10, let's use MU_R and MU_M to represent the marginal utility of rooms and restaurant meals, respectively, and ΔQ_R and ΔQ_M to represent the changes in room and meal consumption, respectively. In general, the change in total utility caused by a small change in consumption of a good is equal to the change in consumption multiplied by the *marginal utility* of that good. This means that we can calculate the change in Ingrid's total utility generated by a change in her consumption bundle using the following equations:

(11-3) Change in total utility arising from a change in consumption of
restaurant meals = $MU_M \times \Delta Q_M$

and

(11-4) Change in total utility arising from a change in consumption of rooms
= $MU_R \times \Delta Q_R$

So we can write Equation 11-2 in symbols as

(11-5) *Along the indifference curve:* $-MU_M \times \Delta Q_M = MU_R \times \Delta Q_R$

Note that the left-hand side of Equation 11-5 has a minus sign; it represents minus the loss in total utility from decreased restaurant meal consumption. This must equal the gain in total utility from increased room consumption, represented by the right-hand side of the equation.

What we want, of course, is to know how this translates into the slope of the indifference curve. To find the slope, we divide both sides of Equation 11-5 by ΔQ_R, and again by MU_M, in order to get the ΔQ_M, ΔQ_R terms on one side and the MU_R, MU_M terms on the other. This results in:

(11-6) *Along the indifference curve:* $-\dfrac{\Delta Q_M}{\Delta Q_R} = \dfrac{MU_R}{MU_M}$

The left-hand side of Equation 11-6 is *minus* the slope of the indifference curve; it is the rate at which Ingrid is willing to trade a higher quantity of rooms (the good on the horizontal axis) in place of restaurant meals (the good on the vertical axis). The right-hand side of Equation 11-6 is the ratio of the marginal utility of rooms to the marginal utility of restaurant meals—that is, the ratio of what she gains from one more room to what she gains from one more meal.

Putting all this together, we see that Equation 11-6 shows that, along the indifference curve, the quantity of restaurant meals Ingrid is willing to give up in return for a room, $\Delta Q_M / \Delta Q_R$, is exactly equal to the ratio of the marginal utility of a room to that of a meal, MU_R / MU_M. Only when this condition is met will her total utility level remain constant as she consumes more rooms and fewer restaurant meals.

Economists have a special name for the ratio of the marginal utilities found in the right-hand side of Equation 11-6: it is called the **marginal rate of substitution,** or **MRS,** of rooms (the good on the horizontal axis) in place of restaurant meals (the good on the vertical axis). That's because as we slide down Ingrid's indifference curve, we are substituting more rooms in place of fewer restaurant meals in her consumption bundle. As we'll see shortly, the marginal rate of substitution plays an important role in finding the optimal consumption bundle.

Recall that indifference curves get flatter as you move down them to the right. The reason, as we've just discussed, is diminishing marginal utility: as Ingrid consumes more housing and fewer restaurant meals, her marginal utility from housing falls and her marginal utility from restaurant meals rises. So her marginal rate of substitution, which is equal to minus the slope of her indifference curve, falls as she moves down the indifference curve.

The flattening of indifference curves as you slide down them to the right—which reflects the same logic as the principle of diminishing marginal utility—is known as the principle of **diminishing marginal rate of substitution.** It says that an individual who consumes only a little bit of good R and a lot of good M will be willing to trade off a lot of M in return for one more unit of R; an individual who already consumes a lot of R and not much of M will be less willing to make that trade-off.

The **marginal rate of substitution,** or **MRS**, of good R in place of good M is equal to MU_R / MU_M, the ratio of the marginal utility of R to the marginal utility of M.

The principle of **diminishing marginal rate of substitution** states that the more of good R a person consumes in proportion to good M, the less M he or she is willing to substitute in place of another unit of R.

We can illustrate this point by referring back to Figure 11-5. At point *V*, a bundle with a high proportion of restaurant meals to rooms, Ingrid is willing to forgo 10 restaurant meals in return for 1 room. But at point *Y*, a bundle with a low proportion of restaurant meals to rooms, she is willing to forgo only 2 restaurant meals in return for 1 room.

From this example we can see that, in Ingrid's utility function, rooms and restaurant meals possess the two additional properties that characterize ordinary goods. Ingrid requires additional rooms to compensate her for the loss of a meal, and vice versa; so her indifference curves for these two goods are downward sloping. And her indifference curves are convex: the slope of her indifference curve—*minus* the marginal rate of substitution—becomes flatter as we move down it. In fact, an indifference curve is convex only when it has diminishing marginal rate of substitution—these two conditions are equivalent.

With this information we can define **ordinary goods,** which account for the great majority of goods in any consumer's utility function. A pair of goods are ordinary goods in a consumer's utility function if they possess two properties: the consumer requires more of one good to compensate for less of the other, and the consumer experiences a diminishing marginal rate of substitution when substituting one good for the other.

Next we will see how to determine Ingrid's optimal consumption bundle using indifference curves.

> Two goods, *R* and *M*, are **ordinary goods** in a consumer's utility function when (1) the consumer requires additional units of *R* to compensate for less *M*, and vice versa; and (2) the consumer experiences a diminishing marginal rate of substitution in substituting one good for another.

The Tangency Condition

Now let's put some of Ingrid's indifference curves on the same diagram as her budget line, to get an alternative way of representing her optimal consumption choice. Figure 11-6 shows Ingrid's budget line, *BL*, when her income is $2,400 per month, housing costs $150 per room each month, and restaurant meals cost $30 each. What is her optimal consumption bundle?

To answer this question, we show several of Ingrid's indifference curves: I_1, I_2, and I_3. Ingrid would like to achieve the total utility level represented by I_3, the highest of the three curves, but she cannot afford to because she is constrained by her income: no consumption bundle on her budget line yields that much total utility. But she shouldn't

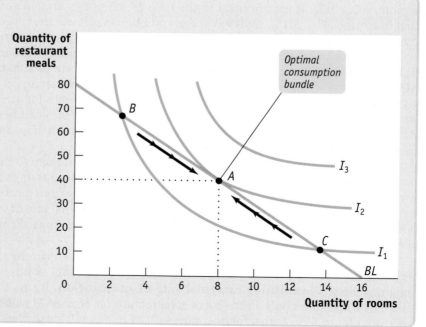

Figure 11-6

The Optimal Consumption Bundle

The budget line, *BL*, shows Ingrid's possible consumption bundles given an income of $2,400 per month, when rooms cost $150 per month and restaurant meals cost $30 each. I_1, I_2, and I_3 are indifference curves. Consumption bundles such as *B* and *C* are not optimal because Ingrid can get onto a higher indifference curve. The optimal consumption bundle is at *A*, where the budget line is just tangent to the highest possible indifference curve. **>web...**

settle for the level of total utility generated by B, which lies on I_1: there are other bundles on her budget line, such as A, that clearly yield higher total utility than B.

In fact, A—a consumption bundle consisting of 8 rooms and 40 restaurant meals per month—is Ingrid's optimal consumption choice. The reason is that A lies on the highest indifference curve Ingrid can reach given her income.

At the optimal consumption bundle A, Ingrid's budget line just touches the relevant indifference curve—the budget line is *tangent* to the indifference curve. This **tangency condition** between the indifference curve and the budget line applies to the optimal consumption bundle when the indifference curves have the typical convex shape: *At the optimal consumption bundle, the budget line just touches the indifference curve.*

To see why, let's look more closely at how we know that a consumption bundle that *doesn't* satisfy the tangency condition can't be optimal. Re-examining Figure 11-6, we can see that the consumption bundles B and C are both affordable because they lie on the budget line. However, neither is optimal. Both of them lie on the indifference curve I_1, which cuts through the budget line at both points. But because I_1 cuts through the budget line, Ingrid can do better: she can move down the budget line from B or up the budget line from C, as indicated by the arrows. In each case this allows her to get onto a higher indifference curve, I_2, which increases her total utility.

Ingrid cannot, however, do any better than I_2: any other indifference curve either cuts through her budget line or doesn't touch it at all. And the bundle that allows her to achieve I_2 is, of course, her optimal consumption bundle, A.

Prices and the Marginal Rate of Substitution

Let's note one final point about the optimal consumption bundle shown in Figure 11-6. At point A, the slope of the indifference curve is just equal to the slope of the budget line.

From rearranging Equation 11-6 we know that the slope of the indifference curve at any point is equal to minus the marginal rate of substitution:

(11-7) Slope of indifference curve $= -\dfrac{MU_R}{MU_M}$

But what is the slope of the budget line? As in Chapter 10, let's use the symbol N to represent Ingrid's income. As we saw in Chapter 10, the horizontal intercept of her budget line—the number of rooms she can afford if she spends all her income on rooms—is N/P_R. The vertical intercept of her budget line—the number of restaurant meals she can afford if she spends all her income on restaurant meals—is N/P_M. So the slope of her budget line when R is measured on the horizontal axis and M is measured on the vertical axis is:

(11-8) Slope of budget line $= -\dfrac{N/P_M}{N/P_R} = -\dfrac{P_R}{P_M}$

The quantity P_R/P_M is known as the **relative price** of rooms in terms of restaurant meals (to distinguish it from an ordinary price in terms of dollars). Because giving up one room allows you to buy P_R/P_M quantity of restaurant meals, or 5 meals, we can interpret the relative price P_R/P_M as the rate at which a room trades for restaurant meals in the market.

Putting Equations 11-7 and 11-8 together, we arrive at the **relative price rule,** which says:

(11-9) *At the optimal consumption bundle:* $\dfrac{MU_R}{MU_M} = \dfrac{P_R}{P_M}$

That is, at the optimal consumption bundle, the marginal rate of substitution of one good in place of another is equal to the ratio of their prices. Or to put it in a more intuitive way, at Ingrid's optimal consumption bundle, the rate at which she would trade a room in exchange for having more restaurant meals along her indifference curve, MU_R/MU_M, is *equal* to the rate at which rooms are traded for restaurant meals in the market, P_R/P_M.

The **tangency condition** between the indifference curve and the budget line holds when the indifference curve and the budget line just touch. This condition determines the optimal consumption bundle when the indifference curves have the typical convex shape.

The **relative price** of good R in terms of good M is equal to P_R/P_M.

The **relative price rule** says that at the optimal consumption bundle, the marginal rate of substitution of one good in place of another is equal to the relative price.

Figure 11-7

Understanding the Relative Price Rule

The *relative price* of rooms in terms of restaurant meals is equal to minus the slope of the budget line. The *marginal rate of substitution* of rooms in place of restaurant meals is equal to minus the slope of the indifference curve. The *relative price rule* says that at the optimal consumption bundle, the marginal rate of substitution must equal the relative price. This point can be demonstrated by considering what happens when the marginal rate of substitution is not equal to the relative price. At consumption bundle *B*, the marginal rate of substitution is larger than the relative price; Ingrid can increase her total utility by moving down her budget line, *BL*. At *C*, the marginal rate of substitution is smaller than the relative price, and Ingrid can increase her total utility by moving up the budget line. Only at *A*, where the relative price rule holds, is her total utility maximized, given her budget constraint.

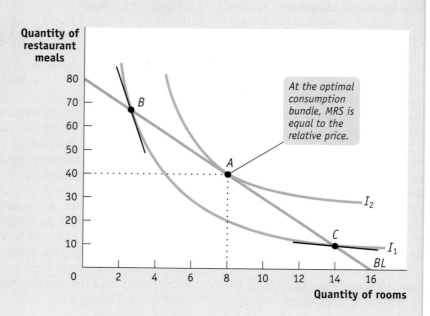

What would happen if this equality did not hold? We can see by examining Figure 11-7. There, at point *B*, the slope of the indifference curve, $-MU_R/MU_M$, is greater in absolute value than the slope of the budget line, $-P_R/P_M$. This means that, at *B*, Ingrid values an additional room in place of meals *more* than it costs her to buy an additional room and forgo some meals. As a result, Ingrid would be better off moving down her budget line toward *A*, consuming more rooms and fewer restaurant meals—and that *B* could not have been her optimal bundle! Likewise, at *C*, the slope of Ingrid's indifference curve is less than the slope of the budget line. The implication is that, at *C*, Ingrid values additional meals in place of a room *more* than it costs her to buy additional meals and forgo a room. Again, Ingrid would be made better off by moving along her budget line—consuming more restaurant meals and fewer rooms—until she reaches *A*, her optimal consumption bundle.

But suppose that we do the following transformation to Equation 11-9: divide both sides by P_R and multiply both by MU_M. Then the relative price rule becomes:

(11-10) *At the optimal consumption bundle:* $\dfrac{MU_R}{P_R} = \dfrac{MU_M}{P_M}$

which is the *optimal consumption rule,* from Chapter 10, Equation 10-5. So using either the optimal consumption rule (from Chapter 10) or the relative price rule (from this chapter), we find the same optimal consumption bundle.

Preferences and Choices

Now that we have seen how to represent optimal consumption choice in an indifference curve diagram, we can turn briefly to the relationship between consumer preferences and consumer choices.

When we say that two consumers have different preferences, we mean that they have different utility functions. This in turn means that they will have indifference curve maps with different shapes. And those different maps will translate into different consumption choices, even among consumers with the same income who face the same prices.

To see this, suppose that Ingrid's friend Lars also consumes only housing and restaurant meals. However, Lars has a stronger preference for restaurant meals and a

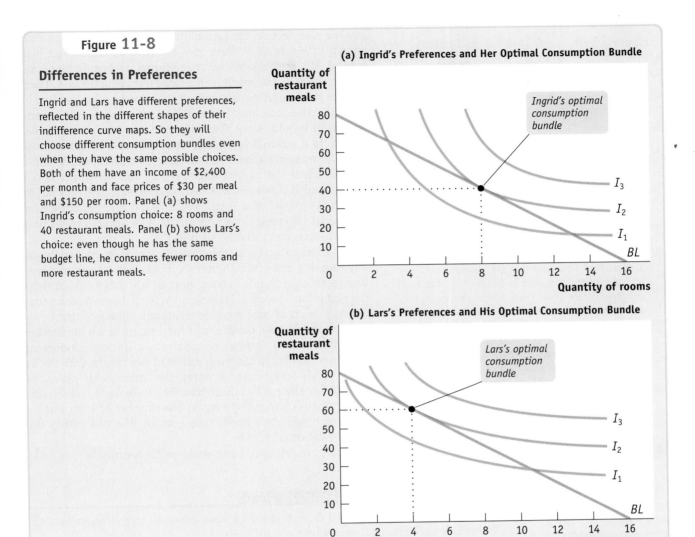

Figure 11-8

Differences in Preferences

Ingrid and Lars have different preferences, reflected in the different shapes of their indifference curve maps. So they will choose different consumption bundles even when they have the same possible choices. Both of them have an income of $2,400 per month and face prices of $30 per meal and $150 per room. Panel (a) shows Ingrid's consumption choice: 8 rooms and 40 restaurant meals. Panel (b) shows Lars's choice: even though he has the same budget line, he consumes fewer rooms and more restaurant meals.

(a) Ingrid's Preferences and Her Optimal Consumption Bundle

Ingrid's optimal consumption bundle

(b) Lars's Preferences and His Optimal Consumption Bundle

Lars's optimal consumption bundle

weaker preference for housing. This difference in preferences is shown in Figure 11-8, which shows *two* sets of indifference curves: panel (a) shows Ingrid's preferences and panel (b) shows Lars's preferences. Note the difference in their shapes.

Suppose, as before, that rooms cost $150 per month and restaurant meals cost $30. Let's also assume that both Ingrid and Lars have incomes of $2,400 per month, giving them identical budget lines. Nonetheless, because they have different preferences, they will make different consumption choices, as shown in Figure 11-8. Ingrid will choose 8 rooms and 40 restaurant meals; Lars will choose 4 rooms and 60 restaurant meals.

economics in action

Rats and Rational Choice

Let's admit it: the theory of consumer choice does not bear much resemblance to the way most of us think about our consumption decisions. The purpose of the theory is, however, to help economists think systematically about how a rational consumer would behave. The practical question is whether consumers actually behave rationally.

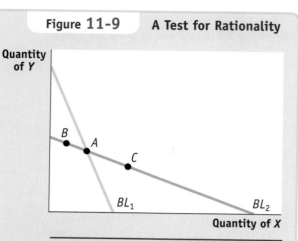

Figure 11-9   A Test for Rationality

Suppose that a consumer has the budget line BL_1 and chooses the consumption bundle A. If that consumer is now given a new budget line such as BL_2, it would be irrational to choose a bundle such as B; the consumer could have afforded that bundle before but chose A instead. A rational consumer would always at least stay at A or choose a new consumption bundle that was not affordable before, such as C. It's difficult to test people in this way—but it works for rats!

One simple test for rationality would look like the one shown in Figure 11-9. First, give a consumer the budget line labeled BL_1, and observe what consumption bundle the consumer chooses; the result is indicated in the figure as A. Then change the budget constraint, so that the new budget line is BL_2. Here the consumer is still able to afford the original consumption bundle A but also has some new choices available.

Would a rational consumer then choose a bundle like B? No. The reason is that B lies *inside* the original budget line—that is, when the budget line was BL_1, the consumer could have afforded it but chose A instead. It would be irrational to choose it now, when A is still available. So the new choice for a rational consumer must be either A or some bundle that has just become available, such as C.

It's hard to perform experiments like this on people—at any rate, it's not ethical (though more indirect experiments do suggest that people behave more or less rationally in their consumption choices). However, there is clear evidence that animals, such as rats, are able to make rational choices!

Economists have conducted experiments in which rats are presented with a "budget constraint"—a limited number of times per hour they can push either of two levers. One of the levers yields small cups of water; the other yields pellets of food. After the rat's choices have been observed, the budget constraint is changed by varying the number of lever pushes required to get each good. Sure enough, the rats satisfy the rule for rational choice.

If rats are rational, can people be far behind? ∎

< < < < < < < < < < < < < < < < < < < <

>> CHECK YOUR UNDERSTANDING 11-2

1. Lucinda and Kyle each consume 3 comic books and 6 video games. Lucinda's marginal rate of substitution of books in place of games is 2 and Kyle's is 5.
   a. For each person, find another consumption bundle that yields the same total utility as the current bundle. Who is less willing to trade games for books? In a diagram with books on the horizontal axis and games on the vertical axis, how would this be reflected in differences in the shapes of their indifference curves?
   b. Find the relative price of books in terms of games at which Lucinda's current bundle is optimal. Is Kyle's bundle optimal given this relative price? If not, how should Kyle rearrange his consumption?

Solutions appear at back of book.

Using Indifference Curves: Substitutes and Complements

Now that we've seen how to analyze consumer choice using indifference curves, we can get some payoffs from our new technique. First up is a new insight into the distinction between *substitutes* and *complements*.

Way back in Chapter 3 we pointed out that the price of one good often affects the demand for another but that the direction of this effect can go either way: a rise in the price of tea increases the demand for coffee, but a rise in the price of cream reduces the demand for coffee. Tea and coffee are substitutes; cream and coffee are complements.

But what determines whether two goods are substitutes or complements? It depends on the shape of a consumer's indifference curves. This relationship can be illustrated with two extreme cases: the cases of *perfect substitutes* and *perfect complements*.

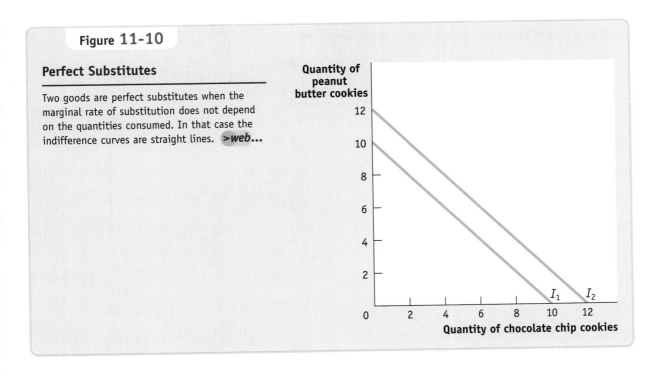

Figure 11-10

Perfect Substitutes

Two goods are perfect substitutes when the marginal rate of substitution does not depend on the quantities consumed. In that case the indifference curves are straight lines. **>web**...

Perfect Substitutes

Consider Cokie, who likes cookies. She isn't particular: it doesn't matter to her whether she has 3 peanut butter cookies and 7 chocolate chip cookies, or vice versa. What would her indifference curves between peanut butter and chocolate chip cookies look like?

The answer is that they would be straight lines like I_1 and I_2 in Figure 11-10. For example, I_1 shows that any combination of peanut butter cookies and chocolate chip cookies that adds up to 10 cookies yields Cokie the same utility.

A consumer whose indifference curves are straight lines is always willing to substitute the same amount of one good for one unit of the other, regardless of how much of either good he or she consumes. Cokie, for example, is always willing to accept one fewer peanut butter cookie in exchange for one more chocolate chip cookie, making her marginal rate of substitution *constant*.

When indifference curves are straight lines, we say that goods are **perfect substitutes**. When two goods are perfect substitutes, there is only one relative price at which consumers will be willing to purchase both goods; a slightly higher or lower relative price will cause consumers to buy only one of the two goods.

Figure 11-11 illustrates this point. The indifference curves are the same as those in Figure 11-10, but now we include Cokie's budget line, *BL*. In each panel we assume that Cokie has $12 to spend. In panel (a) we assume that chocolate chip cookies cost $1.20 and peanut butter cookies cost $1.00. Cokie's optimal consumption bundle is then at point *A*: she buys 12 peanut butter cookies and no chocolate chip cookies. In panel (b) the situation is reversed: chocolate chip cookies cost $1.00 and peanut butter cookies cost $1.20. In this case her optimal consumption is at point *B*, where she consumes only chocolate chip cookies.

Why does such a small change in the price cause Cokie to switch all her consumption from one good to the other? Because her marginal rate of substitution doesn't depend on the composition of her consumption bundle. If the relative price of chocolate chip cookies is more than the marginal rate of substitution, she buys only peanut butter cookies; if it is less, she buys only chocolate chip. And if the relative price of chocolate chip cookies is equal to the marginal rate of substitution, Cokie can maximize her utility by buying any bundle on her budget line. That is, she will be

Two goods are **perfect substitutes** if the marginal rate of substitution of one good in place of the other good is constant, regardless of how much of each an individual consumes.

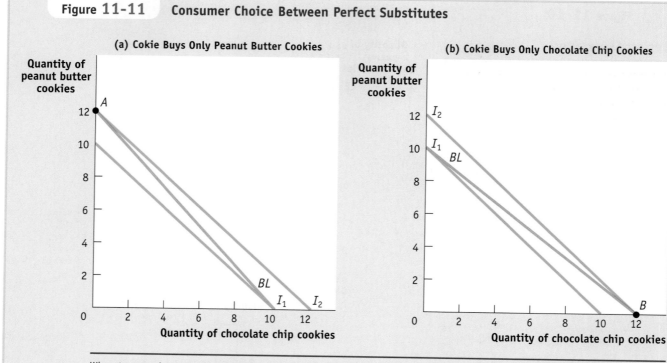

Figure 11-11 **Consumer Choice Between Perfect Substitutes**

(a) Cokie Buys Only Peanut Butter Cookies

(b) Cokie Buys Only Chocolate Chip Cookies

When two goods are perfect substitutes, small price changes can lead to large changes in the consumption bundle. In panel (a), the relative price of chocolate chip cookies is slightly higher than the marginal rate of substitution of chocolate chip in place of peanut butter cookies; this is enough to induce Cokie to choose consumption bundle A, which consists entirely of peanut butter cookies. In panel (b), the relative price of chocolate chip cookies is slightly lower than the marginal rate of substitution; this induces Cokie to choose bundle B, consisting entirely of chocolate chip cookies.

equally happy with any combination of chocolate chip cookies and peanut butter cookies that she can afford. In that case, we cannot predict which particular bundle she will choose among all the bundles that lie on her budget line.

Perfect Complements

> Two goods are **perfect complements** when a consumer wants to consume the goods in the same ratio regardless of their relative price.

The case of perfect substitutes represents one extreme form of consumer preferences; the case of perfect complements represents the other. Goods are **perfect complements** when a consumer wants to consume two goods in the same ratio, regardless of their relative price.

Suppose that Aaron likes cookies and milk—but only together. An extra cookie without an extra glass of milk yields no utility; neither does an extra glass of milk without another cookie. In this case, his indifference curves will form right angles, as shown in Figure 11-12.

To see why, consider the three bundles labeled A, B, and C. At B, on I_4, Aaron consumes 4 cookies and 4 glasses of milk. At A, directly above B, he consumes 4 cookies and 5 glasses of milk; but the extra glass of milk adds nothing to his utility. So A is on the same indifference curve as B, I_4. Similarly, at C he consumes 5 cookies and 4 glasses of milk, but this yields the same total utility as 4 cookies and 4 glasses of milk. So C is also on the same indifference curve, I_4.

Also shown in Figure 11-12 is a budget line that would allow Aaron to choose bundle B. The important point is that the slope of the budget line has no effect on his

Figure 11-12

Perfect Complements

When two goods are perfect complements, a consumer wants to consume the goods in the same ratio regardless of their relative price. Indifference curves take the form of right angles. In this case, Aaron will choose to consume 4 glasses of milk and 4 cookies (bundle B) regardless of the slope of the budget line passing through B. The reason is that neither an additional glass of milk without an additional cookie (bundle A) nor an additional cookie without an additional glass of milk (bundle C) adds to his total utility.

>web...

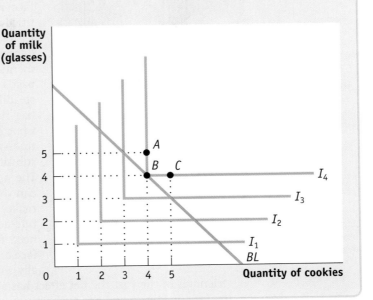

relative consumption of cookies and milk. This means that he will always consume the two goods in the same proportions regardless of prices—which makes the goods perfect complements.

You may be wondering what happened to the marginal rate of substitution in Figure 11-12. That is, exactly what is Aaron's marginal rate of substitution between cookies and milk, given that he is unwilling to make any substitutions between them? The answer is that in the case of perfect complements, the marginal rate of substitution is *undefined* because an individual's preferences don't allow *any* substitution between goods.

Less Extreme Cases

There are real-world examples of pairs of goods that are very close to being perfect substitutes. For example, the list of ingredients on a package of Bisquick pancake mix says that it contains "soybean and/or cottonseed oil": the producer uses whichever is cheaper, since consumers can't tell the difference. There are other pairs of goods that are very close to being perfect complements—for example, cars and tires.

In most cases, however, the possibilities for substitution lie somewhere between these extremes. In some cases, as illustrated by the following Economics in Action, it isn't easy to be sure whether goods are substitutes or complements.

economics in action

Who Needs Fleshmeets?

In the information technology community, "fleshmeet" is slang for a face-to-face (sorry, F2F) meeting, as opposed to an electronic interaction. Clearly the term is meant to be a bit derogatory; actually getting together with someone in the same room is so, well, twentieth-century—a crude, old-fashioned way of doing business.

Video conferencing might cut your commute time, but there's really no substitute for being there.

But are electronic communication and face-to-face meetings really substitutes? In a 1996 paper titled "Information Technology and the Future of Cities," the economists Jess Gaspar and Edward Glaeser argued that they might well be complements. Gaspar and Glaeser pointed out that over the past century the cost of telecommunications has steadily fallen and the quality of the communication has risen: long-distance phone calls, for example, went from being impossible to being cheap and routine—yet activities you might have thought were substitutes, like business travel, continued to boom. The authors suggested that although a phone call can sometimes replace a business trip, the ability to make inexpensive phone calls also generates more interaction among businesses and therefore more need for communication—both on the phone and face to face. (Think of the way that cell phones actually encourage people to get together with their friends.) In the past the net effect has actually been to increase the demand for face-to-face meetings, and the authors suggested that newer technologies will continue to be complements rather than substitutes for direct personal interaction.

Some futurists believe that we are heading for a world in which people live wherever they please and interact via the Internet; in such a world not only business travel but also big cities, which exist mainly to facilitate face-to-face interaction, would lose much of their purpose. Gaspar and Glaeser argued, however, that this remains unlikely for the foreseeable future. ■

< < < < < < < < < < < < < < < < < <

> **QUICK REVIEW**

➤ When two goods are *perfect substitutes*, the marginal rate of substitution is constant and the indifference curves are straight lines.

➤ When two goods are *perfect complements*, the indifference curves form right angles and the marginal rate of substitution is undefined.

➤ The relationship between most goods for most people falls somewhere between these two extremes.

>> **CHECK YOUR UNDERSTANDING 11-3**

In each of the following cases, determine whether the two goods are perfect substitutes, perfect complements, or ordinary goods. Explain your answer, paying particular attention to the marginal rate of substitution of one good in place of the other good.

1. Sanjay cares only about the number of jelly beans he receives and not about whether they are banana-flavored or pineapple-flavored.

2. Hillary's marginal utility of cherry pie goes up as she has more scoops of vanilla ice cream to go with each slice. But she is willing to consume some cherry pie without any vanilla ice cream.

3. Despite repeated reductions in price, customers won't buy software programs made by Omnisoft Corporation unless the company also sells the computer operating system that enables a computer to read these software programs.

4. Darnell works part time at the campus bookstore. The manager has asked him to work additional hours this week. Darnell is willing to do additional work, but he finds that the more hours he has already worked, the less willing he is to work yet another hour. (*Hint:* Think of the goods in question as being income and leisure time.)

Solutions appear at back of book.

Prices, Income, and Demand

Let's now return to Ingrid's consumption choices. In the situation we've considered, her income was $2,400 per month, housing cost $150 per room, and restaurant meals cost $30 each. Her optimal consumption bundle, as seen in Figure 11-7 on page 264, contained 8 rooms and 40 restaurant meals.

Let's now ask how her consumption choice would change if either the rent per room or her income changed. As we'll see, we can put these pieces together to deepen our understanding of consumer demand.

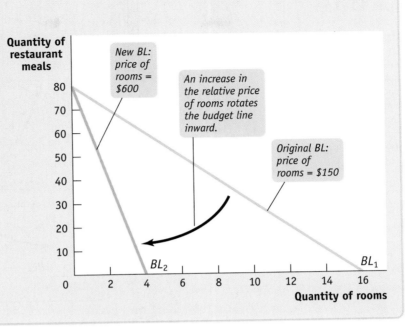

Figure 11-13

Effects of a Price Increase on the Budget Line

An increase in the price of rooms, holding the price of restaurant meals constant, increases the relative price of rooms in terms of restaurant meals. As a result, Ingrid's original budget line, BL_1, rotates inward to BL_2. Her maximum possible purchase of restaurant meals is unchanged, but her maximum possible purchase of rooms is reduced.

>web...

New BL: price of rooms = $600

An increase in the relative price of rooms rotates the budget line inward.

Original BL: price of rooms = $150

The Effects of a Price Increase

Suppose that for some reason there is a sharp increase in housing prices. Ingrid must now pay $600 per room instead of $150. Meanwhile, the price of restaurant meals and her income remain unchanged. How does this change affect her consumption choices?

When the price of rooms rises, the relative price of rooms in terms of restaurant meals rises; as a result, Ingrid's budget line changes (for the worse—but we'll get to that). She responds to that change by choosing a new consumption bundle.

Figure 11-13 shows Ingrid's original (BL_1) and new (BL_2) budget lines—again, under the assumption that her income remains constant at $2,400 per week. With housing costing $150 per room and a restaurant meal costing $30, her budget line, BL_1, intersected the horizontal axis at 16 rooms and the vertical axis at 80 restaurant meals. After the price of a room rises to $600 per room, the budget line, BL_2, still hits the vertical axis at 80 restaurant meals, but it hits the horizontal axis at only 4 rooms. Her budget line has rotated inward, reflecting the new, higher relative price of a room in terms of restaurant meals.

Figure 11-14, on page 272, shows how Ingrid responds to her new circumstances. Her original optimal consumption bundle consists of 8 rooms and 40 meals. After her budget line rotates in response to the change in relative price, she finds her new optimal consumption bundle by choosing the point on BL_2 that brings her to as high an indifference curve as possible. At the new optimal consumption bundle, C, she consumes fewer rooms and more restaurant meals than before: 1 room and 60 restaurant meals.

PITFALLS

"OTHER THINGS EQUAL," REVISITED

One of the biggest sources of confusion and error in economics—both in the classroom and in the real world—is failure to keep in mind the principle that all economic relationships are defined "other things equal." You may recall from Chapter 3 that a demand curve shows the effect of a good's price on its quantity demanded, *other things equal*—that is, all other things that influence demand being unchanged. Among those "other things" are the prices of other goods and the incomes of consumers.

To see how important it is to be clear about what is being held constant, let's compare two experiments. First, what happens to Ingrid's budget line if we increase the price of rooms, holding the price of restaurant meals and Ingrid's income constant? Second, what happens to her budget line if we increase the price of housing and *at the same time also increase the price of restaurant meals and Ingrid's income*?

We've just seen the effects of raising the price of rooms from $150 per month to $600. But now imagine that the price of restaurant meals also quadruples from $30 to $120 and that Ingrid's income quadruples from $2,400 to $9,600 per month. How does her budget line change?

The answer (check it yourself) is that quadrupling all three numbers—the price of rooms, the price of restaurant meals, and Ingrid's income—has *no* effect on her budget line. Because the relative price is unchanged, it won't affect her consumption choice. So the law of demand, which says that increasing the price of a good reduces the quantity demanded, is only an "other things equal" proposition; a higher price results in a lower quantity demanded, holding other prices and income constant.

Figure 11-14

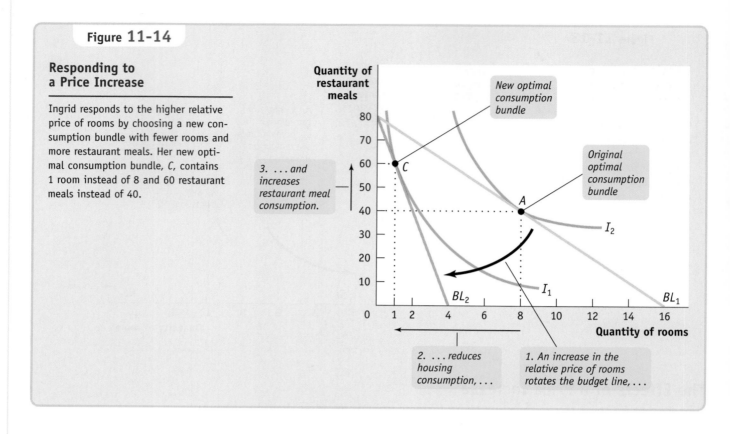

Responding to a Price Increase

Ingrid responds to the higher relative price of rooms by choosing a new consumption bundle with fewer rooms and more restaurant meals. Her new optimal consumption bundle, *C*, contains 1 room instead of 8 and 60 restaurant meals instead of 40.

New optimal consumption bundle

Original optimal consumption bundle

3. . . . and increases restaurant meal consumption.

2. . . . reduces housing consumption, . . .

1. An increase in the relative price of rooms rotates the budget line, . . .

Why does Ingrid's consumption of rooms fall? Part—but only part—of the reason is that the rise in the price of rooms reduces her purchasing power, making her poorer. That is, the higher relative price of rooms rotates her budget line inward towards the origin, reducing her consumption possibilities and putting her on a lower indifference curve. In a sense, when she faces a higher price of housing, it's as if her income declined.

To understand this effect, and to see why it isn't the whole story, let's consider a different change in Ingrid's circumstances: a change in her income.

Income and Consumption

In Chapter 10 we learned about the individual demand curve, which shows how a consumer's consumption choice will change as the price of one good changes, holding income and the prices of other goods constant. That is, movement along the individual demand curve shows the substitution effect—how quantity consumed changes in response to changes in the *relative price* of the two goods. But we can also ask how the consumption choice will change if *income* changes, holding relative price constant.

In the previous section we considered an example in which a rise in the price of housing put Ingrid on a lower indifference curve. As we noted, it was as if her income had fallen. In this section we will consider how Ingrid responds to a direct change in income—that is, a change in her income level holding relative price constant. Figure 11-15 compares Ingrid's budget line and

Figure 11-15

Income and Consumption: Normal Goods

At a monthly income of $2,400, Ingrid chooses bundle A, consisting of 8 rooms and 40 restaurant meals. When relative price remains unchanged, a fall in income shifts her budget line inward to BL_2. At a monthly income of $1,200, she chooses bundle B, consisting of 4 rooms and 20 restaurant meals. Since Ingrid's consumption of both restaurant meals and rooms falls when her income falls, both goods are normal goods.

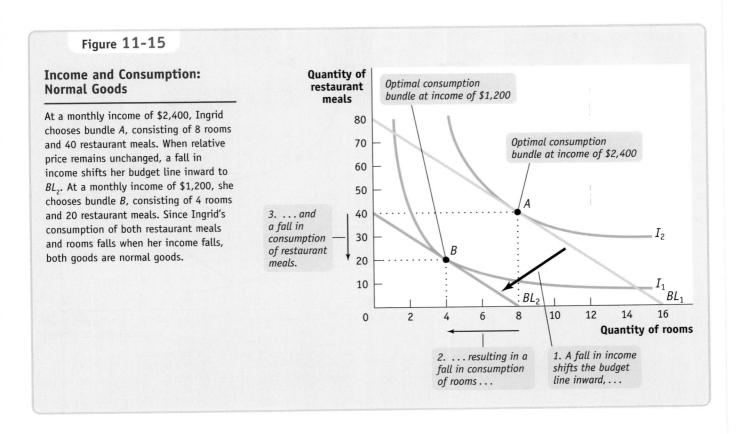

optimal consumption choice with an income of $2,400 per month ($BL_1$) with her budget line and optimal consumption choice with an income of $1,200 per month ($BL_2$), while keeping prices constant at $150 per room and $30 per restaurant meal. A is Ingrid's optimal consumption bundle at an income of $2,400 and B is her optimal consumption bundle at an income of $1,200. In each case, her optimal consumption bundle is given by the point at which the budget line is tangent to the indifference curve. As you can see, at the lower income her budget line shifts *inward* compared to her budget line at the higher income but maintains the same slope because relative price has not changed. This means that she must reduce her consumption of either housing or restaurant meals, or both. As a result she is at a lower level of total utility, represented by a lower indifference curve.

As it turns out, Ingrid chooses to consume less of both goods when her income falls: as her income goes from $2,400 to $1,200, her consumption of housing falls from 8 to 4 rooms and her consumption of restaurant meals falls from 40 to 20. This is because in her utility function both goods are *normal goods*, as defined in Chapter 5: goods for which demand increases when income rises and for which demand decreases when income falls.

Although most goods are normal goods, we also pointed out in Chapter 5 that some goods are *inferior goods*, goods for which demand moves in the opposite direction to the change in income: demand decreases when income rises, and demand increases when income falls. An example might be second-hand furniture. Whether a good is an inferior good depends on the consumer's indifference curve map. Figure 11-16 on page 274 illustrates such a case, where second-hand furniture is measured on the horizontal axis and restaurant meals are measured on the vertical axis. Note that when Ingrid's income falls from $2,400 ($BL_1$) to $1,200 ($BL_2$), and her optimal consumption bundle goes from D to E, her consumption of second-hand furniture increases—implying that second-hand furniture is an inferior good. Simultaneously, her consumption of restaurant meals decreases—implying that restaurant meals are a normal good.

Figure 11-16

Income and Consumption: An Inferior Good

When Ingrid's income falls from $2,400 to $1,200, her optimal consumption bundle changes from *D* to *E*. Her consumption of second-hand furniture increases, implying that second-hand furniture is an inferior good. In contrast, her consumption of restaurant meals falls, implying that restaurant meals are a normal good.
>web...

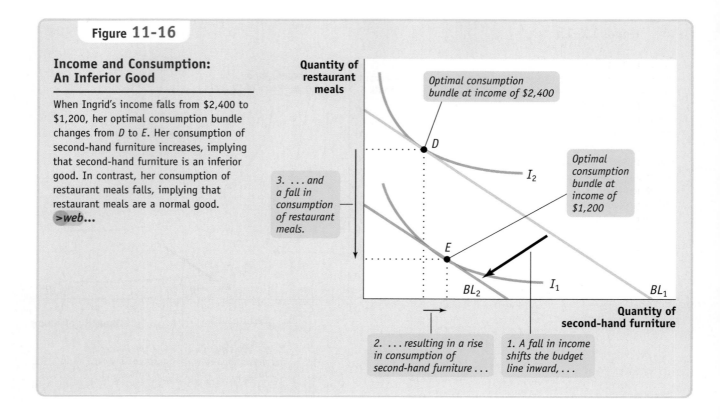

Quantity of restaurant meals

Optimal consumption bundle at income of $2,400

Optimal consumption bundle at income of $1,200

3. ... and a fall in consumption of restaurant meals.

I_2

I_1

BL_2

BL_1

Quantity of second-hand furniture

2. ... resulting in a rise in consumption of second-hand furniture ...

1. A fall in income shifts the budget line inward, ...

Income and Substitution Effects

Now that we have examined the effects of a change in income, we can return to the issue of a change in price—and show in a more specific way that the effect of a higher price on demand has an income component.

Figure 11-17 shows, once again, Ingrid's original (BL_1) and new (BL_2) budget lines and consumption choices with a monthly income of $2,400. At a housing price of $150 per room, Ingrid chooses the consumption bundle at *A*; at a housing price of $600 per room, she chooses the consumption bundle at *C*.

Let's notice again what happens to Ingrid's budget line. It continues to hit the vertical axis at 80 restaurant meals; that is, if Ingrid were to spend all her income on restaurant meals, the increase in the price of housing would not affect her. But the new budget line hits the horizontal axis at only 4 rooms. So the budget line has rotated, *shifting inward* and *becoming steeper*, as a consequence of the rise in the relative price of rooms.

We already know what happens: Ingrid's consumption of housing falls from 8 rooms to 1 room. But the figure suggests that there are *two* reasons for the fall in Ingrid's housing consumption. One reason she consumes fewer rooms is that, because of the higher relative price of rooms, the opportunity cost of a room measured in restaurant meals—the quantity of restaurant meals she must give up to consume an additional room—has increased. This change in opportunity cost, which is reflected in the steeper slope of the budget line, gives her an incentive to substitute restaurant meals in place of rooms in her consumption.

But the other reason Ingrid consumes fewer rooms after their price increases is that the rise in the price of rooms makes her *poorer*. True, her money income hasn't changed. But she must pay more for rooms, and as a result her budget line has rotated inward. So she cannot reach the same level of total utility as before. That is why she ends up on a lower indifference curve.

In the real world these effects—an increase in the price of a good raises its opportunity cost, and also makes consumers poorer—usually go together. But in our

Figure 11-17

Income and Substitution Effects

The movement from Ingrid's original optimal consumption bundle when the price of rooms is $150, *A*, to her new optimal consumption bundle when the price of rooms is $600, *C*, can be decomposed into two parts. The movement from *A* to *B*—the movement along the original indifference curve, I_2, as relative price changes—is the pure substitution effect. It captures how her consumption would change if she were given a hypothetical increase in income that just compensates her for the increase in the price of rooms. The movement from *B* to *C*, the change in consumption when we remove that hypothetical income compensation, is the income effect of the price increase—how her consumption changes as a result of the fall in her purchasing power.

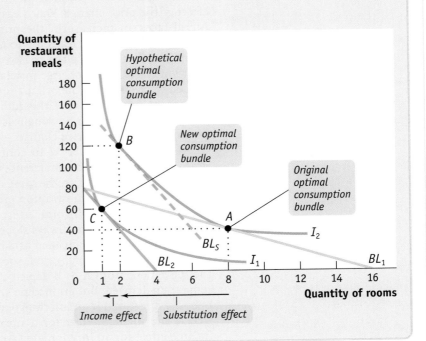

imagination we can separate them. In Chapter 10 we introduced the distinction between the *substitution effect* of a price change (the change in consumption that arises from the substitution of the good that is now relatively cheaper in place of the good that is now relatively more expensive) and the *income effect* (the change in consumption caused by the change in purchasing power arising from a price change). Now we can show these two effects more clearly.

To isolate the substitution effect, let's temporarily change the story about why Ingrid faces an increase in rent: it's not that housing has become more expensive, it's the fact that she has moved from Cincinnati to San Jose, where the rents are higher. But let's consider a hypothetical scenario—let's suppose momentarily that she earns more in San Jose and that the higher income is just enough to *compensate* her for the higher price of housing, so that her total utility is exactly the same as before.

Figure 11-17 shows her situation before and after the move. The bundle labeled *A* represents Ingrid's original consumption choice: 8 rooms, 40 restaurant meals. When she moves to San Jose, she faces a higher price of housing, so her budget line becomes steeper. But we have just assumed that her move increases her income by just enough to compensate for the higher price of housing—that is, just enough to let her reach the original indifference curve. So her new *hypothetical* optimal consumption bundle is at *B*, where the steeper dashed hypothetical budget line (BL_S) is just tangent to the original indifference curve (I_2). By assuming that we have compensated Ingrid for the loss in purchasing power due to the increase in the price of housing, we isolate the *pure substitution* effect of the change in relative price on her consumption.

At *B*, Ingrid's consumption bundle contains 2 rooms and 120 restaurant meals. This costs $4,800 (2 rooms at $600 each, and 120 meals at $30). So if Ingrid faces an increase in the price of housing from $150 to $600 per room, but also experiences a rise in her income from $2,400 to $4,800 per month, she ends up with the same level of total utility.

The movement from *A* to *B* is the pure substitution effect of the price change. It is the effect on Ingrid's consumption choice when we change the relative price of housing while keeping her total utility constant.

Now that we have isolated the substitution effect, we can bring back the income effect of the price change. That's easy: we just go back to the original story, in which Ingrid faces an increase in the price of housing *without* any rise in income. We already know that this leads her to C in Figure 11-17. But we can think of the move from A to C as taking place in two steps. First, Ingrid moves from A to B, the substitution effect of the change in relative price. Then we take away the extra income needed to keep her on the original indifference curve, causing her to move to C. The movement from B to C is the additional change in Ingrid's demand that results because the increase in housing prices actually does reduce her utility. So this is the income effect of the price change.

We can use Figure 11-17 to confirm that restaurant meals and rooms are both normal goods in Ingrid's preferences. For normal goods, the income effect and the substitution effect work in the same direction: a price increase induces a fall in quantity consumed by the substitution effect (the move from A to B) and a fall in quantity consumed by the income effect (the move from B to C). That's why demand curves for normal goods always slope downward.

What would have happened as a result of the increase in the price of housing if, instead of being a normal good, rooms had been an inferior good for Ingrid? First, the movement from A to B depicted in Figure 11-17, the substitution effect, would remain unchanged. But an income change causes quantity consumed to move in the opposite direction for an inferior good. So the movement from B to C shown in Figure 11-17, the income effect for a normal good, would no longer hold. Instead, the income effect for an inferior good would cause Ingrid's quantity of rooms consumed to *increase* from B—say, to a bundle consisting of 3 rooms and 20 restaurant meals.

In the end, the demand curves for inferior goods normally slope downward: if Ingrid consumes 3 rooms after the increase in the price of housing, it is still 5 fewer rooms than she consumed before. So although the income effect moves in the opposite direction of the substitution effect in the case of an inferior good, in this example the substitution effect is stronger than the income effect.

But what if there existed a type of inferior good in which the income effect is so strong that it dominates the substitution effect? Would a demand curve for that good then slope upward—that is, would quantity demanded increase when price increases? The answer is yes: you have encountered such a good already—it is called a *Giffen good,* and it was described in For Inquiring Minds on page 248 of Chapter 10. As we noted there, Giffen goods are rare creatures, but they cannot be ruled out.

Is the distinction between income and substitution effects important in practice? For analyzing the demand for goods, the answer is that it usually isn't that important. However, in Chapter 12 we'll discuss how individuals make decisions about how much of their labor to supply to employers. In that case income and substitution effects work in opposite directions, and the distinction between them becomes crucial.

economics in action

How Much Housing?

To illustrate the substitution effect, we offered a hypothetical example in which Ingrid moves from Cincinnati to San Jose, gaining a higher income but facing a higher price of housing. We made up the numbers for that example, but the real comparison between the two cities is not that different.

As we mentioned at the beginning of this chapter, the website bestplaces.net reports that household incomes are more than twice as high in San Jose as they are in Cincinnati but that housing is also far more expensive. The website also offers an estimate of the cost of living—that is, an estimate of how much income a family would need to achieve a "typical" level of utility. According to this estimate, the cost of living in San Jose is also about twice that in Cincinnati. So, on average, families live about as well in the two metropolitan areas.

But they don't live the same way because relative prices are different. Houses are somewhat smaller in San Jose, with fewer rooms and fewer square feet. Most noticeably, the great majority of new homes in the Cincinnati area are single-family houses on big lots; in San Jose, people are much more likely to live in townhouses or apartments. ■

> > > > > > > > > > > > > > > > > > >

>>CHECK YOUR UNDERSTANDING 11-4

1. Sammy has $60 in weekly income, the current price of clams is $5 per pound, and the current price of potatoes is $1 per pound. Both are normal goods for Sammy. For each of the following situations, construct a diagram that, like Figure 11-17, shows the substitution effect alone and also shows the substitution and income effects together. Put the quantity of clams (in pounds) on the horizontal axis and the quantity of potatoes (in pounds) on the vertical axis.
   a. The price of a pound of clams falls from $5 to $2.50 and the price of a pound of potatoes remains at $1.
   b. The price of a pound of clams rises from $5 to $10 and the price of a pound of potatoes remains at $1.

Solutions appear at back of book.

• A LOOK AHEAD •

With the end of this chapter, our analysis of consumer behavior is complete. Chapters 8 and 9 present a complete analysis of producer behavior under perfect competition. Next we turn to the study of factor markets, which allocate factors of production such as physical capital and labor to various producers. In Chapter 12, we will see that producer and consumer behaviors are much like flip-sides of the same coin. For example, a producer decides whether or not to hire another worker based on a comparison of the worker's cost, the wage rate, to the value of what that worker can produce. Meanwhile, an individual decides whether or not to work based on a comparison of the wage rate to the value that he or she places on leisure. The study of factor markets initiates a higher level of analysis, a first step on the path toward understanding how the market coordinates economic activity in order to, in most cases, bring about the best outcome possible.

>>QUICK REVIEW

➤ The change in a consumer's optimal consumption bundle caused by a change in price can be decomposed into two effects: the substitution effect, due to the change in relative price, and the income effect, due to the change in purchasing power.
➤ The substitution effect refers to the substitution of the good that is now relatively cheaper in place of the good that is now relatively more expensive, holding the utility level constant. It is represented by a movement along the original indifference curve.
➤ When a price change alters a consumer's purchasing power, the resulting change in consumption is the income effect. It is represented by a movement to a different indifference curve, keeping the relative price unchanged.
➤ For normal goods, the income and substitution effects work in the same direction; so their demand curves always slope downward. Although these effects work in opposite directions for inferior goods, their demand curves usually slope downward as well because the substitution effect is typically stronger than the income effect. The exception is the case of a Giffen good.

SUMMARY

1. Preferences can be represented by an **indifference curve map,** a series of **indifference curves.** Each curve shows all the consumption bundles that yield a given level of total utility. Indifference curves have two general properties: they never cross; and greater distance from the origin indicates higher total utility levels. The indifference curves of ordinary goods have two additional properties: they are downward sloping and are *convex* in shape.

2. The **marginal rate of substitution,** or **MRS,** of R in place of M—the rate at which a consumer is willing to substitute more R for less M—is equal to MU_R/MU_M and is also equal to minus the slope of the indifference curve. Convex indifference curves get flatter as you move to the right along the horizontal axis and steeper as you move upward along the vertical axis because of *diminishing marginal utility*: a consumer requires more and more units of

R to substitute for a forgone unit of M as the amount of R consumed relative to the amount of M consumed rises.

3. Most goods are **ordinary goods,** goods for which a consumer requires additional units of some other good as compensation for giving up some of the good, and for which there is **diminishing marginal rate of substitution.**

4. A consumer maximizes utility by getting on the highest indifference curve his or her budget constraint allows. Using the **tangency condition,** the consumer chooses the bundle at which the indifference curve just touches the budget line. At this point, the **relative price** of R in terms of M, P_R/P_M (which is equal to minus the slope of the budget line when R is on the horizontal axis and M is on the vertical axis), is equal to the marginal rate of substitution of R in place of M, MU_R/MU_M (which is equal to minus the slope of the indifference curve). This gives us

the **relative price rule:** at the optimal consumption bundle, the relative price is equal to the marginal rate of substitution. Rearranging this equation also gives us the optimal consumption rule of Chapter 10. Two consumers faced with the same prices and income, but with different preferences and therefore different indifference curve maps, will make different consumption choices.

5. When the marginal rate of substitution is constant, two goods are **perfect substitutes** and indifference curves are straight lines: there is only one relative price at which the consumer is willing to purchase both goods. When a consumer wants to consume the two goods in the same ratio, regardless of the relative price, the goods are **perfect complements.** In this case the indifference curves form right angles and the marginal rate of substitution is

undefined. The relationship between most goods for most people lies between these two extremes.

6. The effect of a change in relative price on consumer choice can be decomposed into the substitution effect and the income effect. The substitution effect is shown by the movement along the original indifference curve in response to the change in relative price, as the consumer substitutes more of the cheaper good in place of the more expensive good. The income effect is shown by a change to a new indifference curve, reflecting the fact that a change in a good's price alters the purchasing power of a given level of income.

7. The income and substitution effects work in the same direction for normal goods, ensuring that demand curves slope downward.

KEY TERMS

Indifference curve, p. 255
Indifference curve map, p. 256
Marginal rate of substitution (*MRS*), p. 261
Diminishing marginal rate of substitution,
   p. 261

Ordinary goods, p. 262
Tangency condition, p. 263
Relative price, p. 263

Relative price rule, p. 263
Perfect substitutes, p. 267
Perfect complements, p. 268

PROBLEMS

1. For each of the following situations, draw a diagram containing three of Isabella's indifference curves.

   a. For Isabella, cars and tires are perfect complements, but in a ratio of 1:4; that is, for each car, Isabella wants exactly four tires. Be sure to label and number the axes of your diagram. Place tires on the horizontal axis and cars on the vertical axis.

   b. Isabella gets utility only from her caffeine intake. She can consume Valley Dew or cola, and Valley Dew contains twice as much caffeine as cola. Be sure to label and number the axes of your diagram. Place cola on the horizontal axis and Valley Dew on the vertical axis.

   c. Isabella gets utility from consuming two goods: leisure time and income. Both have diminishing marginal utility. Be sure to label the axes of your diagram. Place leisure on the horizontal axis and income on the vertical axis.

   d. Isabella can consume two goods: skis and bindings. For each ski she wants exactly one binding. Be sure to label and number the axes of your diagram. Place bindings on the horizontal axis and skis on the vertical axis.

   e. Isabella gets utility from consuming soda. But she gets no utility from consuming water: any more, or any less, water leaves her utility level unchanged. Be sure to label the axes of your diagram. Place water on the horizontal axis and soda on the vertical axis.

2. Use the four properties of indifference curves for ordinary goods illustrated in Figure 11-4 to answer the following questions.

   a. Can you rank the following two bundles? If so, which property of indifference curves helps you rank them?

   > Bundle *A*: 2 movie tickets and 3 cafeteria meals
   > Bundle *B*: 4 movie tickets and 8 cafeteria meals

   b. Can you rank the following two bundles? If so, which property of indifference curves helps you rank them?

   > Bundle *A*: 2 movie tickets and 3 cafeteria meals
   > Bundle *B*: 4 movie tickets and 3 cafeteria meals

   c. Can you rank the following two bundles? If so, which property of indifference curves helps you rank them?

   > Bundle *A*: 12 videos and 4 bags of chips
   > Bundle *B*: 5 videos and 10 bags of chips

   d. Suppose you are indifferent between the following two bundles:

   > Bundle *A*: 10 breakfasts and 4 dinners
   > Bundle *B*: 4 breakfasts and 10 dinners

   Now compare bundle *A* and the following bundle:

   > Bundle *C*: 7 breakfasts and 7 dinners

   Can you rank bundle *A* and bundle *C*? If so, which property of indifference curves helps you rank them? (*Hint:* It may help if you draw this, placing dinners on the horizontal axis and breakfasts on the vertical axis. And remember that breakfasts and dinners are ordinary goods.)

3. The four properties of indifference curves for ordinary goods illustrated in Figure 11-4 rule out certain indifference curves. Determine whether those general properties allow each of the following indifference curves. If not, state which of the general principles rules out the curves.

a.

b.

c.

d.

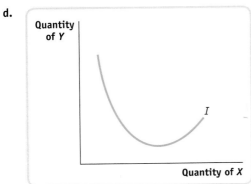

4. Kory has an income of $50, which she can spend on two goods: CDs and cups of hot chocolate. Both are normal goods for her; each CD costs $10, and each cup of hot chocolate costs $2. For each of the following situations, decide whether this is Kory's optimal consumption bundle. If not, what should Kory do to achieve her optimal consumption bundle?

   a. Kory is thinking about buying 4 CDs and 5 cups of hot chocolate. At that bundle, her marginal rate of substitution of CDs in place of hot chocolate is 1; that is, she would be just willing to exchange 1 fewer cup of hot chocolate for 1 more CD.

   b. Kory is thinking about buying 2 CDs and 15 cups of hot chocolate. Kory's marginal utility of the second CD is 25, and her marginal utility of the fifteenth cup of hot chocolate is 5.

   c. Kory is thinking about buying 1 CD and 10 cups of hot chocolate. At that bundle, her marginal rate of substitution of CDs in place of hot chocolate is 5; that is, she would be just willing to exchange 5 cups of hot chocolate for 1 CD.

5. Raul has 4 Cal Ripken and 2 Nolan Ryan baseball cards. The prices of these baseball cards are $24 for Cal and $12 for Nolan. Raul, however, would be willing to exchange 1 Cal card for 1 Nolan card.

   a. What is Raul's marginal rate of substitution of Cal Ripken in place of Nolan Ryan baseball cards?

   b. Can Raul buy and sell baseball cards to make himself better off? How?

   c. Suppose Raul has traded baseball cards and now no longer wants to make any more trades. What is his marginal rate of substitution of Cal Ripken in place of Nolan Ryan cards now?

6. Ralph and Lauren are talking about how much they like going to the gym and how much they like eating out at their favorite restaurant. A session at the gym costs the same as a meal at the restaurant. Ralph says that, for his current consumption of gym sessions and restaurant meals, he values one more meal twice as much as he values one more session at the gym. Lauren is studying economics, and she tells him that he cannot be choosing his optimal consumption bundle.

   a. Is Lauren right? Why or why not? Draw a diagram of Ralph's budget line and the indifference curve that he is on by making his current consumption choice. Place restaurant meals on the horizontal axis and gym sessions on the vertical axis.

   b. How should Ralph adjust his consumption so that it is optimal? Illustrate an optimal choice in your diagram.

7. Sabine can't tell the difference between Coke and Pepsi—the two taste exactly the same to her.

   a. What is Sabine's marginal rate of substitution of Coke in place of Pepsi?

   b. Draw a few of Sabine's indifference curves for Coke and Pepsi. Place Coke on the horizontal axis and Pepsi on the vertical axis.

   c. Sabine has $6 to spend on cola this week. Coke costs $1.50 per six-pack and Pepsi costs $1.00 per six-pack.

Draw Sabine's budget line for Coke and Pepsi on the same diagram.

d. What is Sabine's optimal consumption bundle? Show this on your diagram.

e. If the price of Coke and Pepsi is the same, what combination of Coke and Pepsi will Sabine buy?

8. For Norma, both nachos and salsa are normal goods. Although she likes consuming them together, they are not perfect complements (her indifference curves are convex-shaped, not right angle–shaped). The price of nachos rises, while the price of salsa remains unchanged.

a. Can you determine definitively whether she consumes more or fewer nachos? Explain with a diagram, placing nachos on the horizontal axis and salsa on the vertical axis.

b. Can you determine definitively whether she consumes more or less salsa? Explain with a diagram, placing nachos on the horizontal axis and salsa on the vertical axis.

9. Tyrone is a utility maximizer. His income is $100, which he can spend on cafeteria meals and on notepads. Each meal costs $5, and each notepad costs $2. At these prices Tyrone chooses to buy 16 cafeteria meals and 10 notepads.

a. Draw a diagram that shows Tyrone's choice using an indifference curve and his budget line, placing notepads on the vertical axis and cafeteria meals on the horizontal axis. Label the indifference curve I_1 and the budget line BL_1.

b. The price of notepads falls to $1; the price of cafeteria meals remains the same. On the same diagram, draw Tyrone's budget line with the new prices and label it BL_H.

c. Lastly, Tyrone's income falls to $90. On the same diagram, draw his budget line with this income and the new prices and label it BL_2. Is he worse off, better off, or equally as well off with these new prices and lower income than compared to the original prices and higher income? (Hint: Determine whether Tyrone can afford to buy his original consumption bundle of 16 meals and 10 notepads with the lower income and new prices.) Illustrate your answer using an indifference curve and label it I_2.

d. Give an intuitive explanation of your answer to (c).

10. Gus spends his income on gas for his car and food. The government raises the tax on gas, thereby raising the price of gas. But the government also lowers the income tax, thereby increasing Gus's income. And this rise in income is just enough to place Gus on the same indifference curve as the one he was on before the price of gas rose. Will Gus buy more, less, or the same amount of gas as before these changes?

11. Pam spends her money on bread and Spam, and her indifference curves obey the four properties of indifference curves for ordinary goods. Suppose that, for Pam, Spam is an inferior, but not a Giffen, good; bread is a normal good. Bread costs $2 per loaf, and Spam costs $2 per can. Pam has $20 to spend.

a. Draw a diagram of Pam's budget line, placing Spam on the horizontal axis and bread on the vertical axis. Suppose

her optimal consumption bundle is 4 cans of Spam and 6 loaves of bread. Illustrate that bundle also, and draw the indifference curve on which it lies.

b. The price of Spam falls to $1; the price of bread remains the same. Pam now buys 7 loaves of bread and 6 cans of Spam. Illustrate her new budget line and new optimal consumption bundle in your diagram. Also draw the indifference curve on which this bundle lies.

c. In your diagram, show the income and substitution effects from this fall in the price of Spam. Remember that Spam is an inferior good for Pam.

12. Katya commutes to work. She can either use public transport or her own car. Her indifference curves obey the four properties of indifference curves for ordinary goods.

a. Draw Katya's budget line with car travel on the vertical axis and public transport on the horizontal axis. Suppose that Katya consumes some of both goods. Draw an indifference curve that helps you illustrate that optimal consumption bundle.

b. Now the price of public transport falls. Draw Katya's new budget line.

c. For Katya, public transport is an inferior, but not a Giffen, good. Draw an indifference curve that illustrates her optimal consumption bundle after the price of public transport has fallen. Is Katya consuming more or less public transport?

d. Show the income and substitution effects from this fall in the price of public transport.

13. For Crandall, cheese cubes and crackers are perfect complements: he wants to consume exactly 1 cheese cube with each cracker. He has $2.40 to spend on cheese and crackers. One cheese cube costs 20 cents, and 1 cracker costs 10 cents. Draw a diagram, with crackers on the horizontal axis and cheese cubes on the vertical axis, to answer the following questions.

a. Which bundle will Crandall consume?

b. The price of crackers rises to 20 cents. How many cheese cubes and how many crackers will Crandall consume?

c. In your diagram, show the income and substitution effects from this price rise.

14. Carmen consumes nothing but cafeteria meals and CDs. Her indifference curves exhibit the four general properties of indifference curves. Cafeteria meals cost $5 each, and CDs cost $10. Carmen has $50 to spend.

a. Draw Carmen's budget line and an indifference curve that illustrates her optimal consumption bundle. Place cafeteria meals on the horizontal axis and CDs on the vertical axis. You do not have enough information to know the specific tangency point, so choose one arbitrarily.

b. Now Carmen's income rises to $100. Draw her new budget line on the same diagram, as well as an indifference curve that illustrates her optimal consumption bundle. Assume that cafeteria meals are an inferior good.

c. Can you draw an indifference curve showing that cafeteria meals and CDs are both inferior goods?

Factor Markets and the Distribution of Income

THE VALUE OF A DEGREE

DOES HIGHER EDUCATION PAY? YES, IT does: in the modern economy, employers are willing to pay a premium for workers with more education. And the size of that premium has increased a lot over the last few decades. Back in 1973 workers with advanced degrees, such as law degrees or MBAs, earned only 76 percent more than those who had only graduated from high school. By 2003 the premium for an advanced degree had risen to 120 percent.

Who decided that the wages of workers with advanced degrees would rise so much compared with those of high school grads? The answer, of course, is that nobody decided it. Wage rates are prices, the prices of different kinds of labor; and they are decided, like other prices, by supply and demand.

Still, there is a difference between the wage rate of high school grads and the price of used textbooks: the wage rate isn't the price of a *good*, it's the price of a *factor of production*. And although markets for factors of production are in many ways similar to those for goods, there are also some important differences.

In this chapter, we examine *factor markets*, the markets in which factors of production such as labor are traded. Factor markets, like markets for goods and services, play a crucial role in the economy: they allocate productive resources to producers and help ensure that those resources are used efficiently.

This chapter begins by describing the major factors of production. Then we consider the demand for factors of production, which leads us to a crucial insight: the *marginal productivity theory of income distribution*.

If you've ever had doubts about attending college, consider this: factory workers with only high school degrees will make much less than college grads. The present discounted value of the difference in lifetime earnings is as much as $300,000.

We then consider some challenges to the marginal productivity theory. The final section of the chapter looks at the supply of the most important factor, labor.

What you will learn in this chapter:

➤ How factors of production—resources like land, labor, and both **physical capital** and **human capital**—are traded in factor markets, determining the **factor distribution of income**

➤ How the demand for factors leads to the **marginal productivity theory of income distribution**

➤ An understanding of the sources of wage disparities and the role of discrimination

➤ The way in which a worker's decision about **time allocation** gives rise to labor supply

The Economy's Factors of Production

You may recall that we defined a *factor of production* in Chapter 2 in the context of the circular-flow model; it is any resource that is used by firms to produce *goods* and *services,* items that are consumed by households. Factors of production are bought and sold in *factor markets,* and the prices in factor markets are known as *factor prices*.

What are these factors of production, and why do factor prices matter?

The Factors of Production

As we learned in Chapter 2, economists divide factors of production into four principal classes: land, labor, physical capital, and human capital. *Land* is a resource provided by nature; *labor* is the work done by human beings.

In Chapter 7 we defined *capital;* it is the assets that are used by a firm in producing its output. There are two broad types of capital. **Physical capital**—often referred to simply as "capital"—consists of manufactured resources such as buildings and machines.

In the modern economy, **human capital,** the improvement in labor created by education and knowledge, and embodied in the workforce, is at least equally significant. The importance of human capital has been greatly increased by the progress of technology, which has made a high level of technical sophistication essential to many jobs—one cause of the increased premium paid for workers with advanced degrees.

Why Factor Prices Matter: The Allocation of Resources

Factor markets and factor prices play a key role in one of the most important processes that must take place in any economy: the allocation of resources among producers.

Consider the example of Florida in 1992, in the aftermath of Hurricane Andrew, which was the costliest hurricane to hit the U.S. mainland to date. The state had an urgent need for workers in the building trades—carpenters, plumbers, and so on—to repair or replace damaged homes and businesses. What ensured that those needed workers actually came? The high demand for construction workers in Florida drove up their wages, which led large numbers of workers with the right skills to move temporarily to the state to do the work. In other words, the market for a factor of production—construction workers—allocated that factor of production to where it was needed.

In this sense factor markets are similar to markets for goods and services, which allocate goods and services among consumers. But there are two features that make factor markets somewhat special. Unlike in a market for a good or service, demand in a factor market is what we call *derived demand*. That is, demand for the factor is derived from the firm's output choice. The second feature is that factor markets are where most of us get the largest shares of our income (government transfers being the next largest source of income in the economy).

Factor Incomes and the Distribution of Income

Most American families get most of their income in the form of wages and salaries—that is, they get their income by selling labor. Some people, however, get most of their income from physical capital: when you own stock in a company, what you really own is a share of that company's physical capital. And some people get much of their income from the rents on land they own.

Obviously, then, the prices of factors of production have a major impact on how the economic "pie" is sliced among different groups. For example, a higher wage rate, other things equal, means that more of the income in the economy goes to people who derive their income from labor, as opposed to capital. Economists refer to how the economic pie is sliced as the "distribution of income."

Specifically, factor prices determine the **factor distribution of income**—how the total income of the economy is divided among labor, land, and capital.

Physical capital—often referred to simply as "capital"—consists of manufactured resources such as buildings and machines.

Human capital is the improvement in labor created by education and knowledge that is embodied in the workforce.

PITFALLS

WHAT IS A FACTOR, ANYWAY?

Imagine a business that produces shirts. The business will make use of workers and machines—that is, of labor and capital. But it will also use other inputs, such as electricity and cloth. Are all of these inputs factors of production? No: labor and capital are factors of production, but cloth and electricity are not.

The key distinction is that a factor of production earns income from the selling of its services over and over again but an input cannot. For example, a worker earns income over time from repeatedly selling his or her efforts; the owner of a machine earns income over time from repeatedly selling the use of that machine. So a factor of production, such as labor and capital, represents an enduring source of income. An input like electricity or cloth, however, is used up in the production process. Once exhausted, it cannot be a source of future income for its owner.

The **factor distribution of income** is the division of total income among labor, land, and capital.

THE FACTOR DISTRIBUTION OF INCOME AND SOCIAL CHANGE IN THE INDUSTRIAL REVOLUTION

Have you read any novels by Jane Austen? How about Charles Dickens? If you've read both, you probably noticed that they seem to be describing quite different societies. Austen's novels, set around 1800, describe a world in which the leaders of society are land-owning aristocrats. Dickens, writing about 50 years later, describes a world in which businessmen, especially factory owners, seem to be in control.

This literary shift reflects a dramatic transformation in the factor distribution of income. The Industrial Revolution, which took place between the late

By altering how people lived and worked, the Industrial Revolution led to huge economic and social changes.

eighteenth century and the middle of the nineteenth century, changed England from a mainly agricultural country, in which land earned a fairly substantial share of income, to an urbanized and industrial one, in which land rents were dwarfed by capital income. Recent estimates by the economist Nancy Stokey show that between 1780 and 1850 the share of land represented in national income fell from 20 to 9 percent, while the share represented by capital rose from 35 to 44 percent. That shift changed everything—even literature.

As the following Economics in Action explains, the factor distribution of income in the United States has been quite stable over the past few decades. In other times and places, however, large changes have taken place in the factor distribution. One notable example: during the Industrial Revolution, the share of total income earned by land owners fell sharply, while that earned by capital owners rose. As explained in For Inquiring Minds, this shift had a profound effect on society.

economics in action

The Factor Distribution of Income in the United States

When we talk about the factor distribution of income, what are we talking about in practice?

In the United States, as in all advanced economies, payments to labor account for most of the economy's total income. Figure 12-1 shows the factor distribution of income in the United States in 2004: in that year, 71 percent of total income in the economy took the form of "compensation of employees"—a number that includes both

Figure 12-1

Factor Distribution of Income in the United States in 2004

In 2004, compensation of employees accounted for most income earned in the United States—71 percent of the total. Most of the remainder—consisting of earnings paid in the form of interest, corporate profits, and rent—went to owners of physical capital. Finally, proprietors' income—9 percent of the total—went to individual owners of businesses as compensation for their labor and capital expended in their businesses.

Source: Bureau of Economic Analysis.

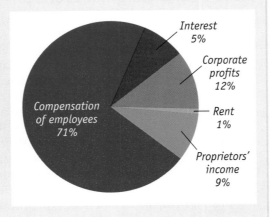

wages and benefits such as health insurance. This number has been quite stable over the long run; roughly 30 years earlier, in 1971, compensation of employees was very similar, at 73 percent of total income.

However, measured wages and benefits don't capture the full income of "labor" because a significant fraction of total income in the United States (usually between 8 and 9 percent) is "proprietors' income"—the earnings of people who own their own businesses. Part of that income should be considered wages these business owners pay themselves. So the true share of labor in the economy is probably a few percentage points higher than the "compensation of employees" share.

But much of what we call compensation of employees is really a return on human capital. A surgeon isn't just supplying the services of a pair of ordinary hands (at least the patient hopes not!): that individual is also supplying the result of many years and hundreds of thousands of dollars invested in training and experience. We can't directly measure what fraction of wages is really a payment for education and training, but many economists believe that human capital has become *the* most important factor of production in modern economies. ■

< < < < < < < < < < < < < < < < < < <

> ## > QUICK REVIEW
>
> ➤ Economists usually divide the economy's factors of production into four principal categories: labor, land, *physical capital,* and *human capital.*
>
> ➤ The demand for a factor is a derived demand. Factor prices, which are set in factor markets, determine the *factor distribution of income.* Labor receives the bulk—more than 70 percent—of the income in the modern U.S. economy. Although the exact share is not directly measurable, much of what is called compensation of employees is a return to human capital.

>>CHECK YOUR UNDERSTANDING 12-1

1. Suppose that the government places price controls on the market for college professors, imposing a wage that is lower than the market wage. Describe the effect of this policy on the production of college degrees. What sectors of the economy do you think will be adversely affected by this policy? What sectors of the economy might benefit?

Solutions appear at back of book.

Marginal Productivity and Factor Demand

All economic decisions are about comparing costs and benefits—and usually about comparing marginal costs and marginal benefits. This goes both for a consumer, deciding whether to buy another pound of fried clams, and for a producer, deciding whether to hire an additional worker.

Although there are some important exceptions, most factor markets in the modern American economy are perfectly competitive, meaning that buyers and sellers of a given factor are price-takers. And in a competitive labor market, it's clear how to define an employer's marginal cost of a worker: it is simply the worker's wage rate. But what is the marginal benefit of that worker? To answer that question, we return to a concept first introduced in Chapter 8: the *production function,* which relates inputs to output. And as in Chapter 9, we will assume throughout this chapter that all producers are price-takers—they operate in a perfectly competitive industry.

Value of the Marginal Product

Figure 12-2 reproduces Figures 8-1 and 8-2, which showed the production function for wheat on George and Martha's farm. Panel (a) uses the total product curve to show how total wheat production depends on the number of workers employed on the farm; panel (b) shows how the *marginal product* of labor, the increase in output from employing one more worker, depends on the number of workers employed. Table 12-1, which reproduces the table in Figure 8-1, shows the numbers behind the figure.

Assume that George and Martha want to maximize their profit, that workers must be paid $200 each, and that wheat sells for $20 per bushel. What is their optimal number of workers? That is, how many workers should they employ to maximize profit?

In Chapters 8 and 9 we showed how to answer this question in several steps. In Chapter 8 we used information from the producer's production function to derive the firm's total cost and its marginal cost. And in Chapter 9 we derived the *price-taking firm's optimal output rule:* a price-taking firm's profit is maximized by producing the

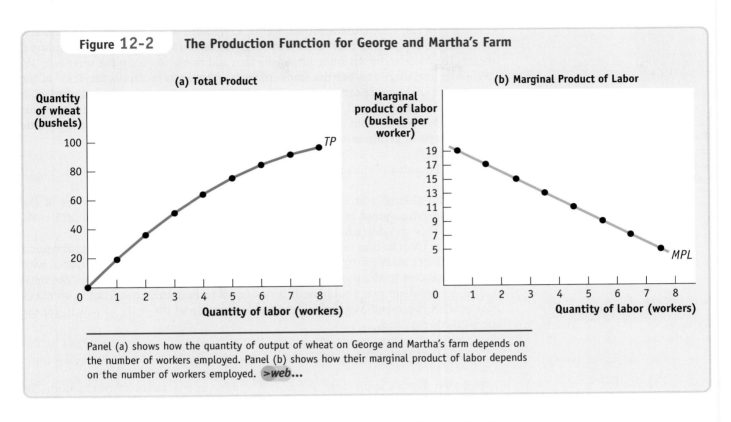

Figure 12-2   **The Production Function for George and Martha's Farm**

(a) Total Product

(b) Marginal Product of Labor

Panel (a) shows how the quantity of output of wheat on George and Martha's farm depends on the number of workers employed. Panel (b) shows how their marginal product of labor depends on the number of workers employed. >*web*...

quantity of output at which the marginal cost of the last unit produced is equal to the market price. Having determined the optimal quantity of output, we can go back to the production function and find the optimal number of workers—it is simply the number of workers needed to produce the optimal quantity of output.

There is, however, another way to find the number of workers that maximizes a producer's profit. We can go directly to the question of what level of employment maximizes profit. This alternative approach is equivalent to the approach we outlined in the preceding paragraph—it's just a different way of looking at the same thing, which gives us more insight into the demand for factors as opposed to the supply of goods.

TABLE 12-1

Employment and Output for George and Martha's Farm

Quantity of labor L (workers)	Quantity of wheat Q (bushels)	Marginal product of labor $MPL = \dfrac{\Delta Q}{\Delta L}$ (bushels per worker)
0	0	
		19
1	19	
		17
2	36	
		15
3	51	
		13
4	64	
		11
5	75	
		9
6	84	
		7
7	91	
		5
8	96	

To see how this alternative approach works, let's return to the example of George and Martha and suppose that they are considering whether or not to employ an additional worker. The increase in *cost* from employing that additional worker is the wage rate, *W*. The *benefit* to George and Martha from employing that extra worker is the value of the extra output that worker can produce. What is this value? It is the marginal product of labor, *MPL*, multiplied by the price per unit of output, *P*. This quantity—the extra value of output that comes from employing one more unit of labor—is known as the **value of the marginal product** of labor, or *VMPL*:

> The **value of the marginal product** of a factor is the value of the additional output generated by employing one more unit of that factor.

(12-1)   Value of the marginal product of labor = $VMPL = P \times MPL$

So should George and Martha hire that extra worker? The answer is yes, if the value of the extra output is more than the cost of the worker—that is, if $VMPL > W$. Otherwise they shouldn't hire that worker.

So the decision to hire labor is a marginal decision, in which the marginal benefit to the producer from hiring an additional worker (*VMPL*) should be compared with the marginal cost to the producer (*W*). And as with any marginal decision, the optimal choice is where marginal benefit is just equal to marginal cost. That is, to maximize profit George and Martha will employ workers up to the point at which, for the last worker employed,

(12-2) $VMPL = W$

This rule doesn't apply only to labor; it applies to any factor of production. The value of the marginal product of any factor is its marginal product times the price of the good it produces. The general rule is that *a profit-maximizing price-taking producer employs each factor of production up to the point at which the value of the marginal product of the last unit of the factor employed is equal to that factor's price.*

It's important to realize that this rule doesn't conflict with our analysis in Chapters 8 and 9. There we saw that a profit-maximizing producer of a good chooses the level of output at which the price of that good is equal to the marginal cost of production. It's just a different way of looking at the same rule. If the level of output is chosen so that price equals marginal cost, then it is also true that at that output level the value of the marginal product of labor will equal the wage rate.

Now let's look more closely at why choosing the level of employment at which the value of the marginal product of the last worker employed is equal to the wage rate works—and at how it helps us understand factor demand.

Value of the Marginal Product and Factor Demand

> The **value of the marginal product curve** of a factor shows how the value of the marginal product of that factor depends on the quantity of the factor employed.

Table 12-2 calculates the value of the marginal product of labor on George and Martha's farm, on the assumption that the price of wheat is $20 per bushel. In Figure 12-3 the horizontal axis shows the number of workers employed; the vertical axis measures the value of the marginal product of the last worker employed *and* the wage rate. The curve shown is the **value of the marginal product curve** of labor. This curve, like the marginal product of labor curve, is downward sloping due to diminishing returns to labor in production. That is, the value of the marginal product of each worker is less than that of the preceding worker, because the marginal product of each worker is less than that of the preceding worker.

We have just seen that to maximize profit, George and Martha must hire workers up to the point at which the wage rate is equal to the value of the marginal product of the last worker employed. Let's use the example to see that this principle really works.

Assume that George and Martha currently employ 3 workers and that workers must be paid the market wage rate of $200. Should they employ an additional worker?

TABLE 12-2

Value of the Marginal Product of Labor for George and Martha's Farm

Quantity of labor L (workers)	Marginal product of labor MPL (bushels per worker)	Value of the marginal product of labor $VMPL = P \times MPL$
0		
	19	$380
1		
	17	340
2		
	15	300
3		
	13	260
4		
	11	220
5		
	9	180
6		
	7	140
7		
	5	100
8		

Looking at Table 12-2, we see that if George and Martha currently employ 3 workers, the value of the marginal product of an additional worker is $260. So if they employ an additional worker, they will increase the value of their production by $260 but increase their cost by only $200, yielding an increase of $60 in the farm's profit. In fact, a producer can always increase profit by employing one more unit of a factor of production as long as the value of the marginal product produced by that unit exceeds the factor price.

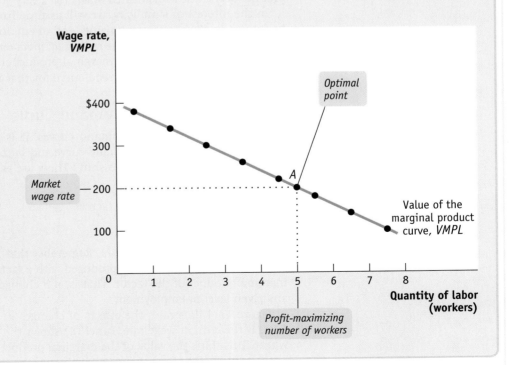

Figure 12-3

The Value of the Marginal Product Curve

This curve shows how the value of the marginal product of labor depends on the number of workers employed. It is downward sloping due to diminishing returns to labor in production. To maximize profit, George and Martha choose the level of employment at which the value of the marginal product of labor is equal to the market wage rate. For example, at a wage rate of $200 the profit-maximizing level of employment is 5 workers, shown by point A. The value of the marginal product curve for a factor is the producer's individual demand curve for that factor. >web...

Alternatively, suppose that George and Martha employ 8 workers. By reducing the number of workers to 7, they can save $200 in wages. Meanwhile, the value of the marginal product of that last worker was only $100. So, by reducing employment by one worker they can increase profit by $100. A producer can always increase profit by employing one less unit of a factor of production as long as the value of the marginal product produced by that unit is less than the factor price.

Using this method, we can see from Table 12-2 that the profit-maximizing employment level is 5 workers given a wage rate of $200. The value of the marginal product of the 5th worker is $220, so adding that worker results in $20 of additional profit. But George and Martha should not hire more than 5 workers: the value of the marginal product of the 6th worker is only $180, $20 less than the cost of that worker. So, to maximize profit, George and Martha should employ workers up to but not beyond the point at which the value of the marginal product of the last worker employed is equal to the wage rate.

Now look again at the value of the marginal product curve in Figure 12-3. To determine the profit-maximizing level of employment, we set the price of labor—$200 per worker—equal to the value of the marginal product of labor. This means that the profit-maximizing level of employment is at point A, corresponding to an employment level of 5 workers. If the price of labor were higher or lower, we would simply move up or down the curve.

In this example, George and Martha have a small farm in which the potential employment level varies from 0 to 8 workers, and they hire workers up to the point where the value of the marginal product of the last worker is no less than the wage rate. Suppose, however, that the firm in question is large and has the potential of hiring many workers. When there are many employees, the value of the marginal product of labor falls only slightly when an additional worker is employed. As a result, there will be some worker whose value of the marginal product almost exactly equals the wage rate. (In keeping with the George and Martha example, this means that some worker has a value of the marginal product of approximately $200.) In this case, the firm maximizes profit by choosing a level of employment at which the value of the marginal product of the last worker hired *equals* (to a very good approximation) the wage rate.

In the interest of simplicity, we will assume from now on that firms use this rule to determine the profit-maximizing level of employment. *This means that the value of the marginal product curve is the individual producer's labor demand curve.* And in general, a producer's value of the marginal product curve for any factor of production is that producer's individual demand curve for that factor of production.

Shifts of the Factor Demand Curve

As in the case of ordinary demand curves, it is important to distinguish between *movements along* the factor demand curve and *shifts of* the factor demand curve. What causes factor demand curves to shift? There are three main causes:

- Changes in prices of goods
- Changes in supply of other factors
- Changes in technology

Changes in Prices of Goods   Remember that factor demand is derived demand: if the price of the good that is produced with a factor changes, so will the value of the marginal product of the factor. That is, if P changes, $VMPL = P \times MPL$ will change at any given level of employment.

Figure 12-4 illustrates the effects of changes in the price of wheat, assuming that $200 is the current wage rate. Panel (a) shows the effect of an *increase* in the price of wheat. This shifts the value of the marginal product curve upward, because *VMPL* rises at any given level of employment. If the wage rate remains unchanged at $200, the optimal point moves from A to B: the profit-maximizing level of employment rises.

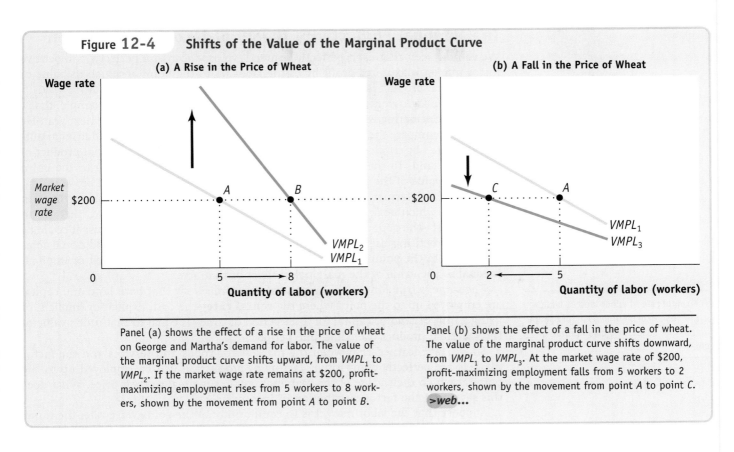

Figure 12-4   **Shifts of the Value of the Marginal Product Curve**

(a) A Rise in the Price of Wheat

Wage rate

Market wage rate $200

A   B

VMPL₂
VMPL₁

0   5 ——→ 8

Quantity of labor (workers)

(b) A Fall in the Price of Wheat

Wage rate

$200

C   A

VMPL₁
VMPL₃

0   2 ←—— 5

Quantity of labor (workers)

Panel (a) shows the effect of a rise in the price of wheat on George and Martha's demand for labor. The value of the marginal product curve shifts upward, from *VMPL₁* to *VMPL₂*. If the market wage rate remains at $200, profit-maximizing employment rises from 5 workers to 8 workers, shown by the movement from point *A* to point *B*.

Panel (b) shows the effect of a fall in the price of wheat. The value of the marginal product curve shifts downward, from *VMPL₁* to *VMPL₃*. At the market wage rate of $200, profit-maximizing employment falls from 5 workers to 2 workers, shown by the movement from point *A* to point *C*.
>*web*...

Panel (b) shows the effect of a *decrease* in the price of wheat. This shifts the value of the marginal product curve downward. If the wage rate remains unchanged at $200, the optimal point moves from *A* to *C*: the profit-maximizing level of employment falls.

Changes in Supply of Other Factors   Suppose that George and Martha acquire more land to cultivate—say, by clearing a woodland on their property. Each worker could then produce more wheat because each one would have more land to work with. So the marginal product of labor on the farm would rise at any given level of employment. This would have the same effect as an increase in the price of wheat, which we have already seen in panel (a) of Figure 12-4: the value of the marginal product curve would shift upward, and at any given wage rate the profit-maximizing level of employment would increase. Similarly, if George and Martha cultivate less land, the marginal product of labor at any given employment level would fall—each worker would produce less wheat because of having less land to work with. As a result, the value of the marginal product curve would shift downward—as in panel (b) of Figure 12-4—and the profit-maximizing level of employment would decrease.

Changes in Technology   In general, the effect of technological progress on the demand for any given factor can go either way: improved technology can either increase or decrease the demand for a given factor of production.

How can technological progress decrease factor demand? Consider horses, which were once an important factor of production. The development of substitutes for horse power, such as automobiles and tractors, greatly reduced the demand for horses.

The usual effect of technological progress, however, is to increase factor demand. In particular, although there have been persistent fears that machinery would reduce the demand for labor, over the long run the U.S. economy has seen both large wage increases and large increases in employment, suggesting that technological progress has greatly increased labor demand.

The Marginal Productivity Theory of Income Distribution

We've now seen that each perfectly competitive producer in a perfectly competitive factor market maximizes profit by hiring labor up to the point at which its value of the marginal product is equal to its price—that is, to the point where $VMPL = W$.

The same logic works for other factors of production. Suppose, for example, that a farmer is considering whether to rent an additional acre of land for the next year. He or she will compare the cost of renting that acre with the value of the additional output generated by employing an additional acre—the value of the marginal product of an acre of land. To maximize profit, the farmer must employ land up to the point where the value of the marginal product of an acre is equal to the rent per acre.

What if the farmer already owns the land? We already saw the answer back in Chapter 7, which dealt with economic decisions: even if you own land, there is an implicit cost—the opportunity cost—of using it for a given activity, because it could be used for something else. So a profit-maximizing producer will employ additional acres of land up to the point where the cost of the last acre employed, explicit or implicit, is equal to the value of the marginal product of that acre.

The same is true for capital. In general, economists say that both land and capital are employed up to the point where the **rental rate**—the cost, explicit or implicit, of using a unit of land or capital for a set period of time—is equal to that unit's value of the marginal product over that time period.

So we have learned that when the markets for goods and services and the factor markets are perfectly competitive, factors of production will be employed up to the point at which their value of the marginal product is equal to their price. What does this say about the factor distribution of income?

Suppose that the labor market is in equilibrium: at the going wage rate, the number of workers that producers want to employ is equal to the number of workers willing to work. Then all employers will pay the *same* wage rate, and *each* employer, whatever he or she is producing, will employ labor up to the point where the value of the marginal product of one more worker is equal to that wage rate.

This situation is illustrated in Figure 12-5, which shows the value of the marginal product curves of two producers—Farmer Jones, who produces wheat, and Farmer

> The **rental rate** of either land or capital is the cost, explicit or implicit, of using a unit of that asset for a given period of time.

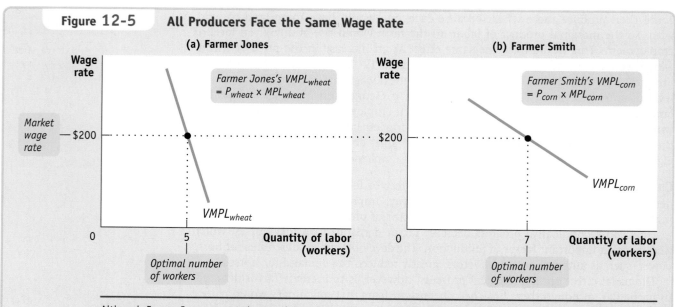

Figure 12-5   **All Producers Face the Same Wage Rate**

Although Farmer Jones grows wheat and Farmer Smith grows corn, they both compete in the same market for labor and must therefore pay the same wage rate, $200.

Each producer hires labor up to the point at which *VMPL* = $200: 5 workers for Jones, 7 workers for Smith.

Smith, who produces corn. Despite the fact that they produce different products, they compete for the same workers, and so must pay the same wage rate, $200. So when both farmers maximize profit, both hire labor up to the point where its value of the marginal product is equal to the wage rate. In the figure, this corresponds to employment of 5 workers by Jones and 7 by Smith.

Figure 12-6 illustrates the general situation in the labor market as a whole. The *market labor demand curve,* like the market demand curve for a good (shown in Figure 10-6), is the horizontal sum of all the individual labor demand curves—which is the same as each producer's value of the marginal product curve. For now, let's simply assume an upward-sloping supply curve for labor; we'll discuss labor supply later in this chapter. Then the equilibrium wage rate is the wage rate at which the quantity of labor supplied is equal to the quantity of labor demanded. In Figure 12-6, this equilibrium wage rate is W^* and the corresponding equilibrium employment level is L^*.

And as we showed in the examples of the farms of George and Martha and of Farmer Jones and Farmer Smith (where the equilibrium wage rate corresponds to $200), each firm will hire labor up to the point at which the value of the marginal product of labor is equal to the equilibrium wage rate. This means that, in equilibrium, the marginal product of labor will be the same for all employers. So the equilibrium (or market) wage rate is equal to the **equilibrium value of the marginal product** of labor—the additional value produced by the last unit of labor employed in the labor market as a whole. It doesn't matter where that additional unit is employed, since VMPL is the same for all producers.

What we have just learned, then, is that the market wage rate is equal to the equilibrium value of the marginal product of labor. And the same is true of each factor of production: in a perfectly competitive market economy, the market price of each factor is equal to its equilibrium value of the marginal product.

The theory that each factor is paid the value of the output generated by the last unit employed in the factor market as a whole is known as the **marginal productivity theory of income distribution**.

The **equilibrium value of the marginal product** of a factor is the additional value produced by the last unit of that factor employed in the factor market as a whole.

According to the **marginal productivity theory of income distribution**, every factor of production is paid its equilibrium value of the marginal product.

Figure 12-6

Equilibrium in the Labor Market

The market labor demand curve is the horizontal sum of the individual labor demand curves of all producers. Here the equilibrium wage rate is W^*, the equilibrium employment level is L^*, and every producer hires labor up to the point at which VMPL = W^*. So labor is paid its equilibrium value of the marginal product, the value of the marginal product of the last worker hired in the labor market as a whole. **>web...**

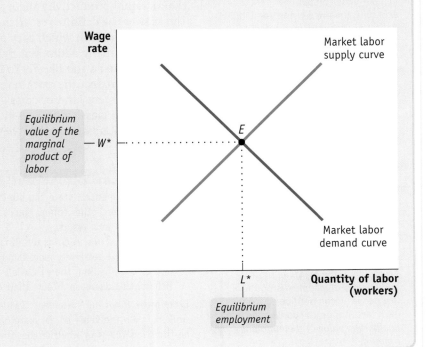

To understand why the marginal productivity theory of income distribution is an important theory, take a look back at Figure 12-1, which showed the factor distribution of income in the United States, and ask yourself this question: who or what decided that labor would get 71 percent of total U.S. income? Why not 90 percent or 50 percent?

The answer, according to the marginal productivity theory of income distribution, is that the division of income among the economy's factors of production isn't arbitrary: it is determined by each factor's marginal productivity at the economy's equilibrium. The wage rate earned by *all* workers in the economy is equal to the increase in the value of output generated by the last worker employed in the economy-wide labor market.

Here we have assumed that all workers are of the same ability. But in reality workers may differ considerably in ability. Rather than thinking of one labor market for all workers in the economy, we can instead think of different markets for different types of workers, where workers are of equivalent ability within each market. For example, the market for computer programmers is different from the market for pastry chefs. And in the market for computer programmers, all participants are assumed to have equal ability; likewise for the market for pastry chefs. In this scenario, the marginal productivity theory of income distribution still holds. That is, when the labor market for computer programmers is in equilibrium, the wage rate earned by all computer programmers is equal to the market's equilibrium value of the marginal product—the value of the marginal product of the last computer programmer hired in that market.

economics in action

Star Power

If you want to be rich, don't become a classical musician or an opera singer. Most musical artists earn quite little considering the many years of training required.

There are, however, a handful of performers who command very large fees, in the vicinity of $30,000 for a single performance. Can the fees paid to stars be explained by the marginal productivity theory of income distribution?

The answer is a definite yes. High fees for stars reflect a careful calculation by managers of the theaters in which they perform. These managers know—with considerable precision—how many additional tickets they will sell, and how much they can raise ticket prices, when a star like Yo-Yo Ma is performing. The high fees paid to these classical superstars reflect the extra revenues they will generate from ticket sales.

All this may seem kind of crass—aren't we talking about art and beauty here? Yes, but music—even classical music—is also a business, and the principles of economics apply to opera stars as much as they do to fast-food workers. ■

< < < < < < < < < < < < < < < < < <

▶▶CHECK YOUR UNDERSTANDING 12-2

1. In the following cases, state the direction of the shift of the demand curve for labor and what will happen, other things equal, to the market equilibrium wage rate and quantity of labor employed as a result.
   a. Service industries, such as retailing and banking, experience an increase in demand. These industries use relatively more labor than nonservice industries.
   b. Due to over-fishing, there is a fall in the amount of fish caught per day by commercial fishers; this decrease affects their demand for workers.

2. Explain the following statement: "When firms in different industries all compete for the same workers, then the value of the marginal product of the last worker hired will be equal across all firms regardless of whether they are in different industries."

Solutions appear at back of book.

Is the Marginal Productivity Theory of Income Distribution Really True?

Although the marginal productivity theory of income distribution is a well-established part of economic theory, closely linked to the analysis of markets in general, it is a source of some controversy. There are two main objections to it.

First, in the real world we see large disparities in income between factors of production that, in the eyes of some observers, should receive the same payment. Perhaps the most conspicuous examples in the United States are the large differences in the average wages between women and men and among various racial and ethnic groups. Do these wage differences really reflect differences in marginal productivity, or is something else going on?

Second, many people wrongly believe that the marginal productivity theory of income distribution gives a *moral* justification for the distribution of income, implying that the existing distribution is fair and appropriate. (We'll explain in Chapter 13 why this is a misconception.) This misconception sometimes leads people who believe that the current distribution of income is unfair to reject marginal productivity theory.

To address these controversies, we'll start by looking at income disparities across gender and ethnic groups. Then we'll ask what factors might account for these disparities and whether these explanations are consistent with the marginal productivity theory of income distribution.

Wage Disparities in Practice

Wage rates in the United States cover a very wide range. In 2004, hundreds of thousands of workers received the legal federal minimum of $5.15 per hour. At the other extreme, the chief executives of several companies were paid more than $100 million, which is $20,000 per hour even if they worked 100-hour weeks. Even leaving out these extremes, there is a huge range of wage rates. Are people really that different in their marginal productivities?

A particular source of concern is the existence of systematic wage differences across gender and ethnicity. Figure 12-7 compares annual median earnings in 2004 of workers 25 years old and over classified by gender and ethnicity. As a group, white males

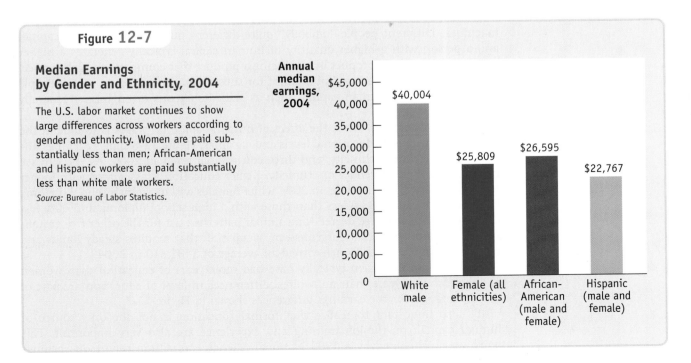

Figure 12-7

Median Earnings by Gender and Ethnicity, 2004

The U.S. labor market continues to show large differences across workers according to gender and ethnicity. Women are paid substantially less than men; African-American and Hispanic workers are paid substantially less than white male workers.

Source: Bureau of Labor Statistics.

had the highest earnings. The data show that women (averaging across all ethnicities) earned only about 65% as much; African-American workers (male and female combined) only 66% as much; Hispanic workers only 57 percent as much.

We are a nation founded on the belief that all men are created equal—and if the Constitution were rewritten today, we would say that *all people* are created equal. So why do they receive such unequal pay? Let's start with the marginal productivity explanations, then look at other influences.

Marginal Productivity and Wage Inequality

A large part of the observed inequality in wages can be explained by considerations that are consistent with the marginal productivity theory of income distribution. In particular, there are three well-understood sources of wage differences across occupations and individuals.

First is the existence of **compensating differentials:** across different types of jobs, wages are often higher or lower depending on how attractive or unattractive the job is. Workers with unpleasant or dangerous jobs demand a higher wage in comparison to workers with jobs that require the same skill and effort but lack the unpleasant or dangerous qualities. For example, truckers who haul hazardous loads are paid more than truckers who haul normal loads. But for any *given* job, the marginal productivity theory of income distribution generally holds true. For example, hazardous-load truckers are paid a wage equal to the equilibrium value of the marginal product of the last person employed in the market for hazardous-load truckers.

A second reason for wage inequality that is clearly consistent with marginal productivity theory is differences in talent. People differ in their abilities: a high-ability person, by producing a better product that commands a higher price compared to a lower-ability person, generates a higher value of the marginal product. And these differences in the value of the marginal product translate into differences in earning potential. We all know that this is true in sports: practice is important, but 99.99 percent (at least) of the population just doesn't have what it takes to hit golf balls like Tiger Woods or skate like Michelle Kwan. The same is true, though less obvious, in other fields of endeavor.

A third, very important reason for wage differences is differences in the quantity of *human capital*. Recall that human capital—education and training—is at least as important in the modern economy as physical capital in the form of buildings and machines. Different people "embody" quite different quantities of human capital, and a person with a higher quantity of human capital typically generates a higher value of the marginal product by producing a product that commands a higher price. So differences in human capital account for substantial differences in wages. People with high levels of human capital, such as skilled surgeons or engineers, generally receive high wages.

The most direct way to see the effect of human capital on wages is to look at the relationship between educational levels and earnings. Figure 12-8 shows earnings differentials by gender, ethnicity, and three educational levels in 2004. As you can see from it, regardless of gender or ethnicity, higher education is associated with higher median earnings. For example, in 2004 white females without a high school diploma had median earnings 33% less than those with a high school diploma and 60% less than those with a college degree—and similar patterns exist for the other five groups. Additional data show that surgeons—an occupation that requires steady hands and many years of formal training—earned an average of $181,610 in 2004.

Because even now men typically have had more years of education than women and whites more years than nonwhites, differences in level of education are part of the explanation for the earnings differences shown in Figure 12-7.

It's also important to realize that formal education is not the only source of human capital; on-the-job training and experience are also very important. This point was highlighted by a 1999 National Science Foundation report on earnings

Compensating differentials are wage differences across jobs that reflect the fact that some jobs are less pleasant than others.

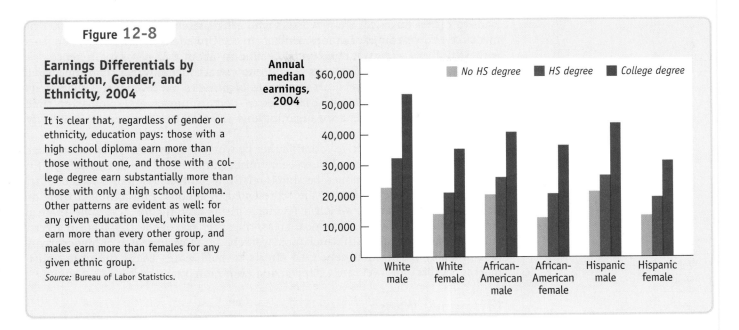

Figure 12-8

Earnings Differentials by Education, Gender, and Ethnicity, 2004

It is clear that, regardless of gender or ethnicity, education pays: those with a high school diploma earn more than those without one, and those with a college degree earn substantially more than those with only a high school diploma. Other patterns are evident as well: for any given education level, white males earn more than every other group, and males earn more than females for any given ethnic group.

Source: Bureau of Labor Statistics.

differences between male and female engineers. The study was motivated by concerns over the male–female earnings gap: on average, men with engineering degrees earn about 25 percent more than women with equivalent degrees. The study found that women in engineering are, on average, younger than men and have considerably less experience than their male counterparts. This difference in age and experience, according to the study, explained most of the earnings differential. Differences in job tenure and experience can partly explain one notable aspect of Figure 12-8: that, across all ethnicities, women's median earnings are less than men's median earnings for any given education level.

But it's also important to emphasize that earnings differences that arise from differences in human capital are not necessarily "fair." A society in which nonwhite children typically receive a poor education because they live in underfunded school districts, then go on to earn low wages because they are poorly educated, may have labor markets that are well described by marginal productivity theory (and would be consistent with the earnings differentials across ethnic groups shown in Figure 12-7). Yet many people would still consider the resulting distribution of income unfair.

Still, many observers think that actual wage differentials cannot be entirely explained by compensating differentials, differences in talent, and human capital. They believe that market power, *efficiency wages,* and discrimination also play an important role. We will examine these forces next.

Market Power

The marginal productivity theory of income distribution is based on the assumption that factor markets are perfectly competitive. In such markets we can expect workers to be paid the equilibrium value of their marginal product, regardless of who they are. But how valid is this assumption?

We haven't yet studied markets that are *not* perfectly competitive (we'll get there in Chapter 14), but let's touch briefly on the ways in which labor markets may deviate from the competitive assumption.

One undoubted source of differences in wages between otherwise similar workers is the role of **unions**—organizations that try to raise wages and improve working conditions for their members. Labor unions, when they are successful, replace one-on-one wage deals between workers and employers with "collective bargaining," in which the employer must negotiate wages with union representatives. Without question, this

Unions are organizations of workers that try to raise wages and improve working conditions for their members.

leads to higher wages for those workers who are represented by unions. In 2004 the median weekly earnings of union members in the United States were $781, compared with $612 for workers not represented by unions—about a 22 percent difference.

Just as workers can sometimes organize to extract higher wages than they would otherwise receive, employers can sometimes organize to pay *lower* wages than would result from competition. Health care workers—doctors, nurses, and so on—sometimes argue that health maintenance organizations (HMOs) are engaged in a collective effort to hold down their wages.

How much does collective action, either by workers or by employers, affect wages in the modern United States? Most economists think that it is a fairly minor influence. To begin with, union membership is relatively limited: less than 9 percent of the employees of private businesses are represented by unions. And although there are fields like health care in which a few large firms account for a sizeable share of employment in certain geographical areas, the sheer size of the U.S. labor market is enormous and the ease with which most workers can move in search of higher-paying jobs probably means that concerted efforts to hold wages below the unrestrained market equilibrium level rarely happen and even more rarely succeed.

Efficiency Wages

A second source of wage inequality is the phenomenon of *efficiency wages*—a type of incentive scheme to motivate workers to work hard and reduce worker turnover used by employers. Suppose that a worker performs a job that is extremely important but in which the employer can observe only at infrequent intervals how well the job is being performed—say, serving as a caregiver for the employer's child. Then it often makes sense for the employer to pay more than the worker could earn in an alternative job—that is, more than the equilibrium wage. Why? Because earning a premium makes losing this job and having to take the alternative job quite costly for the worker. So a worker who happens to be observed performing poorly and is therefore fired is now worse off for having to accept a lower-paying job. The threat of losing a job that pays a premium motivates the worker to perform well and avoid being fired. Likewise, paying a premium also reduces worker turnover—the frequency with which an employee leaves a job voluntarily. Despite the fact that it may take no more effort and skill to be a child's caregiver than to be an office worker, efficiency wages show why it often makes economic sense for a parent to pay a caregiver more than the equilibrium wage of an office worker.

> According to the **efficiency-wage model**, some employers pay an above-equilibrium wage as an incentive for better performance.

The **efficiency-wage model** explains why we may observe wages offered above their equilibrium level. Like the price floors that we studied in Chapter 4—and, in particular, much like the minimum wage—this phenomenon leads to a surplus of labor supplied in the markets for labor that are characterized by the efficiency wage model. This surplus of labor translates into unemployment—some workers are actively searching for a high-paying efficiency-wage job but are unable to get one, and other more fortunate but no more deserving workers are able to acquire one. As a result, two workers with exactly the same profile—the same skills and same job history—may earn unequal wages: the worker who is lucky enough to get an efficiency-wage job earns more than the worker who gets a standard job (or who remains unemployed while searching for a higher-paying job). Efficiency wages are a type of market failure that arises from the fact that some employees don't always perform as well as they should and are able to hide that fact. As a result, employers use nonequilibrium wages in order to motivate their employees, leading to an inefficient outcome.

Discrimination

It is a real and ugly fact that throughout history there has been discrimination against workers who are considered to be the wrong race, ethnicity, or gender. How does this fit into our economic models?

The main insight economic analysis offers is that discrimination is *not* a natural consequence of market competition. On the contrary, market forces tend to work against discrimination. To see why, consider the incentives that would exist if social convention dictated that women be paid, say, 30 percent less than men with equivalent qualifications and experience. A company whose management was itself unbiased would then be able to reduce its costs by hiring women rather than men—and such companies would have an advantage over other companies that hired men despite their higher cost. The result would be to create an excess demand for female workers, which would tend to drive up their wages.

But if market competition works against discrimination, how is it that so much discrimination has taken place? The answer is twofold. First, when labor markets don't work well, employers may have the ability to discriminate without hurting their profits. For example, market interferences (such as unions or minimum-wage laws) or market failures (such as efficiency wages) can lead to wages that are above their equilibrium levels. In these cases, there are more job applicants than there are jobs—leaving employers free to discriminate among applicants. In research published in 2003, two economists, Marianne Bertrand and Sendhil Mullainathan, documented discrimination in hiring by sending fictitious résumés to prospective employers on a random basis. Applicants with "white-sounding" names such as Emily Walsh were 50 percent more likely to be contacted than applicants with "African-American-sounding" names such as Lakisha Washington. Also, applicants with white-sounding names and good credentials were much more likely to be contacted than those without such credentials. By contrast, potential employers seemed to ignore the credentials of applicants with African-American-sounding names.

Second, discrimination has sometimes been institutionalized in government policy. This institutionalization of discrimination has made it easier to maintain it against market pressure, and historically it is the form that discrimination has typically taken. For example, at one time in the United States, African-Americans were barred from attending "whites-only" public schools and universities in many parts of the country and forced to attend inferior schools. So although market competition tends to work against *current* discrimination, it is not a remedy for past discrimination, which typically has had an impact on the education and experience of its victims and thereby reduces their income. Economics in Action below illustrates the way in which government policy enforced discrimination in the world's most famous racist regime, that of South Africa.

So Does Marginal Productivity Theory Work?

The main conclusion you should draw from this discussion is that marginal productivity theory is not a perfect description of how factor incomes are determined but that it works pretty well. The deviations are important. But, by and large, in a modern economy with well-functioning labor markets, factors of production are paid the equilibrium value of the marginal product—the value of the marginal product of the last unit employed in the market as a whole.

It's important to emphasize, once again, that this does not mean that the factor distribution of income is morally justified. We'll turn to issues of fairness and equity in Chapter 13.

economics in action

The Economics of Apartheid

The Republic of South Africa is the richest nation in Africa, but it also has a harsh political history. Until the peaceful transition to majority rule in 1994, the country was controlled by its white minority, Afrikaners, the descendants of European (mainly Dutch) immigrants. This minority imposed an economic system known as apartheid, which overwhelmingly favored white interests over those of native Africans and other groups considered "nonwhite," such as Asians.

South Africa is a democracy now, but the human legacy of apartheid persists.

The origins of apartheid go back to the early years of the twentieth century, when large numbers of white farmers began moving into South Africa's growing cities. There they discovered, to their horror, that they did not automatically earn higher wages than other races. But they had the right to vote—and nonwhites did not. And so the South African government instituted "job-reservation" laws designed to ensure that only whites got jobs that paid well. The government also set about creating jobs for whites in government-owned industries. As Allister Sparks notes in *The Mind of South Africa* (1990), in its efforts to provide high-paying jobs for whites, the country "eventually acquired the largest amount of nationalized industry of any country outside the Communist bloc."

In other words, racial discrimination was possible because it was backed by the power of the government, which prevented markets from following their natural course.

A postscript: in 1994, in one of the political miracles of modern times, the white regime ceded power and South Africa became a full-fledged democracy. Apartheid was abolished. Unfortunately, large racial differences in earnings remain. The main reason is that apartheid created huge disparities in human capital, which will persist for many years to come. ■

< < < < < < < < < < < < < < < < < < < <

> **CHECK YOUR UNDERSTANDING 12-3**

1. Assess each of the following statements. Do you think they are true, false, or ambiguous? Explain.
   a. The marginal productivity theory of income distribution is inconsistent with the presence of income disparities associated with gender, race, or ethnicity.
   b. Companies that engage in workplace discrimination but whose competitors do not are likely to have lower profits as a result of their actions.
   c. Workers who are paid less because they have less experience are not the victims of discrimination.

Solutions appear at back of book.

The Supply of Labor

Up to this point we have focused on the demand for factors, which determines the quantities demanded of labor, capital or land by producers as a function of their factor prices. What about the supply of factors?

In this section we focus exclusively on the supply of labor. We do this for two reasons. First, in the modern U.S. economy, labor is the most important factor of production, accounting for most of factor income. Second, as we'll see, labor supply is the area in which factor markets look most different from markets for goods and services.

Work Versus Leisure

In the labor market, the roles of firms and households are the reverse of what they are in markets for goods and services. On the one hand, a good such as wheat is supplied by firms and demanded by households; on the other hand, labor is demanded by firms and supplied by households. How do people decide how much labor to supply?

As a practical matter, most people have limited control over their work hours: either you take a job that involves working a set number of hours per week, or you don't get the job at all. To understand the logic of labor supply, however, it helps to put realism to one side for a bit and imagine an individual who can choose to work as many or as few hours as he or she likes.

Why wouldn't such an individual work as many hours as possible? Because workers are human beings, too, and have other uses for their time. An hour spent on the job is an hour not spent on other, presumably more pleasant, activities. So the decision about how much labor to supply involves making a decision about **time allocation**—how many hours to spend on different activities.

Decisions about labor supply result from decisions about **time allocation:** how many hours to spend on different activities.

By working, people earn income that they can use to buy goods. The more hours an individual works, the more goods he or she can afford to buy. But this increased purchasing power comes at the expense of a reduction in **leisure,** the time spent not working. (Leisure doesn't necessarily mean time goofing off. It could mean time spent with one's family, pursuing hobbies, exercising, and so on). And though purchased goods yield utility, so does leisure. Indeed, we can think of leisure itself as a normal good, which most people would like to consume more of as their incomes increase.

How does a rational individual decide how much leisure to consume? By making a marginal comparison, of course. In analyzing consumer choice, we asked how a utility-maximizing consumer uses a marginal *dollar*. In analyzing labor supply, we ask how an individual uses a marginal *hour*.

Consider Clive, an individual who likes both leisure and the goods money can buy. And suppose that his wage rate is $10 per hour. In deciding how many hours he wants to work, he must compare the marginal utility of an additional hour of leisure with the additional utility he gets from $10 worth of goods. If $10 worth of goods adds more to his total utility than an additional hour of leisure, he can increase his total utility by giving up an hour of leisure in order to work an additional hour. If an extra hour of leisure adds more to his total utility than $10 in income, he can increase his total utility by working one fewer hour in order to gain an hour of leisure.

At Clive's optimal labor supply choice, then, his marginal utility of one hour of leisure is equal to the marginal utility he gets from the goods that his hourly wage can purchase. This is very similar to the *optimal consumption rule* we encountered in Chapter 10, except that it is a rule about time rather than money.

Our next step is to ask how Clive's decision about time allocation is affected when his wage rate changes.

Wages and Labor Supply

Suppose that Clive's wage rate doubles, from $10 to $20 per hour. How will he change his time allocation?

You could argue that Clive will work longer hours, because his incentive to work has increased: by giving up an hour of leisure, he can now gain twice as much money as before. But you could equally well argue that he will work less, because he doesn't need to work as many hours to generate the income to pay for the goods he wants.

As these opposing arguments suggest, the quantity of labor Clive supplies can either rise or fall when his wage rate rises. To understand why, let's recall the distinction between *substitution effects* and *income effects* that we learned in Chapters 10 and 11. We saw there that a price change affects consumer choice in two ways: by changing the opportunity cost of a good in terms of other goods (the substitution effect) and by making the consumer richer or poorer (the income effect).

Now think about how a rise in Clive's wage rate affects his demand for leisure. On the one hand, the opportunity cost of leisure—the amount of money he gives up by taking an hour off instead of working—rises. That substitution effect gives him an incentive, other things equal, to consume less leisure and work longer hours. But on the other hand, a higher wage rate makes Clive richer—and this income effect leads him, other things equal, to want to consume *more* leisure and supply less labor, because leisure is a normal good.

So in the case of labor supply, the substitution effect and the income effect work in opposite directions. If the substitution effect is so powerful that it dominates the income effect, an increase in Clive's wage rate leads him to supply more hours of labor. If the income effect is so powerful that it dominates the substitution effect, an increase in the wage rate leads him to supply *fewer* hours of labor.

We see, then, that the **individual labor supply curve**—the relationship between the wage rate and the number of hours of labor supplied by an individual worker—is not necessarily upward sloping. If the income effect dominates, a higher wage rate will reduce the quantity of labor supplied.

Leisure is time available for purposes other than earning money to buy marketed goods.

The **individual labor supply curve** shows how the quantity of labor supplied by an individual depends on that individual's wage rate.

Figure 12-9 **The Individual Labor Supply Curve**

(a) The Substitution Effect Dominates

Wage rate

Individual labor supply curve

$20

10

0   40 → 50

Quantity of labor (hours)

(b) The Income Effect Dominates

Wage rate

$20

10

0   30 ← 40

Individual labor supply curve

Quantity of labor (hours)

When the substitution effect of a wage increase dominates the income effect, the individual labor supply curve is upward sloping as in panel (a). Here a rise in the wage rate from $10 to $20 per hour increases the number of hours worked from 40 to 50.

But when the income effect of a wage increase dominates the substitution effect, the individual labor supply curve is downward sloping as in panel (b). Here the same rise in the wage rate reduces the number of hours worked from 40 to 30. **>web**...

Figure 12-9 illustrates the two possibilities for labor supply. If the substitution effect dominates the income effect, the individual labor supply curve slopes upward; panel (a) shows an increase in the wage rate from $10 to $20 per hour leading to a rise in the number of hours worked from 40 to 50. However, if the income effect dominates, the quantity of labor supplied goes down when the wage rate increases. Panel (b) shows the same rise in the wage rate leading to a *fall* in the number of hours worked from 40 to 30. (Economists refer to an individual labor supply curve that contains both upward-sloping and downward-sloping segments as a "backward-bending labor supply curve"— a concept that we analyze in detail in this chapter's appendix.)

Is a negative response of the quantity of labor supplied to the wage rate a real possibility? Yes: many labor economists believe that income effects on the supply of labor may be somewhat stronger than substitution effects. The most compelling piece of evidence for this belief comes from Americans' increasing consumption of leisure over the past century. At the end of the nineteenth century, wages adjusted for inflation

FOR INQUIRING MINDS

WHY YOU CAN'T FIND A CAB WHEN IT'S RAINING

Everyone says that you can't find a taxi in New York when you really need one—say, when it's raining. That could be because everyone else is trying to get a taxi at the same time. But according to a study published in the *Quarterly Journal of Economics*, it's more than that: cab drivers actually go home early when it's raining.

The reason is that the hourly wage rate of a taxi driver depends on the weather:

when it's raining, drivers get more fares and therefore earn more per hour. And it seems that the income effect of this higher wage rate outweighs the substitution effect.

This behavior leads the authors of the study to question drivers' rationality. They point out that if taxi drivers thought in terms of the long run, they would realize that rainy days and nice days tend to average out and that their high earnings on a

rainy day don't really affect their long-run income very much. Indeed, experienced drivers (who have probably figured this out) are less likely than inexperienced drivers to go home early on a rainy day. But leaving such issues to one side, the study does seem to show clear evidence of a labor supply curve that slopes downward instead of upward, thanks to income effects. (See source note on copyright page.)

were only about one-eighth what they are today; the typical work week was 70 hours, and very few workers retired at 65. Today the typical work week is less than 40 hours, and most people retire at 65 or earlier. So it seems that Americans have chosen to take advantage of higher wages in part by consuming more leisure.

Shifts of the Labor Supply Curve

Now that we have examined how income and substitution effects shape the individual labor supply curve, we can turn to the market labor supply curve. In any labor market, the market supply curve is the horizontal sum of the individual labor supply curves of all workers in that market. A change in any factor *other than the wage* that alters workers' willingness to supply labor causes a shift of the labor supply curve. A variety of factors can lead to such shifts, including changes in preferences and social norms, changes in population, changes in opportunities, and changes in wealth.

Changes in Preferences and Social Norms Changes in preferences and social norms can lead workers to increase or decrease their willingness to work at any given wage. A striking example of this phenomenon is the large increase in the number of employed women—particularly married employed women—that has occurred in the United States since the 1960s. Until that time, women who could afford to largely avoided working outside the home. Changes in preferences and norms in post–World War II America (helped along by the invention of labor-saving home appliances such as washing machines, increasing urbanization of the population, and higher female education levels) have induced large numbers of American women to join the workforce—a phenomenon often repeated in other countries that experience similar social and technological forces.

Changes in Population Changes in the population size generally lead to shifts of the labor supply curve. A larger population tends to shift the labor supply rightward as more workers are available at any given wage; a smaller population tends to shift the labor supply curve leftward. Currently the size of the U.S. labor force grows by approximately 1 percent per year, a result of immigration from other countries and, in comparison to other developed countries, a relatively high U.S. birth rate. As a result, many labor markets in the United States are experiencing rightward shifts of their labor supply curves.

Changes in Opportunities At one time, teaching was the only occupation considered suitable for well-educated women. However, as opportunities in other professions opened up to women starting in the 1960s, many women left teaching and potential female teachers chose other careers. This generated a leftward shift of the supply curve for teachers, reflecting a fall in the willingness to work at any given wage and forcing school districts to pay more to maintain an adequate teaching staff. These events illustrate a general result: when superior alternatives arise for workers in another labor market, the supply curve in the original labor market shifts leftward as workers move to the new opportunities. Similarly, when opportunities diminish in one labor market—say, layoffs in the manufacturing industry occur because of increased foreign competition—the supply in alternative labor markets increases as workers move to these other markets.

Changes in Wealth A person whose wealth increases will buy more normal goods, including leisure. So when a class of workers experiences a general rise in their wealth levels—say, due to a stock market boom—the income effect from the wealth increase will shift the labor supply curve associated with those workers leftward as workers consume more leisure and work less. Note that *the income effect caused by a change in wealth shifts the labor supply curve,* but *the income effect from a wage increase*—as we discussed in the case of the individual labor supply curve—*is a movement along the labor supply curve.* The following Economics in Action illustrates how such a change in the wealth levels of many families during the late 1990s led to a shift of the market labor supply curve associated with their employable children.

economics in action

The Decline of the Summer Job

In the summer of 2000, according to the *New York Times,* the New Jersey resort town of Ocean City found itself facing a serious shortage of lifeguards. Traditionally lifeguard positions, together with many other seasonal jobs, have been filled mainly by high school and college students. But in recent years a growing number of young Americans have chosen not to take summer jobs. In 1979, 71 percent of Americans between the ages of 16 and 19 were in the summer workforce. Twenty years later that number had fallen to 63 percent; and by 2005, it was 55 percent. Data show that it was young men in particular who became much less willing to take summer jobs during the 1990s.

One explanation for the decline in summer labor supply is that more students feel that they should devote their summers to additional study. But an important factor in the decline, according to the article, was that an economic and stock market boom in the late 1990s had made many more American families affluent—affluent enough that their children no longer felt pressure to make a financial contribution by working all summer.

In short, the income effect led to a reduced labor supply. ■

< < < < < < < < < < < < < < < < < < < <

>> QUICK REVIEW

➤ The choice of how much labor to supply is a problem of *time allocation:* a choice between work and *leisure.*

➤ A rise in the wage rate causes both an income and a substitution effect on an individual's labor supply. The substitution effect of a higher wage rate induces longer work hours, other things equal. This is countered by the income effect: higher income leads to a higher demand for leisure, a normal good. If the income effect dominates, a rise in the wage rate can actually cause the *individual labor supply curve* to slope the "wrong" way: downward.

➤ The market labor supply curve is the horizontal sum of the individual supply curves of all workers in that market. It shifts for four main reasons: changes in preferences and social norms, changes in population, changes in opportunities, and changes in wealth.

>>CHECK YOUR UNDERSTANDING 12-4

1. Formerly, Clive was free to work as many or as few hours per week as he wanted. But a new law limits the maximum number of hours he can work per week to 35. Explain under what circumstances, if at all, he is made:
   a. Worse off
   b. Equally as well off
   c. Better off

2. Explain in terms of the income and substitution effects how a fall in Clive's wage can induce him to work more hours than before.

Solutions appear at back of book.

• A LOOK AHEAD •

We have now put together all the pieces for understanding how a perfectly competitive market economy works. We've seen how supply and demand determine market prices, how profit maximization gives rise to the supply curve for each good, and how utility maximization gives rise to the demand curve. We've also just seen how factor markets determine the prices of factors of production and therefore the factor incomes of individuals.

But the ultimate purpose of an economy is to provide people with what they want. How well does a market economy do that job? In the next chapter we finally examine the *efficiency* of a market economy and the related but different question of *equity.*

SUMMARY

1. Just as there are markets for goods and services, there are markets for factors of production, including labor, land, and both **physical capital** and **human capital.** These markets determine the **factor distribution of income.**

2. Profit-maximizing price-taking producers will employ a factor up to the point at which its price is equal to its **value of the marginal product**—the marginal product of the factor multiplied by the price of the good. The **value of the marginal product curve** is therefore the individual price-taking producer's demand curve for a factor.

3. The market demand curve for labor is the sum of the individual demand curves of producers in that market. It shifts for three main reasons: changes in output price, changes in the supply of other factors, and technological changes.

4. When a competitive labor market is in equilibrium, the market wage is equal to the **equilibrium value of the marginal product** of labor, the additional value produced by the last worker hired in the labor market as a whole. The same principle applies to other factors of production: the **rental rate** of land or capital is equal to the equilibrium value of the marginal products. This insight leads to the **marginal productivity theory of income distribution,** according to which each factor is paid the value of the marginal product of the last unit of that factor employed in the factor market as a whole.

5. Large disparities in wages raise questions about the validity of the marginal productivity theory of income distribution. Many disparities can be explained by **compensating differentials** and by differences in talent, job experience, and human capital across workers. Market interference in the forms of **unions** and collective action by employers also creates wage disparities. The **efficiency-wage model,** which arises from a type of market failure, shows how wage disparities can arise from employers' attempts to increase worker performance. Free markets tend to diminish dis-

crimination, but discrimination remains a real source of wage disparity. Discrimination is typically maintained either through problems in labor markets or (historically) through institutionalization in government policies.

6. Labor supply is the result of decisions about **time allocation,** where each worker faces a trade-off between **leisure** and work. An increase in the hourly wage rate tends to increase work hours by the substitution effect but to reduce work hours by the income effect. If the net result is that a worker increases the quantity of labor supplied in response to a higher wage, the **individual labor supply curve** slopes upward. If the net result is that a worker reduces their work hours, the individual labor supply curve—unlike supply curves for goods and services—slopes downward.

7. The market labor supply curve is the sum of the individual labor supply curves of all workers in that market. It shifts for four main reasons: changes in preferences and social norms, changes in population, changes in opportunities, and changes in wealth.

KEY TERMS

Physical capital, p. 282
Human capital, p. 282
Factor distribution of income, p. 282
Value of the marginal product, p. 286
Value of the marginal product curve, p. 286
Rental rate, p. 290

Equilibrium value of the marginal product, p. 291
Marginal productivity theory of income distribution, p. 291
Compensating differentials, p. 294
Unions, p. 295

Efficiency-wage model, p. 296
Time allocation, p. 298
Leisure, p. 299
Individual labor supply curve, p. 299

PROBLEMS

1. In 2001, national income in the United States was $8,122.0 billion. In the same year, 135 million workers were employed, at an average wage of $43,518 per worker per year.

   a. How much compensation of employees was paid in the United States in 2001?

   b. Analyze the factor distribution of income. What percentage of national income was received in terms of compensation of employees in 2001?

   c. Suppose that a huge wave of corporate downsizing leads many terminated employees to open their own businesses. What is the effect on the factor distribution of income?

   d. Suppose the supply of labor rises due to an increase in the retirement age. What happens to the percentage of national income received in terms of compensation of employees?

2. Marty's Frozen Yogurt has the production function per day shown in the accompanying table. The equilibrium wage rate for a worker is $80 per day. Each cup of frozen yogurt sells for $2.

Quantity of labor (workers)	Quantity of frozen yogurt (cups)
0	0
1	110
2	200
3	270
4	300
5	320
6	330

   a. Calculate the marginal product of labor for each worker and the value of the marginal product per worker.

   b. How many workers should Marty employ?

3. Patty's Pizza Parlor has the production function per hour shown in the accompanying table. The hourly wage rate for each worker is $10. Each pizza sells for $2.

Quantity of labor (workers)	Quantity of pizza
0	0
1	9
2	15
3	19
4	22
5	24

a. Calculate the marginal product of labor for each worker and the value of the marginal product per worker.

b. Draw the value of the marginal product curve. Use your diagram to determine how many workers Patty should employ.

c. Now the price of pizza increases to $4. Calculate the value of the marginal product per worker, and draw the new value of the marginal product curve into your diagram. Use your diagram to determine how many workers Patty should employ now.

4. The production function for Patty's Pizza Parlor is given in the table in Problem 3. The price of pizza is $2, but the hourly wage rate rises from $10 to $15. Use a diagram to determine how Patty's demand for workers responds as a result of this wage rate increase.

5. Patty's Pizza Parlor initially had the production function given in the table in Problem 3. A worker's hourly wage rate was $10, and pizza sold for $2. Now Patty buys a new high-tech pizza oven that allows her workers to become twice as productive as before. That is, the first worker now produces 18 pizzas per hour instead of 9, and so on.

a. Calculate the new marginal product of labor and the new value of the marginal product of labor.

b. Use a diagram to determine how Patty's hiring decision responds to this increase in the productivity of her workforce.

6. Jameel runs a driver education school. The more driving instructors he hires, the more driving lessons he can sell. But because he owns a limited number of training automobiles, each additional driving instructor adds less to Jameel's output of driving lessons. The accompanying table shows Jameel's production function per day. Each driving lesson can be sold at $35 per hour.

Quantity of labor (driving instructors)	Quantity of driving lessons (hours)
0	0
1	8
2	15
3	21
4	26
5	30
6	33

Determine Jameel's labor demand schedule (his demand schedule for driving instructors) for each of the following daily wage rates for driving instructors: $160, $180, $200, $220, $240, and $260.

7. Dale and Dana work at a self-service gas station and convenience store. Dale opens up everyday and Dana arrives later to help stock the store. They are both paid the current market wage of $9.50 per hour. But Dale feels he should be paid much more because the revenue generated from the gas pumps he turns on every morning is much higher than the revenue generated by the items that Dana stocks. Assess this argument.

8. In the Shire, farmers can rent land for $100 per acre per year. All the acres are identical. Merry Brandybuck rents 30 acres on which he grows carrots. Pippin Took rents 20 acres on which he grows corn. They sell their produce in a perfectly competitive market. Merry boasts that his value of the marginal product of land is twice as large as Pippin's. Pippin replies that, if this is true and if Merry wants to maximize his profit, Merry is renting too much land. Is Pippin right? Explain your answer.

9. For each of the following situations in which similar workers are paid different wages, give the most likely explanation for these wage differences.

a. Test pilots for new jet aircraft earn higher wages than airline pilots.

b. College graduates usually have higher earnings in their first year on the job than workers without college degrees have in their first year on the job.

c. Full professors command higher salaries than assistant professors for teaching the same class.

d. Unionized workers are generally better paid than non-unionized workers.

10. Research consistently finds that despite nondiscrimination policies, African-American workers on average receive lower wages than white workers do. What are the possible reasons for this? Are these reasons consistent with marginal productivity theory?

11. Greta is an enthusiastic amateur gardener and spends a lot of her free time working in her yard. She also has a demanding and well-paid job as a freelance advertising consultant. The advertising business is going through a difficult time and the hourly consulting fee Greta can charge falls. Greta decides to spend more time gardening and less time consulting. Explain her decision in terms of income and substitution effects.

12. Wendy works at a fast-food restaurant. When her wage rate was $5 per hour, she worked 30 hours per week. When her wage rate rose to $6 per hour, she decided to work 40 hours. But when her wage rate rose further to $7, she decided to work only 35 hours.

a. Draw Wendy's individual labor supply curve.

b. Is Wendy's behavior irrational, or can you find a rational explanation? Explain your answer.

13. You are the governor's economic policy adviser. The governor wants to put in place policies that encourage employed people to work more hours at their jobs and that encourage unemployed people to find and take jobs. Assess each of the following policies in terms of reaching that goal. Explain your reasoning in terms of income and substitution effects, and indicate when the impact of the policy may be ambiguous.

a. The state income tax rate is lowered, which has the effect of increasing workers' after-tax wage rate.

b. The state income tax rate is increased, which has the effect of decreasing workers' after-tax wage rate.

c. The state property tax rate is increased, which reduces workers' after-tax income.

>web... To continue your study and review of concepts in this chapter, please visit the Krugman/Wells website for quizzes, animated graph tutorials, web links to helpful resources, and more.

www.worthpublishers.com/krugmanwells

>> Chapter 12 Appendix: Indifference Curve Analysis of Labor Supply

In the body of this chapter, we explained why the labor supply curve can slope downward instead of upward: the substitution effect of a higher wage rate, which provides an incentive to work longer hours, can be outweighed by the income effect of a higher wage rate, which may lead individuals to consume more leisure. In this appendix we show how this analysis can be carried out using the *indifference curves* introduced in Chapter 11.

The Time Allocation Budget Line

Let's return to the example of Clive, who likes leisure but also likes having money to spend. We now assume that Clive has a total of 80 hours per week that he could spend either working or enjoying as leisure time. (The remaining hours in his week, we assume, are taken up with necessary activities, mainly sleeping). Let's also assume, initially, that his hourly wage rate is $10.

A **time allocation budget line** shows an individual's trade-offs between consumption of leisure and the income that allows consumption of marketed goods.

His consumption possibilities are defined by the **time allocation budget line** in Figure 12A-1, a budget line that shows Clive's trade-offs between consumption of leisure and income. Hours of leisure per week are measured on the horizontal axis, and the money he earns from working is measured on the vertical axis.

The horizontal intercept, point X, is at 80 hours: if Clive didn't work at all, he would have 80 hours of leisure per week but would not earn any money. The vertical intercept, point Y, is at $800: if Clive worked all the time, he would earn $800 per week.

Why can we use a budget line to describe Clive's time allocation choice? The budget lines found in Chapters 10 and 11 represented the trade-offs facing consumers deciding how to allocate their income among different goods. Here, instead of asking how

Figure 12A-1

The Time Allocation Budget Line

Clive's time allocation budget line shows his tradeoff between work, which pays a wage rate of $10 per hour, and leisure. At point X he allocates all his time, 80 hours, to leisure but has no income. At point Y he allocates all his time to work, earning $800, but consumes no leisure. His hourly wage rate of $10, the opportunity cost of an hour of leisure, is equal to minus the slope of the time allocation budget line. We have assumed that point A, at 40 hours of leisure and $400 in income, is Clive's optimal time allocation. It obeys the optimal time allocation rule: the additional utility Clive gets from one more hour of leisure must equal the additional utility he gets from the goods he can purchase with one hour's wages.

Clive allocates his income, we ask how he allocates his *time*. But the principles under-lying the allocation of income and the allocation of time are the same: each involves allocating a fixed amount of a resource (80 hours of time in this case) with a constant trade-off (Clive must forgo $10 for each additional hour of leisure). So using a budget line is just as appropriate for time allocation as it is for income allocation.

As in the case of ordinary budget lines, opportunity cost plays a key role. The opportunity cost of an hour of leisure is what Clive must forgo by working one less hour—$10 in income. This opportunity cost is, of course, Clive's hourly wage rate and is equal to minus the slope of his time allocation budget line. You can verify this by noting that the slope is equal to minus the vertical intercept, point *Y*, divided by the horizontal intercept, point *X*—that is, −$800/(80 hours) = −$10 per hour.

To maximize his utility, Clive must choose the optimal point on the time alloca-tion budget line in Figure 12A-1. In Chapter 10 we saw that a consumer who allo-cates spending to maximize utility finds the point on the budget line that satisfies the *optimal consumption rule:* the marginal utility per dollar spent on two goods must be equal. Although Clive's choice involves allocating time rather than money, the same principles apply.

Since Clive "spends" time rather than money, the counterpart of the optimal con-sumption rule is the **optimal time allocation rule:** the marginal utility Clive gets from the extra money earned from an additional hour spent working must equal the marginal utility of an additional hour of leisure.

> The **optimal time allocation rule** says that an individual should allocate time so that the marginal utility per hour spent working is equal to the marginal utility of an additional hour of leisure.

The Effect of a Higher Wage Rate

Depending on his tastes, Clive's utility-maximizing choice of hours of leisure and income could lie anywhere on the time allocation budget line in Figure 12A-1. Let's assume that his optimal choice is point *A*, at which he consumes 40 hours of leisure and earns $400. Now we are ready to link the analysis of time allocation to labor supply.

When Clive chooses a point like *A* on his time allocation budget line, he is also choosing the quantity of labor he supplies to the labor market. By choosing to con-sume 40 of his 80 available hours as leisure, he has also chosen to supply the other 40 hours as labor.

Now suppose that Clive's wage rate doubles, from $10 to $20 per hour. The effect of this increase in his wage rate is shown in Figure 12A-2 on page 308. His time allo-cation budget line rotates outward: the vertical intercept, which represents the amount he could earn if he devoted all 80 hours to work, shifts upward from point *Y* to point *Z*. As a result of the doubling of his wage, Clive would earn $1,600 instead of $800 if he devoted all 80 hours to working.

But how will Clive's time allocation actually change? As we saw in the chapter, this depends on the *income effect* and *substitution effect* that we learned about in Chapters 10 and 11.

The substitution effect of an increase in the wage rate works as follows. When the wage rate increases, the opportunity cost of an hour of leisure increases; this induces Clive to consume less leisure and work more hours—that is, to substitute hours of work in place of hours of leisure as the wage rate rises. If the substitution effect were the whole story, the individual labor supply curve would look like any ordinary supply curve and would always be upward sloping—a higher wage rate leads to a greater quan-tity of labor supplied.

What we learned in our analysis of demand was that for most consumer goods, the income effect isn't very important because most goods account for only a very small share of a consumer's spending. In addition, in the few cases of goods where the income effect is significant—for example, major purchases like housing—it usual-ly reinforces the substitution effect: most goods are normal goods, so when a price increase makes a consumer poorer, he or she buys less of that good.

Figure 12A-2

An Increase in the Wage Rate

The two panels show Clive's initial optimal choice, point A, on BL_1 the time allocation budget line corresponding to a wage rate of $10. After his wage rate rises to $20, his budget line rotates out to the new budget line, BL_2: if he spends all his time working, the amount of money he earns rises from $800 to $1,600, reflected in the movement from Y to Z. This generates two opposing effects: the substitution effect pushes him to consume less leisure and to work more hours; the income effect pushes him to consume more leisure and to work fewer hours. Panel (a) shows the change in time allocation when the substitution effect is stronger: Clive's new optimal choice is point B, representing a decrease in hours of leisure to 30 hours and an increase in hours of labor to 50 hours. In this case the individual labor supply curve slopes upward. Panel (b) shows the change in time allocation when the income effect is stronger: point C is the new optimal choice, representing an increase in hours of leisure to 50 hours and a decrease in hours of labor to 30 hours. Now the individual labor supply curve slopes downward.

(a) The Substitution Effect Dominates

(b) The Income Effect Dominates

In the labor/leisure choice, however, the income effect takes on a new significance, for two reasons. First, most people get the great majority of their income from wages. This means that the income effect of a change in the wage rate is *not* small: an increase in the wage rate will generate a significant increase in income. Second, leisure is a normal good: when income rises, other things equal, people tend to consume more leisure and work fewer hours.

So the income effect of a higher wage rate tends to *reduce* the quantity of labor supplied, working in opposition to the substitution effect, which tends to *increase* the quantity of labor supplied. So the net effect of a higher wage rate on the quantity of labor Clive supplies could go either way—depending on his preferences, he might choose to supply more labor, or he might choose to supply less labor. The two panels of Figure 12-A2 illustrate these two outcomes. In each panel, point A represents Clive's initial consumption choice. Panel (a) shows the case in which Clive works more hours in response to a higher wage rate. An increase in the wage rate induces him to move from point A to point B, where he consumes less leisure than

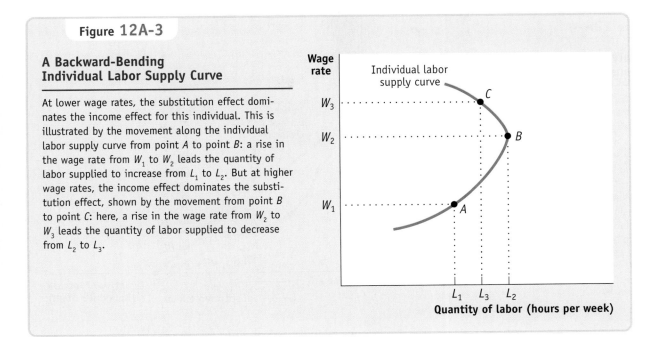

Figure 12A-3

A Backward-Bending Individual Labor Supply Curve

At lower wage rates, the substitution effect dominates the income effect for this individual. This is
illustrated by the movement along the individual
labor supply curve from point A to point B: a rise in
the wage rate from W_1 to W_2 leads the quantity of
labor supplied to increase from L_1 to L_2. But at higher
wage rates, the income effect dominates the substitution effect, shown by the movement from point B
to point C: here, a rise in the wage rate from W_2 to
W_3 leads the quantity of labor supplied to decrease
from L_2 to L_3.

at A and therefore works more hours. Here the substitution effect prevails over the
income effect. Panel (b) shows the case in which Clive works fewer hours in
response to a higher wage rate. Here, he moves from A to C, where he consumes
more leisure and works *fewer* hours than at A. Here the income effect prevails over
the substitution effect.

When the income effect of a higher wage rate is stronger than the substitution
effect, the individual labor supply curve, which shows how much labor an individual
will supply at any given wage rate, slopes the "wrong" way—downward: a higher wage
rate leads to a smaller quantity of labor supplied.

Economists believe that the substitution effect usually dominates the income
effect in the labor supply decision when an individual's wage rate is low. An individual labor supply curve is typically upward sloping for lower wage rates as people
work more in response to rising wage rates. But they also believe that many individuals have stronger preferences for leisure and will choose to cut back the number of
hours worked as their wage rate continues to rise. For these individuals, the income
effect eventually dominates the substitution effect as the wage rate rises, leading
their individual labor supply curves to change slope and to "bend backward" at high
wage rates. An individual labor supply curve with this feature, called a **backward-
bending individual labor supply curve,** is shown in Figure 12A-3. Although an
individual labor supply curve may bend backward, *market* labor supply curves are
almost always upward sloping over their entire range as higher wage rates draw more
new workers into the labor market.

> A **backward-bending individual labor
> supply curve** is an individual labor sup-
> ply curve that is upward sloping at low
> to moderate wage rates and is
> downward sloping at higher wage rates.

Indifference Curve Analysis

In Chapter 11, we showed that consumer choice can be represented using the concept of *indifference curves*, which provide a "map" of consumer preferences. If you
have covered Chapter 11, you may find it interesting to learn that indifference curves
are also useful for addressing the issue of labor supply. In fact, this is one place where
they are particularly helpful.

Figure 12A-4

Labor Supply Choice: The Indifference Curve Approach

Point A, on BL_1, is Clive's initial optimal choice. After a wage rate increase his income and utility level increase: his new time allocation budget line is BL_2 and his new optimal choice is point C. This change can be decomposed into the substitution effect—the fall in the hours of leisure from point A to point S, and the income effect—the increase in the number of hours of leisure from point S to point C. As shown here, the income effect dominates the substitution effect: the net result of an increase in the wage rate is an increase in the hours of leisure consumed and a decrease in the hours of labor supplied.

Using indifference curves, Figure 12A-4 shows how an increase in the wage rate can lead to a fall in the quantity of labor supplied. Point A is Clive's initial optimal choice, given an hourly wage rate of $10. It is the same as point A in Figure 12A-2; this time, however, we include an indifference curve to show that it is a point at which the budget line is tangent to the highest possible indifference curve.

Now consider the effect of a rise in the wage rate to $20. Imagine, for a moment, that at the same time Clive was offered a higher wage, he was told that he had to start repaying his student loan and that the good-news/bad-news combination left his utility unchanged. Then he would find himself at point S: on the same indifference curve as at A, but tangent to a steeper budget line, the dashed line BL_S in Figure 12A-4, which is parallel to BL_2. The move from A to S is the substitution effect of his wage increase: it leads him to consume less leisure and therefore supply more labor.

But now cancel the repayment on the student loan, and Clive is able to move to a higher indifference curve. His new optimum is at C, which corresponds to C in panel (b) of Figure 12A-2. The move from S to C is the income effect of his wage increase. And we see that this income effect can outweigh the substitution effect: at C he consumes more leisure, and therefore supplies less labor, than he did at A.

PROBLEMS

1. Leandro has 16 hours per day that he can allocate to work or leisure. His job pays a wage rate of $20. Leandro decides to consume 8 hours of leisure. His indifference curves have the usual shape: they are downward sloping, they do not cross, and they have the characteristic convex shape.

   a. Draw Leandro's time allocation budget line for a typical day. Then illustrate the indifference curve at his optimal choice.

   Now Leandro's wage rate falls to $10.

   b. Draw Leandro's new budget line.

   c. Suppose that Leandro now works only 4 hours as a result of his reduced wage rate. Illustrate the indifference curve at his new optimal choice.

   d. Leandro's decision to work less as the wage rate falls is the result of a substitution effect and an income effect. In your diagram, show the income effect and the substitution effect from this reduced wage rate. Which effect is stronger?

2. Florence is a highly paid fashion consultant who earns $100 per hour. She has 16 hours per day that she can allocate to work or leisure, and she decides to work for 12 hours.

a. Draw Florence's time allocation budget line for a typical day, and illustrate the indifference curve at her optimal choice.

One of Florence's clients is featured on the front page of *Vague*, an influential fashion magazine. As a result, Florence's consulting fee now rises to $500 per hour. Florence decides to work only 10 hours per day.

b. Draw Florence's new time allocation budget line, and illustrate the indifference curve at her optimal choice.

c. In your diagram, show the income effect and the substitution effect from this increase in the wage rate. Which effect is stronger?

3. Tamara has 80 hours per week that she can allocate to work or leisure. Her job pays a wage rate of $20 per hour, but Tamara is being taxed on her income in the following way. On the first $400 that Tamara makes, she pays no tax. That is, for the first 20 hours she works, her net wage—what she takes home after taxes—is $20 per hour. On all income above $400, Tamara pays a 75% tax. That is, for all hours above the first 20 hours, her net wage rate is only $5 per hour. Tamara

decides to work 30 hours. Her indifference curves have the usual shape.

a. Draw Tamara's time allocation budget line for a typical week. Also illustrate the indifference curve at her optimal choice.

The government changes the tax scheme. Now only the first $100 of income are tax-exempt. That is, for the first 5 hours she works, Tamara's net wage rate is $20 per hour. But the government reduces the tax rate on all other income to 50%. That is, for all hours above the first 5 hours, Tamara's net wage rate is now $10. After these changes, Tamara finds herself exactly equally as well off as before. That is, her new optimal choice is on the same indifference curve as her initial optimal choice.

b. Draw Tamara's new time allocation budget line on the same diagram. Also illustrate her optimal choice. Bear in mind that she is equally as well off (on the same indifference curve) as before the tax changes occurred.

c. Will Tamara work more or less than before the changes to the tax scheme? Why?

>web... To continue your study and review of concepts in this chapter, please visit the Krugman/Wells website for quizzes, animated graph tutorials, web links to helpful resources, and more.

www.worthpublishers.com/krugmanwells

>> Efficiency and Equity

AFTER THE FALL

WHEN THE BERLIN WALL CAME down in 1989, Western observers got their first good look at the centrally planned economy of East Germany. What they found was a stunningly inefficient system. Although investment had been lavished on politically favored industries such as energy production, producers of consumer goods and services were starved for capital. And the consumer goods that were produced were often not what consumers wanted to buy.

The revelation of East German inefficiency showed how badly such a planned economy worked compared with a market economy, like that of West Germany.

But even after the wall had come down, the government of the newly unified Federal Republic of Germany was not willing to let the free market run its course. Instead, both industry and individuals in East Germany received huge amounts of financial aid. The goal was to prevent the emergence of a politically unacceptable level of inequality between the former East Germans, many of whom lost their jobs in the aftermath of reunification, and West Germans.

Over time, many economists have come to believe that this aid actually delayed the reconstruction of the East German economy. They argue that the aid reduced incentives for workers to relocate to areas where more jobs were available or to learn new skills. But German officials insist that the price was well worth paying: sometimes a sense of fairness, they argue, is more important than efficiency.

Germany's experience reminds us that although we want our economy to be efficient, we also want it to be fair. In this chapter we will address both concerns. We begin by discussing the *efficiency* of a competitive market economy—the effectiveness of a competitive market economy at producing the goods and services that people want to consume. We then turn to the less well-defined

What you will learn in this chapter:

➤ How the overall concept of efficiency can be broken down into three components—**efficiency in consumption, efficiency in production,** and **efficiency in output levels**

➤ How a perfectly competitive market for a single good achieves efficiency in all three components

➤ Why an economy consisting of many perfectly competitive markets is typically, but not always, efficient

➤ The limits of the concept of efficiency—in particular, why efficiency is about how to achieve goals but not about which goals are chosen

Pierre Merimme/Corbis

Getty Images

Goods produced in centrally planned economies (consider the East German–produced Trabant at left) are notorious for their poor quality compared to stylish, high-quality goods produced in market economies (consider the West German–produced Mercedes at right).

but equally important issue of *equity*—is the distribution of consumption among individuals "fair"? As we'll see, there is no generally accepted definition of *fairness;* nonetheless, societies often choose to sacrifice some efficiency in the pursuit of equity.

Supply, Demand, and the Virtues of the Market

Back in Chapter 6 we introduced the concepts of *consumer surplus* and *producer surplus*. Recall that consumer surplus is the difference between what buyers are willing to pay for a good and what they actually pay; it measures the gains to consumers from participating in the market. Similarly, producer surplus is the difference between the price that sellers of a good receive and their cost; it measures the gains to producers from participating in the market. The sum of consumer and producer surplus, *total surplus,* measures the gains from trade: the total benefits to buyers and sellers from participating in the market.

What we learned in that chapter was a remarkable fact: in equilibrium, a perfectly competitive market—a market in which both buyers and sellers are price-takers—is usually efficient. That is, in most cases such a market *maximizes total surplus.* Except in cases of market failure, there is no way to increase the gains from trade once a market has done its work.

But why is this true, and what are the conditions that make it possible?

To answer these questions, let's briefly look at this story again. It will set the stage for our discussion of efficiency in the economy as a whole.

Why a Market Maximizes Total Surplus

In Chapter 6 we showed that a market maximizes total surplus by considering the alternatives. That is, any attempt to rearrange consumption or production from the market equilibrium reduces total surplus.

How did we demonstrate this result? Figure 13-1 shows, once again, the example of a market in used textbooks. In this example the equilibrium is at *E*, where the price

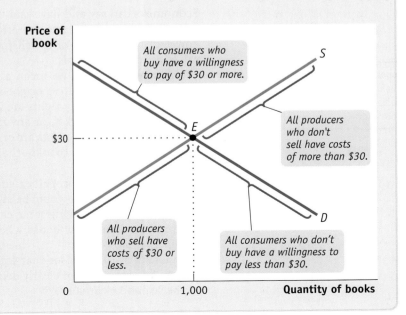

Figure 13-1

Why a Market Maximizes Total Surplus

How do we know that total surplus is maximized at the equilibrium price of $30 per book and the equilibrium quantity of 1,000? First, books go to the "right" consumers: every consumer who buys a book has a willingness to pay of $30 or more, and every potential consumer who does *not* buy a book has a willingness to pay less than $30. Second, books are supplied by the "right" producers: every seller who supplies a book has a cost of $30 or less, and every potential seller who does *not* supply a book has a cost of more than $30. Finally, the "right" quantity of 1,000 books are bought and sold: any additional books would cost more than $30 to produce but would be worth less than $30 to the consumers who receive them. If any fewer books were bought and sold, some consumers would be willing to pay more than it costs producers to supply these books. >*web*...

Price of book

All consumers who buy have a willingness to pay of $30 or more.

S

E

All producers who don't sell have costs of more than $30.

$30

All producers who sell have costs of $30 or less.

All consumers who don't buy have a willingness to pay less than $30.

D

0   1,000   **Quantity of books**

is $30, and the quantity bought and sold is 1,000 books. We then laid out the three ways in which you might try to improve on this equilibrium and showed that none of them will succeed:

■ *Reallocating consumption.* You might try to increase total surplus by giving books to different consumers. But in equilibrium every consumer who gets a book is to the left of *E* on the demand curve, and every consumer who does not get a book is to the right of *E*. That is, every consumer who gets a book has a higher willingness to pay than every consumer who does not get a book. So any reallocation of consumption away from the market equilibrium would reduce the total surplus.

■ *Reallocating production.* You might try to increase total surplus by getting different people to sell books. (For simplicity, let's think of sellers as "producing" the books.) But every potential seller who sells a book is to the left of *E* on the supply curve, and every potential seller who does not sell a book is to the right of *E*. That is, every potential seller who sells a book has a lower cost than every potential seller who does not. So any reallocation of production away from the market equilibrium would reduce the total surplus.

■ *Changing the level of production.* You might try to increase total surplus by either increasing or decreasing the number of books sold. But at point *E*, the willingness to pay of the last buyer is just equal to the cost of the last seller. So any change in production means either producing a book that is not worth as much to the buyer as it costs to provide or *not* producing a book that is worth more to a consumer than it costs.

So we saw in Chapter 6 that when an individual competitive market is in equilibrium, the consumers who are willing to pay the most for a good are the ones who get it; the producers with the lowest cost are the ones who produce it; and the quantity produced and consumed is right, in the sense that producing either more or less would reduce total surplus.

As we'll see in the next section, a similar case for efficiency applies to the economy as a whole. But before we lay out that case, let's look at the reasons why a market manages to get so much right.

Why Markets Work So Well: Property Rights

Economists can say and have said volumes about why markets are an effective way to organize an economy. But the effectiveness of markets comes down largely to the power of two features of a well-functioning market: *property rights* and the role of prices as *economic signals*.

Property rights are the rights of owners of valuable items, whether resources or goods, to dispose of those items as they choose.

By **property rights** we mean a system in which valuable items in the economy—whether they are resources or goods—have specific owners who can dispose of them as they choose. Property rights are what make the mutually beneficial transactions in the used-textbook market, or any market, possible.

To see why property rights are crucial, imagine that students do not have full property rights in their textbooks—that they are not allowed to resell books when the semester is over.

This restriction on property rights would prevent many mutually beneficial transactions. Some students would be stuck with textbooks they do not plan to reread and would be happier receiving some cash instead. Other students would be forced to pay full price for shiny new books when they would be happier getting slightly battered copies at a lower price.

In Chapter 20, we'll see that some of the major ways in which markets go wrong have to do with a lack of clearly defined property rights in valuable goods such as fish in the sea and clean air.

Why Markets Work So Well: Prices as Economic Signals

Because well-defined property rights give individuals the right to engage in mutually beneficial trades, the second necessary feature of well-functioning markets—economic signals—tell individuals *which* trades are mutually beneficial. An **economic signal** is any piece of information that helps people make better economic decisions. There are thousands of signals that businesses watch in the real world. For example, business forecasters say that sales of cardboard boxes are a good early indicator of changes in industrial production: if businesses are buying lots of cardboard boxes, you can be sure that they will soon increase their production.

But prices are far and away the most important signals in a market economy, because they convey essential information about other people's costs and their willingness to pay. If the equilibrium price of used books is $30, this in effect tells everyone both that there are consumers willing to pay $30 and up and that there are producers with a cost of $30 or less.

The signal given by the market price is what ensures that total surplus is maximized, by telling people whether to buy or sell books. If the price of a book is $30, any consumer who would not be willing to pay $30 knows that there are other consumers who are willing to pay more; any producer whose cost is more than $30 knows that there are other producers with lower costs. And consumers who *are* willing to pay $30 or more, like producers with costs of $30 or less, are in effect told that it is a good idea for them to consume and produce.

An **economic signal** is any piece of information that helps people make better economic decisions.

Why Markets Sometimes Don't Work Well: Market Failure

We'll want to keep these two crucial features of competitive markets—property rights and prices as economic signals—in mind in later chapters when we analyze in detail how markets sometimes fail. It's worth revisiting the caution found in Chapter 6 about cases of market failure—the situation in which a market fails to maximize total surplus. First, markets can fail when one party, in an attempt to capture more resources, prevents mutually beneficial trades from occurring. Second, markets can fail when actions have side effects on others that aren't properly taken into account by the market—side effects like pollution. Finally, markets can fail because some goods, by their very nature, are unsuited for efficient management by markets. We will see in the next section how all three of these cases can be interpreted as instances in which prices give incorrect signals—that is, they fail to help people make better economic decisions. And as we will discover shortly, the failure of a particular market in an economy has implications for how well the entire economy operates.

economics in action

Smoothing Out the Bumps

The area around the departure gate is crowded, so it's obvious the plane will be full. In fact, it turns out that it's more than full. The gate agent announces that the flight is overbooked and asks for volunteers to give up their seats in return for rebooking on a later flight plus additional incentives, such as $200 toward a future ticket. If not enough volunteers come forward immediately, the incentives are increased.

This scene is familiar to any frequent flier. But it didn't always work that way. In fact, it took a couple of economists to teach the airlines how to deal efficiently with overbooking.

On busy flights, airlines have always sold tickets for more seats than actually exist. There's a good reason for this: some people with reservations always fail to show up, and an empty seat is a seat wasted. But sometimes fewer people than expected are no-shows, and a flight ends up overbooked. What happens then?

Until 1978, airlines simply "bumped" some of their passengers—informed them that their reservations had been canceled. There were no uniform rules about who got bumped; some airlines, for example, bumped older passengers because they were less likely to complain. Needless to say, those who got bumped were not happy.

In 1968, however, the economist Julian Simon proposed a market approach, in which airlines would treat a flight reservation as if a seat were a property right given to the passenger, so that the airlines would have to buy that right back if the plane was overbooked. Airlines didn't think this idea was practical. But in 1978 another economist, Alfred Kahn, was appointed to head the Civil Aeronautics Board, which regulated airlines at that time. He required airlines to use an auction system to deal with overbooking, resulting in the familiar process of asking for volunteers.

What's the advantage of this voluntary, market solution? Under the old system, someone who urgently needed to get on the scheduled flight was as likely to get bumped as someone who could easily take a later connection. Since 1978, those who absolutely have to make the flight don't volunteer; those who aren't that anxious to board get something that's worth more to them. The airline pays a cost to get passengers to give up their reserved seats but more than makes up for it in higher overall customer satisfaction. In short, everyone gains. By using property rights to create a market, Simon and Kahn moved that piece of the economy toward efficiency. ∎

< < < < < < < < < < < < < < < < < < <

>> CHECK YOUR UNDERSTANDING 13-1

1. Imagine that eMarkets! is a company that implements a competitive market in MP3 players. Based on information it gathers, it tells producers what the equilibrium price will be so that they can decide how much to produce. And once production has occurred, it allocates output to consumers based on the price and their willingness to pay.
   a. What information would they need to know from consumers and producers in order to find the equilibrium price and quantity of MP3 players?
   b. Suppose that eMarkets! has determined that, once production occurs and trading happens, the equilibrium price will be $199 and the equilibrium quantity will be 10,000 units. But also suppose that due to a computer glitch, it informs some producers that the price will be $299, while it informs some producers that the price will be $99. How will producer surplus be affected? Can you determine the effect on the quantity produced—will it be equal to, less than, or more than the equilibrium quantity?
   c. Also suppose that due to the computer glitch, some consumers with a willingness to pay of $299 are told that the price is $399. An equal number of consumers who have a willingness to pay of $119 are allowed to buy the good at a price of $99. How will consumer surplus be affected?

Solutions appear at back of book.

Efficiency in the Economy as a Whole

We've seen how the equilibrium outcome of an individual competitive market usually maximizes the total surplus of participants in that market. Is there an equivalent result for the economy as a whole? That is, is there a corresponding concept of equilibrium for the whole economy? And if so, does this equilibrium outcome maximize the welfare of the economy's participants?

The economy as a whole consists not of one but of many, many markets, all interrelated in two ways:

■ On the consumption side, the demand for each good is affected by the prices of other goods.

■ On the production side, producers of different goods compete for the same factors of production.

To think about the economy as a whole, then, we have to think of many markets, for both goods and factors. A **competitive market economy** is an economy in which all of these markets are perfectly competitive, with equilibrium prices determined by

A **competitive market economy** is an economy in which all markets, for goods and for factors, are perfectly competitive.

supply and demand. In each market both the supply and demand curves are likely to be affected by events in other markets.

When all markets have reached equilibrium—when the quantity of each good and factor demanded is equal to the quantity of each good and factor supplied at the going market prices—we say that the economy is in **general equilibrium.** To put it another way, general equilibrium is the economy-wide counterpart of ordinary equilibrium in a single market.

Our next task is to show that, as with an individual competitive market in equilibrium, a competitive market economy in general equilibrium is usually *efficient*—that is, it is efficient except in certain well-defined cases. What do we mean by saying that the economy as a whole is efficient? Actually, we defined efficiency way back in Chapter 1. We will start by revisiting that definition to see why it is the right approach to analyzing the economy as a whole. Next, we will describe the three criteria that an economy as a whole must satisfy in order to be efficient. Finally, we will learn how failures of individual markets can lead to inefficiency in the economy as a whole—failures we can view as cases in which prices fail to perform as economic signals.

> An economy is in **general equilibrium** when the quantity supplied is equal to the quantity demanded in all markets.

Efficiency, Revisited

When economists discuss efficiency in an individual market, they usually use the concepts of consumer and producer surplus, which measure costs and benefits in monetary terms. This makes sense when you are talking about the market for just one good, because you can take the prices of other goods—and therefore the value of a dollar—as given. When we are analyzing the economy as a whole, however, measuring costs and benefits in dollar terms no longer makes sense, because all prices are "to be determined."

FOR INQUIRING MINDS

DEFINING ECONOMIC EFFICIENCY

The economist's definition of *efficiency*—that an economy is efficient if nobody can be made better off without making others worse off—may seem to be oddly indirect. Why can't we define efficiency in terms of a positive achievement rather than the absence of something?

Many other definitions of efficiency have been proposed, but none of them have survived careful scrutiny—all of them turn out either to be incomplete or to involve unacceptable implications. A good example is the fate of the principle known as utilitarianism, proposed by the nineteenth-century English philosopher Jeremy Bentham.

Bentham offered a simple principle: "the greatest good for the greatest number." In effect, he argued that society should try to maximize the total utility of its members. This sounded persuasive but eventually ran into two problems. First, how do we add up the utility of different people? We may loosely say that Ms. Martineau is happier than Mr. Ricardo, but is she twice as happy or three

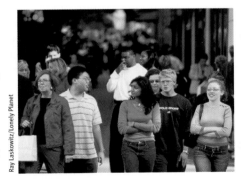

Whose util counts more? Efficiency has been difficult to define because we can't compare utility across people.

times as happy? You may argue that it makes no sense even to ask that question—but in that case Bentham's principle becomes meaningless because we have no way to add up the total utility of all members of society.

Second, even if we imagine that it is somehow possible to add up the utility of different people, critics of Bentham point out that his doctrine has the disturbing

implication that we should cater to the tastes of "utility monsters"—people who derive especially high pleasure from excessive consumption. Bentham's criterion implies that if Martineau really likes owning luxury automobiles and going to fancy restaurants but Ricardo is a modest sort who can make do with a bicycle and macaroni-and-cheese dinners, we should take money from Ricardo and give it to Martineau—even if Ricardo is a hard worker and Martineau notably lazy. This doesn't seem right.

Because of these difficulties, Bentham's principle has pretty much vanished from economic thought. The same is true of other ideas, such as the Marxist slogan "from each according to his ability, to each according to his needs." The only definition of efficiency that has managed to survive practical and logical criticism is the negative one: an economy is inefficient if there is a way to make at least one person better off without making others worse off, and it is efficient if it is not inefficient.

Instead, economists focus on the basic definition of efficiency. Recall from Chapter 1: an economy is efficient if it does not pass up any opportunities to make some people better off without making other people worse off.

To achieve efficiency, an economy must meet three criteria, which closely parallel the three features ensuring that total surplus is maximized in an individual market. The economy must be *efficient in consumption, efficient in production,* and *efficient in output levels.* Let's look at these criteria and see how a competitive market economy satisfies them.

Efficiency in Consumption

An economy is **efficient in consumption** if there is no way to redistribute goods among consumers that makes some consumers better off without making others worse off.

An economy is **efficient in consumption** if there is no way to redistribute goods among consumers that makes some consumers better off without making others worse off.

To see what efficiency in consumption involves, it helps to imagine scenarios for inefficiency. Imagine, for example, an economy that produces both cornflakes and shredded wheat but that provides those who prefer shredded wheat with cornflakes, and vice versa. Then it would be possible to make at least one person better off without making anyone else worse off by redistributing the goods, giving people the breakfast cereal they prefer.

The first piece of good news is that as long as prices perform properly as economic signals, this kind of inefficiency won't occur in a competitive market economy. We've seen this already in the case of market equilibrium in one individual market: the consumers who actually receive a good at the market equilibrium are those with the greatest willingness to pay—thanks to the role prices play in helping people make the right economic decisions. Consumers who prefer an additional box of cornflakes will be willing to pay more for that box than consumers who would rather have an additional box of shredded wheat. So if the markets for cornflakes and shredded wheat are both in equilibrium, there won't be any way to make at least one consumer better off without making others worse off by redistributing the available quantities of breakfast cereals.

In other words, prices in goods markets ensure that you can't increase total surplus in a single market by taking a good away from one person and giving it to another. Similarly, prices also ensure that when all markets in an economy are in perfectly competitive general equilibrium, there is no way to redistribute goods that makes some consumers better off without making others worse off.

It's important, however, to realize the limitations of that statement: even though an economy is efficient, you can always make *some* consumers better off if you are willing to make others worse off. We'll come back to that point shortly.

Efficiency in Production

An economy is **efficient in production** if there is no way to produce more of some goods without producing less of other goods.

Economists say that an economy is **efficient in production** if it is not possible to produce more of some goods without producing less of others.

We can use the *production possibility frontier* model from Chapter 2 to understand this. This model uses a diagram like Figure 13-2 to illustrate the economy's trade-offs: the more wheat it produces, the less corn it can produce, and vice versa. If the economy produces the quantities at either point *A* or point *B* on the production possibility frontier, it is efficient in production: it is possible to produce more corn than the economy produces at *A*, but only by producing less wheat; it is possible to produce more wheat than the economy produces at *B*, but only by producing less corn. The economy is not efficient in production, however, if it produces at point *C*: it is possible to produce more wheat *and* more corn than the economy does at that point.

An economy has an **efficient allocation of resources** if there is no way to reallocate factors of production among producers to produce more of some goods without producing less of others.

An economy will be efficient in production if it has an **efficient allocation of resources**—if there is no way to reallocate factors of production among producers to produce more of some goods without producing less of others. This is an important result: *An economy that is efficient in allocation of resources is efficient in production, and vice versa.*

Here is another way to think about Figure 13-2: at point *A* the economy can produce more corn only by taking resources away from wheat production. Similarly, at

Figure 13-2

The Production Possibility Frontier and Efficiency in Production

An economy is efficient in production if it cannot produce more of one good without producing less of other goods. Equivalently, an economy is efficient in production if it is on its production possibility frontier. Here *A* and *B* are efficient production points—at each point the economy can produce more of one good only by producing less of the other. *C* is not an efficient production point because more corn *and* more wheat can be produced. **>web...**

point *B* the economy can produce more wheat only by taking resources away from corn production.

Just as in the case of efficiency in consumption, it helps to imagine scenarios for inefficiency. In the United States, land in Iowa is ideally suited for growing corn, land in Minnesota is much better suited for growing wheat, and most land in Maine isn't suitable for growing either. It would clearly be inefficient if good land in the Midwest were left idle but farmers struggled with the stony soil of Maine; it would also be inefficient if Iowa farms grew wheat and Minnesota farms grew corn.

The second piece of good news is that, just as in the case of consumption, the role of prices as economic signals ensures that a competitive market economy in general equilibrium achieves efficiency in production. The logic is similar, but this time it applies to prices in factor markets rather than prices in goods markets. Corn farmers are willing to pay more for Iowa land than wheat farmers; wheat farmers are willing to pay more for Minnesota land than are corn farmers. And much of New England is no longer farmed but has returned to forest, because labor and capital can be more productively employed on richer lands elsewhere. In short, when factor markets are competitive, resources are allocated to the producers that can make the best use of them, and the economy is indeed efficient in production.

Notice, however, that this does not say *what* the economy produces. Both *A* and *B* in Figure 13-2 represent efficient production. We still need to ask whether the economy produces at the "right" place on the production possibility frontier—or, rather, *a* right place, because there may be many efficient outcomes. But let's hold off on that for a moment and finish our description of efficiency in the competitive market economy as a whole.

Efficiency in Output Levels

Suppose that a competitive market economy is efficient in production—it cannot produce more of some goods without producing less of others. Suppose also that it is efficient in consumption—there is no way to redistribute the goods produced that will make some consumers better off without making others worse off. There is still the question of whether the competitive market economy is producing the *right mix* of goods to start with. For example, suppose that point *A* in Figure 13-3 on page 320 corresponds to producing enough wheat to let everyone have shredded wheat five times a week and cornflakes two times a week. This will still be inefficient if everyone prefers to have shredded wheat only three times a week but cornflakes four times a week—*and* if point *B* would allow them to do so. In that case, moving from *A* to *B*—that is, shifting resources into corn production—would make everyone better off. Our third criterion for efficiency, then, is that the economy be **efficient in output levels:** there must not be a different mix of output that would make some people better off without making others worse off.

The third and final piece of good news about the general equilibrium of a competitive market economy is that it will be efficient in output levels when prices perform properly as economic signals.

How do we know this? We already saw that in an individual competitive market producers produce the quantity of output that maximizes total surplus. The reason is that consumers and producers face the same price—the market price is an economic signal telling producers what one more unit of output is worth to consumers. This signal induces producers to produce that extra unit of output if the cost of the resources they would need to produce it is less than the market price.

In the economy as a whole, producers learn how much consumers are willing to pay for a bit more of one good versus a bit more of another when market prices operate as economic signals. This process ensures that a competitive market economy in general equilibrium produces the right mix of goods.

To see how this happens, imagine an economy in which the only resource that can be shifted between industries is labor, and all producers are hiring from the same labor market. (We'll also assume there are no complications like compensating differentials that make wages differ.) Imagine that right now consumers would prefer more corn and less wheat than the economy is currently producing. The economy can provide what consumers want by transferring labor from wheat production to corn production—by forgoing some wheat output in order to produce more corn. But will this adjustment take place?

Yes, it will, because consumers are willing to pay more for the additional corn that one more worker employed in corn production can produce than they are willing to pay for the wheat forgone by employing one fewer worker in wheat production. We can express this algebraically. The extra corn that a unit of labor can produce is MPL_{corn}, the marginal product of labor in corn. The wheat that unit of labor would have produced is MPL_{wheat}, the marginal product of labor in wheat. When we say that

---

Figure **13-3**

Efficiency in Output Levels

The output levels *A* and *B* are both efficient in production. However, suppose that *B* represents a mix of quantities of corn and wheat that everyone prefers to the mix at *A*—at *A* everyone prefers more corn and less wheat. Then the economy that produces output mix *A* is not efficient in output levels.

consumers are willing to pay more for the extra corn than for the wheat, we are saying that at the current employment and output levels in the corn and wheat sectors

(13-1) $P_{corn} \times MPL_{corn} > P_{wheat} \times MPL_{wheat}$

where P_{corn} and P_{wheat} are the prices of corn and wheat respectively.

We've already seen the expressions in Equation 13-1 in Chapter 12. $P_{corn} \times MPL_{corn}$ is the *value of the marginal product* of labor in corn production, and $P_{wheat} \times MPL_{wheat}$ is the value of the marginal product of labor in wheat production. So we can restate Equation 13-1 as

(13-2) $VMPL_{corn} > VMPL_{wheat}$

This expression says that the value produced by an additional unit of labor employed in corn production is greater than that of an additional unit of labor employed in wheat production when consumers prefer more corn and less wheat than is being produced.

Can this be an equilibrium? No; we learned in Chapter 12 that producers maximize profits by hiring labor up until the point that $VMPL = W$, where W is the wage rate. That is, a producer hires labor until the value of the output produced by the last worker employed is equal to the current market wage rate. In this example, corn producers and wheat producers hire workers from the same labor market. So the direct implication of $VMPL_{corn} > VMPL_{wheat}$ is that, at current employment levels, corn producers are willing to pay a higher wage rate than wheat producers. Corn producers will hire workers away from wheat producers.

When will this process stop? When the wage rate that corn producers are willing to pay is equal to the wage rate that wheat producers are willing to pay; that is, when $VMPL_{corn} = VMPL_{wheat}$. The evolution of this process is illustrated in Figure 13-4.

Figure 13-4   **How an Economy Achieves Efficiency in Output Levels**

(a) A Corn Producer Hires More Workers

(b) A Wheat Producer Lays Off Workers

If at current employment levels $VMPL_{corn} > VMPL_{wheat}$, then corn producers will increase their profits by hiring workers away from wheat producers, who will, in turn, increase their profits by laying off workers. This process is illustrated for a corn producer in panel (a). As a corn producer hires workers, she increases her corn production and moves down her $VMPL$ curve until she reaches her optimal employment level, the number of workers at which $VMPL_{corn} = W$, the market wage rate. Panel (b) shows the corresponding changes for a wheat producer:

he decreases his wheat production and moves up his $VMPL$ curve as he lays off workers. He also reaches his optimal employment level at $VMPL_{wheat} = W$. Workers cease moving between sectors once $VMPL_{corn} = VMPL_{wheat}$. It is an equilibrium because at that point the value of the additional output produced by a worker in the corn sector no longer exceeds the value of the additional output produced by a worker in the wheat sector and corn producers are no longer willing to pay a higher wage than wheat producers. **>web...**

In panel (a), a corn producer starts at a $VMPL_{corn}$ greater than the current market wage rate. She increases her profits by hiring more workers and moves down her $VMPL$ curve until she reaches her optimal employment level, at which $VMPL_{corn} = W$.

Where are these new workers in the corn sector coming from? They are coming from the wheat sector. This is illustrated in panel (b), where a wheat producer is losing workers and in the process is moving up his $VMPL$ curve. He increases his profits by laying off workers, letting them go until he reaches his optimal employment level, at which $VMPL_{wheat} = W$.

So as labor in the economy is reallocated from wheat production to corn production, the output of corn rises and the output of wheat falls. Eventually, workers cease moving from the wheat sector to the corn sector when $VMPL_{corn} = VMPL_{wheat}$. At this point the value of the additional output produced by a worker in the corn sector no longer exceeds the value of the additional output produced by a worker in the wheat sector. That is, we have finally reached an equilibrium.

This example helps us understand that, in a market economy, markets for goods and services are linked via the factor markets. Or to put it a slightly different way, any change in the amount of one good or service produced will ultimately affect the amounts of other goods and services as factors of production shift from one sector to another. Figure 13-5 helps us make sense of the interconnectedness of markets for goods and services and factor markets in a market economy. To appreciate its signifi-

---

Figure 13-5 **Efficiency in Output Levels in a Circular-Flow Framework**

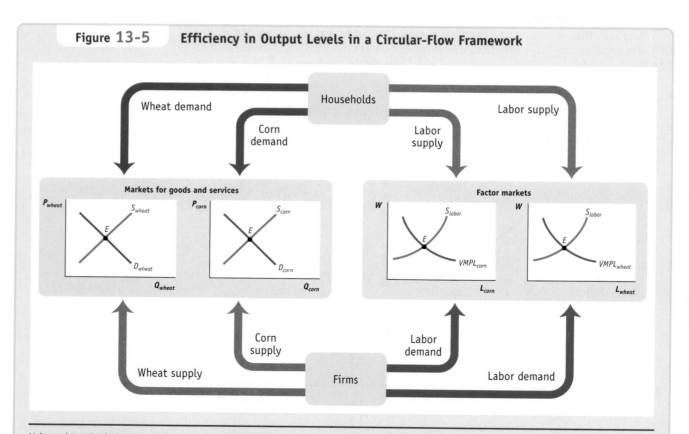

Using a hypothetical economy in which corn and wheat are the only goods and labor is the only factor of production, we can see how the markets for goods and services are linked via the factor markets. The factor markets bring the supply of labor from households and the demand for labor by firms into equilibrium, and the markets for goods and services bring the supply of goods and services from firms and the demand for goods and services by households into equilibrium. But supply and demand in all these markets are interrelated: households' earnings in the labor market determine their demand for goods and services, and vice versa; firms' profits from hiring labor in the labor market and producing output determine their supply of goods and services, and vice versa. Any change in one market will ultimately generate corresponding changes in all the other markets. When every market for goods and services and every factor market in the economy is in equilibrium, the economy as a whole is in general equilibrium.

cance, it may help recalling the circular-flow diagram of Chapter 2. There we saw how firms and households are linked via the factor markets and the markets for goods and services through flows of money. That is, in the factor markets, firms pay households for factors of production; in the markets for goods and services, households pay firms for goods and services.

Figure 13-5 presents an alternative and richer version of the same phenomenon, this time expressed in terms of the forces of supply and demand for resources that underlie the money flows of the circular-flow diagram. Here, we imagine that the only goods in the economy are corn and wheat and that labor is the only factor of production. The right portion of the figure represents how the supply of labor from households and the demand for labor from firms meet and are brought into equilibrium in the factor markets. But supply and demand in the labor market are themselves affected by supply and demand in the markets for goods and services: firms' demand for labor is derived from the demand for their goods and services, and households' supply of labor is determined by the earnings required for purchases in the markets for goods and services.

Similarly, the left portion of Figure 13-5 represents how the supply of goods and services from firms and the demand for goods and services from households meet and are brought into equilibrium in the markets for goods and services. Again, there is an interrelationship between the market for goods and services and factor markets: households' demand for goods and services is determined by the wages they earn in the labor market, and firms' supply of goods and services is determined by the returns they generate from hiring labor in the labor market.

Moreover, any change in the demand for a good will initiate a cascade of events that will ripple through the entire economy as resources shift among various sectors in response. So, for example, an increase in demand for corn relative to wheat causes a rightward shift of the demand for corn and a leftward shift in the demand for wheat. This results in an increase in the equilibrium quantity of corn supplied and a decrease in the equilibrium quantity of wheat supplied, which in turn causes an increase in the equilibrium employment level in the corn sector and a decrease in the equilibrium employment in the wheat sector. So the incentives in a competitive market economy in which prices perform properly as economic signals will lead the economy to produce the mix of goods that consumers prefer—that is, the economy will indeed be efficient in output levels. When each market for goods and services and each factor market is in equilibrium, the economy as a whole is in general equilibrium.

How does a competitive market economy achieve this amazing result? It comes down to the point we have emphasized throughout this discussion: the role of prices as *economic signals*. The fact that everyone faces the same prices ensures that goods and services are efficiently allocated among consumers, that factors of production are efficiently allocated among producers, and that the mix of goods and services produced reflects what people want.

Inefficiency in the Economy: When Prices Go Astray

The efficiency of a competitive market economy, however, is not something we should take for granted. Just as individual markets can fail, the general equilibrium of a competitive market economy may be inefficient. When this happens, some mutually beneficial trades will go unexploited. That is, there is some reallocation of consumption or production, or some change in output levels, that would make someone better off without making others worse off.

Why is a competitive market economy sometimes inefficient? For the same three reasons that individual markets sometimes fail. And when markets fail, prices fail to serve as economic signals.

First, recall that a market fails when attempts by one party to capture more resources prevents mutually beneficial transactions from occurring. We can illustrate this phenomenon by returning to our Chapter 4 example of quotas and New York taxi licenses. Recall that the current quota on taxi licenses in New York City results in a shortage of taxi rides compared to the unrestricted competitive market equilibrium. As a result, existing owners of taxi licenses gain (earning higher returns than they would have otherwise), but mutually beneficial transactions in taxi rides go unexploited. If the quota didn't exist, the fact that the market price of a ride exceeds the unrestricted competitive market price would draw new taxi drivers into the market. So supply would increase until the willingness to pay of the last rider in the market is equal to the cost of the last driver in the market, and the market would achieve efficiency. Or, to put it slightly differently, the quota prevents the market price from operating as an economic signal that would draw new taxi drivers into the market to eliminate the shortage. As a result, the larger economy (of which the New York City taxi ride market is a part) is inefficient. It's not efficient in consumption because some riders with a higher willingness to pay can't get a taxi but some with a lower willingness to pay are able to. It is not efficient in production because some drivers with higher costs have licenses but some with lower costs do not, implying that output could be increased without using more resources by reallocating production to those drivers with the lowest cost. And it is not efficient in output levels because there are too few taxi rides provided relative to other goods. We will study a similar kind of inefficiency in detail in Chapter 14, where we investigate monopoly, an industry that has only a single seller.

The second source of market failure is the side effects of actions that aren't properly accounted for in the existing markets. For example, consider the pollution caused by a large poultry farm whose wastes foul nearby streams and reduce the welfare of nearby residents. The cost savings that the farm gains by dumping its waste rather than having it properly disposed of are smaller in value than the discomfort experienced by its neighbors—that is, what the neighbors would be willing to pay to get rid of the pollution. But a mutually beneficial trade between the farm and the neighbors is going unexploited. Efficiency could be achieved if there were a "market for pollution"—if either the farm could purchase from the residents the right to dump so many barrels of waste or the residents could purchase from the farm the right to water of a certain purity. Either way, efficiency would be achieved: consumers would buy and the seller would sell until the willingness to pay for the last unit bought and sold equals the seller's cost of producing it. The problem here arises because the relevant market doesn't exist—there is no market for either pollution rights or water-purity rights. As a result, there is no relevant market price that can function as an economic signal to direct individuals to buy and sell. This economy is inefficient: the total welfare of individuals in the economy would be higher if less pollution and, correspondingly, less poultry were produced. We will analyze these side effects, called *externalities,* in detail in Chapter 19. There we will see how governments can intervene in ways that assure that market prices do indeed provide the proper economic signals.

The third and final reason that markets fail is that some goods, by their nature, are unsuited for efficient management by markets. Consider a song that can be downloaded from the Internet. Once the song is recorded, the marginal cost to the record company of allowing someone to download it is virtually zero. So efficiency implies that people should be allowed to download the song until the last downloader's willingness to pay is equal to zero. That is, efficiency is achieved only if there is free and unrestricted downloading of music. But an inconvenient fact arises at this point: if the record company can't charge for downloads, then it won't have revenues to pay its artists. And if it can't pay its artists, then artists won't record in the first place. And that, too, is inefficient. The problem here lies in the nature of the good itself, called an *information good,* which is the subject of Chapter 22. For information goods, efficiency in consumption means that the price to consumers must be zero, but efficiency in output levels means that the price received by producers must be greater than zero. For these goods, inefficiency is simply unavoidable. A similar inefficiency arises for what are called *public goods* and *common resources*—goods for which, by their nature, the producer cannot charge consumers. We will study public goods and common resources in Chapter 20.

In most cases, however, market failures can be corrected. Indeed, although it is important to understand how they occur, this analysis isn't a reason to reject markets. Instead, the analysis of market failures tells policy makers how to correct them and take advantage of the remarkable ability of a competitive market economy to allocate resources efficiently.

economics in action

A Great Leap—Backward

We began this chapter with the observation that the planned economy of East Germany did not, as its founders had hoped, surpass the market economies of the West. But possibly the most compelling example of inefficiency in a planned economy comes from China.

In the late 1950s, China's leader Mao Zedong put into effect an ambitious plan, the so-called Great Leap Forward, to speed up the nation's industrialization. Key to this plan was a shift from urban to rural manufacturing: farming villages were supposed to start producing such heavy industrial goods as steel.

Unfortunately, this plan backfired. Diverting farmers from their usual work led to a sharp fall in food production. Meanwhile, because raw materials like coal and iron ore were sent to ill-equipped and inexperienced rural producers rather than to urban factories, industrial output declined as well. The plan, in short, led to a fall in the production of everything.

Because China was a very poor nation to start with, the results were catastrophic. The famine that followed is estimated to have reduced China's population by as much as 30 million. ■

> > > > > > > > > > > > > > > > > > > >

>> CHECK YOUR UNDERSTANDING 13-2

1. In the small country of Bountiful, labor is the only factor of production, all workers are paid the same wage, all food is produced domestically, and all markets are perfectly competitive. Imagine that, due to health concerns, each Bountifullian experiences a greater demand for breakfast cereals and a lower demand for sausage.
   a. Explain how the change in preferences will lead to a reallocation of labor between the sausage and breakfast cereal industries. Use the concepts of $VMPL_S$, $VMPL_C$, and wage rate in your answer (the subscript S refers to sausage and C to cereal).
   b. How will you know that the Bountiful economy has fully adjusted to the change in preferences? Use the three conditions of efficiency in your answer.

Solutions appear at back of book.

Efficiency and Equity

We have now shown why a perfectly competitive market economy is typically efficient: there is no way to make some people better off without making others worse off.

This conclusion refutes the claims of would-be economic planners, who insist that markets are disorganized free-for-alls and that centralized decision making would be more efficient. But we need to be careful: it is easy to get carried away with the idea that markets get it right and to then draw inappropriate conclusions about economic policy.

It's important to remember that efficiency is about *how to achieve goals;* it does not say anything about what your goals should be. Saying that the market outcome is efficient doesn't mean that that outcome is necessarily desirable. In fact, in some circumstances a well-thought-out economic policy may deliberately choose an outcome that is *not* efficient.

When can an outcome be efficient without being desirable? When it's not fair.

FOR INQUIRING MINDS

THEORIES OF JUSTICE

In 1971 the philosopher John Rawls published *A Theory of Justice*, which represents the most famous attempt to date to develop a theory of economic fairness. He asked readers to imagine deciding economic and social policies behind a "veil of ignorance" about their identity. That is, suppose that you knew you would be a human being but you did not know whether you would be rich or poor, healthy or sick, and so on. What kind of policies would you want?

Rawls answered that you would probably choose policies that placed a high weight on the utility of the worst-off members of society: after all, you might end up being one of

them. And because of diminishing marginal utility, having a few dollars more would do you a lot of good if you find yourself poor, but having a few dollars less wouldn't do you much harm if you find yourself well-off.

Although no nation has ever made this theory the basis for its economic policy, Rawls-type arguments do play an important role in the debate over economic and social policy. For example, when Congress debated a plan to cut tax rates on large estates—those valued at over $1.3 million—from their 2000 rate of 55 percent, Bill Gates, Sr., father of the Microsoft billionaire, offered a defense of the existing tax based

on a Rawlsian view of fairness. He made his case by asking people to imagine traveling back to the moment of their birth. At that point, you get to decide, for a price, where you are going to be born—the hugely rich United States or impoverished Ethiopia. The price for choosing Ethiopia is zero; the price for choosing the United States is 55 percent of the value of your estate should it exceed $1.3 million when you die. Or to put it another way, imagine that the price of being born in the United States instead of Ethiopia is your commitment to pay the current level of the U.S. estate tax. What would you choose?

What's Fair?

Imagine an economy in which a dictator controls everything, keeping almost everything the economy produces for himself and allowing his subjects only the bare minimum they need to survive. Could such an economy be efficient?

Yes, it could. If there is no way to make one of the suffering citizens better off without making the dictator worse off, then the economy is efficient. But that doesn't mean we have to approve of it. The situation is clearly unjust; the contrast between the dictator's wealth and his subjects' poverty isn't fair.

This extreme example shows that we want something more than efficiency from an economy. We also want *equity*: we want the distribution of utility among individuals to be reasonably fair.

But what exactly is "fair"? That turns out to be a very hard question to answer. To see why it's such a tricky question, let's consider how plausible ideas about fairness become problematic when you start to think about them carefully.

"FAIR IS FAIR... IF IT'S TURN-OFF-YOUR-TV WEEK FOR ME, THEN IT'S UNPLUG-YOUR-E-MAIL WEEK FOR YOU."

First, you sometimes hear that people should be given an equal chance at the starting line—that is, at birth, or maybe at the age of 18, everyone should have the same opportunities to be successful in life. That sounds fair—but what about the natural desire of parents to do well by their children? Shouldn't parents who own their own businesses have the right to appoint their children to executive positions in those businesses? Shouldn't parents who can afford to do so have the right to send their children to expensive private schools? It seems unfair that children of successful parents should have an advantage over children whose parents don't have the same resources. Yet it would also seem unfair to prevent successful parents from helping their children. How do you resolve this contradiction?

Another familiar concept is that people should be rewarded for the work they do. And that, too seems reasonable: if you are a skilled worker, with twice my marginal product, it seems only fair that you should receive twice my wage. But what about someone who suffers an injury and cannot work? To say that that person should go without any income seems unfair.

The attempt to define fairness has led to some fascinating debates among philosophers; we describe the views of one influential thinker, John Rawls, in For Inquiring Minds on page 326. However, those debates have not led to any generally accepted definition.

Do we need a definition of *fairness*? Not necessarily—virtually everyone agrees that some outcomes, like our hypothetical dictator-dominated economy, are unfair, and in other cases we can agree to differ. But sometimes the lack of agreement on fairness means that economic analysis alone cannot be used to decide between alternative policies. To see why, let's introduce a new concept, the *utility possibility frontier*.

The Utility Possibility Frontier

Let's think of an economy that contains only two kinds of people, Easterners and Westerners. In Figure 13-6, the horizontal axis measures the total utility of the typical Westerner and the vertical axis measures the total utility of the typical Easterner.

An efficient outcome in this economy would be one in which there was no way to make either Easterners or Westerners better off without making members of the other group worse off. But there may be many such possible outcomes. In the figure we show what the possibilities might look like by drawing a **utility possibility frontier,** which shows how well-off each group *could* be given the economy's resources and the total utility of the other. Any point on the utility possibility frontier is efficient—that is, once you are on the frontier, the only way to make some people better off is to make others worse off. Any point inside the frontier is inefficient.

So suppose that you were asked to choose between two sets of economic policies—one that would bring the economy to point A and one that would bring it to point B. For example, suppose there is a question of who should receive ownership of some disputed land. As long as the property rights are clearly defined, the economy will be efficient, but Westerners would prefer that they get the rights, and Easterners would prefer the reverse. So which outcome is better?

A **utility possibility frontier** shows how well-off one individual or group could be for each given total utility level of another individual or group.

Figure 13-6

The Utility Possibility Frontier

The utility possibility frontier reminds us that there may be many efficient outcomes for an economy. The utility possibility frontier shows the maximum level of total utility of a typical Easterner, given the level of total utility of a typical Westerner. Any point on the curve is efficient because at such a point there is no way to make a typical Easterner better off without making a typical Westerner worse off, and vice versa. But this means that we cannot decide on economic grounds alone whether point A or B is better. >web...

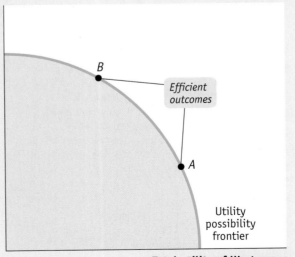

The answer is that it's a matter of taste. Westerners would, of course, prefer *A*; Easterners would prefer *B*. For government officials trying to decide how to assign the property rights, the answer would depend on what relative weight they give to the welfare of the two groups. The question of whether *A* or *B* is better is, in other words, a question of values that economics cannot answer.

Notice, by the way, that *A* and *B* don't differ just in how goods and services are distributed to individuals; they might well involve producing a different mix of goods and services. If Westerners like cornflakes but Easterners prefer shredded wheat, the economy probably produces more corn and less wheat at *B* than at *A*. Is it more efficient to produce corn or wheat? There is no answer to this question, because both can be efficient, depending on our goals.

The point that efficiency is a means to achieve goals, not a goal in itself, can be further illustrated by considering what is wrong with *inefficient* policies. Figure 13-7 shows the same utility possibility frontier as Figure 13-6 but now also shows point *C*—an inefficient outcome, one that lies inside the frontier. You might think of *C* as the result of a policy that favors Easterners in an inefficient way. In fact, many economists believe that the actual policies the newly reunited Germany followed to help the former East Germans were poorly designed, providing them with few incentives to take new jobs or acquire new skills. That is, many economists believe that Germany as a whole ended up at a point like *C*.

Is there any reason why you might want to choose an inefficient point such as *C*? Not if better choices are genuinely available: there are points on the utility possibility frontier that are better than *C* whatever relative weight you give to the welfare of the two groups. For example, *B* is better than *C* by any standard.

But what if the real choices are limited to *A* or *C*? Should you as a voter prefer the efficient policies proposed by the Western party?

Not necessarily. *A* is efficient, and *C* is not; but it is still true that Easterners are better off at *C* than they are at *A*. So if the utility of Easterners matters enough to you, you might well prefer *C* to *A* even though you would prefer *B* to either. As economists say, it is often—but by no means always—worth trading less efficiency for more equity.

So it's important to remember what efficiency is *not*. Efficiency is not a goal in itself, to be pursued at the expense of other goals. It is only a way to achieve our goals more effectively—whatever those goals may be.

Figure 13-7

Efficiency Versus Equity

Suppose that for some reason the policy choices that are available are restricted: you can choose only between the efficient outcome *A* and the inefficient outcome *C*. Does this mean that *A* is preferable? Not necessarily. If you place a high enough weight on the utility of Easterners, you may be willing to trade *efficiency* for *equity*: even though the economy is not efficient at *C*, the utility of Easterners is higher at *C* than at *A*.

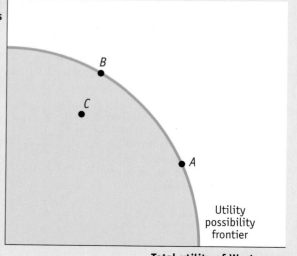

economics in action

Death and Taxes

Earlier, we used the example of parents giving their children a head start by paying for expensive private schooling to show how simple questions of fairness can give conflicting answers. In fact, inheritance is one of those areas in which differing notions of fairness translate directly into different policy conclusions.

One notion of fairness focuses on individual positions at the starting line: it says that it is unfair that some children should inherit large sums but others get nothing. The natural conclusion from this notion is that inheritances should be heavily taxed. This has, in fact, been the policy of many countries, including to some extent the United States.

The alternative notion of fairness focuses on the right of people to choose what to do with their money: it says that it is unfair to deny parents the right to pass on their savings to their children.

These competing notions are reflected in different names for the "estate tax," the tax levied on the assets individuals leave behind them at death. Politicians who focus on the starting line call it the "inheritance tax," emphasizing the position of the heirs. Politicians who focus on individual choice call it the "death tax," emphasizing the position of the parents.

Who's right? Economic analysis can't say. However, legislation passed in 2001 will eliminate the estate tax by 2010. ∎

> >

>>CHECK YOUR UNDERSTANDING 13-3

1. Explain why it is easier to determine whether an economy is efficient than to determine whether it is fair.

2. Explain why the following statements are problematic to use in determining whether or not a society is fair.
   a. In a fair society, each person contributes to society according to his or her means, and each person receives benefits according to his or her needs.
   b. In a fair society, a person is rewarded in proportion to how hard he or she works.

Solutions appear at back of book.

• A LOOK AHEAD •

We have now answered the first of the big questions we raised in the Introduction: *Why does a competitive market economy generally work so well?* Part of the answer involved defining what it means to work "well": an economy works badly if it misses opportunities to make at least one person better off without making others worse off, and it works well if it does not miss those opportunities.

What we've now seen is that in a well-functioning competitive market economy in general equilibrium, consumers can buy as much or as little as they choose at the same price, and producers can sell as much or as little as they choose, also at the same price. And this means that all the opportunities to make at least one person better off without making others worse off—whether by redistributing goods among consumers, rearranging output among producers, or changing what the economy produces—will *already have been taken.*

One question down, another to go. Why do things sometimes go wrong? Why do market economies sometimes work badly? The short answer, as we saw in Chapter 6, is "market failure." The long answer will require a few more chapters!

SUMMARY

1. Except in cases of market failure, an individual competitive market in equilibrium maximizes total surplus, the sum of consumer and producer surplus. Rearranging consumption, rearranging production, or changing the level of output will all reduce total surplus.

2. **Property rights** and prices as **economic signals** are two features of competitive markets that are crucial to their ability to work well. The three causes of market failure—mutually beneficial transactions that are unexploited due to attempts to capture surplus, side effects that are not accounted for in the market, and goods whose nature prevents their efficient management by markets—can all be linked to the failure of prices to perform properly as economic signals.

3. When we turn to the performance of the economy as a whole, we use the economic definition of efficiency: the **general equilibrium** of a **competitive market economy** is efficient if there is no way to make some people better off without making others worse off.

4. Economic efficiency requires **efficiency in consumption**—there is no way to redistribute goods and services that makes some consumers better off without making others worse off. It requires **efficiency in production,** which arises from an **efficient allocation of**

resources—there is no way to reallocate resources that allows the economy to produce more of some goods and services without producing less of others. And it requires **efficiency in output levels**—there is no other choice of output mix that makes some people better off without making others worse off. In the same way in which a competitive market maximizes total surplus, the general equilibrium of a competitive market economy as a whole is efficient—in consumption, in production, and in output levels—when prices perform properly as market signals. In cases of market failure, however, prices fail to lead people to exploit all mutually beneficial transactions; as a result, when markets fail, the economy as a whole is inefficient.

5. It is not enough for an economy to be efficient. We also want it to deliver an outcome that is "fair" in terms of the distribution of utility among individuals. Economic fairness is known as equity.

6. Unfortunately, there is no generally accepted definition of *fairness*. The ambiguity this sometimes creates for evaluating economic policy can be illustrated with the **utility possibility frontier,** which shows the trade-offs between the utility achieved by one individual or group and that achieved by other individuals or groups.

KEY TERMS

PROBLEMS

1. The Medici family in Florence produces all the wool in Italy. The five Medici children each have a factory in which they can produce one pound of wool per day. Their costs of producing each pound of wool are given on the left side of the accompanying table. Wool is demanded by the Visconti family in Milan. Each of the five Visconti children can demand one pound of wool per day. Their willingness to pay is given on the right side of the table.

Medici family		Visconti family	
Name	**Cost (per pound)**	**Name**	**Willingness to pay (per pound)**
Lucrezia	$8	Ennio	$14
Bianca	10	Lucchino	13
Luisa	12	Matteo	12
Contessina	14	Giovanni	11
Maddalena	16	Filippo	10

a. The market in wool is perfectly competitive. What will the equilibrium price be?

b. Does the equilibrium price lead to efficiency in this market?

c. The Visconti family argues that the price of wool should be fixed at a maximum of $10 so that all their operations can buy wool. Is this efficient? Why or why not?

2. Lakshmi and Sam have a cake that they want to divide in an efficient way, and the cake is the only good in their little economy. Both Lakshmi and Sam like cake and would always prefer to have more of it. Using the standard of efficiency in consumption, determine whether the following ways of dividing the cake are efficient.

a. Lakshmi and Sam each get half of the cake.

b. Lakshmi and Sam each get one-third of the cake and one-third is thrown away.

c. Lakshmi gets the whole cake and Sam gets nothing.

3. A city block with 25 residents has a garden in the center. Some of the residents are very busy, but others have lots of leisure time. And their preferences also differ: some enjoy yard work, others don't. The garden requires a total of 1,000 hours of work per year—planting, mowing grass, and so on. One resident suggests that each resident should contribute 40 hours per year to maintain the garden. Another resident, an economist, objects that this will be inefficient.

a. Explain why the economist thinks that the proposal will be inefficient.

b. Describe how a market in which residents can trade hours of yard work leads to an efficient allocation of yard work among residents.

4. In the town of Rockport, only two goods are produced: left shoes and right shoes. And this economy produces on the production possibility frontier. That is, there is no way of producing more left shoes without producing fewer right shoes, and vice versa. What else would you need to know, if anything, to determine whether the economy of Rockport as a whole is efficient? That is, does it satisfy efficiency in production, efficiency in consumption, and efficiency in output levels? Explain your answer.

5. The economy of Dunk, IN, produces only two goods, bagels and doughnuts, using labor as the only factor of production. There are 8 workers in Dunk and all are paid the same wage. The accompanying table shows the amount of output that can be produced with a certain number of workers.

Quantity of labor in doughnut production (workers)	Quantity of doughnuts	Quantity of labor in bagel production (workers)	Quantity of bagels
0	0	0	0
1	34	1	50
2	40	2	86
3	46	3	92
4	49	4	98
5	52	5	104
6	53	6	106

a. Suppose that the price of a doughnut is $0.50 and the price of a bagel is also $0.50. There are 2 workers producing doughnuts and 3 workers producing bagels. The other 3 workers are unemployed. Given what you know about the relationship between the value of the marginal products and efficiency, determine whether this economy is efficient in the production of doughnuts versus the production of bagels—that is, is the economy efficient in output levels? Also determine whether the economy is efficient in production—that is, is it producing on the production possibility frontier?

b. Suppose that the price of doughnuts is $0.20, and the price of bagels is $0.10. There are 4 workers producing doughnuts and 4 workers producing bagels, and nobody is unemployed. Is this economy efficient in production? Is it efficient in output levels?

c. Initially, the price of doughnuts is $0.20, the price of bagels is $0.10, and there are 4 workers producing doughnuts and 4 workers producing bagels, just as in part b. Now consumers' tastes change: due to health concerns, consumers are now willing to pay $0.75 per bagel but only $0.10 per doughnut. These new prices act as signals of consumers' preferences. In response to this change, will the allocation of workers to bagel or doughnut production change?

6. Land in the Shire can be used for growing carrots or potatoes, and the only variable input into production is labor (land is fixed). All workers are paid the same wage. There are two farmers: Sam grows carrots, and the marginal product of labor on his farm is 30 pounds of carrots per month. Merry grows potatoes, and the marginal product of labor on his farm is 44 pounds of potatoes per month. Each experiences diminishing returns to labor. The price of carrots is $3 per pound, and the price of potatoes is $2 per pound.

a. Calculate the value of the marginal product of labor in carrots and in potatoes to assess whether the economy of the Shire is efficient in output levels. Is the economy in general equilibrium?

b. Do the prices of carrots and potatoes signal that farmers should produce more or less of their crops? In which direction will employment levels adjust in response to the market prices for the two crops? Describe how the economy reaches general equilibrium.

7. The economy of Leisureville, CO, produces only two goods: skis and bikes. Labor is the only variable input into production, there are diminishing returns to labor, and all workers are paid the same wage. All markets are competitive, and initially the economy is in general equilibrium. Now, due to a change in tastes, consumers' preferences change away from skis and toward bikes.

a. What will happen to consumers' willingness to pay for bikes and for skis? What will therefore happen to the market prices for bikes and skis?

b. As the prices adjust, what will happen to the value of the marginal product of labor in bikes and in skis? What will happen to bike producers' and ski producers' willingness to pay for workers?

c. As adjustments are made in employment, what happens to the output of bikes and of skis? How does the marginal product of labor in bikes and in skis respond? What therefore happens to the value of the marginal product of labor in bikes and in skis?

d. At what point does this process stop?

8. Gulliver travels to a country in which there are two types of creatures, the Houyhnhnms and the Yahoos, and there are equally as many Houyhnhnms as there are Yahoos. The accompanying table lists the possible combinations of utility levels. That is, the points in the table lie on this economy's utility possibility frontier.

Point	Total utility of Houyhnhnms (utils)	Total utility of Yahoos (utils)
A	200	0
B	180	30
C	140	60
D	80	90
E	0	120

a. Draw the utility possibility frontier. When Gulliver arrives, he notices that the Houyhnhnms have a utility of 120 and the Yahoos have a utility of 50. Is this an efficient outcome?

b. Gulliver remembers that Jeremy Bentham argued that the best outcome is the one that maximizes the sum of everyone's utility. Which of the points A through E on the utility frontier would Bentham have chosen as the best outcome?

c. Gulliver then recalls that John Rawls argued that the best outcome is the one that gives the most utility to whoever happens to be the worst-off member in society. Which of the points A through E would Rawls have chosen?

9. Consider the utility possibility frontier in the accompanying diagram.

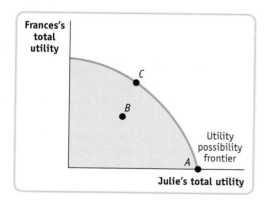

a. Is point A efficient? Would you describe point A as fair? Why or why not?

b. Is point B efficient?

c. Is point C better than point B? Why or why not?

d. Is point A better than point B? Why or why not?

10. The table shows how much total Jeremy and John Stuart experience from various amounts of income.

Jeremy's income	Jeremy's total utility (utils)	John Stuart's income	John Stuart's total utility (utils)
$0	0	$0	0
1	12	1	12
2	22	2	22
3	30	3	30
4	36	4	36
5	40	5	40
6	42	6	42

a. There are $6 that we can distribute between Jeremy and John Stuart. Suppose that Jeremy and John Stuart live in a utilitarian society that tries to distribute income in such a way as to create the greatest sum of the total utility of each member. How can we distribute $6 between Jeremy and John Stuart so that the sum of their total utilities is the greatest?

b. Now Jeremy falls ill, and his illness requires expensive treatment. As a result, the utility he gets from each dollar of income is now only half of what the table above shows. If our aim is to distribute income in such a way as to create the greatest sum of the total utility of both Jeremy and John Stuart, how should we distribute the $6 now? Does this seem fair to you?

11. The minimum wage raises workers' wage above the equilibrium wage. Is this efficient? Do you think it is fair?

>**web**... To continue your study and review of concepts in this chapter, please visit the Krugman/Wells website for quizzes, animated graph tutorials, web links to helpful resources, and more.

www.worthpublishers.com/krugmanwells

>> Monopoly

EVERYBODY MUST GET STONES

A FEW YEARS AGO DE BEERS, THE world's main supplier of diamonds, ran an ad urging men to buy their wives diamond jewelry. "She married you for richer, for poorer," read the ad. "Let her know how it's going."

Crass? Yes. Effective? No question. For generations diamonds have been a symbol of luxury, valued not only for their appearance but also for their rarity.

But geologists will tell you that diamonds aren't all that rare. In fact, according to the *Dow Jones-Irwin Guide to Fine Gems and Jewelry*, diamonds are "more common than any other gem-quality colored stone. They only seem rarer . . ."

Why do diamonds seem rarer than other gems? Part of the answer is a brilliant marketing campaign (We'll talk more about marketing and product differentiation in Chapter 16.) But mainly diamonds seem rare because De Beers *makes* them rare: the company controls most of the world's diamond mines and limits the quantity of diamonds supplied to the market.

Got stones?

Up to now we have concentrated exclusively on perfectly competitive markets—markets in which the producers are perfect competitors. But De Beers isn't like the producers we've studied so far: it is a *monopolist*, the sole (or almost sole) producer of a good. Monopolists behave differently from producers in perfectly competitive industries: whereas perfect competitors take the price at which they can sell their output as given, monopolists know that their actions affect market prices and take that effect into account when deciding how much to produce. Before we begin our analysis, let's step back and look at monopoly and perfect competition as parts of a broader system for classifying markets.

Perfect competition and monopoly are particular types of *market structure*. They are particular categories in a system economists use to classify markets and industries according to two main dimensions. This chapter begins with a brief overview of types of market structure. It will help us here and in subsequent chapters to understand on a deeper level why markets differ and why producers in those markets behave quite differently.

What you will learn in this chapter:

➤ The significance of **monopoly**, where a single **monopolist** is the only producer of a good

➤ How a monopolist determines its profit-maximizing output and price

➤ The difference between monopoly and perfect competition, and the effects of that difference on society's welfare

➤ How policy makers address the problems posed by monopoly

➤ What **price discrimination** is, and why it is so prevalent when producers have **market power**

Types of Market Structure

In the real world, there is a mind-boggling array of different markets. We observe widely different behavior patterns by producers across markets: in some markets producers are extremely competitive; in others, they seem somehow to coordinate their actions to avoid competing with one another; and, as we have just described, some markets are monopolies in which there is no competition at all. In order to develop principles and make predictions about markets and how producers will behave in them, economists have developed four principal models of market structure: *perfect competition, monopoly, oligopoly,* and *monopolistic competition.*

This system of market structures is based on two dimensions:

- The number of producers in the market (one, few, or many)
- Whether the goods offered are identical or *differentiated*

Differentiated goods are goods that are different but considered somewhat substitutable by consumers (think Coke versus Pepsi).

Figure 14-1 provides a simple visual summary of the types of market structure classified according to the two dimensions. In *monopoly,* a single producer sells a single, undifferentiated product. In *oligopoly,* a few producers—more than one but not a large number—sell products that may be either identical or differentiated. In *monopolistic competition,* many producers each sell a differentiated product (think of producers of economics textbooks). And finally, as we know, in *perfect competition* many producers each sell an identical product.

You might wonder what determines the number of firms in a market: whether there is one (monopoly), few (oligopoly), or many (perfect competition and monopolistic competition). We won't answer that question here, because it will be covered in detail later in this chapter and in Chapters 15 and 16, which analyze oligopoly and monopolistic competition. We will just briefly note that in the long run it depends on whether there are conditions that make it difficult for new firms to enter the market, such as government regulations that discourage entry, economies of scale in production, technological superiority, or control of necessary resources or inputs. When these conditions are present, industries tend to be monopolies or oligopolies; when they are not present, industries tend to be perfectly competitive or monopolistically competitive.

You might also wonder why some markets have differentiated products but others have identical ones. The answer is that it depends on the nature of the good and consumers' preferences. Some goods—soft drinks, economics textbooks, breakfast cereals—

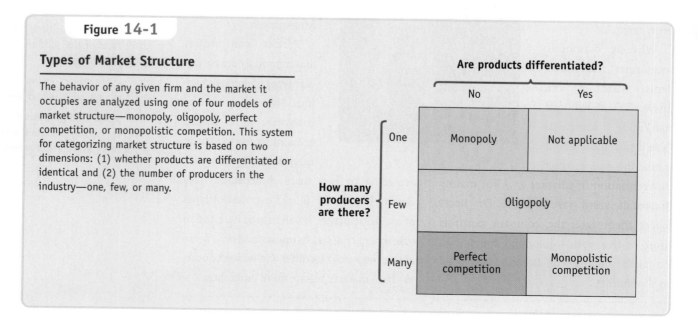

Figure 14-1

Types of Market Structure

The behavior of any given firm and the market it occupies are analyzed using one of four models of market structure—monopoly, oligopoly, perfect competition, or monopolistic competition. This system for categorizing market structure is based on two dimensions: (1) whether products are differentiated or identical and (2) the number of producers in the industry—one, few, or many.

Are products differentiated?

How many producers are there?	No	Yes
One	Monopoly	Not applicable
Few	Oligopoly	
Many	Perfect competition	Monopolistic competition

can readily be made into different varieties in the eyes and tastes of consumers. Other goods—hammers, for example—are much less easy to differentiate.

Although this chapter is devoted to monopoly, important aspects of monopoly carry over to other market structures—to oligopoly and monopolistic competition. In the next section, we will define monopoly and review the conditions that make it possible. These same conditions, in less extreme form, also give rise to oligopoly. We then show how a monopolist can increase profit by limiting the quantity supplied to a market—behavior that also occurs in oligopoly and monopolistic competition. As we'll see, this kind of behavior is good for the producer but bad for consumers; it also causes inefficiency. An important topic of study will be the ways in which public policy tries to limit the damage. Finally, we turn to one of the surprising effects of monopoly—one that is very often present in oligopoly and monopolistic competition as well: the fact that different consumers often pay different prices for the same good.

The Meaning of Monopoly

The De Beers monopoly of South Africa was created in the 1880s by Cecil Rhodes, a British businessman. By 1880 mines in South Africa already dominated the world's supply of diamonds. There were, however, many mining companies, all competing with each other. During the 1880s Rhodes bought the great majority of those mines and consolidated them into a single company, De Beers. By 1889 De Beers controlled almost all of the world's diamond production.

De Beers, in other words, became a **monopolist.** A producer is a monopolist if it is the sole supplier of a good that has no close substitutes. When a firm is a monopolist, the industry is a **monopoly.**

> A **monopolist** is a firm that is the only producer of a good that has no close substitutes. An industry controlled by a monopolist is known as a **monopoly.**

Monopoly: Our First Departure from Perfect Competition

As we saw in the Chapter 9 section "Defining Perfect Competition," the supply and demand model of a market is not universally valid. Instead, it's a model of perfect competition, which is only one of several different types of market structure.

Back in Chapter 9 we learned that a market will be perfectly competitive only if there are many producers, all of whom produce the same standardized product. Monopoly is the most extreme departure from perfect competition.

In practice, true monopolies are hard to find in the modern American economy, partly because of legal obstacles. A contemporary entrepreneur who tried to consolidate all the firms in an industry the way that Rhodes did would soon find himself in court, accused of breaking *antitrust* laws, which are intended to prevent monopolies from emerging. Oligopoly, a market structure in which there is a small number of large producers, is much more common. In fact, most of the goods and services you buy, from autos to airline tickets, are supplied by oligopolies, which we will examine in detail in Chapter 15.

Monopolies do, however, play an important role in some sectors of the economy, such as pharmaceuticals. Furthermore, our analysis of monopoly will provide a foundation for our later analysis of other departures from perfect competition, such as oligopoly and monopolistic competition.

What Monopolists Do

Why did Rhodes want to consolidate South African diamond producers into a single company? What difference did it make to the world diamond market?

Figure 14-2 (on page 336) offers a preliminary view of the effects of monopoly. It shows an industry in which the supply curve under perfect competition intersects the demand curve at C, leading to the price P_C and the output Q_C.

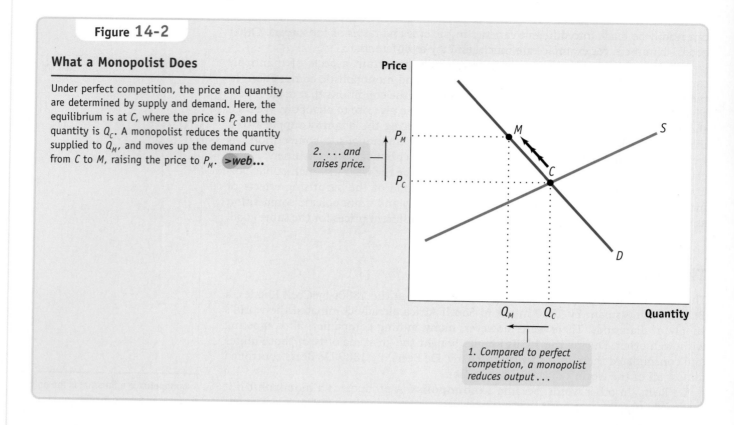

Figure 14-2

What a Monopolist Does

Under perfect competition, the price and quantity are determined by supply and demand. Here, the equilibrium is at *C*, where the price is P_C and the quantity is Q_C. A monopolist reduces the quantity supplied to Q_M, and moves up the demand curve from *C* to *M*, raising the price to P_M. **>web...**

2. ...and raises price.

1. Compared to perfect competition, a monopolist reduces output ...

Suppose that this industry is consolidated into a monopoly. The monopolist *moves up the demand curve* by reducing quantity supplied to a point like *M*, at which the quantity produced, Q_M, is lower and the price P_M, is higher than under perfect competition.

The ability of a monopolist to raise its price above the competitive level by reducing output is known as **market power.** And market power is what monopoly is all about. A wheat farmer who is one of 100,000 wheat farmers has no market power: he or she must sell wheat at the going market price. Your local cable TV company, though, does have market power: it can raise prices and still keep many (though not all) of its customers, because they have nowhere else to go. In short, it's a monopolist.

The reason a monopolist reduces output and raises price compared to the perfectly competitive industry levels is to increase profit. Cecil Rhodes consolidated the diamond producers into De Beers because he realized that the whole would be worth more than the sum of its parts—the monopoly would generate more profit than the sum of the profits of the individual competitive firms. In fact, we saw in Chapter 9 that under perfect competition economic profits normally vanish in the long run. Under monopoly the profits don't go away—a monopolist is able to continue earning profits in the long run.

In fact, monopolists are not the only types of firms that possess market power. In the next chapter we will study *oligopolists*, firms that can have market power as well. Under certain conditions, oligopolists can earn positive economic profits in the long run by restricting output like monopolists do.

But why don't profits get competed away? What allows monopolists to be monopolists?

Market power is the ability of a producer to raise prices.

Why Do Monopolies Exist?

A monopolist making profits will not go unnoticed by others. But won't other firms crash the party, grab a piece of the action, and drive down prices and profits in the long run? For a profitable monopoly to persist, something must keep others from going into the same business; that "something" is known as a **barrier to entry.** There are four principal types of barriers to entry: control of a scarce resource or input, economies of scale, technological superiority, and government-created barriers.

Control of a Scarce Resource or Input A monopolist that controls a resource or input crucial to an industry can prevent other firms from entering its market. Cecil Rhodes created the De Beers monopoly by establishing control over the mines that produced the great bulk of the world's diamonds.

Economies of Scale Many Americans have natural gas piped into their homes, for cooking and heating. Invariably, the local gas company is a monopolist. But why don't rival companies compete to provide gas?

In the early nineteenth century, when the gas industry was just starting up, companies did compete for local customers. But this competition didn't last long; soon local gas supply became a monopoly in almost every town because of the large fixed costs involved in providing a town with gas lines. Since the cost of laying gas lines didn't depend on how much gas a company sold, firms with a larger volume of sales had a cost advantage: because they were able to spread the fixed costs over a larger volume, they had lower average total costs than smaller firms.

Local gas supply is an industry in which average total cost always falls as output increases. As we learned in Chapter 8, this phenomenon is called *economies of scale.* There we learned that when average total cost falls as output increases, firms tend to grow larger. In an industry characterized by economies of scale, larger companies are more profitable and drive out smaller ones. For the same reason, established companies have a cost advantage over any potential entrant—a potent barrier to entry. So economies of scale can both give rise to and sustain monopoly.

A monopoly created and sustained by economies of scale is called a **natural monopoly.** The defining characteristic of a natural monopoly is that it possesses economies of scale over the range of output that is relevant for the industry. This is illustrated in Figure 14-3, showing the firm's average total cost curve and the market demand curve. Here we can see that the natural monopolist's *ATC* curve declines over the output levels at which price is greater than or equal to average total cost. So the

> To earn profits, a monopolist must be protected by a **barrier to entry**—something that prevents other firms from entering the industry.

> A **natural monopoly** exists when economies of scale provide a large cost advantage to having all of an industry's output produced by a single firm.

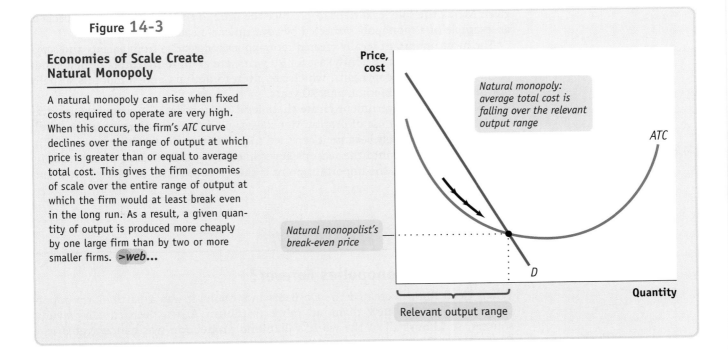

Figure 14-3

Economies of Scale Create Natural Monopoly

A natural monopoly can arise when fixed costs required to operate are very high. When this occurs, the firm's *ATC* curve declines over the range of output at which price is greater than or equal to average total cost. This gives the firm economies of scale over the entire range of output at which the firm would at least break even in the long run. As a result, a given quantity of output is produced more cheaply by one large firm than by two or more smaller firms. **>web...**

natural monopolist has economies of scale over the entire range of output for which any firm would want to remain in the industry—the range of output at which the firm would at least break even in the long run. The source of this condition is large fixed costs: when large fixed costs are required to operate, a given quantity of output is produced at lower average total cost by one large firm than by two or more smaller firms.

The most visible natural monopolies in the modern economy are local utilities—water, gas, electricity, local phone service, and cable television. As we'll see later in this chapter, natural monopolies pose a special challenge to public policy.

Technological Superiority A firm that maintains a consistent technological advantage over potential competitors can establish itself as a monopolist. For example, from the 1970s through the 1990s the chip manufacturer Intel was able to maintain a consistent advantage over potential competitors in both the design and the production of microprocessors, the chips that run computers. But technological superiority is typically a short-run, not a long-run, barrier to entry: over time competitors will invest in upgrading their technology to match that of the technology leader. In fact, in the last few years Intel found its technological superiority eroded by a competitor, Advanced Micro Devices (also known as AMD), which now produces chips approximately as fast and as powerful as Intel chips.

We should note, however, that in certain high-tech industries, technological superiority is not a guarantee of success against competitors. Some high-tech industries are characterized by *network externalities*, a condition that arises when the value to the consumer of a good rises as the number of people who also use the good rises. In these industries, the firm possessing the largest network—the largest number of consumers currently using its product—has an advantage over its competitors in attracting new customers, an advantage that may allow it to become a monopolist. Microsoft is often cited as an example of a company with a technologically inferior product—its computer operating system—that grew into a monopolist through the phenomenon of network externalities. (You can read more about network externalities in Chapter 22.)

Government-Created Barriers In 1998 the pharmaceutical company Merck introduced Propecia, a drug effective against baldness. Despite the fact that Propecia was very profitable and other drug companies had the know-how to produce it, no other firms challenged Merck's monopoly. That's because the U.S. government had given Merck the sole legal right to produce the drug in the United States. Propecia is an example of a monopoly protected by government-created barriers.

The most important legally created monopolies today arise from *patents* and *copyrights*. Patents, which currently last for 20 years, are given to inventors of new products, such as drugs; copyrights, which are given to authors and composers, usually last for the creator's lifetime plus 70 years.

Why does the government create these legal monopolies? To encourage innovation through the promise of profits. Merck was willing to invest large sums in developing Propecia precisely because it expected to profit from the resulting monopoly. In Chapter 22, we'll go into the reasons governments use this method of encouraging innovation. For now, the important point is that in some cases the government creates monopolies.

economics in action

Are Diamond Monopolies Forever?

When Cecil Rhodes created the De Beers monopoly, it was a particularly opportune moment. The new diamond mines in South Africa dwarfed all previous sources, so almost all of the world's diamond production was concentrated in a few square miles.

Since that time, however, diamond deposits similar to those in South Africa have been found in a number of places—other African countries, Russia, and Australia, which is now the largest producer. So how does De Beers remain a monopolist?

Until quite recently De Beers was able to extend its control of resources even as new mines were opened. De Beers either bought out new producers or entered into agreements with local governments which controlled some of the new mines, effectively making them part of the De Beers monopoly. The most remarkable of these was an agreement with the former Soviet Union, which ensured that Russian diamonds would be marketed through De Beers, preserving its ability to control world supplies.

In recent years, however, the spread of diamond production—together with competition from synthetic diamonds, which are becoming better substitutes for natural stones—has led to some erosion of De Beers's control, and prices have even dropped somewhat. De Beers is arguably the most successful monopolist in history—but even diamond monopolies may not be forever. ■

> >

>>QUICK REVIEW

➤ A *monopolist* has *market power* and as a result will charge higher prices and produce less output than a perfectly competitive industry. This generates profit for the monopolist in the short run and long run.

➤ Profits will not persist in the long run unless there is a *barrier to entry*. This can take the form of control of a natural resource or input, economies of scale, technological superiority, or legal restrictions imposed by governments, including patents and copyrights.

➤ A *natural monopoly* arises when average total cost is declining over the output range relevant for the industry. This creates a barrier to entry because an established monopolist has lower average total cost than any smaller firm.

>>CHECK YOUR UNDERSTANDING 14-1

1. Currently, Texas Tea Oil Co. is the only local supplier of home heating oil in Frigid, Alaska. This winter residents were shocked that the cost of a gallon of heating oil had doubled and believed that they were the victims of market power. Explain which of the following pieces of evidence support or undermine that conclusion.
   a. There is a national shortage of heating oil, and Texas Tea could procure only a limited amount.
   b. Last year, Texas Tea and several other competing local oil-supply firms merged into a single firm.
   c. The cost to Texas Tea of purchasing heating oil from refineries has gone up significantly.
   d. Recently, some nonlocal firms have begun to offer heating oil to Texas Tea's regular customers at a price much lower than Texas Tea's.
   e. Texas Tea has acquired an exclusive government license to draw oil from the only heating oil pipeline in the state.

Solutions appear at back of book.

How a Monopolist Maximizes Profit

As we've suggested, once Cecil Rhodes consolidated the competing diamond producers of South Africa into a single company, the industry's behavior changed: the quantity supplied fell and the market price rose. In this section we will learn how a monopolist increases its profits by reducing output. And we will see the crucial role that market demand plays in leading a monopolist to behave differently from a perfectly competitive industry.

The Monopolist's Demand Curve and Marginal Revenue

In Chapter 9 we derived the producer's optimal output rule: a profit-maximizing producer produces the quantity of output at which the marginal cost of producing the last unit of output equals marginal revenue—the change in total revenue generated by that last unit of output. That is, $MR = MC$ at the profit-maximizing quantity of output. Although the optimal output rule holds for *all* producers, we will see shortly that its application leads to different profit-maximizing output levels for a monopolist compared to a perfectly competitive producer—that is, a price-taking producer. The source of that difference lies in the comparison of the demand curve faced by a monopolist to the demand curve faced by an individual, perfectly competitive producer.

In addition to the optimal output rule, we also learned in Chapter 9 that even though the *market* demand curve is always downward sloping, each of the producers that make up a perfectly competitive industry faces a horizontal, *perfectly elastic* demand curve, like D_C in panel (a) of Figure 14-4 (on page 340). Any attempt by an individual producer in a perfectly competitive industry to charge more than the going market price will cause it to lose all its sales. It can, however, sell as much as it likes at the market price. As we saw

Figure 14-4 **Comparing the Demand Curves of a Perfectly Competitive Producer and a Monopolist**

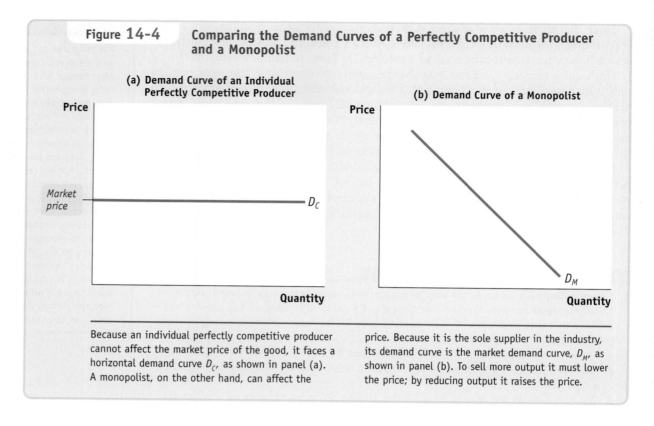

Because an individual perfectly competitive producer cannot affect the market price of the good, it faces a horizontal demand curve D_C, as shown in panel (a). A monopolist, on the other hand, can affect the price. Because it is the sole supplier in the industry, its demand curve is the market demand curve, D_M, as shown in panel (b). To sell more output it must lower the price; by reducing output it raises the price.

in Chapter 9, the marginal revenue of a perfectly competitive producer is simply the market price. As a result, the price-taking firm's optimal output rule is to produce the output level at which the marginal cost of the last unit produced is equal to the market price.

A monopolist, in contrast, is the sole supplier of its good. So its demand curve is simply the market demand curve, which is downward sloping, like D_M in panel (b). This downward slope creates a "wedge" between the price of the good and the marginal revenue of the good—the change in revenue generated by producing one more unit.

Table 14-1 shows this wedge between price and marginal revenue for a monopolist, by calculating the monopolist's total revenue and marginal revenue schedules from its demand schedule.

The first two columns of Table 14-1 show a hypothetical demand schedule for De Beers diamonds. For the sake of simplicity, we assume that all diamonds are exactly alike. And to make the arithmetic easy, we suppose that the number of diamonds sold is far smaller than is actually the case. For instance, at a price of $500 per diamond, we assume that only 10 diamonds are sold. The demand curve implied by this schedule is shown in panel (a) of Figure 14-5 on page 342.

The third column of Table 14-1 shows De Beers's total revenue from selling each quantity of diamonds—the price per diamond multiplied by the number of diamonds sold. The last column calculates marginal revenue, the change in total revenue from producing and selling one more diamond.

Clearly, after the 1st diamond, the marginal revenue a monopolist receives from selling one more unit is less than the price at which that unit is sold. For example, if De Beers sells 10 diamonds, the price at which the 10th diamond is sold is $500. But the marginal revenue—the change in total revenue in going from 9 to 10 diamonds—is only $50.

Why is the marginal revenue from that 10th diamond less than the price? An increase in production by a monopolist has two opposing effects on revenue:

■ *A quantity effect.* One more unit is sold, increasing total revenue by the price at which the unit is sold (in this case, $500).

- *A price effect.* In order to sell that last unit, the monopolist must cut the market price on *all* units sold. This decreases total revenue (in this case, by 9 × (−$50) = −$450).

The quantity effect and the price effect are illustrated by the two shaded areas in panel (a) of Figure 14-5 on page 342. Increasing diamond sales from 9 to 10 means moving down the demand curve from *A* to *B*, reducing the price per diamond from $550 to $500. The green-shaded area represents the quantity effect: De Beers sells the 10th diamond at a price of $500. This is offset, however, by the price effect, represented by the orange-shaded area. In order to sell that 10th diamond, De Beers must reduce the price on all its diamonds from $550 to $500. So it loses 9 × $50 = $450 in revenue, the orange-shaded area. So, as point *C* indicates, the total effect on revenue of selling one more diamond—the marginal revenue—derived from an increase in diamond sales from 9 to 10 is only $50.

Point *C* lies on the monopolist's marginal revenue curve, labeled *MR* in panel (a) of Figure 14-5 and taken from the last column of Table 14-1. The crucial point about the monopolist's marginal revenue curve is that it is always *below* the demand curve.

TABLE 14-1

Demand, Total Revenue, and Marginal Revenue for the De Beers Monopoly

Price of diamond P	Quantity of diamonds Q	Total revenue $TR = P \times Q$	Marginal revenue $MR = \Delta TR/\Delta Q$
$1,000	0	$0	
			$950
950	1	950	
			850
900	2	1,800	
			750
850	3	2,550	
			650
800	4	3,200	
			550
750	5	3,750	
			450
700	6	4,200	
			350
650	7	4,550	
			250
600	8	4,800	
			150
550	9	4,950	
			50
500	10	5,000	
			−50
450	11	4,950	
			−150
400	12	4,800	
			−250
350	13	4,550	
			−350
300	14	4,200	
			−450
250	15	3,750	
			−550
200	16	3,200	
			−650
150	17	2,550	
			−750
100	18	1,800	
			−850
50	19	950	
			−950
0	20	0	

Figure 14-5

A Monopolist's Demand, Total Revenue, and Marginal Revenue Curves

Panel (a) shows the monopolist's demand and marginal revenue curves for diamonds from Table 14-1. The marginal revenue curve lies below the demand curve. To see why, consider point *A* on the demand curve, where 9 diamonds are sold at $550 each, generating total revenue of $4,950. To sell a 10th diamond, the price on all 10 diamonds must be cut to $500, as shown by point *B*. As a result, total revenue increases by the green area (the quantity effect: $500) but decreases by the orange area (the price effect: –$450). So the marginal revenue from the 10th diamond is $50 (the difference between the green and orange areas) which is much lower than its price, $500.

Panel (b) shows the monopolist's total revenue curve for diamonds. As output goes from 0 to 10 diamonds, total revenue increases. It reaches its maximum at 10 diamonds—the level at which marginal revenue is equal to 0—and declines thereafter. The quantity effect dominates the price effect when total revenue is rising; the price effect dominates the quantity effect when total revenue is falling. **>web...**

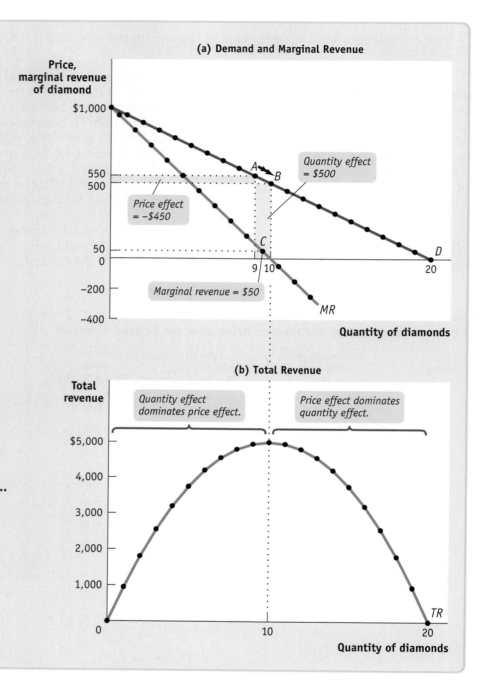

That's because of the price effect, which means that a monopolist's marginal revenue from selling an additional unit is always less than the price the monopolist receives for that unit. It is the price effect that creates the wedge between the monopolist's marginal revenue curve and the demand curve: in order to sell an additional diamond, De Beers must cut the market price on all units sold.

In fact, this wedge exists for any firm that possesses market power, such as oligopolists. Having market power means that the firm faces a downward-sloping demand curve. As a result, there will always be a price effect from an increase in its output. So for a firm with market power, the marginal revenue curve always lies below its demand curve.

Take a moment to compare the monopolist's marginal revenue curve with the marginal revenue curve for a perfectly competitive producer, one without market power. For such a producer there is no price effect from an increase in output: its marginal revenue curve is simply its horizontal demand curve. So for a perfectly competitive producer, market price and marginal revenue are always equal.

To emphasize how the quantity and price effects offset each other for a producer with market power, De Beers's total revenue curve is shown in panel (b) of Figure 14-5. Notice that it is hill-shaped: as output rises from 0 to 10 diamonds, total revenue increases. This reflects the fact that *at low levels of output, the quantity effect is stronger than the price effect:* as the monopolist sells more, it has to lower the price on only very few units, so the price effect is small. As output rises beyond 10 diamonds, total revenue actually falls. This reflects the fact that *at high levels of output, the price effect is stronger than the quantity effect:* as the monopolist sells more, it now has to lower the price on many units of output, making the price effect very large. Correspondingly, the marginal revenue curve lies below zero at output levels above 10 diamonds. For example, an increase in diamond production from 11 to 12 yields only $400 for the 12th diamond, simultaneously reducing the revenue from diamonds 1 through 11 by $550. As a result, the marginal revenue of the 12th diamond is −$150.

The Monopolist's Profit-Maximizing Output and Price

To complete the story of how a monopolist maximizes profit, we now bring in the monopolist's marginal cost. Let's assume that there is no fixed cost of production, and we'll also assume that the marginal cost of producing an additional diamond is constant at $200, no matter how many diamonds De Beers produces. Then marginal cost will always equal average total cost and the marginal cost curve (and the average total cost curve) is a horizontal line at $200, as shown in Figure 14-6.

Figure 14-6

The Monopolist's Profit-Maximizing Output and Price

This figure shows the demand, marginal revenue, and marginal cost curves. Marginal cost per diamond is $200, so the marginal cost curve is horizontal at $200. According to the optimal output rule, the profit-maximizing quantity of output for the monopolist is at $MR = MC$, shown by point A, where the marginal cost and marginal revenue curves cross at an output of 8 diamonds. The price De Beers can charge per diamond is found by going to the point on the demand curve directly above point A, which is point B here—a price of $600 per diamond. It makes a profit of $400 × 8 = $3,200. A perfectly competitive industry produces the output level at which $P = MC$, given by point C, where the demand curve and marginal cost curves cross. So a competitive industry produces 16 diamonds, sells at a price of $200, and makes zero profit.

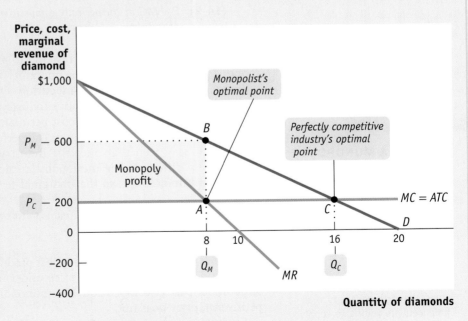

FINDING THE MONOPOLY PRICE

In order to find the *profit-maximizing quantity of output* for a monopolist, you look for the point where the marginal revenue curve crosses the marginal cost curve. Point *A* in Figure 14-6 is an example.

However, it's important not to fall into a common error: imagining that point *A* also shows the *price* at which the monopolist sells its output. It doesn't: it shows the *marginal revenue* received by the monopolist, which we know is less than the price.

To find the monopoly price, you have to go up vertically from *A* to the demand curve. There you find the price at which consumers demand the profit-maximizing quantity. So the profit-maximizing price–quantity combination is always a point on the demand curve, like *B* in Figure 14-6.

To maximize profit, the monopolist compares marginal cost with marginal revenue. If marginal revenue exceeds marginal cost, De Beers increases profit by producing more; if marginal revenue is less than marginal cost, De Beers increases profit by producing less. So the monopolist maximizes its profit by using the optimal output rule:

(14-1) *MR = MC at the monopolist's profit-maximizing quantity of output*

The monopolist's optimal point is shown in Figure 14-6. At *A*, the marginal cost curve, *MC*, crosses the marginal revenue curve, *MR*. The corresponding output level, 8 diamonds, is the monopolist's profit-maximizing quantity of output, Q_M. The price at which consumers demand 8 diamonds is $600, so the monopolist's price, P_M, is $600—corresponding to point *B*. The cost of producing each diamond is $200, so the monopolist earns a profit of $600 − $200 = $400 per diamond, and total profit is 8 × $400 = $3,200, as indicated by the shaded area.

Monopoly versus Perfect Competition

When Cecil Rhodes consolidated many independent diamond producers into De Beers, he converted a perfectly competitive industry into a monopoly. We can now use our analysis to see the effects of such a consolidation.

Let's look again at Figure 14-6 and ask how this same market would work if, instead of being a monopoly, the industry were perfectly competitive. We will continue to assume that there is no fixed cost, and that marginal cost is constant, so average total cost and marginal cost are equal.

If the diamond industry consists of many perfectly competitive firms, each of those producers takes the market price as given. That is, each producer acts as if its marginal revenue is equal to the market price. So each firm within the industry uses the price-taking firm's optimal output rule:

(14-2) *P = MC at the perfectly competitive firm's profit-maximizing quantity of output*

In Figure 14-6, this would correspond to producing at *C*, where the price per diamond, P_C, is $200, equal to the marginal cost of production. Profit-maximizing industry output under perfect competition, Q_C, is therefore 16 diamonds.

But does the perfectly competitive industry earn any profits at *C*? No: the price of $200 is equal to the production cost per diamond. So there are no economic profits for this industry when it produces at the perfectly competitive output level.

We've already seen that once the industry is consolidated into a monopoly, the result is very different. The monopolist's calculation of marginal revenue takes the price effect into account, so that marginal revenue is less than the price. That is,

(14-3) *P > MR = MC at the monopolist's profit-maximizing quantity of output*

As we've already seen, the monopolist produces less than the competitive industry— 8 diamonds rather than 16. The price under monopoly is $600, compared with only $200 under perfect competition. The monopolist earns a positive profit, but the competitive industry does not.

So, just as we suggested earlier, we see that compared with a competitive industry, a monopolist does the following:

- Produces a smaller quantity: $Q_M < Q_C$
- Charges a higher price: $P_M > P_C$
- Earns a profit

IS THERE A MONOPOLY SUPPLY CURVE?

Given how a monopolist applies the optimal output rule, you might be tempted to ask what this implies for the supply curve of a monopolist. But this is a meaningless question: *monopolists don't have supply curves.*

Remember that a supply curve shows the quantity that producers are willing to supply for any given market price. A monopolist, however, does not take the price as given; it chooses a profit-maximizing quantity, taking into account its own ability to influence the price.

MONOPOLY BEHAVIOR AND THE PRICE ELASTICITY OF DEMAND

A monopolist faces marginal revenue that is less than the market price. But how much lower? The answer depends on the *price elasticity of demand*.

Remember from Chapter 5 that the price elasticity of demand determines how *total revenue* from sales changes when the price falls. If the price elasticity is greater than 1, a fall in the price increases total revenue, because the rise in the quantity demanded outweighs the lower price of each unit sold. If the elasticity is less than 1, a lower price reduces total revenue.

When a monopolist increases output by one unit, it must reduce the market price in order to sell that unit. If the price elasticity of demand is less than 1, this will actually reduce revenue—that is, marginal revenue will be negative. The monopolist can only increase

revenue by producing more if the price elasticity of demand is greater than 1; the higher the elasticity, the closer the additional revenue is to the initial market price.

What this tells us is that the difference between monopoly behavior and perfect competition depends on the price elasticity of demand. A monopolist that faces highly elastic demand will behave almost like a firm in a perfectly competitive industry.

For example, Amtrak has a monopoly of intercity passenger service in the Northeast Corridor, but it has very little ability to raise prices: potential train travelers will switch to cars and planes. In contrast, a monopolist that faces less elastic demand—like most cable TV companies—will behave very differently from a perfect competitor: it will charge much higher prices and restrict output more.

Monopoly: The General Picture

Figure 14-6 involved specific numbers and assumed that the marginal cost curve was a horizontal line. Figure 14-7 shows a more general picture of monopoly in action: *D* is the market demand curve; *MR*, the marginal revenue curve; *MC*, the marginal cost curve; and *ATC*, the average total cost curve. Here we return to the usual assumption that the marginal cost curve has a "swoosh" shape and the average total cost curve is U-shaped.

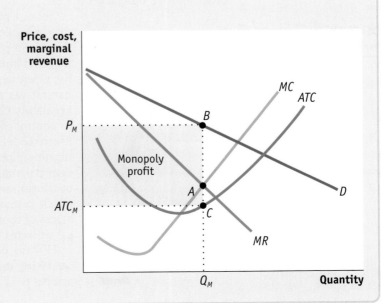

Figure 14-7

The Monopolist's Profit

In this case, the marginal cost curve has a "swoosh" shape and the average total cost curve is U-shaped. The monopolist maximizes profit by producing the level of output at which $MR = MC$, given by point A, generating quantity Q_M. It finds its monopoly price, P_M, from the point on the demand curve directly above point A, point B here. The average total cost of Q_M is shown by point C. Profit is given by the area of the shaded rectangle. **>web...**

Applying the optimal output rule, we see that the profit-maximizing level of output is the output at which marginal revenue equals marginal cost, indicated by point A. The profit-maximizing quantity of output is Q_M, and the price charged by the monopolist is P_M. At the profit-maximizing level of output, the monopolist's average total cost is ATC_M, shown by point C.

Recalling how we calculated profit in Equation 9-5 on page 215, profit is equal to the difference between total revenue and total cost. So we have

(14-4) $\text{Profit} = TR - TC$
$$= (P_M \times Q_M) - (ATC_M \times Q_M)$$
$$= (P_M - ATC_M) \times Q_M$$

Profit is equal to the area of the shaded rectangle in Figure 14-7, with a height of $P_M - ATC_M$ and a width of Q_M.

In Chapter 9 we learned that a perfectly competitive industry can have profits *in the short run but not in the long run*. In the short run price can exceed average total cost, allowing a perfectly competitive firm to make a profit. But we also know that this cannot persist. In the long run, any profit in a perfectly competitive industry will be competed away as new firms enter the market. In contrast, a monopolist will make profits in both the short run and the long run.

economics in action

California Power Play?

The winter of 2000–2001 was a grim time for California, as power shortages gripped the state. One factor involved was the soaring price of natural gas, especially in the southern part of the state.

The strange thing was that natural gas prices in California were much higher than in Texas, the source of most of the state's natural gas. That is, the marginal cost of supplying natural gas to California—the cost of buying it in Texas, plus the small expense of shipping it across state lines—was much less than the price of California gas. So why wasn't more gas supplied?

The answer appears to have been that natural gas is transported via interstate pipelines and that the El Paso Corporation, which held a near-monopoly of pipelines supplying southern California, deliberately restricted the quantity of gas available in order to drive up market prices.

Because pipelines tend to be monopolies, they are subject to *price regulation*, discussed later in this chapter. As a result, the price a pipeline company can charge for shipping natural gas is limited. However, El Paso, in addition to running the pipelines, also has an unregulated subsidiary that sells natural gas in California. A judge at the Federal Energy Regulatory Commission concluded that the company used its control of the pipeline to drive up the prices received by its marketing subsidiary. It did this by reducing output—by running pipelines at low pressure and by scheduling nonessential maintenance during periods of peak demand. This conclusion was partly based on internal memos at El Paso, which seemed to say that the company was "idling large blocks of transport" to widen price spreads between natural gas delivered to Texas and to California.

El Paso denied the charges and has never admitted exercising market power. In 2003, however, the company agreed to a settlement in which it paid the state of

The STRUGGLING U.S. Postal Service takes a LESSON from the POWER COMPANIES...

WHOOPS! STAMP SHORTAGE! NOW THEY'RE TWO BUCKS EACH

California $1.7 billion. Many analysts—including the staff at the Federal Energy Regulatory Commission—believe that El Paso's exercise of market power in the natural gas market was part of a broad pattern of market manipulation that played a key role in California's energy crisis during 2000–2001. ∎

> > > > > > > > > > > > > > > > > > >

>>CHECK YOUR UNDERSTANDING 14-2

1. Use the accompanying total revenue schedule of Emerald, Inc., a monopoly producer of 10-carat emeralds, to calculate the answers to parts a–d. Then answer part e.

   a. The demand schedule
   b. The marginal revenue schedule
   c. The quantity effect component of marginal revenue per output level
   d. The price effect component of marginal revenue per output level
   e. What additional information is needed to determine Emerald, Inc.'s profit-maximizing output?

Quantity of emeralds demanded	Total revenue
1	$100
2	186
3	252
4	280
5	250

2. Use Figure 14-6 to show what happens to the following when the marginal cost of diamond production rises from $200 to $400.

   a. Marginal cost curve
   b. Profit-maximizing quantity
   c. Profit of the monopolist
   d. Perfectly competitive industry profits

Solutions appear at back of book.

>>QUICK REVIEW

➤ The crucial difference between a producer with market power, such as a monopolist, and a producer in a perfectly competitive industry is that perfectly competitive producers are price-takers that face horizontal demand curves, but a producer with market power faces a downward-sloping demand curve.

➤ Due to the price effect of an increase in output, the marginal revenue curve of a producer with market power always lies below its demand curve. So a profit-maximizing monopolist chooses the output level at which marginal cost is equal to marginal revenue—*not* to price.

➤ As a result, the monopolist produces less and sells its output at a higher price than a perfectly competitive industry would. It earns a profit in the short run and the long run.

Monopoly and Public Policy

It's good to be a monopolist, but it's not so good to be a monopolist's customer. A monopolist, by reducing output and raising prices, benefits at the expense of consumers. But buyers and sellers always have conflicting interests. Is the conflict of interest under monopoly any different than it is under perfect competition?

The answer is yes, because monopoly is a source of inefficiency: the losses to consumers from monopoly behavior are larger than the gains to the monopolist. Because monopoly leads to net losses for the economy, governments often try either to prevent the emergence of monopolies or to limit their effects. In this section we will see why monopoly leads to inefficiency and examine the policies governments adopt in an attempt to prevent this inefficiency.

Welfare Effects of Monopoly

By restricting output below the level at which marginal cost is equal to the market price, a monopolist increases its profit but hurts consumers. To assess whether this is a net benefit or loss to society, we must compare the monopolist's gain in profit to the consumer loss. And what we learn is that the consumer loss is larger than the monopolist's gain. Monopoly causes a net loss for the economy.

To see why, let's return to the case where the marginal cost curve is horizontal and there is no fixed cost, as shown in the two panels of Figure 14-8 on page 348. Here the marginal cost curve is *MC*, the demand curve is *D*, and, in panel (b), the marginal revenue curve is *MR*.

Panel (a) shows what happens if this industry is perfectly competitive. Equilibrium output is Q_C; the price of the good, P_C, is equal to marginal cost, and marginal cost is also equal to average total cost because there is no fixed cost and marginal cost is constant. Each firm is earning exactly its cost per unit of output, so there is no producer surplus in this equilibrium. The consumer surplus generated by the market is equal to the area of the blue-shaded triangle CS_C shown in panel (a). Since there is no producer surplus when the industry is perfectly competitive, CS_C also represents the total surplus.

Figure 14-8   Monopoly Causes Inefficiency

(a) Total Surplus with Perfect Competition

(b) Total Surplus with Monopoly

Panel (a) depicts a perfectly competitive industry: output is Q_C and market price, P_C, is equal is to MC. Since price is exactly equal to each producer's cost of production per unit, there is no producer surplus. Total surplus is therefore equal to consumer surplus, the entire shaded area. Panel (b) depicts the industry under monopoly: the monopolist decreases output to Q_M and charges P_M.

Consumer surplus (blue area) has shrunk because a portion of it is has been captured as profit (green area). Total surplus falls: the deadweight loss (orange area) represents the value of mutually beneficial transactions that do not occur because of monopoly behavior. **>web...**

Panel (b) shows the results for the same market, but this time assuming that the industry is a monopoly. The monopolist produces the level of output, Q_M, at which marginal cost is equal to marginal revenue, and it charges the price P_M. The monopolist now earns profit—which is also the producer surplus—equal to the area of the green rectangle, PS_M. Note that this profit is surplus that has been captured from consumers as consumer surplus shrinks to the area of the blue triangle, CS_M.

By comparing panels (a) and (b), we see that in addition to the redistribution of surplus from consumers to the monopolist, another important change has occurred: the sum of profit and consumer surplus—total surplus—is *smaller* under monopoly than under perfect competition. That is, the sum of CS_M and PS_M is less than the area CS_C in panel (a). In Chapter 6, we analyzed the concept of *deadweight loss*, the net loss caused by government policies such as taxes. Here we show that monopoly creates a deadweight loss to society equal to the area of the orange triangle, DL. So monopoly produces a net loss for the economy.

This net loss exists because some mutually beneficial transactions do not occur. There are people for whom an additional unit of the good is worth more than the marginal cost of producing it, but who don't consume it because they are not willing to pay P_M.

Those who recall our discussion of the deadweight loss from taxes in Chapter 6 will notice that the deadweight loss from monopoly looks quite similar. Indeed, by driving a wedge between price and marginal cost, monopoly acts much like a tax on consumers and produces the same kind of inefficiency.

So monopoly hurts the welfare of society as a whole and is a source of market failure. Is there anything government policy can do about it?

Preventing Monopoly

Policy toward monopoly depends crucially on whether or not the industry in question is a natural monopoly, one in which economies of scale ensure that bigger producers have lower average total cost. If the industry is *not* a natural monopoly, the best policy is to prevent monopoly from arising or break it up if it already exists. Let's focus on that case first, then turn to the more difficult problem of dealing with natural monopoly.

The De Beers monopoly on diamonds didn't have to happen. Diamond production is not a natural monopoly: the industry's costs would be no higher if it consisted of a number of independent, competing producers (as is the case, for example, in gold production).

So if the South African government had been worried about how a monopoly would have affected consumers, it could have blocked Cecil Rhodes in his drive to dominate the industry or broken up his monopoly after the fact. Today, governments often try to prevent monopolies from forming and break up existing ones.

De Beers is a rather unique case: for complicated historical reasons, it was allowed to remain a monopoly. But over the last century, most similar monopolies have been broken up. The most celebrated example in the United States is Standard Oil, founded by John D. Rockefeller in 1870. By 1878 Standard Oil controlled almost all U.S. oil refining; but in 1911 a court order broke the company into a number of smaller units, including the companies that later became Exxon and Mobil (and more recently merged to become ExxonMobil).

The government policies used to prevent or eliminate monopolies are known as *antitrust policy*, which we will discuss in the next chapter.

Dealing with Natural Monopoly

Breaking up a monopoly that isn't natural is clearly a good idea: the gains to consumers outweigh the loss to the producer. But it's not so clear whether a natural monopoly, one in which large producers have lower average total costs than small producers, should be broken up, because this would raise average total cost. For example, a town government that tried to prevent a single company from dominating local gas supply—which, as we've discussed, is almost surely a natural monopoly—would raise the cost of providing gas to its residents.

Yet even in the case of a natural monopoly, a profit-maximizing monopolist acts in a way that causes inefficiency—it charges consumers a price that is higher than marginal cost, and therefore prevents some potentially beneficial transactions. Also, it can seem unfair that a firm that has managed to establish a monopoly position earns large profits at the expense of consumers.

What can public policy do about this? There are two common answers.

Public Ownership In many countries, the preferred answer to the problem of natural monopoly has been **public ownership.** Instead of allowing a private monopolist to control an industry, the government establishes a public agency to provide the good and protect consumers' interests. For example, before 1984 in Britain, telephone service was provided by the state-owned British Telecom, and before 1987 airline travel was provided by the state-owned British Airways. (These companies still exist, but they have been privatized, competing with other firms in their respective industries.)

There are some examples of public ownership in the United States. Passenger rail service is provided by the public company Amtrak; regular mail delivery is provided by the U.S. Postal Service; some cities, including Los Angeles, have publicly owned electric power companies.

The advantage of public ownership, in principle, is that a publicly owned natural monopoly can set prices based on the criterion of efficiency rather than profit maximization. In a perfectly competitive industry, profit-maximizing behavior *is* efficient, because producers set prices equal to marginal cost; that is why there is no economic argument for public ownership of, say, wheat farms.

Experience suggests, however, that public ownership as a solution to the problem of natural monopoly often works badly in practice. One reason is that publicly owned firms are often less eager than private companies to keep costs down or offer high-quality products. Another is that publicly owned companies all too often end up serving political

> In **public ownership** of a monopoly, the good is supplied by the government or by a firm owned by the government.

interests—providing contracts or jobs to people with the right connections. For example, Amtrak has notoriously provided train service at a loss to destinations that attract few passengers—but that are located in the districts of influential members of Congress.

Regulation In the United States, the more common answer has been to leave the industry in private hands but subject it to regulation. In particular, most local utilities like electricity, telephone service, natural gas, and so on are covered by **price regulation** that limits the prices they can charge.

Price regulation limits the price that a monopolist is allowed to charge.

We saw in Chapter 4 that imposing a *price ceiling* on a competitive industry is a recipe for shortages, black markets, and other nasty side effects. Doesn't imposing a limit on the price that, say, a local gas company can charge have the same effects?

Not necessarily: a price ceiling on a monopolist need not create a shortage—in the absence of a price ceiling, a monopolist would charge a price that is higher than its marginal cost of production. So even if forced to charge a lower price—as long as that price is above *MC* and the monopolist at least breaks even on total output—the monopolist still has an incentive to produce the quantity demanded at that price.

Figure 14-9 shows an example of price regulation of a natural monopoly—a highly simplified version of a local gas company. The company faces a demand curve *D*, with an associated marginal revenue curve *MR*. For simplicity, we assume that the firm's total cost consists of two parts: a fixed cost and a variable cost that is incurred at a constant proportion to output. So marginal cost is constant in this case, and the marginal cost curve (which here is also the average variable cost curve) is a horizontal line at *MC*. The average total cost curve is the downward-sloping curve *ATC*; it is downward sloping because the higher the output, the lower the average fixed cost (the fixed cost per unit of output). Because average total cost is downward sloping over the range of output relevant for market demand, this is a natural monopoly.

Figure 14-9 **Regulated and Unregulated Natural Monopoly**

(a) Total Surplus with an Unregulated Natural Monopolist

(b) Total Surplus with a Regulated Natural Monopolist

This figure shows the case of a natural monopolist. In panel (a), if the monopolist is allowed to charge P_M, it makes a profit, shown by the green area; consumer surplus is shown by the blue area. If it is regulated and must charge the lower price P_R, output increases from Q_M to Q_R, and consumer surplus increases.

Panel (b) shows what happens when the monopolist must charge a price equal to average total cost, the price P_R^*. Output expands to Q_R^*, and consumer surplus is now the entire blue area. The monopolist makes zero profit. This is the greatest consumer surplus possible when the monopolist is allowed to at least break even, making P_R^* the best regulated price.

Panel (a) illustrates a case of natural monopoly without regulation. The unregulated natural monopolist chooses the monopoly output Q_M and charges the price P_M. Since the monopolist receives a price greater than its average total cost, it earns a profit. This profit is exactly equal to the producer surplus in this market, represented by the green-shaded rectangle. Consumer surplus is given by the blue-shaded triangle.

Now suppose that regulators impose a price ceiling on local gas deliveries—one that falls below the monopoly price P_M but above *ATC*, say, at P_R in panel (a). At that price the quantity demanded is Q_R.

Does the company have an incentive to produce that quantity? Yes. If the price at which the monopolist can sell its product is fixed by regulators, the firm's output no longer affects the market price—so it ignores the *MR* curve and is willing to expand output to meet the quantity demanded as long as the price it receives for the next unit is greater than marginal cost and the monopolist at least breaks even on total output. So with price regulation, the monopolist produces more, at a lower price.

Of course, the monopolist will not be willing to produce at all if the imposed price means producing at a loss. That is, the price ceiling has to be set high enough to allow the firm to cover its average total cost. Panel (b) shows a situation in which regulators have pushed the price down as far as possible, at the level where the average total cost curve crosses the demand curve. At any lower price the firm loses money. The price here, P_R^*, is the best regulated price: the monopolist is just willing to operate and produces Q_R^*, the quantity demanded at that price. Consumers and society gain as a result.

The welfare effects of this regulation can be seen by comparing the shaded areas in the two panels of Figure 14-9. Consumer surplus is increased by the regulation, with the gains coming from two sources. First, profits are eliminated and added instead to consumer surplus. Second, the larger output and lower price leads to an overall welfare gain—an increase in total surplus.

This all looks terrific: consumers are better off, profits are eliminated, and overall welfare increases. Unfortunately, things are rarely that easy in practice. The main problem is that regulators don't have the information required to set the price exactly at the level at which the demand curve crosses the average total cost curve. Sometimes they set it too low, creating shortages; at other times they set it too high. Also, regulated monopolies, like publicly owned firms, tend to exaggerate their costs to regulators and to provide inferior quality to consumers.

Must Monopoly Be Controlled?   Sometimes the cure is worse than the disease. Some economists have argued that the best solution, even in the case of natural monopoly, may be to live with it. The case for doing nothing is that attempts to control monopoly will, one way or another, do more harm than good—for example, by the politicization of pricing, which leads to shortages or by the creation of opportunities for political corruption.

The following Economics in Action describes the case of cable television, a natural monopoly that has been alternately regulated and deregulated as politicians change their minds about the appropriate policy.

economics in action

Cable Dilemmas

Most price regulation in the United States goes back a long way: electricity, local phone service, water, and gas have been regulated in most places for generations. But cable television is a relatively new industry. Until the late 1970s only rural areas too remote to support local broadcast stations were served by cable. After 1972 new technology and looser rules made it profitable to offer cable service to major metropolitan areas; new networks like HBO and CNN emerged to take advantage of the possibilities.

But local cable TV is clearly a natural monopoly: there are large fixed costs to running cable through a town that don't depend on how many people actually subscribe, so that having more than one cable company would involve a lot of wasteful duplication. But if the local cable company is a monopoly, should its prices be regulated?

At first most local governments thought so, and cable TV was subject to price regulation. In 1984, however, Congress passed a law prohibiting most local governments from regulating cable prices. (The law was the result both of widespread skepticism about whether price regulation was actually a good idea and of intensive lobbying by the cable companies.)

After the law went into effect, however, cable television rates increased sharply. The resulting consumer backlash led to a new law, in 1992, which once again allowed local governments to set limits on cable prices.

Was the new regulation a success? As measured by the prices of "basic" cable service, it was: after rising rapidly during the period of deregulation, the cost of basic service leveled off.

However, price regulation in cable applies only to "basic" service. Cable operators can try to evade the restrictions by charging more for premium channels like HBO or by offering fewer channels in the "basic" package. So some skeptics have questioned whether the regulation has actually been effective.

The story of cable television shows that making policy for natural monopolies is harder than the simplified model suggests. It also shows that sometimes governments have a hard time making up their minds! ∎

< < < < < < < < < < < < < < < < < < <

▶▶CHECK YOUR UNDERSTANDING 14-3

1. What policy should the government adopt in the following cases? Explain.
   a. Internet service in Anytown, OH, is provided by cable. Customers feel they are being overcharged, but the cable company claims it must charge prices that let it recover the costs of laying cable.
   b. The only two airlines that currently fly to Alaska need government approval to merge. Other airlines wish to fly to Alaska but need government-allocated landing slots to do so.

2. True or false? Explain your answer.
   a. Society's welfare is lower under monopoly because some consumer surplus is transformed into profit for the monopolist.
   b. A monopolist causes inefficiency because there are consumers who are willing to pay a price greater than or equal to marginal cost but less than the monopoly price.

3. Suppose a monopolist mistakenly believes that its marginal revenue is always equal to the market price. Assuming constant marginal cost and no fixed cost, draw a diagram comparing the level of profit, consumer surplus, total surplus, and deadweight loss for this misguided monopolist compared to a smart monopolist.

Solutions appear at back of book.

Price Discrimination

Up to this point we have considered only the case of a **single-price monopolist,** one who charges all consumers the same price. As the term suggests, not all monopolists do this. In fact, many if not most monopolists find that they can increase their profits by charging different customers different prices for the same good: they engage in **price discrimination.**

The most striking example of price discrimination most of us encounter regularly involves airline tickets. Although there are a number of airlines, most routes in the United States are serviced by only one or two carriers, which, as a result, have market power and can set prices. So any regular airline passenger quickly becomes aware that

A **single-price monopolist** offers its product to all consumers at the same price.

Sellers engage in **price discrimination** when they charge different prices to different consumers for the same good.

the question "How much will it cost me to fly there?" rarely has a simple answer. If you are willing to buy a nonrefundable ticket a month in advance and stay over a Saturday night, the round trip may cost only $150—or less if you are a senior citizen or a student. But if you have to go on a business trip tomorrow, which happens to be Tuesday, and come back on Wednesday, the round trip might cost $550. Yet the business traveler and the visiting grandparent receive the same product—the same cramped seat, the same awful food.

You might object that airlines are not usually monopolists—that the airline industry is an oligopoly. In fact, price discrimination takes place under oligopoly and monopolistic competition as well as monopoly. But it doesn't happen under perfect competition. And once we've seen why monopolists sometimes price discriminate, we'll be in a good position to understand why it happens in other cases, too.

The Logic of Price Discrimination

To get a preliminary view of why price discrimination might be more profitable than charging all consumers the same price, imagine that Air Sunshine offers the only nonstop flights between Bismarck, North Dakota, and Ft. Lauderdale, Florida. Assume that there are no capacity problems—the airline can fly as many planes as the number of passengers warrants. Also assume that there is no fixed cost. The marginal cost to the airline of providing a seat is $125, however many passengers it carries.

Further assume that the airline knows there are two kinds of potential passengers. First, there are business travelers, 2,000 of whom want to travel between the destinations each week. Second, there are students, 2,000 of whom also want to travel each week.

Will potential passengers take the flight? It depends on the price. The business travelers, it turns out, really want to fly; they will take the plane as long as the price is no more than $550. The students, however, have less money and more time; if the price goes above $150, they will take the bus.

So what should the airline do? If it has to charge everyone the same price, its options are limited. It could charge $550; that way it would get as much as possible out of the business travelers but lose the student market. Or it could charge only $150; that way it would get both types of travelers but would not make as much money on the business travelers as it might have.

We can quickly calculate the profits from each of these alternatives. If the airline charged $550, it would sell 2,000 tickets to the business travelers, getting total revenues of 550 × 2,000 = $1.1 million and incurring costs of 125 × 2,000 = $250,000; so its profit would be $850,000. If the airline charged only $150, it would sell 4,000 tickets, receiving revenue of 4,000 × 150 = $600,000 and incurring costs of 4,000 × 125 = $500,000; so its profit would be $100,000. If the airline must charge everyone the same price, charging the higher price is clearly more profitable.

What the airline would really like to do, however, is charge the business travelers the full $550 but offer $150 tickets to the students. That's a lot less than the price paid by business travelers, but it's still above marginal cost; so if the airline could sell those extra 2,000 tickets to students, it would make an additional $50,000 in profit.

In this example we assume that cutting the price below $550 will not lead to *any* additional business travel and that at a price above $150 *no* students will fly. The implied demand curve is shown in Figure 14-10 on page 354.

It would be more realistic to suppose that there is some "give" in the demand of each group. But this, it turns out, does not do away with the argument for price discrimination. The important point is that the two groups of consumers differ in their *sensitivity to price*—that a high price has a larger effect in discouraging purchases by students than by business travelers. As long as different groups of customers respond differently to the price, a monopolist will find that it can capture more consumer surplus and increase its profit by charging them different prices.

Figure 14-10

Two Types of Airline Customers

Air Sunshine has two types of customers, business travelers willing to pay $550 per ticket and students willing to pay $150 per ticket. There are 2,000 of each kind of customer. Air Sunshine has constant marginal cost of $125 per seat. If Air Sunshine could charge these two types of customers different prices, it would maximize its profit by charging business travelers $550 and students $150 per ticket. It would capture all of the consumer surplus as profit.
>web...

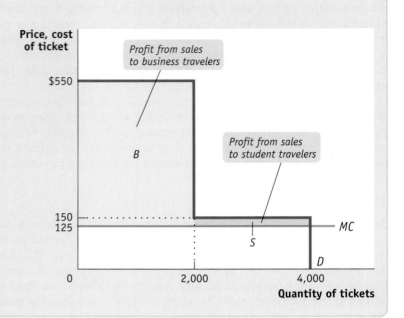

Price Discrimination and Elasticity

A more realistic description of the demand that airlines face would not specify particular prices at which different types of travelers would choose to fly. Instead, it would distinguish between the groups on the basis of their sensitivity to the price—their price elasticity of demand.

Suppose that a company sells its product to two easily identifiable groups of people—business travelers and students. It just so happens that business travelers are very insensitive to the price: there is a certain amount of the product they just have to have whatever the price, but they cannot be persuaded to buy much more than that no matter how cheap it is. Students, though, are more flexible: offer a good enough price and they will buy quite a lot, but raise the price too high and they will switch to something else. What should the company do?

The answer is the one already suggested by our simplified example: the company should charge business travelers, with their low price elasticity of demand, a higher price than it charges students, with their high price elasticity of demand.

The actual situation of the airlines is very much like this hypothetical example. Business travelers typically place a high priority on being at the right place at the right time and are not too sensitive to the price. But nonbusiness travelers faced with a high price might take the bus, drive to another airport to get a lower fare, or skip the trip altogether.

So why doesn't an airline simply announce different prices for business and nonbusiness customers? First, this would probably be illegal (U.S. law places severe limits on the ability of companies to practice open price discrimination). Second, even if it were legal, it would be a hard policy to enforce: business travelers might be willing to wear casual clothing and claim they were visiting family in Ft. Lauderdale in order to save $400.

So what the airlines do—quite successfully—is impose rules that indirectly have the effect of charging business and nonbusiness travelers different fares. Business travelers usually

On many airline routes, the fare you pay depends on the type of traveller you are.

Mark Peterson/Corbis

travel during the week and want to be home on the weekend; so the round-trip fare is much higher if you don't stay over a Saturday night. The requirement of a weekend stay for a cheap ticket effectively separates business from nonbusiness travelers. Similarly, business travelers often visit several cities in succession rather than make a simple round trip; so round-trip fares are much lower than twice the one-way fare. Many business trips are scheduled on short notice; so fares are much lower if you book far in advance. Fares are also lower if you travel standby, taking your chances on whether you actually get a seat—business travelers have to make it to that meeting; people visiting their relatives don't. And by requiring customers to show their ID upon check-in, airlines make sure there are no resales of tickets between the two groups that would undermine their ability to price-discriminate—students can't buy cheap tickets and resell them to business travelers. Look at the rules that govern ticket-pricing, and you will see an ingenious implementation of profit-maximizing price discrimination.

Perfect Price Discrimination

Let's return to the example of business travelers and students traveling between Bismarck and Ft. Lauderdale, illustrated in Figure 14-10, and ask what would happen if the airline could distinguish between the two groups of customers in order to charge each a different price.

Clearly, the airline would charge each group its willingness to pay—that is, as we learned in Chapter 6, the maximum that each group is willing to pay. For business travelers, the willingness to pay is $550, and it is $150 for students. As we have assumed, the marginal cost is $125 and does not depend on output, so that the marginal cost curve is a horizontal line. We can easily read off the airline's profit: it is the sum of the areas of the rectangle B and the rectangle S.

In this case, the consumers do not get any consumer surplus! The entire surplus is captured by the monopolist in the form of profit. When a monopolist is able to capture the entire surplus in this way, we say that it achieves **perfect price discrimination.**

In general, the greater the number of different prices a monopolist is able to charge, the closer it can get to perfect price discrimination. Figure 14-11 on page 356 shows a monopolist facing a downward-sloping demand curve; we suppose that this monopolist is able to charge different prices to different groups of consumers, with the consumers who are willing to pay the most being charged the most. In panel (a) the monopolist charges two different prices; in panel (b) the monopolist charges three different prices. Two things are apparent:

- The greater the number of prices the monopolist charges, the lower the lowest price—that is, some consumers will pay prices that approach marginal cost.
- The greater the number of prices the monopolist charges, the more money it extracts from consumers.

With a very large number of different prices, the picture would look like panel (c), a case of perfect price discrimination. Here, consumers least willing to buy the good pay marginal cost, and the entire consumer surplus is extracted as profit.

Both our airline example and the example in Figure 14-11 can be used to make another point: a monopolist that can engage in perfect price discrimination doesn't cause any inefficiency! The reason is that the source of inefficiency is eliminated: there are no potential consumers who would be willing to purchase the good at a price equal to or above marginal cost but do not get the chance to do so. Instead, the monopolist manages to "scoop up" these consumers by offering them lower prices than it charges others.

Perfect price discrimination is probably never possible in practice. At a fundamental level, the inability to achieve perfect price discrimination is a problem of prices as economic signals, a phenomenon we noted in Chapter 13. When prices work as economic signals, they convey the information needed to ensure that all mutually beneficial transactions will indeed occur: the market price signals the seller's cost, and a

Perfect price discrimination takes place when a monopolist charges each consumer his or her willingness to pay—the maximum that consumer is willing to pay.

Figure 14-11   Price Discrimination

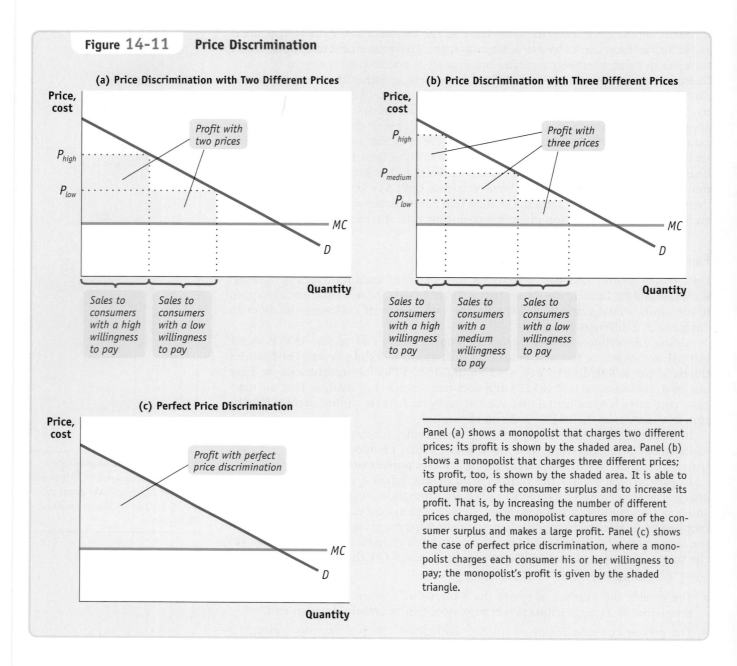

(a) Price Discrimination with Two Different Prices

Profit with two prices

P_{high}
P_{low}

MC

D

Price, cost

Quantity

Sales to consumers with a high willingness to pay | Sales to consumers with a low willingness to pay

(b) Price Discrimination with Three Different Prices

Profit with three prices

P_{high}
P_{medium}
P_{low}

MC

D

Price, cost

Quantity

Sales to consumers with a high willingness to pay | Sales to consumers with a medium willingness to pay | Sales to consumers with a low willingness to pay

(c) Perfect Price Discrimination

Profit with perfect price discrimination

MC

D

Price, cost

Quantity

Panel (a) shows a monopolist that charges two different prices; its profit is shown by the shaded area. Panel (b) shows a monopolist that charges three different prices; its profit, too, is shown by the shaded area. It is able to capture more of the consumer surplus and to increase its profit. That is, by increasing the number of different prices charged, the monopolist captures more of the consumer surplus and makes a large profit. Panel (c) shows the case of perfect price discrimination, where a monopolist charges each consumer his or her willingness to pay; the monopolist's profit is given by the shaded triangle.

consumer signals willingness to pay by purchasing the good whenever that willingness to pay is at least as high as the market price. The problem in reality, however, is that prices are often not perfect signals: a consumer's true willingness to pay can be disguised, as by a business traveler who claims to be a student when buying a ticket in order to obtain a lower fare. When such disguises work, a monopolist cannot achieve perfect price discrimination. However, monopolists do try to move in the direction of perfect price discrimination through a variety of pricing strategies. Common techniques for price discrimination include the following:

- *Advance purchase restrictions.* Prices are lower for those who purchase well in advance (or in some cases for those who purchase at the last minute). This separates those who are likely to shop for better prices from those who won't.

- *Volume discounts.* Often the price is lower if you buy a large quantity. For a consumer who plans to consume a lot of a good, the cost of the last unit—the marginal cost to the consumer—is considerably less than the average price. This separates those who plan to buy a lot and are therefore likely to be more sensitive to price from those who don't.

- *Two-part tariffs.* In a discount club like Sam's Club (which is not a monopolist but a monopolistic competitor), you pay an annual fee in addition to the cost of the items you purchase. So the cost of the first item you buy is in effect much higher than that of subsequent items, thereby making the two-part tariff behave like a volume discount.

Our discussion also helps explain why government policies on monopoly typically focus on preventing deadweight losses, not preventing price discrimination—unless it causes serious issues of equity. Compared to a single-price monopolist, price discrimination—even when it is not perfect—can increase the efficiency of the market. If sales to consumers formerly priced out of the market but now able to purchase the good at a lower price generate enough surplus to offset the loss in surplus to those now facing a higher price and no longer buying the good, then total surplus increases when price discrimination is introduced. An example of this might be a drug that is disproportionately prescribed to senior citizens, who are often on fixed incomes and so are very sensitive to price. A policy that allows a drug company to charge senior citizens a low price and everyone else a high price may indeed increase total surplus compared to a situation in which everyone is charged the same price. But price discrimination that creates serious concerns about equity is likely to be prohibited—for example, an ambulance service that charges patients based on the severity of their emergency.

economics in action

Sales, Factory Outlets, and Ghost Cities

Have you ever wondered why department stores occasionally hold sales, offering their merchandise for considerably less than the usual prices? Or why, driving along America's highways, you sometimes encounter clusters of "factory outlet" stores, often a couple of hours' drive from the nearest city? These familiar features of the economic landscape are actually rather peculiar if you think about them: why should sheets and towels be suddenly cheaper for a week each winter, or raincoats be offered for less in Freeport, Maine, than in Boston? In each case the answer is that the sellers—who are often oligopolists or monopolistic competitors—are engaged in a subtle form of price discrimination.

Why hold regular sales of sheets and towels? Stores are aware that some consumers buy these goods only when they discover that they need them; they are not likely to put a lot of effort into searching for the best price and so have a relatively low price elasticity of demand. So the store wants to charge high prices for customers who come in on an ordinary day. But shoppers who plan ahead, looking for the lowest price, will wait until there is a sale. So by scheduling such sales only now and then, the store is in effect able to discriminate between high-elasticity and low-elasticity customers.

An outlet store serves the same purpose: by offering merchandise for low prices, but only a considerable distance away from downtown, a seller is able to establish a separate market for those customers who are willing to make a significant effort to search out lower prices—and who therefore have a relatively high price elasticity of demand.

Finally, let's return to airline tickets to mention one of the truly odd features of their prices. Often a flight from one major destination to another—say, from Chicago to Los Angeles—is cheaper than a much shorter flight to a smaller city—say, from Chicago to Salt Lake City. Again, the reason is a difference in the price elasticity of demand: customers have a choice of many airlines between Chicago and Los Angeles, so the demand for any one flight is quite elastic; customers have very little choice in flights to a small city, so the demand is much less elastic.

But often there is a flight between two major destinations that makes a stop along the way—say, a flight from Chicago to Los Angeles with a stop in Salt Lake. In these cases, it is sometimes cheaper to fly to the more distant city than to the city that is a stop along the way. For example, it may be cheaper to purchase a ticket to Los Angeles and get off in Salt Lake City than to purchase a ticket to Salt Lake City! It sounds ridiculous but makes perfect sense given the logic of monopoly pricing.

So why don't passengers simply buy a ticket from Chicago to Los Angeles, but get off at Salt Lake? Well, some do—but the airlines, understandably, make it difficult for customers to find out about such "ghost cities." In addition, the airline will not allow you to check baggage only part of the way if you have a ticket for the final destination. (And airlines refuse to honor tickets for return flights when a passenger has not completed all the legs of the outbound flight.) All these restrictions are meant to enforce the separation of markets necessary to allow price discrimination. ■

< < < < < < < < < < < < < < < < < < < <

>>CHECK YOUR UNDERSTANDING 14-4

1. True or false? Explain your answer.
 a. A single-price monopolist sells to some customers that a price-discriminating monopolist refuses to.
 b. A price-discriminating monopolist creates more inefficiency than a single-price monopolist because it captures more of the consumer surplus.
 c. Under price discrimination, a customer with highly elastic demand will pay a lower price than a customer with inelastic demand.

2. Which of the following are cases of price discrimination and which are not? In the cases of price discrimination, identify the consumers with high and those with low price elasticity of demand.
 a. Damaged merchandise is marked down.
 b. Restaurants have senior citizen discounts.
 c. Food manufacturers place discount coupons for their merchandise in newspapers.
 d. Airline tickets cost more during the summer peak flying season.

Solutions appear at back of book.

• A LOOK AHEAD •

We've now taken one large step away from the world of perfect competition. As we have seen, a monopoly behaves quite differently from a perfectly competitive industry.

But pure monopoly is actually quite rare in the modern economy. More typical are industries in which there is some competition, but not perfect competition—that is, where there is *imperfect competition*. In the next two chapters we examine two types of imperfect competition: oligopoly and monopolistic competition.

You might expect an oligopoly to act something like a cross between a monopoly and a perfectly competitive industry, but it turns out that oligopoly raises issues that arise neither in perfect competition nor in monopoly, issues of *strategic interaction* and *collusion* between firms. Likewise, monopolistic competition creates yet another set of issues, such as tastes, product differentiation, and advertising.

SUMMARY

1. There are four main types of market structure based on number of firms in the industry and product differentiation: perfect competition, monopoly, oligopoly, and monopolistic competition.

2. A **monopolist** is a producer who is the sole supplier of a good without close substitutes. An industry controlled by a monopolist is a **monopoly.**

3. The key difference between a monopoly and a perfectly competitive industry is that an individual, perfectly competitive firm faces a horizontal demand curve but a monopolist faces a downward-sloping demand curve. This gives the monopolist **market power,** the ability to raise the market price by reducing output compared to a perfectly competitive industry.

4. To persist, a monopoly must be protected by a **barrier to entry.** This can take the form of control of natural resources or inputs, economies of scale that give rise to **natural monopoly,** technological advantage, or government rules that prevent entry by other firms.

5. The marginal revenue of a monopolist is composed of a quantity effect (the price received from the additional unit) and a price effect (the reduction in the price at which all units are sold). Because of the price effect, a monopolist's marginal revenue is always less than the market price, and the marginal revenue curve lies below the demand curve.

6. At the monopolist's profit-maximizing quantity of output, marginal cost equals marginal revenue, which is less than market price. At the perfectly competitive firm's profit-maximizing quantity of output, marginal cost equals the market price. So in comparison to perfectly competitive industries, monopolies produce less, charge higher prices, and earn higher profits in both the short run and the long run.

7. A monopoly creates deadweight loss by charging a price above marginal cost: the loss in consumer surplus exceeds the monopolist's profit. Thus monopolies are a source of market failure and should be prevented or broken up, except in the case of natural monopolies.

8. Natural monopolies can still cause deadweight losses. To limit these losses, governments sometimes impose **public ownership** and at other times impose **price regulation.** A price ceiling on a monopolist, as opposed to a perfectly competitive industry, need not cause shortages and can increase total surplus.

9. Not all monopolists are **single-price monopolists.** Monopolists, as well as oligopolists and monopolistic competitors, often engage in **price discrimination** to make higher profits, using various techniques to differentiate consumers based on their sensitivity to price and charging those with less elastic demand higher prices. A monopolist that achieves **perfect price discrimination** charges each consumer a price equal to his or her willingness to pay and captures the total surplus in the market. Although perfect price discrimination creates no inefficiency, it is practically impossible to implement.

KEY TERMS

Monopolist, p. 335
Monopoly, p. 335
Market power, p. 336
Barrier to entry, p. 337

Natural monopoly, p. 337
Public ownership, p. 349
Price regulation, p. 350
Single-price monopolist, p. 352

Price discrimination, p. 352
Perfect price discrimination, p. 355

PROBLEMS

1. Each of the following firms possesses market power. Explain its source.

   a. Merck, the producer of the patented cholesterol-lowering drug Zetia

   b. Verizon, a provider of local telephone service

   c. Chiquita, a supplier of bananas and owner of most banana plantations

2. Skyscraper City has a subway system, for which a one-way fare is $1.50. There is pressure on the mayor to reduce the fare by one-third, to $1.00. The mayor is dismayed, thinking that this will mean Skyscraper City is losing one-third of its revenue from sales of subway tickets. The mayor's economic adviser reminds her that she is focusing only on the price effect and ignoring the quantity effect. Explain why the mayor's estimate of a one-third loss of revenue is likely to be an overestimate. Illustrate with a diagram.

3. Consider an industry with the demand curve and marginal cost (MC) curve shown in the accompanying diagram. There is no fixed cost. If the industry is a single-price monopoly, the monopolist's marginal revenue curve would be MR. Answer the following questions by naming the appropriate points or areas.

   a. If the industry is perfectly competitive, what will be the total quantity produced? At what price?

b. Which area reflects consumer surplus under perfect competition?

c. If the industry is a single-price monopoly, what quantity will the monopolist produce? Which price will it charge?

d. Which area reflects the single-price monopolist's profit?

e. Which area reflects consumer surplus under single-price monopoly?

f. Which area reflects the deadweight loss to society from single-price monopoly?

g. If the monopolist can price-discriminate perfectly, what quantity will the perfectly price-discriminating monopolist produce?

4. Bob, Bill, Ben, and Brad Baxter have just made a documentary movie about their basketball team. They are thinking about making the movie available for download on the Internet, and they can act as a single-price monopolist if they choose to. Each time the movie is downloaded, their Internet service provider charges them a fee of $4. The Baxter brothers are arguing about which price to charge customers per download. The accompanying table shows the demand schedule for their film.

Price of download	Quantity of downloads demanded
$10	0
8	1
6	3
4	6
2	10
0	15

a. Calculate the total revenue and the marginal revenue per download.

b. Bob is proud of the film and wants as many people as possible to download it. Which price would he choose? How many downloads would be sold?

c. Bill wants as much total revenue as possible. Which price would he choose? How many downloads would be sold?

d. Ben wants to maximize profit. Which price would he choose? How many downloads would be sold?

e. Brad wants to charge the efficient price. Which price would he choose? How many downloads would be sold?

5. Jimmy has a room that overlooks, from some distance, a major league baseball stadium. He decides to rent a telescope for $50.00 a week and charge his friends and classmates to use it to peep at the game for 30 seconds. He can act as a single-price monopolist for renting out "peeps." For each person who takes a 30-second peep, it costs Jimmy $0.20 to clean the eyepiece. The accompanying table shows the information Jimmy has gathered about the demand for the service.

Price of peep	Quantity of peeps demanded
$1.20	0
1.00	100
0.90	150
0.80	200
0.70	250
0.60	300
0.50	350
0.40	400
0.30	450
0.20	500
0.10	550

a. For each price in the table, calculate the total revenue from selling peeps and the marginal revenue per peep.

b. At what quantity will Jimmy's profit be maximized? What price will he charge? What will his total profit be?

c. Jimmy's landlady complains about all the visitors coming into the building and tells Jimmy to stop selling peeps. Jimmy discovers, however, that if he gives the landlady $0.20 for every peep he sells, she will stop complaining. What effect does the $0.20-per-peep bribe have on Jimmy's marginal cost per peep? What is the new profit-maximizing quantity of peeps? What effect does the $0.20-per-peep bribe have on Jimmy's total profit?

6. Suppose that De Beers is a single-price monopolist in the market for diamonds. De Beers has five potential customers: Raquel, Jackie, Joan, Mia, and Sophia. Each of these customers will buy at most one diamond—and only if the price is just equal to, or lower than, her willingness to pay. Raquel's willingness to pay is $400; Jackie's, $300; Joan's, $200; Mia's, $100; and Sophia's, $0. De Beers's marginal cost per diamond is $100. This leads to the demand schedule for diamonds shown in the accompanying table.

Price of diamond	Quantity of diamonds demanded
$500	0
400	1
300	2
200	3
100	4
0	5

a. Calculate De Beers's total revenue and its marginal revenue. From your calculation, draw the demand curve and the marginal revenue curve.

b. Explain why De Beers faces a downward-sloping demand curve.

c. Explain why the marginal revenue from an additional diamond sale is less than the price of the diamond.

d. Suppose De Beers currently charges $200 for its diamonds. If it lowered the price to $100, how large is the price effect? How large is the quantity effect?

e. Draw the marginal cost curve into your diagram and determine which quantity maximizes De Beers's profit and which price De Beers will charge.

7. Use the demand schedule for diamonds given in Problem 6. The marginal cost of producing diamonds is constant at $100. There is no fixed cost.

a. If De Beers charges the monopoly price, how large is the individual consumer surplus that each buyer experiences? Calculate total consumer surplus by summing the individual consumer surpluses. How large is producer surplus?

Suppose that upstart Russian and Asian producers enter the market and the market becomes perfectly competitive.

b. What is the perfectly competitive price? What quantity will be sold in this perfectly competitive market?

c. At the competitive price and quantity, how large is the consumer surplus that each buyer experiences? How large is total consumer surplus? How large is producer surplus?

d. Compare your answer to part c to your answer to part a. How large is the deadweight loss associated with monopoly in this case?

8. Use the demand schedule for diamonds given in Problem 6. De Beers is a monopolist, but it can now price-discriminate perfectly among all five of its potential customers. De Beers's marginal cost is constant at $100. There is no fixed cost.

a. If De Beers can price-discriminate perfectly, to which customers will it sell diamonds and at what prices?

b. How large is each individual consumer surplus? How large is total consumer surplus? Calculate producer surplus by summing the producer surplus generated by each sale.

9. Download Records decides to release an album by the group Mary and the Little Lamb. It produces the album with no fixed cost, but the total cost of downloading an album to a CD and paying Mary her royalty is $6 per album. Download Records can act as a single-price monopolist. Its marketing division finds that the demand schedule for the album is as shown in the accompanying table.

Price of album	Quantity of albums demanded
$22	0
20	1,000
18	2,000
16	3,000
14	4,000
12	5,000
10	6,000
8	7,000

a. Calculate the total revenue and the marginal revenue per album.

b. The marginal cost of producing each album is constant at $6. To maximize profit, what level of output should Download Records choose, and which price should it therefore charge?

c. Mary renegotiates her contract and now needs to be paid a royalty of $14 per album. So the marginal cost rises to be constant at $14. To maximize profit, what level of output should Download Records now choose, and which price should it charge for each album?

10. The accompanying diagram illustrates your local electricity company's natural monopoly. The diagram shows the demand curve for kilowatt-hours (kWh) of electricity, the company's marginal revenue (MR) curve, the marginal cost (MC) curve, and its average total cost (ATC) curve. The government wants to regulate the monopolist by imposing a price ceiling.

a. If the government does not regulate this monopolist, which price will it charge? Illustrate the inefficiency this creates by shading the deadweight loss from monopoly.

b. If the government imposes a price ceiling equal to the marginal cost, $0.30, will the monopolist make profits or lose money? Shade the area of profit (or losses) for the monopolist. If the government does impose this price ceiling, do you think the firm will continue to produce in the long run?

c. If the government imposes a price ceiling of $0.50, will the monopolist make a profit or lose money?

11. The movie theater in Collegetown serves two kinds of customers: students and professors. There are 900 students and 100 professors in Collegetown. Each student's willingness to pay for a movie ticket is $5. Each professor's willingness to pay for a movie ticket is $10. Each will buy at most one ticket. The movie theater's marginal cost per ticket is constant at $3, and there is no fixed cost.

a. Suppose the movie theater cannot price-discriminate and needs to charge both students and professors the same price per ticket. If the movie theater charges $5, who will buy tickets and what will the movie theater's profit be? How large is consumer surplus?

b. If the movie theater charges $10, who will buy movie tickets and what will the movie theater's profit be? How large is consumer surplus?

c. Now suppose that, if it chooses to, the movie theater can price-discriminate between students and professors by requiring students to show their student ID. If the movie theater charges students $5 and professors $10, how much profit will the movie theater make? How large is consumer surplus?

12. A monopolist knows that if it expands the quantity of output it produces from 8 to 9 units, that will lower the price of its output from $2 to $1. Calculate the quantity effect and the price effect. Use these results to calculate the monopolist's marginal revenue of producing the 9th unit. The marginal cost of producing the 9th unit is positive. Is is a good idea for the monopolist to produce the 9th unit?

>web... To continue your study and review of concepts in this chapter, please visit the Krugman/Wells website for quizzes, animated graph tutorials, web links to helpful resources, and more.

www.worthpublishers.com/krugmanwells

>> Oligopoly

CAUGHT IN THE ACT

THE AGRICULTURAL PRODUCTS COMPANY Archer Daniels Midland (also known as ADM) likes to describe itself as "supermarket to the world." Its name is familiar to many Americans not only because of its important role in the economy but also because of its advertising and sponsorship of public television programs. But on October 25, 1993, ADM itself was on camera.

On that day executives from ADM and its Japanese competitor Ajinomoto met at the Marriott Hotel in Irvine, California, to discuss the market for lysine, an additive used in animal feed. (How is lysine produced? It's excreted by genetically engineered bacteria.) In this and subsequent meetings, the two companies joined with several other competitors to set targets for the market price of lysine. Each company agreed to limit its production in order to achieve those targets. Agreeing on specific limits would be their biggest challenge—or so they thought.

What the participants in the meeting didn't know was that they had a bigger problem: the FBI had bugged the room and was filming them with a camera hidden in a lamp.

What the companies were doing was illegal. To understand why it was illegal and why the companies were doing it anyway, we need to examine the issues posed by industries that are neither perfectly competitive nor pure monopolies. In this chapter we focus on *oligopoly*, an industry in which there are only a few producers. As we'll see, oligopoly is a very important reality—much more important, in fact, than monopoly and arguably more typical of modern economies than perfect competition.

Although much that we have learned about both perfect competition and monopoly is relevant to oligopoly, oligopoly

AP/Wide World Photos

The law catches up with a colluding oligopolist.

also raises some entirely new issues. Among other things, firms in an oligopoly are often tempted to engage in the kind of behavior that got ADM, Ajinomoto, and other lysine producers into trouble with the

What you will learn in this chapter:

➤ The meaning of **oligopoly,** and why it occurs

➤ Why **oligopolists** have an incentive to act in ways that reduce their combined profit, and why they can benefit from **collusion**

➤ How our understanding of oligopoly can be enhanced by using **game theory,** especially the concept of the **prisoners' dilemma**

➤ How repeated interactions among oligopolists can help them achieve **tacit collusion**

➤ How oligopoly works in practice, under the legal constraints of **antitrust policy** law. For example, in 2002 five of the largest music companies and three of the largest music retailers in the United States settled government charges that they worked together to keep the prices of CDs artificially high during the 1990s.

We will begin by examining what oligopoly is and why it is so important. Then we'll turn to the behavior of oligopolistic industries. Finally, we'll look at *antitrust policy*, which is primarily concerned with trying to keep oligopolies "well behaved."

The Prevalence of Oligopoly

At the time of that elaborately bugged meeting, no one company controlled the world lysine industry, but there were only a few major producers. An industry with only a few sellers is known as an **oligopoly**; a firm in such an industry is known as an **oligopolist**.

Oligopolists obviously compete with each other for sales. But ADM and Ajinomoto weren't like firms in a perfectly competitive industry, which take the price at which they can sell their product as given. Each of these firms knew that its decision about how much to produce would affect the market price. That is, like monopolists, each of the firms had some *market power*. So the competition in this industry wasn't "perfect."

Economists refer to a situation in which firms compete but also possess market power—which enables them to affect market prices—as **imperfect competition.** As we saw in Chapter 14, there are actually two important forms of imperfect competition: oligopoly and *monopolistic competition*. Of these, oligopoly is probably the more important in practice.

Although lysine is a multibillion-dollar business, it is not exactly a product familiar to most consumers. However, many familiar goods and services are supplied by only a few competing sellers, which means the industries in question are oligopolies. For example, most air routes are served by only two or three airlines: in recent years, regularly scheduled shuttle service between New York and either Boston or Washington, D.C. has been provided only by Delta and US Airways. Similarly, most long-distance telephone service is supplied by one of three carriers: AT&T, MCI, or Sprint. Most cola beverages are sold by Coca-Cola and Pepsi. This list could go on for many pages.

It's important to realize that an oligopoly isn't necessarily made up of large firms. What matters isn't size per se; the question is how many competitors there are. When a small town has only two grocery stores, grocery service there is just as much an oligopoly as air shuttle service between New York and Washington.

Why are oligopolies so prevalent? Essentially, oligopoly is the result of the same factors that sometimes produce monopoly, but in somewhat weaker form. Probably the most important source of oligopoly is the existence of *economies of scale*, which give bigger producers a cost advantage over smaller ones. When these economies of scale are very strong, they lead to monopoly, but when they are not that strong they lead to competition among a small number of firms. For example, larger grocery stores typically have lower costs than smaller stores. But the advantages of large scale taper off once grocery stores are reasonably large, which is why two or three stores often survive in small towns.

If oligopoly is so common, why has most of this book focused on competition in industries where the number of sellers is very

> An **oligopoly** is an industry with only a small number of producers. A producer in such an industry is known as an **oligopolist.**

> When no one firm has a monopoly, but producers nonetheless realize that they can affect market prices, an industry is characterized by **imperfect competition.**

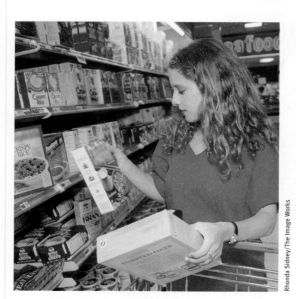

Froot Loops or Wheaties? Four firms control nearly 83 percent of the breakfast cereal market.

Rhonda Sidney/The Image Works

large? And why did we study monopoly, which is relatively uncommon, first? The answer has two parts. First, much of what we learn from the study of perfectly competitive markets—about costs, entry and exit, and efficiency—remains valid despite the fact that many industries are not perfectly competitive. Second, the analysis of oligopoly turns out to present some puzzles for which there is no easy solution. It is almost always a good idea—in exams and in life—first to deal with the questions you can answer, then to puzzle over the harder ones. We have simply followed the same strategy, developing the relatively clear-cut theories of perfect competition and monopoly first, and only then turning to the puzzles presented by oligopoly.

economics in action

Some Oligopolistic Industries

In practice, it is not always easy to determine an industry's market structure just by looking at the number of sellers. Many oligopolistic industries contain a number of small "niche" producers, which don't really compete with the major players. For example, the U.S. airline industry includes a number of regional airlines like Shuttle America, which flies propeller planes between places like Trenton, New Jersey, and Bedford, Massachusetts; if you count these carriers, the U.S. airline industry contains dozens of sellers, which doesn't sound like competition among a small group. But there are only a handful of national competitors like American and United, and on many routes, as we've seen, there are only two or three competitors.

To get a better picture of market structure, economists often use the "four-firm concentration ratio," which asks what share of industry sales is accounted for by the top four firms. (Why four? The federal government normally doesn't release data on share of industry sales by individual firms within the top four, lest it be accused of giving away corporate secrets.)

TABLE 15-1

Four-Firm Concentration Ratios

Industry	Concentration ratio	Largest firms
1. Cigarettes	98.9	Philip Morris, R. J. Reynolds, Lorillard, Brown and Williamson
2. Batteries	90.1	Duracell, Energizer, Rayovac
3. Breweries	89.7	Anheuser-Busch, Miller, Coors, Stroh's
4. Light bulbs	88.9	General Electric, Sylvania, Philips
5. Breakfast cereals	82.9	Kellogg's, General Mills, Post, Quaker Oats
6. Automobiles	79.5	General Motors, Ford, DaimlerChrysler

Source: U.S. Census Bureau.

Table 15-1 shows some industries with very high four-firm concentration ratios, along with the names of the largest firms in each industry. These names are familiar— not only because these are big companies but also because they advertise a lot. And that is not an accident. As we will see shortly, oligopolistic firms often choose *not* to compete much on price, trying to win customers in other ways—such as through ad campaigns. ∎

>> QUICK REVIEW

➤ In addition to perfect competition and monopoly, *oligopoly* and monopolistic competition are also important types of market structure. They are forms of *imperfect competition*.

➤ Oligopoly is a common market structure. It arises from the same forces that lead to monopoly, except in weaker form.

1. Explain why each of the following industries is an oligopoly, not a perfectly competitive industry.
   a. The world oil industry, where a few countries near the Persian Gulf control much of the world's oil reserves
   b. The microprocessor industry, where two firms, Intel and its bitter rival AMD, dominate the technology
   c. The wide-bodied passenger jet industry, composed of the American firm Boeing and the European firm Airbus, where production is characterized by extremely large fixed cost

Solutions appear at back of book.

Understanding Oligopoly

How much will a firm produce? Up to this point we have always answered: the quantity that maximizes its profit. The assumption that firms maximize profit is enough to determine their output when they are perfect competitors or when the industry is a monopoly.

When it comes to oligopoly, however, we run into some difficulties. Indeed, economists often describe the behavior of oligopolistic firms as a "puzzle."

A Duopoly Example

Let's begin looking at the puzzle of oligopoly with the simplest version, an industry in which there are only two producing firms—a **duopoly**—and each is known as a **duopolist.**

Going back to our opening story, imagine that ADM and Ajinomoto are the only two producers of lysine. To make things even simpler, suppose that once a company has incurred the fixed cost needed to produce lysine, the marginal cost of producing another pound is zero. So the companies are concerned only with the revenue they receive from sales.

Table 15-2 shows a hypothetical demand schedule for lysine and the total revenue of the industry at each price–quantity combination.

If this were a perfectly competitive industry, each firm would have an incentive to produce more as long as the market price was above marginal cost. Since the

> An oligopoly consisting of only two firms is a **duopoly.** Each firm is known as a **duopolist.**

TABLE 15-2

Demand Schedule for Lysine

Price of lysine (per pound)	Quantity of lysine demanded (millions of pounds)	Total revenue (millions)
$12	0	$0
11	10	110
10	20	200
9	30	270
8	40	320
7	50	350
6	60	360
5	70	350
4	80	320
3	90	270
2	100	200
1	110	110
0	120	0

marginal cost is assumed to be zero, this would mean that at equilibrium lysine would be provided free. Firms would produce until price equals zero, yielding a total output of 120 million pounds and zero revenue for all firms.

However, surely the firms would not be that stupid. With only two firms in the industry, each would realize that by producing more it would drive down the market price. So each firm would, like a monopolist, realize that profits would be higher if it limited its production.

So how much will the two firms produce?

One possibility is that the two companies will engage in **collusion**—they will cooperate to raise each other's profits. The strongest form of collusion is a **cartel,** an arrangement that determines how much each firm is allowed to produce. The world's most famous cartel is the Organization of Petroleum Exporting Countries, described in Economics in Action on page 377. As its name indicates, it's actually an agreement among governments rather than firms. There's a reason this most famous of cartels is an agreement among governments: cartels among firms are illegal in the United States and many other jurisdictions. But let's ignore the law for a moment (which is, of course, what ADM and Ajinomoto did in real life—to their own detriment).

So suppose that ADM and Ajinomoto were to form a cartel and that this cartel decided to act as if it were a monopolist, maximizing total industry profits. It's obvious from Table 15-2 that in order to maximize the combined profits of the firms, this cartel should set total industry output at 60 million pounds of lysine, which would sell at a price of $6 per pound, leading to revenue of $360 million, the maximum possible. Then the only question would be how much of that 60 million pounds each firm gets to produce. A "fair" solution might be for each firm to produce 30 million pounds.

But even if the two firms agreed on such a deal, they might have a problem: each of the firms would have an incentive to break its word and produce more than the agreed-upon quantity.

> Sellers engage in **collusion** when they cooperate to raise each others' profits. A **cartel** is an agreement by several producers that increases their combined profits by telling each one how much to produce.

Collusion and Competition

Suppose that the presidents of ADM and Ajinomoto were to agree that each would produce 30 million pounds of lysine over the next year. Both would understand that this plan maximizes their combined profits. And both would have an incentive to cheat.

To see why, consider what would happen if Ajinomoto honored its agreement, producing only 30 million pounds, but ADM ignored its promise and produced 40 million pounds. This increase in total output would drive the price down from $6 to $5 per pound, the price at which 70 million pounds are demanded. The industry's total revenue would fall from $360 million ($6 × 60 million pounds) to $350 million ($5 × 70 million pounds). However, ADM's revenue would *rise*, from $180 million to $200 million. Since we are assuming a marginal cost of zero, this would mean a $20 million increase in ADM's profits.

But Ajinomoto's president might make exactly the same calculation. And if *both* firms were to produce 40 million pounds of lysine, the price would drop to $4 per pound. So each firm's profits would fall, from $180 million to $160 million.

Why do individual firms have an incentive to produce more than the quantity that maximizes their joint profits? Because neither firm has as strong an incentive to limit its output as a true monopolist would.

Let's go back for a minute to the theory of monopoly. We know that a profit-maximizing monopolist sets marginal cost (which in this case is zero) equal to marginal revenue. But what is marginal revenue? Producing an additional unit of a good has two effects:

1. A positive *quantity* effect: one more unit is sold, increasing total revenue by the price at which that unit is sold.

2. A negative *price* effect: in order to sell one more unit, the monopolist must cut the market price on *all* units sold.

The negative price effect is the reason marginal revenue for a monopolist is less than the market price. But when considering the effect of increasing production, a firm is concerned only with the price effect on its own units of output, not those of its fellow oligopolists. Both ADM and Ajinomoto suffer a negative price effect if ADM decides to produce extra lysine and so drives down the price. But ADM cares only about the negative price effect on the units it produces, not about the loss to Ajinomoto.

This tells us that an individual firm in an oligopoly faces a smaller price effect from an additional unit of output than a monopolist; therefore, the marginal revenue that such a firm calculates is higher. So it will seem to be profitable for any one company in an oligopoly to increase production, even if that increase reduces the profits of the industry as a whole. But if everyone thinks that way, the result is that everyone earns a lower profit!

Until now, we have been able to analyze producer behavior by asking what a producer should do to maximize profits. But even if ADM and Ajinomoto are both trying to maximize profits, what does this predict about their behavior? Will they engage in collusion, reaching and holding to an agreement that maximizes their combined profits? Or will they engage in **noncooperative behavior,** with each firm acting in its own self-interest, even though this has the effect of driving down everyone's profits? Both strategies sound like profit maximization. Which will actually describe their behavior?

Now you see why oligopoly presents a puzzle: there are only a small number of players, making collusion a real possibility. If there were dozens or hundreds of firms, it would be safe to assume they would behave noncooperatively. When there are only a handful of firms in an industry, however, it's hard to determine whether collusion will actually materialize.

Since collusion is ultimately more profitable than noncooperative behavior, firms have an incentive to collude if they can. One way to do so is to formalize it—sign an agreement (maybe even make a legal contract) or establish some financial incentives for the companies to set their prices high. But in the United States and many other nations, you can't do that—at least not legally. Companies cannot make a legal contract to keep prices high: not only is the contract unenforceable, but writing it is a one-way ticket to jail. Neither can they sign a gentlemen's agreement, which lacks the force of law but perhaps exerts moral force—that's illegal, too. In fact, executives from rival companies rarely meet without lawyers present, who make sure that the conversation does not stray into inappropriate territory. Even hinting at how nice it would be if prices were higher can bring you an unwelcome interview with the Justice Department or the Federal Trade Commission, both of which enforce the laws against oligopolistic collusion. For example, at the time of writing, the Justice Department had begun to consider whether to open a formal inquiry into a series of meetings held between Monsanto and Pioneer Hi-Bred International, two companies that account for 60 percent of the U.S. market in maize and soybean seed. The two companies, parties to a licensing agreement involving genetically modified seed, claimed that no illegal discussions of price fixing occurred in those meetings. But the fact that the two firms discussed prices as part of the licensing agreement is enough to ensure, according to some experts, that a formal investigation will eventually be launched.

Sometimes, as we've seen, oligopolists just ignore the rules. But more often they find ways to achieve collusion without a formal agreement. As we'll see in the next section, one important factor in determining how hard it is to achieve collusion without a formal agreement is how easy it is for a firm to increase its output quickly in order to capture sales from its rival.

Competing in Prices versus Competing in Quantities

In our duopoly example, we've assumed that firms choose a quantity of output and sell that output at whatever the market price turns out to be. That's actually a pretty good description of the way the lysine market works. But in other industries, such as automobiles, firms don't choose a level of output; they choose a *price* and sell as much as they can at that price. Does this make any difference?

Yes, it does, at least when we analyze noncooperative behavior. In choosing what to do, an oligopolist must always be concerned about whether a noncooperative rival firm will respond by *undercutting* her. The oligopolist must be concerned that a rival firm will take some action that allows it to steal some of her sales and capture a larger share of the market. And, it turns out, the answer to whether a rival is willing to engage in undercutting behavior depends on how difficult it is for him to increase output to satisfy the additional customers he gains by his undercutting.

Let's consider a hypothetical example using Airbus and Boeing, duopolists in the large passenger aircraft industry, to gain some intuition. For these firms, deciding their production capacity—how much output they can produce over, say, the next two or three years—is their most important decision. Why? Passenger aircraft are very large and are built in batches, a few planes at a time, in huge hangars. The determining factor in how many planes can be built at any given time is the size of the company's existing production facilities, which can take years to build.

So this means that when Airbus, for example, sets its maximum production capacity at 50 planes per year, Boeing can feel comfortably assured that Airbus won't easily be able to increase this number anytime soon. This, in turn, has important implications for Boeing's actions. If Boeing also sets its production capacity at 50 planes per year, it can safely assume that Airbus's production capacity is *given* and that, as a result, the market will be split 50–50 between the two manufacturers. Airbus won't be able to quickly increase its output and steal some of Boeing's customers by offering them a lower price. The end result is that the total output of the industry is less than the output under perfect competition, and each firm earns a profit. Economists refer to this kind of behavior as *quantity competition* or *Cournot behavior,* after the nineteenth-century French economist who devised the model. The basic insight of the Cournot model is that when firms are restricted in how much they can produce, it is easier for them to avoid excessive competition and to "divvy up" the market, thereby pricing above marginal cost and earning profits. It is easier for them to achieve an outcome that looks like collusion without a formal agreement.

But how does the behavior of oligopolists change when they are not constrained by limited production capacity? Let's assume that American Airlines and British Airways are duopolists and that they have exclusive rights to fly the Chicago–London route. When the economy is strong and lots of people want to fly between Chicago and London, American Airlines and British Airways are likely to find the number of passengers they can carry constrained by their production capacity—for example, the number of landing slots available. So in this environment they are likely to behave according to the Cournot model and price above marginal cost—say, charging $800 per round trip. But when the business climate is poor, the two airlines are likely to find that they have lots of empty seats at a fare of $800 and that capacity constraints are no longer an issue. What will they do?

Recent history tells us they will engage in a price war by slashing ticket prices. They are no longer able to maintain Cournot behavior because at the ticket price of $800, each has excess capacity. If American Airlines were to try to maintain a price of $800, it would soon find itself undercut by British Airways, which would charge $750 and steal all its customers. In turn, American Airlines would undercut British Airways by charging $700—and so on. As long as each firm finds that it can make additional sales by cutting price, each will continue cutting until price is equal to marginal cost. (Going any lower would cause them to incur an avoidable loss.) This type of behavior is known as *price competition* or *Bertrand* behavior, after another nineteenth-century French economist. The logic behind the Bertrand model is that when firms produce perfect substitutes and have sufficient capacity to satisfy demand when price is equal to marginal cost, then each firm will be compelled to engage in competition by undercutting its rival's price until the price reaches marginal cost—that is, perfect competition.

Oligopolists would, understandably, prefer to avoid Bertrand behavior because it earns them zero profits. Lacking an environment that imposes constraints on their output capacity, firms try other means to avoid direct price competition—such as producing products that are not perfect substitutes but are instead differentiated. We'll examine this strategy in more detail later in this chapter, just noting here that producing differentiated products allows oligopolists to cultivate a loyal set of customers and to charge prices higher than marginal cost.

Even in the absence of limitations on production capacity, firms are often able to maintain collusive behavior (although it may be somewhat harder to do). In the next section, we'll see why such informal collusion often works but sometimes fails.

economics in action

The Great Vitamin Conspiracy

It was a bitter pill to swallow. In late 1999 some of the world's largest drug companies (mainly European and Japanese) agreed to pay billions of dollars in damages to customers after being convicted of a huge conspiracy to rig the world vitamin market.

The conspiracy began in 1989 when the Swiss company Roche and the German company BASF began secret talks about raising prices for vitamins. Soon a French company, Rhone-Poulenc, joined in, followed by several Japanese companies and other companies around the world. The members of the group, which referred to itself as "Vitamins Inc.," met regularly—sometimes at hotels, sometimes at the private homes of executives—to set prices and divide up markets for "bulk" vitamins (like vitamin A, vitamin C, and so on). These bulk vitamins are sold mainly to other companies, such as animal feed makers, food producers, and so on, which include them in their products. Indeed, it was the animal feed companies that grew suspicious about the prices they were being charged, which led to a series of investigations. The case eventually broke open when Rhone-Poulenc made a deal with U.S. officials to provide evidence about the conspiracy. The French company was concerned that rumors about price-fixing would lead U.S. officials to block its planned merger with another company.

This was a huge conspiracy—it makes the lysine case look like, well, chicken feed. How could it have happened?

The main answer probably lies in different national traditions about how to treat oligopolists. The United States has a long tradition of taking tough legal action against price-fixing, as we have just described. European governments, however, have historically been much less stringent. Indeed, in the past some European governments have actually encouraged major companies to form cartels. Modern European law on competition is not that different from that in the United States, but the European cultural tradition of viewing conspiracies to raise prices as normal business practice has not entirely died out. ∎

< < < < < < < < < < < < < < < < < <

> > QUICK REVIEW

➤ Some of the key issues in oligopoly can be understood by looking at the simplest case, a *duopoly*.

➤ By acting as if they were a single monopolist, oligopolists can maximize their combined profits. So there is an incentive to form a *cartel*.

➤ However, each firm has an incentive to cheat—to produce more than it is supposed to under the cartel agreement. So there are two principal outcomes: successful *collusion* or behaving *noncooperatively* by cheating.

➤ It is likely to be easier to achieve informal collusion when firms in an industry face capacity constraints.

> > CHECK YOUR UNDERSTANDING 15-2

1. Which of the following factors increase the likelihood that an oligopolist will collude with other firms in the industry? The likelihood that an oligopolist will act noncooperatively and raise output? Explain your answers.
   a. The firm's initial market share is small.
   b. The firm has a cost advantage over its rivals.
   c. The firm's customers face additional costs when they switch from the use of one firm's product to another firm's product.
   d. The firm and its rivals are currently operating at maximum production capacity, which cannot be altered in the short run.

Solutions appear at back of book.

Games Oligopolists Play

In our duopoly example and in real life, each oligopolist realizes both that its profit depends on what its competitor does and that its competitor's profit depends on what it does. That is, the two firms are in a situation of **interdependence.**

In effect, the two firms are playing a "game" in which the profit of each player depends not only on its own actions but on those of the other player. The area of study of such games, known as **game theory,** has many applications, not just to economics but also to military strategy, politics, and other social sciences.

Let's see how game theory helps us understand oligopoly.

> When the decisions of two or more firms significantly affect each others' profits, they are in a situation of **interdependence.**
>
> The study of behavior in situations of interdependence is known as **game theory.**

The Prisoners' Dilemma

Game theory deals with any situation in which the reward to any one player—the **pay-off**—depends not only on his or her own actions but also on those of other players in the game. In the case of oligopolists, the payoff is simply each firm's profit.

When there are only two players, as in a duopoly, the interdependence between the players can be represented with a **payoff matrix** like that shown in Figure 15-1. Each row corresponds to an action by one player (in this case, ADM); each column corresponds to an action by the other (in this case, Ajinomoto). For simplicity, let's assume that ADM can pick only one of two alternatives: produce 30 million pounds of lysine or produce 40 million pounds. Ajinomoto has the same pair of choices.

The matrix contains four boxes, each divided by a diagonal line. Each box shows the payoff to the two firms that results from a pair of choices; the number below the diagonal shows ADM's profits, the number above the diagonal shows Ajinomoto's profits.

These payoffs show what we concluded from our earlier analysis: the combined profit of the two firms is maximized if they each produce 30 million pounds. Either firm can, however, increase its own profits by producing 40 million pounds while the

> The reward received by a player in a game, such as the profit earned by an oligopolist, is that player's **payoff.**
>
> A **payoff matrix** shows how the payoff to each of the participants in a two-player game depends on the actions of both. Such a matrix helps us analyze interdependence.

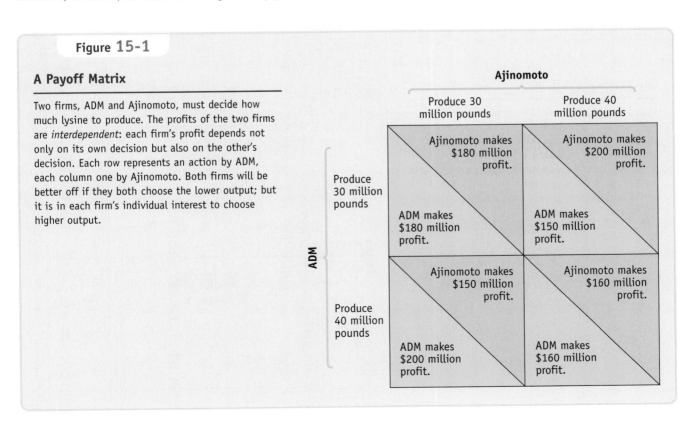

Figure 15-1

A Payoff Matrix

Two firms, ADM and Ajinomoto, must decide how much lysine to produce. The profits of the two firms are *interdependent*: each firm's profit depends not only on its own decision but also on the other's decision. Each row represents an action by ADM, each column one by Ajinomoto. Both firms will be better off if they both choose the lower output; but it is in each firm's individual interest to choose higher output.

		Ajinomoto	
		Produce 30 million pounds	Produce 40 million pounds
ADM	Produce 30 million pounds	Ajinomoto makes $180 million profit. / ADM makes $180 million profit.	Ajinomoto makes $200 million profit. / ADM makes $150 million profit.
	Produce 40 million pounds	Ajinomoto makes $150 million profit. / ADM makes $200 million profit.	Ajinomoto makes $160 million profit. / ADM makes $160 million profit.

other produces only 30 million pounds. But if both produce the larger quantity, both will have lower profits than if they had both held their output down.

The particular situation shown here is a version of a famous—and seemingly paradoxical—case of interdependence that appears in many contexts. Known as the **prisoners' dilemma,** it is a type of game in which the payoff matrix implies the following:

- Each player has an incentive, regardless of what the other player does, to cheat—to take an action that benefits him or her at the other's expense.
- When both players cheat, both are worse off than they would have been if neither had cheated.

The original illustration of the prisoners' dilemma occurred in a fictional story about two accomplices in crime—let's call them Thelma and Louise—who have been caught by the police. The police have enough evidence to put them behind bars for 5 years. They also know that the pair have committed a more serious crime, one that carries a 20-year sentence; unfortunately, they don't have enough evidence to convict the women on that charge. To do so, they would need each of the prisoners to implicate the other in the second crime.

So the police put the miscreants in separate cells and say the following to each: "Here's the deal: If neither of you confesses, you know that we'll send you to jail for 5 years. If you confess and implicate your partner, and she doesn't do the same, we'll reduce your sentence from 5 years to 2. But if your partner confesses and you don't, you'll get the maximum 20 years. And if both of you confess, we'll give you both 15 years."

Figure 15-2 shows the payoffs that face the prisoners, depending on the decision of each to remain silent or to confess. (Usually the payoff matrix reflects the players' payoffs, and higher payoffs are better than lower payoffs. This case is an exception: a higher number of years in prison is bad, not good!) Let's assume that the prisoners have no way to communicate and that they have not sworn an oath not to harm each other or anything of that sort. So each acts in her own self-interest. What will they do?

Prisoners' dilemma is a game based on two premises: (1) Each player has an incentive to choose an action that benefits him or herself at the other player's expense. (2) When both players act in this way, both are worse off than if they had chosen different actions.

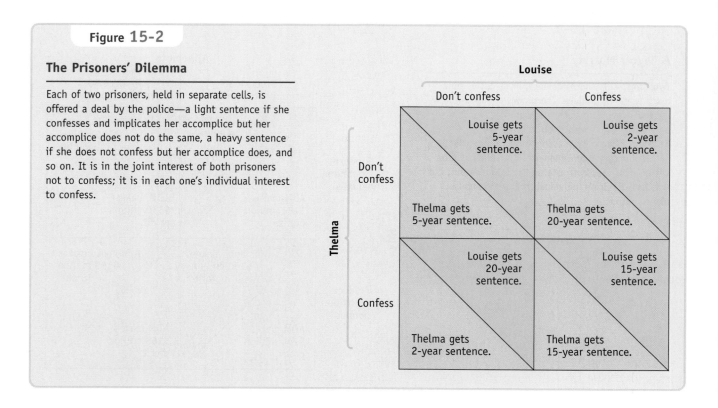

Figure 15-2

The Prisoners' Dilemma

Each of two prisoners, held in separate cells, is offered a deal by the police—a light sentence if she confesses and implicates her accomplice but her accomplice does not do the same, a heavy sentence if she does not confess but her accomplice does, and so on. It is in the joint interest of both prisoners not to confess; it is in each one's individual interest to confess.

The answer is clear: both will confess. Look at it first from Thelma's point of view: she is better off confessing, regardless of what Louise does. If Louise doesn't confess, Thelma's confession reduces her own sentence from 5 years to 2. If Louise *does* confess, Thelma's confession reduces her sentence from 20 to 15 years. Either way, it's clearly in Thelma's interest to confess. And because she faces the same incentives, it's clearly in Louise's interest to confess, too. To confess in this situation is a type of action that economists call a *dominant strategy*. An action is a **dominant strategy** when it is the player's best action regardless of what action the other player takes. It's important to note that not all games have a dominant strategy—it depends on the structure of payoffs in the game. But in the case of Thelma and Louise, it is clearly in the interest of the police to structure the payoffs so that confessing is a dominant strategy for each person. So as long as the two prisoners have no way to make an enforceable agreement that neither will confess (something they can't do if they can't communicate, and the police certainly won't allow them to do because the police want to compel each one to confess), Thelma and Louise will each act in a way that hurts the other.

So if each prisoner acts rationally in her own interest, both will confess. Yet if neither of them had confessed, both would have received a much lighter sentence! In a prisoners' dilemma, each player has a clear incentive to act in a way that hurts the other player—but when both make that choice, it leaves both of them worse off.

When Thelma and Louise both confess, they reach an *equilibrium* of the game. We have used the concept of equilibrium many times in this book; it is an outcome in which no individual or firm has any incentive to change his or her action. In game theory, this kind of equilibrium, in which each player takes the action that is best for her given the actions taken by other players, and vice versa, is known as a **Nash equilibrium,** after the mathematician and Nobel Laureate John Nash. (Nash's life was chronicled in the best-selling biography *A Beautiful Mind*, which was made into a movie.) Because the players in a Nash equilibrium do not take into account the effect of their actions on others, this is also known as a **noncooperative equilibrium.**

Now look back at Figure 15-1; ADM and Ajinomoto are in the same situation as Thelma and Louise. Each firm is better off producing the higher output, regardless of what the other firm does. Yet if both produce 40 million pounds, both are worse off than if they had followed their agreement and produced only 30 million pounds. In both cases, then, the pursuit of individual self-interest—the effort to maximize profits or to minimize jail time—has the perverse effect of hurting both players.

Prisoners' dilemmas appear in many situations. The For Inquiring Minds on page 374 describes an example from the days of the Cold War. Clearly, the players in any prisoners' dilemma would be better off if they had some way of enforcing cooperative behavior—if Thelma and Louise had both sworn to a code of silence, or if ADM and Ajinomoto had signed an enforceable agreement not to produce more than 30 million pounds of lysine.

But in the United States an agreement setting the output levels of two oligopolists isn't just unenforceable, it's illegal. So it seems that the undesirable noncooperative equilibrium is the only possible outcome. Or is it?

Overcoming the Prisoners' Dilemma: Repeated Interaction and Tacit Collusion

Thelma and Louise in their cells are playing what is known as a *one-shot* game—that is, they play the game with each other only once. They get to choose once and for all whether to confess or hang tough, and that's it. However, most of the games that

An action is a **dominant strategy** when it is a player's best action regardless of the action taken by the other player.

A **Nash equilibrium,** also known as a **noncooperative equilibrium,** is the result when each player in a game chooses the action that maximizes his or her payoff given the actions of other players, ignoring the effects of his or her action on the payoffs received by those other players.

FOR INQUIRING MINDS

PRISONERS OF THE ARMS RACE

Between World War II and the late 1980s, the United States and the Soviet Union were locked in a seemingly endless struggle that never broke out into open war. During this Cold War, both countries spent huge sums on arms, sums that were a significant drain on the U.S. economy and eventually proved a crippling burden for the Soviet Union, whose underlying economic base was much weaker. Yet neither country was ever able to achieve a decisive military advantage.

As many people pointed out, both nations would have been better off if they had both spent less on arms. Yet the arms race continued for 40 years.

Why? As political scientists were quick to notice, one way to explain the arms race was to suppose that the two countries were locked in a classic prisoners' dilemma. Each government would have

TASS/Soufoto

Caught in the prisoners' dilemma: heavy military spending hastened the collapse of the Soviet Union.

liked to achieve decisive military superiority, and each feared military inferiority. But both would have preferred a stalemate with low military spending to one with high spending. However, each government rationally chose to engage in high spending. If its rival did not spend heavily, this would lead to military superiority; *not* spending heavily would lead to inferiority if the other government continued its arms buildup. So the countries were trapped.

The answer to this trap could have been an agreement not to spend as much; indeed, the two sides tried repeatedly to negotiate limits on some kinds of weapons. But these agreements weren't very effective. In the end the issue was resolved as heavy military spending hastened the collapse of the Soviet Union in 1991.

---

oligopolists play aren't one-shot; instead, they expect to play the game repeatedly with the same competitors. An oligopolist usually expects to be in business for many years, and it knows that its decision today about whether to cheat is likely to affect the way other firms treat it in the future. So a smart oligopolist doesn't just decide what to do based on the effect on profit in the short run. Instead, he or she engages in **strategic behavior,** taking account of the effects of the action he or she chooses today on the future actions of other players in the game. And under some conditions oligopolists that behave strategically can manage to behave as if they had a formal agreement to collude.

Suppose that ADM and Ajinomoto expect to be in the lysine business for many years and therefore expect to play the game of cheat versus collude shown in Figure 15-1 many times. Would they really betray each other time and again?

Probably not. Suppose that ADM considers two strategies. In one strategy it always cheats, producing 40 million pounds of lysine each year, regardless of what Ajinomoto does. In the other strategy, it starts off with good behavior, producing only 30 million pounds in the first year, and watches to see what its rival does. If Ajinomoto also keeps its production down, ADM will stay cooperative, producing 30 million pounds again for the next year. But if Ajinomoto produces 40 million pounds, ADM will take the gloves off and also produce 40 million pounds next year. This latter strategy—start off behaving cooperatively, but thereafter do whatever the other player did in the previous period—is generally known as **tit for tat**.

"Tit for tat" is a form of strategic behavior, which we have just defined as behavior intended to influence the future actions of other players. "Tit for tat" offers a reward to the other player for cooperative behavior—if you behave cooperatively, so will I. It also provides a punishment for cheating—if you cheat, don't expect me to be nice in the future.

The payoff to ADM of each of these strategies would depend on which strategy Ajinomoto chooses. Consider the four possibilities, shown in Figure 15-3:

A firm engages in **strategic behavior** when it attempts to influence the future behavior of other firms.

A strategy of **tit for tat** involves playing cooperatively at first, then doing whatever the other player did in the previous period.

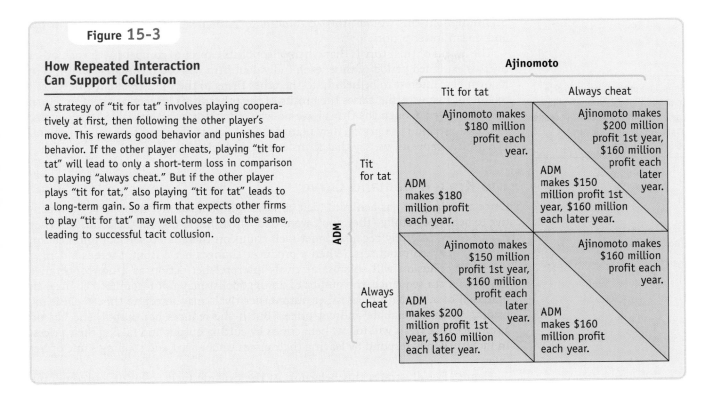

Figure 15-3

How Repeated Interaction Can Support Collusion

A strategy of "tit for tat" involves playing cooperatively at first, then following the other player's move. This rewards good behavior and punishes bad behavior. If the other player cheats, playing "tit for tat" will lead to only a short-term loss in comparison to playing "always cheat." But if the other player plays "tit for tat," also playing "tit for tat" leads to a long-term gain. So a firm that expects other firms to play "tit for tat" may well choose to do the same, leading to successful tacit collusion.

1. If ADM plays "tit for tat" and so does Ajinomoto, both firms will make a profit of $180 million each year.

2. If ADM plays "always cheat" but Ajinomoto plays "tit for tat," ADM makes a profit of $200 million the first year but only $160 million per year thereafter.

3. If ADM plays "tit for tat" but Ajinomoto plays "always cheat," ADM makes a profit of only $150 million in the first year but $160 million per year thereafter.

4. If ADM plays "always cheat" and Ajinomoto does the same, both firms will make a profit of $160 million each year.

Which strategy is better? In the first year, ADM does better playing "always cheat," whatever its rival's strategy: it assures itself that it will get either $200 million or $160 million (which of the two payoffs it actually receives depends upon whether Ajinomoto plays "always cheat" or "tit for tat"). This is better than what it would get in the first year if it played "tit for tat": either $180 million or $150 million. But by the second year, a strategy of "always cheat" gains ADM only $160 million per year for the second and all subsequent years, regardless of Ajinomoto's actions. This amount is inferior to the amount ADM would gain by playing "tit for tat": for the second and all subsequent years, it would never get any less than $160 million and would get as much as $180 million if Ajinomoto played "tit for tat" as well. So which strategy is more profitable depends on two things: how many years ADM expects to play the game and what strategy its rival follows.

If ADM expects the lysine business to end in the near future, it is in effect playing a one-shot game. So it might as well grab what it can. Even if ADM expects to remain in the lysine business for many years (therefore to find itself repeatedly playing this game with Ajinomoto) and expects, for some reason, Ajinomoto always to cheat, it should also always cheat. That is, ADM should follow the old rule "Do unto others before they do unto you."

But if ADM expects to be in the business for a long time and thinks Ajinomoto is likely to play "tit for tat," it will make more profits over the long run by playing "tit for tat," too. It could have made some extra short-term profits by cheating at the beginning, but this would provoke Ajinomoto into cheating too, and would, in the end, mean lower profits.

The lesson of this story is that when oligopolists expect to compete with each other over an extended period of time, each individual firm will often conclude that it is in its own best interest to be helpful to the other firms in the industry. So it will restrict its output in a way that raises the profits of the other firms, expecting them to return the favor. Even though the firms have no way of making an enforceable agreement to limit output and raise prices, they manage to act "as if" they had such an agreement. When this happens, we say that firms engage in **tacit collusion.**

> When firms limit production and raise prices in a way that raises each others' profits, even though they have not made any formal agreement, they are engaged in **tacit collusion**.

The Kinked Demand Curve

Once an oligopoly has achieved tacit collusion, individual producers have an incentive to behave carefully—they don't want to do anything to disrupt the collusion. They must behave carefully because under tacit collusion there is no safe communication channel between producers. When a producer changes her output, there is a danger that tacit collusion will collapse as rivals interpret her action as a noncooperative move. As a consequence, the output of an oligopolist may not respond to changes in marginal cost. If she increases her output, her rivals may interpret this as cheating, leading them to retaliate and cut prices. But if she reduces her output, she has no assurance that rivals will follow her actions by cutting output and raising their prices. In fact, they may respond by leaving their prices unchanged and stealing some of her sales.

Figure 15-4 illustrates this behavior. At the original tacit collusion outcome, the oligopolist produces the quantity Q^* and receives the price P^*, located on her demand curve, D. This demand curve shows how the price she receives for her good varies as she changes her output. As you can see, this demand curve has a special shape—it is *kinked* at the price and quantity combination associated with the tacit collusion outcome, P^* and Q^*.

Figure 15-4

The Kinked Demand Curve

This oligopolist believes that her demand curve is kinked at the tacit collusion price and quantity levels, P^* and Q^*. That is, she believes that if she increases her output and lowers her price her rivals will retaliate, increasing their output and lowering their prices as well, leading to only a small gain in sales. So her demand curve is very steep to the right of Q^*. But the oligopolist believes that if she lowers her output and raises her price her rivals will refuse to reciprocate and will steal a substantial number of her customers, leading to a large fall in sales. So her demand curve is very flat to the left of Q^*. The kink in the demand curve leads to the break XY in the marginal revenue curve. As shown by the marginal cost curves, MC_1 and MC_2, any marginal cost curve that lies within the break leads the oligopolist to produce the same output level, Q^*. So starting at the tacit collusion outcome, changes in marginal cost within a certain range will leave the firm's output unchanged. But large changes in marginal cost—changes that cause the marginal cost curve to cut the marginal revenue curve in the segment WX or the segment YZ—will lead to changes in output. **>web...**

On one side, the demand curve slopes steeply downward at output quantities greater than Q^*. The reason is that the oligopolist believes that if she produces more than Q^*, and lowers her price, she will gain very few sales because her rivals will retaliate by also producing more and cutting their prices.

On the other side, the demand curve is very flat. If the oligopolist reduces her output below Q^*, she does not expect rivals to reduce their output as well. Consequently, she will lose a relatively large number of sales if she lowers her output and raises her price as her rivals capture a substantial share of her customers. You might ask why the industry can't reestablish tacit collusion at a higher price and lower output after our oligopolist cuts her output and raises her price. It is possible, but by no means assured, that the industry can reestablish tacit collusion. So it is reasonable for an oligopolist to fear that tacit collusion will not be reestablished and to behave as if her demand curve is kinked as in Figure 15-4.

Now that we have explained the source of the oligopolist's **kinked demand curve,** let's examine how this affects her response to a change in marginal cost. The kink in the demand curve D generates a break in the oligopolist's marginal revenue curve, MR, shown by the gap between the points X and Y. Two marginal cost curves pass through that break in the marginal revenue curve: MC_1 corresponds to a situation of higher marginal cost, and MC_2 corresponds to a situation of lower marginal cost.

Recall that according to the optimal output rule, a firm will maximize profits by producing the output quantity at which marginal revenue is equal to marginal cost. But given the break between X and Y in the oligopolist's marginal revenue curve, any marginal cost curves that lie within that break—like MC_1 and MC_2—will generate the same output quantity, Q^*. To put it in a slightly different way, starting from the tacit collusive output quantity Q^*, the oligopolist's output level is unresponsive to changes in marginal cost within a certain range. If marginal cost falls substantially, the oligopolist is more likely to risk a breakdown in collusion and increase her output; in this case, the marginal cost curve cuts the marginal revenue curve in the segment YZ. And if marginal cost rises substantially, shifting the marginal cost curve up so that it cuts the marginal revenue curve in the segment WX, then the oligopolist is likely to reduce output and raise her price despite the risk of losing significant sales to rivals. But if marginal cost changes within a limited range—the range defined by XY—the producer will leave her output quantity unchanged rather than risk a breakdown in tacit collusion.

The behavior described by the kinked demand curve appears justified when a producer believes that she alone is facing a change in marginal cost—that is, when the change is unique to her. But when the change in marginal cost is clearly shared throughout the industry, this behavior is much less plausible. In that case, each producer knows that a change in a rival's output quantity and price is just a response to a change in the general level of marginal cost, not a hostile act of noncooperation. Consequently, all the producers in the industry are likely to respond to a change in marginal cost by adjusting their output and prices and thereby maintain collusion.

> An oligopolist who believes she will lose a substantial number of sales if she reduces output and increases her price but will gain only a few additional sales if she increases output and lowers her price, away from the tacit collusion outcome, faces a **kinked demand curve.**

economics in action

The Rise and Fall and Rise of OPEC

Call it the cartel that does not need to meet in secret. The Organization of Petroleum Exporting Countries, usually referred to as OPEC, includes 11 national governments (Algeria, Indonesia, Iran, Iraq, Kuwait, Libya, Nigeria, Qatar, Saudi Arabia, United Arab Emirates, and Venezuela). Two other oil-exporting countries, Norway and Mexico, are not formally part of the cartel but act as if they were. (Russia, also an important oil exporter, has not yet become part of the club.) Unlike corporations, which are often legally prohibited by governments from reaching agreements about production and prices, national governments can talk about whatever they feel like. OPEC members routinely meet to try to set targets for production.

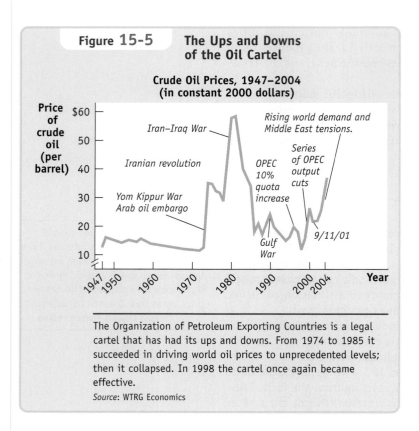

Figure 15-5 The Ups and Downs of the Oil Cartel

The Organization of Petroleum Exporting Countries is a legal cartel that has had its ups and downs. From 1974 to 1985 it succeeded in driving world oil prices to unprecedented levels; then it collapsed. In 1998 the cartel once again became effective.

Source: WTRG Economics

These nations are not particularly friendly with one another. Indeed, OPEC members Iraq and Iran fought a spectacularly bloody war with each other in the 1980s. And, in 1990, Iraq invaded another member, Kuwait. (A mainly American force based in yet another OPEC member, Saudi Arabia, drove the Iraqis out of Kuwait.)

Yet the members of OPEC, like one another or not, are effectively players in a game with repeated interactions. In any given year it is in their combined interest to keep output low and prices high. But it is also in the interest of any one producer to cheat and produce more than the agreed-upon quota—unless that producer believes that this action will bring future retaliation.

So how successful is the cartel? Well, it's had its ups and downs.

Figure 15-5 shows the price of oil in constant dollars (that is, the value of a barrel of oil in terms of other goods) since 1947. OPEC first demonstrated its muscle in 1974: in the aftermath of a war in the Middle East, several OPEC producers limited their output—and they liked the results so much that they decided to continue the practice. Following a second wave of turmoil in the aftermath of Iran's 1979 revolution, prices shot still higher.

By the mid-1980s, however, there was a growing glut of oil on world markets, and cheating by cash-short OPEC members became widespread. The result, in 1985, was that producers who had tried to play by the rules—especially Saudi Arabia, the largest producer—got fed up, and collusion collapsed.

The cartel began to act effectively again at the end of the 1990s, thanks largely to the efforts of Mexico's oil minister to orchestrate output reductions. To assure greater adherence to production targets, OPEC meets very frequently—seven times in 2003 alone—seeking to keep the price of a barrel of oil in the range of $22 to $28. And this discipline appears to be paying off; a decrease of 900,000 barrels per day in late 2003 coupled with rising demand from China and production difficulties in Iraq resulted in oil prices above $50 a barrel in 2004. ■

< < < < < < < < < < < < < < < < < <

>> CHECK YOUR UNDERSTANDING 15-3

1. Find the Nash (noncooperative) equilibrium actions for the accompanying payoff matrix. Which actions maximize the total payoff of Nikita and Margaret? Why is it unlikely that they will choose those actions without some communication?

2. Which factors make it more likely that oligopolists will play noncooperatively? Which make it more likely that they will engage in tacit collusion? Explain.
   a. Each oligopolist expects several new firms to enter the market in the future.
   b. It is very difficult for a firm to detect whether another firm has raised output.
   c. The firms have coexisted while maintaining high prices for a long time.

>> QUICK REVIEW

➤ Economists use *game theory* to study firms' behavior when there is *interdependence* between their *payoffs*. The game can be represented with a *payoff matrix*. Depending on the payoffs, a player may or may not have a *dominant strategy*.

➤ When each firm has an incentive to cheat, but both are worse off if both cheat, the situation is known as a *prisoners' dilemma*.

➤ Players who don't take their interdependence into account arrive at a *Nash*, or *noncooperative*, *equilibrium*. But if a game is played repeatedly, players may engage in *strategic behavior*, sacrificing short-run profit to influence future behavior.

➤ In repeated prisoners' dilemma games, *tit for tat* is often a good strategy, leading to successful *tacit collusion*.

➤ The *kinked demand curve* illustrates how tacit collusion can make an oligopolist unresponsive to changes in marginal cost within a certain range when those changes are unique to her.

Oligopoly in Practice

In Economics in Action on page 370 we described the cartel known as "Vitamins Inc.," which effectively promoted collusion for many years. The conspiratorial dealings of the vitamin makers were not, fortunately, the norm. But how do oligopolies usually work in practice? The answer depends both on the legal framework that limits what firms can do and on the underlying ability of firms in a given industry to cooperate without formal agreements.

The Legal Framework

To understand oligopoly pricing in practice, we must be familiar with the legal constraints under which oligopolistic firms operate. In the United States, oligopoly first became an issue during the second half of the nineteenth century, when the growth of railroads—themselves an oligopolistic industry—created a national market for many goods. Large firms producing oil, steel, and many other products soon emerged. The industrialists quickly realized that profits would be higher if they could limit price competition. So many industries formed cartels—that is, they signed formal agreements to limit production and raise prices. Until 1890, when the first federal legislation against such cartels was passed, this was perfectly legal.

However, although these cartels were legal, they weren't legally *enforceable*—members of a cartel couldn't ask the courts to force a firm that was violating its agreement to reduce its production. And firms often did violate their agreements, for the reason already suggested by our duopoly example: there is always a temptation for each firm in a cartel to produce more than it is supposed to.

In 1881 clever lawyers at John D. Rockefeller's Standard Oil Company came up with a solution—the so-called *trust*. In a trust, shareholders of all the major companies in an industry placed their shares in the hands of a board of trustees who controlled the companies. This, in effect, merged the companies into a single firm that could then engage in monopoly pricing. In this way, the Standard Oil Trust established what was essentially a monopoly of the oil industry, and it was soon followed by trusts in sugar, whiskey, lead, cottonseed oil, and linseed oil.

Eventually there was a public backlash, driven partly by concern about the economic effects of the trust movement, partly by fear that the owners of the trusts were simply becoming too powerful. The result was the Sherman Antitrust Act of 1890, which was intended both to prevent the creation of more monopolies and to break up existing ones. At first this law went largely unenforced. But over the decades that followed, the federal government became increasingly committed to making it difficult for oligopolistic industries either to become monopolies or to behave like them. Such efforts are known to this day as **antitrust policy.**

One of the most striking early actions of antitrust policy was the breakup of Standard Oil in 1911. (Its components formed the nuclei of many of today's large oil companies—Standard Oil of New Jersey became Exxon, Standard Oil of New York became Mobil, and so on.) In the 1980s a long-running case led to the breakup of Bell Telephone, which once had a monopoly of both local and long-distance phone service in the United States.

The details of antitrust policy can be exceedingly complex, especially because corporations can and do fight costly legal battles against decisions they dislike. The core of what antitrust means in practice can, however, be understood by turning, once again, to our lysine example. In that example, there are two obvious ways for the companies to avoid getting trapped in the prisoners' dilemma. One is the solution they actually tried: for the companies to meet with each other to agree to produce less and get higher prices. The other is to eliminate conflict by combining the two companies into one—let one company buy the other, or let them exchange their shares and merge.

Antitrust policy refers to the efforts of the government to prevent oligopolistic industries from becoming or behaving like monopolies.

Antitrust law makes both of these solutions illegal. If the executives meet to collude on prices, they can be sent to jail and their companies fined. If the companies try to merge, the Justice Department or the Federal Trade Commission will tell them that they cannot.

So what's an oligopolist to do?

Tacit Collusion and Price Wars

If a real industry were as simple as our lysine example, it probably wouldn't be necessary for the company presidents to meet or do anything that could land them in jail. Both firms would realize that it was in their mutual interest to restrict output to 30 million pounds each and that any short-term gains to either firm from producing more would be much less than the later losses as the other firm retaliated. So even without any explicit agreement, the firms would probably achieve the tacit collusion needed to maximize their combined profits.

Real industries are nowhere near that simple; nonetheless, in most oligopolistic industries, most of the time, the sellers do appear to succeed in keeping prices above their noncooperative level. Tacit collusion, in other words, is the normal state of oligopoly.

Although tacit collusion is common, it rarely allows an industry to push prices all the way up to their monopoly level; collusion is usually far from perfect. A variety of factors make it hard for an industry to coordinate on high prices.

Large Numbers

Suppose that there were three instead of two firms in the lysine industry and that each was currently producing only 20 million pounds. You can confirm for yourself that in that case any one firm that decided to produce an extra 10 million pounds would gain more in short-term profits—and lose less once another firm responded in kind—than in our original example. The general point is that the more firms there are in an oligopoly, the less is the incentive of any one firm to behave cooperatively, taking into account the impact of its actions on the profits of the other firms. Large numbers of firms in an industry typically are an indication that there are low barriers to entry.

Complex Products and Pricing Schemes

In our lysine example the two firms produce only one product. In reality, however, oligopolists often sell thousands or even tens of thousands of different products. Under these circumstances, keeping track of what other firms are producing and what prices they are charging is difficult. This makes it hard to determine whether a firm is cheating on the tacit agreement.

Differences in Interests

In the lysine example, a tacit agreement for the firms to split the market equally is a natural outcome, probably acceptable to both firms. In real industries, however, firms often differ both in their perceptions about what is fair and in their real interests.

For example, suppose that Ajinomoto was a long-established lysine producer and ADM a more recent entrant to the industry. Ajinomoto might feel that it deserved to continue producing more than ADM, but ADM might feel that it was entitled to 50 percent of the business. (A disagreement along these lines was one of the contentious issues in those meetings the FBI was filming.)

Alternatively, suppose that ADM's marginal costs were lower than Ajinomoto's. Even if they could agree on market shares, they would then disagree about the profit-maximizing level of output.

Bargaining Power of Buyers

Often oligopolists sell not to individual consumers but to large buyers—other industrial enterprises, nationwide chains of stores, and so on. These large buyers are in a position to bargain for lower prices from the oligopolists: they can ask for a discount from an oligopolist, and warn that they will go to a competitor if they don't get it. An important reason why large retailers like Wal-Mart are able to offer lower prices to customers than small retailers is precisely their ability to use their size to extract lower prices from their suppliers.

These difficulties in enforcing tacit collusion have sometimes led companies to defy the law and create illegal cartels. We've already examined the cases of the lysine industry and the bulk vitamin industry. An older, classic example was the U.S. electrical equipment conspiracy of the 1950s, which led to the indictment of and jail sentences for some executives. The industry was one in which tacit collusion was especially difficult because of all the reasons just mentioned. There were many firms—40 companies were indicted. They produced a very complex array of products, often more or less custom-built for particular clients. They differed greatly in size, from giants like General Electric to family firms with only a few dozen employees. And the customers in many cases were large buyers like electrical utilities, which would normally try to force suppliers to compete for their business. Tacit collusion just didn't seem practical—so executives met secretly and illegally to decide who would bid what price for which contract.

The following For Inquiring Minds describes yet another price-fixing conspiracy: the one between the very posh auction houses Sotheby's and Christie's.

FOR INQUIRING MINDS

THE ART OF CONSPIRACY

If you want to sell a valuable work of art, there are really only two places to go: Christie's, the London-based auction house, or Sotheby's, its New York counterpart and competitor. Both are classy operations—literally: many of the employees of Christie's come from Britain's aristocracy, and many of Sotheby's come from blue-blooded American families that might as well have titles. They're not the sort of people you would expect to be seeking plea bargains from prosecutors.

But on October 6, 2000, Diana D. Brooks, the very upper-class former president of Sotheby's, pleaded guilty to a conspiracy. With her counterpart at Christie's, she had engaged in the illegal practice of price-fixing—agreeing on the fees they would charge people who sold artwork through either house. As part of her guilty plea, and in an effort to avoid going to jail, she agreed to help in the investigation of her boss, the former chairman of Sotheby's.

Why would such upper-crust types engage in illegal practices? For the same reasons that respectable electrical equipment industry executives did. By definition, no two works of art are alike; it wasn't easy for the two houses to collude tacitly, because it was too hard to determine what commissions they were charging on any given transaction. To increase profits, then, the companies felt that they needed to reach a detailed agreement. They did, and they got caught.

Because tacit collusion is often hard to achieve, most oligopolies charge prices that are well below what the same industry would charge if it were controlled by a single firm—or what they would charge if they were able to collude explicitly. In addition, sometimes collusion breaks down and there is a **price war.** A price war sometimes involves simply a collapse of prices to their noncooperative level. Sometimes they even go *below* that level, as sellers try to put each other out of business or at least punish what they regard as cheating.

> A **price war** occurs when tacit collusion breaks down and prices collapse.

Product Differentiation and Price Leadership

Lysine is lysine: there was no question in anyone's mind that ADM and Ajinomoto were producing the same good and that consumers would make their decision about which company's lysine to buy based on the price.

In many oligopolies, however, firms produce products that consumers regard as similar but not identical. A $10 difference in the price won't make many customers switch from a Ford to a Chrysler, or vice versa. Sometimes the differences between products are real, like differences between Froot Loops and Wheaties; sometimes, like differences between brands of vodka (which is *supposed* to be tasteless), they exist mainly in the minds of consumers. Either way, the effect is to reduce the intensity of the competition among the firms: consumers will not all rush to buy whichever product is cheapest.

Firms engage in **product differentiation** when they try to convince buyers that their product is different from the products of other firms in the industry.

As you might imagine, oligopolists welcome the extra market power that comes when consumers think that their product is different from that of competitors. So in many oligopolistic industries, firms make considerable efforts to create the perception that their product is different—that is, they engage in **product differentiation.**

A firm that tries to differentiate its product may do so by altering what it actually produces, adding "extras," or choosing a different design. It may also use advertising and marketing campaigns to create a differentiation in the minds of consumers, even though its product is more or less identical to the products of rivals.

A classic case of how products may be perceived as different even when they are really pretty much the same is over-the-counter medication. For many years there were only three widely sold pain relievers—aspirin, ibuprofen, and acetaminophen. Yet these generic pain relievers were marketed under a number of brand names, each brand using a marketing campaign implying some special superiority (one classic slogan was "contains the pain reliever doctors recommend most"—that is, aspirin).

Whatever the nature of product differentiation, oligopolists producing differentiated products often reach a tacit understanding not to compete on price. For example, during the years when the great majority of cars sold in the United States were produced by the Big Three auto companies, there was a sort of unwritten rule that none of the three companies would try to gain market share by making its cars noticeably cheaper than those of the other two.

But then who would decide on the overall price of cars? The answer was normally that General Motors, the biggest of the three, would announce its prices for the year first; then the other companies would match it. This pattern of behavior, in which some company tacitly sets prices for the industry as a whole, is known as **price leadership.**

In **price leadership**, one firm sets its price first, and other firms then follow.

Firms that have a tacit understanding not to compete on price often engage in intense **nonprice competition**, using advertising and other means to try to increase their sales.

Interestingly, firms that have a tacit agreement not to compete on price often engage in vigorous **nonprice competition**—adding new features to their products, spending large sums on ads that proclaim the inferiority of their rivals' offerings, and so on.

Perhaps the best way to understand the mix of cooperation and competition in such industries is with a political analogy. During the long Cold War between the United States and the Soviet Union, the two countries engaged in intense rivalry for global influence. They not only provided financial and military aid to their allies; they sometimes supported forces trying to overthrow governments allied with their rival (as the Soviet Union did in Vietnam in the 1960s and early 1970s, and as the United States did in Afghanistan from 1979 until the collapse of the Soviet Union in 1991). They even sent their own soldiers to support allied governments against rebels (as the United States did in Vietnam and the Soviet Union did in Afghanistan). But they did *not* get into direct military confrontations with each other; open warfare between the two superpowers was regarded by both as too dangerous—and tacitly avoided.

Price wars aren't as serious as shooting wars, but the principle is the same.

economics in action

Air Wars

The first time Robert Crandall, then CEO of American Airlines, tried to collude on prices, he was blunt: in 1983 he called the head of rival Braniff (now defunct) and proposed in so many words (many of them unprintable) that the two airlines both raise fares 20 percent. Alas for Crandall, the conversation was being taped.

Eight years later, Crandall tried a more legal approach: declaring himself a "statesman," he raised American's fares in the hopes that rivals would follow suit. But they didn't, and the airline lost many passengers.

On both occasions the airline industry was in the midst of a price war. Indeed, price wars—in which fares fall 50 percent or more for a time, then soar again—are something of an industry specialty.

Why are airlines so prone to price wars? There are at least three reasons, all bearing on the problems of tacit collusion we have just discussed. First, although each airline tries to differentiate its product, creating a perception among consumers that it offers better service, most fliers choose airlines on the basis of schedule and price—period. So competition is intense. Second, airline pricing is complex: as discussed in Chapter 14, airlines engage in complex price-discrimination schemes that make it hard to figure out when tacit collusion is being broken. Third, airlines often differ in their interests: many of the most severe price wars have been set off by attempts of a new competitor to break into established markets. And this indicates yet another source of airline price wars: low barriers to entry. ∎

> > > > > > > > > > > > > > > > > > >

>> **CHECK YOUR UNDERSTANDING 15-4**

1. Which of the following factors are likely to support the conclusion that there is tacit collusion in this industry? Which are not? Explain.
   a. For many years the price in the industry has changed infrequently, and all the firms in the industry charge the same price. The largest firm publishes a catalog containing a "suggested" retail price. Changes in price coincide with changes in the catalog.
   b. There has been considerable variation in the market shares of the firms in the industry over time.
   c. Firms in the industry build into their products unnecessary features that make it hard for consumers to switch from one company's products to another's.
   d. Firms meet yearly to discuss their annual sales forecasts.
   e. Firms tend to adjust their prices upward at the same times.

Solutions appear at back of book.

How Important Is Oligopoly?

We have seen that, across industries, oligopoly is far more common than either perfect competition or monopoly. When we try to analyze oligopoly, the economist's usual way of thinking—asking how self-interested individuals would behave, then analyzing their interaction—does not work as well as we might hope, because we do not know whether rival firms will engage in noncooperative behavior or manage to engage in some kind of collusion. Given the prevalence of oligopoly, then, is the analysis we developed in earlier chapters, which was based on perfect competition, still useful?

The conclusion of the great majority of economists is yes. For one thing, important parts of the economy are fairly well described by perfect competition. And even though many industries are oligopolistic, in many cases the limits to collusion keep prices relatively close to marginal costs—in other words, the industry behaves "almost" as if it were perfectly competitive.

It is also true that predictions from supply and demand analysis are often valid for oligopolies. For example, in Chapter 4 we saw that price controls will produce shortages. Strictly speaking, this conclusion is certain only for perfectly competitive industries. But in the 1970s, when the U.S. government imposed price controls on the definitely oligopolistic oil industry, the result was indeed to produce shortages and lines at the gas pumps.

So how important is it to take account of oligopoly? Most economists adopt a pragmatic approach. As we have seen in this chapter, the analysis of oligopoly is far more difficult and messy than that of perfect competition; so in situations where they do not expect the complications associated with oligopoly to be crucial, economists prefer to adopt the working assumption of perfectly competitive markets. They always keep in mind the possibility that oligopoly might be important; they recognize that there are important issues, from antitrust policies to price wars, where trying to understand oligopolistic behavior is crucial.

We will follow the same approach in the chapters that follow.

• A LOOK AHEAD •

We're not yet done with our investigation of market structures other than perfect competition. There are quite a few industries that don't seem to fit either the definition of oligopoly or the definition of perfect competition. Consider, for example, the restaurant business. There are many restaurants, so it's not an oligopoly. But restaurants aren't price-takers, like wheat farmers, so it's not perfectly competitive. What is it?

The answer lies in the next chapter, which turns to the concept of *monopolistic competition.*

SUMMARY

1. Many industries are **oligopolies:** there are only a few sellers. In particular, a **duopoly** has only two sellers. Oligopolies exist for more or less the same reasons that monopolies exist, but in weaker form. They are characterized by **imperfect competition:** firms compete but possess market power.

2. Predicting the behavior of **oligopolists** poses something of a puzzle. The firms in an oligopoly could maximize their combined profits by acting as a **cartel,** setting output levels for each firm as if they were a single monopolist; to the extent that firms manage to do this, they engage in **collusion.** But each individual firm has an incentive to produce more than it would in such an arrangement—to engage in **noncooperative behavior.** Informal collusion is likely to be easier to achieve in industries in which firms face capacity constraints.

3. The situation of **interdependence,** in which each firm's profit depends noticeably on what other firms do, is the subject of **game theory.** In the case of a game with two players, the **payoff** of each player depends both on its own actions and on the actions of the other; this interdependence can be represented as a **payoff matrix.** Depending upon the structure of payoffs in the payoff matrix, a player may have a **dominant strategy**—an action that is always the best regardless of the other player's actions.

4. **Duopolists** face a particular type of game known as a **prisoners' dilemma;** if each acts independently in its own interest, the resulting **Nash equilibrium** or **noncooperative equilibrium** will be bad for both. However, firms that expect to play a game repeatedly tend to engage in **strategic behavior,** trying to influence each other's future actions. A particular strategy that seems to work well in such situations is **tit for tat,** which often leads to **tacit collusion.**

5. The **kinked demand curve** illustrates how an oligopolist who faces unique changes in her marginal cost within a certain range may choose not to adjust her output and price in order to avoid a breakdown in tacit collusion.

6. In order to limit the ability of oligopolists to collude and act like monopolists, most governments pursue an **antitrust policy** designed to make collusion more difficult. In practice, however, tacit collusion is widespread.

7. A variety of factors make tacit collusion difficult: large numbers of firms, complex products and pricing, differences in interests, and bargaining power of buyers. When tacit collusion breaks down, there is a **price war.** Oligopolists try to avoid price wars in various ways, such as through **product differentiation** and through **price leadership,** in which one firm sets prices for the industry. Another is through **nonprice competition,** like advertising.

KEY TERMS

PROBLEMS

1. The accompanying table shows the demand schedule for vitamin D. Suppose that the marginal cost of producing vitamin D is zero.

Price of vitamin D (per ton)	Quantity of vitamin D demanded (tons)
$8	0
7	10
6	20
5	30
4	40
3	50
2	60
1	70

a. Assume that BASF is the only producer of vitamin D and acts as a monopolist. It currently produces 40 tons of vitamin D at $4 per ton. If BASF were to produce 10 tons more, what would be the price effect for BASF? What would be the quantity effect? Would BASF therefore have an incentive to produce those 10 additional tons?

b. Now assume that Roche enters the market by also producing vitamin D and the market is now a duopoly. BASF and Roche agree to produce 40 tons of vitamin D in total, 20 tons each. BASF cannot be punished for deviating from the agreement with Roche. If BASF, on its own, were to deviate from that agreement and produce 10 tons more, what would be the price effect for BASF? What would be the quantity effect for BASF? Would BASF have an incentive to produce those 10 additional tons?

2. The market for olive oil in New York City is controlled by two families, the Sopranos and the Contraltos. Both families will ruthlessly eliminate any other family that attempts to enter the New York City olive oil market. The marginal cost of producing olive oil is constant and equal to $40 per gallon. There is no fixed cost. The accompanying table gives the market demand schedule for olive oil.

Price of olive oil (per gallon)	Quantity of olive oil demanded (gallons)
$100	1,000
90	1,500
80	2,000
70	2,500
60	3,000
50	3,500
40	4,000
30	4,500
20	5,000
10	5,500

a. Suppose the Sopranos and the Contraltos form a cartel. For each of the quantities given in the table, calculate the total revenue for their cartel and the marginal revenue for each additional gallon. How many gallons of olive oil would the cartel sell in total and at what price? The two families share the market equally (each produces half of the total output of the cartel). How much profit does each family make?

b. Uncle Junior, the head of the Soprano family, breaks the agreement and sells 500 more gallons of olive oil than under the cartel agreement. Assuming the Contraltos maintain the agreement, how does this affect the price for olive oil and the profits earned by each family?

c. Anthony Contralto, the head of the Contralto family, decides to punish Uncle Junior by increasing his sales by 500 gallons as well. How much profit does each family earn now?

3. In France, the market for bottled water is controlled by two large firms, Perrier and Evian. Each firm has a fixed cost of €1 and a constant marginal cost of €2 per liter of bottled water (€ = 1 euro). The accompanying table gives the market demand schedule for bottled water in France.

Price of bottled water (per liter)	Quantity of bottled water demanded (liters)
€10	0
9	1
8	2
7	3
6	4
5	5
4	6
3	7
2	8
1	9

a. Suppose the two firms form a cartel and act as a monopolist. Calculate marginal revenue for the cartel. What will the monopoly price and output be? Assuming the firms divided the output evenly, how much will each produce and what will each firm's profits be?

b. Now suppose Perrier decides to increase production by 1 liter. Evian doesn't change its production. What will the new market price and output be? What is Perrier's profit? What is Evian's profit?

c. What if Perrier increases production by 3 liters? Evian doesn't change its production. What would its output and profits be relative to those in part b?

d. What do your results tell you about the likelihood of cheating on such agreements?

4. To preserve the North Atlantic fish stocks, it is decided that only two fishing fleets, one from the United States and the

other from the European Union (EU) can fish in those waters. The accompanying table shows the market demand schedule per week for fish from these waters. The only costs are fixed costs, so fishing fleets maximize profit by maximizing revenue.

Price of fish (per pound)	Quantity of fish demanded (pounds)
$17	1,800
16	2,000
15	2,100
14	2,200
12	2,300

a. If both fishing fleets collude, what is the revenue-maximizing output for the North Atlantic fishery? What price will a pound of fish sell for?

b. If both fishing fleets collude and share the output equally, what is the revenue to the EU fleet? To the U.S. fleet?

c. Suppose the EU fleet cheats by expanding its own catch by 100 pounds per week. The U.S. fleet doesn't change its catch. What is the revenue to the U.S. fleet? To the EU fleet?

d. In retaliation for the cheating by the EU fleet, the U.S. fleet also expands its catch by 100 pounds per week. What is the revenue to the U.S. fleet? to the EU fleet?

5. Suppose that the fisheries agreement in Problem 4 breaks down, so that the fleets behave noncooperatively. Assume that the U.S. and the EU each can send out either one or two fleets. Also assume that the more fleets in the area, the more fish they catch in total but the lower the catch of each fleet. The accompanying matrix shows the profit (in dollars) per week earned by the two sides.

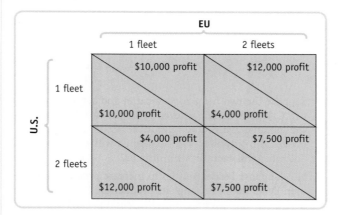

a. What is the noncooperative Nash equilibrium? Will each side choose to send out one or two fleets?

b. Suppose that the fish stocks are being depleted. Each region considers the future and comes to a "tit-for-tat" agreement whereby each side will send only one fleet out as long as the other does the same. If either of them breaks the agreement and sends out a second fleet, the other will also send out two and will continue to do so until its competitor sends out only one fleet. If both play

this "tit for tat" strategy, how much profit will each make every week?

6. Untied and Air 'R' Us are the only two airlines operating flights between Collegeville and Bigtown. That is, they operate in a duopoly. Each airline can charge either a high price or a low price for a ticket. The accompanying matrix shows their payoffs, in profits per seat (in dollars), for any choice that the two airlines can make.

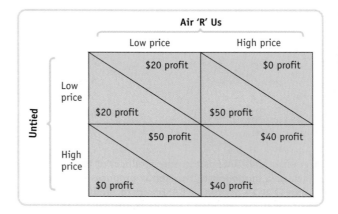

a. Suppose the two airlines play a one-shot game—that is, they interact only once and never again. What will be the Nash (noncooperative) equilibrium in this one-shot game?

b. Now suppose the two airlines play this game twice. And suppose each airline can play one of two strategies: it can play either "always charge the low price" or "tit for tat"— that is, it starts off charging the high price in the first period, and then in the second period it does whatever the other airline did in the previous period. Write down the payoffs to Untied from the following four possibilities:

   i. Untied plays "always charge the low price" when Air 'R' Us also plays "always charge the low price."

   ii. Untied plays "always charge the low price" when Air 'R' Us plays "tit for tat."

   iii. Untied plays "tit for tat" when Air 'R' Us plays "always charge the low price."

   iv. Untied plays "tit for tat" when Air 'R' Us also plays "tit for tat."

7. Suppose that Coke and Pepsi are the only two producers of cola drinks, so they are duopolists. Both companies have zero marginal cost and a fixed cost of $100,000.

a. Assume first that consumers regard Coke and Pepsi as perfect substitutes. Currently both are sold for $0.20 per can, and at that price each company sells 4 million cans per day.

   i. How large is Pepsi's profit?

   ii. If Pepsi were to raise its price to $0.30 cents per can, what would happen to its profit?

b. Now suppose that each company advertises to differentiate its product from the other company's. As a result of advertising, Pepsi realizes that if it raises or lowers its price, it will sell less or more of its product, as shown by the demand schedule in the accompanying table.

Price of Pepsi (per can)	Quantity of Pepsi demanded (millions of cans)
$0.10	5
0.20	4
0.30	3
0.40	2
0.50	1

If Pepsi now were to raise its price to $0.30 per can, what would happen to its profit?

c. Comparing your answer to part a(i) and to part b, what is the maximum amount Pepsi would be willing to spend on advertising?

8. Philip Morris and R.J. Reynolds spend huge sums of money each year to advertise their tobacco products in an attempt to steal customers from each other. Suppose each year Philip Morris and R.J. Reynolds have to decide whether or not they want to spend money on advertising. If neither firm advertises, each will earn a profit of $2 million. If they both advertise, each will earn a profit of $1.5 million. If one firm advertises and the other does not, the firm that advertises will earn a profit of $2.8 million and the other firm will earn $1 million.

a. Use a payoff matrix to depict this problem.

b. Suppose Philip Morris and R.J. Reynolds can write an enforceable contract about what they will do. What is the cooperative solution to this game?

c. What is the Nash equilibrium without an enforceable contract? Explain why this is the likely outcome.

9. Over the last 30 years the Organization of Petroleum Exporting Countries (OPEC) has had varied success in forming and maintaining its cartel agreements. Explain how the following factors may contribute to the difficulty of forming and/or maintaining its price and output agreements.

a. New oil fields are discovered and increased drilling is undertaken in the Gulf of Mexico and the North Sea by nonmembers of OPEC.

b. Crude oil is a product that is differentiated by sulfur content: it costs less to refine low-sulfur crude oil into gasoline. Different OPEC countries possess oil reserves of different sulfur content.

c. Cars powered by hydrogen are developed.

10. Suppose you are an economist working for the Antitrust Division of the Department of Justice. In each of the following cases you are given the task of determining whether the behavior warrants an antitrust investigation for possible illegal acts, or is just an example of undesirable, but not illegal, tacit collusion. Explain your reasoning.

a. Two companies dominate the industry for industrial lasers. Several people sit on the boards of directors of both companies.

b. Three banks dominate the market for banking in a given state. Their profits have been going up recently as they add new fees for customer transactions. Advertising among the banks is fierce, and new branches are springing up in many locations.

c. The two oil companies that produce most of the petroleum for the western half of the United States have decided to forgo building their own pipelines and to share a common pipeline, the only means of transporting petroleum products to that market.

d. The two major companies that dominate the market for herbal supplements have each created a subsidiary that sells the same product as the parent company in large quantities but with a generic name.

e. The two largest credit card companies, Passport and OmniCard, have required all banks and retailers who accept their cards to agree to limit their use of rival credit cards.

11. The industry for small, single-engine airplanes is oligopolistic, and it has achieved tacit collusion. Each firm currently sells 10 airplanes at a price of $200,000 each. Each firm believes that it will sell 1 fewer airplane if it raises the price by $5,000. And each firm also believes that it can sell 1 more airplane if it lowers the price by $10,000. That is, each firm has a kinked demand curve.

a. How much additional revenue will a firm generate if it produces 1 more (the 11th) airplane?

b. How much revenue will a firm lose if it produces 1 fewer airplane?

c. If the marginal cost of producing an airplane is $120,000, how many airplanes will each firm produce, and at what price?

d. If the marginal cost of producing an airplane is $140,000, how many airplanes will each firm produce, and at what price?

>web... To continue your study and review of concepts in this chapter, please visit the Krugman/Wells website for quizzes, animated graph tutorials, web links to helpful resources, and more.

www.worthpublishers.com/krugmanwells

16

>> Monopolistic Competition and Product Differentiation

FAST-FOOD DIFFERENTIATION

What you will learn in this chapter:

➤ The meaning of **monopolistic competition**

➤ Why oligopolists and monopolistically competitive firms **differentiate** their products

➤ How prices and profits are determined in monopolistic competition in the short run and the long run

➤ Why monopolistic competition poses a trade-off between lower prices and greater product diversity

➤ The economic significance of advertising and brand names

A RECENT BEST-SELLING BOOK TITLED *Fast Food Nation* offered a fascinating if rather negative report on the burgers, pizza, tacos, and fried chicken that make up so much of the modern American diet. According to the book, all fast-food chains produce and deliver their food in pretty much the same way. In particular, a lot of the taste of your fast food—whatever kind of fast food it is—comes from food additives manufactured in New Jersey.

But each fast-food provider goes to great lengths to convince you that it has something special to offer. Everyone recognizes Ronald McDonald the clown, a symbol of McDonald's carefully cultivated image as the place kids love. Rival Wendy's took a bite out of McDonald's market share with a little old lady yelling "Where's the beef?", a campaign that emphasized Wendy's somewhat bigger burgers.

So how would you describe the fast-food industry? On the one hand, it clearly isn't a monopoly. When you go to a fast-food court, you have a choice among vendors, and there is real competition between the different burger outlets and between the burgers and

the fried chicken. On the other hand, in a way each vendor *does* possess some aspects of a monopoly: at one point McDonald's had the slogan "Nobody does it like McDonald's." That was literally true—though McDonald's competitors would say that they did it *better*. In any case, the point is that each fast-food provider offers a product that is *differentiated* from its rivals' products.

Competing for your tastebuds.

In the fast-food industry, many firms compete to satisfy more or less the same demand—the desire of consumers for something tasty but quick. But each firm offers to satisfy that demand with a distinctive, differentiated product—products that consumers typically view as close but not perfect substitutes. When there are many firms offering competing, differentiated products, as there are in the fast-food industry, economists say that the industry is characterized by *monopolistic competition*.

This is the fourth and final market structure that we will discuss, after perfect competition, monopoly, and oligopoly.

We'll start by defining monopolistic competition more carefully and explain its characteristic features. Then we'll explore how firms differentiate their products; this will allow us to analyze how monopolistic competition works. The chapter concludes with a discussion of some ongoing controversies about product differentiation—in particular, the question of why advertising is effective.

The Meaning of Monopolistic Competition

Joe manages the Wonderful Wok stand in the food court of a big shopping mall. He offers the only Chinese food there, but there are more than a dozen alternatives, from Bodacious Burgers to Pizza Paradise. When deciding what to charge for a meal, Joe knows that he must take those alternatives into account: even people who normally prefer stir-fry won't order a $15 lunch from Joe when they can get a burger, fries, and drink for $4.

But Joe also knows that he won't lose all his business even if his lunches cost a bit more than the alternatives. Chinese food isn't the same thing as burgers or pizza. Some people will really be in the mood for Chinese that day, and they will buy from Joe even if they could have dined more cheaply on burgers. Of course, the reverse is also true: even if Chinese is a bit cheaper, some people will choose burgers instead. In other words, Joe does have some market power: he has *some* ability to set his own price.

So how would you describe Joe's situation? He definitely isn't a price-taker, so he isn't in a situation of perfect competition. But you wouldn't exactly call him a monopolist, either. Although he's the only seller of Chinese food in that food court, he does face competition from other food vendors.

Yet it would also be wrong to call him an oligopolist. Oligopoly, remember, involves competition among a small number of firms in an industry protected by some—albeit limited—barriers to entry and whose profits are highly interdependent. This interdependence provides an incentive for oligopolists to try to find a way to collude, if only tacitly. But in Joe's case there are *lots* of vendors in the shopping mall, too many to make tacit collusion feasible.

Economists describe Joe's situation as one of **monopolistic competition.** Monopolistic competition is particularly common in service industries like restaurants and gas stations, but it also exists in some manufacturing industries. It involves three conditions: large numbers of competing producers, differentiated products, and free entry into and exit from the industry in the long run. In a monopolistically competitive industry, each producer has some ability to set the price of her differentiated good. But exactly how high she can set it is limited by the competition she faces from other existing and potential producers that produce close, but not identical, products.

> **Monopolistic competition** is a market structure in which there are many competing producers in an industry, each producer sells a differentiated product, and there is free entry into and exit from the industry in the long run.

Large Numbers

In a monopolistically competitive industry there are many producers. Such an industry does not look either like a monopoly, where the firm faces no competition, or an oligopoly, where each firm has only a few rivals. Instead, each seller has many competitors. There are many vendors in a big food court, many gas stations along a major highway, and many hotels in a popular beach resort.

Differentiated Products

In a monopolistically competitive industry, each producer has a product that consumers view as somewhat distinct from the products of competing firms but at the same time are considered close substitutes. If Joe's food court contained 15 vendors selling exactly the same kind and quality of food, there would be perfect competition: any seller who tried to charge a higher price would have no customers. But suppose that Wonderful Wok is the only Chinese food vendor, Bodacious Burgers is the only hamburger stand, and so on. The result of this differentiation is that each seller has some ability to set his own price: each producer has some—albeit limited—market power.

Free Entry and Exit in the Long Run

In monopolistically competitive industries, new producers, with their own distinct products, can enter the industry freely in the long run. For example, other food vendors would open outlets in the shopping mall if they thought it would be profitable to do so. In addition, firms will exit the industry if they find they are not covering their costs in the long run.

Monopolistic competition, then, differs from the three market structures we have examined so far. It's not the same as perfect competition: firms have some power to set prices. It's not pure monopoly: firms face some competition. And it's not the same as oligopoly: because there are many firms and free entry, the potential for collusion so important in oligopoly no longer exists.

We'll see in a moment how prices, output, and the number of products available are determined in monopolistically competitive industries. But first, let's look a little more closely at what it means to have differentiated products.

Product Differentiation

We pointed out in Chapter 15 that product differentiation often plays an important role in oligopolistic industries. In such industries, product differentiation reduces the intensity of competition between firms when tacit collusion cannot be achieved. Product differentiation plays an even more crucial role in monopolistically competitive industries. Because tacit collusion is virtually impossible when there are many producers, product differentiation is the only way monopolistically competitive firms can acquire some market power.

How do firms in the same industry—such as fast-food vendors, gas stations, or chocolate companies—differentiate their products? Sometimes the difference is mainly in the minds of consumers rather than in the products themselves. We'll discuss the role of advertising and the importance of brand names in achieving this kind of product differentiation later in the chapter. But, in general, firms differentiate their products by—surprise!—actually making them different.

The key to product differentiation is that consumers have different preferences and that each producer can carve out a market niche by producing something that caters to the particular preferences of some group of consumers better than the products of other firms. There are three important forms of product differentiation: differentiation by style or type, differentiation by location, and differentiation by quality.

Differentiation by Style or Type

The sellers in Joe's food court offer different types of fast food: hamburgers, pizza, Chinese food, Mexican food, and so on. Each consumer arrives at the food court with some preference for one or another of these offerings. This preference may depend on the consumer's mood, her diet, or what she has already eaten that day. These preferences will not make consumers indifferent to price: If Wonderful Wok were to charge $15 for an egg roll, everybody would go to Bodacious Burgers or Pizza Paradise instead. But, some people will choose a more expensive meal if that type of food is closer to their preference. So the products of the different vendors are substitutes, but they aren't *perfect* substitutes—they are *imperfect* substitutes.

BUCKS FOR STARBUCKS

The coffee shop industry has always been monopolistically competitive, with each local shop selling a somewhat differentiated product. Until the middle of the 1980s, however, products were mainly differentiated by location: customers chose a coffee shop because it was near their workplace or on the way to work. There was also a bit of differentiation by quality—some places made better coffee than others—but that was it. After all, coffee was coffee.

That is, coffee was coffee until it started becoming cappuccino, latte, frappuccino, and other more or less Italian-style beverages. Call it the Starbucks revolution: the Seattle-based chain led the transformation of America's caffeine intake, growing from 15 stores in Seattle in 1987 to more than 9,000 around the world by 2005.

Is this a true expansion of the choices available to consumers? Are the coffee varieties now available really different? Yes, they are. The authors are old enough to remember what typical coffee shop coffee tasted like in the dark ages: things really have improved. Is the

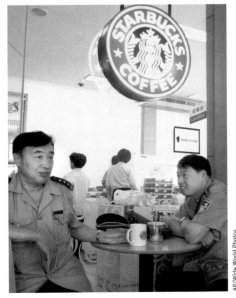

Mocha lattes served here—the Starbucks revolution comes to Beijing.

improvement worth the price of a Starbucks latte? Well, people are willing to pay those prices, and the customer is always right.

Vendors in a food court aren't the only sellers who differentiate their offerings by type. Clothing stores concentrate on women's or men's clothes, on business attire or sportswear, on trendy or classic styles, and so on. Auto manufacturers offer sedans, minivans, sport-utility vehicles, and sports cars, each type aimed at drivers with different needs and tastes.

Books offer yet another example of differentiation by type and style. Mysteries are differentiated from romances; among mysteries, we can differentiate among hard-boiled detective stories, whodunits, and police procedurals. And no two writers of hard-boiled detective stories are exactly alike: Raymond Chandler and Sue Grafton each have their devoted fans.

In fact, product differentiation is characteristic of most consumer goods. As long as people differ in their tastes, producers find it possible and profitable to produce a range of varieties.

Differentiation by Location

Gas stations along a road offer differentiated products. True, the gas may be exactly the same. But the location of the stations is different, and location matters to consumers: it's more convenient to stop for gas near your home, near your workplace, or near wherever you are when the gas gauge gets low.

In fact, many monopolistically competitive industries supply goods differentiated by location. This is especially true in service industries, from dry cleaners to hairdressers, where customers often choose the seller who is closest rather than cheapest.

Differentiation by Quality

Do you have a craving for chocolate? How much are you willing to spend on it? You see, there's chocolate and then there's chocolate: although ordinary chocolate may not be very expensive, gourmet chocolate can cost dollars for every bite.

With chocolate, as with many goods, there is a range of possible qualities. You can get a usable bicycle for less than $100; you can get a much fancier bicycle for 10 times as much. It all depends on how much the additional quality matters to you and how much you will miss the other things you could have purchased with that money.

Because consumers vary in what they are willing to pay for higher quality, producers can differentiate their products by quality—some offering lower-quality, inexpensive products and others offering higher-quality products at a higher price.

Product differentiation, then, can take several forms. Whatever form it takes, however, there are two important features of industries with differentiated products: *competition among sellers* and *value in diversity*.

Competition among sellers means that even though sellers of differentiated products are not offering identical goods, they are to some extent competing for a limited market. If more businesses enter the market, each will find that it sells less quantity at any given price. For example, if a new gas station opens along a road, each of the existing gas stations will sell a bit less.

Value in diversity refers to the gain to consumers from the proliferation of differentiated products. A food court with eight vendors makes consumers happier than one with only six vendors, even if the prices are the same, because some customers will get a meal that is closer to what they had in mind. A road on which there is a gas station every two miles is more convenient for motorists than a road where gas stations are five miles apart. When a product is available in many different qualities, fewer people are forced to pay for more quality than they need or to settle for lower quality than they want. There are, in other words, benefits to consumers from a greater diversity of available products.

As we'll see next, competition among the sellers of differentiated products is the key to understanding how monopolistic competition works.

economics in action

Any Color, So Long as It's Black

The early history of the auto industry offers a classic illustration of the power of product differentiation.

The modern automobile industry was created by Henry Ford, who first introduced assembly-line production. This technique made it possible for him to offer the famous Model T at a far lower price than anyone else was charging for a car; by 1920, Ford dominated the automobile business.

Ford's strategy was to offer just one style of car, which maximized his economies of scale but made no concessions to differences in taste. He supposedly declared that customers could get the Model T in "any color, so long as it's black."

This strategy was challenged by Alfred P. Sloan, who had merged a number of smaller automobile companies into General Motors. Sloan's strategy was to offer a range of car types, differentiated by quality and price. Chevrolets were basic cars that directly challenged the Model T, Buicks were bigger and more expensive, and so on up to Cadillacs. And you could get each model in several different colors.

By the 1930s the verdict was clear: customers preferred a range of styles, and General Motors, not Ford, became the dominant auto manufacturer for the rest of the twentieth century. ■

< < < < < < < < < < < < < < < < <

1. Each of the following goods and services are differentiated products. Which are differentiated as a result of monopolistic competition and which are not? Explain.
   a. Ladders
   b. Soft drinks
   c. Department stores
   d. Steel

2. You must determine which of two types of market structure best describes an industry, but you are allowed to ask only one question about the industry. What question should you ask to determine if an industry is:
   a. Perfectly competitive or monopolistically competitive?
   b. Monopoly or monopolistically competitive?

Solutions appear at back of book.

Understanding Monopolistic Competition

Suppose an industry is monopolistically competitive: it consists of many producers, all competing for the same consumers but offering differentiated products. How does such an industry behave?

As the term *monopolistic competition* suggests, this market structure combines some features typical of monopoly with others typical of perfect competition. Because each firm is offering a distinct product, it is in a way like a monopolist: it faces a downward-sloping demand curve and has some market power—the ability within limits to determine the price of its product. However, unlike a pure monopolist, a monopolistically competitive firm does face competition: the amount of its product it can sell depends on the prices and products offered by other firms in the industry.

The same, of course, is true of an oligopoly. In a monopolistically competitive industry, however, there are *many* producers, as opposed to the small number that defines an oligopoly. This means that the "puzzle" of oligopoly—will firms collude or will they behave noncooperatively?—does not arise in the case of monopolistically competitive industries. True, if all the gas stations or all the restaurants in a town could agree—explicitly or tacitly—to raise prices, it would be in their mutual interest to do so. But such collusion is virtually impossible when the number of firms is large and, by implication, there are no barriers to entry. So in situations of monopolistic competition, we can safely assume that firms behave noncooperatively and ignore the potential for collusion.

Monopolistic Competition in the Short Run

We introduced the distinction between short-run and long-run equilibrium back in Chapter 9. The short-run equilibrium of an industry takes the number of firms as given. The long-run equilibrium, by contrast, is reached only after enough time has elapsed for firms to enter or exit the industry. To analyze monopolistic competition, we focus first on the short run and then on how an industry moves from the short run to the long run.

Panels (a) and (b) of Figure 16-1 on page 394 show two possible situations that a typical firm in a monopolistically competitive industry might face in the short run. In each case the firm looks like any monopolist: it faces a downward-sloping demand curve, which implies a downward-sloping marginal revenue curve.

We assume that every firm has an upward-sloping marginal cost curve but that it also faces some fixed costs, so that its average total cost curve is U-shaped. This assumption doesn't matter in the short run, but, as we'll see shortly, it is crucial to understanding the long-run equilibrium.

In each case the firm, in order to maximize profit, sets marginal revenue equal to marginal cost. So how do these two figures differ? In panel (a) the firm is profitable; in panel (b) it is unprofitable.

| Figure 16-1 | The Monopolistically Competitive Firm in the Short Run |

(a) A Profitable Firm

(b) An Unprofitable Firm

The firm in panel (a) can be profitable for some output quantity: the quantity at which its average total cost curve, *ATC*, lies below its demand curve, D_P. The profit-maximizing output quantity is Q_P, the output at which marginal revenue, MR_P, is equal to marginal cost, *MC*. The firm charges price P_P and earns a profit, represented by the area of the shaded rectangle. The

firm in panel (b), however, can never be profitable because its average total cost curve lies above its demand curve, D_U, for every output quantity. The best that it can do if it produces at all is to produce quantity Q_U and charge price P_U. This generates a loss, indicated by the area of the shaded rectangle. Any other output quantity results in a greater loss. **>web...**

In panel (a) the firm faces the demand curve D_P and the marginal revenue curve MR_P. It produces the profit-maximizing output Q_P, the quantity at which marginal revenue is equal to marginal cost, and sells it at the price P_P. This price is above the average total cost at this output, ATC_P. The firm's profit is indicated by the area of the shaded rectangle.

In panel (b) the firm faces the demand curve D_U and the marginal revenue curve MR_U. It chooses the quantity Q_U at which marginal revenue is equal to marginal cost. However, in this case the price P_U is *below* the average total cost ATC_U; so at this quantity the firm loses money. Its loss is equal to the area of the shaded rectangle. Since Q_U is the profit-maximizing quantity—which means, in this case, the loss-minimizing quantity—there is no way for a firm in this situation to make a profit. We can confirm this by noting that at *any* quantity of output, the average total cost curve in panel (b) lies above the demand curve D_U. Because $ATC > P$ at all quantities of output, this firm always suffers a loss.

As this comparison suggests, the key to whether a firm with market power is profitable or unprofitable in the short run lies in the relationship between its demand curve and its average total cost curve. In panel (a) the demand curve D_P crosses the average total cost curve, meaning that some of the demand curve lies above the average total cost curve. So there are some price–quantity combinations available at which price is higher than average total cost, indicating that the firm can choose a quantity at which it makes positive profit.

In panel (b), by contrast, the demand curve D_U does not cross the average total cost curve—it always lies below it. So the price corresponding to each quantity demanded is always less than the average total cost of producing that quantity. There is no quantity at which the firm can avoid losing money.

These figures, showing firms facing downward-sloping demand curves and their associated marginal revenue curves, look just like ordinary monopoly analysis. The "competition" aspect of monopolistic competition comes into play, however, when we move from the short run to the long run.

Monopolistic Competition in the Long Run

Obviously, an industry in which existing firms are losing money, like the one in panel (b) of Figure 16-1, is not in long-run equilibrium. When existing firms are losing money, some firms will *exit* the industry. The industry will not be in long-run equilibrium until the persistent losses have been eliminated by the exit of some firms.

It may be less obvious that an industry in which existing firms are earning profits, like the one in panel (a) of Figure 16-1, is also not in long-run equilibrium. Given there is *free entry* into the industry, persistent profits by the firms already existing will lead to the entry of additional producers. The industry will not be in long-run equilibrium until the persistent profits have been eliminated by the entry of new producers.

How will entry or exit by other firms affect the profits of a typical existing firm? Because the differentiated products offered by firms in a monopolistically competitive industry compete for the same set of customers, entry or exit by other firms will affect the demand curve facing every existing producer. If new gas stations open along a highway, each of the existing gas stations will sell less gas at any given price. So, as illustrated in panel (a) of Figure 16-2, entry of additional producers into a monopolistically competitive industry will lead to a *leftward* shift of the demand curve and the marginal revenue curve facing a typical existing producer.

Figure 16-2 **Entry and Exit Shift Each Firm's Demand Curve and Marginal Revenue Curve**

(a) Effects of Entry

Price, marginal revenue

Entry shifts the firm's demand curve and its marginal revenue curve leftward.

MR_2 MR_1 D_2 D_1

Quantity

(b) Effects of Exit

Price, marginal revenue

Exit shifts the firm's demand curve and its marginal revenue curve rightward.

MR_1 MR_2 D_1 D_2

Quantity

Entry will occur in the long run when existing firms are profitable. In panel (a), entry causes each existing firm's demand curve and marginal revenue curve to shift to the left. The firm receives a lower price for every unit it sells, and its profit falls. Entry will cease when firms make zero profit. Exit will occur in the long run when existing firms are unprofitable. In panel (b), exit out of the industry shifts each remaining firm's demand curve and marginal revenue curve to the right. The firm receives a higher price for every unit it sells, and profit rises. Exit will cease when the remaining firms make zero profit.

Conversely, suppose that some of the gas stations along the highway close. Then each of the remaining stations will sell more gasoline at any given price. So as illustrated in panel (b), exit of firms from an industry leads to a *rightward* shift of the demand curve and marginal revenue curve facing a typical remaining producer.

The industry will be in long-run equilibrium when there is neither entry nor exit. This will occur only when every firm earns zero profit. So in the long run, a monopolistically competitive industry will end up in **zero-profit equilibrium,** in which firms just manage to cover their costs at their profit-maximizing output quantities.

We have seen that a firm facing a downward-sloping demand curve will earn positive profits if any part of that demand curve lies above its average total cost curve; it will incur a loss if its demand curve lies everywhere below its average total cost curve. So in zero-profit equilibrium, the firm must be in a borderline position between these two cases; its demand curve must just touch its average total cost curve. That is, it must be just *tangent* to it at the firm's profit-maximizing output quantity—the output quantity at which marginal revenue equals marginal cost.

If this is not the case, the firm operating at its profit-maximizing quantity will find itself making either a profit or loss, as illustrated in the panels of Figure 16-1. But we also know that free entry and exit means that this cannot be a long-run equilibrium. Why? In the case of a profit, new firms will enter the industry, shifting the demand curve of every existing firm leftward until all profits are extinguished. In the case of a loss, some existing firms exit and so shift the demand curve of every remaining firm to the right until all losses are extinguished. All entry and exit ceases only when every existing firm makes zero profit at its profit-maximizing quantity of output.

Figure 16-3 shows a typical monopolistically competitive firm in such a zero-profit equilibrium. The firm produces Q_{MC}, the output at which $MR = MC$, and charges price P_{MC}. At this price and quantity, represented by point Z, the demand curve is just tangent to its average total cost curve. The firm earns zero profit because price, P_{MC}, is equal to average total cost, ATC_{MC}.

The normal long-run condition of a monopolistically competitive industry, then, is that each producer is in the situation shown in Figure 16-3. Each producer acts like a monopolist, setting marginal cost equal to marginal revenue so as to maximize profits. But this is just enough to achieve zero economic profit. The producers in the industry are like monopolists without monopoly profits.

> In the long run, a monopolistically competitive industry ends up in **zero-profit equilibrium:** each firm makes zero profit at its profit-maximizing quantity.

Figure 16-3

The Long-Run Zero-Profit Equilibrium

If existing firms are profitable, entry will occur and shift each existing firm's demand curve leftward. If existing firms are unprofitable, each remaining firm's demand curve shifts rightward as some firms exit the industry. Entry and exit will cease when every existing firm makes zero profit at its profit-maximizing quantity. So, in long-run zero-profit equilibrium, the demand curve of each firm is tangent to its average total cost curve at its profit-maximizing quantity: at the profit-maximizing quantity, Q_{MC}, price, P_{MC}, equals average total cost, ATC_{MC}. A monopolistically competitive firm is like a monopolist without monopoly profits. **>web...**

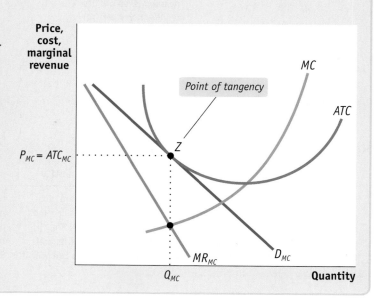

FOR INQUIRING MINDS

FOR INQUIRING MINDS

HITS AND FLOPS

On the face of it, the movie business seems to meet the criteria for monopolistic competition. Movies compete for the same consumers; each movie is different from the others; new companies can and do enter the business. But where's the zero-profit equilibrium? After all, some movies are enormously profitable.

The key is to realize that for every successful blockbuster, there are several flops—and that the movie studios don't know in advance which will be which. (One observer of Hollywood summed up his conclusions as follows: "Nobody knows anything.") And by the time it becomes clear that a movie will be a flop, it's too late to cancel it.

The difference between movie-making and the type of monopolistic competition we model in this chapter is that the fixed costs of making a movie are also *sunk costs*—once they've been incurred, they can't be recovered.

Yet there is still, in a way, a zero-profit equilibrium. If movies on average were highly profitable, more studios would enter the industry and more movies would be made. If movies on average lost money, fewer movies would be made. In fact, as you might expect, the movie industry on average earns just about enough to cover the cost of production—that is, it earns roughly zero economic profit.

This kind of situation—in which firms earn zero profit on average but have a mixture of highly profitable hits and money-losing flops—can be found in other industries, characterized by high, up-front sunk costs. A notable example is the pharmaceutical industry, where many research projects lead nowhere, but a few lead to highly profitable drugs.

economics in action

Bagels from Boom to Bust

Bagels have always been big in New York City, but in the mid-1990s they suddenly became popular across the entire country. Nobody was quite sure why. One factor may have been health consciousness (bagels are low in fat and cholesterol—until you smother them in cream cheese). Another may have been the popularity of New York-based TV shows, like *Seinfeld*. In any case, bagel consumption surged. Those who already owned bagel shops suddenly found their businesses highly profitable.

The fresh-bagel sector fits the definition of monopolistic competition quite well: there are many shops, all competing with one another, but the shops are differentiated by location as well as by style (some shops offer traditional bagels; others offer new items like bagels with blueberries or jalapenos). Each has some market power—it will not lose all its business if it charges slightly higher prices than other shops. And the industry is also characterized by free entry. Sure enough, once bagel shops became highly profitable, many new competitors entered the business. This, in turn, reduced the profitability of every bagel shop. By the end of the 1990s bagels were no longer a highly profitable business. Indeed, quite a few companies dropped out of the business or went bankrupt.

Meanwhile, a similar story seems to be emerging among specialty coffee shops: Starbucks is the most visible company but by no means the only one. When Americans developed a taste for espresso-based drinks like lattes, the business became highly profitable, and many firms entered the industry. In 1991 there were only 500 high-end coffee shops in the United States, but today there are more than 10,000. Demand for specialty coffee is still going up, but thanks to the rapid growth in the number of coffee shops, experts no longer think that the business offers easy opportunities for high profits. ■

> > > > > > > > > > > > > > > > > > > >

> **QUICK REVIEW**

> ➤ Like a monopolist, each firm in a monopolistically competitive industry faces a downward-sloping demand curve and marginal revenue curve. In the short run, it may earn a profit or incur a loss at its profit-maximizing quantity.

> ➤ If the typical firm earns positive profit, new firms will enter the industry in the long run, shifting each existing firm's demand curve to the left. If the typical firm incurs a loss, some existing firms will exit the industry in the long run, shifting the demand curve of each remaining firm to the right.

> ➤ In the long-run equilibrium of a monopolistically competitive industry, the *zero-profit equilibrium*, firms just break even. The typical firm's demand curve is tangent to its average total cost curve at its profit-maximizing quantity.

1. Currently a monopolistically competitive industry, composed of firms with U-shaped average total cost curves, is in long-run equilibrium. Describe how the industry adjusts, in both the short and long run, in each of the following situations.
   a. A technological change that increases fixed cost for every firm in the industry
   b. A technological change that decreases marginal cost for every firm in the industry
2. Why, in the long run, is it impossible for firms in a monopolistically competitive industry to create a monopoly by joining together to form a single firm?

Solutions appear at back of book.

Monopolistic Competition versus Perfect Competition

In a way, long-run equilibrium in a monopolistically competitive industry looks a lot like long-run equilibrium in a perfectly competitive industry. In both cases, there are many firms; in both cases, profits have been competed away; in both cases, the price received by every firm is equal to the average total cost of production.

However, the two versions of long-run equilibrium are different—in ways that are economically significant.

Price, Marginal Cost, and Average Total Cost

Figure 16-4 compares the long-run equilibrium of a typical firm in a perfectly competitive industry with that of a typical firm in a monopolistically competitive industry. Panel (a) shows a perfectly competitive firm facing a market price equal to its minimum average total cost; panel (b) reproduces Figure 16-3. Comparing the panels, we see two important differences.

First, in the case of the perfectly competitive firm shown in panel (a), the price, P_C, received by the firm at the profit-maximizing quantity, Q_C, is equal to the firm's marginal cost of production, MC_C, at that quantity of output. By contrast, at the profit-maximizing quantity chosen by the monopolistically competitive firm in panel (b), Q_{MC}, the price, P_{MC}, is *higher* than the marginal cost of production, MC_{MC}.

This difference translates into a difference in the attitude of firms toward consumers. A wheat farmer, who can sell as much wheat as he likes at the going market price, would not get particularly excited if you offered to buy some wheat at the market price. Since he has no desire to produce more at that price and can sell the wheat to someone else, you are not doing him a favor.

But if you decide to fill up your tank at Jamil's gas station rather than at Katy's, you are doing Jamil a favor. He is not willing to cut his price to get more customers—he's already made the best of that trade-off. But if he gets a few more customers than he expected at the *posted* price, that's good news: an additional sale at the posted price increases his revenue more than it increases his costs because the posted price exceeds marginal cost.

The fact that monopolistic competitors, unlike perfect competitors, want to sell more at the going price is crucial to understanding why they engage in activities like advertising that help increase sales.

The other difference between monopolistic competition and perfect competition that is visible in Figure 16-4 involves the position of each firm on its average total cost curve. In panel (a), the perfectly competitive firm produces at point Q_C, at the bottom of the U-shaped average total cost curve. That is, each firm produces the quantity at which average total cost is minimized—the *minimum-cost output*. As a consequence, the total cost of industry output is also minimized.

Under monopolistic competition, in panel (b), the firm produces at Q_{MC}, on the *downward-sloping* part of the U-shaped *ATC* curve: it produces less than the quantity

Figure 16-4 **Comparing Long-Run Equilibrium in Perfect Competition and Monopolistic Competition**

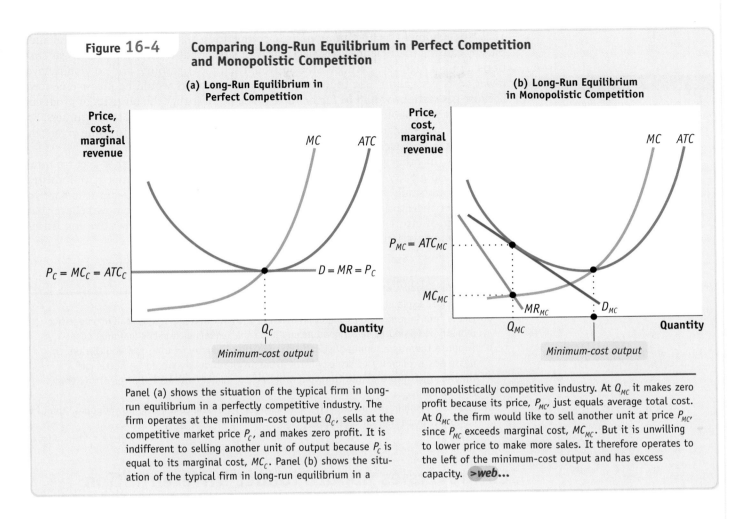

(a) Long-Run Equilibrium in Perfect Competition

(b) Long-Run Equilibrium in Monopolistic Competition

Panel (a) shows the situation of the typical firm in long-run equilibrium in a perfectly competitive industry. The firm operates at the minimum-cost output Q_C, sells at the competitive market price P_C, and makes zero profit. It is indifferent to selling another unit of output because P_C is equal to its marginal cost, MC_C. Panel (b) shows the situation of the typical firm in long-run equilibrium in a monopolistically competitive industry. At Q_{MC} it makes zero profit because its price, P_{MC}, just equals average total cost. At Q_{MC} the firm would like to sell another unit at price P_{MC}, since P_{MC} exceeds marginal cost, MC_{MC}. But it is unwilling to lower price to make more sales. It therefore operates to the left of the minimum-cost output and has excess capacity. >**web**...

that would minimize average total cost. This failure to produce enough to minimize average total cost is sometimes described as the **excess capacity** issue. The typical vendor in a food court or gas station along a road is not big enough to take maximum advantage of available cost savings. So, the total cost of industry output is not minimized in the case of a monopolistically competitive market.

Some people have argued that, because every monopolistic competitor has excess capacity, monopolistically competitive industries are inefficient. But the issue of efficiency under monopolistic competition turns out to be a subtle one that does not have a clear answer.

> Firms in a monopolistically competitive industry have **excess capacity**: they produce less than the output at which average total cost is minimized.

Is Monopolistic Competition Inefficient?

A monopolistic competitor, like a monopolist, charges a price that is above marginal cost. As a result, some people are willing to pay at least as much for an egg roll at Wonderful Wok as it costs to produce it, but who are deterred from doing so. In monopolistic competition, some mutually beneficial transactions go unexploited.

Furthermore, it is often argued that monopolistic competition is subject to a further kind of inefficiency: that the excess capacity of every monopolistic competitor implies *wasteful duplication*: monopolistically competitive industries offer too many varieties. According to this argument, it would be better if there were only two or three vendors in the food court, not six or seven. If there were fewer vendors, they would each have lower average total costs and so could offer food more cheaply.

Is this argument against monopolistic competition right—that it lowers total surplus by causing inefficiency? Not necessarily. It's true that if there were fewer gas stations along a highway, each gas station would sell more gasoline and so would have lower costs per gallon. But there is a drawback: motorists would be inconvenienced because gas stations would be farther apart. The point is that the diversity of products offered in a monopolistically competitive industry is itself beneficial to consumers. So the higher price consumers pay because of excess capacity is offset to some extent by the value they receive from greater diversity.

There is, in other words, a trade-off: more producers means higher average total costs but also greater product diversity. Does a monopolistically competitive industry arrive at the socially optimal point on this trade-off? Probably not—but it is hard to say whether there are too many firms or too few! Most economists now believe that duplication of effort and excess capacity in monopolistically competitive industries are not important issues in practice. ■

< < < < < < < < < < < < < < < < < < <

>>CHECK YOUR UNDERSTANDING 16-3

1. True or false? Explain your answer.
  a. Like a firm in a perfectly competitive industry, a firm in a monopolistically competitive industry is willing to sell a good at any price that equals or exceeds marginal cost.
  b. Suppose there is a monopolistically competitive industry in long-run equilibrium that possesses economies of scale. All the firms in the industry would be better off if they merged into a single firm, but whether consumers are made better off by this is ambiguous.
  c. Fads and fashions are more likely to arise in monopolistic competition or oligopoly than in monopoly or perfect competition.

Solutions appear at back of book.

Controversies about Product Differentiation

Up to this point, we have assumed that products are differentiated in a way that corresponds to some real desire of consumers. There is real convenience in having a gas station in your neighborhood; Chinese food and Mexican food are really different from each other.

In the real world, however, some instances of product differentiation can seem puzzling if you think about them. What is the real difference between the long-distance phone service of AT&T and MCI? Between Energizer and Duracell batteries? Or a Marriot and a Ramada hotel room? Most people would be hard-pressed to answer any of these questions. Yet the producers of these goods make considerable efforts to convince consumers that their products are different from and better than those of their competitors.

No discussion of product differentiation is complete without spending at least a bit of time on the two related issues—and puzzles—of *advertising* and *brand names*.

The Role of Advertising

Wheat farmers don't advertise their wares on TV; car dealers do. That's not because farmers are shy and car dealers are outgoing; it's because advertising is worthwhile only in industries in which firms have at least some market power. The purpose of advertisements is to get people to buy more of a seller's product at the going price. A perfectly competitive firm, which can sell as much as it likes at the going market price, would have no incentive to spend money convincing consumers to buy more. Only a firm that has some market power, and which therefore charges a price that is above marginal cost, can gain from advertising. (Industries that are more or less perfectly competitive, like the milk industry, do advertise—but these ads are sponsored by an association on behalf of the industry as a whole, not on behalf of the milk that comes from the cows on a particular farm.)

Given that advertising "works," it's not hard to see why firms with market power would spend money on it. But the big question about advertising is *why* it works. A related question is whether advertising is, from society's point of view, a waste of resources.

Not all advertising poses a puzzle. Much of it is straightforward: it's a way for sellers to inform potential buyers about what they have to offer (or, occasionally, for buyers to inform potential sellers about what they want). Nor is there much controversy about the economic usefulness of ads that provide information: the real estate ad that declares "sunny, charming, 2 br, 1 ba, a/c" tells you things you need to know (even if a few euphemisms are involved—"charming," of course, means "small").

But what information is being conveyed when a TV actress proclaims the virtues of one or another long-distance telephone service or a sports hero declares that some company's batteries are better than those inside that pink mechanical rabbit? Surely nobody believes that the sports star is an expert on batteries—or that he chose the company that he personally believes makes the best batteries, as opposed to the company that offered to pay him the most. Yet companies believe, with good reason, that money spent on such promotions increases their sales—and that they would be in big trouble if they stopped advertising but their competitors continued to do so.

Why are consumers influenced by ads that do not really provide any information about the product? One answer is that consumers are not as rational as economists typically assume. Perhaps consumers' judgments, or even their tastes, can be influenced by things that economists think ought to be irrelevant, such as which company has hired the most charismatic celebrity to endorse its product. And there is surely some truth to this. Consumer rationality is a useful working assumption; it is not an absolute truth.

However, another answer is that consumer response to advertising is not entirely irrational, because ads can serve as indirect "signals" in a world where consumers don't have good information about products. Suppose, to take a common example, that you need to avail yourself of some local service that you don't use regularly—body work on your car, say, or furniture moving. You turn to the Yellow Pages, where you see a number of small listings and several large display ads. You know that those display ads are large because the firms paid extra for them; still, it may be quite rational to call one of the firms with a big display ad. After all, the big ad probably means that it's a relatively large, successful company—otherwise, the company wouldn't have found it worth spending the money for the larger ad.

The same principle may partly explain why ads feature celebrities. You don't really believe that the supermodel prefers that watch; but the fact that the watch manufacturer is willing and able to pay her fee tells you that it is a major company that is likely to stand behind its product. According to this reasoning, an expensive advertisement serves to establish the quality of a firm's products in the eyes of consumers.

The possibility that it is rational for consumers to respond to advertising also has some bearing on the question of whether advertising is a waste of resources. If ads only work by manipulating the weak-minded, the $128 billion U.S. businesses spent on advertising in 2003 would have been an economic waste—except to the extent that ads sometimes provide entertainment. To the extent that advertising conveys important information, however, it is an economically productive activity after all.

Brand Names

You've been driving all day, and you decide that it's time to find a place to sleep. On your right, you see a sign for the Bates Motel; on your left, you see a sign for a Motel 6, or a Best Western, or some other national chain. Which one do you choose?

Unless they were familiar with the area, most people would head for the chain. In fact, most motels in the United States are members of major chains; the same is true of most fast-food restaurants and many, if not most, stores in shopping malls.

Motel chains and fast-food restaurants are only one aspect of a broader phenomenon: the role of **brand names,** names owned by particular companies that differentiate their products in the minds of consumers. In many cases, a company's brand name is the most important asset it has: clearly, McDonald's is worth far more than the sum of the deep-fat fryers and hamburger grills the company owns.

In fact, companies often go to considerable lengths to defend their brand names, suing anyone else who uses them without permission. You may talk about blowing your nose on a kleenex or xeroxing a term paper, but unless the product in question comes from Kleenex or Xerox, the seller must describe it as a facial tissue or a photocopier.

As with advertising, with which they are closely linked, the social usefulness of brand names is a source of dispute. Does the preference of consumers for known brands reflect consumer irrationality? Or do brand names convey real information? That is, do brand names create unnecessary market power, or do they serve a real purpose?

As in the case of advertising, the answer is probably some of both. On the one hand, brand names often do create unjustified market power. Consumers often pay more for brand-name goods in the supermarket even though consumer experts assure us that the cheaper store brands are equally good. Similarly, many common medicines, like aspirin, are cheaper—with no loss of quality—in their generic form.

On the other hand, for many products the brand name does convey information. A traveler arriving in a strange town can be sure of what awaits in a Holiday Inn or a McDonald's; a tired and hungry traveler may find this preferable to trying an independent hotel or restaurant that might be better—but might be worse.

In addition, brand names offer some assurance that the seller is engaged in repeated interaction with its customers and so has a reputation to protect. If a traveler eats a bad meal at a restaurant in a tourist trap and vows never to eat there again, the restaurant owner may not care, since the chance is small that the traveler will be in the same area again in the future. But if that traveler eats a bad meal at McDonald's and vows never to eat at a McDonald's again, that matters to the company. This gives McDonald's an incentive to provide consistent quality and so gives travelers some assurance that quality controls are in place.

*A **brand name** is a name owned by a particular firm that distinguishes its products from those of other firms.*

economics in action

Absolut Irrationality

Advertising often serves a useful function. Among other things, it can make consumers aware of a wider range of alternatives, which leads to increased competition and lower prices. Indeed, in some cases the courts have viewed industry agreements *not* to advertise as violations of antitrust law. For example, in 1995 the California Dental Association was convicted of conspiracy to prevent competition by discouraging its members from advertising. It had, according to the judge, "withheld from the public information about prices, quality, superiority of service, guarantees, and the use of procedures to allay patient anxiety."

Conversely, advertising sometimes creates product differentiation and market power where there is no real difference in the product. Consider, in particular, the spectacularly successful advertising campaign of Absolut vodka.

In *Twenty Ads That Shook the World*, James B. Twitchell puts it this way: "The pull of Absolut's magnetic advertising is curious because the product itself is so bland. Vodka is aquavit, and aquavit is the most unsophisticated of alcohols. . . . No taste, no smell. . . . In fact, the Swedes, who make the stuff, rarely drink Absolut. They prefer cheaper brands such as Explorer, Renat Brannwinn, or Skane. That's because Absolut can't advertise in Sweden, where alcohol advertising is against the law."

But here's a metaphysical question: if Absolut doesn't really taste any different from other brands, but advertising convinces consumers that they are getting a distinctive product, who are we to say that they aren't? Isn't distinctiveness in the mind of the beholder? ∎

> > > > > > > > > > > > > > > > > > >

>>CHECK YOUR UNDERSTANDING 16-4

1. In which of the following cases is advertisement likely to be economically useful? Economically wasteful? Explain.
   a. Advertisements on the benefits of aspirin
   b. Advertisements for Bayer aspirin
   c. Advertisements on the benefits of drinking orange juice
   d. Advertisements for Tropicana orange juice
   e. Advertisements that state how long a plumber or an electrician has been in business

2. Some industry analysts have stated that a successful brand name is like a barrier to entry. Explain.

Solutions appear at back of book.

• A LOOK AHEAD •

Over the last three chapters we have taken the basic analysis of a perfectly competitive market and extended it in one important direction: to include other kinds of *market structures*. Next we turn to a different kind of extension: to different kinds of *markets*. We begin by asking how economic analysis changes when a national economy can exchange goods and services with other national economies. Next stop: international trade.

SUMMARY

1. **Monopolistic competition** is a market structure in which there are many competing producers, each producing a differentiated product, and there is free entry and exit in the long run. Product differentiation takes three main forms: by style or type, by location, or by quality. Products of competing sellers are considered imperfect substitutes, and each firm has its own downward-sloping demand curve and marginal revenue curve.

2. Short-run profits will attract entry of new firms. This reduces the quantity each existing producer sells at any given price and shifts its demand curve to the left. Short-run losses will induce exit by some firms. This shifts the demand curve of each remaining firm to the right.

3. In the long run, a monopolistically competitive industry is in **zero-profit equilibrium:** at its profit-maximizing quantity, the demand curve for each existing firm is tangent to its average total cost curve. There are zero profits in the industry and no entry or exit.

4. In long-run equilibrium, firms in a monopolistically competitive industry sell at a price greater than marginal cost. They also have **excess capacity** because they produce less than the minimum-cost output; as a result, they have higher costs than firms in a competitive industry. Whether or not monopolistic competition is inefficient is ambiguous because consumers value the diversity of products that it creates.

5. A monopolistically competitive firm will always prefer to make an additional sale at the going price, so it will engage in advertising to increase demand for its product and enhance its market power. Advertising and **brand names** that provide useful information to consumers are economically valuable. But they are economically wasteful when their only purpose is to create market power. In reality, advertising and brand names are likely to be some of both: economically valuable and economically wasteful.

KEY TERMS

Monopolistic competition, p. 389
Zero-profit equilibrium, p. 396

Excess capacity, p. 399

Brand name, p. 402

PROBLEMS

1. Use the three conditions for monopolistic competition discussed in the chapter to decide which of the following firms are likely to be operating as monopolistic competitors. If they are not monopolistically competitive firms, are they monopolists, oligopolists, or perfectly competitive firms?

   a. A local band that plays for weddings, parties, and so on

   b. Minute Maid, a producer of individual-serving juice boxes

   c. Your local dry cleaner

   d. A farmer who produces soybeans

2. You are thinking of setting up a coffee shop. The market structure for coffee shops is monopolistic competition. There are three Starbucks shops, and two other coffee shops very much like Starbucks, in your town already. In order for you to have some degree of market power, you may want to differentiate your coffee shop. Thinking about the three different ways in which products can be differentiated, explain how you would decide whether you should copy Starbucks or whether you should sell coffee in a completely different way.

3. The restaurant business in town is a monopolistically competitive industry in long-run equilibrium. One restaurant owner asks for your advice. She tells you that, each night, not all tables in her restaurant are full. She also tells you that if she lowered the prices on her menu, she would attract more customers and that doing so would lower her average total cost. Should she lower her prices? Draw a diagram showing the demand curve, marginal revenue curve, marginal cost curve, and average total cost curve for this restaurant to explain your advice. Show in your diagram what would happen to the restaurant owner's profit if she were to lower the price so that she sells the minimum-cost output.

4. The structure of the local gas station industry is monopolistic competition. Suppose that currently each gas station incurs a loss. Draw a diagram for a typical gas station to show this short-run situation. Then, in a separate diagram, show what will happen to the typical gas station in the long run. Explain your reasoning.

5. The local hairdresser industry has the structure of monopolistic competition. Your hairdresser boasts that he is making a profit and that if he continues to do so, he will be able to retire in five years. Use a diagram to illustrate your hairdresser's current situation. Do you expect this to last? In a separate diagram, draw what you expect to happen in the long run. Explain your reasoning.

6. Magnificent Blooms is a florist in a monopolistically competitive industry. It is a successful operation, producing the quantity that minimizes its average total cost and making a profit. The owner also boasts that at its current level of output, its marginal cost is above marginal revenue. Illustrate the current situation of Magnificent Blooms in a diagram. Answer the following questions by illustrating with a diagram.

   a. In the short run, could Magnificent Blooms increase its profit?

   b. In the long run, could Magnificent Blooms increase its profit?

7. "In the long run, there is no difference between monopolistic competition and perfect competition." True, false, or ambiguous? Discuss this statement with respect to the following:

   a. The price charged to consumers

   b. The average total cost of production

   c. The efficiency of the market outcome

   d. The typical firm's profit in the long run

8. "In both the short run and in the long run, the typical firm in monopolistic competition and a monopolist each make a profit." Do you agree with this statement? Explain your reasoning.

9. The market for clothes has the structure of monopolistic competition. What impact will fewer firms in this industry have on you as a consumer? Address the following issues:

   a. Variety of clothes

   b. Differences in quality of service

   c. Price

10. For each of the following situations, decide whether advertising is directly informative about the product or simply an indirect signal of its quality. Explain your reasoning.

    a. Golf champion Tiger Woods drives a Buick in a TV commercial and claims that he prefers it to any other car.

    b. A newspaper ad states "For sale: 1989 Honda Civic, 160,000 miles, new transmission."

    c. McDonald's spends millions of dollars on an advertising campaign that proclaims: "I'm lovin' it."

    d. Subway advertises one of its sandwiches claiming that it contains 6 grams of fat and fewer than 300 calories.

11. In each of the following cases, explain how the advertisement functions as a signal to a potential buyer. Explain what information the buyer lacks that is being supplied by the advertisement and how the information supplied by the advertisement is likely to affect the buyer's willingness to buy the good.

    a. "Looking for work. Excellent references from previous employers available."

    b. "Electronic equipment for sale. All merchandise carries a one-year, no-questions-asked warranty."

    c. "Car for sale by original owner. All repair and maintenance records available."

12. McDonald's spends millions of dollars each year on legal protection of its brand name, thereby preventing any unauthorized use of it. Explain what information this conveys to you as a consumer about the quality of McDonald's products.

> **web...** To continue your study and review of concepts in this chapter, please visit the Krugman/Wells website for quizzes, animated graph tutorials, web links to helpful resources, and more.
> ## www.worthpublishers.com/krugmanwells

17

>> International Trade

A ROSE BY ANY OTHER NATION

GIVING YOUR BELOVED ROSES ON Valentine's Day is a well-established tradition in the United States. But in the past it was a very expensive gesture: in the northern hemisphere, Valentine's Day falls not in summer, when roses are in bloom, but in the depths of winter. Until recently, that meant that the roses in the florist's shop were grown at great cost in heated greenhouses. Nowadays, however, most of the Valentine's Day roses sold in this country are flown in from South America, mainly from Colombia, where growing a rose in February is no trouble at all.

Is it a good thing that we now buy our winter roses from abroad? The vast majority of economists say yes: international trade, in which countries specialize in producing different goods and trade those goods with each other, is a source of mutual benefit to the countries involved. In Chapter 2 we laid out the basic principle that there are *gains from trade*; it's a principle that applies to countries as well as individuals.

But politicians and the public are often not convinced. In fact, during the 1996 presidential campaign one contender used the occasion of Valentine's Day to visit a flower-growing greenhouse in New Hampshire, where he denounced imports of South American roses as a threat to U.S. jobs.

Up to now this book has analyzed the economy as if it were self-sufficient, as if the economy produced all the goods and services it consumes, and vice versa. This is, of course, true of the world economy as a whole. But it is not true of any individual country. It's true that 40 years ago the United States exported only a small fraction of what it produced and imported only a

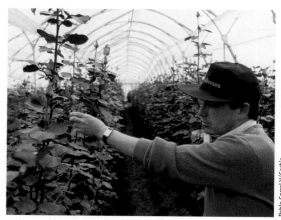

What do these sweethearts and this rose farmer have in common? They are enjoying the mutual benefits of international trade.

What you will learn in this chapter:

➤ How comparative advantage leads to mutually beneficial international trade

➤ The sources of international comparative advantage

➤ Who gains and who loses from international trade, and why the gains exceed the losses

➤ How **tariffs** and **import quotas** cause inefficiency and reduce total surplus

➤ Why governments often engage in **trade protection** to shelter domestic industries from imports and how **international trade agreements** counteract this small fraction of what it consumed. Since then, however, both U.S. imports and U.S. exports have grown much faster than the U.S. economy as a whole. And other countries engage in far more foreign trade, relative to the size of their economies, than does the United States. To have a full picture of how national economies work, we must understand international trade.

This chapter examines the economics of international trade. We start from the model of comparative advantage, which, as we saw in Chapter 2, explains why there are gains from international trade. It's also important, however, to understand how some individuals can be hurt by international trade and the effects of trade policies that countries use to limit imports or promote exports.

Comparative Advantage and International Trade

The United States buys roses—and many other goods and services—from other countries. At the same time, it sells many goods and services to other countries. Goods and services purchased from abroad are **imports;** goods and services sold abroad are **exports.**

As illustrated by the opening story, imports and exports have taken on an increasingly important role in the U.S. economy. Over the last 40 years, both imports into the United States and exports from the United States have grown faster than the U.S. economy; panel (a) of Figure 17-1 shows how the values of imports and exports have grown as a percentage of gross domestic product. As panel (b) demonstrates, foreign trade is even more important for many other countries than for the United States.

To understand why international trade occurs and why economists believe it is beneficial to the economy, we will first review the concept of comparative advantage.

> Goods and services purchased from other countries are **imports;** goods and services sold to other countries are **exports.**

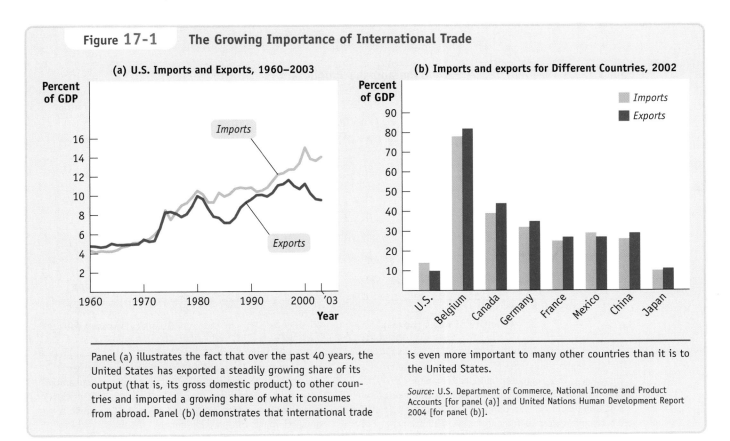

Figure 17-1   The Growing Importance of International Trade

Panel (a) illustrates the fact that over the past 40 years, the United States has exported a steadily growing share of its output (that is, its gross domestic product) to other countries and imported a growing share of what it consumes from abroad. Panel (b) demonstrates that international trade is even more important to many other countries than it is to the United States.

Source: U.S. Department of Commerce, National Income and Product Accounts [for panel (a)] and United Nations Human Development Report 2004 [for panel (b)].

Production Possibilities and Comparative Advantage, Revisited

To grow Valentine's Day roses, any country must use resources—labor, energy, capital, and so on—that could have been used to produce other things. The potential production of other goods a country must forgo to produce a rose is the opportunity cost of that rose.

It's a lot easier to grow Valentine's Day roses in Colombia, where the weather in January and February is nearly ideal, than it is in the United States. Conversely, other goods are not produced as easily in Colombia as in the United States. For example, Colombia doesn't have the base of skilled workers and technological know-how that makes the United States so good at producing high-technology goods. So the opportunity cost of a Valentine's Day rose, in terms of other goods such as computers, is much less in Colombia than it is in the United States.

And so we say that Colombia has a comparative advantage in producing roses. Let's repeat the definition of comparative advantage from Chapter 2: *a country has a comparative advantage in producing a good if the opportunity cost of producing the good is lower for that country than for other countries.*

Figure 17-2 provides a hypothetical numerical example of comparative advantage in international trade. We assume that only two goods are produced and consumed, roses and computers, and there are only two countries in the world, the United States and Colombia. We also assume that roses are shipped in standard refrigerated boxes, each containing 100 roses. The figure shows hypothetical production possibility frontiers for the United States and Colombia. As in Chapter 2, we simplify the model by assuming that the production possibility frontiers are straight lines, rather than the more realistic bowed-out shape shown in Figure 2-1. The straight-line shape implies that the opportunity cost of a box of roses in terms of computers in each country is constant—it does not depend on how many units of each good the country produces. The analysis of international trade under the assumption that opportunity costs are constant and therefore production possibility frontiers are

Figure 17-2　**Comparative Advantage and the Production Possibility Frontier**

The U.S. opportunity cost of a box of roses in terms of a computer is 2: 2 computers must be forgone for every additional box of roses produced. The Colombian opportunity cost of a box of roses in terms of a computer is 0.5: only 0.5 computer must be forgone for every additional box of roses produced. Therefore, Colombia has a comparative advantage in roses and the United States has a comparative advantage in computers. In autarky, C_{US} is the U.S. production and consumption bundle and C_{CO} is the Colombian production and consumption bundle. **>web...**

TABLE 17-1

Production Possibilities

| (a) United States | Production | |
	One possibility	Another possibility
Quantity of roses (boxes)	1,000	0
Quantity of computers	0	2,000

| (b) Colombia | Production | |
	One possibility	Another possibility
Quantity of roses (boxes)	2,000	0
Quantity of computers	0	1,000

straight lines is known as the **Ricardian model of international trade,** named after the English economist David Ricardo, who introduced this analysis in the early nineteenth century.

Table 17-1 presents the same information that is shown in Figure 17-2. We assume that the United States can produce 1,000 boxes of roses if it produces no computers or 2,000 computers if it produces no roses. The slope of the production possibility frontier in panel (a) is −2,000/1,000, or −2: to produce an additional box of roses, the United States must forgo the production of 2 computers.

Similarly, we assume that Colombia can produce 2,000 boxes of roses if it produces no computers or 1,000 computers if it produces no roses. The slope of the production possibility frontier in panel (b) is −1,000/2,000, or −0.5: to produce an additional box of roses, Colombia must forgo the production of 0.5 computer.

Economists use the term **autarky** to describe a situation in which a country cannot trade with other countries. We assume that in autarky the United States would choose to produce and consume 500 boxes of roses and 1,000 computers. This autarky production and consumption bundle is shown by point C_{US} in panel (a) of Figure 17-2. We also assume that in autarky Colombia would choose to produce and consume 1,000 boxes of roses and 500 computers, shown by point C_{CO} in panel (b). The outcome in autarky is summarized in Table 17-2, where world production and consumption is the sum of U.S. and Colombian production and consumption.

If the countries trade with each other, they can do better than they can in autarky. In this example, Colombia has a comparative advantage in the production of roses. That

The **Ricardian model of international trade** analyzes international trade under the assumption that opportunity costs are constant.

Autarky is a situation in which a country cannot trade with other countries.

TABLE 17-2

Production and Consumption Under Autarky

(a) United States	Production	Consumption
Quantity of roses (boxes)	500	500
Quantity of computers	1,000	1,000

(b) Colombia	Production	Consumption
Quantity of roses (boxes)	1,000	1,000
Quantity of computers	500	500

(c) World (United States and Colombia)	Production	Consumption
Quantity of roses (boxes)	1,500	1,500
Quantity of computers	1,500	1,500

is, the opportunity cost of roses is lower in Colombia than in the United States: 0.5 computer per box of roses in Columbia versus 2 computers per box of roses in the United States. Conversely, the United States has a comparative advantage in the production of computers: to produce an additional computer, the United States must forgo the production of 0.5 box of roses, but producing an additional computer in Colombia requires forgoing the production of 2 boxes of roses. International trade allows each country to specialize in producing the good in which it has a comparative advantage: computers in the United States, roses in Colombia. And that leads to gains for both when they trade.

The Gains from International Trade

Figure 17-3 illustrates how both countries gain from specialization and trade. Again, panel (a) represents the United States and panel (b) represents Colombia. As a result of international trade, the United States produces at point Q_{US}: 2,000 computers but no roses. Colombia produces at Q_{CO}: 2,000 boxes of roses but no computers. The new production choices are given in the second column of Table 17-3.

By comparing Table 17-3 with Table 17-2, you can see that specialization increases total world production of *both* goods. In the absence of specialization, total world production consists of 1,500 computers and 1,500 boxes of roses. After specialization, total world production rises to 2,000 computers and 2,000 boxes of roses. These goods can now be traded, with the United States consuming roses produced in Colombia and Colombia consuming computers produced in the United States. The result is that each country can consume more of *both* goods than it did in autarky.

In addition to showing production under trade, Figure 17-3 shows one of many possible pairs of consumption bundles for the United States and Colombia, which is also given in Table 17-3. In this example, the United States moves from its autarky consumption of 1,000 computers and 500 boxes of roses, shown by C_{US}, to consumption after trade of 1,250 computers and 750 boxes of roses, represented by C'_{US}. Colombia moves from its autarky consumption of 500 computers and 1,000 boxes of

Figure 17-3   The Gains from International Trade

(a) U.S. Production and Consumption

(b) Colombian Production and Consumption

Trade increases world production of both goods, allowing both countries to consume more. Here, each country specializes its production as a result of trade: the United States produces at Q_{US} and Colombia produces at Q_{CO}. Total world production of computers has risen from 1,500 to 2,000

and of roses from 1,500 boxes to 2,000 boxes. The United States can now consume bundle C'_{US}, and Colombia can now consume bundle C'_{CO}—consumption bundles that were unattainable without trade.

TABLE 17-3

Production and Consumption After International Trade

(a) United States

	Production	Consumption
Quantity of roses (boxes)	0	750
Quantity of computers	2,000	1,250

(b) Colombia

	Production	Consumption
Quantity of roses (boxes)	2,000	1,250
Quantity of computers	0	750

(c) World (United States and Columbia)

	Production	Consumption
Quantity of roses (boxes)	2,000	2,000
Quantity of computers	2,000	2,000

roses, shown by C_{CO}, to consumption after trade of 750 computers and 1,250 boxes of roses, shown by C'_{CO}.

What makes this possible is the fact that with international trade countries are no longer required to consume the same bundle of goods that they produce. Each country produces at one point (Q_{US} for the United States, Q_{CO} for Colombia) but consumes at a different point (C'_{US} for the United States, C'_{CO} for Colombia). The difference reflects imports and exports: the 750 boxes of roses the United States consumes are imported from Colombia; the 750 computers Colombia consumes are imported from the United States.

In this example we have simply assumed the post-trade consumption bundles of the two countries. In fact, just as in the case of individual consumption choices, the consumption choices of countries reflect both the preferences of its residents and the *relative prices* in international markets—the prices of one good in terms of another. Although we have not explicitly given the price of computers in terms of roses, that price is implicit in our example: Colombia exports 750 boxes of roses and receives 750 computers in return, so that each box of roses is traded for 1 computer. This tells us that the price of a computer on world markets must be equal to the price of a box of roses in our example.

What determines the actual relative prices in international trade? The answer is supply and demand—and we'll turn to supply and demand in international trade in the next section. However, first let's look behind the production possibility frontiers and ask what determines a country's comparative advantage.

Sources of Comparative Advantage

International trade is driven by comparative advantage, but where does comparative advantage come from? Economists who study international trade have found three main sources of comparative advantage: international differences in *climate*, international differences in *factor endowments*, and international differences in *technology*.

Differences in Climate A key reason the opportunity cost of producing a Valentine's Day rose in Colombia is less than in the United States is that nurseries in Colombia can grow roses outdoors all year

---

PITFALLS

THE PAUPER LABOR FALLACY

One common argument about international trade goes as follows: it's true that Bangladesh (to pick an example) can produce some goods, such as clothing, more cheaply than we can—but that cost advantage is based only on lower wages. In fact, it takes *fewer* hours of labor to produce a shirt in the United States than in Bangladesh. So importing goods produced by "pauper labor" (workers who are paid very low wages), goes the argument, reduces the American standard of living.

Why is this a misconception? Because it confuses *comparative advantage* with *absolute advantage*. Yes, it takes less labor to produce a shirt in the United States than it does in Bangladesh. But what determines comparative advantage is not the amount of resources used to produce a good but the opportunity cost of that good—the quantity of other goods forgone in order to produce a shirt.

Low wages in countries such as Bangladesh reflect low productivity of labor across the board. Because labor productivity in other Bangladeshi industries is very low, using a lot of labor to produce a shirt does not require forgoing the production of large quantities of other goods. But in the United States, the opposite is true: very high productivity in other industries (such as high-technology goods) means that producing a shirt in the United States requires sacrificing lots of other goods. So the opportunity cost of producing a shirt is less in Bangladesh than in the United States. Despite its lower labor productivity, Bangladesh has a comparative advantage in clothing production, although the United States has an absolute advantage. As a result, importing clothing from Bangladesh actually raises the standard of living in the United States.

round but nurseries in the United States can't. In general, differences in climate are a significant source of international trade. Tropical countries export tropical products like coffee, sugar, and bananas. Countries in the temperate zones export crops like wheat and corn. Some trade is even driven by the difference in seasons between the northern and southern hemispheres: winter deliveries of Chilean grapes and New Zealand apples have become commonplace in U.S. and European supermarkets.

Differences in Factor Endowments Canada is a major exporter of forest products—lumber and products derived from lumber, like pulp and paper—to the United States. These exports don't reflect the special skill of Canadian lumberjacks. Instead, Canada has a comparative advantage in forest products because its forested area is much greater compared to the size of its labor force than the ratio of forestland to the labor force in the United States.

Forestland, like labor and capital, is a factor of production. Due to history and geography, the mix of available factors of production differs among countries, providing an important source of comparative advantage. The relationship between comparative advantage and factor availability is found in an influential model of international trade, the *Heckscher–Ohlin model* (developed by two Swedish economists in the first half of the twentieth century).

A key concept in the model is *factor intensity*. Producers use different ratios of factors of production in the production of different goods. For example, at any given wage rate and rental rate of capital, oil refineries will use much more capital per worker than clothing factories. Economists use the term **factor intensity** to describe this difference among goods: oil refining is capital-intensive, because it tends to use a high ratio of capital to labor, but clothing manufacture is labor-intensive, because it tends to use a high ratio of labor to capital.

According to the **Heckscher–Ohlin model,** a country will have a comparative advantage in a good whose production is intensive in the factors that are abundantly available in that country. So a country that has an abundance of capital will have a comparative advantage in capital-intensive industries such as oil refining, but a country that has an abundance of labor will have a comparative advantage in labor-intensive industries such as clothing production. The basic intuition behind this result is simple and based on opportunity cost. The opportunity cost of a given factor—the value that the factor would generate in alternative uses—is low for a country when it possesses an abundance of that factor. (For example, in rainy parts of the United States, the opportunity cost of water for residences is low because there is a plentiful supply for other uses, such as agriculture.) So the opportunity cost of producing goods that are intensive in the use of an abundantly available factor is also low.

> The **factor intensity** of production of a good is a measure of which factor is used in relatively greater quantities than other factors in production.
>
> According to the **Heckscher–Ohlin model,** a country has a comparative advantage in a good whose production is intensive in the factors that are abundantly available in that country.

FOR INQUIRING MINDS

DOES TRADE HURT POOR COUNTRIES?

It's a good bet that the clothes you are wearing right now were produced in a labor-abundant country such as Bangladesh or Sri Lanka. If so, the workers who produced those clothes were paid very low wages by Western standards: in 2002 (the most recent data available) workers in Sri Lankan factories were paid an average of $0.33 an hour. Doesn't this mean that Sri Lankan workers are getting a bad deal?

The answer of most economists is that it doesn't. The wages paid to export workers in poor countries should be compared not to what workers get in rich countries but to what they would get if those export jobs weren't available. The reason Sri Lankans are willing to work for so little is that in an underdeveloped economy, with lots of labor but very little of other factors of production like capital, the opportunities available to workers are very limited. It's almost certain that international trade makes Sri Lanka and other low-wage countries *less* poor than they would be otherwise and raises workers'

wages relative to what they would be without international trade.

Nonetheless, many people in advanced countries—students in particular—are disturbed by the thought that their consumer goods are produced by such poorly paid workers and want to see those workers receive higher pay and better working conditions. The dilemma is whether it is possible to insist on higher wages and better working conditions without eliminating the job altogether, thereby choking off the benefits of international trade.

The most dramatic example of the validity of the Heckscher–Ohlin model is world trade in clothing. Clothing production is a labor-intensive activity: it doesn't take much physical capital, nor does it require a lot of human capital in the form of highly educated workers. So you would expect labor-abundant countries such as China and Bangladesh to have a comparative advantage in clothing production. And they do.

That much international trade is the result of differences in factor endowments helps explain another fact: international specialization of production is often *incomplete.* That is, a country often maintains some domestic production of a good that it imports. A good example of this is the United States and oil. Saudi Arabia exports oil to the United States because Saudi Arabia has an abundant supply of oil relative to its other factors of production; the United States exports medical devices to Saudi Arabia because it has an abundant supply of medical technical expertise relative to its other factors of production. But the United States also produces some oil domestically because the size of its domestic oil reserves make it economical to do so. In our demand and supply analysis in the next section, we'll consider incomplete specialization by a country to be the norm. We should emphasize, however, that the fact that countries often incompletely specialize does not in any way change the conclusion that there are gains from trade.

Differences in Technology In the 1970s and 1980s, Japan became by far the world's largest exporter of automobiles, selling large numbers to the United States and the rest of the world. Japan's comparative advantage in automobiles wasn't the result of climate. Nor can it easily be attributed to differences in factor endowments: aside from a scarcity of land, Japan's mix of available factors is quite similar to that in other advanced countries. Instead, Japan's comparative advantage in automobiles was based on the superior production techniques developed by that country's manufacturers, which allowed them to produce more cars with a given amount of labor and capital than their American or European counterparts.

Japan's comparative advantage in automobiles was a case of comparative advantage caused by differences in technology—the techniques used in production.

The causes of differences in technology are somewhat mysterious. Sometimes they seem to be based on knowledge accumulated through experience—for example, Switzerland's comparative advantage in watches reflects a long tradition of watchmaking. Sometimes they are the result of a set of innovations that for some reason occur in one country but not in others. Technological advantage is also often transitory. American auto manufacturers have now closed much of the gap in productivity with their Japanese competitors; Europe's aircraft industry has closed a similar gap with the U.S. aircraft industry. At any given point in time, however, differences in technology are a major source of comparative advantage.

FOR INQUIRING MINDS

INCREASING RETURNS AND INTERNATIONAL TRADE

Most analysis of international trade focuses on how differences between countries—differences in climate, factor endowments, and technology—create national comparative advantage. However, economists have also pointed out another reason for international trade: the role of *increasing returns.*

Production of a good is characterized by increasing returns if the productivity of labor and other resources rises with the quantity of output. For example, in an industry characterized by increasing returns, increasing output by 10 percent might require only 8 percent more labor and 9 percent more raw materials. Increasing returns (sometimes also called economies of scale) can give rise to monopoly, because they give large firms an advantage over small firms.

But increasing returns can also give rise to international trade. The logic runs as follows: if production of a good is characterized by increasing returns, it makes sense to concentrate production in only a few locations, so as to achieve a high level of production in each location. But that also means that the good is produced in only a few countries, which export that good to other countries. A commonly cited example is the North American auto industry: although both the United States and Canada produce automobiles and their components, each particular model or component tends to be produced in only one of the two countries and exported to the other. Increasing returns probably play a large role in the trade in manufactured goods between advanced countries, which is about 25 percent of the total value of world trade.

In the United States, an abundance of engineering know-how has led to a comparative advantage in aircraft.

economics in action

The Comparative Advantage of the United States

The United States is a country of superlatives: a nation richly endowed with many resources, human and natural, it has an *absolute* advantage in almost everything—that is, it is better at producing almost everything than anyone else. But what is its *comparative* advantage?

In 1953 the economist Wassily Leontief made a surprising discovery. Until his work, many economists had assumed that because U.S. workers were clearly better-equipped with machinery than their counterparts in other countries, the production of U.S. exports was more capital-intensive than the production of U.S. imports. That is, they expected that U.S. exports were more capital-intensive than U.S. imports. But Leontief's work showed that this wasn't true: in fact, goods that the United States exported were slightly less capital-intensive than goods the country imported. The "Leontief paradox" led to a sustained effort to make sense of U.S. trade patterns.

The main resolution of this paradox, it turns out, depends on the definition of capital. U.S. exports aren't intensive in *physical* capital—machines and buildings. Instead, they are intensive in *human* capital. U.S. exporting industries use a substantially higher ratio of highly educated workers to other workers than is found in U.S. industries that compete against imports. For example, one of America's biggest export sectors is aircraft; the aircraft industry employs large numbers of engineers and other people with graduate degrees relative to the number of manual laborers. Conversely, we import a lot of clothing, which is often produced by workers with little formal education. ∎

< < < < < < < < < < < < < < < < < <

>>CHECK YOUR UNDERSTANDING 17-1

1. In the United States, the opportunity cost of 1 ton of corn is 50 bicycles. In China, the opportunity cost of 1 bicycle is 0.01 ton of corn.
   a. Determine the pattern of comparative advantage.
   b. In autarky, the United States can produce 200,000 bicycles if no corn is produced, and China can produce 3,000 tons of corn if no bicycles are produced. Draw each country's production possibility frontier assuming constant opportunity cost, with tons of corn on the vertical axis and bicycles on the horizontal axis.
   c. With trade, each country specializes its production. The United States consumes 1,000 tons of corn and 200,000 bicycles; China consumes 3,000 tons of corn and 100,000 bicycles. Indicate the production and consumption points on your diagrams, and use them to explain the gains from trade.

2. Explain the following patterns of trade using the Heckscher–Ohlin model:
   a. France exports wine to the United States, and the United States exports movies to France.
   b. Brazil exports shoes to the United States, and the United States exports shoe-making machinery to Brazil.

Solutions appear at back of book.

Supply, Demand, and International Trade

Simple models of comparative advantage are helpful for understanding the fundamental causes of international trade. However, to analyze the effects of international trade at a more detailed level and to understand trade policy, it helps to return to the supply and demand model. We'll start by looking at the effects of imports on domestic producers and consumers, then turn to the effect of exports.

The Effects of Imports

Figure 17-4 shows the U.S. market for roses, ignoring international trade for a moment. It introduces a few new concepts: the *domestic demand curve*, the *domestic supply curve*, and the *domestic* or *autarky* price.

The **domestic demand curve** shows how the quantity of a good demanded by residents of a country depends on the price of that good. Why "domestic"? Because people living in other countries may demand the good, too. Once we introduce international trade, we need to distinguish between purchases of a good by domestic consumers and purchases by foreign consumers. So the domestic demand curve reflects only the demand of residents of our own country. Similarly, the **domestic supply curve** shows how the quantity of a good supplied by producers inside a country depends on the price of that good. Once we introduce international trade, we need to distinguish between the supply of domestic producers and foreign supply—supply brought in from abroad.

In autarky, with no international trade in roses, the equilibrium in this market would be determined by the intersection of the domestic demand and domestic supply curves, point *A*. The equilibrium price of roses would be P_A, and the equilibrium quantity of roses produced and consumed would be Q_A. As always, both consumers and producers would gain from the existence of the domestic market. Consumer surplus would be equal to the area of the upper shaded triangle in Figure 17-4. Producer surplus would be equal to the area of the lower shaded triangle. And total surplus would be equal to the sum of these two shaded triangles.

Now let's imagine opening up this market to imports. To do this, we must make some assumption about the supply of imports. The simplest assumption, which we will adopt here, is that unlimited quantities of roses can be purchased from abroad at a fixed price, known as the **world price** of roses. Figure 17-5 on page 416 shows a situation in which the world price of roses, P_W, is lower than the price of roses that would prevail in the domestic market in autarky, P_A.

Given the world price of roses is below the domestic price of roses, it is profitable for importers to buy roses abroad and resell them domestically. The imported roses increase the supply of roses to the domestic market, driving down the domestic market price. Roses will continue to be imported until the domestic price falls to a level equal to the world price.

The result is shown in Figure 17-5. Because of imports, the domestic price of roses falls from P_A to P_W. The quantity of roses demanded by domestic consumers rises from Q_A to C_T, and the quantity supplied by domestic producers falls from Q_A to Q_T.

The **domestic demand curve** shows how the quantity of a good demanded by domestic consumers depends on the price of that good.

The **domestic supply curve** shows how the quantity of a good supplied by domestic producers depends on the price of that good.

The **world price** of a good is the price at which that good can be bought or sold abroad.

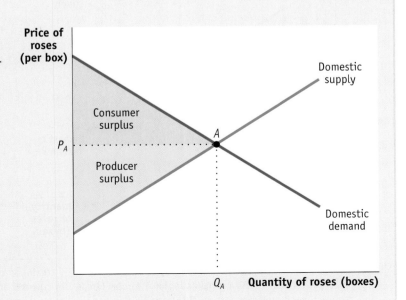

Figure 17-4

Consumer and Producer Surplus in Autarky

In the absence of trade, domestic price is P_A, the autarky price at which the domestic supply curve and the domestic demand curve intersect. The quantity produced and consumed domestically is Q_A. Consumer surplus is represented by the blue-shaded area, and producer surplus is represented by the red-shaded area.

>web...

Figure 17-5

The Domestic Market with Imports

Here the world price of roses, P_W, is below the autarky price, P_A. When the economy is opened to international trade, imports enter the domestic market, and the domestic price falls from the autarky price, P_A, to the world price, P_W. As the price falls, the domestic quantity demanded rises from Q_A to C_T and domestic production falls from Q_A to Q_T. The difference between domestic quantity demanded and domestic quantity supplied at P_W, the quantity $C_T - Q_T$, is filled by imports.

>web...

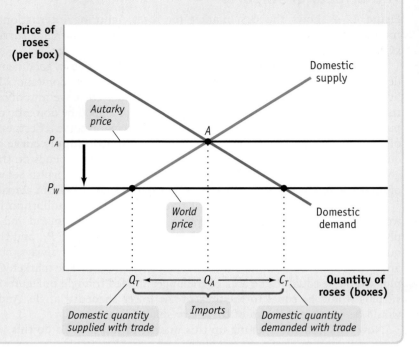

The difference between the domestic quantity demanded and the domestic quantity supplied, $C_T - Q_T$, is filled by imports.

Now let's turn to the effects of imports on consumer surplus and producer surplus. Because imports of roses lead to a fall in their domestic price, consumer surplus rises and producer surplus falls. Figure 17-6 shows how this works. We label four areas: W,

Figure 17-6 The Effects of Imports on Surplus

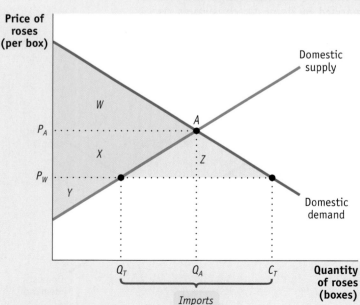

	Changes in surplus	
	Gain	**Loss**
Consumer surplus	$X + Z$	
Producer surplus		$-X$
Change in total surplus	**+Z**	

When the domestic price falls to P_W as a result of international trade, consumers gain additional surplus (areas $X + Z$) and producers lose surplus (area X). Because the gains to consumers outweigh the losses to producers, there is an increase in the total surplus in the economy as a whole (area Z).

X, Y, and Z. The autarky consumer surplus we identified in Figure 17-4 corresponds to W, and the autarky producer surplus corresponds to the sum of X and Y. The fall in the domestic price to the world price leads to an increase in consumer surplus; it increases by the areas X and Z, so that it now equals the sum of W, X, and Z. At the same time, producers lose the area X in surplus, so that producer surplus now equals only Y.

The table in Figure 17-6 summarizes the changes in consumer and producer surplus when the rose market is opened to imports. Consumers gain surplus equal to the area X + Z. Producers lose surplus equal to the area X. So the sum of producer and consumer surplus—the total surplus generated in the rose market—increases by the area Z. As a result of trade, consumers gain and producers lose, but the gain to consumers exceeds the loss to producers.

This is an important result. We have just shown that opening up a market to imports leads to a net gain in total surplus, which is what we should have expected given the proposition that there are gains from international trade. However, we have also learned that although the country as a whole gains, some groups—in this case, domestic producers of roses—lose as a result of international trade. As we'll see shortly, the fact that international trade typically creates losers as well as winners is crucial for understanding the politics of trade policy.

We turn next to the case in which a country exports a good.

The Effects of Exports

Figure 17-7 shows the effects on a country when it exports a good, in this case computers. For this example, we assume that unlimited quantities of computers can be sold abroad at a given world price, P_W, which is higher than the price that would prevail in the domestic market in autarky, P_A.

The higher world price makes it profitable for exporters to buy computers domestically and sell them overseas. The purchases of domestic computers drives the domestic price up until the domestic price is equal to the world price. As a result, the quantity demanded by domestic consumers falls from Q_A to C_T, and the quantity supplied by domestic producers rises from Q_A to Q_T. This difference between domestic production and domestic consumption, $Q_T - C_T$, is exported.

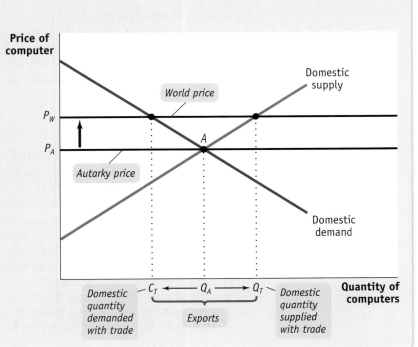

Figure 17-7

The Domestic Market with Exports

Here the world price, P_W, is greater than the autarky price, P_A. When the economy is opened to international trade, some of the domestic supply is now exported. The domestic price rises from the autarky price, P_A, to the world price, P_W. As the price rises, the domestic quantity demanded falls from Q_A to C_T and domestic production rises from Q_A to Q_T. The remainder of the domestic quantity supplied, $Q_T - C_T$, is exported.

>web...

Figure 17-8   **The Effects of Exports on Surplus**

		Changes in surplus	
		Gain	**Loss**
Consumer surplus			$-X$
Producer surplus		$X + Z$	
Change in total surplus		**+Z**	

When the domestic price rises to P_W as a result of trade, producers gain additional surplus (areas $X + Z$) but consumers lose surplus (area X). Because the gains to producers outweigh the losses to consumers, there is an increase in the total surplus in the economy as a whole (area Z).

Like imports, exports lead to an overall gain in total surplus for the exporting country, but also create losers as well as winners. Figure 17-8 shows the effects of computer exports on producer and consumer surplus. In the absence of trade, the price of computers would be P_A. Consumer surplus in the absence of trade is the sum of the areas W and X, and producer surplus would be the area Y. As a result of trade, price rises from P_A to P_W, consumer surplus falls to W, and producer surplus rises to $Y + X + Z$. So producers gain $X + Z$, consumers lose X, and, as shown in the table accompanying the figure, the economy as a whole gains total surplus in the amount of Z.

We have learned, then, that imports of a particular good hurt domestic producers of that good but help domestic consumers, whereas exports of a particular good hurt domestic consumers but help domestic producers of that good. In each case, the gains are larger than the losses.

International Trade and Factor Markets

So far we have focused on the effects of international trade on producers and consumers in a particular industry. For many purposes this is a very helpful approach. But to understand the long-run effects of international trade on income distribution, this approach can be inadequate, because factors of production move between industries.

To see the problem, consider the position of Maria, a trained accountant who currently works for a U.S. company that grows flowers. If the economy is opened up to imports of roses from South America, the domestic rose-growing industry will contract, and it will hire fewer accountants. But accounting is a profession with employment opportunities in many industries, and Maria might well find a better job in the computer industry, which expands as a result of international trade. So it may not be appropriate to think of her as a producer of flowers who is hurt by competition from imported roses. Rather, what matters to her is the effect of international trade on the salaries of accountants, wherever they are employed. In other words, sometimes it is important to analyze the effect of trade on *factor prices*.

Earlier in this chapter we described the Heckscher–Ohlin model of trade, which states that comparative advantage is determined by a country's factor endowment. This model also suggests how international trade affects factor prices in a country: compared to autarky, international trade tends to raise the prices of factors that are abundantly available and reduce the prices of factors that are scarce.

We won't work this out in detail, but the idea is intuitively simple. Think of a country's industries as consisting of two kinds: **exporting industries,** which produce goods and services that are sold abroad, and **import-competing industries,** which produce goods and services that are also imported. Compared with autarky, international trade leads to higher production in exporting industries and lower production in import-competing industries. This indirectly increases the demand for the factors used by exporting industries and decreases the demand for factors used by import-competing industries. In addition, the Heckscher–Ohlin model says that a country tends to export goods that are intensive in its abundant factors and to import goods that are intensive in its scarce factors. *So international trade tends to increase the demand for factors that are abundant in our country compared with other countries, and to decrease the demand for factors that are scarce in our country compared with other countries. As a result, the prices of abundant factors tend to rise, and the prices of scarce factors tend to fall.*

The Economics in Action on page 414 pointed out that U.S. exports tend to be human-capital-intensive and U.S. imports tend to be unskilled-labor-intensive. This suggests that the effect of international trade on U.S. factor markets is to raise the wage rate of highly educated workers and to reduce the wage rate of unskilled workers.

This effect has been a source of some concern in recent years. Wage inequality—the gap between the wages of highly paid and low-paid workers—has increased substantially over the last 25 years. Some economists believe that growing international trade is an important factor in that trend. If international trade has the effects predicted by the Heckscher–Ohlin model, it raises the wages of highly educated workers, who already have relatively high wages, and lowers the wages of less educated workers, who already have relatively low wages.

How important are these effects? In some historical episodes, the impacts of international trade on factor prices have been very large. As we explain in the Economics in Action that follows, the opening of transatlantic trade in the late nineteenth century had a large negative impact on land rents in Europe, hurting landowners but helping workers and owners of capital. The effects of trade on wages in the United States have generated considerable controversy in recent years. Most economists who have studied the issue agree that growing imports of labor-intensive products from newly industrializing economies, and the export of high-technology goods in return, have helped cause a widening wage differential between highly educated and less educated workers in this country. However, other forces, especially technological change, are probably more important in explaining growing wage inequality.

> **Exporting industries** produce goods and services that are sold abroad.
>
> **Import-competing industries** produce goods and services that are also imported.

economics in action

Trade, Wages, and Land Prices in the Nineteenth Century

Beginning around 1870, there was an explosive growth of world trade in agricultural products, based largely on the steam engine. Steam-powered ships could cross the ocean much more quickly and reliably than sailing ships. Until about 1860, steamships had higher costs than sailing ships, but after that rates dropped sharply. At the same time, steam-powered rail transport made it possible to bring grain and other bulk goods cheaply from the interior to ports. The result was that land-abundant countries—the United States, Canada, Argentina, Australia—began shipping large quantities of agricultural goods to the densely populated, land-scarce countries of Europe.

An economy has **free trade** when the government does not attempt either to reduce or to increase the levels of exports and imports that occur naturally as a result of supply and demand.

Policies that limit imports are known as **trade protection** or simply as **protection.**

A **tariff** is a tax levied on imports.

This opening up of international trade led to higher prices of agricultural products, such as wheat, in exporting countries and a decline in their prices in importing countries. Notably, the difference between wheat prices in the midwestern United States and England plunged.

The change in agricultural prices created both winners and losers on both sides of the Atlantic as factor prices adjusted. In England, land prices fell by half compared with average wages; landowners found their purchasing power sharply reduced, but workers benefited from cheaper food. In the United States, the reverse happened: land prices doubled compared with wages. Landowners did very well, but workers found the purchasing power of their wages dented by rising food prices. ∎

< < < < < < < < < < < < < < < < < < <

>>CHECK YOUR UNDERSTANDING 17-2

1. Due to a strike by truckers, trade in food between the United States and Mexico is halted. In autarky, the price of Mexican grapes is lower than that of U.S grapes. Using a diagram of the U.S. domestic demand curve and the U.S domestic supply curve for grapes, explain the effect of these events on the following:
   a. U.S grape consumers' surplus
   b. U.S grape producers' surplus
   c. U.S total surplus

2. What effect do you think these events have on Mexican grape producers? Mexican grape pickers? Mexican grape consumers? U.S. grape pickers?

Solutions appear at back of book.

The Effects of Trade Protection

Ever since David Ricardo laid out the principle of comparative advantage in the early nineteenth century, most economists have advocated **free trade.** That is, they have argued that government policy should not attempt either to reduce or to increase the levels of exports and imports that occur naturally as a result of supply and demand. Despite the free-trade arguments of economists, however, many governments use taxes and other restrictions to limit imports. Much less frequently, governments offer subsidies to encourage exports. Policies that limit imports, usually with the goal of protecting domestic producers in import-competing industries from foreign competition, are known as **trade protection** or simply as **protection.**

Let's look at the two most common protectionist policies, tariffs and import quotas, then turn to the reasons governments follow these policies.

The Effects of a Tariff

A **tariff** is a form of excise tax, one that is levied only on sales of imported goods. For example, the U.S. government could declare that anyone bringing in roses from Colombia must pay a tariff of $2 per rose, or $200 per box of 100 roses. In the distant past, tariffs were an important source of government revenue because they were relatively easy to collect. But in the modern world, tariffs are usually intended to discourage imports and protect import-competing domestic producers rather than as a source of government revenue.

The effect of a tariff is to raise both the price received by domestic producers and the price paid by domestic consumers. Suppose, for example, that our country imports roses, and a box of 100 roses is available on the world market at $400. As we saw earlier, under free trade the domestic price would also be $400. But if a tariff of $200 per box is imposed, the domestic price will rise to $600, and it won't be profitable to import roses unless the price in the domestic market is high enough to compensate importers for the cost of paying the tariff.

Figure 17-9 illustrates the effects of a tariff on rose imports. As before, we assume that P_W is the world price of roses. Before the tariff is imposed, imports have driven the domestic price down to P_W, so that pre-tariff domestic production is Q_1, pre-tariff domestic consumption is C_1, and pre-tariff imports are $C_1 - Q_1$.

Now suppose that the government imposes a tariff on each box of roses imported. As a consequence, it is no longer profitable to import roses unless the domestic price

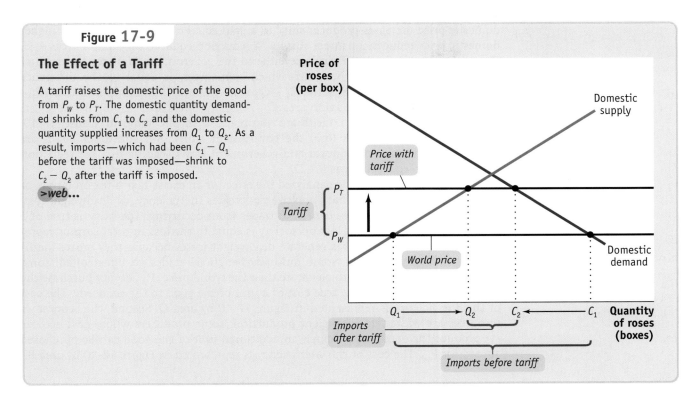

Figure 17-9

The Effect of a Tariff

A tariff raises the domestic price of the good from P_W to P_T. The domestic quantity demanded shrinks from C_1 to C_2 and the domestic quantity supplied increases from Q_1 to Q_2. As a result, imports—which had been $C_1 - Q_1$ before the tariff was imposed—shrink to $C_2 - Q_2$ after the tariff is imposed.

>web...

received by the importer is greater than or equal to the world price *plus* the tariff. So the domestic price rises to P_T, which is equal to the world price, P_W, plus the tariff. Domestic production rises to Q_2, domestic consumption falls to C_2, and imports fall to $C_2 - Q_2$.

A tariff, then, raises domestic prices, and leads to increased domestic production and reduced domestic consumption compared to the situation under free trade. Figure 17-10 shows the effects on surplus. There are three effects. First, the higher

Figure 17-10   A Tariff Reduces Total Surplus

	Changes in surplus	
	Gain	Loss
Consumer surplus		$-(A+B+C+D)$
Producer surplus	A	
Government revenue	C	
Change in total surplus		$-(B+D)$

When the domestic price rises as a result of a tariff, producers gain additional surplus (area A), the government gains revenue (area C), and consumers lose surplus (areas $A + B + C + D$). Because the losses to consumers outweigh the gains to producers and the government, the economy as a whole loses surplus (areas $B + D$). **>web...**

domestic price increases producer surplus, a gain equal to area *A*. Second, the higher domestic price reduces consumer surplus, a reduction equal to the sum of areas *A*, *B*, *C*, and *D*. Finally, the tariff yields revenue to the government. How much revenue? The government collects the tariff—which, remember, is equal to the difference between P_T and P_W on each of the $C_2 - Q_2$ roses imported. So total revenue is $(P_T - P_W) \times (C_2 - Q_2)$. This is equal to area *C*.

The welfare effects of a tariff are summarized in the table in Figure 17-10. Producers gain, consumers lose, the government gains. But consumer losses are greater than the sum of producer and government gains, leading to a net reduction in total surplus equal to areas *B* + *D*.

Recall that in Chapter 4 we analyzed the effect of an excise tax—a tax on buyers or sellers of a good. We saw that an excise tax creates inefficiency, or deadweight loss, because it prevents mutually beneficial trades from occurring. The same is true of a tariff, where its deadweight loss on society is equal to the loss in total surplus represented by areas *B* + *D*. Tariffs generate deadweight losses because they create inefficiencies in two ways. First, some mutually beneficial trades go unexploited: some consumers who are willing to pay more than the world price, P_W, do not purchase the good, even though P_W is the true cost of a unit of the good to the economy. The cost of this inefficiency is represented in Figure 17-10 by area *D*. Second, the economy's resources are wasted on inefficient production: some producers whose cost exceeds P_W produce the good, even though an additional unit of the good can be purchased abroad for P_W. The cost of this inefficiency is represented in Figure 17-10 by area *B*.

The Effects of an Import Quota

An **import quota** is a legal limit on the quantity of a good that can be imported.

An **import quota,** another form of trade protection, is a legal limit on the quantity of a good that can be imported. For example, a U.S. import quota on Colombian roses might limit the number imported each year to 50 million. Import quotas are usually administered through licenses: a number of licenses are issued, each giving the license-holder the right to import a limited quantity of the good each year.

We discussed quotas in Chapter 4, where we saw that a quota on sales has the same effect as an excise tax, with one difference: the money that would otherwise have accrued to the government as tax revenue under an excise tax becomes quota rents to license-holders under a quota. Similarly, an import quota has the same effect as a tariff, with one difference: the money that would otherwise have been government revenue becomes quota rents to license-holders. Look again at Figure 17-10. An import quota that limits imports to $C_2 - Q_2$ will raise the domestic price of roses by the same amount as the tariff we considered previously. That is, it will raise the domestic price from P_W to P_T. However, area *C* will now represent quota rents rather than government revenue.

Who receives import licenses and so collects the quota rents? In the case of U.S. import protection, the answer may surprise you: the most important import licenses—mainly for clothing, to a lesser extent for sugar—are granted to foreign governments.

Because the quota rents for most U.S. import quotas go to foreigners, the cost to the nation of such quotas is larger than that of a comparable tariff (a tariff that leads to the same level of imports). In Figure 17-10 the net loss to the United States from such an import quota would be equal to *B* + *C* + *D*, the difference between consumer losses and producer gains.

economics in action

Trade Protection in the United States

The United States today generally follows a policy of free trade, at least in comparison with other countries and also in comparison with its own past. Most manufactured goods are subject either to no tariff or to a low tariff. However, there are two areas in which the United States does significantly limit imports.

One is agriculture. The typical U.S. policy here is something called a "tariff quota." A certain amount of the imports are subject to a low tariff rate; this acts like an import quota because an importer is allowed to pay the low rate only if she has a license. Any additional imports are subject to a much higher tariff rate. We have tariff quotas on beef, dairy products, sugar, peanuts, and other things. For Inquiring Minds on page 424 discusses the sugar quota in the context of worldwide sugar policy.

The other area in which the United States significantly limits imports is clothing and textiles, where the government applies an elaborate system of import quotas.

The peculiar thing about U.S. trade protection is that in most cases quota licenses are assigned to foreigners, often foreign governments. For example, rights to sell clothing in the United States are allotted to various exporting countries, which can then hand those rights out as they see fit. This means that the quota rents go overseas, greatly increasing the cost to the United States of the import limitations. In fact, according to some estimates, about 70 percent of the total cost of U.S. import restrictions comes not from deadweight loss but from the transfer of quota rents to foreigners. ■

> >

>>CHECK YOUR UNDERSTANDING 17-3

1. Suppose that the world price of butter is $0.50 per pound and the domestic price in autarky is $1.00 per pound. Use a diagram similar to Figure 17-9 to show the following:
   a. If there is free trade, domestic butter producers want the government to impose a tariff of no less than $0.50 per pound.
   b. What happens if a tariff greater than $0.50 per pound is imposed.
2. Suppose the government imposes an import quota rather than a tariff on butter. What quota limit would generate the same quantity of imports as a tariff of $0.50 per pound?

Solutions appear at back of book.

The Political Economy of Trade Protection

We have seen that international trade produces mutual benefits to the countries that engage in it. We have also seen that tariffs and import quotas, although they produce winners as well as losers, reduce total surplus. Yet many countries continue to impose tariffs and import quotas, and to enact other protectionist measures.

To understand why trade protection takes place, we will first look at some common justifications for protection. Then we will look at the politics of trade protection. Finally, we will look at an important feature of trade protection in today's world: tariffs and import quotas are the subject of international negotiation and are policed by international organizations.

Arguments for Trade Protection

Advocates of tariffs and import quotas offer a variety of arguments. Three common arguments are *national security*, *job creation*, and the *infant industry argument*.

The national security argument is based on the proposition that overseas sources of goods are vulnerable to disruption in times of international conflict; therefore a country should protect domestic suppliers of crucial goods with the aim to be self-sufficient in those goods. In the 1960s, the United States—which had begun to import oil as domestic oil reserves ran low—had an import quota on oil, justified on national

>>QUICK REVIEW

➤ Most economists advocate *free trade*, although many governments engage in *trade protection* of import-competing industries. The two most common protectionist policies are tariffs and import quotas. In rare instances, governments subsidize export industries.

➤ A *tariff* is a tax on imports. It raises the domestic price above the world price, leading to a fall in trade and total consumption and a rise in domestic production. Domestic producers and the government gain, but consumer losses more than offset this gain, leading to deadweight loss in total surplus.

➤ An *import quota* is a legal quantity limit on imports. Its effect is like that of a tariff, except that revenues—the quota rents—accrue to the license-holder, not to the government.

BITTERSWEET

If there's one good in which we can be absolutely sure that neither the European Union nor the United States has a comparative advantage, it's sugar. The cheapest way to produce sugar is by growing sugar cane, a crop that requires a tropical climate. A few places in the United States can grow cane sugar (basically along the Gulf of Mexico and in Hawaii), but they are no match for the sugar-growing capacity of genuinely tropical countries. And it's almost impossible to grow sugar cane in Western Europe.

Yet Europe is a net *exporter* of sugar, and the United States imports only a fraction of its consumption. How is this possible, and why does it happen?

It's possible because there is another less efficient way to produce sugar: sugar beets can survive even in cold climates. On both sides of the Atlantic, sugar producers receive huge amounts of government support. In the United States, an import quota keeps prices on average at twice world levels. In Europe, import restrictions are supplemented by huge government subsidies to farmers.

What's the rationale for this trade protection? Governments hardly even bother to make excuses: on both sides of the Atlantic, there's a powerful farm lobby. In fact, agriculture in industrial countries is heavily subsidized, at the expense of both consumers and taxpayers.

The really sad thing is that some of the protected goods—sugar in particular— would be major exports of poor countries (and major sources of income for their poor farmers) if it weren't for the import quotas and subsidies in advanced countries.

---

security grounds. Some people have argued that we should again have policies to discourage imports of oil, especially from the Middle East.

The job creation argument points to the additional jobs created in import-competing industries as a result of trade protection. Economists argue that these jobs are offset by the jobs lost elsewhere, such as industries that use imported inputs and now face higher input costs. But noneconomists don't always find this argument persuasive.

Finally, the infant industry argument, often raised in newly industrializing countries, holds that new industries require a temporary period of trade protection to get established. For example, in the 1950s many countries in Latin America imposed tariffs and import quotas on manufactured goods, in an effort to switch from their traditional role as exporters of raw materials to a new status as industrial countries.

The Politics of Trade Protection

In reality, much trade protection has little to do with the arguments just described. Instead, it reflects the political influence of import-competing producers.

We've seen that a tariff or import quota leads to gains for import-competing producers and losses for consumers. Producers, however, usually have much more influence over trade policy decisions. The producers who compete with imports of a particular good are usually a smaller, more cohesive group than the consumers of that good.

An example is trade protection for sugar, discussed in For Inquiring Minds above. The United States has an import quota on sugar, which on average leads to a domestic price about twice the world price. This quota is difficult to rationalize in terms of any economic argument. However, consumers rarely complain about the quota because they are unaware that it exists: Because no individual consumer buys large amounts of sugar, the cost of the quota is only a few dollars per family each year, not enough to attract notice. But there are only a few thousand sugar growers in the United States. They are very aware of the benefits they receive from the quota and make sure that their representatives in Congress are aware of their interest in the matter.

Given these political realities, it may seem surprising that trade is as free as it is. As explained in Economics in Action on page 425, the United States has low tariffs, and its import quotas are mainly confined to clothing and a few agricultural products. It would be nice to say that the main reason trade protection is so limited is that economists have convinced governments of the virtues of free trade. A more important reason, however, is the role of *international trade agreements*.

International Trade Agreements and the World Trade Organization

When a country engages in trade protection, it hurts two groups. We've already emphasized the adverse effect on domestic consumers, but protection also hurts foreign export industries. This means that countries care about each others' trade policies: the Canadian lumber industry has a strong interest in keeping U.S. tariffs on forest products low.

Because countries care about each others' trade policies, they engage in **international trade agreements:** treaties in which a country promises to engage in less trade protection against the exports of another country in return for a promise by the other country to do the same for its exports. Most world trade is now governed by such agreements.

Some international trade agreements involve just two countries or a small group of countries. In 1993, the U.S. Congress approved the North American Free Trade Agreement (NAFTA) between the United States, Canada, and Mexico. Once fully implemented, this agreement will remove all barriers to trade among the three nations. Free trade has already been implemented among the 25 nations of the European Union.

There are also global trade agreements, covering most of the world. Such global agreements are overseen by the **World Trade Organization,** or WTO, which plays two roles. First, it provides the framework for the massively complex negotiations involved in a major international trade agreement (the full text of the last major agreement, approved in 1994, was 24,000 pages long). Second, the WTO resolves disputes between members. These disputes typically arise when one country claims that another country's policies violate its previous agreements.

Here are two examples that illustrate the WTO's role. First, in 1999 the WTO ruled that the European Union's import restrictions on bananas, which discriminate in favor of producers in former European colonies and against Central American producers, are in violation of international trade rules. The banana dispute had threatened to become a major source of conflict between the European Union and the United States because the United States has taken the side of the Central American countries. Europe is currently in the process of revising its system. In 2002 the United States was on the losing side of a WTO decision: the European Union complained that a provision in U.S. tax law, intended to help exporting companies, is in effect an export subsidy—which is not allowed according to international agreements. The WTO ruled in Europe's favor and the United States is now obliged to revise its tax law.

The WTO is sometimes, with great exaggeration, described as a world government. In fact, it has no army, no police, and no direct enforcement power. The grain of truth in that description is that when a country joins the WTO, it agrees to accept the organization's judgments—and these judgments apply not only to tariffs and import quotas but also to domestic policies that, according to the organization, are in effect trade protection under another name. So in joining the WTO a country does give up a bit of its sovereignty.

> **International trade agreements** are treaties in which a country promises to engage in less trade protection against the exports of other countries in return for a promise by other countries to do the same for its own exports.

> The **World Trade Organization** oversees international trade agreements and rules on disputes between countries over those agreements.

economics in action

Declining Tariffs

The United States began basing its trade policy on international agreements in the 1930s, and global trade negotiations began soon after World War II. The success of these agreements in reducing trade protection is illustrated by Figure 17-11 on page 426 which shows the average U.S. tariff rate on imports subject to tariffs since the 1920s.

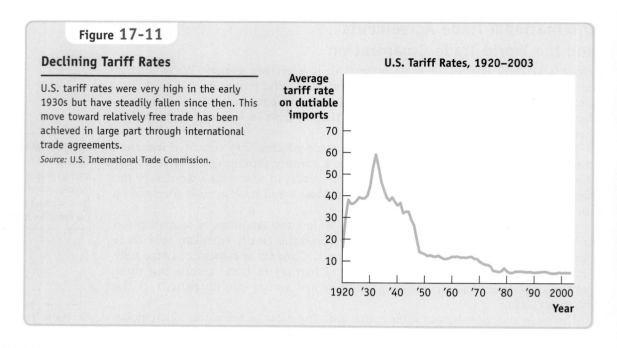

Figure 17-11

Declining Tariff Rates

U.S. tariff rates were very high in the early 1930s but have steadily fallen since then. This move toward relatively free trade has been achieved in large part through international trade agreements.

Source: U.S. International Trade Commission.

U.S. Tariff Rates, 1920–2003

Tariffs reached a peak in the early 1930s after the passage of a very protectionist bill, known as the Smoot-Hawley tariff, in 1930. (Some people blame Smoot-Hawley for causing the Great Depression of the 1930s, though few economists think it was *that* bad.) From then on, tariff rates have steadily ratcheted down, with U.S. moves matched in other advanced countries, and later in many poorer countries as well.

At this point world trade in manufactured goods is subject to low tariffs and relatively few import quotas, with clothing the main exception. Agricultural products are subject to many more restrictions, reflecting the political power of farmers in advanced countries. ∎

< < < < < < < < < < < < < < < < < < <

>>CHECK YOUR UNDERSTANDING 17-4

1. In 2002 the U.S. imposed tariffs on steel imports, which are an input in a large number and variety of U.S. industries. Explain why political lobbying to eliminate these tariffs is more likely to be effective than political lobbying to eliminate tariffs on consumer goods such as sugar or clothing.

2. Over the years, the WTO has increasingly found itself adjudicating trade disputes that involve not just tariffs or quota restrictions but also restrictions based on quality, health, and environmental considerations. Why do you think this has occurred? What method would you, as a WTO official, use to decide whether a quality, health, or environmental restriction is in violation of a free-trade agreement?

Solutions appear at back of book.

• A LOOK AHEAD •

As we move ahead to new topics, it is important that we carry with us the insights learned here about the logic of comparative advantage and the gains from international trade. They will provide us with a deeper understanding of what drives the world economy and of the reasons countries differ economically. In addition, the study of international trade teaches us how economic policies can create both winners and losers despite the fact that society as a whole gains, an important consideration in any study of how policies are actually made.

SUMMARY

1. International trade is of growing importance to the United States and of even greater importance to most other countries. International trade, like trade among individuals, arises from comparative advantage: the opportunity cost of producing an additional unit of a good is lower in some countries than in others. Goods and services purchased abroad are **imports;** those sold abroad are **exports.**

2. The **Ricardian model of international trade** assumes that opportunity costs are constant. It shows that there are gains from trade: two countries are better off with trade than in **autarky.**

3. In practice, comparative advantage reflects differences between countries in climate, factor endowments, and technology. The **Heckscher–Ohlin model** shows how differences in factor endowments determine comparative advantage: goods differ in **factor intensity,** and countries tend to export goods that are intensive in the factors they have in abundance.

4. The **domestic demand curve** and the **domestic supply curve** determine the price of a good in autarky. When international trade occurs, the domestic price is driven to equality with the **world price,** the price at which the good may be bought or sold abroad.

5. If the world price is below the autarky price, a good is imported. This leads to an increase in consumer surplus, a fall in producer surplus, and a gain in total surplus. If the world price is above the autarky price, a good is exported. This leads to an increase in producer surplus, a fall in consumer surplus, and a gain in total surplus.

6. International trade leads to expansion in **exporting industries** and contraction in **import-competing industries.** This raises the domestic demand for abundant factors of production, reduces the demand for scarce factors, and so affects factor prices.

7. Most economists advocate **free trade,** but in practice many governments engage in **trade protection.** The two most common forms of **protection** are tariffs and quotas; in rare occasions, export industries are subsidized.

8. A **tariff** is a tax levied on imports. It raises the domestic price above the world price, hurting consumers, benefiting domestic producers, and generating government revenue. As a result, total surplus falls. An **import quota** is a legal limit on the quantity of a good that can be imported. It has the same effects as a tariff, except that the revenue goes not to the government but to those who receive import licenses.

9. Although several popular arguments have been made in favor of trade protection, in practice the main reason for protection is probably political: import-competing industries are well organized and well informed about how they gain from trade protection, while consumers are unaware of the costs they pay. Still, U.S. trade is fairly free, mainly because of the role of **international trade agreements,** in which countries agree to reduce trade protection against each others' exports. Trade negotiations are overseen, and the resulting agreements are enforced, by the **World Trade Organization.**

KEY TERMS

Imports, p. 407
Exports, p. 407
Ricardian model of international trade, p. 409
Autarky, p. 409
Factor intensity, p. 412
Heckscher–Ohlin model, p. 412

Domestic demand curve, p. 415
Domestic supply curve, p. 415
World price, p. 415
Exporting industries, p. 419
Import-competing industries, p. 419
Free trade, p. 420
Trade protection, p. 420

Protection, p. 420
Tariff, p. 420
Import quota, p. 422
International trade agreements, p. 425
World Trade Organization, p. 425

PROBLEMS

1. Assume Saudi Arabia and the United States face the production possibilities for oil and cars shown in the accompanying table.

Saudi Arabia		United States	
Quantity of oil (millions of barrels)	Quantity of cars (millions)	Quantity of oil (millions of barrels)	Quantity of cars (millions)
0	4	0	10.0
200	3	100	7.5
400	2	200	5.0
600	1	300	2.5
800	0	400	0

a. What is the opportunity cost of producing a car in Saudi Arabia? In the United States? What is the opportunity cost of producing a barrel of oil in Saudi Arabia? In the United States?

b. Which country has the comparative advantage in producing oil? In producing cars?

c. Suppose that in autarky, Saudi Arabia produces 200 million barrels of oil and 3 million cars; and that the United States produces 300 million barrels of oil and 2.5 million cars. Without trade, can Saudi Arabia produce more oil *and* more cars? Without trade, can the United States produce more oil *and* more cars?

2. The production possibilities for the United States and Saudi Arabia are given in Problem 1. Suppose now that each country specializes in the good in which it has the comparative advantage, and the two countries trade. Also assume that for each country the value of imports must equal the value of exports.

a. What is the total quantity of oil produced? What is the total quantity of cars produced?

b. Is it possible for Saudi Arabia to consume 400 million barrels of oil and 5 million cars, and for the United States to consume 400 million barrels of oil and 5 million cars?

c. Suppose that, in fact, Saudi Arabia consumes 300 million barrels of oil and 4 million cars and the United States consumes 500 million barrels of oil and 6 million cars. How many barrels of oil does the United States import? How many cars does the United States export? Suppose a car costs $10,000 on the world market. How much, then, does a barrel of oil cost on the world market?

3. Both Canada and the United States produce lumber and music CDs with constant opportunity costs. The United States can produce either 10 tons of lumber and no CDs, or 1,000 CDs and no lumber, or any combination in between. Canada can produce either 8 tons of lumber and no CDs, or 400 CDs and no lumber, or any combination in between.

a. Draw the U.S. and Canadian production possibility frontiers in two separate diagrams, with CDs on the horizontal axis and lumber on the vertical axis.

b. In autarky, if the United States wants to consume 500 CDs, how much lumber can it consume at most? Label this point *A* in your diagram. Similarly, if Canada wants to consume 1 ton of lumber, how many CDs can it consume in autarky? Label this point *C* in your diagram.

c. Which country has the absolute advantage in lumber production?

d. Which country has the comparative advantage in lumber production?

Suppose each country specializes in the good in which it has the comparative advantage, and there is trade.

e. How many CDs does the United States produce? How much lumber does Canada produce?

f. Is it possible for the United States to consume 500 CDs and 7 tons of lumber? Label this point *B* in your diagram. Is it possible for Canada at the same time to consume 500 CDs and 1 ton of lumber? Label this point *D* in your diagram.

4. For each of the following trade relationships, explain the likely source of the comparative advantage of each of the exporting countries.

a. The United States exports software to Venezuela, and Venezuela exports oil to the United States.

b. The United States exports airplanes to China, and China exports clothing to the United States.

c. The United States exports wheat to Colombia, and Colombia exports coffee to the United States.

5. Shoes are labor-intensive and satellites are capital-intensive to produce. The United States has abundant capital. China has abundant labor. According to the Heckscher–Ohlin model, which good will China export? Which good will the United States export? In the United States, what will happen to the price of labor (the wage) and to the price of capital?

6. Before the North American Free Trade Agreement (NAFTA) gradually eliminated import tariffs on goods, the autarky price of tomatoes in Mexico was below the world price and in the United States was above the world price. Similarly, the autarky price of poultry in Mexico was above the world price and in the United States was below the world price. Draw diagrams with domestic supply and demand curves for each country and each of the two goods. As a result of NAFTA, the United States now imports tomatoes from Mexico and the United States now exports poultry to Mexico. How would you expect the following groups to be affected?

a. Mexican and U.S. consumers of tomatoes. Illustrate the effect on consumer surplus in your diagram.

b. Mexican and U.S. producers of tomatoes. Illustrate the effect on producer surplus in your diagram.

c. Mexican and U.S. tomato workers.

d. Mexican and U.S. consumers of poultry. Illustrate the effect on consumer surplus in your diagram.

e. Mexican and U.S. producers of poultry. Illustrate the effect on producer surplus in your diagram.

f. Mexican and U.S. poultry workers.

7. The accompanying table indicates the U.S. domestic demand schedule and domestic supply schedule for commercial jet airplanes. Suppose that the world price of a commercial jet airplane is $100 million.

Price of jet (millions)	Quantity of jets demanded	Quantity of jets supplied
$120	100	1,000
110	150	900
100	200	800
90	250	700
80	300	600
70	350	500
60	400	400
50	450	300
40	500	200

a. In autarky, how many commercial jet airplanes does the United States produce, and at what price are they bought and sold?

b. With trade, what will the price for commercial jet airplanes be? Will the United States import or export airplanes? How many?

8. The accompanying table shows the U.S. domestic demand schedule and domestic supply schedule for oranges. Suppose that the world price of oranges is $0.30 per orange.

Price of orange	Quantity of oranges demanded (thousands)	Quantity of oranges supplied (thousands)
$1.00	2	11
0.90	4	10
0.80	6	9
0.70	8	8
0.60	10	7
0.50	12	6
0.40	14	5
0.30	16	4
0.20	18	3

a. Draw the U.S. domestic supply curve and domestic demand curve.

b. With free trade, how many oranges will the United States import or export?

Suppose that the U.S. government imposes a tariff on oranges of $0.20 per orange.

c. How many oranges will the United States import or export after introduction of the tariff?

d. In your diagram, shade the gain or loss to the economy as a whole from the introduction of this tariff.

9. The U.S. domestic demand schedule and domestic supply schedule for oranges was given in Problem 8. Suppose that the world price of oranges is $0.30. The United States introduces an import quota of 3,000 oranges. Draw the domestic demand and supply curves and answer the following questions.

a. What will the domestic price of oranges be after introduction of the quota?

b. What is the value of the quota rents that importers of oranges receive?

10. The accompanying diagram illustrates the U.S. domestic demand curve and domestic supply curve for beef.

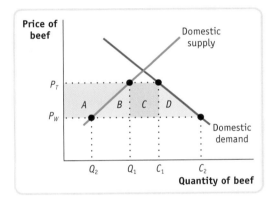

The world price of beef is P_W. The United States currently imposes an import tariff on beef, so the price of beef is P_T. Congress decides to eliminate the tariff. In terms of the areas marked in the diagram, answer the following questions.

a. What is the gain/loss in consumer surplus?

b. What is the gain/loss in producer surplus?

c. What is the gain/loss to the government?

d. What is the gain/loss to the economy as a whole?

11. As the United States has opened up to trade, it has lost many of its low-skill manufacturing jobs, but it has gained jobs in high-skill industries, such as the software industry. Explain whether the United States as a whole has been made better off by trade.

12. The United States is highly protective of its agricultural industry, imposing import tariffs, and sometimes quotas, on imports of agricultural goods. The chapter has presented three arguments for trade protection. For each argument, discuss whether it is a valid justification for trade protection of U.S. agricultural products.

13. In World Trade Organization (WTO) negotiations, if a country agrees to reduce trade barriers (tariffs or quotas), it usually refers to this as a *concession* to other countries. Do you think that this terminology is appropriate?

14. Producers in import-competing industries often make the following argument: "Other countries have an advantage in production of certain goods purely because workers abroad are paid lower wages. In fact, American workers are much more productive than foreign workers. So import-competing industries need to be protected." Is this a valid argument? Explain your answer.

>web... To continue your study and review of concepts in this chapter, please visit the Krugman/Wells website for quizzes, animated graph tutorials, web links to helpful resources, and more.

www.worthpublishers.com/krugmanwells

Uncertainty, Risk, and Private Information

AFTER THE FLOOD

IN MARCH 1998 THE FLINT RIVER OVER-flowed its banks and flooded the town of Albany, Georgia. It was a catastrophe. The town's residents were especially distraught because many of them had no flood insurance—they had dropped their coverage after a similar flood in 1994 led insurance companies to raise their *premiums*.

The case of Albany's floods reminds us that uncertainty is an important feature of real-world economies. Up to this point, we have assumed that people make decisions with knowledge of exactly how those decisions will affect their welfare. In reality, people often make economic decisions—such as whether to build a house near a river—without full knowledge of their future consequences. As the residents of Albany learned, making decisions when the future is uncertain carries with it the *risk* of loss.

Yet it is often possible for individuals to use markets to reduce the risk they face. The Flint River flood made head-lines because it's unusual for so many victims of a disaster to be without insurance. In fact, through insurance and other devices, the modern economy offers many ways for individuals to reduce their exposure to risk.

Does this mean that a market economy can solve all the problems created by uncertainty? Alas, no. Markets do very well at coping with situations in which nobody knows what will happen. But they run into trouble when some people know things that others do not—a situation known as *private information*. We'll see that private information can cause ineffi-ciency by preventing mutually beneficial transactions.

By failing to maintain their flood insurance, these Albany, Georgia, homeowners incurred huge losses in 1998.

What you will learn in this chapter:

➤ That **risk** is an important feature of the economy, and that most people are **risk-averse**—they would like to avoid risk

➤ Why diminishing marginal utility makes people risk-averse and determines the **premium** they are willing to pay to reduce risk

➤ How risk can be traded, with risk-averse people paying others to assume part of their risk

➤ How exposure to risk can be reduced through **diversification** and **pooling**

➤ The special problems posed by **private information**—situations in which some people know things that other people do not

In this chapter we'll examine the economics of risk and private information. We'll start by looking at why people dislike risk. Then we'll explore how a market economy allows people to reduce risk, at a price. Finally, we'll turn to the special problems created when some people have information that others don't.

The Economics of Risk Aversion

In general, people don't like risk and are willing to pay a price to avoid it. Just ask the U.S. insurance industry, which collects more than $1 trillion in premiums every year. But what exactly is risk? And why don't people like it? To answer these questions, we need to look briefly at the concept of *expected value* and the meaning of uncertainty. Then we can turn to why people dislike *risk*.

Expectations and Uncertainty

The Lee family doesn't know how big its medical bills will be next year. If all goes well, it won't have any medical expenses at all. Let's assume that there's a 50 percent chance of that happening. But if family members require hospitalization or expensive drugs, they will face medical expenses of $10,000. Let's assume that there's also a 50 percent chance that these high medical expenses will materialize.

In this example—which is designed to illustrate a point, rather than to be realistic—the Lees' medical expenses for the coming year are a **random variable,** a variable that has an uncertain future value. No one can predict which of its possible values, or outcomes, a random variable will take. But that doesn't mean we can say nothing about the Lees' future medical expenses. On the contrary, an actuary (a person trained in evaluating uncertain future events) could calculate the **expected value** of expenses next year—the weighted average of all possible values, where the weights on each possible value correspond to the probability of that value occurring. In this example, the expected value of the Lees' medical expenses is $(0.5 \times \$0) + (0.5 \times \$10,000) = \$5,000$.

To derive the general formula for the expected value of a random variable, we imagine that there are a number of different **states of the world,** possible future events. Each state is associated with a different realized value—the value that actually occurs—of the random variable. You don't know which state of the world will actually occur, but you can assign probabilities, one for each state of the world. Let's assume that P_1 is the probability of state 1, P_2 the probability of state 2, and so on. And you know the realized value of the random value in each state of the world: S_1 in state 1, S_2 in state 2, and so on. Let's also assume that there are N possible states. Then the expected value of the random variable is:

(18-1) *Expected value of a random variable*
$$EV = (P_1 \times S_1) + (P_2 \times S_2) + \dots + (P_N \times S_N)$$

In the case of the Lee family, there are only two possible states of the world, each with a probability of 0.5.

Notice, however, that the Lee family doesn't actually expect to pay $5,000 in medical bills next year, regardless of what occurs. That's because in this example there is no state of the world in which the family pays exactly $5,000. Either the family pays nothing, or it pays $10,000. So the Lees face considerable uncertainty about their future medical expenses.

But what if the Lee family can buy health insurance that will cover its medical expenses, whatever they turn out to be? Suppose, in particular, that the family can pay $5,000 up front in return for full coverage of whatever medical expenses actually arise during the coming year. Then the Lees' future medical expenses are no longer uncer-

---

A **random variable** is a variable with an uncertain future value.

The **expected value** of a random variable is the weighted average of all possible values, where the weights on each possible value correspond to the probability of that value occurring.

A **state of the world** is a possible future event.

tain *for them*: in return for $5,000—an amount equal to the expected value of the medical expenses—the insurance company assumes all responsibility for paying those medical expenses. Would this be a good deal from the Lees' point of view?

Yes, it would—or at least most families would think so. Most people prefer, other things equal, to reduce **risk**—uncertainty about future outcomes. (We'll focus here on **financial risk,** in which the uncertainty is about monetary outcomes, as opposed to uncertainty about outcomes that can't be assigned a monetary value.) In fact, most people are willing to pay a substantial price to reduce their risk; that's why we have an insurance industry. But before we study the market for insurance, we need to understand why people feel that risk is a bad thing, an attitude that economists call *risk aversion*. The answer, as we'll now see, is a concept we first encountered in our analysis of consumer demand, back in Chapter 10: *diminishing marginal utility*.

Risk is uncertainty about future outcomes. When the uncertainty is about monetary outcomes, it becomes **financial risk**.

The Logic of Risk Aversion

To understand how diminishing marginal utility gives rise to risk aversion, we need to look not only at the Lees' medical costs but also at how those costs affect the income the family has left after medical expenses. Let's assume that the family knows that it will have an income of $30,000 next year. If the family has no medical expenses, it will be left with all of that income. If its medical expenses are $10,000, its income after medical expenses will be only $20,000. Since we have assumed that there is an equal chance of these two outcomes, the expected value of the Lees' income after medical expenses is (0.5 × $30,000) + (0.5 × $20,000) = $25,000. At times we will simply refer to this as *expected income*.

But as we'll now see, if the family's utility function has the shape typical of most families', its **expected utility**—the expected value of its total utility given uncertainty about future outcomes—is less than it would be if the family didn't face any risk and knew with certainty that its income after medical expenses would be $25,000.

Expected utility is the expected value of an individual's total utility given uncertainty about future outcomes.

To see why, we need to look at how total utility depends on income. Panel (a) of Figure 18-1 on page 434 shows a hypothetical utility function for the Lee family, where total utility depends on income—the amount of money the Lees have available for consumption of goods and services (after they have paid any medical bills). The table within the figure shows how the family's total utility varies over the income range of $20,000 to $30,000. As usual, the utility function is upward sloping, because more income leads to higher total utility. Notice as well that the curve gets flatter as we move up and to the right, which reflects diminishing marginal utility.

In Chapter 10 we applied the principle of diminishing marginal utility to individual goods and services: each successive unit of a good or service that a consumer purchases adds less to his or her total utility. The same principle applies to income used for consumption: each successive dollar of income adds less to total utility than the previous dollar. Panel (b) shows how marginal utility varies with income, confirming that marginal utility of income falls as income rises. As we'll see in a moment, diminishing marginal utility is the key to understanding the desire of individuals to reduce risk.

To analyze how a person's utility is affected by risk, economists start from the assumption that individuals facing uncertainty maximize their *expected* utility. We can use the data in Figure 18-1 to calculate the Lee family's expected utility. We'll first do the calculation assuming that the Lees have no insurance, and then we'll recalculate it assuming that they have purchased insurance.

Without insurance, if the Lees are lucky and don't incur any medical expenses, they will have an income of $30,000, generating total utility of 1,080 utils. But if they have no insurance and are unlucky, incurring $10,000 in medical expenses, they will have just $20,000 of their income to spend on consumption and total utility of only 920 utils. So *without insurance*, the family's expected utility is (0.5 × 1,080) + (0.5 × 920) = 1,000 utils.

Now let's suppose that an insurance company offers to pay whatever medical expenses the family incurs during the next year in return for a **premium**—a payment

A premium is a payment to an insurance company in return for the insurance company's promise to pay a claim in certain states of the world.

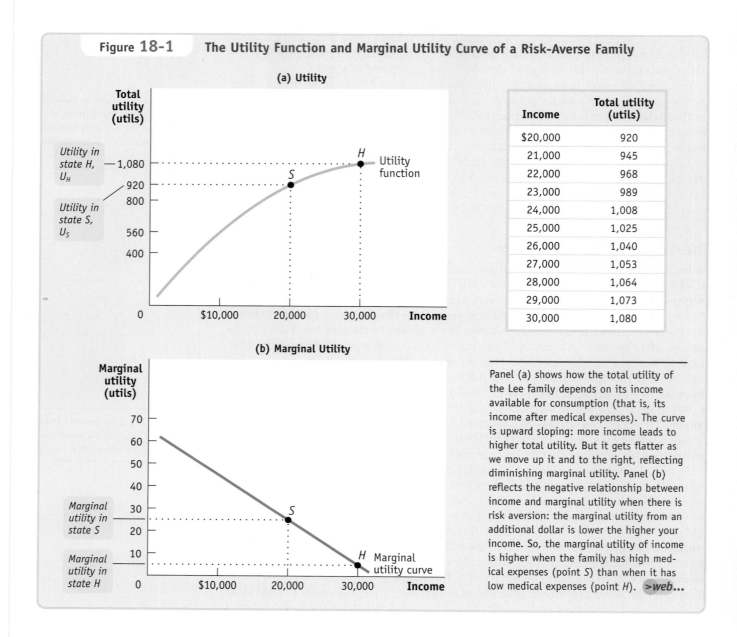

Figure 18-1 The Utility Function and Marginal Utility Curve of a Risk-Averse Family

(a) Utility

Income	Total utility (utils)
$20,000	920
21,000	945
22,000	968
23,000	989
24,000	1,008
25,000	1,025
26,000	1,040
27,000	1,053
28,000	1,064
29,000	1,073
30,000	1,080

(b) Marginal Utility

Panel (a) shows how the total utility of the Lee family depends on its income available for consumption (that is, its income after medical expenses). The curve is upward sloping: more income leads to higher total utility. But it gets flatter as we move up it and to the right, reflecting diminishing marginal utility. Panel (b) reflects the negative relationship between income and marginal utility when there is risk aversion: the marginal utility from an additional dollar is lower the higher your income. So, the marginal utility of income is higher when the family has high medical expenses (point S) than when it has low medical expenses (point H). **>web...**

---

to the insurance company—of $5,000. Note that the amount of the premium in this case is equal to the expected value of the Lees' medical expenses—the expected value of their future claim against the policy. An insurance policy with this feature, for which the premium is equal to the expected value of the claim, has a special name— a **fair insurance policy.**

If the family purchases this fair insurance policy, the expected value of its income available for consumption is the *same* as it would be without insurance: $25,000— that is, $30,000 minus the $5,000 premium. But the family's risk has been eliminated: the family has an income available for consumption of $25,000 *for sure*, which means that it receives the total utility associated with an income of $25,000. Reading from the table in Figure 18-1, we see that this total utility is 1,025 utils. Or to put it a slightly different way, their expected utility with insurance is $1 \times 1,025 = 1,025$ utils, because with insurance they will receive a total utility of 1,025 utils with a probability of 1. And this is higher than the expected utility without insurance—only 1,000 utils. So by eliminating risk through the purchase of a fair insurance policy, the family increases its expected utility even though its expected income hasn't changed.

TABLE 18-1

The Effect of Fair Insurance on the Lee Family's Income Available for Consumption and Expected Utility

	Income in different states of the world			
	$0 in medical expenses (0.5 probability)	$10,000 in medical expenses (0.5 probability)	Income available for consumption	Expected utility
Without insurance	$30,000	$20,000	(0.5 × $30,000) + (0.5 × $20,000) = $25,000	(0.5 × 1,080 utils) + (0.5 × 920 utils) = 1,000 utils
With fair insurance	$25,000	$25,000	(0.5 × $25,000) + (0.5 × $25,000) = $25,000	(0.5 × 1,025 utils) + (0.5 × 1,025 utils) = 1,025 utils

The calculations for this example are summarized in Table 18-1. This example shows that the Lees, like most people in real life, are **risk-averse:** they will choose to reduce the risk they face when the cost of that reduction leaves the expected value of their income or wealth unchanged. So the Lees, like most people, will be willing to buy fair insurance.

> **Risk-averse** individuals will choose to reduce the risk they face when that reduction leaves the expected value of their income or wealth unchanged.

You might think that this result depends on the specific numbers we have chosen. In fact, however, the proposition that purchase of a fair insurance policy increases expected utility depends on only one assumption: diminishing marginal utility. The reason is that *with diminishing marginal utility, a dollar gained when income is low adds more to utility than a dollar lost when income is high.* That is, having an additional dollar matters more when you are facing hard times than when you are facing good times. And as we will shortly see, a fair insurance policy is desirable because it transfers a dollar from high-income states (where it is valued less) to low-income states (where it is valued more).

But first, let's see how diminishing marginal utility leads to risk aversion by examining expected utility more closely. In the case of the Lee family, there are two states of the world; let's call them H and S, for healthy and sick. In state H the family has no medical expenses; in state S it has $10,000 in medical expenses. Let's use the symbols U_H and U_S to represent the Lee family's utility in each state. Then the family's expected utility is

(18-2)   Expected utility = (Probability of state H × Total utility in state H) +
                     (Probability of state S × Total utility in state S)
             = $(0.5 \times U_H) + (0.5 \times U_S)$

The fair insurance policy *reduces* the family's income available for consumption in state H by $5,000, but it *increases* it in state S by the same amount. As we've just seen, we can use the utility function to directly calculate the effects of these changes on expected utility. But as we have also seen in many other contexts, we gain more insight into individual choice by focusing on *marginal* utility.

To use marginal utility to analyze the effects of fair insurance, let's imagine introducing the insurance a bit at a time, say in 5,000 small steps. At each of these steps, we reduce income in state H by $1 and simultaneously increase income in state S by $1. At each of these steps, utility in state H falls by the marginal utility of income in that state but utility in state S rises by the marginal utility of income in that state.

Now look again at panel (b) of Figure 18-1, which shows how marginal utility varies with income. Point S shows marginal utility when the Lee family's income is $20,000; point H shows marginal utility when income is $30,000. Clearly, marginal utility is higher when income after medical expenses is low. Because of diminishing marginal utility, an additional dollar of income adds more to utility when the family has low income (point S) than when it has high income (point H).

This tells us that the gain in expected utility from increasing income in state S is larger than the loss in expected utility from reducing income in state H. So at each step of the process of reducing risk, by transferring $1 of income from state H to state S, expected utility increases. This is the same as saying that the family is risk-averse; that is, risk aversion is a result of diminishing marginal utility.

Almost everyone is risk-averse, because almost everyone has diminishing marginal utility. But the degree of risk aversion varies among individuals—some people are more risk-averse than others. To illustrate this point, Figure 18-2 compares two individuals, Danny and Mel. We suppose that each of them earns the same income now but is confronted with the possibility of earning either $1,000 more or $1,000 less. Panel (a) shows how each individual's total utility would be affected by the change in income. Danny would gain very few utils from a rise in income, which moves him from N to H_D, but lose a large number of utils from a fall in income, which moves him from N to L_D. That is, he is highly risk-averse. This is reflected in the lower part of the figure by his steeply declining marginal utility curve. Mel, though, would gain almost as

Figure 18-2

Differences in Risk Aversion

Danny and Mel have different utility functions. Danny is highly risk-averse: a gain of $1,000 in income, which moves him from N to H_D, adds only a few utils to his total utility, but a $1,000 fall in income, which moves him from N to L_D, reduces his total utility by a large number of utils. By contrast, Mel gains almost as many utils from a $1,000 rise in income (the movement from N to H_M) as he loses from a $1,000 fall in income (the movement from N to L_M). This difference—reflected in the differing slopes of the two men's marginal utility curves—means that Danny would be willing to pay much more than Mel for insurance.

>web...

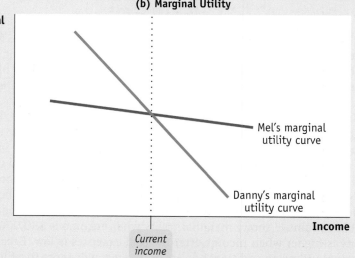

If most people are risk-averse and risk-averse individuals won't take a fair gamble, how come Las Vegas, Atlantic City, and other places where gambling is legal do so much business?

After all, a casino doesn't even offer gamblers a fair gamble: all the games in any gambling facility are designed so that, on average, the casino makes money. So why would anyone play their games?

You might argue that the gambling industry caters to the minority of people who are actually the opposite of risk-averse: risk-loving. But a glance at the

Gambling: Enjoyment or addiction?

customers of Las Vegas hotels quickly refutes that hypothesis: most of them aren't daredevils who also sky-dive and

hang-glide. Instead, most of them are ordinary people who have health and life insurance and who wear seat belts. In other words, they are risk-averse like the rest of us.

So why do people gamble? Presumably because they enjoy the experience.

Also, gambling may be one of those areas where the assumption of rational behavior goes awry. Psychologists have concluded that gambling can be addictive in ways that are not that different from the addictive effects of drugs. Taking dangerous drugs is irrational; so is excessive gambling. Alas, both happen all the same.

many utils from higher income, which moves him from N to H_M, as he would lose from lower income, which moves him from N to L_M. He is barely risk-averse at all. This is reflected in his marginal utility curve, which is almost horizontal. So other things equal, Danny will gain a lot more utility from insurance than Mel will.

Individuals differ in risk aversion for two main reasons: differences in preferences and differences in initial income or wealth.

- *Differences in preferences.* Other things equal, people simply differ in how much their marginal utility is affected by their level of income. Someone whose marginal utility does not depend very much on income won't be highly risk-averse.

- *Differences in initial income or wealth.* The possible loss of $1,000 makes a big difference to a family living below the poverty line; it makes very little difference to someone who earns $1 million a year. In general, people with high incomes or high wealth will be less risk-averse.

Differences in risk aversion have an important consequence: they affect how much an individual is willing to pay to avoid risk.

Paying to Avoid Risk

The risk-averse Lee family is clearly better off taking out a fair insurance policy—a policy that leaves their expected income unchanged but eliminates their risk. Unfortunately, real insurance policies are rarely fair: because insurance companies have to cover other costs, such as salaries for salespeople and actuaries, they charge more than they expect to pay in claims. Will the Lee family still want to purchase an "unfair" insurance policy—one for which the premium is larger than the expected claim?

It depends on the size of the premium. Look again at Table 18-1. We know that without insurance expected utility is 1,000 utils and that insurance costing $5,000 raises expected utility to 1,025 utils. If the premium were $6,000, the Lees would be left with an income of $24,000, which, as you can see from Figure 18-1, would give them a total utility of 1,008 utils—which is still higher than their expected utility if they had no insurance at all. So the Lees would be willing to buy insurance with a $6,000 premium. But they wouldn't be willing to pay $7,000, which would reduce their income to $23,000 and their total utility to 989 utils.

This example shows that risk-averse individuals are willing to make deals that reduce their expected income but also reduce their risk: they are willing to pay a premium that exceeds their expected claim. The more risk-averse they are, the higher the premium they are willing to pay. That willingness to pay is what makes the insurance industry possible.

economics in action

Warranties

Many expensive consumer goods—stereos, major appliances, cars—come with some form of *warranty*. Typically, the manufacturer guarantees to repair or replace the item if something goes wrong with it during some specified period after purchase—usually six months or one year.

Why do manufacturers offer warranties? Part of the answer is that warranties *signal* to consumers that the goods are of high quality (see the discussion of private information later in this chapter). But mainly warranties are a form of consumer insurance. For many people, the cost of repairing or replacing an expensive item like a refrigerator—or, worse yet, a car—would be a serious burden. If they were obliged to come up with the cash, their consumption of other goods would be restricted; as a result, their marginal utility of income would be higher than if they didn't have to pay for repairs.

So a warranty that covers the cost of repair or replacement increases the consumer's expected utility, even if the cost of the warranty is greater than the expected future claim paid by the manufacturer. ∎

< < < < < < < < < < < < < < < < < < <

>>CHECK YOUR UNDERSTANDING 18-1

1. In which of the following circumstances would you be more likely to buy car insurance?
   a. You must work to pay your living expenses, and you need a car to get to work.
   b. Your parents are wealthy and can easily buy you another car if you need it.

2. Karma's income next year is uncertain: there is a 60% probability she will make $22,000 and a 40% probability she will make $35,000. The accompanying table shows some income and utility levels for Karma:

Income	Total utility (utils)
$22,000	850
25,000	1,014
26,000	1,056
35,000	1,260

   a. What is Karma's expected income? her expected utility?
   b. What certain income level leaves her equally as well off as her uncertain income? What does this imply about Karma's attitudes toward risk? Explain.
   c. Would Karma be willing to pay some amount of money greater than zero for an insurance policy that guarantees her an income of $26,000? Explain.

Solutions appear at back of book.

Buying, Selling, and Reducing Risk

Lloyd's of London is the oldest existing commercial insurance company, and it is an institution with an illustrious past. Originally formed in the eighteenth century as a commercial venture to help merchants cope with the risks of commerce, it grew in the heyday of the British Empire into a mainstay of imperial trade.

The basic idea of Lloyd's was simple. In the eighteenth century, shipping goods via sailing vessels was risky: the chance that a ship would sink in a storm or be captured by pirates was fairly high. The merchant who owned the ship and its cargo could easily be ruined financially by such an event. Lloyd's matched shipowners seeking insurance with wealthy investors who promised to compensate a merchant if his ship was lost. In return, the merchant paid the investor a fee in advance; if his ship *didn't* sink, the investor still kept the fee. In effect, the merchant paid a price to relieve himself of risk. By matching people who wanted to purchase insurance with people who wanted to provide it, Lloyd's performed the functions of a market. The fact that British merchants could use Lloyd's to reduce their risk made many more people in Britain willing to undertake merchant trade.

Insurance companies have changed quite a lot from the early days of Lloyd's. They no longer consist of wealthy individuals deciding on insurance deals over port and boiled mutton. But asking why Lloyd's worked to the mutual benefit of merchants and investors is a good way to understand how the market economy as a whole "trades" and thereby transforms risk.

The insurance industry rests on two principles. The first is that trade in risk, like trade in any good or service, can produce mutual gains. In this case, the gains come when people who are less willing to bear risk transfer it to people who are more willing to bear it. The second is that some risk can be made to disappear through *diversification*. Let's consider each principle in turn.

Trading Risk

It may seem a bit strange to talk about "trading" risk. After all, risk is a bad thing—and aren't we supposed to be trading goods and services?

But people often trade away things they don't like to other people who dislike them less. Suppose you have just bought a house for $100,000, the average price for a house in your community. But you have now learned, to your horror, that the building next door is being turned into an all-night disco. You want to sell the house immediately and are willing to accept $95,000 for it. But who will now be willing to buy it? The answer: a person who doesn't really mind late-night noise. Such a person might be willing to pay up to $100,000. So there is an opportunity here for a mutually beneficial deal—you are willing to sell for as little as $95,000, and the other person is willing to pay as much as $100,000, so any price in between will benefit both of you.

The key point is that the two parties have different sensitivities to noise, which enables those who most dislike noise, in effect, to pay other people to make their lives quieter. Trading risk works exactly the same way: people who want to reduce the risk they face can pay other people who are less sensitive to risk to take some of their risk away.

As we saw in the previous section, individual preferences account for some of the variations in people's attitudes toward risk, but differences in income and wealth are probably the principal reason behind different risk sensitivities. Lloyd's made money by matching wealthy investors who were more risk-tolerant with less wealthy and therefore more risk-averse shipowners.

Suppose, staying with our Lloyd's of London story, that a merchant whose ship went down would lose £1,000, and that there was a 10% chance of such a disaster. The expected loss in this case, then, would be $0.10 \times £1,000 = £100$. But the merchant, whose whole livelihood was at stake, might have been willing to pay £150 to be compensated in the amount of £1,000 if the ship sank. Meanwhile, a wealthy investor for whom the loss of £1,000 was no big deal would have been willing to take this risk for a return only slightly better than the expected loss—say, £110. Clearly, there is room for a mutually beneficial deal here: the merchant pays something less than £150 and more than £110—say, £130—in return for compensation if the ship goes down. In effect, he has paid a less risk-averse individual to bear the burden of his risk. Everyone has been made better off by this transaction.

The funds that an insurer places at risk when providing insurance is called his or her **capital at risk**.

An **efficient allocation of risk** is an allocation of risk in which those who are most willing to bear risk are those who end up bearing it.

The funds that an insurer places at risk when providing insurance are called his or her **capital at risk.** In our example, the wealthy Lloyd's investor places capital of £1,000 at risk in return for a premium of £130. In general, the amount of capital that potential insurers are willing to place at risk depends, other things equal, on the premium offered. If every ship is worth £1,000 and has a 10% chance of going down, nobody would offer insurance for less than a £100 premium, equal to the expected claim. In fact, only an investor who isn't risk-averse at all would be willing to offer a policy at that price, because accepting a £100 premium would leave the insurer's expected income unchanged while increasing his or her risk. Suppose there is one investor who isn't risk-averse; but the next most willing investor is slightly risk-averse and insists on a £105 premium. The next investor, being somewhat more risk-averse, demands a premium of £110, and so on. By varying the premium and asking how many insurers would be willing to provide insurance at that premium, we can trace out a supply curve for insurance, as shown in Figure 18-3. As the premium increases as we move up the supply curve, more risk-averse investors are induced to provide coverage.

Meanwhile, potential buyers will consider their willingness to pay a given premium, defining the demand curve for insurance. In Figure 18-4, the highest premium that any shipowner is willing to pay is £200. Who's willing to pay this? The most risk-averse shipowner, of course. A slightly less risk-averse shipowner might be willing to pay £190, an even slightly less risk-averse ship owner is willing to pay £180, and so on.

Now imagine a market in which there are thousands of shipowners and potential insurers, so that the supply and demand curves for insurance are smooth lines. In this market, as in markets for ordinary goods and services, there will be an equilibrium price and quantity. Figure 18-5 illustrates such a market equilibrium at a premium of £130, with a total quantity of 5,000 policies bought and sold, representing a total capital at risk of £5,000,000.

Notice that in this market risk is transferred from the people who most want to get rid of it (the most risk-averse shipowners) to the people least bothered by risk (the least risk-averse investors). So just as markets for goods and services typically produce an efficient allocation of resources, markets for risk also typically lead to an **efficient allocation of risk**—an allocation of risk in which those who are most willing to bear

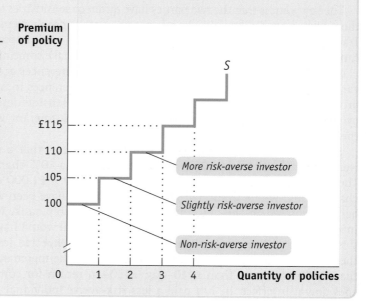

Figure 18-3

The Supply of Insurance

This is the supply of insurance policies to provide £1,000 in coverage to a merchant ship that has a 10% chance of being lost. Each investor has £1,000 of capital at risk. The lowest possible premium at which a policy is offered is £100, equal to the expected claim, and only a non-risk-averse investor is willing to supply this policy. As the premium increases, investors who are more risk-averse are induced to supply policies to the market, increasing the quantity of policies supplied.

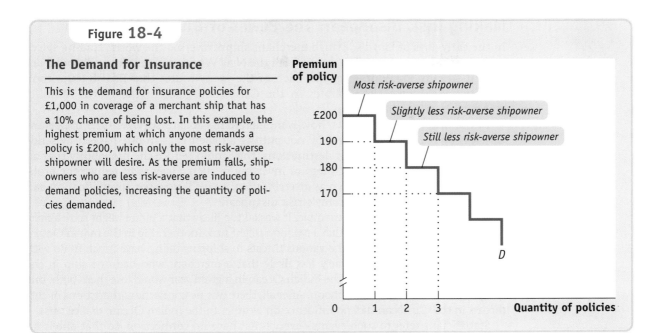

Figure 18-4

The Demand for Insurance

This is the demand for insurance policies for £1,000 in coverage of a merchant ship that has a 10% chance of being lost. In this example, the highest premium at which anyone demands a policy is £200, which only the most risk-averse shipowner will desire. As the premium falls, shipowners who are less risk-averse are induced to demand policies, increasing the quantity of policies demanded.

risk are those who end up bearing it. But as in the case of the markets for goods and services, there is an important qualification to this result: there are well-defined cases in which the market for risk fails to achieve efficiency. These arise from the presence of private information, an important topic that we will cover in the next section.

The trading of risk between individuals who differ in their degree of risk aversion plays an extremely important role in the economy, but it is not the only way that markets can help people cope with risk. Under some circumstances, markets can perform a sort of magic trick: they can make some (though rarely all) of the risk that individuals face simply disappear.

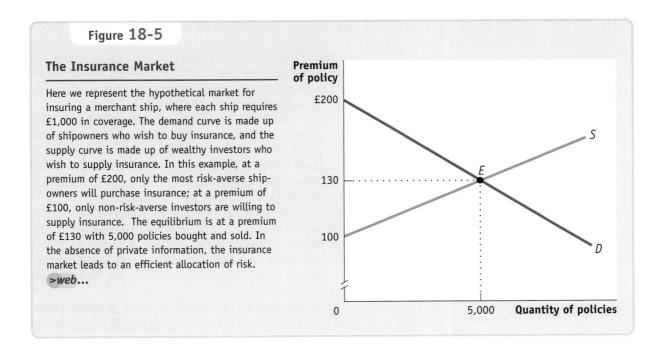

Figure 18-5

The Insurance Market

Here we represent the hypothetical market for insuring a merchant ship, where each ship requires £1,000 in coverage. The demand curve is made up of shipowners who wish to buy insurance, and the supply curve is made up of wealthy investors who wish to supply insurance. In this example, at a premium of £200, only the most risk-averse shipowners will purchase insurance; at a premium of £100, only non-risk-averse investors are willing to supply insurance. The equilibrium is at a premium of £130 with 5,000 policies bought and sold. In the absence of private information, the insurance market leads to an efficient allocation of risk.

>web...

Making Risk Disappear: The Power of Diversification

In the early days of Lloyd's, British merchant ships traversed the world, trading spices and silk from Asia, tobacco and rum from the New World, and textiles and wool from Britain, among many other goods. Each of the many routes that British ships took had its own unique risks—pirates in the Caribbean, gales in the North Atlantic, typhoons in the Indian Ocean.

In the face of all these risks, how were merchants able to survive? One important way was by reducing their risks by not putting all their eggs in one basket: by sending different ships to different destinations, they could reduce the probability that all their ships would be lost. A strategy of investing in such a way as to reduce the probability of severe losses is known as *diversification*. As we'll now see, diversification can often make some of the economy's risk disappear.

Let's stay with our shipping example. It was all too likely that a pirate might seize a merchant ship in the Caribbean or that a typhoon might sink another ship in the Indian Ocean. But the key point here is that the various threats to shipping didn't have much to do with each other. So it was considerably less likely that a merchant who had one ship in the Caribbean and another ship in the Indian Ocean in a given year would lose them both, one to a pirate and the other to a typhoon. After all, there was no connection: the actions of cutthroats in the Carribean had no influence on weather in the Indian Ocean, or vice versa.

Two possible events are **independent events** if each of them is neither more nor less likely to happen if the other one happens.

Statisticians refer to such events—events that have no connection, so that one is no more likely to happen if the other does than if it does not—as **independent events.** Many unpredictable events are independent of each other. If you toss a coin twice, the probability that it will come up heads on the second toss is the same whether it came up heads or tails on the first toss. If your house burns down today, it does not affect the probability that my house will burn down the same day (unless we live next door to each other or share the services of the same incompetent electrician.)

There is a simple rule for calculating the probability that two independent events will both happen: multiply the probability that one event would happen on its own by the probability that the other event would happen on its own. If you toss a coin once, the probability that it will come up heads is 0.5; if you toss the coin twice, the probability that it will come up heads *both* times is $0.5 \times 0.5 = 0.25$.

But what did it matter to shipowners or Lloyd's investors that ship losses in the Caribbean and ship losses in the Indian Ocean were independent events? The answer is that by spreading their investments across different parts of the world, shipowners or Lloyd's investors could make some of the riskiness of the shipping business simply disappear.

Let's suppose that Joseph Moneypenny, Esq., is wealthy enough to outfit two ships—and let's ignore for a moment the possibility of insuring his ships. Should Mr. Moneypenny equip two ships for the Caribbean trade and send them off together? Or should he send one ship to Barbados and one to Calcutta?

Assume that both voyages will be equally profitable if successful, yielding £1,000 if the voyage is completed. Also assume that there is a 10% chance both that a ship sent to Barbados will run into a pirate or that a ship sent to Calcutta will be sunk by a typhoon. And if two ships travel to the same destination, we will assume that they share the same fate. So if Mr. Moneypenny were to send both his ships to either destination, he would face a probability of 10% of losing all his investment.

But if Mr. Moneypenny were instead to send one ship to Barbados and one to Calcutta, the probability that he would lose both of them would be only $0.1 \times 0.1 = 0.01$, or just 1%. As we will see shortly, his expected payoff would be the same—but the chance of losing it all would be much less. So by engaging in **diversification**—investing in several different things, where the possible losses are independent events—he could make some of his risk disappear.

An individual can engage in **diversification** by investing in several different things, so that the possible losses are independent events.

Table 18-2 summarizes Mr. Moneypenny's options and their possible consequences. If he sends both ships to the same destination, he runs a 10% chance of los-

TABLE 18-2

How Diversification Reduces Risk

(a) If both ships sent to the same destination

State	Probability	Payoff	Expected payoff
Both ships arrive	0.9 = 90%	£2,000	(0.9 × £2,000) + (0.1 × £0) = £1,800
Both ships lost	0.1 = 10%	0	

(b) If one ship sent east, one west

State	Probability	Payoff	Expected payoff
Both ships arrive	0.9 × 0.9 = 81%	£2,000	(0.81 × £2,000) + (0.01 × £0) + (0.18 × £1,000) = £1,800
Both ships lost	0.1 × 0.1 = 1%	0	
One ship arrives	(0.1 × 0.9) + (0.1 × 0.9) = 18%	1,000	

ing them both. If he sends them to different destinations, there are three possible outcomes. Both ships could arrive safely: because there is a 0.9 probability of either one making it, the probability that both will make it is 0.9 × 0.9 = 81%. Both could be lost—but the probability of that happening is only 0.1 × 0.1 = 1%. Finally, there are two ways that only one ship can arrive. The probability that the first ship arrives and the second ship is lost is 0.9 × 0.1 = 9%. The probability that the first ship is lost but the second ship arrives is 0.1 × 0.9 = 9%. So the probability that only one ship makes it is 9% + 9% = 18%.

You might think that diversification is a strategy available only to those with a lot of money to begin with. How could Mr. Moneypenny have diversified if he were able to finance only one ship? But there are ways for even small investors to diversify. Even if Mr. Moneypenny were only wealthy enough to equip one ship, he could enter a partnership with another merchant. They could jointly outfit two ships, agreeing to share the profits equally, and then send those ships to different destinations. That way each would face less risk than if he equipped one ship on his own.

In the modern economy, diversification is made much easier for investors by the fact that they can easily buy shares in many companies by using the *stock market*. The owner of a **share** in a company is the owner of part of that company—typically a very small part, one-millionth or less. An individual who put all of his or her wealth in shares of a single company would lose all of that wealth if the company went bankrupt. But most investors hold shares in many companies, which makes the chance of losing all their investment very small.

> A **share** in a company is a partial ownership of that company.

In fact, Lloyd's of London wasn't just a way to trade risks; it was also a way for investors to diversify. To see how this worked, let's introduce Lady Penelope Smedley-Smythe, a wealthy aristocrat, who decides to increase her income by placing £1,000 of her capital at risk via Lloyd's. She could use that capital to insure just one ship. But more typically she would enter a "syndicate," a group of investors, who would jointly insure a number of ships going to different destinations, agreeing to share the cost if any one of those ships went down. Because it would be much less likely for all the ships insured by the syndicate to sink than for any one of them to go down, Lady Smedley-Smythe would be at much less risk of losing her entire capital.

In some cases, an individual can make risk almost entirely disappear by taking a small share in many

"Your mother called to remind you to diversify."

Pooling is a strong form of diversification in which an individual takes a small share in many independent events. This produces a payoff with very little risk.

independent events. This strategy is known as **pooling.** Consider the case of a health insurance company, which has millions of policyholders, with thousands of them requiring expensive treatment each year. The insurance company can't know whether any given individual will, say, require a heart bypass operation. But heart problems for two different individuals are pretty much independent events. And when there are many possible independent events, it is possible, using statistical analysis, to predict with great accuracy *how many* events of a given type will happen. For example, if you toss a coin 1,000 times, it will come up heads about 500 times—and it is very unlikely to be more than a percent or two off that figure. So a company offering fire insurance can predict very accurately how many of its clients' homes will burn down in a given year; a company offering health insurance can predict very accurately how many of its clients will need heart surgery in a given year; a life insurance company can predict how many of its clients will . . . Well, you get the idea.

When an insurance company is able to take advantage of the predictability that comes from looking at large numbers of independent events, it is said to engage in *pooling of risks.* And this pooling often means that even though insurance companies protect people from risk, the owners of the insurance companies may not themselves face much risk.

Lloyd's of London wasn't just a way for wealthy individuals to get paid for taking on some of the risks of less wealthy merchants. It was also a vehicle for pooling some of those risks. The effect of that pooling was to shift the supply curve in Figure 18-5 rightward: to make people willing to accept more risk, at a lower price, than would otherwise have been possible.

FOR INQUIRING MINDS

401(k) FOLLIES

It's important to save for your retirement. In the United States, many people save using what is known as a 401(k) plan—a plan that puts aside part of their salary in a special account, which can only be drawn down after retirement. The name comes from a special provision of the tax law, which exempts money set aside in these plans from income tax until the money is withdrawn.

The money in a 401(k) plan can be invested in stocks and other financial assets. Of course, this exposes the worker to the risk of losing some of his or her savings if the value of the stock falls.

The sensible thing is therefore to diversify 401(k) investments. But in 2001 and 2002, when the prices of some stocks plunged, it became clear that in some cases workers had been persuaded to invest most or all of their retirement savings in the stock of the companies that employed them. Most spectacularly, many employees at Enron, a seemingly solid company that suddenly collapsed in 2001, had their entire retirement savings in Enron stock—and were left with nothing. Other stock prices also fell at the time, but a broadly diversified 401(k) would have lost no more than 20 percent of its value in those years.

The Limits of Diversification

Diversification can reduce risk. In some cases it can eliminate it. But these cases are not typical, because there are important limits to diversification. We can see the most important reason for these limits by returning to Lloyd's one more time.

During the period when Lloyd's was creating its legend, there was one important hazard facing British shipping other than pirates or storms: war. Between 1690 and 1815, Britain fought a series of wars, mainly with France (which, among other things, went to war with Britain in support of the American Revolution). Each time, France would sponsor "privateers"—basically pirates with official backing—to raid British shipping and thus indirectly damage Britain's war effort.

Whenever war broke out between Britain and France, losses of British merchant ships would suddenly increase. Unfortunately, merchants could not protect themselves against this eventuality by sending ships to different ports: the privateers would prey on British ships anywhere in the world. So the loss of a ship to French privateers in the Caribbean and the loss of another ship to French privateers in the Indian Ocean would *not* be independent events. It would be quite likely that they would happen in the same year.

When an event is more likely to occur if some other event occurs, these two events are said to be **positively correlated.** And like the risk of having a ship seized by French privateers, many financial risks are, alas, positively correlated.

Here are some of the positively correlated financial risks that investors in the modern world face:

- *Severe weather*. Within any given region of the United States, losses due to weather are definitely not independent events. When a hurricane hits Florida, a lot of Florida homes will suffer hurricane damage. To some extent, insurance companies can diversify away this risk by insuring homes in many states. But events like El Niño (a recurrent temperature anomaly in the Pacific Ocean that disrupts weather around the world) can cause simultaneous flooding across the United States.

- *Political events*. Modern governments do not, thankfully, license privateers— although submarines served much the same function during World War II. Even today, however, some kinds of political events—say, a war or revolution in a key raw-material-producing area—can damage business around the globe.

- *Business cycles*. The causes of *business cycles*, fluctuations in the output of the economy as a whole, are a subject for macroeconomics. What we can say here is that if one company suffers a decline in business because of a nationwide economic slump, many other companies will also suffer such declines. So these events will be positively correlated.

When events are positively correlated, the risks they pose cannot be diversified away. An investor can protect herself from the risk that any one company will do badly by investing in many companies; she cannot use the same technique to protect against an economic slump in which *all* companies do badly. An insurance company can protect itself against the risk of losses from local flooding by insuring houses in many different places; but a global weather pattern that produces floods in many places will defeat this strategy.

So institutions like insurance companies and stock markets cannot make risk go away completely. There is always an irreducible core of risk that cannot be diversified. Markets for risk, however, do accomplish two things: First, they enable the economy to eliminate the risk that can be diversified. Second, they allocate the risk that remains to the people most willing to bear it.

> Two events are **positively correlated** if each event is more likely to occur if the other event also occurs.

economics in action

When Lloyd's Almost Llost It

At the end of the 1980s, the venerable institution of Lloyd's found itself in severe trouble. Investors who had placed their capital at risk, believing that the risks were small and the return on their investments more or less assured, found themselves required to make large payments to satisfy enormous claims. A number of investors, including members of some very old aristocratic families, found themselves pushed into bankruptcy.

What happened? Part of the answer is that ambitious managers at Lloyd's had persuaded investors to take on risks that were much larger than the investors realized. (Or to put it a different way, the premiums the investors accepted were too small for the true level of risk contained in the policies.)

But the biggest single problem was that many of the events against which Lloyd's had become a major insurer were *not* independent. In the 1970s and 1980s, Lloyd's had become a major provider of corporate liability insurance in the United States: it protected American corporations against the possibility that they might be sued for selling defective or harmful products. Everyone expected such suits to be more or less independent events. Why should one company's legal problems have much to do with another's?

The answer turned out to lie in one word: asbestos. For decades, this fireproofing material had been used in many products, which meant that many companies were responsible for its use. Then it turned out that asbestos can cause severe damage to the lungs, especially in children. The result was a torrent of lawsuits by people who believed they were injured by asbestos and billions of dollars in damage awards—many of them ultimately paid by Lloyd's investors. ∎

< < < < < < < < < < < < < < < < < <

>>CHECK YOUR UNDERSTANDING 18-2

1. Explain how each of the following events would change the equilibrium premium and quantity of insurance in the market, indicating any shifts in the supply and demand curves.
   a. An increase in the number of ships traveling the same trade routes and so facing the same kinds of risks
   b. An increase in the number of trading routes, with the same number of ships traveling a greater variety of routes and so facing different kinds of risk
   c. An increase in the degree of risk aversion among the ship-owners in the market
   d. An increase in the degree of risk aversion among the investors in the market
   e. An increase in the risk affecting the economy as a whole
   f. A fall in the wealth levels of investors in the market

Solutions appear at back of book.

Private Information: What You Don't Know Can Hurt You

Markets do very well at dealing with risk due to uncertainty: situations in which nobody knows what is going to happen, whose house will be flooded, or who will get sick. However, markets have much more trouble with situations in which *some people know things that other people don't know*—situations of **private information.** As we will see, private information can distort economic decisions and sometimes prevent mutually beneficial economic transactions from taking place. (Sometimes economists use the term *asymmetric information* rather than private information, but they are equivalent.)

Why is some information private? The most important reason is that people gen-erally know more about themselves than other people do. You know whether or not you are a careful driver; but unless you have already been in several accidents, your insurance company does not. You also probably know more about objects you deal with regularly than anyone else. So if you are selling me your used car, you are more likely to be aware of any problems with it than I am.

But why should such differences in who knows what be a problem? It turns out that there are two distinct sources of trouble: *adverse selection,* which arises from hav-ing private information about the way things are, and *moral hazard,* which arises from having private information about what people do.

Adverse Selection: The Economics of Lemons

Suppose that someone offers to sell you an almost brand-new car—purchased just three months ago, with only 2,000 miles on the odometer and no dents or scratches. Will you be willing to pay almost the same for it as for a car direct from the dealer?

Probably not, for one main reason: you cannot help but wonder why this car is being sold. Is it because the owner has discovered that something is wrong with it—that it is a "lemon"? Having driven the car for a while, the owner knows more about it than you do—and people are more likely to sell cars that give them trouble.

You might think that the fact that sellers of used cars know more about them than the buyers do represents an advantage to the sellers. But potential buyers know that potential sellers are likely to offer them lemons—they just don't know exactly which car is a lemon. Because potential buyers of a used car know that potential sellers are more likely to sell lemons than good cars, buyers will offer a lower price than they would if they had a guarantee of the car's quality. Worse yet, this poor opinion of used cars tends to be self-reinforcing, precisely because it depresses the prices that buyers offer. Used cars sell at a discount because buyers expect a disproportionate share of those cars to be lemons. Even a used car that is not a lemon would sell only at a large discount, because buyers don't know whether it's a lemon or not. But potential sellers who have good cars are unwilling to sell them at a deep discount, except under exceptional circumstances. So good used cars are rarely offered for sale; and used cars that are offered for sale have a strong tendency to be lemons. (This is why people who have a compelling reason to sell a car, such as moving overseas, make a point of revealing that information to potential buyers—as if to say "This car is not a lemon!")

The end result, then, is not only that used cars sell for low prices and that there are a large number of used cars with hidden problems. Equally important, many potentially beneficial transactions—sales of good cars by people who would like to get rid of them to people who would like to buy them—end up being frustrated by the inability of potential sellers to convince potential buyers that their cars are actually worth the higher price demanded. So some mutually beneficial trades between those who want to sell used cars and those who want to buy them go unexploited.

Although economists sometimes refer to situations like this as the "lemons problem" (the issue was introduced in a famous 1970 paper by economist and Nobel Laureate George Akerlof entitled "The Market for Lemons"), the more formal name of the problem is **adverse selection.** The reason for the name is obvious: because the potential sellers know more about the quality of what they are selling than the potential buyers, they have an incentive to select the worst things to sell.

Adverse selection does not apply only to used cars. It is a problem for many parts of the economy—most notably for insurance companies. Suppose that an insurance company were to offer a standard policy for repairing cars after accidents, with the same premium for all drivers. This premium would reflect the *average* risk of accidents across all drivers. But that would make the policy look very expensive to drivers who know they are particularly careful or skillful and so less likely than the average driver to have an accident. So safe drivers would be less likely than less-safe drivers to buy this policy, leaving the insurance company with exactly the customers it doesn't want: people who have a higher-than-average risk of having accidents. Mutually beneficial transactions between safe drivers and insurance companies go unexploited because when drivers possess private information about their risk characteristics, the insurance company cannot set premiums according to the true riskiness of the driver. Safe drivers would get "priced out" of the market.

In practice, people or firms faced with the problem of adverse selection follow one of several well-established strategies for dealing with it. One strategy is **screening:** using observable information to make inferences about private information. Auto insurance provides a very good example. An insurance company may not know whether you are a careful driver, but it has statistical data on the accident rates of people who resemble your profile—and it uses those data in setting premiums. A 19-year-old male who drives a sports car and has already had a fender-bender is likely to pay a very high premium. A 40-year-old female who drives a minivan and has

Adverse selection occurs when an individual knows more about the way things are than other people do. Private information leads buyers to expect hidden problems in items offered for sale, leading to low prices and the best items being kept off the market.

Adverse selection can be reduced through **screening:** using observable information about people to make inferences about their private information.

never had an accident is likely to pay much less. In some cases, this may be quite unfair: some adolescent males are very careful drivers, and some mature women drive their minivans as if they were F-16s. But nobody can deny that the insurance companies are right on average.

Another strategy is for people who are good prospects to do something **signaling** their private information—taking some action that wouldn't be worth taking unless they were indeed good prospects. Reputable used-car dealers often offer warranties—promises to repair any problems with the cars they sell that arise within a given amount of time. This isn't just a way of insuring their customers against possible expenses; it's a way of credibly showing that they are not selling lemons. As a result, more sales occur and dealers can command higher prices for their used cars.

Finally, in the face of adverse selection, it can be very valuable to establish a good **reputation:** a used-car dealer will often advertise how long it has been in business to show that it has continued to satisfy its customers. New customers, therefore, will be willing to purchase cars and to pay more for that dealer's cars.

> Adverse selection can be diminished by people **signaling** their private information through actions that credibly reveal what they know.

> A long-term **reputation** allows an individual to reassure others that he or she isn't concealing adverse private information.

Moral Hazard

In the late 1970s, New York and other major cities experienced an epidemic of "suspicious" fires—fires that appeared to be deliberately set. Some of the fires were probably started by teenagers on a lark, others by gang members struggling over turf. But investigators eventually became aware of patterns in a number of the fires. Particular landlords, who owned several buildings, seemed to have an unusually large number of their buildings burn down. Although it was difficult to prove, police had few doubts that most of these "fire-prone" landlords were hiring professional arsonists to torch their own properties.

Why burn your own building? These buildings were typically in declining neighborhoods, where rising crime and middle-class flight had led to a decline in property values. But the insurance policies on the buildings were written to compensate owners based on historical property values, and so would actually pay the owner of a destroyed building more than the building was worth in the current market. For an unscrupulous landlord who knew the right people, this presented a profitable opportunity.

The arson epidemic became less severe during the 1980s, partly because insurance companies began making it difficult to overinsure properties, and partly because a boom in real estate values made many previously arson-threatened buildings worth more unburned.

The episode makes it clear that it is a bad idea for insurance companies to let customers insure buildings for more than their value—it gives the customers some destructive incentives. You might think, however, that the incentive problem goes away as long as the insurance is no more than 100 percent of the value of what is being insured.

But, unfortunately, anything close to 100 percent insurance still distorts incentives—it induces policyholders to behave differently than they would in the absence of insurance. The reason is that preventing fires requires effort and cost on the part of a building's owner. Fire alarms and sprinkler systems have to be kept in good repair, fire safety rules have to be strictly enforced, and so on. All of this takes time and money—time and money that the owner may not find worth spending if the insurance policy will provide close to full compensation for any losses.

Of course, the insurance company could specify in the policy that it won't pay if basic safety precautions have not been taken. But it isn't always easy to tell how careful a building's owner has been—the owner knows, but the insurance company does not.

The point is that the building's owner has private information about his or her own actions, about whether he or she has really taken all appropriate precautions. As a result, the insurance company is likely to face greater claims than if it were able to determine exactly how much effort a building owner exerts to prevent a loss. The problem of distorted incentives arises when an individual has private information about his own actions but someone else bears the costs of a lack of care or effort. This is known as **moral hazard.**

> **Moral hazard** occurs when an individual knows more about his or her own actions than other people do. This leads to a distortion of incentives to take care or to exert effort when someone else bears the costs of the lack of care or effort.

To deal with moral hazard, it is necessary to give individuals with private information some personal stake in what happens, a stake that gives them a reason to exert effort even if others cannot verify that they have done so. Moral hazard is the reason salespeople in many stores receive a commission on sales: it's hard for managers to be sure how hard the salespeople are really working, and if they were paid only straight salary, they would not have an incentive to exert effort to make those sales. As described in the Economics in Action below, similar logic explains why many stores and restaurants, even if they are part of national chains, are actually franchises, licensed outlets owned by the people who run them.

Insurance companies deal with moral hazard by requiring a **deductible:** they compensate for losses only above a certain amount, so that coverage is always less than 100 percent. The insurance on your car, for example, may pay for repairs only after the first $500 in loss. This means that a careless driver who gets into a fender-bender will end up paying $500 for repairs even if he is insured, which provides at least some incentive to be careful and reduce moral hazard.

> A **deductible** in an insurance policy is a sum that the insured individual must pay before being compensated for a claim.

In addition to reducing moral hazard, deductibles provide a partial solution to the problem of adverse selection. Your insurance premium often drops substantially if you are willing to accept a large deductible. This is an attractive option to people who know they are low-risk customers; it is less attractive to people who know they are high-risk—and so are likely to have an accident and end up paying the deductible. By offering a menu of policies with different premiums and deductibles, insurance companies can screen their customers, inducing them to sort themselves out on the basis of their private information.

As the example of deductibles suggests, moral hazard limits the ability of the economy to allocate risks efficiently. You generally can't get full (100 percent) insurance on your home or car, even though you would like to buy it, and you bear the risk of large deductibles even though you would prefer not to. The following Economics in Action illustrates how in some cases moral hazard limits the ability of investors to diversify their investments.

economics in action

Franchise Owners Try Harder

When Americans go out for a quick meal, they often end up at one of the fast-food chains—McDonald's, Burger King, and so on. Because these are large corporations, most customers probably imagine that the people who serve them are themselves employees of large corporations. But usually they aren't. Most fast-food restaurants—for example, 85 percent of McDonald's outlets—are franchises. That is, some individual has paid the parent company for the right to operate a restaurant selling its product; he or she may look like an arm of a giant company but is in fact a small-business owner.

Becoming a franchisee is not a guarantee of success. You must put up a large amount of money, both to buy the license and to set up the restaurant itself (to open a Taco Bell, for example, cost $1 million in 1997). And although McDonald's takes care that its franchises are not too close to each other, they often face stiff competition from rival chains and even from a few truly independent restaurants. Becoming a franchise owner, in other words, involves taking on quite a lot of risk.

But why should people be willing to take these risks? Didn't we just learn that it is better to diversify, to spread your wealth among many investments? The logic of diversification would seem to say that it's better for someone with $1 million to invest in a wide range of stocks rather than put it all into one Taco Bell. This implies that Taco Bell would find it hard to attract franchisees: nobody would be willing to be a franchisee unless they expected to earn considerably more than they would as a simple hired manager having invested their wealth in a diversified portfolio of stocks. So wouldn't it be more profitable for McDonald's or Taco Bell simply to hire managers to run their restaurants?

It turns out that it isn't, because the success of a restaurant depends a lot on how hard the manager works, on the effort he or she puts into choosing the right employees, on keeping the place clean and attractive to customers, and so on. Could McDonald's get the right level of effort from a salaried manager? Probably not. The problem is moral hazard: the manager knows whether he or she is really putting 100 percent into the job; but company headquarters, which bears the costs of a poorly run restaurant, does not. So a salaried manager, who gets a salary even without doing everything possible to make the restaurant a success, does not have the incentive to do that extra bit—an incentive the owner does have because he or she has a substantial personal stake in the success of the restaurant.

In other words, there is a moral hazard problem when a salaried manager runs a McDonald's, where the private information is how hard the manager works. Franchising resolves this problem. A franchisee, whose wealth is tied up in the business and who stands to profit personally from its success, has every incentive to work extremely hard.

The result is that fast-food chains rely mainly on franchisees to operate their restaurants, even though the contracts with these owner-managers allow the franchisees on average to make much more than it would have cost the companies to employ store managers. The higher earnings of franchisees compensate them for the risk they accept, and the companies are compensated by higher sales that lead to higher license fees. In addition, franchisees are forbidden by the licensing agreement with the company from reducing their risk by taking actions such as selling shares of the franchise to outside investors and using the proceeds to diversify. It's an illustration of the fact that moral hazard prevents the elimination of risk through diversification. ∎

< < < < < < < < < < < < < < < < < < <

>> **CHECK YOUR UNDERSTANDING 18-3**

1. Your car insurance premiums are lower if you have had no moving violations for several years. Explain how this feature tends to decrease the potential inefficiency caused by adverse selection.

2. A common feature of home construction contracts is that when it costs more to construct a building than was originally estimated, the contractor must absorb the additional cost. Explain how this feature reduces the problem of moral hazard but also forces the contractor to bear more risk than she would like.

3. True or false? Explain your answer, stating what concept analyzed in this chapter accounts for the feature.
   People with higher deductibles on their auto insurance:
   a. Generally drive more carefully
   b. Pay lower premiums
   c. Generally are wealthier

Solutions appear at back of book.

• **A LOOK AHEAD** •

We began this chapter with a discussion of yet another thing markets can do right: they allow individuals to trade risk, to their mutual benefit. But our discussion of private information shows that markets have difficulty handling some problems.

In the next two chapters, we will begin discussing in earnest the problem of *market failure*—situations in which markets, left to themselves, can lead to inefficient outcomes. As we'll see, one of the key roles of government is to correct market failure.

SUMMARY

1. The **expected value** of a **random variable** is the weighted average of all possible values, where the weight corresponds to the probability of a given value occurring.

2. **Risk** is uncertainty about future events or **states of the world**. It is **financial risk** when the uncertainty is about monetary outcomes.

3. Under uncertainty, people maximize **expected utility**. A **risk-averse** person will choose to reduce risk when that reduction leaves the expected value of his or her income or wealth unchanged. A **fair insurance policy** has that feature: the **premium** is equal to the expected value of the claim.

4. Risk aversion arises from diminishing marginal utility: an additional dollar of income generates higher marginal utility in low-income states than in high-income states. A fair insurance policy increases a risk-averse person's utility because it transfers a dollar from a high-income state (a state when no loss occurs) to a low-income state (a state when a loss occurs).

5. Differences in preferences and income or wealth lead to differences in risk aversion. Depending on the size of the premium, a risk-averse person is willing to purchase unfair insurance, a policy for which the premium exceeds the expected value of the claim. The greater your risk aversion, the higher the premium you are willing to pay.

6. There are gains from trade in risk, leading to an **efficient allocation of risk:** those who are most willing to bear risk put their **capital at risk** to cover the losses of those least willing to bear risk.

7. Risk can also be reduced through **diversification,** investing in several different things that correspond to **independent events.** The stock market, where **shares** in companies are traded, offers one way to diversify. Insurance companies can engage in **pooling,** insuring many independent events so as to eliminate almost all risk. But when the underlying events are **positively correlated,** all risk cannot be diversified away.

8. **Private information** can cause inefficiency in the allocation of risk. One problem is **adverse selection,** private information about the way things are. It creates the "lemons problem" in used car markets where sellers of high-quality cars drop out of the market. Adverse selection can be limited in several ways—through **screening** of individuals, through **signaling** that people use to reveal their private information, and through the building of a **reputation.**

9. A related problem is **moral hazard:** individuals have private information about their actions, which distorts their incentives to exert effort or care when someone else bears the costs of that lack of effort or care. It limits the ability of markets to allocate risk efficiently. Insurance companies try to limit moral hazard by imposing **deductibles,** placing more risk on the insured.

KEY TERMS

PROBLEMS

1. For each of the following situations, calculate the expected value.

   a. Tanisha owns one share of IBM stock, which is currently trading at $80. There is a 50% chance that the share price will rise to $100 and a 50% chance that the share price will fall to $70. What is the expected value of the future share price?

   b. Sharon buys a ticket in a small lottery. There is a probability of 0.7 that she will win nothing, of 0.2 that she will win $10, and of 0.1 that she will win $50. What is the expected value of Sharon's winnings?

   c. Aaron is a farmer whose rice crop depends on the weather. If the weather is favorable, he will make a profit of $100. If the weather is unfavorable, he will make a profit of −$20 (that is, he will lose money). The weather forecast reports that the probability of weather being favorable is 0.9 and the probability of weather being unfavorable is 0.1. What is the expected value of Aaron's profit?

2. Vicky N. Vestor is considering investing some of her money in a start-up company. She currently has income of $4,000, and she is considering investing $2,000 of that in the company. There is a 0.5 probability that the company will succeed and

will pay out $8,000 to Vicky (her original investment of $2,000 plus $6,000 of the company's profits). And there is a 0.5 probability that the company will fail and Vicky will get nothing (and lose her investment). The accompanying table illustrates Vicky's utility function.

Income	Total utility (utils)
$0	0
1,000	50
2,000	85
3,000	115
4,000	140
5,000	163
6,000	183
7,000	200
8,000	215
9,000	229
10,000	241

a. Calculate Vicky's marginal utility of income for each income level. Is Vicky risk-averse?

b. Calculate the expected value of Vicky's income from this investment.

c. Calculate Vicky's expected utility from making the investment.

d. What is Vicky's utility from not making the investment? Will Vicky therefore invest in the company?

3. Vicky N. Vestor's utility function was given in Problem 2. As in Problem 2, Vicky currently has income of $4,000. She is considering investing in a start-up company, but the investment now costs $4,000 to make. If the company fails, Vicky will get nothing from the company. But if the company succeeds, she will get $10,000 from the company (her original investment of $4,000 plus $6,000 of the company's profits). Each event has a 0.5 probability of occurring. Will Vicky invest in the company?

4. You have $1,000 that you can invest. If you buy Ford stock, you face the following returns and probabilities from holding the stock for one year: with a probability of 0.2 you will get $1,500; with a probability of 0.4 you will get $1,100; and with a probability of 0.4 you will get $900. If you put the money into the bank, in one year's time you will get $1,100 for certain.

a. What is the expected value of your earnings from investing in Ford stock?

b. Suppose you are risk-averse. Can we say for sure whether you will invest in Ford stock or put your money into the bank?

5. You have $1,000 that you can invest. If you buy General Motors stock, then, in one year's time: with a probability of 0.4 you will get $1,600; with a probability of 0.4 you will get $1,100; and with a probability of 0.2 you will get $800. If you put the money into the bank, in one year's time you will get $1,100 for certain.

a. What is the expected value of your earnings from investing in General Motors stock?

b. Suppose you prefer putting your money into the bank to investing it in General Motors stock. What does that tell us about your attitude to risk?

6. Wilbur is an airline pilot who currently has income of $60,000. If he gets sick and loses his flight medical certificate, he loses his job and has only $10,000 income. His probability of staying healthy is 0.6, and his probability of getting sick is 0.4. Wilbur's utility function is given in the accompanying table.

Income	Total utility (utils)
$0	0
10,000	60
20,000	110
30,000	150
40,000	180
50,000	200
60,000	210

a. What is the expected value of Wilbur's income?

b. What is Wilbur's expected utility?

Wilbur thinks about buying "loss-of-license" insurance that will compensate him if he loses his flight medical certificate.

c. One insurance company offers Wilbur full compensation for his income loss (that is, the insurance company pays Wilbur $50,000 if he loses his flight medical certificate), and it charges a premium of $40,000. That is, regardless of whether he loses his flight medical certificate, Wilbur's income after insurance will be $20,000. What is Wilbur's utility? Will he buy the insurance?

d. What is the highest premium Wilbur would just be willing to pay for full insurance (insurance that completely compensates him for the income loss)?

7. Hugh's income is currently $5,000. His utility function is shown in the accompanying table.

Income	Total utility (utils)
$0	0
1,000	100
2,000	140
3,000	166
4,000	185
5,000	200
6,000	212
7,000	222
8,000	230
9,000	236
10,000	240

a. Calculate Hugh's marginal utility of income. What is his attitude toward risk?

b. Hugh is thinking about gambling in a casino. With a probability of 0.5 he loses $4,000, and with a probability of 0.5 he wins $4,000. What is the expected value of Hugh's income? What is Hugh's expected utility? Will he decide to gamble? (Suppose that he gets no extra utility from going to the casino.)

c. Suppose that the "spread" (how much he can win versus how much he can lose) of the gamble narrows, so that with a probability of 0.5 Hugh loses $2,000, and with a probability of 0.5 he wins $2,000. What is the expected value of Hugh's income? What is his expected utility? Is this gamble better for him than the gamble in part b? Will he decide to gamble?

8. Eva is risk-averse. Currently she has $50,000 to invest. She faces the following choice: she can invest in the stock of a dot-com company, or she can invest in IBM stock. If she invests in the dot-com company, then with probability 0.5 she will lose $30,000, but with probability 0.5 she will gain $50,000. If she invests in IBM stock, then with probability 0.5 she will lose only $10,000, but with probability 0.5 she will gain only $30,000. Can you tell which investment she will prefer to make?

9. Suppose you have $1,000 that you can invest in Ted and Larry's Ice Cream Parlor and Ethel's House of Cocoa. The price of a share of stock in either company is $100. The fortunes of each company are closely linked to the weather. When it is warm, the value of Ted and Larry's stock rises to $150 but the value of Ethel's stock falls to $60. When it is cold, the value of Ethel's stock rises to $150 but the value of Ted and Larry's stock falls to $60. There is an equal chance of the weather being warm or cold.

a. If you invest all your money in Ted and Larry's, what is your expected stock value? What if you invest all your money in Ethel's?

b. Suppose you diversify and invest half of your $1,000 in each company. How much will your total stock be worth if the weather is warm? What if it is cold?

c. Suppose you are risk-averse. Would you prefer to put all your money in Ted and Larry's, as in part a? Or would you prefer to diversify, as in part b? Explain your reasoning.

10. You are considering buying a second-hand Volkswagen. From reading car magazines, you know that half of all Volkswagens have problems of some kind (they are "lemons") and the other half run just fine (they are "plums"). If you knew that you were getting a plum, you would be willing to pay $10,000 for it: this is how much a plum is worth to you. You would also be willing to buy a lemon, but only if its price was no more than $4,000: this is how much a lemon is worth to you. And someone who owns a plum would be willing to sell it at any price above $8,000. Someone who owns a lemon would be willing to sell it for any price above $2,000.

a. For now, suppose that you can immediately tell whether the car that you are being offered is a lemon or a plum. Suppose someone offers you a plum. Will there be trade?

Now suppose that the seller has private information about the car she is selling: the seller knows whether she has a lemon or a plum. But when the seller offers you a Volkswagen, you do not know whether it is a lemon or a plum. So this is a situation of adverse selection.

b. Since you do not know whether you are being offered a plum or a lemon, you base your decision on the expected value to you of a Volkswagen, assuming you are just as likely to buy a lemon as a plum. Calculate this expected value.

c. Suppose, from driving the car, the seller knows she has a plum. However, you don't know whether this particular car is a lemon or a plum, so the most you are willing to pay is your expected value. Will there be trade?

11. You own a company that produces chairs, and you are thinking about hiring one more employee. Each chair produced gives you revenue of $10. There are two potential employees, Fred Ast and Sylvia Low. Fred is a fast worker who produces ten chairs per day, creating revenue for you of $100. Fred knows that he is fast and so will work for you only if you pay him more than $80 per day. Sylvia is a slow worker who produces only five chairs per day, creating revenue for you of $50. Sylvia knows that she is slow and so will work for you if you pay her more than $40 per day. Although Sylvia knows she is slow and Fred knows he is fast, you do not know who is fast and who is slow. So this is a situation of adverse selection.

a. Since you do not know which type of worker you get, you think about what the expected value of your revenue will be if you hire one of the two. What is that expected value?

b. Suppose you offered to pay a daily wage equal to the expected revenue you calculated in part a. Who would you be able to hire: Fred, or Sylvia, or either?

12. For each of the following situations, do the following: First describe whether it is a situation of moral hazard or of adverse selection. Then explain what inefficiency can arise from this situation and explain how the proposed solution reduces the inefficiency.

a. When you buy a second-hand car, you do not know whether it is a lemon (low quality) or a plum (high quality), but the seller knows. A solution is for sellers to offer a warranty with the car that pays for repair costs.

b. Some people are prone to see doctors unnecessarily for minor complaints like headaches and health maintenance organizations do not know how urgently you need a doctor. A solution is for insurees to have to make a co-payment of a certain dollar amount (for example, $10) each time they visit a health care provider. All insurees are risk-averse.

c. When airlines sell tickets, they do not know whether a buyer is a business traveler (who is willing to pay a lot for a seat), or a leisure traveler (who has a low willingness to pay). A solution for a profit-maximizing airline is to offer an expensive ticket that is very flexible (it allows date and route changes) and a cheap ticket that is very inflexible (it has to be booked in advance and cannot be changed).

d. A company does not know whether workers on an assembly line work hard or whether they shirk. A solution is to pay the workers "piece rates," that is, pay them according to how much they have produced each day. All workers are risk-averse while the company is not risk-averse.

e. When making a decision about hiring you, prospective employers do not know whether you are a productive or unproductive worker. A solution is for productive workers to provide potential employers with references from previous employers.

13. Kory owns a house that is worth $300,000. If the house burns down, she loses all $300,000. If the house does not burn down, she loses nothing. Her house burns down with a probability of 0.02. Kory is risk-averse. What would a fair insurance policy cost?

a. Suppose that an insurance company offers to insure her fully against the loss from the house burning down, at a premium of $1,500. Can you say for sure whether Kory will or will not take the insurance?

b. Suppose that an insurance company offers to insure her fully against the loss from the house burning down, at a premium of $6,000. Can you say for sure whether Kory will or will not take the insurance?

c. Suppose that an insurance company offers to insure her fully against the loss from the house burning down, at a premium of $9,000. Can you say for sure whether Kory will or will not take the insurance?

>web... To continue your study and review of concepts in this chapter, please visit the Krugman/Wells website for quizzes, animated graph tutorials, web links to helpful resources, and more.

www.worthpublishers.com/krugmanwells

>> Externalities

WHO'LL STOP THE RAIN?

MILLIONS OF PEOPLE IN THE NORTH-eastern United States can think of no better way to relax than fishing in one of the region's thousands of lakes. But in the 1960s avid fishermen noticed something alarming: lakes that had formerly teemed with fish were now almost empty. What had happened?

The answer turned out to be acid rain, caused mainly by coal-burning power plants. When coal is burned, it releases sulfur dioxide and nitric oxide into the atmosphere; these gases react with water, producing sulfuric acid and nitric acid. The result in the Northeast, downwind from the nation's industrial heartland, was rain sometimes as acidic as lemon juice. Acid rain didn't just kill fish; it also damaged trees and crops and in time even began to dissolve limestone buildings.

You'll be glad to hear that the acid rain problem today is much less serious than it was in the 1960s. Power plants have reduced their emissions by switching to low-sulfur coal and installing scrubbers in their smokestacks. But they didn't do this out of the goodness of their hearts; they did it in response to government

policy. Without such intervention, power companies would have had no incentive to take the environmental effects of their actions into account.

When individuals impose costs on or provide benefits for others, but don't have an economic incentive to take those costs or benefits into account, economists say that the situation includes *externalities*. You may recall that we briefly noted this phenomenon in Chapters 1, 6, and 13. There we stated that one of the principal sources of market failure are actions that create *side effects* that are not

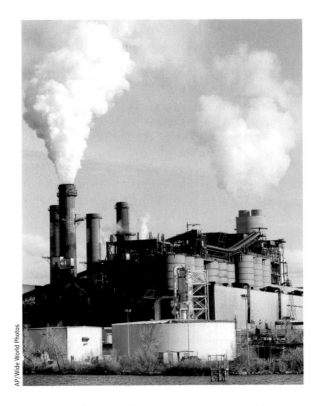
For many polluters, acid rain is someone else's problem.

What you will learn in this chapter:

➤ What **externalities** are and why they can lead to inefficiency in a market economy and support for government intervention

➤ The difference between **negative** and **positive externalities**

➤ The importance of the **Coase theorem,** which explains how private individuals can sometimes solve externalities

➤ Why some government policies to deal with externalities, such as **emissions taxes, tradable permits,** or **Pigouvian subsidies,** are efficient, although others, like **environmental standards,** are inefficient

➤ How positive externalities give rise to arguments for **industrial policy** properly taken into account—that is, externalities. In this chapter, we'll examine the economics of externalities, seeing how they can get in the way of economic efficiency and lead to market failure, why they provide a reason for government intervention in markets, and how economic analysis can be used to guide government policy.

Because externalities arise from the side effects of actions, we need to study them from two slightly different vantage points. First, we consider the situation in which the side effect—that is, pollution—can be directly observed and quantified. Whenever an activity can be directly observed and quantified, it can be regulated: by imposing direct controls on it, by taxing it, or by subsidizing it. As we will see, government intervention in this case should be aimed directly at moving the market to the right quantity of the side effect.

But in many situations, only the original activity, not its side effect, can be observed. For example, we can't observe the congestion caused by a single car, so the government is unable to implement policies that control the side effect directly. What it can do is employ policies that affect the *original* activity—driving. So in the second part of our analysis we will consider how governments can indirectly achieve the right quantity of the side effect through influencing the activity that generates it. In a fundamental way, however, the two approaches are equivalent: each one involves, at the margin, setting the benefit of doing a little bit more of something equal to the cost of doing that little bit more.

The Economics of Pollution

Pollution is a bad thing. Yet most pollution is a side effect of activities that provide us with good things: our air is polluted by power plants generating the electricity that lights our cities, and our rivers are damaged by fertilizer runoff from farms that grow our food. Why don't we accept a certain amount of pollution as the cost of a good life?

Actually, we do. Even highly committed environmentalists don't think that we can or should completely eliminate pollution—even an environmentally conscious society would accept *some* pollution as the cost of producing useful goods and services. What environmentalists argue is that unless there is a strong and effective environmental policy, our society will generate *too much* pollution—too much of a bad thing. And the great majority of economists agree.

To see why, we need a framework that lets us think about how much pollution a society *should* have. We'll then be able to see why a market economy, left to itself, will produce more pollution than it should. We'll start by adopting the simplest framework to study the problem—assuming that the amount of pollution emitted by a polluter is directly observable and controllable.

Costs and Benefits of Pollution

How much pollution should society allow? We learned in Chapter 7 that "how much" decisions always involve comparing the marginal benefit from an additional unit of something with the marginal cost of that additional unit. The same is true of pollution.

The **marginal social cost of pollution** is the additional cost imposed on society as a whole by an additional unit of pollution. For example, acid rain damages fisheries, crops, and forests, and each additional ton of sulfur dioxide released into the atmosphere increases the damage.

The **marginal social cost of pollution** is the additional cost imposed on society as a whole by an additional unit of pollution.

PITFALLS

SO HOW DO YOU MEASURE THE MARGINAL SOCIAL COST OF POLLUTION?

It might be confusing to think of marginal *social* cost—after all, we have up to this point always defined marginal cost as being incurred by an individual or a firm, not society as a whole. But it is easily understandable once we link it to the familiar concept of willingness to pay: the marginal social cost of a unit of pollution is equal to the *highest willingness to pay among all members of society* to avoid that unit of pollution. But calculating the true cost to society of pollution—marginal or average—is a difficult matter, requiring a great deal of scientific knowledge, as the Economics in Action on page 461 illustrates. As a result, society often underestimates the true marginal social cost of pollution.

The **marginal social benefit of pollution**—the additional gain to society from an additional unit of pollution—may seem like a confusing concept. What's good about pollution? However, avoiding pollution requires using scarce resources that could have been used to produce other goods and services. For example, to reduce the quantity of sulfur dioxide they emit, power companies must either buy expensive low-sulfur coal or install special scrubbers to remove sulfur from their emissions. The more sulfur dioxide they are allowed to emit, the lower these extra costs. Suppose that we can calculate how much money the power industry would save if it were allowed to emit an additional ton of sulfur dioxide. That saving is the marginal benefit to society of emitting an extra ton of sulfur dioxide.

Using hypothetical numbers, Figure 19-1 shows how we can determine the **socially optimal quantity of pollution**—the quantity of pollution society would choose if all its costs and benefits were fully accounted for. The upward-sloping marginal social cost curve, *MSC*, shows how the marginal cost to society of an additional ton of pollution emissions varies with the quantity of emissions. (An upward slope is likely because nature can often safely handle low levels of pollution but is increasingly harmed as pollution reaches high levels.) The marginal social benefit curve, *MSB*, is downward sloping because it is progressively harder, and therefore more expensive, to achieve a further reduction in pollution as the total amount of pollution falls—increasingly more expensive technology must be used. As a result, as pollution falls, the cost savings to a polluter of being allowed to emit one more ton rises.

The socially optimal quantity of pollution in this example isn't zero. It's Q_{OPT}, the quantity corresponding to point *O*, where *MSB* crosses *MSC*. At Q_{OPT}, the marginal social benefit from an additional ton of emissions and its marginal social cost are equalized at $200.

But will a market economy, left to itself, arrive at the socially optimal quantity of pollution? No, it won't.

> The **marginal social benefit of pollution** is the additional gain to society as a whole from an additional unit of pollution.

> The **socially optimal quantity of pollution** is the quantity of pollution that society would choose if all the costs and benefits of pollution were fully accounted for.

PITFALLS

SO HOW DO YOU MEASURE THE MARGINAL SOCIAL BENEFIT OF POLLUTION?

Similar to the problem of measuring the marginal social cost of pollution, the concept of willingness to pay helps us understand the marginal social benefit of pollution in contrast to the marginal benefit to an individual or firm. The marginal social benefit of a unit of pollution is simply equal to the highest willingness to pay for the right to emit that unit across all polluters. But unlike the marginal social cost of pollution, the value of the marginal social benefit of pollution is a number likely to be known—to polluters, that is.

Figure 19-1

The Socially Optimal Quantity of Pollution

Pollution yields both costs and benefits. Here the curve *MSC* shows how the marginal cost to society as a whole from emitting one more ton of pollution emissions depends on the quantity of emissions. The curve *MSB* shows how the marginal benefit to society as a whole of emitting an additional ton of pollution emissions depends on the quantity of pollution emissions. The socially optimal quantity of pollution is Q_{OPT}; at that quantity, the marginal social benefit of pollution is equal to the marginal social cost, corresponding to $200.

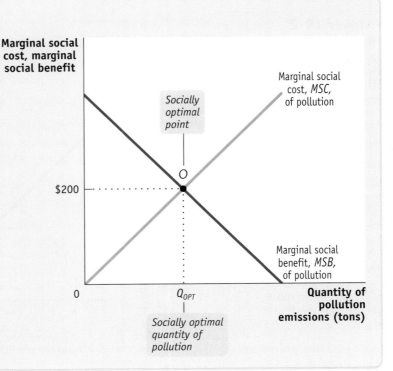

Pollution: An External Cost

Pollution yields both benefits and costs to society. But in a market economy without government intervention, those who benefit from pollution—like the owners of power companies—decide how much pollution occurs. They have no incentive to take into account the costs of pollution that they impose on others.

To see why, remember the nature of the benefits and costs from pollution. For polluters, the benefits take the form of monetary savings: by emitting an extra ton of sulfur dioxide, any given polluter saves the cost of buying expensive, low-sulfur coal or installing pollution-control equipment. So the benefits of pollution accrue directly to the polluters.

The costs of pollution, though, fall on people who have no say in the decision about how much pollution takes place: people who fish in northeastern lakes do not control the decisions of power plants.

Figure 19-2 shows the result of this asymmetry between who reaps the benefits and who pays the costs. In a market economy without government intervention to protect the environment, only the benefits of pollution are taken into account in choosing the quantity of pollution. So the quantity of emissions won't be at the socially optimal quantity Q_{OPT}; it will be Q_{MKT}, the quantity at which the marginal social benefit of an additional ton of pollution is zero, but the marginal social cost of that additional ton is much larger—$400. The quantity of pollution in a market economy without government intervention will be higher than its socially optimal quantity. (The Pigouvian tax noted in Figure 19-2 will be explained shortly.)

The reason is that in the absence of government intervention, those who derive the benefits from pollution—in this case, the owners of power plants—don't have to compensate those who bear the costs. So the marginal cost of pollution to any given polluter is zero: polluters have no incentive to limit the amount of emissions. For example, before the Clean Air Act of 1970, midwestern power plants used the cheapest type of coal available, regardless of how much pollution it caused, and did nothing to scrub their emissions.

The environmental costs of pollution are the best-known and most important example of an **external cost**—an uncompensated cost that an individual or firm

> An **external cost** is an uncompensated cost that an individual or firm imposes on others.

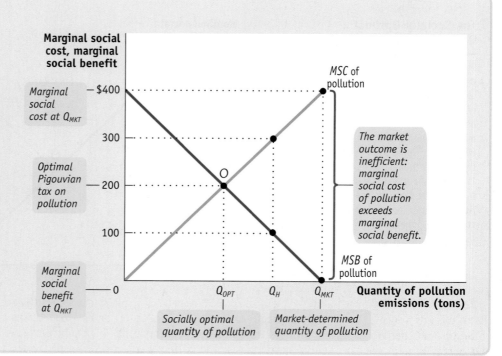

Figure 19-2

Why a Market Economy Produces Too Much Pollution

In the absence of government intervention, the quantity of pollution will be Q_{MKT}, the level at which the marginal social benefit of pollution to polluters is zero. This is an inefficiently high quantity of pollution: the marginal social cost, $400, greatly exceeds the marginal social benefit, $0. An optimal Pigouvian tax of $200, the value of the marginal social cost of pollution when it equals the marginal social benefit of pollution, can move the market to the socially optimal quantity of pollution, Q_{OPT}.

>web...

TALKING AND DRIVING

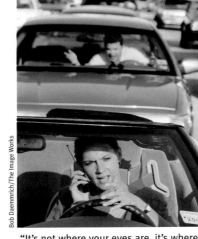

Why is that woman in the car in front of us driving so erratically? Is she drunk? No, she's talking on her cell phone.

Traffic safety experts take the risks posed by driving while talking very seriously. Using hands-free, voice-activated phones doesn't seem to help much because the main danger is distraction. As one traffic safety consultant put it, "It's not where your eyes are; it's where your head is." And we're not talking about a trivial problem. One estimate suggests that people who talk on their cell phones while driving may be responsible for 600 or more traffic deaths each year.

The National Safety Council urges people not to use phones while driving. But a growing

"It's not where your eyes are, it's where your head is."

number of people say that voluntary standards aren't enough; they want the use of cell phones while driving made illegal, as it already is in Japan, Israel, and several other countries.

Why not leave the decision up to the driver? Because the risk posed by driving while talking isn't just a risk to the driver; it's also a safety risk to others—especially people in other cars. Even if you decide that the benefit to you of taking that call is worth the cost, you aren't taking into account the cost to other people. Driving while talking, in other words, generates a serious—sometimes fatal—negative externality.

imposes on others. There are many other examples of external costs besides pollution. Another important, and certainly very familiar, external cost is traffic congestion—an individual who chooses to drive during rush hour increases congestion and so increases the travel time of other drivers.

We'll see later in this chapter that there are also important examples of **external benefits,** benefits that individuals or firms confer on others without receiving compensation. External costs and benefits are jointly known as **externalities,** with external costs called **negative externalities** and external benefits called **positive externalities.**

As we've already suggested, externalities can lead to individual decisions that are not optimal for society as a whole. Let's take a closer look at why, focusing on the case of pollution.

> An **external benefit** is a benefit that an individual or firm confers on others without receiving compensation.
>
> External costs and benefits are known as **externalities;** external costs are **negative externalities,** and external benefits are **positive externalities.**

The Inefficiency of Excess Pollution

We have just shown that in the absence of government action, the quantity of pollution will be *inefficient:* polluters will pollute up to the point at which the marginal social benefit of pollution is zero, as shown by the pollution quantity Q_{MKT} in Figure 19-2. Recall that an outcome is inefficient if some people could be made better off without making others worse off. In Chapter 6 we showed why the market equilibrium quantity in a perfectly competitive market is the efficient quantity of the good, the quantity that maximizes total surplus. Here, we can use a variation of that analysis to show how the presence of a negative externality upsets that result.

Because the marginal social benefit of pollution is zero at Q_{MKT}, reducing the quantity of pollution by one ton would subtract very little from the total social benefit from pollution. In other words, the benefit to polluters from that last unit of pollution is very low—virtually zero. Meanwhile, the marginal social cost imposed on the rest of society from that last ton of pollution at Q_{MKT} is quite high—$400. This means that by reducing the quantity of pollution at Q_{MKT} by one ton, the total social cost of pollution falls by $400, while total social benefits fall by virtually zero. So total surplus rises by approximately $400 if the quantity of pollution at Q_{MKT} is reduced by one ton.

If the quantity of pollution is reduced further, there will be more gains in total surplus, though they will be smaller. For example, if the quantity of pollution is Q_H in Figure 19-2, the marginal social benefit of a ton of pollution is $100, but the marginal social cost is still $300. This means that reducing the quantity of pollution by one ton leads to a net gain in total surplus of approximately $300 − $100 = $200. This tells us that Q_H is still an inefficiently high quantity of pollution. Only if the quantity of pollution is reduced to Q_{OPT}, where the marginal social cost and the marginal social benefit of an additional ton of pollution are both $200, is the outcome efficient.

Private Solutions to Externalities

Can the private sector solve the problem of externalities without government intervention? Bear in mind that when an outcome is inefficient, there is potentially a deal that makes people better off. Why don't individuals find a way to make that deal?

In an influential 1960 article, the economist and Nobel laureate Ronald Coase pointed out that in an ideal world the private sector could indeed deal with all externalities. According to the **Coase theorem,** even in the presence of externalities an economy can always reach an efficient solution provided that the costs of making a deal are sufficiently low. The costs of making a deal are known as **transaction costs.**

To get a sense of Coase's argument, imagine two neighbors, Mick and Britney, who both like to barbecue in their backyards on summer afternoons. Mick likes to play golden oldies on his boombox while barbecuing; but this annoys Britney, who can't stand that kind of music.

Who prevails? You might think that it depends on the legal rights involved in the case: if the law says that Mick has the right to play whatever music he wants, Britney just has to suffer; if the law says that Mick needs Britney's consent to play music in his backyard, Mick has to live without his favorite music while barbecuing.

But as Coase pointed out, the outcome need not be determined by legal rights, because Britney and Mick can make a private deal. Even if Mick has the right to play his music, Britney could pay him not to. Even if Mick can't play the music without an OK from Britney, he can offer to pay her to give that OK. These payments allow them to reach an efficient solution, regardless of who has the legal upper hand. If the benefit of the music to Mick exceeds its cost to Britney, the music will go on; if the benefit to Mick is less than the cost to Britney, there will be silence.

The implication of Coase's analysis is that externalities need not lead to inefficiency because individuals have an incentive to make mutually beneficial deals—deals that lead them to take externalities into account when making decisions. When individuals *do* take externalities into account when making decisions, economists say that they **internalize the externality.** If externalities are fully internalized, the outcome is efficient even without government intervention.

Why can't individuals always internalize externalities? Our barbecue example implicitly assumes the transaction costs are low enough for Mick and Britney to be able to make a deal. In many situations involving externalities, however, transaction costs prevent individuals from making efficient deals. Examples of transaction costs include the following:

- The costs of communication among the interested parties—costs that may be very high if many people are involved

- The costs of making legally binding agreements—costs that may be high if the employment of expensive lawyers is required

- Costly delays involved in bargaining—even if there is a potentially beneficial deal, both sides may hold out in an effort to extract more favorable terms, leading to increased effort and forgone utility

---

According to the **Coase theorem,** even in the presence of externalities an economy can always reach an efficient solution as long as **transaction costs**—the costs to individuals of making a deal—are sufficiently low.

When individuals take external costs or benefits into account, they **internalize the externality.**

In some cases, people do find ways to reduce transaction costs, allowing them to internalize externalities. For example, many people live in private communities that set rules for home maintenance and behavior, making bargaining between neighbors unnecessary. But in many other cases, transaction costs are too high to make it possible to deal with externalities through private action. For example, tens of millions of people are adversely affected by acid rain. It would be prohibitively expensive to try to make a deal among all those people and all those power companies.

When transaction costs prevent the private sector from dealing with externalities, it is time to look for government solutions. We turn to public policy in the next section.

economics in action

Thank You for Not Smoking

New Yorkers call them the "shiver-and-puff people"—the smokers who stand outside their workplaces, even in the depths of winter, to take a cigarette break. Over the past couple of decades, rules against smoking in spaces shared by others have become ever stricter. This is partly a matter of personal dislike—nonsmokers really don't like to smell other people's cigarette smoke—but it also reflects concerns over the health risks of second-hand smoke. As the Surgeon General's warning on many packs says, "Smoking causes lung cancer, heart disease, emphysema, and may complicate pregnancy." And there's no question that being in the same room as someone who smokes exposes you to at least some health risk.

Second-hand smoke, then, is clearly an example of a negative externality. But how important is it? Putting a dollar-and-cents value on it—that is, measuring the marginal social cost of cigarette smoke—requires not only estimating the health effects but putting a value on these effects. Despite the difficulty, economists have tried. A paper published in 1993 in the *Journal of Economic Perspectives* surveyed the research on the external costs of both cigarette smoking and alcohol consumption.

According to this paper, valuing the health costs of cigarettes depends on whether you count the costs imposed on members of smokers' families, including unborn children, in addition to costs borne by smokers. If you don't, the external costs of second-hand smoke have been estimated at about only $0.19 per pack smoked. (Using this method of calculation, $0.19 corresponds to the *average* social cost of smoking per pack at the current level of smoking in society.) If you include effects on smokers' families, the number rises considerably—family members who live with smokers are exposed to a lot more smoke. (They are also exposed to the risk of fires, which alone is estimated at $0.09 per pack.) If you include the effects of smoking by pregnant women on their unborn children's future health, the cost is immense—$4.80 per pack, which is more than twice the wholesale price charged by cigarette manufacturers. ∎

(See source note on the copyright page.)

> > > > > > > > > > > > > > > > > >

>> **CHECK YOUR UNDERSTANDING 19-1**

1. Waste water runoff from large poultry farms adversely affects their neighbors. Explain the following:
   a. The nature of the external cost imposed
   b. The outcome in the absence of government intervention or a private deal
   c. The socially optimal outcome

2. According to Yasmin, any student who borrows a book from the university library and fails to return it on time imposes a negative externality on other students. He claims that rather than charging a modest fine for late returns, the library should charge a huge fine, so that borrowers will never return a book late. Is Yasmin's economic reasoning correct?

Solutions appear at back of book.

Policies Toward Pollution

Before 1970, there were no rules governing the amount of sulfur dioxide power plants in the United States could emit—which is why acid rain got to be such a problem. After 1970, the Clean Air Act set rules about sulfur dioxide emissions—and the acidity of rainfall declined significantly. Economists argued, however, that a more flexible system of rules that exploited the effectiveness of markets could achieve lower pollution at less cost. In 1990 this theory was put into effect with a modified version of the Clean Air Act. And guess what? The economists were right!

In this section we'll look at the policies governments use to deal with pollution and at how economic analysis has been used to improve those policies.

Environmental Standards

The most serious external costs in the modern world are surely those associated with actions that damage the environment—air pollution, water pollution, habitat destruction, and so on. Protection of the environment has become a major role of government in all advanced nations. In the United States, the Environmental Protection Agency is the principal enforcer of environmental policies at the national level, supported by the actions of state and local governments.

> **Environmental standards** are rules that protect the environment by specifying actions by producers and consumers.

How does a country protect its environment? At present the main policy tools are **environmental standards,** rules that protect the environment by specifying actions by producers and consumers. A familiar example is the law that requires almost all vehicles to have catalytic converters, which reduce the emission of chemicals that can cause smog and lead to health problems. Other rules require communities to treat their sewage, factories to avoid or limit certain kinds of pollution, and so on.

Environmental standards came into widespread use in the 1960s and 1970s, and they have had considerable success in reducing pollution. For example, since the United States passed the Clean Air Act in 1970, overall emission of pollutants into the air has fallen by more than a third, even though the population has grown by a third and the size of the economy has more than doubled. Even in Los Angeles, still famous for its smog, the air has improved dramatically: in 1988 ozone levels in the South Coast Air Basin exceeded federal standards on 178 days; in 2003, on only 68 days.

Despite these successes, economists believe that when regulators can control a polluter's emissions directly, there are more efficient ways than environmental standards to deal with pollution. By using methods grounded in economic analysis, society can achieve a cleaner environment at lower cost. Most current environmental standards are inflexible and don't allow reductions in pollution to be achieved at minimum cost. For example, Plant A and Plant B might be ordered to reduce pollution by the same percentage, even if their costs of achieving that objective are very different.

How does economic theory suggest that pollution should be directly controlled? There are actually two approaches: taxes and tradable permits. As we'll see, either approach can achieve the efficient outcome at the minimum feasible cost.

Emissions Taxes

> An **emissions tax** is a tax that depends on the amount of pollution a firm produces.

One way to deal with pollution directly is to charge polluters an **emissions tax.** Emissions taxes are taxes that depend on the amount of pollution a firm produces. For example, power plants might be charged $200 for every ton of sulfur dioxide they emit.

Look again at Figure 19-2, which shows that the socially optimal quantity of pollution is Q_{OPT}. At that quantity of pollution, the marginal social benefit and marginal social cost of an additional ton of emissions are equal at $200. But in the absence of government intervention, power companies have no incentive to limit pollution to the socially optimal quantity Q_{OPT}; instead, they will push pollution up to the quantity Q_{MKT}, at which marginal social benefit is zero.

It's now easy to see how an emissions tax can solve the problem. If power companies are required to pay a tax of $200 per ton of emissions, they now face a marginal cost of $200 per ton and have an incentive to reduce emissions to Q_{OPT}, the socially optimal quantity. This illustrates a general result: an emissions tax equal to the marginal social cost at the socially optimal quantity of pollution induces polluters to internalize the externality—to take into account the true cost to society of their actions.

Why is an emissions tax an efficient way (that is, a cost-minimizing way) to reduce pollution but environmental standards are generally not? Because an emissions tax ensures that the marginal benefit of pollution is equal for all sources of pollution but an environmental standard does not. Figure 19-3 shows a hypothetical industry consisting of only two plants, Plant A and Plant B. We'll assume that Plant A uses newer technology than plant B and so has a lower cost of reducing pollution. Reflecting this difference in costs, Plant A's marginal benefit of pollution curve, MB_A, lies below Plant B's marginal benefit of pollution curve, MB_B. Because it is more costly for Plant B to reduce its pollution at any output quantity, an additional ton of pollution is worth more to Plant B than to Plant A.

In the absence of government action, we know that polluters will pollute until the marginal social benefit of an additional unit of emissions is equal to zero. Recall that

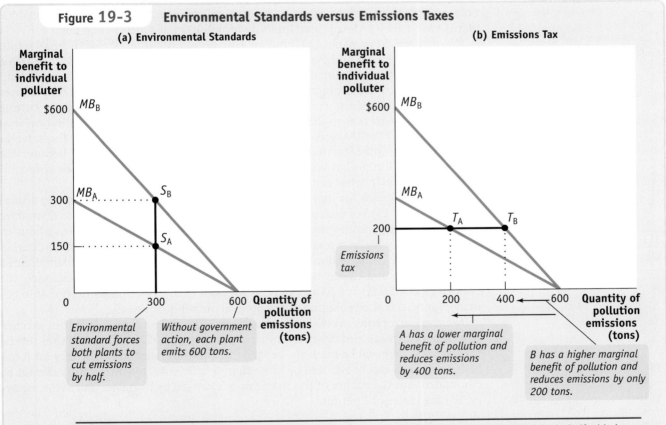

Figure 19-3   Environmental Standards versus Emissions Taxes

In both panels, MB_A shows the marginal benefit of pollution to Plant A and MB_B shows the marginal benefit of pollution to Plant B. In the absence of government intervention, each plant would emit 600 tons. However, the cost of reducing emissions is lower for Plant A, as shown by the fact that MB_A lies below MB_B. Panel (a) shows the result of an environmental standard that requires both plants to cut emissions in half; this is inefficient, because it leaves the marginal benefit of pollution higher for Plant B than for Plant A. Panel (b) shows that an emissions tax achieves the same quantity of overall pollution efficiently: faced with an emissions tax of $200 per ton, both plants reduce pollution to the point where its marginal benefit is $200. **>web...**

the marginal social benefit of pollution is the cost savings, at the margin, to polluters of an additional unit of pollution. This means that without government intervention each plant will pollute until its own marginal benefit of pollution is equal to zero. This corresponds to an emissions quantity of 600 tons each for Plants A and B—the quantity of pollution at which MB_A and MB_B are each equal to zero. So although Plant A and Plant B value a ton of emissions differently, without government action they will each choose to emit the same amount of pollution.

Now suppose that the government decides that overall pollution from this industry should be cut in half, from 1,200 tons to 600 tons. Panel (a) of Figure 19-3 shows how this might be achieved with an environmental standard that requires each plant to cut its emissions in half, from 600 to 300 tons. The standard has the desired effect of reducing overall emissions from 1,200 to 600 tons but accomplishes it in an inefficient way. As you can see from panel (a), the environmental standard leads Plant A to produce at point S_A, where its marginal benefit of pollution is $150, but Plant B produces at point S_B, where its marginal benefit of pollution is twice as high, $300.

This difference in marginal benefits between the two plants tells us that the same quantity of pollution can be achieved at lower total cost by allowing Plant B to pollute more than 300 tons but inducing Plant A to pollute less. In fact, the efficient way to reduce pollution is to ensure that at the industry-wide outcome, the marginal benefit of pollution is the same for all plants. When each plant values a unit of pollution equally, there is no way to re-arrange pollution reduction among the various plants that achieves the optimal quantity of pollution at a lower total cost.

We can see from panel (b) how an emissions tax achieves exactly that result. Suppose both Plant A and Plant B pay an emissions tax of $200 per ton, so that the marginal cost of an additional ton of emissions to each plant is now $200 rather than zero. As a result, Plant A produces at T_A and Plant B produces at T_B. So Plant A reduces its pollution more than it would under an inflexible environmental standard, cutting its emissions from 600 to 200 tons; meanwhile, Plant B reduces its pollution less, going from 600 to 400 tons. In the end, total pollution—600 tons—is the same as under the environmental standard, but total surplus is higher. That's because the reduction in pollution has been achieved efficiently, allocating most of the reduction to Plant A, the plant that can reduce emissions at lower cost.

The term *emissions tax* may convey the misleading impression that taxes are a solution to only one kind of external cost, pollution. In fact, taxes can be used to discourage any activity that generates negative externalities, such as driving during rush hour or operating a noisy bar in a residential area. In general, taxes designed to reduce external costs are known as **Pigouvian taxes,** after the economist A. C. Pigou, who emphasized their usefulness in a classic 1920 book, *The Economics of Welfare*. In our example, the optimal Pigouvian tax is $200; as you can see from Figure 19-2, this corresponds to the marginal social cost of pollution at the optimal output quantity, Q_{OPT}.

Are there any problems with emissions taxes? The main concern is that in practice government officials usually aren't sure how high the tax should be set. If they set the tax too low, there will be too little improvement in the environment; if they set it too high, emissions will be reduced by more than is efficient. This uncertainty cannot be eliminated, but the nature of the risks can be changed by using an alternative strategy, issuing emissions permits.

> Taxes designed to reduce external costs are known as **Pigouvian taxes.**

Tradable Emissions Permits

> **Tradable emissions permits** are licenses to emit limited quantities of pollutants that can be bought and sold by polluters.

Tradable emissions permits are licenses to emit limited quantities of pollutants that can be bought and sold by polluters. They are usually issued to polluting firms according to some formula reflecting their history. For example, each power plant might be issued permits equal to 50 percent of its emissions before the system went into effect. The more important point, however, is that these permits are *tradable*. Firms with differing costs of reducing pollution can now engage in mutually beneficial transactions: those that find it easier to reduce pollution will sell some of their permits to those that find it more difficult. In other words, firms will use transactions in permits to re-allocate pollution reduction among themselves, so that in the end those with the lowest cost will reduce their pollution the most, while those with the highest cost will reduce their pollution the least. Using our original example, this means that Plant A will find it profitable to sell 100 of its 300 government-issued licenses to Plant B. The effect of a tradable permit system is to create a market in rights to pollute.

Just like emissions taxes, tradable permits provide polluters with an incentive to take the marginal social cost of pollution into account. To see why, suppose that the market price of a permit to emit one ton of sulfur dioxide is $200. Then every plant has an incentive to limit its emissions of sulfur dioxide to the point where the marginal benefit of emissions is $200. This is obvious for plants that buy rights to pollute: if a plant must pay $200 for the right to emit an additional ton of sulfur dioxide, it faces the same incentives as a plant facing an emissions tax of $200 per ton. But it's equally true for plants that have more permits than they plan to use: by *not* emitting a ton of sulfur dioxide, a plant frees up a permit that it can sell for $200, so the opportunity cost of a ton of emissions to the plant's owner is $200.

In short, tradable emissions permits have the same cost-minimizing advantage as emissions taxes over environmental standards: either system ensures that those who can reduce pollution most cheaply are the ones who do so. The socially optimal quantity of pollution shown in Figure 19-2 could be efficiently achieved either way: by imposing an emissions tax of $200 per ton of pollution or by issuing tradable permits to emit Q_{OPT} tons of pollution. If regulators choose to issue Q_{OPT} permits, where one permit allows the release of one ton of emissions, then the equilibrium market price of a permit among polluters will indeed be $200. Why? You can see from Figure 19-2 that at Q_{OPT}, only polluters with a marginal benefit of pollution of $200 or more will buy a permit. And the last polluter who buys—who has a marginal benefit of exactly $200—sets the market price.

It's important to realize that emissions taxes and tradable permits do more than induce polluting industries to reduce their output. They also provide incentives to create and use less-polluting technology. In fact, the main effect of the permit system for sulfur dioxide has been to change *how* electricity is produced rather than to reduce the nation's electricity output. For example, power companies have shifted to the use of alternative fuels such as low-sulfur coal and natural gas; they have also installed scrubbers that take much of the sulfur dioxide out of a power plant's emissions.

The main problem with tradable emissions permits is the flip-side of the problem with emissions taxes: because it is difficult to determine the optimal quantity of pollution, governments can find themselves either issuing too many permits—that is, they don't reduce pollution enough, or issuing too few—that is, they reduce pollution too much.

In practice, after first relying on rigid environmental standards, the U.S. government has turned to a system of tradable emissions permits to control acid rain, and current proposals would extend that system to other major sources of pollution. The Economics in Action that follows describes how the system has worked in practice.

economics in action

Controlling Acid Rain

The Clean Air Act of 1970 instituted what even the Environmental Protection Agency (EPA) calls a "command-and-control" regime, in which businesses and individuals were given detailed instructions about what to do to reduce air pollution. When the act was revised in 1990, however, the EPA made an effort to move in the direction of market-based remedies. The most notable of these is the program designed to reduce sulfur dioxide emissions from coal-burning electric power plants, the major source of acid rain.

The sulfur dioxide program issues "allowances" to power plants based on their historical consumption of coal. Each allowance is the right to emit one ton of sulfur dioxide during or after a specified year. Power companies are free to buy or sell allowances. However, they must present the EPA with enough allowances to cover their own emissions. So plants with extra allowances can sell them, but plants without enough allowances must buy the difference.

Since the program began in 1994, the price per allowance has fluctuated, sometimes going below $100 and sometimes above $200; in 2004 it was $260. This is well below the price most analysts expected, and some environmentalists have taken the low price as a sign that the government should seek further reductions in pollution levels.

Economists who have analyzed the system believe it has led to large savings compared with what would have been the costs of achieving the same quantity of pollution under a regulatory rule that did not allow the power companies to trade. ∎

< < < < < < < < < < < < < < < < < < <

>> CHECK YOUR UNDERSTANDING 19-2

1. Some opponents of tradable emissions permits object to them on the ground that polluters that sell their permits benefit monetarily from their contribution to polluting the environment. Assess this argument.

2. Explain the following:
   a. Why an emissions tax smaller than or greater than the marginal social cost at Q_{OPT} reduces total surplus
   b. Why a system of tradable emissions permits that sets the total quantity of allowable pollution higher or lower than Q_{OPT} reduces total surplus

Solutions appear at back of book.

Production, Consumption, and Externalities

Nobody imposes external costs like pollution out of malice. Pollution, traffic congestion, and other harmful externalities are side effects of activities, like electricity generation or driving, that are otherwise desirable. We've just learned how government regulators can move the market to the socially optimal quantity when the side effect can be directly controlled. But as we cautioned earlier, in some cases it's not possible to directly control the side effect; only the original activity can be influenced. As we'll see shortly, government policies in these situations must instead be geared to changing the quantity of the original activity, which in turn changes the quantity of the side effect produced.

This approach, although slightly more complicated, has several advantages. First, it gives us a clear understanding of how the quantity of the original, desirable activity is altered by policies designed to manage its side effects (which will, in fact, typically occur both when the side effect can be directly controlled and when it can't). Second, it lets us evaluate arguments against environmental policy—arguments that arise from the fact that desirable activities are unavoidably impeded by policies intended to control their negative side effects. Finally, it helps us think about a phenomenon that is different but related to the problem of external costs: what should be done when an activity generates external *benefits*.

Private versus Social Costs

Given current technology, there is no affordable way to breed and raise livestock on a commercial scale without hurting the environment. Whatever it is—cows, pigs, chicken, sheep, or salmon—livestock farming produces prodigious amounts of what is euphemistically known as "muck." But that's not all: scientists estimate that the amount of methane gas produced by livestock (the same gas produced when a person—heaven forbid!—belches) currently rivals the pollution caused by the burning of fossil fuels in the creation of greenhouses gases. From the point

Muck and methane gas: the costly side effects of producing a side of bacon.

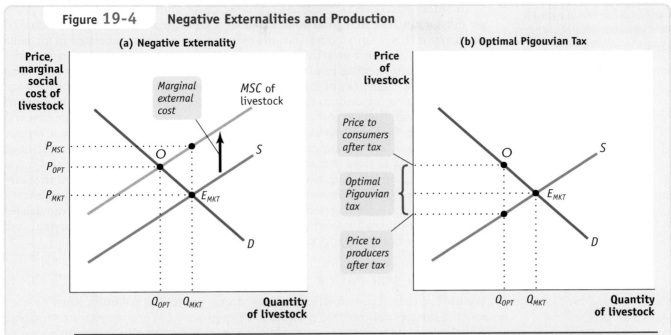

Figure 19-4   Negative Externalities and Production

(a) Negative Externality

Price, marginal social cost of livestock

Marginal external cost

MSC of livestock

P_{MSC}

P_{OPT}

P_{MKT}

O

S

E_{MKT}

D

Q_{OPT} Q_{MKT}

Quantity of livestock

(b) Optimal Pigouvian Tax

Price of livestock

Price to consumers after tax

Optimal Pigouvian tax

Price to producers after tax

O

S

E_{MKT}

D

Q_{OPT} Q_{MKT}

Quantity of livestock

Livestock production generates external costs, so the marginal social cost curve of livestock, *MSC*, corresponds to the supply curve, *S*, shifted upward by the marginal external cost. Panel (a) shows that without government action, the market produces the quantity Q_{MKT}. It is greater than the socially optimal quantity of livestock production, Q_{OPT}, the quantity at which *MSC* crosses the demand curve, *D*. At Q_{MKT}, the market price, P_{MKT}, is less than P_{MSC}, the true marginal cost to society of livestock production. Panel (b) shows how an optimal Pigouvian tax on livestock production, equal to its marginal external cost, moves the production to Q_{OPT}, resulting in lower output and a higher price to consumers. **>web...**

of view of society as a whole, then, the cost of livestock farming includes both direct production costs to the farmer (payments for factors of production and inputs such as animal feed) and the external environmental costs imposed as a by-product. In the absence of government intervention, however, livestock farmers have no incentive to take into account the environmental costs of their production decisions. As a result, in the absence of government intervention, livestock farmers will produce too much output.

Panel (a) of Figure 19-4 illustrates this point. The market demand curve for livestock by consumers is represented by the curve *D*; the market, or industry, supply curve is given by the curve *S*. In the absence of government intervention, market equilibrium will be at point E_{MKT}, yielding the amount produced and consumed Q_{MKT} and the market price P_{MKT}. At that point, the marginal benefit to society of another unit of livestock (measured by the market price) is equal to the marginal cost *incurred by the industry* for producing that unit.

Let's look a little more closely at the supply curve. Assuming that the livestock industry is competitive, we know from Chapter 9 that the industry supply curve corresponds to the horizontal sum of all the individual supply curves of producers in the industry. In addition, we know that each individual producer's supply curve corresponds to its marginal cost curve. These two facts taken together imply that the industry supply curve is the horizontal sum of the individual producers' marginal cost curves: a given point on *S* corresponds to the total industry-wide marginal cost at the corresponding output level. But we also know from our earlier discussion that this estimation of marginal cost does not include the external cost that production imposes on others. In other words, when external costs are present, the industry supply curve does not reflect the true cost to society of production of the good.

> The **marginal social cost of a good or activity** is equal to the marginal cost of production plus its marginal external cost.

In order to account for the true cost to society of an additional unit of the good, we must define the **marginal social cost of a good or activity,** which is equal to the marginal cost of production plus the marginal external cost generated by an additional unit of the good or activity. It captures the increase in production cost to the industry *and* the increase in external cost to the rest of society caused by producing one more unit. Panel (a) of Figure 19-4 shows the marginal social cost of livestock curve, *MSC*; it corresponds to the industry supply curve *shifted upward* by the amount of the marginal external cost. With the marginal social cost curve and the demand curve, we can find the socially optimal quantity of a good or activity that creates external costs: it is the quantity Q_{OPT}, the quantity corresponding to O, the point at which *MSC* and *D* cross. Reflecting the proper accounting for external cost, Q_{OPT} is less than Q_{MKT}. So left to its own, a market will result in too much of a good that carries external costs being produced and consumed. Correspondingly, without government action, the price to consumers of such a good is too low: at the output level Q_{MKT}, the unregulated market price P_{MKT} is lower than P_{MSC}, the true marginal cost to society of a unit of livestock.

Environmental Policy, Revisited

We have already seen two efficient methods for controlling pollution when government regulators can control it directly: an emissions tax and a system of tradable emissions permits. Are there similar methods that lead to an efficient quantity of pollution when regulators can target only the original activity or good, such as livestock production? Yes, there are—although they will take the form of a tax on livestock sales or a license to produce a unit of livestock rather than on the pollution created. These methods will move the market to the optimal quantity by compelling producers to internalize the externality caused by livestock production in their decisions.

Consider first the case of a Pigouvian tax on livestock transactions. Once such a tax is in effect, the cost to a livestock farmer of producing an additional unit of livestock includes both the marginal cost of production and the tax. If the tax is set at the right amount, it is exactly equal to the marginal external cost. As shown in panel (b) of Figure 19-4, the optimal Pigouvian tax will move the market outcome to the optimal point O.

A system of tradable production permits that restricts the industry-wide quantity of livestock produced to the optimal quantity has the same effect. Suppose that in order to produce an additional unit of livestock, a farmer must purchase a permit. The cost of this permit behaves like a Pigouvian tax, and once again external costs are completely internalized in the private decisions of producers. Even if the farmer already possesses the permit, its opportunity cost—the price it could command in the market for permits—acts like a Pigouvian tax.

So Q_{OPT}, the optimal quantity of livestock produced and consumed, corresponds to the optimal quantity of pollution generated by livestock production. You might ask yourself at this point how this analysis, in terms of the optimal quantity of a good or activity that gives rise to an external cost, relates to our earlier analysis of the optimal quantity of pollution. Except for the effect that emissions taxes and tradable emissions permits have on the creation and adoption of less-polluting production methods, the two approaches are equivalent: the difference between the two comes down to a matter of units. The first analysis was carried out in units of pollution and the second in units of a good or activity that yields pollution. But regardless of the framework we use, the underlying method is the same: to find the level at which society's marginal benefit from another unit equals society's marginal cost.

But our second analysis does create additional insights: we see how consumption choices are affected by policies designed to counteract external costs. Note that in panel (b) of Figure 19-4, consumers consume less livestock (in the form of meat purchased at supermarkets and restaurants) and pay a higher market price at the socially optimal quantity. (We know from Chapter 5 that exactly how the burden of the tax is allocated between producers and consumers depends on the price elasticities of demand and supply.) Moreover, this shows us that criticisms of environmental policies made exclusively on the basis that they "hurt consumers" are misguided.

Finally, you might ask which method a regulator would choose if a choice existed between policies that target pollution directly and policies that target production of the original good or activity. Generally, whenever feasible it is a good idea to target the pollution directly. The main reason, as we mentioned earlier, is that it gives incentives for the creation and adoption of less-polluting production methods. This, in turn, lessens the disincentive to produce the good (something, after all, that people want) when the good is targeted rather than when pollution is targeted.

As this book goes to press, an example of this phenomenon is being reported. A Florida-based company, Agcert, has developed technology whereby methane from pig-waste tanks can be drawn off and either burnt or used as "biofuel" to generate electricity. The company claims that this technology can achieve an average emissions reduction of one ton of methane gas per pig per year, a sizable savings in an industry where farms can have as many as 10,000 animals. Farmers could then be granted "credits" for their emissions reductions, which they could sell to producers in other industries who want to purchase a license to pollute. Such credits could be a lucrative source of income for farmers, given that the current market price for a one-ton credit for emissions is about $7 to $8. Agcert is currently valued at around $128 million. As some have commented, this invention has given new life to an old saying among plumbers and sewer workers: "Where there's muck, there's gold."

Private versus Social Benefits

Not all externalities are negative. In some important cases, an economic activity creates external benefits—that is, individual actions provide benefits to other people for which the producers are not compensated.

The most important source of external benefits in the modern economy probably involves creation of knowledge. In high-tech industries like semiconductors, innovations by one firm are quickly emulated and improved upon both by rival firms in the same industry and by firms in other industries. Such spreading of knowledge among individuals and firms is known as a **technology spillover.** Such spillovers often take place through face-to-face contact. As Economics in Action on page 471 explains, bars and restaurants in California's Silicon Valley are famed for their technical gossip, and the need to keep tabs on the latest innovations is a major reason so many high-tech firms are clustered near each other.

> A **technology spillover** is an external benefit that results when knowledge spreads among individuals and firms.

In Chapter 22 we'll discuss the economics of goods whose value lies principally in the knowledge or information they embody. For now, let's just look at the implications of external benefits in general for economic efficiency and economic policy. Suppose that the production of some good—say, semiconductor chips—yields positive externalities. How does this affect our analysis of the chip market, and does it create a justification for government intervention?

Just as external costs cause the marginal social *cost* of producing a good to exceed the industry's marginal cost, when there are external benefits from a good, the marginal social *benefit* exceeds consumers' marginal benefit. This is illustrated in panel (a) of Figure 19-5 on page 470, which shows the market for semiconductor chips. Since there are no external costs in this case, the industry supply curve, S, represents the true marginal social cost to society of production. The demand curve, D, represents the marginal benefit that accrues to *consumers of the good:* each point on the demand curve corresponds to the willingness to pay of the last consumer to purchase the good at the corresponding price. But it does not incorporate the benefits to society as a whole from production of the good—the technological spillover an additional unit provides to the economy as a whole.

To explore this phenomenon we need a new concept, the **marginal social benefit of a good or activity**—the marginal benefit that accrues to consumers from an additional unit of the good or activity, plus the marginal external benefit to society

> The **marginal social benefit of a good or activity** is equal to the marginal benefit that accrues to consumers plus its marginal external benefit.

Figure 19-5   Positive Externalities and Production

(a) Positive Externality

Price, marginal social benefit of chip

Marginal external benefit

P_{MSB}
P_{OPT}
P_{MKT}

S

O

E_{MKT}

MSB of chips

D

Q_{MKT} Q_{OPT}

Quantity of chips

(b) Optimal Pigouvian Subsidy

Price of chip

Price to producers after subsidy

Optimal Pigouvian subsidy

Price to consumers after subsidy

S

O

E_{MKT}

D

Q_{MKT} Q_{OPT}

Quantity of chips

Semiconductor chip production generates external benefits, so the marginal social benefit curve of chips, *MSB*, corresponds to the demand curve, *D*, shifted upward by the marginal external benefit. Panel (a) shows that without government action, the market produces Q_{MKT}. It is lower than the socially optimal quantity of production, Q_{OPT}, the quantity at which

MSB crosses the supply curve, *S*. At Q_{MKT}, the market price, P_{MKT}, is less than P_{MSB}, the true marginal benefit to society of semiconductor chip production. Panel (b) shows how an optimal Pigouvian subsidy to chip producers, equal to its marginal external benefit, moves the production to Q_{OPT}, resulting in higher output and a higher price to producers. **>web...**

from an additional unit. As you can see from panel (a) of Figure 19-5, the marginal social benefit curve, *MSB*, corresponds to the demand curve *D shifted upward* by the amount of the marginal external benefit.

The analysis in this case is very similar to that of external costs. Left to itself, the market will reach an equilibrium at E_{MKT}, the point at which the demand curve *D* crosses the supply curve *S* at a market price P_{MKT}. But the quantity of output at this equilibrium, Q_{MKT}, is inefficiently low: at that output level, the marginal social benefit of an additional unit, P_{MSB}, exceeds the industry's marginal cost of producing that unit, P_{MKT}. The optimal quantity of production and consumption is Q_{OPT}, the quantity at which marginal cost is equal to marginal social benefit.

How can the economy be induced to produce Q_{OPT} chips? The answer is a **Pigouvian subsidy:** a payment designed to encourage activities that yield external benefits. The optimal Pigouvian subsidy, shown in panel (b) of Figure 19-5, is equal to the marginal external benefit of producing an additional unit. Producers receive the price paid by consumers plus the per-unit subsidy, inducing them to produce more output. Such a subsidy is an example of an **industrial policy,** a general term for a policy of supporting industries believed to yield positive externalities.

Although the strict economic logic supporting such efforts is impeccable, economists are generally less enthusiastic about industrial policies to promote positive externalities than they are about fees and permit schemes to discourage negative externalities. This lack of enthusiasm reflects a mixture of practical and political judgments. First, positive externalities—which most often involve the creation of knowledge and new technologies—are typically much harder to identify and measure than negative externalities. (A simple sensor can keep track of how many tons of sulfur dioxide come out of a smokestack. But how do you tell whether and when a new product embodies a technology that will benefit other producers and consumers?) In

A **Pigouvian subsidy** is a payment designed to encourage activities that yield external benefits.

An **industrial policy** is a policy that supports industries believed to yield positive externalities.

addition, producers gain monetarily from subsidies: they receive a higher price than they otherwise would. So many economists also fear, with some historical justification, that a program intended to promote industries that yield positive externalities will degenerate into a program that promotes industries with political pull.

However, there is one activity that is widely believed to generate positive externalities and is provided with considerable subsidies: education!

economics in action

Spillovers in Silicon Valley

The author Tom Wolfe is best known for his social essays, like "Radical Chic," and his novels, like *Bonfire of the Vanities*. But his article "The Tinkerings of Robert Noyce: How the Sun Rose on the Silicon Valley," published in *Esquire* in 1983, is one of the best descriptions ever written of technological spillovers at work.

Wolfe emphasized the role of informal contact in spreading useful knowledge: "Every year there was some place, the Wagon Wheel, Chez Yvonne, Rickey's, the Roundhouse, where members of this esoteric fraternity, the young men and women of the semiconductor industry, would head after work to have a drink and gossip and brag and trade war stories about contacts, burst modes, bubble memories, pulse trains, bounceless modes, slow-death episodes, RAMs, NAKs, MOSes, PCMs, PROMs, PROM blowers, PROM blasters, and teramagnitudes, meaning multiples of a million millions." If you don't know what he's talking about, that's the point: the way to find out what all this was about, and keep in touch with the latest technologies, was to hang around in the right places. The informal spread of knowledge Wolfe described was and is the key to Silicon Valley's success. ■

>> **CHECK YOUR UNDERSTANDING 19-3**

1. Explain how the London congestion charge described in Chapter 3 (pages 62-63), in which cars entering central London during business hours must pay a fee of £5, can be an optimal policy to manage inner-city pollution and congestion.

2. In each of the following cases, determine whether an external cost or an external benefit is imposed and what an appropriate policy response would be.
   a. Trees planted in urban areas improve air quality and lower summer temperatures.
   b. Water-saving toilets reduce the need to pump water from rivers and aquifers. The cost of a gallon of water to homeowners is virtually zero.
   c. Old computer monitors contain toxic materials that pollute the environment when improperly disposed of.

Solutions appear at back of book.

• A LOOK AHEAD •

Externalities are an important justification for government intervention in the economy. As we've seen, government programs such as emissions taxes or tradable permit systems may be necessary to bring individual incentives in line with social costs or benefits.

In the next chapter, we'll turn to some related justifications for government intervention: the problems of *public goods* like lighthouses, which won't be provided in the absence of government action, and *common resources* like fish in the sea, which will be overused in the absence of government action.

SUMMARY

1. When pollution can be directly observed and controlled, government policies should be geared directly to producing the **socially optimal quantity of pollution,** the quantity at which the **marginal social cost of pollution** is equal to the **marginal social benefit of pollution.** In the absence of government intervention, a market produces too much pollution because polluters take only their benefit from polluting into account, not the costs imposed on others.

2. The costs to society of pollution are an example of an **external cost;** in some cases, however, economic activities yield **external benefits.** External costs and benefits are jointly known as **externalities,** with external costs called **negative externalities** and external benefits called **positive externalities.**

3. According to the **Coase theorem,** individuals can find a way to **internalize the externality,** making government intervention unnecessary, as long as **transaction costs—** the costs of making a deal—are sufficiently low. However, in many cases transaction costs are too high to permit such deals.

4. Governments often deal with pollution by imposing **environmental standards,** a method, economists argue, that is usually an inefficient way to reduce pollution. Two efficient (cost-minimizing) methods for reducing pollution are **emissions taxes,** a form of **Pigouvian tax,** and **tradable emissions permits.** The optimal Pigouvian tax on pollution is equal to its marginal social cost at the socially optimal quantity of pollution. These

methods also provide incentives for the creation and adoption of less-polluting production technologies.

5. When only the original good or activity can be controlled, government policies are geared to influencing how much of it is produced. When there are external costs from production, the **marginal social cost of a good or activity** exceeds its marginal cost to producers, the difference being the marginal external cost. Without government action, the market produces too much of the good or activity. The optimal Pigouvian tax on production of the good or activity is equal to its marginal external cost, yielding lower output and a higher price to consumers. A system of tradable production permits for the right to produce the good or activity can also achieve efficiency at minimum cost.

6. When a good or activity yields external benefits, such as **technology spillovers,** the **marginal social benefit of the good or activity** is equal to the marginal benefit accruing to consumers plus its marginal external benefit. Without government intervention, the market produces too little of the good or activity. An optimal **Pigouvian subsidy** to producers, equal to the marginal external benefit, moves the market to the socially optimal quantity of production. This yields higher output and a higher price to producers. It is a form of **industrial policy,** a policy to support industries that are believed to generate positive externalities. Economists are often skeptical of industrial policies because external benefits are hard to measure and they motivate producers to lobby for lucrative benefits.

KEY TERMS

Marginal social cost of pollution, p. 456
Marginal social benefit of pollution, p. 457
Socially optimal quantity of pollution, p. 457
External cost, p. 458
External benefit, p. 459
Externalities, p. 459
Negative externalities, p. 459

Positive externalities, p. 459
Coase theorem, p. 460
Transaction costs, p. 460
Internalize the externality, p. 460
Environmental standards, p. 462
Emissions tax, p. 462
Pigouvian taxes, p. 464
Tradable emissions permits, p. 464

Marginal social cost of a good or activity, p. 468
Technology spillover, p. 469
Marginal social benefit of a good or activity, p. 469
Pigouvian subsidy, p. 470
Industrial policy, p. 470

PROBLEMS

1. What type of externality (positive or negative) is described in each of the following examples? Is the marginal social benefit of the activity greater than or equal to the marginal benefit to the individual? Is the marginal social cost of the activity greater than or equal to the marginal cost to the individual? Consequently, without intervention, will there be too little or too much (relative to what would be socially optimal) of this activity?

a. Mrs. Chau plants lots of colorful flowers in her front yard.

b. Anna Crombie and Fritz, a popular clothing store, opens in a mall, attracting more shoppers who also visit other stores.

c. The fraternity next to your dorm plays loud music, keeping you from studying.

d. Maija, who lives next to an apple orchard, decides to keep bees to produce honey.

e. Justine buys a large SUV that consumes a lot of gasoline.

2. The loud music coming from the sorority next to your dorm is a negative externality that can be directly quantified. The table below shows the marginal social benefit and the marginal social cost per decibel (dB, a measure of volume) of music.

Volume of music (dB)	Marginal social benefit of dB	Marginal social cost of dB
90		
	$36	$0
91		
	30	2
92		
	24	4
93		
	18	6
94		
	12	8
95		
	6	10
96		
	0	12
97		

a. Draw the marginal social benefit curve and the marginal social cost curve. Use your diagram to determine the socially optimal volume of music.

b. Only the members of the sorority benefit from the music and they bear none of the cost. Which volume of music will they choose?

c. The college imposes a Pigouvian tax of $3 per decibel of music played. From your diagram, determine the volume of music the sorority will now choose.

3. Many dairy farmers in California are adopting a new technology that allows them to produce their own electricity from methane gas captured from animal wastes. (One cow can produce up to 2 kilowatts a day.) This practice reduces the amount of methane gas released into the atmosphere. In addition to reducing their own utility bills, the farmers are allowed to sell any electricity they produce at favorable rates.

a. Explain how the ability to earn money from capturing and transforming methane gas behaves like a Pigouvian tax on methane gas pollution and can lead dairy farmers to emit the efficient amount of methane gas pollution.

b. Suppose some dairy farmers have lower costs of transforming methane into electricity than others. Explain how this system leads to an efficient allocation of emissions reduction among farmers.

4. The accompanying table shows the total social benefit from steel production and the total cost to steel producers of producing steel. Producing a ton of steel imposes a marginal external cost of $60 per ton.

Quantity of steel (tons)	Total social benefit	Total cost to producers
1	$115	$10
2	210	30
3	285	60
4	340	100
5	375	150

a. Calculate the marginal social benefit per ton of steel and the marginal cost per ton of steel to steel producers. Then calculate the marginal social cost per ton of steel.

b. What is the market equilibrium quantity of steel production?

c. What is the socially optimal quantity of steel production?

d. If you wanted to impose a Pigouvian tax to remedy the problem created by the negative externality, how high would the Pigouvian tax have to be per ton of steel?

5. Education is an example of a positive externality: acquiring more education benefits the individual student and having a more highly educated work force is good for the economy as a whole. The accompanying table illustrates the marginal benefit to Sian per year of education and the marginal cost per year of education. Each year of education has a marginal external benefit to society equal to $8,000. Assume that the marginal social cost is the same as the marginal cost paid by an individual student.

Quantity of education (years)	Sian's marginal benefit per year	Sian's marginal cost per year
9		
	$20,000	$15,000
10		
	19,000	16,000
11		
	18,000	17,000
12		
	17,000	18,000
13		
	16,000	19,000
14		
	15,000	20,000
15		
	14,000	21,000
16		
	13,000	22,000
17		

a. Find Sian's market equilibrium number of years of education.

b. Calculate the marginal social benefit schedule. What is the socially optimal number of years of education?

c. You are in charge of education funding. Would you use a Pigouvian tax or a Pigouvian subsidy to induce Sian to choose the socially optimal amount of education? How high would you set this tax or subsidy per year of education?

6. Getting a flu shot reduces not only your chance of getting the flu but also the chance that you will pass it on to someone else.

   a. Draw a diagram showing the supply and demand curves of inoculating different proportions of the population. Assume that the marginal cost of each flu shot is constant and is equal to the marginal social cost, and that the demand curve is downward sloping.

   b. Will the marginal social benefit curve be higher, lower, or the same as the demand curve? Why? Draw the marginal social benefit curve into your diagram.

   c. In your diagram, show the market equilibrium quantity and the socially optimal quantity of flu shots. Is the market equilibrium quantity of flu shots socially efficient? Why or why not?

   d. Many university health centers offer free flu shots to students and employees. Does this solution necessarily achieve efficiency? Explain, using your diagram.

7. Draw a diagram of the supply and demand curves for telephone service. The marginal cost of connecting another household to the telephone network is increasing, as it is more costly to connect another household as the size of the network grows larger. Assume that the demand curve is downward sloping.

   a. Label the market equilibrium in your diagram E_{MKT}.

Telephone service is a positive externality (sometimes called a "network externality"). There is a marginal external benefit to connecting one more household to the telephone network, the benefit to everybody else of being able to call the newly connected household.

   b. Draw the marginal social benefit curve into your diagram, find the socially optimal point, and label it O.

   c. Explain why the market equilibrium E_{MKT} is inefficient.

   d. Governments subsidize phone service for rural households. Describe how such a Pigouvian subsidy eliminates the inefficiency.

8. According to a report from the U.S. Census "the average [lifetime] earnings of a full-time, year round worker with a high school education are about $1.2 million compared with $2.1 million for a college graduate." This indicates that there is a considerable benefit to a graduate from investing in his or her own education. Tuition at most state universities covers only about two-thirds to three-quarters of the cost, so the state applies a Pigouvian subsidy to college education.

If a Pigouvian subsidy is appropriate, is the externality created by a college education a positive or a negative externality? What does this imply about the differences between the costs and benefits to students compared to social costs and benefits? What are some reasons for the differences?

9. Fishing for sablefish has been so intensive that sablefish were threatened with extinction. After several years of banning such fishing, the government is now proposing to introduce tradable vouchers, each of which entitles its holder to a catch of a certain size. Explain how fishing is a negative externality and how the voucher scheme may overcome the inefficiency created by this externality.

10. The two dry-cleaning companies in Collegetown, College Cleaners and Big Green Cleaners, are a major source of air pollution. Together they currently produce 350 units of air pollution, which the town wants to reduce to 200 units. The accompanying table shows the current pollution level produced by each company and each company's marginal cost of reducing its pollution. The marginal cost is constant.

Companies	Initial pollution level (units)	Marginal cost of reducing pollution (per unit)
College Cleaners	230	$5
Big Green Cleaners	120	$2

   a. Suppose that Collegetown were to pass an environmental standards law that limits each company to 100 units of pollution. What would be the total cost to the two companies of each reducing its pollution emissions to 100 units?

Suppose instead that Collegetown issues 100 pollution vouchers to each company, each entitling the company to one unit of pollution, and that these vouchers can be traded.

   b. How much is each pollution voucher worth to College Cleaners? to Big Green Cleaners? (That is, how much would each company, at most, be willing to pay for one more voucher?)

   c. Who will sell vouchers and who will buy them? How many vouchers will be traded?

   d. What is the total cost to the two companies of the pollution controls under this voucher system?

11. Ronald owns a cattle farm at the source of a long river. His cattle's waste flows into the river, and down many miles to where Carla lives. Carla gets her drinking water from the river. By allowing his cattle's waste to flow into the river, Ronald imposes a negative externality on Carla. In each of the two following cases, do you think that through negotiation, Ronald and Carla can find an efficient solution? What might this solution look like?

   a. There are no telephones, and for Carla to talk to Ronald, she has to travel for two days on a rocky road.

   b. Carla and Ronald both have e-mail access, making it costless for them to communicate.

> **>web...** To continue your study and review of concepts in this chapter, please visit the Krugman/Wells website for quizzes, animated graph tutorials, web links to helpful resources, and more.
>
> **www.worthpublishers.com/krugmanwells**

THE GREAT STINK

BY THE MIDDLE OF THE NINETEENTH century, London had become the world's largest city, with close to 2.5 million inhabitants. Unfortunately, all those people produced a lot of waste—and there was no place for the stuff to go except the Thames, the river flowing through the city. Nobody with a working nose could ignore the results. And the river didn't just smell bad—it carried waterborne diseases like cholera and typhoid. London neighborhoods close to the Thames had death rates from cholera more than six times greater than the neighborhoods farthest away. And the great majority of Londoners drew their drinking water from the Thames.

What the city needed, said reformers, was a sewage system that would carry waste away from the river. Yet no private individual was willing to build such a system, and influential people were opposed to the idea that the government should take responsibility for the problem. For example, the magazine *The Economist* weighed in against proposals for a government-built sewage system, declaring that "suffering and evil are nature's admonitions—they cannot be got rid of."

But the hot summer of 1858 brought what came to be known as the Great Stink, which was so bad that one health journal reported "men struck down with the stench." Even the privileged and powerful suffered: Parliament met in a building next to the river. After unsuccessful efforts to stop the smell by covering the windows with chemical-soaked curtains, Parliament

PUNCH, OR THE LONDON CHARIVARI. June 18, 1859.

THE LONDON BATHING SEASON.
"COME, MY DEAR! COME TO ITS OLD THAMES, AND HAVE A NICE BATH."

London's River Thames then . . .

. . . and the same river now, thanks to government intervention.

What you will learn in this chapter:

➤ A way to classify goods that predicts whether a good can be efficiently provided by markets

➤ What **public goods** are, and why markets fail to supply them

➤ What **common resources** are, and why they are overused

➤ What **artificially scarce goods** are, and why they are underconsumed

➤ How government intervention in the production and consumption of these types of goods can make society better off

➤ Why finding the right level of government intervention is difficult finally approved a plan for an immense system of sewers and pumping stations to direct sewage away from the city. The system, opened in 1865, brought dramatic improvement in the city's quality of life; cholera and typhoid epidemics, which had been regular occurrences, completely disappeared. The Thames was turned from the filthiest to the cleanest metropolitan river in the world, and the sewage system's principal engineer, Sir Joseph Bazalgette, was lauded as having "saved more lives than any single Victorian public official." It was estimated at the time that Bazalgette's sewer system added 20 years to the life span of the average Londoner.

The story of the Great Stink and the policy response that followed illustrate two important reasons for government intervention in the economy. London's new sewage system was a clear example of a *public good*—a good that benefits many people, whether or not they have paid for it, and whose benefits to any one individual do not depend on how many others also benefit. As we will see shortly, public goods differ in important ways from the *private goods* we have studied so far—and these differences mean that public goods cannot be efficiently supplied by the market.

In addition, clean water in the Thames is an example of a *common resource*, a good that many people can consume whether or not they have paid for it but whose consumption by each person reduces the amount available to others. Such goods tend to be overused by individuals in a market system unless the government takes action.

In earlier chapters, we saw that markets sometimes fail to deliver efficient levels of production and consumption of a good or activity. We saw how inefficiency can arise from market power, which leads producers to charge prices that are higher than marginal cost, thereby preventing mutually beneficial transactions from occurring. We also saw how inefficiency can arise from externalities, which cause a divergence between the costs and benefits of an individual's or industry's actions and the costs and benefits of those actions borne by society as a whole, and from private information, which distorts incentives and leads to market failure.

In this chapter, we will take a somewhat different approach to the question of why markets sometimes fail. Here we focus on how the characteristics of goods often determine whether markets can deliver them efficiently. When goods have the "wrong" characteristics, the resulting market failures resemble those associated with externalities or market power. This alternative way of looking at sources of inefficiency deepens our understanding of why markets sometimes don't work well, and how government can serve a useful purpose.

Private Goods—and Others

What's the difference between installing a new bathroom in a house and building a municipal sewage system? What's the difference between growing wheat and fishing in the open ocean?

These aren't trick questions. In each case there is a basic difference in the characteristics of the goods involved. Bathroom appliances and wheat have the characteristics needed to allow markets to work efficiently. Sewage systems and fish in the sea do not.

Let's look at these crucial characteristics and why they matter.

Characteristics of Goods

Goods like bathroom fixtures or wheat have two characteristics that, as we'll soon see, are essential if a good is to be efficiently provided by a market economy.

- They are **excludable:** suppliers of the good can prevent people who don't pay from consuming it.
- They are **rival in consumption:** the same unit of the good cannot be consumed by more than one person at the same time.

When a good is both excludable and rival in consumption, it is called a **private good.** Wheat is an example of a private good. It is *excludable:* the farmer can sell a bushel to one consumer without having to provide wheat to everyone in the county. And it is *rival in consumption:* if I eat bread baked with a farmer's wheat, that bread can no longer be eaten by someone else.

But not all goods have these two characteristics. Some goods are **nonexcludable**—the supplier cannot prevent consumption of the good by people who do not pay for it. Fire protection is one example: a fire department that puts out fires before they spread protects the whole city, not just people who have made contributions to the Firemen's Benevolent Association. An improved environment is another: the city of London couldn't have ended the Great Stink for some residents while leaving the River Thames foul for others.

Nor are all goods rival in consumption. Goods are **nonrival in consumption** if more than one person can consume the same unit of the good at the same time. TV programs are nonrival in consumption: your decision to watch a show does not prevent other people from watching the same show.

Because goods can be either excludable or nonexcludable, rival or nonrival in consumption, there are four types of goods, illustrated by the matrix in Figure 20-1:

- *Private goods*, which are excludable and rival in consumption, like wheat
- *Public goods*, which are nonexcludable and nonrival in consumption, like a public sewer system
- *Common resources*, which are nonexcludable but rival in consumption, like clean water in a river
- *Artificially scarce goods*, which are excludable but nonrival in consumption, like pay-per-view movies on cable TV

There are, of course, many other characteristics that distinguish between types of goods—necessities versus luxuries, normal versus inferior, and so on. Why focus on whether goods are excludable and rival in consumption?

A good is **excludable** if the supplier of that good can prevent people who do not pay from consuming it.

A good is **rival in consumption** if the same unit of the good cannot be consumed by more than one person at the same time.

A good that is both excludable and rival in consumption is a **private good.**

When a good is **nonexcludable,** the supplier cannot prevent consumption by people who do not pay for it.

A good is **nonrival in consumption** if more than one person can consume the same unit of the good at the same time.

Figure 20-1

Four Types of Goods

There are four types of goods. The type of a good depends on (1) whether or not it is excludable—whether a producer can prevent someone from consuming it; and (2) whether or not it is rival in consumption—whether it is impossible for the same unit of a good to be consumed by more than one person at the same time.

	Rival in consumption	**Nonrival in consumption**
Excludable	**Private goods** • Wheat • Bathroom fixtures	**Artificially scarce goods** • Pay-per-view movies • Computer software
Non-excludable	**Common resources** • Clean water • Biodiversity	**Public goods** • Public sanitation • National defense

Why Markets Can Supply Only Private Goods Efficiently

A market economy, as we learned in earlier chapters, is an amazing system for delivering goods and services. But it cannot supply goods and services efficiently unless they are private goods—excludable and rival in consumption.

To see why excludability is crucial, suppose that a farmer had only two choices: either produce no wheat or provide a bushel of wheat to every resident of the county who wants it, whether or not that resident pays for it. It seems unlikely that anyone would grow wheat under those conditions.

Yet the operator of a municipal sewage system faces pretty much the same problem as our hypothetical farmer. A sewage system makes the whole city cleaner and healthier—but that benefit accrues to all the city's residents, whether or not they pay the system operator. That's why no private entrepreneur came forward with a plan to end London's Great Stink.

The general point is that if a good is nonexcludable, rational consumers won't be willing to pay for it—they will take a "free ride" on anyone who *does* pay. So there is a **free-rider problem.** Examples of the free-rider problem are familiar from daily life. One example you may have encountered happens when students are required to do a group project. There is often a tendency of some members of the group to shirk, relying on others in the group to get the work done. The shirkers *free-ride* on someone else's effort.

Because of the free-rider problem, the forces of self-interest alone do not lead to an efficient level of production for a nonexcludable good. Even though consumers would benefit from increased production of the good, no one individual is willing to pay for more, and so no producer is willing to supply it. The result is that nonexcludable goods suffer from *inefficiently low production* in a market economy. In fact, in the face of the free-rider problem, self-interest may not ensure that any amount of the good—let alone the efficient quantity—is produced.

Goods that are excludable and nonrival in consumption, like pay-per-view movies, suffer from a different kind of inefficiency. As long as a good is excludable, it is possible to earn a profit by making the good available only to those who pay. But the marginal cost of letting an additional viewer watch a pay-per-view movie is zero because it is nonrival in consumption. So the efficient price to the consumer is also zero—or, to put it another way, individuals should watch TV movies up to the point where their marginal benefit is zero. But if the cable company actually charges viewers $4, viewers will consume the good only up to the point where their marginal benefit is $4. When consumers must pay a price greater than zero for a good that is nonrival in consumption, the price they pay is higher than the marginal cost of allowing them to consume that good, which is zero. So in a market economy goods that are nonrival in consumption suffer from *inefficiently low consumption.*

Now we can see why private goods are the only goods that can be efficiently produced and consumed in a competitive market. (That is, a private good will be efficiently produced and consumed in a market free of market power, externalities, or private information.) Because private goods are excludable, producers can charge for them and so have an incentive to produce them. And because they are also rival in consumption, it is efficient for consumers to pay a positive price—a price equal to the marginal cost of production. If one or both of these characteristics are lacking, a market economy will not lead to efficient production and consumption of the good.

Fortunately for the market system, most goods are private goods. Food, clothing, shelter, and most other desirable things in life are excludable and rival in consumption, so markets can provide us with most things. Yet there are crucial goods that don't meet these criteria—and in most cases, that means that the government must step in.

Goods that are nonexcludable suffer from the **free-rider problem:** individuals have no incentive to pay for their own consumption and instead will take a "free ride" on anyone who does pay.

PITFALLS

MARGINAL COST OF WHAT EXACTLY?

In the case of a good that is nonrival in consumption, it's easy to confuse the marginal cost of *producing* a unit of the good with the marginal cost of *allowing* a unit of the good *to be consumed.* For example, your local cable company incurs a marginal cost in making a movie available to its subscribers that is equal to the cost of the resources it uses to produce and broadcast that movie. However, *once that movie is being broadcast,* no marginal cost is incurred by letting an additional family watch it. In other words, no costly resources are "used up" when one more family consumes a movie that has already been produced and is being broadcast.

This complication does not arise, however, when a good is rival in consumption. In that case, the resources used to produce a unit of the good are "used up" by a person's consumption of it—they are no longer available to satisfy someone else's consumption. So when a good is rival in consumption the marginal cost to society of allowing an individual to consume a unit is equal to the resource cost of producing that unit—that is, equal to the marginal cost of producing it.

economics in action

A Policeman's Lot

We tend to think of crime prevention as a function of government, yet individuals take their own measures to prevent theft: homeowners put locks on their doors, and many businesses hire their own security guards.

Why, then, do we also have public police departments? Because law enforcement, as opposed to self-protection, is a public good. The benefits of keeping a potential thief off your own property are rival and excludable. But the benefits of tracking down criminals and bringing them to justice, and of policing public areas, accrue to all law-abiding citizens.

The beginning of modern police departments can be traced to two eighteenth-century institutions that concentrated on these clearly public-good aspects of crime prevention: the Bow Street Runners, an early detective agency that concentrated on finding and catching criminals, and the Thames River Police, who patrolled the dock areas. In 1829 Sir Robert Peel, building on the lessons from these institutions, oversaw the creation of a unified London police force, which served as a model for police forces throughout the world. To this day British police officers are known, after Sir Robert, as "bobbies." ■

> > > > > > > > > > > > > > > > > > > >

>> **CHECK YOUR UNDERSTANDING 20-1**

1. Classify each of the following goods according to whether they are excludable and whether they are rival in consumption. What kind of good is each?
   a. Use of a public space such as a park
   b. A cheese burrito
   c. Information from a website that is password-protected
   d. Publicly announced information on the path of an incoming hurricane

2. Which of the goods in Question 1 will be provided by a competitive market? Which will not be? Explain.

Solutions appear at back of book.

Public Goods

A **public good** is the exact opposite of a private good: it is a good that is both nonexcludable and nonrival in consumption. A sewage system is an example of a public good: you can't keep a river clean without making it clean for everyone who lives near its banks, and my protection from great stinks does not come at my neighbor's expense.

Here are some other examples of public goods:

- *Disease prevention.* When doctors act to stamp out the beginnings of an epidemic before it can spread, they protect people around the world.
- *National defense.* A strong military protects all citizens.
- *Scientific research.* More knowledge benefits everyone.

Because these goods are nonexcludable, they suffer from the free-rider problem, so no private firm would be willing to produce them. And because they are nonrival in consumption, it would be inefficient to charge people for consuming them. As a result, society must find nonmarket methods for providing these goods.

Providing Public Goods

Public goods are provided through a variety of means. The government doesn't always get involved—in many cases a nongovernmental solution has been found for the free-rider problem. But these solutions are usually imperfect in some way.

A **public good** is both nonexcludable and nonrival in consumption.

Some public goods are supplied through voluntary contributions. For example, private donations support a considerable amount of scientific research. But private donations are insufficient to finance huge, socially important projects like basic medical research.

Some public goods are supplied by self-interested individuals or firms because those who produce them are able to make money in an indirect way. The classic example is broadcast television, which in the United States is supported entirely by advertising. The downside of such indirect funding is that it skews the nature and quantity of the public goods that are supplied, as well as imposing additional costs on consumers. TV stations show the programs that yield the most advertising revenue (that is, programs best suited for selling antacids, hair-loss remedies, antihistamines, and the like to the segment of the population that buys them), which are not necessarily the programs people most want to see. And viewers must also endure many commercials.

On the prowl: a British TV detection van at work.

Some potentially public goods are deliberately made excludable and therefore subject to charge, like pay-per-view movies. In the U.K., where most television programming is paid for by a yearly license fee assessed on every television owner, television viewing is made artificially excludable by the use of "television detection vans": vans that roam neighborhoods in an attempt to detect televisions in nonlicensed households and fine them. However, as noted earlier, when suppliers charge a price greater than zero for a nonrival good, consumers will consume an inefficiently low quantity of that good.

In small communities, a high level of social encouragement or pressure can be brought to bear on people to contribute money or time to provide the efficient level of a public good. Volunteer fire departments, which depend both on the volunteered services of the firefighters themselves and on contributions from local residents, are a good example. But as communities grow larger and more anonymous, social pressure is increasingly difficult to apply, so that larger towns and cities must depend on salaried firefighters.

As this last example suggests, when these other solutions fail, it is up to the government to provide public goods. Indeed, the most important public goods—national defense, the legal system, disease control, fire protection in large cities, and so on—are provided by government and paid for by taxes. Economic theory tells us that the provision of public goods is one of the crucial roles of government.

How Much of a Public Good Should Be Provided?

In some cases, provision of a public good is an "either–or" decision: London would either have a sewage system—or not. But in most cases, governments must decide not only whether to provide a public good but also *how much* of that public good to provide. For example, street cleaning is a public good—but how often should the streets be cleaned? Once a month? Twice a month? Every other day?

Imagine a city in which there are only two residents, Ted and Alice. Assume that the public good in question is street cleaning and that Ted and Alice truthfully tell the government how much they value a unit of the public good, where a unit is equal to one street cleaning per month. Specifically, each of them tells the government *his or her willingness to pay for another unit of the public good supplied*—an amount that corresponds to that *individual's marginal benefit* of another unit of the public good.

Using this information plus information on the cost of providing the good, the government can use marginal analysis to find the efficient level of providing the public good: the level at which the *marginal social benefit* of the public good is equal to the marginal cost of producing it. Recall from Chapter 19 that the marginal social benefit of a good is the benefit that accrues to society as a whole from the consumption of one additional unit of the good.

But what is the marginal social benefit of another unit of a public good—a unit that generates utility for *all* consumers, not just one consumer, because it is nonexcludable and nonrival in consumption? This question leads us to an important principle: *in the special case of a public good, the marginal social benefit of a unit of the good is equal to the sum of the individual marginal benefits that are enjoyed by all consumers of that unit.* Or to consider it from a slightly different angle, if a consumer could be compelled to pay for a unit before consuming it (the good is made excludable), then the marginal social benefit of a unit is equal to the *sum* of each consumer's willingness to pay for that unit. Using this principle, the marginal social benefit of an additional street cleaning per month is equal to Ted's individual marginal benefit from that additional cleaning *plus* Alice's individual marginal benefit.

We all benefit when someone does the cleaning up.

Why? Because a public good is nonrival in consumption—Ted's benefit from a cleaner street does not diminish Alice's benefit from that same clean street, and vice versa. Because people can all simultaneously consume the same unit of a public good, the marginal social benefit of an additional unit of that good is the *sum* of the individual marginal benefits of all who enjoy the public good. And the efficient quantity of a public good is the quantity at which the marginal social benefit is equal to the marginal cost of providing it.

Figure 20-2 on page 482 illustrates the efficient provision of a public good, showing three marginal benefit curves. Panel (a) shows Ted's individual marginal benefit curve of street cleanings, MB_T: he would be willing to pay $25 for the city to clean its streets once per month, an additional $18 to have it done a second time, and so on. Panel (b) shows Alice's individual marginal benefit curve of street cleanings, MB_A. Panel (c) shows the marginal social benefit curve of street cleanings, MSB: it is the vertical sum of Ted's and Alice's individual marginal benefit curves, MB_T and MB_A.

To maximize society's welfare, the government should clean the street up to the level at which the marginal social benefit of an additional cleaning is no longer greater than the marginal cost. Suppose that the marginal cost of street cleaning is $6 per cleaning. Then the city should clean its streets 5 times per month, because the marginal social benefit of going from 4 to 5 cleanings is $8, but going from 5 to 6 cleanings would yield a marginal social benefit of only $2.

Figure 20-2 can help reinforce our understanding of why we cannot rely on individual self-interest to yield provision of an efficient quantity of public goods. Suppose that the city did one fewer street cleaning than the efficient quantity and that either Ted or Alice was asked to pay for the last cleaning. Neither one would be willing to pay for it! Ted would personally gain only the equivalent of $3 in utility from adding one more street cleaning—so he wouldn't be willing to pay the $6 marginal cost of another cleaning. Alice would personally gain the equivalent of $5 in utility—so she wouldn't be willing to pay either. The point is that the marginal social benefit of one more unit of a public good is always greater than the individual marginal benefit to any one individual. That is why no individual is willing to pay for the efficient quantity of the good.

Does this description of the public good problem, in which the marginal social benefit of an additional unit of the public good is greater than any individual's marginal benefit, sound a bit familiar? It should: we encountered a somewhat similar situation in our discussion of *positive externalities.* Remember that in the case of a positive externality, the marginal social benefit accruing to all consumers of another unit of the good is greater than the producer's marginal benefit of producing that unit and the market alone produces too little of the good. In the case of a public good, the individual marginal benefit of a consumer plays the same role that the producer's marginal benefit plays in the case of positive externalities. So the problem of providing public goods is very similar to the problem of dealing with positive externalities; in both cases there is a market failure that calls for government intervention. One basic rationale for the existence of government is that it provides a way for citizens to tax themselves in order to provide public goods—particularly a vital public good like national defense.

Of course, if society really consisted of only two individuals, they would probably manage to strike a deal to provide the good. But imagine a city with a million residents, each of whose individual marginal benefit from provision of the good is only a tiny fraction of the marginal social benefit. It would be impossible for people to reach a voluntary

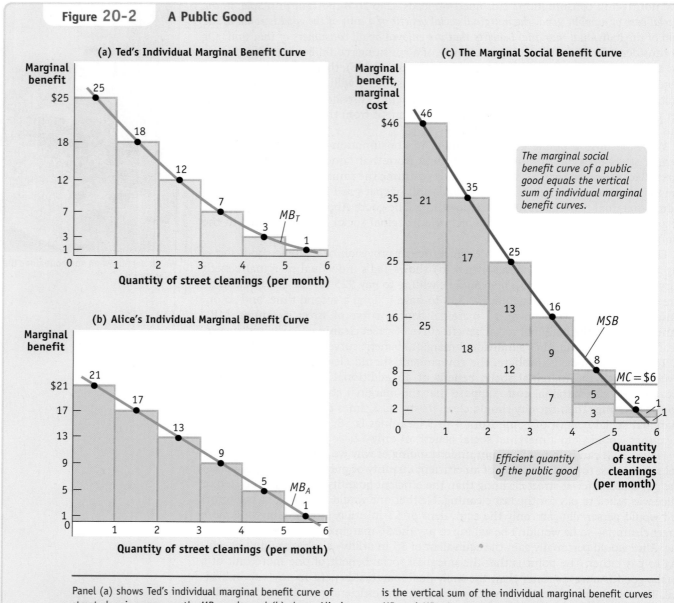

Figure 20-2 **A Public Good**

(a) Ted's Individual Marginal Benefit Curve

(b) Alice's Individual Marginal Benefit Curve

(c) The Marginal Social Benefit Curve

The marginal social benefit curve of a public good equals the vertical sum of individual marginal benefit curves.

Efficient quantity of the public good

Panel (a) shows Ted's individual marginal benefit curve of street cleanings per month, MB_T, and panel (b) shows Alice's individual marginal benefit curve, MB_A. Panel (c) shows the marginal social benefit of the public good, equal to the *sum* of the individual marginal benefits to all consumers (in this case, Ted and Alice). The marginal social benefit curve, MSB, is the vertical sum of the individual marginal benefit curves MB_T and MB_A. At a constant marginal cost of $6, there should be 5 street cleanings per month, because the marginal social benefit of going from 4 to 5 cleanings is $8 ($3 for Ted plus $5 for Alice), but the marginal social benefit of going from 5 to 6 cleanings is only $2. **>web...**

agreement to pay for the efficient quantity of street cleaning—the potential for free-riding makes it too difficult to make and enforce an agreement among so many people. But they could and would vote to tax themselves to pay for a citywide sanitation department.

Cost-Benefit Analysis

Governments engage in **cost-benefit analysis** when they estimate the social costs and social benefits of providing a public good.

How do governments decide in practice how much of a public good to provide? Sometimes policy makers just guess—or do whatever they think will get them reelected. However, responsible governments try to estimate both the social benefits and the social costs of providing a public good, a process known as **cost-benefit analysis.**

VOTING AS A PUBLIC GOOD

It's a sad fact that many Americans who are eligible to vote don't bother to. As a result their interests tend to be ignored by politicians. But what's even sadder is that this self-defeating behavior may be completely rational.

As the economist Mancur Olson pointed out in a famous book titled *The Logic of Collective Action*, voting is a public good, one that suffers from severe free-rider problems.

Imagine that you are one of a million people who would stand to gain the equivalent of $100 each if some plan is passed in a statewide referendum—say, a plan to improve public schools. And sup-

pose that the opportunity cost of the time it would take you to vote is $10. Will you be sure to go to the polls and vote for the referendum? If you are rational, the answer is no! The reason is that it is very unlikely that your vote will decide the issue, either way. If the measure passes, you benefit, even if you don't bother to vote—the benefits are nonexcludable. If the measure doesn't pass, your vote would not have changed the outcome. Either way, by not voting—by free-riding on those who do vote—you save $10.

Of course, many people do vote out of a sense of civic duty. But because political action is a public good, in general people

devote too little effort to defending their own interests.

The result, Olson pointed out, is that when a large group of people share a common political interest, they are likely to exert too little effort promoting their cause and so will be ignored. Conversely, small, well-organized interest groups that act on issues narrowly targeted in their favor tend to have disproportionate power.

Is this a reason to distrust democracy? Winston Churchill said it best: "Democracy is the worst form of government, except for all the other forms that have been tried."

It's straightforward to estimate the cost of supplying a public good. Estimating the benefit is harder. In fact, it is a very difficult problem.

Now you might wonder why governments can't figure out the marginal social benefit of a public good just by asking people their willingness to pay for it (their individual marginal benefit). But it turns out that it's hard to get an honest answer.

This is not a problem with private goods: we can determine how much an individual is willing to pay for one more unit of a private good by looking at his or her actual choices. But because people don't actually pay for public goods, the question of willingness to pay is always hypothetical.

Worse yet, it's a question that people have an incentive not to answer truthfully. People naturally want more rather than less. Because they cannot be made to pay for whatever quantity of the public good they use, when asked how much they desire a public good people are apt to overstate their true feelings. For example, if street cleaning were scheduled according to the stated wishes of homeowners alone, the streets would be cleaned every day—an inefficient level of provision. So governments must be aware that they cannot simply rely on the public's statements when deciding how much of a public good to provide—if they do, they are likely to provide too much. In contrast, as the For Inquiring Minds explains above, relying on the public to indicate how much of the public good they want through voting has problems as well—and is likely to lead to too little of the public good being provided.

economics in action

Old Man River

It just keeps rolling along—but now and then it decides to roll in a different direction. In fact, the Mississippi River changes its course every few hundred years. Sediment carried downstream gradually clogs the river's route to the sea, and eventually the river breaches its banks and opens a new channel. Over the millennia the mouth of the Mississippi has swung back and forth along an arc some 200 miles wide.

So when is the Mississippi due to change course again? Oh, about 35 years ago.

The Mississippi currently runs to the sea past New Orleans; but by 1950 it was apparent that the river was about to shift course, taking a new route to the sea. If the Army Corps of Engineers hadn't gotten involved, the shift would probably have happened by 1970.

A shift in the Mississippi would have severely damaged the Louisiana economy. A major industrial area would have lost good access to the ocean, and salt water would have contaminated much of its water supply. So the Army Corps of Engineers has kept the Mississippi in its place with a huge complex of dams, walls, and gates known as the Old River Control Structure. At times the amount of water released by this control structure is five times the flow at Niagara Falls.

The Old River Control Structure is a dramatic example of a public good. No individual would have had an incentive to build it, yet it protects many billions of dollars' worth of private property. The history of the Army Corps of Engineers, which handles water-control projects across the United States, illustrates the problems with government provision of public goods. Everyone wants a project that benefits his or her own property—if other people are going to pay for it. So there is a systematic tendency for potential beneficiaries of Corps projects to overstate the benefits. And the Corps has become notorious for undertaking expensive projects that cannot be justified with any reasonable cost-benefit analysis.

In other countries the counterparts of the Army Corps of Engineers are even more prone to overspending. In Japan, almost every river now runs through a concrete channel, and an amazing 60 percent of the coastline is now "armored" with concrete barriers. ■

< < < < < < < < < < < < < < < < < < <

>>CHECK YOUR UNDERSTANDING 20-2

1. The town of Centreville, population 16, has two types of residents, Homebodies and Revelers. Using the accompanying table, the town must decide how much to spend on its New Year's Eve party. No individual resident expects to directly bear the cost of the party.

   a. Suppose there are 10 Homebodies and 6 Revelers. Determine the marginal social benefit schedule of money spent on the party. What is the efficient level of spending?

   b. Suppose there are 6 Homebodies and 10 Revelers. How do your answers to part a change? Explain.

   c. Suppose that the individual marginal benefit schedules are known but no one knows the true numbers of Homebodies and Revelers. Individuals are asked their preferences. What is the likely outcome? Why is it likely to result in an inefficiently high level of spending? Explain.

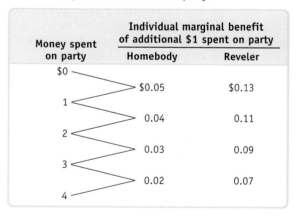

Money spent on party	Individual marginal benefit of additional $1 spent on party	
	Homebody	Reveler
$0		
	$0.05	$0.13
1		
	0.04	0.11
2		
	0.03	0.09
3		
	0.02	0.07
4		

Solutions appear at back of book.

Common Resources

A **common resource** is a good that is nonexcludable but is rival in consumption. An example is the stock of fish in a limited fishing area, like the fisheries off the coast of New England. Traditionally, anyone who had a boat could go out to sea and catch fish—fish in the sea were a nonexcludable good. Yet because the total number of fish is limited, the fish that one person catches are no longer available to be caught by someone else. So fish in the sea are rival in consumption.

A **common resource** is nonexcludable and rival in consumption: you can't stop me from consuming the good, and more consumption by me means less of the good available for you.

Other examples of common resources are clean air and water as well as the diversity of animal and plant species on the planet (biodiversity). In each of these cases the fact that the good, though rival in consumption, is nonexcludable poses a serious problem.

The Problem of Overuse

Because common resources are nonexcludable, individuals cannot be charged for their use. Yet, because they are rival in consumption, an individual who uses a unit depletes the resource by making that unit unavailable to others. As a result, a common resource is subject to **overuse**: an individual will continue to use it until his or her marginal benefit of its use is equal to zero, ignoring the cost that this action inflicts on society as a whole. As we will see shortly, the problem of overuse of a common resource is similar to a problem we studied in Chapter 19: the problem of a good that generates a negative externality, such as pollution-creating electricity generation or livestock farming.

Fishing is a classic example of a common resource. In heavily fished waters, my fishing imposes a cost on others by reducing the fish population and making it harder for others to catch fish. But I have no personal incentive to take this cost into account, since I cannot be charged for fishing. As a result, from society's point of view, I catch too many fish. Traffic congestion is another example of overuse of a common resource. A major highway during rush hour can accommodate only a certain number of vehicles per hour. If I decide to drive alone to work rather than carpool or work at home, I make the commute of many other people a bit longer; but I have no incentive to take these consequences into account.

In the case of a common resource, the *marginal social cost* of my use of that resource is higher than my *individual marginal cost*, the cost to me of using an additional unit of the good.

Figure 20-3 illustrates the point. It shows the demand curve for fish, which measures the marginal benefit of fish—the benefit to consumers when an additional unit of fish is caught and consumed. It also shows the supply curve for fish, which measures the marginal cost of production of the fishing industry. We know from Chapter 9 that the industry supply curve is the horizontal sum of each individual

> Common resources left to the market suffer from **overuse**: individuals ignore the fact that their use depletes the amount of the resource remaining for others.

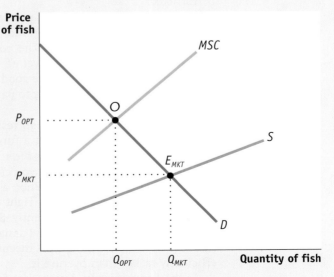

Figure 20-3

A Common Resource

The supply curve *S*, which shows the marginal cost of production of the entire fishing industry, is composed of the individual supply curves of the individual fishermen. But each fisherman's individual marginal cost does not include the cost that his or her actions impose on others: the depletion of the common resource. As a result, the marginal social cost curve, *MSC*, lies above the supply curve; in an unregulated market, the quantity of the common resource used, Q_{MKT}, exceeds the efficient quantity of use, Q_{OPT}.

fisherman's supply curve—equivalent to his or her individual marginal cost curve. The fishing industry supplies the quantity where its marginal cost is equal to the price, the quantity Q_{MKT}. But the efficient outcome is to catch the quantity Q_{OPT}, the quantity of output that equates the marginal benefit to the marginal social cost, not to the fishing industry's marginal cost of production. The market outcome results in overuse of the common resource.

As we noted, there is a close parallel between the problem of managing a common resource and the problem posed by negative externalities. In the case of an activity that generates a negative externality, the marginal social cost of production is greater than the industry's marginal cost of production, the difference being the marginal external cost imposed on society. Here, the loss to society arising from a fisherman's depletion of the common resource plays the same role as the external cost plays when there is a negative externality. In fact, many negative externalities (such as pollution) can be thought of as involving common resources (such as clean air).

The Efficient Use and Maintenance of a Common Resource

Because common resources pose problems similar to those created by negative externalities, the solutions are also similar. To ensure efficient use of a common resource, society must find a way of getting individual users of the resource to take into account the costs they impose on other users. This is basically the same principle as that of getting individuals to internalize a negative externality that arises from their actions.

There are three fundamental ways to induce people who use common resources to internalize the costs they impose on others.

- Tax or otherwise regulate the use of the common resource
- Create a system of tradable licenses for the right to use the common resource
- Make the common resource excludable and assign property rights to some individuals

Like activities that generate negative externalities, use of a common resource can be reduced to the efficient quantity by imposing a Pigouvian tax. For example, some countries have imposed "congestion charges" on those who drive during rush hour, in effect charging them for use of the common resource of highway space. Likewise, visitors to national parks must pay a fee and the number of visitors to any one park is restricted.

A second way to correct the problem of overuse is to create a system of tradable licenses for the use of the common resource much like the systems designed to address negative externalities. The policy maker issues the number of licenses that corresponds to the efficient level of use of the good. Making the licenses tradable assures that the right to use the good is allocated efficiently—that is, those who end up using the good (those willing to pay the most for a license) are those who gain the most from its use.

But when it comes to common resources, often the most natural solution is simply to assign property rights. At a fundamental level, common resources are subject to overuse because *nobody owns them*. The essence of ownership of a good—the *property right* over the good—is that you can limit who can and cannot use the good, and how much of it can be used. When a good is nonexcludable, in a very real sense no one owns it because a property right cannot be enforced—and consequently no one has an incentive to use it efficiently. So one way to correct the problem of overuse is to make the good excludable and assign property rights over it to someone. The good now has an owner who has an incentive to protect the value of the good—to use it efficiently rather than overuse it.

As the Economics in Action that follows shows, a system of tradable licenses has been a successful strategy in some fisheries.

economics in action

A Tale of Two Fisheries

On August 27, 2000, the *New York Times Magazine* carried a story titled "A Tale of Two Fisheries," which compared the lives of lobstermen in two places: Port Judith, Rhode Island, and Port Lincoln, Australia.

Port Judith used to call itself the "tuna capital of the world," but tuna—along with swordfish, cod, halibut, and other species that used to be plentiful offshore—are now hard to find anywhere in the vicinity. Fishermen in the United States have been free to catch as many fish as they like; as a result of overfishing, the once-great fisheries of New England have largely collapsed. This includes lobsters, except for some areas of Maine where "lobster gangs" have protected the common resource by sabotaging the boats of outsiders. As lobster stocks have plunged, life for the lobstermen of Port Judith has gotten increasingly difficult.

In Australia, however, a different system prevails. To set a lobster trap, you must have a license, and only a limited number of licenses have been issued. A license now sells for about $21,000. At first Australian lobstermen were skeptical of a system that limited their fishing. But they now support the system enthusiastically, because it sustains the value of their licenses—and also sustains their livelihood.

The system is popular because it works: an Australian lobster trap typically comes up with more and bigger lobsters than its American counterpart. As a result, the lobstermen of Port Lincoln, Australia, are far more prosperous than those of Port Judith, Rhode Island.

By the way, we don't want to give the impression that establishing property rights over common resources is un-American. The New Jersey clam fishery, which was in serious trouble in the late 1980s, now operates under a license system similar to that of the Australian lobster fishery. And both the clams and the New Jersey clam industry have staged a spectacular comeback. ∎

> > > > > > > > > > > > > > > > > > > >

>> CHECK YOUR UNDERSTANDING 20-3

1. Rocky Mountain Forest is a government-owned forest in which private citizens were allowed in the past to harvest as much timber as they wanted free of charge. State in economic terms why this is problematic from society's point of view.

2. You are the new Forest Service Commissioner and have been instructed to come up with ways to preserve the forest for the general public. Name three different methods you could use to maintain the efficient level of tree harvesting and explain how each would work. For each method, what information would you need to know in order to achieve an efficient outcome?

Solutions appear at back of book.

Artificially Scarce Goods

An **artificially scarce good** is a good that is excludable but nonrival in consumption. As we've already seen, pay-per-view movies are a familiar example. The marginal cost to society of allowing an individual to watch the movie is zero, because one person's viewing doesn't interfere with other people's viewing. Yet cable companies prevent an individual from seeing a movie if he or she hasn't paid. Many *information goods* like computer software are also artificially scarce; we will discuss the economics of information goods at greater length in Chapter 22.

As we've already seen, markets will supply artificially scarce goods: because they are excludable, the producers can charge people for consuming them.

But artificially scarce goods are nonrival in consumption, which means that the marginal cost of an individual's consumption is zero. So the price that the supplier of an artificially scarce good charges exceeds marginal cost. Because the efficient price

An **artificially scarce good** is excludable but nonrival in consumption.

Figure 20-4

An Artificially Scarce Good

An artificially scarce good is excludable and nonrival in consumption. It is made artificially scarce because producers charge a positive price but the marginal cost of allowing one more person to consume the good is zero. In this example the market price of a pay-per-view movie is $4 and the quantity demanded at that price is Q_{MKT}. But the efficient level of consumption is Q_{OPT}, the quantity demanded when the price is zero. The efficient quantity, Q_{OPT}, exceeds the quantity demanded in an unregulated market, Q_{MKT}. The shaded area represents the loss in total surplus from charging a price of $4. >*web*...

is equal to the marginal cost of zero, the good is "artificially scarce," and consumption of the good is inefficiently low. However, unless the producer can somehow earn revenue for producing and selling the good, he or she will be unwilling to produce at all—an outcome that leaves society even worse off than it would otherwise be with positive but inefficiently low consumption.

Figure 20-4 illustrates the loss in total surplus caused by artificial scarcity. The demand curve shows the quantity of pay-per-view movies watched at any given price. The marginal cost of allowing an additional person to watch the movie is zero; so the efficient quantity of movies viewed is Q_{OPT}. The cable company charges a positive price, in this case $4, to unscramble the signal, and as a result only Q_{MKT} pay-per-view movies will be watched. This leads to a deadweight loss equal to the area of the shaded triangle.

Does this look familiar? Like the problems that arise with public goods and common resources, the problem created by artificially scarce goods is similar to something we have already seen: in this case, it is the problem of *natural monopoly*. A natural monopoly, you will recall, is an industry in which average total cost is above marginal cost for the relevant output range. In order to be willing to produce output, the producer must charge a price at least as high as average total cost—that is, a price above marginal cost. But a price above marginal cost leads to inefficiently low consumption.

economics in action

Blacked-Out Games

It's the night of the big game for your local team—a game that is being nationally televised by one of the major networks. So you flip to the local channel that is an affiliate of that network—but the game isn't on. Instead, you get some other show with a message scrolling across the bottom of the screen that this game has been blacked out in your area. What the message probably doesn't say, though you understand quite well, is that this blackout is at the insistence of the team's owners, who don't want people who might have paid for tickets staying home and watching the game on TV instead.

So the good in question—watching the game on TV—has been made artificially scarce. Because the game is being broadcast anyway, no scarce resources would be used to make it available in its immediate locality as well. But it isn't available—which means a loss in welfare to those who would have watched the game on TV but are not willing to pay the price, in time and money, to go to the stadium. ■

> > > > > > > > > > > > > > > > > > >

>>CHECK YOUR UNDERSTANDING 20-4

1. Xena is a software program produced by Xenoid. Each year Xenoid produces an upgrade that costs $300,000 to produce. It costs nothing to allow customers to download it from the company's website. The demand schedule for the upgrade is shown in the accompanying table.
   a. What is the efficient price to a consumer of this upgrade? Explain.
   b. What is the lowest price at which Xenoid is willing to produce and sell the upgrade? Draw the demand curve and show the loss of total surplus that occurs when Xenoid charges this price compared to the efficient price.

Price of upgrade	Quantity of upgrades demanded
$180	1,700
150	2,000
120	2,300
90	2,600
0	3,500

Solutions appear at back of book.

• A LOOK AHEAD •

In 2003 the various levels of U.S. government—federal, state, and local—spent about $3 trillion. Where did the money go?

The answer, in large part, is that it went to provide public goods. National defense and homeland security took a big chunk; so did education, which is widely regarded as a public good. Then there was spending on highways, public health, fire prevention, and so on.

Not all government spending is on items that can easily be described as public goods. As we'll see in Chapter 21, much spending at the federal level goes for *social insurance,* programs intended to help individuals and families in trouble. But providing public goods is still a central feature of government budgets.

And that brings us to the next question: where does the money that pays for public goods come from? The answer, of course, is that it comes from tax revenue. But taxes, in turn, have economic effects, because they change incentives.

In the next chapter we'll take a deeper look at how taxes affect a market economy. We'll also look at the related effects of social insurance.

SUMMARY

1. Goods may be classified according to whether or not they are **excludable** and whether or not they are **rival in consumption.**

2. Free markets can deliver efficient levels of production and consumption for **private goods,** which are both excludable and rival in consumption. When goods are nonexcludable, nonrival in consumption, or both, free markets cannot achieve efficient outcomes.

3. When goods are **nonexcludable,** there is a **free-rider problem:** consumers will not pay for the good, leading to inefficiently low production. When goods are **non-**

rival in consumption, they should be free, and any positive price leads to inefficiently low consumption.

4. A **public good** is nonexcludable and nonrival in consumption. In most cases a public good must be supplied by the government. The marginal social benefit of a public good is equal to the sum of the individual marginal benefits to each consumer. The efficient quantity of a public good is the quantity at which marginal social benefit equals marginal cost. Like a positive externality, marginal social benefit is greater than any one individual's marginal benefit, so no individual is willing to provide the efficient quantity.

5. One rationale for the presence of government is that it allows citizens to tax themselves in order to provide public goods. Governments use **cost-benefit analysis** to determine the efficient provision of a public good. Such analysis is difficult, however, because individuals have an incentive to overstate the good's value to them.

6. A **common resource** is rival in consumption but nonexcludable. It is subject to **overuse,** because an individual does not take into account the fact that his or her use depletes the amount available for others. This is similar to the problem of a negative externality: the marginal social cost of use of an individual's common resource is always higher than his or her individual marginal cost. Pigouvian taxes, the creation of a system of tradable licenses, or the assignment of property rights are possible solutions.

7. **Artificially scarce goods** are excludable but nonrival in consumption. Because no marginal cost arises from allowing another individual to consume the good, the efficient price is zero. A positive price compensates the producer for the cost of production but leads to inefficiently low consumption. The problem of an artificially scarce good is similar to that of a natural monopoly.

KEY TERMS

Excludable, p. 477
Rival in consumption, p. 477
Private good, p. 477
Nonexcludable, p. 477

Nonrival in consumption, p. 477
Free-rider problem, p. 478
Public good, p. 479
Cost-benefit analysis, p. 482

Common resource, p. 484
Overuse, p. 485
Artificially scarce good, p. 487

PROBLEMS

1. The government is involved in providing many goods and services. For each of the goods or services listed, determine whether it is rival or nonrival in consumption and whether it is excludable or nonexcludable. What type of good is it? Without government involvement, would the quantity provided be efficient, inefficiently low, or inefficiently high?

   a. Street signs

   b. Amtrak rail service

   c. Regulations limiting pollution

   d. An interstate highway without tolls

   e. A lighthouse on the coast

2. An economist gives the following advice to a museum director: "You should introduce 'peak pricing': at times when the museum has few visitors, you should admit visitors for free. And at times when the museum has many visitors, you should charge a higher admission fee."

   a. When the museum is quiet, is it rival or nonrival in consumption? Is it excludable or nonexcludable? What type of good is the museum at those times? What would be the efficient price to charge visitors during that time, and why?

   b. When the museum is busy, is it rival or nonrival in consumption? Is it excludable or nonexcludable? What type of good is the museum at those times? What would be the efficient price to charge visitors during that time, and why?

3. In many planned communities, various aspects of community living are subject to regulation by a homeowners' association. These rules can regulate house architecture; require snow removal from sidewalks; excluded of outdoor equipment, such as backyard swimming pools; require appropriate conduct in shared spaces such as the community clubhouse; and so on. There has been some conflict, as some homeowners feel that some of the regulations are overly intrusive. You have been called in to mediate. Using economics, how would you decide what types of regulations are warranted and what types are not?

4. A residential community has 100 residents who are concerned about security. The accompanying table gives the total cost of hiring a 24-hour security service as well as each individual resident's total benefit.

Quantity of security guards	Total cost	Total individual benefit to each resident
0	$0	$0
1	150	10
2	300	16
3	450	18
4	600	19

   a. Explain why the security service is a public good for the residents of the community.

   b. Calculate the marginal cost, the individual marginal benefit for each resident, and the marginal social benefit.

   c. If an individual resident were to decide about hiring and paying for security guards on his or her own, how many guards would that resident hire?

d. If the residents act together, how many security guards will they hire?

5. The accompanying table shows Tanisha's and Ari's individual marginal benefit of different amounts of street cleanings per month. Suppose that the marginal cost of street cleanings is constant at $9 each.

Quantity of street cleanings per month	Tanisha's individual marginal benefit	Ari's individual marginal benefit
0		
	$10	$8
1		
	6	4
2		
	2	1
3		

a. If Tanisha had to pay for street cleaning on her own, how many street cleanings would there be?

b. Calculate the marginal social benefit of street cleaning. What is the optimal number of street cleanings?

c. Consider the optimal number of street cleanings. The last street cleaning of that number costs $9. Is Tanisha willing to pay for that last cleaning on her own? Is Ari willing to pay for that last cleaning on his own?

6. Anyone with a radio receiver can listen to public radio, which is funded largely by donations.

a. Is public radio excludable or nonexcludable? Is it rival in consumption or nonrival? What type of good is it?

b. Should the government support public radio? Explain your reasoning.

c. In order to finance itself, public radio decides to transmit only to satellite radios, for which users have to pay a fee. What type of good is public radio then? Will the quantity of radio listening be efficient? Why or why not?

7. The village of Upper Bigglesworth has a village "commons," a piece of land on which each villager, by law, is free to graze his or her cows. Use of the commons is measured in units of the number of cows grazing on it. Assume that each resident has a constant marginal cost of sending cows to graze (that is, the marginal cost is the same, whether 1 or 10 cows are grazing). But each additional cow grazed means less grass available for others, and the damage done by overgrazing of the commons increases as the number of cows grazing increases. Finally, assume that the benefit to the villagers of each additional cow grazing on the commons declines as more cows graze, since each additional cow has less grass to eat than the previous one.

a. Is the commons excludable or nonexcludable? Is it rival in consumption or nonrival? What kind of good is the commons?

b. Draw a diagram, with the quantity of cows that graze on the commons on the horizontal axis. How does the quantity of cows grazing in the absence of government intervention compare to the efficient quantity? Show both in your diagram.

c. The villagers hire you to tell them how to achieve an efficient use of the commons. You tell them that there are three possibilities: a Pigouvian tax, the assignment of property rights over the commons, and a system of tradable licenses for the right to graze a cow. Explain how each one of these options would lead to an efficient use of the commons. Draw a diagram that shows the Pigouvian tax.

8. The accompanying table shows six consumers' willingness to pay (his or her individual marginal benefit) for one MP3 file copy of a Dr. Dre album. The marginal cost of making the file accessible to one additional consumer is constant, at zero.

Consumer	Individual marginal benefit
Adriana	$2
Bhagesh	15
Chizuko	1
Denzel	10
Emma	5
Frank	4

a. What would be the efficient price to charge for a download of the file?

b. All six consumers are able to download the file for free from a file-sharing service, Pantster. Which consumers will download the file? What will be the total consumer surplus to those consumers?

c. Pantster is shut down for copyright law infringement. In order to download the file, consumers now have to pay $4.99 at a commercial music site. Which consumers will download the file? What will be the total consumer surplus to those consumers? How much producer surplus accrues to the commercial music site? What is the total surplus? What is the deadweight loss from the new pricing policy?

9. Butchart Gardens is a very large garden in Victoria, British Columbia, renowned for its beautiful plants. It is so large that it could hold many times more visitors than currently visit it. The garden charges an admission fee of $10. At this price, 1,000 visitors visit the garden each day. If admission were free, 2,000 visitors would visit the garden each day.

a. Are visits to Butchart Gardens excludable or nonexcludable? Are they rival in consumption or nonrival? What type of good is it?

b. In a diagram, illustrate the demand curve for visits to Butchart Gardens. Indicate the situation when Butchart Gardens charges an admission fee of $10. Also indicate the situation when Butchart Gardens charges no admission fee.

c. Illustrate the deadweight loss from charging a $10 admission fee. Explain why charging a $10 admission fee is inefficient.

10. In developing a vaccine for a new virus called SARS, a pharmaceutical company incurs a very high fixed cost. The marginal cost of delivering the vaccine to patients, however, is negligible (consider it to be equal to zero). The pharmaceutical company holds the exclusive patent to the vaccine. You are a regulator who must decide what price the pharmaceutical company is allowed to charge.

a. Draw a diagram that shows the price for the vaccine that would arise if the company is unregulated, and label it P_M.

What is the efficient price for the vaccine? Show the deadweight loss that arises from the price P_M.

b. On another diagram, show the lowest price that the regulator can enforce that would still induce the pharmaceutical company to develop the vaccine. Label it P^*. Show the deadweight loss that arises from this price. How does it compare to the deadweight loss that arises from the price P_M?

c. Suppose you have accurate information about the pharmaceutical company's fixed cost. How could you use price regulation of the pharmaceutical company, combined with a subsidy to the company, to have the efficient quantity of the vaccine provided at the lowest cost to the government?

>web... To continue your study and review of concepts in this chapter, please visit the Krugman/Wells website for quizzes, animated graph tutorials, web links to helpful resources, and more.

www.worthpublishers.com/krugmanwells

>>Taxes, Social Insurance, and Income Distribution

A TAX RIOT

ON MARCH 31, 1990, HUNDREDS OF thousands of British citizens marched across London, protesting a new tax that had been introduced by Prime Minister Margaret Thatcher. As some protesters clashed with police, the initially peaceful demonstration turned into a riot, with hundreds injured. The violence came as a surprise, but maybe it shouldn't have: the tax had aroused angry opposition throughout Britain. Later that year, Mrs. Thatcher was forced to resign, and many observers believed that the tax controversy was the prime cause of her fall.

The tax at issue was officially known as the "Community Charge" but was popularly known as the "poll tax." Until 1989 local public services like street cleaning and trash collection had been financed with "the rates," a tax that depended on the value of people's homes. (Most local services in the United States are financed with similar property-based taxes.) Mrs. Thatcher, however, replaced these property taxes with a payment from each individual over the age of 18. Although the amount of the poll tax varied from town to town, every adult in a given town owed the same amount, regardless of income or the value of his or her property.

Supporters of the poll tax argued that it was more efficient than the tax it replaced. Because the old tax depended on the value of property, it discouraged people both from buying more expensive homes and from improving the homes they had. Supporters also argued that the poll tax was fair, because the cost of providing local public services depended mainly on how many people lived in a town, not on how rich those people were.

But opponents argued that the poll tax was extremely unfair because it did not take into account differences in people's ability to pay— a single mother who worked as a waitress and

Margaret Thatcher and these protesters differed sharply over the fairness of the poll tax.

a millionaire stockbroker owed the same amount if they lived in the same town.

One moral of the story is that making tax policy isn't easy—in fact, if you are a politician, it can be dangerous to your professional health. But the deeper moral is that making tax policy always involves striking a balance between the pursuit of efficiency and the pursuit of perceived fairness. Or, as economists say, there is a *trade-off between equity and efficiency*. In this chapter we will show why this trade-off exists and how attempts to make the best of the trade-off influence the design of actual tax systems.

Principles of Tax Policy

A tax system achieves **tax efficiency** when it minimizes the direct and indirect costs to the economy of tax collection.

A tax system achieves **tax fairness,** or **tax equity,** when the "right" people actually bear the burden of taxes.

Tax policy always has two goals. On the one hand, governments strive to achieve **tax efficiency:** they try to minimize the direct and indirect costs to the economy of tax collection. On the other hand, governments also seek **tax fairness,** or **tax equity:** they try to ensure that the "right" people actually bear the burden of taxes. The central dilemma in tax policy—the dilemma that led to London's poll tax riot—is that an efficient tax may not seem fair, and a seemingly fair tax may not be efficient. So there is a fundamental trade-off between equity and efficiency.

The Burden of Taxes: A Quick Review

We analyzed some of the basic economics of taxation in Chapter 6. Here we briefly revisit the results of that analysis. As in Chapter 6, we'll assume here that there are no market failures, such as negative externalities or common resources, that make a tax efficiency enhancing (that is, make it a Pigouvian tax) rather than efficiency diminishing. Figure 21-1 shows the effects of an excise tax—a tax on sales—imposed on some good, in this case automobiles. Excise taxes are only one part of the U.S. tax system, but the principles suggested by this analysis apply to all taxes.

In the absence of a tax, the equilibrium price of autos would be P_E and the quantity bought and sold would be Q_E. Once a tax is imposed on the purchase or sale of an automobile, it *drives a wedge* between the price paid by consumers and that received by pro-

---

Figure 21-1

The Deadweight Loss of a Tax

Here an excise tax of the amount $T = P_C - P_P$ is imposed per auto sold. The quantity transacted falls from Q_E to Q_T, and there is a deadweight loss equal to the shaded area. The tax creates a wedge between the price paid by consumers, P_C, and the price received by producers, P_P. As a result, incentives are distorted and inefficiency arises: consumers consume less than is efficient and producers produce less than is efficient.
>web...

ducers. In this case, a tax of T per unit is imposed. In the new equilibrium the price paid by consumers rises to P_C and the price received by producers falls to P_P. The difference, $P_C - P_P$, is equal to the tax. As a result of the tax, the quantity bought and sold falls from Q_E to Q_T. So the tax changes people's behavior: less of the good is bought and sold.

Our analysis in Chapter 6 revealed three key results:

1. Consumers are hurt by the tax to the extent that the price they pay rises, and producers are hurt to the extent that the price they receive falls. But how much P_C rises and how much P_P falls does not depend on who pays the tax to the government—in fact, in Figure 21-1 we have not even specified whether this is a tax on producers or on consumers. So the incidence of a tax—who actually bears the burden—cannot be determined simply by looking at who pays the money to the government.

2. The price elasticities of supply and demand determine the incidence of the tax. The higher the price elasticity of supply, the more the price paid by consumers rises as a result of the tax and the greater the tax burden on consumers. The higher the price elasticity of demand, the more the price received by producers falls and the greater the tax burden on producers. The party with the lower price elasticity (producers or consumers) will bear the greater burden of the tax. If demand is relatively inelastic compared with supply, then consumers will bear a greater tax burden because quantity demanded is relatively insensitive to an increase in the price paid. If supply is relatively inelastic compared with demand, then producers will bear a greater share of the tax burden because quantity supplied is relatively insensitive to the decrease in the price received.

3. The tax causes a loss in efficiency—a deadweight loss—by creating a wedge between the price paid by consumers and the price received by producers. At Q_T in Figure 21-1, the marginal benefit of an additional unit of consumption is greater than the marginal cost of producing that additional unit. This means that the economy loses the potential gain from greater production and consumption of the good. The total deadweight loss from the tax can be measured by the area of the shaded triangle. This deadweight loss represents the *excess burden* of the tax—the cost to society over and above the tax revenue the government collects.

A tax system causes deadweight losses because taxes *distort incentives:* the incentives at the margin for producers to produce and consumers to consume are different from what they would have been without the tax, so people change their behavior. As a result, the tax that distorts incentives the least also minimizes any deadweight losses. So if the goal, in choosing whom to tax, is to minimize deadweight loss, then taxes should be imposed on those who have the most inelastic response—people who will change their behavior the least in response to the tax. (Unless they have a tendency to riot, of course.)

In considering the efficiency of a tax, we must also take into account something not shown in Figure 21-1: the resources actually used both to collect the tax and to pay it. These are called the **administrative costs** of the tax. The most familiar administrative cost of the U.S. tax system is the time individuals spend filling out their tax forms or the money they spend on accountants to do their taxes for them. (The costs of operating the Internal Revenue Service are actually quite small by comparison.)

The **administrative costs** of a tax are the resources used both to collect the tax and to pay it.

If maximizing efficiency is the only goal, a tax system should be designed to minimize the sum of its deadweight loss and its administrative costs. But tax policy is not driven by efficiency alone, because the voters who must approve a tax system also care about fairness, or equity. As we will see, fairness in a tax system usually comes at the expense of efficiency.

Tax Fairness

We have just seen how economic analysis can be used to determine who bears the burden of a tax. But who *should* bear the burden? Governments have wide discretion in choosing what to tax and how to tax it. How should they exercise this discretion?

One answer is that the tax system should be fair. But what exactly does fairness mean? We could say that fairness, like beauty, is often in the eyes of the beholder. However, most debates about taxes rely on one of two principles of tax fairness: the *benefits principle* and the *ability-to-pay principle*.

According to the **benefits principle** of tax fairness, those who benefit from public spending should bear the burden of the tax that pays for that spending. For example, those who benefit from a road should pay for that road's upkeep, those who fly on airplanes should pay for air traffic control, and so on. The benefits principle is the basis for some parts of the U.S. tax system. For example, revenue from the federal tax on gasoline is specifically reserved for the maintenance and improvement of federal roads, including the Interstate Highway System. In this way motorists, who benefit from the highway system, also pay for it.

The benefits principle is attractive from an economic point of view because it matches well with one of the major justifications for public spending—the theory of public goods. If government's role is to provide people with goods that could not otherwise be made available, it seems natural to charge each person in proportion to the benefits he or she gets from those goods.

Practical considerations, however, make it impossible to base the entire tax system on the benefits principle. It would be too cumbersome to have a specific tax for each of the many distinct programs that the government offers. Also, attempts to base taxes on the benefits principle often conflict with the other major principle of tax fairness: the **ability-to-pay principle,** according to which those with greater ability to pay a tax should pay more.

The ability-to-pay principle is usually interpreted to mean that high-income individuals should pay more in taxes than low-income individuals. Often the ability-to-pay principle is used to argue not just that high-income individuals should pay more taxes but that they should pay a higher *percentage* of their income in taxes. We'll consider the issue of how taxes vary as a percentage of income later.

The London protest described at the beginning of this chapter was basically a protest against the failure of the poll tax to take the ability-to-pay principle into account. In some parts of Britain, the poll tax was as high as £550 (equivalent to around $900) per adult per year. For highly paid executives or professionals, £550 was not a lot of money. But for struggling British families, £550 per year was a crushing burden. It's not surprising that many people were upset that the new tax completely disregarded the ability-to-pay principle.

Equity versus Efficiency

Margaret Thatcher's poll tax was an example of a **lump-sum tax,** a tax that is the same for everyone regardless of any actions people take. It was widely perceived as much less fair than the tax structure it replaced, in which local taxes were proportional to property values. Under the old system, the highest local taxes were paid by the people with the most expensive houses; because these people tended to be wealthy, they were also best able to bear the burden.

But the old system definitely distorted incentives. People who were considering home improvements knew that such improvements, by making their property more valuable, would increase their tax bills. The result, surely, was that some home improvements that would have taken place without the tax did not take place because of it.

In contrast, a lump-sum tax does not distort incentives. Because people have to pay the same tax regardless of their situation, it does not lead them to avoid doing things that would raise their taxes. So lump-sum taxes, although unfair, are better than other taxes at promoting economic efficiency.

The example of the poll tax debate illustrates a general point. Unless a tax system is badly designed, it can be made fairer only by sacrificing efficiency; conversely, it can be made more efficient only by making it less fair. So there is normally a **trade-off between equity and efficiency**.

According to the **benefits principle** of tax fairness, those who benefit from public spending should bear the burden of the tax that pays for that spending.

According to the **ability-to-pay principle** of tax fairness, those with greater ability to pay a tax should pay more tax.

A **lump-sum tax** is the same for everyone, regardless of any actions people take.

In a well-designed tax system, there is a **trade-off between equity and efficiency:** the system can be made more efficient only by making it less fair, and vice versa.

POLL TAXES AND REVOLTING PEASANTS

Perhaps Margaret Thatcher wouldn't have tried to impose a poll tax if she had remembered her English history. For it was the tripling of an existing poll tax that set off the great English peasant rebellion of 1381.

In that rebellion, peasants under the leadership of Wat Tyler marched on London to demand a repeal of the tax. One of their slogans was "The first thing to do is to kill all the lawyers." (Lawyers at that time were responsible for enforcing the tax.) The rebels did kill quite a few lawyers and tax collectors; they also burned part of London and

A lesson from history: in 1381, English peasants revolted over unfair taxes.

HIP/Scala/Art Resource, NY

came close to taking King Richard II hostage. However, they dispersed after the king promised some concessions—a promise he promptly broke. After all, in 1381 royal promises to peasants didn't count: as the king declared before hanging Wat Tyler and the other rebel leaders, "Villeins ye are, and villeins ye shall remain." (*Villein* is a fourteenth-century English term for a peasant.)

Nonetheless, the fact that the rebellion came so close to success struck terror into the hearts of the nobility, and it remained a cautionary tale for centuries.

Economic analysis cannot say how much weight a tax system should give to equity and how much to efficiency. That choice is a value judgment, one we make through the political process.

economics in action

Federal Tax Philosophy

What is the principle underlying the federal tax system? (By federal, we mean taxes collected by the federal government, as opposed to the taxes collected by state and local governments.) The answer is that it depends on the tax.

The best-known federal tax, accounting for about half of all federal revenue, is the income tax. The structure of the income tax reflects the ability-to-pay principle: families with low incomes pay little or no income tax. In fact, some families pay negative income tax: a program known as the Earned Income Tax Credit "tops up" or adds to the earnings of workers who receive low wages. Meanwhile, those with high incomes not only pay a lot of income tax but must pay a larger share of their income in income taxes than the average family.

The second most important federal tax, however, is set up very differently. The payroll tax, a tax on an employee's paid earnings, was originally introduced in 1935 to pay for Social Security, a program that guarantees retirement income to qualifying older Americans and also provides benefits to workers who become disabled and to family members of workers who die. (Part of the payroll tax is now also used to pay for Medicare, a program that pays most medical bills of older Americans.) The Social Security system was set up to resemble a private insurance program: people pay into the system during their working years, then receive benefits based on their payments. And the tax more or less reflects the benefits principle: because the benefits of Social Security are mainly intended to assist lower- and middle-income people, and don't increase substantially for the rich, the Social Security tax is levied only on incomes up to a maximum level—$90,000 in 2005. (The Medicare portion of the payroll tax

TABLE 21-1

Share of Income and Federal Income Taxes, by Quintile, 2002

Quintile of income group	Percent of total pre-tax income received	Percent of total federal income tax paid	Percent of total payroll tax paid
Lowest	4.2%	−2.6%	3.9%
Second	9.3	−0.2	9.9
Third	14.7	5.3	15.8
Fourth	21.2	14.8	25.6
Top	51.5	82.8	44.6

Source: Congressional Budget Office

continues to be levied on incomes over $90,000.) As a result, a high-income family doesn't pay much more in payroll taxes than a middle-income family.

Table 21-1 illustrates the difference in the two taxes, using data from a Congressional Budget Office study. The study divided American families into quintiles: the lowest quintile is the poorest 20% of families, the second quintile is the next poorest 20%, and so on. The second column shows the share of total U.S. pre-tax income received by each quintile. The third column shows the share of total federal income tax collected that is paid by each quintile. As you can see, low-income families actually paid negative income tax, and even middle-income families paid a substantially smaller share of total income taxes collected than their share of total income. In contrast, the top quintile, the richest 20% of families, pays a much higher share of total income taxes collected compared with their share of total income. The fourth column shows the share of total payroll tax collected that is paid by each quintile, and the results are very different: the share of total payroll taxes paid by the top quintile is substantially *less* than their share of total income. ■

< < < < < < < < < < < < < < < < < < < <

>> CHECK YOUR UNDERSTANDING 21-1

1. Assess each of the following taxes in terms of the benefits principle versus the ability-to-pay principle. What, if any, actions are distorted by the tax? Assume for simplicity in each case that the purchaser of the good bears 100% of the burden of the tax.
   a. A federal tax of $500 for each new car purchased that finances highway safety programs
   b. A local tax of 20% on hotel rooms that finances local government expenditures
   c. A local tax of 1% of the assessed value of homes that finances local schools
   d. A 1% sales tax on food that pays for government food safety regulation and inspection programs

Solutions appear at back of book.

Understanding the Tax System

An excise tax is the easiest tax to analyze, making it a good vehicle for understanding the general principles of tax analysis. However, in the United States today, excise taxes are actually a relatively minor source of government revenue. In this section, we develop a framework for understanding more general forms of taxation and look at some of the major taxes used in the United States.

Tax Bases and Tax Structure

Every tax consists of two pieces: a *base* and a *structure*. The **tax base** is the measure or value that determines how much tax an individual pays. It is usually a monetary measure, like income or property value. The **tax structure** specifies how the tax depends on the tax base. It is usually expressed in percentage terms; for example,

The **tax base** is the measure or value, such as income or property value, that determines how much tax an individual pays.

The **tax structure** specifies how the tax depends on the tax base.

homeowners in some areas might pay taxes equal to 2 percent of the value of their homes.

Some important taxes and their tax bases are as follows:

- **Income tax:** a tax that depends on the income of an individual or family from wages and investments
- **Payroll tax:** a tax that depends on the earnings an employer pays to an employee
- **Sales tax:** a tax that depends on the value of goods sold (also known as an excise tax)
- **Profits tax:** a tax that depends on a firm's profits
- **Property tax:** a tax that depends on the value of property, such as the value of a home
- **Wealth tax:** a tax that depends on an individual or family's wealth

Once the tax base has been defined, the next question is how the tax depends on the base. The simplest tax structure is a **proportional tax,** also sometimes called a *flat tax,* which is the same percentage of the base regardless of the taxpayer's income or wealth. For example, a property tax that is set at 2 percent of the value of the property, whether the property is worth $10,000 or $10,000,000, is a proportional tax. Many taxes, however, are not proportional. Instead, different people pay different percentages, usually because the tax law tries to take account either of the benefits principle or the ability-to-pay principle.

Because taxes are ultimately paid out of income, economists classify taxes according to how they vary with the income of individuals. A tax that rises *more* than in proportion to income, so that high-income taxpayers pay a larger percentage of their income than low-income taxpayers, is a **progressive tax.** A tax that rises *less* than in proportion to income, so that higher-income taxpayers pay a smaller percentage of their income than low-income taxpayers, is a **regressive tax.** A proportional tax on income would be neither progressive nor regressive.

Figure 21-2 illustrates the relationship between tax payment and income for proportional, progressive, and regressive taxes with three curves, one corresponding to each type of tax. In the case of a proportional tax, plotting the tax due against income yields a tax schedule that is a straight line from the origin. For a progressive tax, the curve gets steeper as income increases; for a regressive tax, the curve gets flatter as income increases.

The U.S. tax system contains a mixture of progressive and regressive taxes, though it is somewhat progressive overall.

An **income tax** is a tax on an individual's or family's income.

A **payroll tax** is a tax on the earnings an employer pays to an employee.

A **sales tax** is a tax on the value of goods sold.

A **profits tax** is a tax on a firm's profits.

A **property tax** is a tax on the value of property, such as the value of a home.

A **wealth tax** is a tax on an individual's wealth.

A **proportional tax** is the same percentage of the tax base regardless of the taxpayer's income or wealth.

A **progressive tax** takes a larger share of the income of high-income taxpayers than of low-income taxpayers.

A **regressive tax** takes a smaller share of the income of high-income taxpayers than of low-income taxpayers.

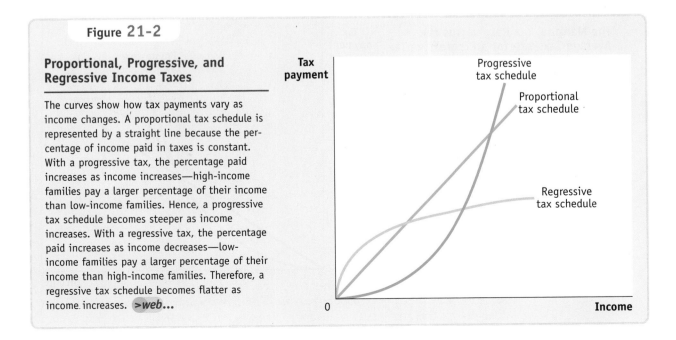

Figure 21-2

Proportional, Progressive, and Regressive Income Taxes

The curves show how tax payments vary as income changes. A proportional tax schedule is represented by a straight line because the percentage of income paid in taxes is constant. With a progressive tax, the percentage paid increases as income increases—high-income families pay a larger percentage of their income than low-income families. Hence, a progressive tax schedule becomes steeper as income increases. With a regressive tax, the percentage paid increases as income decreases—low-income families pay a larger percentage of their income than high-income families. Therefore, a regressive tax schedule becomes flatter as income increases. >web...

Equity, Efficiency, and Progressive Taxation

Most, though not all, people view a progressive tax system as fairer than a regressive system. The reason is the ability-to-pay principle: a high-income family that pays 35 percent of its income in taxes is still left with a lot more money than a low-income family that pays only 15 percent in taxes. But attempts to make taxes strongly progressive run up against the trade-off between equity and efficiency.

Figure 21-3 shows once again a progressive tax schedule on income. Consider a particular individual whose income is N; given that income, he will find himself at point A on the tax schedule and will pay taxes equal to T. His **average tax rate on income** is the ratio of tax payment to income, equal to T/N. As shown in Figure 21-3, it is equal to the slope of a line from the origin to point A.

But what effect does the tax have on his incentive to earn income—say, by working longer hours, or by investing? The answer depends on his **marginal tax rate on income,** the additional tax he pays if his income goes up by $1. It is the marginal tax rate, not the average tax rate, that affects an individual's incentives to earn another $1.

In Figure 21-3, the marginal tax rate of an individual with income N is the slope of a line tangent to the tax schedule at point A. Clearly, in this example the marginal tax rate is higher than the average tax rate. This is always true in the case of a progressive tax: *when a tax is progressive, the marginal tax rate is higher than the average tax rate at every income level.*

To deepen our understanding of this point, let's consider a simplified tax system. Imagine that income taxes work as follows: families pay no tax on the first $40,000 of income but pay a 50 percent tax rate on any income over $40,000. This system would be strongly progressive: families with less than $40,000 in income will pay no taxes, but families with high incomes will pay up to 50 percent of their income in taxes.

At the same time, this system will lead to a high marginal tax rate for many families, even if their *average* tax rates aren't very high. Consider a family with an income of $50,000. It will pay taxes only on the last $10,000 of that income, so its average tax rate will be $5,000/$50,000, or 10 percent. However, the family will pay $0.50 in taxes for each additional $1 it earns; its marginal tax rate is 50 percent.

In fact, the federal income tax works a lot like that. Family income below a certain amount (the amount depends on the size of the family and other criteria) isn't taxed. Income above that amount is taxed at a rate of 10 percent, up to another threshold

The **average tax rate on income** is the ratio of income taxes paid by an individual to his or her income.

The **marginal tax rate on income** is the additional tax an individual pays if his or her income goes up by $1.

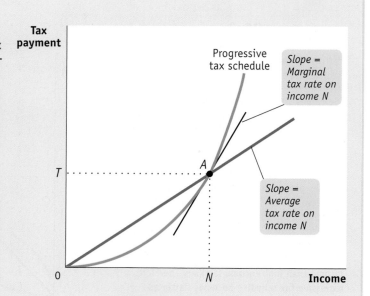

Figure 21-3

The Marginal Tax Rate versus the Average Tax Rate for a Progressive Tax

Under the progressive tax schedule shown here, a taxpayer with income N finds himself at point A on the tax schedule and pays taxes of T. His average tax rate at income N is the total tax paid divided by the total income, T/N, which is equal to the slope of the line connecting the origin to A. His marginal tax rate at income N is the tax rate paid on an additional $1 of income at point A. This is equal to the slope of the line tangent to the tax schedule at A. As shown, for a progressive tax the marginal tax rate is greater than the average tax rate. As a result, compared to a proportional or regressive tax, progressive taxes result in reduced incentives for higher-income people to work and invest. **>web...**

at which the tax rate rises to 15 percent, and so on. In 2003 the average federal income tax rate was about 11 percent, but taxpayers faced marginal rates as high as 35 percent. In the past, marginal rates in the United States have been as high as 94 percent, and the highest marginal rate stayed above 50 percent until the 1980s.

The excess burden of a tax comes from its effect on marginal incentives. Suppose that a highly progressive tax system implied a marginal tax rate of 70 percent on successful businesspeople. An entrepreneur might look at that rate and decide that the risk and effort of expanding her business just wasn't worth it. So high marginal tax rates distort incentives, reducing the incentive to earn more income by working more or investing money rather than spending it. In short, the ability-to-pay principle pushes governments toward a highly progressive tax system, but efficiency considerations push them the other way.

Taxes in the United States

Table 21-2 shows the revenue raised by some major taxes in the United States in fiscal year 2003. (For reasons not worth going into, fiscal years start on October 1 of the preceding calendar year.) Some of the taxes are collected by the federal government, the others by state and local governments.

TABLE 21-2

Revenue from Major Taxes in the United States, Fiscal Year 2003 (billions of dollars)

Federal	State and local
Income tax: $793.7	Sales tax: $340.5
Payroll tax: 713.0	Income tax: 205.4
Profits tax: 131.8	Property tax: 304.0
	Profits tax: 37.2

Source: *Statistical Abstract of the United States,* 2003

There is a major tax corresponding to five of the six tax bases we identified earlier. There are income taxes, profits taxes, payroll taxes, sales taxes, and property taxes, all playing an important role in the overall tax system. The only item missing is a wealth tax. In fact, the United States does have a wealth tax, the *estate tax,* which depends on the value of someone's estate after he or she dies. But at the time of writing, the current law phases out the estate tax over a few years, and in any case it raises much less money than the taxes shown in the table.

In addition to the taxes shown, state and local governments collect substantial revenue from other sources as varied as driver's license fees and sewer charges. These fees and charges are an important part of the burden of taxes but very difficult to summarize or analyze.

Are the taxes in Table 21-2 progressive or regressive? It depends on the tax. The personal income tax is strongly progressive. The payroll tax, which, except for the Medicare portion, is paid only on earnings up to $90,000, is somewhat regressive. Sales taxes are generally regressive, because higher-income families save more of their income and thus spend a smaller share of it on taxable goods than do lower-income families. In addition, there are other taxes principally levied at the state and local level that are typically quite regressive: it costs the same amount to get a new driver's license no matter what your income is.

Overall, the taxes collected by the federal government are quite progressive. Table 21-3 on page 502 shows estimates by the Congressional Budget Office of the average federal tax rate paid by families at different levels of income earned in 2002. These estimates don't just count the money families pay directly; they also attempt to estimate the incidence of

TABLE **21-3**

Federal Taxes Paid as a Percentage of Average Family Pre-tax Income, by Quintile, 2002

Quintile of income group	Average pre-tax family income	Average tax rate
Lowest	$14,400	4.6%
Second	33,600	10.8
Third	51,100	14.4
Fourth	75,900	18.7
Top	175,900	26.1

Source: Congressional Budget Office

taxes directly paid by business, like the tax on corporate profits, which ultimately falls on individual shareholders. The table shows that the federal tax system is indeed progressive, with low-income families paying a relatively small share of their income in federal taxes and high-income families paying a greater share of their income.

Since 2000, the federal government has cut taxes for most families. The largest cuts, both as a share of income and as a share of federal taxes collected have gone to families with high income. As a result, the federal system is less progressive (at the time of this writing) than it was in 2000, and it will become even less progressive over the next few years, as some delayed pieces of the post-2000 tax cut legislation take effect. However, even after those changes, the federal tax system will remain progressive.

As Table 21-4 shows, however, taxes at the state and local level are generally regressive. That's because the sales tax, the largest source of revenue for states, is somewhat regressive, and other items, such as vehicle licensing fees, are strongly regressive.

Different Taxes, Different Principles

Why are some taxes progressive but others regressive? Can't the government make up its mind?

There are two main reasons for the mixture of regressive and progressive taxes in the U.S. system: the difference between levels of government, and the fact that different taxes are based on different principles.

TABLE **21-4**

State and Local Taxes as a Percentage of Income, by Income Category, 2002

Lowest quintile	11.4%
Second quintile	10.4
Third quintile	9.9
Fourth quintile	9.4
Next 15 percent	8.9
Next 4 percent	8.1
Top 1 percent	7.3

Source: Institute for Taxation and Economic Policy.

FOR INQUIRING MINDS

TAXING INCOME VERSUS TAXING CONSUMPTION

The federal government in the United States taxes people mainly on the money they *make*, not on the money they spend. Yet most tax experts argue that this distorts incentives. If someone earns income, and then invests that income for the future, she gets taxed twice: once when she earns the original sum, and again on any earnings she makes on her investment. So a system that taxes income discourages people from saving and investing and provides them with an incentive to spend their income today.

Moving from a system that taxes income to one that taxes consumption would solve this problem. In fact, the governments of many countries get much of their revenue from a value-added tax, or VAT, which acts like a national sales tax. In some countries VAT rates are very high; in Sweden, for example, the rate is 25 percent.

The United States does not have a value-added tax for two main reasons. One is that it is difficult, though not impossible, to make a consumption tax progressive. The other is that although VATs may not distort incentives as much as income taxes, they typically have quite high administrative costs.

State and especially local governments generally do not make much effort to apply the ability-to-pay principle. This is largely because they are subject to *tax competition*: a state or local government that tried to impose high taxes on people with high incomes might find those people moving to other locations where taxes are lower. This is much less of a concern at the national level, although a handful of very rich people have given up their U.S. citizenship to avoid paying U.S. taxes.

Although the federal government is in a better position than state or local governments to apply principles of fairness, it applies different principles to different taxes. We already saw this in Economics in Action on page 497. The most important tax, the income tax, is strongly progressive, reflecting the ability-to-pay principle. But the second most important tax, the payroll tax, is somewhat regressive, because most of it is linked to specific programs—Social Security and Medicare—and, reflecting the benefits principle, is levied more or less in proportion to the benefits received from these programs.

economics in action

Marginal Tax Rates in the United States

Congress keeps fiddling with the federal income tax. There were nine major revisions of the tax between 1980 and 2003. Tax rates on high-income families, for example, were cut during the 1980s, raised again in the 1990s, and cut again after 2000.

Although the politics of the income tax constantly seesaws, there has been a clear trend toward lower marginal tax rates on income. This trend is driven largely by economic arguments: many politicians have picked up on the idea that high marginal tax rates discourage productive activity.

In 1980 the highest-income families faced a marginal tax rate of no less than 70 percent. Tax cuts in the 1980s brought that down to 28 percent; tax increases in the 1990s pushed it back up again, but only to 39.6 percent. The rate is now 35 percent. Less affluent families never paid that high a marginal rate, but at almost all income levels marginal rates are considerably lower now than they were in 1980. Currently, families in the middle of the income distribution—about 60 percent of families, who earn $30,000 to $80,000 a year—typically pay a marginal rate of either 10 or 15 percent, depending on income and the number of deductions they can take.

The U.S. tax system still imposes a substantial wedge between the pre-tax earnings of families and their after-tax income. But the wedge is considerably smaller than it was a generation ago. ■

> > > > > > > > > > > > > > > > > > > >

>>CHECK YOUR UNDERSTANDING 21-2

1. A wealth tax taxes 1% of the first $10,000 of wealth and 2% on all wealth above $10,000. Show that the average rate is smaller than the marginal rate for someone with wealth of $20,000.

2. When comparing households at different income levels, economists find that consumption spending grows more slowly than income. Assume that when income grows by 50%, from $10,000 to $15,000, consumption spending grows by 25%, from $8,000 to $10,000. Compare the percent of income paid in taxes by a family with $15,000 in income to that paid by a family with $10,000 in income under a 1% tax on consumption purchases. Is this tax a proportional, progressive, or regressive tax?

3. True or false? Explain your answers.
   a. Payroll taxes do not affect a person's incentive to take a job because they are paid by employers.
   b. A lump-sum tax is a proportional tax because it is the same amount for each person.

Solutions appear at back of book.

Understanding Government Spending

One way or another, governments in the United States collected 27 percent of total U.S. income in 2003. And that's actually low by international standards: Canada collects more than 35 percent total of Canadian income, and European countries on average collect more than 40 percent of national income. Where does all the money go?

It's easy to make fun of government spending; everyone has a favorite story of wasted money, and some of those stories are even true. But most government spending is done for reasons that seem sensible to a large fraction of the electorate. Let's take a look at the major types of spending in the United States.

Types of Spending

Broadly speaking, governments spend money for three reasons: to provide *public goods,* to provide *social insurance,* and to engage in *income redistribution.*

We defined public goods in Chapter 20. They are goods that are nonexcludable so that people cannot be forced to pay for consuming them, and nonrival in consumption so that people *should* not have to pay. As a result many public goods are provided by the government. One public good in particular—national defense—has traditionally been the largest component of spending by the federal government (although this is no longer true).

Social insurance is government spending intended to protect people against financial risks.

Much modern government spending is not for public goods but for **social insurance:** programs intended to protect people against some of the financial risks in life. The clearest examples are government programs that pay for medical care. When someone needs expensive medical treatment, the cost can be a severe burden; indeed, sometimes people cannot afford the treatment at all. This is widely viewed as unfair—the ability-to-pay principle again. So many governments provide some kind of national health insurance that covers many medical bills. The United States offers extensive health insurance for people 65 and older, although not for younger people unless they are indigent. The concept of social insurance can be extended more broadly to include items like unemployment insurance, which provides temporary income to people who have lost their jobs, and programs that support people after retirement.

Governments engage in **redistribution of income** when they tax the well-off and use the money to support those less well-off.

Finally, most governments also engage in **redistribution of income:** taking money via taxes from the relatively well-off and using it either to provide income for the poor or to provide the poor with benefits like housing and medical care. The case for redistribution can be made in a couple of different ways. One is to think of it as an extension of the ability-to-pay principle: the poor, you could argue, are not only less able to pay taxes than the affluent—they could actually use some help with other expenses.

Alternatively, you can think of poverty reduction as a sort of public good. Most of us prefer to live in a society where everyone has enough to eat, decent housing, and so on; these sentiments motivate us to give to charity. But each of us is tempted to free-ride on the positive effects of charitable giving by others. So just as most people agree that they should be taxed to provide for national defense, many agree that they should be taxed to provide aid to the poor.

This raises the question of what we mean by saying that people are "poor." How do we define poverty? We'll discuss that question in the next section, where we also look at poverty trends in the United States.

A **transfer payment** is money that an individual receives from the government but for which no good or service is produced for the government in exchange.

Means-tested government programs are available only to those with sufficiently low income.

How do we draw the line between social insurance and redistribution? Both typically involve **transfer payments:** money that an individual receives from the government for which no good or service is produced for the government in exchange. A transfer payment is the opposite of a tax. And don't social insurance programs often help the poor? Aren't programs for the poor a sort of social insurance for those of us who might end up poor one day?

The answer is that the line between social insurance and income redistribution is a fuzzy one. However, one way economists often draw that line is by distinguishing between programs that are *means-tested* and those that are not. A **means-tested** program is available only to an individual who can show that he or she has a sufficiently low income to qualify; such programs clearly redistribute income. Programs that aren't means-tested are more generally viewed as social insurance.

Spending in the United States

Figure 21-4 shows the composition of federal spending in fiscal year 2004. Let's consider how the categories shown here fit into the categories of spending we have just described.

National defense is, of course, the budget of the U.S. military. It is clearly a public good: the government can't defend some people without defending others, and my security doesn't come at your expense.

The category labeled "nondefense discretionary" consists of everything from running the court system and medical research to highway construction and education. Broadly speaking, it also fits the definition of public goods.

Social Security and Medicare are the two major social insurance programs. Both benefit older Americans: Medicare covers most of their medical bills, and Social Security provides retirement income. In 2003, Congress added a significant new benefit to Medicare, so that starting in 2006 the program will cover some of the cost of prescription drugs for older Americans. The category "other mandatory" includes unemployment insurance, pensions for federal workers, and a variety of other expenses; by and large they can be regarded as social insurance.

Finally, Medicaid is a means-tested program that provides health insurance for low-income families, and "other means-tested" spending includes such programs as food stamps and housing subsidies. These programs are best viewed as income redistribution.

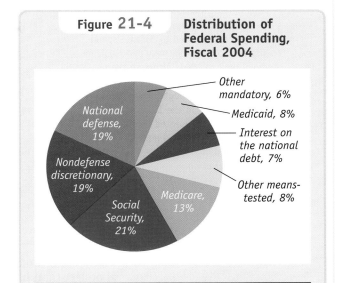

Figure 21-4   **Distribution of Federal Spending, Fiscal 2004**

This pie chart shows how the federal government spent money in fiscal year 2004. National defense and "nondefense discretionary" can be considered spending on public goods. Social Security, Medicare, and "other mandatory" (which includes unemployment insurance) are social insurance programs. Medicaid, which provides medical insurance for people with low incomes, and "other means-tested" (which includes food stamps) are best viewed as income redistribution. (Due to rounding error, percentages do not add up to 100%.)

Source: Congressional Budget Office

Comparisons Across Time and Space

Politicians invariably denounce "big government"—unless they are demanding more government spending on themselves or their constituents. Economic analysis cannot tell us whether the government spends too much or too little. But it is useful to have some sense both of how the level of government spending in the United States compares with its level in the past, and of how spending here compares with spending in other advanced nations.

Figure 21-5 on page 506 shows federal spending as a percentage of *gross domestic product* (GDP) over the past four decades. GDP is a measure of all the income generated in the economy in a year—the sum of payments to all factors of production like labor, land, and capital.

The basic message of Figure 21-5 is that the overall size of the federal government compared with the economy hasn't changed much for a long time. It has fluctuated, but the share of federal spending as a percentage of GDP was only slightly higher in 2003 than it was in the early 1960s. (State and local spending grew somewhat faster, from about 7% of GDP in the early 1960s to about 10% in 2003.)

Although federal spending has stayed roughly constant as a share of the economy, its composition has changed. Figure 21-5 also shows two components of federal spending. One curve shows defense spending as a percentage of GDP. In the 1960s defense spending, at 9% of GDP, accounted for about half of federal spending. After the collapse of the Soviet Union in 1991, the huge military forces that the United States maintained to guard against the Soviet threat were downsized, and defense spending fell to only 3% of GDP. Since the terrorist attacks on September 11, 2001,

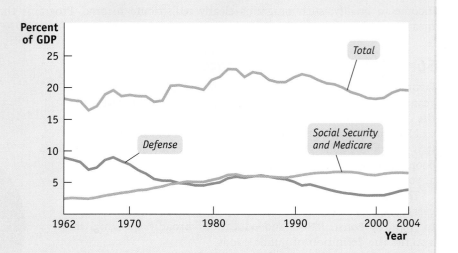

Figure 21-5

Total U.S. Federal Government Spending, 1962–2004

This graph shows the percent of GDP devoted to total federal spending and the percent devoted to defense spending and to Social Security and Medicare from 1962 to 2004. Although the percent of GDP represented by total federal spending was roughly the same in 2004 as it was in the 1960s, the percent of GDP represented by defense spending has declined markedly over that period.

Source: Office of Management and Budget

defense spending has risen rapidly, but it still plays a much smaller role in the federal budget than it did at the height of the Cold War.

Given the decline in defense spending, why hasn't the share of government spending in the economy decreased? The answer is growth in social insurance spending, mainly on Social Security (established in 1935) and Medicare (established in 1965). As the curve in Figure 21-5 shows, combined spending on Social Security and Medicare has risen steadily as a share of GDP. We have gone from a government that spent tax dollars mainly on public goods to one that now spends heavily on social insurance. In 2002 one senior official at the Treasury Department described the U.S. government as "a gigantic insurance company with a sideline business in national defense and homeland security."

However, the United States spends *less* on social insurance as a share of GDP than most other advanced nations. As a result, U.S. government spending actually makes up a smaller share of GDP than that of any other major economy. Figure 21-6 compares government spending (state and local as well as federal) as the share of GDP for the world's seven largest economies in 2002. The United States was at the bottom of the list.

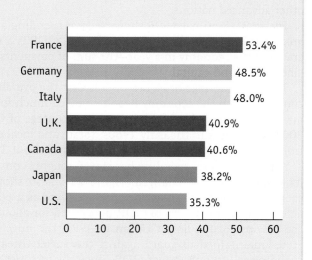

Figure 21-6

Government Spending as a Percent of GDP in 2002

In 2002, France devoted the largest share of its GDP to government spending among the major industrial countries: 53.4%. The United States devoted the smallest share among these countries: 35.3%. Canada appears to have been around average, at about 40.6%.

Source: OECD Economic Outlook

Country	Percent
France	53.4%
Germany	48.5%
Italy	48.0%
U.K.	40.9%
Canada	40.6%
Japan	38.2%
U.S.	35.3%

economics in action

Greedy Geezers?

In 1998 *The New Republic* startled many readers with a cover bearing the slogan "greedy geezers." Although the title was shocking, the story did draw attention to a substantive point: programs providing benefits to older Americans have become increasingly important as a share of both federal spending and the total economy. In 1970 Medicare and Social Security combined cost 3.5 percent of GDP, less than half as much as that year's defense budget. In 2004 the two programs combined cost 6.5 percent of GDP, almost twice the current defense budget.

Why has spending on older Americans grown more rapidly than the economy or the overall budget? One reason is demographics: the percentage of Americans age 65 and over has steadily risen for the past 30 years. This demographic trend will become dramatic after 2011, when members of the "baby-boom" generation become old enough to receive Social Security and Medicare benefits.

Jose Luis Pelaez, Inc.

Spending on older Americans has grown more rapidly than the economy or the overall budget. One of the main reasons is the rising cost of medical care.

The other main reason for rising spending on the elderly is that medical care has become much more expensive. Experts in health economics say that this is not mainly because the costs of medical care have risen. Instead, it is because progress in medicine has made it possible to do much more for the elderly. Many treatments that are now common, such as heart bypass surgery, were experimental, rare, or not yet developed 30 years ago. So Medicare now spends more because there are more useful ways to spend money on health care than ever before.

So should rising spending on the elderly be viewed as a burden on the budget or as a sign of progress? Probably both. ∎

> > > > > > > > > > > > > > > > > > > >

>>QUICK REVIEW

➤ There are three main types of government spending: spending on public goods, *social insurance*, and *redistribution of income*.

➤ Although the line between social insurance and redistribution is somewhat blurry, a program that is *means-tested* is usually considered redistribution and one that is not means-tested is considered social insurance.

➤ The U.S. government spends substantial sums on all three types of programs. Historically, spending on defense—a public good—was the largest component of federal spending. But today spending on social insurance, especially for older Americans, is considerably larger.

>>CHECK YOUR UNDERSTANDING 21-3

1. Unemployment insurance is financed by taxes on employed workers, who collect benefits if they become unemployed. Suppose that workers in Alaska are unemployed and workers in Florida are employed during even-numbered years, but the opposite is true during odd-numbered years. Explain why workers in these two states can benefit from an unemployment insurance program that covers both states.

2. Classify the following programs according to whether they redistribute income or provide social insurance.
   a. Natural disaster emergency relief
   b. Heating cost assistance for low-income families
   c. Health care for people over 65
   d. Aid grants to low income students

Solutions appear at back of book.

Poverty and Public Aid

Public aid—government spending that is means-tested and is intended to reduce poverty—is a relatively small part of government spending compared with social insurance. But it is the subject of intense debate, not only about how much public aid should be given but about the criteria for aid and its effect on society. Let's look at how poverty is defined, how it has changed over time, and how it is affected by public policy.

Defining Poverty

The **poverty line** is a minimum annual income that the government defines as adequate. Families whose income falls below the poverty line are considered poor.

What does it mean to be "poor"? Any definition is somewhat arbitrary. Since 1965, however, the U.S. government has maintained an official definition of the **poverty line:** a minimum annual income that is considered adequate. Families whose income falls below the poverty line are considered poor. The history of this official definition is described in For Inquiring Minds on page 509.

The poverty line depends on the size and composition of a family: in 2005 the poverty line for an adult living alone was $9,570, whereas the poverty line for a family of 4 was $19,350. Also, the official poverty line is adjusted each year to reflect changes in the cost of living. Contrary to some popular misconceptions, however, the poverty line has *not* been adjusted upwards over time to reflect the long-term rise in the average standard of living. This means that as the economy grows, and average incomes rise, you might expect the percentage of the population living below the poverty line to decline steadily. Has this actually happened?

Trends in Poverty

The **poverty rate** is the percentage of the population living below the poverty line.

Figure 21-7 shows the U.S. **poverty rate**—the percentage of the population living below the poverty line—from 1959 to 2004. As you can see, the poverty rate fell steeply during the 1960s and early 1970s. But since then progress has been much more questionable. The poverty rate rose from 1973 until 1993, then fell in the boom economy of the 1990s. But even at the end of that boom, in 2001, the poverty rate was no lower than it had been almost 30 years earlier.

The failure of the country to make clear progress against poverty has led to widespread debate both about the causes of poverty and about the nature and effectiveness of public aid. We turn first to the question of who is poor.

A Portrait of the Poor

Many Americans probably have in their minds a stereotyped image of poverty: an African-American or Hispanic family with no husband present, and the female head of household unemployed at least part of the time. This picture isn't completely off-base: poverty is disproportionately high among African-Americans and Hispanics as well as among female-headed households. But a majority of the poor don't fit the stereotype.

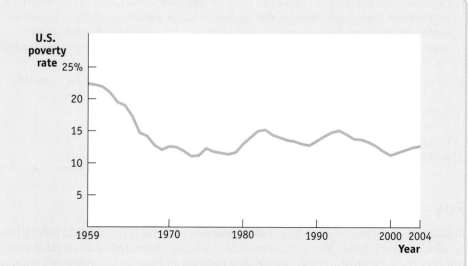

Figure 21-7

Trends in the U.S. Poverty Rate, 1959–2004

Poverty fell sharply from the 1960s to the early 1970s but has not shown a clear downward trend since then.
Source: U.S. Census Bureau

WHO DEFINED POVERTY?

Who decided how much income an American family needs to escape poverty? Mollie Orshansky! Orshansky, a research analyst at the Social Security Administration, developed initial estimates of the poverty line in 1963–1964.

Orshansky started by estimating the cost of buying an inexpensive but nutritionally adequate diet. She then observed that families with children spent about one-third of their income on food; so she argued that any family earning less than three times the cost of purchasing an adequate diet did not have adequate income.

Was this the right measure of poverty? When it was created, Orshansky's calculation made a lot of sense, and it has been the basis for U.S. poverty statistics ever since. But many experts now think that this measure of poverty is badly outdated because the composition of spending by low-income families has changed significantly since the 1960s. On average, the share of income expended on food has fallen to less than 20%, while the share spent on things such as housing, health care, transportation, and child care has risen. Many state governments have recognized this trend and now use an income benchmark of 150% to 200% of the poverty line to determine a family's eligibility for assistance programs (and some states use a benchmark as high as 275% to 300% of the poverty line).

In 2004, about 37 million Americans were in poverty—12.7 percent of the population. About one-quarter of the poor were African-American and a roughly equal number Hispanic. Among these two groups, poverty rates were well above the national average: 25 percent among blacks, 22 percent among Hispanics. But there was also widespread poverty among non-Hispanic whites, who had a poverty rate of 9 percent.

Female-headed families with no husband present had a very high poverty rate: 28 percent. Married couples were much less likely to be poor, with a poverty rate of only 6 percent; still, about 41 percent of poor families were married couples.

What really stands out from the data, however, is the association between poverty and lack of adequate employment. Adults who work full time are very unlikely to be poor (only 2.8 percent in 2004). Adults who work part time or have no work at all during the course of a year make up the great majority of the adult poor. Many industries, particularly in the retail and service sectors, now rely primarily on part-time workers. In addition to lacking benefits such as health plans, paid vacation days, and retirement benefits, most part-time work pays a lower hourly wage than comparable full-time work. As a result, many of the poor are *working poor*: workers whose income falls at or below the poverty line.

The Origins and Consequences of Poverty

Educational attainment clearly has a strong effect on income level—those with more education earn, on average, higher incomes than those with less education. And those with less education have, as a group, seen their fortunes decline over time: the average young, male non-college-educated worker now earns 25 percent less than someone in a similar situation in 1973. For females, the comparable number is 13 percent.

Like lack of education, lack of proficiency in English can create a barrier to higher income. For example, Mexican-born workers in the United States—two-thirds of whom have not graduated from high school and many of whom have poor English skills—earn less than half of what native-born men earn.

Although discrimination is less pervasive today than it was 30 years ago, it still generates a formidable barrier to advancement for many Americans. Nonwhites with comparable levels of education earn less and are less likely to be employed than whites. Women with similar qualifications earn lower incomes than men. Studies find that African-American males suffer persistent discrimination by employers in favor of whites, African-American women, and Hispanic immigrants.

In addition, one important source of poverty that should not be overlooked is bad luck coupled with the lack of a safety net. Without adequate health care coverage or savings, many families find themselves impoverished when a wage-earner loses a job or a family member falls seriously ill.

The consequences of poverty are often severe, particularly for children. More than 17 percent of children in the United States live in poverty. For their families, health care is often erratic, leading to further health problems that erode the ability to work. Affordable housing is frequently a problem that leads poor families to move often, disrupting school and work schedules. Because parental income is the single most important factor influencing children's later socioeconomic attainment, children raised in poverty have a greater likelihood of living in poverty as adults than do those raised in nonpoor families. Low income is strongly correlated with a low level of pre-school ability, and low preschool ability often leads to lower test scores in elementary school and higher high school dropout rates. Low-income children are at higher risk of mental health problems and behavioral disorders than the children of parents with higher income. And lower-income children are less likely to be covered by health insurance, leading to higher rates of illness and hospitalization. Poverty, in short, is not good for children.

Antipoverty Programs

Welfare is monetary aid to poor families.

Aid to the poor takes three main forms: *welfare, in-kind transfers,* and *negative income tax.* **Welfare** refers to monetary aid to poor families. The main welfare program in the United States is Temporary Assistance for Needy Families. This program does not aid simply anyone who is poor; it is available only to poor families with children and only for a limited time.

Critics of welfare have long argued that it creates perverse incentives for the poor. First, they argue that it tends to encourage family breakup, because a family with both spouses present may not qualify for aid. Second, they argue that it encourages out-of-wedlock births, because a single woman alone will not qualify for aid. These claims are hotly disputed by other analysts.

In any case, welfare is a generally unpopular program, and this has been reflected in public policy changes over time. Because payments to welfare recipients have not kept up with inflation, in real terms benefits are considerably less generous today than they were a generation ago. Also, welfare programs now contain time limits, so that welfare recipients—even single parents—must eventually seek work.

In-kind transfers provide poor families with specific goods and services.

In-kind transfers provide the poor not with cash but with specific goods and services. The most important in-kind transfers are *food stamps*, which can be used only to purchase food; *Medicaid*, which provides health insurance; and *housing subsidies*, which generally take the form of subsidies for rent.

A **negative income tax** is a program that supplements the earnings of low-income families.

Finally, economists use the term **negative income tax** for a program that supplements the earnings of low-income working families. The United States has a program known as the Earned Income Tax Credit (EITC), which provides additional income to millions of workers. Only workers who earn income are eligible for the EITC, and over a certain range of incomes the amount of EITC a worker receives increases with his or her earnings. That is, for low-wage workers the EITC acts as a negative income tax.

In 2003, married couples with two children earning less than $10,500 per year received payments from the government equal to 40 percent of their earnings. (Payments were slightly lower for single-parent families or workers without children.) At higher incomes the EITC is phased out, disappearing at an income of $34,692.

Taken together, these three programs provide substantial aid to poor families. This does not mean that there is a consensus about the size and nature of antipoverty programs. Some critics argue that the programs distort incentives and perpetuate poverty; we discuss this further in Economics in Action below. Others note that U.S. antipoverty programs are considerably less generous than comparable programs in other advanced countries.

economics in action

Old Poor, Young Poor

Over the past 30 years, the overall poverty rate has been roughly constant. But in some ways this stability is misleading: poverty has fallen for some groups but risen for others. The most striking difference involves age. Traditionally, poverty has been most common among two groups: the elderly, who often cannot work, and families with children, who often have difficulty making ends meet. As a result, poverty rates among the young and old have usually been higher than those for the population at large. As Table 21-5 shows, this traditional pattern was still true in 1973. Since then, however, the poverty rate for Americans age 65 and older has fallen sharply and is now below the average for the entire population. But the poverty rate for Americans under age 18 has risen.

Why this divergence? There are a number of reasons, but one important cause is the change in the nature of government spending over time. The items in the national bud-get that have experienced the most growth over time are Social Security and Medicare—programs that benefit older Americans and often help keep them above the poverty line. Public aid programs, which are more likely to benefit families with children, have received much less funding and have failed to keep pace with the rate of inflation. ■

TABLE 21-5

Poverty Rates in the United States

	1973	2003	2004
All Americans	11.1%	12.5%	12.7%
Americans under age 18	14.4	17.6	17.8
Americans age 65 and older	16.3	10.2	9.8

Source: U.S. Census Bureau

> >

>>CHECK YOUR UNDERSTANDING 21-4

1. Explain why the poverty rate has fallen for Americans over 65 since 1973 but has risen for Americans under 18.

2. Do you think that the introduction of a negative income tax makes it more or less likely that unemployed low-income adults will become employed? Explain.

3. The current U.S. poverty rate is no lower than it was in 1973 despite the fact that the poverty line has not been adjusted to take into account the long-term rise in the standard of living in the country since 1973. What does this imply about the change over time in the gap between the living standards of a family living at the poverty line and the living standards of the average family above the poverty line?

Solutions appear at back of book.

>> QUICK REVIEW

> Families are considered poor if their income falls below the *poverty line*. The overall *poverty rate* in the United States fell steadily until 1973, but since then it has moved up and down, with no clear trend.

> The most important factors contributing to poverty are lack of education, discrimination, and adverse events. The consequences of poverty are often severe, particularly for children.

> Families below the poverty line receive three main types of government aid: *welfare, in-kind transfers,* and *negative income taxes.*

The Big Debate: Taxes, Transfers, and Income Distribution

The great majority of Americans agree that the ability-to-pay principle should be given some weight in tax and spending policy—that high-income individuals should pay more in taxes than low-income individuals and that at least some public aid should be offered to the poor. But *how much* weight should ability to pay be given?

That is not a question of economic analysis; it is a political question, perhaps *the* political question. Roughly speaking, conservatives believe that at present the United States gives too much weight to the ability-to-pay principle, that taxes are excessively progressive, and that is too much redistribution of income. Liberals believe the opposite.

Although we can't resolve this debate, we can shed some light on it by clarifying the issues involved.

The Distribution of Income

A starting point for the big debate is to have a sense of how much families differ in their ability to pay—that is, of the distribution of income among families. Look back at Table 21-1: the second column summarizes the distribution of income among U.S. families in 2002. The numbers show a considerable amount of inequality: the poorest 20% of families received only 4.2% of the income, and the richest 20% received more than half of total U.S. income. Recent estimates suggest that the top 1% of families receive about 18% of total income. The average income among the top 1% is 18 times as high as the overall average income and 90 times as high as the average income of the poorest 20% of families.

Economists are in general agreement that these numbers overstate the true degree of inequality in America, for several reasons. One is that the incomes of individual families fluctuate over time: many of those near the bottom in any given year are having an unusually bad year and many of those at the top are having an unusually good one. Over time, their incomes will revert to a more normal level. So a table showing average incomes over, say, a 10-year period would not be quite as striking. Also, a family's income tends to vary over its life cycle: most people start off earning considerably less than they will later in life, then experience a considerable drop in income when they retire. The numbers in Table 21-1, which combine young workers, mature workers, and retirees all in the same pool, would therefore show considerable inequality even if all families had similar incomes at the same points in their lives.

Nonetheless, there is a considerable amount of genuine inequality in the United States. And for the last quarter-century the degree of inequality has been increasing. The causes of this increase in inequality are a subject of some controversy, but probably the most important cause is rapid technological change, which has increased the demand for highly skilled or talented workers more rapidly than the demand for other workers. Growing international trade may have contributed to inequality by allowing the United States to import labor-intensive products from low-wage countries rather than making them for itself. This depresses the wages of domestic workers employed in industries that compete with imports. Rising immigration may also be a source of growing inequality. On average, immigrants have lower education levels than native-born workers and increase the supply of low-skilled labor while depressing low-skilled wages.

Figure 21-8 shows one indicator of growing inequality: the percentage increase in average income within each quintile between 1979 and 2003. The average income of the poorest fifth of families rose 3.5%; that of families in the middle fifth rose 12.5%; that of families in the top fifth rose 45.7%. Not shown in the figure: the average income of families in the top 5% rose 68%. Clearly, the gap between the best-off and the worst-off families increased.

The fact that some people in the United States are extremely well-off—indeed, better off than ever before—but others remain quite poor leads advocates of income redistribution to argue for higher taxes on those with high incomes and greater aid to those with low incomes. Let's look briefly at their argument and then at the arguments that others make against redistribution.

The Case for Redistribution

Those who advocate more progressive taxation and redistribution of income to people in the lower part of the income distribution base their position on an extended version of the ability-to-pay principle. High-income families should pay high taxes, they argue, because they will still have after-tax income that is higher than average. Low-income families not only should not pay taxes, they should

Figure 21-8 Percentage Increases in Household Income by Income Group, 1979–2003

This graph shows that income inequality increased from 1979 to 2003: the incomes of higher-income households grew faster during this period than the incomes of lower-income families. The first quintile is the 20% of families with the lowest income, the second quintile the next poorest 20%, and so on. From 1979 to 2003, average income in the lowest quintile rose, but by only 3.5%. Meanwhile, average income in the top quintile rose by 45.7%.

Source: U.S. Census Bureau.

receive aid from the government, because even with that aid they will have incomes lower than average. So the redistribution is justified because the money transferred adds more to the welfare of the recipients than it subtracts from the welfare of the taxpayers.

Wouldn't the logical conclusion of this argument be that the government should tax away any income above the average and top up the income of anyone who makes less than the average? No, because even the most ardent advocates of progressive taxes and redistribution recognize that there is a trade-off between equity and efficiency—that the taxing and spending policies of the government must take care not to do too much damage to incentives. That brings us to the case, or rather cases, against income redistribution.

Arguments Against Income Redistribution

There are two different kinds of arguments against income redistribution. One is based on philosophical concerns about the proper role of government. Some political theorists believe that redistributing income is not a legitimate role of government—that government's role should be limited to maintaining the rule of law, providing public goods, and controlling externalities. We cannot go into this debate at length, but because it is an influential point of view, you should be aware that it exists.

The more conventional argument against taxing the rich and making transfers to the poor involves the trade-off between efficiency and equity. We've already seen part of this argument: a tax system that tries to put all of the burden on the very well off will have to be highly progressive. A highly progressive system implies high marginal tax rates, and high marginal tax rates reduce the incentive to work hard or otherwise increase a family's income. As a result, a highly progressive tax system makes society as a whole poorer, and may hurt even those who pay little or no tax. That's why even economists who strongly favor progressive taxation don't support a return to the extremely progressive system that prevailed in the 1950s, when the top marginal rate was more than 90 percent.

A similar trade-off between equity and efficiency occurs as a result of programs that aid people with low incomes. Consider the following example: suppose there is some means-tested benefit, worth $1,000 per year, that is available only to individuals with earnings of less than $10,000 per year. Now suppose that an individual is currently earning $9,800 per year and is deciding whether to take a new job that will raise his income to $10,200. He will actually make himself worse off by taking the job because he will lose the $1,000 government benefit.

This situation, in which earning more actually leaves an individual worse off, is known as a *notch*. It is a well-known problem with programs that aid the poor, and behaves much like a high marginal rate on income. Most programs are designed to avoid creating a notch. This is typically done by setting a sliding scale for benefits, so that they fall off gradually as the recipient's income rises rather than coming to an abrupt end. Even so, as Economics in Action on page 515 illustrates, means-tested programs have indeed led to high effective marginal tax rates for low-income workers.

The Politics of Equity and Efficiency

In the real world, however, decisions about how much efficiency to trade off for equity and vice versa aren't based on philosophical discussions. They're the result of elections in which political parties try to convince voters that their policies are in the voters' interests. But voters differ in their interests: a tax and spend policy that maximizes the welfare of a family earning $15,000 per year will look very different from a policy that maximizes the welfare of a family earning $1.5 million a year.

Generally speaking, voters toward the bottom of the income distribution favor highly progressive taxes and strong redistribution, with voters toward the top of the distribution favoring less progressive taxes and less generous redistribution. There are, of course, many exceptions—there are billionaires who, on principle, favor high taxes and generous poverty programs, and there are people with low income who strongly believe that redistribution undermines self-reliance. Still, there are clear differences in the interests of different voters. Whose interests prevail?

Let's suppose that voters can be lined up in order of the policy they prefer. In each panel of Figure 21-9, the horizontal axis shows the preferred share of government spending in national income; this share will be larger if the government engages in more redistribution and smaller if it engages in less redistribution. (We put higher government spending on the left of each panel, reflecting the long tradition under which politicians who favor redistribution are considered to the "left" of politicians who don't.) On the vertical axis are hypothetical percentages of voters who prefer a given level of government spending. For example, reading from left to right, 1% of voters are willing to sacrifice a lot of efficiency in order to increase equity and favor government spending equal to 50% of total income. Another 3% prefer spending of 45% of total income, and so on. (Such preferences typically reflect voters' own financial positions, but that's not necessary for the argument.) A famous result called the *median voter theorem* says that if voter preferences can be represented this way, and that if two parties compete for votes, actual policies will reflect the preferences of the *median voter*—the voter in the middle of our left-right lineup. In both panels of Figure 21-9, the median voter prefers government spending equal to 30% of total income.

The two panels of Figure 21-9 illustrate how the median voter argument works. In panel (a), we suppose that party D stakes out a position that is well to the left of the median voter's preferences, advocating spending equal to 45% of total income. If a rival party, R, advocates a position slightly to D's right, it can get the votes of all those

Figure 21-9   The Median Voter Theorem

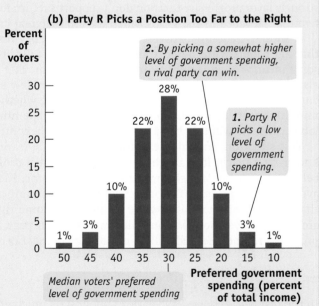

In this hypothetical example, voters have preferences about the level of government spending as a share of total income, measured from high levels on the left to low levels on the right. In both panels, the height of each bar represents the percent of voters who prefer a given level of spending. The median voter prefers spending equal to 30% of total income. In panel (a), party D picks a position—spending equal to 45% of total income—that is well to the left of the median voter's preferences. A rival party can easily win by picking a policy that is closer to the center, leaving D with only the voters represented by blue bars. In panel (b), party R picks a position that is well to the right of the median voter's preferences. Again, a rival party can win by picking a position closer to the center, leaving R with only the voters represented by red bars.

voters who prefer a smaller level of government spending. D will get only the voters indicated by the blue bars—4% of the electorate—and R will get the other 96%, indicated by the red bars. So party D, by choosing a position to the left of the median voter, makes it easy for R to win.

Panel (b) shows the opposite case: R stakes out a position well to the right of the median voter, advocating spending equal to only 15% of total income. By choosing a position slightly to R's left, D can ensure that R gets only the voters indicated by the red bars—and win. Clearly, then, the only way parties can avoid giving their opponents an easy way to win elections is to pick positions close to the middle—positions that reflect the preferences of the median voter. We can summarize the result as follows: in an election by majority rule where voters decide how much of a given policy action should be taken, the **median voter theorem** says that actual policies will most closely reflect the preferences of the median voter.

In practice, however, things are a bit more complicated. Politics isn't one-dimensional: parties can compete on other issues, such as foreign policy. Also, political activists and interest groups within each party tend to pull parties' political positions away from the center. In the United States, statistical studies by political scientists suggest that the two major parties held similar positions on economic issues a generation ago but have diverged since then: Republicans are currently well to the right of Democrats on economic policy. Still, the median voter theory is a useful model for understanding how democracies resolve the trade-off between equity and efficiency.

> In an election by majority rule where voters decide how much of a given policy action should be taken, the **median voter theorem** says that actual policies will most clearly reflect the preferences of the median voter.

economics in action

Effective Marginal Tax Rates on the Poor

Because means-tested programs are available only to families with sufficiently low incomes, families that manage to increase their earnings find that they lose benefits. So in effect they face a high marginal tax rate on their earnings, although the stated marginal tax rate is quite low.

The importance of this effect was emphasized in a 2002 study by Laurence Kotlikoff, an economist at Boston University, and two of his students. This study tried to calculate how much hypothetical couples with different levels of income get to keep of an additional dollar of income once the whole range of tax and benefits policies are taken into account.

They found that almost all couples in the United States face an effective marginal tax rate of more than 50 percent. The highest rates—up to 70 percent—aren't at the top of the income distribution; they're toward the lower end, where families find that higher income leads to reductions in means-tested benefits. ■

> >

>> CHECK YOUR UNDERSTANDING 21-5

1. Suppose that the government offered free health care to families with incomes of less than $15,000 per year, but no health care assistance for families with incomes of $15,000 per year or more.
   a. What problem would this program create for incentives? Explain this problem in terms of a marginal tax rate.
   b. How would you restructure the program to make the problem less severe? Again, explain in terms of a marginal tax rate.
2. Describe the trade-off between equity and efficiency in the following programs:
   a. A program that supplements the income of farmers during poor crop years
   b. A program that pays rent for low-income families

Solutions appear at back of book.

Economists and the Tax System

As the opening story of Britain's poll tax suggested, tempers often run high when it comes to tax policy. The same is true when it comes to government spending for social insurance or income redistribution. What makes these disputes especially hard to resolve is that there is *no right answer*: there is always a trade-off between equity and efficiency, and two people who agree about that trade-off can disagree about what weight to give to each goal.

What role can economics play in this eternal debate? First, the economist can try to keep the debate honest. Politics being politics, those who advocate policy changes that will increase equity are always tempted to deny that their proposals will come at the expense of efficiency, and vice versa. It is the job of economists to point out when a proposed change in taxes or spending is being offered under false pretenses.

The other job of economists is to point out opportunities for clear improvement. An ideal tax system would offer no way to improve efficiency without reducing equity. Real tax systems probably can be made better, allowing progress toward both goals, and economic analysis should be used to show the way.

• A LOOK AHEAD •

We have now almost completed our study of microeconomics. We've learned a lot about how the economy works and about the role of government policy.

But do the models we have studied—models that reflect a couple of centuries of economic analysis and observation—still apply? In recent years there have been dramatic changes on the economic scene, as information technology has transformed the way we live and work. Some people talk of a "new economy" whose rules differ drastically from those of the past. In the next chapter, we'll look at how technology changes microeconomics—and how it doesn't.

SUMMARY

1. **Tax efficiency** is achieved when the costs of a tax—the sum of the deadweight loss or excess burden due to distorted incentives and the **administrative costs** of the tax—are minimized. However, **tax fairness,** or **tax equity,** ensuring that the right people pay taxes, is also a goal of tax policy.

2. There are two major principles of tax fairness, the **benefits principle** and the **ability-to-pay principle.** The most efficient tax, a **lump-sum tax,** does not distort incentives but performs badly in terms of fairness. The fairest taxes in terms of the ability-to-pay principle, however, distort incentives the most and perform badly on efficiency grounds. So in a well-designed tax system, there is a **trade-off between equity and efficiency.**

3. Every tax consists of a **tax base,** which defines what is taxed, and a **tax structure.** Different tax bases give rise to different taxes—the **income tax, payroll tax, sales tax, profits tax, property tax,** and **wealth tax.** A **proportional tax** is the same percentage of the tax base for all taxpayers.

4. A tax is **progressive** if higher-income people pay a higher percentage of their income in taxes than lower income people, and **regressive** if they pay a lower percentage. Progressive

taxes are often justified by the ability-to-pay principle. However, a progressive tax on income can distort incentives to work, save, and invest because the **marginal tax rate on income** is higher than the **average tax rate on income.**

5. Money raised in taxes is spent in three main ways: for **social insurance** and for **redistribution of income** (which are implemented through **transfer payments** to individuals) and for public goods. Defense spending, a public good, used to be the biggest item, but now social insurance, largely for older residents, is the largest item.

6. The **poverty line** is an estimate of the minimum annual income needed to achieve an acceptable standard of living. The **poverty rate** is the fraction of the population with incomes below the poverty line. Despite rising average incomes, the poverty rate in the United States has shown no clear trend over the past 30 years.

7. The most important causes of poverty are lack of education, discrimination, and adverse events. The effects of poverty are often severe, particularly for children.

8. Aid to the poor takes three main forms: **welfare,** cash payments to the poor; **in-kind transfers** such as food stamps, Medicaid, and housing subsidies; and **negative income taxes.**

9. Income redistribution is often justified by the inequality of income distribution. But a highly progressive tax system makes society as a whole poorer, a fact that limits the level of progressivity that supporters advocate. Like progressive taxation, redistribution forces a trade-off between equity and efficiency. An example of this is a **means-tested** program, which places high effective marginal tax rate on low-income families.

10. According to the **median voter theorem,** in an election by majority rule where voters decide how much of a given policy action to undertake, the outcome will most closely reflect the preferences of the median voter. Consequently, parties will choose positions close to the one preferred by the median voter. But for various reasons, this result has not happened in recent American politics.

KEY TERMS

Tax efficiency, p. 494
Tax fairness, p. 494
Tax equity, p. 494
Administrative costs, p. 495
Benefits principle, p. 496
Ability-to-pay principle, p. 496
Lump-sum tax, p. 496
Trade-off between equity and efficiency, p. 496
Tax base, p. 498
Tax structure, p. 498

Income tax, p. 499
Payroll tax, p. 499
Sales tax, p. 499
Profits tax, p. 499
Property tax, p. 499
Wealth tax, p. 499
Proportional tax, p. 499
Progressive tax, p. 499
Regressive tax, p. 499
Average tax rate on income, p. 500
Marginal tax rate on income, p. 500

Social insurance, p. 504
Redistribution of income, p. 504
Transfer payment, p. 504
Means-tested, p. 504
Poverty line, p. 508
Poverty rate, p. 508
Welfare, p. 510
In-kind transfers, p. 510
Negative income tax, p. 510
Median voter theorem, p. 515

PROBLEMS

1. Assume that the demand for gasoline is inelastic. The government imposes a sales tax on gasoline. The tax revenue is used to fund research into clean fuel alternatives to gasoline, which will improve the air we all breathe.

   a. Who bears more of the excess burden of this tax: consumers or producers? Show in a diagram who bears how much of the excess burden.

   b. Is this tax based on the benefits principle or the ability-to-pay principle? Explain.

2. Assess the following three taxes in terms of the benefits principle versus the ability-to-pay principle.

   a. A tax on gasoline that finances maintenance of state roads

   b. An 8% tax on imported goods valued in excess of $800 per household brought in on passenger flights

   c. Airline-flight landing fees that pay for air-traffic control

3. Consider the following deductions, which reduce the amount of income tax an individual must pay. Can they be justified on the basis of the ability-to-pay principle?

   a. Amount of charitable contributions

   b. Amount of interest paid on a mortgage

   c. Number of dependent children

4. You are advising the government on how to pay for national defense. There are two proposals for a tax system to fund national defense. Under both proposals, the tax base is an individual's income. Under proposal A, all citizens pay exactly the same lump-sum tax, regardless of income. Under proposal B, individuals with higher income pay a greater proportion of their income in taxes.

   a. Is the tax in proposal A progressive, proportional, or regressive? What about the tax in proposal B?

   b. Is the tax in proposal A based on the ability-to-pay principle or on the benefits principle? What about the tax in proposal B?

   c. In terms of efficiency, which tax is better? Explain.

5. Each of the following tax proposals has income as the tax base. In a diagram with the tax base—income, ranging from $0 to $50,000—on the horizontal axis and the taxes paid on the vertical axis, draw the income tax for each of the following tax proposals. For an individual who earns $25,000, what is the marginal tax rate under each proposal? What is the average tax rate for that individual? Is the marginal tax rate higher than, lower than, or equal to the average tax rate? Accordingly, classify the tax as being proportional, progressive, or regressive.

   a. All income is taxed at 20%.

   b. All income up to $10,000 is tax-free. All income above $10,000 is taxed at a constant rate of 20%.

   c. All income between $0 and $10,000 is taxed at 10%. All income between $10,000 and $20,000 is taxed at 20%. All income higher than $20,000 is taxed at 30%.

   d. Each individual who earns more than $10,000 pays a lump-sum tax of $10,000. If the individual's income is less than $10,000, that individual pays in tax exactly what his or her income is.

6. In Transylvania the basic income tax system is fairly simple. The first 40,000 sylvers (the official currency of Transylvania) earned each year are free of income tax. Any additional income is taxed at a rate of 25%. In addition, every individual pays a social security tax, which is calculated as follows: all income up to 80,000 sylvers is taxed at an additional 20%, but there is no additional social security tax on income above 80,000 sylvers.

   a. Calculate the average and the marginal tax rates for Transylvanians with the following levels of income: 20,000 sylvers, 40,000 sylvers, 80,000 sylvers, and 120,000 sylvers.

   b. For each of the income levels in part (a), is the tax system progressive, regressive, or proportional?

7. You work for the Council of Economic Advisers, providing economic advice to the White House. The president wants to overhaul the income tax system and asks your advice. Suppose that the current income tax system consists of a proportional tax of 10% on all income and that there is one person in the country who earns $110 million; everyone else earns less than $100 million. The president proposes a tax cut targeted at the very rich so that the new tax system would consist of a proportional tax of 10% on all income up to $100 million and a marginal tax rate of 0% (no tax) on income above $100 million. You are asked to evaluate this tax proposal.

   a. For incomes of $100 million or less, is this tax system progressive, regressive, or proportional? For incomes of more than $100 million? Explain.

   b. Would this tax system create more or less tax revenue, other things equal? Is this tax system more or less efficient than the current tax system? Explain.

8. In the city of Metropolis, there are 100 residents, each of whom lives until age 75. Residents of Metropolis have the following incomes over their lifetime: Through age 14, they earn nothing. From age 15 until age 29, they earn 200 metros (the currency of Metropolis) per year. From age 30 to age 49, they earn 400 metros. From age 50 to age 64, they earn 300 metros. And finally at age 65 they retire and are paid a pension of 100 metros per year until they die at age 75. Everyone consumes each year whatever their income is that year (that is, there is no saving and no borrowing). Currently, 20 residents are 10 years old, 20 residents are 20 years old, 20 residents are 40 years old, 20 residents are 60 years old, and 20 residents are 70 years old.

   a. Study the income distribution among all residents of Metropolis. Split the population into quintiles according to their income. How much income does a resident in the lowest quintile have? in the second, third, fourth, and top

quintiles? Which share of total income of all residents goes to the residents in each quintile? Construct a table showing the share of total income that goes to each quintile. Does this income distribution show inequality?

   b. Now look only at the 20 residents of Metropolis who are currently 40 years old, and study the income distribution among only those residents. Split those 20 residents into quintiles according to their income. How much income does a resident in the lowest quintile have? in the second, third, fourth, and top quintiles? Which share of total income of all 40-year-olds goes to the residents in each quintile? Does this income distribution show inequality?

   c. What is the relevance of these examples for assessing data on the distribution of income in any country?

9. The country of Marxland has the following income tax and social insurance system. Each citizen's income is taxed at an average tax rate of 100%. A social insurance system then provides transfers to each citizen such that each citizen's after-tax income is exactly equal. That is, each citizen gets (through a government transfer payment) an equal share of the income tax revenue. What is the incentive for one individual citizen to work and earn income? What will the total tax revenue in Marxland be? What will be the after-tax income (including the transfer payment) for each citizen? Do you think such a tax system that creates perfect equality will work?

10. In the city of Notchingham, each worker is paid a wage rate of $10 per hour. Notchingham administers its own unemployment benefit, which is structured as follows: If you are unemployed (that is, if you do not work at all), you get unemployment benefits (a transfer from the government) of $50 per day. As soon as you work for only one hour, the unemployment benefit is completely withdrawn. That is, there is a "notch" in the benefit system.

   a. How much income does an unemployed person have per day? How much daily income does an individual have who works four hours per day? How many hours do you need to work to earn just the same as if you were unemployed?

   b. Will anyone ever accept a part-time job that requires working four hours per day, rather than being unemployed?

   c. Suppose that Notchingham now changes the way in which the unemployment benefit is withdrawn. For each additional dollar that an individual earns, $0.50 of the unemployment benefit is withdrawn. How much daily income does an individual now have who works four hours per day? Is there an incentive now to work four hours per day rather than being unemployed?

>**web...** To continue your study and review of concepts in this chapter, please visit the Krugman/Wells website for quizzes, animated graph tutorials, web links to helpful resources, and more.

www.worthpublishers.com/krugmanwells

>> Technology, Information Goods, and Network Externalities

SUING CHILDREN

IN SEPTEMBER 2003, THE RECORDING Industry Association of America—a group representing big record labels—sued Brianna Lahara, a 12-year-old schoolgirl, for copyright infringement. Her mother settled the case for $2,000.

Was Brianna in the music piracy business? Not exactly. All she did was participate in Kazaa, a file-swapping network whose members use the Internet to download digitized music, among other things, from each others' computers. But recordings of musical performances are copyrighted—and by swapping files of these recordings with other Kazaa members, Brianna was indeed breaking the law. By the way, the reason the recording industry went after individuals like Brianna was that the company behind

Kazaa—chastened by the legal action brought against Napster, the company that made file-swapping famous—insisted that it bore no responsibility for what other people did with its software.

But what about the economics of the case? Are people who swap music files truly engaged in theft? File-swappers and the companies whose software facilitates their activities say no—they're not making off with physical goods, and they aren't doing anyone any harm. If I listen to a bootleg recording of my favorite band, I don't make the band's music any less available to you. Or do I?

The fight over file-swapping flared up just two years after another high-tech legal drama. In 2001 a federal judge ordered the

What you will learn in this chapter:

➤ The growing importance of goods embodying new technology and the unique economic problems they pose

➤ How the economics of **information goods** differs from that of other goods

➤ The importance of **network externalities** and why they lead a consumer to prefer the good used by most other consumers

➤ Why information goods can lead to **critical mass** effects, in which a market suddenly explodes in size, or to **tipping,** in which the market swings to favor one good over another

➤ The special dilemmas information goods pose for antitrust policy

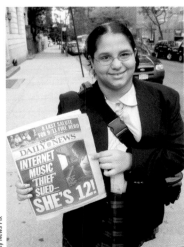

Photographer's Choice

Daily News Pix

New technology has changed the way we access music, but it has also created new economic challenges. Brianna Lahara (shown at right) learned this the hard way.

breakup of Microsoft, the producer of the Windows software that runs most personal computers, only to have his ruling thrown out on appeal. Both cases vividly illustrate the extent to which changing technology—and in particular the growing importance of digital products—is changing the economic landscape and presenting new problems for economic policy.

Why does technology change the landscape? Because products like software and music files, unlike most of the goods and services traded in an economy, are *information goods:* their value comes not from their physical attributes but from the information they embody. They are also goods whose value to a consumer depends in large part on how many other consumers use the same good. As we'll see, the growing importance of information goods takes some issues we have discussed in earlier chapters—monopoly, positive externalities, and the dilemmas of antitrust policy—to a new and higher level.

The Economics of Information Goods

Even now most workers in the U.S. economy are employed in the production of conventional goods and services: cars, houses, haircuts, and so on. But considerable resources are now also devoted to producing **information goods**—products whose value comes not from their physical characteristics but from the information they embody.

An **information good** is a good whose value comes from the information it contains.

There is no sharp line dividing information goods from other goods. A computer file is clearly an information good, but conventional goods also contain information. For example, the value of a piece of furniture is partly the result of the knowledge of the furniture-maker, embodied in its form. But although almost all recordings sold these days are in digital form and can be sent over the Internet, many consumers still prefer a physical CD to a downloadable file. By any definition, however, the importance of information goods in the economy has clearly been increasing. As we'll see next, this creates some new challenges for a market economy.

Producing and Selling Information Goods

The fight over file-swapping is widely seen as a landmark dispute, with significance that goes well beyond the music industry. Why? Because the dispute poses, in a very clear way, the question of how society should deal with the production, sale, and distribution of information goods.

To understand why this is an issue, let's start by examining the production costs for an information good. It seems clear that the marginal cost of producing an additional unit of an information good is very low. For example, once the master of a recording has been created, the cost of making an additional digital copy—or burning a copy onto a compact disc—is very small. Similarly, it costs Microsoft very little to produce and ship another copy of Windows. Indeed, many information goods have nearly zero marginal cost.

But that doesn't mean that an information good is costless to produce. A master recording requires many hours of work by songwriters, musicians, audio technicians, producers, and so on, many of them working with expensive equipment. Producing a large software program may require tens of thousands of hours of work by highly skilled and highly paid programmers. These costs are, however, *fixed*—they are the same regardless of how many copies of the product are sold. Whether a recording goes multiple platinum or is never released, the costs of making it are the same. So the characteristic cost structure of information goods involves *high fixed cost* and *very low marginal cost*. This means that information goods have the kind of cost structure we discussed in our analysis of natural monopolies in Chapter 14.

Figure 22-1 illustrates the typical cost structure of an information good and its consequences. Here we imagine that Def Ear Ventures, a record company, is considering producing a new recording by a group that has a large but not huge potential audience. If the recording is made, Def Ear will have a monopoly on its sales, since it owns the copyright. But the company must decide whether the recording is worth producing.

Def Ear's management believes that the demand curve for the new recording is shown by the demand schedule in Figure 22-1: at a price of $10, sales are zero, but if the recording were free, 1 million people would take it. The graph in Figure 22-1 shows the demand curve D, along with its associated marginal revenue curve MR. (Remember from Chapter 14 that a monopolist's marginal revenue curve is always below the demand curve.)

Figure 22-1

The Profit-Maximizing Quantity of an Information Good

An information good such as a musical recording has high fixed cost and low marginal cost, a situation similar to natural monopoly. Here, Def Ear's fixed cost is $1.5 million, and the marginal cost of manufacturing a single recording is zero. As a result, the average total cost curve, ATC, is downward sloping. Given the demand curve, D, with its associated marginal revenue curve, MR, the profit-maximizing quantity of output is 500,000 recordings, the quantity at which marginal revenue equals marginal cost, as indicated by the optimal point M. The profit-maximizing price, P_M, is $5, the average total cost, ATC_M, is $3, resulting in a per-unit profit of $2. **>web...**

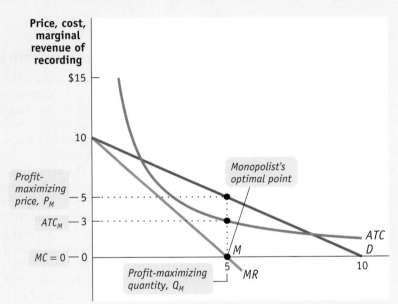

Demand for Recording		Production Cost of Recording		
Price of recording	Quantity of recordings demanded (hundreds of thousands)	Quantity of recordings produced (hundreds of thousands)	Fixed cost (millions)	Average total cost
$10	0	0	$1.5	—
9	1	1	1.5	$15.00
8	2	2	1.5	7.50
7	3	3	1.5	5.00
6	4	4	1.5	3.75
5	5	5	1.5	3.00
4	6	6	1.5	2.50
3	7	7	1.5	2.14
2	8	8	1.5	1.88
1	9	9	1.5	1.67
0	10	10	1.5	1.50

The company also believes that it will cost $1.5 million to produce the master recording, but that no additional costs will arise from distributing it. This cost structure is also shown in Figure 22-1. Average total cost is equal to $1.5 million divided by the number of recordings sold; so average total cost falls as the number of recordings sold increases, leading to the downward-sloping average total cost curve *ATC*. When only 100,000 recordings are sold, the average total cost per recording is $15, but the average total cost is $1.50 when 1,000,000 recordings are sold. Marginal cost, though, is always zero.

We can apply the *optimal output rule* from Chapters 9 and 14 to find Def Ear's profit-maximizing quantity. The company should produce the quantity at which marginal revenue equals marginal cost, as indicated by the optimal point *M*. Because marginal cost is zero, the profit-maximizing quantity, Q_M, is 500,000 recordings, the quantity at which marginal revenue is equal to zero.

The price at this profit-maximizing quantity, P_M, is $5 per recording and the average total cost, ATC_M, is $3 per recording. So the recording is profitable: Def Ear earns $2 per recording sold, generating a profit of $1 million on sales of 500,000 recordings.

Pricing Problems for Information Goods

The economic analysis we just applied to Def Ear's recording is standard monopoly theory. So what makes an information good different from any other good?

The answer is illustrated by the problem of file-swapping. Suppose that a music-copying technology, such as the one exploited by file-swappers, allows some potential buyers to download copies of Def Ear's new recording for free. Is this good or bad from an economic perspective?

It depends on whether the recording would still be produced. If Def Ear, knowing that some customers will make free copies, still produces the recording, free downloading increases total surplus. Remember, the marginal cost to the company of producing one more copy is zero. So inefficiency arises whenever anyone decides not to buy the recording because the price is greater than zero. If a person who wouldn't have bought the recording downloads a free copy, the music company doesn't lose anything, the listener gains something, and total surplus increases.

Figure 22-2 shows the gains to total surplus from free copying, compared with the original monopoly outcome: they are equal to the area of the triangle labeled *E*, the gain in consumer surplus from letting those who would not otherwise have bought the recording listen to the music for free. Q_O, 1 million copies, is the socially optimal quantity of output because at Q_O, the marginal benefit to the consumer of the last copy (the millionth copy) is equal to marginal cost—that is, zero. Those who defend file-swapping are in effect basing their argument on these potential gains to total surplus represented by the area *E*.

This analysis may look familiar: it is basically the same as the analysis of *artificially scarce goods* in Chapter 20. These are goods that are nonrival in consumption, so the marginal cost of allowing an additional individual to consume the good is zero. For such goods, efficiency is achieved when the price to consumers is zero.

But you may already have seen the problem: consumers can't download music that hasn't been produced. If Def Ear expects many listeners to download its recording for free—not just those who would not otherwise have bought the recording, but some or all of those who *would* have bought one—producing the master recording won't be profitable in the first place.

MOZART DIED PENNILESS.

BUMMER. WAS EVERYONE GETTIN' HIS TUNES FREE OFF 'NAPSTER'?

MIKE LUCKOVICH
ATLANTA CONSTITUTION©

By permission of Mike Luckovich and Creators Syndicate, Inc.

The Problem of Achieving Efficiency with an Information Good

The profit-maximizing record company behaves like a monopolist and will produce 500,000 recordings, Q_M, leading to consumer surplus of area A and profit or producer surplus of area B. Area C represents the producer's total cost. But the efficient quantity is 1 million recordings, Q_O, the quantity at which price is equal to marginal cost. Offering the good for free leads to a gain in total surplus of area E. Knowing, however, that it will be forced to provide the good for free is likely to lead the music company to forgo producing the good altogether. **>web...**

And if the recording isn't produced, both Def Ear and its potential consumers are worse off than if the recording were produced, even if it is priced above marginal cost. In Figure 22-2, if Def Ear is able to charge the profit-maximizing monopoly price of $5, it earns enough to cover its total cost, measured by the area of the rectangle C, and earn profits equal to the area of the rectangle B. The profits represented by the area B are the producer surplus compared to a situation in which the good is not produced at all. In addition, consumers receive the consumer surplus measured by the area of the triangle A. So if the company is deterred from producing the recording, both producer and consumer surplus (the sum of areas A and B) are sacrificed.

Clearly, then, information goods create a special tension. Monopoly is a bad thing, other things equal: it is inefficient to charge a price that is above marginal cost. But the expectation of monopoly profits is necessary to induce the company to produce the good at all. Indeed, economists generally agree that when it comes to information goods, a *temporary* monopoly may be the necessary price of progress.

Why temporary? As we will now see, both law and natural forces tend to limit the duration of the monopolies associated with information goods.

Property Rights in Information

The conundrum we have just seen is not new; indeed, it has plagued inventors for centuries. Some, like Samuel Morse, who invented the telegraph in 1837, were criticized for allowing their inventions to become the source of monopoly power. Others, like Eli Whitney, who invented the cotton gin in 1793, couldn't make money from their inventions. (Whitney's design was easy to copy, and he was never able to enforce his patent.) But the growing importance of information goods has made the dilemma more critical today than ever before. How has it been dealt with?

To make it worthwhile for people to incur the cost of producing information goods, they must be given some kind of property rights to the information the goods embody that, in turn, allows them to earn revenue. Traditionally this has been done through

A **patent** gives an inventor a temporary monopoly in the use or sale of an invention; a **copyright** similarly gives the creator of a literary or artistic work sole rights to profit from that work.

two closely related legal instruments: **patents** and **copyrights.** Both instruments give creators of knowledge property rights to the knowledge. Patents give inventors the sole right to make, use, or sell their invention for a period that in most countries lasts between 16 and 20 years. Copyrights give the creators of literary or artistic works a similar monopoly for a longer period. One of the strange aspects of the digital revolution, by the way, is the blurring of the distinction between items subject to patent law and those subject to copyright law. Is a piece of software, which takes the form of thousands of lines of program code, an invention or a literary work? Because copyrights last much longer than patents, millions or even billions of dollars depend on how that question is answered.

The justification for patent and copyright law is clear from our earlier discussion. If inventors were not protected by patents, they would gain little reward from their efforts: as soon as a valuable invention was made public, other people would copy it and sell products based on it. And if inventors could not expect to profit from their inventions, they would not incur the costs of invention in the first place. So the law gives a temporary monopoly through the creation of temporary property rights to encourage invention. In effect, the law tries to ensure that the gains measured by the areas *A* and *B* in Figure 22-2 take place.

But why are patents temporary? Again, Figure 22-2 illustrates the logic that underlies the law. As long as production of an information good is assured, it is efficient to set its price at marginal cost. But granting a permanent monopoly means creating a permanent gap between price and marginal cost. As a result, the gains from making the invention freely available, measured by the area *E*, would be permanently forgone.

Patent and copyright laws try to strike a compromise. Inventors are granted a temporary monopoly, which, it is hoped, will compensate them for the cost of invention. Because the monopoly eventually ends, the gap between marginal cost and marginal benefit is ultimately eliminated.

Because the length of the temporary monopoly cannot be tailored to specific cases, this system is imperfect and leads to some missed opportunities. Although some potential inventions are not created because the property rights don't last long enough, some monopolies go on longer than necessary. So the length of patents involves a trade-off. Furthermore, it's not clear whether the actual duration of patents makes the best of this trade-off.

FOR INQUIRING MINDS
PROTECTING MICKEY MOUSE

Until 1998 copyright law in the United States gave individual authors the sole right to publish their works for their lives, plus 50 years. Works of corporate ownership received 75 years of protection. But the Sonny Bono Copyright Term Extension Act of 1998 (yes, that's its real name) extended copyrights to 70 years beyond the life of the author and 95 years for corporate creations.

As we've explained, setting the duration of patents and copyrights involves a trade-off: nobody knows whether the new, longer copyrights are better or worse for the economy. But economists and consumer advocates were outraged at the 1998 act because it made the copyright extension *retroactive:* existing copyrights, including many that would have expired in the near future, suddenly got a new lease on life.

This made no sense from an economic point of view. The fixed costs on a decades-old artistic creation had already been incurred, so extending the copyright wouldn't lead to more creation. The only effect was to prolong the inefficiency of monopoly—and, of course, to sustain the monopoly profits of the copyright's owner.

Not surprisingly, the act was passed in large part because of lobbying from big entertainment companies, especially Disney. You see, Mickey Mouse was introduced as a character in 1928; without the act, he would have entered the public domain in 2003; now he is scheduled to enter the public domain in 2023. Critics of the 1998 bill often refer to it as "the Mickey Mouse protection act."

In any case, the effectiveness of patents and copyrights varies, depending on the characteristics of the product and industry. In some industries, patents are a highly effective protection for innovators and are the principal incentive for invention. Economics in Action below describes one such industry, pharmaceuticals. In other industries, however, innovations are less easy to patent. For example, the innovation may not be a discrete, patentable invention as much as a combination of existing ideas. A case in point is Wal-Mart, which became the nation's number-one retailer by, among other things, building large stores away from traditional downtowns, and using information technology to manage inventories efficiently. Nothing in that system could be patented, yet the combination gave Wal-Mart a huge cost advantage over competitors. Or it may be possible for competitors to engage in what is known as "reverse engineering": taking a patented product apart, figuring out how it works and how it was made, then developing something similar that avoids violating the letter (but perhaps not the spirit) of the patent.

Even in cases where innovations cannot be patented, however, innovators often have "first-mover" advantages over potential rivals that allow them to establish temporary monopoly positions. The innovating firm's head start in production can give it a technological advantage. If reputation is important to consumers, the first firm into a market can establish brand-name recognition. And in an industry characterized by *network externalities,* which we describe later in this chapter, the first firm in an industry can have a powerful advantage. All of these first-mover advantages arise because reverse engineering and other forms of copying take time.

A good, relatively recent example of first-mover advantage is Amazon.com, the first large-scale online book retailer. Its leadership is based not on patents—other online booksellers offer similar services—but on the advantages of size and name recognition among book buyers.

Such first-mover created monopoly positions, unlike those created by patents, are real even though they have no legal standing. Despite the fact that companies don't have legal property rights to their innovation, they are able to use their head start to gain a privileged market position. Even so, the monopoly positions established by innovators tend to erode over time, much as if patents were expiring. There are two reasons for this. One is that eventually competitors manage to duplicate the innovation. The other is that newer innovators come up with products that make the original innovation obsolete. For example, in the late 1990s AOL dominated the residential market for Internet access, which at that time relied almost completely on dial-up connections. But its position has rapidly eroded in recent years as broadband access via DSL and cable has become widely available at home.

So temporary monopoly tends to be the norm for many kinds of innovation, including those that cannot be effectively protected by patents.

economics in action

Drugs on the Market

The trade-off between the good aspects of a monopoly (it encourages innovation) and the bad aspects (it discourages consumption) is vividly illustrated by the pharmaceutical industry.

It may not be apparent that prescription drugs are information goods. But once they have been developed, most drugs are relatively inexpensive to manufacture. Most of their cost comes from the resources required for research and development. In other words, the drug embodies the information created by researchers, which gives it a high fixed cost but a low marginal cost.

How high are these fixed costs? One study, conducted in 2001, found that developing a successful drug costs, on average, about $800 million. Another study, which included spending on failed drugs (for every successful drug, several unsuccessful ones are developed) and marketing campaigns, came up with an average cost of $1.7 billion per successful drug.

Drugs are protected by patents, which give the producer a temporary monopoly. As with other patents, this monopoly lasts 20 years. But in the case of drugs, a 20-year patent length is misleading. Pharmaceutical companies normally receive a patent after laboratory testing suggests that a drug might be medically useful. However, before a company can sell a drug it must go through a series of clinical tests on groups of human subjects to demonstrate that the drug is safe and effective. These tests often take more than a decade—and sometimes as much as 14 years. So the actual period during which a drug company can make use of its monopoly can be as short as 6 years. After that, it will face competition from other companies that produce versions of the drug. So some observers have wondered whether the 20-year patent life on drugs is too short because it does not give enough incentive for research and development.

Still, the monopoly position of a patent holder means that many patients end up paying high prices for medicine that is actually cheap to produce. In some cases, this means that people can't afford medicine that might be significant to their well-being, and even save their lives. ∎

—< < < < < < < < < < < < < < < < <

1. Which of the following are information goods? Which are not? Explain your answer.
   a. A premium cable show delivered to cable viewers
   b. A winter coat made from a newly developed high-tech fabric
   c. A newspaper
   d. A car that contains a new, highly fuel-efficient motor
2. It is often said that "bigger is better" in industries in which the good has the characteristics of an information good. Explain this statement.

Solutions appear at back of book.

Network Externalities

Suppose you owned the only fax machine in the world. What would it be worth to you?

The answer, of course, is nothing. A fax machine derives its value only from the fact that other people also possess fax machines so that you and they can exchange faxes. And in general the more people who have fax machines, the more valuable a fax machine is to you.

This phenomenon, in which a good's value to an individual is greater when many other people own or use the same good, is common in technology-driven sectors of the economy. This is called a **network externality** because the most obvious versions of the "fax machine effect" occur when the goods involved form some kind of communications or transportation network. But the phenomenon is considerably more widespread than that.

Network externalities play a key role both in the modern economy and in a number of policy controversies. Let's look at where and how network externalities occur and then at some of the issues they raise.

Types of Network Externality

The most obvious examples of network externalities involve communications. At different points in history the prime examples have been telegraphs, telephones, fax machines, and e-mail accounts. In each case the value of the good is derived entirely from its ability to link many people possessing the same good. As a result, the marginal benefit of the good to any one individual depends on the number of other individuals who use it.

However, network externalities can also arise in less dramatic ways. For example, network externalities can exist when other users are not strictly necessary for the use of a good, as long as they enhance its usefulness. In the early days of railroad development, a railroad from New York to Chicago would have had considerable

---

A good is subject to a **network externality** when the value of the good to an individual is greater when a large number of other people also use that good.

value all by itself, as would a railroad from Kansas City to Chicago. However, each line was worth more given the existence of the other, because once both were in place, goods could be shipped via Chicago between New York and Kansas City. In the modern world, a scheduled flight between two airports becomes more valuable if one or both of those airports is a hub with connections to other places.

Even this kind of direct link need not be necessary to create important network externalities. Any way in which other people's consumption of a good increases your own marginal benefit from consumption of that good can give rise to network effects.

Perhaps the classic case of indirect network externalities is that of computer operating systems. The operating system of a computer is the underlying software that runs the machine's basic operations, underpinning and coordinating the various programs—word processors, spreadsheets, e-mail programs, and so on—that the user runs. Most personal computers around the world run on Windows, the system sold by Microsoft—although a significant minority of users own computers produced by Apple, which has its own operating system. And a growing number of computers run on Linux, a system designed by programmers who believe that operating systems should not be corporate property.

Why is Windows so dominant? Is a personal computer running Windows like a fax machine, which is useful only to the extent that other people possess the same good? Not in a direct sense: a computer can be used to type a term paper, do calculations on a spreadsheet, even send and receive e-mail regardless of how many other people have computers running the same operating system. So there isn't a literal network issue making Windows the preferred system.

Nonetheless, the dominance of Windows turns out to be self-reinforcing, for at least two indirect reasons. First, it is easier for a Windows user to get help and advice from other computer users than for someone using a less popular system. So it's a good idea, if possible, to use the same system that your colleague in the next office uses. Second, because Windows is used so widely, it attracts more attention from software developers. As a result, there are more programs that run on Windows than on any other operating system.

Network externalities in this broad sense occur for many goods. Even your choice of a car is influenced by a form of network externalities. Most people would be reluctant to switch to a car that does not run on ordinary gasoline—for example, a vehicle that runs on natural gas—if only because fueling the car would be difficult: very few gas stations offer alternative fuels. But the reason they do not offer alternative fuels is, of course, that few people drive anything other than gasoline-powered cars. Or to take a less drastic example, people who live in small towns are reluctant to drive an unusual imported vehicle: Where would they find a mechanic who knows how to fix it? So the circularity that makes one person choose Windows because everyone else uses Windows also applies to non-high-tech goods like cars.

Nonetheless, experience suggests that network externalities are more important for information goods than for other goods. And network externalities lead to two characteristic features of markets for information goods: *positive feedback* and *tipping*.

Positive Feedback

When a good is subject to a network externality, it is likely to be subject to **positive feedback.** If large numbers of people buy the good, other people become more likely to buy it. If people *don't* buy the good, others become less likely to buy it. So both success and failure tend to be self-reinforcing.

Because of positive feedback, certain "story lines" recur in the history of information good industries. One of these is the story of a small network that suddenly takes off when it reaches *critical mass*. Another is that of competition between two alternative technologies, neither obviously better than the other, that is resolved decisively through market *tipping*. Let's look at each story line in turn.

> Goods subject to network externalities experience **positive feedback:** success breeds success, failure breeds failure.

Critical Mass and Industry Takeoffs Fax machines have existed for a remarkably long time. The basic technology was developed by the Scottish inventor Alexander Bain in 1843, and AT&T introduced a wire photo service using fax technology in 1925. Really widespread use of fax machines, however, began only in the 1980s. And the rise was sudden indeed. Sharp introduced the first low-priced fax machine in 1984 and sold 80,000 that first year. In 1987 a million fax machines were sold, and by 1989 they were everywhere.

E-mail and the Internet present a similar picture. The first e-mail message was sent in 1969, but at the beginning of the 1990s only a relative handful of people were online; by about 1996, e-mail had become essential to business, and tens of millions of people had access to the Internet.

What accounts for these sudden explosions? In each case the technology improved: low-priced high-quality fax machines like the one Sharp introduced in 1984 were made possible by the rapid progress of microelectronics. But the explosive growth of fax machine use wasn't just because the technology improved; it also resulted from the network externality in fax use.

To see why, let's consider a simplified description of the decision to acquire a fax machine. We assume that there are two types of potential buyers. First, there are "unconditional" fax users—people who will want a fax machine regardless of how many other people have them. (An example might be corporations, who use faxes to send documents between their own branches.) Second, there are "conditional" users, who will want a fax machine only if the network of fax machines is large enough—that is, if enough other people already have them. In addition, both the number of unconditional users and the level of fax machine ownership that would persuade the conditional users to buy machines depend on how much the machines cost and how well they work.

Suppose that there are 1 million potential fax machine users, the total number of conditional and unconditional users. Suppose also that given the current technology and price of fax machines, 100,000 of them are unconditional users. But the other 900,000 potential users will find it worthwhile to buy a machine only if the number of machines already out there exceeds a **threshold network size** of 300,000. That is, they will buy machines only if 300,000 other people (the unconditional users) have machines because they won't have enough occasions to send or receive faxes otherwise.

> In a market subject to network externalities, the **threshold network size** for a given individual is the smallest number of current members of the network that leads the individual to join the network.

The initial situation of the demand for fax machines is shown in panel (a) of Figure 22-3. Here we assume for simplicity that all fax machines are produced with the same technology so that all consumers face the same price and quality. On the horizontal axis is the quantity of fax machines currently in use at the given price and quality. On the vertical axis is the quantity of fax machines demanded—the number of people who *want* fax machines. The two blue lines show what we have assumed about the demand for fax machines. The blue line on the left shows that there is an unconditional demand for 100,000 fax machines—100,000 people will acquire fax machines regardless of how many other people have them. The blue line on the right shows that if the number of fax machines in use reaches 300,000, the number of users suddenly increases to 1 million. (In this case we have assumed that all conditional users have the *same* threshold network size, but the story would stay the same as long as they have sufficiently similar thresholds.)

How many people will acquire fax machines in this situation? There are two possible equilibria, represented by points L and H. The point labeled L, at which 100,000 people acquire fax machines is a possible equilibrium—each individual is making his or her best choice given what everyone else is doing. The point labeled H, with 1 million fax machines in use, is also a possible equilibrium. But if, as is typically the case, machines built with the original technology are relatively expensive given the quality, you would expect the number of unconditional users to be relatively small. So we can safely assume that L is indeed the initial equilibrium in this market, and not H.

Now suppose that improved technology makes faxes cheaper and better. This will both increase the number of unconditional users and reduce the threshold network

Figure 22-3   A Network Externality

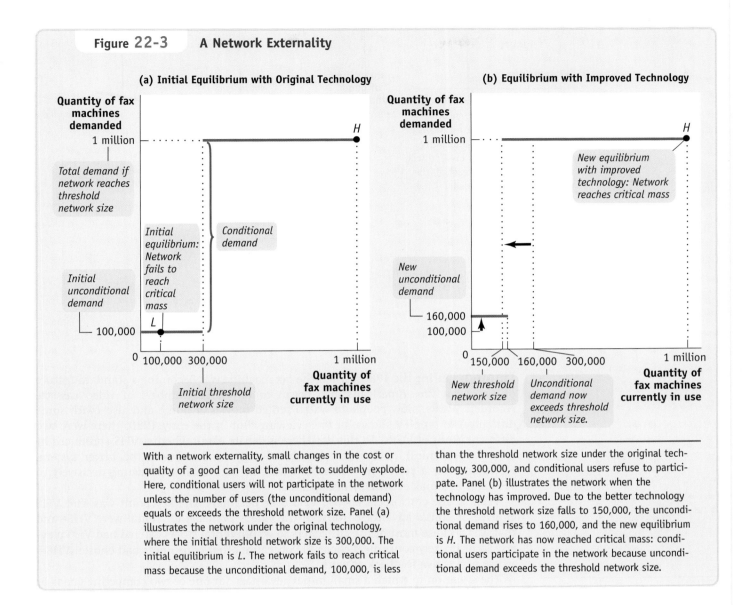

(a) Initial Equilibrium with Original Technology

Quantity of fax machines demanded

1 million — Total demand if network reaches threshold network size

Initial unconditional demand — 100,000

Initial equilibrium: Network fails to reach critical mass

Conditional demand

L *H*

0   100,000 300,000   1 million

Initial threshold network size

Quantity of fax machines currently in use

(b) Equilibrium with Improved Technology

Quantity of fax machines demanded

1 million

New equilibrium with improved technology: Network reaches critical mass

New unconditional demand — 160,000   100,000

H

0 150,000 160,000 300,000   1 million

New threshold network size

Unconditional demand now exceeds threshold network size.

Quantity of fax machines currently in use

With a network externality, small changes in the cost or quality of a good can lead the market to suddenly explode. Here, conditional users will not participate in the network unless the number of users (the unconditional demand) equals or exceeds the threshold network size. Panel (a) illustrates the network under the original technology, where the initial threshold network size is 300,000. The initial equilibrium is *L*. The network fails to reach critical mass because the unconditional demand, 100,000, is less than the threshold network size under the original technology, 300,000, and conditional users refuse to participate. Panel (b) illustrates the network when the technology has improved. Due to the better technology the threshold network size falls to 150,000, the unconditional demand rises to 160,000, and the new equilibrium is *H*. The network has now reached critical mass: conditional users participate in the network because unconditional demand exceeds the threshold network size.

size for conditional users. If the improvement in technology is substantial enough, the new number of unconditional users will equal or exceed the threshold network size and the fax machine industry will take off.

Panel (b) of Figure 22-3 shows how this might happen. Due to the cheaper and better machines, the number of unconditional users rises from 100,000 to 160,000, and the threshold network size drops from 300,000 to 150,000. The number of current users now exceeds the threshold network size, leading the 840,000 conditional users to jump in and buy fax machines. The network quickly expands and a new equilibrium is reached at *H*.

The moral of this story is that improvements in the technology of goods subject to network externalities may at first lead to only gradual increases in the size of the network. But when the network reaches a certain size—a **critical mass**—it suddenly explodes.

Because of the critical mass effect, industries subject to network externalities often exhibit the pattern of growth shown in Figure 22-4 on page 530: a long period of slow growth, followed by a sudden, rapid expansion, with growth leveling off again once the conditional buyers have been brought in.

The **critical mass** of a network is the size at which it suddenly begins to grow rapidly.

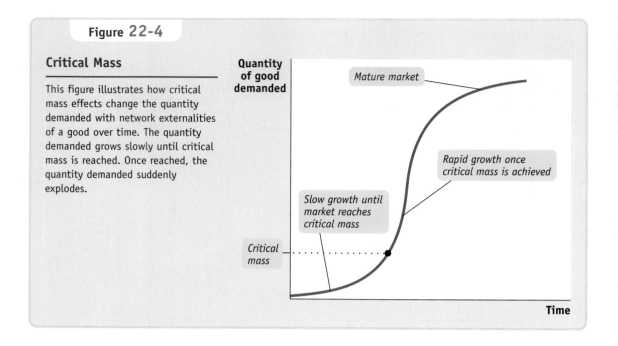

Figure 22-4

Critical Mass

This figure illustrates how critical mass effects change the quantity demanded with network externalities of a good over time. The quantity demanded grows slowly until critical mass is reached. Once reached, the quantity demanded suddenly explodes.

Tipping During the 1980s, when the fax machine was becoming a standard feature of American life, Americans also began to buy large numbers of video cassette recorders. VCRs allow people to watch rented movies at home and also (with some difficulty) to tape TV shows for later viewing. But in the early 1980s there were two different kinds of VCRs. To this day there is debate about whether VHS (produced by several companies) or Betamax (produced only by Sony) was the better system. However, after a period in which both were in use, consumers swung decisively to VHS and Betamax eventually disappeared.

What made consumers choose VHS over Betamax? The key point was that VHS enjoyed an initial advantage. Most of the videos available for rental were VHS—and that was because most of the customers to whom rental stores catered had VHS players. So ultimately consumers chose VHS because other consumers had chosen VHS—a case of positive feedback at work.

Tipping occurs when positive feedback due to network externalities causes consumers to swing to one of two competing goods or technologies.

The situation in which a small initial advantage for one of two competing goods or technologies proves self-reinforcing, eventually driving the other competitor out of the market, is known as **tipping.** Tipping is similar in its logic to the critical mass effect on sales of a single good. And it leads to somewhat similar patterns of change over time. Figure 22-5 shows the characteristic path of a market subject to tipping. On the horizontal axis is time; on the vertical axis is the quantity of a good demanded. A good that has a substantial but not dominant share of the market may stay in that range for an extended period. Then, quite suddenly, and often for no obvious reason, the market tips either for or against it, and the good either becomes dominant or fades away.

Competition in the Face of Network Externalities

Companies that produce information goods are aware of the importance of network externalities. But how do these effects change the behavior of firms? The general answer is that when companies believe that their products are subject to strong network externalities, they typically place a strong emphasis on building their sales network, even at the expense of short-term profits. This strategy is sometimes reflected by saying that in information industries you need to lose money to make money.

To see why, consider the case of a good subject to a critical mass effect—say, camera phones that also allow speakers to see each other. If only a few companies

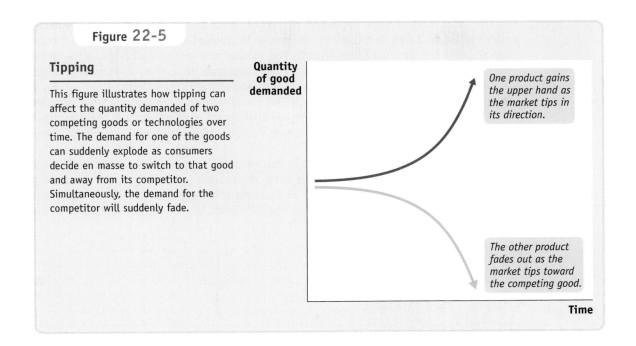

Figure 22-5

Tipping

This figure illustrates how tipping can affect the quantity demanded of two competing goods or technologies over time. The demand for one of the goods can suddenly explode as consumers decide en masse to switch to that good and away from its competitor. Simultaneously, the demand for the competitor will suddenly fade.

Quantity of good demanded

One product gains the upper hand as the market tips in its direction.

The other product fades out as the market tips toward the competing good.

Time

are supplying those phones, it is clearly in their interest to get the industry to critical mass—to get the explosion of sales that will occur when many people feel that they should have camera phones because so many other people have them. But how can these companies get the industry to critical mass? One way is to sell the product cheaply—perhaps at a loss—in order to increase the size of the network. So we often see companies introducing new high-technology products at a price well below production cost.

FOR INQUIRING MINDS

WHOSE NETWORK IS IT, ANYWAY?

Suppose that Sharp, when it introduced the first cheap fax machine, had engineered it so that it could send and receive faxes only from other Sharp machines. That would not have been good for the fax network—but it might have been very good for Sharp.

Sound implausible? Consider the case of America Online and instant messaging.

AOL is a sort of Internet within the Internet—subscribers can access all the usual web pages and also have special access to services only AOL offers. And at the end of the 1990s, AOL introduced a new service: instant messaging, e-mail that pops up immediately on the recipient's screen. This was supposed to be available only between AOL subscribers: the company viewed it as an additional selling point that would increase the number of subscribers. But AOL subscribers wanted to be able to send instant messages to

non-AOL subscribers, and vice versa. So a sort of arms race developed, as programmers wrote software that allowed non-AOL users to send instant messages and to receive them from AOL users, to which AOL responded by introducing countermeasures, to which the programmers responded with new software, and so on.

Who was serving the public interest? As in the case of file-sharing, the answer is ambiguous. Instant messaging is more useful if it's available to everyone; but companies like AOL won't make innovations unless they believe that they can profit from them. So although AOL eventually opened up their instant messaging service to non-AOL users after it became the subject of antitrust scrutiny, the original belief that sales would be increased by the threat of excluding non-AOL users made the innovation possible.

The same kind of logic applies in markets subject to tipping. Because a company wants to do all it can to induce the market to tip toward its product, it has an incentive to offer the product cheaply until the market has swung decisively in its favor. Of course, firms offering rival products have the same incentive, so the early stages of competition in information goods often involve rival firms offering their products for very little—in some cases nothing. The most famous case may be the "browser wars" of the 1990s. A browser is software used to access the Internet; the two main competitors—Netscape Navigator and Microsoft Internet Explorer—were both available for free.

In the real world, of course, nobody can be quite sure if a new product will ever achieve critical mass or if it is possible to tip the market toward a product by offering it cheaply. The result is that there are many cases of attempts to launch products that seem foolish in retrospect: goods sold cheaply, with lots of money lost, that never took off.

economics in action

Apple's Big Mistake

In 1984 Apple Computer introduced the Macintosh, a personal computer that co-founder Steve Jobs described as "insanely great." Many observers agreed. Before the Mac, personal computers were operated by typing in cumbersome commands or possibly by choosing a command from a menu. The Mac introduced the much more powerful graphical user interface, also known as point-and-click: you use a mouse to move an arrow to an image on the screen, then click a button. Graphical user interfaces have now become standard for all personal computers.

But sales of the Mac were never as good as Apple expected. And even though Apple's computers were clearly technologically superior to the alternatives well into the 1990s (devotees say they still are), they have remained a small part of the market.

What happened? At the time the Mac was introduced, most computer users had PCs that ran on DOS, an operating system created by Microsoft. Apple knew that its product was better and so charged a premium price. This kept Apple's customer base relatively small. Apple failed to recognize the strength of the network externality that caused many users to stick with an inferior product that was widely used, especially given the fact that the superior alternative was considerably more expensive.

Over time, Microsoft developed its own version of a graphical user interface, Windows. Windows, especially in its early versions, was still technologically inferior to Apple's system: it took a long time to boot, and it was notoriously vulnerable to crashes. (The joke went around that if Microsoft made cars, they would take five minutes to start and would occasionally stop suddenly for no apparent reason.) But again, the network externalities already achieved by DOS induced many people to stay with the technologically inferior Microsoft system.

In retrospect, it seems likely that if Apple had understood the force of network externalities and priced the Macintosh lower, it would have come to dominate the industry. ∎

< < < < < < < < < < < < < < < < < <

>> CHECK YOUR UNDERSTANDING 22-2

1. For each of the following goods explain the nature of the network externality present.
   a. Appliances using a particular voltage, such as 110 volt versus 220 volt
   b. 8½-by-11-inch paper versus 8-by-12½-inch paper

2. Suppose there are two competing companies in an industry that has critical mass effects. Explain why the market is likely to tip to the company that can sustain the largest initial losses.

Solutions appear at back of book.

Policy Toward Information Goods

Does the growing importance of information goods require new kinds of economic policy? Most economists would answer with a qualified no. The principles of economics remain the same as ever, and the issues raised by information goods are not new. Still, the emphasis shifts: issues that may have seemed unimportant in the past become very important in this new world.

Let's look at two types of policy concerns raised by the growing importance of information goods: antitrust policy and standards.

Antitrust Policy

We saw in Chapters 14 and 15 that market power creates problems for economic efficiency. As a result, the government attempts both to limit the growth of monopolies and to keep oligopolies from behaving like monopolies. But how should antitrust policy be conducted in information goods industries?

As we saw earlier in this chapter, monopoly is a natural outcome in industries with high fixed costs but low marginal costs, which is the case for information goods. Furthermore, it is the hope of achieving a monopoly that leads potential producers to incur those high fixed costs in the first place.

However the antitrust laws do not, strictly speaking, forbid monopoly. Rather, they only prohibit "monopolization"—efforts to create a monopoly. If you just happen to end up ruling an industry, that's okay, but if you take actions designed to drive out competition, that's not okay. So we could argue that monopolies in information goods, because they occur naturally, should not pose legal problems.

Unfortunately, it isn't that simple. Firms investing in new technologies are clearly trying to establish monopoly positions. Furthermore, in the face of positive feedback, firms have an incentive to engage in aggressive strategies to push their goods to critical mass, or to tip the market in their direction. So what is the dividing line between legal and illegal actions?

At this point the rules are somewhat in flux. In the Microsoft antitrust case, described in the Economics in Action on pages 534–535, reasonable economists and legal experts disagreed sharply both about whether the company had broken the law by pursuing a monopoly position, and whether the company should be broken up to diminish its ability to tip new markets in its favor.

Setting Standards

The United States, though at the technological cutting edge in most respects, lags noticeably behind other advanced countries in one area: cell phones. As one Boston-based computer expert put it in 2003, "After two days of touring Wales, a country that apparently has yet to discover the mixing faucet [a single faucet combining hot and cold water], it has become apparent that there is better mobile phone coverage in the remotest sheep pasture or coastal outcrop than in downtown Boston." Why?

The answer has to do with the European decision, at the end of the 1980s, to adopt a common **standard** for digital cellular phones—a set of rules for operation that induced competing cell phone companies to form a common network—so that every cellular phone would work everywhere on the continent. A GSM (General Standard for Mobiles) phone works equally well anywhere in Europe; because of the common standard, supporting antennas are plentiful and there is good coverage almost everywhere. In the United States, by contrast, there is no common standard among competing cell phone companies: some use the GSM, but others use alternative standards. Even if there is a transmission tower near you, it may not carry a signal your phone can use. (At the time of writing, the authors had a GSM cell phone that worked fine even in remote European locations but received no signal in or near their New Jersey home.)

A **standard** is a set of rules for operation that induces competing goods to operate as a single network.

Standards are by no means a new issue. In the nineteenth century the most important choice of standard was the gauge of railroads—how far apart the rails of a track were. The problems created when two railroads with different gauges met were obvious, yet in 1860 there were no fewer than seven different railroad gauges in use in the United States. (The two main versions were the 4-foot-8½-inch gauge used in most of the North and the 5-foot gauge used in most of the South.) The South finally switched to the "standard" 4-foot-8½-inch gauge in a coordinated move, taking place over two days in 1886.

Both the old railroad example and the modern cell phone example suggest that the need for common standards creates a justification for government intervention in the economy. Left to itself, the market may fail to converge on a common standard. And as in the case of early U.S. railroads or contemporary U.S. cell phones, an industry may suffer from avoidable inefficiency because of failure to converge. So the government can play a useful role by prodding the private sector into that convergence, as it did in the case of European cell phones.

An important point about standards is that getting *some* standard is often more important than *which* standard is chosen. For example, American railroads would have done equally well with a 5-foot gauge, as long as they had all coordinated on it. And it isn't always necessary for the government to enforce a standard. Sometimes industries do it voluntarily. A number of companies agreed on the standard for digital video discs (DVDs), which are rapidly replacing video cassettes. In other cases a standard simply evolves as firms try to match each other.

But do unplanned standards—standards that arise as a natural market outcome—get it right? In some cases, different standards will lead to different results: one standard may lead to lower costs or superior quality than another, and there is no guarantee that the market will choose the better standard. So could an industry get "stuck" with one standard when some other standard is clearly better?

Economists have long debated this issue, which has come to be known as the **QWERTY problem**. The name comes from the top row on a standard keyboard, which reads QWERTYUIOP. Why are keyboards laid out that way? Basically because they started out with that layout, which was chosen partly because it helped prevent keys on a mechanical typewriter from jamming—not a concern on a computer—and partly because it allowed salesmen to quickly pick out the letters "TYPEWRITER," which are all in the top row of the QWERTY keyboard. So that is what typists learn, and that is what typewriter manufacturers, and more recently computer keyboard manufacturers, provide—it's a self-reinforcing loop.

The question is whether QWERTY is the best keyboard layout. Might there be a better layout, one that would allow faster typing, that nobody uses because network externalities have locked us into the standard layout?

The evidence on keyboards is mixed. Other layouts seem to be somewhat better. But a computer can be easily reprogrammed to use a different keyboard layout, so if the gains from a switch were really large we would expect a widespread move away from the QWERTY layout; this hasn't happened. Nonetheless, in principle government intervention might be useful in moving an industry to a superior standard.

An industry that gets stuck using an inferior standard suffers from the **QWERTY problem**.

economics in action

The Microsoft Case

In 2000 the Justice Department took on Microsoft in one of the most watched antitrust cases in history. By that time, Microsoft had become the world's most valuable corporation, and its founder, Bill Gates, was the world's richest man. What the government sought was nothing less than the breakup of the company.

The case involved almost all of the issues raised by information goods. Microsoft was, by any reasonable definition, a monopoly: leaving aside the niches of Apple customers and Linux users, just about all personal computers ran the Windows operating system. The key fact sustaining the Windows system was the force of a network externality: people used Windows because other people used Windows.

The government did not, however, challenge the Windows monopoly itself (although some economists urged it to). Basically, everyone agreed that monopoly per se is a natural thing in such industries and should not be prevented. What the government claimed, however, was that Microsoft had used its monopoly position in operating systems to give its products an advantage over competitors in other markets. For example, by including Internet Explorer as part of the Windows system, it was alleged, Microsoft was giving itself an unfair advantage over its rival Netscape in the browser software market.

The Microsoft case involved almost all of the issues raised by information goods.

Why was this considered harmful? The government argued both that monopolies were being created unnecessarily and that Microsoft was discouraging innovation. Potential innovators in software, the government claimed, were unwilling to invest large sums out of fear that Microsoft would use its control of the operating system to take away any market they might win by producing a competing product that would then be sold as a bundle with the operating system. For its part, Microsoft argued that by setting the precedent that companies would be punished for success, the government was the real opponent of innovation.

At first the case went against Microsoft, when a judge ordered the company split in two—into an operating-system company and a company selling the firm's other products. But this judgment was overturned on appeal. In November 2001, the government reached a settlement with Microsoft in which the company agreed to provide other companies with the technology to develop products that interacted seamlessly with Microsoft's software, thus removing the company's special advantage acquired through bundling its products.

Competitors complained bitterly that this settlement had far too many loopholes, and that Microsoft's ability to exploit its monopoly position would remain. And by early 2004, the government agreed: antitrust lawyers from the Justice Department reported to the judge who negotiated the original settlement that they were increasingly uneasy about the plan's ability to spur competition. A particular concern was a rumored Microsoft move to take over the market in publishing software, in which Adobe Acrobat was the current leader. ∎

> > > > > > > > > > > > > > > > > > > >

>>**CHECK YOUR UNDERSTANDING 22-3**

1. As described in the For Inquiring Minds on page 531, America Online (AOL), the biggest Internet service provider in the United States, was at one time the subject of antitrust scrutiny of its instant messaging service. In the original form of the program, when an AOL customer sent a message to another AOL customer, the message instantly popped up on the receiver's screen. But AOL did not allow non-AOL senders to access the service when they sent messages to an AOL customer. Was this an antitrust violation on AOL's part? Give arguments pro and con.

Solution appears at back of book.

SUMMARY

1. **Information goods**—goods whose value derives mainly from the information they embody—are increasingly important in the economy.

2. Information goods typically have high fixed costs but low or zero marginal costs. This means that once an information good has been created, efficiency requires that it be free or almost free to consumers. But innovators must have some way to earn back their fixed costs if the good is to be produced at all.

3. To enhance efficiency, governments have created **patents** and **copyrights,** which give innovators a temporary monopoly. But these temporary monopolies often arise naturally due to first-mover advantages from innovation.

4. Many information goods are also characterized by **network externalities:** the value of the good to an individual is greater when a large number of people also use the good. Network externalities cause **positive feedback,** in which either initial success or initial failure is self-reinforcing.

5. Because consumers may have a **threshold network size** at which they are willing to purchase a good, information goods may have a **critical mass,** a market size at which growth explodes. Or they may experience **tipping,** in which a small advantage to one of two competing goods leads it to become dominant. These features often lead firms to price their goods or technologies very low in the hope of greatly increasing sales.

6. Information goods pose difficulties for antitrust policy because firms investing in new technologies may engage in aggressive tactics to establish monopolies, tactics that may or may not be legal.

7. To facilitate network externalities, industries must coordinate on **standards** that let competing goods work together. Government can play a useful role both in helping an industry establish a standard and in helping it avoid getting trapped in an inferior standard, known as the **QWERTY problem.**

KEY TERMS

Information goods, p. 520
Patents, p. 524
Copyrights, p. 524
Network externalities, p. 526

Positive feedback, p. 527
Threshold network size, p. 528
Critical mass, p. 529

Tipping, p. 530
Standard, p. 533
QWERTY problem, p. 534

PROBLEMS

1. Information goods are characterized by high fixed cost and very low or zero marginal cost. Suppose the government grants the producer of an information good a patent so that the producer is the only seller of that good.

   a. If the government forces the producer to charge a price equal to marginal cost, would the firm's profit be greater than, equal to, or less than zero?

   b. If the government forces the producer to charge a price equal to average total cost, would the firm's profit be greater than, equal to, or less than zero?

2. Werck, a pharmaceutical company, is developing a new AIDS drug. The demand schedule for the drug, once it has been developed, is shown in Table 2a. If Werck can act as a monopolist, its marginal revenue from selling the drug will be as given in Table 2b.

Table 2a

Price of dose	Quantity of doses demanded (thousands)
$100	0
90	20
80	40
70	60
60	80
50	100
40	120
30	140
20	160
10	180
0	200

Table 2b

Quantity of doses (thousands)	Marginal revenue (per dose)
0	
	$90
20	
	70
40	
	50
60	
	30
80	
	10
100	
	−10
120	

Werck's fixed cost in developing the drug is $4 million. The marginal cost of producing the drug is zero.

a. If Werck develops the drug and can act as a monopolist, which quantity of output will it choose to produce? What will its profit be? Does Werck therefore have an incentive to engage in the costly development of the drug?

b. Suppose now that the government announces that in order to make AIDS drugs more widely available, it will force the producer to sell the drug at marginal cost. If Werck develops the drug, what will the price be and how much of the drug will be sold? What will its profit be? Does Werck have an incentive to engage in the costly development of the drug?

3. British Biotech is developing a new cancer drug. The demand schedule for the drug, once the drug has been developed, is shown in Table 3a. If British Biotech can act as a monopolist, its marginal revenue from selling the drug will be as shown in Table 3b.

Table 3a

Price of dose	Quantity of doses demanded (millions)
$50	0
45	1
40	2
35	3
30	4
25	5
20	6
15	7
10	8
5	9
0	10

Table 3b

Quantity of doses (millions)	Marginal revenue (per dose)
0	
	$45
1	
	35
2	
	25
3	
	15
4	
	5
5	
	−5
6	

British Biotech's fixed cost of developing the drug is $750 million. Its marginal cost is zero.

a. If British Biotech is granted a monopoly for one year, what will its revenue be that year?

b. If British Biotech does not have a monopoly, other drug makers will copy its product without incurring any development cost and the price will fall to marginal cost. What will British Biotech's yearly revenue be in that case?

c. If the government sets the length of British Biotech's patent at four years so that British Biotech is a monopolist for four years and then other firms can imitate the product (and therefore after four years the price falls to marginal cost), what will British Biotech's revenue be over those four years? Is this enough to cover British Biotech's fixed cost of developing the drug? (Ignore the issue of discounting over time.)

d. How long would the patent have to be for British Biotech to cover its fixed cost and so want to invest in development of the drug?

4. Explain the following situations.

a. In Europe, many cell phone service providers give away for free what would otherwise be very expensive cell phones when a service contract is purchased. Why might a company want to do that?

b. In the United Kingdom, the country's antitrust authority banned one cell phone service provider (Vodaphone) from offering a plan that gave customers free calls to other customers of Vodaphone. Why might Vodaphone have wanted to offer these calls for free? Why might a government want to step in and ban this practice? Why might it not be a good idea for the government to interfere in this way?

5. A new company providing cellular telephone service, Springulizon, has identified 10 million potential subscribers to its new cellular telephone network. The network operates on a new standard that will allow Springulizon subscribers to only talk to other Springulizon subscribers. 1 million of these potential users are unconditional users: they will buy a Springulizon phone regardless of how many other subscribers there are. The remaining 9 million potential users are conditional users: they will only buy a Springulizon phone if the network reaches a certain threshold network size. Suppose that the threshold network size is 2 million. Springulizon starts service, and initially 1 million unconditional users subscribe to Springulizon service.

a. In the current situation, will conditional users also want to subscribe to Springulizon service?

b. Springulizon gives away 1 million free phones (complete with service contracts) to 1 million conditional users in a large-scale advertising campaign. Will the remaining 8 million conditional users now want to join the network?

c. Suppose each phone (complete with service contract) costs $100. How much did it cost Springulizon to give away the free phones? How much additional revenue did it create by doing so? Therefore, was this advertising campaign worth it?

>web... To continue your study and review of concepts in this chapter, please visit the Krugman/Wells website for quizzes, animated graph tutorials, web links to helpful resources, and more.

www.worthpublishers.com/krugmanwells

>> Macroeconomics: The Big Picture

DISAPPOINTED GRADUATES

2000 WAS A VERY GOOD YEAR TO BE a new graduate of an American university or college. As one newspaper put it, companies were "tripping over themselves to entice graduating seniors with fat salaries and other perks." 2000 was a particularly good year for students graduating with an MBA degree. But events were not nearly as kind to those who graduated just two years later. For many members of the class of 2002 at American business schools, graduation was not the happy occasion they had expected—a golden ticket to a well-paying job and success. Even at top business schools, such as Harvard, the University of Pennsylvania, and Stanford, students and faculty watched in disbelief as recruiters reneged on job offers that had already been extended to hundreds of newly graduated MBAs. Months after commencement, many graduates still had not landed jobs. As shown in Table 23-1, graduates who did find jobs typically received lower salaries than those of graduates just two years earlier. (If you rank salaries from high to low, the median salary is the salary right at the middle.)

There was nothing wrong with the new MBAs in 2002; they were every bit as talented and motivated as the graduates two years earlier. And the phenomenon wasn't limited to business school graduates. The difference was that in the spring of 2000 the economy was booming, and employers were anxious to hire more people. In the spring of 2002 the economy was weak. Many firms were laying off employees and were in no hurry to hire more. As you can see from Table 23-1, by 2004 job prospects had improved somewhat; however, starting salaries still lagged behind the levels MBA graduates enjoyed in the spring of 2000.

The alternation between boom and bust—between years in which jobs are plentiful and years in which jobs are hard to find—is known as the *business cycle*. But why is there a business cycle, and can anything be done to smooth it out? That's one question addressed by *macroeconomics*, the area of

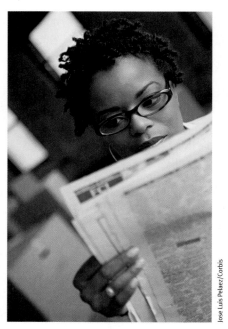

Even the best students had a tough time finding a job in 2002.

Jose Luis Pelaez/Corbis

TABLE 23-1

Median Starting Salaries of New MBAs from Selected Schools in 2000, 2002, and 2004

School	2000 starting salary	2002 starting salary	2004 starting salary
Stanford	$165,500	$138,100	$150,000
Harvard	160,000	134,600	147,500
Pennsylvania	156,000	124,500	144,000
Columbia	142,500	123,600	142,500
Dartmouth	149,500	122,100	135,000

Source: *Business Week* Graduate Survey, October 18, 2004.

economics that focuses on the behavior of the economy as a whole.

In contrast, *microeconomics* is concerned with the production and consumption decisions of consumers and producers and with the allocation of scarce resources among industries. Returning to our example of business school graduates, a typical question for microeconomics would be why different industries—say, investment banking versus marketing—pay different salaries to new graduates. Macroeconomics is concerned with developments in the national economy, such as the total output level, the overall level of prices, and the total level of employment. In addition, macroeconomics analyzes how the behavior of the economy depends on and is affected by the workings of the global economy.

Another element of Table 23-1 should strike you: new MBAs get paid an awful lot of money. Most Americans don't earn as much as MBAs from elite business schools do. Still, the incomes of Americans in almost all walks of life are much higher than those typical in previous generations. The average starting salary for Stanford's MBA class of 1968 was only $12,000. A dollar doesn't go as far today as it did in the 1960s, but even after you adjust for *inflation*—a rise in the overall price level—MBA salaries in 2002 were more than twice as high as they were in 1968. This comparison touches on *long-run growth*, another fundamental area

of study in macroeconomics. Long-run growth is the sustained upward trend in the economy's overall output, and is a critical factor in a country's ability to achieve higher incomes and a higher standard of living. The main reason MBAs were paid so much more in 2002 than in 1968 is that output per person in the United States had doubled over those years. As this comparison suggests, economists measure long-run growth by looking at the economy's performance over several decades—long enough to show, in retrospect, that the increase in output was a permanent trend rather than the result of a temporary boom in the economy. Historical evidence shows that over an extended period of time, long-run growth is much more important than the *business cycle*—short-run fluctuations in the economy's performance—in determining a country's living standards. The average graduate of the class of 2002, even though facing disappointing job prospects and a lower salary, would have had an enormously higher standard of living than a comparable graduate in 1968.

Earlier chapters have given you a grasp of some fundamental microeconomic concepts and principles. To understand the scope and sweep of macroeconomics, let's begin by looking more carefully at the difference between microeconomics and macroeconomics. Following that, we'll present an overview of the four main areas of macroeconomic study.

Microeconomics versus Macroeconomics

Table 23-2 lists some questions that are often asked in economics. A microeconomic version of the question appears on the left paired with a similar macroeconomic question on the right. By comparing the questions, you can begin to get a sense of the difference between microeconomics and macroeconomics.

As you can see, microeconomics focuses on how decisions are made by individuals and firms and the consequences of those decisions. For example, we use microeconomics to determine how much it would cost a university or college to offer a new course—a cost that includes the instructor's salary, the cost of class materials, and so on. The school can then decide whether or not to offer the course by weighing the costs and benefits. Macroeconomics, in contrast, examines the *aggregate* behavior of the economy—how the actions of all the individuals and firms in the economy interact to produce a particular economy-wide level of economic performance. For example, macroeconomics is concerned with the overall level of prices in the economy and how high or how low they are relative to prices last year, rather than focusing on the price of one particular good or service.

TABLE 23-2

Microeconomic versus Macroeconomic Questions

Microeconomic Questions	Macroeconomic Questions
Should I go to business school or take a job right now?	How many people are employed in the economy as a whole this year?
What determines the salary offered by Citibank to Cherie Camajo, a new Columbia MBA?	What determines the overall salary levels paid to workers in a given year?
What determines the cost to a university or college of offering a new course?	What determines the overall level of prices in the economy as a whole?
What government policies should be adopted to make it easier for low-income students to attend college?	What government policies should be adopted to promote employment and growth in the economy as a whole?
What determines whether Citibank opens a new office in Shanghai?	What determines the overall trade in goods, services, and financial assets between the United States and the rest of the world?

You might imagine that macroeconomic questions can be answered simply by adding up microeconomic answers. For example, the model of supply and demand we introduced in Chapter 3 tells us how the equilibrium price of an individual good or service is determined in a competitive market. So you might think that applying supply and demand analysis to every good and service in the economy, then summing the results, is the way to understand the overall level of prices in the economy as a whole.

But that turns out not to be the case: although basic concepts such as supply and demand are as essential to macroeconomics as they are to microeconomics, answering macroeconomic questions requires an additional set of tools and an expanded frame of reference. We will develop the required tools in the chapters ahead. We'll start by developing the wider viewpoint that characterizes macroeconomics, and we'll consider four principal ways in which macroeconomics differs from microeconomics.

Macroeconomics: The Whole Is Greater Than the Sum of Its Parts

If you occasionally drive on a highway, you probably know what a "rubber-necking" traffic jam is and why it is so annoying. Someone pulls over to the side of the road for something minor, such as changing a flat tire, and, pretty soon, a long traffic jam occurs as drivers slow down to take a look. What makes it so annoying is that the length of the traffic jam is greatly out of proportion to the minor event that precipitated it. Because some drivers hit their brakes in order to "rubber-neck," the drivers behind them must also hit their brakes, those behind them must do the same, and so on. The accumulation of all the individual tappings of brakes eventually leads to a long, wasteful traffic jam as each driver slows down a little bit more than the driver in front of him or her.

Understanding a rubber-necking traffic jam gives us some insight into one very important way in which macroeconomics is different from microeconomics: many thousands or millions of individual actions accumulate to produce an outcome that is larger than the simple sum of those individual actions. Consider, for example, what macroeconomists call the "Paradox of Thrift": when families and businesses are worried about the possibility of economic hard times, they prepare by cutting their spending. This reduction in spending depresses the economy as consumers spend less and businesses react by laying off workers. As a result, families and businesses may end up worse off than if they hadn't tried to act responsibly by cutting their spending. This is called a paradox because seemingly virtuous behavior—cautiously preparing for hard times by saving more—ends up harming everyone. And there is a flip-side to this story: when families and businesses are feeling optimistic about the future, they spend more today. This stimulates the economy, leading businesses to hire more workers, which further expands the economy. Seemingly profligate behavior leads to good times for all.

A key insight into macroeconomics is that in the short run—a time period consisting of several years but typically less than a decade—the combined effect of individual decisions can have effects that are very different from what any one individual intended, effects that are sometimes perverse. The behavior of the macroeconomy is, indeed, greater than the sum of individual actions and market outcomes.

Macroeconomic Policy

The fact that the sum of individual decisions can sometimes lead to bad results for the macroeconomy leads us to another critical difference between microeconomics and macroeconomics: the role of government policy. Careful study of how markets work has led microeconomists to the conclusion that government should typically leave markets alone. Except in certain well-defined cases, government intervention in markets usually leaves society as a whole worse off. There are, to be sure, important tasks for microeconomic policy—ensuring that markets perform well and intervening appropriately in the well-defined cases in which markets don't work well. But the area of microeconomics, in general, suggests a limited role for government intervention.

In contrast, economists generally believe there is a much wider role for government to play in macroeconomics—most importantly, to manage short-term fluctuations and adverse events in the economy. Like the highway police who work to prevent or reduce the effects of rubber-necking traffic jams, government policy makers work to prevent or reduce the effects of adverse events on the macroeconomy.

The widely held view that the government should take an active role in the management of the macroeconomy dates back to the Great Depression of the 1930s, a pivotal event in world economic history. A global event in which output plunged, banks failed, companies went bust, and workers were laid off en masse, it was as if the world economic engine had been thrown sharply into reverse. Lasting more than a decade, from 1929 through the end of the 1930s, it caused a thorough rethinking of the principles and aims of macroeconomics. During and after the Great Depression, economists developed the modern macroeconomic toolkit—*fiscal policy,* control of government spending and taxation, and *monetary policy,* control over interest rates and the quantity of money in circulation—now used to manage the performance of the macroeconomy.

Long-Run Growth

Why, in the United States, are we able to drive at high speeds to distant destinations on well-built and (usually) well-maintained highways? For that matter, why are we able to drive at all, rather than having to rely on horses or our own two feet? The reason is long-run growth. Another fundamental area of difference between microeconomics and macroeconomics is the latter's study of long-run growth. In macroeconomics we consider questions such as: What factors lead to a higher long-run growth rate? Are there government policies capable of increasing the long-run growth rate?

Microeconomics, in contrast, focuses on problems that take the amount of ouput the economy is capable of producing as given. For example, it might consider a question like, "Given the extent of national broadband Internet access, how should access be priced so that it is used as efficiently as possible?" That is, microeconomics asks how to use a given set of resources as efficiently as possible. Macroeconomics, though, examines the longer-run problem of how a society can *increase* the total amount of productive resources so that it can achieve higher rates of growth and a higher standard of living. Moreover, what governments should or shouldn't do to promote long-run growth is also an important area of study.

You might ask why long-run growth is considered a part of macroeconomics rather than microeconomics. The reason is that the subject of long-run growth fundamentally depends on the use of *economic aggregates*. As we'll see shortly, the study of aggregates is the last of the four principal ways in which macroeconomics differs from microeconomics.

Economic Aggregates

> **Economic aggregates** are economic measures that summarize data across different markets for goods, services, workers, and assets.

A distinctive feature of modern macroeconomics is that both its theory and policy implementation focus on **economic aggregates**—economic measures that summarize data across many different markets for goods, services, workers, and *assets*. (Assets are items that serve as a store of value, like cash or real estate.) For example, macroeconomics analyzes the performance of the economy by studying *aggregate output*, the total output of the economy over a given time period, and the *aggregate price level*, a measure of the overall level of prices in the economy. Using these aggregate measures, we will study the business cycle and how fiscal policy and monetary policy can be used to manage the business cycle. As the lucky and unlucky business school grads discovered, these fluctuations affect *unemployment*, a measure of the total number of unemployed workers in the economy. We'll also see how the business cycle and long-run growth are affected by *investment spending*, additions to the economy's supply of productive *physical capital*, including machines, buildings, and inventories, as well as by *savings*, the amount that households and the government save in a given year. And we'll see how economic interactions with other countries are analyzed using the *current account*, the total net amount of goods and services exported abroad, and the *financial account*, the total net amount of assets sold to foreigners.

In the remainder of this chapter and in Chapter 24, we'll focus on how many of these economic aggregates are calculated and measured. In subsequent chapters, we'll also define these aggregates more precisely.

Now that we have an idea of how macroeconomics and microeconomics differ, we're ready to begin learning about some of the key features of modern macroeconomics, starting with the business cycle. Before we do that, however, let's take a moment to look at the episode that created macroeconomics as we know it—and almost destroyed civilization as we know it.

economics in action

The Great Depression

Historians agree that the Great Depression, which began in 1929 and lasted through the 1930s, was one of the great defining moments in American history. And its effect wasn't just limited to the United States; the catastrophe was felt in virtually all the world's market economies—in Europe, Latin America, Japan, Canada, and Australia. Germany had one of the hardest-hit economies. Historians agree that this was a major reason for the rise of Nazism, which ultimately led to World War II.

The Great Depression was also *the* defining moment for modern macroeconomics: if we had to express in a few words the central mission of modern macroeconomics, it is to prevent anything like the Great Depression from ever happening again.

The Depression began in August 1929 with a mild fall in aggregate output. This, in turn, contributed to the single event most associated with the Great Depression—the famous stock market crash of October 1929. If the economic effects had been limited to the fallout from the stock market crash, then the economy would probably have experienced a short-term downturn. But what made the Depression a long-term disaster was the catastrophic rise in unemployment and huge decline in aggregate output that occurred after the market crash. In 1929, the *unemployment rate*—loosely speaking, the percentage of the working population unable to find jobs—was only 3.2%, as shown in panel (a) of Figure 23-1. By 1933 it was 24.9%: one American worker in four was out of work, with many people forced to rely on soup kitchens and other forms of charity simply to eat. Families were evicted from their homes, and shantytowns—enclaves with dwellings made from cast-off materials—

Much of modern macroeconomics arose as a way to understand the economic devastation caused by the Great Depression. Shown here is the family of an unemployed Appalachian coal miner in 1938.

arose across the country. Labor strife was pervasive because workers felt abandoned by the market economy. (In one famous example, World War I veterans, called "Bonus Marchers," erected a shantytown on the Mall in Washington, D.C. They were driven off by the U.S. Army after they made large and vocal demands for a government-paid bonus.) Along with the collapse in employment came an extraordinary collapse in *real gross domestic product* (or *real GDP*)—a measure of aggregate output. Real GDP fell 27% from 1929 to 1933, as panel (b) of Figure 23-1 shows. It was a time of incredible, unexpected misery, all the more shocking because the previous decade, the "Roaring Twenties," had been a time of unprecedented growth and prosperity. By the 1930s, many people felt that even democracy in America was at risk.

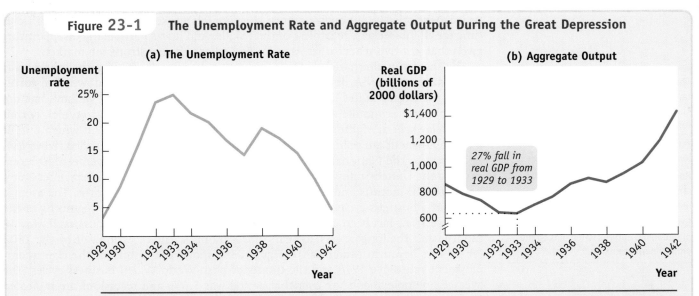

Figure 23-1   The Unemployment Rate and Aggregate Output During the Great Depression

(a) The Unemployment Rate

(b) Aggregate Output

27% fall in real GDP from 1929 to 1933

The economic slump that began in 1929 led to a drastic rise in the unemployment rate, shown in panel (a), and a drastic fall in aggregate output, shown in panel (b). Aggregate output, as measured by real GDP in 2000 dollars (we'll explain what "2000 dollars" are in Chapter 24), didn't rise above its 1929 level until 1937. The unemployment rate didn't return to single digits until 1941.

Source: U.S. Census Bureau. **>web...**

Although the economy eventually recovered, it took a very long time. In 1939, after a full decade of policy attempts to reverse the downturn, the unemployment rate was 17%—far higher than anything seen since. Real GDP did not get above its 1929 level until 1936, and it took until 1941 for the unemployment rate to drop back into single digits. Only with the coming of World War II did economic prosperity return.

The Great Depression led to a feverish effort by economists to understand what had happened and what could be done about it. This led to a breakthrough in economic measurement, and many of the statistics we now rely on to track the economy's performance first began to be collected during the 1930s. Economic theory changed dramatically with the 1936 publication of *The General Theory of Employment, Interest, and Money* by the British economist John Maynard Keynes—a book that ranks in influence with Adam Smith's *The Wealth of Nations*. Keynes's work, and the interpretations and critiques of his work by other economists, gave rise to both the field of macroeconomics and macroeconomic policy-making as we know it. ∎

< < < < < < < < < < < < < < < < < <

>>CHECK YOUR UNDERSTANDING 23-1

1. Which of the following questions is appropriate to the study of microeconomics? Of macroeconomics? Explain your answers.
   a. How much profit is gained by installing a new piece of equipment in the Otis Furniture Factory?
   b. How does the overall level of sales of manufactured goods change as the state of the economy changes?
   c. What types of investment spending lead to a higher growth rate of the economy over time?
   d. Should Melanie buy a new car or not?

2. Explain why there is typically less scope for government intervention in microeconomics than in macroeconomics.

Solutions appear at back of book.

The Business Cycle

As we mentioned in our opening story, the poor job market of 2002 created a difficult time for all job-seekers, regardless of their skills. And it was particularly disappointing given that just two years earlier America had enjoyed a very strong job market.

The short-run alternation between economic downturns and upturns is known as the **business cycle**. A **depression** is a very deep and prolonged downturn; fortunately, the United States hasn't had one since the 1930s. But what we have had are less prolonged economic downturns known as **recessions,** periods in which output and *employment* are falling. In contrast, economic upturns, periods in which output and employment are rising, are known as **expansions** (sometimes called *recoveries*). According to the National Bureau of Economic Research there have been 10 recessions in the United States since World War II. Over that period the average recession has lasted 10 months and the average expansion has lasted 57 months. The average length of a business cycle, from the beginning of a recession to the beginning of the next recession, has been 5 years and 7 months. The shortest business cycle was 18 months and the longest was 10 years and 8 months. The recession felt by the 2002 job-seekers began in March 2001. Figure 23-2 shows the history of the U.S. unemployment rate since 1948 and the timing of post–World War II business cycles. The average unemployment rate over that period was 5.6%, and recessions are indicated in the figure by the shaded areas.

What happens during a business cycle, and what can be done about it? Let's look at three issues: the effects of recessions and expansions on unemployment; the effects on aggregate output; and the possible role of government policy.

The **business cycle** is the short-run alternation between economic downturns, known as recessions, and economic upturns, known as expansions.

A **depression** is a very deep and prolonged downturn.

Recessions are periods of economic downturns when output and employment are falling.

Expansions, or recoveries, are periods of economic upturns when output and employment are rising.

DEFINING RECESSIONS AND EXPANSIONS

Some readers may be wondering exactly how recessions and expansions are defined. The answer is that there is no exact definition!

In many countries, economists adopt the rule that a recession is a period of at least two consecutive quarters (a quarter is 3 months), during which aggregate output falls. The two-consecutive-quarter requirement is designed to avoid classifying brief hiccups in the economy's performance, with no lasting significance, as recessions. Sometimes, however, this definition seems too strict. For example, an economy that has three months of sharply declining output,

then three months of slightly positive growth, then another three months of rapid decline, should surely be considered to have endured a nine-month recession.

In the United States, we try to avoid such misclassifications by assigning the task of determining when a recession begins and ends to an independent panel of experts at the National Bureau of Economic Research (NBER). This panel looks at a variety of economic indicators, with the main focus on employment and production. But, ultimately, the panel makes a judgment call.

Sometimes this judgment is controversial. In fact, there is lingering controversy over the 2001 recession. According to the NBER, that recession began in March 2001 and ended in November 2001 when output began rising. Some critics argue, however, that the recession really began several months earlier, when industrial production began falling. Other critics argue that the recession didn't really end in 2001 because employment continued to fall and the job market remained weak for another year and a half.

Figure 23-2

The Unemployment Rate and Recessions Since 1948

The unemployment rate normally rises during recessions and falls during expansions. As shown here, there were large fluctuations in the U.S. unemployment rate during the period after World War II. Shaded areas show periods of recession; unshaded areas are periods of expansion. Over the entire period from 1948 to 2004, the unemployment rate averaged 5.6%.

Source: Bureau of Labor Statistics; National Bureau of Economic Research.

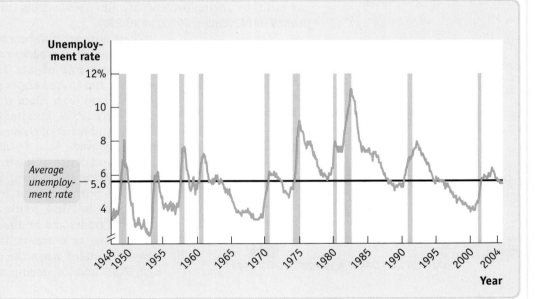

Employment and Unemployment

Although not as severe as a depression, a recession is clearly an undesirable event. Like a depression, a recession leads to higher unemployment, reduced output, reduced incomes, and lower living standards.

To understand unemployment and how it relates to the adverse effects of recessions, we need to understand something about how the labor force is structured. **Employment** is the total number of people currently employed, and **unemployment** is the total number of people who are actively looking for work but aren't currently employed. A country's **labor force** is the sum of employment and unemployment. The official labor force doesn't include **discouraged workers,** people who are capable of working but have given up looking for jobs because they don't think they will find

Employment is the number of people currently employed in the economy.

Unemployment is the number of people who are actively looking for work but aren't currently employed.

The **labor force** is equal to the sum of employment and unemployment.

Discouraged workers are nonworking people who are capable of working but have given up looking for a job.

Underemployment is the number of people who work during a recession but receive lower wages than they would during an expansion due to fewer number of hours worked, lower-paying jobs, or both.

The **unemployment rate** is the percentage of the total number of people in the labor force who are unemployed.

them. Labor statistics don't include information on **underemployment,** the number of people who work during a recession but receive lower wages than they would during an expansion due to a smaller number of hours worked, lower-paying jobs, or both.

The **unemployment rate** is the percentage of the total number of people in the labor force who are unemployed. It is calculated as follows:

$$\text{(23-1)} \quad \frac{\text{Unemployment}}{\text{rate}} = \frac{\text{Number of unemployed workers}}{\text{Number of unemployed workers} + \text{Number of employed workers}} \times 100$$

The unemployment rate is usually a good indicator of what conditions are like in the job market: a high unemployment rate signals a poor job market in which jobs are hard to find; a low unemployment rate indicates a good job market in which jobs are relatively easy to find. (Exactly what makes for "high" or "low" has changed quite a bit over time in the United States, something we will discuss more fully in Chapter 32.) In general, during recessions the unemployment rate is rising; during expansions it is falling.

Look again at Figure 23-2, which shows the monthly unemployment rate from 1948 through 2004. The average unemployment rate for the whole period was 5.6%, but there were large fluctuations around that average. In fact, even in the most prosperous times there is some unemployment. In Chapter 32 we'll see why zero unemployment is not a realistic possibility and should not be a goal of policy makers. A booming economy, like that of the late 1960s or late 1990s, can push the unemployment rate down to 4% or even lower. But a severe recession, like that of 1981–1982, can push the unemployment rate into double digits (unemployment in that recession peaked in November 1982, at 10.8%).

"WOULD YOU LIKE A COPY OF MY MASTERS THESIS WITH THAT?"

Jim Borgman

These abstract numbers translate into enormous differences in personal experiences. For example, the 10.8% unemployment rate of late 1982 meant nearly 12 million people in the United States were actively seeking work but couldn't find jobs. More recently, as unemployment rose in the early 1990s, hundreds of thousands of workers were laid off, and many of those who did find jobs were severely underemployed. As a result, the nation was gripped by malaise and doubt. (One influential book at the time was titled *America: What Went Wrong?*) But at the end of the 1990s, as unemployment fell to 30-year lows, businesses scrambled to find workers and even students with mediocre grades and minimal experience got very good job offers. Alas, as is the nature of the business cycle, this happy era ended when the economy hit a rough patch in early 2001 and the unemployment rate rose again.

Aggregate Output

Rising unemployment is the most painful consequence of a recession, and falling unemployment the most urgently desired feature of an expansion. But the business cycle isn't just about jobs—it's also about output. Over the business cycle, the economy's level of output and its unemployment rate move in opposite directions.

Aggregate output is the economy's total production of final goods and services for a given time period.

Formally, **aggregate output** is the economy's total production of *final goods and services* for a given time period—usually a year. It excludes goods and services that are produced as inputs for the production of other goods (inputs are often called *intermediate goods*). Steel manufactured for the purpose of producing a car is not counted in aggregate output, but the car is. Real GDP is the actual numerical measure of aggregate output typically used by economists. We'll see how real GDP is calculated in Chapter 24. For now, the important point is that aggregate output normally falls in recessions but rises during expansions.

Panel (a) of Figure 23-3 shows the annual growth rate of U.S. real GDP from 1948 to 2004. That is, it plots the percent change in aggregate output from 1947 to 1948, from 1948 to 1949, and so on. On average, aggregate output grew 3.5% per year. As you can see, however, the actual growth rate fluctuated widely around that average, going as high as 8.7% in 1950 and as low as −1.9% in 1982. Comparison of panel (a) of Figure 23-3 to Figure 23-2 shows that the year in which aggregate output had its steepest post–World War II decline, 1982, was also the year in which the unemployment rate hit its post–World War II peak.

Panel (b) of Figure 23-3 shows the growth of U.S. real GDP over the same period, from 1948 to 2004. As you can see from the sustained upward trend line, declines in real GDP that occurred during recessions have been temporary events. Over the post–World War II period, real GDP has grown by more than 500% in the United States. We'll soon learn more about this long-run upward trend in aggregate output that is independent of the business cycle. For right now, however, let's learn more about the business cycle.

Figure 23-3

Growth in Aggregate Output, 1948–2004

Real GDP is a numerical measure of aggregate output, the output of the economy as a whole. Panel (a) shows the annual rate of growth of U.S. real GDP from 1948 to 2004, which averaged 3.5% over that period. Although real GDP rose in most years, the actual growth rate fluctuated with the business cycle, with real GDP actually falling in some years. Panel (b) shows the same data presented in a different form: it shows real GDP from 1948 to 2004. From it we see that when viewed from a period of time long enough to be independent of the business cycle, real GDP has grown substantially.

Source: Bureau of Economic Analysis.

(a) The Annual Growth Rate of Real GDP

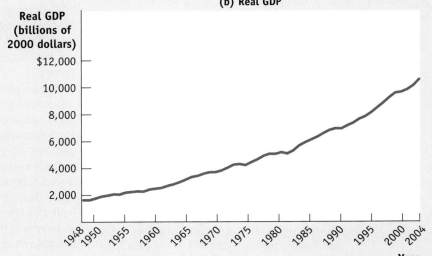

(b) Real GDP

Taming the Business Cycle

As we've explained, one of the key missions of macroeconomics is to understand why recessions happen and what, if anything, can be done about them. In addition, we'll learn in Chapter 27 that another major macroeconomic concern is inflation, a rise in the overall price level that often results from an excessively strong expansion.

Policy efforts undertaken to reduce the severity of recessions or to rein in excessively strong expansions are called **stabilization policy.** Stabilization policy is based on two main tools—monetary policy and fiscal policy. **Monetary policy** attempts to stabilize the economy through changes in the quantity of money in circulation or in interest rates, or both. **Fiscal policy** attempts to stabilize the economy through changes in taxation or in government spending, or both. We'll examine these tools in Chapters 29 and 31, where we'll see how they can diminish the length and severity of recessions as well as dampen overly robust expansions. But we'll also see in those chapters why they don't work perfectly—that is, fiscal policy and monetary policy can't eliminate fluctuations in the economy altogether. So, in the end, the business cycle is still with us.

Although the business cycle is one of the main concerns of macroeconomics and historically played a crucial role in fostering the development of the field, macroeconomists are also concerned with other issues. We turn next to the question of long-run growth.

> Policy efforts undertaken to reduce the severity of recessions and to rein in excessively strong expansions are called **stabilization policy.**
>
> **Monetary policy** is a type of stabilization policy that involves changes in the quantity of money in circulation or in interest rates, or both.
>
> **Fiscal policy** is a type of stabilization policy that involves changes in taxation or in government spending, or both.

economics in action

Has the Business Cycle Been Tamed?

Macroeconomics as we know it came into existence during the Great Depression, created by economists determined to prevent anything like that from happening again. From the evidence, it appears that U.S. policy makers and economists have been successful: the United States has not suffered any downturn severe enough to be considered a depression since then. But have we succeeded in the related task of taming the business cycle?

Sort of. Figure 23-4 shows the average annual U.S. unemployment rate going all the way back to 1900. The figure is dominated by the huge rise in unemployment during the 1930s; since World War II the United States has managed to avoid anything comparably severe. Macroeconomists believe that part of the reason is that since World War II macroeconomic policies have been smarter because they are based on better macroeconomic theory.

Economists have learned, however, to be wary of pronouncements that the business cycle has been brought under control and that recessions are a thing of the past. Such pronouncements were common during the long expansion of the 1960s, but two severe recessions that drove unemployment to post–World War II highs followed. Claims that the business cycle was no more arose again during the long expansion of the 1990s, only to be belied by the recession of 2001.

In recent times other countries have suffered economic downturns almost as severe as the Great Depression. For example, between 1998 and 2002 Argentina suffered an 18% fall in its aggregate output. The unemployment rate rose to 24%, and many middle-class families were

Figure 23-4 **The Unemployment Rate Since 1900**

Has progress in macroeconomics made the economy more stable? This figure shows average annual U.S. unemployment rates since 1900. Clearly, nothing like the Great Depression—the huge surge in unemployment that dominates the figure—has happened since. But economists who argued during the 1960s that the business cycle had been tamed were proven wrong by severe recessions in the 1970s and early 1980s.

Source: U.S. Census Bureau; Bureau of Labor Statistics.

plunged into poverty. These downturns inspired some humility in macroeconomists. Although they believe they know enough to prevent another Great Depression, the task of economic stabilization remains far from complete. ■

> >

>>CHECK YOUR UNDERSTANDING 23-2

1. Why do the unemployment rate and aggregate output move in opposite directions over the business cycle?

2. Describe some of the costs to society of having a high unemployment rate.

3. What are likely signs that a stabilization policy has been successful over a period of time?

Solutions appear at back of book.

Long-Run Economic Growth

Although 2002 was a difficult year for all new graduates seeking jobs, the jobs actually on offer paid extremely well by historical standards. The pay package of an average U.S. worker in 2002, even after correcting for higher prices of goods and services, was worth almost three times as much as the pay of an average worker in 1948.

In fact, the purchasing power of the average American worker's wage, the average family's income, and just about any other measure of what ordinary people can afford, has been rising steadily since at least the middle of the nineteenth century. The reason is that aggregate output, despite occasional declines, has trended powerfully upward over the long run—and has grown at a much faster rate than the population.

Recall from panel (a) of Figure 23-3 that the average growth rate of aggregate output from 1948 to 2004 was 3.5%. Over that same period, the U.S. population grew at an average rate of only 1.3% each year. So the size of the economic pie per person, or per capita, grew an average of 2.2% each year, equal to the 3.5% annual growth rate of aggregate output minus the 1.3% annual growth rate of the population. That's enough to allow every American's standard of living to double every 35 years. And that, roughly speaking, is what happened.

The sustained upward trend in aggregate output is known as **secular long-run growth,** or **long-run growth** for short. The word *secular,* in this context, is used to distinguish long-run growth from the expansion phase of business cycles, which lasts less than five years on average. Secular long-run growth refers to the growth of the economy over several decades. You can get an idea of just how powerful a force long-run growth is by looking at Figure 23-5, which shows annual figures for U.S.

Secular long-run growth, or **long-run growth,** is the sustained upward trend in aggregate output over several decades.

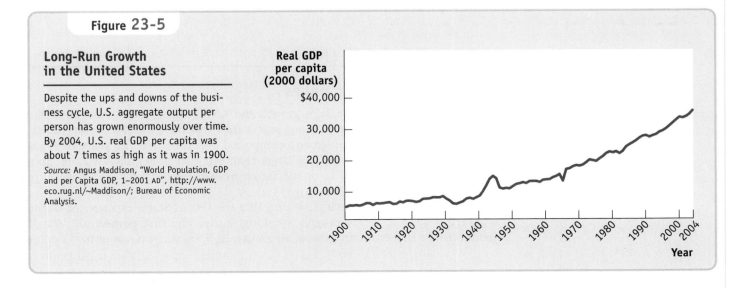

Figure 23-5

Long-Run Growth in the United States

Despite the ups and downs of the business cycle, U.S. aggregate output per person has grown enormously over time. By 2004, U.S. real GDP per capita was about 7 times as high as it was in 1900.

Source: Angus Maddison, "World Population, GDP and per Capita GDP, 1–2001 AD", http://www.eco.rug.nl/~Maddison/; Bureau of Economic Analysis.

Real GDP per capita (2000 dollars)

FOR INQUIRING MINDS

WHEN DID LONG-RUN GROWTH START?

We've seen that over the long run aggregate output rises steadily. In the United States it grew by more than 20-fold over the past 100 years. But did it grow that much in the previous 100 years? How far back does this process go?

The answer is that long-run growth is a relatively modern phenomenon. The U.S. economy was already growing steadily by the mid-nineteenth century—think railroads. But if you go back to the period before 1800, you find a world economy that grew extremely slowly by contemporary standards. Between the years 1000 and 1800, according to the best available estimates, the world economy grew less than 0.2% per year. Furthermore, population grew almost as fast, meaning that there was hardly any increase in aggregate output per capita. This economic stagnation was matched by unchanging living standards. For example, it's not clear that peasants in eighteenth-century Europe lived any better than Egyptian peasants in the age of the pharaohs. From examining historical records of birth and death rates, demographers know that in both periods human beings were living right on the edge of subsistence.

real GDP per capita from 1900 to 2004. As a result of this long-run growth, the U.S. economy's aggregate output per person was about 7 times as large in 2004 as it was in 1900. (Note that there was a 7-fold increase in real GDP per capita over the same period in which there was a 20-fold increase in real GDP. The difference in these two numbers is due to there being a much larger U.S. population in 2004 than in 1900.)

Long-run growth is fundamental to many of the most pressing economic questions today. In particular, *long-run growth per capita*—a sustained upward trend in aggregate output *per person*—is the key to higher wages and a rising standard of living. A major concern of macroeconomics—and the theme of Chapter 25—is trying to understand the long-run growth rate. Why was the average annual U.S. output growth rate 3.5% from 1948 to 2004? Could something have been done to make the growth rate higher?

These questions are even more urgent in poorer, less developed countries. In these countries, which would like to achieve a higher standard of living, the question of how to increase their growth rates is the central concern of economic policy.

As we'll see, macroeconomists don't use the same models to think about long-run growth that they use to think about the business cycle. It's always important to keep both sets of models in mind, because what is good in the long run can be bad in the short run, and vice versa. For example, the Paradox of Thrift shows that an attempt by households to increase their savings can be bad for the economy in the short run. But an economy's level of savings, as we'll see in Chapter 26, plays a crucial role in encouraging long-run economic growth.

economics in action

The Difference a Point Makes

What's the difference between 2.5% growth and 3.5% growth? It may not sound like much, and over the course of only one year it isn't that big a difference. But the effects of differences in long-run growth compound over time: after 25 years an economy that grows at 3.5% will be 30% larger than one that only grows at 2.5%. So a percentage point or so added to or subtracted from the growth rate can have huge economic implications over time.

A case in point is the growth slowdown that the United States experienced in the 1970s. From 1948 to 1973—roughly speaking, during the first post–World War II generation—the U.S. economy grew at an average of 3.9% per year, about half a point faster than its long-run average. For most people that meant an unprecedented rise in living standards, a general sense of miraculous prosperity.

From 1973 to 1995, however, the growth rate fell, averaging only 2.7%. The reasons for this slowdown remain disputed, but the consequences were clear: although the economic pie continued to grow, it was no longer growing fast enough to make everyone feel satisfied. Blue-collar workers believed that their wages were not keeping up with inflation, leading to a decline in their purchasing power. And investors were disappointed with company profits.

After 1995 there was a pickup in economic growth, again for reasons that remain in dispute. Many economists now believe that the U.S. economy has returned to a state in which growth may average 3.5% or so per year, that is, comparable to the miracle post–World War II generation. Let's hope that they are right! ∎

> >

>> QUICK REVIEW

➤ From 1948 to 2004, on average, the United States experienced *secular long-run growth* (or simply *long-run growth*) of real GDP of 3.5% per year, and of real GDP per capita of 2.2% per year, yielding a doubling of the American standard of living approximately every 35 years.
➤ A country can achieve a permanent increase in the standard of living of its citizens only through long-run growth. So a central concern of macroeconomics is what determines long-run growth.

>> CHECK YOUR UNDERSTANDING 23-3

1. In the United States the 1950s and 1960s were considered times of great optimism and accomplishment on a national scale. In contrast, the 1970s and 1980s were thought of as periods of retrenchment, pessimism, and diminished expectations. Explain the economic source of the different outlooks.

2. Many poor countries have high rates of population growth. What does this imply about the long-run growth rates of aggregate output that they must achieve in order to generate a higher standard of living per person?

Solutions appear at back of book.

Inflation and Deflation

Earlier we said that the average worker in 2002 earned about three times as much as the average worker in 1948, *after correcting for higher prices of goods and services.* That's an important qualification. If we don't correct for the higher prices of goods and services, the rise in wages from 1948 to 2002 appears much larger—increasing by a factor of 20 rather than by a factor of only 3.

This example illustrates an important distinction in macroeconomics: the distinction between *nominal* versus *real*. A **nominal** measure of something, such as nominal wages, is a measure that has not been adjusted for changes in prices over time. So we say that *nominal wages* have increased by a factor of 20 from 1948 to 2002. By comparison, a **real** measure of something is a measure that has been adjusted for changes in prices over time. So we say that *real wages* have increased by a factor of 3 from 1948 to 2002. Economists typically express wages in real terms because the real wage is a better indicator of the actual change in workers' purchasing power over time: it captures how much wages have changed over and above the change in the prices of goods and services that workers buy. So although nominal wages rose by a factor of 20 in those 55 years, workers could buy only 3 times as much in goods and services rather than 20 times as much. To say this another way, an average worker's wage in 2002, expressed in *2002 dollars*—the amount of goods and services that an average worker's wage from 2002 would buy in 2002—was 3 times higher than the wage in 1948 when it is expressed in *2002 dollars*—the amount of goods and services that an average worker's wage from 1948 would buy in 2002.

We refer to the overall price level of all final goods and services in the economy—that is, the price level of aggregate output—as the **aggregate price level.** When this price level rises, we say that the economy is experiencing **inflation.** When it falls, the economy is experiencing **deflation.**

As we'll explain in Chapter 24, there are two widely used measures of the aggregate price level—the *GDP deflator* and the *consumer price index,* or *CPI.* Figure 23-6 on page 552 shows the consumer price index from 1913 to 2004.

A **nominal** measure is a measure that has not been adjusted for changes in prices over time.

A **real** measure is a measure that has been adjusted for changes in prices over time.

The **aggregate price level** is the overall price level for final goods and services in the economy.

A rising aggregate price level is **inflation.**

A falling aggregate price level is **deflation.**

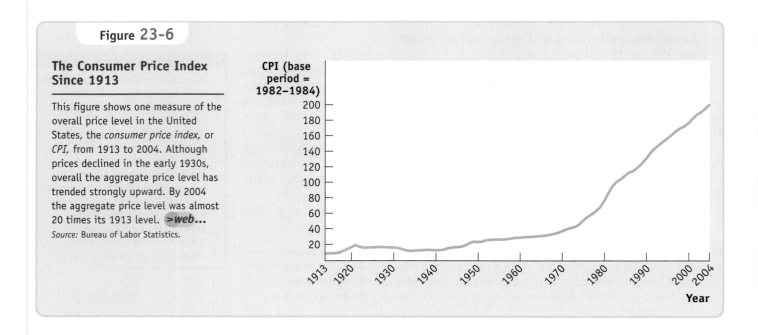

Figure 23-6

The Consumer Price Index Since 1913

This figure shows one measure of the overall price level in the United States, the *consumer price index,* or *CPI,* from 1913 to 2004. Although prices declined in the early 1930s, overall the aggregate price level has trended strongly upward. By 2004 the aggregate price level was almost 20 times its 1913 level. **>web...**

Source: Bureau of Labor Statistics.

CPI (base period = 1982–1984)

The economy has **price stability** when the aggregate price level is changing only slowly.

The **inflation rate** is the annual percent change in the aggregate price level.

You can see from the figure that the aggregate price level, like aggregate output (see Figure 23-5), has risen substantially over time. Overall prices were almost 20 times higher in 2004 than they were in 1913. Unlike the upward trend in aggregate output, however, the upward trend in prices is not a necessary feature of a well-performing economy. Nor is it necessarily a good thing.

Both inflation and deflation can pose problems for the economy, although these problems are subtler than those associated with recession. Here are two examples: Inflation discourages people from holding on to cash, because cash loses value over time if the aggregate price level is rising. This raises the cost of making purchases and sales for which cash is required. In extreme cases, people stop holding cash altogether and turn to barter. Deflation can cause the reverse problem. If the price level is falling, holding on to cash, which gains value over time, can become more attractive than investing in new factories and other productive assets. This can deepen a recession. We'll describe other costs of inflation and deflation in Chapter 33. For now, let's just note that in general economists regard **price stability**—in which the aggregate price level is changing, if at all, only slowly—as a desirable goal. (We say "changing slowly" instead of "not changing" because many macroeconomists believe that an inflation rate of 2 or 3% per year does little harm and may even do some good. We'll explain why in Chapter 33.) Price stability is a goal that seemed far out of reach for much of the post–World War II period but has been achieved to most macroeconomists' satisfaction in recent years.

The annual percent change in the aggregate price level is known as the **inflation rate** (which is negative in the case of deflation). Figure 23-7 shows the annual inflation rate in the United States from 1929 to 2004, measured as percent changes in the CPI. There were two brief bursts of inflation associated with World War II—one at the beginning, before the government imposed price controls, and one at the end, when the controls came off. Aside from those events, three main things stand out. First, there was sharp deflation in the early 1930s, associated with the onset of the Great Depression. Second, there was a prolonged period of high inflation in the 1970s and early 1980s. Finally, in the 1990s the aggregate price level returned to near-stability.

Macroeconomists have devoted a lot of effort to understanding the causes of inflation and deflation and to providing advice to governments on how to steer a path between the two undesirable extremes.

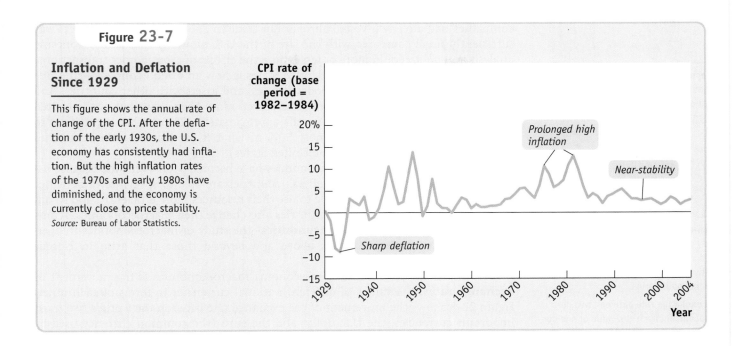

Figure 23-7

Inflation and Deflation Since 1929

This figure shows the annual rate of change of the CPI. After the deflation of the early 1930s, the U.S. economy has consistently had inflation. But the high inflation rates of the 1970s and early 1980s have diminished, and the economy is currently close to price stability.

Source: Bureau of Labor Statistics.

CPI rate of change (base period = 1982–1984)

Prolonged high inflation

Near-stability

Sharp deflation

Year

economics in action

A Fast (Food) Measure of Inflation

The original McDonald's opened in 1954. It offered fast service—it was, indeed, the original fast-food restaurant—and it was also very inexpensive. Hamburgers cost only $0.15; $0.25 with fries. Today a hamburger at a typical McDonald's costs five times as much—between $0.70 and $0.80. Has McDonald's lost touch with its fast-food roots? Have burgers become luxury cuisine?

No—in fact, a burger is, compared with other consumer goods, a better bargain today than it was in 1954. Burger prices have risen about 400%, from $0.15 to about $0.75, over the last half century. But the overall CPI has increased more than 600%. If McDonald's had matched the overall price-level increase, a hamburger would now cost between $0.90 and $1.00.

Inflation subsided in the 1990s—that is, the rate of increase in the aggregate price level slowed. And the same was true of burger prices—in fact, in 1997 McDonald's actually cut the price of many of its items, including the signature Big Mac. ∎

> > > > > > > > > > > > > > > > > > > >

>>CHECK YOUR UNDERSTANDING 23-4

1. Suppose your wages rose by 10% over the past year. In each of the following cases, determine whether you are better or worse off in comparison to the year before. Explain your answers.
   a. The yearly inflation rate was 5%.
   b. The yearly inflation rate was 15%.
   c. The economy experienced deflation, with prices falling at a rate of 2% per year.

Solutions appear at back of book.

The Open Economy

In 1954, when the original McDonald's was selling hamburgers for $0.15, the United States was very close to being a **closed economy**—an economy that does not trade goods, services, or assets with other countries. It wasn't literally closed, of course: even then the United States imported its coffee and bananas, and some U.S.

A **closed economy** is an economy that does not trade goods, services, or assets with other countries.

An **open economy** is an economy that trades goods, services, and assets with other countries.

Open-economy macroeconomics is the study of those aspects of macroeconomics that are affected by movements of goods, services, and assets across national boundaries.

The **exchange rate** between two national currencies is the value of one currency in terms of the other.

A country's **trade balance** is the difference between the value of the goods and services it sells to other countries and the value of the goods and services it buys from other countries.

companies had already invested abroad. But trade in goods, services, and assets was sufficiently small compared with the size of the U.S. economy that macroeconomic analysis and policy could more or less ignore the effects of cross-border transactions.

That is no longer the case. The United States is now an **open economy**—an economy that does a lot of trade in goods, services, and assets with other countries. And the economies of most other countries are even more open than that of the United States. For example, while the U.S. sells approximately 12% of what it produces to other countries, Canada sells almost 50% of what it produces to other countries (mainly, though not entirely, to the United States).

As we discussed in Chapter 2, economies have become open over time because international trade is mutually beneficial: countries are able to specialize in activities they do comparatively well, are able to use their resources more efficiently, and so on.

By pursuing gains from trade, countries also change their macroeconomic circumstances. **Open-economy macroeconomics**—the study of macroeconomics in open economies—involves some issues above and beyond those that arise in closed-economy macroeconomics.

One important concern in open-economy macroeconomics is the movement of **exchange rates,** the values of different national currencies in terms of each other. Figure 23-8 shows the movement of the exchange rate between the world's two most important currencies, the U.S. dollar and the euro (the common currency used by many European countries), from 1999 to the beginning of 2005. As you can see, the rate swung between a minimum of $0.85 per euro and a maximum of more than $1.30 per euro. When it cost only $0.85 to buy a euro, European goods looked very cheap to Americans; when the euro rose to $1.30, the reverse was true.

One major effect of swings in exchange rates is that they have an impact on the aggregate price level. Suppose, for example, that a German car costs € 40,000. At an exchange rate of $0.85 per euro, that's $34,000. At an exchange rate of $1.30, that's $52,000. Because the prices of imported goods like foreign cars are included in some measures of the aggregate price level, changes in the exchange rate of the dollar versus other currencies affect those measures of the aggregate price level.

Another important effect of the exchange rate is its influence on the **trade balance,** the difference between the value of the goods and services a country sells to other countries and the value of the goods and services it buys from other countries. When changes in the exchange rate make American goods cheaper to foreigners, the American trade balance becomes more positive or less negative. In Chapter 35 we'll see that this

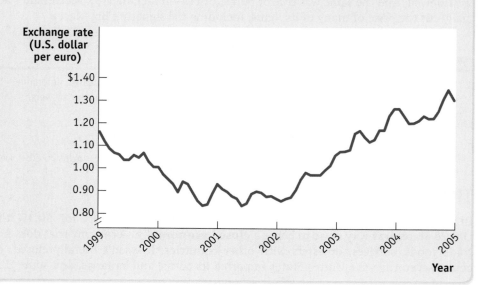

Figure 23-8

U.S. Dollars per Euro Since 1999

The U.S. dollar and Europe's euro are the world's two most important currencies. Over the course of only a few years, the exchange rate moved over a wide range, from $0.85 per euro to more than $1.30 per euro.

Source: Federal Reserve Bank of St. Louis.

increases U.S. aggregate output. When changes in the exchange rate make American goods more expensive to foreigners, the American trade balance becomes more negative or less positive.

Open economies trade goods and services as well as assets. International movements of *financial assets* are known as **capital flows.** We'll see in Chapter 26 how capital flows allow some countries to spend more on additions to their productive capacity than they would have been able to without capital flows. In the long run, this leads to a higher standard of living. We'll also see how capital flows allow international investors to get a higher return on their savings than they would have received in the absence of capital flows—also leading to a higher standard of living for investors.

Perhaps the most profound issue in open-economy macroeconomics involves the very existence of national currencies. Should the Canadian economy, which is closely intertwined with the economy of its much larger southern neighbor, even have its own currency? Or should there be a single currency for both the United States and Canada? This is not an academic question: although the Canadian dollar's independent existence seems assured for the time being, in 1999 most European countries gave up their independent national currencies in exchange for a pan-European currency, the euro. As we'll see, the question of whether other countries should follow Europe's example is the subject of intense debate, with a strong case to be made for both positions.

> **Capital flows** are international movements of financial assets.

economics in action

North of the Border

"At Windsor Crossing we welcome U.S. guests where your dollar buys you more!" So read an advertisement run in 2002 by an outlet mall that was pretty much the same as any outlet mall in the United States. But this one *wasn't* in the United States—it was in Windsor, Canada, just across the border from Detroit. (The U.S. Census considers Detroit and Windsor to be part of the same metropolitan area, even though they are in different countries.) The reason your U.S. dollar bought more was that in Windsor you could buy things with Canadian dollars—and one Canadian dollar, when this ad ran in June 2002, cost only US $0.65 (that is, $0.65 in U.S. dollars).

The Canadian dollar—known as the "loonie" because of the loon engraved on the dollar coin—isn't always that cheap. In fact, the Canadian dollar–U.S. dollar exchange rate has moved up and down significantly over the years. In 1974 a Canadian dollar was worth US $1.04. In 1986 it was down to US $0.71; in 1991 it was back up to US $0.89; in the spring of 2002 it was down to US $0.66; and by the end of 2004 it was back up to US $0.84.

These swings in the Canadian dollar–U.S. dollar exchange rate had strong effects on Canada's economy and some effect on the much larger U.S. economy. Since many of the goods Canadians buy are made in the United States, with prices set in U.S. dollars, a fall in the loonie—which means that it takes more Canadian dollars to buy a U.S. dollar—has the direct effect in Canada of raising consumer prices of goods and services imported from the United States. This sounds as if a *weak* loonie—a loonie that has fallen in value relative to other currencies like the U.S. dollar—is a bad thing for Canada, but there are compensations. Since Canadian wages and prices are largely set in Canadian dollars, a Canadian producer that sells to American customers has a cost advantage over U.S. competitors when the loonie is weak. That's because the price that it receives for its goods, in American dollars, has gone up relative to the production costs that it has to pay, which are in Canadian loonies. So it can lower its price to American customers in U.S. dollars and still make a profit—something its American competitors (whose costs are in U.S. dollars and so have not fallen) cannot match. And it's great news for Windsor's outlet malls. ∎

> >

>> **QUICK REVIEW**

➤ In contrast to a *closed economy,* an *open economy* is able to exploit gains from trade in goods, services, and assets.

➤ An open economy must be studied using the tools of *open-economy macroeconomics.*

➤ Changes in the *exchange rate* can affect the aggregate price level because they alter the prices of imported goods. They can also affect aggregate output through their effect on the *trade balance.*

➤ *Capital flows* of financial assets can also have important effects on aggregate output and raise a country's standard of living in the long run.

>>CHECK YOUR UNDERSTANDING 23-5

1. The euro, the currency of most countries that make up the European Union, went from approximately $1.15 in 1999 to $0.85 in 2001. Assume that over that time the price of European goods in euros, as well as the price of American goods in American dollars, did not change.
   a. Were European goods cheaper or more expensive for Americans in 1999 compared to 2001? Were American goods cheaper or more expensive for Europeans in 1999 compared to 2001?
   b. How do you think the change in the exchange rate of the euro versus the dollar from 1999 to 2001 affected the total value of European goods bought by Americans during this time? The total value of American goods bought by Europeans?

Solutions appear at back of book.

• A LOOK AHEAD •

In the chapters ahead we will examine in depth the issues described so briefly here. We'll start our discussion of macroeconomic models in Part 12 with an analysis of the long run—long-run growth, as well as the markets and institutions that channel savings in investment productive capacity. Part 13 then turns to the short run—the realm of the business cycle. There we learn how business cycles happen and how monetary policy and fiscal policy can be used to stabilize the economy. Part 14 turns to what we describe as the medium run—the period beyond the business cycle but before the long run, in which issues of inflation and deflation become central to the economic story.

Before we begin analyzing macroeconomic models, however, we need to know something about the numbers we are analyzing. How do we actually estimate aggregate output, the aggregate price level, and other key measures of macroeconomic performance?

SUMMARY

1. Macroeconomics is the study of the behavior of the economy as a whole—the total output level, the overall level of prices, total employment, and so on.

2. There are four principal ways in which macroeconomics differs from microeconomics: it focuses on how the accumulated effects of individual actions can lead to unintended macroeconomic outcomes; it allows greater scope for government intervention; it studies long-run growth; and it uses **economic aggregates,** measures that summarize data across various markets for goods, services, workers, and assets. Modern macroeconomics arose from efforts to understand the Great Depression.

3. One key concern of macroeconomics is the **business cycle,** the short-run alternation between **recessions,** periods of falling employment and output, and **expansions,** periods of rising employment and output. Modern macroeconomics arose largely in order to prevent the occurrence of another **depression,** a deep and prolonged economic downturn. The **labor force,** the sum of **employment** and **unemployment,** does not include **discouraged workers,** non-working people capable of working but who have given up looking for a job. Labor statistics also do not contain data on **underemployment,** employed workers who earn less than they would in an expansion due to lower-paying jobs or fewer hours worked. The **unemployment rate,** which is usually a good measure of conditions in the labor market, has risen and fallen repeatedly over time. **Aggregate output,** the total level of output of final goods and services in the economy, moves in the opposite direction of unemployment over the business cycle.

4. **Stabilization policy,** the effort by governments to smooth out the business cycle, has two main tools: **monetary policy,** changes in the quantity of money in circulation or in interest rates, or both; and **fiscal policy,** changes in taxation or in government spending, or both.

5. Another key area of macroeconomic study is **secular long-run growth,** or simply **long-run growth,** the sustained upward trend in aggregate output over several decades. A sustained increase in aggregate output per capita is the key to rising living standards over time.

6. Economists distinguish between **nominal** measures, measures that haven't been adjusted for changing prices, and **real** measures, measures that have been adjusted for changing prices. Changes in real wages are a better measure of changes in workers' purchasing power. The **aggregate price level** is the overall price level for all final goods and services in the economy. The **inflation rate,** the annual percent change in the aggregate price level, is

positive when the aggregate price level is rising (**inflation**) and negative when the aggregate price level is falling (**deflation**). Because inflation and deflation can cause problems, **price stability** is generally preferred. Currently, the U.S. economy is close to price stability.

7. A **closed economy** is an economy that does not trade goods, services, or assets with other countries; an **open economy** trades goods, services, and assets with other countries. The United States has become an increasingly open economy, and **open-economy macroeconomics**

has become increasingly important. One of the main concerns introduced by open-economy macroeconomics is the **exchange rate,** the value of one currency in terms of another. Exchange rates can affect the aggregate price level. They can also affect aggregate output through their effect on the **trade balance,** the difference in value between sales to and purchases from foreigners. Another area of study is **capital flows,** movements of financial assets across borders.

KEY TERMS

Economic aggregates, p. 542
Business cycle, p. 544
Depression, p. 544
Recessions, p. 544
Expansions, p. 544
Employment, p. 545
Unemployment, p. 545
Labor force, p. 545
Discouraged workers, p. 545
Underemployment, p. 546
Unemployment rate, p. 546

Aggregate output, p. 546
Stabilization policy, p. 548
Monetary policy, p. 548
Fiscal policy, p. 548
Secular long-run growth (long-run growth), p. 549
Nominal, p. 551
Real, p. 551
Aggregate price level, p. 551
Inflation, p. 551
Deflation, p. 551

Price stability, p. 552
Inflation rate, p. 552
Closed economy, p. 553
Open economy, p. 554
Open-economy macroeconomics, p. 554
Exchange rate, p. 554
Trade balance, p. 554
Capital flows, p. 555

PROBLEMS

1. Which of the following questions are relevant for the study of macroeconomics and which for microeconomics?

   a. How will Ms. Martin's tips change when a large manufacturing plant near the restaurant where she works closes?

   b. What will happen to spending by consumers when the economy enters a downturn?

   c. How will the price of oranges change when a late frost damages Florida's orange groves?

   d. How will wages at a manufacturing plant change when its workforce is unionized?

   e. What will happen to U.S. exports as the dollar becomes less expensive in terms of other currencies?

   f. What is the relationship between a nation's unemployment rate and its inflation rate?

2. When one person saves, that person's wealth is increased, meaning that he or she can consume more in the future. But when everyone saves, everyone's income falls, meaning that everyone must consume less today. Explain this seeming contradiction.

3. What was the Great Depression? How did it affect the role of government in the economy and the macroeconomic toolkit?

4. Why do we consider a business-cycle expansion different from long-run economic growth? Why do we care about the size of the long-run growth rate of real GDP versus the size of the growth rate of the population?

5. There are 100,000 inhabitants in Macronesia. Among those 100,000 inhabitants, 25,000 are too old to work and 15,000 inhabitants are too young to work. Among the remaining 60,000 inhabitants, 10,000 are not working and have given up looking for work, 45,000 are currently employed, and the remaining 5,000 are looking for work but do not currently have a job.

   a. What is the number of people in the labor force in Macronesia?

   b. What is the unemployment rate in Macronesia?

   c. How many people in Macronesia are discouraged workers?

6. In 1798, Thomas Malthus's "Essay on the Principle of Population" was published. In it, he wrote: "Population, when unchecked, increases in a geometrical ratio. Subsistence increases only in an arithmetical ratio . . . . This implies a strong and constantly operating check on population from the difficulty of subsistence." Malthus was saying that the growth of

the population is limited by the amount of food available to eat; people will live at the subsistence level forever. Why didn't Malthus's description apply to the world after 1800?

7. At the start of 2005 in Macroland, aggregate output was $10 billion ($10,000 million) and the population was 1 million. During 2005, aggregate output increased by 3.5%, the population increased by 2.5%, and the aggregate price level remained constant.

a. What was aggregate output per capita in Macroland at the start of 2005?

b. What was aggregate output in Macroland at the end of 2005?

c. What was the population of Macroland at the end of 2005?

d. What was aggregate output per capita in Macroland at the end of 2005?

e. What was the annual growth rate of aggregate output per capita in Macroland during 2005? *Hint:* the 2005 growth rate is equal to:

$$\frac{\text{Change in aggregate output during 2005}}{\text{Aggregate output at start of 2005}} \times 100$$

8. College tuition has risen significantly in the last few decades. From the 1971–1972 academic year to the 2001–2002 academic year, total tuition, room, and board paid by full-time undergraduate students went from $1,357 to $8,022 at public institutions and from $2,917 to $21,413 at private institutions. This is an average annual tuition increase of 6.1% at public institutions and 6.9% at private institutions. Over the same time, average personal income after taxes rose from $3,860 to $26,156 per year, which is an average annual rate of growth of personal income of 6.6%. Have these tuition increases made it more difficult for the average student to afford college tuition?

9. In May of each year, *The Economist* publishes data on the price of the Big Mac in different countries and exchange rates. The accompanying table shows some data used for the index from 2001 and 2003. Use this information to answer the questions below.

Country	2001		2003	
	Price of Big Mac (in local currency)	Exchange rate (foreign currency per U.S. dollar)	Price of Big Mac (in local currency)	Exchange rate (foreign currency per U.S. dollar)
Argentina	peso2.50	1.00 pesos per US$1	peso4.10	2.88 pesos per US$1
Canada	C$3.33	C$1.56 per US$1	C$3.20	C$1.45 per US$1
Euro area	€2.57	€1.14 per US$1	€2.71	€0.91 per US$1
Japan	¥294	¥124 per US$1	¥262	¥120 per US$1
United States	US$2.54		US$2.71	

a. Where was it cheapest to buy a Big Mac in U.S. dollars in 2001?

b. Where was it cheapest to buy a Big Mac in U.S. dollars in 2003?

c. If the increase in the local currency price of the Big Mac in each country represented the average inflation rate in that country over the two-year period from 2001 to 2003, which nation experienced the most inflation? Did any of the nations experience deflation?

d. For each currency, explain whether the dollar became more or less valuable in terms of that currency from 2001 to 2003.

>*web*... To continue your study and review of concepts in this chapter, please visit the Krugman/Wells website for quizzes, animated graph tutorials, web links to helpful resources, and more.

www.worthpublishers.com/krugmanwells

>>Tracking the Macroeconomy

AFTER THE REVOLUTION

IN DECEMBER 1975 THE GOVERNMENT of Portugal—a provisional government in the process of establishing a democracy—feared that it was facing an economic crisis. Business owners, alarmed by the rise of leftist political parties, were issuing dire warnings about plunging production. Newspapers speculated that the economy had shrunk 10 or even 15% since the 1974 revolution that had overthrown the country's long-standing dictatorship.

In the face of this supposed economic collapse, some Portuguese were pronouncing democracy itself a failure. Others declared that capitalism was the culprit and demanded that the government seize control of the nation's factories to force them to produce more. But how bad was the situation, really?

To answer this question, Portugal's top monetary official invited his old friend Richard Eckaus, an economist at the Massachusetts Institute of Technology, and two other MIT economists to look at the country's national accounts, the set of data collected on the country's economic activity. The

visiting experts had to engage in a lot of educated guesswork: Portugal's economic data collection had always been somewhat incomplete, and it had been further disrupted by political upheavals. For example, the country's statisticians normally tracked construction with data on the sales of structural steel and concrete. But in the somewhat chaotic situation of 1975, these indicators were moving in opposite directions because many builders were ignoring the construction regulations

With accurate economic data, Portugal was able to make the transition from revolution in 1975 to a prosperous democracy today.

What you will learn in this chapter:

➤ How economists use aggregate measures to track the performance of the economy

➤ What **gross domestic product,** or **GDP,** is and the three ways of calculating it

➤ The difference between **real GDP** and **nominal GDP** and why real GDP is the appropriate measure of real economic activity

➤ The significance of the **unemployment rate** and how it moves over the business cycle

➤ What a **price index** is and how it is used to calculate the **inflation rate** and using very little steel. (Travel tip: if you find yourself visiting Portugal, try to avoid being in a 1975-vintage building during an earthquake.)

Still, they went to work with the available data, and within a week they were able to make a rough estimate: aggregate output had declined only 3% from 1974 to 1975. The economy had suffered a serious setback, but its decline was much less drastic than the calamity being portrayed in the newspapers. (Later revisions pushed the decline up to 4.5%, but that was still much less than feared.) The Portuguese government certainly had work to do, but there was no need to abandon either democracy or a market economy. In fact, the economy soon began to recover. Over the past three decades, Portugal—though it has had its problems—has, on the whole, been a success story. A once-backward dictatorship is now a fairly prosperous, solidly democratic member of the European Union.

What's the lesson of this story? It is that economic measurement matters. If the government of Portugal had believed the scare stories some were telling at the time, it might have made major policy mistakes. Good macroeconomic policy depends on good measurement of what is happening in the economy as a whole.

In this chapter, we explain how macroeconomists measure key aspects of the economy—the level of income and aggregate output, the level of employment and unemployment, and the level and rate of change of prices.

The National Accounts

Almost all countries calculate a set of numbers known as the *national income and product accounts*. In fact, the accuracy of a country's accounts is a remarkably reliable indicator of its state of economic development—in general, the more reliable the accounts, the more economically advanced the country. When international economic agencies seek to help a less developed country, typically the first order of business is to send a team of experts to audit and improve the country's accounts.

In the United States, these numbers are calculated by the Bureau of Economic Analysis, a division of the U.S. government's Commerce Department. The **national income and product accounts,** often referred to simply as the **national accounts,** keep track of the spending of consumers, sales of producers, business investment spending, government purchases, and a variety of other flows of money between different sectors of the economy. Let's see how they work.

The **national income and product accounts,** or **national accounts,** keep track of the flows of money between different sectors of the economy.

The Circular-Flow Diagram, Revisited and Expanded

To understand the principles behind the national accounts, it helps to look at Figure 24-1, a revised and expanded *circular-flow diagram* similar to the one we introduced in Chapter 2. Recall that in Figure 2-7 we showed the flows of money, goods and services, and factors of production through the economy. Here we restrict ourselves to flows of money but add extra elements that allow us to show the key concepts behind the national accounts. As in our original version of the circular-flow diagram, the underlying principle is that the flow of money into each market or sector is equal to the flow of money coming out of that market or sector.

Figure 2-7 showed a simplified world containing only two kinds of "inhabitants," households and firms. And it illustrated the circular flow of money between households and firms, which remains visible in Figure 23-1. In the markets for goods and services, households engage in **consumer spending,** buying goods and services from domestic firms and from firms in the rest of the world. Households also own factors of production—

Consumer spending is household spending on goods and services.

Figure 24-1   An Expanded Circular-Flow Diagram: The Flows of Money Through the Economy

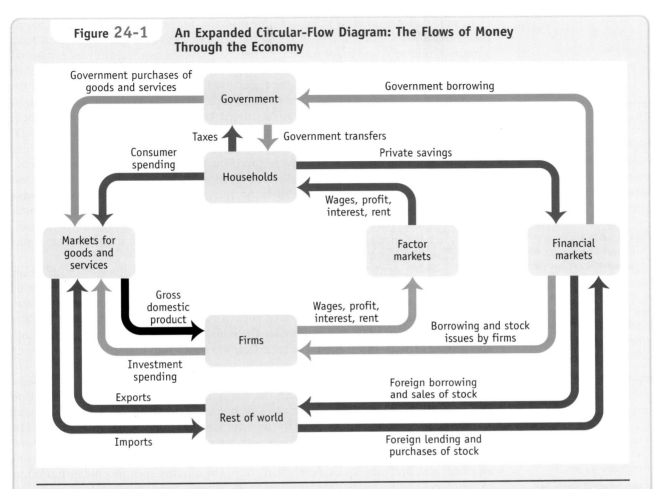

A circular flow of funds connects the four sectors of the economy—households, firms, government, and the rest of the world—via three types of markets: the factor markets, the markets for goods and services, and the financial markets. Funds flow from firms to households in the form of wages, profit, interest, and rent through the factor markets. After paying taxes to the government and receiving government transfers, households allocate the remaining income—disposable income—to private savings and consumer spending. Via the financial markets, private savings and funds from the rest of the world are channeled into investment spending by firms, government borrowing, foreign borrowing and lending, and foreign transactions of stocks. In turn, funds flow from the government and households to firms to pay for purchases of goods and services. Finally, exports to the rest of the world generate a flow of funds into the economy and imports lead to a flow of funds out of the economy. If we add up consumer spending on goods and services, investment spending by firms, government purchases of goods and services, and exports, then subtract the value of imports, the total flow of funds represented by this calculation is total spending on final goods and services produced in the United States. Equivalently, it's the value of all the final goods and services produced in the United States—that is, the gross domestic product of the economy.

labor, land, physical capital, and financial capital. They sell the use of these factors of production to firms, receiving wages, profit, interest payments, and rent in return. Firms buy and pay households for the use of those factors of production in the factor markets. Most households derive the bulk of their income from wages earned by selling labor. But households derive additional income from their indirect ownership of the physical capital used by firms, mainly in the form of **stocks,** shares in the ownership of a company, and **bonds,** borrowing in the form of an IOU that pays interest. So the income households receive from the factor markets includes profit distributed to shareholders, and the interest payments on bonds held by households. Finally, households receive rent in return for allowing firms to use land or structures that they own. So households receive income in the form of wages, profit, interest, and rent via factor markets.

A **stock** is a share in the ownership of a company held by a shareholder.

A **bond** is borrowing in the form of an IOU that pays interest.

Government transfers are payments by the government to individuals for which no good or service is provided in return.

Disposable income, equal to income plus government transfers minus taxes, is the total amount of household income available to spend on consumption and to save.

Private savings, equal to disposable income minus consumer spending, is disposable income that is not spent on consumption.

The banking, stock, and bond markets, which channel private savings and foreign lending into investment spending, government borrowing, and foreign borrowing are known as the **financial markets.**

Government borrowing is the amount of funds borrowed by the government in the financial markets.

Government purchases of goods and services are government expenditures on goods and services.

Goods and services sold to residents of other countries are **exports;** goods and services purchased from residents of other countries are **imports.**

Investment spending is spending on productive physical capital, such as machinery and construction of structures, and on changes to inventories.

In our original, simplified circular-flow diagram, households spent all the income they received via factor markets on goods and services. Figure 24-1, however, illustrates a more complicated and more realistic model. There we see two reasons why goods and services don't in fact absorb all of households' income. First, households don't get to keep all the income they receive via the factor markets. They must pay part of their income to the government in the form of taxes, such as income taxes and sales taxes. In addition, some households receive **government transfers**—payments by the government to individuals for which no good or service is provided in return, such as Social Security benefits and unemployment insurance payments. The total income households have left after paying taxes and receiving government transfers is **disposable income.**

In addition, households normally don't spend all their disposable income on goods and services. Instead, part of their income is typically set aside as **private savings,** which goes into **financial markets** where individuals, banks, and other institutions buy and sell stocks and bonds as well as make loans. As Figure 24-1 shows, the financial markets also receive funds from the rest of the world and provide funds to the government, to firms, and to the rest of the world.

Before going further, we can use the box representing households to illustrate an important general feature of the circular-flow diagram: the total sum of flows of money out of a given box is equal to the total sum of flows of money into that box. It's simply a matter of accounting: what goes in must come out. So, for example, the total flow of money out of households—the sum of taxes paid, consumer spending, and private savings—must equal the total flow of money into households—the sum of wages, profit, interest, rent, and government transfers.

Now let's look at the other types of inhabitants we've added to the circular-flow diagram, including the government and the rest of the world. The government returns part of the money it collects from taxes to households in the form of government transfers. However, it uses much of its tax revenue, plus additional funds borrowed in the financial markets through **government borrowing,** to buy goods and services. **Government purchases of goods and services,** the total purchases by federal, state, and local governments, include everything from the military spending on ammunition to your local public school's spending on chalk, erasers, and teacher salaries.

The rest of the world participates in the U.S. economy in three ways. First, some of the goods and services produced in the United States are sold to residents of other countries. For example, more than half of America's annual wheat and cotton crops are sold abroad. Goods and services sold to other countries are known as **exports.** Export sales lead to a flow of funds from the rest of the world into the United States to pay for them. Second, some of the goods and services purchased by residents of the United States are produced abroad. For example, many consumer goods are made in China. Goods and services purchased from residents of other countries are known as **imports.** Import purchases lead to a flow of funds out of the United States to pay for them. Third, foreigners can participate in U.S. financial markets by making transactions. Foreign lending—lending by foreigners to parties in the United States, and purchases by foreigners of shares of stock in American companies—generates a flow of funds into the United States from the rest of the world. Conversely, foreign borrowing—borrowing by foreigners from U.S. parties and purchases by Americans of stock in foreign companies—leads to a flow of funds out of the United States to the rest of the world.

Finally, let's go back to the markets for goods and services. In Chapter 2 we focused only on purchases of goods and services by households. We now see that there are other types of spending on goods and services, including government purchases, imports, and exports. Notice that firms also buy goods and services in our expanded economy. For example, an automobile company that is building a new factory will buy investment goods, stamping presses, welding robots, and other machines from companies that specialize in producing these items. It will also accumulate an inventory of finished cars in preparation for shipping them to dealers. The national income accounts count this **investment spending**—spending on productive physical capital, such as machinery and construction of structures, and on changes to *inventories*—as part of total spending on goods and services.

You might ask why changes to inventories are included in investment spending—finished cars aren't, after all, used to produce more cars. Additional inventories of finished goods are counted as investment spending because, like machinery, they contribute to greater future sales for a firm. So spending on additions to inventories is a form of investment spending by a firm. Conversely, a drawing-down of inventories is counted as a fall in investment spending because it leads to lower future sales. It's also important to understand that investment spending includes spending on construction of any structure, regardless of whether it is an assembly plant or a new house. Why include construction of homes? Because, like a plant, a new house produces a future stream of services—housing services for its occupants.

Suppose that we add up consumer spending on goods and services, investment spending, government purchases of goods and services, and the value of exports, then subtract the value of imports. That measure has a name: it's a country's *gross domestic product*. But before we can formally define gross domestic product, or GDP, we have to examine an important distinction between classes of goods and services: the difference between *final goods and services* versus *intermediate goods and services*.

Gross Domestic Product

A consumer's purchase of a new car from a dealer is one example of a sale of **final goods and services:** goods and services sold to the final, or end, user. But an automobile manufacturer's purchase of steel from a steel foundry or glass from a glass-maker is an example of purchasing **intermediate goods and services:** goods and services that are inputs for production of final goods and services. In the case of intermediate goods and services, the purchaser—another firm—is *not* the final user.

Gross domestic product, or **GDP**, is the total value of all *final* goods and services produced in an economy during a given period, usually a year. In 2004 the GDP of the United States was $11,734 billion, or about $40,000 per person. So if you are an economist trying to construct a country's national accounts, *one way to calculate GDP is to calculate it directly: survey firms and find out the value of their production of final goods and services.* We'll explain in detail in the next section why intermediate goods, and some other types of goods as well, are not included in the calculation of GDP.

But adding up the total value of final goods and services produced isn't the only way of calculating GDP. Since GDP is equal to the total value of final goods and services produced in the economy, it must also equal the flow of funds received by firms from sales in the goods and services market. If you look again at the circular-flow diagram in Figure 24-1, you will see that the arrow going from markets for goods and services to firms is indeed labeled "Gross domestic product." By our basic rule of accounting, which says that flows out of any box are equal to flows into the box, the flow of funds out of the markets for goods and services to firms is equal to the total flow of funds into the markets for goods and services from other sectors. And as you can see from Figure 24-1, the total flow of funds into the markets for goods and services is total or **aggregate spending** on domestically produced final goods and services—the sum of consumer spending, investment spending, government purchases of goods and services, and exports minus imports. *So a second way of calculating GDP is to add up aggregate spending on domestically produced final goods and services in the economy.*

And there is yet another way of calculating GDP. The flow from firms to the factor markets is the factor income paid out by firms to households in the form of wages, profit, interest, and rent. Again, by accounting rules, the value of the flow of factor income from firms to households must be equal to the flow of money into firms from the markets for goods and services. And this last value, we know, is the total value of production in the economy—GDP. An intuitive explanation of why

Final goods and services are goods and services sold to the final, or end, user.

Intermediate goods and services are goods and services—bought from one firm by another firm—that are inputs for production of final goods and services.

Gross domestic product, or **GDP,** is the total value of all final goods and services produced in the economy during a given year.

Aggregate spending, the sum of consumer spending, investment spending, government purchases, and exports minus imports, is the total spending on domestically produced final goods and services in the economy.

"You wouldn't think there'd be much money in potatoes, chickens, and woodchopping, but it all adds up."

GDP is equal to the total value of factor income paid by firms in the economy to households is the fact that the value of each sale in the economy must accrue to someone as income—either as wages, profit, interest, or rent. *So a third way of calculating GDP is to sum the total factor income earned by households from firms in the economy.*

Calculating GDP

We've just explained that there are in fact three methods for calculating GDP. Government statisticians use all three methods. To explain how these three methods work, we will consider a hypothetical economy, shown in Figure 24-2. This economy consists of three firms—American Motors, Inc., which produces one car per year; American Steel, Inc., which produces the steel that goes into the car; and American Ore, Inc., which mines the iron ore that goes into the steel. This economy produces one car, worth $21,500. So GDP is $21,500. Let's look at how the three different methods of calculating GDP yield the same result.

Measuring GDP as the Value of Production of Final Goods and Services

The first method for calculating GDP is to add up the value of all the final goods and services produced in the economy—a calculation that excludes the value of intermediate goods and services. Why are intermediate goods and services excluded? After all, don't they represent a very large and valuable portion of the economy?

To understand why only final goods and services are included in GDP, look at the simplified economy described in Figure 24-2. Should we measure the GDP of this economy by adding up the total sales of the iron ore producer, the steel producer, and the auto producer? If we did, we would in effect be counting the value of the steel twice—once when it is sold by the steel plant to the auto plant, and again when the steel auto body is sold to a consumer as a finished car. And we would be counting the value of the iron ore *three* times—once when it is mined and sold to the steel company, a second time when it is made into steel and sold to the auto producer, and a third time when the steel is made into a car and sold to the consumer. So counting the full value of each producer's sales would cause us to count the same items several times and artificially inflate the

Figure 24-2

Calculating GDP

In this hypothetical economy consisting of three firms, GDP can be calculated in three different ways: measuring GDP as the value of production of final goods and services, by summing each firm's value added; measuring GDP as aggregate spending on domestically produced final goods and services; and measuring GDP as factor income earned from firms in the economy.

Aggregate spending on domestically produced final goods and services = $21,500

	American Ore, Inc.	American Steel, Inc.	American Motors, Inc.	Total factor income	
Value of sales	$4,200 (ore)	$9,000 (steel)	$21,500 (car)		
Intermediate goods	0	4,200 (iron ore)	9,000 (steel)		
Wages	2,000	3,700	10,000	$15,700	Total
Interest payments	1,000	600	1,000	2,600	payments
Rent	200	300	500	1,000	to factors
Profit	1,000	200	1,000	2,200	= $21,500
Total expenditure by firm	4,200	9,000	21,500		
Value added per firm **=** **Value of sales – cost of intermediate goods**	4,200	4,800	12,500		

Sum of value added = $21,500

An old line says that when a person marries his or her housekeeper or chef, GDP falls. And it's true: when someone provides services for pay, those services are counted as a part of GDP. But the services family members provide to each other are not. Some economists have produced alternative measures that try to "impute" the value of household work—that is, assign an estimate of what the market value of that work would have been if it had been paid for. But the standard measure of GDP doesn't contain that imputation.

GDP estimates do, however, include an imputation for the value of "owner-occupied housing." That is, if you buy the home you were formerly renting, GDP does not go down. It's true that because you no longer pay rent to your landlord, the landlord no longer sells a service to you— namely, use of the house or apartment. But the statisticians make an estimate of what you would have paid if you rented whatever you live in, whether it's an apartment or a house. For the purposes of the statistics,

it's as if you were renting your dwelling from yourself.

If you think about it, this makes a lot of sense. In a homeowning country like the United States, the pleasure we derive from our houses is an important part of the standard of living. So to be accurate, estimates of GDP must take into account the value of housing that is occupied by owners as well as the value of rental housing.

---

calculation of GDP. For example, in Figure 24-2, the total value of all sales, intermediate and final, is $34,700: $21,500 from the sale of the car, plus $9,000 from the sale of the steel, plus $4,200 from the sale of the iron ore. Yet we know that GDP is only $21,500.

The way we avoid double-counting is to count only each producer's **value added** in the calculation of GDP: the difference between the value of its sales and the value of the inputs it purchases from other businesses. In this case, the value added of the auto producer is the dollar value of the cars it manufactures *minus* the cost of the steel it buys, or $12,500. The value added of the steel producer is the dollar value of the steel it produces *minus* the cost of the ore it buys, or $4,800. Only the ore producer, which we have assumed doesn't buy any intermediate inputs, has value added equal to its total sales, $4,200. The sum of the three producers' value added is $21,500, equal to GDP.

The **value added** of a producer is the value of its sales minus the value of its purchases of inputs.

Measuring GDP as Spending on Domestically Produced Final Goods and Services

Another way to calculate GDP is by adding up aggregate spending on domestically produced final goods and services. That is, GDP can be measured by the flow of funds into firms. Like the method that estimates GDP as the value of production, this measurement must be carried out in a way that avoids double-counting. In terms of our steel and auto example, we don't want to count both consumer spending on a car (represented in Figure 24-2 by the sales price of the car) and the auto producer's spending on steel (represented in Figure 24-2 by the price of a car's worth of steel). If we counted both, we would be counting the steel embodied in the car twice. We solve this problem by counting only the value of sales to *final buyers,* such as consumers, firms that purchase investment goods, the government, or foreign buyers. In other words, in order to avoid double-counting of spending, we omit sales of inputs from one business to another when estimating GDP using spending data.

As we've already pointed out, however, the national accounts *do* include investment spending by firms as a part of final spending. That is, an auto company's purchase of steel to make a car isn't considered a part of final spending, but the company's purchase of new machinery for its factory *is* considered a part of final spending. What's the difference? Steel is an input that is used up in production; machinery, although it is used to make cars, will last for a number of years. Since purchases of capital goods, like machinery, that will last for a considerable time aren't closely tied to current production, the national accounts consider such purchases a form of final sales.

In later chapters, we will repeatedly make use of the proposition that GDP is equal to aggregate spending on domestically produced goods and services by final buyers. We will also develop models of how each group of final buyers decides how much to spend. So it is useful at this point to look at a breakdown of the types of spending that make up GDP.

PITFALLS

GDP: WHAT'S IN AND WHAT'S OUT

It's easy to confuse what is included and what isn't included in GDP. So let's stop here for a moment and make sure the distinction is clear. Probably the biggest source of confusion is the difference between investment spending and spending on inputs. Investment spending—spending on investment goods, construction of structures (residential as well as commercial), and changes to inventories—is included in GDP. But spending on inputs is not. Why the difference? Recall from Chapter 2 that we made a distinction between resources that are *used up* and those that are *not used up* in production. An input, like steel, is used up in production. A metal-stamping machine, an investment good, is not; it will last for many years and will be used repeat-

edly to make many cars. Since spending on investment goods and construction of structures is not directly tied to current output, economists consider such spending to be spending on final goods. And spending on changes to inventories, considered a part of investment spending, is also included in GDP. Why? Because, like a machine, additional inventory is an investment in future sales. And when a good is released for sale from inventories, its value is subtracted from the value of inventories and so from GDP. Used goods are not included in GDP because, as with inputs, to include them would be to double-count: counting them once when sold as new and again when re-sold as used. Finally, financial assets such as stocks and bonds are not included in GDP because they don't represent either the pro-

duction or the sale of final goods and services. Rather, a bond represents a promise to repay with interest, and a stock represents a proof of ownership.

Here is a summary of what's included and not included in GDP.

Included
- Domestically produced final goods and services, including capital goods, new construction of structures, and changes to inventories

Not Included
- Intermediate goods and services
- Inputs
- Used goods
- Financial assets like stocks and bonds
- Foreign-produced goods and services

Look again at the markets for goods and services in Figure 24-1, and you will see that one component of sales by firms is consumer spending. Let's denote consumer spending with the symbol *C*. Figure 24-1 also shows three other components of sales: sales of investment spending goods to other businesses, which we will denote by *I*; government purchases of goods and services, which we will denote by *G*; and sales to foreigners—that is, exports—which we will denote by *X*.

But not all of this final spending goes toward domestically produced goods and services: spending on imports, which we will denote by *IM*, "leaks" across national borders. Putting this all together gives us the following equation that breaks GDP down by the four sources of aggregate spending:

(24-1) $\text{GDP} = C + I + G + X - IM$

We'll be seeing a lot of Equation 24-1 in later chapters.

Measuring GDP as Factor Income Earned from Firms in the Economy A final way to calculate GDP is to add up all the income earned by factors of production from firms in the economy—the wages earned by labor; the interest earned by those who lend their savings to firms and the government; the rent earned by those who lease their land or structures to firms; and the profit earned by the shareholders, the owners of the firms' physical capital. This is a valid measure because the money firms earn by selling goods and services must go somewhere; whatever isn't paid as wages, interest, or rent is profit. And part of profit is paid out to shareholders as *dividends*.

Figure 24-2 shows how this calculation works for our simplified economy. The shaded column at far right shows the total wages, interest, and rent paid by all these firms as well as their total profit. Summing up all of these yields total factor income of $21,500—again, equal to GDP.

We won't emphasize factor income as much as the other two methods of calculating GDP. It's important to keep in mind, however, that all the money spent on domestically produced goods and services generates factor income to households—that is, there really is a circular flow.

The Components of GDP Now that we know how GDP is calculated in principle, let's see what it looks like in practice.

Figure 24-3 shows the first two methods of calculating GDP side by side. The height of each bar above the horizontal axis represents the GDP of the U.S. economy in 2004: $11,734 billion. Each bar is divided to show the breakdown of that total in terms of where the value was added and how the money was spent.

GROSS WHAT?

Occasionally you may see references not to gross domestic product but to gross *national* product, or GNP. Is this just another name for the same thing? Not quite.

If you look at Figure 24-1 carefully, you may realize that there's a possibility that is missing from the figure. According to the figure, all factor income goes to domestic households. But what happens when profits are paid to foreigners who own stock in General Motors or Microsoft? And where do the profits earned by American companies operating overseas fit in?

The answer is that they go into GNP but not GDP. GNP is defined as the total factor income earned by residents of a country. It *excludes* factor income earned by foreigners, like profits paid to Japanese investors who own American stocks and payments to Mexican farm workers temporarily in the United States. But it *includes* factor income earned abroad by Americans, like the profits of IBM's European operations that accrue to IBM's American shareholders and the wages of American consultants who work temporarily in Asia.

In the early days of national income accounting, economists usually used GNP rather than GDP as a measure of the economy's size—although the measures were generally very close to each other. They switched to GDP mainly because it's considered a better indicator of short-run movements in production and because data on international flows of factor income are considered somewhat unreliable.

In practice, it doesn't make much difference which measure is used for large economies like that of the United States, where the flows of net factor income to other countries are small. In 2004, America's GNP was about 0.4% larger than its GDP, mainly because of the overseas profit of U.S. companies. For smaller countries, however, GDP and GNP can diverge significantly. For example, much of Ireland's industry is owned by American corporations, whose profit must be deducted from Ireland's GNP. In addition, Ireland has become a host to many temporary workers from poorer regions of Europe, whose wages must also be deducted from Ireland's GNP. As a result, in 2004 Ireland's GNP was only 84% of its GDP.

In the left bar in Figure 24-3, we see the breakdown of GDP by value added according to sector, the first method of calculating GDP. Of the $11,734 billion, $2,300 billion—less than 20%—consisted of the value added by producers of physical goods. Another $7,977 billion, or 68%, consisted of value added by private producers of services. The rest consisted of value added by government, in the form of military,

Figure 24-3

U.S. GDP in 2004: Two Methods of Calculating GDP

The two bars show two equivalent ways of calculating GDP. The height of each bar above the horizontal axis represents $11,734 billion, U.S. GDP in 2004. The left bar shows the breakdown of GDP according to the value added of each sector of the economy. From it we see that slightly less than 20% of GDP in 2004 came from the value added in the production of goods. The rest came from the value added in the production of services. The right bar shows the breakdown of GDP according to the four types of spending: C, I, G, and X − IM. The right bar has a total length of $11,734 billion + $607 billion = $12,341 billion. The $607 billion, shown as the area extending below the horizontal axis, is the amount of total spending absorbed by net imports (negative net exports) in 2004.

Source: Bureau of Economic Analysis.

Components of GDP (billions of dollars)

Value added by government = $1,458 (12.4%)

Value added in services production = $7,977 (68.0%)

Value added in goods production = $2,300 (19.6%)

Value of final goods and services

Government purchases of goods and services G = $2,184 (18.6%)

Investment spending I = $1,927 (16.4%)

Consumer spending C = $8,229 (70.1%)

$C + I + G = $12,341$

Net exports X − IM = −$607 (−5.2%)

Spending on domestically produced final goods and services

education, and other government services. As commentators often emphasize, the United States is now largely a service economy.

The right bar in Figure 24-3 corresponds to the second method of calculating GDP, showing the breakdown by the four types of aggregate spending. The total length of the right bar is longer than the total length of the left bar, a difference of $607 billion (which, as you can see, extends below the horizontal axis). That's because the total length of the right bar represents total spending in the economy, spending on both domestically produced and foreign produced final goods and services. Within the bar, consumer spending (C), which is 70.1% of GDP, dominates the picture. But some of that spending was absorbed by foreign-produced goods and services. In 2004, **net exports,** the difference between the value of exports and the value of imports (X – IM in Equation 24-1) was negative—the United States was a net importer of foreign goods and services. The 2004 value of X – IM was –$607 billion, or –5.2% of GDP. Thus a portion of the right bar extends below the horizontal axis by $607 billion to represent the amount of total spending that was absorbed by net imports and therefore did not lead to higher U.S. GDP. Investment spending (I) constituted 16.4% of GDP, while government purchases of goods and services (G) constituted 18.6% of GDP.

> **Net exports** are the difference between the value of exports and the value of imports.

What GDP Tells Us

Now we've seen the various ways that gross domestic product is calculated. But what does the measurement of GDP tell us?

The most important use of GDP is as a measure of the size of the economy, providing us a scale against which to measure the economic performance of other years, or compare the economic performance of other countries. For example, suppose you want to compare the economies of different nations. A natural approach is to compare their GDPs. In 2004, as we've seen, U.S. GDP was $11,734 billion; Japan's GDP was $4,665 billion; and the combined GDP of the 25 countries that make up the European Union was $12,758 billion. This comparison tells us that Japan, although it has the world's second-largest national economy, carries considerably less economic weight than does the United States. When taken in aggregate, Europe is America's equal.

Still, one must be careful when using GDP numbers, especially when making comparisons over time. That's because part of the increase in the value of GDP over time represents increases in the *prices* of goods and services rather than an increase in output. For example, U.S. GDP was $5,803 billion in 1990 and had roughly doubled to $11,734 billion by 2004. But the U.S. economy didn't actually double in size over that period. To measure actual changes in aggregate output, we need a modified version of GDP that is adjusted for price changes, known as *real GDP*. We'll see next how real GDP is calculated.

economics in action

Creating the National Accounts

The national accounts, like modern macroeconomics, owe their creation to the Great Depression. As the economy plunged into depression, government officials found their ability to respond crippled not only by the lack of adequate economic theories but also by the lack of adequate information. All they had were scattered statistics: railroad freight car loadings, stock prices, and incomplete indexes of industrial production. They could only guess at what was happening to the economy as a whole.

In response to this perceived lack of information, the Department of Commerce commissioned Simon Kuznets, a young Russian-born economist, to develop a set of national income accounts. (Kuznets later won the Nobel Prize in economics for his work.) The first version of these accounts was presented to Congress in 1937 and in a research report titled *National Income, 1929–35.*

There was, at first, some skepticism about the usefulness of such accounts. In 1936 the British economist John Maynard Keynes published *The General Theory of Employment,*

Interest, and Money, the book that created modern macroeconomic theory. Keynes argued against trying to use the concepts of aggregate output or the aggregate price level: "To say that net output to-day is greater, but the price-level lower, than ten years ago or one year ago, is a proposition of a similar character to the statement that Queen Victoria was a better queen but not a happier woman than Queen Elizabeth—a proposition not without meaning and not without interest, but unsuitable as material for the differential calculus." But macroeconomists soon found that the concepts of aggregate output and the aggregate price level, tied to actual measurements of these quantities, were powerful aids to understanding economic developments.

Kuznets's initial estimates fell short of the full modern set of accounts because they focused on income, not production. The push to fill out the national accounts came during World War II, when policy makers were in even more need of comprehensive measures of the economy's performance. The federal government began issuing estimates of gross domestic product and gross national product in 1942.

In January 2000, in its publication *Survey of Current Business,* the Department of Commerce ran an article titled "GDP: One of the Great Inventions of the 20th Century." This may seem a bit over the top, but national income accounting, invented in the United States, has since become a tool of economic analysis and policy making around the world. ■

> >

>> QUICK REVIEW

> A country's *national accounts* track flows of money among economic sectors.
> Households receive factor income in the form of wages, profit from ownership of *stocks*, interest paid on *bonds*, and rent. They also receive *government transfers*.
> Households allocate *disposable income* between *consumer spending* and *private savings*, funds that flow into the *financial markets* and finance *investment spending* and any *government borrowing*.
> *Imports* lead to a flow of funds out of the country. *Exports* lead to a flow of funds into the country.
> *Gross domestic product*, or *GDP*, can be calculated in three different ways: add up the value of production of final goods and services by adding up *value added* of all firms; add up all spending on domestically produced *final goods and services*, an amount equal to *aggregate spending*; or add up all factor income paid by firms. *Intermediate goods and services* are not included in the calculation of GDP.

>> CHECK YOUR UNDERSTANDING 24-1

1. Explain why the three methods of calculating GDP produce the same estimate of GDP.

2. What are the various sectors to which firms make sales? What are the various ways in which households are linked with other sectors of the economy?

3. Consider Figure 24-2 and suppose you mistakenly believed that total value added was $30,500, the sum of the sales price of a car and a car's worth of steel. What items would you be counting twice?

Solutions appear at back of book.

Real GDP and Aggregate Output

Although the commonly cited GDP number is an interesting and useful statistic, it is not a useful measure for tracking changes in aggregate output over time. For example, GDP can rise either because the economy is producing more or simply because the prices of the goods and services it produces have increased. Likewise, GDP can fall either because the economy is producing less or because prices have fallen. In order to separate these possibilities, we must calculate how much the economy has changed in *real* terms over any given period. That is, we need to calculate how much of the change in GDP is due to a change in aggregate output separate from a change in prices. The measure that is used for this purpose is known as *real GDP.* Let's look first at how real GDP is calculated, then at what it means.

Calculating Real GDP

To understand how real GDP is calculated, imagine an economy in which only two goods, apples and oranges, are produced and in which both goods are sold only to final consumers. The outputs and prices of the two fruits for two consecutive years are shown in Table 24-1 on page 570.

The first thing we can say about these data is that the value of sales increased from year 1 to year 2. In the first year, the total value of sales was (2,000 billion × $0.25) + (1,000 billion × $0.50) = $1,000 billion; in the second it was (2,200 billion × $0.30) + (1,200 billion × $0.70) = $1,500 billion, which is 50% larger. But it is also clear from the table that this increase in the dollar value of GDP overstates the real growth in the economy. Although the quantities of both apples and oranges increased, the prices of both apples and oranges also rose. So part of the 50% increase in the dollar value of GDP simply reflects higher prices, not higher production of output.

TABLE 24-1

Calculating GDP and Real GDP in a Simple Economy

	Year 1	Year 2
Quantity of apples (billions)	2,000	2,200
Price of apple	$0.25	$0.30
Quantity of oranges (billions)	1,000	1,200
Price of orange	$0.50	$0.70
GDP (billions of dollars)	$1,000	$1,500
Real GDP (billions of year 1 dollars)	$1,000	$1,150

To estimate the true increase in aggregate output produced, we have to ask the following question: How much would GDP have gone up if prices had *not* changed? To answer this question, we need to find the value of output in year 2 expressed in year 1 prices. In year 1 the price of apples was $0.25 each and the price of oranges $0.50 each. So year 2 output *at year 1 prices* is (2,200 billion × $0.25) + (1,200 billion × $0.50) = $1,150 billion. And output in year 1 at year 1 prices was $1,000 billion. So in this example GDP measured in year 1 prices rose 15%—from $1,000 billion to $1,150 billion.

Now we can define **real GDP:** it is the total value of final goods and services produced in the economy during a year, calculated as if prices had stayed constant at the level of some given base year. A real GDP number always comes with information about what the base year is. A GDP number that has not been adjusted for changes in prices is calculated using the prices in the year in which the output is produced. Economists call this measure **nominal GDP,** GDP at current prices. If we had used nominal GDP to measure the true change in output from year 1 to year 2 in our apples and oranges example, we would have overstated the true growth in output: we would have claimed it to be 50%, when in fact it was only 15%. By comparing output in the two years using a common set of prices—the year 1 prices in this example—we are able to focus solely on changes in the quantity of output by eliminating the influence of changes in prices.

Table 24-2 shows a real-life version of our apples and oranges example. The second column shows nominal GDP in 1996, 2000, and 2004. The third column shows real GDP for each year in 2000 dollars. For 2000 the two numbers are the same. But real GDP in 1996 expressed in 2000 dollars was higher than nominal GDP in 1996, reflecting the fact that prices were in general higher in 2000 than in 1996. Real GDP in 2004 expressed in 2000 dollars, however, was less than nominal GDP in 2004 because prices in 2000 were lower than in 2004.

Real GDP is the total value of all final goods and services produced in the economy during a given year, calculated using the prices of a selected base year.

Nominal GDP is the value of all final goods and services produced in the economy during a given year, calculated using the prices current in the year in which the output is produced.

TABLE 24-2

Nominal versus Real GDP in 1996, 2000, and 2004

	Nominal GDP (billions of current dollars)	Real GDP (billions of 2000 dollars)
1996	$7,817	$8,329
2000	9,817	9,817
2004	11,734	10,842

Source: Bureau of Economic Analysis.

A Technical Detail: "Chained" Dollars

Until the 1990s, the real GDP estimates published by the Bureau of Economic Analysis were calculated in exactly the way we calculated real GDP in Table 24-1: the Bureau picked a base year and calculated each year's real GDP in the base year's prices.

But the U.S. national accounts now report real GDP in "billions of chained 2000 dollars." What does "chained" mean?

You might have noticed that there is an alternative way to calculate real GDP using the data in Table 24-1. Why not measure it using the prices of year 2 rather than year 1 as the base-year prices? This procedure seems equally valid. According to that calculation, real GDP in year 1 at year 2 prices is (2,000 billion × $0.30) + (1,000 billion × $0.70) = $1,300 billion; real GDP in year 2 in year 2 prices is $1,500 billion, the same as nominal GDP in year 2. So using year 2 prices as the base year, the growth in real GDP is equal to ($1,500 billion − $1,300 billion)/$1,300 billion = 0.154, or 15.4%. This is slightly higher than the figure we got from the previous calculation, in which year 1 prices were the base-year prices. In that calculation, we found that real GDP increased by 15%. Neither answer, 15.4% versus 15%, is more "correct" than the other.

Because 15.4% and 15% are pretty close to each other, it doesn't matter much which base year you choose in Table 24-1. But this isn't always true when calculating authentic GDP numbers. In fact, economists estimating the growth in U.S. real GDP during the 1980s and 1990s found that the results differed significantly depending on which year they used as a base. The main reason was the rapid pace of technological progress in computers, which led both to rapid growth in computer output and to falling prices of computers relative to those of other goods and services. When economists used an early base year, a year when computers were still expensive, their calculations produced a higher rate of real GDP growth than if they used a later base year, a year when computers were cheap. Because there was such a huge increase in output of computers, the two calculations produced very different estimates for real GDP.

As a result, the government economists who put together the U.S. national income accounts have adopted a method known as "chain-linking," which splits the difference between using early base years and late base years. We won't go into the details of that procedure; for the purposes of this book, we can think of calculating real GDP in the prices of a single base year.

What Real GDP Doesn't Measure

GDP is a measure of a country's aggregate output. Other things equal, a country with a larger population will have higher GDP simply because there are more people working. So if we want to compare GDP across countries but want to eliminate the effect of differences in population size, we use the measure **GDP per capita**—GDP divided by the size of the population, equivalent to the average GDP per person. Correspondingly, real GDP per capita is the average real GDP per person.

> **GDP per capita** is GDP divided by the size of the population; it is equivalent to the average GDP per person.

Although real GDP per capita can be a useful measure in some circumstances, it has well-known limitations as a measure of a country's living standards. Every once in a while economists are accused of believing that growth in real GDP per capita is the only thing that matters—of thinking that increasing real GDP per capita is a goal in itself. In fact, economists rarely make that mistake; the idea that economists care only about real GDP per capita is a sort of urban legend. Let's take a moment to be clear about why a country's real GDP per capita is not a sufficient measure of human welfare in that country and why growth in real GDP per capita is not an appropriate policy goal in itself.

One way to think about this issue is to say that an increase in real GDP means an expansion in the economy's production possibility frontier. Because the economy has increased its productive capacity, there are more things that society can achieve. But whether society actually makes good use of that increased potential to improve living standards is another matter. To put it in a slightly different way, your income may be higher this year than last year, but whether you use that higher income to actually improve your quality of life is your choice.

The United Nations produces an annual document, the *Human Development Report,* that tries to rank countries by measures other than real GDP per capita. These measures include data on infant mortality, life expectancy, and literacy. It compiles these measures into the Human Development Index, which is an effort to determine how well societies are doing, aside from how much they produce. The index suggests that real GDP per capita is one of many important determinants of human welfare—but by no means the only one. Countries with high real GDP per capita—like the United States, European nations, and Japan—also score very well on just about every other indicator of human welfare. But there are some relatively poor countries—like Costa Rica—that have remarkably high literacy and life expectancy along with low infant mortality. And there are some relatively rich countries—especially countries with valuable natural resources—that score quite low on these criteria.

So let's say it again: real GDP per capita is a measure of an economy's average aggregate output per person—and so of what it *can* do. It is not a sufficient goal in itself because it doesn't address how a country uses that output to affect living standards. A country with a high GDP can afford to be healthy, to be well-educated, and in general to have a good quality of life. But there is not a one-to-one match between GDP and the quality of life.

economics in action

Good Decades, Bad Decades

How important is the distinction between nominal GDP and real GDP? If you are trying to interpret U.S. economic history, the answer is that it is very important indeed. Figure 24-4 tells the tale.

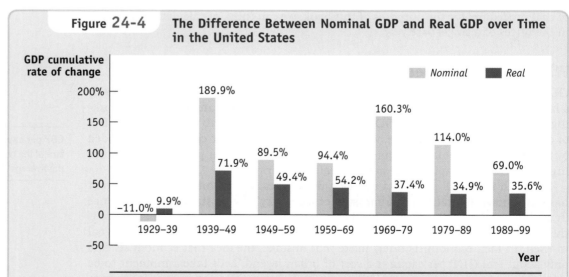

Figure 24-4 **The Difference Between Nominal GDP and Real GDP over Time in the United States**

To illustrate the difference between nominal GDP and real GDP, this figure shows the percent change in both measures over successive decades within the United States. (Real GDP was calculated using chained 2000 dollars.) The years 1929–1939 show the effect of deflation on the difference between nominal and real GDP: U.S. nominal GDP in 1939 was 11% lower than in 1929, but U.S. aggregate output as measured by real GDP was nearly 10% higher. The remaining years show the effect of inflation on the difference between the two measures: relatively high growth of U.S. nominal GDP in the years 1969–1979 and 1979–1989 contrast with relatively low growth of U.S. real GDP during those same periods. Those years experienced high levels of inflation and a simultaneous slowdown in real GDP growth. **>web...**
Source: Bureau of Economic Analysis.

Figure 24-4 shows the cumulative percent change in both U.S. nominal GDP and U.S. real GDP over successive decades since national income accounting began. That is, we show percent changes from 1929 to 1939, 1939 to 1949, and so on. In each pair, the bar on the left shows the percent change in U.S. nominal GDP over the time period, and the bar on the right shows the percent change in U.S. real GDP over the same period. (Real GDP was calculated using chained 2000 dollars.)

What we see right away is the effect of deflation during the 1930s: nominal GDP and real GDP actually moved in opposite directions during the Great Depression. Due to a falling price level, U.S. nominal GDP in 1939 was 11% lower than in 1929, but U.S. aggregate output as measured by real GDP was nearly 10% higher. After that, both nominal and real GDP rose every decade, but at different rates due to the influence of a changing price level. For example, U.S. nominal GDP grew much faster than U.S. real GDP for the years 1969–1979 and 1979–1989. The explanation is that those years saw high levels of inflation. ∎

> >

>>QUICK REVIEW
> To determine the actual growth in aggregate output, we calculate *real GDP* using prices from some given base year. In contrast, *nominal GDP* refers to the value of aggregate output calculated with current prices.
> Real *GDP per capita* is a measure of the average aggregate output per person. But it is not a sufficient measure of human welfare, nor is it an appropriate goal in itself, because it does not reflect important aspects of living standards within an economy.

>>CHECK YOUR UNDERSTANDING 24-2

1. Assume there are only two goods in the economy, french fries and onion rings. In 2004, 1,000,000 servings of french fries were sold at $0.40 each and 800,000 servings of onion rings at $0.60 each. From 2004 to 2005, the price of french fries rose by 25% and the servings sold fell by 10%; the price of onion rings fell by 15% and the servings sold rose by 5%.
   a. Calculate the nominal GDP in 2004 and 2005. Calculate real GDP in 2005 using 2004 as the base year.
   b. Why would an assessment of growth using nominal GDP be misguided?

2. From 1990 to 2000, the price of electronic equipment fell dramatically and the price of housing rose dramatically. What are the implications of this in deciding whether to use 1990 or 2000 as the base year in calculating 2005 real GDP?

Solutions appear at back of book.

The Unemployment Rate

In addition to measures of GDP, a number of other measures help us track the performance of the economy. As we learned in Chapter 23, one extremely important statistic for economic policy is the unemployment rate because unemployment leads to lost output and lower social welfare. Cases of very high unemployment, such as in a depression, often lead to political unrest. What exactly does the unemployment rate tell us about the economy?

Understanding the Unemployment Rate

Every month, the U.S. Census Bureau carries out the Current Population Survey, which involves interviewing a random sample of 60,000 American families. People are asked whether they are currently employed. If they are not employed, they are asked whether they have been looking for a job during the past four weeks. As you may recall from Chapter 23, the labor force is equal to the total of those who are either working or have recently been seeking employment; it does not include discouraged workers, those who have given up actively looking for a job. Those who are actively looking for work but have not, or at least not yet, found a job are classified as unemployed. The unemployment rate, which we showed how to calculate in Chapter 23, is the percent of the labor force that is unemployed.

What does the unemployment rate tell us? It indicates how easy or difficult it is to find a job given the current state of the economy. When the unemployment rate is low, nearly everyone who wants a job can find one. When the unemployment rate is high, jobs are hard to find. As an illustration, recall the story that we told at the beginning of Chapter 23: in the spring of 2000, when the U.S. unemployment rate was only about 4%, potential employers were anxiously wooing potential employees.

Two years later, when the unemployment rate had risen to 6%, new graduates found their job search much more difficult.

Although the unemployment rate is a good indicator of current conditions in the job market, it should not be taken literally as a measure of the percentage of people who want to work but can't find jobs. In some ways the unemployment rate exaggerates the difficulty people have in finding work. In other ways, the opposite is true: low measured unemployment can conceal deep frustration felt by discouraged workers.

Let's start with the argument that the measured unemployment rate is an overstatement of the percentage of people who want to work but can't find jobs. It's normal for someone searching for work to take at least a few weeks to find a suitable job. Yet a worker who is quite confident of getting a job, but has not yet accepted a position, is counted as unemployed. This means that even in boom times, when jobs are very easy to find, the unemployment rate does not fall to zero. As we've seen, the spring of 2000 was a very good time to be looking for a job, yet the unemployment rate was still 4%. We'll discuss in Chapter 32 why measured unemployment persists even when jobs are plentiful.

Meanwhile, an individual who has given up looking for a job for the time being—say, a laid-off steelworker in a deeply depressed steel town—isn't counted as unemployed because he or she has not been searching for work during the previous four weeks. Because it does not count discouraged workers, the measured unemployment rate may understate the percentage of people who want to work but are unable to find jobs.

Finally, it's important to realize that the unemployment rate varies greatly among demographic groups. Figure 24-5 shows unemployment rates for different groups in January 2005, when the overall unemployment rate of 5.2% was low by historical standards. As you can see, in January 2005 the unemployment rate for African-American workers was more than twice the national average, the unemployment rate for white teenagers was more than three times the national average, and the unemployment rate for African-American teenagers, at more than 30%, was almost seven times the national average. So even at a time when the overall unemployment rate was relatively low, jobs were hard to find for some groups. We'll examine the causes of persistent unemployment in Chapter 32.

So you should interpret the unemployment rate as an indicator of labor market conditions, not as a literal measure of the percentage of people unable to find jobs. Still, the

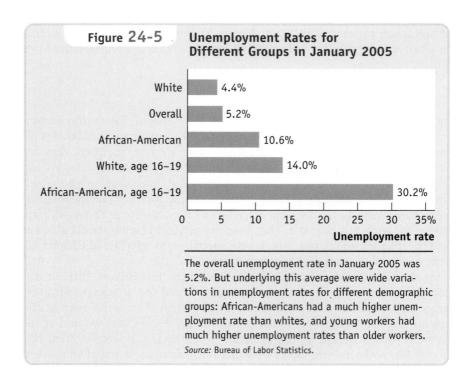

Figure 24-5 **Unemployment Rates for Different Groups in January 2005**

The overall unemployment rate in January 2005 was 5.2%. But underlying this average were wide variations in unemployment rates for different demographic groups: African-Americans had a much higher unemployment rate than whites, and young workers had much higher unemployment rates than older workers.
Source: Bureau of Labor Statistics.

ups and downs of the unemployment rate have a significant impact on people's lives. What causes these fluctuations? We already saw, in Chapter 23, that the unemployment rate rises and falls with the business cycle. Now we can be more specific: there is a close relationship between the unemployment rate and the growth rate of real GDP.

Growth and Unemployment

Figure 24-6 is a scatter diagram showing observations of the growth rate of real GDP and changes in the unemployment rate over time in the United States. Each dot represents one year over the period 1949–2004. The horizontal axis measures the annual rate of growth in real GDP—the percent by which each year's real GDP changed compared to the previous year's real GDP. The vertical axis measures the *change* in the unemployment rate over the previous year in percentage points. For example, the average unemployment rate fell from 4.2% in 1999 to 4.0% in 2000; this is shown as a value of –0.2 along the vertical axis for the year 2000. Over the same period, real GDP grew by 3.7%; this is the value shown along the horizontal axis for the year 2000.

From the downward trend of the scatter points in Figure 24-6, it's clear that, in general, there is a negative relationship between growth in the economy and the rate of unemployment. Years of high growth in real GDP were years in which the unemployment rate fell, and years of low or negative growth in real GDP were years in which the unemployment rate rose. The average growth rate of real GDP over the period from 1949 to 2004 was 3.5%, and for reference we've included a dashed vertical line

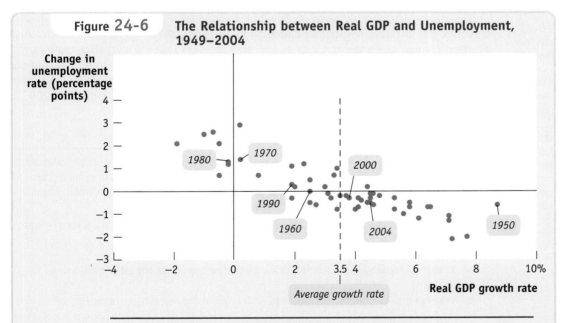

Figure 24-6   The Relationship between Real GDP and Unemployment, 1949–2004

The horizontal axis measures the annual growth rate of real GDP, the vertical axis measures the *change* in the unemployment rate over the previous year, and each dot represents one year over the period 1949–2004. The data show that there is typically a negative relationship between growth in the economy and the change in the rate of unemployment. The vertical dashed line is drawn at a value of 3.5%, the average growth rate of real GDP from 1949 to 2004. Points lying to the right of the vertical dashed line indicate that years of above-average growth were typically years of a falling unemployment rate. Points lying to the left show that years of below-average growth were typically years of a rising unemployment rate. The downward trend of the scatter points shows that there is, in general, a negative relationship between the real GDP growth rate and the change in the unemployment rate. **>web...**

Source: Bureau of Economic Analysis; Bureau of Labor Statistics.

indicating that value. You can see from examining the points lying to the right of the dashed vertical line that, with few exceptions, years when the economy grew faster than average were also years of a falling unemployment rate. For those years, the value on the vertical axis is negative. Points lying to the left of the dashed vertical line show that years when the economy grew more slowly than average were typically years with a rising unemployment rate. This relationship helps us understand why recessions, periods when real GDP falls, are so painful. As illustrated by the points to the left of the vertical axis in Figure 24-6, falling real GDP is always associated with a rising rate of unemployment, causing a great deal of hardship to families.

Our next and final subject in this chapter will be *price indexes*, which are measures of the aggregate price level.

economics in action

Jobless Recoveries

During recessions real GDP falls and the unemployment rate always rises. During expansions real GDP rises. Does the unemployment rate automatically fall?

Not necessarily. Look again at Figure 24-6. The data suggest that unemployment falls when growth is *above average* (the points lying to the right of the dashed vertical line), where the average growth rate of real GDP has been about 3.5% per year. If the economy grows at a positive rate, but below 3.5% per year, can the unemployment rate rise even as the economy grows? Put another way, can the unemployment rate rise when the economy grows at a below-average rate?

Yes, it can. The combination of slow but positive growth in real GDP with a rising unemployment rate is sometimes called a jobless recovery. It's not a usual occurrence. Normally, once an expansion gets going, growth picks up to a level that reduces unemployment. But jobless recoveries have happened. In fact, one occurred during the most recent economic expansion: the recession of 2001 officially ended in November of that year, but the unemployment rate continued to rise until the summer of 2003. ∎

< < < < < < < < < < < < < < < < < < <

>> CHECK YOUR UNDERSTANDING 24-3

1. Suppose the advent of employment websites enables job-seekers to find a suitable job more quickly. What effect will this have on the unemployment rate over time? Also suppose that these websites encourage job-seekers who had given up their search to begin looking again. What effect will this have on the unemployment rate?

2. Which of the following are consistent with the observed relationship between growth in real GDP and changes in the unemployment rate? Which are not?
   a. A rise in the unemployment rate accompanies a fall in real GDP.
   b. A business recovery is associated with a greater percentage of the labor force being employed.
   c. Negative real GDP growth is associated with a fall in the unemployment rate.

Solutions appear at back of book.

Price Indexes and the Aggregate Price Level

As we noted in Chapter 23, both inflation and deflation can pose problems for the economy. For that reason, we must have a way of measuring changes in the economy's overall price level over time. The aggregate price level, a single number, is supposed to be a measure of the overall price level of final goods and services. But a huge variety of goods and services are produced and consumed within the economy. How can we summarize the prices of all these goods and services with a single number? The answer lies in the concept of a *price index*—a concept best introduced with an example.

Market Baskets and Price Indexes

Suppose that a frost in Florida destroys most of the citrus harvest. As a result, the price of oranges rises from $0.20 each to $0.40 each, the price of grapefruit rises from $0.60 to $1.00, and the price of lemons rises from $0.25 to $0.45. How much has the price of citrus fruit increased?

One way to answer that question is to state three numbers, the changes in prices for oranges, grapefruit, and lemons. But this is a very cumbersome method. Rather than having to recite three numbers every time someone asks what has happened to the prices of citrus fruit, we would prefer to have some kind of overall measure of the *average* price increase.

Economists measure average price changes for consumer goods and services by asking how much more or less a typical consumer would have to spend to buy his or her previous *consumption bundle*—the typical basket of goods and services purchased before the price changes. Suppose that before the frost a typical consumer bought 200 oranges, 50 grapefruit, and 100 lemons over the course of a year. The average individual might change that pattern of consumption after the price changes caused by the frost. But we can still ask how much it would cost if he or she were to buy the same mix of fruit. A hypothetical consumption bundle, used to measure changes in the overall price level, is known as a **market basket.**

Table 24-3 shows the pre-frost and post-frost cost of the market basket. Before the frost, it cost $95. After the frost, the same bundle of goods cost $175. Since $175/$95 = 1.842, the post-frost basket costs 1.842 times the cost of the pre-frost basket, an increase in cost of 84.2%. So in this case we would say that the average price of citrus fruit increased 84.2% since the base year as a result of the frost.

A **market basket** is a hypothetical set of consumer purchases of goods and services.

TABLE 24-3

Calculating the Cost of a Market Basket

	Pre-frost	Post-frost
Price of orange	$0.20	$0.40
Price of grapefruit	$0.60	$1.00
Price of lemon	$0.25	$0.45
Cost of market basket (200 oranges, 50 grapefruit, 100 lemons)	(200 × $0.20) + (50 × $0.60) + (100 × $0.25) = $95.00	(200 × $0.40) + (50 × $1.00) + (100 × $0.45) = $175.00

Economists use the same method to measure changes in the overall price level: they track changes in the cost of buying a given market basket. In addition, economists perform another simplification in order to avoid having to keep track of the information that the market basket cost, for example, $95 in such-and-such a year. They *normalize* the measure of the aggregate price level so that it is equal to 100 in some given base year. A normalized measure of the overall price level is known as a **price index,** and it is always cited along with the year for which the aggregate price level is being measured and the base year. A price index can be calculated using the following formula:

A **price index** measures the cost of purchasing a given market basket in a given year, where that cost is normalized so that it is equal to 100 in the selected base year.

(24-2) Price index in a given year = $\dfrac{\text{Cost of market basket in a given year}}{\text{Cost of market basket in base year}} \times 100$

For example, our citrus fruit market basket cost $95 before the frost; so we would define the price index for citrus fruit as (current cost of market basket/$95) × 100. This yields an index of 100 for the period before the frost and 184.2 for the period afterward. You should note that applying Equation 24-2 to calculate the price index for the base year always results in a price index equal to 100. That is, the price index in the base year is equal to: (cost of market basket in base year/cost of market basket in base year) × 100 = 100.

The price index makes it clear that the average price of citrus has risen 84.2% as a consequence of the frost. Because of its simplicity and intuitive appeal, this method is used to calculate a variety of price indexes to track the average price change among different groups of goods and services. For example, the *consumer price index* is the most widely used measure of the aggregate price level, the overall price level of final consumer goods and services across the economy. Price indexes are also the basis for measuring inflation. The **inflation rate** is the annual percent change in a price index. The inflation rate from year 1 to year 2 is calculated using the following formula:

$$\text{(24-3)} \quad \text{Inflation rate} = \frac{\text{Price index in year 2} - \text{Price index in year 1}}{\text{Price index in year 1}} \times 100$$

Typically, a news report that cites "the inflation rate" is referring to the annual percent change in the consumer price index.

The **inflation rate** is the percent change per year in a price index—typically the consumer price index.

The Consumer Price Index

The **consumer price index,** or **CPI,** measures the cost of the market basket of a typical urban American family.

The most widely used measure of prices in the United States is the **consumer price index** (often referred to simply as the **CPI**), which is intended to show how the cost of all purchases by a typical urban family has changed over time. It is calculated by surveying market prices for a market basket that is constructed to represent the consumption of a typical family of four living in a typical American city. The base period for the index is currently 1982–1984; that is, the index is calculated so that the average of consumer prices in 1982–1984 is 100.

The market basket used to calculate the CPI is far more complex than the three-fruit market basket we described above. In fact, to calculate the CPI, the Bureau of Labor Statistics sends its employees out to survey supermarkets, gas stations, hardware stores, and so on—some 21,000 retail outlets in 85 cities. Every month it tabulates about 90,000 prices, on everything from Romaine lettuce to video rentals. Figure 24-7 shows the makeup of the market basket underlying the current consumer price index by broad categories. The largest component, housing, includes all the costs of owning or renting a residence, including heating and electricity.

Figure 24-8 shows how the CPI has changed over the past 90 years. Since 1940 the CPI has risen steadily, although its annual percent increases in recent years have been much smaller than those of the 1970s and early 1980s. A proportional scale is used so that equal percent changes in the CPI appear the same.

The United States is not the only country that calculates a consumer price index. In fact, nearly every country has one. As you might expect, the market baskets that make up these indexes differ quite a lot from country to country. In poor countries, where people must spend a high proportion of their income just to feed themselves, food makes up a large share of the price index. Among high-income countries, differences in consumption patterns lead to differences in the price indexes: the Japanese price index puts a larger weight on raw fish and a smaller weight on beef than ours does, and the French price index puts a larger weight on wine.

Figure 24-7   The Makeup of the Consumer Price Index in 2004

Education and communication 6%
Other goods and services 4%
Recreation 6%
Medical care 6%
Food and beverages 15%
Transportation 17%
Housing 42%
Apparel 4%

Housing—all the costs of owning or renting a residence—is the largest component of the market basket underlying the 2004 CPI, followed by transportation and food.
Source: Bureau of Labor Statistics.

The CPI, 1913–2004

Since 1940 the CPI has risen steadily. But the annual percent increases in recent years have been much smaller than those of the 1970s and early 1980s. (The vertical axis is measured in log scale so that equal percent changes in the CPI appear the same.) **>web...**

Source: Bureau of Labor Statistics.

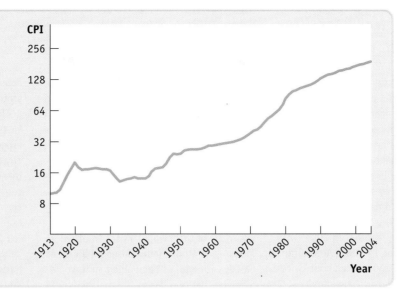

Other Price Measures

There are two other price measures that are also widely used to track economy-wide price changes. One is the **producer price index** (or PPI, which used to be known as the *wholesale price index*). As its name suggests, the producer price index measures the cost of a typical basket of goods and services—containing raw commodities such as steel, electricity, coal, and so on—purchased by producers. Because commodity producers are relatively quick to raise prices when they perceive a change in overall demand for their goods, the PPI often responds to inflationary or deflationary pressures more quickly than the CPI. As a result, the PPI is often regarded as an "early warning signal" of changes in the inflation rate.

The other widely used price measure is the *GDP deflator;* it isn't exactly a price index, although it serves the same purpose. Recall how we distinguished between nominal GDP (GDP in current prices), and real GDP (GDP calculated using the prices of a base year). The **GDP deflator** for a given year is equal to 100 times the ratio of nominal GDP for that year to real GDP for that year expressed in prices of a selected base year. Since real GDP is currently expressed in 2000 dollars, the GDP deflator for 2000 is equal to 100. If nominal GDP doubles but real GDP does not change, the GDP deflator indicates that the aggregate price level doubled.

Perhaps the most important point about the different inflation rates generated by these three measures of prices is that they usually move closely together (although the

> The **producer price index**, or **PPI**, measures changes in the prices of goods purchased by producers.

> The **GDP deflator** for a given year is 100 times the ratio of nominal GDP to real GDP in that year.

Figure 24-9

The CPI, the PPI, and the GDP Deflator

As the figure shows, these three different measures of inflation usually move closely together. Each reveals a drastic acceleration in the inflation rate during the 1940s and the 1970s and a return to relative price stability in the 1990s.

Source: Bureau of Economic Analysis; Bureau of Labor Statistics.

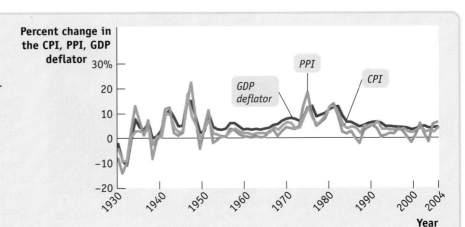

The U.S. government takes considerable care in measuring consumer prices. Nonetheless, many—but not all—economists believe that the consumer price index systematically overstates the actual rate of inflation. Because many government payments are tied to the CPI, this is an important fact if true.

What do we mean by saying that the CPI overstates inflation? Imagine comparing two families: one in 1983, with an after-tax income of $20,000, and another in 2004, with an after-tax income of $40,000. According to the CPI, prices in 2004 were about twice as high as in 1983, so those two families should have about the same standard of living. Many economists argue, however, that the 2004 family would have a higher standard of living for two reasons.

One reason is the fact that the CPI measures the cost of buying a given market basket, when in fact consumers typically alter the mix of goods and services they buy away from products that have become relatively more expensive and toward products that have become relatively cheaper. For example, suppose that the price of hamburgers were to double suddenly. Americans currently eat a lot of burgers, but in the face of such a price rise many of them would switch to other foods—and a price index based on a market basket with a lot of hamburgers in it would overstate the true rise in the cost of living.

Actual changes in prices and in the mix of goods and services Americans consume are usually less dramatic than our hypothetical example. But the changing mix of consumption probably leads to some overstatement of inflation by the CPI.

The second reason arises from innovation. In 1983 many goods we now take for granted, especially those using information technology, didn't exist: there was no Internet and there were no iPods. By widening the range of consumer choice, innovation makes a given amount of money worth more. That is, innovation is like a fall in consumer prices.

For both these reasons, many economists believe that the CPI somewhat overstates inflation when we think of inflation as measuring the actual change in the cost of living of a typical urban American family. But there is no consensus on how large the bias is, and for the time being the official CPI remains the basis for most estimates of inflation.

---

producer price index tends to fluctuate more than either of the other two measures). Figure 24-9 on page 579 shows the annual percent changes in the three indexes since 1930. By all three measures, the U.S. economy experienced deflation during the early years of the Great Depression, wartime inflation, accelerating inflation during the 1970s, and a return to relative price stability in the 1990s.

economics in action

Indexing to the CPI

Although GDP is a very important number for shaping economic policy, official statistics on GDP don't have a direct effect on people's lives. The CPI, by contrast, has a direct and immediate impact on millions of Americans. The reason is that many payments are tied or "indexed" to the CPI—the amount paid rises or falls when the CPI rises or falls.

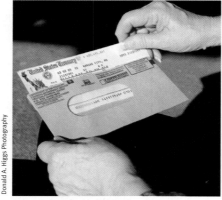

A small change in the CPI has large consequences for those dependent on Social Security payments.

The practice of indexing payments to consumer prices goes back to the dawn of the United States as a nation. In 1780 the Massachusetts state legislature recognized that the pay of its soldiers fighting the British needed to be increased because of inflation that occurred during the Revolutionary War. The legislature adopted a formula that made a soldier's pay proportional to the cost of a market basket, consisting of 5 bushels of corn, 68^{4}/$_{7}$ pounds of beef, 10 pounds of sheep's wool, and 16 pounds of sole leather.

Today, 48 million people, most of them old or disabled, receive checks from Social Security, a national retirement program that accounts for almost a quarter of current total federal spending—more than the defense budget. The amount of an individual's check is determined by a formula that reflects his or her previous payments into the system as well as other factors. In addition, all Social Security payments are adjusted each year to offset any increase in consumer prices over the previous year. The CPI is used to calculate the official estimate of the inflation rate used to adjust these payments yearly. So every percentage point added to the official estimate of the rate of inflation adds 1% to the checks received by tens of millions of individuals.

Other government payments are also indexed to the CPI. In addition, income tax brackets, the bands of income levels that determine a taxpayer's income tax rate, are also indexed to the CPI. (An individual in a higher income bracket pays a higher income tax rate in a progressive tax system like ours.) Indexing also extends to the private sector, where many private contracts, including some wage settlements, contain cost-of-living allowances (called COLAs) that adjust payments in proportion to changes in the CPI.

Because the CPI plays such an important and direct role in people's lives, it's a politically sensitive number. The Bureau of Labor Statistics, which calculates the CPI, takes great care in collecting and interpreting price and consumption data. They use a complex method in which households are surveyed to determine what they buy and where they shop and a carefully selected sample of stores are surveyed to get representative prices.

As explained in For Inquiring Minds on p. 580, however, there is still considerable controversy about whether the CPI accurately measures inflation. ■

> >

>>CHECK YOUR UNDERSTANDING 24-4

1. Consider Table 24-3 but suppose that the market basket is composed of 100 oranges, 50 grapefruit, and 200 lemons. How does this change the pre-frost and post-frost price indexes? Explain. Generalize your explanation to how the construction of the market basket affects the price index.

2. Using what you have learned from Question 1, explain the effect of each of the following events on how well a CPI based on a market basket determined 10 years ago functions in measuring the change in prices today.
   a. A typical family owns more cars than it would have a decade ago. Over that time, the average price of a car has increased more than the average prices of other goods.
   b. Virtually no households had broadband Internet access a decade ago. Now, many households have it, and the price has regularly fallen each year.

3. The consumer price index in the United States (base period 1982–1984) was 184.0 in 2003 and 188.9 in 2004. Calculate the inflation rate from 2003 to 2004.

Solutions appear at back of book.

• A LOOK AHEAD •

We have now seen how economists put actual numbers to key macroeconomic variables such as aggregate output, the unemployment rate, and the aggregate price level. Now we can turn to the actual study of macroeconomics—analyzing how the values of those key macroeconomic variables are determined in the real world.

As we will learn, our analysis will depend on whether we are considering the long-run behavior of the economy or the short-run ups and downs of the business cycle. In the next two chapters we will set the short run to one side and focus on the long run. Our next topic will be the determinants of aggregate output in the long run—that is, the story behind *long-run growth*.

>> QUICK REVIEW

➤ Changes in the aggregate price level are measured by the cost of buying a particular *market basket* during different years. A *price index* for a given year is the cost of the market basket in that year normalized so that the price index equals 100 in a selected base year.
➤ The *inflation rate* is calculated as the percent change in a price index. The most commonly used price index is the *consumer price index*, or *CPI*, which tracks the cost of a basket of consumer goods and services. The *producer price index* does the same for goods and services used as inputs by firms. The *GDP deflator* measures the aggregate price level as the ratio of nominal to real GDP times 100. These three measures normally behave quite similarly.

SUMMARY

1. Economists keep track of the flows of money between sectors with the **national income and product accounts,** or **national accounts.** Households earn income via the factor markets from wages, interest on **bonds,** profit accruing to owners of **stocks,** and rent on land. In addition, they receive **government transfers** from the government. **Disposable income,** total household income minus taxes plus government transfers, is allocated to **consumer spending** (C) and **private savings.** Via the **financial markets,** private savings and foreign lending are channeled to **investment spending** (I), government borrowing, and foreign borrowing. **Government purchases of goods and services** (G) are paid for by tax revenues and any **government borrowing. Exports** (X) generate an inflow of funds into the country from the rest of the world, but **imports** (IM) lead to an outflow of funds to the rest of the world. Foreigners can also buy stocks and bonds in the U.S. financial markets.

2. **Gross domestic product,** or **GDP,** measures the value of all **final goods and services** produced in the economy. It does not include the value of **intermediate goods and services.** It can be calculated in three ways: add up the **value added** by all producers; add up all spending on domestically produced final goods and services, leading to the equation $GDP = C + I + G + X - IM$; or add up all the income paid by domestic firms to factors of production. These three methods are equivalent because in the economy as a whole, total income paid by domestic firms to factors of production must equal total spending on domestically produced final goods and services. $(X - IM)$, exports minus imports, is often called **net exports.**

3. **Real GDP** is the value of the final goods and services produced calculated using the prices of a selected base year. Except in the base year, real GDP is not the same as **nominal GDP,** aggregate output calculated using current prices. Analysis of the growth rate of aggregate output must use real GDP because doing so eliminates any change in the value of aggregate output due solely to price changes. Real **GDP per capita** is a measure of average aggregate output per person, but is not in itself an appropriate policy goal.

4. The unemployment rate is an indicator of the state of the labor market, but it should not be taken literally as a measure of the percentage of people who want to work but can't find jobs. It may overstate the true level of unemployment because a person typically spends time unemployed while searching for a job. It may also understate the true level of unemployment because it does not include discouraged workers.

5. There is a strong negative relationship between growth in real GDP and changes in the unemployment rate: when growth is above average, the unemployment rate falls; when it is below average, the unemployment rate rises.

6. To measure the aggregate price level, economists calculate the cost of purchasing a **market basket.** A **price index** is the ratio of the current cost of that market basket to the cost in a selected base year, multiplied by 100.

7. The **inflation rate** is the yearly percent change in a price index, typically based on the **consumer price index,** or **CPI,** the most common measure of the aggregate price level. A similar index for goods and services purchased by firms is the **producer price index.** Finally, economists also use the **GDP deflator,** which measures the price level by calculating the ratio of nominal to real GDP times 100.

KEY TERMS

PROBLEMS

1. At right is a simplified circular-flow diagram for the economy of Micronia.

   a. What is the value of GDP in Micronia?

   b. What is the value of net exports?

   c. What is the value of disposable income?

   d. Does the total flow of money out of households—the sum of taxes paid, consumer spending, and private savings—equal the total flow of money into households?

   e. How does the government of Micronia finance its purchases of goods and services?

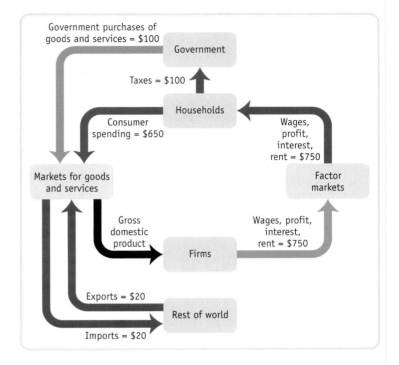

2. A more complex circular-flow diagram for the economy of Macronia is shown at right.

   a. What is the value of GDP in Macronia?

   b. What is the value of net exports?

   c. What is the value of disposable income?

   d. Does the total flow of money out of households—the sum of taxes paid, consumer spending, and private savings—equal the total flow of money into households?

   e. How does the government finance its spending?

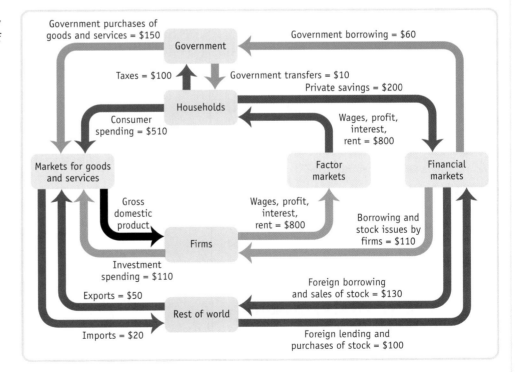

3. The small economy of Pizzania produces three goods (bread, cheese, and pizza), each produced by a separate company. The bread and cheese companies produce all the inputs they need to make bread and cheese, respectively; the pizza company uses the bread and cheese from the other companies to make its pizzas. All three companies employ labor to help produce their goods, and the difference between the value of goods sold and the sum of labor and input costs is the firm's profit. This table summarizes the activities of the three companies when all the bread and cheese produced are sold to the pizza company as inputs in the production of pizzas.

	Bread company	Cheese company	Pizza company
Cost of inputs	$0	$0	$50 Bread
			35 Cheese
Wages	15	20	75
Value of output	50	35	200

a. Calculate GDP as the value added in production.

b. Calculate GDP as spending on final goods and services.

c. Calculate GDP as factor income.

4. In the economy of Pizzania (from Problem 3), bread and cheese produced are sold both to the pizza company for inputs in the production of pizzas and to consumers as final goods. The accompanying table summarizes the activities of the three companies.

	Bread company	Cheese company	Pizza company
Cost of inputs	$0	$0	$50 Bread
			35 Cheese
Wages	25	30	75
Value of output	100	60	200

a. Calculate GDP as the value added in production.

b. Calculate GDP as spending on final goods and services.

c. Calculate GDP as factor income.

5. Which of the following transactions will be included in GDP for the United States?

a. Coca-Cola builds a new bottling plant in the United States.

b. Delta sells one of its existing airplanes to Korean Air.

c. Ms. Moneybags buys an existing share of Disney stock.

d. A California winery produces a bottle of Chardonnay and sells it to a customer in Montreal, Canada.

e. An American buys a bottle of French perfume.

f. A book publisher produces too many copies of a new book; the books don't sell this year, so the publisher adds the surplus books to inventories.

6. The economy of Britannica produces three goods: computers, DVDs, and pizza. The accompanying table shows the prices and output of the three goods for the years 2002, 2003, and 2004.

	Computers		DVDs		Pizza	
Year	Price	Quantity	Price	Quantity	Price	Quantity
2002	$900	10	$10	100	$15	2
2003	1,000	10.5	12	105	16	2
2004	1,050	12	14	110	17	3

a. What is the percent change in production of each of the goods from 2002 to 2003 and from 2003 to 2004?

b. What is the percent change in prices of each of the goods from 2002 to 2003 and from 2003 to 2004?

c. Calculate nominal GDP in Britannica for each of the three years. What is the percent change in nominal GDP from 2002 to 2003 and from 2003 to 2004?

d. Calculate real GDP in Britannica using 2002 prices for each of the three years. What is the percent change in real GDP from 2002 to 2003 and from 2003 to 2004?

7. The accompanying table shows data on nominal GDP (in billions of dollars), real GDP (in billions of dollars) using 2000 as the base year, and population (in thousands) of the U.S. in 1960, 1970, 1980, 1990, 2000, and 2004, years in which the U.S. price level consistently rose.

Year	Nominal GDP (billions of dollars)	Real GDP (billions of 2000 dollars)	Population (thousands)
1960	$526.4	$2,501.8	180,671
1970	1,038.5	3,771.9	205,052
1980	2,789.5	5,161.7	227,726
1990	5,803.1	7,112.5	250,132
2000	9,817.0	9,817.0	282,388
2004	11,734.0	10,841.9	293,907

a. Why is real GDP greater than nominal GDP for all years before 2000 and lower for 2004? Does nominal GDP have to equal real GDP in 2000?

b. Calculate the percent change in real GDP from 1960 to 1970, 1970 to 1980, 1980 to 1990, and 1990 to 2000. Which period had the highest growth rate?

c. Calculate real GDP per capita for each of the years in the table.

d. Calculate the percent change in real GDP per capita from 1960 to 1970, 1970 to 1980, 1980 to 1990, and 1990 to 2000. Which period had the highest growth rate?

e. How do the percent change in real GDP and the percent change in real GDP per capita compare? Which is larger? Do we expect them to have this relationship?

8. This table shows the Human Development Index (HDI) and real GDP per capita in U.S. dollars for six nations in 2002.

	HDI	Real GDP per capita
Brazil	0.775	$7,770
Canada	0.943	29,480
Japan	0.938	26,940
Mexico	0.802	8,970
Saudi Arabia	0.768	12,650
United States	0.939	35,750

Rank the nations according to HDI and according to real GDP per capita. Why do the two vary?

9. In general, how do changes in the unemployment rate vary with changes in real GDP? After several quarters of a severe recession, explain why we might observe a decrease in the official unemployment rate. Could we see an increase in the official unemployment rate after several quarters of a strong expansion?

10. Each month, usually on the first Friday of the month, the Bureau of Labor Statistics releases the Employment Situation Summary for the previous month. Go to www.bls.gov and find the latest report. (On the Bureau of Labor Statistics home page, click on "National unemployment rate" and then choose "Employment Situation Summary.") How does the unemployment rate compare to the rate one year earlier? What percentage of unemployed workers are long-term unemployed workers?

11. Eastland College is concerned about the rising price of textbooks that students must purchase. To better identify the increase in the price of textbooks, the dean asks you, the Economics Department's star student, to create an index of textbook prices. The average student purchases three English, two math, and four economics textbooks. The prices of these books are given in the accompanying table.

   a. Create the price index for these books for all years with a base year of 2002.

	2002	2003	2004
English textbook	$50	$55	$57
Math textbook	70	72	74
Economics textbook	80	90	100

   b. What is the percent change in the price of an English textbook from 2002 to 2004?

   c. What is the percent change in the price of a math textbook from 2002 to 2004?

   d. What is the percent change in the price of an economics textbook from 2002 to 2004?

   e. What is the percent change in the market index from 2002 to 2004?

12. The consumer price index, or CPI, measures the cost of living for the average consumer by multiplying the price for each category of expenditure (housing, food, and so on) times a meas-

ure of the importance of that expenditure in the average consumer's market basket and summing over all categories. However, using data from the consumer price index, we can see that changes in the cost of living for different types of consumers can vary a great deal. Let's compare the cost of living for a hypothetical retired person and a hypothetical college student. Let's assume that the market basket of a retired person is allocated in the following way: 10% on housing, 15% on food, 5% on transportation, 60% on medical care, 0% on education, and 10% on recreation. The college student's market basket is allocated as follows: 5% on housing, 15% on food, 20% on transportation, 0% on medical care, 40% on education, and 20% on recreation. The accompanying table shows the December 2004 CPI for each of the relevant categories.

	CPI, December 2004
Housing	190.7
Food	188.9
Transportation	164.8
Medical care	314.9
Education	112.6
Recreation	108.5

Calculate the overall CPI for the retired person and for the college student by multiplying the CPI for each of the categories by the relative importance of that category to the individual and then summing each of the categories. The CPI for all items in December 2004 was 190.3. How do your calculations for a CPI for the retired person and the college student compare to the overall CPI?

13. Each month the Bureau of Labor Statistics releases the Consumer Price Index Summary for the previous month. Go to www.bls.gov and find the latest report. (On the Bureau of Labor Statistics home page, click on "CPI" under "Latest Numbers" and then choose "Consumer Price Index Summary.") What was the CPI for the previous month? How did it change from the previous month? How does the CPI compare to the same month one year ago?

14. The accompanying table contains two price indexes for the years 2002, 2003, and 2004: the GDP deflator and the CPI. For each price index, calculate the inflation rate from 2002 to 2003 and from 2003 to 2004.

Year	GDP deflator	CPI
2002	104.1	179.9
2003	106.0	184.0
2004	108.3	188.9

25

>> Long-Run Economic Growth

THE BAD OLD DAYS

What you will learn in this chapter:

➤ How long-run growth can be measured by the increase in real GDP per capita, how this measure has changed over time, and how it varies across countries

➤ Why **productivity** is the key to long-run growth, and how productivity is driven by **physical capital, human capital,** and **technological progress**

➤ The factors that explain why growth rates differ so much among countries

➤ How growth has varied among several important regions of the world and why the **convergence hypothesis** applies to economically advanced countries

I N 1999 BRITAIN'S CHANNEL 4TV carried out an experiment in time travel. They filmed a documentary about a modern English family, the Bowlers, who spent three months living exactly the way an upper-middle-class family lived in the year 1900. That meant living in a house without electricity or modern appliances, doing the laundry took two days of hard, hot work, and most of their food was boiled on a coal-burning stove. There was no shampoo, toothpaste, packaged or frozen food, and frequently there was insufficient hot water for a bath. The toilet was an outdoor privy in the garden. Not surprisingly, the Bowlers found life very difficult. (At a point of desperation in the battle to stay clean, the family broke the rules and purchased a bottle of modern shampoo.) As one reviewer said, "[Viewing this] should kill any feelings of nostalgia [for the old days] once and for all."

The documentary, called *1900 House*, vividly illustrated the huge improvement in living standards that has taken place in Britain over the past century. Nowadays the vast majority of people in Britain, even those considered poor, have comforts that were not available even to well-off families in 1900. The same is true in the United States. For example, a century ago most American families didn't even have indoor plumbing.

Yet old-fashioned discomfort isn't ancient history. Today, most of the world's population still has a standard of living far worse than that of the Bowlers in their 1900 house. In fact, billions of people still lack access to clean water and don't get enough to eat.

Why do residents of countries such as the United States, Canada, Japan, Britain, and others live so much better than they did a century ago? Why is the standard of living so much lower in countries such as India or Nigeria? The answer to both questions is that some, but not all, countries have been highly successful at achieving long-run economic

The Bowlers: a late-20th-century family that found life in the year 1900 very trying indeed.

growth: their economies produce far more goods and services per capita than they did 100 years ago, which makes it possible to have a much higher average standard of living. The world's poorer countries have not yet matched this achievement.

Many economists have argued that long-run growth—why it happens and how to achieve it—is the single most important issue in macroeconomics. In this chapter, we present some facts about long-run growth, look at the factors that economists believe determine the pace at which long-run growth takes place, and examine how government policies can help or hinder growth.

Comparing Economies Across Time and Space

Before we analyze the sources of long-run economic growth, it's useful to have a sense of just how much the U.S. economy has grown over time and how large the gaps are between wealthy countries like the United States and countries that have yet to match our growth record. So let's take a look at the numbers.

Real GDP per Capita

The key statistic used to track economic growth is *real GDP per capita*—real GDP divided by the population. We focus on GDP because, as we learned in Chapter 24, GDP measures the total value of an economy's production of final goods and services as well as the income earned in that economy in a given year. We use *real* GDP because we want to separate changes in the quantity of goods and services from the effects of a rising price level. We focus on real GDP *per capita* because we want to isolate the effect of a change in the population. For example, other things equal, an increase in the population lowers the standard of living for the average person—there are now more people to share a given amount of real GDP. A rise in real GDP that only matches population growth leaves the average standard of living unchanged.

Although we learned in Chapter 24 that growth in real GDP per capita should not be a policy goal in and of itself, it does serve as a very useful summary measure of a

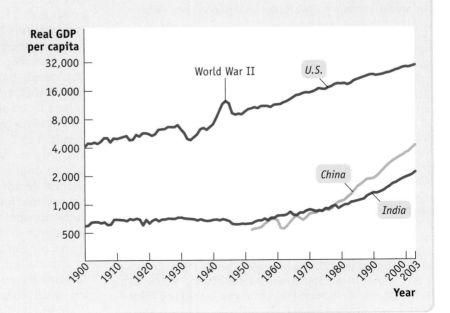

Figure 25-1

The Growth of Real GDP per Capita

Over the past century, U.S. real GDP per capita rose by nearly 600%, representing an average annual growth rate of real GDP per capita of 1.9% since 1900. Despite recent increases in growth, China and India are still poorer than the United States was in 1900.

Source: 1900–2001 data: Angus Maddison, *The World Economy: Historical Statistics* (Paris: OECD, 2003); 2002–2003 data: World Bank.

country's economic progress over time. Figure 25-1 on page 187 shows real GDP per capita for the United States, India, and China, in 2002 dollars, from 1900 to 2003. (We'll talk about India and China in a moment.) The vertical axis is drawn in a proportional scale so that equal percentage changes in real GDP per capita across countries are the same size in the graph.

To give a sense of how much the U.S. economy has grown, Table 25-1 shows real GDP per capita at 20-year intervals, expressed two ways: as a percentage of the 1900 level and as a percentage of the 2000 level. By 1920, the U.S. economy already produced 136% as much per person as it did in 1900. By 2000, it produced 688% as much per person as it did in 1900, or nearly seven times as much in output per person. Alternatively, in 1900 the U.S. economy produced only 14.5% as much per person as it did in 2000.

TABLE 25-1

U.S. Real GDP per Capita

Year	Real GDP per capita (2002 dollars)	Percentage of 1900 real GDP per capita	Percentage of 2000 real GDP per capita
1900	$5,219	100%	14.5%
1920	7,083	136	19.7
1940	8,943	171	24.9
1960	14,452	277	40.3
1980	23,700	454	66.0
2000	35,887	688	100.0

Source: Angus Maddison, *The World Economy: Historical Statistics* (Paris: OECD, 2003), adjusted using GDP deflator.

PITFALLS

CHANGE IN LEVELS VERSUS RATE OF CHANGE

When studying economic growth, it's vitally important to understand the difference between a change in level and a rate of change. When we say that real GDP "grew," we mean that the level of real GDP increased. For example, we might say that U.S. real GDP grew during 2005 by $15 billion.

If we knew the level of U.S. real GDP in 2004, we could also represent the amount of 2005 growth in terms of a rate of change. For example, if U.S. real GDP in 2004 was $485 billion, then U.S. real GDP in 2005 was $485 billion + $15 billion = $500 billion. We could calculate the rate of change, or the growth rate, of U.S. real GDP during 2005 as: (($500 billion − $485 billion)/ $485 billion) × 100 = ($15 billion/$485 billion) × 100 = 0.0309, or 3.09%. Statements about economic growth over a period of years almost always refer to changes in the growth rate.

When talking about growth or growth rates, economists often use phrases that appear to mix the two concepts and so can be confusing. For example, when we say that "U.S. growth fell during the 1970s," we are really saying that the U.S. growth rate of real GDP was lower in the 1970s in comparison to the 1960s. When we say that "growth accelerated during the early 1990s," we are saying that the growth rate increased year after year in the early 1990s—for example, going from 3% to 3.5% to 4%.

The income of the typical family normally grows in proportion to per capita income. For example, a 1% increase in real GDP per capita corresponds, roughly, to a 1% increase in the income of the median or typical family—a family in the center of the income distribution. In 2000, the median American family had an income of about $44,000. Since Table 25-1 tells us that real GDP per capita in 1900 was only 14.5% of its 2000 level, a typical family in 1900 probably had a purchasing power only 14.5% as large as the purchasing power of a typical family in 2000. That's around $6,000 in today's dollars, representing a standard of living that we would now consider severe poverty. Much like the Bowlers discovered, today's typical American family, if transported back to the United States of 1900, would feel quite a lot of deprivation.

Still many people in the world have yet to achieve the standard of living the United States had a century ago. That's the message about China and India in Figure 25-1: despite dramatic economic growth in China over the last two decades and a less dramatic acceleration of economic growth in India, as of 2003 the world's two most populous nations were still poorer than the United States was in 1900. And much of the world is poorer than China or India.

You can get a sense of how poor much of the world remains by looking at Figure 25-2, a map of the world in which countries are classified according to their 2003 levels of real gross national income per capita, a

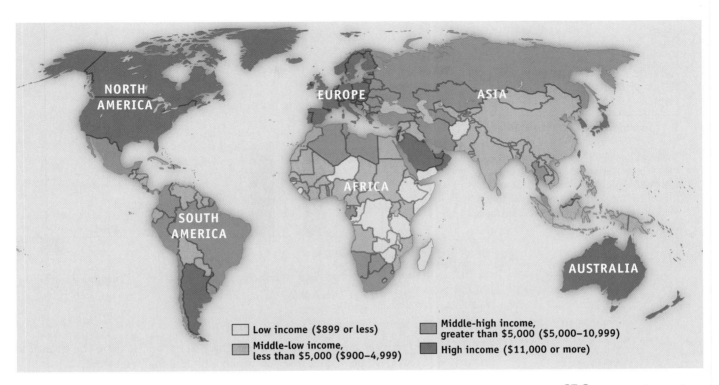

Low income ($899 or less)

Middle-low income,
less than $5,000 ($900–4,999)

Middle-high income,
greater than $5,000 ($5,000–10,999)

High income ($11,000 or more)

measure very close to real GDP per capita. As you can see, large parts of the world have very low incomes. Generally speaking, the countries of Europe and North America, as well as a few in the Pacific, have high incomes. The rest of the world, containing most of its population, is dominated by countries with real GDP less than $5,000 per capita—and often much less. In fact, today more than 50% of the world's people live in countries poorer than the United States was in 1900.

Figure 25-2 Income Around the World Income varies greatly among nations. More than half the world's population lives in countries that are poorer than the U.S. was in 1900.
Source: World Bank.

Growth Rates

How did the United States manage to produce nearly seven times more per person in 2000 than in 1900, a nearly 600% increase in real GDP per capita? A little bit at a time. Long-run economic growth is normally a gradual process, in which real GDP per capita grows at most a few percent per year. During the twentieth century, real GDP per capita in the United States increased an average of 1.9% each year.

To have a sense of the relationship between the annual growth rate of real GDP per capita and the long-run change in real GDP per capita, it's helpful to keep in mind the **Rule of 70,** a mathematical formula that tells us how long it takes real GDP per capita, or any other variable that grows gradually over time, to double. The approximate answer is:

The **Rule of 70** tells us that the time it takes a variable that grows gradually over time to double is approximately 70 divided by that variable's annual growth rate.

$$\textbf{(25-1)}\ \text{Number of years for variable to double} = \frac{70}{\text{Annual growth rate of variable}}$$

(Note that the rule of 70 can only be applied to a positive growth rate.) So if real GDP per capita grows at 1% per year, it will take 70 years to double. If it grows at 2% per year, it will take only 35 years to double. In fact, U.S. real GDP per capita rose on average 1.9% per year over the last century. Applying the Rule of 70 to this information implies that it should have taken 37 years for real GDP per capita to double; it would have taken 111 years—three periods of 37 years each—for U.S. real GDP per capita to double three times. That is, the Rule of 70 implies that over the course of 111 years U.S. real GDP per capita should have increased by a factor of $2 \times 2 \times 2 = 8$. And this does turn out to be a pretty good approximation to reality, once we

Figure 25-3

Average Annual Growth Rates of Real GDP per Capita, 1975–2003

Some countries, such as China and Ireland, have been very successful at achieving a rapid rise in real GDP per capita. Others, such as Argentina, have been much less successful. Still others, such as the countries of the former U.S.S.R., have slid backward. (Data for the former U.S.S.R. are for the period 1975–2001.)

Source: World Bank.

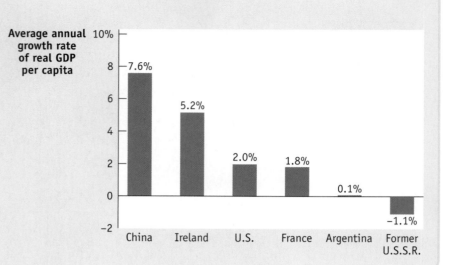

adjust for the fact that a century is a bit less than 111 years. During the twentieth century, U.S. real GDP per capita rose sevenfold, a bit less than eightfold.

Figure 25-3 shows the average annual rate of growth of real GDP per capita for selected countries from 1975 to 2003. (Data for the former U.S.S.R. are for the period 1975–2001.) Some countries were notable success stories: for example, China, though still quite a poor country, has made spectacular progress. Ireland did very well, too, as discussed in the following Economics in Action.

Some countries, though, have had very disappointing growth. Argentina was once considered a wealthy nation—in the early years of the twentieth century, it was in the same league as the United States and Canada. But since then it has lagged far behind more dynamic economies. In 2003 it was not significantly richer than it was in 1975. The countries that made up the former U.S.S.R. suffered a severe economic decline after the Soviet Union broke up in 1991 and have not yet recovered.

What explains these differences in growth rates? To answer that question, we need to examine the sources of long-run growth.

economics in action

The Luck of the Irish

In the nineteenth century, Ireland was desperately poor, so poor that millions of its residents fled poverty and hunger by emigrating to the United States and other countries. Even as late as the 1970s, Ireland remained one of the poorest countries in Western Europe, poorer than Latin American countries such as Argentina and Venezuela.

But that was then. As Figure 25-3 shows, for the last few decades real GDP per capita has grown almost as fast in Ireland as in China, and all that growth has made Ireland *richer* than most of Europe: Irish real GDP per capita is now higher than in the United Kingdom, France, and Germany. Not surprisingly, the Irish no longer emigrate in search of a better life. In fact, these days German workers sometimes go to Ireland in search of better-paying jobs.

Why has Ireland, after centuries of poverty, done so well? That's getting a bit ahead of our story. Let's just say that economists attribute Ireland's economic performance in large part to a very good *infrastructure* and *human capital.* For example, Ireland has a very good education system, very good airports, and excellent telecommunications and shipping facilities—all of which have attracted a lot of investment by American and Japanese companies. ■

> >

1. Why do economists use real GDP per capita to measure economic progress rather than some other measure, such as nominal GDP per capita or real GDP?

2. Apply the Rule of 70 to the data in Figure 25-3 to determine how long it will take each of the countries listed there, except the former U.S.S.R., to double its real GDP per capita. Would Ireland's real GDP per capita exceed that of the United States in the future if growth rates remain the same? Why or why not?

Solutions appear at back of book.

The Sources of Long-Run Growth

Long-run economic growth depends almost entirely on one ingredient: rising *productivity*. However, a number of factors affect the growth of productivity. Let's look at why productivity is the key ingredient, and then examine what affects it.

The Crucial Importance of Productivity

Sustained economic growth occurs only when the amount of output produced by the average worker increases steadily. The term **labor productivity,** or **productivity** for short, refers to output per worker. (Where data are available, productivity is defined as output *per hour*. This is often a useful statistic for comparing countries' productivities because the number of hours worked by an average worker often differs across countries.) For the economy as a whole, productivity is simply real GDP divided by the number of people working.

You might wonder why we say that higher productivity is the only source of long-run growth. Can't an economy also increase its real GDP per capita by putting more of the population to work? The answer is "Yes, but." For short periods of time an economy can experience a burst of growth in output per capita by putting a higher percentage of the population to work. That's what happened in the United States during World War II, when millions of women entered the paid workforce. The percentage of adult civilians employed outside the home rose from 50% in 1941 to 58% in 1944, and you can see the resulting bump in real GDP per capita during those years in Figure 25-1.

But over the longer run the rate of employment growth is never very different from the rate of population growth. Over the course of the twentieth century, for example, the population of the United States rose at an average rate of 1.3% per year and employment rose 1.5% per year. Real GDP per capita rose 1.9% per year; of that, 1.7%—that is, almost 90% of the total—was the result of rising productivity. In general, overall real GDP can grow because of population growth, but any large increase in real GDP *per capita* must be the result of increased output *per worker*. That is, it must be due to higher productivity.

So increased productivity is the key to long-run economic growth. But what leads to higher productivity?

Explaining Growth in Productivity

There are three main reasons why the average U.S. worker today produces far more than his or her counterpart a century ago. First, the modern worker has far more *physical capital*, such as machinery and office space, to work with. Second, the modern worker is much better educated and so possesses much more *human capital.*

Labor productivity, often referred to simply as **productivity,** is output per worker.

Finally, modern firms have the advantage of a century's accumulation of technical advancements reflecting a great deal of *technological progress*.

Let's look at each of these factors in turn.

Physical Capital

Economists define **physical capital** as human-made resources such as buildings and machines. Physical capital makes workers more productive. For example, a worker operating a backhoe can dig a lot more feet of trench per day than one equipped only with a shovel.

The average U.S. worker today is backed up by around $110,000 worth of physical capital—far more than a U.S. worker had 100 years ago and far more than the average worker in most other countries has today.

Human Capital

It's not enough for a worker to have good equipment—he or she must also know what to do with it. **Human capital** refers to the improvement in labor created by the education and knowledge embodied in the workforce.

The human capital of the United States has increased dramatically over the past century. A century ago, although most Americans were able to read and write, very few had an extensive education. In 1910, only 13.5% of Americans over 25 had graduated from high school and only 3% had four-year college degrees. By 2003, the percentages were 85% and 27%, respectively. It would be impossible to run today's economy with a population as poorly educated as that of a century ago.

Statistical analysis comparing economic growth rates in different countries suggests that education—and its effect on productivity—is an even more important determinant of growth than increases in physical capital.

Physical capital consists of human-made resources such as buildings and machines.

Human capital is the improvement in labor created by the education and knowledge embodied in the workforce.

Technology is the technical means for the production of goods and services.

I SHALL BE SO GLAD WHEN THEY INVENT THE INTERNET AND THIS STUFF CAN GO STRAIGHT ON TO OUR WEBSITE

Roger Beale

Technology

Probably the most important driver of productivity growth is progress in **technology,** which is broadly defined as the technical means for the production of goods and services. We'll see shortly how economists measure the impact of technology on growth.

Workers today are able to produce more than those in the past, even with the same amount of physical and human capital, because technology has advanced over time. It's important to realize that economically important technological progress need not be flashy or rely on cutting-edge science. Historians have noted that past economic growth has been driven not only by major inventions, such as the railroad or the semiconductor chip, but also by thousands of modest innovations, such as the flat-bottomed paper bag, patented in 1870, which made packing groceries and many other goods much easier, and the Post-it® Note, introduced in 1981, which has had surprisingly large benefits for office productivity. As For Inquiring Minds on page 593 points out, experts attribute much of the productivity surge that took place in the United States late in the twentieth century to new technology adopted by retail companies like Wal-Mart rather than to high-technology companies.

Accounting for Growth: The Aggregate Production Function

Productivity is higher, other things equal, when workers are equipped with more physical capital, more human capital, better technology, or any combination of the three. But can we put numbers to these effects? To do this, economists make use of estimates of the **aggregate production function,** which shows how productivity depends on the quantities of physical capital per worker and human capital per worker as well as the state of technology. The aggregate production function is a hypothetical relationship of the general form shown in Equation 25-2:

The **aggregate production function** is a hypothetical function that shows how productivity (real GDP per worker) depends on the quantities of physical capital per worker and human capital per worker as well as the state of technology.

(25-2) *Aggregate production function:* $Y/L = f(K/L, H/L, T)$

where $f(\cdot)$ means a function of the variables within the parentheses. Here, Y is real GDP produced, and L is the number of workers employed, so that Y/L is real GDP produced per worker; K/L is the quantity of physical capital per worker; H/L is the quantity of human capital per worker; and T is a measure of the state of the technology used in production.

In analyzing historical economic growth, economists have discovered a crucial fact about the estimated aggregate production function: it exhibits **diminishing returns to physical capital**. That is, when the amount of human capital per worker and the state of technology are held fixed, each successive increase in the amount of physical capital per worker leads to a smaller increase in productivity. Table 25-2 gives a hypothetical example of how the level of physical capital per worker might affect the level of real GDP per worker, holding human capital per worker and the state of technology fixed. In this example, we measure the quantity of physical capital in dollars.

As you can see from the table, there is a big payoff for the first $15,000 of physical capital: real GDP per worker rises by $30,000. The second $15,000 of physical capital also raises productivity, but not by as much: real GDP per worker goes up only $15,000. The third $15,000 of physical capital raises real GDP per worker by only $10,000.

An aggregate production function exhibits **diminishing returns to physical capital** when, holding the amount of human capital and the state of technology fixed, each successive increase in the amount of physical capital leads to a smaller increase in productivity.

TABLE 25-2

A Hypothetical Example: How Physical Capital per Worker Affects Productivity Holding Human Capital and Technology Fixed

Physical capital per worker	Real GDP per worker
$0	$0
15,000	30,000
30,000	45,000
45,000	55,000

To see why the relationship between physical capital per worker and productivity exhibits diminishing returns, think about how having farm equipment affects the productivity of farm workers. A little bit of equipment makes a big difference: a worker equipped with a tractor can do much more than a worker without one. And a worker using more expensive equipment will, other things equal, be more productive: a worker with a $30,000 tractor will normally be able to cultivate more farmland in a given amount of time than a worker with a $15,000 tractor because the more expensive machine will be more powerful, perform more tasks, or both.

PITFALLS

IT MAY BE DIMINISHED . . . BUT IT'S STILL POSITIVE

It's important to understand what diminishing returns to physical capital means and what it doesn't mean. As we've already explained, it's an "other things equal" statement: holding the amount of human capital per worker and the technology fixed, each successive increase in the amount of physical capital per worker results in a smaller increase in real GDP per worker. But this doesn't mean that real GDP per worker eventually falls as more and more physical capital is added. It's just that the *increase* in real GDP per worker gets smaller and smaller, albeit remaining at or above zero. So an increase in physical capital per worker will never reduce productivity. But due to diminishing returns, at some point increasing the amount of physical capital per worker no longer produces an economic payoff: at some point the increase in output is so small that it is not worth the cost of the additional physical capital.

But will a worker with a $30,000 tractor, holding human capital and technology constant, be twice as productive as a worker with a $15,000 tractor? Probably not: the second $15,000 worth of equipment won't raise productivity as much as the first $15,000 worth. And we can be sure that a worker with a $150,000 tractor won't be 10 times as productive: a tractor can be improved only so much. Because the same is true of other kinds of equipment, the aggregate production function shows diminishing returns to physical capital.

Diminishing returns to physical capital imply a relationship between physical capital per worker and output per worker like the one shown in Figure 25-4. As the curve illustrates, more physical capital per worker leads to more output per worker. But each $30,000 increment in physical capital per worker adds less to productivity. By comparing points A, B, and C you can also see that as physical capital per worker rises, output per worker rises but at a diminishing rate. Starting at point A, a $30,000 increase in physical capital per worker leads to an increase of $20,000 in real GDP per worker. At point B, an additional $30,000 increase in physical capital per worker leads to an increase of only $10,000 in real GDP per worker.

It's important to realize that diminishing returns to physical capital is an "other things equal" phenomenon: additional amounts of physical capital are less productive *when the amount of human capital and the technology are held fixed*. Diminishing returns may disappear if we increase the amount of human capital, or improve the technology, or both, at the same time the amount of physical capital is increased. For example, a worker with a $30,000 tractor who has also been trained in the most advanced cultivation techniques may in fact be more than twice as productive as a worker with only a $15,000 tractor and no additional human capital. But diminishing returns to any one input—regardless of whether it is physical capital, human capital, or number of workers—is a

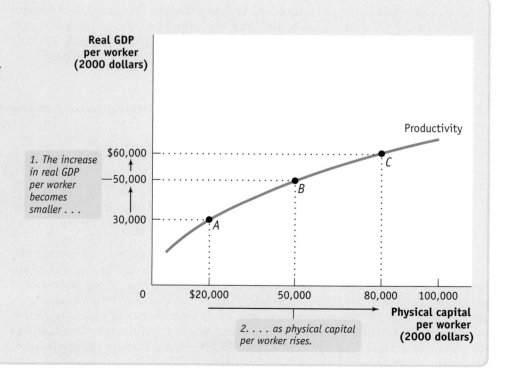

Figure 25-4

Physical Capital and Productivity

Other things equal, a greater quantity of physical capital per worker leads to higher real GDP per worker, but is subject to diminishing returns: each successive addition to physical capital per worker produces a smaller increase in productivity. Starting at point A, with $20,000 in physical capital per worker, a $30,000 increase in physical capital per worker leads to an increase of $20,000 in real GDP per worker. At point B, with $50,000 in physical capital per worker, a $30,000 increase in physical capital per worker leads to an increase of only $10,000 in real GDP per worker. >**web...**

pervasive characteristic of production. Typical estimates suggest that in practice a 1% increase in the quantity of physical capital per worker increases output per worker by only ⅓ of 1%, or 0.33%.

In practice, all the factors contributing to higher productivity rise during the course of economic growth: both physical capital and human capital per worker increase, and technology advances as well. To disentangle the effects of these factors, economists use **growth accounting,** which estimates the contribution of each major factor in the aggregate production function to economic growth. For example, suppose the following are true:

> **Growth accounting** estimates the contribution of each major factor in the aggregate production function to economic growth.

- The amount of physical capital per worker grows 3% a year.
- According to estimates of the aggregate production function, each 1% rise in physical capital per worker, holding human capital and technology constant, raises output per worker by ⅓ of 1%, or 0.33%.

In that case, we would estimate that growing physical capital per worker is responsible for 3% × 1/3 = 1 percentage point of productivity growth per year. A similar but more complex procedure is used to estimate the effects of growing human capital. The procedure is more complex because there aren't simple dollar measures of the quantity of human capital.

Growth accounting allows us to calculate the effects of greater physical and human capital on economic growth. But how can we estimate the effects of technological progress? We do so by estimating what is left over after the effects of physical and human capital have been taken into account. For example, let's imagine that there was no increase in human capital per worker so that we can focus on changes in physical capital and in technology. In Figure 25-5, the lower curve shows the same hypothetical relationship between physical capital per worker and output per worker shown in Figure 25-4.

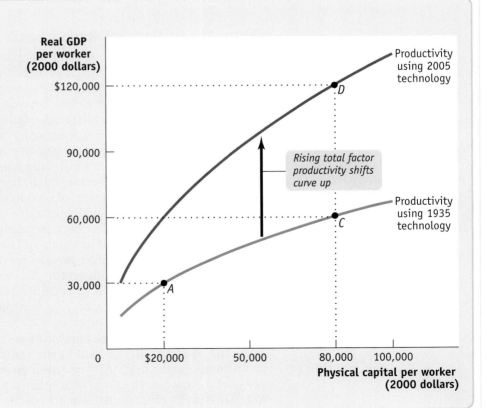

Figure 25-5

Technological Progress and Productivity Growth

Technological progress shifts the productivity curve upward. Here we hold human capital per worker fixed. We assume that the lower curve (the same curve as in Figure 25-4) reflects technology in 1935, and the upper curve reflects technology in 2005. Holding technology and human capital fixed, quadrupling physical capital per worker from $20,000 to $80,000 leads to a doubling of real GDP per worker, from $30,000 to $60,000. This is shown by the movement from point *A* to point *C,* reflecting an approximately 1% per year rise in real GDP per worker. In reality, technological progress shifted the productivity curve upward and the actual rise in real GDP per worker is shown by the movement from point *A* to point *D*. Real GDP per worker grew 2% per year, leading to a quadrupling during the period. The extra 1% in growth of real GDP per worker is due to higher total factor productivity.

Let's assume that this was the relationship given the technology available in 1935. The upper curve also shows a relationship between physical capital per worker and productivity, but this time given the technology available in 2005. (We've chosen a 70-year stretch to make the numerical example easier to understand.) The 2005 curve is shifted up compared to the 1935 curve because technologies developed over the previous 70 years make it possible to produce more output for a given amount of physical capital per worker than was possible with the technology available in 1935.

Let's assume that between 1935 and 2005 the amount of physical capital per worker rose from $20,000 to $80,000. If this increase in physical capital per worker had taken place without any technological progress, the economy would have moved from A to C: output per worker would have risen, but only from $30,000 to $60,000, or 1% per year (remember the Rule of 70). In fact, however, the economy moved from A to D: output rose from $30,000 to $120,000, or 2% per year. There was both an increase in physical capital per worker and technological progress, which shifted the aggregate production function.

In this case, 50% of the annual 2% increase in productivity—that is, 1% in productivity growth—is due to higher **total factor productivity,** the amount of output that can be produced with a given amount of factor inputs. So when total factor productivity increases, the economy can produce more output with the same quantity of physical capital, human capital, and labor.

Most estimates find that increases in total factor productivity are central to a country's economic growth. We believe that observed increases in total factor productivity do in fact measure the economic effects of technological progress. All of this implies that technological change is crucial to economic growth. The Bureau of Labor Statistics estimates the growth rate of both labor productivity and total factor productivity for nonfarm business in the United States. According to the bureau's estimates, over the period from 1948 to 2004 American labor productivity rose 2.3% per year. Only 48% of that rise is explained by increases in physical and human capital per worker; the rest is explained by rising total factor productivity—that is, by technological progress.

What About Natural Resources?

In our discussion so far, we haven't mentioned natural resources, which certainly have an effect on productivity. Other things equal, countries that are abundant in valuable natural resources, such as highly fertile land or rich mineral deposits, have higher real GDP per capita than less fortunate countries. The most obvious modern example is the Middle East, where enormous oil deposits have made a few sparsely populated countries very rich. For example, Kuwait has about the same level of real GDP per capita as South Korea, but Kuwait's wealth is based on oil, not manufacturing, the source of South Korea's high output per worker.

But other things are often not equal. In the modern world, natural resources are a much less important determinant of productivity than human or physical capital for the great majority of countries. For example, some nations with very high real GDP per capita, such as Japan, have very few natural resources. Some resource-rich nations, such as Nigeria (which has sizable oil deposits), are very poor.

Historically, natural resources played a much more prominent role in determining productivity. In the nineteenth century, the countries with the highest real GDP per capita were those abundant in rich farmland and mineral deposits: the United States, Canada, Argentina, and Australia. As a consequence, natural resources figured prominently in the development of economic thought. In a famous book published in 1798, *An Essay on the Principle of Population,* the English economist Thomas Malthus made the fixed quantity of land in the world the basis of a pessimistic prediction about future productivity. As population grew, he pointed out, the amount of land per worker would decline. And this, other things equal, would cause productivity to fall. His view, in fact, was that improvements in technology or increases in physical

---

Total factor productivity is the amount of output that can be achieved with a given amount of factor inputs.

capital would lead to only temporary improvements in productivity because they would always be offset by the pressure of rising population and more workers on the supply of land. In the long run, he concluded, the great majority of people were condemned to living on the edge of starvation. Only then would death rates be high enough and birth rates low enough to prevent rapid population growth from outstripping productivity growth.

It hasn't turned out that way, although many historians believe that Malthus's prediction of falling or stagnant productivity was valid for much of human history. Population pressure probably did prevent large productivity increases until the eighteenth century. But in the time since Malthus wrote his book, any negative effects on productivity from population growth have been far outweighed by other, positive factors—advances in technology, increases in human and physical capital, and the opening up of enormous amounts of cultivatable land in the New World.

economics in action

The Information Technology Paradox

From the early 1970s through the mid-1990s, the United States went through a slump in productivity growth. Figure 25-6 shows the annual growth rate of U.S. labor productivity on a 10-year basis—that is, the number for 1957 is the average annual growth rate from 1947 to 1957, the number for 1958 is the average annual growth rate from 1948 to 1958, and so on. As you can see, there was a large fall in the productivity growth rate beginning in the early 1970s. Because higher output per worker is the key to long-run growth, the economy's overall growth was also disappointing, leading to a widespread sense that economic progress had ground to a halt.

Many economists were puzzled by the slowdown in the U.S. growth rate of labor productivity—a fall from an average annual growth rate of 3% in the late 1960s to slightly less than 1% in the mid-1980s. This was surprising given that there appeared to be rapid progress in technology. Modern information technology really began with the development of the first microprocessor—a computer on a chip—in 1971. In the 25 years that followed, a series of inventions that seemed revolutionary became standard equipment in the business world: fax machines, desktop computers, cell phones, and e-mail. Yet the rate of growth of productivity remained stagnant. In a famous remark, MIT economics professor and Nobel laureate Robert Solow, a pioneer in the analysis of economic growth, declared that the information technology revolution could be seen everywhere except in the economic statistics.

Why didn't information technology show large rewards? Paul David, a Stanford economic historian, offered a theory and a prediction. He pointed out that 100 years earlier another miracle technology—electric power—had spread through the economy, again with surprisingly little impact on productivity growth at first. The reason, he suggested, was that a new technology doesn't yield its full potential if you use it in old ways.

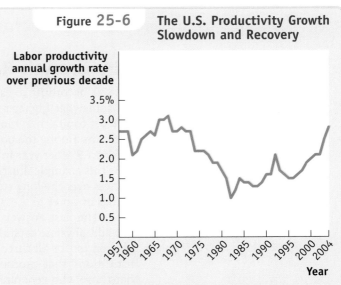

Figure 25-6   The U.S. Productivity Growth Slowdown and Recovery

Labor productivity annual growth rate over previous decade

Year

This curve shows the 10-year rate of growth of productivity in the United States. For example, the point for 1960 is the average annual productivity growth rate from 1950 to 1960. The productivity growth rate fell in the 1970s and 1980s, despite what appeared to be rapid technological progress. However, the productivity growth rate rose again in the 1990s.
Source: Bureau of Labor Statistics.

For example, a traditional factory around 1900 was a multistory building, with the machinery tightly crowded together and designed to be powered by a steam engine in the basement. This design had problems: it was very difficult to move people and materials around. Yet owners who electrified their factories initially maintained the multistory, tightly packed layout. Only with the switch to spread-out, one-story factories that took advantage of the flexibility of electric power—most famously Henry Ford's auto assembly line—did productivity take off.

David suggested that the same phenomenon was happening with information technology. Productivity, he predicted, would take off when people really changed their way of doing business to take advantage of the new technology—such as, replacing letters and phone calls with electronic communications. Sure enough, productivity growth accelerated dramatically in the second half of the 1990s. And, as For Inquiring Minds on page 593 suggested, a lot of that may have been due to the discovery by companies like Wal-Mart of how to effectively use information technology. ∎

< < < < < < < < < < < < < < < < < < <

>>CHECK YOUR UNDERSTANDING 25-2

1. Explain the effect of each of the following events on the growth rate of productivity.
   a. The amounts of physical and human capital per worker are unchanged, but there is significant technological progress.
   b. The amount of physical capital per worker grows, but the level of human capital per worker and technology are unchanged.

2. Multinomics, Inc., is a large company with many offices around the country. It has just adopted a new computer system that will affect virtually every function performed within the company. Why might a period of time pass before employees' productivity is improved by the new computer system? Why might there be a temporary decrease in employees' productivity?

Solutions appear at back of book.

Why Growth Rates Differ

In 1820, according to estimates by the economic historian Angus Maddison, Mexico had somewhat higher real GDP per capita than Japan. Today, Japan has higher real GDP per capita than most European nations and Mexico is a poor country, though by no means among the poorest. The difference? Over the long run, real GDP per capita grew at 1.9% per year in Japan but at only 1.2% per year in Mexico.

As this example illustrates, even small differences in growth rates have large consequences over the long run. But why do growth rates differ across countries and across periods of time?

The simplest answer is that economies with rapid growth tend to be economies that add physical capital, increase their human capital, experience rapid technological progress, or all three, on a sustained basis. The deeper answer lies in policies and institutions that promote economic growth—policies and institutions that ensure that those who generate additions to physical or human capital, or to technological progress, are rewarded for their efforts.

Savings and Investment Spending

To increase the physical capital available to workers, an economy must engage in investment spending. There are two ways to do this. One way is for its residents to engage in saving—that is, for them to put aside some of their income rather than using it for consumer spending. Such domestic savings can be generated by private households saving some of their disposable income, by the government spending less than its tax revenues, or both. The other source of funds for investment spending is foreign savings from residents of other countries. Let's focus first on domestic savings, those generated by a country's own residents.

Both the amount of savings and the ability of an economy to direct savings into productive investment spending depend on the economy's institutions, notably its financial system. In particular, a well-functioning banking system is very important for economic growth because in most countries it is the principal way in which savings are channeled into business investment spending. If a country's citizens trust their banks, they will place their savings in bank deposits, which the banks will then lend to their business customers. But if people don't trust their banks, they will hoard gold or foreign currency, keeping their savings in safe deposit boxes or under the mattress, where it cannot be turned into productive investment spending. As we'll discuss in Chapter 30, a well-functioning financial system requires appropriate government regulation that assures depositors that their funds are protected.

Government policy has an effect on savings and investment spending in two other important ways. As we'll see in Chapter 26, the government can engage in saving by taking in more in taxes than it spends. By doing so, the government effectively makes more funds available for investment spending. But what happens if the government spends more than it collects, requiring it to borrow money? One major concern of economists is whether government borrowing, if it is sufficiently large, "crowds out" private investment spending. In other words, does government borrowing absorb resources that would otherwise have promoted economic growth and by doing so lower investment spending compared to what it would have been without the borrowing? We'll explore the economics of savings and investment spending, the working of the financial system, and the role of government borrowing in Chapter 26.

Another way in which governments can adversely affect savings and investment spending is through irresponsible conduct of monetary policy—specifically, by generating excessive inflation. As we'll see in Chapter 33, high inflation erodes the value of many financial assets. As a result, people in countries with a history of inflation are often reluctant to save—or at least to place their savings in assets whose real value might be hurt by inflation.

Foreign Investment

A country's investment spending can be either more or less than its domestic savings because of foreign investment: residents of some countries invest part of their savings in other countries. The United States is currently a net recipient of foreign investment. In fact, foreign savings fund a large fraction of our investment spending, allowing the United States to have a quantity of investment spending higher than domestic savings. This continues a national tradition of foreign investment that goes back to the nineteenth century, when British investors financed much of the country's railroad construction.

Investors expect and normally receive a return on their investment. If a country's residents, like Americans, have borrowed from foreigners, they have to pay interest on those loans. And if foreign companies build new factories or purchase existing factories in a country, the foreign owners are entitled to receive any profits those factories earn. Still, economists argue that the increase in real GDP generated by foreign investment is usually greater than the interest and profits paid to foreigners. So, the country benefits overall from foreign investment.

In many cases there is an additional payoff to the recipient country when foreign companies invest in a country by building or purchasing factories. They often bring with them new technology that diffuses through the recipient economy, raising productivity in many sectors. In Asian nations such as Malaysia, investments in factories by U.S., European, and Japanese companies have brought modern production techniques that local Asian businesses have learned to emulate. Even U.S. businesses can learn a thing or two. In the 1980s, Japanese companies had developed production techniques, especially in the auto industry, that were superior to those used in the United States. In the 1990s, the United States closed the gap, largely by learning from Japanese-owned factories located here.

Education

An economy's physical capital is created mainly through investment spending by individuals and private companies. Much of an economy's human capital, in contrast, is the result of government spending on education. Governments pay for the great bulk of primary and secondary education, although individuals pay a significant share of the costs of higher education. The quality of education a country provides for its citizens has a large impact on its economic growth rate.

Like the Irish success story, the "East Asian economic miracle," described later in this chapter, is a case in point. Many analysts believe that the most important reason certain Asian nations did so well in the last few decades of the twentieth century is that, even when poor, they provided a very good basic education to their residents.

Infrastructure

Roads, power lines, ports, information networks, and other underpinnings for economic activity are known as **infrastructure**.

The term **infrastructure** refers to roads, power lines, ports, information networks, and other parts of an economy's physical capital that provide an underpinning, or foundation, for economic activity. Although some infrastructure is provided by private companies, much of it is either provided by the government or requires a great deal of government regulation and support. As we pointed out in Economics in Action on page 590, excellent infrastructure played a significant role in Ireland's rapid growth.

Poor infrastructure—for example, a power grid that often fails, cutting off electricity to homes and businesses—is a major obstacle to economic growth in some countries. To provide good infrastructure, an economy must be able to afford it, but it must also have the political discipline to maintain it and provide for the future.

Perhaps the most crucial infrastructure is something we rarely think about: basic public health measures in the form of a clean water supply and disease control. As we'll see in the next section, poor health infrastructure is a major problem for economic growth in poor countries, especially those in Africa.

Research and Development

Research and development is spending to create and implement new technologies.

The advance of technology is a key force behind economic growth. What drives technology?

Scientific advances make new technologies possible. To take the most spectacular example in today's world, the semiconductor chip—which is the basis for all modern information technology—could not have been developed without the theory of quantum mechanics in physics.

But science alone is not enough: scientific knowledge must be translated into useful products and processes. And that often requires devoting a lot of resources to **research and development,** R&D, spending to create new technologies and prepare them for practical use.

Much research and development is paid for by the private sector. The United States became the world's leading economy in large part because American businesses were among the first to make systematic research and development a part of their operations. For Inquiring Minds on the next page describes how Thomas Edison created the first modern industrial research laboratory.

But much important R&D is done by government agencies. In Economics in Action on page 601, we describe Brazil's recent agricultural boom. This boom was made possible by government researchers who discovered that adding crucial nutrients would allow crops to be grown on previously unusable land and also developed new varieties of soybeans and breeds of cattle that flourish in Brazil's tropical climate.

INVENTING R&D

Thomas Edison is best known as the inventor of the light bulb and the phonograph. But his biggest invention may surprise you: he invented research and development.

Before Edison's time, there had, of course, been many inventors. Some of them worked in teams. But in 1875 Edison created something new: his Menlo Park, New Jersey, laboratory. It employed 25 men full-time to generate new products and processes for business. In other words, he did not set out to

pursue a particular idea and then cash in. He created an organization whose purpose was to create new ideas year after year.

Edison's Menlo Park lab is now a museum. "To name a few of the products that were developed in Menlo Park," says the museum's website, "we can list the following: the carbon button mouthpiece for the telephone, the phonograph, the incandescent light bulb and the electrical distribution system, the electric train, ore separation, the

Edison effect bulb, early experiments in wireless, the grasshopper telegraph, and improvements in telegraphic transmission."

You could say that before Edison's lab, technology just sort of happened: people came up with ideas, but businesses didn't plan to make continuous technological progress. Now R&D operations, often much bigger than Edison's original team, are standard practice throughout the business world.

Political Stability, Property Rights, and Excessive Government Intervention

There's not much point in investing in a business if rioting mobs are likely to destroy it or saving your money if someone with political connections can steal it. Political stability and protection of property rights are crucial ingredients in long-run economic growth.

Long-run economic growth in successful economies, like that of the United States, has been possible because there are good laws, institutions that enforce those laws, and a stable political system that maintains those institutions. The law must say that your property is really yours so that someone else can't take it away. The courts and the police must be honest so that they can't be bribed to ignore the law. And the political system must be stable so that the law doesn't change capriciously.

Americans take these preconditions for granted, but they are by no means guaranteed. Aside from the disruption caused by war or revolution, many countries find that their economic growth suffers due to corruption among the government officials who should be enforcing the law. For example, until 1991 the Indian government imposed many bureaucratic restrictions on businesses, which often had to bribe government officials to get approval for even routine activities—a tax on business, in effect. Economists have argued that a reduction in this burden of corruption is one reason Indian growth has been much faster in recent years than it was in the first 40 years after India gained independence in 1947.

Even when governments aren't corrupt, excessive government intervention can be a brake on economic growth. If large parts of the economy are supported by government subsidies, protected from imports, or otherwise insulated from competition, productivity tends to suffer because of a lack of incentives. As we'll see in the next section, excessive government intervention is one often-cited explanation for slow growth in Latin America.

economics in action

The Brazilian Breadbasket

A wry Brazilian joke says that "Brazil is the country of the future—and always will be." The world's fifth most populous country has often been seen as a possible major economic power, yet has never fulfilled that promise.

In recent years, however, Brazil's economy has made a better showing, especially in agriculture. This success depends on exploiting a natural resource, the tropical savanna land known as the *cerrado*. But until a quarter-century ago, the land was considered unsuitable for farming. A combination of three factors changed that: technological progress due to research and development, improved economic policies, and greater physical capital.

The Brazilian Enterprise for Agricultural and Livestock Research, a government-run agency, developed the crucial technologies. It showed that adding lime and phosphorus made *cerrado* land productive and developed breeds of cattle and varieties of soybeans suited for the climate. (Now they're working on wheat.) Also, until the 1980s, Brazilian international trade policies discouraged exports, as did an overvalued exchange rate that made the country's goods more expensive to foreigners. After economic reform, investing in Brazilian agriculture became much more profitable and companies began putting in place the farm machinery, buildings, and other forms of physical capital needed to exploit the land.

What limits Brazil's growth? Infrastructure. According to a report in the *New York Times,* Brazilian farmers are "concerned about the lack of reliable highways, railways and barge routes, which adds to the cost of doing business." But the Brazilian government is investing in infrastructure, and Brazilian agriculture is continuing to expand. The country has already overtaken the United States as the world's largest beef exporter and may not be far behind in soybeans.

< < < < < < < < < < < < < < < < < <

▶▶CHECK YOUR UNDERSTANDING 25-3

1. In recent years the United States has had a very low savings rate (the percentage of GDP that is saved nationally in a given year) but has attracted much foreign investment. Some economists say this is a danger to long-run growth, but others disagree. Why might both sides be right?

2. U.S. centers of academic biotechnology research have closer connections with private biotechnology companies than their European counterparts. What effect might this have on the pace of creation and development of new drugs in the United States versus Europe?

3. During the 1990s in the former U.S.S.R., a lot of property was seized and controlled by those in power. How might this have affected the country's growth rate?

4. Many countries that once shunned foreign-owned factories now welcome them. Explain this change of attitude.

Solutions appear at back of book.

Success, Disappointment, and Failure

As we've seen, rates of long-run economic growth differ quite a lot around the world. We conclude this chapter with a look at three regions of the world that have had quite different experiences with economic growth over the last few decades.

Figure 25-7 shows trends since 1960 in real GDP per capita for three countries: Argentina, Ghana, and South Korea. (As in Figure 25-1, the vertical axis is drawn in

Figure 25-7

Success, Disappointment, and Failure

South Korea and some other East Asian countries have been highly successful at achieving economic growth. Argentina, like much of Latin America, had relatively high real GDP per capita in the early twentieth century but has achieved little growth in real GDP per capita over the past half-century. Like most of Africa, Ghana's economy has stagnated over time.

Source: World Bank.

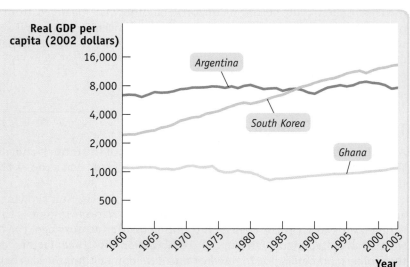

proportional scale.) We have chosen these countries because each is a particularly striking example of what has happened in its region. South Korea's amazing rise is part of a broad "economic miracle" in East Asia. Argentina's stagnant real GDP per capita is more or less typical of the disappointment that has characterized Latin America. And Ghana's unhappy story—despite some recovery since the mid-1980s, real GDP per capita is still lower than it was in 1960—is, unfortunately, typical of Africa's experience.

The East Asian Miracle

In 1960 South Korea was a very poor country. In fact, in 1960 its real GDP per capita was lower than that of India today. But, as you can see from Figure 25-7, beginning in the early 1960s South Korea began an extremely rapid economic ascent: real GDP per capita grew about 7% per year for more than 30 years. Today South Korea, though still somewhat poorer than Europe or the United States, looks very much like an economically advanced country.

South Korea's economic growth is unprecedented in history: it took the country only 35 years to achieve growth that required centuries elsewhere. Yet South Korea is only part of a broader phenomenon, often referred to as the East Asian economic miracle. High growth rates first appeared in South Korea, Taiwan, Hong Kong, and Singapore but then spread across the region, most notably to China. Since 1975 the whole region has increased real GDP per capita by 6% per year, three times America's historical rate of growth.

How have the Asian countries achieved such high growth rates? The answer is that all of the sources of productivity growth have been firing on all cylinders. Very high savings rates, the percentage of GDP that is saved nationally in any given year, have allowed the countries to significantly increase the amount of physical capital per worker. Very good basic education has permitted a rapid improvement in human capital. And these countries have experienced substantial technological progress.

Why hasn't any economy achieved this kind of growth in the past? Most economic analysts think that East Asia's growth spurt was possible because of its *relative* backwardness. That is, by the time that East Asian economies began to move into the modern world, they could benefit from adopting the technological advances that had been generated in technologically advanced countries such as the United States. In 1900, the United States could not have moved quickly to a modern level of productivity because much of the technology that powers the modern economy, from jet planes to computers, hadn't been invented yet. In 1970, South Korea probably still had lower labor productivity than the United States had in 1900, but it could rapidly upgrade its productivity by adopting technology that had been developed in the United States, Europe, and Japan over the previous century.

The East Asian experience demonstrates that economic growth can be especially fast in countries that are playing catch-up to other countries with higher GDP per capita. On this basis many economists have suggested a general principle known as the **convergence hypothesis.** It says that differences in real GDP per capita among countries tend to narrow over time because countries that start with lower real GDP per capita tend to have higher growth rates. We'll look at the evidence on the convergence hypothesis in the Economics in Action on page 605.

Even before we get to that evidence, however, we can say right away that starting with a relatively low level of real GDP per capita is no guarantee of rapid growth, as the examples of Latin America and Africa both demonstrate.

China's high rate of economic growth is rapidly raising Chinese living standards.

According to the **convergence hypothesis,** international differences in real GDP per capita tend to narrow over time.

Latin America's Disappointment

In 1900, Latin America was not regarded as an economically backward region. Natural resources, including both cultivatable land and minerals, were abundant. Some countries, notably Argentina, attracted millions of immigrants from Europe, people in search of a better life. Measures of real GDP per capita in Argentina, Uruguay, and southern Brazil were comparable to that in economically advanced countries.

Since about 1920, however, growth in Latin America has been disappointing. As Figure 25-7 shows in the case of Argentina, it has remained disappointing to this day. The fact that South Korea is now much richer than Argentina would have seemed inconceivable a few generations ago.

Why has Latin America stagnated? Comparisons with East Asian success stories suggest several factors. The rates of savings and investment spending in Latin America have been much lower than in East Asia, partly as a result of irresponsible government policy that has eroded savings through high inflation, bank failures, and other disruptions. Education—especially broad basic education—has been underemphasized: even Latin American nations rich in natural resources often failed to channel that wealth into their educational systems. And political instability, leading to irresponsible economic policies, has taken a toll.

In the 1980s, many economists came to believe that Latin America was suffering from excessive government intervention in markets. They recommended opening the economies to imports, selling off government-owned companies and, in general, freeing up individual initiative. The hope was that this would produce an East Asian-type economic surge. So far, however, only one Latin American nation, Chile, has achieved really rapid growth. It now seems that pulling off an economic miracle is harder than it looks.

Africa's Troubles

Africa south of the Sahara is home to about 600 million people, more than twice the population of the United States. On average they are very poor, nowhere close to U.S. living standards 100 or even 200 years ago. Worst of all, Africa's economies have been moving backward: average real GDP per capita in 2003 was 11% lower than in 1974.

The consequence of this poor growth performance has been intense and worsening poverty. In 1970, 42% of Africans lived on less than $1 a day in today's prices. By 2001, that number was 46%.

This is a very disheartening picture. What explains it?

Several factors are probably crucial. Perhaps first and foremost is the problem of political instability. In the years since 1975, large parts of Africa have experienced savage civil wars (often with outside powers backing rival sides) that have killed millions of people and made productive investment spending impossible. The threat of war and general anarchy has also inhibited other important preconditions for growth, such as education and provision of necessary infrastructure.

Property rights are also a problem. The lack of legal safeguards means that property owners are often subject to extortion because of government corruption, making them averse to owning property or improving it. This is especially damaging in a country that is very poor.

Although many economists see political instability and government corruption as the leading causes of underdevelopment in Africa, some—most notably Jeffrey Sachs of Columbia University and the United Nations—believe the opposite. They argue that Africa is politically unstable because Africa is poor. And Africa's poverty, they go on to claim, stems from its extremely unfavorable geographic conditions—much of the continent is landlocked, hot, infested with tropical diseases, and cursed with poor soil.

Sachs, along with economists from the World Health Organization, has highlighted the importance of health problems in Africa. In poor countries, worker productivity is often severely hampered by malnutrition and disease. In particular, tropical diseases such as malaria can only be controlled with an effective public health infrastructure, something that is lacking in much of Africa. At the time of writing, within regions of Africa, economists are studying whether modest amounts of aid given directly to residents for the purposes of increasing crop yields, reducing malaria, and increasing school attendance can produce self-sustaining gains in living standards.

Although the example of African countries represents a warning that long-run economic growth cannot be taken for granted, there are some signs of hope. Mauritius has developed a successful textile industry. Several African countries that are dependent on commodities such as coffee and oil have benefited from the recent sharp rise in the prices of commodities. And Ghana has managed to maintain an increase in real GDP per capita for several years now.

economics in action

Are Economies Converging?

In the 1950s, much of Europe seemed quaint and backward to American visitors, and Japan seemed very poor. Today, a visitor to Paris or Tokyo sees a city that looks about as rich as New York. Although real GDP per capita is still somewhat higher in the United States, the differences in the standards of living among the United States, Europe, and Japan are relatively small.

Many economists have argued that this convergence in living standards is normal; the convergence hypothesis says that relatively poor countries should have higher rates of growth of real GDP per capita than relatively rich countries. And if we look at today's relatively well-off countries, the convergence hypothesis seems to be true. Panel (a) of Figure 25-8 shows data for a number of today's wealthy economies. On

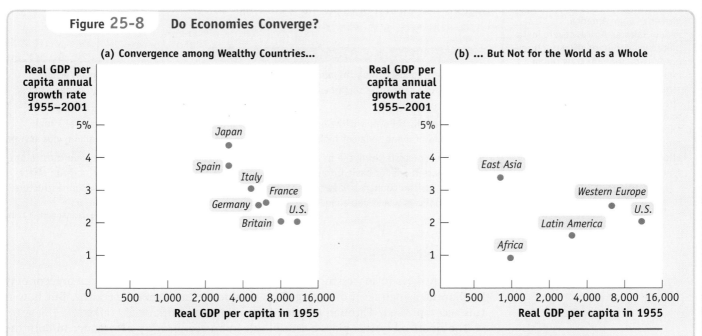

Figure 25-8   Do Economies Converge?

Data on today's wealthy economies seem to support the convergence hypothesis. In panel (a) we see that among wealthy countries, those that had low levels of real GDP per capita in 1955 have had high growth rates since then, and vice versa. But for the world as a whole, there has been little sign of convergence. Panel (b) shows real GDP per capita in 1955 and subsequent growth rates in major world regions. Poorer regions did not consistently have higher growth rates than richer regions: poor Africa turned in the worst performance, and relatively wealthy Europe and grew faster than Latin America. *>web...*

Source: Angus Maddison, *The World Economy: Historical Statistics,* (Paris: OECD, 2003).

the horizontal axis is real GDP per capita in 1955; on the vertical axis is the growth rate of real GDP per capita from 1955 to 2001. There is a clear negative relationship. The United States was the richest country in this group in 1955 and had the slowest rate of growth. Japan and Spain were the poorest countries in 1955 and had the fastest rate of growth. These data suggest that the convergence hypothesis is true.

But economists who looked at similar data realized that these results depend on the countries selected. If you look at successful economies that have a high standard of living today, you find that real GDP per capita has converged. But looking across the world as a whole, including countries that remain poor, there is little evidence of convergence. Panel (b) of Figure 25-8 illustrates this point using data for regions rather than individual countries (other than the United States). In 1955, East Asia and Africa were both very poor regions. Over the next 45 years, the East Asian regional economy grew quickly, as the convergence hypothesis would have predicted, but the African regional economy grew very slowly. In 1955, Western Europe had substantially higher real GDP per capita than Latin America. But, contrary to the convergence hypothesis, the Western European regional economy grew more quickly over the next 45 years, widening the gap between the regions.

So is the convergence hypothesis all wrong? No: economists still believe that countries with relatively low real GDP per capita tend to have higher rates of growth than countries with relatively high real GDP per capita, *other things equal.* But other things—education, infrastructure, rule of law, and so on—are often not equal. Statistical studies find that when you adjust for differences in these other factors, poorer countries do tend to have higher growth rates. This result is known as *conditional convergence.*

Because other factors differ, however, there is no clear tendency toward convergence in the world economy as a whole. Western Europe, North America, and parts of Asia are becoming more similar in real GDP per capita, but the gap between these regions and the rest of the world is growing.

< < < < < < < < < < < < < < < < < < <

>> **QUICK REVIEW**

➤ East Asia's spectacular growth was generated by high savings and investment spending rates, emphasis on education, and adoption of technological advances from other countries.

➤ Poor education, political instability, and irresponsible government policies are major factors in the slow growth of Latin America.

➤ In sub-Saharan Africa, severe instability, war, and poor infrastructure—particularly that affecting public health—have resulted in a catastrophic failure of growth.

➤ The *convergence hypothesis* seems to hold only when other things—such as education, infrastructure, property rights, and so on—that affect economic growth are held equal.

>>CHECK YOUR UNDERSTANDING 25-4

1. Some economists think the high rates of growth of productivity achieved by many Asian economies cannot be sustained. Why might they be right? What would have to happen for them to be wrong?

2. Which of the following is the better predictor of a future high long-run growth rate: a high standard of living today or high levels of savings and investment spending? Explain your answer.

3. Some economists think the best way to help African countries is for wealthier countries to provide more funds for basic infrastructure. Others think this policy will have no long-run effect unless African countries have the financial and political means to maintain this infrastructure. What policies would you suggest?

Solutions appear at back of book.

• A LOOK AHEAD •

One of the keys to successful long-run economic growth is the ability of an economy to channel a high level of savings into productive investment spending. But how is this accomplished? Through policies, institutions, and financial markets.

The financial system plays a crucial role in an economy's performance in both the long run and the short run. In the next chapter, we examine how that system works.

SUMMARY

1. Levels of real GDP per capita vary greatly around the world: more than half the world's population lives in countries that are still poorer than the United States was in 1900. Over the course of the twentieth century, real GDP per capita in the United States increased by nearly 600%.

2. Growth rates of real GDP per capita also vary widely. According to the **Rule of 70,** the number of years it takes for real GDP per capita to double is equal to 70 divided by the annual growth rate of real GDP per capita.

3. The key to long-run growth is rising **labor productivity,** or just **productivity,** which is output per worker. Increases in productivity arise from increases in **physical capital** per worker and **human capital** per worker as well as advances in **technology.** The **aggregate production function** shows how real GDP per worker depends on these three factors. Other things equal, there are **diminishing returns to physical capital:** each successive addition to physical capital yields a smaller increase in productivity than the one before. Equivalently, more physical capital per worker results in a lower, but still positive, growth rate of productivity. **Growth accounting,** which estimates the contribution of each factor to a country's economic growth, has shown that rising **total factor productivity,** the amount of output produced from a given amount of factor inputs, is key to long-run growth. It is usually interpreted as the effect of technological progress. In contrast to earlier times, natural resources are a less significant source of productivity growth in most countries today.

4. A number of factors influence differences among countries in their growth rates. These are government policies and institutions that increase savings and investment spending, foreign investment, **infrastructure, research and development,** as well as foster political stability and the protection of property rights.

5. The world economy contains examples of success and failure in the effort to achieve long-run economic growth. East Asian economies have done many things right and achieved very high growth rates. In Latin America, where some important conditions are lacking, growth has generally been disappointing. In Africa, real GDP per capita has declined for several decades, although there are some signs of progress now. The growth rates of economically advanced countries have converged, but not the growth rates of countries across the world. This has led economists to believe that the **convergence hypothesis** fits the data only when factors that affect growth, such as education, infrastructure, and favorable policies and institutions, are held equal across countries.

KEY TERMS

Rule of 70, p. 589
Labor productivity, p. 591
Productivity, p. 591
Physical capital, p. 592
Human capital, p. 592

Technology, p. 592
Aggregate production function, p. 592
Diminishing returns to physical capital, p. 593
Growth accounting, p. 595

Total factor productivity, p. 596
Infrastructure, p. 600
Research and development, p. 600
Convergence hypothesis, p. 603

PROBLEMS

1. The accompanying table shows data from the Penn World Table, Version 6.1, for real GDP per capita in 1996 U.S. dollars for Argentina, Ghana, South Korea, and the United States for 1960, 1970, 1980, 1990, and 2000.

a. Complete the table by expressing each year's real GDP per capita as a percentage of its 1960 and 2000 levels.

b. How does the growth in living standards from 1960 to 2000 compare across these four nations? What might account for these differences?

	Argentina			Ghana			South Korea			United States		
Year	Real GDP per capita (1996 dollars)	Percentage of 1960 real GDP per capita	2000 real GDP per capita	Real GDP per capita (1996 dollars)	Percentage of 1960 real GDP per capita	2000 real GDP per capita	Real GDP per capita (1996 dollars)	Percentage of 1960 real GDP per capita	2000 real GDP per capita	Real GDP per capita (1996 dollars)	Percentage of 1960 real GDP per capita	2000 real GDP per capita
1960	$7,395	?	?	$832	?	?	$1,571	?	?	$12,414	?	?
1970	9,227	?	?	1,275	?	?	2,777	?	?	16,488	?	?
1980	10,556	?	?	1,204	?	?	4,830	?	?	21,337	?	?
1990	7,237	?	?	1,183	?	?	9,959	?	?	26,470	?	?
2000	10,995	?	?	1,349	?	?	15,881	?	?	33,308	?	?

2. The accompanying table shows the average annual growth rate in real GDP per capita for Argentina, Ghana, and South Korea using data from the Penn World Table, Version 6.1, for the past few decades.

	Average annual growth rate of real GDP per capita		
Years	Argentina	Ghana	South Korea
1960–1970	2.24%	4.36%	5.86%
1970–1980	1.35	−0.57	5.69
1980–1990	−3.70	−0.18	7.51
1990–2000	4.27	1.33	4.78

a. For each decade and for each country, use the Rule of 70 where possible to calculate how long it would take for that country's real GDP per capita to double.

b. Suppose that the average annual growth rate that each country achieved over the period 1990–2000 continues indefinitely into the future. Starting from 2000, use the Rule of 70 to calculate, where possible, the year in which a country will have doubled its real GDP per capita.

3. You are hired as an economic consultant to the countries of Albernia and Brittania. Each country's current relationship between physical capital per worker (K/L) and output per worker (Y/L) is given by the curve labeled Productivity$_1$ in the accompanying diagram. Albernia is at point A and Brittania is at point B.

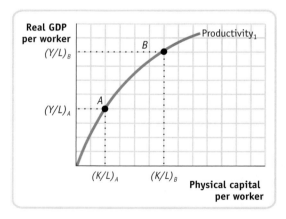

a. In the relationship depicted by the curve Productivity$_1$, what factors are held fixed? Do these countries experience diminishing returns to physical capital per worker?

b. Assuming that the amount of human capital per worker and the technology are held fixed in each country, can you recommend a policy to generate a doubling of real GDP per capita in each country?

c. How would your policy recommendation change if the amount of human capital per worker and the technology were not fixed? Draw a curve on the diagram that represents this policy for Albernia.

4. Why would you expect real GDP per capita in California and Pennsylvania to exhibit convergence but not in California and Baja California, a state of Mexico that borders the United States? What changes would allow California and Baja California to converge?

5. The economy of Profunctia has estimated its aggregate production function, when holding human capital per worker and technology constant, as

$$\frac{Y}{L} = 100 \times \sqrt{\frac{K}{L}}$$

Y is real GDP, L is the number of workers, and K is the quantity of physical capital. Given that Profunctia has 1,000 workers, calculate real GDP per worker and the quantity of physical capital per worker for the differing amounts of physical capital shown in the accompanying table.

K	L	K/L	Y/L
$0	1,000	?	?
10	1,000	?	?
20	1,000	?	?
30	1,000	?	?
40	1,000	?	?
50	1,000	?	?
60	1,000	?	?
70	1,000	?	?
80	1,000	?	?
90	1,000	?	?
100	1,000	?	?

a. Plot the aggregate production function for Profunctia.

b. Does the aggregate production function exhibit diminishing returns to physical capital? Explain your answer.

6. The Bureau of Labor Statistics regularly releases the "Productivity and Costs" report for the previous month. Go to www.bls.gov and find the latest report. (On the Bureau of Labor Statistics home page, click on "Productivity" under Latest Numbers and then choose the latest "Productivity and Costs" report.) What were the percent changes in business and nonfarm business productivity for the previous quarter? How does the percent change in that quarter's productivity compare to previous data?

7. What roles do physical capital, human capital, technology, and natural resources play in influencing long-run economic growth of aggregate output per capita?

8. Through its policies and institutions, how has the United States influenced U.S. long-run economic growth? Why might persistently large borrowing by the U.S. government ultimately limit long-run economic growth in the future?

9. Over the next 100 years, real GDP per capita in Groland is expected to grow at an average annual rate of 2.0%. In Sloland, however, growth is expected to be somewhat slower, at an average annual growth rate of 1.5%. If both countries have a real GDP per capita today of $20,000, how will their real GDP per capita differ in 100 years? (*Hint:* A country that has a real GDP today of x and grows at y% per year will achieve a real GDP of $x \times (1 + 0.0y)^z$ in z years.

10. The accompanying table shows data from the Penn World Table, Version 6.1, for real GDP per capita (1996 U.S. dollars) in France, Japan, the United Kingdom, and the United States in 1950 and 2000. Complete the table. Have these countries converged economically?

	1950		2000	
	Real GDP per capita (1996 dollars)	Percentage of U.S. real GDP per capita	Real GDP per capita (1996 dollars)	Percentage of U.S. real GDP per capita
France	$5,561	?	$22,254	?
Japan	2,445	?	24,495	?
United Kingdom	7,498	?	22,849	?
United States	10,601	?	33,308	?

11. The accompanying table shows data from the Penn World Table, Version 6.1, for real GDP per capita (1996 U.S. dollars) for Argentina, Ghana, South Korea, and the United States in 1960 and 2000. Complete the table. Have these countries converged economically?

	1960		2000	
	Real GDP per capita (1996 dollars)	Percentage of U.S. real GDP per capita	Real GDP per capita (1996 dollars)	Percentage of U.S. real GDP per capita
Argentina	$7,395	?	$10,995	?
Ghana	832	?	1,349	?
South Korea	1,571	?	15,881	?
United States	12,414	?	33,308	?

> **web...** To continue your study and review of concepts in this chapter, please visit the Krugman/Wells website for quizzes, animated graph tutorials, web links to helpful resources, and more.
>
> **www.worthpublishers.com/krugmanwells**

26

>> Savings, Investment Spending, and the Financial System

A HOLE IN THE GROUND

BETWEEN 1987 AND 1994, A LARGE international group of private investors threw $15 billion into a hole in the ground. But this was no ordinary hole: it was the Channel Tunnel, popularly known as the Chunnel. Engineers had dreamed for centuries about linking Britain directly to France so that travelers would no longer have to cross the often-stormy seas of the English Channel. The Chunnel fulfills that dream, allowing passengers to take a comfortable fast train (and ship their cars, too) underneath the 31-mile-wide strait.

Everyone agrees that the Chunnel is a big improvement on the previously available alternatives. It's much faster than taking a ferry. Even flying from London to Paris can easily be an all-day affair, what with getting to and from the airports and air traffic delays. The *Eurostar,* the express train through the Chunnel, gets you from downtown London to downtown Paris in three hours.

How could such a massive investment be financed? The French and British governments could have built the Chunnel but chose to leave it to private initiative. Yet the size of the required investment was beyond the means of any individual. So how was the money raised?

The answer: the Eurotunnel Corporation, the company formed to build the Chunnel, was able to turn to the financial markets. It raised $4 billion by selling stock to thousands of people, who then became part-owners of the Chunnel, and an additional $12 billion through bank loans. Raising this much money was an incredible feat, in a way as incredible as the engineering required in the construction of the Chunnel.

What you will learn in this chapter:

➤ The relationship between savings and investment spending

➤ Aspects of the **loanable funds market,** which shows how savers are matched with borrowers

➤ The purpose of the four principal types of **financial assets:** stocks, bonds, **loans,** and **bank deposits**

➤ How **financial intermediaries** help investors achieve **diversification**

➤ Some competing views of what determines stock prices and why stock market fluctuations can be a source of macroeconomic instability

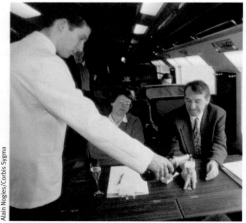

A quick and luxurious ride from London to Paris beneath the English Channel was made possible by the savings of millions of people.

Yet modern economies do this sort of thing all the time. The long-run growth we analyzed in Chapter 25 depends crucially on a set of markets and institutions, collectively known as the *financial system,* that channels the funds of savers into productive investment spending. Without this system, businesses would not be able to purchase much of the physical capital that is such an important source of productivity growth. And savers would be forced to accept a lower return on their funds. Historically, financial systems channeled funds into investment projects such as railroads, factories, electrification, and so on. Today, financial systems channel funds into sources of growth such as telecommunications, advanced technology, and investments in human capital. Without a well-functioning financial system, a country will suffer stunted economic growth.

In this chapter, we begin by focusing on the economy as a whole. We examine the relationship between savings and investment spending at the macroeconomic level. Next, we go behind this relationship and analyze the financial system, the means by which savings is transformed into investment spending. We'll see how the financial system works by creating assets, markets, and institutions that increase the welfare of both savers (those with funds to invest) and borrowers (those with investment projects to finance). Finally, we close by examining the behavior of financial markets and why that behavior often resists economists' attempts to explain it.

Matching Up Savings and Investment Spending

We learned in Chapter 25 that two of the essential ingredients in economic growth are increases in the economy's levels of *human capital* and *physical capital*. Human capital is largely provided by government through public education. (In countries with a large private education sector, like the United States, private post-secondary education is also an important source of human capital.) But physical capital, with the exception of infrastructure, is mainly created through private investment spending—that is, spending by firms rather than by the government.

Investment spending must be financed out of savings. There are two sources of savings. One source is domestic savings, created by a country's own residents. The second source is foreign savings, generated by foreigners. We'll begin with the simplest case, a *closed economy*—an economy in which there is no economic interaction with the rest of the world. There are no exports, no imports, and no capital flows. In a closed economy, the second source of acquiring savings is unavailable; so, all investment spending must come from domestic savings. However, modern economies aren't closed. So we'll follow with a discussion of an *open economy*—an economy in which there is economic interaction with the rest of the world. In an open economy, both sources of investment funds—domestic savings and foreign savings—are available.

In both a closed and an open economy, our first step in understanding the process of investment spending is to clarify the relationship between savings and investment spending. Then we can look at how savings is allocated among various investment spending projects available in the economy.

The Savings–Investment Spending Identity

The most basic point to understand about savings and investment spending is that they are always equal, regardless of whether an economy is open or closed. This is not a theory; it's a fact of accounting called the **savings–investment spending identity.**

According to the **savings–investment spending identity,** savings and investment spending are always equal for the economy as a whole.

To see why the savings–investment spending identity must be true, let's look again at the national income accounting that we examined in Chapter 24. Recall that GDP is equal to total spending on final goods and services produced in the economy and that we can write the following equation:

(26-1) $GDP = C + I + G + X - IM$

where C is spending by consumers, I is investment spending, G is government purchases of goods and services, X is the value of exports to other countries, and IM is spending on imports from other countries.

The Savings–Investment Spending Identity in a Closed Economy In a closed economy, there are no exports or imports. So $X = 0$ and $IM = 0$, which makes Equation 26-1 simpler:

(26-2) $GDP = C + I + G$

Let's rearrange Equation 26-2, putting investment spending on one side and everything else on the other. It looks like this:

(26-3) $I = GDP - C - G$

That is, investment spending is equal to GDP minus consumer spending minus government purchases of goods and services in a closed economy.

Now let's derive savings for the total economy. We know from Chapter 24 that private savings is equal to disposable income (household income, including government transfers, net of taxes) minus consumer spending:

(26-4) $S_{Private} = GDP + TR - T - C$

where $S_{Private}$ is private savings, TR is government transfers, and T is taxes paid.

But households are not the only parties that can save in an economy. In any given year the government can save, too, if it collects more tax revenue than it spends. When this occurs, the difference is called a **budget surplus** and is equivalent to savings by government. If, alternatively, government spending exceeds tax revenue, there is a **budget deficit**—a negative surplus. In this case we often say that the government is "dissaving": by spending more than its tax revenues, the government is engaged in the opposite of saving. We'll define the term **budget balance,** $S_{Government}$, to refer to both cases, with the understanding that the budget balance can be positive (a budget surplus) or negative (a budget deficit). Then we have:

(26-5) $S_{Government} = T - TR - G$

In general, as we'll see in Chapter 29, responsible governments run deficits when faced with difficult times, such as wars or recessions, then run surpluses later to pay off the debt incurred during those deficit periods.

Putting together Equations 26-4 and 26-5 we arrive at an expression for total savings generated within the economy as a whole, called **national savings,** or NS:

(26-6) $NS = S_{Private} + S_{Government}$
$= (GDP + TR - T - C) + (T - TR - G)$
$= GDP - C - G$

At this point we can see that the right-hand sides of Equations 26-3 and 26-6 are identical. Combining these two equations brings us to our final step in showing the savings–investment spending identity in a closed economy:

(26-7) $I = NS$

or

Investment spending = National savings in a closed economy

The **budget surplus** is the difference between tax revenue and government spending when tax revenue exceeds government spending.

The **budget deficit** is the difference between tax revenue and government spending when government spending exceeds tax revenue.

The **budget balance** is the difference between tax revenue and government spending.

National savings, the sum of private savings and the budget balance, is the total amount of savings generated within the economy.

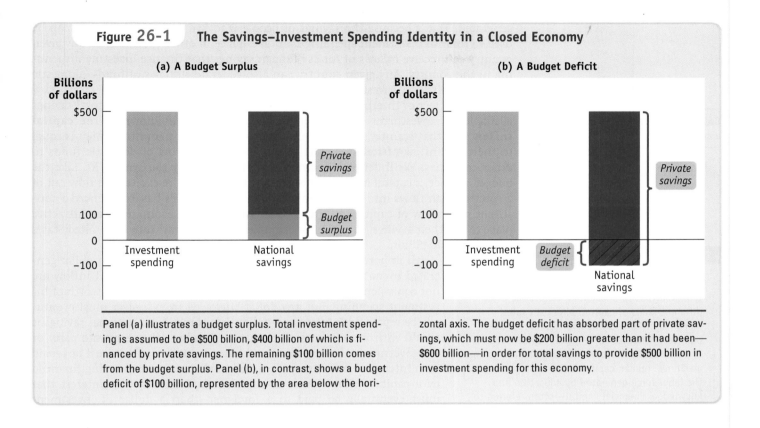

Figure 26-1   **The Savings–Investment Spending Identity in a Closed Economy**

Panel (a) illustrates a budget surplus. Total investment spending is assumed to be $500 billion, $400 billion of which is financed by private savings. The remaining $100 billion comes from the budget surplus. Panel (b), in contrast, shows a budget deficit of $100 billion, represented by the area below the horizontal axis. The budget deficit has absorbed part of private savings, which must now be $200 billion greater than it had been—$600 billion—in order for total savings to provide $500 billion in investment spending for this economy.

So the closed-economy version of the savings–investment spending identity is that investment spending is always equal to national savings.

Figure 26-1 illustrates how this works by considering a hypothetical closed economy, where we have broken national savings, *NS*, into its two components, $S_{Private}$, private savings, and $S_{Government}$, the budget balance (a budget surplus or deficit, as the case may be). In each panel, the height of the bar on the left represents the amount of investment spending, *I*, which is $500 billion. Because national savings equals investment spending in a closed economy, the bar representing investment spending must be matched by the height of the bar on the right, which represents national savings, *NS*. In panel (a), we show an economy in which the government runs a budget surplus of $100 billion and private savings is equal to $400 billion. The areas representing private savings and the budget surplus are stacked to create the overall pool of national savings of $500 billion, which is available for investment spending. In panel (b), we show an economy in which the government runs a budget deficit of $100 billion, represented by the area below the horizontal axis. Here part of private savings has been offset by the budget deficit. As a result, private savings must now be $200 billion greater than before—$600 billion—in order for national savings to provide $500 billion in investment spending for this economy.

We've just learned that investment spending in a closed economy is equal to national savings; that is, investment spending is equal to private savings plus the budget balance, the government's contribution to savings or dissavings, as the case may be. Now we'll examine the savings–investment spending identity when the economy is open.

The Savings–Investment Spending Identity in an Open Economy An *open economy* is an economy in which goods and money can flow into and out of the country. This changes the savings–investment spending identity because savings need not be spent on physical capital located in the same country in which the savings are

---

Capital inflow is net inflow of funds into a country.

---

generated. That's because the savings of people who live in any one country can be used to finance investment spending that takes place in other countries. So any given country can receive *inflows* of funds—foreign savings that finance investment spending in the country. Any given country can also generate *outflows* of funds—domestic savings that finance investment spending in another country.

The net effect of international inflows and outflows of funds on the total savings available for investment spending in any given country is known as the **capital inflow** into that country. It is the net inflow of funds into a country, which is equal to the total inflow of foreign funds minus the total outflow of domestic funds to other countries. We'll denote a country's capital inflow by the symbol *KI*. Like the budget balance, a capital inflow can be negative—that is, more capital can flow out of a country than flows into it. In recent years the United States has experienced a consistent net inflow of capital from foreigners, who view our economy as an attractive place to put their savings. In 2004, for example, capital inflows into the United States exceeded $600 billion.

PITFALLS

THE DIFFERENT KINDS OF CAPITAL

It's important to understand clearly the three different kinds of capital: physical capital, human capital, and financial capital. As we explained in Chapter 25, physical capital consists of manufactured resources such as buildings and machines; human capital is the improvement in the labor force generated by education and knowledge. Financial capital—often referred to simply as "capital" in macroeconomics—is funds from savings that are available for investment spending. So a country that has a "capital inflow" is experiencing a flow of funds into the country from abroad for the purpose of investment spending.

It's important to note that, from a national perspective, a dollar generated by national savings and a dollar generated by capital inflow are not equivalent. Yes, they can both finance the same dollar's worth of investment spending. But any dollar borrowed from a saver must eventually be repaid with interest. A dollar that comes from national savings is repaid with interest to someone domestically—either a private party or the government. But a dollar that comes as capital inflow must be repaid with interest to a foreigner. So a dollar of investment spending financed by a capital inflow comes at a higher *national* cost—the interest that must eventually be paid to a foreigner—than a dollar of investment spending financed by national savings.

The fact that a net capital inflow represents funds borrowed from foreigners is an important aspect of the savings–investment spending identity in an open economy. Consider an individual who spends more than his or her income; that person must borrow the difference from others. Similarly, a country that spends more on imports than it earns from exports must borrow the difference from foreigners. And that difference, the amount of funds borrowed from foreigners, is equal to the country's capital inflow. As we will explain at greater length in Chapter 35, this means that the capital inflow into a country is equal to the difference between imports and exports:

$$\textbf{(26-8)} \quad KI = IM - X$$

We can now go back to Equation 26-1 to derive the savings–investment spending identity for an open economy. By rearranging Equation 26-1, we get:

$$\textbf{(26-9)} \quad I = (GDP - C - G) + (IM - X)$$

Using Equation 26-6, we can break (GDP − C − G) into private savings and the budget balance, yielding for an open economy:

$$\textbf{(26-10)} \quad I = S_{Private} + S_{Government} + (IM - X)$$
$$= NS + KI$$

or

Investment spending = National savings + Capital inflow in an open economy

So the savings–investment spending identity for an open economy means that investment spending is equal to savings, where savings is equal to national savings *plus*

capital inflow. That is, in an open economy with a positive capital inflow, some investment spending is funded by the savings of foreigners. And in an open economy with a
negative capital inflow (a net outflow), some portion of national savings is funding investment spending in other countries. In the United States in 2004, investment spending totaled $2,307 billion. Private savings were $1,927 billion, offset by a budget deficit
of $358 billion and supplemented by capital inflows of $636 billion. Notice that these
numbers don't quite add up; because data collection isn't perfect, there is a "statistical
discrepancy" of $102 billion. But we know that this is an error in the data and not in
the theory because the savings–investment spending identity must hold in reality.

Figure 26-2 shows what this identity actually looked like in 2003 for the world's
two largest economies, those of the United States and Japan. To make the two
economies easier to compare, we've measured savings and investment spending as
percentages of GDP. As in Figure 26-1, in each panel the bars on the left show total
investment spending and those on the right show the components of savings. U.S. investment spending was 18.4% of GDP, financed by a combination of private savings
(18.2% of GDP) and capital inflows (4.8% of GDP) and partly offset by government
dissaving (–4.6% of GDP). Japanese investment spending was higher as a percentage
of GDP, at 24.2%. It was financed by a higher level of private savings as a percentage
of GDP (35.3%) and was offset by both a capital outflow (–3.2% of GDP) and a relatively high budget deficit (–7.9% of GDP).

The economy's savings, then, finance its investment spending. But how are these
funds available for investment spending allocated among various projects? That is,
what determines which projects get financed (such as the Chunnel) and which don't
(such as a new jetliner that would fly close to the speed of sound, which Boeing recently declined to fully develop and produce). We'll see shortly that funds get allocated
to investment projects using a familiar method: by the market, via supply and demand.

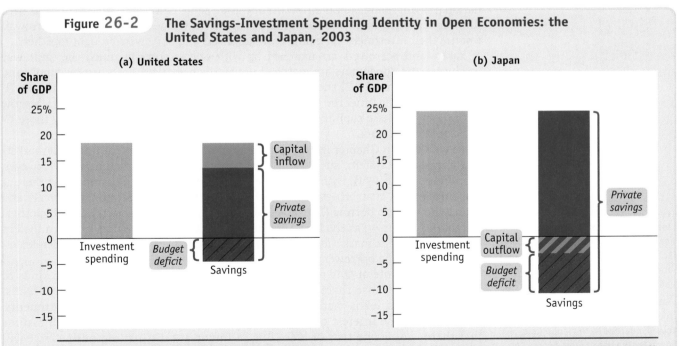

**Figure 26-2   The Savings-Investment Spending Identity in Open Economies: the
United States and Japan, 2003**

U.S. investment spending in 2003 (equal to 18.4% of GDP) was
financed by private savings (18.2% of GDP) and capital inflows
(4.8% of GDP), which were partially offset by a budget deficit
(–4.6% of GDP). Japanese investment spending in 2003 was
higher as a percentage of GDP (24.2%). It was financed by a

higher level of private savings as a percentage of GDP (35.3%),
which was offset by both a capital outflow (–3.2% of GDP) and
a relatively high budget deficit (–7.9% of GDP).

Source: Bureau of Economic Analysis; OECD.

The savings–investment spending identity is a fact of accounting. By definition, savings equal investment spending for the economy as a whole. But who enforces the arithmetic? For example, what happens if the amount that businesses want to invest in capital equipment is less than the amount households want to save?

The short answer is that actual and *desired* investment spending aren't always equal. Suppose that households suddenly decide to save more by spending less. The immediate effect will be that unsold goods pile up in stores and warehouses. And this increase in inventory counts as investment spending, albeit unintended. So the savings–investment spending identity still holds, because businesses end up engaging in more investment spending than

they intended to. Similarly, if households suddenly decide to save less and spend more, inventories will drop—and this will be counted as *negative* investment spending.

A real-world example occurred in 2001. Savings and investment spending, measured at an annual rate, both fell by $126 billion between the second and the fourth quarter of 2001. But on the investment spending side, $71 billion of that fall took the form of negative inventory investment spending.

Of course, businesses respond to changes in their inventories by changing their production. The inventory reduction in late 2001 prepared the ground for a spurt in output in early 2002. We'll examine the special role of inventories in economic fluctuations in later chapters.

The Market for Loanable Funds

For the economy as a whole, savings always equals investment spending. In a closed economy, savings is equal to national savings. In an open economy, savings is equal to national savings plus capital inflow. At any given time, however, savers, the people with funds to lend, are usually not the same as borrowers, the people who want to borrow to finance their investment spending. How are savers and borrowers brought together?

Savers and borrowers are matched up with one another in much the same way producers and consumers are matched up: through markets governed by supply and demand. In Figure 24-1, the expanded circular-flow diagram, we noted that the *financial markets* channel the savings of households to businesses that want to borrow in order to purchase capital equipment. It's now time to take a look at how those financial markets work.

As we noted in Chapter 24, there are a large number of different financial markets in the financial system, such as the bond market and the stock market. However, economists often work with a simplified model in which they assume that there is just one market that brings together those who want to lend money (savers) and those who want to borrow (firms with investment spending projects). This hypothetical market is known as the **loanable funds market.** The price that is determined in the loanable funds market is the **interest rate,** denoted by r, the return a lender receives for allowing borrowers the use of a dollar for one year.

We should note at this point that there are, in reality, many different kinds of interest rates because there are many different kinds of loans—short-term loans, long-term loans, loans made to corporate borrowers, loans made to governments, and so on. In the interest of simplicity, we'll ignore those differences and assume that there is only one type of loan. But an important distinction, one that we will explore in Chapter 33, is between the *real interest rate*—the interest rate adjusted for changes in prices over the length of the loan, and the *nominal interest rate*—the interest rate unadjusted for such price changes. In the context of the hypothetical loanable funds market, we'll keep things simple by assuming that there are no price changes and that, as a result, there is no difference between the real and the nominal interest rate.

The **loanable funds market** is a hypothetical market that examines the market outcome of the demand for funds generated by borrowers and the supply of funds provided by lenders.

The **interest rate** is the price, calculated as a percentage of the amount borrowed, charged by the lender to a borrower for the use of their savings for one year.

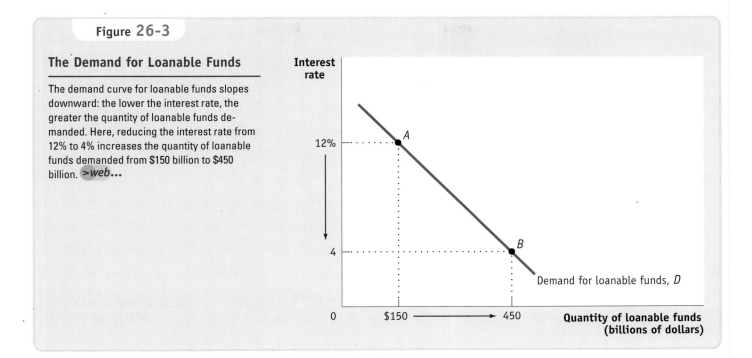

Figure 26-3

The Demand for Loanable Funds

The demand curve for loanable funds slopes downward: the lower the interest rate, the greater the quantity of loanable funds demanded. Here, reducing the interest rate from 12% to 4% increases the quantity of loanable funds demanded from $150 billion to $450 billion. **>web...**

Figure 26-3 illustrates the hypothetical demand for loanable funds, represented by a downward-sloping demand curve. Imagine that there are many businesses, each of which has one potential investment project. How does a given business decide whether or not to borrow money to finance its project? The decision depends on the interest rate the business faces and the **rate of return** of its project—the profit earned on the project expressed as a percentage of its cost. This can be expressed in a formula as:

The **rate of return** of a project is the profit earned on the project expressed as a percentage of its cost.

$$\text{(26-11)} \quad Rate\ of\ return = \frac{(Revenue\ from\ project - Cost\ of\ project)}{Cost\ of\ project} \times 100$$

A business will want a loan when the rate of return on its project is at least as great as the interest rate. So, for example, at an interest rate of 12%, only businesses with projects that yield a rate of return greater than or equal to 12% will want a loan. The demand curve in Figure 26-3 shows that if the interest rate is 12%, businesses will want to borrow $150 billion (point A); if the interest rate is only 4%, businesses will want to borrow a larger amount, $450 billion (point B). That's a consequence of our assumption that the demand curve slopes downward: the lower the interest rate, the larger the total quantity of loanable funds demanded. Why do we make that assumption? Because, in reality, the number of potential investment projects that yield at least 4% is always greater than the number that yield at least 12%.

Figure 26-4 on page 618 shows the hypothetical supply of loanable funds. Savers have an opportunity cost for the funds that they could lend to a business; they could instead be spent on consumption—say, a nice vacation. Whether a given saver becomes a lender by making funds available to borrowers depends on the interest rate received in return. By saving your money today and earning interest on it, you are rewarded with higher consumption in the future when your loan is repaid with interest. So it is a good assumption that more people are willing to forgo current consumption and make a loan when the interest rate is higher. As a result, our hypothetical supply curve of loanable funds slopes upward. In Figure 26-4, lenders will supply $150 billion to the loanable funds market at an interest rate of 4% (point X); if the interest rate rises to 12%, the quantity of loanable funds supplied will rise to $450 billion (point Y).

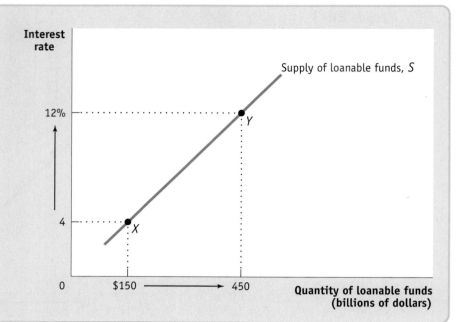

Figure 26-4

The Supply of Loanable Funds

The supply curve for loanable funds slopes upward: the higher the interest rate, the greater the quantity of loanable funds supplied. Here, increasing the interest rate from 4% to 12% increases the quantity of loanable funds supplied from $150 billion to $450 billion. **>web...**

The equilibrium interest rate is the interest rate at which the quantity of loanable funds supplied equals the quantity of loanable funds demanded. As you can see in Figure 26-5, the equilibrium interest rate, r^*, and the total quantity of lending, Q^*, are determined by the intersection of the supply and demand curves, at point E. Here, the equilibrium interest rate is 8%, at which $300 billion is lent and borrowed. Investment spending projects with a rate of return of 8% or more are funded; projects with a rate of return of less than 8% are not. Correspondingly, only lenders who are willing to accept an interest rate of 8% or less will have their offers to lend funds accepted. Potential lenders who demand an interest rate higher than 8% have a higher opportunity

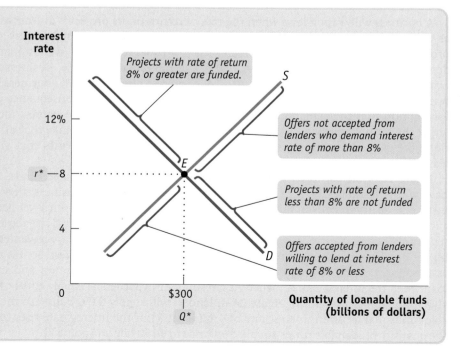

Figure 26-5

Equilibrium in the Loanable Funds Market

At the equilibrium interest rate, the quantity of loanable funds supplied equals the quantity of loanable funds demanded. Here the equilibrium interest rate is 8%, with $300 billion of funds lent and borrowed. Investment spending projects with a rate of return of 8% or higher receive financing; those with a lower rate of return do not. Lenders who demand an interest rate of 8% or lower have their offers of loans accepted; those who demand a higher interest rate do not.

cost of their funds. Their offers to lend will be turned down in the loanable funds market, and their funds will remain uninvested.

In Chapter 5 we learned that a market for an ordinary good, such as used textbooks, is usually efficient. The same is true of the hypothetical market for loanable funds. The investment spending projects that are actually financed have higher rates of return than those that do not get financed. The potential savers who actually lend funds are willing to lend for lower interest rates than those who do not. In other words, the loanable funds market maximizes the gains from trade between lenders and borrowers. Savings are allocated efficiently to investment projects throughout the economy. This result, although drawn from a highly simplified model, has important implications for real life. As we'll see shortly, it is the reason that a well-functioning financial system increases an economy's long-run economic growth rate.

Savings, Investment Spending, and Government Policy

Our model of the loanable funds market is very simple, yet it is enough to give us some preliminary insight into the source of concern about the effect of government policy on economic growth.

Consider first the impact of the government's budget. When the government runs a budget deficit, it must borrow funds to cover the gap between tax revenue and government spending—the government becomes a borrower in the loanable funds market. And we'll make an assumption, consistent with real government behavior, that the amount of government borrowing does not depend on the interest rate. At any given interest rate, private (non-government) borrowers still want to borrow as much as before the emergence of the budget deficit. But now, at any given interest rate, the government makes additional demand for funds. Figure 26-6 shows what happens. The demand curve for loanable funds shifts rightward by the amount of the government's borrowing. As a result, the equilibrium moves from E_1 to E_2. The interest rate and the total amount of borrowing rise. Because of the higher interest rate, however, the amount of private borrowing falls from Q_1 to Q_2, as shown by the movement up the demand curve D_1.

This decrease in private borrowing means that as a result of the budget deficit, businesses will engage in less investment spending than they otherwise would have.

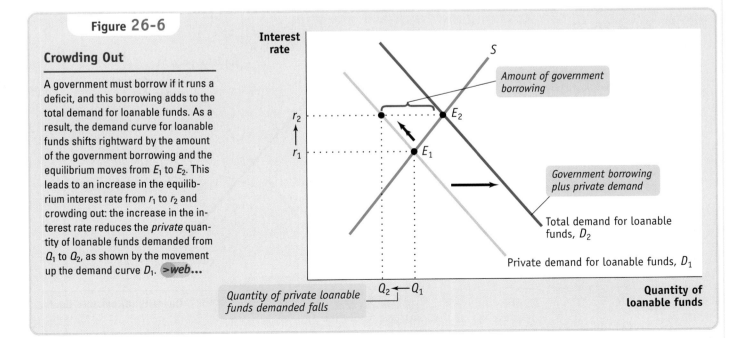

Figure 26-6

Crowding Out

A government must borrow if it runs a deficit, and this borrowing adds to the total demand for loanable funds. As a result, the demand curve for loanable funds shifts rightward by the amount of the government borrowing and the equilibrium moves from E_1 to E_2. This leads to an increase in the equilibrium interest rate from r_1 to r_2 and crowding out: the increase in the interest rate reduces the *private* quantity of loanable funds demanded from Q_1 to Q_2, as shown by the movement up the demand curve D_1. >*web*...

Quantity of private loanable funds demanded falls

Crowding out is the negative effect of budget deficits on private investment.

This negative effect of budget deficits on private investment spending is called **crowding out.** When a budget deficit causes crowding out, the economy adds less private physical capital each year than it would if the budget were balanced or in surplus. And since private physical capital is one of the sources of productivity growth, budget deficits, *other things equal*, lead to lower long-run growth.

But this should not be interpreted to mean that government spending is necessarily bad for economic growth! It depends on what the government is spending its money on. In fact, as we learned in Chapter 25, much government spending is essential to growth. For example, the court system must be kept running to enforce contracts, and the public health system must be maintained to prevent the spread of disease. Governments also do quite a lot of investment spending themselves—for example, building and maintaining necessary infrastructure such as roads, schools, and airports. Our analysis of crowding out is an "other things equal" result: When government spending has *already* created the things that enhance growth (such as a court system and roads), *further* government spending that results in budget deficits reduces private investment spending and lowers growth. So we cannot say unambiguously that government spending that results in a budget deficit either decreases or increases economic growth.

Government borrowing is not the only policy that affects the loanable funds market. Many economists have argued for changes in the tax system that they believe would lead to higher private savings and lower current consumption but would generate the same amount of total tax revenue. An example would be reducing the tax on investment income (such as interest on bonds and dividends on stocks) but increasing the sales tax on consumption of goods and services. A reduction in the tax on investment income motivates people to save more because it raises the net return earned on savings after taxes are paid, while an increase in the sales taxes motivates people to consume less by making the total cost of goods and services higher. Figure 26-7 shows what would happen if their proposals were adopted and if they turned out to be right. The supply of funds to the loanable funds market would increase—that is, the supply curve would shift to the right. The equilibrium would move from E_1 to E_2, the interest rate would fall from r_1 to r_2, and private borrowing would increase from Q_1 to Q_2. So a tax reform that increases private savings would lead to higher private investment spending and, as a result, to higher long-run economic growth.

Figure 26-7

Increasing Private Savings

Some economists have urged reforms in the tax system and adoption of other policies that would, they say, increase private savings but keep tax revenue unchanged. If they are correct, the effect would be to shift the supply curve of loanable funds to the right, leading to a reduction in the equilibrium interest rate and a larger quantity of funds lent and borrowed. Private investment spending in the economy would rise and so, ultimately, would long-run economic growth.

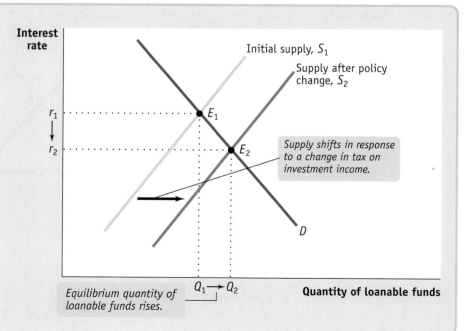

The loanable funds model is a good way to think about many issues involving savings and investment spending. Although very simple, it illustrates the trade-off involved in deciding whether to save and lend or whether to consume as well as the trade-off involved in deciding whether or not to borrow and undertake an investment spending project. It also illustrates how an interest rate moves to equalize the supply and demand for loanable funds. In reality, though, the actual markets that channel savings into investment spending are more complex than that. We turn next to an examination of those markets.

economics in action

Budgets and Investment Spending in the 1990s

Do government budget deficits really crowd out private investment spending? Does moving from deficit to surplus really encourage private investment spending? These questions aren't just academic; they have a direct bearing on political issues such as the spending priorities of the government. So what does the evidence say?

Federal, state, and local governments in the United States moved from a combined deficit of 4.2% of GDP in 1990 to a combined surplus of 1.6% of GDP in 2000. Over the same period private investment spending rose from 14.8% to 17.7% of GDP. Did the move from deficit to surplus, accompanied by a boom in private investment spending, demonstrate that deficits really do crowd out private investment spending?

The answer is that it's not clear because there was another reason for the rise in private investment spending: a sharp rise in capital inflows, which rose from 1.2% of GDP in 1990 to 4.0% of GDP in 2000. Meanwhile, private savings as a percent of GDP were falling. The increase in capital inflows, 2.8% of GDP, was almost equal to the rise in private investment spending, 2.9% of GDP. So you could say that the investment spending boom of the 1990s was basically foreign-financed.

There are two morals to this story. First, although the data don't show it unambiguously, from our model we can conclude that the move from budget deficit to budget surplus in the late 1990s made private investment spending *greater than it would have been* if there had been no increase in the budget balance. Second, we must be careful about jumping to conclusions about the impact of government policies on the basis of observed data—lots of other things tend to be happening at the same time as policy changes, and those other things may be the real story. ■

> >

>> QUICK REVIEW

➤ According to the *savings–investment spending identity*, savings is equal to investment spending for the economy as a whole.

➤ The government is a source of savings when it runs a positive *budget balance*, also known as a *budget surplus*. It is a source of dissavings when it runs a *budget deficit*.

➤ In a closed economy, savings is equal to *national savings*. In an open economy, savings is equal to national savings plus *capital inflow*.

➤ The hypothetical *loanable funds market* matches savers to borrowers. In equilibrium, only investment spending projects with a *rate of return* greater than or equal to the equilibrium *interest rate* are funded.

➤ Budget deficits can cause *crowding out* of private investment spending. It is unclear whether crowding out raises or lowers economic growth.

>>CHECK YOUR UNDERSTANDING 26-1

1. Suppose the government's deficit becomes a budget surplus. Using a diagram like Figure 26-6, show the effects on private investment spending and the equilibrium interest rate.

2. Illustrate with a diagram of the loanable funds market the effect of the following events on the equilibrium interest rate and investment spending.
   a. A closed economy becomes an open one. A capital inflow occurs.
   b. Retired people generally save less than working people at any interest rate. The proportion of retired people in the population goes up.

3. Explain what is wrong with the following statement: "Savings and investment spending may not be equal in the economy as a whole because when the interest rate rises, households will want to save more money than businesses will want to invest."

Solutions appear at back of book.

The Financial System

A well-functioning financial system that brought together the funds of British, French, and other international investors made the Chunnel possible. But to think that this is an exclusively modern phenomenon is misguided. Financial markets raised the funds that were used to develop colonial markets in India, to build canals across Europe, and to finance the Napoleonic wars in the eighteenth century. Capital inflows financed the early economic development of the United States, funding investment spending in mining, railroads, and canals. In fact, many of the principal features of financial markets and assets have been well understood in Europe and the United States since the eighteenth century. However, these features are no less relevant today. So let's begin by understanding exactly what is traded in financial markets.

Financial markets are where households invest their current savings and their accumulated savings, or **wealth,** by purchasing *financial assets*. A **financial asset** is a paper claim that entitles the buyer to future income from the seller. For example, when a saver lends funds to a company, the loan is a financial asset sold by the company that entitles the lender (the buyer) to future income from the company. A household can also invest its current savings or wealth by purchasing a **physical asset,** a claim on a tangible object, such as a preexisting house or preexisting piece of equipment. It gives the owner the right to dispose of the object as he or she wishes (for example, rent it or sell it). Recall from Pitfalls on page 611 that the purchase of a financial or physical asset is typically called investing. So if you purchase a preexisting piece of equipment—say, a used airliner—you are engaging in investing in a physical asset. But if you spend funds that *add* to the stock of physical capital in the economy—say, purchasing a newly manufactured airplane—you are engaging in investment spending.

If you were to go to your local bank and get a loan—say, to buy a new car—you and the bank would be creating a financial asset—your loan. A *loan* is one important kind of financial asset in the real world, one that is owned by the lender—in this case, your local bank. In creating that loan, you and the bank would also be creating a **liability,** a requirement to pay income in the future. So although your loan is a financial asset from the bank's point of view, it is a liability from your point of view: a requirement that you repay the loan, including any interest. In addition to loans, there are three other important kinds of financial assets: stocks, bonds, and *bank deposits*. Because a financial asset is a claim to future income that someone has to pay, it is also someone else's liability. We'll explain in detail shortly who bears the liability for each type of financial asset.

These four types of financial assets exist because the economy has developed a set of specialized markets, like the stock market and the bond market, and specialized institutions, like banks, that facilitate the flow of funds from lenders to borrowers. In Chapter 24, in the context of the circular-flow diagram, we defined the financial markets and institutions that make up the financial system. A well-functioning financial system is a critical ingredient in achieving long-run growth because it encourages greater savings and investment spending; it also ensures that savings and investment spending are undertaken efficiently. To understand how this occurs, we first need to know what tasks the financial system needs to accomplish. Then we can see how the job gets done.

> A household's **wealth** is the value of its accumulated savings.
>
> A **financial asset** is a paper claim that entitles the buyer to future income from the seller.
>
> A **physical asset** is a claim on a tangible object that gives the owner the right to dispose of the object as he or she wishes.
>
> A **liability** is a requirement to pay income in the future.

Three Tasks of a Financial System

Our earlier analysis of the loanable funds market ignored three important problems facing borrowers and lenders: *transaction costs*, *risk*, and the desire for *liquidity*. The three tasks of a financial system are to reduce these problems in a cost-effective way. Doing so enhances the efficiency of financial markets: it makes it more likely that lenders and borrowers will make mutually beneficial trades—trades that increase society's welfare. We'll turn now to examining how financial assets are designed and how institutions are developed to cope with these problems.

Reducing Transaction Costs **Transaction costs** are the expenses of actually putting together and executing a deal. For example, arranging a loan requires spending time and money negotiating the terms of the deal, verifying the borrower's ability to pay, drawing up and executing legal documents, and so on. Suppose a large business decided that it

> **Transaction costs** are the expenses of negotiating and executing a deal.

wanted to raise $100 million for investment spending. No individual would be willing to lend that much. And negotiating individual loans from thousands of different people, each willing to lend a modest amount, would impose very large total costs because each individual transaction would incur a cost. Total costs would be so large that the entire deal would probably be unprofitable for the business.

Fortunately, that's not necessary: when large businesses want to borrow money, they either go to a bank or sell bonds in the bond market. Obtaining a loan from a bank avoids large transaction costs because it involves only a single borrower and a single lender. We'll explain more about how bonds work in the next section. For now, it is enough to know that the principal reason there is a bond market is that it allows companies to borrow large sums of money without incurring large transaction costs.

Reducing Risk A second problem that real-world borrowers and lenders face is **financial risk,** uncertainty about future outcomes that involve financial losses and gains. Financial risk (which from now on we'll simply call "risk") is a problem because the future is uncertain, typically containing the potential for losses as well as gains. For example, owning and driving a car entails the financial risk of a costly accident. Most people view potential losses and gains in an *asymmetrical* way: the total loss in individual welfare from losing a given amount of money is considered larger than the total gain in welfare from gaining the same amount of money. A person who values potential losses and gains in this asymmetrical way is called *risk-averse*. This attitude toward risk is illustrated in panel (a) of Figure 26-8. Here, we show an example of a typical risk-averse person who is faced with the prospect of losing $1,000 or gaining $1,000. The bar on the left, which represents the loss in welfare from losing $1,000, is longer than the bar on the right, which represents the gain in welfare from gaining $1,000. The difference in the lengths of these two bars illustrates risk aversion: a person experiences a $1,000 loss as a significant hardship (equivalent to a $2,000 loss in welfare) and a $1,000 gain as a much less significant benefit (equivalent to a $1,000 gain in welfare). To put it a slightly different way, if you are risk-averse, you are willing to expend more

> **Financial risk** is uncertainty about future outcomes that involve financial losses and gains.

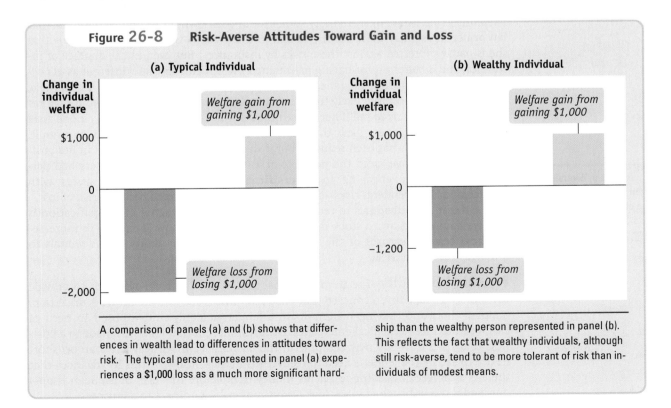

Figure 26-8 **Risk-Averse Attitudes Toward Gain and Loss**

(a) Typical Individual

Change in individual welfare

Welfare gain from gaining $1,000

$1,000

0

Welfare loss from losing $1,000

−2,000

(b) Wealthy Individual

Change in individual welfare

Welfare gain from gaining $1,000

$1,000

0

−1,200

Welfare loss from losing $1,000

A comparison of panels (a) and (b) shows that differences in wealth lead to differences in attitudes toward risk. The typical person represented in panel (a) experiences a $1,000 loss as a much more significant hardship than the wealthy person represented in panel (b). This reflects the fact that wealthy individuals, although still risk-averse, tend to be more tolerant of risk than individuals of modest means.

resources to avoid losing $1,000 (say, by buying an auto insurance policy) than you are willing to expend to gain $1,000 (say, by hunting around to find the cheapest mechanic when your car needs a major repair).

Most people are risk-averse, although to differing degrees. For example, people who are wealthy are typically less risk-averse than those who are not so well-off. As panel (b) shows, a wealthy person—while still risk-averse—would consider the loss of $1,000 a lot less of a hardship than would a person of modest means. Such a loss would be experienced as only a $1,200 loss in welfare by a wealthy individual, compared to a $2,000 loss in welfare by a typical individual.

A well-functioning financial system helps people reduce their exposure to risk, which risk-averse people would like to do. Suppose the owner of a business expects to make a greater profit if she buys additional capital equipment but isn't completely sure that this will indeed happen. She could pay for the equipment by using her savings or selling her house. But if the profit is significantly less than expected, she will have lost her savings, or her house, or both. That is, she would be exposing herself to a lot of risk arising from how well or poorly the business performs. (This is why business owners, who typically have a significant portion of their own personal wealth tied up in their businesses, are usually people who are more tolerant of risk than the average person.) So, being risk-averse, this business owner wants to share the risk of purchasing new capital equipment with someone even if that requires sharing some of the profit if all goes well. How can she do this? By selling shares of her company to other people and using the money she receives from selling shares, rather than money from the sale of her other assets, to finance the equipment purchase. By selling shares in her company, she reduces her personal losses if the profit is less than expected: she won't have lost her other assets. But if things go well, the shareholders earn a share of the profit as a return on their investment.

By selling a share of her business, the owner has achieved *diversification:* she has been able to invest in several things in a way that lowers her total risk. She has maintained her investment in her bank account, a financial asset; in ownership of her house, a physical asset; and in ownership of the unsold portion of her business, also a physical asset. These investments are likely to carry some risk of their own; for example, her bank may fail or her house may burn down (though in the modern United States it is likely that she is partly protected against these risks by insurance.) But even in the absence of insurance, she is better off for having maintained investments in these different assets because their different risks are *unrelated,* or *independent, events.* This means, for example, that her house is no more likely to burn down if her business does poorly, and that her bank is no more likely to fail if her house burns down. To put it another way, if one asset performs poorly, it is very likely that her other assets will be unaffected and, as a result, her total risk of loss has been reduced. But if she had invested all her wealth in her business, she would have faced the prospect of losing everything if the business had performed poorly. By engaging in **diversification**—investing in several assets with unrelated, or independent, risks—our business owner has lowered her total risk of loss.

An individual can engage in **diversification** by investing in several different things so that the possible losses are independent events.

The desire of individuals to reduce their total risk by engaging in diversification is why we have stocks and a stock market. In the next section, we'll explain in more detail how certain features of the stock market increase the ability of individuals to manage and reduce risk.

Providing Liquidity   The third and final task of the financial system is to provide investors with *liquidity,* a concern that—like risk—arises because the future is uncertain. Suppose that, once having made a loan, a lender suddenly finds himself in need of cash—say, to meet a medical emergency. Unfortunately, if that loan was made to a business that used it to buy new equipment, the business cannot repay the loan on short notice to satisfy the lender's need to recover his money. Knowing this in advance—that there is a danger of needing to get his money back before the term of the loan is up—our lender might be reluctant to lock up his money by lending it to a business.

An asset is **liquid** if it can be quickly converted into cash, without much loss of value, and it is **illiquid** if it cannot. As we'll see, stocks and bonds are a partial answer to the problem of liquidity. Banks provide a further way for individuals to hold liquid assets and still finance illiquid investments.

To help lenders and borrowers make mutually beneficial deals, then, the economy needs ways to reduce transaction costs, to reduce and manage risk through diversification, and to provide liquidity. How does it achieve these tasks?

Types of Assets

In the modern economy there are four main types of financial assets: loans, bonds, stocks, and bank deposits. Each serves a somewhat different purpose. We'll examine loans, bonds, and stocks now, reserving our discussion of bank deposits until the following section.

Loans A **loan** is a lending agreement between a particular lender and a particular borrower. Most people encounter loans in the form of bank loans to finance the purchase of a car or a house. And small businesses usually use bank loans to buy new equipment.

The good aspect of loans is that a given loan is usually tailored to the needs of the borrower. Before a small business can get a loan, it usually has to discuss its business plans, its profits, and so on with the lender. This results in a loan that meets the borrower's needs and ability to pay.

The bad aspect of loans is that making a loan to an individual person or a business typically involves a lot of transaction costs, such as the cost of negotiating the terms of the loan, investigating the borrower's credit history and ability to repay, and so on. To minimize these costs, large borrowers such as major corporations and governments often take a more streamlined approach: they sell (or issue) bonds.

Bonds As we learned in Chapter 24, a bond is a promise by the seller to pay interest each year and to repay the principal to the owner of the bond on a particular date. So a bond is a financial asset from its owner's point of view and a liability from its issuer's point of view. A bond issuer sells a number of bonds with a given interest rate and maturity date to whomever is willing to buy them, a process that avoids costly negotiation of the terms of a loan with many individual lenders.

Bond purchasers can acquire information free of charge on the quality of the bond issuer, such as the bond issuer's credit history, from *bond-rating agencies* rather than having to incur the expense of investigating it themselves. As a result, bonds can be sold on the bond market as a more or less standardized product—a product with clearly defined terms and quality.

Another important advantage of bonds is that they are easy to resell. This provides liquidity to bond purchasers. Indeed, a bond will often pass through many hands before it finally comes due. Loans, in contrast, are much more difficult to resell because, unlike bonds, they are not standardized: they differ in size, quality, terms, and so on. This makes them a lot less liquid than bonds.

"Damn it, I don't want to know about my love life. Tell me about the bond market."

Stocks As we learned in Chapter 24, a stock is a share in the ownership of a company. A share of stock is a financial asset from its owner's point of view and a liability from the the company's point of view. Not all companies sell shares of their stock; "privately held" companies are owned by an individual or a few partners, who get to keep all of the company's profit. Most large companies, however, do sell stock. For example, Microsoft has nearly 11 billion shares outstanding; if you buy one of those shares, you are entitled to one eleven-billionth of the company's profit, as well as 1 of 11 billion votes on company decisions.

An asset is **liquid** if it can be quickly converted into cash without much loss of value.

An asset is **illiquid** if it cannot be quickly converted into cash without much loss of value.

A **loan** is a lending agreement between a particular lender and a particular borrower.

Why does Microsoft, historically a very profitable company, allow you to buy a share in its ownership? Why don't Bill Gates and Paul Allen, the two founders of Microsoft, keep ownership for themselves and just sell bonds for their investment spending needs? The reason, as we have just learned, is risk: few individuals are risk-tolerant enough to face the risk involved in being the owners of a large company.

Reducing the risk that business owners face, however, is not the only way in which the existence of stocks improves society's welfare: it also improves the welfare of investors who buy stocks. Shareowners are able to enjoy the higher returns over time that stocks generally offer in comparison to bonds. Over the past century, stocks have typically yielded about 7% after adjusting for inflation; bonds have yielded only about 2%. But as investment companies warn you, "past performance is no guarantee of future performance." And there is a downside: owning the stock of a given company is riskier than owning a bond issued by the same company. Why? Loosely speaking, a bond is a promise while a stock is a hope: by law, a company must pay what it owes its lenders before it distributes any profit to its shareholders. And if the company should fail (that is, be unable to pay its interest obligations and declare bankruptcy), its physical and financial assets go to its bondholders—its lenders—while its shareholders generally receive nothing. So although a stock generally provides a higher return to an investor than a bond, it also carries higher risk.

But the financial system has devised ways to help investors as well as business owners both manage risk and enjoy somewhat higher returns. It does that through the services of institutions known as *financial intermediaries*.

Financial Intermediaries

A **financial intermediary** is an institution that transforms funds gathered from many individuals into financial assets. The most important types of financial intermediaries are *mutual funds, pension funds, life insurance companies*, and *banks*. About three-quarters of the financial assets Americans own are held through these intermediaries rather than directly.

Mutual Funds As we've explained, owning shares of a company entails risk in return for a higher potential reward. But it should come as no surprise that stock investors can lower their total risk by engaging in diversification. By owning a *diversified portfolio* of stocks—a group of stocks in which risks are unrelated to or offset one another—rather than concentrating investment in the shares of a single company or a group of related companies, investors can reduce their risk. In addition, financial advisers, aware that most people are risk-averse, almost always advise their clients to diversify not only their stock portfolio but also their entire wealth by holding other assets in addition to stocks, such as bonds, real estate, and cash. (And, for good measure, to have plenty of insurance in case of accidental losses!)

However, for individuals who don't have a large amount of money to invest—say $1 million or more—building a diversified stock portfolio can incur high transaction costs (particularly fees paid to stock brokers) because they are buying a few shares of a lot of companies. Fortunately for such investors, mutual funds solve the problem of achieving diversification without high transaction costs. A **mutual fund** is a financial intermediary that creates a stock portfolio by buying and holding shares in companies and then reselling *shares of the stock portfolio* to individual investors. By buying these shares, investors with a relatively small amount of money to invest can indirectly hold a diversified portfolio, achieving a better return for any given level of risk than they could otherwise achieve. Table 26-1 shows an example of a diversified mutual fund, the State Street Global Advisors S&P 500 Index Fund. It shows the percentage of investors' money invested in the stocks of the largest companies in the mutual fund's portfolio.

Many mutual funds also perform *market research* on the companies they invest in. This is important because there are thousands of stock-issuing U.S. companies (not to mention foreign companies), each differing in terms of its likely profitability, dividend payments, and so on. It would be extremely time-consuming and costly for an

A **financial intermediary** is an institution that transforms the funds it gathers from many individuals into financial assets.

A **mutual fund** is a financial intermediary that creates a stock portfolio and then resells shares of this portfolio to individual investors.

TABLE 26-1

State Street Global Advisors S&P 500 Index Fund, Top Holdings (as of March 31, 2005)

Company	Percent of mutual fund assets invested in company
General Electric	3.53%
Exxon Mobil	3.52
Microsoft	2.26
Citigroup	2.17
Johnson & Johnson	1.85
Pfizer	1.81
Bank of America	1.65
Wal-Mart Stores	1.57
IBM	1.38
Intel	1.34

Source: State Street Global Advisors.

individual investor to do adequate research on even a small number of companies. Mutual funds save transaction costs by doing this research for their customers.

The mutual fund industry represents a huge portion of the modern U.S. economy, not just of the U.S. financial system. The largest mutual fund at the end of 2004 was State Street Global Advisors, which managed $1.4 trillion in funds.

Pension Funds and Life Insurance Companies In addition to mutual funds, many Americans have holdings in **pension funds,** nonprofit institutions that collect the savings of their members and invest those funds in a wide variety of assets, providing their members with income when they retire. Although pension funds are subject to some special rules and receive special treatment for tax purposes, they function much like mutual funds. They invest in a diverse array of financial assets, allowing their members to achieve more cost-effective diversification and market research than they would be able to achieve individually. Pension funds in the United States hold more than $8 trillion in assets.

A **pension fund** is a type of mutual fund that holds assets in order to provide retirement income to its members.

Americans also have substantial holdings in the policies of **life insurance companies,** which guarantee a payment to the policyholder's beneficiaries (typically, the family) when the policyholder dies. By enabling policyholders to cushion their beneficiaries from financial hardship arising from their death, life insurance companies also improve welfare by reducing risk.

A **life insurance company** sells policies that guarantee a payment to a policyholder's beneficiaries when the policyholder dies.

Banks Recall the problem of liquidity: other things equal, people want assets that can be readily converted into cash. Bonds and stocks are much more liquid than physical assets or loans, yet the transaction cost of selling bonds or stocks to meet a sudden expense can be large. Furthermore, for many small and moderate-size companies, the cost of issuing bonds and stocks is too large given the modest amount of money they seek to raise. A *bank* is an institution that helps resolve the conflict between lenders' needs for liquidity and the financing needs of borrowers who don't want to use the stock or bond markets.

A bank works by first accepting funds from *depositors:* when you put your money in a bank, you are essentially becoming a lender by lending the bank your money. In return, you receive credit for a **bank deposit**—a claim on the bank, which is obliged to give you your cash if and when you demand it. So a bank deposit is a financial asset owned by the depositor and a liability of the bank that holds it.

A **bank deposit** is a claim on a bank that obliges the bank to give the depositor his or her cash when demanded.

A bank, however, keeps only a fraction of its customers' deposits in the form of ready cash. Most of its deposits are lent out to businesses, buyers of new homes, and other borrowers. These loans come with a long-term commitment by the bank to the

A **bank** is a financial intermediary that provides liquid assets in the form of bank deposits to lenders and uses those funds to finance the illiquid investments or investment spending needs of borrowers.

borrower: as long as the borrower makes his or her payments on time, the loan cannot be recalled by the bank and converted into cash. So a bank enables those who wish to borrow for long lengths of time to use the funds of those who wish to lend but simultaneously want to maintain the ability to get their cash back on demand. More formally, a **bank** is a financial intermediary that provides liquid financial assets in the form of deposits to lenders and uses their funds to finance the illiquid investments or investment spending needs of borrowers.

In essence, a bank is engaging in a kind of mismatch: lending for long periods of time but also subject to the condition that its depositors could demand their funds back at any time. How can it manage that?

The bank counts on the fact that, on average, only a small fraction of its depositors will want their cash at the same time. On any given day, some people will make withdrawals and others will make new deposits; these will roughly cancel each other out. So the bank needs to keep only a limited amount of cash on hand to satisfy its depositors. In addition, if a bank becomes financially incapable of paying its depositors, individual bank deposits are guaranteed to depositors up to $100,000 by the Federal Deposit Insurance Corporation, or FDIC, a federal agency. This reduces the risk to a depositor of holding a bank deposit, and thereby reduces the incentive to withdraw funds if concerns about the financial state of the bank should arise. So, under normal conditions, banks need hold only a fraction of their depositors' cash.

By reconciling the needs of savers for liquid assets with the needs of borrowers for long-term financing, banks play a key economic role. As the following Economics in Action explains, the creation of a well-functioning banking system was a key turning point in South Korea's economic success.

economics in action

Banks and the South Korean Miracle

As we discussed in Chapter 25, South Korea is one of the great success stories of economic growth. In the early 1960s, it was a very poor nation. Then it experienced spectacularly high rates of economic growth. South Korean banks had a lot to do with it.

In the early 1960s, South Korea's banking system was a mess. Interest rates on deposits were very low at a time when the country was experiencing a lot of inflation. So savers didn't want to save by putting money in a bank, fearing that much of their purchasing power would be eroded by rising prices. Instead, they engaged in current consumption by spending their money on goods and services or used their wealth to buy physical assets such as real estate and gold. And because savers refused to make bank deposits, businesses found it very hard to borrow money to finance investment spending.

In 1965 the South Korean government reformed the country's banks and increased interest rates to a level that was attractive to savers. Over the next five years the value of bank deposits increased 600%, and the national savings rate—the percentage of GDP going into national savings—more than doubled. The rejuvenated banking system made it possible for South Korean businesses to launch a great investment boom, a key element in the country's growth surge.

Many other factors besides banking were involved in South Korea's success, but the country's experience does show how important a good financial system is to economic growth. ∎

< < < < < < < < < < < < < < < < < <

1. Rank the following assets in terms of (i) level of transaction costs, (ii) level of risk, (iii) level of liquidity.
   a. A bank deposit with a guaranteed interest rate
   b. A share of a highly diversified mutual fund, which can be quickly sold
   c. A share of the family business, which can be sold only if you find a buyer and all other family members agree to the sale

---

>> **QUICK REVIEW**

➤ Households can invest their current savings or their *wealth* by purchasing either *financial assets* or *physical assets*. A financial asset is a *liability* from the point of view of its seller.

➤ A well-functioning financial system reduces *transaction costs*, reduces *financial risk* by enabling *diversification*, and provides *liquid* assets, which investors prefer to *illiquid* assets.

➤ The four main types of financial assets are *loans*, bonds, stocks, and *bank deposits*.

➤ The most important types of *financial intermediaries* are *mutual funds*, *pension funds*, *life insurance companies*, and *banks*.

➤ A bank accepts bank deposits, which obliges it to return depositors' cash on demand, and lends those funds to borrowers for long lengths of time.

2. What relationship would you expect to find between the level of development of a country's financial system and its level of economic development? Explain in terms of the country's level of savings and level of investment spending.

Solutions appear at back of book.

Financial Fluctuations

We've learned that the financial system is an essential part of the economy; without stock markets, bond markets, and banks, long-run economic growth would be hard to achieve. Yet the news isn't entirely good: the financial system sometimes doesn't function well and instead is a source of instability. For evidence, we need look no further than the pivotal event of modern macroeconomics, the Great Depression. The worst economic slump in American history is closely identified with the U.S. stock market crash of 1929. And the 2001 U.S. recession was preceded by a sharp decline in stock prices in 2001. In Chapter 27 we'll learn about the channel by which changes in stock prices influence macroeconomic performance—how changes in households' wealth caused by asset market fluctuations alter their demand for goods and services.

We could easily write a whole book on asset market fluctuations. In fact, many people have. Here, we briefly discuss the causes of stock price fluctuations.

The Demand for Stocks

Once a company issues shares of stock to investors, those shares can then be re-sold to other investors in the stock market. And these days, thanks to cable TV and the Internet, you can easily spend all day watching stock market fluctuations—the movement up and down of the prices of individual stocks as well as the indexes. These fluctuations reflect changes in supply and demand by investors. But what causes the supply and demand for stocks to shift?

Remember that stocks are financial assets: they are shares in the ownership of a company. Unlike a good or service, whose value to its owner comes from its consumption, the value of an asset comes from its ability to generate higher *future consumption* of goods or services. A financial asset allows higher future consumption in two ways. It can generate future income through paying interest or dividends. But many companies don't pay dividends, instead retaining their earnings to finance future investment spending. Investors purchase non-dividend-paying stocks in the belief that they will earn future income from selling the stock in the future at a profit, the second way of generating higher future income. Even in the cases of a bond or a dividend-paying stock, investors will not want to purchase an asset that they believe will sell for less in the future than today because such an asset will reduce their wealth when they sell it. So the value of a financial asset today depends on investors' beliefs about the *future value* or *price* of the asset. That is, if investors believe that it will be worth more in the future, they will demand more of the asset today at any given price. As a consequence, today's equilibrium price of the asset will rise. Conversely, if investors believe the asset will be worth less in the future, they will demand less today at any given price. As a consequence, today's equilibrium price of the asset will fall. In summary, today's stock prices will change according to changes in investors' expectations about future stock prices.

Suppose an event occurs that leads to a rise in the expected future price of a company's shares—say, for example, Apple announces that it expects higher profitability due to torrential sales of its iPods. Demand for Apple shares will increase. At the same time, existing shareholders will be less willing to supply their shares to the market at any given price, leading to a decrease in the supply of Apple shares. And as we know from Chapter 3, an increase in demand or a decrease in supply (or both) leads to a rise in price. Alternatively, suppose that an event occurs that leads to a fall in the expected future price of a company's shares—say, Krispy Kreme announces that it expects lower profitability due to the popularity of low-carb diets. Demand for Krispy Kreme shares will decrease. At the same time, supply will increase because existing shareholders will

Financial news reports often lead with the day's stock market action, as measured by changes in the Dow Jones Industrial Average, the S&P 500, and the NASDAQ. What are these numbers, and what do they tell us?

All three are stock market *indexes*. Like the consumer price index, they are numbers constructed as a summary of average prices—in this case, prices of stocks. The Dow, created by the financial analysis company Dow Jones (owner of the *Wall Street Journal*), is an index of the prices of stock in 30 leading companies, such as Microsoft, Wal-Mart, and General Electric. The S&P 500 is an index of 500 companies, created by Standard and Poor's, another financial company. The NASDAQ is compiled by the National Association of Securities Dealers, which trades the stocks of smaller new companies, like the satellite radio companies Sirius and XM.

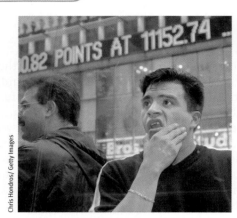

It's unexpected news, not expected news, that makes for a busy day in the financial markets.

Because these indexes contain different groups of stocks, they track somewhat different things. The Dow, because it contains only 30 of the largest companies, tends to reflect the "old economy," the traditional business powerhouses. The NASDAQ is heavily influenced by technology stocks. The S&P 500, a broad measure, is in between.

Why are these indexes important? Because the movement in an index gives investors a quick, snapshot view of how stocks from certain sectors of the economy are doing. As we'll explain shortly, the price of a stock at a given point in time embodies investors' expectations about the future prospects of the underlying company. By implication, an index composed of stocks drawn from companies in a particular sector embodies investors' expectations of the future prospects of that sector of the economy. So a day on which the NASDAQ moves up but the Dow moves down implies that, on that day, prospects appear brighter for the high-tech sector than for the old economy sector. The movement in the indexes reflects the fact that investors are acting on their beliefs by selling stocks in the Dow and buying stocks in the NASDAQ.

be more willing to supply their Krispy Kreme shares to the market. Both changes lead to a fall in the stock price. So stock prices are determined by supply and demand—which, in turn, depend on investors' expectations about the future stock price.

Stock prices are also affected by changes in the attractiveness of substitute assets, like bonds. As we learned in Chapter 3, the demand for a particular good decreases when purchasing a substitute good becomes more attractive—say, due to a fall in its price. The same lesson holds true for stocks: when purchasing a bond becomes more attractive due to a rise in interest rates, stock prices will fall. And when purchasing a bond becomes less attractive due to a fall in interest rates, stock prices will rise.

But we haven't yet fully answered the question of what determines the price of a share of stock, because we haven't explained what determines investors' *expectations* about future stock prices.

Stock Market Expectations

There are two principal competing views about how stock price expectations are determined. One view, which comes from traditional economic analysis, emphasizes the rational reasons why expectations *should* change. The other, widely held by market participants and also supported by some economists, emphasizes the irrationality of market participants.

The Efficient Markets Hypothesis Suppose you were trying to assess what Krispy Kreme stock is really worth. To do this, you would look at the *fundamentals*, the underlying determinants of the company's future profits. These would include factors like the changing tastes of the American public and the price of sugar. You would also want to compare the earnings you could expect to receive from Krispy Kreme with the likely returns on other financial assets, such as bonds.

According to one view of asset prices, the value you would come up with after a careful study of this kind would, in fact, turn out to be the price at which Krispy Kreme stock is already selling in the market. Why? Because all publicly available information about Krispy Kreme's fundamentals is already embodied in its stock price. Any difference between the market price and the value suggested by a careful analysis of the underlying fundamentals would indicate a profit opportunity to smart investors, who would sell Krispy Kreme stock if it looked overpriced and buy it if it looked underpriced. The **efficient markets hypothesis** is the general form of this view; it means that asset prices always embody all publicly available information. An implication of the efficient markets hypothesis is that at any point in time stock prices are fairly valued: they reflect all currently available information about fundamentals. So they are neither overpriced nor underpriced.

> The **efficient markets hypothesis** says that asset prices embody all publicly available information.

One implication of the efficient markets hypothesis is that the prices of stocks and other assets should change only in response to new information about the underlying fundamentals. Since new information is by definition unpredictable—if it were predictable, it wouldn't be new information—movements in asset prices are also unpredictable. As a result, the movement of, say, stock prices will follow a **random walk**—the general term for the movement over time of an unpredictable variable.

> A **random walk** is the movement over time of an unpredictable variable.

The efficient markets hypothesis plays an important role in understanding how financial markets work. Most investment professionals and many economists, however, regard it as an oversimplification. Investors, they claim, aren't that rational.

Irrational Markets? Many people who actually play the markets, such as individual investors and professional money managers, are skeptical of the efficient markets hypothesis. They believe that markets often behave irrationally and that a smart investor can engage in successful "market timing"—buying stocks when they are underpriced and selling them when they are overpriced.

Although economists are generally skeptical about claims that there are sure-fire ways to outsmart the market, many have also challenged the efficient markets hypothesis. It's important to understand, however, that finding particular examples where the market got it wrong does not disprove the efficient markets hypothesis. If the price of Krispy Kreme stock plunges from $40 to $10 because of a sudden change in eating habits, this doesn't mean that the market was inefficient in originally pricing the stock at $40. The fact that eating habits were about to change wasn't publicly available information, so it wasn't embodied in the earlier stock price.

Serious challenges to the efficient markets hypothesis focus instead either on evidence of systematic misbehavior of market prices or on evidence that individual investors don't behave in the way the theory suggests. For example, some economists believe they have found strong evidence that stock prices fluctuate more than can be explained by news about fundamentals. Others believe they have strong evidence that individual investors behave in systematically irrational ways. For example, people seem to expect that a stock that has risen in the past will keep on rising, even though the efficient markets hypothesis tells us there is no reason to expect this.

Stock Prices and Macroeconomics

How do macroeconomists and policy makers deal with the fact that stock prices fluctuate a lot and that these fluctuations can have important economic effects? The short answer is that, for the most part, they adopt an open-minded but watchful attitude.

The efficient markets hypothesis suggests that policy makers shouldn't assume that the stock market is wrong—either that stock prices are too high or too low. The best guess is always that any information that is publicly available is already accounted for in stock prices.

At the same time, policy makers shouldn't assume that stock prices will be reasonably stable and consistent with rational investor behavior. Sudden rises or falls in the market can happen for no obvious reason, and these fluctuations can have major macroeconomic effects. Policy makers have to be prepared to deal with them.

The question of how much to trust financial markets isn't academic. As the following Economics in Action explains, it was a hot issue during the 1990s.

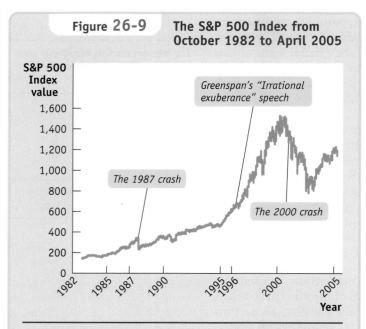

Figure 26-9 **The S&P 500 Index from October 1982 to April 2005**

Greenspan's "Irrational exuberance" speech

The 1987 crash

The 2000 crash

From 1982 to 1995 the stock market rose steadily with only a few setbacks, the most notable being the 1987 crash. In 1995, however, the market began growing at a much faster pace, and in 1996 Alan Greenspan cautioned that the market might be suffering from "irrational exuberance." The market, however, continued to rise for another four years—until 2000, when stock prices in general, and the prices of technology stocks in particular, suffered a large fall.

Source: Yahoo! Finance.

economics in action

"Irrational Exuberance"

Robert Shiller is an economist at Yale University and one of the best-known critics of the efficient markets hypothesis. In 1996 he gave a briefing to Alan Greenspan, the chairman of the Federal Reserve, that gave rise to a famous phrase: "irrational exuberance."

Figure 26-9 provides some background for the story. It shows the value, since October 1982, of the S&P 500, the broadest of the stock indexes we discussed in For Inquiring Minds on page 630. As you can see, from 1982 to 2000 the stock market rose steadily, with only a few setbacks.

One of those setbacks was the sudden crash in 1987, shown in the figure. There was no obvious fundamental reason for that crash. After the fact, some economists began coming up with reasons why a sudden fall in stock prices might have made sense. Shiller, however, actually surveyed investors *while* the market was crashing and found that they were selling simply because other people were selling. That is, it looked like mob psychology, not the working of an efficient market.

In 1996, when Shiller briefed Greenspan, the market was rising to unprecedented heights—and Shiller questioned whether this rise made sense. Greenspan shared his doubts and, in a famous speech, wondered whether the market was suffering from "irrational exuberance."

The big question, though, was whether Greenspan would do something about it, such as raising interest rates to discourage people from buying stocks. He didn't: he wasn't willing to second-guess the market to that extent. And, as you can see, stock prices continued to rise for another four years.

Starting in 2000, there was a large fall in stock prices, especially those of technology stocks, and many people now think that by the late 1990s, if not necessarily when Greenspan said it, there really was irrational exuberance in the market. Specifically, it's now widely accepted that there was a stock market *bubble*—a large upward movement in asset prices not based on rational factors such as fundamentals. But should Greenspan have done something about it? That's still very much a matter of debate; we'll revisit this question in Chapter 34. ■

< < < < < < < < < < < < < < < < < <

>>CHECK YOUR UNDERSTANDING 26-3

1. What is the likely effect of each of the following events on the stock price of a company? Explain your answers.
   a. The company announces that while profit is low this year, it has discovered a new line of business that will generate a high profit next year.
   b. The company announces that although it had a high profit this year, that profit will be less than had been previously announced.

c. Other companies in the same industry announce that sales are unexpectedly slow this year.

d. The company announces that it is on track to meet its previously forecast profit target.

2. Assess the following statement: "Although many investors may be irrational, it is unlikely that over time they will behave irrationally in exactly the same way—such as always buying stocks the day after the Dow has risen by 1%."

Solutions appear at back of book.

• A LOOK AHEAD •

At this point we've completed our study of why savings and investment spending are a critical component of long-run economic growth. We've examined how savings and investment spending are generated in the economy and how they are allocated by a well-functioning financial system. Now it's time for us to turn to the business cycle—that is, to understand the short-run fluctuations around the trend in long-run growth. Our next step, then, is to develop the Aggregate Supply–Aggregate Demand model, which we will use to analyze how the behavior of producers, consumers, and the government influences the economy's short-run performance.

SUMMARY

1. Investment in physical capital is necessary for long-run economic growth. So in order for an economy to grow, it must channel savings into investment spending.

2. According to the **savings–investment spending identity,** savings and investment spending are always equal for the economy as a whole. The government is a source of savings when it runs a positive **budget balance,** also known as a **budget surplus;** it is a source of dissavings when it runs a negative budget balance, also known as a **budget deficit.** In a closed economy, savings is equal to **national savings,** the sum of private savings plus the budget balance. In an open economy, savings is equal to national savings plus **capital inflow** of foreign savings. A capital outflow, or negative capital inflow, occurs when savings flow abroad.

3. The hypothetical **loanable funds market** shows how loans from savers are allocated among borrowers with investment spending projects. In equilibrium, only those projects with a **rate of return** greater than or equal to the equilibrium **interest rate** will be funded. By showing how gains from trade between lenders and borrowers are maximized, the loanable funds market shows why a well-functioning financial system leads to greater long-run economic growth. It also shows how government borrowing to cover a budget deficit can lead to **crowding out** of private investment spending and, other things equal, lower economic growth.

4. Households invest their current savings or **wealth**—their accumulated savings—by purchasing assets. Assets come in the form of either a **financial asset,** a paper claim that entitles the buyer to future income from the seller, or a **physical asset,** a claim on a tangible object that gives the owner the right to dispose of it as desired. A financial asset is also a **liability** from the point of view of its seller. There are four main types of financial assets: **loans,** bonds, stocks, and **bank deposits.** Each of them serves a different purpose in addressing the three fundamental tasks of a financial system: reducing **transaction costs**—the cost of making a deal; reducing **financial risk**—uncertainty about future outcomes that involves financial gains and losses; and providing **liquid** assets—assets that can be quickly converted into cash without much loss of value (in contrast to **illiquid** assets, which can't).

5. Although many small and moderate-size borrowers use bank loans to fund investment spending, larger companies typically issue bonds. Business owners reduce their risk by selling stock. Although stocks usually generate a higher return than bonds, investors typically wish to reduce their risk by engaging in **diversification,** owning a wide range of assets whose returns are based on unrelated, or independent, events. Most people are risk-averse, viewing the loss of a given amount of money as a significant hardship while viewing the gain of an equal amount of money as a much less significant benefit.

6. **Financial intermediaries**—institutions such as **mutual funds, pension funds, life insurance companies,** and **banks**—are critical components of the financial system. Mutual funds and pension funds do allow small investors to diversify; and life insurance companies reduce risk.

7. A bank allows individuals to hold liquid bank deposits that are then used to finance illiquid loans. Banks can perform this mismatch because on average only a small fraction of depositors withdraw their savings at any one time. Banks are a key ingredient of long-run economic growth.

8. Financial market fluctuations can be a source of macro-economic instability. Stock prices are determined by supply and demand as well as the desirability of competing assets, like bonds: when the interest rate rises, stock prices generally fall and vice versa. Expectations drive the supply of and demand for stocks: expectations of higher future prices push today's stock prices higher and expectations of lower future prices drive them lower. One view of how expectations are formed is the **efficient markets hypothesis,** which holds that the prices of financial assets embody all publicly available information. It implies that fluctuations are inherently unpredictable—they follow a **random walk.**

9. Many market participants and economists believe that, based on actual evidence, financial markets are not as rational as the efficient markets hypothesis claims. Such evidence includes the fact that stock price fluctuations are too great to be driven by fundamentals alone. Policy makers assume neither that markets always behave rationally nor that they can outsmart them.

KEY TERMS

Savings–investment spending identity, p. 611
Budget surplus, p. 612
Budget deficit, p. 612
Budget balance, p. 612
National savings, p. 612
Capital inflow, p. 614
Loanable funds market, p. 616
Interest rate, p. 616
Rate of return, p. 617

Crowding out, p. 620
Wealth, p. 622
Financial asset, p. 622
Physical asset, p. 622
Liability, p. 622
Transaction costs, p. 622
Financial risk, p. 623
Diversification, p. 624
Liquid, p. 625
Illiquid, p. 625

Loan, p. 625
Financial intermediary, p. 626
Mutual fund, p. 626
Pension fund, p. 627
Life insurance company, p. 627
Bank deposit, p. 627
Bank, p. 628
Efficient markets hypothesis, p. 631
Random walk, p. 631

PROBLEMS

1. Given the following information about the closed economy of Brittania, what is the level of investment spending and private savings, and what is the budget balance? What is the relationship among the three? Is national savings equal to investment spending? There are no government transfers.

   GDP = $1,000 million T = $50 million
   C = $850 million G = $100 million

2. Given the following information about the open economy of Regalia, what is the level of investment spending and private savings, and what are the budget balance and capital inflow? What is the relationship among the four? There are no government transfers.

   GDP = $1,000 million G = $100 million
   C = $850 million X = $100 million
   T = $50 million IM = $125 million

3. The accompanying table shows the percentage of GDP accounted for by private savings, investment spending, and capital inflow in the economies of Capsland and Marsalia. Capsland is currently experiencing a net capital inflow and Marsalia, a net capital outflow. What is the budget balance (as a percentage of GDP) in both countries? Are Capsland and Marsalia running a budget deficit or surplus?

	Capsland	Marsalia
Investment spending as a percentage of GDP	20%	20%
Private savings as a percentage of GDP	10	25
Capital inflow as a percentage of GDP	5	–2

4. Assume the economy is open. Answer each of the following questions.

   a. X = $125 million
   IM = $80 million
   $S_{Government}$ = – $200 million
   I = $350 million
   Calculate $S_{Private}$.

   b. X = $85 million
   IM = $135 million
   $S_{Government}$ = $100 million
   $S_{Private}$ = $250 million
   Calculate I.

   c. X = $60 million
   IM = $95 million
   $S_{Private}$ = $325 million
   I = $300 million
   Calculate $S_{Government}$.

   d. $S_{Private}$ = $325 million
   I = $400 million
   $S_{Government}$ = $10 million
   Calculate $IM – X$.

5. Use the market for loanable funds shown in the accompanying diagram to explain what happens to private savings, private investment spending, and the rate of interest if the following events occur. Assume the economy is closed.

   a. The government reduces the size of its deficit to zero.

   b. At any given interest rate, consumers decide to save more. Assume the budget balance is zero.

   c. At any given interest rate, businesses become very optimistic about the future profitability of investment spending. Assume the budget balance is zero.

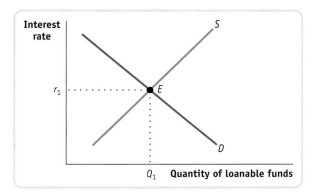

6. The government is running a budget balance of zero when it decides to increase education spending by $200 billion and finance the spending by selling bonds. The accompanying diagram shows the market for loanable funds before the government sells the bonds. Assume the economy is closed. How will the equilibrium interest rate and the equilibrium quantity of loanable funds change? Is there any crowding out in the market?

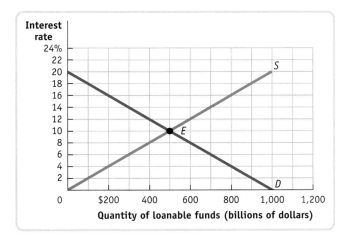

7. Explain why equilibrium in the loanable funds market maximizes efficiency.

8. How would you respond to a friend who claims that the government should eliminate all purchases that are financed by borrowing because such borrowing crowds out private investment spending?

9. Which of the following are examples of investment spending, investing in financial assets, or investing in physical assets?

   a. Rupert Moneybucks buys 100 shares of existing Coca-Cola stock.

   b. Rhonda Moviestar spends $10 million to buy a mansion built in the 1970s.

   c. Ronald Basketballstar spends $10 million to build a new mansion with a view of the Pacific Ocean.

   d. Rawlings builds a new plant to make catcher's mitts.

   e. Russia buys $100 million in U.S. government bonds.

10. Explain how a well-functioning financial system increases savings and investment spending, holding the budget balance and any capital flows fixed.

11. What are the important types of financial intermediaries in the U.S. economy? What are the primary assets of these intermediaries, and how do they facilitate investment spending and saving?

12. Explain the effect on a company's stock price today of the following events, other things held constant.

   a. The interest rate on bonds falls.

   b. Several companies in the same sector announce surprisingly slow sales.

   c. A change in the tax law passed last year reduces this year's profit.

   d. The company unexpectedly announces that due to an accounting error, it must amend last year's accounting statement and reduce last year's reported profit by $5 million. It also announces that this change has no implications for future profits.

>web... To continue your study and review of concepts in this chapter, please visit the Krugman/Wells website for quizzes, animated graph tutorials, web links to helpful resources, and more.

www.worthpublishers.com/krugmanwells

>>Aggregate Supply and Aggregate Demand

SHOCKS TO THE SYSTEM

What you will learn in this chapter:

► How the **aggregate supply curve** illustrates the relationship between the aggregate price level and the quantity of aggregate output supplied in the economy

► Why the aggregate supply curve is different in the short run compared to the long run

► How the **aggregate demand curve** illustrates the relationship between the aggregate price level and the quantity of aggregate output demanded in the economy

► The importance of the **multiplier**, which determines the total change in aggregate output arising from a shift of the aggregate demand curve

► How the *AS–AD* **model** is used to analyze economic fluctuations

► How monetary policy and fiscal policy can stabilize the economy

O N NOVEMBER 4, 1979, MILITANT Iranian students seized the U.S. embassy in Tehran, taking 66 Americans hostage. For the next 444 days the news was dominated by the plight of the hostages, the threat of U.S. military action, and the resulting political instability. The home front was further shaken by a quadrupling of the price of oil, another repercussion of the hostage crisis in the Persian Gulf. Price controls on gasoline, which limited its price at the pump and had been imposed in response to an earlier jump in the price of oil, led to gasoline shortages and long lines. Next came a severe recession, the worst since the Great Depression. The industrial Midwest, experiencing a catastrophic loss in the number of jobs, became known as the Rust Belt. In Michigan,

ground zero of the hard-hit auto industry, the unemployment rate rose to over 16%.

But if the economic slump that followed the Persian Gulf crisis looked in many ways like a small-scale repeat of the Great Depression, it was very different in one important respect. During the Great Depression, from 1929 to 1933, the U.S. economy experienced severe *deflation*—a falling aggregate price level. During the slump from 1979 to 1982, the economy experienced severe *inflation*—a rising aggregate price level—reaching a peak rate of more than 13%. Many people were as upset by the high inflation as by the job losses because they saw the purchasing power of their incomes shrinking. And the emergence of *stagflation,* the combination of inflation and rising unemployment, also shook the confidence of economists and

In the late 1970s and early 1980s, energy price increases arising from events in the Middle East led to recession and inflation here at home.

policy makers in their ability to manage the economy.

Why did the recession of 1979–1982 look different from the slump at the beginning of the Great Depression? Because it had a different cause. Indeed, the lesson of the 1970s was that recessions can have different causes and that the appropriate policy response depends on the cause. The Great Depression was caused by a crisis of confidence that led businesses and consumers to spend less, exacerbated by a banking crisis. This led to a combination of recession and deflation, which policy makers at that time didn't know how to respond to. But today we think we know what they should have done: pump cash into the economy, fighting the slump and stabilizing prices.

But the recession of 1979–1982, like the earlier recession of 1973–1975, was largely caused by events in the Middle East that led to sudden cuts in world oil production and soaring prices for oil and other fuels. These energy price increases led to a combination of recession and inflation. They also led to a dilemma: should economic policy fight the slump by pumping cash *into* the economy, or should it fight inflation by pulling cash *out* of the economy?

In this chapter, we'll develop a model that shows us how to distinguish between different types of short-run economic fluctuations—*demand shocks,* like the Great Depression, and *supply shocks,* like those of the 1970s. This model is our first step toward understanding short-run macroeconomics and macroeconomic policy.

To develop this model, we'll proceed in three steps. First, we'll develop the concept of *aggregate supply.* Then we'll turn to the parallel concept of *aggregate demand.* Finally, we'll put them together in the *AS–AD model.*

Aggregate Supply

Between 1929 and 1933, the demand curve for almost every good produced in the United States shifted to the left—the quantity demanded at any given price fell. We'll turn to the reasons for that decline in the next section, but let's focus first on the effects on producers.

One consequence of the economy-wide decline in demand was a fall in the prices of most goods and services. By 1933 the GDP deflator, one of the price indexes we defined in Chapter 24, was 26% below its 1929 level, and other indexes were down by similar amounts. A second consequence was a decline in the output of most goods and services: by 1933 real GDP was 27% below its 1929 level. A third consequence, closely tied to the fall in real GDP, was a surge in the unemployment rate from 3% to 25%.

The association between the plunge in real GDP and the plunge in prices wasn't an accident. Between 1929 and 1933, the U.S. economy was moving down its **aggregate supply curve,** which shows the relationship between the economy's aggregate price level (the overall price level of final goods and services in the economy) and the total quantity of final goods and services, or aggregate output, producers are willing to supply. (As we learned in Chapter 24, we use real GDP to measure aggregate output. So we'll often use the two terms interchangeably.) More specifically, between 1929 and 1933 the U.S. economy moved down its *short-run aggregate supply curve.*

The **aggregate supply curve** shows the relationship between the aggregate price level and the quantity of aggregate output supplied.

The Short-Run Aggregate Supply Curve

The period from 1929 to 1933 demonstrated that there is a positive relationship in the short run between the aggregate price level and the quantity of aggregate output supplied. That is, a rise in the aggregate price level leads to a rise in the quantity of aggregate output supplied, other things equal; a fall in the aggregate price level leads to a fall in the quantity of aggregate output supplied, other things equal. To understand why this positive relationship exists, let's think about the most basic question facing a producer: is producing a unit of output profitable or not? The answer depends on whether the price the producer receives for a unit of output, such as a bushel of corn, is greater or less than the cost of producing that unit of output. That is,

(27-1)   Profit per unit output =
            Price per unit output − Production cost per unit output

At any given point in time, many of the costs producers face are fixed and can't be changed for an extended period of time. Typically, the largest source of inflexible production cost is the wages paid to workers. *Wages* here refers to all forms of worker compensation, such as employer-paid health care and retirement benefits in addition to earnings. Wages are typically an inflexible production cost because the dollar amount of any given wage paid, called the **nominal wage,** is often determined by contracts that were signed several years earlier. And even when there are no formal contracts, there are often informal agreements between management and workers, reflecting reluctance by companies to change wages in response to economic conditions. For example, companies usually will not reduce wages during poor economic times—unless the downturn has been particularly long and severe—for fear of generating worker resentment. Correspondingly, they typically won't raise wages during better economic times—until they are at risk of losing workers to competitors—because they don't want to encourage workers to routinely demand higher wages. So as a result of both formal and informal agreements, nominal wages are "sticky": slow to fall even in the face of high unemployment, and slow to rise even in the face of labor shortages. We'll discuss the reasons for this stickiness in greater detail in Chapter 32. It's important to note, however, that nominal wages cannot be sticky forever: ultimately, formal contracts and informal agreements will be renegotiated to take into account changed economic circumstances. As the Pitfalls on page 645 explains, how long it takes for nominal wages to become flexible is an integral component of what distinguishes the short run from the long run.

Let's return to the question of the positive relationship between the aggregate price level and the quantity of aggregate output supplied in the short run. Imagine that, for some reason, the aggregate price level falls, which means that the price received by the typical producer of a final good or service falls. Because many production costs are fixed in the short run, production cost per unit of output doesn't fall by the same proportion as the fall in the price of output. So the profit per unit of output declines, leading producers to reduce the quantity supplied in the short run. In the economy as a whole, when the aggregate price level falls, aggregate output falls in the short run.

Now consider what would happen if, for some reason, the aggregate price level rises. As a result, the typical producer receives a higher price for his or her final good or service. Because many production costs are fixed in the short run, production cost per unit of output doesn't rise by the same proportion as the rise in the price of a unit. So profit per unit of output rises, the producer increases output, and aggregate output increases in the short run.

The positive relationship between the aggregate price level and the quantity of aggregate output producers are willing to supply during the time period when many production costs, particularly nominal wages, can be taken as fixed is illustrated by **the short-run aggregate supply curve.** The positive relationship between the aggregate price level and aggregate output in the short run gives the short-run aggregate supply curve its upward slope. Figure 27-1 shows a hypothetical short-run aggregate supply curve, *SRAS*, which matches actual U.S. data for 1929 and 1933.

The **nominal wage** is the dollar amount of the wage paid.

The **short-run aggregate supply curve** shows the relationship between the aggregate price level and the quantity of aggregate output supplied that exists in the short run, the time period when many production costs can be taken as fixed.

Figure 27-1

The Short-Run Aggregate Supply Curve

The short-run aggregate supply curve shows the relationship between the aggregate price level and the quantity of aggregate output supplied in the short run, the period in which many production costs such as nominal wages are fixed. It is upward-sloping because a higher aggregate price level leads to higher profit per unit of output and higher aggregate output given fixed nominal wages. Here we show numbers corresponding to the Great Depression, from 1929 to 1933: when deflation occurred and the aggregate price level fell from 11.9 (in 1929) to 8.9 (in 1933), firms responded by reducing the quantity of aggregate output supplied from $865 billion to $636 billion measured in 2000 dollars.

On the horizontal axis is aggregate output (or, equivalently, real GDP)—the total quantity of final goods and services supplied in the economy—measured in 2000 dollars. On the vertical axis is the aggregate price level as measured by the GDP deflator, with the value for year 2000 equal to 100. In 1929, the aggregate price level was 11.9 and real GDP was $865 billion. In 1933, the aggregate price level was 8.9 and real GDP was only $636 billion. The movement down the SRAS curve corresponds to the deflation and fall in aggregate output experienced over those years.

FOR INQUIRING MINDS

WHAT'S TRULY FLEXIBLE, WHAT'S TRULY STICKY

Most macroeconomists agree that the basic picture shown in Figure 27-1 is correct: there is, other things equal, a positive short-run relationship between the aggregate price level and aggregate output. But many would argue that the details are a bit more complicated.

So far we've stressed a difference in the behavior of the aggregate price level and the behavior of nominal wages. That is, we've said that the aggregate price level is flexible but nominal wages are sticky in the short run. Although this assumption is a good way to explain why the short-run aggregate supply curve is upward-sloping, empirical data on wages and prices don't wholly support a sharp distinction between flexible

prices of final goods and services and sticky nominal wages. On one side, some nominal wages are in fact flexible even in the short run because some workers are not covered by a contract or informal agreement with their employers. Since some nominal wages are sticky but others are flexible, we observe that the *average nominal wage*—the nominal wage averaged over all workers in the economy—falls when there is a steep rise in unemployment. For example, nominal wages fell substantially in the early years of the Great Depression. On the other side, some prices of final goods and services are sticky rather than flexible. For example, some firms, particularly the makers of luxury or

name-brand goods, are reluctant to cut prices even when demand falls. Instead they prefer to cut output even if their profit per unit hasn't declined.

These complications, as we've said, don't change the basic picture. When the aggregate price level falls, some producers cut output because the nominal wages they pay are sticky. And some producers don't cut their prices in the face of a falling aggregate price level, preferring instead to reduce their output. In both cases the positive relationship between the aggregate price level and aggregate output is maintained. So, in the end, the short-run aggregate supply curve is still upward-sloping.

Shifts of the Short-Run Aggregate Supply Curve

In Chapter 3, where we introduced the analysis of supply and demand in the market for an individual good, we stressed the importance of the distinction between *movements along* the supply curve and *shifts of* the supply curve. The same distinction applies to the aggregate supply curve. Figure 27-1 shows a *movement along* the short-run aggregate supply curve, as the aggregate price level and aggregate output fell from 1929 to 1933. But there can also be *shifts of* the short-run aggregate supply curve, as shown in Figure 27-2. Panel (a) shows a *decrease in short-run aggregate supply*—a leftward shift of the short-run aggregate supply curve. Aggregate supply decreases when producers reduce the quantity of aggregate output they are willing to supply at any given aggregate price level. Panel (b) shows an *increase in short-run aggregate supply*—a rightward shift of the short-run aggregate supply curve. Aggregate supply increases when producers increase the quantity of aggregate output they are willing to supply at any given aggregate price level.

To understand why the short-run aggregate supply curve can shift, it's important to recall that producers make output decisions based on their profit per unit of output. The short-run aggregate supply curve illustrates the relationship between the aggregate price level and aggregate output: because some production costs are fixed in the short run, a change in the aggregate price level leads to a change in producers' profit per unit of output and, in turn, leads to a change in aggregate output. But there are other factors besides the aggregate price level that can affect profit per unit and, in turn, aggregate output. It is changes in these other factors that will shift the short-run aggregate supply curve.

To develop some intuition, suppose that something happens that raises production costs—say an increase in the price of oil. At any given price of output, a producer now earns a smaller profit per unit of output. As a result, producers reduce the quantity supplied at any given aggregate price level, and the short-run aggregate supply curve shifts to the left. If, in contrast, something happens that lowers production costs—say a fall in the nominal wage—a producer now earns a higher profit per unit of output at any given price of output. This leads producers to increase the quantity

Figure 27-2   **Shifts of the Short-Run Aggregate Supply Curve**

Panel (a) shows a decrease in short-run aggregate supply: the short-run aggregate supply curve shifts leftward from SRAS₁ to SRAS₂, and the quantity of aggregate output supplied at any given aggregate price level falls. Panel (b) shows an increase in short-run aggregate supply: the short-run aggregate supply curve shifts rightward from SRAS₁ to SRAS₂, and the quantity of aggregate output supplied at any given aggregate price level rises.

of aggregate output supplied at any given aggregate price level, and the short-run aggregate supply curve shifts to the right.

Now we'll discuss some of the other important factors that affect producers' profit per unit and so can lead to shifts of the short-run aggregate supply curve.

Changes in Commodity Prices In this chapter's opening story, we described how a surge in the price of oil caused problems for the U.S. economy in 1979. Oil is a commodity, a standardized input bought and sold in bulk quantities. An increase in the price of a commodity—oil—raised production costs across the economy and reduced the quantity of aggregate output supplied at any given aggregate price level, shifting the short-run aggregate supply curve to the left. Conversely, a decline in commodity prices will reduce production costs, leading to an increase in the quantity supplied at any given aggregate price level and a rightward shift of the short-run aggregate supply curve.

Why isn't the influence of commodity prices already captured by the short-run aggregate supply curve? Because commodities—unlike, say, soft drinks—are not a final good, their prices are not included in the calculation of the aggregate price level. Further, commodities represent a significant cost of production to most suppliers, just like nominal wages do. So changes in commodity prices have large impacts on production costs. And in contrast to non-commodities, the prices of commodities can sometimes change drastically due to industry-specific shocks to supply—such as wars in the Middle East.

Changes in Nominal Wages At any given point in time, the dollar wages of many workers are fixed because they are set by contracts or informal agreements made in the past. Nominal wages can change, however, once enough time has passed for contracts and informal agreements to be renegotiated. Suppose, for example, that there is an economy-wide rise in the cost of health care insurance premiums paid by employers as part of employees' wages. From the employers' perspective, this is equivalent to a rise in nominal wages because it is an increase in employer-paid compensation. So this rise in nominal wages increases production costs and shifts the short-run aggregate supply curve to the left. Conversely, suppose there is an economy-wide fall in the cost of such premiums. This is equivalent to a fall in nominal wages from the point of view of employers; it reduces production costs and shifts the short-run aggregate supply curve to the right.

An important historical fact is that during the 1970s the surge in the price of oil had the indirect effect of also raising nominal wages. This "knock-on" effect occurred because many wage contracts included *cost-of-living allowances* that automatically raised the nominal wage when consumer prices increased. Through this channel, the surge in the price of oil—which led to an increase in overall consumer prices—ultimately caused a rise in nominal wages. So the economy, in the end, experienced two leftward shifts of the aggregate supply curve: the first generated by the initial surge in the price of oil, the second generated by the induced increase in nominal wages. The negative effect on the economy of rising oil prices was greatly magnified through the cost-of-living allowances in wage contracts. Today, cost-of-living allowances in wage contracts are rare.

Changes in Productivity An increase in productivity means that a worker can produce more units of output with the same quantity of inputs. For example, the introduction of bar-code scanners in retail stores greatly increased the ability of a single worker to stock, inventory, and resupply store shelves. As a result, the cost to a store of "producing" a dollar of sales fell and profit rose. And, correspondingly, the quantity supplied increased. (Think of Wal-Mart and the increase in the number of its stores as an increase in aggregate supply.) So a rise in productivity, whatever the source, increases producers' profits and shifts the short-run aggregate supply curve to the right. Conversely, a fall in productivity—say, due to new regulations that require workers to spend more time filling out forms—reduces the number of units of output a worker can produce with the same quantity of inputs. Consequently, the cost per unit of output rises, profit falls, and quantity supplied falls. This shifts the short-run aggregate supply curve to the left.

The Long-Run Aggregate Supply Curve

We've just seen that in the short run a fall in the aggregate price level leads to a decline in the quantity of aggregate output supplied because nominal wages are sticky in the short run. But, as we mentioned earlier, contracts and informal agreements are renegotiated in the long run. So in the long run, nominal wages—like the aggregate price level—are flexible, not sticky. This fact greatly alters the long-run relationship between the aggregate price level and aggregate supply. In fact, in the long run the aggregate price level has *no* effect on the quantity of aggregate output supplied.

To see why, let's conduct a thought experiment. Imagine that you could wave a magic wand—or maybe a magic bar-code scanner—and cut *all prices* in the economy in half at the same time. By "all prices" we mean the prices of all inputs, including nominal wages, as well as the prices of final goods and services. What would happen to aggregate output, given that the aggregate price level has been halved and all input prices, including nominal wages, have been halved?

The answer is: nothing. Consider Equation 27-1 again: each producer would receive a lower price for his or her product, but costs would fall by the same proportion. As a result, every unit of output profitable to produce before the change in prices would still be profitable to produce after the change in prices. So a halving of *all* prices in the economy has no effect on the economy's aggregate output. In other words, changes in the aggregate price level now have no effect on the quantity of aggregate output supplied.

In reality, of course, no one can change all prices by the same proportion at the same time. But in the long run, when all prices are fully flexible, inflation or deflation has the same effect as someone changing all prices by the same proportion. *As a result, changes in the aggregate price level do not change the quantity of aggregate output supplied in the long run.* That's because changes in the aggregate price level will, in the long run, be accompanied by equal proportional changes in *all* input prices, including nominal wages.

The **long-run aggregate supply curve,** illustrated in Figure 27-3 by the curve *LRAS*, shows the relationship between the aggregate price level and the quantity of aggregate output supplied that would exist if all prices, including nominal wages, were fully flexible. The long-run aggregate supply curve is vertical because changes in the aggregate price level have *no* effect on aggregate output in the long run. At an aggregate price level of 15.0, the quantity of aggregate output supplied is $800 billion in 2000 dollars. If the aggregate price level falls by 50% to 7.5, the quantity of aggregate output supplied is unchanged in the long run at $800 billion in 2000 dollars.

The **long-run aggregate supply curve** shows the relationship between the aggregate price level and the quantity of aggregate output supplied that would exist if all prices, including nominal wages, were fully flexible.

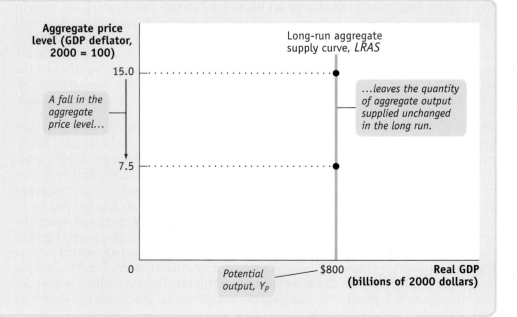

Figure 27-3

The Long-Run Aggregate Supply Curve

The long-run aggregate supply curve shows the quantity of aggregate output supplied when all prices, including nominal wages, are flexible. It is vertical at potential output, Y_P, because in the long run a change in the aggregate price level has no effect on the quantity of aggregate output supplied.

It's important to understand not only that the *LRAS* curve is vertical but also that its position along the horizontal axis represents a significant measure. The horizontal intercept in Figure 27-3, where *LRAS* touches the horizontal axis ($800 billion in 2000 dollars), is the economy's **potential output,** Y_P: the level of real GDP the economy would produce if all prices, including nominal wages, were fully flexible.

In reality, the actual level of real GDP is almost always either above or below potential output. We'll see why later in this chapter, when we discuss the *AS-AD* model. Still, an economy's potential output is an important number because it defines the trend around which actual aggregate output fluctuates from year to year.

In the United States, the Congressional Budget Office (CBO) estimates annual potential output for the purpose of federal budget analysis. Panel (a) of Figure 27-4 shows the CBO's estimates of U.S. potential output from 1989 to 2004 and the actual values of U.S. real GDP over the same period. Purple-shaded years correspond to periods in which potential output exceeded actual aggregate output; green-shaded years to periods in which actual aggregate output exceeded potential output.

As you can see in panel (a), U.S. potential output has risen steadily over time—implying a series of rightward shifts of the *LRAS* curve. What has caused these rightward shifts? The answer lies in the factors related to long-run growth that we discussed in Chapter 25, such as increases in physical capital and human capital as well as technological progress. Over the long run, as the size of the labor force and the productivity of labor both rise, the level of real GDP that the economy is capable of producing also rises. Indeed, one way to think about long-run economic growth is that it is the

> **Potential output** is the level of real GDP the economy would produce if all prices, including nominal wages, were fully flexible.

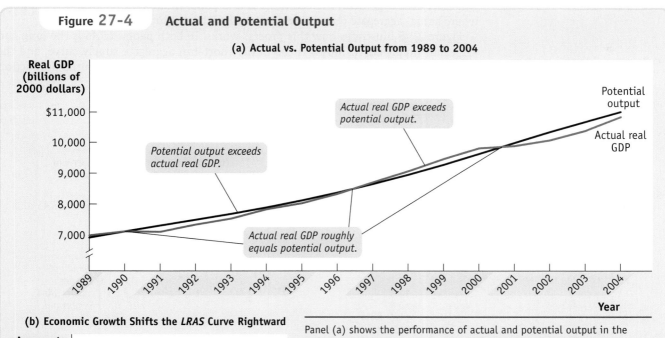

Figure 27-4   Actual and Potential Output

(a) Actual vs. Potential Output from 1989 to 2004

(b) Economic Growth Shifts the *LRAS* Curve Rightward

Panel (a) shows the performance of actual and potential output in the United States from 1989 to 2004. The black line shows estimates of U.S. potential output, produced by the Congressional Budget Office, and the blue line shows actual aggregate output. The purple-shaded years are periods in which actual aggregate output fell below potential output, and the green-shaded years are periods in which actual aggregate output exceeded potential output. As shown, significant shortfalls occurred in the recessions of the early 1990s and after 2000. Actual aggregate output was significantly above potential output in the boom of the late 1990s. Panel (b) shows how economic growth has shifted the long-run aggregate supply curve, *LRAS*, rightward over time.

growth in the economy's potential output. As illustrated in panel (b) of Figure 27-4, we generally think of the long-run aggregate supply curve as shifting to the right over time as an economy experiences long-run growth.

From the Short Run to the Long Run

As you can see in panel (a) of Figure 27-4, the economy almost always produces more or less than potential output: in only three periods during the years from 1989 to 2004 did actual aggregate output roughly equal potential output (the three years at which the two lines cross). The economy is almost always on its short-run aggregate supply curve—producing an aggregate output level more than or less than potential output—not on its long-run aggregate supply curve. So why is the long-run curve relevant? Does the economy ever move from the short run to the long run? And if so, how?

The first step to answering these questions is to understand that the economy is always in one of only two states with respect to the short-run and long-run aggregate supply curves. It can be on both curves simultaneously by being at a point where the curves cross (as in the three periods in panel (a) of Figure 27-4 in which actual aggregate output and potential output roughly coincide). Or it can be on the short-run aggregate supply curve but not the long-run aggregate supply curve (as in the years in panel (a) of Figure 27-4 in which actual aggregate output and potential output *did not* coincide). But that is not the end of the story. If the economy is on the short-run but not the long-run aggregate supply curve, the short-run aggregate supply curve will shift over time until the economy is at a point where both curves cross—a point where actual aggregate output is equal to potential output.

Figure 27-5 illustrates how this process works. In both panels *LRAS* is the long-run aggregate supply curve, $SRAS_1$ is the initial short-run aggregate supply curve, and the aggregate price level is at P_1. In panel (a) the economy starts at the initial production

Figure 27-5   From the Short Run to the Long Run

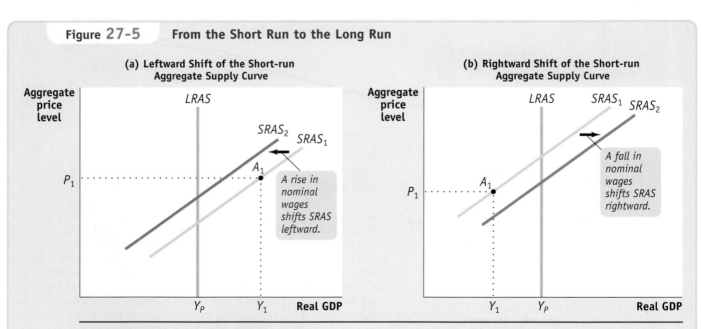

In panel (a), the initial short-run aggregate supply curve is $SRAS_1$. At the aggregate price level, P_1, the quantity of aggregate output supplied, Y_1, exceeds potential output, Y_P. Eventually, low unemployment will cause nominal wages to rise, leading to a leftward shift of the short-run aggregate supply curve from $SRAS_1$ to $SRAS_2$. In panel (b), the reverse happens: at the aggregate price level, P_1, the quantity of aggregate output supplied is less than potential output. High unemployment eventually leads to a fall in nominal wages over time and a rightward shift of the short-run aggregate supply curve.

point, A_1, which corresponds to a quantity of aggregate output supplied, Y_1, that is higher than potential output, Y_P. Producing an aggregate output level (such as Y_1) that is higher than potential output (Y_P) is possible only because nominal wages haven't yet fully adjusted upward. Until this upward adjustment in nominal wages occurs, producers are earning high profits and producing a high level of output. But a level of aggregate output higher than potential output means a low level of unemployment. Because jobs are abundant and workers are scarce, nominal wages will rise over time, gradually shifting the short-run aggregate supply curve leftward. Eventually it will be in a new position, such as $SRAS_2$. (Later in this chapter we'll show where the short-run aggregate supply curve ends up. As we'll see, that depends on the aggregate demand curve as well.)

In panel (b) of Figure 27-5, the initial production point, A_1, corresponds to the aggregate output level, Y_1, that is lower than potential output, Y_P. Producing an aggregate output level (such as Y_1) that is lower than potential output (Y_P) is possible only because nominal wages haven't yet fully adjusted downward. Until this downward adjustment occurs, producers are earning low (or negative) profits and producing a low level of output. An aggregate output level lower than potential output means high unemployment. Because workers are abundant and jobs are scarce, nominal wages will fall over time, shifting the short-run aggregate supply curve gradually to the right. Eventually it will be in a new position, such as $SRAS_2$.

We'll see shortly that these shifts of the short-run aggregate supply curve will return the economy to potential output in the long run. To explain why, however, we first need to introduce the concept of the *aggregate demand curve*.

PITFALLS

ARE WE THERE YET? WHAT THE LONG RUN REALLY MEANS

We've used the term *long run* in two different contexts. In Chapter 25 we focused on *long-run economic growth*: growth that takes place over decades. In this chapter we introduced the *long-run aggregate supply curve*, which depicts the economy's potential output: the level of aggregate output that the economy would produce if all prices, including nominal wages, were fully flexible. It might seem that we're using the same term, *long run*, for two different concepts. But we aren't: these two concepts are really the same thing.

Because the economy always tends to return to potential output in the long run, actual aggregate output *fluctuates around* potential output, rarely getting too far from it. As a result, the economy's rate of growth over long periods of time—say, decades—is very close to the rate of growth of potential output. And potential output growth is determined by the factors we analyzed in Chapter 25. So that means that the "long run" of long-run growth and the "long run" of the long-run aggregate supply curve coincide.

economics in action

Prices and Output During the Great Depression

Figure 27-6 shows the actual track of the aggregate price level, as measured by the GDP deflator, and real GDP, from 1929 to 1942. As you can see, aggregate output and the aggregate price level fell together from 1929 to 1933 and rose together during 1933 to 1937. This is what we'd expect to see if the economy were moving down the

Figure 27-6

Prices and Output During the Great Depression

From 1929 to 1933, prices and aggregate output fell together. And from 1933 to 1937, prices and aggregate output rose together. That is, during the period of 1929 to 1937, the economy behaved as if it were first moving down and then up the short-run aggregate supply curve. By the late 1930s, however, aggregate output was above 1929 levels even though the aggregate price level was still lower than it was in 1929. This reflects the fact that the short-run aggregate supply curve had shifted to the right during this period, due to both the short-run adjustment process in the economy and to a rightward shift of the long-run aggregate supply curve.

short-run aggregate supply curve from 1929 to 1933 and moving up it (with a brief reversal in 1937–1938) thereafter.

But even in 1942 the aggregate price level was still lower than it was in 1929; yet real GDP was much higher. What happened?

The answer is that the short-run aggregate supply curve shifted to the right over time. This shift partly reflected rising productivity—a rightward shift of the underlying long-run aggregate supply curve. But since the U.S. economy was producing below potential output and had high unemployment during this period, the rightward shift of the short-run aggregate supply curve also reflected the adjustment process shown in panel (b) of Figure 27-5. So the movement of aggregate output from 1929 to 1942 reflected both movements along and shifts of the short-run aggregate supply curve. ■

< < < < < < < < < < < < < < < < < < <

>> CHECK YOUR UNDERSTANDING 27-1

1. Determine the effect on short-run aggregate supply of each of the following events. Explain whether it represents a movement along the *SRAS* curve or a shift of the *SRAS* curve.
   a. A rise in the consumer price index (CPI) leads producers to increase output.
   b. A fall in the price of oil leads producers to increase output.
   c. A rise in legally mandated retirement benefits paid to workers leads producers to reduce output.

2. Suppose the economy is initially at potential output and the quantity of aggregate output supplied increases. What information would you need to determine whether this was due to a movement along the *SRAS* curve or a shift of the *LRAS* curve?

Solutions appear at back of book.

Aggregate Demand

The **aggregate demand curve** shows the relationship between the aggregate price level and the quantity of aggregate output demanded by households, businesses, the government, and the rest of the world.

Just as the aggregate supply curve shows the relationship between the aggregate price level and the quantity of aggregate output supplied by producers, the **aggregate demand curve** shows the relationship between the aggregate price level and the quantity of aggregate output demanded by households, firms, the government, and the rest of the world. Figure 27-7 shows an aggregate demand curve, *AD*. One point on

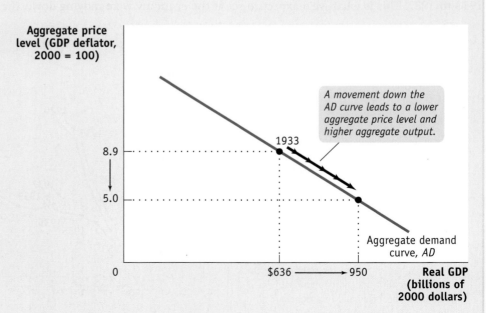

Figure 27-7

The Aggregate Demand Curve

The aggregate demand curve shows the relationship between the aggregate price level and the quantity of aggregate output demanded. The curve is downward-sloping due to the wealth effect of a change in the aggregate price level and the interest rate effect of a change in the aggregate price level. Corresponding to the actual 1933 data, here the total quantity of goods and services demanded at an aggregate price level of 8.9 is $636 billion in 2000 dollars. According to our hypothetical curve, however, if the aggregate price level had been only 5.0, the quantity of aggregate output demanded would have risen to $950 billion.

Aggregate price level (GDP deflator, 2000 = 100)

A movement down the AD curve leads to a lower aggregate price level and higher aggregate output.

1933

8.9

5.0

Aggregate demand curve, *AD*

0   $636 ⟶ 950   **Real GDP (billions of 2000 dollars)**

the curve corresponds to actual data for 1933, when the aggregate price level was 8.9 and the total quantity of domestic final goods and services purchased was $636 billion in 2000 dollars. *AD* is downward-sloping, indicating a negative relationship between the aggregate price level and the quantity of aggregate output demanded. A higher aggregate price level, other things equal, reduces the quantity of aggregate output demanded; a lower aggregate price level, other things equal, increases the quantity of aggregate output demanded. According to Figure 27-7, if the price level in 1933 had been 5.0 instead of 8.9, the total quantity of domestic final goods and services demanded would have been $950 billion in 2000 dollars instead of $636 billion.

Why Is the Aggregate Demand Curve Downward-Sloping?

In Figure 27-7, the curve *AD* is downward-sloping. Why? Recall the basic equation of national income accounting:

(27-2) $GDP = C + I + G + X - IM$

where *C* is consumer spending, *I* is investment spending, *G* is government purchases of goods and services, *X* is exports to other countries, and *IM* is imports. If we measure these variables in constant dollars—that is, in prices of a base year—then *C* + *I* + *G* + *X* − *IM* is the quantity of domestically produced final goods and services demanded during a given period. *G* is decided by the government, but the other variables are private-sector decisions. To understand why the aggregate demand curve slopes downward, we need to understand why a rise in the aggregate price level reduces *C, I,* and *X* − *IM*.

You might think that the downward slope of the aggregate demand curve is a natural consequence of the *law of demand* we defined back in Chapter 3. That is, since the demand curve for any one good is downward-sloping, isn't it natural that the demand curve for aggregate output is downward-sloping? This turns out to be a misleading parallel. The demand curve for any individual good shows how the quantity demanded depends on the price of that good, *holding the prices of other goods and services constant*. The main reason the quantity of a good demanded falls when the price of that good rises is that people switch their consumption to other goods and services.

But when we consider movements up or down the aggregate demand curve, we're considering *a simultaneous change in the prices of all final goods and services*. Furthermore, changes in the composition of goods and services in consumer spending aren't relevant to the aggregate demand curve: if consumers decide to buy fewer clothes but more cars, this doesn't necessarily change the total quantity of final goods and services they demand.

Why, then, does a rise in the aggregate price level lead to a fall in the quantity of all domestically produced final goods and services demanded? There are two main reasons: the *wealth effect* and the *interest rate effect* of a change in the aggregate price level.

The Wealth Effect   An increase in the aggregate price level, other things equal, reduces the purchasing power of many assets. Consider, for example, someone who has $5,000 in a bank account. If the aggregate price level were to rise by 25%, that $5,000 would buy only as much as $4,000 would have bought previously. With the loss in purchasing power, the owner of that bank account would probably scale back his or her consumption plans, leading to a fall in spending on final goods and services. The **wealth effect of a change in the aggregate price level** is the effect on consumer spending caused by the effect of a change in the aggregate price level on the purchasing power of consumers' assets. Because of it, consumer spending, *C,* falls when the aggregate price level rises, leading to a downward-sloping aggregate demand curve.

> The **wealth effect of a change in the aggregate price level** is the effect on consumer spending caused by the effect of a change in the aggregate price level on the purchasing power of consumers' assets.

The Interest Rate Effect Economists use the term *money* in its narrowest sense to refer to cash and bank deposits on which people can write checks. People and firms hold money because it reduces the cost and inconvenience of making transactions. An increase in the aggregate price level, other things equal, reduces the purchasing power of a given amount of money holdings. To purchase the same basket of goods and services as before, people and firms now need to hold more money. So, in response to an increase in the aggregate price level, the public tries to increase its money holdings, either by borrowing more or by selling other assets such as bonds. This reduces the funds available for lending to other borrowers and has the effect of driving interest rates up. In Chapter 26 we learned that a rise in the interest rate reduces investment spending because it makes the cost of borrowing higher. It also reduces consumer spending as households save more of their disposable income. So a rise in the aggregate price level depresses investment spending, *I,* and consumer spending, *C,* through its effect on the purchasing power of money holdings, an effect known as the **interest rate effect of a change in the aggregate price level.** This also leads to a downward-sloping aggregate demand curve.

> The **interest rate effect of a change in the aggregate price level** is the effect on consumer spending and investment spending caused by the effect of a change in the aggregate price level on the purchasing power of consumers' and firms' money holdings.

We'll have a lot more to say about money and interest rates in Chapter 31. We'll also see, in Chapter 35, that a higher interest rate indirectly tends to reduce exports (*X*) and increase imports (*IM*). For now, the important point is that the aggregate demand curve is downward-sloping due to both the wealth effect and the interest rate effect of a change in the aggregate price level.

Shifts of the Aggregate Demand Curve

When we talk about an increase in aggregate demand, we mean a shift of the aggregate demand curve to the right, as shown in panel (a) of Figure 27-8 by the shift from AD_1 to AD_2. A rightward shift occurs when the quantity of aggregate output demanded increases at any given aggregate price level. A decrease in aggregate demand means that *AD* shifts to the left, as in panel (b). A leftward shift implies that the quantity of aggregate output demanded falls at any given aggregate price level.

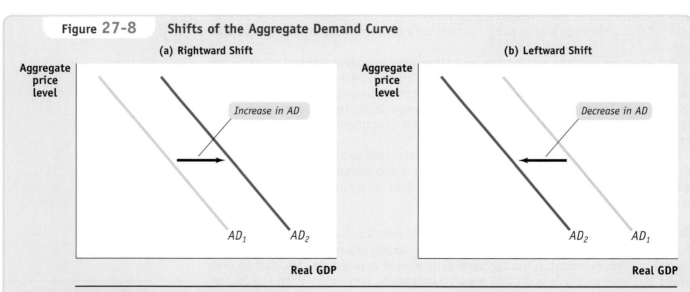

Figure 27-8   **Shifts of the Aggregate Demand Curve**

(a) Rightward Shift

Aggregate price level

Increase in AD

AD_1 AD_2

Real GDP

(b) Leftward Shift

Aggregate price level

Decrease in AD

AD_2 AD_1

Real GDP

Panel (a) shows the effect of events that increase the quantity of aggregate output demanded at any given aggregate price level, such as improvements in business and consumer expectations or increased government spending. Such changes shift the aggregate demand curve to the right, from AD_1 to AD_2. Panel (b) shows the effect of events that decrease the quantity of aggregate output demanded at any given price level, such as a fall in wealth caused by a stock market decline. This shifts the aggregate demand curve leftward from AD_1 to AD_2.

A number of factors can shift the aggregate demand curve. Among the most important factors are changes in expectations, changes in wealth, and changes in the stock of physical capital. In addition, both fiscal and monetary policy can shift the aggregate demand curve.

Changes in Expectations Both consumer spending and investment spending depend in part on people's expectations about the future. Consumers base their spending not only on the income they have now but also on the income they expect to have in the future. Firms base their investment spending not only on current conditions but also on the sales they expect to make in the future. As a result, changes in expectations can push consumer spending and investment spending up or down. If consumers and firms become more optimistic, spending rises; if they become more pessimistic, spending falls. In fact, short-run economic forecasters pay careful attention to surveys of consumer and business sentiment. In particular, forecasters watch the Consumer Confidence Index, a monthly measure calculated by the Conference Board, and the Michigan Consumer Sentiment Index, a similar measure calculated by the University of Michigan.

"CONSUMER CONFIDENCE CRISIS IN AISLE THREE!"

Changes in Wealth Consumer spending depends in part on the value of household assets. When the real value of these assets rises, the purchasing power they embody also rises, leading to an increase in aggregate demand. For example, in the 1990s there was a significant rise in the stock market that shifted aggregate demand. And when the real value of household assets falls—for example, because of a stock market crash—the purchasing power they embody is reduced and aggregate demand also falls. The stock market crash of 1929 was one factor in the Great Depression. Similarly, a sharp decline in the stock market in the United States after 2000 was an important factor in the 2001 recession.

Changes in the Stock of Physical Capital Firms engage in investment spending to add to their stock of physical capital. Their incentive to spend depends in part on how much physical capital they already have: the more they have, the less they will feel a need to add more, other things equal. Investment spending fell in 2000–2001 partly because high investment spending over the previous few years had left companies with more of certain kinds of capital, such as computers and fiber-optic cable, than they needed at that time.

Government Policies and Aggregate Demand

One of the key insights of macroeconomics is that the government can have a powerful influence on aggregate demand and that, in some circumstances, this influence can be used to improve economic performance.

The two main ways the government can influence the aggregate demand curve are through fiscal policy and monetary policy. We'll briefly discuss their influence on aggregate demand, pending full-length discussions in Chapter 29 and Chapter 31.

> ### PITFALLS
>
> #### CHANGES IN WEALTH: A MOVEMENT ALONG VERSUS A SHIFT OF THE AGGREGATE DEMAND CURVE
>
> In the last section we explained that one reason that the *AD* curve was downward-sloping was due to the wealth effect of a change in the aggregate price level: a higher aggregate price level reduces the purchasing power of households' assets and leads to a fall in consumer spending, *C*. But in this section we've just explained that changes in wealth lead to a shift of the *AD* curve. Aren't those two explanations contradictory? Which one is it—does a change in wealth move the economy along the *AD* curve or does it shift the *AD* curve? The answer is both: it depends on the *source* of the change in wealth. A movement along the *AD* curve occurs when a change in the aggregate price level changes the purchasing power of consumers' existing wealth (the real value of their assets). This is the *wealth effect of a change in the aggregate price level*—a change in the aggregate price level is the source of the change in wealth. For example, a fall in the aggregate price level increases the purchasing power of consumers' assets and leads to a movement down the *AD* curve. In contrast, a change in wealth *independent of a change in the aggregate price level* shifts the *AD* curve. For example, a rise in the stock market or a rise in real estate values leads to an increase in the real value of consumers' assets at any given aggregate price level. In this case, the source of the change in wealth is a change in the values of assets without any change in the aggregate price level—that is, a change in asset values holding the prices of all final goods and services constant.

Fiscal Policy As we learned in Chapter 23, fiscal policy is the use of either government spending—government purchases of final goods and services and government transfers—or tax policy to stabilize the economy. In practice, governments often respond to recessions by increasing spending, cutting taxes, or both. They often respond to inflation by reducing spending or increasing taxes.

The effect of government purchases of final goods and services, G, on the aggregate demand curve is *direct* because government purchases are themselves a component of aggregate demand. So an increase in government purchases shifts the aggregate demand curve to the right and a decrease shifts it to the left. History's most dramatic example of how increased government purchases affect aggregate demand was the effect of wartime government spending during World War II. Because of the war, U.S. federal purchases surged 400%. This increase in purchases is usually given the credit for ending the Great Depression. In the 1990s Japan used large public works projects—such as government-financed construction of roads, bridges, and dams—in an effort to increase aggregate demand in the face of a slumping economy. In contrast, government transfers affect aggregate demand indirectly: by changing disposable income, they change consumer spending.

In contrast, changes in tax rates (like changes in transfers) influence the economy *indirectly* through their effect on disposable income. A lower tax rate means that consumers get to keep more of what they earn, increasing their disposable income. This increases consumer spending and shifts the aggregate demand curve to the right. A higher tax rate reduces the amount of disposable income received by consumers. This reduces consumer spending and shifts the aggregate demand curve to the left.

Monetary Policy In Chapter 23 we defined monetary policy as the use of changes in the quantity of money or the interest rate to stabilize the economy. We've just discussed how a rise in the aggregate price level, by reducing the purchasing power of money holdings, causes a rise in the interest rate. That, in turn, reduces both investment spending and consumer spending.

But what happens if the quantity of money in the hands of households and firms changes? In modern economies, the quantity of money in circulation is largely determined by the decisions of a *central bank* created by the government. (As we'll learn in Chapter 30, the Federal Reserve, the U.S. central bank, is a special institution that is neither exactly part of the government nor exactly a private institution.) When the central bank increases the quantity of money in circulation, people have more money, which they are willing to lend out. The effect is to drive the interest rate down at any given aggregate price level and to increase investment spending and consumer spending. That is, increasing the quantity of money shifts the aggregate demand curve to the right. Reducing the quantity of money has the opposite effect: people have less money than before, leading them to borrow more and lend less. This raises the interest rate, reduces investment spending and consumer spending, and shifts the aggregate demand curve to the left.

economics in action

Moving Along the Aggregate Demand Curve, 1979–1980

When looking at data, it's often hard to distinguish between changes in spending that represent *movements along* the aggregate demand curve and *shifts of* the aggregate demand curve. One telling exception, however, is what happened right after the oil crisis of 1979, which we described in this chapter's opening story. Faced with a sharp increase in the aggregate price level—the rate of consumer price inflation reached 14.8% in March of 1980—the Federal Reserve stuck to a policy of increasing the quantity of money slowly. The aggregate price level was rising steeply, but the quantity of money going into the economy was growing slowly. The net result was that the purchasing power of the quantity of money in circulation in the economy fell.

This led to an increase in the demand for borrowing and a surge in interest rates. The *prime rate,* which is the interest rate banks charge their best customers, went above 20%. High interest rates, in turn, caused both consumer spending and investment spending to fall: in 1980 purchases of durable consumer goods like cars fell by 5.3% and real investment spending fell by 8.9%.

In other words, in 1979–1980 the economy responded just as we'd expect if it were moving along the aggregate demand curve: due to the wealth effect and the interest rate effect of a change in the aggregate price level, the quantity of aggregate output demanded fell as the aggregate price level rose. In the section "The *AS–AD* Model" we'll see that although this interpretation of the events in 1979–1980 is correct, the facts are a bit more complicated. There was indeed a movement along the aggregate demand curve. And the cause of this shift of the aggregate demand curve was a shift of the short-run aggregate supply curve. ∎

> >

>> CHECK YOUR UNDERSTANDING 27-2

1. Determine the effect on aggregate demand of each of the following events. Explain whether it represents a movement along the aggregate demand curve (up or down) or a shift of the curve (leftward or rightward).
   a. A rise in the interest rate caused by a change in monetary policy
   b. A fall in the real value of money in the economy due to a higher aggregate price level
   c. Expectations of a poor job market next year
   d. A fall in tax rates
   e. A rise in the real value of assets in the economy due to a lower aggregate price level
   f. A rise in the real value of assets in the economy due to a surge in real estate values

Solutions appear at back of book.

The Multiplier

Suppose that businesses become more optimistic about future sales and increase investment spending by $50 billion. This shifts the aggregate demand curve rightward—increasing the quantity of aggregate output demanded at any given aggregate price level. But suppose that we want to know *how much* the aggregate demand curve will shift to the right. To answer that question we use the concept of the *multiplier,* which plays an important role in the analysis of economic policy.

When we ask how far to the right a $50 billion autonomous increase in investment spending shifts the aggregate demand curve, what we really want to know is the magnitude of the shift shown in Figure 27-9 on page 652: the increase in the quantity of aggregate output demanded at a *given* aggregate price level, P*. So we will hold the aggregate price level constant. (This means, among other things, that there is no difference between changes in *nominal* GDP and changes in *real* GDP.) We'll also make some additional simplifying assumptions: we'll hold the interest rate constant, and we'll ignore the roles of taxes and foreign trade, reserving those issues for later chapters.

Assuming a constant aggregate price level and a fixed interest rate, you might be tempted to say that a $50 billion increase in investment spending will shift the aggregate demand curve to the right by $50 billion. That, however, is an underestimate. It's true that an increase in investment spending leads firms that produce investment goods to increase output. If the process stopped there, then the rightward shift of the *AD* curve would indeed be $50 billion.

But the process doesn't stop there. The increase in output leads to an increase in disposable income that flows to households in the form of profits and wages. The increase in households' disposable income leads to a rise in consumer spending, which, in turn, induces firms to increase output yet again. This generates another rise in disposable income, which leads to another round of consumer spending increases, and so on. So there are multiple rounds of increases in aggregate output.

How large is the total effect on aggregate output if we sum the effect from all these rounds of spending increases? To answer this question, we need to introduce the concept of the **marginal propensity to consume,** or *MPC:* the increase in consumer

>> QUICK REVIEW

➤ The *aggregate demand curve,* the relationship between the aggregate price level and the quantity of aggregate output demanded, is downward-sloping because of the *wealth effect of a change in the aggregate price level* and the *interest rate effect of a change in the aggregate price level.*

➤ Changes in consumer spending caused by changes in wealth and expectations about the future shift the aggregate demand curve. Changes in investment spending caused by changes in expectations and in the stock of physical capital also shift the aggregate demand curve.

➤ Fiscal policy affects aggregate demand directly through government purchases and indirectly through changes in taxes or government transfers. Monetary policy affects aggregate demand indirectly through changes in the interest rate.

The **marginal propensity to consume,** or *MPC,* is the increase in consumer spending when disposable income rises by $1.

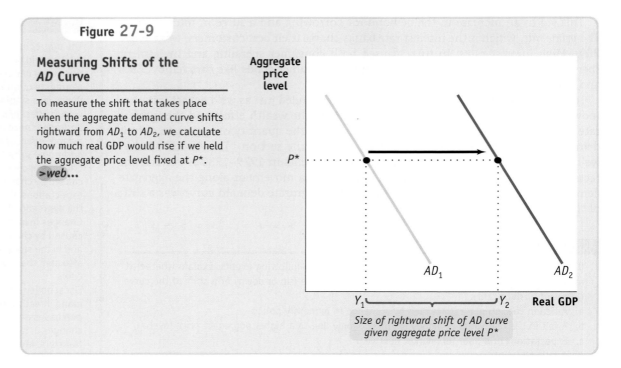

Figure 27-9

Measuring Shifts of the AD Curve

To measure the shift that takes place when the aggregate demand curve shifts rightward from AD_1 to AD_2, we calculate how much real GDP would rise if we held the aggregate price level fixed at $P*$.
>web...

Size of rightward shift of AD curve given aggregate price level P*

spending when disposable income rises by $1. When consumer spending changes because of a rise or fall in disposable income, *MPC* is the change in consumer spending divided by the change in disposable income:

(27-3) $MPC = \dfrac{\Delta \text{ Consumer spending}}{\Delta \text{ Disposable income}}$

For example, if consumer spending goes up by $6 billion when disposable income goes up by $10 billion, *MPC* is $6 billion/$10 billion = 0.6.

Because consumers normally spend part but not all of an additional dollar of disposable income, *MPC* is a number between 0 and 1. The additional disposable income that consumers don't spend is saved; the **marginal propensity to save,** or **MPS** is the fraction of an additional dollar of disposable income that is saved, and it is equal to $1 - MPC$.

Since we're ignoring taxes for now, we can assume that each $1 increase in real GDP raises real disposable income by $1. So the $50 billion increase in investment spending initially raises real GDP by $50 billion. This leads to a second-round increase in consumer spending, which raises real GDP by a further $MPC \times \$50$ billion. It is followed by a third-round increase in consumer spending of $MPC \times MPC \times \$50$ billion, and so on for several more rounds. The total effect on real GDP is:

> The **marginal propensity to save,** or **MPS,** is the increase in household savings when disposable income rises by $1.

Increase in investment spending	$=$	$50 billion
+ Second-round increase in consumer spending	$= MPC$	$\times \$50$ billion
+ Third-round increase in consumer spending	$= MPC^2$	$\times \$50$ billion
+ Fourth-round increase in consumer spending	$= MPC^3$	$\times \$50$ billion
⋮	⋮	

Total increase in real GDP $= (1 + MPC + MPC^2 + MPC^3 + \ldots) \times \$50$ billion

So the initial $50 billion increase in investment spending arising from more optimistic expectations sets off a chain reaction in the economy. The net result of this chain reaction is that a $50 billion increase in investment spending leads to a change in real GDP that is a *multiple* of the size of that initial change in spending.

How large is this multiple? It's a mathematical fact that a series of the form $1 + x + x^2 + x^3 + \ldots$, where x is between 0 and 1, is equal to $1/(1 - x)$. So the total effect of a $50 billion increase in investment spending, taking into account all the subsequent increases in consumer spending (and assuming no taxes and no trade), is given by:

(27-4)   Total increase in real GDP from $50 billion rise in I

$$= \$50 \text{ billion} \times \frac{1}{1 - MPC}$$

Let's consider a numerical example in which $MPC = 0.6$: each $1 in additional disposable income causes a $0.60 rise in consumer spending. In that case, a $50 billion increase in investment spending raises real GDP by $50 billion in the first round. The second-round increase in consumer spending raises real GDP by another $0.6 \times \$50$ billion, or $30 billion. The third-round increase in consumer spending raises real GDP by another $0.6 \times \$30$ billion, or $18 billion. Table 27-1 shows the successive stages of increases, where "$\ldots$" means the process goes on an infinite number of times. In the end, real GDP rises by $125 billion as a consequence of the initial $50 billion rise in investment spending. We know that is true by Equation 27-4:

$$\$50 \text{ billion} \times \frac{1}{1 - 0.6} = \$50 \text{ billion} \times 2.5 = \$125 \text{ billion}$$

Notice that even though there are an infinite number of rounds of expansion of real GDP, the total rise in real GDP is limited to $125 billion. The reason is that at each stage some of the rise in disposable income "leaks out" because it is saved. How much of an additional dollar of disposable income is saved depends on MPS, the marginal propensity to save.

Figure 27-10 illustrates the effect of the increase in investment spending on the aggregate demand curve. Panel (a) shows the successive rounds of increasing real

TABLE 27-1

Rounds of Increases of Real GDP

	Increase in real GDP (billions of dollars)	Total increase in real GDP (billions of dollars)
First round	$50	$50
Second round	30	80
Third round	18	98
Fourth round	10.8	108.8
...	...	...
Final round	0	125

Figure 27-10   The Multiplier

(a) Rounds of Cumulative Increases in Real GDP

(b) The Corresponding Effect on Aggregate Demand

A change in expectations that leads to a rise in investment spending shifts the aggregate demand curve rightward for two reasons. Holding the aggregate price level constant, there is an initial increase in real GDP from the rise in I. Then there are subsequent increases in real GDP as rising disposable income leads to higher consumer spending. Panel (a) shows how the rise in real GDP at a given aggregate price level takes place. Panel (b) shows how this shifts the aggregate demand curve.

GDP from Table 27-1. Panel (b) shows the corresponding effect on aggregate demand: the total amount of the rightward shift of the AD curve, from AD_1 to AD_2, is $125 billion, the sum of the initial increase in investment spending, $50 billion, plus the subsequent rise in consumer spending, $75 billion.

We've described the effects of a change in investment spending arising from a change in expectations, but the same analysis can be applied to other causes of a shift in the aggregate demand curve. Since there is no foreign trade in this simple economy, we'll focus on domestic aggregate spending in the economy, the sum of consumer spending, C, investment spending, I, and government purchases of goods and services, G. Shifts in the aggregate demand curve can arise from autonomous changes in any of those three components of aggregate spending. The important thing is to distinguish between the initial change in aggregate spending, before real GDP rises, and the additional change in aggregate spending caused by the change in real GDP as the chain reaction unfolds. For example, suppose that total wealth in the economy increases for some reason. This will lead to an initial rise in consumer spending, before real GDP rises. But it will also lead to second and later rounds of higher consumer spending as real GDP rises.

An initial rise or fall in aggregate spending at a given level of real GDP is called an **autonomous change in aggregate spending**. It's autonomous—which means "self-governing"—because it's the cause, not the result, of the chain reaction we've just described. The **multiplier** is the ratio of the total change in real GDP caused by an autonomous change in aggregate spending to the size of that autonomous change. If we let ΔAAS stand for autonomous change in aggregate spending and ΔY stand for the change in real GDP, then the multiplier is equal to $\Delta Y/\Delta AAS$. And we've already seen from Equation 27-4 how to find the value of the multiplier. Assuming no taxes and no trade, it's

$$(27\text{-}5) \quad \text{Multiplier} = \frac{1}{1 - MPC} = \frac{\Delta Y}{\Delta AAS}$$

Accordingly, the multiplier lets us calculate the change in real GDP that arises from an autonomous change in aggregate spending. Re-arranging Equation 10-5 we get:

$$(27\text{-}6) \quad \Delta Y = \frac{1}{1 - MPC} \times \Delta AAS$$

Notice that the size of the multiplier—and so the size of the shift in the aggregate demand curve resulting from any given initial change in aggregate spending—depends on MPC. If the marginal propensity to consume is high, so is the multiplier. This is true because the size of MPC determines how large each round of expansion is compared with the previous round. To put it another way, the higher MPC is, the less disposable income "leaks out" into savings at each round of expansion.

In later chapters we'll use the concept of the multiplier to analyze the effects of fiscal and monetary policies. We'll also see that the formula for the multiplier changes when we introduce various complications, including taxes and foreign trade.

< < < < < < < < < < < < < < < < < < <

An **autonomous change in aggregate spending** is an initial change in the desired level of spending by firms, households, and government at a given level of real GDP.

The **multiplier** is the ratio of the total change in real GDP caused by an autonomous change in aggregate spending to the size of that autonomous change.

> **QUICK REVIEW**

> ➤ A change in investment spending arising from a change in expectations starts a chain reaction in which the initial change in real GDP leads to changes in consumer spending, leading to further changes in real GDP, and so on. The total shift in the aggregate demand curve is a multiple of the initial change in investment spending.

> ➤ Any *autonomous change in aggregate spending*, a change in *C*, *I*, or *G* that shifts the aggregate demand curve, generates the same chain reaction. The total size of the change in real GDP depends on the size of the *multiplier*. Assuming that there are no taxes and no trade, the multiplier is equal to $1/(1 - MPC)$, where *MPC* is the *marginal propensity to consume*. The total change in real GDP, ΔY, is equal to $1/(1 - MPC) \times \Delta AAS$.

> **CHECK YOUR UNDERSTANDING 27-3**

1. Explain why a decline in investment spending, caused by a change in business expectations, would also lead to a fall in consumer spending.

Solution appears at back of book.

The *AS–AD* Model

From 1929 to 1933, the U.S. economy moved down the short-run aggregate supply curve as the aggregate price level fell. In contrast, from 1979 to 1980 the U.S. economy moved up the aggregate demand curve as the aggregate price level rose. In each case, the cause of the movement along the curve was a shift of the other curve. In 1929–1933, it was a leftward shift of the aggregate demand curve—a major fall in consumer spending. In 1979–1980, it was a leftward shift of the short-run aggregate supply curve—a dramatic fall in short-run aggregate supply caused by the oil price shock.

So to understand the behavior of the economy, we must put the aggregate supply curve and the aggregate demand curve together. The result is the **AS–AD model,** the basic model we use to understand economic fluctuations.

Short-Run Macroeconomic Equilibrium

We'll begin our analysis by focusing on the short run. Figure 27-11 shows the aggregate demand curve and the short-run aggregate supply curve on the same diagram. The point at which the AD and $SRAS$ curves intersect, E_{SR}, is the **short-run macroeconomic equilibrium:** the point at which the quantity of aggregate output supplied is equal to the quantity demanded by domestic households, businesses, the government, and the rest of the world. The aggregate price level at E_{SR}, P_E, is the **short-run equilibrium aggregate price level.** The level of aggregate output at E_{SR}, Y_E, is the **short-run equilibrium aggregate output.**

In the supply and demand model of Chapter 3 we saw that a shortage of any individual good causes its market price to rise but a surplus of the good causes its market price to fall. These forces ensure that the market reaches equilibrium. The same logic applies to short-run macroeconomic equilibrium. If the aggregate price level is above its equilibrium level, the quantity of aggregate output supplied exceeds the quantity demanded. This leads to a fall in the aggregate price level and pushes it toward its equilibrium level. If the aggregate price level is below its equilibrium level, the quantity of aggregate output supplied is less than the quantity demanded. This leads to a rise in the aggregate price level, again pushing it toward its equilibrium level. In the discussion that follows, we'll assume that the economy is always in short-run macroeconomic equilibrium.

We'll also make another important simplification based on the observation that in reality there is a long-term upward trend in both aggregate output and the aggregate price level. We'll assume that a fall in either variable really means a fall compared to the long-run trend. For example, if the aggregate price level normally rises 4% per year, a year in which the aggregate price level rises only 3% would count, for

> In the **AS–AD model,** the aggregate supply curve and the aggregate demand curve are used together to analyze economic fluctuations.

> The economy is in **short-run macroeconomic equilibrium** when the quantity of aggregate output supplied is equal to the quantity demanded.

> The **short-run equilibrium aggregate price level** is the aggregate price level in the short-run macroeconomic equilibrium.

> **Short-run equilibrium aggregate output** is the quantity of aggregate output produced in the short-run macroeconomic equilibrium.

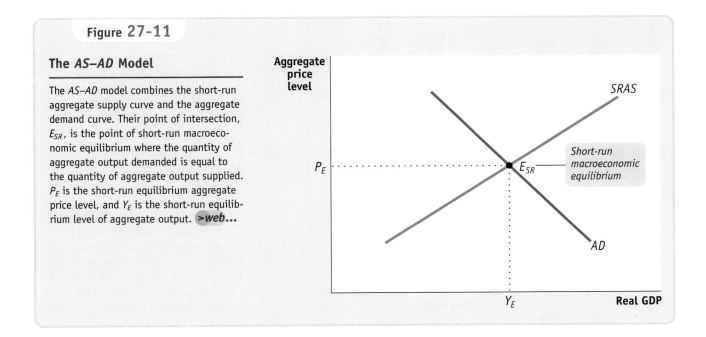

Figure 27-11

The *AS–AD* Model

The *AS–AD* model combines the short-run aggregate supply curve and the aggregate demand curve. Their point of intersection, E_{SR}, is the point of short-run macroeconomic equilibrium where the quantity of aggregate output demanded is equal to the quantity of aggregate output supplied. P_E is the short-run equilibrium aggregate price level, and Y_E is the short-run equilibrium level of aggregate output. **>web...**

our purposes, as a 1% decline. In fact, since the Great Depression there have been very few years in which the aggregate price level of any major nation actually declined—Japan's deflation after about 1995 is one of the few exceptions. We'll explain why in Chapter 33. There have, however, been many cases in which the aggregate price level fell relative to the long-run trend.

Short-run equilibrium aggregate output and the short-run equilibrium aggregate price level can change either because of shifts of the *SRAS* curve or because of shifts of the *AD* curve. Let's look at each case in turn.

Shifts of the *SRAS* Curve

An event that shifts the short-run aggregate supply curve is a **supply shock**.

An event that shifts the short-run aggregate supply curve, such as a change in commodity prices, nominal wages, or productivity, is known as a **supply shock.** A *negative* supply shock raises production costs and reduces the quantity producers are willing to supply at any given aggregate price level, leading to a leftward shift of the short-run aggregate supply curve. The U.S. economy experienced severe negative supply shocks following disruptions to world oil supplies in 1973 and 1979. In contrast, a *positive* supply shock reduces production costs and increases the quantity supplied at any given aggregate price level, leading to a rightward shift of the short-run aggregate supply curve. The United States experienced a positive supply shock between 1995 and 2000, when the increasing use of the Internet and other information technologies caused productivity growth to surge.

The effects of a negative supply shock are shown in panel (a) of Figure 27-12. The initial equilibrium is at E_1, with aggregate price level P_1 and aggregate output Y_1. The disruption in the oil supply causes the short-run aggregate supply curve to shift to the left, from $SRAS_1$ to $SRAS_2$. As a consequence, aggregate output falls and the aggregate price level rises, a movement up along the *AD* curve. At the new equilibrium,

Figure 27-12   Supply Shocks

(a) A Negative Supply Shock

A negative supply shock...

...leads to lower aggregate output and a higher aggregate price level.

(b) A Positive Supply Shock

A positive supply shock...

...leads to higher aggregate output and a lower aggregate price level.

A supply shock shifts the short-run aggregate supply curve, moving the aggregate price level and aggregate output in opposite directions. Panel (a) shows a negative supply shock, which shifts the short-run aggregate supply curve leftward and causes stagflation—lower aggregate output and a higher aggregate price level. Here the short-run aggregate supply curve shifts from $SRAS_1$ to $SRAS_2$, and the economy moves from E_1 to E_2. The aggregate price level rises from P_1 to P_2, and aggregate output falls from Y_1 to Y_2. Panel (b) shows a positive supply shock, which shifts the short-run aggregate supply curve rightward, generating higher aggregate output and a lower aggregate price level. The short-run aggregate supply curve shifts from $SRAS_1$ to $SRAS_2$, and the economy moves from E_1 to E_2. The aggregate price level falls from P_1 to P_2, and aggregate output rises from Y_1 to Y_2.

E_2, the equilibrium aggregate price level, P_2, is higher, and the equilibrium aggregate output level, Y_2, is lower than before.

The combination of inflation and falling aggregate output shown in panel (a) has a special name: **stagflation,** for "stagnation plus inflation." When an economy experiences stagflation, it's very unpleasant: falling aggregate output leads to rising unemployment, and people feel that their purchasing power is squeezed by rising prices. Stagflation in the 1970s led to a mood of national pessimism. It also, as we'll see shortly, poses a dilemma for policy makers.

A positive supply shock, shown in panel (b), has exactly the opposite effects. A rightward shift of the *SRAS* curve from $SRAS_1$ to $SRAS_2$ results in a rise in aggregate output and a fall in the aggregate price level, a movement down along the *AD* curve. The favorable supply shocks of the late 1990s led to a combination of full employment and declining inflation. That is, the aggregate price level fell compared with the long-run trend. This combination produced, for a time, a great wave of national optimism.

The distinctive feature of supply shocks, both negative and positive, is that they cause the aggregate price level and aggregate output to move in *opposite* directions.

> **Stagflation** is the combination of inflation and falling aggregate output.

Shifts of Aggregate Demand: Short-Run Effects

An event that shifts the aggregate demand curve, such as a change in expectations, wealth, the stock of physical capital, or the use of fiscal or monetary policy, is known as a **demand shock.** The Great Depression was caused by a negative demand shock, the collapse of wealth and of business and consumer confidence that followed the stock market crash of 1929 and the banking crisis of 1930–1931. The Depression was ended by a positive demand shock—the huge increase in government purchases during World War II. In 2001 the U.S. economy experienced another significant negative demand shock as the stock market boom of the 1990s turned into a bust and nervous businesses drastically scaled back their investment spending.

> An event that shifts the aggregate demand curve is a **demand shock**.

Figure 27-13 shows the short-run effects of negative and positive demand shocks. A negative demand shock shifts the aggregate demand curve, *AD,* to the left, from AD_1 to AD_2, as shown in panel (a). The economy moves down along the *SRAS* curve from

Figure 27-13 Demand Shocks

A demand shock shifts the aggregate demand curve, moving the aggregate price level and aggregate output in the same direction. In panel (a) a negative demand shock shifts the aggregate demand curve leftward from AD_1 to AD_2, reducing the aggregate price level from P_1 to P_2 and aggregate output from Y_1 to Y_2. In panel (b) a positive demand shock shifts the aggregate demand curve rightward, increasing the aggregate price level from P_1 to P_2 and aggregate output from Y_1 to Y_2.

E_1 to E_2, leading to lower equilibrium aggregate output and a lower equilibrium aggregate price level. A positive demand shock shifts the aggregate demand curve, AD, to the right, as shown in panel (b). Here, the economy moves up along the $SRAS$ curve, from E_1 to E_2. This leads to higher equilibrium aggregate output and a higher equilibrium aggregate price level. In contrast to supply shocks, demand shocks cause aggregate output and the aggregate price level to move in the *same* direction.

There's another important contrast between supply shocks and demand shocks. As we've seen, monetary policy and fiscal policy enable the government to shift the AD curve, meaning that governments are in a position to create the kinds of shocks shown in Figure 27-13. Are there good policy reasons to do this? We'll turn to that question soon. First, however, let's look at the difference between short-run macroeconomic equilibrium and long-run macroeconomic equilibrium.

Long-Run Macroeconomic Equilibrium

Figure 27-14 combines the aggregate demand curve with both the short-run and long-run aggregate supply curves. The aggregate demand curve, AD, crosses the short-run aggregate supply curve, $SRAS$, at E_{LR}. Here we assume that enough time has elapsed that the economy is also on the long-run aggregate supply curve, $LRAS$. As a result, E_{LR} is at the intersection of all three curves, $SRAS$, $LRAS$, and AD. So short-run equilibrium aggregate output is equal to potential output, Y_P. Such a situation, in which the point of short-run macroeconomic equilibrium is on the long-run aggregate supply curve, is known as **long-run macroeconomic equilibrium.**

> The economy is in **long-run macroeconomic equilibrium** when the point of short-run macroeconomic equilibrium is on the long-run aggregate supply curve.

To see the significance of long-run macroeconomic equilibrium, let's consider what happens if a demand shock moves the economy away from long-run macroeconomic equilibrium. In Figure 27-15, we assume that the initial aggregate demand curve is AD_1 and the initial short-run aggregate supply curve is $SRAS_1$. So the initial macroeconomic equilibrium is at E_1, which lies on the long-run aggregate supply curve, $LRAS$. The economy, then, starts from a point of short-run and long-run macroeconomic equilibrium, and short-run equilibrium aggregate output equals potential output at Y_1.

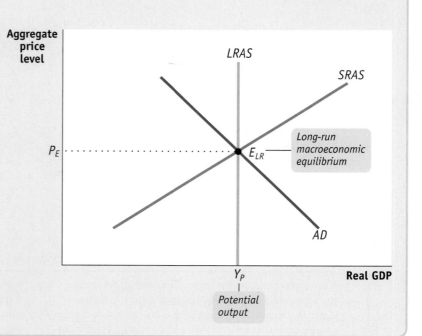

Figure 27-14

Long-Run Macroeconomic Equilibrium

Here the point of short-run macroeconomic equilibrium also lies on the long-run aggregate supply curve, *LRAS*. As a result, short-run equilibrium aggregate output is equal to potential output, Y_P. The economy is in long-run macroeconomic equilibrium at E_{LR}. **>web...**

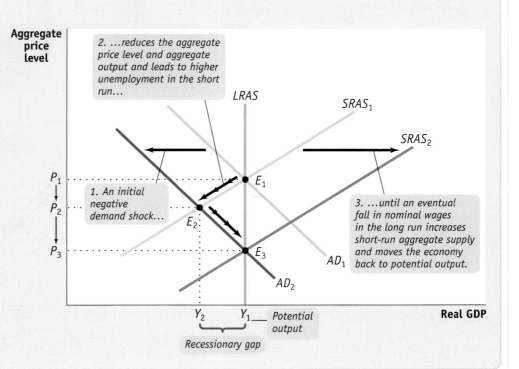

Figure 27-15

Short-Run versus Long-Run Effects of a Negative Demand Shock

In the long run the economy is self-correcting: demand shocks have only a short-run effect on aggregate output. Starting at E_1, a negative demand shock shifts AD_1 leftward to AD_2. In the short run the economy moves to E_2 and a recessionary gap arises: the aggregate price level declines from P_1 to P_2, aggregate output declines from Y_1 to Y_2, and unemployment rises. But in the long run nominal wages fall in response to high unemployment at Y_2, and $SRAS_1$ shifts rightward to $SRAS_2$. Aggregate output rises from Y_2 to Y_1, and the aggregate price level declines again, from P_2 to P_3. Long-run macroeconomic equilibrium is eventually restored at E_3.

Now suppose that for some reason—such as a sudden worsening of business and consumer expectations—aggregate demand falls and the aggregate demand curve shifts leftward to AD_2. This results in a lower equilibrium aggregate price level at P_2 and a lower equilibrium aggregate output level at Y_2 as the economy settles in the short run at E_2. The short-run effect of such a fall in aggregate demand is what the U.S. economy experienced in 1929–1933: a falling aggregate price level and falling aggregate output.

Aggregate output in this new short-run equilibrium, E_2, is below potential output. When this happens, the economy faces a **recessionary gap.** In the real world, a recessionary gap inflicts a great deal of pain because it corresponds to high unemployment. The large recessionary gap that opened up in the United States by 1933 caused intense social and political turmoil. And the devastating recessionary gap that opened up in Germany at the same time played an important role in Hitler's rise to power.

But this isn't the end of the story. In the face of high unemployment, nominal wages eventually fall, as do any other sticky prices, ultimately leading producers to increase output. As a result, a recessionary gap causes the short-run aggregate supply curve to gradually shift to the right over time. This process continues until $SRAS_1$ reaches its new position at $SRAS_2$, bringing the economy to equilibrium at E_3, where AD_2, $SRAS_2$, and $LRAS$ all intersect. At E_3, the economy is back in long-run macroeconomic equilibrium; it is back at potential output Y_1 but at a lower aggregate price level, P_3, reflecting a long-run fall in the aggregate price level. In the end, the economy is *self-correcting* in the long run.

What if, instead, there were an increase in aggregate demand? The results are shown in Figure 27-16 on page 660, where we again assume that the initial aggregate demand curve is AD_1, and the initial short-run aggregate supply curve is $SRAS_1$, so that the initial macroeconomic equilibrium, at E_1, lies on the long-run aggregate supply curve, $LRAS$. Initially, then, the economy is in long-run macroeconomic equilibrium.

Now suppose that aggregate demand rises, and the AD curve shifts rightward to AD_2. This results in a higher aggregate price level, at P_2, and a higher aggregate output

There is a **recessionary gap** when aggregate output is below potential output.

Figure 27-16

Short-Run versus Long-Run Effects of a Positive Demand Shock

Starting at E_1 a positive demand shock shifts AD_1 rightward to AD_2, and the economy moves to E_2 in the short run. This results in an inflationary gap as aggregate output rises from Y_1 to Y_2, the aggregate price level rises from P_1 to P_2, and unemployment falls to a low level. In the long run, $SRAS_1$ shifts leftward to $SRAS_2$ as nominal wages rise in response to low unemployment at Y_2. Aggregate output falls back to Y_1, the aggregate price level rises again to P_3, and the economy self-corrects as it returns to long-run macro-economic equilibrium at E_3.

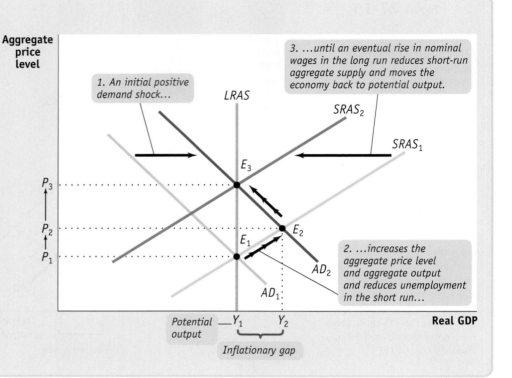

1. An initial positive demand shock...

3. ...until an eventual rise in nominal wages in the long run reduces short-run aggregate supply and moves the economy back to potential output.

2. ...increases the aggregate price level and aggregate output and reduces unemployment in the short run...

Inflationary gap

There is an **inflationary gap** when aggregate output is above potential output.

level, at Y_2, as the economy settles in the short run at E_2. Aggregate output in this new short-run equilibrium is above potential output, and unemployment is low in order to produce this higher level of aggregate output. When this happens, the economy experiences an **inflationary gap.** As in the case of a recessionary gap, this isn't the end of the story. In the face of low unemployment, nominal wages will rise, as will other sticky prices. An inflationary gap causes the short-run aggregate supply curve to shift gradually to the left as producers reduce output in the face of rising nominal wages. This process continues until $SRAS_1$ reaches its new position at $SRAS_2$, bringing the economy to equilibrium at E_3, where AD_2, $SRAS_2$, and $LRAS$ all intersect. At E_3, the economy is back in long-run macroeconomic equilibrium. It is back at potential output, but at a higher price level, P_3, reflecting a long-run rise in the aggregate price level. Again, the economy is self-correcting in the long run.

There is an important lesson about the macroeconomy to be learned from this analysis. When there is a recessionary gap, nominal wages eventually fall, moving the economy back to potential output. And when there is an inflationary gap, nominal wages eventually rise, also moving the economy back to potential output. So in the long run the economy is **self-correcting:** shocks to aggregate demand affect aggregate output in the short run but not in the long run.

In the long run the economy is **self-correcting:** shocks to aggregate demand affect aggregate output in the short run but not the long run.

economics in action

Supply Shocks versus Demand Shocks in Practice

How often do supply shocks and demand shocks, respectively, cause recessions? The verdict of most, though not all, macroeconomists is that recessions are mainly caused by demand shocks. But when a negative supply shock does happen, the resulting recession tends to be particularly nasty.

Let's get specific. Officially there have been ten recessions in the United States since World War II. However, two of these, in 1979–1980 and 1981–1982, are often treated as a single "double-dip" recession, bringing the total number down to nine. Of these nine recessions, only two—the recession of 1973–1975 and the double-dip recession of 1979–1982—showed the distinctive combination of falling aggregate output and a surge in the price level that we call stagflation. In each case, the cause of the supply shock was political turmoil in the Middle East—the Arab–Israeli war of 1973 and the Iranian revolution of 1979—that disrupted world oil supplies and sent oil prices skyrocketing. In fact, economists sometimes refer to the two slumps as "OPEC I" and "OPEC II," after the Organization of Petroleum Exporting Countries, the world oil cartel.

So seven of nine postwar recessions were the result of demand shocks, not supply shocks. The two supply-shock recessions, however, were the two worst as measured by the unemployment rate. Figure 27-17 shows the U.S. unemployment rate since 1948, with the dates of the 1973 Arab–Israeli war and the 1979 Iranian revolution marked on the graph. The two highest unemployment rates since World War II came after these two big negative supply shocks.

There's a reason the aftermath of a supply shock is particularly nasty: macroeconomic policy has a much harder time dealing with supply shocks than with demand shocks. We'll see why in a minute.

Figure 27-17   Negative Supply Shocks Are Relatively Rare But Nasty

Only two of nine postwar recessions seem to fit the profile of a recession caused by a negative supply shock: the recession that followed the increase in oil prices after the 1973 Arab–Israeli war and the recession that followed another surge in oil prices after the Iranian revolution. These two recessions were, however, the worst in terms of unemployment.

> >

>>CHECK YOUR UNDERSTANDING 27-4

1. Describe the short-run effects of each of the following shocks on the aggregate price level and on aggregate output.
   a. The government sharply increases the minimum wage, raising the wages of many workers.
   b. Solar energy firms launch a major program of investment spending.
   c. Congress raises taxes and cuts spending.
   d. Severe weather destroys crops around the world.

2. A rise in productivity increases potential output, but some worry that demand for the additional output will be insufficient even in the long run. How would you respond?

Solutions appear at back of book.

>>QUICK REVIEW

➤ *Short-run macroeconomic equilibrium* occurs at the intersection of the short-run aggregate supply and aggregate demand curves.

➤ A *supply shock*, a shift of the *SRAS* curve, causes the aggregate price level and aggregate output to move in opposite directions. A *demand shock*, a shift of the *AD* curve, causes them to move in the same direction. *Stagflation* is the consequence of a negative supply shock.

➤ The economy is *self-correcting* in the long run. A fall in nominal wages occurs in response to a *recessionary gap*, and a rise in nominal wages occurs in response to an *inflationary gap*. Both move the economy to *long-run macroeconomic equilibrium*, where the *AD*, *SRAS*, and *LRAS* curves intersect.

Macroeconomic Policy

We've just seen that the economy is self-correcting in the long run: it will eventually trend back to potential output. Most macroeconomists believe, however, that the process of self-correction takes several years—typically a decade or more. In particular, if aggregate output is below potential output, the economy can suffer an extended period of depressed aggregate output and high unemployment before it returns to normal.

This belief is the background to one of the most famous quotations in economics: John Maynard Keynes's declaration, "In the long run we are all dead." We explain the context in which he made this remark in For Inquiring Minds on page 662.

F O R   I N Q U I R I N G   M I N D S

KEYNES AND THE LONG RUN

The British economist Sir John Maynard Keynes (1883–1946), probably more than any other single economist, created the modern field of macroeconomics. We'll look at his role, and the controversies that still swirl around some aspects of his thought, in Chapter 34. But for now let's just look at his most famous quote.

In 1923 Keynes published *A Tract on Monetary Reform,* a small book on the economic problems of Europe after World War I. In it he decried the tendency of many of his colleagues to focus on how things work out in the long run—as in the long-run macroeconomic equilibrium we have just analyzed—while ignoring the often very painful and possibly disastrous things that can happen along the way. Here's a fuller version of the quote:

> This *long run* is a misleading guide to current affairs. *In the long run* we are all dead. Economists set themselves too easy, too useless a task if in tempestuous seasons they can only tell us that when the storm is long past the sea is flat again.

Economists usually interpret Keynes as having recommended that governments not wait for the economy to correct itself. Instead, it is argued by many economists, but not all, that the government should use monetary and fiscal policy to get the economy back to potential output in the aftermath of a shift of the aggregate demand curve. This is the rationale for an active stabilization policy, which we defined in Chapter 23 as the use of government policy to reduce the severity of recessions and rein in excessively strong expansions.

Can stabilization policy improve the economy's performance? If we reexamine Figure 27-4, the answer certainly appears to be yes. Under active stabilization policy, the U.S. economy returned to potential output in 1996 after an approximately six-year recessionary gap. Likewise, in 2001 it also returned to potential output after an approximately four-year inflationary gap. These periods are much shorter than the decade or more that economists believe it would take for the economy to self-correct in the absence of active stabilization policy. However, as we'll see shortly, the ability to improve the economy's performance is not always guaranteed. It depends on the kinds of shocks the economy faces.

Policy in the Face of Demand Shocks

Imagine that the economy experiences a negative demand shock, like the one shown in Figure 27-15. As we've discussed in this chapter, monetary and fiscal policy shift the aggregate demand curve. If policy makers react quickly to the fall in aggregate demand, they can use monetary or fiscal policy to shift the aggregate demand curve back to the right. And if policy were able to perfectly anticipate shifts of the aggregate demand curve, it could short-circuit the whole process shown in Figure 27-15. Instead of going through a period of low aggregate output and falling prices, the government could manage the economy so that it would stay at E_1.

Why might a policy that short-circuits the adjustment shown in Figure 27-15, and maintains the economy at its original equilibrium, be desirable? For two reasons. First, the temporary fall in aggregate output that would happen without policy intervention is a bad thing, particularly because such a decline is associated with high unemployment. Second, as we explained briefly in Chapter 23 and will explain at greater length in Chapter 33, *price stability* is generally regarded as a desirable goal. So preventing deflation—a fall in the aggregate price level—is a good thing.

Does this mean that policy makers should always act to offset declines in aggregate demand? Not necessarily. Some policy measures to increase aggregate demand, especially those that increase budget deficits, may have long-term costs in terms of lower long-run growth, such as the crowding out of private investment spending. Furthermore, in the real world policy makers aren't perfectly informed, and the effects of their policies aren't perfectly predictable. This creates the danger that stabilization policy will do more harm than good; that is, that attempts to stabilize the economy may end up creating more instability. We'll describe the long-running debate over macroeconomic policy in Chapter 34. Despite these qualifications, most economists believe that a good case can be made for using macroeconomic policy to offset major negative shocks to the *AD* curve.

Should policy makers also try to offset positive shocks to aggregate demand? It may not seem obvious that they should. After all, even though inflation may be a bad thing, aren't more output and lower unemployment a good thing? Not necessarily. As we'll see in Chapter 33, most economists now believe that any short-run gains from an inflationary gap must be paid back later. So policy makers today usually try to offset positive as well as negative demand shocks. We can see evidence of this in panel (a) of Figure 27-4. For reasons we'll explain in Chapter 34, attempts to eliminate recessionary gaps and inflationary gaps usually rely on monetary rather than fiscal policy. During the recessionary gap of the early 1990s the Federal Reserve cut interest rates to stimulate consumer and investment spending. And it raised interest rates during the inflationary gap of the late 1990s to generate the opposite effect.

But how should macroeconomic policy respond to supply shocks?

Responding to Supply Shocks

We've now come full circle to the story that began this chapter. We can now explain why the stagflationary recessions of the 1970s posed such a policy puzzle.

Back in panel (a) of Figure 27-12 we showed the effects of a negative supply shock: in the short run such a shock leads to lower aggregate output but a higher aggregate price level. As we've noted, policy makers can respond to a negative *demand* shock by using monetary and fiscal policy to return aggregate demand to its original level. But what can or should they do about a negative *supply* shock?

In contrast to the aggregate demand curve, there are no easy policies that shift the short-run aggregate supply curve. That is, there is no government policy that can easily affect producers' profitability and so compensate for shifts of the short-run aggregate supply curve. So the policy response to a negative supply shock cannot be simply to try to push the curve that shifted back to its original position.

And if you consider using monetary or fiscal policy to shift the aggregate demand curve in response to a supply shock, the right response isn't obvious. Two bad things are happening simultaneously: a fall in aggregate output *and* a rise in the aggregate price level. Any policy that shifts the aggregate demand curve helps one problem only by making the other worse. If the government acts to increase aggregate demand, it reduces the decline in output but causes more inflation. If it acts to reduce aggregate demand, it curbs inflation but causes a further decline in output.

It's a nasty trade-off. In the end, as we'll see in Chapter 34, the United States and other economically advanced nations suffering from the supply shocks of the 1970s chose to stabilize prices. But being an economic policy maker in the 1970s meant facing even harder choices than usual.

economics in action

The End of the Great Depression

In 1939, a full decade after the 1929 stock market crash, the U.S. economy remained deeply depressed, with 17% of the labor force unemployed. But then the economy began a rapid recovery, growing an amazing 12% per year until 1944. By 1943 the unemployment rate had fallen below 2%.

Library of Congress, Washington, DC

A spectacular rise in government spending on arms during World War II spurred women to enter the workforce in droves and was the catalyst that ended the Great Depression.

What caused this turnaround? The answer, without question, was the huge increase in aggregate demand caused by World War II.

Although World War II began in September 1939, the United States didn't become a combatant until the attack on Pearl Harbor in December 1941. But the war boosted aggregate demand before the United States became involved in the fighting. A U.S. military buildup began as soon as the risk of war was apparent. In addition, Britain began buying large amounts of U.S. military equipment and other goods during 1940, boosting U.S. exports. And once the United States was directly involved, government spending on arms increased at a spectacular rate.

Did the behavior of prices match the predictions of the *AS–AD* model? Yes. At the height of the war, many goods were subject to price controls and rationing. Still, the aggregate price level as measured by the GDP deflator rose 30% during the war years and shot up further after the war as controls were removed. ∎

< < < < < < < < < < < < < < < < < <

>>CHECK YOUR UNDERSTANDING 27-5

1. Suppose someone says, "Expansionary monetary or fiscal policy does nothing but temporarily overstimulate the economy—you get a brief high, but then you have the pain of inflation."
   a. Explain what this means in terms of the *AS–AD* model.
   b. Is this a valid argument against stabilization policy? Why or why not?

Solutions appear at back of book.

• A LOOK AHEAD •

The *AS-AD* model is a powerful tool for understanding both economic fluctuations and the ways economic policy can sometimes fight adverse shocks. But in order to present the basic idea, we've been somewhat sketchy about the details.

In the next three chapters we'll put some flesh on these economic bones. We'll begin with a more detailed analysis of the factors that determine aggregate demand, then move on to how fiscal and monetary policy actually work.

SUMMARY

1. The **aggregate supply curve** shows the relationship between the aggregate price level and the quantity of aggregate output supplied.

2. The **short-run aggregate supply curve** is upward-sloping because **nominal wages** are sticky in the short run: a higher aggregate price level leads to higher profit per unit output and increased aggregate output in the short run. Changes in commodity prices, nominal wages, and productivity lead to changes in producers' profits and shift the short-run aggregate supply curve.

3. In the long run, all prices, including nominal wages, are flexible and the economy produces at its **potential output.** If actual aggregate output exceeds potential output, nominal wages will eventually rise in response to low unemployment and aggregate output will fall. If potential output exceeds actual aggregate output, nominal wages will eventually fall in response to high unemployment and aggregate output will rise. So the **long-run aggregate supply curve** is vertical at potential output.

4. The **aggregate demand curve** shows the relationship between the aggregate price level and the quantity of aggregate output demanded. It is downward-sloping for two reasons. The first is the **wealth effect of a change in the aggregate price level**—a higher aggregate price level reduces the purchasing power of households' wealth and reduces consumer spending. The second is the **interest rate effect of a change in the aggregate price level**—a higher aggregate price level reduces the purchasing power of households' and firms' money holdings, leading to a rise in interest rates and a fall in investment spending and consumer spending. The aggregate demand curve shifts because of changes in expectations, changes in wealth not due to changes in the aggregate price level, and changes in the stock of physical capital. Policy makers can use fiscal policy and monetary policy to shift the aggregate demand curve.

5. An **autonomous change in aggregate spending** leads to a chain reaction in which the total change in real GDP is equal to the **multiplier** times the initial change in aggregate spending. The size of the multiplier, $1/(1 - MPC)$, depends on the **marginal propensity to consume,** MPC, the fraction of an additional dollar of disposable income spent on consumption. The larger the MPC, the larger the multiplier and the larger the change in real GDP for any given autonomous change in aggregate spending. The **marginal propensity to save,** MPS, is equal to $1 - MPC$.

6. In the *AS–AD* **model,** the intersection of the short-run aggregate supply curve and the aggregate demand curve is the point of **short-run macroeconomic equilibrium.** It determines the **short-run equilibrium aggregate price level** and the level of **short-run equilibrium aggregate output.**

7. Economic fluctuations occur because of a shift of the short-run aggregate supply curve (a *supply shock*) or the aggregate demand curve (a *demand shock*). A **supply shock** causes the aggregate price level and aggregate output to move in opposite directions as the economy moves along the aggregate demand curve . A particularly nasty occurrence is **stagflation**—inflation and falling aggregate output—which is caused by a negative supply shock. A **demand shock** causes them to move in the same direction as the economy moves along the short-run aggregate supply curve.

8. Demand shocks have only short-run effects on aggregate output because the economy is **self-correcting** in the long run. In a **recessionary gap,** an eventual fall in nominal wages moves the economy to **long-run macroeconomic equilibrium,** where aggregate output is equal to potential output. In an **inflationary gap,** an eventual rise in nominal wages moves the economy to long-run macroeconomic equilibrium.

9. The high cost—in terms of unemployment—of a recessionary gap and the future adverse consequences of an inflationary gap lead many economists to advocate active stabilization policy: using fiscal or monetary policy to offset demand shocks. Fiscal policy affects aggregate demand directly through government purchases and indirectly through changes in taxes or government transfers that affect consumer spending. Monetary policy affects aggregate demand indirectly through changes in the interest rate that affect consumer and investment spending. There can be drawbacks, however, because such policies may contribute to a long-term rise in the budget deficit and crowding out of private investment, leading to lower long-run growth. Also, erroneous predictions can increase economic instability.

10. Negative supply shocks pose a policy dilemma: a policy that counteracts the fall in aggregate output by increasing aggregate demand will lead to higher inflation, but a policy that counteracts inflation by reducing aggregate demand will deepen the output slump.

KEY TERMS

Aggregate supply curve, p. 637
Nominal wage, p. 638
Short-run aggregate supply curve,
    p. 638
Long-run aggregate supply curve, p. 642
Potential output, p. 643
Aggregate demand curve, p. 646
Wealth effect of a change in the aggregate
    price level, p. 647
Interest rate effect of a change in the
    aggregate price level, p. 648

Marginal propensity to consume (MPC),
    p. 651
Marginal propensity to save (MPS), p. 652
Autonomous change in aggregate spending,
    p. 654
Multiplier, p. 654
AS–AD model, p. 655
Short-run macroeconomic equilibrium,
    p. 655
Short-run equilibrium aggregate price level,
    p. 655

Short-run equilibrium aggregate output,
    p. 655
Supply shock, p. 656
Stagflation, p. 657
Demand shock, p. 657
Long-run macroeconomic equilibrium,
    p. 658
Recessionary gap, p. 659
Inflationary gap, p. 660
Self-correcting, p. 660

PROBLEMS

1. Your study partner is confused by the upward-sloping short-run aggregate supply curve and the vertical long-run aggregate supply curve. How would you explain why these slopes differ?

2. Suppose that in Wageland all workers sign annual wage contracts each year on January 1. No matter what happens to prices of final goods and services during the year, all workers earn the wage specified in their annual contract. This year, prices of final goods and services fall unexpectedly after the contracts are signed. Answer the following questions using a diagram and assume that the economy starts at potential output.

   a. In the short run, how will the quantity of aggregate output supplied respond to the fall in prices?

   b. What will happen when firms and workers renegotiate their wages?

3. In each of the following cases, in the short run, determine whether the events cause a shift of a curve or a movement along a curve. Determine which curve is involved and the direction of the change.

   a. As a result of an increase in the value of the dollar in relation to other currencies, American producers now pay less in dollar terms for foreign steel, a major commodity used in production.

   b. An increase in the quantity of money by the Federal Reserve increases the quantity of money that people and firms wish to lend, lowering interest rates.

   c. Greater union activity leads to higher nominal wages.

   d. A fall in the aggregate price level increases the purchasing power of households' money holdings. As a result, they borrow less and lend more.

4. A fall in the value of the dollar against other currencies makes U.S. final goods and services cheaper to foreigners even though the U.S. aggregate price level stays the same. As a result, foreigners demand more American aggregate output. Your study partner says that this represents a movement down the aggregate demand curve because foreigners are demanding more in response to a lower price. You, however, insist that this represents a rightward shift of the aggregate demand curve. Who is right? Explain.

5. Suppose that local, state, and federal governments were obliged to cut government purchases whenever consumer spending falls. Then suppose that consumer spending falls due to a fall in the stock market. Draw a diagram and explain the full effect of the fall in the stock market on the aggregate demand curve and on the economy. How is this similar to the experience of stagflation in the 1970s?

6. Due to an increase in consumer wealth, there is a $40 billion autonomous increase in consumer spending in the economies of Westlandia and Eastlandia. Assuming that the aggregate price level is constant, the interest rate is fixed in both countries, and there are no taxes and no foreign trade, complete the accompanying tables to show the various rounds of increased spending that will occur in both economies if the marginal propensity to consume is 0.5 in Westlandia and 0.75 in Eastlandia. What do your results indicate about the relationship between the size of the marginal propensity to consume and the multiplier?

Westlandia

Rounds	Incremental change in GDP		Total change in GDP
1	$\Delta C = \$40$ billion		?
2	$MPC \times \Delta C =$	?	?
3	$MPC \times MPC \times \Delta C =$	?	?
4	$MPC \times MPC \times MPC \times \Delta C =$	?	?
. . .		. . .	. . .
Total change in GDP	$(1/(1 - MPC)) \times \Delta C =$		?

Eastlandia

Rounds	Incremental change in GDP	Total change in GDP
1	$\Delta C = \$40$ billion	?
2	$MPC \times \Delta C =$?	?
3	$MPC \times MPC \times \Delta C =$?	?
4	$MPC \times MPC \times MPC \times \Delta C =$?	?
. . .	. . . . . .	
Total change in GDP	$(1/(1 - MPC)) \times \Delta C =$	?

7. Assuming that the aggregate price level is constant, the interest rate is fixed, and there are no taxes and no foreign trade, how much will the aggregate demand curve shift and in what direction if the following events occur?

   a. An autonomous increase in consumer spending of $25 billion; the marginal propensity to consume is 2/3.

   b. Firms reduce investment spending by $40 billion; the marginal propensity to consume is 0.8.

   c. The government increases its purchases of military equipment by $60 billion; the marginal propensity to consume is 0.6.

8. The economy is at point A in the accompanying diagram. Suppose that the aggregate price level rises from P_1 to P_2. How will aggregate supply adjust in the short run and in the long run to the increase in the aggregate price level?

9. Suppose that all households hold all their wealth in assets that automatically rise in value when the aggregate price level rises (an example of this is what is called an "inflation-indexed bond"—a bond whose interest rate, among other things, changes one-for-one with the inflation rate). What happens to the wealth effect of a change in the aggregate price level as a result of this allocation of assets? What happens to the slope of the aggregate demand curve? Will it still slope downward? Explain.

10. Suppose that the economy is currently at potential output. Also suppose that you are an economic policy maker and that a college economics student asks you to rank, if possible, your most preferred to least preferred type of shock: positive demand shock, negative demand shock, positive supply shock, negative supply shock. How would you rank them and why?

11. Explain whether the following government policies affect the aggregate demand curve or the short-run aggregate supply curve and how.

    a. The government reduces the minimum nominal wage.

    b. The government increases Temporary Assistance to Needy Families (TANF) payments, government transfers to families with dependent children.

    c. To reduce the budget deficit, the government announces that households will pay much higher taxes beginning next year.

    d. The government reduces military spending.

12. In Wageland, all workers sign an annual wage contract each year on January 1. In late January, a new computer operating system is introduced that increases labor productivity dramatically. Explain how Wageland will move from one short-run macroeconomic equilibrium to another. Illustrate with a diagram.

13. Using aggregate demand, short-run aggregate supply, and long-run aggregate supply curves, explain the process by which each of the following economic events will move the economy from one long-run macroeconomic equilibrium to another. Illustrate with diagrams. In each case, what are the short-run and long-run effects on the aggregate price level and aggregate output?

    a. There is a decrease in households' wealth due to a decline in the stock market.

    b. The government lowers taxes, leaving households with more disposable income, with no corresponding reduction in government purchases.

14. Using aggregate demand, short-run aggregate supply, and long-run aggregate supply curves, explain the process by which each of the following government policies will move the economy from one long-run macroeconomic equilibrium to another. Illustrate with diagrams. In each case, what are the short-run and long-run effects on the aggregate price level and aggregate output?

    a. There is an increase in taxes on households.

    b. There is an increase in the quantity of money.

    c. There is an increase in government purchases.

15. The economy is in short-run macroeconomic equilibrium at point E_1 in the accompanying diagram.

a. Is the economy facing an inflationary or a recessionary gap?

b. What policies can the government implement that might bring the economy back to long-run macroeconomic equilibrium? Illustrate with a diagram.

c. If the government did not intervene to close this gap, would the economy return to long-run macroeconomic equilibrium? Explain and illustrate with a diagram.

d. What are the advantages and disadvantages of the government's implementing policies to close the gap?

16. In the accompanying diagram, the economy is in long-run macroeconomic equilibrium at point E_1 when an oil shock shifts the short-run aggregate supply curve to $SRAS_2$.

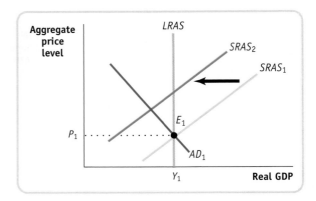

a. How do the aggregate price level and aggregate output change in the short run as a result of the oil shock? What is this phenomenon known as?

b. What fiscal or monetary policies can the government use to address the effects of the negative supply shock? Use a diagram that shows the effect of policies chosen to address the change in real GDP. Use another diagram to show the effect of policies chosen to address the change in the aggregate price level.

c. Why do negative supply shocks present a dilemma for government policy makers?

17. The late 1990s in the United States were characterized by substantial economic growth with low inflation; that is, real GDP increased with little, if any, increase in the aggregate price level. Explain this experience using aggregate demand and aggregate supply curves. Illustrate with a diagram.

28

>>Income and Expenditure

BE A PATRIOT AND SPEND

AFTER THE TERRORIST ATTACKS ON September 11, 2001, many leading figures in American life made speeches urging the shocked nation to show fortitude—and keep buying consumer goods. "Do your business around the country. Fly and enjoy America's great destination spots," urged President Bush. "Go shopping," said former president Clinton.

Such words were a far cry from British prime minister Winston Churchill's famous 1940 declaration, in the face of an imminent Nazi invasion of the United Kingdom, that he had nothing to offer but "blood, toil, tears, and sweat." But there was a reason politicians of both parties called for spending, not sacrifice. The economy was already in recession, mainly because of a 14% drop in real investment spending. A plunge in consumer spending would have greatly deepened the recession. Fortunately, that didn't happen: American consumers bought less of some goods and services, such as air travel, but bought more of others.

As we explained in Chapter 27, the source of most, but not all, recessions since World War II has been negative demand shocks, leftward shifts of the aggregate demand curve. Over the course of this and the next three chapters, we'll continue to focus on the short-run behavior of the economy, looking in detail at the factors that cause such shifts of the aggregate demand curve. In this chapter, we begin by looking at the determinants of consumer

After 9/11, Americans traveled less but shopped more for goods that they could enjoy at home like barbecue grills and swimming pools.

What you will learn in this chapter:

➤ The meaning of the **aggregate consumption function,** which shows how current disposable income affects consumer spending

➤ How expected future income and aggregate wealth affect consumer spending

➤ The determinants of investment spending, and the distinction between **planned investment spending** and **unplanned inventory investment**

➤ How the inventory adjustment process moves the economy to a new equilibrium after a demand shock

➤ Why investment spending is considered a leading indicator of the future state of the economy

669

spending and investment spending. We'll examine in further detail the multiplier process discussed in Chapter 27, the process by which slumps or booms in aggregate spending are amplified throughout the economy over a period of time. We'll see how changes in investment spending are crucial to the multistage multiplier process that eventually moves the economy to a new equilibrium. Through this analysis we'll come to understand why investment spending and inventory levels are considered to be key indicators of the future state of the economy.

Consumer Spending

Should you splurge on a restaurant meal or save money by eating at home? Should you buy a new car and, if so, how expensive a model? Should you redo that bathroom or live with it for another year? In the real world, households are constantly confronted with such choices—not just about the consumption mix but about how much to spend in total. These choices, in turn, have a powerful effect on the economy: consumer spending normally accounts for two-thirds of total spending on final goods and services. So changes in consumer spending can produce significant shifts of the aggregate demand curve. And as we know from Chapter 27, the position of the aggregate demand curve, along with the position of the short-run aggregate supply curve, determines the economy's aggregate output and aggregate price level in the short run.

But what determines how much consumers spend? In Chapter 27, we learned that consumer spending is affected by wealth and by the interest rate. Here, we'll focus on two additional significant factors, current disposable income and expected future disposable income, in addition to exploring further the effect of wealth.

Current Disposable Income and Consumer Spending

The most important factor affecting a family's consumer spending is its current disposable income—income after taxes are paid and government transfers are received. It's obvious from daily life that people with high disposable incomes on average drive more expensive cars, live in more expensive houses, and spend more on meals and clothing than people with lower disposable incomes. And the relationship between current disposable income and spending is clear in the data.

The Bureau of Labor Statistics (BLS) collects annual data on family income and spending. Families are grouped by levels of before-tax income, and after-tax income for each group is also reported. Since the income figures include transfers from the government, what the BLS calls a household's after-tax income is equivalent to its current disposable income.

Figure 28-1 is a scatter diagram illustrating the relationship between household current disposable income and household consumer spending for American households by income group in 2003. For example, point A shows that among the group with an annual income of $40,000 to $49,999, average household current disposable income was $42,842 and average household consumer spending was $39,757 in 2003. It's clear that households with higher current disposable income had higher consumer spending.

It's very useful to represent the relationship between an individual household's current disposable income and its consumer spending with an equation. The **consumption function** is an equation showing how an individual household's consumer spending varies with the household's current disposable income. The simplest version of a consumption function is a linear equation:

(28-1) $c = a + MPC \times yd$

where lowercase letters indicate variables measured for an individual household.

The **consumption function** is an equation showing how an individual household's consumer spending varies with the household's current disposable income.

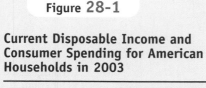

Figure 28-1

Current Disposable Income and Consumer Spending for American Households in 2003

For each income group of households, average current disposable income in 2003 is plotted versus average consumer spending in 2003. For example, point A shows that among the group with an annual income of $40,000 to $49,999, a household's average current disposable income was $42,842 and average household consumer spending was $39,757. The data clearly show a positive relationship between current disposable income and consumer spending: families with higher current disposable income have higher consumer spending.

Source: Bureau of Labor Statistics.

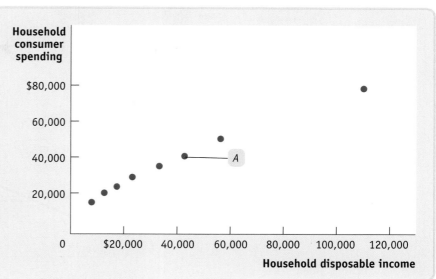

In this equation, c is individual household consumer spending and yd is individual household current disposable income. As we learned in Chapter 27, MPC, the marginal propensity to consume, is the amount by which consumer spending rises if current disposable income rises by $1. Finally, a is a constant term—individual household *autonomous consumer spending,* the amount of spending a household would do if it had zero disposable income. We assume that a is greater than zero because a household with zero disposable income is able to fund some consumption by borrowing or using its savings.

Recall Equation 27-3, which expressed MPC as the ratio of a change in consumer spending to the change in current disposable income. We've rewritten it for an individual household as Equation 28-2:

(28-2) $MPC = \Delta c / \Delta yd$

Multiplying both sides of Equation 28-2 by Δyd, we get:

(28-3) $MPC \times \Delta yd = \Delta c$

Equation 28-3 tells us that when yd goes up by $1, c goes up by $MPC \times$ $1. Notice, by the way, that we're using y for income. That's standard practice in macroeconomics, even though *income* isn't actually spelled "yncome." The reason is that I is reserved for investment spending.

Figure 28-2 on page 672 shows what Equation 28-1 looks like graphically, plotting yd on the horizontal axis and c on the vertical axis. Individual household autonomous consumer spending, a, is the value of c when yd is zero—it is the vertical *intercept* of the consumption function, cf. MPC is the *slope* of the line, measured by rise over run. If current disposable income rises by Δyd, household consumer spending, c, rises by Δc. Since MPC is defined as $\Delta c / \Delta yd$, the slope of the consumption function is:

(28-4) Slope of consumption function
   = Rise over run
   = $\Delta c / \Delta yd$
   = MPC

In reality, actual data never fit Equation 28-1 perfectly, but the fit can be pretty good. Figure 28-3 on page 672 shows the data from Figure 28-1 again, together with a line drawn to fit the data as closely as possible. According to the data on households' consumer spending and current disposable income, the best estimate of a is $14,184 and of MPC is 0.597. So the consumption function fitted to the data is:

$$c = \$14,184 + 0.597 \times yd$$

Figure 28-2

The Consumption Function

The consumption function relates a household's current disposable income to its consumer spending. The vertical intercept, *a,* is individual household autonomous consumer spending: the amount of a household's consumer spending if its current disposable income is zero. The slope of the consumption function line, *cf,* is the marginal propensity to consume, or *MPC:* of every additional $1 of current disposable income, *MPC* × $1 is spent.

That is, the data suggest a marginal propensity to consume of approximately 0.6. This implies that the marginal propensity to save (*MPS*)—the amount of an additional $1 of disposable income that is saved—is approximately 0.4.

It's important to realize that Figure 28-3 shows a *microeconomic* relationship between the current disposable income of individual families and their spending on goods and services. However, macroeconomists assume that a similar relationship holds *for the economy as a whole*: that there is a relationship, called the **aggregate consumption function,** between aggregate current disposable income and aggregate consumer spending. So we'll assume that it has the same form as the household-level consumption function: $C = A + MPC \times YD$. Here, *C* is aggregate consumer spending (called just "consumer spending"); *YD* is aggregate current disposable income (called just "disposable income"); and *A* is aggregate autonomous consumer spending, the amount of consumer spending when *YD* equals zero. This is the relationship represented in Figure 28-4 by *CF*, analogous to *cf* in Figure 28-3.

The **aggregate consumption function** is the relationship for the economy as a whole between aggregate current disposable income and aggregate consumer spending.

Figure 28-3

A Consumption Function Fitted to Data

The data from Figure 28-1 are reproduced here, along with a line drawn to fit the data as closely as possible. For American households in 2003, the best estimate of the average household's autonomous consumer spending, *a,* is $14,184 and the best estimate of *MPC* is 0.597, or approximately 0.6.

Source: Bureau of Labor Statistics.

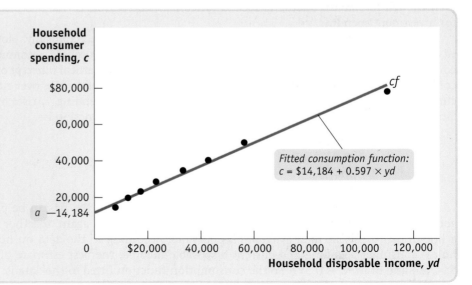

Shifts of the Aggregate Consumption Function

The aggregate consumption function shows the relationship between disposable income and consumer spending for the economy as a whole, other things equal. When things other than disposable income change, the aggregate consumption function shifts. There are two principal causes of shifts of the aggregate consumption function: changes in expected future disposable income and changes in aggregate wealth.

Changes in Expected Future Disposable Income Suppose you land a really good, well-paying job on graduating from college—but the job, and the paychecks, won't start until September. So your disposable income hasn't risen yet. Even so, it's likely that you will start spending more on final goods and services right away—maybe buying nicer work clothes than you originally planned—because you know that the income is coming.

Conversely, suppose you have a good job but learn that the company is planning to downsize your division, raising the possibility that you may lose your job and have to take a lower-paying one somewhere else. Even though your disposable income hasn't gone down yet, you might well cut back on spending even while still employed, to save for a rainy day.

Both of these examples show how expectations about future disposable income can affect consumer spending. The two panels of Figure 28-4, which plot disposable income against consumer spending, show how changes in expected future disposable income affect the aggregate consumption function. In both panels, CF_1 is the initial aggregate consumption function. Panel (a) shows the effect of good news: information that leads consumers to expect higher disposable income in the future than they

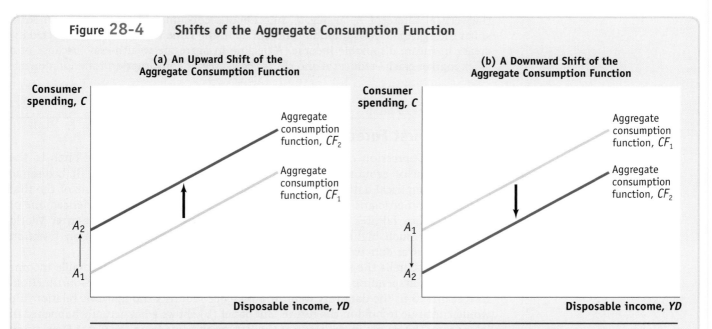

Figure 28-4 **Shifts of the Aggregate Consumption Function**

Panel (a) illustrates the effect of an increase in expected future disposable income. Consumers will spend more at every given level of current disposable income, YD. As a result, the initial aggregate consumption function CF_1, with aggregate autonomous consumer spending A_1, shifts up to a new position at CF_2 and aggregate autonomous consumer spending A_2. An increase in aggregate wealth will also shift the aggregate consumption function up. Panel (b), in contrast, illustrates the effect of a reduction in expected future disposable income. Consumers will spend less at every given level of current disposable income, YD. Consequently, the initial aggregate consumption function CF_1, with aggregate autonomous consumer spending A_1, shifts down to a new position at CF_2 and aggregate autonomous consumer spending A_2. A reduction in aggregate wealth will have the same effect.

did before. Consumers will now spend more at any given level of current disposable income YD, corresponding to an increase in A, aggregate autonomous consumer spending, from A_1 to A_2. The effect is to shift the aggregate consumption function up, from CF_1 to CF_2. Panel (b) shows the effect of bad news: information that leads consumers to expect lower disposable income in the future than they did before. Consumers will now spend less at any given level of current disposable income YD, corresponding to a fall in A from A_1 to A_2. The effect is to shift the aggregate consumption function down, from CF_1 to CF_2.

Changes in Aggregate Wealth As we discussed in Chapter 27, a household's wealth influences how much of its disposable income it spends. This observation is part of an economic model of how consumers make choices about spending versus saving, called the *life-cycle hypothesis*. According to this hypothesis, consumers plan their spending over a lifetime, not just in response to their current disposable income. As a result, people try to *smooth* their consumption over their lifetimes—they save some of their current disposable income during their years of peak earnings (typically occurring during a worker's 40s and 50s) and live off the wealth they have accumulated while working during their retirement. We won't go into the details of this hypothesis but will simply point out that it implies an important role for wealth in determining consumer spending. For example, a middle-aged couple who have accumulated a lot of wealth—who have paid off the mortgage on their house and already own plenty of stocks and bonds—will, other things equal, spend more on goods and services than a couple who have the same current disposable income but still need to save for their retirement.

Because wealth affects household consumer spending, changes in wealth across the economy can shift the aggregate consumption function. A rise in aggregate wealth—say, because of rising housing values, which make homeowners wealthier—increases the vertical intercept A, aggregate autonomous consumer spending. This, in turn, shifts the aggregate consumption function up in the same way as does an expected increase in future disposable income. A decline in aggregate wealth—say, because of a stock market crash—reduces A and shifts the aggregate consumption function down.

economics in action

Famous First Forecasting Failures

The Great Depression created modern macroeconomics. It also gave birth to the modern field of econometrics—the use of statistical techniques to fit economic models to empirical data. The aggregate consumption function was one of the first things econometricians studied. And, sure enough, they quickly experienced one of the first major failures of economic forecasting: consumer spending after World War II was much higher than estimates of the aggregate consumption function based on prewar data would have predicted.

Figure 28-5 tells the story. Panel (a) shows aggregate data on disposable income and consumer spending from 1929 to 1941. A simple linear consumption function, CF_1, seems to fit the data very well. And many economists thought this relationship would continue to hold in the future. But panel (b) shows what actually happened in later years. The points in the circle at the left are the data from the Great Depression shown in panel (a). The points in the circle at the right are data from 1946 to 1960. (Data from 1942 to 1945 aren't included because rationing during World War II prevented consumers from spending normally.) The solid line in the figure, CF_1, is the consumption function fitted to 1929–1941 data. As you can see, post–World War II consumer spending was much higher than the relationship from the Depression years would have predicted. For example, in 1960 consumer spending was 13.5% higher than the level predicted by CF_1.

Why was extrapolating from the earlier relationship so misleading? The answer is that from 1946 onward both expected future disposable income and aggregate

Figure 28-5 Changes in the Aggregate Consumption Function Over Time

(a) A Simple Aggregate Consumption Function Fits Data from the Great Depression Years Quite Well...

$C = \$175 + 0.7 \times YD$

CF_1

Consumer spending, *C*

Disposable income, *YD*

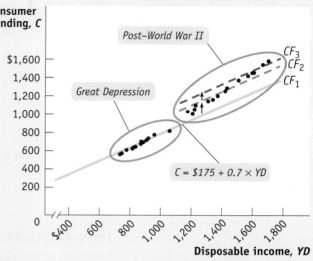

(b) ...but Greatly Underestimates Consumer Spending After the War.

Post–World War II

Great Depression

CF_3
CF_2
CF_1

$C = \$175 + 0.7 \times YD$

Consumer spending, *C*

Disposable income, *YD*

Panel (a) is a scatter diagram of observations of American households' annual disposable income measured in billions of 2000 dollars versus annual consumer spending, also in billions of 2000 dollars, during the period 1929–1941. A simple consumption function, CF_1 of the form $C = \$175 + 0.7 \times YD$, fits the data quite well and suggests that during the Great Depression the marginal propensity to consume was 0.7.

Panel (b) contains the same data as panel (a) and the same consumption function, as well as observations from the post–World War II period. CF_1 lies below the postwar observations and does not fit the data from those years well. In fact, the consumption function shifted up over time, as shown in the figure by the dashed lines, CF_2 and CF_3. **>web...**
Source: Commerce Department.

wealth were steadily rising. Consumers grew increasingly confident that the Great Depression wouldn't reemerge and that the post–World War II economic boom would continue. At the same time, wealth was steadily increasing. As indicated by the dashed lines in panel (b), CF_2 and CF_3, the increases in expected future disposable income and in aggregate wealth shifted the aggregate consumption function up a number of times.

In macroeconomics, failure—whether of economic policy or of economic prediction—often leads to intellectual progress. The embarrassing failure of early estimates of the aggregate consumption function to predict post–World War II consumer spending led to important progress in our understanding of consumer behavior. ∎

> >

>>CHECK YOUR UNDERSTANDING 28-1

1. Suppose the economy consists of three people: Angelina, Felicia, and Marina. The table shows how their consumer spending varies as their current disposable income rises by $10,000.
   a. Derive each individual person's consumption function, where *MPC* is calculated for a $10,000 change in current disposable income.
   b. Derive the aggregate consumption function.

2. Suppose that problems in the capital markets make consumers unable to borrow or save.
   What implication does this have for the effects of expected future disposable income on consumer spending?

Current disposable income	Consumer spending		
	Angelina	Felicia	Marina
$0	$8,000	$6,500	$7,250
10,000	12,000	14,500	14,250

Solutions appear at back of book.

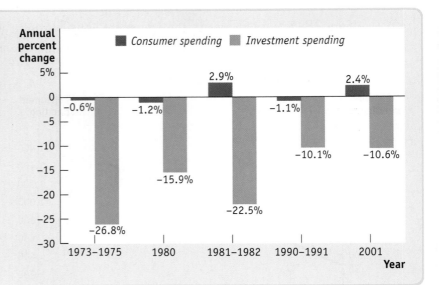

Figure 28-6

Fluctuations in Investment Spending and Consumer Spending

The bars illustrate the annual percent change in investment spending and consumer spending during the last five recessions. As the lengths of the bars show, swings in investment spending were much larger in percentage terms than those in consumer spending. This pattern has led economists to believe that recessions typically originate as a slump in investment spending.

Investment Spending

A major reason economists were so concerned about a possible fall in consumer spending after 9/11 was that there was no clear alternative source of aggregate demand that would offset a fall in consumer spending and keep the economy from plunging. At the time of the attacks, investment spending was in the midst of an 18-month slump and showed few signs of bouncing back. An increase in government spending would take too long to legislate and implement. And there was no feasible way to stimulate foreigners' demand for American goods and services.

Most economists viewed the ongoing slump in investment spending as the cause of the recession that had begun six months earlier in March 2001. As we know from the *AS-AD* model in Chapter 27, a fall in investment spending shifts the aggregate demand curve leftward, leading to a recession. In fact, most recessions originate as a fall in investment spending. Figure 28-6 illustrates this point; it shows the annual percent change of investment spending and consumer spending in the United States, both measured in 2000 dollars, during the last five recessions. As you can see, swings in investment spending are much more dramatic than those in consumer spending. In addition, due to the multiplier process introduced in Chapter 27, economists believe that declines in consumer spending are usually the result of a process that begins with a slump in investment spending. We'll examine very soon how a slump in investment spending generates a fall in consumer spending through the multiplier process. Before we do that, however, let's analyze the factors that determine investment spending, which are somewhat different from those that determine consumer spending. The most important ones are the interest rate and expected future real GDP. We'll also revisit a fact that we noted in For Inquiring Minds on page 616 in Chapter 26: the level of investment spending businesses *actually* carry out is sometimes not the same as the level they had *planned* to undertake.

The Interest Rate and Investment Spending

Planned investment spending is the investment spending that businesses intend to undertake during a given period.

Planned investment spending is the investment spending that firms intend to undertake during a given period, in contrast to investment spending that occurs but is *unplanned*. Planned investment spending depends on three principal factors: the interest rate, the expected future level of real GDP, and the current level of production capacity. First, we'll analyze the effect of the interest rate.

Let's begin by recalling the loanable funds model of Chapter 26, which showed how those with funds to lend are matched with those who wish to borrow. Potential lenders are households that are deciding whether to save some of their disposable income and lend it out to earn interest, or to spend it on consumption. The supply curve of loanable funds is upward-sloping: as the interest rate rises, households are more willing to forgo consumption and lend their funds out. On the other side are potential borrowers, firms with investment spending projects. They will choose to borrow in order to fund a project only if the rate of return on the project equals or exceeds the interest rate charged on the loan. Otherwise, the firm would incur a loss. The demand curve for loanable funds is downward-sloping: as the interest rate rises, the number of projects with a rate of return that equals or exceeds the interest rate falls. Equilibrium in the loanable funds market is determined by the intersection of the demand and supply curves for loanable funds: at the equilibrium interest rate, the quantity of loanable funds demanded is equal to the quantity supplied. Investment projects with a rate of return equal to or exceeding the equilibrium interest rate are funded; projects with a rate of return less than the equilibrium interest rate are not.

You might think that the trade-off a firm faces is different if it can fund its investment project with its past profits rather than through borrowing. Past profits used to finance investment spending are called *retained earnings*. But even if a firm pays for investment spending out of retained earnings, the trade-off it must make in deciding whether or not to fund a project remains the same because it must take into account the opportunity cost of its funds. For example, instead of purchasing new equipment, the firm could lend out the funds and earn interest. The forgone interest earned is the opportunity cost of using retained earnings to fund an investment project. So the trade-off the firm faces when comparing a project's rate of return to the market interest rate has not changed when it uses retained earnings rather than borrowed funds.

The upshot is that regardless of whether a firm funds investment spending through borrowing or retained earnings, a rise in the market interest rate makes any given investment project less profitable. (And if it had been unprofitable before, it is even more unprofitable after a rise in the interest rate.) For example, consider a rise in the interest rate caused by a leftward shift of the supply curve of loanable funds—say, due to fear of a banking crisis that leads households to refuse to deposit their savings in banks that then lend the funds to businesses. Some projects that would have been funded under the initial, lower interest rate will not be funded now; their rates of return are now below the now-higher interest rate. Conversely, a fall in the interest rate makes some investment projects that were unprofitable before now profitable at the now lower interest rate. Some projects that had been unfunded before will be funded now.

So planned investment spending—spending on investment projects that firms voluntarily decide whether or not to undertake—is negatively related to the interest rate. Other things equal, a higher interest rate leads to a lower level of planned investment spending.

Expected Future Real GDP, Production Capacity, and Investment Spending

Suppose a firm has enough capacity to continue to produce the amount it is currently selling but doesn't expect its sales to grow in the future. Then it will engage in investment spending only to replace equipment and structures that are worn out or have been rendered obsolete by new technologies. But if, instead, the firm expects its sales to grow rapidly in the future, it will find its existing production capacity insufficient for its future production needs. So the firm will undertake investment spending to meet those needs. This implies that, other things equal, firms will undertake more investment spending when they expect their sales to grow.

Now suppose that the firm currently has considerably more capacity than necessary to meet current production needs. Even if it expects sales to grow, it won't have to undertake investment spending for a while—not until the growth in sales catches up with its excess capacity. This illustrates the fact that, other things equal, the current level of productive capacity has a negative effect on investment spending: other things equal, the higher the current capacity, the lower investment spending is.

If we put together the effects on investment spending of growth in expected future sales and the size of current production capacity, we can see one situation in which we can be reasonably sure that firms will undertake high levels of investment spending: when their sales are growing very rapidly. In that case, even excess production capacity will soon be used up, leading firms to resume investment spending.

What is an indicator of a high level of sales growth? It's the rate of growth of real GDP. A higher growth rate of real GDP results in a higher level of investment spending while a lower growth rate of real GDP leads to lower planned investment spending. This relationship is summarized in a proposition known as the **accelerator principle.** As we explain in the following Economics in Action, the effects of the accelerator principle play an important role in *investment spending slumps,* periods of low investment spending.

Inventories and Unplanned Investment Spending

Most firms maintain **inventories,** stocks of goods held to satisfy future sales. Firms hold inventories so they can quickly satisfy buyers—a consumer can purchase an item off the shelf rather than waiting for it to be manufactured. In addition, businesses often hold inventories of their inputs to be sure they have a steady supply of necessary materials and spare parts. In 2004 the overall value of inventories in the U.S. economy was estimated at $1.7 trillion, about 13% of GDP for that year.

As we explained in Chapter 24, a firm that increases its inventories is engaging in a form of investment spending. Suppose, for example, that the U.S. auto industry produces 800,000 cars per month but sells only 700,000. The remaining 100,000 cars are added to the inventory at auto company warehouses or car dealerships, ready to be sold in the future. **Inventory investment** is the value of the change in total inventories held in the economy during a given period. Unlike other forms of investment spending, inventory investment can actually be negative. If, for example, the auto industry reduces its inventory over the course of a month, we say that it has engaged in negative inventory investment.

To understand inventory investment, think about a manager stocking the canned goods section of a supermarket. The manager tries to keep the store fully stocked so that shoppers can almost always find what they're looking for. But the manager does not want the shelves too heavily stocked because shelf space is limited and products can spoil. Similar considerations apply to many firms and typically lead them to manage their inventories carefully. However, sales fluctuate. And because firms cannot always accurately predict sales, they often find themselves holding more or less inventories than they had intended. These unintended swings in inventories due to unforeseen changes in sales are called **unplanned inventory investment.** They represent investment spending, positive or negative, that occurred but was unplanned.

So in any given period, **actual investment spending** is equal to planned investment spending plus unplanned inventory investment. If we let $I_{Unplanned}$ represent unplanned inventory investment, $I_{Planned}$ represent planned investment spending, and I represent actual investment spending, then the relationship among all three can be represented as:

(28-5) $I = I_{Unplanned} + I_{Planned}$

To see how unplanned inventory investment can occur, let's continue to focus on the auto industry and make the following assumptions. First, let's assume that the industry must determine each month's production volume in advance, before it knows the volume of actual sales. Second, let's assume that it anticipates selling 800,000 cars next month and that it plans neither to add to nor subtract from existing inventories. In that case, it will produce 800,000 cars to match anticipated sales.

Now imagine that next month's actual sales are less than expected, only 700,000 cars. As a result, the value of 100,000 cars will be added to investment spending as unplanned inventory investment.

According to the **accelerator principle**, a higher growth rate of GDP leads to higher planned investment spending, and a lower growth rate of real GDP leads to lower planned investment spending.

Inventories are stocks of goods held to satisfy future sales.

This lot full of cars is inventory awaiting the arrival of eager car buyers.

Inventory investment is the value of the change in total inventories held in the economy during a given period.

Unplanned inventory investment occurs when actual sales are more or less than businesses expected, leading to unplanned changes in inventories.

Actual investment spending is the sum of planned investment spending and unplanned inventory investment.

The auto industry will, of course, eventually adjust to this slowdown in sales and the resulting unplanned inventory investment. It is likely that it will cut next month's production volume in order to reduce inventories. In fact, economists who study macroeconomic variables in an attempt to determine the future path of the economy pay careful attention to changes in inventory levels. Rising inventories typically indicate positive unplanned inventory investment and a slowing economy, as sales are less than had been forecast. Falling inventories typically indicate negative unplanned inventory investment and a growing economy, as sales are greater than forecast. In the next section, we will see how production adjustments in response to fluctuations in sales and inventories ensure that the value of final goods and services actually produced is equal to desired purchases of those final goods and services.

economics in action

A Tale of Two Investment Spending Slumps

At the beginning of the 1980s there was a prolonged slump in investment spending, which played a key role in the two recessions—often treated as a single episode—of 1980 and 1981–1982. At the beginning of the twenty-first century there was another prolonged investment spending slump, which played a key role in the 2001 recession and the disappointing "jobless recovery" of the next two years.

But these investment spending slumps were very different. The 1980s slump was mainly in housing; nonresidential investment spending remained fairly strong. The slump that began in 2001 was entirely in nonresidential investment spending; by 2003 there was actually a boom in housing construction.

Figure 28-7 tells the tale. Panel (a) shows the behavior of the level of nonresidential and residential (housing) investment spending, measured in 2000 dollars, during the slump of the early 1980s. The levels of both types of investment spending are measured in real terms as an index number, with 1979 fourth-quarter real values set equal to 100. You can see that the early 1980s slump was concentrated in residential, that is, housing,

Figure 28-7   Two Investment Spending Slumps and the Mortgage Interest Rate for Housing

(a) Real Investment Spending (1979 Q4 = 100)

(b) Real Investment Spending (2000 Q4 = 100)

(c) 30-year Conventional Mortgage Rate

Panels (a) and (b) show the quantities of nonresidential and residential (housing) investment spending during two investment slumps. In each case, quantities are measured as index numbers, with the level just before the slump equal to 100. The slump of the early 1980s was concentrated in residential investment spending, but residential investment spending rose after 2000, and eventually turned into a boom. Panel (c) shows the source of the difference: the interest rate on 30-year mortgages, loans that many people use to buy homes, soared in the early 1980s but fell after 2000.

Source: Commerce Department.

investment spending. Panel (b) shows the same comparison starting in the fourth quarter of 2000, measured so that 2000 fourth-quarter real values equal 100. In this case, the investment spending slump was entirely concentrated in nonresidential investment spending; housing investment spending remained high through the recession, then went up from there.

This difference in residential investment spending was due to interest rates, which shot up during the early 1980s but fell during the years after 2000. Panel (c) shows the interest rate on 30-year home mortgage loans. The rate soared to its highest level ever in the early 1980s; it fell to its lowest level in decades after 2000.

So why did nonresidential investment spending fall 15% during 2001 and 2002? It was high during the late 1990s in large part because of the accelerator principle: firms believed the economy would grow rapidly, and this encouraged investment spending. When firms became somewhat less optimistic in 2000–2001, this led to a fall in planned investment spending. Also, the high investment spending of the late 1990s left some firms with larger production capacities than they needed. This was especially true in telecommunications, where companies found themselves with lots of "dark fiber": fiber-optic cables (used to transmit phone calls and other data) that turned out not to be needed, at least for the time being. So firms cut back sharply on investment spending, waiting for demand to catch up with capacity. ∎

< < < < < < < < < < < < < < < < < <

> ► QUICK REVIEW

➤ *Planned investment spending* is negatively related to the interest rate and positively related to expected future real GDP. According to the *accelerator principle*, there is a positive relationship between planned investment spending and the expected future growth rate of real GDP.

➤ Firms hold *inventories* to sell in the future. *Inventory investment*, a form of investment spending, can be positive or negative.

➤ When actual sales are more or less than expected, *unplanned inventory investment* occurs. *Actual investment spending* is equal to planned investment spending plus unplanned inventory investment.

>> CHECK YOUR UNDERSTANDING 28-2

1. For each event, explain whether planned investment spending or unplanned inventory investment will change and in what direction.
   a. An unexpected increase in consumer spending.
   b. A sharp rise in the cost of business borrowing.
   c. A sharp increase in the economy's growth rate of real GDP.
   d. An unanticipated fall in sales.

2. Historically, investment spending has experienced more extreme upward and downward swings than consumer spending. Why do you think this is so? (*Hint*: Consider the marginal propensity to consume and the accelerator principle.)

3. Consumer demand was sluggish during 2002 and economists worried that an *inventory overhang*—a high level of unplanned inventory investment throughout the economy—would make it difficult for the economy to recover anytime soon. Explain why an inventory overhang might, like the existence of too much production capacity, depress economic activity.

Solutions appear at back of book.

Behind Shifts of the Aggregate Demand Curve: The Income-Expenditure Model

We began this chapter by describing the concern voiced by American politicians about a possible slump in consumer spending after 9/11. We can understand that concern in terms of the analysis of short-run economic fluctuations we developed in Chapter 27. There we learned that most, though not all, recessions are caused by negative *demand shocks*—leftward shifts of the aggregate demand curve. What people feared after 9/11, then, was another negative demand shock.

We also learned in Chapter 27 how to use the multiplier to answer the question of how much the aggregate demand curve shifts in response to a demand shock. We saw that due to the multistage process of a change in aggregate demand leading to changes in real GDP, disposable income, and consumer spending, the magnitude of the shift of the aggregate demand curve is several multiples of the size of the original demand shock. In this section, we will examine this multistage process more closely. We'll see that the multiple rounds of changes in real GDP are accomplished through changes in the amount of output produced by firms—changes that they make in response to changes in their inventories. And we'll come to understand why inventories play a central role in macroeconomic models of the economy in the short run, and why economists pay particular attention to the behavior of firms' inventories when trying to understand the likely future state of the economy.

Before we begin, let's quickly recap the assumptions underlying the multiplier process.

1. *The aggregate price level is fixed.* In other words, we'll analyze the determination of aggregate output as if the short-run aggregate supply curve, *SRAS*, is horizontal at a given aggregate price level. This is in contrast to the upward-sloping short-run aggregate supply curve of the *AS–AD* model. A fixed aggregate price level also implies that there is no difference between nominal GDP and real GDP. As a result, we can use the two terms interchangeably in this chapter.

2. *The interest rate is fixed.* We'll take the interest rate as predetermined and unaffected by the factors we analyze in the model. As in the case of the aggregate price level, what we're really doing here is leaving the determinants of the interest rate outside the model. As we'll see, the model can still be used to study the effects of a change in the interest rate.

3. *Taxes, government transfers, and government purchases are all zero.*

4. *There is no foreign trade.*

The Chapter 29 Appendix addresses how taxes affect the multiplier process. In all subsequent chapters we will drop the assumption that the aggregate price level is fixed. We'll explain how the interest rate is determined in Chapter 31 and bring foreign trade back into the picture in Chapter 17.

Planned Aggregate Spending and Real GDP

In an economy with no government and no foreign trade, there are only two sources of aggregate demand: consumer spending, *C*, and investment spending, *I*. And since we assume that there are no taxes or transfers, aggregate disposable income is equal to GDP (which, since the aggregate price level is fixed, is the same as real GDP): the total value of final sales of goods and services ultimately accrues to households as income. So in this highly simplified economy, there are two basic equations of national income accounting:

(28-6) $GDP = C + I$

(28-7) $YD = GDP$

As we learned earlier in this chapter, the *aggregate consumption function* shows the relationship between disposable income and consumer spending. Let's continue to assume that the aggregate consumption function is of the form:

(28-8) $C = A + MPC \times YD$

In our simplified model, we will also assume planned investment spending, $I_{Planned}$, is fixed.

We need one more concept before putting the model together: **planned aggregate spending,** the total amount of planned spending in the economy. Unlike firms, households don't take unintended actions. So planned aggregate spending is equal to the sum of consumer spending and planned investment spending. We denote planned aggregate spending by $AE_{Planned}$, so

> **Planned aggregate spending** is the total amount of planned spending in the economy.

(28-9) $AE_{Planned} = C + I_{Planned}$

The level of planned aggregate spending in a given year depends on the level of real GDP in that year. To see why, let's look at a specific example, shown in Table 28-1 on page 682. We assume that the aggregate consumption function is

(28-10) $C = 300 + 0.6 \times YD$

TABLE 28-1

Real GDP	YD	C	$I_{Planned}$	$AE_{Planned}$
		(billions of dollars)		
$0	$0	$300	$500	$800
500	500	600	500	1,100
1,000	1,000	900	500	1,400
1,500	1,500	1,200	500	1,700
2,000	2,000	1,500	500	2,000
2,500	2,500	1,800	500	2,300
3,000	3,000	2,100	500	2,600
3,500	3,500	2,400	500	2,900

Real GDP, YD, C, $I_{Planned}$, and $AE_{Planned}$ are all measured in billions of dollars, and we assume that the level of planned investment, $I_{Planned}$, is fixed at $500 billion per year. The first column shows possible levels of real GDP. The second column shows disposable income, YD, which in our simplified model is equal to real GDP. The third column shows consumer spending, C, equal to $300 billion plus 0.6 times disposable income, YD. The fourth column shows planned investment spending, $I_{Planned}$, which we have assumed is $500 billion regardless of the level of real GDP. Finally, the last column shows planned aggregate spending, $AE_{Planned}$, the sum of aggregate consumer spending, C, and planned investment spending, $I_{Planned}$. (To economize on notation, we'll assume that it is understood from now on that all the variables in Table 28-1 are measured in billions of dollars per year.) As you can see, a higher level of real GDP leads to a higher level of disposable income: every 500 increase in real GDP raises YD by 500, which in turn raises C by $500 \times 0.6 = 300$ and $AE_{Planned}$ by 300.

Figure 28-8 illustrates the information in Table 28-1 graphically. Real GDP is measured on the horizontal axis. CF is the aggregate consumption function; it shows how consumer spending depends on real GDP. $AE_{Planned}$, the planned aggregate spending line, corresponds to the aggregate consumption function shifted up by 500 (the amount of $I_{Planned}$). It shows how planned aggregate spending depends on real GDP. Both lines have a slope of 0.6, equal to MPC, the marginal propensity to consume.

But this isn't the end of the story. Table 28-1 reveals that at all but one level of real GDP, when real GDP equals 2,000, planned aggregate spending, $AE_{Planned}$, doesn't equal the corresponding level of real GDP. Is that possible? Didn't we learn in Chapter 24, with the circular-flow diagram, that total spending on final goods and services in the economy is equal to the total value of output of final goods and services? The answer is that for *brief* periods of time, planned aggregate spending can differ from real GDP because of the role of *unplanned* aggregate spending—$I_{Unplanned}$, unplanned inventory investment. But as we'll see in the next section, the economy moves over time to a situation in which there is no unplanned inventory investment, called *income–expenditure equilibrium*. And when the economy is in income–expenditure equilibrium, planned aggregate spending on final goods and services equals aggregate output.

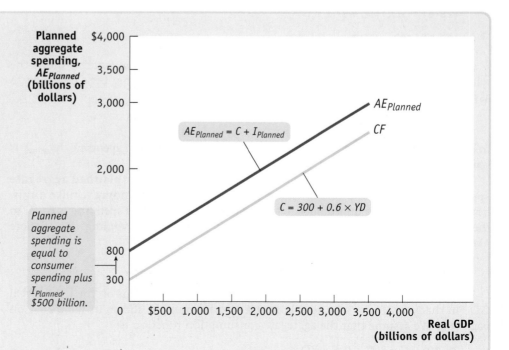

Figure 28-8

The Aggregate Consumption Function and Planned Aggregate Spending

The lower line, *CF*, is the aggregate consumption function constructed from the data in Table 28-1. The upper line, $AE_{Planned}$, is the planned aggregate spending line, also constructed from the data in Table 28-1. It is equivalent to the aggregate consumption function shifted up by $500 billion, the amount of planned investment spending, $I_{Planned}$. >web...
>web...

Income–Expenditure Equilibrium

For all but one value of real GDP shown in Table 28-1, real GDP is either more or less than $AE_{Planned}$, the sum of consumer spending and *planned* investment spending. For example, when real GDP is 1,000, consumer spending C is 900 and planned investment spending is 500, making planned aggregate spending 1,400. This is 400 *more* than the corresponding level of real GDP. Now consider what happens when real GDP is 2,500; consumer spending C is 1,800 and planned investment spending is 500, making planned aggregate spending only 2,300, 200 *less* than real GDP.

As we've just explained, planned aggregate spending can be different from real GDP only if there is unplanned inventory investment, $I_{Unplanned}$, in the economy. Let's examine Table 28-2, which includes the numbers for real GDP and for planned aggregate spending from Table 28-1. It also includes the levels of unplanned inventory investment, $I_{Unplanned}$, that each combination of real GDP and planned aggregate spending implies. For example, if real GDP is 2,500, planned aggregate spending is only 2,300. This 200 excess of real GDP over $AE_{Planned}$ must consist of positive unplanned inventory investment. This can happen only if firms have overestimated sales and produced too much, leading to unintended additions to inventories. More generally, any level of real GDP in excess of 2,000 corresponds to a situation in which firms are producing more than consumers and other firms want to purchase, creating an unintended increase in inventories.

Conversely, a level of real GDP below 2,000 implies that planned aggregate spending is *greater* than real GDP. For example, when real GDP is 1,000, planned aggregate spending is much larger, at 1,400. The 400 excess of $AE_{Planned}$ over real GDP corresponds to negative unplanned inventory investment of –400. More generally, any level of real GDP below 2,000 implies that firms have underestimated sales, leading to a negative level of unplanned inventory investment in the economy.

By putting together Equations 28-5, 28-6, and 28-9, we can summarize the general relationship among real GDP, planned aggregate spending, and unplanned inventory investment:

(28-11) $GDP = C + I$
$$= C + I_{Planned} + I_{Unplanned}$$
$$= AE_{Planned} + I_{Unplanned}$$

So whenever real GDP exceeds $AE_{Planned}$, $I_{Unplanned}$ is positive; whenever real GDP is less than $AE_{Planned}$, $I_{Unplanned}$ is negative.

But firms will act to correct their mistakes: they will reduce production if they have experienced an unintended rise in inventories or increase production if they have experienced an unintended fall in inventories. And these responses will eventually eliminate the unanticipated changes in inventories and move the economy to a point at which real GDP is equal to planned aggregate spending. Staying with our example, if real GDP is 1,000, negative unplanned inventory investment will lead firms to increase production, leading to a rise in real GDP. In fact, this will happen whenever real GDP is less than 2,000—that is, whenever real GDP is less than planned aggregate spending. Conversely, if real GDP is 2,500, positive unplanned inventory investment will lead firms to reduce production, leading to a fall in real GDP. This will happen whenever real GDP is greater than planned aggregate spending.

The only situation in which firms won't have an incentive to change output in the next period is when aggregate output, measured by real GDP, is equal to planned aggregate spending in the current period, an outcome known as **income–expenditure equilibrium**. In Table 28-2, income–expenditure equilibrium is achieved when real GDP is 2,000, the only level of real GDP at which unplanned inventory investment is zero. From now on, we'll denote the real GDP level at which income–expenditure equilibrium occurs as Y* and call it the **income–expenditure equilibrium GDP.**

Figure 28-9 on page 684 illustrates the concept of income–expenditure equilibrium graphically. Real GDP is on the horizontal axis and planned aggregate spending, $AE_{Planned}$, is on the vertical axis. There are two lines in the figure. The solid line is the

TABLE 28-2

Real GDP	$AE_{Planned}$	$I_{Unplanned}$
(billions of dollars)		
$0	$800	–$800
500	1,100	–600
1,000	1,400	–400
1,500	1,700	–200
2,000	2,000	0
2,500	2,300	200
3,000	2,600	400
3,500	2,900	600

The economy is in **income–expenditure equilibrium** when aggregate output, measured by real GDP, is equal to planned aggregate spending.

Income–expenditure equilibrium GDP is the level of real GDP at which real GDP equals planned aggregate spending.

Figure 28-9

Income–Expenditure Equilibrium

Income–expenditure equilibrium occurs at E, the point where the planned aggregate spending line, $AE_{Planned}$, crosses the 45-degree line. At E, the economy produces real GDP of $2,000 billion per year, the only point at which real GDP equals planned aggregate spending, $AE_{Planned}$, and unplanned inventory investment, $I_{Unplanned}$, is zero. This is the level of income–expenditure equilibrium GDP, Y^*. At any level of real GDP less than Y^*, $AE_{Planned}$ exceeds real GDP. As a result, unplanned inventory investment, $I_{Unplanned}$, is negative and firms respond by increasing production. At any level of real GDP greater than Y^*, real GDP exceeds $AE_{Planned}$. Unplanned inventory investment, $I_{Unplanned}$, is positive and firms respond by reducing production. **>web...**

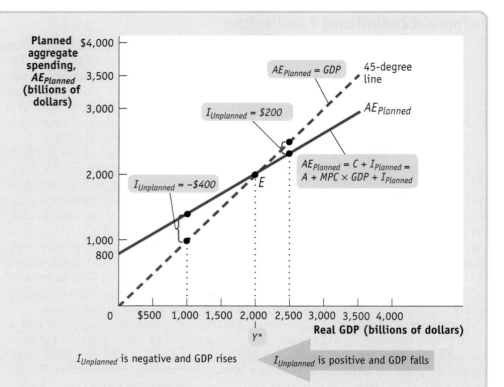

$I_{Unplanned}$ is negative and GDP rises $I_{Unplanned}$ is positive and GDP falls

---

INCOME–EXPENDITURE EQUILIBRIUM VERSUS SHORT-RUN MACROECONOMIC EQUILIBRIUM

In Chapter 27 we developed the concept of short-run macroeconomic equilibrium using the AS–AD model. Using it, we determined the equilibrium level of real GDP as the level at which the quantity of aggregate output supplied in the short run is equal to the quantity of aggregate output demanded. Here we've introduced another concept, the income–expenditure equilibrium process. Using it, we've defined income–expenditure equilibrium GDP to be the level of real GDP at which planned aggregate spending equals real GDP. So are these concepts of equilibrium in conflict with each other? That is, do they lead to two different and therefore conflicting definitions of what real GDP is when the economy is in short-run macroeconomic equilibrium?

Definitely not. Recall that what we're doing in the income–expenditure model is analyzing how real GDP would change *holding all prices fixed*. To derive the full short-run macroeconomic equilibrium, we need to bring the flexible aggregate price level back in. So income–expenditure equilibrium is a step on the way to calculating macroeconomic equilibrium—one that allows us to closely examine the inventory adjustment process behind a shift of the aggregate demand curve—not an alternative concept.

The **Keynesian cross** diagram identifies income–expenditure equilibrium as the point where the planned aggregate spending line crosses the 45-degree line.

planned aggregate spending line. It shows how $AE_{Planned}$, equal to $C + I_{Planned}$, depends on real GDP; it has a slope of 0.6, equal to the marginal propensity to consume, MPC, and a vertical intercept equal to $A + I_{Planned}$ (300 + 500 = 800). The dashed line, which goes through the origin with a slope of 1 (often called a 45-degree line), shows all the possible points at which planned aggregate spending is equal to real GDP. This line allows us to easily spot the point of income-expenditure equilibrium, which must lie on both the 45-degree line and the planned aggregate spending line. So the point of income-expenditure equilibrium is at E, where the two lines cross. And the income-expenditure equilibrium GDP, Y^*, is 2,000—the same outcome we derived in Table 28-2.

Now consider what happens if the economy isn't in income-expenditure equilibrium. We can see from Figure 28-9 that whenever real GDP is less than Y^*, the planned aggregate spending line lies above the 45-degree line and $AE_{Planned}$ exceeds real GDP. In this situation, $I_{Unplanned}$ is negative: as shown in the figure, at a real GDP of 1,000, $I_{Unplanned}$ is −400. As a consequence, real GDP will rise. In contrast, whenever real GDP is greater than Y^*, the planned aggregate expenditure line lies below the 45-degree line. Here, $I_{Unplanned}$ is positive: as shown, at a real GDP of 2,500, $I_{Unplanned}$ is 200. The unanticipated accumulation of inventory leads to a fall in real GDP.

The type of diagram shown in Figure 28-9, which identifies income–expenditure equilibrium as the point at which the planned aggregate spending line crosses the 45-degree line, has a special place in the history of economic thought. Known as the **Keynesian cross,** it was developed by Paul Samuelson, one of the greatest economists of the twentieth century (as well as a Nobel Prize winner), to explain the ideas of John Maynard Keynes, the founder of macroeconomics as we know it.

The Multiplier Process and Inventory Adjustment

We've just learned about a very important feature of the macroeconomy: when planned spending by households and firms does not equal the current aggregate output by firms, there is a self-adjustment process in the economy that moves real GDP over time to the point at which real GDP and planned aggregate spending are equal. And that self-adjustment mechanism operates through inventories. That's why, as we mentioned earlier, changes in inventories are considered a leading indicator of future economic activity.

Now that we understand how real GDP moves to achieve income–expenditure equilibrium for a given level of planned aggregate spending, let's turn to understanding what happens when there is *a shift of the planned aggregate spending line*. How does the economy move from the initial point of income–expenditure equilibrium to a new point of income–expenditure equilibrium? And what are the possible sources of changes in planned aggregate spending?

In our simple model there are only two possible sources of a shift of the planned aggregate spending line: a change in planned investment spending, $I_{Planned}$, or a shift of the consumption function, C. For example, a change in $I_{Planned}$ can occur because of a change in the interest rate. (Remember, we're assuming that the interest rate is fixed by factors that are outside the model. But we can still ask what happens when the interest rate changes.) A shift of the consumption function (that is, a change in its vertical intercept, A) can occur because of a change in aggregate wealth—say, due to a rise in housing values. When the planned aggregate spending line shifts—when there is a change in the level of planned aggregate spending at any given level of real GDP—there is an autonomous change in planned aggregate spending. Recall from Chapter 27 that an autonomous change in planned aggregate spending is a change in the desired level of spending by firms, households, and government at any given level of real GDP (although we've assumed away the government for the time being). How does an autonomous change in planned aggregate spending affect real GDP in income–expenditure equilibrium?

Table 28-3 and panel (a) of Figure 28-10 on page 286 start from the same numerical example we used in Table 28-2 and Figure 28-9. They also show the effect of an autonomous increase in planned aggregate spending of 400—what happens when planned aggregate spending is 400 higher at each level of real GDP. Look first at Table 28-3. Before the autonomous increase in planned aggregate spending, the level of real GDP at which planned aggregate spending is equal to real GDP, Y^*, is 2,000. After the autonomous change, Y^* has risen to 3,000. The same result is visible in panel (a) of Figure 28-10. The initial income–expenditure equilibrium is at E_1, where Y_1^* is 2,000. The autonomous rise in planned aggregate spending shifts the planned aggregate spending line up, leading to a new income–expenditure equilibrium at E_2, where Y_2^* is 3,000.

The fact that the rise in income–expenditure equilibrium GDP, from 2,000 to 3,000, is much larger than the autonomous increase in aggregate spending, which is only 400, has a familiar explanation: the multiplier process. In the specific example we have just described, an autonomous increase in planned aggregate spending of 400 leads to an increase in Y^* from 2,000 to 3,000, a rise of 1,000. So the multiplier in this example is $1,000/400 = 2.5$.

We can examine in detail what underlies the multistage multiplier process by continuing to use panel (a) of Figure 28-10. First, starting from E_1, the autonomous increase in planned aggregate spending leads to a gap between planned aggregate spending and real GDP. This is represented by the vertical distance between X, at 2,400, and E_1, at 2,000. This gap illustrates an unplanned fall in inventory investment: $I_{Unplanned} = -400$. Firms respond by increasing production, leading to a rise in real GDP from Y_1^*. The rise in real GDP translates into an increase in disposable income, YD. That's the first stage in the chain reaction. But it doesn't stop there—the increase in YD leads to a rise in consumer spending, C, which sets off a second-round rise in real GDP. This in turn leads to a further rise in disposable income and consumer spending, and so on. And we could play this process in reverse: an autonomous fall in

TABLE 28-3

Real GDP	$AE_{Planned}$ before autonomous change	$AE_{Planned}$ after autonomous change
	(billions of dollars)	
$0	$800	$1,200
500	1,100	1,500
1,000	1,400	1,800
1,500	1,700	2,100
2,000	2,000	2,400
2,500	2,300	2,700
3,000	2,600	3,000
3,500	2,900	3,300
4,000	3,200	3,600

Figure 28-10

The Multiplier

Panel (a) illustrates the change in Y^* caused by an autonomous increase in planned aggregate spending. The economy is initially at equilibrium point E_1 with an income–expenditure equilibrium GDP, Y_1^*, equal to 2,000. An autonomous increase in $AE_{Planned}$ of 400 shifts the planned aggregate spending line upward by 400. The economy is no longer in income–expenditure equilibrium: real GDP is equal to 2,000 but $AE_{Planned}$ is now 2,400, represented by point X. The vertical distance between the two planned aggregate spending lines, equal to 400, represents $I_{Unplanned} = -400$—the negative inventory investment that the economy now experiences. Firms respond by increasing production, and the economy eventually reaches a new income–expenditure equilibrium at E_2 with a higher level of income–expenditure equilibrium GDP, Y_2^*, equal to 3,000. Panel (b) shows the corresponding rightward shift of the AD curve generated by the increase in $AE_{Planned}$. At the conclusion of the multiplier process, $AE_{Planned}$ will have risen by a total of 1,000, 2.5 times as much as the initial increase of 400.

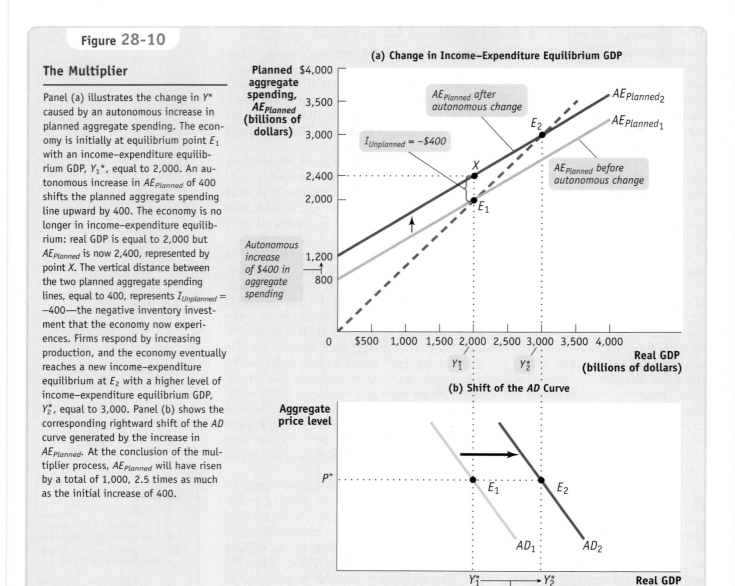

(a) Change in Income–Expenditure Equilibrium GDP

(b) Shift of the AD Curve

Change in quantity demanded of real GDP at aggregate price level P^*

aggregate spending will lead to a chain reaction of reductions in real GDP and consumer spending.

We can summarize these results in an equation, where ΔAAE represents the autonomous change in $AE_{Planned}$:

(28-12) $\quad \Delta Y^* = \text{Multiplier} \times \Delta AAE_{Planned}$

$$= \frac{1}{1 - MPC} \times \Delta AAE_{Planned}$$

Like Equation 27-6, Equation 28-12 tells us that the change in income–expenditure equilibrium GDP, ΔY^*, is several times as large as the autonomous change in planned aggregate spending, $\Delta AAE_{Planned}$. Equation 28-12 also helps us recall an important point: because the marginal propensity to consume is less than 1, each increase in disposable income and each corresponding increase in consumer spending is smaller than in the previous round. That's because at each round some of the increase in disposable income leaks out into savings. As a result, although real GDP grows at each round, the increase in real GDP diminishes from each round to the next. At some point the increase in real GDP is negligible, and the economy converges to a new income–expenditure equilibrium GDP at Y_2^*.

Now we're in a position to tie the inventory adjustment that underlies the multiplier process to the question of how much the aggregate demand curve shifts in response to a slump or a boom in consumer spending or investment spending. Panel (b) of Figure 28-10 shows the corresponding shift of the aggregate demand curve generated by the events illustrated in panel (a). At a *fixed aggregate price level*, given here by P^*, the change in the quantity of aggregate output demanded is equal to the change in income–expenditure equilibrium GDP that arises from the autonomous change in $AE_{Planned}$ plus the multiplier effect. Again, we see the importance of the multiplier: the larger the multiplier, the larger the shift of the *AD* curve at any given aggregate price level.

The Paradox of Thrift You may recall that in Chapter 23 we mentioned the Paradox of Thrift to illustrate the fact that, in macroeconomics, the outcome of many individual actions can generate a result that is different and worse than the simple sum of those individual actions. In the Paradox of Thrift, households and firms cut their spending in anticipation of future tough economic times. These actions depress the economy, leaving households and firms worse off than if they hadn't acted virtuously to prepare for tough times. It is called a paradox because what's usually "good" (saving to provide for your family in hard times) is "bad" (because it can make everyone worse off).

Using the multiplier, we can now see exactly how this scenario unfolds. Suppose that there is a slump in consumer spending or investment spending, or both, which causes a fall in income–expenditure equilibrium GDP that is several times larger than the original fall in spending. The fall in real GDP leaves consumers and producers worse off than they would have been if they hadn't cut their spending. Conversely, prodigal behavior is rewarded: if consumers or producers increase their spending, the resulting multiplier process makes the increase in income–expenditure equilibrium GDP several times larger than the original increase in spending. So prodigal spending makes consumers and producers better off than if they had been cautious spenders.

It's important to realize that setting the multiplier equal to $1/(1 - MPC)$ depends on the simplifying assumption that there are no taxes or transfers, so that disposable income is equal to real GDP. In the Appendix to Chapter 29 we'll bring taxes into the picture, which makes the expression for the multiplier more complicated and the multiplier itself smaller. But the general principle we have just learned—an autonomous change in planned aggregate spending leads to a change in income–expenditure equilibrium GDP, both directly and through an induced change in consumer spending—remains valid.

As we noted earlier in this chapter, declines in planned investment spending are usually the major factor in recessions. So historically they have been the most common source of autonomous reductions in aggregate spending. The tendency of the consumption function to shift upward over time, which we pointed out in Economics in Action on page 674, means that autonomous changes in both planned investment spending and consumer spending play important roles in expansions. But regardless of the source, there are multiplier effects in the economy that magnify the size of the initial change in aggregate spending. Recall our opening story about how political leaders urged consumers to open their wallets and spend after 9/11. As we've now learned, the fears of those leaders were understandable: they were concerned that the shock of the terrorist attacks would lead to a reduction in consumer spending that would, through the multiplier effect, greatly worsen the existing recession. Fortunately for the economy, this didn't happen. American consumers were shocked and saddened, but they didn't stop spending. As a result, the economy began to recover only a few months later.

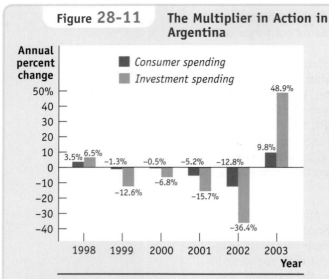

Figure 28-11 **The Multiplier in Action in Argentina**

The most severe recession in recent history was a case of the multiplier at work. The bars show annual rates of change in consumer spending and investment spending in Argentina between 1998 and 2003. A financial crisis led to a plunge in investment spending between 1998 and 2002, leading to a decline in consumer spending. Then an upturn in investment spending led to recovery in consumer spending as well.

economics in action

Bad Times in Buenos Aires

The closest thing the world has seen in recent times to a replay of the Great Depression was the severe recession that hit Argentina from 1998 to 2002. Over that period, Argentina's real GDP fell 18%, and the unemployment rate rose above 20%.

The origins of the Argentine slump lay in a financial crisis: foreign investors lost confidence in the country's ability to repay the debts owed to them, setting in motion a chain reaction that led to bank closings and widespread bankruptcy. But the channel through which the financial crisis caused a recession was the multiplier. Financial difficulties caused by the loss in confidence led to a plunge in planned investment spending. This, in turn, led to a fall in real GDP, both because of the direct effect of the reduction in investment spending and because of the induced fall in consumer spending. Figure 28-11 shows the annual rates of change of real investment spending and real consumer spending in Argentina from 1998 to 2003. As you can see, the slump in investment spending from 1998 to 2002 led to a proportionately smaller decline in consumer spending. Then, when investment spending bounced back in 2003, so did consumer spending. ∎

< < < < < < < < < < < < < < < < < <

>> **CHECK YOUR UNDERSTANDING 28-3**

1. Although economists believe that recessions typically begin as slumps in investment spending, they also believe that consumer spending eventually slumps during a recession. Explain why.

2. a. Use a diagram like Figure 28-10 to show what happens when there is an autonomous fall in planned aggregate spending. Describe how the economy adjusts to a new income–expenditure equilibrium.

 b. Suppose Y^* is originally $500 billion, the autonomous reduction in planned aggregate spending is $300 million ($0.3 billion), and $MPC = 0.5$. Calculate Y^* after such a change.

Solutions appear at back of book.

● A LOOK AHEAD ●

In this chapter we studied the inventory adjustment process that underlies the multiplier. But we used a very simplified model of the determination of aggregate output, leaving out a number of important factors in order to focus our attention on a few key relationships. Now we're ready to bring some of the complications back in—starting with the role of government and government policy.

We begin by introducing taxes, transfers, and government purchases into our model. As we'll see, putting the government in leads us immediately to one of the key insights of macroeconomics: sometimes the government can do something about the business cycle. We'll explore the potential and the difficulties of *fiscal policy*—changes in taxes, transfers, and government purchases designed to affect macroeconomic outcomes—in Chapter 29. Then in Chapters 30 and 31 we'll turn to an even more important tool in the government's hands, *monetary policy*.

SUMMARY

1. The **consumption function** shows how an individual household's consumer spending is determined by its current disposable income. The **aggregate consumption function** shows the relationship for the entire economy. According to the life-cycle hypothesis, households try to smooth their consumption over their lifetime. As a result, the aggregate consumption function shifts in response to changes in expected future disposable income and changes in aggregate wealth.

2. **Planned investment spending** depends negatively on the interest rate and on existing production capacity; it depends positively on expected future real GDP. The **accelerator principle** says that investment spending is greatly influenced by the expected growth rate of real GDP.

3. Firms hold **inventories** of goods so that they can satisfy consumer demand quickly. **Inventory investment** is positive when firms add to their inventories, negative when they reduce them. Often, however, changes in inventories are not a deliberate decision but the result of mistakes in forecasts about sales. The result is **unplanned inventory investment,** which can be either positive or negative. **Actual investment spending** is the sum of planned investment spending and unplanned inventory investment.

4. In **income–expenditure equilibrium, planned aggregate spending,** which in a simplified model with no government and no trade is the sum of consumer spending and planned investment spending, is equal to real GDP. At the **income–expenditure equilibrium GDP,** or Y^*, unplanned inventory investment is zero. When planned aggregate spending is larger than Y^*, unplanned inventory investment is negative; there is an unanticipated reduction in inventories and firms increase production. When planned aggregate spending is less than Y^*, unplanned inventory investment is positive; there is an unanticipated increase in inventories and firms reduce production. The **Keynesian cross** shows how the economy self-adjusts to income–expenditure equilibrium through inventory adjustments.

5. After an autonomous change in planned aggregate spending, the inventory adjustment process moves the economy to a new income–expenditure equilibrium. The change in income–expenditure equilibrium GDP arising from an autonomous change in spending is equal to the multiplier × $\Delta AAE_{Planned}$. Correspondingly, the amount of the shift of the AD curve at any given aggregate price level arising from an autonomous change in investment spending or consumer spending is equal to the multiplier times the autonomous change in spending.

KEY TERMS

Consumption function, p. 670
Aggregate consumption function, p. 672
Planned investment spending, p. 676
Accelerator principle, p. 678
Inventories, p. 678

Inventory investment, p. 678
Unplanned inventory investment, p. 678
Actual investment spending, p. 678
Planned aggregate spending, p. 681
Income–expenditure equilibrium, p. 683

Income–expenditure equilibrium GDP, p. 683
Keynesian cross, p. 684

PROBLEMS

1. Economists observed the only five residents of a very small economy and estimated each one's consumer spending at various levels of current disposable income. The accompanying table shows each resident's consumer spending at three income levels.

Individual consumer spending by	Individual current disposable income		
	$0	$20,000	$40,000
Andre	1,000	15,000	29,000
Barbara	2,500	12,500	22,500
Casey	2,000	20,000	38,000
Declan	5,000	17,000	29,000
Elena	4,000	19,000	34,000

a. What is each resident's consumption function? What is the marginal propensity to consume for each resident?

b. What is the economy's aggregate consumption function? What is the marginal propensity to consume for the economy?

2. From 2000 to 2005, Eastlandia experienced large fluctuations in both aggregate consumer spending and disposable income, but wealth, the interest rate, and expected future disposable income did not change. The accompanying table on page 690 shows the level of aggregate consumer spending and disposable income in millions of dollars for each of these years. Use this information to answer the following questions.

Year	Disposable income (millions of dollars)	Consumer spending (millions of dollars)
2000	$100	$180
2001	350	380
2002	300	340
2003	400	420
2004	375	400
2005	500	500

a. Plot the aggregate consumption function for Eastlandia.

b. What is the aggregate consumption function?

c. What is the marginal propensity to consume? What is the marginal propensity to save?

3. How will each of the following actions affect the aggregate consumption function? Explain whether the event will result in a movement along or a shift of the aggregate consumption function and in which direction.

a. The government grants an unexpected and one-time tax cut to all households.

b. The government announces permanently higher tax rates beginning next year.

c. The Social Security Administration raises the age at which workers who are currently younger than 65 can qualify for Social Security benefits from age 65 to age 75.

4. From the end of 1995 to March 2000, the Standard and Poor's 500 (S&P 500) stock index, a broad measure of stock market prices, rose almost 150%, from 615.93 to a high of 1,527.46. From that time to September 10, 2001, the index fell 28.5% to 1,092.54. How do you think the movements in the stock index influenced both the growth in real GDP in the late 1990s and the concern about maintaining consumer spending after the terrorist attacks on September 11, 2001?

5. How will the interest rate and planned investment spending change as the following events occur?

a. An increase in the quantity of money by the Federal Reserve increases the amount of money that people wish to lend at any interest rate.

b. The U.S. Environmental Protection Agency decrees that corporations must adopt new technology that reduces their emissions of sulfur dioxide.

c. Baby boomers begin to retire in large numbers and reduce their savings.

6. Explain how each of the following actions will affect the level of planned investment spending and unplanned inventory investment. Assume the economy is initially in income-expenditure equilibrium.

a. The Federal Reserve raises the interest rate.

b. There is a rise in the expected growth rate of real GDP.

c. A sizable inflow of foreign funds into the country lowers the interest rate.

7. The accompanying table shows real gross domestic product (GDP), disposable income (YD), consumer spending (C), and planned investment spending ($I_{Planned}$) in an economy. Assume there is no government or foreign sector in this economy. Complete the table by calculating planned aggregate spending ($AE_{Planned}$) and unplanned inventory investment ($I_{Unplanned}$).

GDP	YD	C	$I_{Planned}$	$AE_{Planned}$	$I_{Unplanned}$
		(billions of dollars)			
$0	$0	$100	$300	?	?
400	400	400	300	?	?
800	800	700	300	?	?
1,200	1,200	1,000	300	?	?
1,600	1,600	1,300	300	?	?
2,000	2,000	1,600	300	?	?
2,400	2,400	1,900	300	?	?
2,800	2,800	2,200	300	?	?
3,200	3,200	2,500	300	?	?

a. What is the aggregate consumption function?

b. What is Y*, income–expenditure equilibrium GDP?

c. What is the value of the multiplier?

d. If planned investment spending falls to $200 billion, what will be the new Y*?

e. If autonomous consumer spending rises to $200 billion, what will be the new Y*?

8. In an economy with no government and no foreign sectors, autonomous consumer spending is $250 billion, planned investment spending is $350 billion, and the marginal propensity to consume is 2/3.

a. Plot the aggregate consumption function and planned aggregate spending.

b. What is unplanned inventory investment when real GDP equals $600 billion?

c. What is Y*, income–expenditure equilibrium GDP?

d. What is the value of the multiplier?

e. If planned investment spending rises to $450 billion, what will be the new Y*?

9. An economy has a marginal propensity to consume of 0.5 and Y*, income–expenditure equilibrium GDP, equals $500 billion. Given an autonomous increase in planned investment of $10 billion, show the rounds of increased spending that take place by completing the accompanying table. The first and second rows are filled in for you. In the first row, the increase in planned investment spending of $10 billion raises real GDP and YD by $10 billion, leading to an increase in consumer spending of $5 billion (MPC × change in disposable income) in row 2.

Rounds	Change in $I_{Planned}$ or C	Change in real GDP	Change in YD
	(billions of dollars)		
1	$\Delta I_{Planned} = \$10.00$	$10.00	$10.00
2	$\Delta C = \$ 5.00$	$ 5.00	$ 5.00
3	$\Delta C = ?$	?	?
4	$\Delta C = ?$	?	?
5	$\Delta C = ?$	?	?
6	$\Delta C = ?$	?	?
7	$\Delta C = ?$	?	?
8	$\Delta C = ?$	?	?
9	$\Delta C = ?$	?	?
10	$\Delta C = ?$	?	?

a. What is the total change in real GDP after the 10 rounds? What is the value of the multiplier? What would you expect the total change in Y^* to be based on the multiplier formula? How do your answers to the first and third qestions compare?

b. Redo the table, assuming the marginal propensity to consume is 0.75. What is the total change in real GDP after 10 rounds? What is the value of the multiplier? As the marginal propensity to consume increases, what happens to the value of the multiplier?

10. Although the U.S. is one of the richest nations in the world, it is also the world's largest debtor nation. We often hear that the problem is the nation's low savings rate. Suppose policy makers attempt to rectify this by encouraging greater savings in the economy. What effect will their successful attempts have on real GDP?

>web... To continue your study and review of concepts in this chapter, please visit the Krugman/Wells website for quizzes, animated graph tutorials, web links to helpful resources, and more.

www.worthpublishers.com/krugmanwells

>>Chapter 28 Appendix: Deriving the Multiplier Algebraically

This appendix shows how to derive the multiplier algebraically. First recall that in this chapter planned aggregate spending, $AE_{Planned}$, is the sum of consumer spending, C, which is determined by the consumption function, and planned investment spending, $I_{Planned}$. Rewriting Equation 28-9 to express all its terms fully, we have:

(28A-1) $AE_{Planned} = A + MPC \times YD + I_{Planned}$

Because there are no taxes or government transfers in this model, disposable income is equal to GDP, so Equation 28A-1 becomes:

(28A-2) $AE_{Planned} = A + MPC \times GDP + I_{Planned}$

The income–expenditure equilibrium GDP, Y^*, is equal to planned aggregate spending:

(28A-3) $Y^* = AE_{Planned}$
$= A + MPC \times Y^* + I_{Planned}$
in income–expenditure equilibrium

Just two more steps. Subtract $MPC \times Y^*$ from both sides of Equation 28A-3:

(28A-4) $Y^* - MPC \times Y^* = Y^* \times (1 - MPC) = A + I_{Planned}$

Finally, divide both sides by $(1 - MPC)$:

(28A-5) $Y^* = \dfrac{A + I_{Planned}}{1 - MPC}$

Equation 28A-5 tells us that a \$1 autonomous change in planned aggregate spending—a change in either A or $I_{Planned}$—causes a $\$1/(1 - MPC)$ change in income–expenditure equilibrium GDP, Y^*. The multiplier in our simple model is therefore:

(28A-6) Multiplier $= 1/(1 - MPC)$

PROBLEMS

1. In an economy without government purchases, transfers, or taxes, aggregate autonomous consumer spending is \$500 billion, planned investment spending is \$250 billion, and the marginal propensity to consume is 0.5.

   a. Write the expression for planned aggregate spending as in Equation 28A-1.

   b. Solve for Y^* algebraically.

   c. What is the value of the multiplier?

   d. How will Y^* change if autonomous consumer spending falls to \$450 billion?

2. Complete the following table by calculating the value of the multiplier and identifiying the change in Y^* due to the change in autonomous spending. How does the value of the multiplier change with the marginal propensity to consume?

MPC	Value of multiplier	Change in spending	Change in Y*
0.5	?	$\Delta C = +$ \$50 million	?
0.6	?	$\Delta I = -$ \$10 million	?
0.75	?	$\Delta C = -$ \$25 million	?
0.8	?	$\Delta I = +$ \$20 million	?
0.9	?	$\Delta C = -$ \$2.5 million	?

>>Fiscal Policy

A BRIDGE TO PROSPERITY?

IN 1998 THE JAPANESE GOVERNMENT completed the longest suspension bridge in the world. The 6,500-foot span linking Awaji Island to the city of Kobe cost $7.3 billion to build. Yet as skeptics had predicted, it currently carries very little traffic—about 4,000 cars a day. By comparison, America's longest suspension bridge, the Verrazano Bridge that links New York City's Staten Island to the borough of Brooklyn, carries more than 300,000 cars a day.

In Japan, stories like this are common. During the 1990s the Japanese government spent around $1.4 trillion on infrastructure that included many construction projects of questionable usefulness. But the main purpose of construction spending in Japan wasn't to provide useful infrastructure. It was to prop up aggregate demand.

During the 1990s, the Japanese government built bridges, roads, dams, breakwaters, and even parking garages in an effort to combat persistent shortfalls in aggregate demand. Japan's use of government construction spending to stimulate its economy is an example of *discretionary fiscal policy*—the deliberate use of government spending or taxation to manage aggregate demand. The U.S. government has also tried to spend its way out of economic slumps, though on a smaller scale. Indeed, many countries attempt to manage aggregate demand by using discretionary fiscal policy. Governments also adjust taxes in an attempt to manage aggregate demand. They may reduce taxes to try to stimulate the economy or raise taxes when they believe that aggregate demand is too high.

In this chapter, we will learn how discretionary fiscal policy fits into the model of short-run fluctuations we developed in Chapter 27. We'll see how deliberate changes in government spending and tax policy affect real GDP. We'll also see how

The Akashi Kaikyo Bridge was built by the Japanese government in the 1990s to prop up aggregate demand.

changes in tax revenue caused by short-run fluctuations in GDP—an automatic response that occurs without deliberate changes in policy—help stabilize the economy. Finally, we'll examine long-run consequences of government debt and budget deficits.

What you will learn in this chapter:

➤ What fiscal policy is and why it is an important tool in managing economic fluctuations

➤ Which policies constitute an **expansionary fiscal policy** and which constitute a **contractionary fiscal policy**

➤ Why fiscal policy has a multiplier effect and how this effect is influenced by **automatic stabilizers**

➤ Why governments calculate the **cyclically adjusted budget balance**

➤ Why a large **public debt** may be a cause for concern

➤ Why **implicit liabilities** of the government are also a cause for concern

Fiscal Policy: The Basics

Let's begin with the obvious: modern governments spend a great deal of money and collect a lot in taxes. Figure 29-1 shows government spending and tax revenue as percentages of GDP for a selection of high-income countries in 2003. As you can see, the Swedish government sector is relatively large, representing nearly 60% of the Swedish

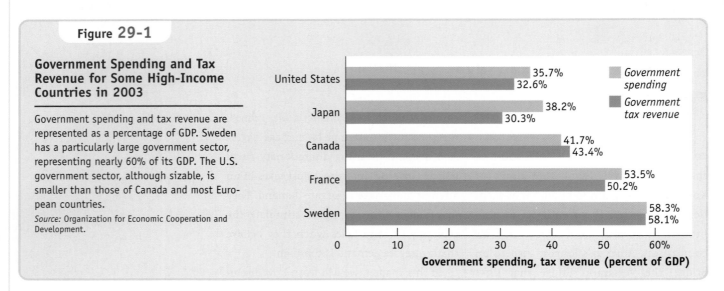

Figure 29-1

Government Spending and Tax Revenue for Some High-Income Countries in 2003

Government spending and tax revenue are represented as a percentage of GDP. Sweden has a particularly large government sector, representing nearly 60% of its GDP. The U.S. government sector, although sizable, is smaller than those of Canada and most European countries.

Source: Organization for Economic Cooperation and Development.

economy. The government of the United States plays a smaller role in the economy than those of Canada or most European countries. But that role is still sizable, meaning that the government plays a major role in the U.S. economy. Changes in the federal budget—changes in government spending or in taxation—can potentially have large effects on the American economy.

To analyze these effects, we begin by showing how taxes and government spending affect the economy's flow of income. Then we can see how changes in spending and tax policy affect aggregate demand.

Taxes, Purchases of Goods and Services, Government Transfers, and Borrowing

In Figure 24-1 we showed the circular flow of income and spending in the economy as a whole. One of the sectors represented in that figure was the government. Funds flow *into* the government in the form of taxes and government borrowing; funds flow *out* in the form of government purchases of goods and services and government transfers to households.

What kinds of taxes do Americans pay, and where does the money go? Figure 29-2 shows the composition of U.S. tax revenue in 2004. Taxes, of course, are required payments to the government. In the United States, taxes are collected at the national level by the federal government; at the state level by each state government; and at the local levels by counties, cities, and towns. At the federal level, the main taxes are income taxes on both personal income and corporate profits as well as *social insurance* taxes, which we'll explain shortly. At the state and local levels, the picture is more complex: these governments rely on a mix of sales taxes,

Figure 29-2   **Sources of Tax Revenue in the United States, 2004**

Personal income taxes, taxes on corporate profits, and social insurance taxes account for most government tax revenue. The rest is a mix of property taxes, sales taxes, and other sources of revenue.

Source: Bureau of Economic Analysis.

property taxes, income taxes, and fees of various kinds. Overall, taxes on personal income and corporate profits accounted for 43% of total government revenue in 2004; social insurance taxes accounted for 28%; and a variety of other taxes, collected mainly at the state and local level, accounted for the rest.

Figure 29-3 shows the composition of total U.S. government spending in 2004, which takes two forms. One form is purchases of goods and services. This includes everything from ammunition for the army to the salaries of public schoolteachers (who are treated in the national accounts as providers of a service—education). The big items here are national defense and education. The large category labeled "other goods and services" consists mainly of state and local spending on a variety of services, from police and firefighters to highway construction and maintenance.

The other form of government spending is government transfers, which are payments by the government to households for which no good or service is provided in return. In the modern United States, as well as in Canada and Europe, government transfers represent a very large proportion of the budget. Most U.S. government spending on transfer payments is accounted for by three big programs:

- Social Security, which provides guaranteed income to older Americans, disabled Americans, and the surviving spouses and dependent children of deceased beneficiaries

- Medicare, which covers much of the cost of health care for Americans over 65

- Medicaid, which covers much of the cost of health care for Americans with low incomes

The term **social insurance** is used to describe government programs that are intended to protect families against economic hardship. These include Social Security, Medicare, and Medicaid, as well as smaller programs such as unemployment insurance and food stamps. In the United States, social insurance programs are largely paid for with special, dedicated taxes on wages—the social insurance taxes we mentioned earlier.

But how do tax policy and government spending affect the economy? The answer is that taxation and government spending have a strong effect on total aggregate spending in the economy.

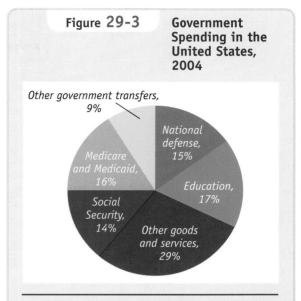

Figure 29-3 **Government Spending in the United States, 2004**

The two types of government spending are purchases of goods and services and government transfers. The big items in government purchases are national defense and education. The big items in government transfers are Social Security and the Medicare and Medicaid health care programs.

Source: Office of Management and Budget.

Social insurance programs are government programs intended to protect families against economic hardship.

The Government Budget and Total Spending

Let's recall the basic equation of national income accounting:

(29-1) $GDP = C + I + G + X - IM$

The left-hand side of this equation is GDP, the value of all final goods and services produced in the economy. The right-hand side is aggregate spending, total spending on final goods and services produced in the economy. It is the sum of consumer spending (C), investment spending (I), government purchases of goods and services (G), and the value of exports (X) minus the value of imports (IM). It includes all the sources of aggregate demand.

The government directly controls one of the variables on the right-hand side of Equation 29-1: government purchases of goods and services (G). But that's not the only effect fiscal policy has on aggregate spending in the economy. Through changes in taxes and transfers, it also influences consumer spending (C) and, in some cases, investment spending (I).

When we discuss changes in taxes in this chapter, we focus mainly on the effects of these changes on consumer spending. However, there is one tool of fiscal policy that is designed to affect investment spending—*investment tax credits*.

An investment tax credit is a tax break given to firms based on their investment spending. For example, a firm might be allowed to deduct $1 from its tax bill for every $10 it spends on investment goods. This increases the incentive for investment spending.

One more thing about investment tax credits: they're often temporary, applying only to investment spending within a specific period. For example, Congress introduced an investment tax credit in 2002 that only applied to investment spending over the next two years. Like department store sales that encourage shoppers to spend a lot while the sale is on, temporary investment tax credits tend to generate a lot of investment spending when they're in effect. Even if a firm doesn't think it will need a new server or lathe for another year or so, it may make sense to buy it while the tax credit is available, rather than wait.

To see why the budget affects consumer spending, recall that *disposable income*, the total income households have available to spend, is equal to the total income they receive from wages, dividends, interest, and rent, *minus* taxes, *plus* government transfers. So either an increase in taxes or a decrease in government transfers *reduces* disposable income. And a fall in disposable income, other things equal, leads to a fall in consumer spending. Conversely, either a decrease in taxes or an increase in government transfers *increases* disposable income. And a rise in disposable income, other things equal, leads to a rise in consumer spending.

The government's ability to affect investment spending is a more complex story, which we won't discuss in detail (but see For Inquiring Minds above). The important point is that the government taxes profits, and changes in the rules that determine how much a business owes can increase or reduce the incentive to spend on investment goods.

Because the government itself is one source of aggregate demand in the economy, and because taxes and transfers can affect spending by consumers and firms, the government can use changes in taxes or government spending to *shift the aggregate demand curve*. And as we saw in Chapter 27, there are sometimes good reasons to shift the aggregate demand curve. For example, the Japanese government has spent trillions of dollars in an effort to increase aggregate demand. Japan's use of massive government construction spending to prop up its economy in the 1990s is a classic example of *fiscal policy:* the use of taxes, government transfers, or government purchases of goods and services to stabilize the economy by shifting the aggregate demand curve.

Expansionary and Contractionary Fiscal Policy

Why would the government want to shift the aggregate demand curve? Because it wants to close either a recessionary gap, created when aggregate output falls below potential output, or an inflationary gap, created when aggregate output exceeds potential output.

Figure 29-4 shows the case of an economy facing a recessionary gap. *SRAS* is the short-run aggregate supply curve, *LRAS* is the long-run aggregate supply curve, and AD_1 is the initial aggregate demand curve. At the initial short-run macroeconomic equilibrium, E_1, aggregate output is Y_1, below potential output, Y_P. What the government would like to do is increase aggregate demand, shifting the aggregate demand curve rightward to AD_2. This would increase aggregate output, making it equal to

Figure 29-4

Expansionary Fiscal Policy Can Close a Recessionary Gap

At E_1 the economy is in short-run macroeconomic equilibrium where the aggregate demand curve AD_1 intersects the $SRAS$ curve. At E_1, there is a recessionary gap of $Y_P - Y_1$. An expansionary fiscal policy—an increase in government purchases, a reduction in taxes, or an increase in government transfers—shifts the aggregate demand curve rightward. It can close the recessionary gap by shifting AD_1 to AD_2, moving the economy to a new short-run macroeconomic equilibrium, E_2, which is also a long-run macroeconomic equilibrium. **>web**...

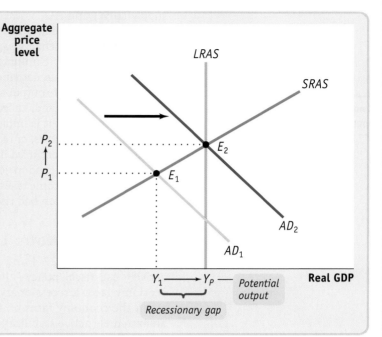

potential output. Fiscal policy that increases aggregate demand, called **expansionary fiscal policy,** normally takes one of three forms:

Expansionary fiscal policy increases aggregate demand.

- An increase in government purchases of goods and services, such as the Japanese government's decision to launch a massive construction program
- A cut in taxes, such as the one the United States implemented in 2001
- An increase in government transfers, such as unemployment benefits

Figure 29-5 shows the opposite case—an economy facing an inflationary gap. Again, $SRAS$ is the short-run aggregate supply curve, $LRAS$ is the long-run aggregate

Figure 29-5

Contractionary Fiscal Policy Can Close an Inflationary Gap

At E_1 the economy is in short-run macroeconomic equilibrium where the aggregate demand curve AD_1 intersects the $SRAS$ curve. At E_1, there is an inflationary gap of $Y_1 - Y_P$. A contractionary fiscal policy—reduced government purchases, an increase in taxes, or a reduction in government transfers—shifts the aggregate demand curve leftward. It can close the inflationary gap by shifting AD_1 to AD_2, moving the economy to a new short-run macroeconomic equilibrium, E_2, which is also a long-run macroeconomic equilibrium.
>web...

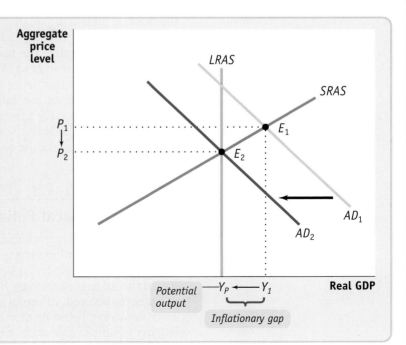

supply curve, and AD_1 is the initial aggregate demand curve. At the initial short-run macroeconomic equilibrium, E_1, aggregate output is Y_1, above potential output, Y_P. As we'll explain in later chapters, policy makers often try to head off inflation by eliminating inflationary gaps. To eliminate the inflationary gap shown in Figure 29-5, fiscal policy must reduce aggregate demand and shift the aggregate demand curve leftward to AD_2. This reduces aggregate output and makes it equal to potential output. Fiscal policy that reduces aggregate demand, called **contractionary fiscal policy,** is the opposite of expansionary fiscal policy. It is implemented by reducing government purchases of goods and services, increasing taxes, or reducing government transfers. A classic example of contractionary fiscal policy occurred in 1968, when U.S. policy makers grew worried about rising inflation. President Lyndon Johnson imposed a temporary 10% surcharge on income taxes—everyone's income taxes were increased by 10%. He also tried to scale back government purchases, which had risen dramatically because of the cost of the Vietnam War.

Contractionary fiscal policy reduces aggregate demand.

A Cautionary Note: Lags in Fiscal Policy

Looking at Figures 29-4 and 29-5, it may seem obvious that the government should actively use fiscal policy—always adopting an expansionary fiscal policy when the economy faces a recessionary gap and always adopting a contractionary fiscal policy when the economy faces an inflationary gap. But many economists caution against an extremely active stabilization policy, arguing that a government that tries too hard to stabilize the economy—through either fiscal policy or monetary policy—can end up making the economy less stable.

We'll leave discussion of the warnings associated with monetary policy to Chapter 34. In the case of fiscal policy, the reason for caution is that there are important *time lags* in its use. To understand the nature of these lags, think about what has to happen before the government increases spending to fight a recessionary gap. First, the government has to realize that the recessionary gap exists: economic data take time to collect and analyze, and recessions are often recognized only months after they have begun. Second, the government has to develop a spending plan, which can itself take months, particularly if politicians take time debating how the money should be spent and passing legislation. Finally, it takes time to spend money. For example, a road construction project begins with activities such as surveying that don't involve spending large sums. It may be quite some time before the big spending begins.

Because of these lags, an attempt to increase spending to fight a recessionary gap may take so long to get going that the recessionary gap may have turned into an inflationary gap by the time the fiscal policy takes effect. In that case, the fiscal policy will make things worse instead of better.

This doesn't mean that fiscal policy should never be actively used. After all, time lags didn't pose a problem for Japanese fiscal policy in the 1990s, which was attempting to fight a recessionary gap that lasted for many years. But the problem of lags makes the actual use of both fiscal and monetary policy harder than you might think from a simple analysis like the one we have just given.

economics in action

Expansionary Fiscal Policy in Japan

"In what may be the biggest public works bonanza since the pharaohs, Japan has spent something like $1.4 trillion trying to pave and build its way back to economic health," began one newspaper report on Japan's efforts to prop up its economy with fiscal policy.

Japan turned to expansionary fiscal policy in the early 1990s. In the 1980s the country's economy boomed, driven in part by soaring values of stocks and real estate, which boosted consumer spending through the wealth effect and also encouraged investment spending. Japanese economists now refer to this period as the "bubble economy," because the rise in stock and land values could not be justified in terms of rational calculations. At the end of the 1980s the bubble burst—stock and land values plunged, and the economy slid into recession as consumer and investment spending fell. Since the early 1990s Japan has relied on large-scale government purchases of goods and services, mainly in the form of construction spending on infrastructure, to prop up aggregate demand. This spending has been scaled back in recent years, but at its peak it was truly impressive. In 1996 Japan spent about $300 billion on infrastructure, compared with only $180 billion spent in the United States, even though Japan has less than half America's population and considerably less than half its GDP. Superb roads run through sparsely populated regions, ferries to small islands have been replaced by bridges, and many of the country's riverbeds have been paved, so that they resemble concrete aqueducts.

Has this policy been a success? Yes and no. Many economists believe that without all that government spending the Japanese economy would have slid into a 1930s-type depression after the bubble in stock and land values burst. Instead, the economy suffered a slowdown but not a severe slump: growth has been sluggish and unemployment has risen, but there has been no depression.

Furthermore, alternative policies weren't readily available. The alternative to using fiscal policy to prop up a slumping economy is using monetary policy, in which the central bank expands the money supply and drives down interest rates. Japan has done that, too; since 1998 short-term interest rates have been approximately zero! Since interest rates can't go below zero, there was no room for further interest rate cuts, yet the economy remained sluggish. So expansionary fiscal policy was the only obvious way to increase aggregate demand.

However, expansionary fiscal policy has not yet produced a full recovery in Japan. And the years of deficit spending have led to a rising government debt–GDP ratio that worries many financial experts. ∎

> >

>>**CHECK YOUR UNDERSTANDING 29-1**

1. In each of the following cases, determine whether the policy is an expansionary or contractionary fiscal policy.
   a. Several military bases around the country, which together employ tens of thousands of people, are closed.
   b. The number of weeks an unemployed person is eligible for unemployment benefits is increased.
   c. The federal tax on gasoline is increased.

2. Explain why federal disaster relief, which quickly disburses funds to victims of natural disasters such as hurricanes, floods, and large-scale crop failures, will stabilize the economy more effectively than relief that must be legislated.

Solutions appear at back of book.

Fiscal Policy and the Multiplier

An expansionary fiscal policy, like Japan's program of public works, pushes the aggregate demand curve to the right. A contractionary fiscal policy, like Lyndon Johnson's tax surcharge, pushes the aggregate demand curve to the left. For policy makers, however, knowing the direction of the shift isn't enough: they need estimates of *how much* the aggregate demand curve is shifted by a given policy. To get these estimates, they use the concept of the multiplier, which we introduced in Chapter 27.

Multiplier Effects of an Increase in Government Purchases of Goods and Services

Suppose that a government decides to spend $50 billion building bridges and roads. The government's purchases of goods and services will directly increase total spending on final goods and services by $50 billion. But as we learned in Chapter 27, there will also be an indirect effect because the government's purchases will start a chain reaction throughout the economy. The firms producing the goods and services purchased by the government will earn revenues that flow to households in the form of wages, profit, interest, and rent. This increase in disposable income will lead to a rise in consumer spending. The rise in consumer spending, in turn, will induce firms to increase output, leading to a further rise in disposable income, which will lead to another round of consumer spending increases, and so on.

In Chapter 27 we introduced the concept of the *multiplier*: the ratio of the change in real GDP caused by an autonomous change in aggregate spending to the size of that autonomous change. We saw there that in the simplest case (where there are no taxes or international trade, so that any change in real GDP accrues entirely to households, and the aggregate price level and the interest rate are fixed) the multiplier is $1/(1 - MPC)$. Recall that MPC is the *marginal propensity to consume,* the fraction of an additional dollar in disposable income that is spent. For example, if the marginal propensity to consume is 0.6, the multiplier is $1/(1 - 0.6) = 1/0.4 = 2.5$.

An increase in government purchases of goods and services is an example of an autonomous increase in aggregate spending. Its effect is illustrated in Figure 29-6. Given a multiplier of 2.5, a $50 billion increase in government purchases of goods and services will shift the AD curve rightward from AD_1 to AD_2, a distance representing an increase in real GDP of $125 billion at a given aggregate price level, P^*. Of that $125 billion, $50 billion is the initial effect from the increase in G, and the remaining $75 billion is the subsequent effect arising from the increase in consumer spending.

What happens if government purchases of goods and services are instead reduced? The math is exactly the same, except that there's a minus sign in front: if government purchases fall by $50 billion and the marginal propensity to consume is 0.6, the AD curve shifts leftward by $125 billion.

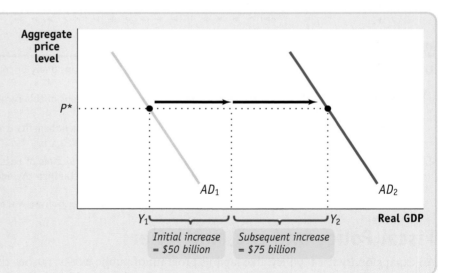

Figure 29-6

The Multiplier Effect of an Increase in Government Purchases of Goods and Services

A $50 billion increase in government purchases of goods and services has the direct effect of shifting the aggregate demand curve to the right by $50 billion. However, this is not the end of the story. The rise in real GDP causes a rise in disposable income, which leads to an increase in consumer spending, which leads to a further rise in real GDP, which leads to a further rise in consumer spending, and so on. The eventual shift, from AD_1 to AD_2, is a *multiple* of the increase in government purchases.

Multiplier Effects of Changes in Government Transfers and Taxes

Expansionary or contractionary fiscal policy need not take the form of changes in government purchases of goods and services. Governments can also change transfer payments or taxes. In general, however, a change in government transfers or taxes shifts the aggregate demand curve by *less* than an equal-sized change in government purchases.

To see why, imagine that instead of spending $50 billion on building bridges, the government simply hands out $50 billion in the form of government transfers. In this case, there is no direct effect on aggregate demand as there was with government purchases of goods and services. Real GDP goes up only because households spend some of that $50 billion. How much will they spend? Because the $50 billion transfer payment increases disposable income, households will engage in a first-round increase in consumer spending of $MPC \times \$50$ billion. For example, if $MPC = 0.6$, the first-round increase in consumer spending will be $30 billion ($0.6 \times \$50$ billion $= \$30$ billion). Like an increase in government purchases, this initial rise in consumer spending will lead to a series of subsequent rounds in which real GDP, disposable income, and consumer spending rise further. In this example, although the transfer costs the government the same amount as the increase in spending on goods and services, the autonomous increase in aggregate spending from the transfer ($30 billion) is smaller than the autonomous increase in aggregate spending from government spending ($50 billion), and the overall effect on real GDP will also be smaller. In general, $1 of transfer payments will increase GDP by $\$MPC/(1 - MPC)$, less than the multiplier for increases in government purchases, which is $\$1/(1-MPC)$. For example, if the marginal propensity to consume is 0.6, $1 of transfer payments raises real GDP by only $\$0.6/(1 - 0.6) = \$1.50$, while a $1 increase in government purchases of goods and services raises real GDP by $\$1/(1 - 0.6) = \$2.50$.

A tax cut has an effect similar to the effect of a transfer. It increases disposable income, leading to a series of increases in consumer spending. But the overall effect is smaller than that of an equal-size increase in government purchases: the autonomous increase in aggregate spending is smaller because households save part of the amount of the tax cut.

We should also note that taxes introduce a further complication: they typically change the size of the multiplier. That's because in the real world governments rarely impose "lump sum" taxes, in which the amount of tax a household owes is independent of its income. Instead, the great majority of tax revenue is raised via taxes that depend positively on the level of real GDP. (The multiplier on tax changes given above, $\$MPC/(1 - MPC)$, is the multiplier on lump-sum taxes.) As we'll discuss shortly, and analyze in detail in the appendix to this chapter, taxes that depend positively on real GDP reduce the size of the multiplier.

In practice, economists often argue that it also matters *who* among the population gets tax cuts or increases in government transfers. For example, compare the effects of an increase in unemployment benefits with a cut in taxes on profits distributed to shareholders as dividends. Consumer surveys indicate that the average unemployed worker will spend a higher share of any increase in his or her disposable income than would the average recipient of dividend income. That is, people who are unemployed tend to have a higher MPC than people who own a lot of stocks because the latter tend to be wealthier and to save more of any increase in disposable income. If that's true, a dollar spent on unemployment benefits increases aggregate demand more than a dollar's worth of dividend tax cuts. As the Economics in Action that follows this section explains, such arguments played an important role in recent policy debates.

How Taxes Affect the Multiplier

When we introduced the analysis of the multiplier in Chapter 27, we simplified matters by assuming that a $1 increase in real GDP raises disposable income by $1. In fact, however, government taxes capture some part of the increase in real GDP that occurs in each round of the multiplier process since most government taxes depend positively on real GDP. As a result, disposable income increases by considerably less than $1 once we include taxes in the model.

The increase in government tax revenue when real GDP rises isn't the result of a deliberate decision or action by the government. It's a consequence of the way the tax laws are written, which causes most sources of government revenue to increase *automatically* when real GDP goes up. For example, income tax receipts increase when real GDP rises because the amount each individual owes in taxes depends positively on his or her income, and households' disposable income rises when real GDP rises. Sales tax receipts increase when real GDP rises because people with more income spend more on goods and services. And corporate profit tax receipts increase when real GDP rises because profits increase when the economy expands.

The effect of these automatic increases in tax revenue is to reduce the size of the multiplier. Remember, the multiplier is the result of a chain reaction in which higher GDP leads to higher disposable income, which leads to higher consumer spending, which leads to further increases in real GDP. The fact that the government siphons off some of any increase in real GDP means that at each stage of this process the increase in consumer spending is smaller than it would be if taxes weren't part of the picture. The result is to reduce the multiplier. The appendix to this chapter shows how to derive the multiplier when taxes that depend positively on real GDP are taken into account.

Many macroeconomists believe it's a good thing that in real life taxes reduce the multiplier. In Chapter 27 we argued that most, though not all, recessions are the result of negative *demand shocks*. The same mechanism that causes tax revenue to increase when the economy expands causes it to decrease when the economy contracts. Since tax receipts decrease when real GDP falls, the effects of these negative demand shocks are smaller than they would be if there were no taxes. The decrease in tax revenue reduces the adverse effect of the initial fall in aggregate demand. By cutting the amount of taxes households pay, the automatic decrease in government tax revenue generated by a fall in real GDP acts like an automatic expansionary fiscal policy implemented in the face of a recession. Similarly, when the economy expands, the government finds itself automatically pursuing a contractionary fiscal policy—a tax increase. Government spending and taxation rules that cause fiscal policy to be expansionary when the economy contracts and contractionary when the economy expands, without requiring any deliberate action by policy makers, are called **automatic stabilizers.**

The rules that govern tax collection aren't the only automatic stabilizers, although they are the most important ones. Some types of government transfers also play a stabilizing role. For example, more people receive unemployment insurance when the economy is depressed than when it is booming. The same is true of Medicaid and food stamps. So transfer payments tend to rise when the economy is contracting and fall when the economy is expanding. Like changes in tax revenue, these changes in transfers tend to reduce the size of the multiplier because the total change in disposable income that results from a given rise or fall in real GDP is smaller.

As in the case of government tax revenue, many macroeconomists believe that it's a good thing that government transfers reduce the multiplier. More generally, expansionary and contractionary fiscal policies that are the result of automatic stabilizers are widely considered helpful to macroeconomic stabilization. But what about fiscal policy that *isn't* the result of automatic stabilizers? **Discretionary fiscal policy** is fiscal policy that is the direct result of deliberate actions by policy makers rather than automatic adjustment. For example, during a recession, the government may pass legislation that cuts taxes and purposely increases government spending in order to stimulate the economy. The use of discretionary fiscal policy to fight recessions and rein in expansions is much more controversial than the role of automatic stabilizers. We'll explain why, and describe the debates among macroeconomists on the appropriate role of fiscal policy, in Chapter 34.

Automatic stabilizers are government spending and taxation rules that cause fiscal policy to be expansionary when the economy contracts and contractionary when the economy expands.

Discretionary fiscal policy is fiscal policy that is the result of deliberate actions by policy makers rather than rules.

An example of a discretionary fiscal policy was the Works Progress Administration (WPA), a relief measure established during the Great Depression. The unemployed were put to work on public works projects, building bridges, roads, buildings, and parks.

economics in action

How Much Bang for the Buck?

In 2001 the U.S. economy experienced a recession, followed by a 2002–2003 "jobless recovery" in which real GDP grew but overall employment didn't. There was widespread agreement among economists that the country needed an expansionary fiscal policy to stimulate aggregate demand. And the government did, in fact, pursue an expansionary fiscal policy: tax cuts combined with increased government spending undoubtedly helped increase aggregate demand and output.

But was the expansionary fiscal policy carried out in the right way? Critics argued that a different mix of policies would have yielded more "bang for the buck"—they would have done more to increase aggregate demand, but led to a smaller rise in the budget deficit.

A particularly clear (and nonpartisan) example of this criticism was an analysis by Mark Zandi, the chief economist of economy.com, a consulting firm. Zandi estimated the multiplier effects of a number of alternative fiscal policies, shown in Table 29-1. He argued that many of the tax cuts enacted between 2001 and 2003 had smaller effects on aggregate demand compared to other types of tax cuts because they went to people who probably wouldn't spend much of the increase in their disposable income. He was particularly critical of tax cuts on dividend income and on the value of inherited estates, arguing that they did very little to raise consumer spending. According to his analysis, an alternative set of fiscal policies that put more disposable income into the hands of unemployed workers, lower-income taxpayers, and cash-strapped state and local governments would have created a larger increase in spending at the same cost. This would have led to both lower budget deficits and a larger increase in real GDP—and so to lower unemployment. This view was shared by many economists, though certainly not by all.

Despite the criticisms, there was widespread agreement that the tax cuts of 2001–2003 helped generate an economic expansion. As Richard Berner, an economist

TABLE 29-1

Differences in the Effect of Expansionary Fiscal Policies

Policy	Estimated increase in real GDP per dollar of fiscal policy	Explanation of policy
Extend emergency federal unemployment insurance benefits	$1.73	Extends the period for unemployment benefits, increasing transfers to the unemployed
10% personal income tax bracket	1.34	Reduces tax rate on some income from 15% to 10%, mainly benefiting middle-income families
State government aid	1.24	Provides financial aid to state governments during recessions so states do not have to raise taxes or cut spending
Child tax credit rebate	1.04	Increases the income tax reduction for each child, mainly benefiting middle- and lower-income families
Marriage tax penalty	0.74	Reduces the "marriage penalty," an increase in combined taxes that can occur when two working people marry
Alternative minimum tax adjustments	0.67	Revises the alternative minimum tax, designed to prevent wealthy people with many deductions from paying too little tax, to exclude those not considered sufficiently wealthy
Personal marginal tax rate reductions	0.59	Reduces tax rates for people in higher income brackets
Business investment writeoff	0.24	Temporarily allows companies to deduct some investment spending from taxable profits
Dividend–capital gain tax reduction	0.09	Reduces taxes on dividends and capital gains
Estate tax reduction	0.00	Reduces the tax paid on the value of assets passed to heirs upon a person's death

Source: economy.com

at the investment firm Morgan Stanley, put it, the tax cuts might not have generated a lot of bang per buck, but they were still effective because they involved a lot of bucks. ∎

< < < < < < < < < < < < < < < < < < <

>>CHECK YOUR UNDERSTANDING 29-2

1. Explain why a $500 million increase in government purchases of goods and services will generate a larger shift in the aggregate demand curve than a $500 million increase in government transfers.

2. Explain why a $500 million reduction in government purchases of goods and services will generate a larger shift in the aggregate demand curve than a $500 million reduction in government transfers.

Solutions appear at back of book.

The Budget Balance

Headlines about the government's budget tend to focus on just one point: whether the government is running a surplus or a deficit and, in either case, how big. People usually think of surpluses as good: when the federal government ran a record surplus in 2000, many people regarded it as a cause for celebration. Conversely, people usually think of deficits as bad: when the federal government ran a record deficit in 2004, many people regarded it as a cause for concern, and the White House promised to bring the deficit down over time.

How do surpluses and deficits fit into the analysis of fiscal policy? Are deficits ever a good thing and surpluses a bad thing? Let's look at the causes and consequences of surpluses and deficits.

The Budget Balance as a Measure of Fiscal Policy

What do we mean by surpluses and deficits? The budget balance, which we defined in Chapter 26, is the difference between the government's income, in the form of tax revenue, and its spending, both on goods and services and on government transfers, in a given year. That is, the budget balance is equal to government savings and is defined by Equation 29-2:

(29-2) $S_{Government} = T - G - TR$

where T is the value of tax revenues, G is government purchases, and TR is the value of government transfers. As we learned in Chapter 26, a budget surplus is a positive budget balance and a budget deficit is a negative budget balance.

Other things equal, expansionary fiscal policies—increased government purchases of goods and services, higher government transfers, or lower taxes—reduce the budget balance for that year. That is, expansionary fiscal policies make a budget surplus smaller or a budget deficit bigger. Conversely, contractionary fiscal policies—reduced government purchases of goods and services, lower government transfers, or higher taxes—increase the budget balance for that year, making a budget surplus bigger or a budget deficit smaller.

You might think this means that changes in the budget balance can be used to measure fiscal policy. In fact, economists often do just that: they use changes in the budget balance as a "quick-and-dirty" way to assess whether current fiscal policy is expansionary or contractionary. But they always keep in mind two reasons this quick-and-dirty approach is sometimes misleading:

- Two different changes in fiscal policy that have equal effects on the budget balance may have quite unequal effects on aggregate demand. As we have already seen, changes in government purchases have a larger effect on aggregate demand than equal-size changes in taxes and government transfers.

- Often, changes in the budget balance are themselves the result, not the cause, of fluctuations in the economy.

To understand the second point, we need to examine the effects of the business cycle on the budget.

The Business Cycle and the Cyclically Adjusted Budget Balance

Historically there has been a strong relationship between the federal government's budget balance and the business cycle. The budget tends to move into deficit when the economy experiences a recession, but deficits tend to get smaller or even turn into surpluses when the economy is expanding. Figure 29-7 shows the federal budget deficit as a percentage of GDP since 1970. Shaded areas indicate recessions; unshaded areas indicate expansions. As you can see, the federal budget deficit increased around the time of each recession and usually declined during expansions. In fact, in the late stages of the long expansion from 1991 to 2000 the deficit actually became negative—the budget deficit became a budget surplus.

The relationship between the business cycle and the budget balance is even clearer if we compare the budget deficit as a percentage of GDP with the unemployment rate, as we do in Figure 29-8 on page 706. The budget deficit almost always rises when the unemployment rate rises and falls when the unemployment rate falls.

Is this relationship between the business cycle and the budget balance evidence that policy makers engage in discretionary fiscal policy, using expansionary fiscal policy during recessions and contractionary fiscal policy during expansions? Not

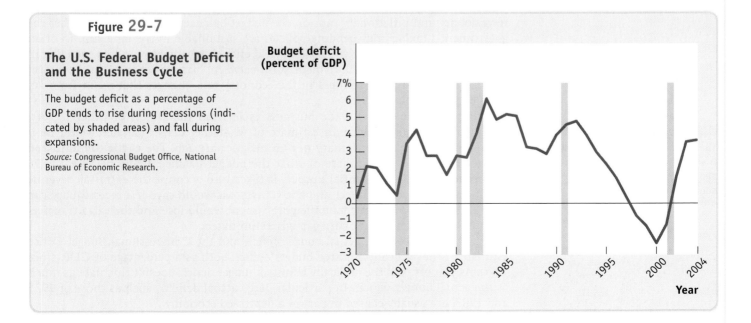

Figure 29-7

The U.S. Federal Budget Deficit and the Business Cycle

The budget deficit as a percentage of GDP tends to rise during recessions (indicated by shaded areas) and fall during expansions.

Source: Congressional Budget Office, National Bureau of Economic Research.

Figure 29-8

The U.S. Federal Budget Deficit and the Unemployment Rate

There is a close relationship between the budget balance and the business cycle: a recession moves the budget balance toward deficit, but an expansion moves it toward surplus. Here, the unemployment rate serves as an indicator of the business cycle, and we should expect to see a higher unemployment rate associated with a higher budget deficit. This is confirmed by the figure: the budget deficit as a percentage of GDP moves closely in tandem with the unemployment rate. **>web...**

Source: Congressional Budget Office, Bureau of Labor Statistics.

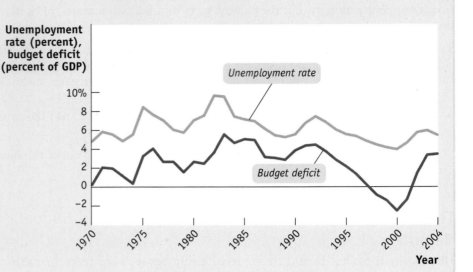

necessarily. To a large extent the relationship in Figure 29-8 reflects automatic stabilizers at work. As we learned in the discussion of automatic stabilizers, government tax revenue tends to rise and some government transfers, like unemployment benefit payments, tend to fall when the economy expands. Conversely, government tax revenue tends to fall and some government transfers tend to rise when the economy contracts. So the budget tends to move toward deficit during recessions and toward surplus during expansions even without any deliberate action on the part of policy makers.

In assessing budget policy, it's often useful to separate changes in the budget balance due to the business cycle from changes due to deliberate policy changes. The former are affected by automatic stabilizers and the latter, by deliberate changes in government purchases, government transfers, or taxes. For one thing, business-cycle effects on the budget balance are temporary: both recessionary gaps (in which real GDP is below potential output) and inflationary gaps (in which real GDP is above potential output) tend to be eliminated in the long run. So taking out the effects of recessionary and inflationary gaps on the budget balance sheds light on whether the government's taxing and spending policies are sustainable in the long run. In other words, do the government's tax policies yield enough revenue to fund its spending in the long run? Also, it's useful to distinguish between "passive" changes in the budget balance that result from changes in the economy and changes that result from actions by policy makers.

To separate the effect of the business cycle from the effects of other factors, many governments produce an estimate of what the budget balance would be if there were neither a recessionary nor an inflationary gap. The **cyclically adjusted budget balance** is an estimate of what the budget balance would be if real GDP were exactly equal to potential output. It takes into account the extra tax revenue the government would collect and the transfers it would save if a recessionary gap were eliminated—or the revenue the government would lose and the extra transfers it would make if an inflationary gap were eliminated.

Figure 29-9 shows the actual budget deficit and the Congressional Budget Office estimate of the cyclically adjusted budget deficit, both as a percentage of GDP, since 1970. As you can see, the cyclically adjusted budget deficit doesn't fluctuate as much as the actual budget deficit. In particular, large actual deficits, such as those of 1975 and 1983, are usually caused in part by a depressed economy.

The **cyclically adjusted budget balance** is an estimate of what the budget balance would be if real GDP were exactly equal to potential output.

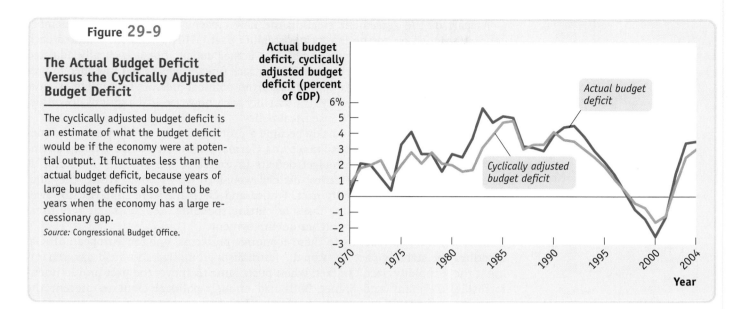

Figure 29-9

The Actual Budget Deficit Versus the Cyclically Adjusted Budget Deficit

The cyclically adjusted budget deficit is an estimate of what the budget deficit would be if the economy were at potential output. It fluctuates less than the actual budget deficit, because years of large budget deficits also tend to be years when the economy has a large recessionary gap.

Source: Congressional Budget Office.

Should the Budget Be Balanced?

As we'll see in the next section, persistent budget deficits can cause problems for both the government and the economy. Yet politicians are always tempted to run deficits because this allows them to cater to voters by cutting taxes without cutting spending or by increasing spending without increasing taxes. As a result, there are occasional attempts by policy makers to force fiscal discipline by introducing legislation—even a constitutional amendment—forbidding the government from running budget deficits. This is usually stated as a requirement that the budget be "balanced"—that revenues at least equal spending each fiscal year. Would it be a good idea to require a balanced budget annually?

Most economists don't think so. They believe that the government should only balance its budget on average—that it should be allowed to run deficits in bad years, offset by surpluses in good years. They don't believe the government should be forced to run a balanced budget *every year* because this would undermine the role of taxes and transfers as automatic stabilizers. As we learned earlier in this chapter, the tendency of tax revenue to fall and transfers to rise when the economy contracts helps to limit the size of recessions. But falling tax revenue and rising transfer payments push the budget toward deficit. If constrained by a balanced-budget rule, the government would have to respond to this deficit with contractionary fiscal policies that would tend to deepen the recession.

Yet policy makers concerned about excessive deficits sometimes feel that rigid rules prohibiting—or at least setting an upper limit on—deficits are necessary. As Economics in Action explains, Europe has had a lot of trouble reconciling rules to enforce fiscal responsibility with the problems of short-run fiscal policy.

economics in action

Stability Pact—or Stupidity Pact?

In 1999 a group of European nations took a momentous step when they adopted a common currency, the euro, to replace their national currencies, such as French francs, German marks, and Italian lira. Along with the introduction of the euro came the creation of the European Central Bank, which sets monetary policy for the whole region.

As part of the agreement creating the new currency, governments of member countries signed on to the European "stability pact." This agreement required each government to keep its budget deficit—its actual deficit, not a cyclically adjusted number—below 3% of the country's GDP or face fines. The pact was intended to prevent irresponsible deficit spending arising from political pressure that might eventually undermine the new currency. The stability pact, however, had a serious downside: it limited a country's ability to use fiscal policy.

In fact, the stability pact quickly became a problem for the two largest economies in the euro zone. In 2002 both France and Germany were experiencing rising unemployment and also running budget deficits in excess of 3% of GDP. Moreover, it seemed likely that both countries' deficits would go up in 2003, which they did. Under the rules of the stability pact, France and Germany were supposed to lower their budget deficits by raising taxes or cutting spending. Yet contractionary fiscal policy would have led to even higher unemployment.

In October 2002, reacting to these economic problems, one top European official described the stability pact as "stupid." Journalists promptly had a field day, renaming it the "stupidity pact." In fact, when push came to shove, the pact proved unenforceable. Germany and France both had enough political clout to prevent the imposition of penalties. Indeed, in March 2005 the stability pact was rewritten to allow "small and temporary" breaches of the 3% limit, with a special clause allowing Germany to describe aid to the former East Germany as a temporary expense.

Before patting themselves on the back over the superiority of their own fiscal rules, Americans should note that the United States has its own version of the stupidity pact. The federal government's budget acts as an automatic stabilizer, but 49 of the 50 states are required by their state constitutions to balance their budgets every year. When recession struck in 2001, most states were forced to—guess what?—slash spending and raise taxes in the face of a recession, exactly the wrong thing from a macroeconomic point of view. Not surprisingly, some states, like some European countries, found ways to cheat. ∎

< < < < < < < < < < < < < < < < < < <

>>**CHECK YOUR UNDERSTANDING 29-3**

1. When your work–study earnings are low, your parents help you out with expenses. When your earnings are high, they expect you to contribute toward your tuition bill. Explain how this arrangement acts like an automatic stabilizer for your economic activity.

2. Explain why states required by their constitutions to balance their budgets are likely to experience more severe economic fluctuations than states not held to that requirement.

Solutions appear at back of book.

Long-Run Implications of Fiscal Policy

The Japanese government built the bridge to Awaji Island as part of a fiscal policy aimed at increasing aggregate demand. As we've seen, that policy was partly successful: although Japan's economy was sluggish during the 1990s, it avoided a severe slump comparable to what happened to many countries in the 1930s. Yet the fact that Japan was running large deficits year after year made many observers uneasy. By 2000 there was a debate among economists about whether Japan's debt was starting to reach alarming levels.

No discussion of fiscal policy is complete if it doesn't take into account the long-run implications of government budget surpluses and deficits. We now turn to those long-run implications.

Deficits, Surpluses, and Debt

When a family spends more than it earns over the course of a year, it has to raise the extra funds either by selling assets or by borrowing. And if a family borrows year after year, it will end up with a lot of debt.

The same is true for governments. With a few exceptions, governments don't raise large sums by selling assets such as national parkland. Instead, when a government spends more than the tax revenue it receives—when it runs a budget deficit—it almost always borrows the extra funds. And governments that run persistent budget deficits end up with substantial debts.

To interpret the numbers that follow, you need to know a slightly peculiar feature of federal government accounting. For historical reasons, the U.S. government does not keep books for calendar years. Instead, budget totals are kept for **fiscal years,** which run from October 1 to September 30 and are named by the calendar year in which they end. For example, fiscal 2004 began on October 1, 2003, and ended on September 30, 2004.

At the end of fiscal 2004, the U.S. federal government had total debt equal to almost $7.4 trillion. However, part of that debt represented special accounting rules specifying that the federal government as a whole owes funds to certain government programs, especially Social Security. We'll explain those rules shortly. For now, however, let's focus on **public debt:** government debt held by individuals and institutions outside the government. At the end of fiscal 2004, the federal government's public debt was "only" $4.3 trillion, or 37% of GDP. If we include the debts of state and local governments, total government public debt was approximately 44% of GDP. Figure 29-10 compares the U.S. public debt–GDP ratio with the public debt–GDP ratios of other wealthy countries in 2003. As of 2003, the U.S. debt level was more or less typical.

U.S. federal government public debt at the end of fiscal 2004 was larger than it was at the end of fiscal 2003, because the federal government ran a budget deficit during fiscal 2004. A government that runs persistent budget deficits will experience a rising level of public debt. But why is this a problem?

PITFALLS

DEFICITS VERSUS DEBT

One common mistake—it happens all the time in newspaper reports—is to confuse *deficits* with *debt*. Let's review the difference.

A *deficit* is the difference between the amount of money a government spends and the amount it receives in taxes over a given period—usually, though not always, a year. Deficit numbers always come with a statement about the time period to which they apply, as in "The U.S. budget deficit *in fiscal 2004* was $412 billion."

A *debt* is the sum of money a government owes at a particular point in time. Debt numbers usually come with a specific date, as in "U.S. public debt *at the end of fiscal 2004* was $4.3 trillion."

Deficits and debt are linked, because government debt grows when governments run deficits. But they aren't the same thing, and they can even tell different stories. At the end of fiscal 2004, U.S. *debt* as a percentage of GDP was fairly low by historical standards, but the *deficit* during fiscal 2004 was considered quite high.

Fiscal years run from October 1 to September 30 and are named by the calendar year in which they end.

Public debt is government debt held by individuals and institutions outside the government.

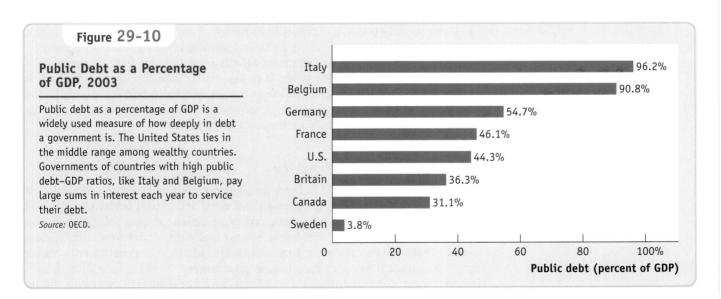

Figure 29-10

Public Debt as a Percentage of GDP, 2003

Public debt as a percentage of GDP is a widely used measure of how deeply in debt a government is. The United States lies in the middle range among wealthy countries. Governments of countries with high public debt–GDP ratios, like Italy and Belgium, pay large sums in interest each year to service their debt.

Source: OECD.

Country	Public debt (percent of GDP)
Italy	96.2%
Belgium	90.8%
Germany	54.7%
France	46.1%
U.S.	44.3%
Britain	36.3%
Canada	31.1%
Sweden	3.8%

Problems Posed by Rising Government Debt

There are two reasons to be concerned when a government runs persistent budget deficits. We described one reason in Chapter 26: when the government borrows funds in the financial markets, it is competing with firms that plan to borrow funds for investment spending. As a result, the government's borrowing may "crowd out" private investment spending and reduce the economy's long-run rate of growth.

But there's also a second reason: today's deficits, by increasing the government's debt, place financial pressure on future budgets. The impact of current deficits on future budgets is straightforward. Like individuals, governments must pay their bills—including interest payments on their accumulated debt. When a government is deeply in debt, those interest payments can be substantial. In fiscal 2004, the U.S. federal government paid 1.4% of GDP—$160 billion—in interest on its debt. The two most heavily indebted governments shown in Figure 29-10 on page 709, Italy and Belgium, each paid interest of more than 5% of GDP in 2004.

Other things equal, a government paying large sums in interest must raise more revenue from taxes or spend less than it would otherwise be able to afford—or it must borrow even more to cover the gap. But a government that borrows to pay interest on its outstanding debt pushes itself even deeper into debt. This process can eventually push a government to the point where lenders question its ability to repay. Like a consumer who has maxed out his or her credit cards, it will find that lenders are unwilling to lend any more funds. The result can be that the government defaults on its debt—it stops paying what it owes. Default is often followed by financial and economic turmoil.

The idea of a government defaulting sounds far-fetched, but it is not impossible. In the 1990s Argentina, a relatively high-income developing country, was widely praised for its economic policies—and it was able to borrow large sums from foreign lenders. By 2002, however, Argentina's interest payments were spiraling out of control, and the country stopped paying the sums that were due. We describe that default in the Economics in Action that follows this section.

Default creates havoc in a country's financial markets and badly shakes public confidence in both the government and the economy. Argentina's debt default was accompanied by a crisis in the country's banking systems and a very severe recession. And even if a highly indebted government avoids default, a heavy debt burden typically forces it to slash spending or raise taxes, politically unpopular measures that can also damage the economy.

One question some people ask is, can't a government that has trouble borrowing just print money to pay its bills? Yes, it can, but this leads to another problem: inflation. In fact, budget problems are the main cause of very severe inflation, as we'll see in Chapter 33. The point for now is that governments do not want to find themselves in a position where the choice is between defaulting on their debts and inflating those debts away.

Concerns about the long-run effects of deficits need not rule out the use of fiscal policy to stimulate the economy when it is depressed. However, these concerns do mean that governments should try to offset budget deficits in bad years with budget surpluses in good years. In other words, governments should run a budget that is approximately balanced over time. Have they actually done so?

Deficits and Debt in Practice

Figure 29-11 shows how the U.S. federal government's budget deficit and its debt have evolved since 1939. Panel (a) shows the federal deficit as a percentage of GDP. As you can see, the federal government ran huge deficits during World War II. It briefly ran surpluses after the war, but it has normally run deficits ever since, especially after 1980. This seems inconsistent with the advice that governments should offset deficits in bad times with surpluses in good times.

However, panel (b) shows that these deficits have not led to runaway debt. To assess the ability of governments to pay their debt, we often use the **debt–GDP ratio,** government debt as a percentage of GDP. We use this measure, rather than simply looking at the size of the debt, because GDP, which measures the size of the economy as a whole, is a good indicator of the potential taxes the government can collect. If the government's debt grows more slowly than GDP, the burden of paying that debt is actually falling compared with the government's potential tax revenue.

What we see from panel (b) is that although the federal debt has grown in almost every year, the debt–GDP ratio fell for 30 years after the end of World War II. This

The **debt–GDP ratio** is government debt as a percentage of GDP.

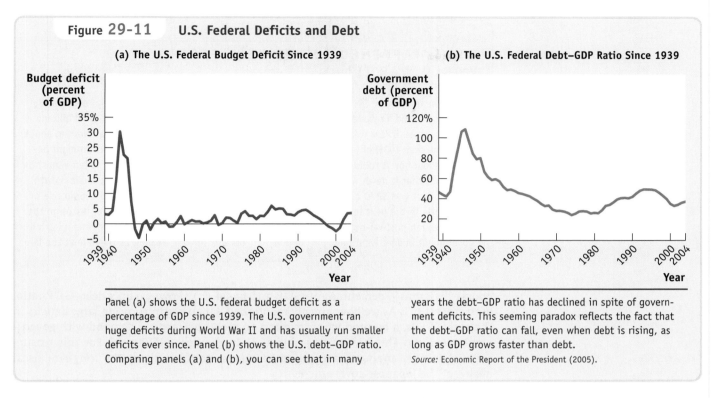

Figure 29-11   **U.S. Federal Deficits and Debt**

(a) The U.S. Federal Budget Deficit Since 1939

(b) The U.S. Federal Debt–GDP Ratio Since 1939

Panel (a) shows the U.S. federal budget deficit as a percentage of GDP since 1939. The U.S. government ran huge deficits during World War II and has usually run smaller deficits ever since. Panel (b) shows the U.S. debt–GDP ratio. Comparing panels (a) and (b), you can see that in many years the debt–GDP ratio has declined in spite of government deficits. This seeming paradox reflects the fact that the debt–GDP ratio can fall, even when debt is rising, as long as GDP grows faster than debt.

Source: Economic Report of the President (2005).

shows that the debt–GDP ratio can fall, even when debt is rising, as long as GDP grows faster than debt. For Inquiring Minds on page 712, which focuses on the large debt the U.S. government ran up during World War II, explains how growth and inflation sometimes allow a government that runs persistent budget deficits to nevertheless have a declining debt–GDP ratio.

Still, a government that runs persistent *large* deficits will have a rising debt–GDP ratio when debt grows faster than GDP. Panel (a) of Figure 29-12 shows Japan's

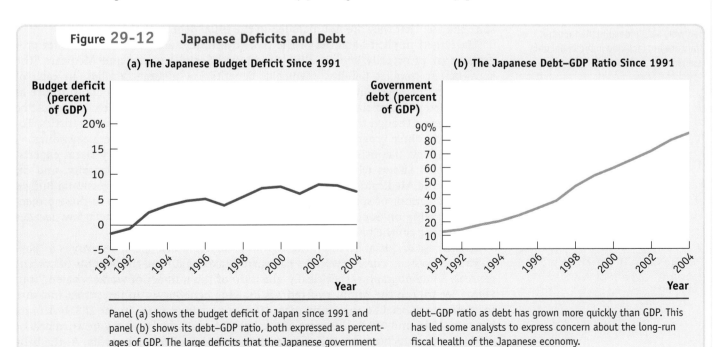

Figure 29-12   **Japanese Deficits and Debt**

(a) The Japanese Budget Deficit Since 1991

(b) The Japanese Debt–GDP Ratio Since 1991

Panel (a) shows the budget deficit of Japan since 1991 and panel (b) shows its debt–GDP ratio, both expressed as percentages of GDP. The large deficits that the Japanese government began running in the early 1990s have led to a rapid rise in its debt–GDP ratio as debt has grown more quickly than GDP. This has led some analysts to express concern about the long-run fiscal health of the Japanese economy.

Source: OECD.

WHAT HAPPENED TO THE DEBT FROM WORLD WAR II?

As you can see from Figure 29-11 on page 711, the U.S. government paid for World War II by borrowing on a huge scale. By the war's end, the public debt was more than 100% of GDP, and many people worried about how it could ever be paid off.

The truth is that it never was paid off. In 1946 public debt was $270 billion; that number dipped slightly in the next few years, as the United States ran postwar budget surpluses, but the government budget went back into deficit in 1950 with the start of the Korean War. By 1956 the debt was back up to $270 billion.

But by that time nobody was worried about the fiscal health of the U.S. government because the debt–GDP ratio had fallen almost by half. The reason? Vigorous economic growth, plus mild inflation, had led to a rapid rise in GDP. The experience was a clear lesson in the peculiar fact that modern governments can run deficits forever, as long as they aren't too large.

budget deficit as a percentage of GDP and panel (b) shows Japan's debt–GDP ratio, both since 1991. As we have already mentioned, Japan began running large deficits in the early 1990s, a by-product of its effort to prop up aggregate demand with government spending. This has led to a rapid rise in the debt–GDP ratio. For this reason, some economic analysts have begun to express concern about the long-run fiscal health of the Japanese government.

Implicit Liabilities

Looking at Figure 29-11 on page 711, you might be tempted to conclude that the U.S. federal budget is in fairly decent shape: the return to budget deficits after 2001 caused the debt–GDP ratio to rise a bit, but that ratio is still low compared with both historical experience and some other wealthy countries. In fact, however, experts on long-run budget issues view the situation of the United States (and other countries such as Japan and Italy) with alarm. The reason is the problem of *implicit liabilities*. **Implicit liabilities** are spending promises made by governments that are effectively a debt despite the fact that they are not included in the usual debt statistics.

The largest implicit liabilities of the U.S. government arise from two transfer programs that principally benefit older Americans: Social Security and Medicare. The third-largest implicit liability, Medicaid, benefits low-income families. In each of these cases the government has promised to provide transfer payments to future as well as current beneficiaries. So these programs represent a future debt that must be honored, even though the debt does not currently show up in the usual statistics. Together, these three programs currently account for about 40% of federal spending.

The implicit liabilities created by these transfer programs worry fiscal experts. Figure 29-13 shows why. It shows current spending on Social Security, and on Medicare and Medicaid as percentages of GDP, together with Congressional Budget Office projections of spending in 2010, 2030, and 2050. According to these projections, spending on Social Security will rise substantially over the next few decades and spending on the two health care programs will soar. Why?

In the case of Social Security, the answer is demography. Social Security is a "pay-as-you-go" system: current workers pay payroll taxes that fund the benefits of current retirees. So demography—specifically, the ratio of the number of workers paying into Social Security to the number of retirees drawing benefits—is an important measure for managing Social Security's finances. There was a huge surge in the U.S. birth rate between 1946 and 1964, the years of the baby boom. Baby boomers are currently of working age—which means they are paying taxes, not collecting benefits. As the baby boomers retire, they will stop earning income that is taxed and start collecting benefits. As a result, the ratio of retirees receiving benefits to workers paying into the So-

Implicit liabilities are spending promises made by governments that are effectively a debt despite the fact that they are not included in the usual debt statistics.

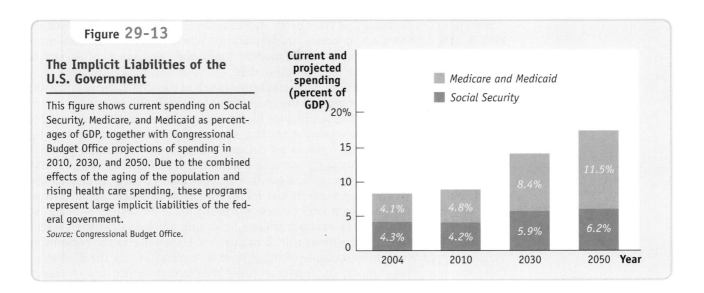

Figure 29-13

The Implicit Liabilities of the U.S. Government

This figure shows current spending on Social Security, Medicare, and Medicaid as percentages of GDP, together with Congressional Budget Office projections of spending in 2010, 2030, and 2050. Due to the combined effects of the aging of the population and rising health care spending, these programs represent large implicit liabilities of the federal government.

Source: Congressional Budget Office.

cial Security system will rise. In 2004 there were 30 retirees receiving benefits for every 100 workers paying into the system. By 2030, according to the Social Security Administration, that number will rise to 46; by 2050 it will rise to 50. This will raise benefit payments relative to the size of the economy.

The aging of the baby boomers, by itself, poses only a moderately sized long-run fiscal problem. The projected rise in Medicare and Medicaid spending is a much more serious concern. The main story behind projections of higher Medicare and Medicaid spending is the long-run tendency of health care spending to rise faster than overall spending, both for government-funded and for privately funded health care.

To some extent, the implicit liabilities of the U.S. government are already reflected in debt statistics. We mentioned earlier that the government had a total debt of $7.4 trillion at the end of 2004, but that only $4.3 trillion of that total was owed to the public. The main explanation for that discrepancy is that both Social Security and part of Medicare (the hospital insurance program) are supported by *dedicated taxes:* their expenses are paid out of special taxes on wages. At times, these dedicated taxes yield more revenue than is needed to pay current benefits. In particular, since the mid-1980s the Social Security system has been taking in more revenue than it currently needs in order to prepare for the retirement of the baby boomers. This surplus in the Social Security system has been used to accumulate a Social Security *trust fund,* which was $1.7 trillion at the end of 2004.

The $1.7 trillion in the trust fund is held in the form of U.S. government bonds, which are included in the $7.4 trillion in total debt. You could say that there's something funny about counting bonds in the Social Security trust fund as part of government debt. After all, they're owed by one part of the government (the government outside the Social Security system) to another part of the government (the Social Security system itself). But the debt corresponds to a real, if implicit, liability: promises by the government to pay future retirement benefits. So many economists argue that the gross debt of $7.4 trillion, the sum of public debt and government debt held by Social Security and other trust funds, is a more accurate indication of the government's fiscal health than the smaller amount owed to the public alone.

economics in action

Argentina's Creditors Take a Haircut

As we mentioned earlier, the idea that a government's debt can reach a level at which the government can't pay its creditors can seem far-fetched. In the United States, government debt is usually regarded as the safest asset there is.

But countries *do* default on their debts—fail to repay the money they borrowed. In 1998 Russia defaulted on its bonds, triggering a worldwide panic in financial markets. In 2001, in the biggest default of modern times, the government of Argentina stopped making payments on $81 billion in debt.

How did the Argentine default happen? During much of the 1990s, the country was experiencing an economic boom and the government was easily able to borrow money from abroad. Although deficit spending led to rising government debt, few considered this a problem. In 1998, however, the country slid into an economic slump that reduced tax revenues, leading to much larger deficits. Foreign lenders, increasingly nervous about the country's ability to repay, became unwilling to lend money except at very high interest rates. By 2001 the country was in a vicious circle: to cover its deficits and pay off old loans as they came due, it was forced to borrow at much higher interest rates, and the escalating interest rates on new borrowing made the deficits even bigger.

Argentine officials tried to reassure lenders by raising taxes and cutting government spending. But they were never able to balance the budget due to the continuing recession and the negative multiplier impact of their contractionary fiscal policies. These strongly contractionary fiscal policies drove the country deeper into recession. Late in 2001, facing popular protests, the Argentine government collapsed, and the country defaulted on its debt.

Creditors can take individuals who fail to pay debts to court. The court, in turn, can seize the debtors' assets and force them to pay part of future earnings to their creditors. But when a country defaults, it's different. Its creditors can't send in the police to seize the country's assets. They must negotiate a deal with the country for partial repayment. The only leverage creditors have in these negotiations is the defaulting government's fear that if it fails to reach a settlement, its reputation will suffer and it will be unable to borrow in the future. (A report by Reuters, the news agency, on Argentina's debt negotiations was headlined "Argentina to unhappy bondholders: so sue.")

It took three years for Argentina to reach an agreement with its creditors because the new Argentine government was determined to strike a hard bargain. And it did. Here's how Reuters described the settlement reached in March 2005: "The deal, which exchanged new paper valued at around 32 cents for every dollar in default, was the biggest 'haircut,' or loss on principal, for investors of any sovereign bond restructuring in modern times." Let's put this into English: Argentina forced its creditors to trade their "sovereign bonds"—debts of a sovereign nation, that is, Argentina—for new bonds worth only 32% as much. Such a reduction in the value of debt is known as a "haircut."

It's important to avoid two misconceptions about this "haircut." First, you might be tempted to think that because Argentina ended up paying only a fraction of the sums it owed, it paid little price for default. In fact, Argentina's default accompanied one of the worst economic slumps of modern times, a period of mass unemployment, soaring poverty, and widespread unrest. Second, it's tempting to dismiss the Argentine story as being of little relevance to countries like the United States. After all, aren't we more responsible than that? But Argentina wouldn't have been able to borrow so much in the first place if its government hadn't been well regarded by international lenders. In fact, as late as 1998 Argentina was widely admired for its economic management. What Argentina's slide into default shows is that concerns about the long-run effects of budget deficits are not at all academic. Due to its large and growing debt–GDP ratio, one recession pushed Argentina over the edge into economic collapse. ∎

< < < < < < < < < < < < < < < < < < <

>>CHECK YOUR UNDERSTANDING 29-4

1. Explain how each of the following events would affect the public debt or implicit liabilities of the U.S. government, other things equal. Would the public debt or implicit liabilities be greater or smaller?
   a. A higher growth rate of real GDP
   b. Retirees live longer
   c. A decrease in tax revenue
   d. Government borrowing to pay interest on its current public debt

2. Suppose the economy is in a slump and the current public debt is quite large. Explain the trade-off of short-run versus long-run objectives that policy makers face when deciding whether or not to engage in deficit spending.

Solutions appear at back of book.

● A LOOK AHEAD ●

Fiscal policy isn't the only way governments can stimulate aggregate demand when the economy is slumping or reduce aggregate demand when it is too high. In fact, although most economists believe that automatic stabilizers play a useful role, many are skeptical about the usefulness of discretionary fiscal policy due to the time lags in its formulation and implementation.

But there's an important alternative: monetary policy. In the next two chapters we'll learn about monetary institutions and see how monetary policy works.

SUMMARY

1. The government plays a large role in the economy, collecting a large share of GDP in taxes and spending a large share both to purchase goods and services and to make transfer payments, largely for **social insurance.** *Fiscal policy* is the use of taxes, government transfers, or government purchases of goods and services to shift the aggregate demand curve. But many economists caution that a very active fiscal policy may in fact make the economy less stable due to time lags in policy formulation and implementation.

2. Government purchases of goods and services directly affect aggregate demand, and changes in taxes and government transfers affect aggregate demand indirectly by changing households' disposable income. **Expansionary fiscal policies** shift the aggregate demand curve rightward, while **contractionary fiscal policies** shift the aggregate demand curve leftward.

3. Fiscal policy has a multiplier effect on the economy. Expansionary fiscal policy leads to an increase in real GDP larger than the initial rise in aggregate spending caused by the policy. Conversely, contractionary fiscal policy leads to a fall in real GDP larger than the initial reduction in aggregate spending caused by the policy. The size of the shift of the aggregate demand curve depends on the type of fiscal policy. The multiplier on changes in government purchases, $1/(1 - MPC)$, is larger than the multiplier on changes in (lump-sum) taxes or transfers, $MPC/(1 - MPC)$, because part of any change in taxes or transfers is absorbed by savings in the first round of spending. So changes in government purchases have a more powerful effect on the economy than equal-size changes in taxes or transfers.

4. Rules governing taxes and some transfers act as **automatic stabilizers,** reducing the size of the multiplier and automatically reducing the size of fluctuations in the business cycle. In contrast, **discretionary fiscal policy** arises from deliberate actions by policy makers rather than from the business cycle.

5. Some of the fluctuations in the budget balance are due to the effects of the business cycle. In order to separate the effects of the business cycle from the effects of discretionary fiscal policy, governments estimate the **cyclically adjusted budget balance,** an estimate of the budget balance if the economy were at potential output.

6. U.S. government budget accounting is calculated on the basis of **fiscal years.** Persistent budget deficits have long-run consequences because they lead to an increase in **public debt.** This can be a problem for two reasons. Public debt may crowd out investment spending, which reduces long-run economic growth. And in extreme cases, rising debt may lead to government default, resulting in economic and financial turmoil.

7. A widely used measure of fiscal health is the **debt–GDP ratio.** This number can remain stable or fall even in the face of moderate budget deficits if GDP rises over time. However, a stable debt–GDP ratio may give a misleading impression that all is well because modern governments often have large **implicit liabilities.** The largest implicit liabilities of the U.S. government come from Social Security, Medicare, and Medicaid, the costs of which are increasing due to the aging of the population and rising medical costs.

KEY TERMS

Social insurance, p. 695
Expansionary fiscal policy, p. 697
Contractionary fiscal policy, p. 698
Automatic stabilizers, p. 702

Discretionary fiscal policy, p. 702
Cyclically adjusted budget balance, p. 706
Fiscal years, p. 709
Public debt, p. 709

Debt–GDP ratio, p. 710
Implicit liabilities, p. 712

PROBLEMS

1. The accompanying diagram shows the current macroeconomic situation for the economy of Albernia. You have been hired as an economic consultant to help the economy move to potential output, Y_E.

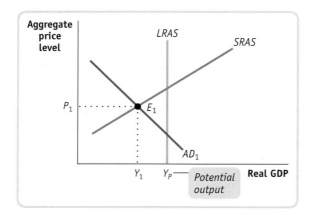

   a. Is Albernia facing a recessionary or inflationary gap?

   b. Which type of fiscal policy—expansionary or contractionary—would move the economy of Albernia to potential output, Y_E? What are some examples of such policies?

   c. Illustrate the macroeconomic situation in Albernia with a diagram after the successful fiscal policy has been implemented.

2. The accompanying diagram shows the current macroeconomic situation for the economy of Brittania; real GDP is Y_1 and the aggregate price level is P_1. You have been hired as an economic consultant to help the economy move to potential output, Y_P.

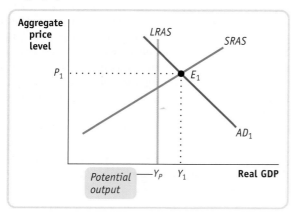

   a. Is Brittania facing a recessionary or inflationary gap?

   b. Which type of fiscal policy—expansionary or contractionary—would move the economy of Brittania to potential output, Y_P? What are some examples of such policies?

   c. Illustrate the macroeconomic situation in Brittania with a diagram after the successful fiscal policy has been implemented.

3. An economy is in long-run macroeconomic equilibrium when each of the following aggregate demand shocks occurs. What kind of gap—inflationary or recessionary—will the economy face after the shock, and what type of fiscal policies would help move the economy back to potential output?

   a. A stock market boom increases the value of stocks held by households.

   b. Firms come to believe that a recession in the near future is likely.

   c. Anticipating the possibility of war, the government increases its purchases of military equipment.

   d. The quantity of money in the economy declines and interest rates increase.

4. Show why a $10 billion decrease in government purchases will have a larger effect on real GDP than a $10 billion reduction in government transfers by completing the table at the top of page 717 for an economy with a marginal propensity to consume (MPC) of 0.6. The first and second rows of the table are filled in for you: in the first row, the $10 billion decrease in government purchases decreases real GDP and disposable income, YD, by $10 billion, leading to a decrease in consumer spending of $6 billion (MPC × change in disposable income) in row 2. However, the $10 billion reduction in transfers has no effect on real GDP in round 1 but does lower YD by $10 billion, resulting in a decrease in consumer spending of $6 billion in round 2.

| | Decrease in G = −$10 billion | | | Decrease in TR = −$10 billion | | |
| | Billions of dollars | | | Billions of dollars | | |
Rounds	Change in G	Change in real GDP	Change in YD	Change in TR	Change in real GDP	Change in YD
1	ΔG = −$10.00	−$10.00	−$10.00	ΔTR = −$10.00	$0.00	−$10.00
2	ΔC = 6.00	−6.00	−6.00	ΔC = −6.00	−6.00	−6.00
3	ΔC = ?	?	?	ΔC = ?	?	?
4	ΔC = ?	?	?	ΔC = ?	?	?
5	ΔC = ?	?	?	ΔC = ?	?	?
6	ΔC = ?	?	?	ΔC = ?	?	?
7	ΔC = ?	?	?	ΔC = ?	?	?
8	ΔC = ?	?	?	ΔC = ?	?	?
9	ΔC = ?	?	?	ΔC = ?	?	?
10	ΔC = ?	?	?	ΔC = ?	?	?

a. When government purchases decrease by $10 billion, what is the sum of the changes in real GDP after the 10 rounds?

b. When the government reduces government transfers by $10 billion, what is the sum of the changes in real GDP after the 10 rounds?

c. Using the formula for the multiplier for changes in government purchases and for changes in transfers, calculate the total change in real GDP due to the $10 billion decrease in government purchases and the $10 billion reduction in government transfers. What explains the difference?

5. In each of the following cases, either a recessionary or inflationary gap exists. Assume that the short-run aggregate supply curve is horizontal so that the change in real GDP arising from a shift of the aggregate demand curve equals the size of the shift of the curve. Calculate both the change in government purchases of goods and services and the change in government transfers necessary to close the gap.

a. Real GDP equals $100 billion, potential output equals $160 billion, and the marginal propensity to consume is 0.75.

b. Real GDP equals $250 billion, potential output equals $200 billion, and the marginal propensity to consume is 0.5.

c. Real GDP equals $180 billion, potential output equals $100 billion, and the marginal propensity to consume is 0.8.

6. Most macroeconomists believe it is a good thing that taxes act as automatic stabilizers and lower the size of the multiplier. However, a smaller multiplier means that the change in government purchases of goods and services, government transfers, or taxes necessary to close an inflationary or recessionary gap is larger. How can you explain this apparent inconsistency?

7. The accompanying table shows how consumers' marginal propensities to consume in a particular economy are related to their level of income:

Income range	Marginal propensity to consume
$0–$20,000	0.9
$20,001–$40,000	0.8
$40,001–$60,000	0.7
$60,001–$80,000	0.6
Above $80,000	0.5

a. What is the "bang for the buck" in terms of the increase in real GDP for an additional $1 of income for consumers in each income range?

b. If the government needed to close a recessionary or inflationary gap, what types of fiscal policies would you recommend to close the gap with the smallest change in either government purchases of goods and services or taxes?

8. The government's budget surplus in Macroland has risen consistently over the past five years. Two government policy makers disagree as to why this has happened. One argues that a rising budget surplus indicates a growing economy; the other argues that it shows that the government is using contractionary fiscal policy. Can you determine which policy maker is correct? If not, why not?

9. Figure 29-9 shows the actual budget deficit and the cyclically adjusted budget deficit as a percentage of real GDP in the United States since 1970. Assuming that potential output was unchanged, use this figure to determine in which years since 1992 the government used discretionary expansionary fiscal policy and in which years it used discretionary contractionary fiscal policy.

10. You are an economic adviser to a candidate for national office. She asks you for a summary of the economic consequences of a balanced-budget rule for the federal government and for your recommendation on whether she should support such a rule. How do you respond?

11. In 2005, the policy makers of the economy of Eastlandia projected the debt–GDP ratio and the deficit–GDP ratio for the economy for the next 10 years under different scenarios for growth in the government's deficit. Real GDP is currently $1,000 billion per year and is expected to grow by 3% per year, the public debt is $300 billion at the beginning of the year, and the deficit is $30 billion in 2005.

Year	Real GDP (billions of dollars)	Debt (billions of dollars)	Budget deficit (billions of dollars)	Debt (percent of real GDP)	Budget deficit (percent of real GDP)
2005	$1,000	$300	$30	?	?
2006	1,030	?	?	?	?
2007	1,061	?	?	?	?
2008	1,093	?	?	?	?
2009	1,126	?	?	?	?
2010	1,159	?	?	?	?
2011	1,194	?	?	?	?
2012	1,230	?	?	?	?
2013	1,267	?	?	?	?
2014	1,305	?	?	?	?
2015	1,344	?	?	?	?

a. Complete the accompanying table to show the debt–GDP ratio and the deficit–GDP ratio for the economy if the government's budget deficit remains constant at $30 billion over the next 10 years. (Remember that the government's debt will grow by the previous year's deficit.)

b. Redo the table to show the debt–GDP ratio and the deficit–GDP ratio for the economy if the government's budget deficit grows by 3% per year over the next 10 years.

c. Redo the table again to show the debt–GDP ratio and the deficit–GDP ratio for the economy if the government's budget deficit grows by 20% per year over the next 10 years.

d. What happens to the debt–GDP ratio and the deficit–GDP ratio for the economy over time under the three different scenarios?

12. Your study partner argues that the distinction between the government's budget deficit and debt is similar to the distinction between consumer savings and wealth. He also argues that if you have large budget deficits, you must have a large debt. In what ways is your study partner correct and in what ways is he incorrect?

13. In which of the following cases does the size of the government's debt and the size of the budget deficit indicate potential problems for the economy?

a. The government's debt is relatively low, but the government is running a large budget deficit as it builds a high-speed rail system to connect the major cities of the nation.

b. The government's debt is relatively high due to a recently ended deficit-financed war, but the government is now running only a small budget deficit.

c. The government's debt is relatively low, but the government is running a budget deficit to finance the interest payments on the debt.

14. How did or would the following affect the current public debt and implicit liabilities of the U.S. government?

a. In 2003, Congress passed and President Bush signed the Medicare Modernization Act, which provides seniors and individuals with disabilities with a prescription drug benefit. Some of the benefits under this law took effect immediately, but others will not begin until sometime in the future.

b. The age at which retired persons can receive full Social Security benefits is raised to age 70 for future retirees.

c. For future retirees, Social Security benefits are limited to those with low incomes.

d. Because the cost of health care is increasing faster than the overall inflation rate, annual increases in Social Security benefits are increased by the annual increase in health care costs rather than the overall inflation rate.

>>Chapter 29 Appendix: Taxes and the Multiplier

In the chapter, we described how taxes that depend positively on real GDP reduce the size of the multiplier and act as an automatic stabilizer for the economy. Let's look a little more closely at the mathematics of how this works.

Specifically, let's assume that the government "captures" a fraction t of any increase in real GDP in the form of taxes, where t, the tax rate, is a fraction between 0 and 1. And let's repeat the exercise we carried out in Chapter 27, where we consider the effects of a $50 billion increase in investment spending.

The $50 billion increase in investment spending initially raises real GDP by $50 billion (the first round). In the absence of taxes, disposable income would rise by $50 billion. But because part of the rise in real GDP is collected in the form of taxes, disposable income only rises by $(1 - t) \times \$50$ billion. The second-round increase in consumer spending, which is equal to the marginal propensity to consume (MPC) multiplied by the rise in disposable income, is $MPC \times (1 - t) \times \$50$ billion. This leads to a third-round increase in consumer spending of $(MPC \times (1 - t)) \times (MPC \times (1 - t)) \times \$50$ billion, and so on. So the total effect on real GDP is

Increase in investment spending $= \$50$ billion
$+$ Second-round increase in consumer spending $= (MPC \times (1 - t)) \times \$50$ billion
$+$ Third-round increase in consumer spending $= (MPC \times (1 - t))^2 \times \$50$ billion
$+$ Fourth-round increase in consumer spending $= (MPC \times (1 - t))^3 \times \$50$ billion
$\vdots$
$\vdots$
$\vdots$

Total change in real GDP $= [1 + (MPC \times (1 - t)) + (MPC \times (1 - t)^2)$
$+ (MPC \times (1 - t)^3) + \ldots] \times \$50$ billion

As we pointed out in Chapter 27, a series of the form $1 + x + x^2 + \ldots$, with $0 < x < 1$, is equal to $1/(1 - x)$. In this example, $x = (MPC \times (1 - t))$. So the total effect of a $50 billion increase in government purchases of goods and services, taking into account all the subsequent increases in consumer spending, is to raise real GDP by

$$\$50 \text{ billion} \times \frac{1}{1 - (MPC \times (1 - t))}$$

When we calculated the multiplier assuming away the effect of taxes, we found that it was $1/(1 - MPC)$. But when we assume that a fraction t of any change in real GDP is collected in the form of taxes, the multiplier is

$$\text{Multiplier} = \frac{1}{1 - (MPC \times (1 - t))}$$

This is always a smaller number than $1/1 - MPC$, and its size diminishes as t grows. Suppose, for example, that $MPC = 0.6$. In the absence of taxes, this implies a multiplier of $1/(1 - 0.6) = 1/0.4 = 2.5$. But now let's assume that $t = 1/3$, that is, that $1/3$ of any increase in real GDP is collected by the government. Then the multiplier is

$$\frac{1}{1 - (0.6 \times (1 - 1/3))} = \frac{1}{1 - (0.6 \times 2/3)} = \frac{1}{1 - 0.4} = \frac{1}{0.6} = 1.667$$

PROBLEMS

1. An economy has a marginal propensity to consume of 0.6, real GDP equals $500 billion, and the government collects 20% of GDP in taxes. If government purchases increase by $10 billion, show the rounds of increased spending that take place by completing the accompanying table. The first and second rows are filled in for you. In the first row, the increase in government purchases of $10 billion raises real GDP by $10 billion, taxes increase by $2 billion, and *YD* increases by $8 billion; in the second row, the increase in *YD* of $8 billion increases consumer spending by $4.80 billion (*MPC* × change in disposable income).

Rounds	Change in G or C	Change in real GDP	Change in taxes	Change in YD
	(billions of dollars)			
1	$\Delta G = \$10.00$	$10.00	$2.00	$8.00
2	$\Delta C = \$4.80$	4.80	0.96	3.84
3	$\Delta C =$?	?	?	?
4	$\Delta C =$?	?	?	?
5	$\Delta C =$?	?	?	?
6	$\Delta C =$?	?	?	?
7	$\Delta C =$?	?	?	?
8	$\Delta C =$?	?	?	?
9	$\Delta C =$?	?	?	?
10	$\Delta C =$?	?	?	?

a. What is the total change in real GDP after the 10 rounds? What is the value of the multiplier? What would you expect the total change in real GDP to be, based on the multiplier formula? How do your two answers compare?

b. Redo the accompanying table, assuming the marginal propensity to consume is 0.75 and the government collects 10% of the rise in real GDP in taxes. What is the total change in real GDP after 10 rounds? What is the value of the multiplier?

2. Calculate the change in government purchases of goods and services necessary to close the recessionary or inflationary gaps in the following cases. Assume that the short-run aggregate supply curve is horizontal so that the change in real GDP arising from a shift of the aggregate demand curve equals the size of the shift of the curve.

a. Real GDP equals $100 billion, potential output equals $160 billion, the government collects 20% of any change in real GDP in the form of taxes, and the marginal propensity to consume is 0.75.

b. Real GDP equals $250 billion, potential output equals $200 billion, the government collects 10% of any change in real GDP in the form of taxes, and the marginal propensity to consume is 0.5.

c. Real GDP equals $180 billion, potential output equals $100 billion, the government collects 25% of any change in real GDP in the form of taxes, and the marginal propensity to consume is 0.8.

>web... To continue your study and review of concepts in this chapter, please visit the Krugman/Wells website for quizzes, animated graph tutorials, web links to helpful resources, and more.

www.worthpublishers.com/krugmanwells

>>Money, Banking, and the Federal Reserve System

A WAGGON-WAY THROUGH THE AIR

THE BIRTH OF ECONOMICS AS A discipline is usually dated to 1776, when Adam Smith published *The Wealth of Nations*. His book is most famous for its early appreciation of the "invisible hand" of markets, which harnesses private interest to the public good. But there's a lot more in *The Wealth of Nations*. Among other things, it contains a passionate defense of what were, in Smith's time, new-fangled inventions: banks and paper money.

Today we take it for granted that we can trade pieces of elaborately printed paper—green paper, in the United States—for almost any good or service. We also take for granted that in many cases we don't even need the pieces of paper: we can write a check or swipe a card, both of which amount to promises that a bank will provide green paper or its equivalent at a later time.

In Adam Smith's time, however, most of the world's business was still conducted with gold or silver coins. Paper money and bank accounts—though well established in his native Scotland—were still regarded with suspicion in much of the world. That's why Smith felt it necessary to explain the virtues of a modern monetary system that would allow a nation to conduct its business

while freeing up that gold and silver for other uses. Using paper money instead of gold and silver coins, he said, was like finding a way to build a road without diverting any land from other uses—building "a sort of waggon-way through the air."

According to an old proverb, "With money in your pocket, you are wise, and you are handsome, and you sing well, too."

In this chapter, we'll look at how a modern monetary system works and at the institutions that sustain and regulate it. This topic is important in itself, and it's also essential background for the understanding of *monetary policy,* which we will examine in Chapter 31.

What you will learn in this chapter:

➤ The various roles **money** plays and the many forms it takes in the economy

➤ How the actions of private banks and the Federal Reserve determine the **money supply**

➤ How the Federal Reserve uses **open-market operations** to change the **monetary base**

The Meaning of Money

In everyday conversation, people often use the word *money* to mean "wealth." If you ask, "How much money does Bill Gates have?" the answer will be something like, "Oh, $40 billion or so, but who's counting?" That is, the number will include the value of the stocks, bonds, real estate, and other assets he owns.

But the economist's definition of money doesn't include all forms of wealth. The dollar bills in your wallet are money; other forms of wealth—such as cars, houses, and stock certificates—aren't money. What, according to economists, distinguishes money from other forms of wealth?

What Is Money?

Money is any asset that can easily be used to purchase goods and services.

Currency in circulation is cash held by the public.

Checkable bank deposits are bank accounts on which people can write checks.

The **money supply** is the total value of financial assets in the economy that are considered money.

Money is defined in terms of what it does: **money** is any asset that can easily be used to purchase goods and services. In Chapter 26 we defined an asset as *liquid* if it can easily be converted into cash. Money consists either of cash itself, which is liquid by definition, or of other assets that are highly liquid.

You can see the distinction between money and other assets by asking yourself how you pay for groceries. The person at the cash register will accept dollar bills in return for milk and frozen pizza—but not stock certificates or a collection of vintage baseball cards. If you want to convert stock certificates into groceries, you have to sell them—trade them for money—and then use the money to buy groceries.

Of course, many stores allow you to write a check on your bank account in payment for goods (or to pay with a debit card that is linked to your bank account). Does that make your bank account money, even if you haven't converted it into cash? Yes. **Currency in circulation**—actual cash in the hands of the public—is considered money. So are **checkable bank deposits**—bank accounts on which people can write checks.

Are currency and checkable bank deposits the only assets that are considered money? It depends. As we'll see later, there are several widely used definitions of the **money supply,** the total value of financial assets in the economy that are considered money. The narrowest definition is the most liquid because it contains only currency in circulation, traveler's checks, and checkable bank deposits. Broader definitions include other assets that are "almost" checkable, such as savings account deposits that can be transferred into a checking account with a phone call. All definitions of the money supply, however, make a distinction between assets that can easily be used to purchase goods and services, and those that can't.

Money plays a crucial role in generating *gains from trade,* because it makes indirect exchange possible. Think of what happens when a cardiac surgeon buys a new refrigerator. The surgeon has valuable services to offer—namely, heart operations. The owner of the store has valuable goods to offer: refrigerators and other appliances. It would be extremely difficult for both parties if, instead of using money, they had to directly barter the goods and services they sell. In a barter system, a cardiac surgeon and an appliance store owner could trade only if the store owner happened to want a heart operation *and* the surgeon happened to want a new refrigerator. This is known as the problem of finding a "double coincidence of wants": in a barter system, two parties can trade only when each wants what the other has to offer. Money solves this problem: individuals can trade what they have to offer for money and trade money for what they want.

Because money makes it easier to achieve gains from trade, it increases welfare, even though it does not directly produce anything. As Adam Smith put it, money "may very properly be compared to a highway, which, while it circulates and carries to market all the grass and corn of the country, produces itself not a single pile of either."

Let's take a closer look at the roles money plays in the economy.

PITFALLS

PLASTIC AND THE MONEY SUPPLY

In twenty-first-century America, many purchases are made with neither cash nor a check, but with cards. These cards come in two varieties. *Debit cards,* like bank ATM cards that can also be used at the supermarket, automatically transfer funds from the buyer's bank account. So debit cards allow you to access your bank account balance, which is part of the money supply.

But what about credit cards? *Credit cards* in effect allow you to borrow money to buy things at the store. Shouldn't these be counted as part of the money supply? The answer is no—the money supply is the value of *financial assets,* and credit cards are not assets. Credit cards access funds you can borrow—a liability, not an asset. Your credit card balance is what you currently owe. Your available credit is the maximum amount you can borrow. Since your credit card balance and your available credit are both liabilities, not assets, neither is part of the money supply.

Both debit and credit cards make it easier for individuals to make purchases. But they don't affect measures of the money supply.

Roles of Money

Money plays three main roles in any modern economy: it is a *medium of exchange,* a *store of value,* and a *unit of account.*

Medium of Exchange   Our cardiac surgeon–refrigerator example illustrates the role of money as a **medium of exchange**—an asset that individuals use to trade for goods and services rather than for consumption. People can't eat dollar bills; rather, they use dollar bills to trade for edible goods and their accompanying services.

In normal times, the official money of a given country—the dollar in the United States, the peso in Mexico, and so on—is also the medium of exchange in virtually all transactions in that country. During troubled economic times, however, other goods or assets often play that role. For example, during economic turmoil other countries' moneys frequently become the medium of exchange: U.S. dollars have played this role in Latin American countries, and euros have done so in Eastern Europe. In a famous example, cigarettes functioned as the medium of exchange in World War II prisoner-of-war camps. Even nonsmokers traded goods and services for cigarettes, because the cigarettes could in turn be easily traded for other items. During the extreme German inflation of 1923, goods such as eggs and lumps of coal became, briefly, mediums of exchange.

A medium of exchange is an asset that individuals acquire for the purpose of trading rather than for their own consumption.

Store of Value   In order to act as a medium of exchange, money must also be a **store of value**—a means of holding purchasing power over time. To see why this is necessary, imagine trying to operate an economy in which ice-cream cones were the medium of exchange. Such an economy would quickly suffer from, well, monetary meltdown: your medium of exchange would often turn into a sticky puddle before you could use it to buy something else. (As we'll see in Chapter 33, one of the problems caused by high inflation is that, in effect, it causes the value of money to "melt.") Of course, money is by no means the only store of value. Any asset that holds its purchasing power over time is a store of value. So the store-of-value role is necessary but not distinctive.

A **store of value** is a means of holding purchasing power over time.

Unit of Account   Finally, money normally serves as a **unit of account**—a measure individuals use to set prices and make economic calculations. A new CD costs about five times as much as a Big Mac, but Amazon.com lists the price of a CD as $14, not five Big Macs.

A **unit of account** is a measure used to set prices and make economic calculations.

Types of Money

In some form or another, money has been in use for thousands of years. For most of that period, people used **commodity money:** the medium of exchange was a good, normally gold or silver, that had other uses. These other uses gave commodity money value independent of its role as a medium of exchange. For example, cigarettes, which served as money in World War II POW camps, were also valuable because many prisoners smoked. Gold was valuable because it was used for jewelry and ornamentation, aside from the fact that it was minted into coins.

Commodity money is a good used as a medium of exchange that has other uses.

By the time Adam Smith wrote *The Wealth of Nations,* most of the money in Scotland consisted of paper notes rather than gold or silver coins. Unlike modern dollar bills, however, those notes were issued by private banks, which promised to exchange their notes for gold or silver coins on demand. That is, the paper currency of 1776 Scotland was a **commodity-backed money,** a medium of exchange with no intrinsic value whose ultimate value was guaranteed by a promise that it could always be converted into valuable goods.

A **commodity-backed money** is a medium of exchange with no intrinsic value whose ultimate value is guaranteed by a promise that it can be converted into valuable goods.

The big advantage of commodity-backed money over gold and silver coins is that it ties up fewer valuable resources. A country in which gold and silver coins have been replaced by paper money can normally rely on the fact that on any given day holders of only a fraction of its paper notes will demand to have them converted into gold or silver coins. So the note-issuing bank needs to keep only a portion of the total value of its notes in circulation in the form of gold and silver in its vaults. It can lend out the remaining gold and silver to those who wish to use it. This allows society to use that gold and silver for other purposes, all with no loss in the ability to achieve gains from trade.

That's what Adam Smith meant by a "waggon-way through the air." Remember his analogy between money and an imaginary highway that did not absorb valuable land beneath it. An actual highway provides a useful service but at a cost: land that could be used to grow crops is instead paved over. If the highway could be built through the air, it wouldn't destroy useful land. As Smith understood, when Scottish banks replaced gold and silver money with paper, they accomplished a similar feat: they reduced the amount of real resources used by society to provide the functions of money.

At this point you may ask, why make any use at all of gold and silver as a medium of exchange in the monetary system? In fact, today's monetary system goes even further than the Scottish system Smith admired. A U.S. dollar bill isn't commodity money, and it isn't even commodity-backed. Its value arises entirely from the fact that it is generally accepted as a means of payment, a role that is ultimately decreed by the U.S. government. Money whose value derives entirely from its official status as a means of exchange is known as **fiat money** because it exists by government *fiat,* a historical term for a policy declared by a ruler.

Fiat money is a medium of exchange whose value derives entirely from its official status as a means of payment.

Measuring the Money Supply

The Federal Reserve (an institution we'll talk about shortly) calculates three **monetary aggregates,** overall measures of the money supply, which differ in how strictly money is defined. The three aggregates are known, rather cryptically, as M1, M2, and M3. M1, the narrowest definition, contains only currency in circulation (also known as cash), traveler's checks, and checkable bank deposits. M2 adds several other kinds of assets, often referred to as **near-moneys**—financial assets that aren't directly usable as a medium of exchange but can be readily converted into cash or checkable bank deposits, such as savings accounts. Examples are deposits that aren't checkable but can be withdrawn at any time with little or no penalty. Most monetary analyses focus on either M1 or M2. There is, however, a third aggregate, M3, which adds yet another group of somewhat more "distant" near-moneys—assets that are somewhat harder to convert into cash or checkable bank deposits, such as deposits that come with larger penalties for early withdrawal. M1 is therefore the most liquid measure of money because currency and checkable deposits are directly usable as a medium of exchange.

A **monetary aggregate** is an overall measure of the money supply.

Near-moneys are financial assets that can't be directly used as a medium of exchange but can be readily converted into cash or checkable bank deposits.

Figure 30-1 shows the makeup of M1 and M2 in June 2005, in billions of dollars. M1, valued at $1,368.4 billion, consisted roughly of half currency in circulation and

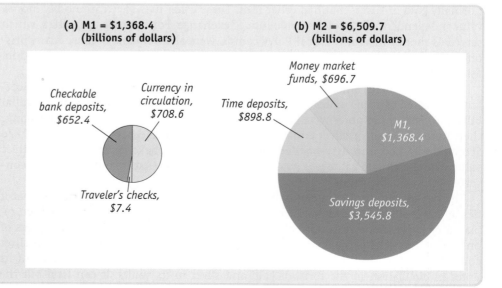

Figure 30-1

Monetary Aggregates, June 2005

The Federal Reserve uses three definitions of the money supply: M1, M2, and M3 (not shown). As panel (a) shows, M1 is almost equally split between currency in circulation and checkable bank deposits. M2, as panel (b) shows, has a much broader definition: it includes M1, plus a range of other deposits and deposit-like assets, making it almost five times as large.

Source: Federal Reserve Bank of St. Louis.

(a) M1 = $1,368.4 (billions of dollars)

Checkable bank deposits, $652.4
Currency in circulation, $708.6
Traveler's checks, $7.4

(b) M2 = $6,509.7 (billions of dollars)

Money market funds, $696.7
Time deposits, $898.8
M1, $1,368.4
Savings deposits, $3,545.8

FOR INQUIRING MINDS

WHAT'S WITH ALL THE CURRENCY?

Alert readers may be a bit startled at one of the numbers in the money supply: more than $700 billion of currency in circulation. That's almost $2,500 in cash for every man, woman, and child in the United States. How many people do you know who carry $2,500 in their wallets? Not many. So where is all that cash?

Part of the answer is that it isn't in individuals' wallets: it's in cash registers. Businesses as well as individuals need to hold cash.

Economists also believe that cash plays an important role in transactions that people want to keep hidden. Small businesses and the self-employed sometimes prefer to be paid in cash so they can hide the income from the Internal Revenue Service. Also, drug dealers and other criminals obviously don't want bank records of their dealings. In fact, some analysts have tried to use cash holdings to infer the amount of illegal activity in the economy.

The most important reason for those huge currency holdings, however, is foreign use of dollars. The Federal Reserve estimates that 60% of U.S. currency is actually held outside the country.

half checkable bank deposits, with a tiny slice of traveler's checks. In turn, M1 made up slightly less than 25% of M2, valued at $6,509.7 billion. The rest of M2 consisted of two types of bank deposits, known as savings deposits and time deposits, which both are considered noncheckable, plus money market funds, which are mutual funds that invest only in liquid assets and bear a close resemblance to bank deposits.

economics in action

The History of the Dollar

U.S. dollar bills are pure fiat money: they have no intrinsic value, and they are not backed by anything that does. But money in America wasn't always like that. In the early days of European settlement, the colonies that would become the United States used commodity money, consisting in part of gold and silver coins. But such coins were scarce on this side of the Atlantic, so the colonists relied on a variety of other forms of commodity money. For example, settlers in Virginia used tobacco as money and settlers in the Northeast used "wampum," a type of clamshell.

Later in American history, commodity-backed paper money came into widespread use. But this wasn't paper money as we now know it, issued by the government and bearing the signature of the Secretary of the Treasury. Before the Civil War, the U.S. government didn't issue paper money at all. Dollar bills were issued by private banks, which promised holders that these bills could be redeemed for silver coins on demand. These promises weren't always credible because sometimes banks failed. People were reluctant to accept currency from banks suspected of being in financial trouble. In other words, some dollars were less valuable than others.

Counting money 1870s style: Iroquois chiefs from the Six Nations Reserve read wampum belts.

A curious legacy of that time was notes issued by the Citizens' Bank of Louisiana, based in New Orleans, that became among the most widely used bank notes in the southern states. These notes were printed in English on one side and French on the other. (At the time, many people in New Orleans, originally a colony of France, spoke French.) Thus, the $10 bill read *Ten* on one side and *Dix,* the French word for "ten," on the other. These $10 bills became known as "dixies," probably the source of the nickname of the U.S. South.

The U.S. government began issuing official paper money, called "greenbacks," during the Civil War. At first greenbacks had no fixed value in terms of commodities. After 1873 the U.S. government guaranteed the value of a dollar in terms of gold, effectively turning dollars into commodity-backed money.

In 1933, when President Franklin D. Roosevelt broke the link between dollars and gold, his own federal budget director declared ominously, "This will be the end of Western civilization." It wasn't. The link between the dollar and gold was restored a few years later, then dropped again—seemingly for good—in August 1971. Despite the warnings of doom, the U.S. dollar is still the world's most widely used currency. ∎

< < < < < < < < < < < < < < < < < < <

>>CHECK YOUR UNDERSTANDING 30-1

1. Suppose you hold a gift certificate, good for certain products at participating stores. Is this gift certificate money? Why or why not?

2. Although most bank accounts pay some interest, depositors can get a higher interest rate by buying a certificate of deposit, or CD. The difference between a CD and a checking account is that the depositor pays a penalty for withdrawing the money before the CD comes due—a period of months or even years. Small CDs are counted in M2, but not in M1. Explain why they are not part of M1.

Solutions appear at back of book.

The Monetary Role of Banks

About half of M1, the narrowest definition of the money supply, consists of currency in circulation—$1 bills, $5 bills, and so on. It's obvious where currency comes from: it's printed by the U.S. Treasury. But the other half consists of bank deposits, and deposits account for the great bulk of M2 and M3, the broader definitions of the money supply. Bank deposits, then, are a major component of the money supply. And this fact brings us to our next topic: the monetary role of banks.

What Banks Do

As we learned in Chapter 26, a bank is a *financial intermediary* that uses liquid assets in the form of bank deposits to finance the illiquid investments of borrowers. Banks can create liquidity because it isn't necessary for a bank to keep all of the funds deposited with it in the form of highly liquid assets. Except in the case of a *bank run*—which we'll get to shortly—all of a bank's depositors won't want to withdraw his or her funds at the same time. So a bank can provide its depositors with liquid assets yet still invest much of the depositors' funds in illiquid assets, such as mortgages and business loans.

Banks don't, however, lend out all the funds placed in their hands by depositors because they do have to satisfy any depositor who wants to withdraw his or her funds. In order to meet these demands, banks keep substantial quantities of liquid assets on hand. In the modern U.S. banking system, these assets take the form either of currency in the banks' vaults or deposits held in the bank's own account at the Federal Reserve. The latter can be, as we'll see shortly, converted into currency more or less instantly. The currency and Federal Reserve deposits held by banks are called **bank reserves.** Because bank reserves are held by banks and the Federal Reserve, and not by the public, they are not considered part of currency in circulation.

To understand the basic role of banks in determining the money supply, let's consider a hypothetical example. Figure 30-2 shows the financial position of First Street

Bank reserves are the currency banks hold in their vaults plus their deposits at the Federal Reserve.

Figure 30-2

Assets and Liabilities of First Street Bank

A T-account summarizes a bank's financial position. The bank's assets, $900,000 in outstanding loans to borrowers and reserves of $100,000, are entered on the left side. Its liabilities, $1,000,000 in bank deposits held for depositors, are entered on the right side. **>web...**

Assets		Liabilities	
Loans	$900,000	Deposits	$1,000,000
Reserves	$100,000		

Bank, which is the repository of $1 million in bank deposits. The bank's financial position is described by the *T-account,* a type of financial spreadsheet, as shown in the figure. On the left side are First Street's *assets*—claims on individuals and businesses, consisting of the value of its outstanding loans—and its reserves. On the right side are the bank's *liabilities*—claims held by individuals and firms against the bank, consisting of the value of bank deposits.

In this example, First Street Bank holds reserves equal to 10% of its bank deposits. The fraction of bank deposits that a bank holds as reserves is its **reserve ratio.** In the modern American system the Federal Reserve—which, among other things, regulates banks—sets a minimum required reserve ratio that banks are required to maintain. To understand why banks are regulated, we need to look at a problem banks can face: *bank runs.*

> The **reserve ratio** is the fraction of bank deposits that a bank holds as reserves.

The Problem of Bank Runs

Banks can lend out most of the funds deposited in their care because all depositors normally won't want to withdraw all their funds at the same time. But what would happen to a bank if, for some reason, all or at least a large fraction of its depositors *did* try to withdraw all their funds during a short period of time, such as a couple of days?

The answer is that the bank wouldn't have enough cash and reserves at the Federal Reserve to meet its depositors' demands for immediate cash withdrawals. The bank would have a hard time coming up with the cash, even if it had invested depositors' funds wisely, because bank loans are relatively illiquid. Bank loans can't easily be converted into cash on short notice. To see why, imagine that First Street Bank has lent $100,000 to Drive-A-Peach Used Cars, a local dealership. To raise cash, First Street can sell its loan to Drive-A-Peach to someone else—another bank or an individual investor. But if First Street tries to sell the loan quickly, potential buyers will be wary: they will suspect that First Street wants to sell the loan because there is something wrong and the loan might not be repaid. As a result, First Street Bank can sell the loan quickly only by offering it for sale at a deep discount, say a discount of 50%, or $50,000.

The upshot is that if First Street's depositors all suddenly decide to withdraw their funds, any effort to raise the necessary cash forces the bank to sell off its assets very cheaply. Inevitably, it will not be able to pay off its depositors in full.

What might start this whole process? That is, what might lead First Street's depositors to rush to pull their money out? A plausible answer is a spreading rumor that the bank is in financial trouble. Even if they aren't sure the rumor is true, depositors are likely to play it safe and get their money out while they still can. And it gets worse: a depositor who simply thinks that *other* depositors are going to panic and try to get their money out will realize that this could "break the bank." So he or she joins the rush. In other words, fear about a bank's financial condition can be a self-fulfilling prophecy: depositors who believe that other depositors will rush for the exit will rush for the exit themselves.

A **bank run** is a phenomenon in which many of a bank's depositors try to withdraw their funds due to fears of a bank failure. Moreover, bank runs aren't bad only for the bank in question and its depositors. Historically, they have often proved contagious, with a run on one bank leading to a loss of faith in other banks, causing additional bank runs. The Economics in Action on the following page describes just such a contagion, the wave of bank runs that swept the United States in the early 1930s. In response to that experience and similar experiences in other countries, the United States and most other modern governments have established a system of bank regulations that protect depositors and prevent bank runs.

> A **bank run** is a phenomenon in which many of a bank's depositors try to withdraw their funds due to fears of a bank failure.

Bank Regulation

Should you worry about losing money in the United States because of a bank run? No. After the banking crises of the 1930s, the United States and most other countries put into place a system designed to protect depositors and the economy as a whole against bank runs. This system has three main features: *deposit insurance, capital requirements,* and *reserve requirements.*

Deposit Insurance Almost all banks in the United States advertise themselves as a "member of the FDIC"—the Federal Deposit Insurance Corporation. As we learned in Chapter 26, it provides **deposit insurance,** a guarantee by the federal government that depositors will be paid even if the bank can't come up with the funds, up to a maximum amount per account. The FDIC currently guarantees the first $100,000 of each account.

> **Deposit insurance** guarantees that a bank's depositors will be paid even if the bank can't come up with the funds, up to a maximum amount per account.

It's important to realize that deposit insurance doesn't just protect depositors if a bank actually fails. The insurance also eliminates the main reason for bank runs: since depositors know their funds are safe even if a bank fails, they have no incentive to rush to pull them out because of a rumor that the bank is in trouble.

FOR INQUIRING MINDS

IS BANKING A CON?

Banks make it possible for any individual depositor to withdraw funds whenever he or she wants. Yet the cash in a bank's vault, and its deposits at the Federal Reserve, wouldn't be enough to satisfy all or even most depositors if they all tried to withdraw funds at the same time. Does this mean that there is something fundamentally dishonest about the banking business?

Many people have thought so; every once in a while a prominent critic of the banking industry demands regulations that would stop banks from making illiquid loans. But an analogy may help explain what banks do and why it's productive.

Think about car-rental agencies. Because of

these agencies, someone who travels, say, from Atlanta to Cincinnati can normally count on having a car when he or she needs one. Yet there are many more potential travelers to Cincinnati than there are cars available to rent; the rent-a-car business depends on the fact that only a fraction of those potential visitors show up in any given week. There's no trickery involved. Travelers believe they can almost always get a car when needed, even though the number of cars actually available is limited—and they are right. Banks do the same thing. Depositors believe they can almost always get cash when they need it, even though the amount of cash actually available is limited—and they are right too.

Capital Requirements Deposit insurance, although it protects the banking system against bank runs, creates a well-known incentive problem. Because depositors are protected from loss, they have no incentive to monitor their bank's financial health. Meanwhile, the owners of banks have an incentive to engage in overly risky investment behavior, such as making risky loans at high interest. If all goes well, the owners profit; and if things go badly, the government covers the losses through federal deposit insurance.

To reduce the incentive for excessive risk taking, regulators require that the owners of banks hold substantially more assets than the value of bank deposits. That way, the bank will still have assets larger than its deposits even if some of its loans go bad, and losses will accrue against the bank owners' assets, not the government. The excess of a bank's assets over its bank deposits and other liabilities is called the bank's capital. In practice, banks' capital is equal to 7% or more of their assets.

Reserve Requirements Another way to reduce the risk of bank runs is to require banks to maintain a higher reserve ratio than they otherwise would. **Reserve requirements** are rules set by the Federal Reserve that determine a bank's minimum reserve ratio. For example, in the United States, the minimum reserve ratio for checkable bank deposits is 10%.

> **Reserve requirements** are rules set by the Federal Reserve that determine the minimum reserve ratio for a bank.

economics in action

It's a Wonderful Banking System

Next Christmas time, it's a sure thing that at least one TV station in your home town will show the 1946 film *It's a Wonderful Life,* featuring Jimmy Stewart as George Bailey, a small-town banker whose life is saved by an angel. The movie's climactic scene is a run on Bailey's bank, as fearful depositors rush to take their funds out.

When the movie was made, such scenes were still fresh in Americans' memories. There was a wave of bank runs in late 1930, a second wave in the spring of 1931, and a third wave in early 1933. By the end, more than a third of the nation's banks had failed. To bring the panic to an end, on March 6, 1933, the newly inaugurated president, Franklin Delano Roosevelt, declared a national "bank holiday," closing all banks for a week.

Since then, regulation has protected the United States and other wealthy countries against bank runs. In fact, the scene in *It's a Wonderful Life* was already out of date when the movie was made. But the last decade has seen several waves of bank runs in developing countries. For example, bank runs played a role in an economic crisis that swept Southeast Asia in 1997–1998 and in the severe economic crisis in Argentina, which began in late 2001. ∎

Diego Guidice/AP Photo

Argentina's economic crisis led to massive bank runs, angry public protests, and despair as many middle- and working-class families lost jobs and savings and were plunged into poverty.

> >

> ➤ Banks hold *bank reserves* of currency plus deposits at the Federal Reserve. The *reserve ratio* is the ratio of reserves to bank deposits.
> ➤ *Bank runs* were a serious problem in the past, but in the contemporary United States, banks and their depositors are protected by *deposit insurance,* capital requirements, and *reserve requirements.*

>>CHECK YOUR UNDERSTANDING 30-2

1. Suppose you are a depositor at First Street Bank. You hear a rumor that the bank has suffered serious losses on its loans. Every depositor knows that the rumor isn't true, but each thinks that most other depositors believe the rumor. Why, in the absence of deposit insurance, could this lead to a bank run? Why does deposit insurance change the situation?

2. A con man has a great idea: he'll open a bank without investing any capital and lend all the deposits at high interest rates to real estate developers. If the real estate market booms, the loans will be repaid and he'll make high profits. If the real estate market goes bust, the loans won't be repaid and the bank will fail—but he will not lose any of his own wealth. How would modern bank regulation frustrate his scheme?

Solutions appear at back of book.

Determining the Money Supply

If banks didn't exist, the quantity of currency in circulation would equal the money supply. And since all U.S. currency in circulation—coins, $1 bills, $5 bills, and so on—is issued by the government, the money supply would be determined directly by whoever controls the minting and printing presses. But banks do exist, and they affect the money supply in two ways. First, they take some currency out of circulation: dollar bills that are sitting in bank vaults, as opposed to sitting in people's wallets, aren't considered part of the money supply. Second, and much more important, is that banks, by offering deposits, create money, allowing the money supply to be larger than the quantity of currency in circulation. Let's look at how banks create money and what determines the amount of money they create.

How Banks Create Money

To see how banks create money, it's useful to examine what happens when someone decides to deposit currency in a bank. So let's consider the example of Silas, a miser, who keeps shoeboxes full of currency under his mattress. Suppose he realizes that it would actually be safer, as well as more convenient, to deposit that cash in the bank and withdraw funds or write checks when necessary. And suppose he takes his money, $1,000 in cash, and deposits it into a checkable account at First Street Bank. What effect will this have on the money supply?

Panel (a) of Figure 30-3 shows the initial effect of his deposit. First Street Bank credits Silas with $1,000 in his account, so checkable bank deposits rise by $1,000. Meanwhile, Silas's cash goes into the vault, so First Street's reserves also rise by $1,000.

This initial transaction has no effect on the money supply. Currency in circulation falls by $1,000, but checkable bank deposits—which are also part of the money supply—rise by the same amount.

Figure 30-3 **Effect on the Money Supply of Turning Cash into a Checkable Deposit at First Street Bank**

(a) Initial Effect Before Bank Makes a New Loan

Assets		Liabilities	
Loans	No change	Checkable deposits	+$1,000
Reserves	+ $1,000		

(b) Effect After Bank Makes a New Loan

Assets		Liabilities
Loans	+ $900	No change
Reserves	− $900	

When Silas deposits $1,000 (which had been stashed under his mattress) into a checkable bank account, there is initially no effect on the money supply: currency in circulation falls by $1,000, but checkable bank deposits rise by $1,000. The corresponding entries on the bank's T-account (panel a) show deposits initially rising by $1,000 and the bank's reserves initially rising by $1,000. In the second stage (panel b), the bank holds 10% of Silas's deposit ($100) as reserves and lends out the rest ($900) to Mary. As a result, its reserves fall by $900 and its loans increase by $900. Its liabilities, including Silas's $1,000 deposit, are unchanged. The money supply, the sum of checkable bank deposits and currency in circulation, has now increased by $900—the $900 now held by Mary.

But this is not the end of the story, because First Street Bank can now lend out part of Silas's deposit. Assume that it holds 10% of the deposit—$100—in reserves and lends the rest out in cash to Silas's neighbor, Mary. The effect of this second stage is shown in panel (b). First Street's deposits remain unchanged, and so does the value of its assets. But the composition of its assets changes. Its reserves are $900 less than if it had not made the loan (and they are $100 more than before Silas deposited his money). And in the place of that $900 it has acquired an IOU, its $900 cash loan to Mary.

By putting Silas's cash back in circulation by lending it to Mary, First Street Bank has, in fact, increased the money supply. That is, the sum of currency in circulation and checkable bank deposits has risen by $900.

And even this may not be the end of the story. Suppose that Mary uses her cash to buy a television and a DVD player from Acme Merchandise. What does Anne Acme, the store's owner, do with the cash? If she holds on to it, the money supply doesn't increase any further. But suppose she deposits the $900 into a checkable bank deposit—say, at Second Street Bank. Second Street Bank, in turn, will keep only part of that deposit in reserves, lending out the rest, creating still more money.

Assume that Second Street Bank, like First Street Bank, keeps 10% of any bank deposit in reserves and lends out the rest. Then it will keep $90 in reserves and lend out $810 of Anne's deposit, further increasing the money supply.

Table 30-1 shows the process of money creation we have described so far. At first the money supply consists only of Silas's $1,000. After he deposits the cash into a checkable bank deposit and the bank makes a loan, the money supply rises to $1,900. After the second deposit and the second loan, the money supply rises to $2,710. And the process will, of course, continue from there. (Although we have considered the case in which Silas places his cash in a checkable bank deposit, the results would be the same if he put it into any type of near-money.)

This process of money creation may sound familiar. In Chapter 27 we described the *multiplier process:* an initial increase in real GDP leads to a rise in consumer spending, which leads to a further rise in real GDP, which leads to a further rise in consumer spending, and so on. What we have here is another kind of multiplier—the *money multiplier*. Let's look at how the size of this multiplier is determined.

TABLE 30-1

How Banks Create Money

	Currency in circulation	Checkable bank deposits	Money supply
First stage (Silas keeps his cash under the mattress)	$1,000	$0	$1,000
Second stage (Silas deposits cash in First Street Bank, which lends out $900 to Mary)	900	1,000	1,900
Third stage (Mary deposits cash loan of $900 in Second Street Bank, which lends out $810 to Anne Acme.	810	1,900	2,710

Reserves, Bank Deposits, and the Money Multiplier

In tracing out the effect of Silas's deposit in Table 30-1, we assumed that the funds a bank lends out always end up being deposited either in the same bank or in another bank—so loans come back to the banking system, even if not to the lending bank itself. In reality, part of the loans may be held by borrowers in the form of currency, and so some of the loaned amount "leaks" out of the banking system because individuals add to their holdings of currency. Such leaks will reduce the size of the money multiplier, just as leaks of real income into savings reduces the size of the standard multiplier. But let's set that complication aside for a moment and consider how the money supply would be determined in a "checkable-deposits-only" monetary system.

Assume, then, that banks are subject to a rule that sets a minimum required reserve ratio. Also assume that banks lend out any of their **excess reserves,** reserves over and above required reserves. Assume, finally, that any money an individual borrows from a bank is deposited into a checkable bank account. Now suppose that for some

Excess reserves are a bank's reserves over and above its required reserves.

reason a bank suddenly finds itself with $1,000 in excess reserves. What happens? The answer is that the bank will lend out that $1,000, which will end up as a checkable bank deposit somewhere in the banking system, launching a money multiplier process very similar to the process shown in Table 30-1.

Let's examine this process more closely by assuming that the required reserve ratio is 10%. In the first stage of the process, the bank with excess reserves lends out $1,000, which becomes a checkable bank deposit somewhere. The bank that receives that deposit keeps 10%, or $100, as reserves, and lends out the remaining 90%, or $900, which again becomes a checkable bank deposit somewhere. The bank receiving this $900 deposit again keeps 10%, which is $90, as reserves, and lends out the remaining $810. The bank receiving this $810 keeps $81 in reserves, and lends out the remaining $729, and so on. As a result of this process, the total increase in checkable bank deposits is equal to a sum that looks like:

$$\$1,000 + \$900 + \$810 + \$729 + \dots$$

We'll use the symbol rr for the reserve ratio. More generally, the total increase in checkable bank deposits that is generated when a bank lends out $1,000 in excess reserves is:

(30-1)   Increase in checkable bank deposits from $1,000 in excess reserves = $\$1,000 + \$1,000 \times (1 - rr) + \$1,000 \times (1 - rr)^2 + \$1,000 \times (1 - rr)^3 + \dots$

As we saw in Equation 10-4 in Chapter 10, this can be simplified to:

(30-2)   Increase in checkable bank deposits from $1,000 in excess reserves = $\$1,000/rr$

Given a reserve ratio of 10%, or 0.1, a $1,000 increase in excess reserves will increase the total value of checkable bank deposits by $\$1,000/0.1 = \$10,000$. In fact, in a checkable-deposits-only monetary system the total value of checkable bank deposits will be equal to the value of bank reserves divided by the reserve ratio. Or to put it a different way, if the reserve ratio is 10%, each dollar of reserves held by a bank supports $\$1/rr = \$1/0.1 = \$10$ of checkable bank deposits.

The Money Multiplier in Reality

In reality, the determination of the money supply is more complicated than our simple model suggests, because it depends not only on the ratio of reserves to bank deposits but also on the fraction of the money supply that individuals choose to hold in the form of currency. In fact, we already saw this in our example of Silas depositing the cash under his bed: when he chose to hold a checkable bank deposit instead of currency, he set in motion an increase in the money supply.

To define the money multiplier in practice, it's important to recognize that the monetary authorities control the *sum* of bank reserves and currency in circulation, but not the allocation of that sum between reserves and currency in circulation. Consider Silas and his deposit one more time: by taking the cash from under his bed and depositing it in a bank, he reduced the quantity of currency in circulation but increased bank reserves by an equal amount. The **monetary base,** which is the quantity the monetary authorities control, is the sum of currency in circulation and reserves held by banks.

The monetary base isn't the same thing as the money supply, for two reasons. First, bank reserves, which are part of the monetary base, aren't considered part of the money supply. A $1 bill in someone's wallet is considered money because it's available for an individual to spend, but a $1 bill held as bank reserves in a bank vault or deposited at the Federal Reserve isn't considered part of the money supply because it's not available for spending. Second, checkable bank deposits aren't part of the monetary base, but they are part of the money supply because they are available for spending.

The **monetary base** is the sum of currency in circulation and bank reserves.

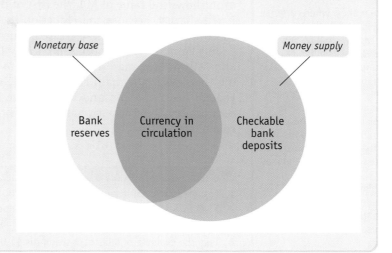

Figure 30-4

The Monetary Base and the Money Supply

The monetary base is equal to bank reserves plus currency in circulation. It is different from the money supply, consisting mainly of checkable or near-checkable bank deposits plus currency in circulation. Each dollar of bank reserves backs several dollars of bank deposits, making the money supply larger than the monetary base.

Monetary base | *Money supply*

Bank reserves | Currency in circulation | Checkable bank deposits

Figure 30-4 shows the two concepts schematically. The circle on the left represents the monetary base, consisting of bank reserves plus currency in circulation. The circle on the right represents the money supply, consisting mainly of currency in circulation plus checkable or near-checkable bank deposits. As the figure indicates, currency in circulation is part of both the monetary base and the money supply. But bank reserves aren't part of the money supply, and checkable or near-checkable bank deposits aren't part of the monetary base. In practice, most of the monetary base actually consists of currency in circulation, which also makes up about half of the money supply.

Now we can formally define the **money multiplier:** it's the ratio of the money supply to the monetary base. The actual money multiplier in the United States, using M1 as our measure of money, is about 1.9. That's a lot smaller than $1/0.1 = 10$, the money multiplier in a checkable-deposits-only system with a reserve ratio of 10% (the ratio for most checkable deposits in the United States). The reason the money multiplier is so small is that a dollar of currency in circulation, unlike a dollar in reserves, doesn't support multiple dollars of the money supply. And as Figure 30-4 illustrates, most of the monetary base is held as currency in circulation.

The **money multiplier** is the ratio of the money supply to the monetary base.

economics in action

Multiplying Money Down

In our hypothetical example illustrating how banks create money, we described Silas the miser deciding to take the currency from under his mattress and turning it into a checkable bank deposit. This led to an increase in the money supply, as banks engaged in successive waves of lending backed by Silas's funds. It follows that if something happened to make Silas revert to old habits, taking his money out of the bank and putting it back under his bed, the result would be less lending and a decline in the money supply. And that's exactly what happened as a result of the bank runs of the 1930s.

Table 30-2 shows what happened between 1929 and 1933, as bank failures shook the public's confidence. The first column shows the public's holdings of currency. This increased sharply, as many Americans decided that money under the bed might be safer than money in the bank after all. The second column shows the value of checkable bank deposits. This fell sharply, through the multiplier process we have just analyzed, when individuals pulled their cash out of banks. (Loans also fell because banks that survived the waves of bank

TABLE 30-2

The Effects of Bank Runs, 1929–1933

	Currency in circulation	Checkable Bank deposits	M1
	(billions of dollars)		
1929	$3.90	$22.74	$26.64
1933	5.09	14.82	19.91
Percent change	+31%	−35%	−25%

Source: U.S Census Bureau (1975), *Historical Statistics of the United States.*

runs increased their excess reserves, just in case another wave began.) The third column shows the value of M1, the first of the monetary aggregates we described earlier. It fell sharply, because the reduction in checkable or near-checkable bank deposits was much larger than the increase in currency in circulation.

In a famous 1963 book, *A Monetary History of the United States,* Anna Schwartz and Milton Friedman drew attention to this drop in the U.S. money supply, arguing that it was the main cause of the Great Depression. They also argued that the Federal Reserve could and should have prevented it. (We should note that many economists disagree with both conclusions.) And that brings us to the nature and role of the Fed. ■

< < < < < < < < < < < < < < < < < <

>>CHECK YOUR UNDERSTANDING 30-3

1. Assume that total reserves are equal to $200 and total checkable bank deposits are equal to $1,000. Also assume that the public does not hold any currency. Now suppose that the required reserve ratio falls from 20% to 10%. Trace out how this leads to an expansion in bank deposits.

2. Take the example of Silas depositing his $1,000 in cash into First Street Bank and assume that the required reserve ratio is 10%. But now assume that each time someone receives a bank loan, he or she keeps half the loan in cash. Trace out the resulting expansion in the money supply.

Solutions appear at back of book.

The Federal Reserve System

Who's in charge of ensuring that banks maintain enough reserves? Who decides how large the monetary base will be? The answer, in the United States, is an institution known as the Federal Reserve (or, informally, as the "Fed").

The Fed: America's Central Bank

A **central bank** is an institution that oversees and regulates the banking system and controls the monetary base.

The Federal Reserve is a **central bank**—an institution that oversees and regulates the banking system, and controls the monetary base. Other central banks include the Bank of England, the Bank of Japan, and the European Central Bank, or ECB. The ECB acts as a common central bank for 12 European countries: Austria, Belgium, Finland, France, Germany, Greece, Ireland, Italy, Luxembourg, the Netherlands, Portugal, and Spain. The world's oldest central bank, by the way, is Sweden's Sveriges Rijksbank, which awards the Nobel Prize in economics.

The legal status of the Fed, which was created in 1913, is unusual: it is not exactly part of the U.S. government, but it is not really a private institution either. Strictly speaking, the Federal Reserve system consists of two parts: the Board of Governors and the 12 regional Federal Reserve Banks.

The Board of Governors, which oversees the system from its offices in Washington, D.C., is set up like a government agency: its seven members are appointed by the president and must be approved by the Senate. However, they are appointed for 14-year terms, to insulate them from political pressure. The chairman is appointed on a more frequent basis, every 4 years, but it's traditional for chairmen to be reappointed and serve much longer terms. William McChesney Martin was chairman of the Fed from 1951 until 1970. Alan Greenspan, appointed in 1987, was still serving as Fed chairman in 2005.

The 12 Federal Reserve Banks each serve a region of the country, providing various banking and supervisory services. For example, they audit the books of private-sector banks, to ensure that they are financially sound. Each regional bank is run by a board of directors chosen from the local banking and business community. The Federal Reserve Bank of New York has a special role: it carries out *open-market operations*, the main tool of monetary policy. Figure 30-5 shows the Federal Reserve districts and the city in which each regional Federal Reserve Bank is located.

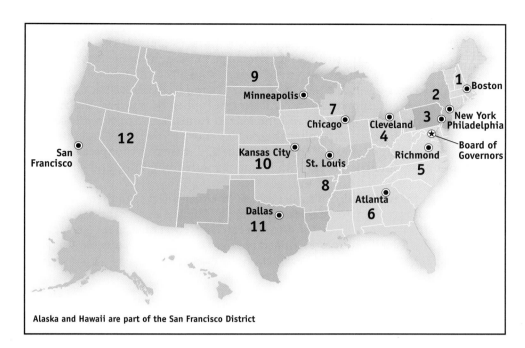

Figure 30-5 The Federal Reserve System The Federal Reserve system consists of the Board of Governors in Washington, D.C., plus regional Federal Reserve Banks, each serving its district. This map shows each of the 12 Federal Reserve districts.
Source: Board of Governors of the Federal Reserve system.

Decisions about monetary policy are made by the Federal Open Market Committee, which consists of the Board of Governors plus five of the regional bank presidents. The president of the Federal Reserve Bank of New York is always on the committee, and the other four seats rotate among the 11 other regional bank presidents. The chairman of the Board of Governors normally also serves as the chairman of the Open Market Committee.

The effect of this complex structure is to create an institution that is ultimately accountable to the voting public, because the Board of Governors is chosen by the president and confirmed by the Senate, all of whom are themselves elected officials. But the long terms served by board members, as well as the indirectness of the process by which they are appointed, largely insulate them from short-term political pressures.

What the Fed Does: Reserve Requirements and the Discount Rate

The Fed has three main policy tools at its disposal: *reserve requirements,* the *discount rate,* and, most importantly, *open-market operations.*

In our discussion of bank runs, we noted that the Fed sets a minimum reserve ratio requirement, currently equal to 10% for checkable bank deposits. Banks that fail to maintain at least the required reserve ratio on average over a two-week period face penalties.

What does a bank do if it looks as if it has insufficient reserves to meet the Fed's reserve requirement? Normally, it borrows additional reserves from other banks. Banks lend money to each other in the **federal funds market,** a financial market that allows banks that fall short of the reserve requirement to borrow reserves—usually just overnight—from banks that hold excess reserves. The interest rate in this market is determined by supply and demand—but the supply and demand are both strongly affected by Federal Reserve actions. As we'll see in Chapter 31, the **federal funds rate,** the interest rate determined in the federal funds market, plays a key role in modern monetary policy.

Alternatively, banks can borrow reserves from the Fed itself. The **discount rate** is the rate of interest the Fed charges on loans to banks. Currently, the discount rate is set 1 percentage point above the federal funds rate in order to discourage banks from turning to the Fed.

The **federal funds market** allows banks that fall short of the reserve requirement to borrow funds from banks with excess reserves.

The **federal funds rate** is the interest rate determined in the federal funds market.

The **discount rate** is the rate of interest the Fed charges on loans to banks.

If it chooses to do so, the Fed can change the reserve requirements or the discount rate, or both. Either change affects the money supply. If the Fed reduces reserve requirements, banks will lend a larger percentage of their deposits, leading to more loans and an increase in the money supply via the money multiplier. If the Fed increases reserve requirements, banks are forced to cut back on loans, reducing the money supply via the money multiplier. If the Fed reduces the spread between the discount rate and the federal funds rate, banks increase their lending because the cost of finding themselves short of reserves wouldn't be as high, and the money supply will increase. If the Fed increases the spread between the discount rate and the Federal funds rate, bank lending falls, and so will the money supply.

In practice, today's Fed doesn't use changes in either reserve requirements or the discount rate to actively manage the money supply. The last significant change in reserve requirements was in 1992. The discount rate, as we've noted, is set 1 percentage point above the federal funds rate. Monetary policy is, instead, conducted using the Fed's third policy tool: open-market operations.

Open-Market Operations

Like the banks it oversees, the Federal Reserve has assets and liabilities. The Fed's assets consist of government debt it holds, mainly short-term U.S. government bonds with a maturity of less than one year, known as U.S. Treasury bills. Remember, the Fed isn't exactly part of the U.S. government, so those U.S. Treasury bills are a liability of the government but an asset of the Fed. Its liabilities consist of currency in circulation and bank reserves (either in bank vaults or in deposits that private banks maintain at regional Federal Reserve Banks). In other words, the Fed's liabilities are the same as the monetary base—currency in circulation plus bank reserves. The assets and liabilities of the Fed are summarized by the T-account in Figure 30-6.

> An **open-market operation** is a purchase or sale of government debt by the Fed.

In an **open-market operation** the Federal Reserve buys or sells some of the existing stock of U.S. Treasury bills, normally through a transaction with *commercial banks*—banks that mainly make business loans, as opposed to home loans. The Fed never buys U.S. Treasury bills directly from the federal government. There's a good reason for this: when central banks lend directly to the government, they are in effect printing money to finance the budget deficit. As we'll see later in the book, this can be a route to disastrous levels of inflation.

The two panels of Figure 30-7 show the changes in the financial position of both the Fed and commercial banks that result from open-market operations. When the Fed buys U.S. Treasury bills, it pays for them by crediting the accounts of these banks with additional deposits, which increases the banks' reserves. This is illustrated in panel (a): the Fed buys $100 million of U.S. Treasury bills from commercial banks, which increases the monetary base by $100 million because it increases bank reserves by $100 million. When the Fed sells U.S. Treasury bills to commercial banks,

Figure 30-6

The Federal Reserve's Assets and Liabilities

The Federal Reserve holds its assets mostly in short-term government bonds called U.S. Treasury bills. Its liabilities are the monetary base—currency in circulation plus bank reserves. >**web**...

Assets	Liabilities
Government debt (Treasury bills)	Monetary base (Currency in circulation + bank reserves)

Figure 30-7   Open-Market Operations by the Federal Reserve

(a) An Open-Market Purchase of $100 Million

	Assets		Liabilities	
Federal Reserve	Treasury bills	+ $100 million	Monetary base	+ $100 million

	Assets		Liabilities
Commercial banks	Treasury bills	− $100 million	No change
	Reserves	+ $100 million	

(b) An Open-Market Sale of $100 Million

	Assets		Liabilities	
Federal Reserve	Treasury bills	− $100 million	Monetary base	− $100 million

	Assets		Liabilities
Commercial banks	Treasury bills	+ $100 million	No change
	Reserves	− $100 million	

In panel (a), the Federal Reserve increases the monetary base by purchasing U.S. Treasury bills from private commercial banks in an open-market operation. Here a $100 million purchase of U.S. Treasury bills by the Federal Reserve is paid for by a $100 million addition to private bank reserves, generating a $100 million increase in the monetary base. This will ultimately lead to an increase in the money supply via the money multiplier as banks lend out some of these new reserves. In panel (b), the Federal Reserve reduces the monetary base by selling U.S. Treasury bills to private commercial banks in an open-market operation. Here a $100 million sale of U.S. Treasury bills leads to a $100 million reduction in private bank reserves, resulting in a $100 million decrease in the monetary base. This will ultimately lead to a fall in the money supply via the money multiplier as banks reduce their loans in response to a fall in their reserves.

it debits the banks' accounts, reducing their reserves. This is shown in panel (b), where the Fed sells $100 million of U.S. Treasury bills. Here, bank reserves and the monetary base decrease.

You might wonder where the Fed gets the funds to purchase U.S. Treasury bills from banks. The answer is that it simply creates them with a stroke of the pen (or, these days, a click of the mouse). Remember, the modern dollar is fiat money, which isn't backed by anything. So the Fed can create additional monetary base at its own discretion.

The increase or decrease in reserves caused by an open-market operation doesn't directly affect the money supply. However, an open-market operation starts the money multiplier in motion. After the $100 million increase in reserves shown in panel (a), commercial banks would lend out the additional reserves, immediately increasing the money supply by $100 million. Some of those loans will be deposited back in the banking system, increasing reserves again and permitting a further round of loans, and so on. So an open-market purchase of U.S. Treasury bills sets the money multiplier in motion, leading to a rise in the money supply. An open-market sale has the reverse effect: bank reserves fall, requiring banks to reduce their loans, leading to a fall in the money supply.

The Federal Open Market Committee, as its name suggests, sets policy on open-market operations—that is, it gives instructions to the New York Fed to buy or sell U.S. Treasury bills.

Economists often say, loosely, that the Fed controls the money supply. Literally, it only controls the monetary base. But by increasing or reducing the monetary base, the Fed can exert a powerful influence on both the money supply and interest rates. This influence is the basis of monetary policy, the subject of our next chapter.

economics in action

Building Europe's Fed

Until the last year of the twentieth century, the Federal Reserve was a giant among central banks. Because the U.S. economy was far larger than any other nation's, no other nation's central bank was remotely comparable in influence. But that all changed in January 1999, when 11 European nations adopted the euro as their common currency, placing their joint monetary policy in the hands of the new European Central Bank, generally referred to as the ECB.

Like the Fed, the ECB has a special status: it's not a private institution, but it's not exactly a government agency either. In fact, it can't be a government agency, because there is no pan-European government! Luckily for puzzled Americans, there are strong analogies between European central banking and the Federal Reserve system.

First of all, the ECB, which is located in the German city of Frankfurt, isn't really the counterpart of the whole Federal Reserve system: it's the equivalent of the Board of Governors in Washington. The European counterparts of regional Federal Reserve Banks are Europe's national central banks: the Bank of France, the Bank of Italy, and so on. Until 1999, each of these national banks was the equivalent of the Fed. For example, the Bank of France controlled the French monetary base. Today these national banks, like regional Feds, provide various financial services to local banks and businesses, and actually carry out open-market operations. That doesn't mean that they are small institutions: together, the national central banks employ more than 50,000 people, while the ECB employs fewer than 1,300.

Each country gets to choose who runs its own central bank. The ECB is run by an executive board that is the counterpart of the Fed's Board of Governors; its members are chosen by unanimous consent of the governments of countries that use the euro. The counterpart of the Federal Open Market Committee is the ECB's Governing Board. Just as the Fed's Open Market Committee consists of the Board of Governors plus a rotating group of regional Fed presidents, the ECB's Governing Board consists of the executive board plus a rotating group of national central bank heads. But there's a special twist: the frequency with which any country's central bank gets a seat at the table is determined by a formula that reflects the size of the country's economy. In other words, Germany, which had a GDP of $2.7 trillion in 2004, gets a seat on the board a lot more often than Greece, which had a GDP of only $205 billion.

In the end, the details probably don't matter much. Like the Fed, the ECB is ultimately answerable to voters but is highly insulated from short-term political pressures. ∎

< < < < < < < < < < < < < < < < < <

>>CHECK YOUR UNDERSTANDING 30-4

1. Assume that any money lent by a bank is deposited back in the banking system as a checkable deposit and that the reserve ratio is 10%. Trace out the effects of a $100 million open-market purchase of U.S. Treasury bills by the Fed on the value of checkable bank deposits.

Solution appears at back of book.

• A LOOK AHEAD •

We have now seen how the monetary system is organized and, in particular, the role of the Federal Reserve in determining the size of the monetary base. But why is this important? Because the actions of the Fed change the money supply and create a powerful effect on interest rates. And through changes in interest rates the Fed has a powerful effect on real GDP and the aggregate price level.

In the next chapter we'll examine how monetary policy affects the economy and how the Fed behaves in practice.

SUMMARY

1. **Money** is any asset that can easily be used to purchase goods and services. **Currency in circulation** and **checkable bank deposits** are both considered part of the **money supply.** Money plays three roles: it is a **medium of exchange** used for transactions, a **store of value** that holds purchasing power over time, and a **unit of account** in which prices are stated.

2. Over time, **commodity money,** which consists of goods possessing value aside from their role as money, such as gold and silver coins, was replaced by **commodity-backed money,** such as paper currency backed by gold. Today the dollar is pure **fiat money,** whose value derives solely from its official role.

3. The United States has several definitions of the money supply. M1 is the narrowest **monetary aggregate,** containing only currency in circulation, traveler's checks, and checkable bank deposits. M2 and M3 include a wider range of assets called **near-moneys,** mainly other forms of bank deposits, that can easily be converted into checkable bank deposits.

4. Banks allow depositors immediate access to their funds, but they also lend out most of the funds deposited in their care. To meet demands for cash, they maintain **bank reserves** composed of both currency held in vaults and deposits at the Federal Reserve. The **reserve ratio** is the ratio of bank reserves to bank deposits.

5. Historically, banks have sometimes been subject to **bank runs,** most notably in the early 1930s. To avert this danger, depositors are now protected by **deposit insurance,** bank owners face capital requirements that reduce the incentive to make overly risky loans with depositors' funds, and banks must satisfy **reserve requirements.**

6. When currency is deposited in a bank, it starts a multiplier process in which banks lend out **excess reserves,** leading to an increase in the money supply—so banks create money. If the entire money supply consisted of checkable bank deposits, the money supply would be equal to the value of reserves divided by the reserve ratio. In reality, much of the **monetary base** consists of currency in circulation, and the **money multiplier** is the ratio of the money supply to the monetary base.

7. The monetary base is controlled by the Federal Reserve, the **central bank** of the United States. The Federal Reserve system combines some aspects of a government agency with some aspects of a private institution. The Fed sets reserve requirements. To meet those requirements, banks borrow and lend reserves in the **federal funds market** at the **federal funds rate.** Banks can also borrow from the Fed at the **discount rate.**

8. **Open-market operations** by the Fed are the principal tool of monetary policy: the Fed can increase or reduce the monetary base by buying U.S. Treasury bills from banks or selling U.S. Treasury bills to banks.

KEY TERMS

Money, p. 722
Currency in circulation, p. 722
Checkable bank deposits, p. 722
Money supply, p. 722
Medium of exchange, p. 723
Store of value, p. 723
Unit of account, p. 723
Commodity money, p. 723
Commodity-backed money, p. 723

Fiat money, p. 724
Monetary aggregate, p. 724
Near-moneys, p. 724
Bank reserves, p. 726
Reserve ratio, p. 727
Bank run, p. 728
Deposit insurance, p. 728
Reserve requirements, p. 729
Excess reserves, p. 731

Monetary base, p. 732
Money multiplier, p. 733
Central bank, p. 734
Federal funds market, p. 735
Federal funds rate, p. 735
Discount rate, p. 735
Open-market operation, p. 736

PROBLEMS

1. For each of the following transactions, what is the effect (increase or decrease) on M1? On M2?

   a. You sell a few shares of stock and put the proceeds into your savings account.

   b. You sell a few shares of stock and put the proceeds into your checking account.

   c. You transfer money from your savings account to your checking account.

   d. You discover $0.25 under the floor mat in your car and deposit it in your checking account.

   e. You discover $0.25 under the floor mat in your car and deposit it in your savings account.

2. There are three types of money: commodity money, commodity-backed money, and fiat money. Which type of money is used in each of the following situations?

   a. Mother-of-pearl seashells were used to pay for goods in ancient China.

   b. Salt was used in many European countries as a medium of exchange.

   c. For a brief time, Germany used paper money (the "Rye Mark") that could be redeemed for a certain amount of grain rye.

   d. The town of Ithaca, New York, prints its own currency, the Ithaca HOURS, which can be used to purchase local goods and services.

3. The table below shows the components of M1 and M2 in billions of dollars for the month of December in the years 1995 to 2004 as published in the *2005 Economic Report of the President*. Complete the table by calculating M1, M2, currency in circulation as a percentage of M1, and currency in circulation as a percentage of M2. What trends or patterns about M1, M2, currency in circulation as a percentage of M1, and currency in circulation as a percentage of M2 do you see? What might account for these trends?

4. Indicate whether each of the following is part of M1, M2, or neither:

   a. $95 on your campus meal card

   b. $0.55 in the change cup of your car

   c. $1,663 in your savings account

   d. $459 in your checking account

   e. 100 shares of stock worth $4,000

   f. A $1,000 line of credit on your Sears credit card

5. Tracy Williams deposits $500 that was in her sock drawer into a checking account at the local bank.

   a. How does the deposit initially change the T-account of the local bank? How does it change the money supply?

   b. If the bank maintains a reserve ratio of 10%, how will it respond to the new deposit?

   c. If every time the bank makes a loan, the loan results in a new checkable bank deposit in a different bank equal to the amount of the loan, by how much could the money supply in the economy expand in total?

   d. If every time the bank makes a loan, the loan results in a new checkable bank deposit in a different bank equal to the amount of the loan and the bank maintains a reserve ratio of 5%, by how much could the money supply expand in response to an initial cash deposit of $500?

6. Ryan Cozzens withdraws $400 from his checking account at the local bank and keeps it in his wallet.

   a. How will the withdrawal change the T-account of the local bank and the money supply?

   b. If the bank maintains a reserve ratio of 10%, how will the bank respond to the withdrawal?

   c. If every time the bank decreases its loans, checkable bank deposits fall by the amount of the loan, by how much could the money supply in the economy contract in total?

   d. If every time the bank decreases its loans, checkable bank deposits fall by the amount of the loan and the bank main-

Year	Currency in circulation	Traveler's checks	Checkable bank deposits	Money market funds	Time deposits smaller than $100,000	Savings deposits	M1	M2	Currency in circulation as a percentage of M1	Currency in circulation as a percentage of M2
1995	$372.1	$9.1	$745.9	$448.8	$931.4	$1,134.0	?	?	?	?
1996	394.1	8.8	676.5	517.4	946.8	1,273.1	?	?	?	?
1997	424.6	8.5	639.5	592.2	967.9	1,399.1	?	?	?	?
1998	459.9	8.5	627.7	732.7	951.5	1,603.6	?	?	?	?
1999	517.7	8.6	597.7	832.5	954.0	1,738.2	?	?	?	?
2000	531.6	8.3	548.1	924.2	1,044.2	1,876.2	?	?	?	?
2001	582.0	8.0	589.3	987.2	972.8	2,308.9	?	?	?	?
2002	627.4	7.8	582.0	915.5	892.1	2,769.5	?	?	?	?
2003	663.9	7.7	621.8	801.1	809.4	3,158.5	?	?	?	?
2004	699.3	7.6	656.2	714.7	814.0	3,505.9	?	?	?	?

tains a reserve ratio of 20%, by how much will the money supply contract in response to a withdrawal of $400?

7. The government of Eastlandia uses measures of monetary aggregates similar to those used by the United States, and the central bank of Eastlandia imposes a required reserve ratio of 10%. Given the following information, answer the questions below.

Bank deposits at the central bank = $200 million
Currency held by public = $150 million
Currency in bank vaults = $100 million
Checkable bank deposits = $500 million
Traveler's checks = $10 million

a. What is M1?

b. What is the monetary base?

c. Are the commercial banks holding excess reserves?

d. Can the commercial banks increase checkable bank deposits? If yes, by how much can checkable bank deposits increase?

8. In Westlandia, the public holds 50% of M1 in the form of currency, and the required reserve ratio is 20%. Estimate how much the money supply will increase in response to a new cash deposit of $500 by completing the table below. (*Hint:* The first row shows that the bank must hold $100 in minimum reserves—20% of the $500 deposit—against this deposit, leaving $400 in excess reserves that can be loaned out. However, since the public wants to hold 50% of the loan in currency, only $400 × 0.5 = $200 of the loan will be deposited in round 2 from the loan granted in round 1.) How does your answer compare to an economy in which the total amount of the loan is deposited in the banking system and the public doesn't hold any of the loan in currency? What does this imply about the relationship between the public's desire for currency and the money multiplier?

Round	Deposits	Required reserves	Excess reserves	Loans	Held as currency
1	$500.00	$100.00	$400.00	$400.00	$200.00
2	200.00	?	?	?	?
3	?	?	?	?	?
4	?	?	?	?	?
5	?	?	?	?	?
6	?	?	?	?	?
7	?	?	?	?	?
8	?	?	?	?	?
9	?	?	?	?	?
10	?	?	?	?	?
Total after 10 rounds	?	?	?	?	?

9. What will happen to the money supply under the following circumstances?

a. The required reserve ratio is 25%, and a depositor withdraws $700 from his checkable bank deposit.

b. The required reserve ratio is 5%, and a depositor withdraws $700 from his checkable bank deposit.

c. The required reserve ratio is 20%, and a customer deposits $750 to her checkable bank deposit.

d. The required reserve ratio is 10%, and a customer deposits $600 to her checkable bank deposit.

10. Although the U.S. Federal Reserve doesn't use changes in reserve requirements to manage the money supply, the central bank of Albernia does. The commercial banks of Albernia have $100 million in reserves and $1,000 million in checkable deposits; the initial required reserve ratio is 10%. The commercial banks follow a policy of holding no excess reserves. The public holds a fixed amount of currency, so all loans create an equal amount of deposits in the banking system.

a. How will the money supply change if the required reserve ratio falls to 5%?

b. How will the money supply change if the minimum reserve ratio rises to 25%?

11. Using Figure 30-5, find the Federal Reserve district in which you live. Go to http://www.federalreserve.gov/bios/pres.htm and identify the president of that Federal Reserve Bank. Go to http://www.federalreserve.gov/fomc/and determine if the president of the Fed is currently a voting member of the Federal Open Market Committee (FOMC).

12. Show the changes to the T-accounts for the Federal Reserve and for commercial banks when the Federal Reserve buys $50 million in U.S. Treasury bills. If the public holds a fixed amount of currency (so that all loans create an equal amount of deposits in the banking system), the minimum reserve ratio is 10%, and banks hold no excess reserves, by how much will deposits in the commercial banks change? By how much will the money supply change? Show the final changes to the T-account for commercial banks when the money supply changes by this amount.

13. Show the changes to the T-accounts for the Federal Reserve and for commercial banks when the Federal Reserve sells $30 million in U.S. Treasury bills. If the public holds a fixed amount of currency (so that all new loans create an equal amount of checkable bank deposits in the banking system) and the minimum reserve ratio is 5%, by how much will checkable bank deposits in the commercial banks change? By how much will the money supply change? Show the final changes to the T-account for the commercial banks when the money supply changes by this amount.

>web... To continue your study and review of concepts in this chapter, please visit the Krugman/Wells website for quizzes, animated graph tutorials, web links to helpful resources, and more.

www.worthpublishers.com/krugmanwells

31

>> Monetary Policy

EIGHT TIMES A YEAR

WHEN THE FOMC TALKS, PEOPLE listen.

Eight times a year, economists and investors around the world wait anxiously for word from the dozen men and women who make up the Federal Open Market Committee of the Federal Reserve. The FOMC controls the *federal funds rate,* the interest rate charged on reserves that banks lend each other to meet reserve requirements. What the world wants to know is the FOMC's decision—whether it has decided to increase the federal funds rate, reduce it, or leave it unchanged. Financial market analysts also carefully read the committee's accompanying statement and wait anxiously for the official minutes of the meeting, released three weeks later.

Why such a high degree of scrutiny? Because the statements of the FOMC, although usually written in jargon, offer clues to the future stance of monetary policy. A careful reading of FOMC statements, where seemingly minor changes in wording can be highly significant, can help predict whether monetary policy will be relatively expansionary (or loose), leading to a fall in interest rates, or relatively contractionary (or tight), leading to a rise in interest rates.

For example, the FOMC statement in December 2003 said, as it had after the past several meetings, that "policy accommodation can be maintained for a considerable period." The phrase "policy accommodation" means "keeping interest rates low." But in January 2004 these words were replaced with slightly different wording: "The Committee believes that it can be patient in removing its policy accommodation." The new wording suggested that the FOMC would soon begin raising the federal funds rate, and stocks and bonds plunged at this news.

The FOMC's decision about interest rates is anxiously watched by traders like these, and by investors around the world.

In Chapter 30 we learned about the structure of the Federal Reserve system and about how its open-market operations affect the money supply. In this chapter, we'll look at how monetary policy works—how actions by the FOMC can turn recession into expansion, and vice versa. We'll start by looking at the *demand for money* by households and firms. Then we'll see how the Fed's ability to change the money supply allows it to raise or reduce interest rates in the short run and, in doing so, shift the aggregate demand curve. Finally, we'll see why monetary policy affects the aggregate price level but doesn't affect aggregate output in the long run.

The Demand for Money

In Chapter 30 we saw that M1, the most commonly used definition of the money supply, consists of currency in circulation (cash) plus checkable bank deposits plus traveler's checks. M2, a broader definition of the money supply, consists of M1 plus deposits that can easily be transferred into checkable deposits. We also saw why people hold money—to make it easier to purchase goods and services. Now we'll go deeper, examining what determines *how much* money individuals and firms want to hold at any given time.

The Opportunity Cost of Holding Money

Individuals and firms hold some of their assets in the form of money because only money can be used to make purchases directly. But there is a price to be paid for holding money: it normally yields a lower rate of return than nonmonetary assets. For most individuals and firms, the relevant choice is between money and less liquid assets, such as short-term bonds, that can be converted fairly quickly into money but yield higher interest rates than money.

The rate-of-return disadvantage of money is obvious in the case of currency, which pays no interest. Most checkable bank deposits pay interest, but the rate is lower than that on other, less convenient assets.

Table 31-1 shows a selection of average interest rates prevailing in two months, May 2004 and March 2005. The top row shows the federal funds rate. The next row shows the rate on one-month Treasury bills, a bond issued by the U.S. government that is paid off in one month. The next row shows the interest rate on interest-bearing zero-maturity bank deposits. These are deposits, including checking account deposits, from which funds can be withdrawn at any time without penalty. The fourth row shows the interest rate on currency, which is, of course, zero.

TABLE **31-1**

Selected Interest Rates

	May 2004	March 2005
Federal funds rate	1.00%	2.63%
One-month Treasury bill	0.91	2.36
Interest-bearing checkable bank deposits*	0.54	1.05
Currency	0.00	0.00
Treasury bill rate minus rate on deposits	0.37	1.31
Treasury bill rate minus rate on currency	0.91	2.36

*Average on all zero-maturity deposits (deposits that can be withdrawn at any time)
Source: Federal Reserve Bank of St. Louis.

As you can see, in both months people received a higher rate of interest on one-month U.S. Treasury bills than they did on either currency or zero-maturity deposits. There is an *opportunity cost* to holding money, which we can measure by the difference between the interest rate on assets that aren't money and the interest rate on assets that are money. The next-to-last row in Table 31-1 shows the difference between the interest rate on one-month Treasury bills and the interest rate on zero-maturity bank deposits. The last row shows the difference between the interest rate on one-month Treasury bills and the interest rate on currency. In May 2004 zero-maturity deposits yielded 0.37 percentage points less at an annual rate than Treasury bills; by March 2005 that difference had risen to 1.31 percentage points. The comparison between one-month Treasury bills and currency is even worse: in May 2004 holding currency meant forgoing 0.91 percentage points at an annual rate; by March 2005 that difference had widened to 2.36 percentage points.

As this example shows, people pay a cost for holding wealth in the form of money as opposed to nonmonetary assets such as Treasury bills. Why, then, does the public hold money? Money provides convenience and reduces the costs of transactions because it can be used immediately for spending, which other assets can't.

As an example of how convenience makes it worth incurring some opportunity costs, consider the fact that even today—with the prevalence of credit cards, debit cards, and ATMs—people continue to keep cash in their wallets rather than leave the funds in an interest-bearing account. They don't want to have to go to the bank to withdraw money every time they want to buy lunch from a place that doesn't accept credit cards at all or won't accept them for small amounts because of the processing fee. The convenience of keeping some cash in your wallet is more valuable than the interest you would earn by keeping that money in the bank.

So how much of your wealth should you hold in the form of money on any given day? Choosing the optimal quantity of money to hold requires a trade-off between the extra convenience of an additional dollar in your wallet against the higher return from keeping it in other financial assets. The terms of this trade-off change when interest rates change. Look again at Table 31-1. Between May 2004 and March 2005, the federal funds rate rose by about 1.63 percentage points. The interest rate on one-month Treasury bills rose by about the same amount. That's not an accident: all **short-term interest rates**—rates on financial assets that come due, or mature, within six months or less—tend to move together. This occurs because Treasury bills, one-month bonds, three-month bonds, and so on are in effect competing for the same business. Why? Investors will move their wealth out of any short-term financial asset that offers a lower-than-average interest rate. The selling of the asset forces the interest rate on that asset up because buyers of the asset must be rewarded with a higher rate in order to induce them to buy it. Conversely, investors will move their wealth into any short-term financial asset that offers an above-average interest rate. The purchase of the asset drives its interest rate down when sellers find they can lower the rate of return on the asset and still find willing buyers. So interest rates on short-term financial assets tend to be roughly the same because no asset will consistently offer a higher-than-average or a lower-than-average interest rate.

But the interest rates on money didn't rise by the same amount. The interest rate on currency remained at zero. The interest rate on zero-maturity bank deposits rose, but by much less than short-term interest rates. As a result, the opportunity cost of holding money increased. This reflects a general result: the higher the short-term interest rate, the higher the opportunity cost of holding money. So the quantity of money the public wants to hold—the quantity of money demanded—depends negatively on short-run interest rates.

Table 31-1 contains only short-term interest rates. At any given moment, **long-term interest rates**—rates of interest on financial assets that mature, or come due, a number of years into the future—may be different from short-term interest rates. The difference between short-term and long-term interest rates is sometimes important

Short-term interest rates are the interest rates on financial assets that mature within six months or less.

Long-term interest rates are interest rates on financial assets that mature a number of years in the future.

as a practical matter. For our current purposes, however, it's useful to ignore the distinction between short-term and long-term rates and assume that there is only one interest rate.

The Money Demand Curve

The relationship between the interest rate and the quantity of money demanded by the public is illustrated by the **money demand curve,** *MD,* in Figure 31-1. This curve is downward-sloping because, other things equal, a higher interest rate increases the opportunity cost of holding money, leading the public to reduce the quantity of money it demands. For example, if the interest rate is very low—say, 1%—the interest forgone by holding money is relatively small. As a result, people will tend to hold relatively large amounts of money to avoid the cost and nuisance of converting other assets into money when making purchases. By contrast, if the interest rate is relatively high—say, 15%, a level it reached in the United States in the early 1980s—the opportunity cost of holding money is high. People will respond by keeping only small amounts in cash and deposits, converting funds into money only when needed.

> The **money demand curve** shows the relationship between the quantity of money demanded and the interest rate.

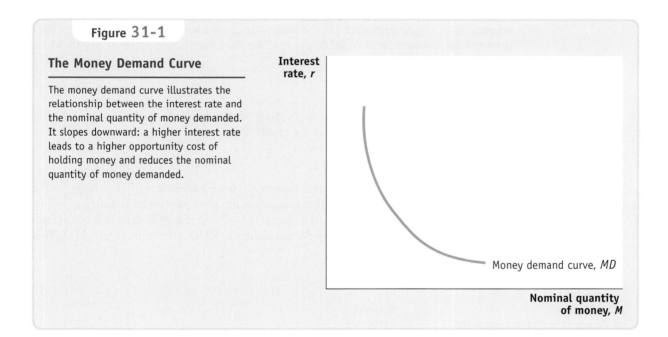

Figure 31-1

The Money Demand Curve

The money demand curve illustrates the relationship between the interest rate and the nominal quantity of money demanded. It slopes downward: a higher interest rate leads to a higher opportunity cost of holding money and reduces the nominal quantity of money demanded.

Interest rate, *r*

Money demand curve, *MD*

Nominal quantity of money, *M*

You might ask why we draw the money demand curve with the interest rate—as opposed to rates of return on other assets, such as stocks or real estate—on the vertical axis. As we noted earlier, for most people the relevant question in deciding how much money to hold is whether to put the funds in the form of other assets that can be turned fairly quickly into money, such as Treasury bills. And the rates of return on assets that are "close to" money—fairly liquid assets like Treasury bills that are relatively good substitutes for money—move closely with short-term interest rates.

Prices and the Demand for Money

Because the horizontal axis in Figure 31-1 measures the *nominal* quantity of money, the money demand curve shows the number of dollars demanded unadjusted for the purchasing power of a dollar. However, economists sometimes focus instead on the **real quantity of money:** the nominal quantity of money divided by the aggregate

> The **real quantity of money** is the nominal quantity of money divided by the aggregate price level.

price level. Using M for the nominal quantity of money and P for the aggregate price level, the *real* quantity of money is M/P. The real quantity of money, M/P, measures the purchasing power of the nominal quantity of money, M.

To see why economists sometimes focus on the real quantity of money, consider the effects of a doubling of the aggregate price level on the nominal quantity of money demanded, as shown in Figure 31-2. An increase in the aggregate price level means consumers must spend more money to buy a given basket of goods and services. This translates into a desire to hold more money at any given interest rate. So a rise in the aggregate price level from P_1 to P_2 shifts the money demand curve rightward from MD_1 to MD_2.

But we can be more specific about the effect of the aggregate price level on money demand: other things equal, the nominal quantity of money demanded is *proportional* to the aggregate price level. That is, a 50% rise in the aggregate price level leads to a 50% rise in the nominal quantity of money demanded at any given interest rate.

We can get a better intuitive understanding of this property with a little algebra. Suppose that the interest rate is constant at r_1 in Figure 31-2. Also suppose that the aggregate price level rises from P_1 to P_2 by a factor k, so that we can express the rise in the aggregate price level as $P_2 = k \times P_1$. Then the fact that nominal money demand is proportional to the aggregate price level means that the nominal quantity of money demanded after the aggregate price change (M_2), and before the price change (M_1) have the following relationship: $M_2 = k \times M_1$. As a result, the ratio of M_2 to M_1 is equal to the ratio of P_2 to P_1:

$$(31\text{-}1) \quad \frac{M_2}{M_1} = \frac{P_2}{P_1}$$

Equation 31-1 can be rearranged by dividing both sides by P_2 and multiplying both sides by M_1. This gives us the following result:

$$(31\text{-}2) \quad \frac{M_2}{P_2} = \frac{M_1}{P_1}$$

The **real money demand curve** shows the relationship between the real quantity of money demanded and the interest rate.

Equation 31-2 tells us that *the real quantity of money demanded after a change in the aggregate price level, M_2/P_2, other things equal, is the same as the real quantity of money demanded before the aggregate price level change, M_1/P_1.* One way to take this result into account is to draw the **real money demand curve,** *RMD*, shown in Figure 31-3. This

Figure 31-2

The Aggregate Price Level and Money Demand

Other things equal, an increase in the aggregate price level leads to an equal percent increase in the nominal quantity of money demanded. In this case, an increase in the aggregate price level causes a rightward shift in the money demand curve from MD_1 to MD_2. The nominal quantity of money demanded at the interest rate r_1 rises from M_1 to M_2, an increase that is proportional to the increase in the aggregate price level.

A rise in the aggregate price level shifts the money demand curve rightward.

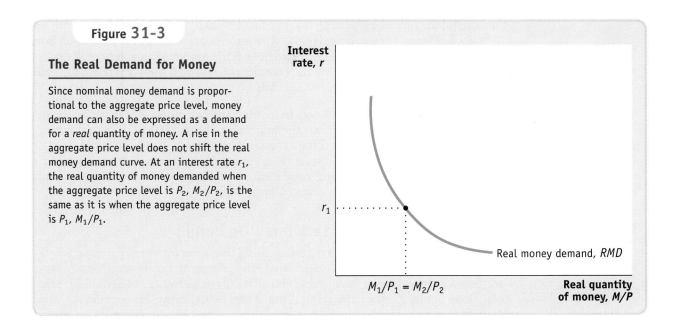

Figure 31-3

The Real Demand for Money

Since nominal money demand is proportional to the aggregate price level, money demand can also be expressed as a demand for a *real* quantity of money. A rise in the aggregate price level does not shift the real money demand curve. At an interest rate r_1, the real quantity of money demanded when the aggregate price level is P_2, M_2/P_2, is the same as it is when the aggregate price level is P_1, M_1/P_1.

curve shows the relationship between the real quantity of money demanded and the interest rate. Unlike the nominal money demand curve, the real money demand curve automatically takes into account the effect of changes in the aggregate price level on the nominal quantity of money demanded. So, for example, at an interest rate r_1, the real quantity of money demanded is equal to both M_1/P_1 and M_2/P_2, shown as the same point on the real money demand curve.

Shifts of the Real Money Demand Curve

By expressing the demand for money in real terms, we take account of the effects of changes in the aggregate price level on the nominal demand for money. A number of factors can shift the real and nominal money demand curves. The most important of these are changes in the level of real aggregate spending, changes in banking technology, and changes in banking institutions.

Changes in Real Aggregate Spending Households and firms hold money as a way to facilitate purchases of goods and services. The larger the quantity of goods and services they plan to buy, the larger the real quantity of money they will want to hold at any given interest rate. So an increase in real aggregate spending will shift the real money demand curve rightward. A fall in real aggregate spending will shift the real money demand curve leftward.

Some economists have argued that the real quantity of money demanded, other things equal, is proportional to real aggregate spending. That is, a 20% rise in real aggregate spending leads to a 20% rise in the real quantity of money demanded. This view leads to a concept known as the *velocity of money,* which we'll turn to shortly.

Changes in Technology There was a time, not so long ago, when withdrawing cash from a bank account required a visit during the bank's hours of operation. And since most people found themselves trying to do their banking during lunch hour, this often meant standing in line. So people limited the number of times they needed to withdraw funds by keeping substantial amounts of cash on hand. Not surprisingly, this tendency diminished greatly with the advent of ATMs in the 1970s.

These events illustrate how changes in technology can affect the real demand for money. In general, advances in information technology have tended to reduce the real demand for money by making it easier for the public to make purchases without holding significant sums of money. ATM machines are only one example of how changes in technology have altered the demand for money. The ability of stores to process credit card transactions via the Internet has widened the acceptance of credit cards and similarly reduced the need for cash.

Changes in Institutions Changes in institutions can increase or decrease the demand for money. For example, until the beginning of the 1980s, U.S. banks weren't allowed to offer interest on checking accounts. As a result, the opportunity cost of holding funds in checking accounts was very high. That disincentive was greatly reduced when a change in banking regulations made interest on checking accounts legal, leading to a rise in the real demand for money.

The Velocity Approach to Money Demand

We have discussed the demand for money using the same framework we use for discussing any demand curve: first we described the reasons the curve slopes downward, and then we discussed the factors that shift the curve rightward or leftward. In some discussions about money demand and monetary policy, however, economists use a different approach, emphasizing a concept known as the *velocity of money.*

The **velocity of money** is defined as nominal GDP divided by the nominal quantity of money. That is,

$$(31\text{-}3) \quad V = \frac{P \times Y}{M}$$

where V is the velocity of money, P is the aggregate price level, Y is aggregate output measured by real GDP (so that $P \times Y$ equals nominal GDP), and M is the nominal quantity of money. This definition is often restated by multiplying both sides of the equation by the quantity of money to yield the **quantity equation:**

$$(31\text{-}4) \quad M \times V = P \times Y$$

It says that the nominal quantity of money multiplied by the velocity of money is equal to nominal GDP.

The intuition behind the concept of velocity is that each unit of money in the economy can be spent several times over the course of a year. For example, someone may use a dollar bill to pay for a cup of coffee at a cafe; the cafe may give that dollar bill as change to someone else who buys a sandwich; that person may use the dollar bill to buy a newspaper; and so on. The value of spending that takes place using a particular dollar bill in a given year depends on the number of times that dollar bill "turns over" during the year. For example, if the dollar bill is spent three times in a year, it is used for $3 worth of spending.

By analogy, aggregate spending in the economy as a whole during a year is equal to the nominal quantity of money in the economy, *M,* multiplied by the number of times the average unit of money is spent—the velocity of money, *V.* And nominal GDP, $P \times Y$, is equal to aggregate spending. So aggregate spending, measured as the number of dollars turned over, is equal to aggregate spending as measured by nominal GDP, giving us the quantity equation.

One way to think about the velocity approach is that it is a special case of the real money demand curve. To see that, let's rewrite the velocity equation, putting the real quantity of money on the left-hand side:

$$(31\text{-}5) \quad \frac{M}{P} = \frac{1}{V} \times Y$$

Equation 31-5 says that the real demand for money, *M/P,* is proportional to real GDP, *Y,* where the constant of proportionality is 1/*V.* But real GDP is, in equilibrium, equal to real aggregate spending. And we already know that the real demand for

---

The **velocity of money** is nominal GDP divided by the nominal quantity of money.

According to the **quantity equation,** the nominal quantity of money multiplied by the velocity of money is equal to nominal GDP.

money depends positively on real aggregate spending. Equation 31-5 says that, in addition to being positive, the relationship is proportional. This is why we noted earlier that some economists believe that the real quantity of money demanded is proportional to real aggregate spending. If this is indeed true, then the effect of changes in the interest rate on real money demand is reflected in changes in the velocity of money, V. For example, a rise in the interest rate, which reduces real money demand, will lead to a fall in $1/V$—or a rise in V—other things equal. Intuitively, a smaller amount of real money holdings, M/P, will now account for the same amount of real aggregate spending, Y, because velocity, V, has increased.

We won't pursue the velocity approach to money demand any further in this chapter. As we'll see in Chapter 34, however, the concept of monetary velocity has played an important role in some debates about macroeconomic policy.

economics in action

A Yen for Cash

Japan, say financial experts, is still a "cash society." Visitors from the United States or Europe are surprised at how little use the Japanese make of credit cards and how

much cash they carry around in their wallets. Yet Japan is an economically and technologically advanced country and, according to some measures, ahead of the United States in the use of telecommunications and information technology. So why do the citizens of this economic powerhouse still do business the way Americans and Europeans did a generation ago? The answer highlights the factors affecting the demand for money.

One reason the Japanese use cash so much is that their institutions never made the switch to heavy reliance on plastic. For complex reasons, Japan's retail sector is still dominated by small mom-and-pop stores, which are reluctant to invest in credit card technology. Japan's banks have also been slow about pushing transaction technology; visitors are often surprised to find that ATMs close early in the evening rather than stay open all night.

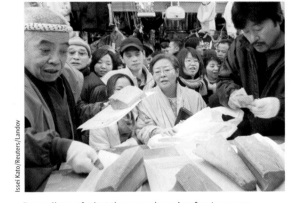

Issei Kato/Reuters/Landov

Regardless of what they are shopping for, Japanese consumers tend to pay with cash rather than plastic.

But there's another reason the Japanese hold so much cash: there's little opportunity cost to doing so. Short-term interest rates in Japan have been below 1% since the mid-1990s. It also helps that the Japanese crime rate is quite low, so you are unlikely to have your wallet full of cash stolen. So why not hold cash? ∎

> >

>> CHECK YOUR UNDERSTANDING 31-1

1. Explain how each of the following would affect the real and nominal quantity of money demanded:
   a. Short-term interest rates rise from 5% to 30%.
   b. All prices fall by 10%.
   c. New wireless technology automatically charges supermarket purchases to credit cards, eliminating the need to stop at the cash register.
   d. For some reason, firms return to the old practice of paying employees in cash rather than with checks.

Solutions appear at back of book.

Money and Interest Rates

"The Federal Open Market Committee decided today to raise its target for the federal funds rate by 25 basis points to 2¾%." So reads the first sentence of the press release from the FOMC after its meeting of March 22, 2005. (A basis point is equal to 0.01 percentage point. So the statement says that the Fed raised the target from 2.50% to 2.75%.) We learned about the federal funds rate in Chapter 30: it's the rate at which banks lend reserves to each other to meet the required reserve ratio. As the statement implies, at each of its eight-times-a-year meetings, the Federal Open Market Committee sets a target value for the federal funds rate. It's then up to Fed officials to achieve that target. This is done by the Open Market Desk at the Federal Reserve Bank of New York, which buys and sells Treasury bills to achieve that target.

Other short-term interest rates, such as the rates on bank loans to businesses, move with the federal funds rate. So when the Fed raised its target for the federal funds rate from 2.50% to 2.75% in March 2005, all short-term interest rates rose as well by about a quarter of a percentage point.

How does the Fed go about achieving a *target federal funds rate?* And more to the point, how is the Fed able to affect interest rates at all?

The Equilibrium Interest Rate

Recall that, for simplicity, we've assumed that there is only one interest rate paid on nonmonetary financial assets, both in the short run and in the long run. To understand how the interest rate is determined, consider Figure 31-4, which illustrates the **liquidity preference model of the interest rate;** this model says that the interest rate is determined by the supply and demand for money in the market for money. Figure 31-4 combines the nominal money demand curve, *MD,* with the **money supply curve,** *MS,* which shows how the nominal quantity of money supplied by the Federal Reserve varies with the interest rate. (From now on we will drop the word *nominal* with the understanding that *MD* and *MS* represent nominal quantities.) In Chapter 13 we learned how the Federal Reserve can increase or decrease the money supply by buying or selling Treasury bills. Let's assume for simplicity that the Fed simply chooses the level of the money

According to the **liquidity preference model of the interest rate,** the interest rate is determined by the supply and demand for money.

The **money supply curve** shows how the nominal quantity of money supplied varies with the interest rate.

Figure 31-4

Equilibrium in the Money Market

The money supply curve, *MS,* is vertical at the money supply chosen by the Federal Reserve, *M̄.* The money market is in equilibrium at the interest rate r_E: the quantity of money demanded by the public is equal to *M̄,* the quantity of money supplied. At a point such as *L,* the interest rate, r_L, is below r_E and the corresponding quantity of money demanded, M_L, exceeds the money supply, *M̄.* In an attempt to shift their wealth out of nonmonetary interest-bearing financial assets and raise their money holdings, investors drive the interest rate up to r_E. At a point such as *H,* the interest rate r_H is above r_E and the corresponding quantity of money demanded, M_H, is less than the money supply *M̄.* In an attempt to shift out of money holdings into nonmonetary interest-bearing financial assets, investors drive the interest rate down to r_E.

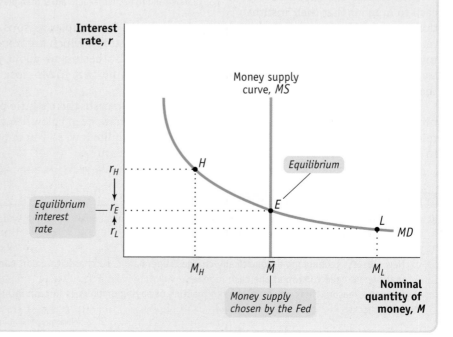

supply that it believes will achieve its interest rate target. Then the money supply curve is a vertical line, *MS*, in Figure 31-4, with a horizontal intercept corresponding to the money supply chosen by the Fed, $\overline{M}$. The money market equilibrium is at *E*, where *MS* and *MD* cross. At this point the quantity of money demanded equals the money supply, $\overline{M}$, leading to an equilibrium interest rate of r_E.

To understand why r_E is the equilibrium interest rate, consider what happens if the money market is at a point like *L*, where the interest rate, r_L, is below r_E. At r_L the public wants to hold the quantity of money M_L, an amount larger than the actual money supply, $\overline{M}$. This means that at point *L*, the public wants to shift some of its wealth out of nonmonetary interest-bearing financial assets such as Treasury bills and into money. This has two implications. One is that the quantity of money demanded is *more* than the quantity of money supplied. The other is that the quantity of nonmonetary interest-bearing financial assets demanded is *less* than the quantity supplied. So those trying to sell interest-bearing assets will find that they have to offer a higher interest rate to attract buyers. As a result, the interest rate will be driven up from r_L until the public wants to hold the quantity of money that is actually available, $\overline{M}$. That is, the interest rate will rise until it is equal to r_E.

Now consider what happens if the money market is at a point such as *H* in Figure 31-4, where the interest rate r_H is above r_E. In that case the quantity of money demanded, M_H, is less than the quantity of money supplied, $\overline{M}$. Correspondingly, the quantity of nonmonetary interest-bearing financial assets demanded is greater than the quantity supplied. Those trying to sell interest-bearing financial assets will find that they can offer a lower interest rate and still find willing buyers. This leads to a fall in the interest rate from r_H. It falls until the public wants to hold the quantity of money that is actually available, $\overline{M}$. Again, the interest rate will end up at r_E.

Two Models of Interest Rates?

At this point you may be a bit puzzled. This is the second time we have discussed the determination of the interest rate. In Chapter 26 we studied the *loanable funds model* of the interest rate; according to that model, the interest rate is determined by the equalization of the supply of funds from lenders and the demand for funds by borrowers in the market for loanable funds. But here we have described a seemingly different model in which the interest rate is determined by the equalization of the supply and demand for money in the money market. Which of these models is correct?

The answer is both. But that will take a little time to explain, something we will do later in this chapter. For now, let's put the loanable funds model to one side and concentrate on the liquidity preference model of the interest rate. The most important insight from this model is that it shows us how monetary policy—actions by the Federal Reserve and other central banks—works.

Monetary Policy and the Interest Rate

Let's examine how the Federal Reserve can use changes in the money supply to change the interest rate. Figure 31-5 on page 752 shows what happens when the Fed increases the money supply from $\overline{M}_1$ to $\overline{M}_2$. The economy is originally in equilibrium at E_1, with an equilibrium interest rate of r_1 and money supply $\overline{M}_1$. An increase in the money supply by the Fed to $\overline{M}_2$ shifts the money supply curve to the right, from MS_1 to MS_2, and leads to a fall in the equilibrium interest rate to r_2. Why? Because r_2 is the only interest rate at which the public is willing to hold the quantity of money actually supplied, $\overline{M}_2$. So an increase in the money supply drives the interest rate down. Similarly, a reduction in the money supply drives the interest rate up. By adjusting the money supply up or down, the Fed can set the interest rate.

PITFALLS

THE TARGET VERSUS THE MARKET
Over the years, the Federal Reserve has changed the details of how it makes monetary policy. At one point, in the late 1970s and early 1980s, it set a target level for the money supply and altered the monetary base to achieve that target. Under this policy, the federal funds rate fluctuated freely. Today the Fed does the reverse, setting a target for the federal funds rate and allowing the money supply to fluctuate as it pursues that target.

A common mistake is to imagine that these changes in the way the Federal Reserve operates alter the way the money market works. That is, you'll sometimes hear people say that the interest rate no longer reflects the supply and demand for money because the Fed sets the interest rate.

In fact, the money market works the same way as always: the interest rate is determined by the supply and demand for money. The only difference is that now the Fed adjusts the supply of money to achieve its target interest rate. It's important not to confuse a change in the Fed's operating procedure with a change in the way the economy works.

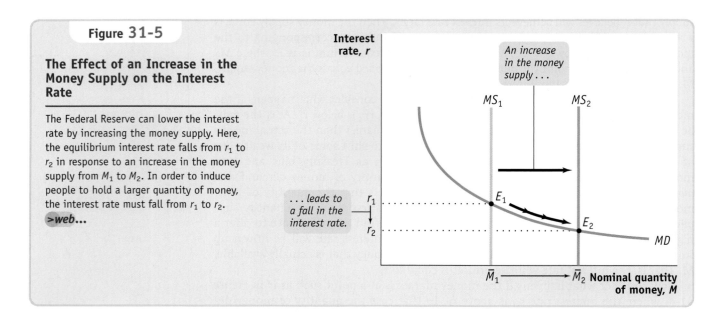

Figure 31-5

The Effect of an Increase in the Money Supply on the Interest Rate

The Federal Reserve can lower the interest rate by increasing the money supply. Here, the equilibrium interest rate falls from r_1 to r_2 in response to an increase in the money supply from M_1 to M_2. In order to induce people to hold a larger quantity of money, the interest rate must fall from r_1 to r_2.

>web...

An increase in the money supply ...

... leads to a fall in the interest rate.

The **target federal funds rate** is the Federal Reserve's desired federal funds rate.

In practice, at each meeting the FOMC decides on the interest rate to prevail for the next six weeks, until its next meeting. The Fed sets a **target federal funds rate,** a desired level for the federal funds rate. The Open Market Desk of the Federal Reserve Bank of New York adjusts the money supply through the purchase and sale of Treasury bills until the actual federal funds rate equals the target rate.

Figure 31-6 shows how this works. In both panels, r_T is the target federal funds rate. In panel (a), the initial money supply curve is MS_1 with money supply $\overline{M}_1$, and

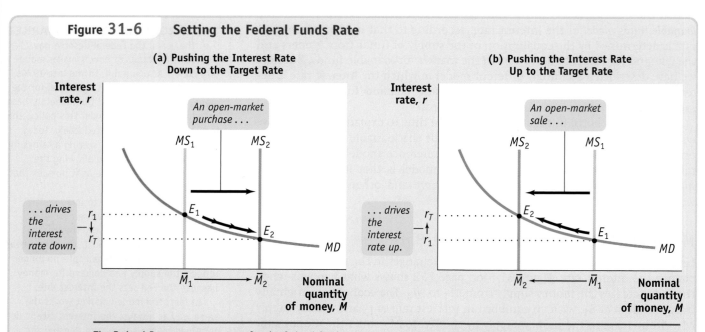

Figure 31-6 **Setting the Federal Funds Rate**

(a) Pushing the Interest Rate Down to the Target Rate

An open-market purchase ...

... drives the interest rate down.

(b) Pushing the Interest Rate Up to the Target Rate

An open-market sale ...

... drives the interest rate up.

The Federal Reserve sets a target for the federal funds rate and uses open-market operations to achieve that target. In both panels the target rate is r_T. In panel (a) the initial equilibrium interest rate, r_1, is above the target rate. The Fed increases the money supply by making an open-market purchase of Treasury bills, pushing the money supply curve rightward from MS_1 to MS_2, and driving the interest rate down to r_T. In panel (b) the initial equilibrium interest rate, r_1, is below the target rate. The Fed reduces the money supply by making an open-market sale of Treasury bills, pushing the money supply curve leftward from MS_1 to MS_2, and driving the interest rate up to r_T.

FOR INQUIRING MINDS

LONG-TERM INTEREST RATES

Earlier in this chapter we mentioned that *long-term interest rates*—rates on bonds or loans that mature in several years—don't necessarily move with short-term interest rates. How is that possible?

Consider the case of Millie, who has already decided to place $1,000 in certificates of deposit (CDs) for the next two years. However, she hasn't decided whether to put the money in a one-year CD, at a 4% rate of interest, or a two-year CD, at a 5% rate of interest.

You might think that the two-year CD is a clearly better deal—but it may not be. Suppose that Millie expects the rate of interest on one-year CDs to rise sharply next year. If she puts her funds in a one-year CD this year, she will be able to reinvest the money at a much higher rate next year. And this could give her a two-year rate of return that is higher than if she put her funds into the two-year CD. For exam-

ple, if the rate of interest on one-year CDs rises from 4% this year to 8% next year, putting her funds in a one-year CD will give her a rate of return over the next two years of about 6%, better than the rate on two-year CDs.

The same considerations apply to investors deciding between short-term and long-term bonds. If they expect short-term interest rates to rise, investors may buy short-term bonds even if long-term bonds offer a higher interest rate. If they expect short-term interest rates to fall, investors may buy long-term bonds even if short-term bonds offer a higher interest rate.

In practice, long-term interest rates reflect the average expectation in the market about what's going to happen to short-term rates in the future. When long-term rates are much higher than short-term rates, as they were in 2003, the market is signaling that it expects short-term rates to rise in the future.

the equilibrium interest rate, r_1, is above the target rate. To lower the interest rate to r_T, the Fed makes an open-market purchase of Treasury bills. As we learned in Chapter 30, an open-market purchase of Treasury bills leads to an increase in the money supply via the money multiplier. This is illustrated in panel (a) by the rightward shift of the money supply curve from MS_1 to MS_2 and an increase in the money supply to $\overline{M}_2$. This drives the equilibrium interest rate down to the target rate, r_T.

Panel (b) shows the opposite case. Again, the initial money supply curve is MS_1 with money supply $\overline{M}_1$. But this time the equilibrium interest rate, r_1, is below the target federal funds rate, r_T. In this case, the Fed will make an open-market sale of Treasury bills, leading to a fall in the money supply to $\overline{M}_2$ via the money multiplier. The money supply curve shifts leftward from MS_1 to MS_2, driving the equilibrium interest rate *up* to the target federal funds rate, r_T.

economics in action

The Fed Takes Action

In January 2001 the Federal Reserve, alarmed by signs of a looming recession, began cutting the target federal funds rate. We'll explain in the next section why the Fed believed this would be the correct response to a recession. But for now, let's focus on the Fed's ability to move interest rates.

Figure 31-7 on page 754 shows the movements of three interest rates between 1999 and 2005: the actual federal funds rate, the *prime rate,* and the 30-year mortgage rate. As you can see, the January 2001 cut in the federal funds rate was followed by several more. In fact, by the end of 2001 the Fed had cut the target federal funds rate 10 times, bringing it down from 6% at the beginning of 2001 to 1.75% at the end of 2001. (This was achieved by making cuts between regular meetings of the FOMC.) In 2002 the Fed cut the target again, to 1.25%; in 2003 it cut the target even further, to just 1%. In 2004, in response to signs of a growing economy, the Fed began gradually raising its target again, by 0.25 percentage points at each meeting.

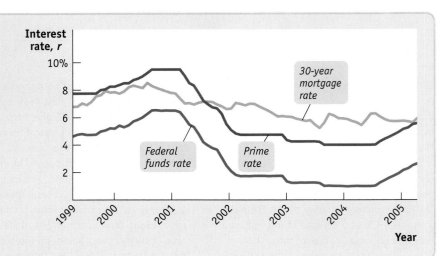

Figure 31-7

The Fed Moves Interest Rates

In early 2001, in response to a weakening economy, the Fed began cutting the federal funds rate. The prime rate—the interest rate on short-term bank loans to their best customers—fell in parallel. The 30-year mortgage rate, which is used by many consumers buying homes, fell, too, though not as much. By 2004, in the face of a growing economy, the Fed began raising the federal funds rate.

Source: Federal Reserve Bank of St. Louis.

The second interest rate shown in Figure 31-7, the prime rate, is the short-term rate that banks charge on loans to their best customers. This is a measure of how much it costs businesses to borrow. It's always above the federal funds rate because lending to a business customer always involves some risk of nonpayment. But the prime rate moves almost perfectly in parallel with the federal funds rate.

The last interest rate in Figure 31-7 is the rate on 30-year mortgages—loans that many people use to buy homes. As you can see, this rate didn't move nearly as much in synch with the federal funds rate as did the prime rate. This illustrates a point we mentioned earlier in this chapter: long-term interest rates don't always move closely together with short-term rates.

Still, mortgage rates did fall significantly as the Fed cut the federal funds rate repeatedly in 2001. And the fall in mortgage rates helped start a housing boom, which had an expansionary effect on the economy. Housing starts—the number of new homes on which construction has begun—rose by one-third, from 1.2 million in 2000 to 1.6 million in 2004. ∎

< < < < < < < < < < < < < < < < < <

>>CHECK YOUR UNDERSTANDING 31-2

1. Assume that there is an increase in the demand for money at every interest rate. Using a diagram, show what effect this will have on the equilibrium interest rate for a given money supply.

2. Now assume that the Fed is following a policy of targeting the federal funds rate. What will the Fed do in the situation described in Question 1 to keep the federal funds rate unchanged? Illustrate with a diagram.

Solutions appear at back of book.

Monetary Policy and Aggregate Demand

In Chapter 29 we saw how fiscal policy can be used to stabilize the economy. Now we will see how monetary policy—changes in the money supply or the interest rate, or both—can play the same role.

Expansionary and Contractionary Monetary Policy

As we have just seen, the Fed moves the interest rate down or up by increasing or decreasing the money supply. Changes in the interest rate, in turn, change aggregate demand. Other things equal, a fall in the interest rate leads to a rise in investment and consumer spending and therefore a rise in aggregate demand. And, other things equal, a rise in the interest rate leads to a fall in investment and consumer spending and therefore a fall in aggregate demand. As a result, monetary policy, like fiscal policy, can be used to close either a recessionary gap or an inflationary gap.

Figure 31-8 shows the case of an economy facing a recessionary gap, where aggregate output is below potential output. *SRAS* is the short-run aggregate supply curve, *LRAS* is the long-run aggregate supply curve, and AD_1 is the initial aggregate demand curve. At the initial short-run macroeconomic equilibrium, E_1, aggregate output is Y_1, below potential output, Y_P. Suppose the Fed would like to increase aggregate demand, shifting the aggregate demand curve rightward to AD_2. This would increase aggregate output to potential output. The Fed can accomplish that goal by increasing the money supply, which drives the interest rate down. A lower interest rate leads to higher investment and consumer spending leading to a rise in aggregate demand. Monetary policy that increases aggregate demand is called **expansionary monetary policy.** Commentators often call an expansionary monetary policy a "loose" monetary policy because it is associated with a loosening of the money supply.

> **Expansionary monetary policy** is monetary policy that increases aggregate demand.

Figure 31-8

Expansionary Monetary Policy to Fight a Recessionary Gap

Here, initial actual aggregate output, Y_1, is below potential output, Y_P. An expansionary monetary policy reduces the interest rate, shifting the aggregate demand curve rightward from AD_1 to AD_2 and eliminating the recessionary gap. **>web...**

An expansionary monetary policy reduces the interest rate and increases aggregate demand.

Recessionary gap

Figure 31-9 on page 756 shows the opposite case—an economy facing an inflationary gap, where actual output is above potential output. *SRAS* is the short-run aggregate supply curve, *LRAS* is the long-run aggregate supply curve, and AD_1 is the initial aggregate demand curve. At the initial short-run macroeconomic equilibrium, aggregate output, Y_1, is above potential output, Y_P. As we've previously mentioned, policy makers often try to head off inflation by eliminating inflationary gaps. To eliminate the inflationary gap illustrated in Figure 31-9, aggregate demand must be reduced. By raising the interest rate, the Fed can cause a leftward shift of the aggregate demand curve, from AD_1 to AD_2, which reduces aggregate output to potential output. Monetary policy that reduces aggregate demand is called **contractionary monetary policy.** Commentators often refer to this as a "tight" monetary policy because it is associated with a restriction of the money supply.

Does monetary policy, like fiscal policy, have a multiplier effect on aggregate demand? Yes, although it's important to have a clear understanding of what is being multiplied.

"I told you the Fed should have tightened."

> **Contractionary monetary policy** is monetary policy that reduces aggregate demand.

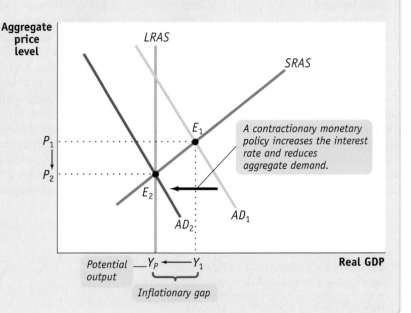

Figure 31-9

Contractionary Monetary Policy to Fight an Inflationary Gap

Here, initial actual aggregate output, Y_1, is above potential output, Y_P. A contractionary monetary policy raises the interest rate, shifting the aggregate demand curve leftward from AD_1 to AD_2 and eliminating the inflationary gap.

A contractionary monetary policy increases the interest rate and reduces aggregate demand.

Monetary Policy and the Multiplier

Suppose the Fed drives down the interest rate, causing a rightward shift of the aggregate demand curve. How expansionary is this? That is, how much does the *AD* curve shift to the right? We'll use the multiplier analysis of Chapter 27 to answer that question. In particular, we'll analyze how monetary policy, via a change in the interest rate, affects aggregate demand. (For the purposes of this analysis, we'll ignore the effect of taxes or foreign trade on the multiplier and hold the aggregate price level constant.)

Figure 31-10 shows the aggregate demand curve shifted to the right due to a fall in the interest rate. As you can see, the quantity of aggregate output demanded at any

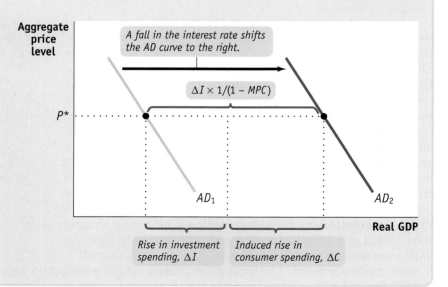

Figure 31-10

Monetary Policy and the Multiplier

An expansionary monetary policy drives down the interest rate, leading to an initial rise in investment spending, ΔI. This raises disposable income, which causes a rise in consumer spending, which further raises disposable income, and so on. In the end, the *AD* curve shifts rightward by a *multiple* of the initial rise in *I*.

A fall in the interest rate shifts the AD curve to the right.

$\Delta I \times 1/(1 - MPC)$

Rise in investment spending, ΔI

Induced rise in consumer spending, ΔC

given aggregate price level increases. To calculate how much the quantity of aggregate output demanded increases, we need to know how much a fall in the interest rate increases real GDP at a given aggregate price level, such as P^*. To keep things simple, we'll focus exclusively on the change in investment spending caused by a change in the interest rate, ignoring the direct effect of a change in the interest rate on consumer spending. Although they are present in reality, they are also likely to be much smaller than the effects on investment spending.

Assume that the initial aggregate demand curve is AD_1, and that the decline in the interest rate increases investment spending at the aggregate price level P^* by an amount ΔI. This is an example of an autonomous rise in aggregate spending, a phenomenon we studied in Chapter 27. From this point on, the analysis is exactly the same as that of any autonomous change in aggregate spending. The initial increase in real GDP translates into an increase in disposable income. This causes a rise in consumer spending, C, and a second-round rise in real GDP. This second-round increase in real GDP leads to yet another rise in consumer spending, and so on. At each round, however, the increase in real GDP is smaller than in the previous round, because some of the increase in disposable income "leaks out" into savings due to the fact that the marginal propensity to save, MPS, is positive. In the end, the AD curve shifts to a new position such as AD_2.

So a fall in the interest rate, r, leads to a rise in investment spending, ΔI. This rise in investment spending leads, in turn, to a rightward shift of the AD curve that reflects both the increase in investment spending, ΔI, and an induced rise in consumer spending, ΔC. As we saw in Chapter 29, the total rise in real GDP, assuming a fixed aggregate price level and no taxes or foreign trade, is a multiple of the initial rise in investment spending:

$$\textbf{(31-6)} \quad \Delta Y = \Delta I \times \frac{1}{1 - MPC}$$

where MPC is the marginal propensity to consume—the increase in consumer spending if disposable income rises by \$1.

Two Models of Interest Rates, Revisited

Earlier in this chapter we developed the liquidity preference model of the interest rate. In this model, the equilibrium interest rate is the rate at which the quantity of money demanded equals the quantity of money supplied. We promised to explain how this is consistent with the loanable funds model of the interest rate we developed in Chapter 26. In this model, the equilibrium interest rate matches the quantity of loanable funds supplied by savers with the quantity of loanable funds demanded for investment spending. We will now take the first of two steps toward providing that explanation, focusing on what happens in the short run.

As we have just discussed, a fall in the interest rate leads to a rise in investment spending, I, which then leads to a rise in both real GDP and consumer spending, C. The rise in real GDP doesn't lead only to a rise in consumer spending, however. As we noted, it also leads to a rise in savings: at each stage of the multiplier process, part of the increase in disposable income is saved. How much do savings rise? In Chapter 26 we introduced the *savings-investment spending identity:* total savings in the economy is always equal to investment spending. This tells us that when a fall in the interest rate leads to higher investment spending, the resulting increase in real GDP generates exactly enough additional savings to match the rise in investment spending. To put it another way, after a fall in the interest rate, the quantity of savings supplied rises exactly enough to match the quantity of savings demanded.

Figure 31-11 on page 758 shows how our two models of the interest rate are reconciled in the short run by the links among changes in the interest rate, changes in real GDP, and changes in savings. Panel (a) represents the liquidity preference model

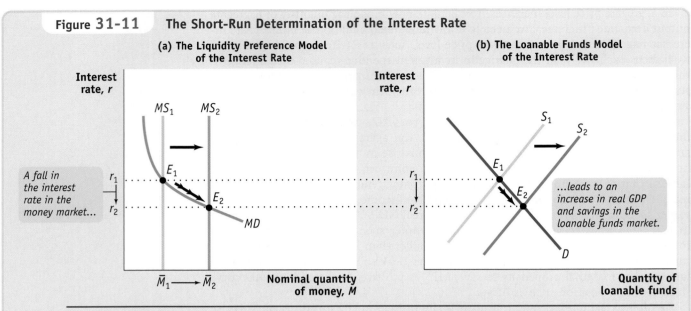

Figure 31-11   The Short-Run Determination of the Interest Rate

(a) The Liquidity Preference Model of the Interest Rate

(b) The Loanable Funds Model of the Interest Rate

Panel (a) shows the liquidity preference model of the interest rate: the equilibrium interest rate matches the money supply to the quantity of money demanded. In the short run, the interest rate is determined in the money market, where an increase in the money supply from $\bar{M}_1$ to $\bar{M}_2$ pushes the equilibrium interest rate down from r_1 to r_2. Panel (b) shows the loanable funds model of the interest rate. The fall in the interest rate in the money market leads, through the multiplier effect, to an increase in real GDP and savings, to a rightward shift of the supply curve of loanable funds, from S_1 to S_2, and to a fall in the interest rate, from r_1 to r_2. As a result, the new equilibrium interest rate in the loanable funds market matches the new equilibrium interest rate in the money market at r_2.

of the interest rate. MS_1 and MD are the initial supply and demand curves for money. According to the liquidity preference model, the equilibrium interest rate in the economy is the rate at which the quantity of money supplied is equal to the quantity of money demanded in the money market. Panel (b) represents the loanable funds model of the interest rate. S_1 is the initial supply curve and D is the demand curve for loanable funds. According to the loanable funds model, the equilibrium interest rate in the economy is the rate at which the quantity of loanable funds supplied is equal to the quantity of loanable funds demanded in the market for loanable funds.

In Figure 31-11 both the money market and the market for loanable funds are initially in equilibrium at the same interest rate, r_1. You might think that this would only happen by accident, but in fact it will always be true. To see why, let's look at what happens when the Fed increases the money supply. This action pushes the money supply curve rightward to MS_2, and the equilibrium interest rate in the market for money falls to r_2. What happens in panel (b), in the market for loanable funds? In the short run, the fall in the interest rate leads to a rise in real GDP, which generates a rise in savings through the multiplier process. This rise in savings shifts the supply curve for loanable funds rightward from S_1 to S_2, reducing the equilibrium interest rate in the loanable funds market, too. And we know that savings rise by exactly enough to match the rise in investment spending. This tells us that the equilibrium rate in the loanable funds market falls to r_2, the same as the new equilibrium interest rate in the money market.

In the short run, then, the supply and demand for money determine the interest rate, and the loanable funds market follows the lead of the money market. When a change in the money supply leads to a change in the interest rate, the resulting change in real GDP causes the supply of loanable funds to change as well. As a result, the equilibrium interest rate in the loanable funds market is the same as the equilibrium interest rate in the money market.

Notice our use of the phrase "in the short run." Recall from Chapter 27 that changes in aggregate demand affect aggregate output only in the short run. In the long run, aggregate output is equal to potential output. So our story about how a fall in the interest rate leads to a rise in aggregate output, which leads to a rise in savings, applies only to the short run. In the long run, as we'll see in the next section, the determination of the interest rate is quite different, because the roles of the two markets are reversed. In the long run, the loanable funds market determines the equilibrium interest rate, and it is the market for money that follows the lead of the loanable funds market.

economics in action

The Fed and the Output Gap, 1985–2004

In Figures 31-8 and 31-9 we showed how monetary policy can play a useful role: expansionary monetary policy can close recessionary gaps, and contractionary monetary policy can close inflationary gaps. A look back at U.S. monetary policy between 1985 and 2004 shows that the Federal Reserve did indeed tend to cut interest rates when the economy had a recessionary gap and raise interest rates when the economy had an inflationary gap.

The vertical axis on the left of Figure 31-12 shows the federal funds rate; the line labeled "federal funds rate" shows the average yearly value of that rate between 1985 and 2004. The vertical axis on the right shows the Congressional Budget Office estimate of the output gap, measured as a percentage of potential output. This number is positive when there is an inflationary gap, as in 1999 and 2000, and negative when there is a recessionary gap, as in 2001 through 2004.

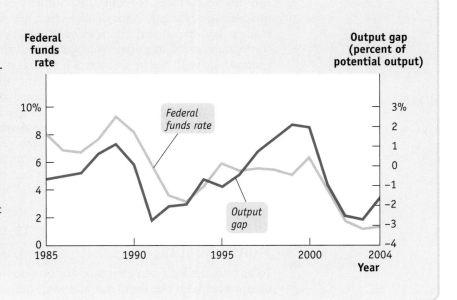

Figure 31-12

Federal Reserve Policy and the Business Cycle

The left vertical axis measures the federal funds rate. The right vertical axis measures the output gap, calculated as the difference between actual and potential output as a percentage of potential output. Over the past 20 years, the Fed has pursued a contractionary monetary policy when the economy was operating above potential output—that is, raising the federal funds rate when there was an inflationary gap. It has pursued an expansionary monetary policy when the economy was operating below potential output—that is, reducing the federal funds rate when there was a recessionary gap.

As you can see, there's a positive association between the federal funds rate and the output gap: the Fed tended to raise interest rates when aggregate output was moving above potential output and to reduce them when aggregate output was moving below potential output. In other words, the Fed was following pretty much the policy illustrated in Figures 31-8 and 31-9.

The two lines aren't perfectly synchronized. As you can see, the Fed did not raise interest rates in 1998 and 1999, even though the economy had developed a substantial inflationary gap. The main reason was that the Federal Reserve wasn't sure at the time that there was an output gap. As we'll see in Chapter 34, some economists believe that the Fed *should* have raised rates during that period. Also, data from years earlier than 1985 look very different. Prior to 1985 the Fed was grappling with the problem of *inflationary expectations,* which we will discuss in Chapter 33.

The important lesson, however, is that over the past two decades the Fed's actual policy has largely followed our basic analysis of how monetary policy should work. ■

< < < < < < < < < < < < < < < < < < <

>> CHECK YOUR UNDERSTANDING 31-3

1. Suppose the economy is currently suffering from a recessionary gap and the Federal Reserve uses an expansionary monetary policy to close that gap. Describe the short-run effect of this policy on the following:
   a. The money supply curve
   b. The equilibrium interest rate
   c. Investment spending
   d. Consumer spending
   e. Aggregate output
   f. The aggregate price level
   g. Savings
   h. The supply curve of loanable funds in the loanable funds market

Solutions appear at back of book.

Money, Output, and Prices in the Long Run

Through its expansionary and contractionary effects, monetary policy can be used to move the economy more quickly to long-run macroeconomic equilibrium. Sometimes, however, there are monetary events that move the economy *away* from long-run macroeconomic equilibrium. Sometimes the central bank simply makes a mistake. For example, it may believe that potential output is higher or lower than it really is and implement a misguided monetary policy. In addition, central banks are sometimes forced to pursue considerations other than stabilizing the economy. For example, as we'll see in Chapter 33, central banks sometimes help the government pay its bills by printing money, an action that increases the money supply.

What happens when a change in the money supply pushes the economy away from, rather than toward, long-run equilibrium? We learned in Chapter 27 that the economy is self-correcting in the long run: a demand shock has only a temporary effect on aggregate output. If the demand shock is the result of a change in the money supply, we can make a stronger statement: in the long run, changes in the quantity of money affect the aggregate price level, but they do not change real aggregate output or the interest rate. To see why, let's look at the case of an increase in the money supply.

Short-Run and Long-Run Effects of an Increase in the Money Supply

To analyze the long-run effects of an increase in the money supply, we recall the distinction between the short-run and long-run aggregate supply curves. The short-run aggregate supply curve slopes upward: in the short run, a higher aggregate price level leads to higher production. The long-run aggregate supply curve, however, is vertical at potential output: in the long run, a rise in prices of final goods and services leads to an equal rise in nominal wages, and real GDP remains equal to potential output.

Figure 31-13 shows the short-run and long-run effects of an increase in the money supply when the economy begins at potential output, Y_1. The initial short-run aggregate supply curve is $SRAS_1$, the long-run aggregate supply curve is *LRAS,* and the initial aggregate demand curve is AD_1. The economy's initial equilibrium is at E_1, a point of both short-run and long-run macroeconomic equilibrium because it is on

Figure 31-13

The Short-Run and Long-Run Effects of an Increase in the Money Supply

An increase in the money supply generates a positive short-run effect, but no long-run effect, on real GDP. Here, the economy begins at E_1, a point of short-run and long-run equilibrium. An increase in the money supply shifts the AD curve rightward, and the economy moves to a new short-run equilibrium at E_2 and a new real GDP of Y_2. But E_2 is not a long-run equilibrium: Y_2 exceeds potential output, Y_1, leading over time to an increase in nominal wages. In the long run, the increase in nominal wages shifts the short-run aggregate supply curve leftward, to a new position at $SRAS_2$. The economy reaches a new short-run and long-run equilibrium at E_3 on the $LRAS$ curve, and output falls back to potential output, Y_1. The only long-run effect of an increase in the money supply is an increase in the aggregate price level to P_3. **>web...**

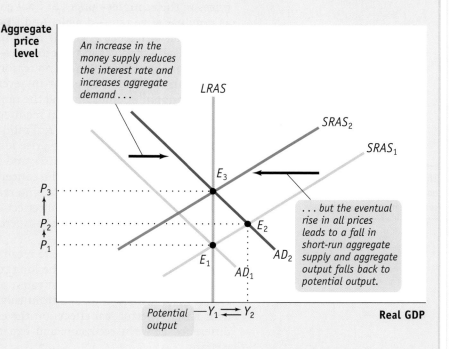

both the short-run and the long-run aggregate supply curves. Real GDP is at potential output, Y_1.

Now suppose there is an increase in the money supply. This shifts the AD curve to the right, to AD_2. In the short run, the economy moves to a new short-run macroeconomic equilibrium at E_2. The price level rises from P_1 to P_2, and real GDP rises from Y_1 to Y_2. That is, both the aggregate price level and aggregate output increase in the short run.

But the aggregate output level Y_2 is above potential output. As a result, nominal wages will rise over time, causing the short-run aggregate supply curve to shift leftward. This process stops only when the $SRAS$ curve ends up at $SRAS_2$ and the economy ends up at point E_3, a point of both short-run and long-run macroeconomic equilibrium. The long-run effect of an increase in the money supply, then, is that the aggregate price level has increased from P_1 to P_3, but aggregate output is back at potential output, Y_1. In the long run, a monetary expansion raises the aggregate price level but has no effect on real GDP.

We won't describe the effects of a monetary contraction in detail, but the same logic applies. In the short run, a fall in the money supply leads to a fall in aggregate output as the economy moves down the short-run aggregate supply curve. In the long run, however, the monetary contraction reduces only the aggregate price level, and real GDP returns to potential output.

Monetary Neutrality

How much does a change in the money supply change the aggregate price level in the long run? A change in the money supply leads to a proportional change in the aggregate price level in the long run. For example, if the money supply falls 25%, the aggregate price level falls 25% in the long run; if the money supply rises 50%, the aggregate price level rises 50% in the long run.

How do we know this? Consider the following thought experiment: suppose all prices in the economy—prices of final goods and services and also factor prices, such as nominal wage rates—double. And suppose the money supply doubles at the same time. What difference does this make to the economy in real terms? The answer is none. All real variables in the economy—including the real value of the money supply—are unchanged, so there is no reason for anyone to behave any differently.

We can state this argument in reverse: if the economy starts out in long-run macroeconomic equilibrium and the nominal money supply changes, restoring long-run macroeconomic equilibrium requires restoring all real values to their original values. This includes restoring the real money supply to its original level. So if the money supply falls 25%, the aggregate price level must fall 25%; if the money supply rises 50%, the price level must rise 50%; and so on.

This analysis demonstrates the concept known as **monetary neutrality,** in which changes in the money supply have no real effects on the economy—no effects on real GDP or its components. The only effect of an increase in the money supply is to raise the aggregate price level by an equal percentage. Economists argue that *money is neutral in the long run.*

This is, however, a good time to recall the dictum of John Maynard Keynes: "In the long run we are all dead." In the long run, changes in the money supply don't have any effect on real GDP, interest rates, or anything else except the price level. But it would be foolish to conclude from this that the Fed is irrelevant. Monetary policy does have powerful real effects on the economy in the short run, often making the difference between recession and expansion. And that matters a lot for society's welfare.

> There is **monetary neutrality** when changes in the money supply have no real effects on the economy.

The Interest Rate in the Long Run

In the short run an increase in the money supply leads to a fall in the interest rate, and a decrease in the money supply leads to a rise in the interest rate. In the long run, however, changes in the money supply don't affect the interest rate.

Figure 31-14 shows why. It is similar to Figure 31-11, but in this case panel (a) shows the *real* money demand curve, RMD. Panel (b), as in Figure 31-11, shows the supply and demand for loanable funds. We assume that in both panels the economy is initially at E, in long-run macroeconomic equilibrium at potential output with the nominal money supply equal to $\overline{M}_1$ and the price level equal to P_1. The demand curve for loanable funds is D, and the initial supply curve for loanable funds is S_1. The initial equilibrium interest rate is r_1.

Now suppose the nominal money supply rises from $\overline{M}_1$ to $\overline{M}_2$. We already know from the neutrality of money that in the long run the aggregate price level rises by the same proportion as the increase in the money supply but that in the short run the price level rises by a smaller amount. So the initial effect of an increase in the nominal money supply is a rise in the *real* money supply, from $\overline{M}_1/P_1$ to $\overline{M}_2/P_2$. Given the real money demand curve, RMD, this reduces the equilibrium interest rate from r_1 to r_2, and the money market moves to X in panel (a). And as we saw earlier, the supply of loanable funds shifts rightward by just enough that the quantity of loanable funds supplied and the quantity of loanable funds demanded are equalized at r_2. Correspondingly, the loanable funds market moves to X in panel (b). X corresponds to an aggregate output greater than potential output because the interest rate at X, r_2, is lower than the interest rate that holds at potential output, r_1.

In the long run, however, the aggregate price level rises further, from P_2 to P_3. As we've already seen, this reduces the real money supply back to its original level: $\overline{M}_2/P_3$ is equal to $\overline{M}_1/P_1$. As a result, the equilibrium interest rate goes back to r_1 and each market moves back to E. Meanwhile, aggregate output also falls back to potential output—which means that savings return to their original level, too. In panel (b), the supply of loanable funds, which initially shifted from S_1 to S_2, shifts back to S_1.

Figure 31-14   The Long-Run Determination of the Interest Rate

(a) The Real Liquidity Preference Model

Interest rate, r

Potential output equilibrium

2. . . . but in the long run, the increase in all prices reduces the real money supply back to its original level . . .

r_1

r_2

E

X

RMD

1. In the short run, an increase in the real money supply reduces the interest rate . . .

$\bar{M}_1/P_1 = \bar{M}_2/P_3 \rightleftarrows \bar{M}_2/P_2$

Real quantity of money, M/P

(b) The Loanable Funds Model

Interest rate, r

Potential output equilibrium

S_1

S_2

r_1

r_2

E

X

3. . . . and reduces the supply of loanable funds to its original level and aggregate output back to potential output.

D

$Q_1 \rightleftarrows Q_2$

Quantity of loanable funds

Panel (a) shows the money market expressed in real terms and panel (b) shows the loanable funds market. Each market starts at point E, where the economy is at potential output. In the short run, an increase in the money supply increases the real money supply from $\bar{M}_1/P_1$ to $\bar{M}_2/P_2$ and reduces the equilibrium interest rate from r_1 to r_2 as the money market moves from point E to point X. The fall in the interest rate leads to higher real GDP and higher savings through the multiplier effect. This shifts the supply curve of loanable

funds rightward, from S_1 to S_2, also moving the market for loanable funds from point E to point X. In the long run, however, the increase in the money supply raises prices: the real money supply returns to its original level, $\bar{M}_2/P_3 = \bar{M}_1/P_1$, and the supply curve of loanable funds shifts back to its initial position, S_1. So in the long run the equilibrium interest rate is determined by the supply and demand for loanable funds that arise at potential output.

In the long run, then, changes in the money supply do not affect the interest rate. So what determines the interest rate in the long run—that is, what determines r_1 in Figure 31-14? The answer is the supply and demand for loanable funds. More specifically, in the long run the equilibrium interest rate matches the supply and demand for loanable funds that arise at potential output.

economics in action

International Evidence of Monetary Neutrality

These days monetary policy is quite similar among wealthy countries. Each major nation (or, in the case of the euro, group of nations) has a central bank that is insulated from political pressure; all of these central banks try to keep the aggregate price level roughly stable, which usually means inflation of at most 2% to 3% per year.

But if we look at a longer period and a wider group of countries, we see large differences in the growth of the money supply. Between 1970 and the present the money supply rose only a few percent per year in some countries, such as Switzerland and the United States, but rose much more rapidly in some poorer countries, such as Bolivia. These differences allow us to see whether it is really true that increases in the money supply lead, in the long run, to equal percentage rises in the aggregate price level.

Figure 31-15 on page 764 shows the annual percentage increases in the money supply and in the aggregate price level for a sample of countries during the period

Figure 31-15

The Long-Run Relationship Between Money and Inflation

The horizontal axis measures the annual percent increase in a country's money supply between 1970 and 2000. The vertical axis measures the annual percent increase in a country's aggregate price level over the same period. Each point represents a specific country. The scatter of points lies close to a 45-degree line, demonstrating that in the long run increases in the money supply lead to roughly equal percent increases in the aggregate price level.

Source: United Nations Statistical Database.

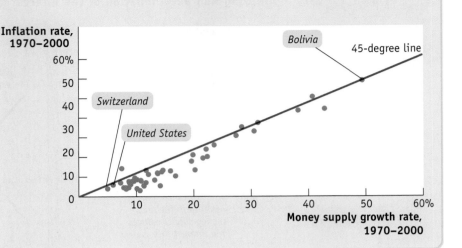

1970–2000, with each point representing a country. If the relationship between increases in the money supply and changes in the aggregate price level were exact, the points would lie precisely on a 45-degree line. In fact, the relationship isn't exact, because other factors besides money affect the aggregate price level. But the scatter of points clearly lies close to a 45-degree line, showing a more or less proportional relationship between money and the aggregate price level. That is, the data support the idea that money is neutral in the long run. ∎

< < < < < < < < < < < < < < < < < <

>>CHECK YOUR UNDERSTANDING 31-4

1. Assume the central bank increases the quantity of money by 25%, even though the economy is initially in both short-run and long-run macroeconomic equilibrium. Describe the effects, in the short run and in the long run (giving numbers where possible), on the following:
   a. Aggregate output
   b. Aggregate price level
   c. Real quantity of money
   d. Interest rate

Solutions appear at back of book.

• A LOOK AHEAD •

Monetary and fiscal policy can be used to help close gaps: a recessionary gap, in which the economy is producing less than potential output, or an inflationary gap, in which it is producing more than potential output. We have not yet explained, however, why closing such gaps is so important.

In the case of a recessionary gap, the answer is that recessionary gaps are associated with high unemployment. To deepen our understanding of that concern, however, we need to look more deeply into the causes and meaning of unemployment. That's the subject of Chapter 32.

The causes and costs of inflation are a more subtle issue, which we deal with in Chapter 33.

SUMMARY

1. The **money demand curve** arises from a trade-off between the opportunity cost of holding money and the liquidity that money provides. The opportunity cost of holding money depends on **short-term interest rates,** not **long-term interest rates.**

2. Other things equal, the nominal quantity of money demanded is proportional to the aggregate price level. So money demand can also be represented using the **real money demand curve.** Changes in real aggregate spending, technology, and institutions shift the real and nominal money demand curves. According to the **quantity equation,** the **real quantity of money** demanded is proportional to real aggregate spending, where the constant of proportionality is one over the **velocity of money.**

3. The **liquidity preference model of the interest rate** says that the interest rate is determined in the money market by the money demand curve and the **money supply curve.** The Federal Reserve can change the interest rate in the short run by shifting the money supply curve. In practice, the Fed uses open-market operations to achieve a **target federal funds rate,** which other interest rates generally track.

4. **Expansionary monetary policy,** which reduces the interest rate and increases aggregate demand by increasing the money supply, is used to close recessionary gaps. **Contractionary monetary policy,** which increases the interest rate and reduces aggregate demand by decreasing the money supply, is used to close inflationary gaps.

5. Like fiscal policy, monetary policy has a multiplier effect, because changes in the interest rate lead to changes in consumer spending and savings as well as investment spending. In the short run, a change in the equilibrium interest rate determined in the money market results in a change in real GDP and in savings through the multiplier effect. The change in savings shifts the supply of loanable funds in the market for loanable funds until it reaches equilibrium at the new equilibrium interest rate.

6. In the long run, changes in the money supply affect the aggregate price level but not real GDP or the interest rate. In fact, there is **monetary neutrality:** changes in the money supply have no real effect on the economy in the long run. So monetary policy is ineffectual in the long run.

7. In the long run, the equilibrium interest rate matches the supply and demand for loanable funds that arise at potential output in the market for loanable funds.

KEY TERMS

Short-term interest rates, p. 744
Long-term interest rates, p. 744
Money demand curve, p. 745
Real quantity of money, p. 745
Real money demand curve, p. 746

Velocity of money, p. 748
Quantity equation, p. 748
Liquidity preference model of the interest rate, p. 750
Money supply curve, p. 750

Target federal funds rate, p. 753
Expansionary monetary policy, p. 755
Contractionary monetary policy, p. 755
Monetary neutrality, p. 762

PROBLEMS

1. Go to the FOMC page of the Federal Reserve Board's website (http://www.federalreserve.gov/FOMC/) to find the statement issued after the most recent FOMC meeting. (Go to the bottom of the web page and click on the most recent statement listed in the calendar.)

   a. What is the target federal funds rate?

   b. Is the target federal funds rate different from the target federal funds rate from the previous FOMC statement? If yes, by how much does it differ?

   c. Does the statement comment on macroeconomic conditions in the United States? How does it describe the U.S. economy?

2. How will the following events affect the nominal demand for money as defined by M1? In each case, specify whether there is a shift of the money demand curve or a movement along the money demand curve and its direction.

   a. There is a fall in the interest rate from 12% to 10%.

   b. Thanksgiving arrives and, with it, the beginning of the holiday shopping season.

   c. McDonald's and other fast-food restaurants begin to accept credit cards.

   d. The Fed engages in an open-market purchase of U.S. Treasury bills.

3. The table on page 766 shows nominal GDP, M1, and M2 in billions of dollars in five-year increments from 1960 to 2000 as published in the *2005 Economic Report of the President.* Complete the table by calculating the velocity of money using both M1 and M2. What trends or patterns in the velocity of money do you see? What might account for these trends?

Year	Nominal GDP (billions of dollars)	M1 (billions of dollars)	M2 (billions of dollars)	Velocity using M1	Velocity using M2
1960	$526.4	$140.7	$312.4	?	?
1965	719.1	167.8	459.2	?	?
1970	1,038.5	214.4	626.5	?	?
1975	1,638.3	287.1	1,016.2	?	?
1980	2,789.5	408.5	1,599.8	?	?
1985	4,220.3	619.8	2,495.7	?	?
1990	5,803.1	824.8	3,279.2	?	?
1995	7,397.7	1,127.0	3,641.2	?	?
2000	9,817.0	1,087.9	4,932.5	?	?

4. The accompanying table shows the annual growth of M1 and nominal GDP in Japan during the early 2000s. What must have been happening to velocity during this time?

Year	M1 growth	Nominal GDP growth
2000	8.2%	2.9%
2001	8.5%	0.4%
2002	27.6%	−0.5%
2003	8.2%	2.5%

5. An economy is facing the recessionary gap shown in the accompanying diagram. To eliminate the gap, should the central bank use expansionary or contractionary monetary policy? How will the interest rate, investment spending, consumer spending, real GDP, and the aggregate price level change as the monetary policy closes the recessionary gap?

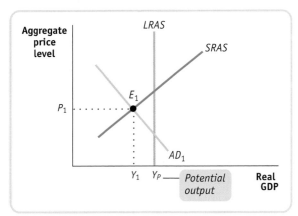

6. An economy is facing the inflationary gap shown in the accompanying diagram. To eliminate the gap, should the central bank use expansionary or contractionary monetary policy? How will the interest rate, investment spending, consumer spending, real GDP, and the aggregate price level change as the monetary policy closes the inflationary gap?

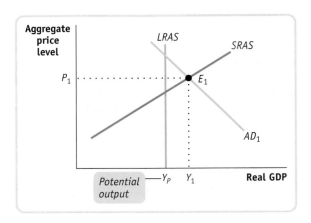

7. In the economy of Eastlandia, the money market is initially in equilibrium when the economy begins to slide into a recession.

a. Using the accompanying diagram, explain what will happen to the interest rate if the central bank of Eastlandia keeps the money supply constant at $\overline{M}_1$.

b. If the central bank is instead committed to maintaining an interest rate target of r_1, how should the central bank react as the economy slides into recession?

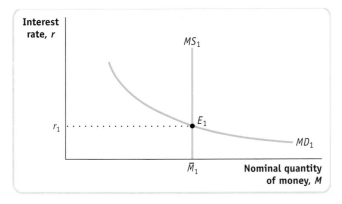

8. An economy is in long-run macroeconomic equilibrium with an unemployment rate of 5% when the government passes a law requiring the central bank to use monetary policy to lower the unemployment rate to 3% and keep it there. How could the central bank achieve this goal in the short run? What would happen in the long run? Illustrate with a diagram.

9. According to the European Central Bank website, the treaty establishing the European Community "makes clear that ensuring price stability is the most important contribution that monetary policy can make to achieve a favourable economic environment and a high level of employment." If price stability is the only goal of monetary policy, explain how monetary policy would be conducted during recessions. Analyze both the case of a recession that is the result of a demand shock and the case of a recession that is the result of a supply shock.

10. The effectiveness of monetary policy depends on how easy it is for changes in the money supply to change interest rates. By changing interest rates, monetary policy affects investment spending and the aggregate demand curve. The economies of Albernia and Brittania have very different money demand curves, as shown in the accompanying diagram. In which economy will changes in the money supply be a more effective policy tool? Why?

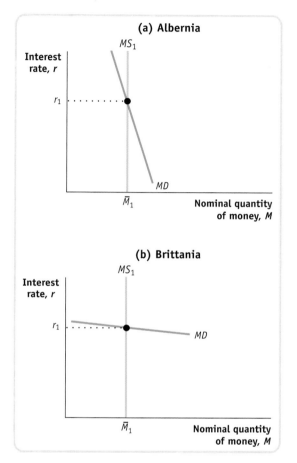

11. During the Great Depression, businesspeople in the United States were very pessimistic about the future of economic growth and reluctant to increase investment spending even when interest rates fell. How did this limit the potential for monetary policy to help alleviate the Depression?

12. Using a figure similar to Figure 31-11, explain how the money market and the loanable funds market react to a reduction in the money supply in the short run.

13. Contrast the short-run effects of an increase in the money supply on the interest rate to the long-run effects of an increase in the money supply on the interest rate. Which market determines the interest rate in the short run? Which market does so in the long run? What are the implications of your answers for the effectiveness of monetary policy in the short run and the long run in influencing real GDP?

>web... To continue your study and review of concepts in this chapter, please visit the Krugman/Wells website for quizzes, animated graph tutorials, web links to helpful resources, and more.

www.worthpublishers.com/krugmanwells

>>Labor Markets, Unemployment, and Inflation

TWO PATHS TO UNEMPLOYMENT

MICHAEL WATSON, A SOFTWARE developer in Colorado Springs, has been moving in and out of unemployment for three years. Ever since his high-tech employer closed its doors in July 2002, Watson has been without a permanent job and traveling to places as far-flung as Virginia and Djibouti to do temporary contract work. He isn't alone: Colorado Springs, home to many high-tech workers, lost nearly 20% of its high-tech jobs between 2000 and 2004. Some workers who lost their jobs have since found new ones in Colorado Springs, others have left the area, and others—like Watson—are still looking for permanent work.

The economy in North Carolina, where textile engineer Tommy Patterson lives, is booming relative to that in the rest of the country. But Patterson, who lost his job at a Charlotte textile mill in November 2004, is still looking for work as a process engineer in the chemical industry. Still, despite sending out between 50 and 75 résumés, he has had few bites to date. In North Carolina there are more jobs than there were a few years ago, but manufacturing and engineering jobs are still hard to come by.

Because both Watson and Patterson are currently jobless and actively seeking employment, they are considered to be unemployed. Both are in professions on the decline or stagnating in their given locations, but each is hesitant to move his family to a new city in search of work. So both men continue to search actively for permanent employment that's a good match for their skills and ambitions.

At any given point in time, millions of Americans are actively pursuing employment but have not found the right match. Others have recently been laid off, and still others have just entered the workforce but haven't yet found jobs. This "natural" churning of the labor force means that at any given point in time some fraction of the population is

What you will learn in this chapter:

➤ The meaning of the **natural rate of unemployment,** and why it isn't zero

➤ Why **cyclical unemployment** changes over the business cycle

➤ How factors such as minimum wages and **efficiency wages** can lead to **structural unemployment**

➤ The reasons that the unemployment rate can be higher or lower than the natural rate for extended periods

➤ The existence of a short-run trade-off between unemployment and inflation, called the **short-run Phillips curve,** that disappears in the long run

➤ Why the **NAIRU,** the **nonaccelerating inflation rate of unemployment,** is an important measure for policy-making

Job loss strikes many kinds of workers, from computer programmers like Michael Watson to process engineers like Tommy Patterson. These two, like the millions of other workers who lose jobs in any given year, would like to see themselves as pictured above: employed again.

unemployed. But the size of that fraction depends on the state of the economy: there are more people in Watson's and Patterson's situation when the economy is depressed than when the economy is booming.

In this chapter, we look more closely at the nature of unemployment, why the unemployment rate goes up and down over time, and what economic policy can and cannot do about it.

The Nature of Unemployment

U.S. government statistics count as unemployed a worker who is actively looking for a job but hasn't found one. Recall from Chapter 23 that the unemployment rate is the ratio of the number of people unemployed to the total number of people in the labor force, where the labor force consists of people who are either currently working or looking for jobs. If everyone who wanted a job had one, the unemployment rate would be 0%. But American public policy considers the unemployment rate at "full employment," which you might think means that everyone who wants to work has a job, to be a number well above 0%. Indeed, as explained in For Inquiring Minds, a famous piece of legislation known as the Humphrey–Hawkins bill was passed by Congress in 1978. It called on the government to seek full employment—but defined full employment to be an unemployment rate of 4%.

Although a 4% unemployment rate may seem like a large number—after all, this implies that even with "full employment" millions of Americans looking for work would be jobless—at the time Humphrey–Hawkins was passed the vast majority of economists considered this target to be unrealistic. In fact, the Congressional Budget Office currently calculates the cyclically adjusted budget balance, the budget balance if the economy were at potential output and, hence, at full employment, under the assumption that full employment means a 5.2% unemployment rate.

To understand why there are so many unemployed workers even when the economy is considered to be at full employment, we need to look at the realities of the labor market.

FOR INQUIRING MINDS
FULL EMPLOYMENT: IT'S THE LAW!

Is there a law requiring the U.S. government to ensure full employment? No, and there never was. But the Full Employment and Balanced Growth Act of 1978, usually referred to as the Humphrey–Hawkins bill, did call on the U.S. government to achieve an unemployment rate of 4% or less through macroeconomic policy.

Nothing in the bill specified penalties for government officials who failed to achieve these goals, and policy makers began ignoring the unemployment target from the start. The only provision that really had teeth was the requirement that the chairman of the Federal Reserve Board of Governors testify about monetary policy before Congress twice a year, a tradition that continues to this day. That

testimony is still often referred to as the "Humphrey–Hawkins testimony," even though the 1978 bill was allowed to lapse in 2000.

Despite the fact that Humphrey–Hawkins never had much direct effect on policy, it came to have symbolic importance. A 4% unemployment rate became the seemingly unattainable goal of economic policy. In late 1998, when the unemployment rate finally (and briefly) dropped toward the elusive goal, columnist Walter Shapiro asked in the online magazine *Slate*, "Where are the ticker-tape parades, the patriotic speeches, the red-white-and-blue fireworks, and the photographs of beautiful women embracing exuberant economists in Times Square?"

Job Creation and Job Destruction

At any given time, most Americans know someone who has lost his or her job recently. On average, about one worker in seven loses his or her job each year (in some cases because of leaving voluntarily) even in good years.

Dave Carpenter

"*They just like to remind you about the job market.*"

There are many reasons for such job loss. One is that industries rise and fall as new technologies emerge and consumers' tastes change. For example, employment in high-tech industries such as telecommunications surged in the late 1990s but slumped severely after 2000. That's a major reason why Michael Watson, the software developer, lost his job in 2002 and has had difficulty finding another. Another reason is that individual companies do well or badly depending on the quality of their management or simply depending on luck: for example, in 2005 General Motors announced plans to close a number of auto plants even as Japanese companies such as Toyota announced plans to open new plants in North America. In addition, individual workers are constantly leaving jobs for personal reasons—family moves, dissatisfaction, better job prospects elsewhere.

This constant churning of the workforce is an inevitable feature of the modern economy. It is also one main reason that there is a considerable amount of unemployment even when the economy is at full employment.

Frictional Unemployment

> Workers who spend time looking for employment are engaged in **job search**.
>
> **Frictional unemployment** is unemployment due to the time workers spend in job search.

When a worker loses a job—or a young worker enters the job market for the first time—he or she often doesn't take the first new job offered. For example, suppose a skilled programmer, laid off because her company's product line was unsuccessful, sees a help-wanted sign in the window of a shop. She might well be able to walk in and get the job—but that would usually be foolish. Instead, she should take the time to look for a job that takes advantage of her skills and pays accordingly.

Economists say that workers who spend time looking for employment are engaged in **job search.** If all workers and all jobs were alike, job search wouldn't be necessary; if information about jobs and workers were perfect, job search would be very quick. In practice, however, it's normal for a worker who loses a job (or a young worker seeking a first job) to spend at least a few weeks searching.

Frictional unemployment is unemployment due to the time workers spend in job search. A certain amount of frictional unemployment is inevitable, for two reasons. One is the constant process of job creation and job destruction, which we have just described. The other is the fact that new workers are always entering the job market. For example, in July 2005, out of 7.8 million workers counted as unemployed, 882,000 were new entrants to the workforce.

A limited amount of frictional unemployment is relatively harmless and may even be a good thing. The economy is more productive if workers take the time to find jobs that are well matched to their skills, and workers who are unemployed for a brief period while searching for the right job don't experience great hardship. In fact, when there is a low unemployment rate, periods of unemployment tend to be quite short, suggesting that much of the unemployment is frictional. Figure 32-1 shows the composition of unemployment in 2000, when the unemployment rate was only 4%. Forty-five percent of the unemployed had been unemployed for less than 5 weeks and only 23% had been unemployed for 15 or more weeks. Just 11% were considered to be "long-term unemployed"—unemployed for 27 or more weeks.

Figure 32-1

Distribution of the Unemployed by Duration of Unemployment, 2000

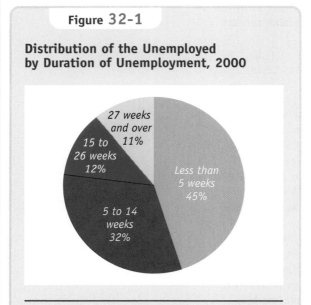

- 27 weeks and over 11%
- 15 to 26 weeks 12%
- 5 to 14 weeks 32%
- Less than 5 weeks 45%

In years when the unemployment rate is low, most unemployed workers are unemployed for only a short period. In 2000, a year of low unemployment, 45% of the unemployed had been unemployed for less than 5 weeks and 77% for less than 15 weeks. The short duration of unemployment for most workers suggests that most unemployment in 2000 was frictional.

Source: Bureau of Labor Statistics.

In periods of higher unemployment, however, workers tend to be jobless for longer periods of time, suggesting that a smaller share of unemployment is frictional. By 2003, for instance, the fraction of workers considered "long-term unemployed" had jumped to 22%.

Structural Unemployment

Frictional unemployment exists even when the number of people seeking jobs is equal to the number of jobs being offered—that is, frictional unemployment doesn't signal a surplus of labor. Sometimes, however, there is a *persistent surplus* of job-seekers in a particular labor market. For example, there may be more workers with a particular skill than there are jobs available using that skill, or there may be more workers in a particular geographic region than there are jobs available in that region. **Structural unemployment** is unemployment that results when there are more people seeking jobs in a labor market than there are jobs available at the current wage rate.

The supply and demand model tells us that the price of a good, service, or factor of production tends to move toward an equilibrium level that matches the quantity supplied with the quantity demanded. This is equally true, in general, of labor markets. Figure 32-2 shows a typical market for labor. The labor demand curve indicates that when the price of labor—the wage rate—increases, employers demand less labor. The labor supply curve indicates that when the price of labor increases, more workers will be willing to supply labor at the prevailing wage rate. These two forces coincide to lead to an equilibrium wage rate for any given type of labor in a particular location. That equilibrium wage rate is shown as W_E.

> **Structural unemployment** is unemployment that results when there are more people seeking jobs in a labor market than there are jobs available at the current wage rate.

Figure 32-2

The Effect of a Minimum Wage on the Labor Market

When the government sets a minimum wage, W_F, that exceeds the market equilibrium wage rate, W_E, the number of workers, Q_S, who would like to work at that minimum wage, is greater than the number of workers, Q_D, demanded at that wage rate. This surplus of labor is considered structural unemployment.

>web...

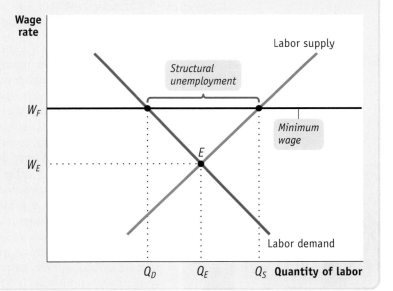

Even at the equilibrium wage rate W_E, there will still be some frictional unemployment. That's because there will always be some workers engaged in job search even when the number of jobs available is equal to the number of workers seeking jobs. But there wouldn't be any structural unemployment in this labor market. *Structural unemployment occurs when the wage rate is, for some reason, persistently above W_E.* There are several factors that can lead to a wage rate in excess of W_E, the most important being minimum wages, labor unions, *efficiency wages*, and the side effects of government policies.

Minimum Wages As we learned in Chapter 4, a minimum wage is a government-mandated floor on the price of labor. In the United States, the national minimum wage in 2005 was $5.15 an hour. For many types of labor, the minimum wage is irrelevant; the market equilibrium wage is well above this price floor. But for some types of labor, the minimum wage may be binding—it affects the wages that people are actually paid.

Figure 32-2 on page 771 shows just such a situation. In this market, there is a legal floor on wages, W_F, which is above the equilibrium wage rate, W_E. This leads to a persistent surplus in the labor market: the quantity of labor supplied, Q_S, is larger than the quantity demanded, Q_D. In other words, more people want to work than can find jobs at the minimum wage, leading to structural unemployment.

Given that minimum wages—that is, binding minimum wages—generally lead to structural unemployment, you might be wondering why governments impose them. The rationale is to help ensure that people who work can earn enough income to afford at least a minimally comfortable lifestyle. However, this comes at a cost, because it forecloses the opportunity to work for some workers who would have willingly worked for lower wages. As illustrated in Figure 32-2, not only are there more sellers of labor than there are buyers, but there are also fewer people working at a minimum wage (Q_D) than there would have been with no minimum wage at all (Q_E).

We should note, however, that although economists broadly agree that a high minimum wage has the employment-reducing effects shown in Figure 32-2, there is some question about whether this is a good description of how the minimum wage works in the United States. As a percentage of average wages, the minimum wage in the United States is quite low by international standards. (See the Economics in Action that follows this section.) Some researchers have produced evidence that increases in the minimum wage actually lead to higher employment when the minimum wage is low compared with average wages. They argue that firms that employ low-skilled workers sometimes restrict their hiring in order to keep wages low and that, as a result, the minimum wage can sometimes be increased without any loss of jobs. Most economists, however, agree that a sufficiently high minimum wage *does* lead to structural unemployment.

Labor Unions The actions of *labor unions* can have effects similar to those of minimum wages, leading to structural unemployment. By bargaining for all a firm's workers collectively, unions can often win higher wages from employers than the market would have otherwise provided when workers bargained individually. This process, known as *collective bargaining,* is intended to tip the scales of bargaining power more to workers and away from employers. Labor unions exercise bargaining power by threatening firms with a *labor strike,* a collective refusal to work. The threat of a strike can be very serious for firms that would have difficulty replacing striking workers. In such cases, workers acting collectively can exercise more power than they could if they acted independently.

When workers have greater bargaining power, they tend to demand and receive higher wages. Unions also bargain over benefits, such as health care and retirement benefits, which we can think of as additional wages. Indeed, economists who study the effects of unions on wages find that unionized workers earn higher wages and benefits than non-union workers with similar skills. The result of these increased wages is the same as the result of a minimum wage: labor unions push the wage that workers receive above the equilibrium wage. Consequently, there are more people willing to work at the wage being paid than there are jobs available. Like a binding minimum wage, this leads to structural unemployment.

Another way in which labor unions lead to unemployment involves the ways in which the labor contracts that result from collective bargaining are structured. Union members tend to have long-term contracts of two or three years duration. Independent of the increased wages associated with unions, these long-term contracts could also lead to structural unemployment. If the demand for labor is falling but employers and

Unions are one reason why wages are sometimes higher than the level that matches the supply and demand for labor.

employees have previously agreed to a higher wage rate, this has the same effect as a floor on wages—leading to more workers being willing to work for the negotiated wage rate than there are jobs available at that wage rate.

If non-unionized firms also commit to a given advertised wage for a period of time, the same effects could occur even without labor unions. The fact that some firms are on a different timetable for negotiating their labor contracts than other firms—a phenomenon known as *wage staggering*—leads the labor market to move slowly from one equilibrium to another when the demand for labor changes. In the meantime, while the labor market is out of equilibrium, structural unemployment can occur. We will turn to this topic again later in this chapter when we explore in more detail why the labor market moves slowly from one equilibrium to another.

Efficiency Wages Actions by firms may also contribute to structural unemployment in the absence of labor unions and wage staggering. Firms may choose to pay **efficiency wages**—wages that employers set above the equilibrium wage rate as an incentive for better performance.

Efficiency wages are wages that employers set above the equilibrium wage rate as an incentive for better performance.

Employers may do this for several reasons. One is that workers know more about their other work opportunities than do their employers. An employer that pays as little as possible risks losing its better workers and retaining more of its lower-quality workers—the ones who wouldn't be able to find better work elsewhere. This is less likely to happen if the firm pays a wage above the equilibrium wage rate. In such a situation, high-quality workers will be less likely to move to a different employer.

Employers may also pay above-market wages in order to ensure a higher degree of worker effort when they can't directly observe how hard an employee works. Employees receiving these higher wages are more likely to maintain a higher level of effort to ensure that they do not suffer a wage reduction by being fired.

If many firms pay wages that are above the market equilibrium wage rate, this will result in a pool of workers who want higher-paying jobs but can't find them. So the use of efficiency wages by firms leads to structural unemployment.

Side Effects of Public Policy In addition, public policy designed to help workers who lose their jobs can lead to structural unemployment as an unintended side effect. Most economically advanced countries provide benefits to laid-off workers as a way to tide them over until they find a new job. In the United States, these benefits typically replace only a small fraction of a worker's income and expire after 26 weeks. In other countries, particularly in Europe, benefits are more generous and last longer. The drawback to this generosity is that it reduces a worker's incentive to seek a new job. Generous unemployment benefits are widely believed to be one of the main causes of "Eurosclerosis," described in Economics in Action on page 776.

The Natural Rate of Unemployment

We can now return to the question of why national goals for unemployment are so modest. Why settle for an unemployment rate of 4% or more?

Because some frictional unemployment is inevitable and many economies also suffer from structural unemployment, a certain amount of unemployment is normal, or "natural," although actual unemployment fluctuates around this normal level. The **natural rate of unemployment** is the normal unemployment rate around which the actual unemployment rate fluctuates. It is the rate of unemployment that arises from the effects of frictional plus structural unemployment. Deviations in the actual rate of unemployment from the natural rate are called **cyclical unemployment.** As the name suggests, cyclical unemployment is unemployment that arises from the business cycle. We'll see later in this chapter that public policy cannot keep the unemployment rate persistently below the natural rate without leading to accelerating inflation. We can summarize the relationships between the various types of unemployment as follows:

The **natural rate of unemployment** is the normal unemployment rate around which the actual unemployment rate fluctuates.

Cyclical unemployment is the deviation in the actual rate of unemployment from the natural rate.

(32-1) Natural unemployment = Frictional unemployment +
Structural unemployment

(32-2) Actual unemployment = Natural unemployment +
Cyclical unemployment

Perhaps because of its name, people often imagine that the natural rate of unemployment is a constant that doesn't change over time and can't be affected by policy. Neither proposition is true. Let's take a moment to stress two facts: the natural rate of unemployment changes over time, and it can be affected by economic policies.

Changes in the Natural Rate of Unemployment

Both private-sector economists and government agencies need estimates of the natural rate of unemployment for forecasts and policy analyses. Almost all these estimates show the U.S. natural rate rising and falling over time. For example, the Congressional Budget Office believes that the natural rate was 5.3% in 1950, rose to 6.3% by the end of the 1970s, then fell to 5.2% by the end of the 1990s. The United States is not alone in its changes in the natural rate of unemployment over time. In fact, Europe has experienced even larger swings in the natural rate of unemployment.

What causes the natural rate of unemployment to change? The most important factors are changes in the characteristics of the labor force, changes in labor market institutions, changes in government policies, and changes in productivity. Let's look briefly at each factor.

Changes in Labor Force Characteristics In 2000, as we've seen, the overall rate of unemployment in the United States was 4%. Young workers, however, had much higher unemployment rates: 13% for teenagers and 7% for workers aged 20 to 24. Workers over 25 had an unemployment rate of only 3%.

In general, unemployment rates tend to be lower for experienced workers than for inexperienced workers. Because experienced workers tend to stay in a given job longer than do inexperienced workers, they have lower frictional unemployment. Also, because older workers are more likely than young workers to be family breadwinners, they have a stronger incentive to find and keep jobs.

One reason the natural rate of unemployment rose during the 1970s was a large rise in the number of new workers—children of the post World War II baby boom entered the labor force, as did a rising percentage of married women. As Figure 32-3 shows, both the percentage of the labor force less than 25 years old and the percentage of women in the labor force surged in the 1970s. By the end of the 1990s, however, the share of women in the labor force had leveled off, and the percentage of

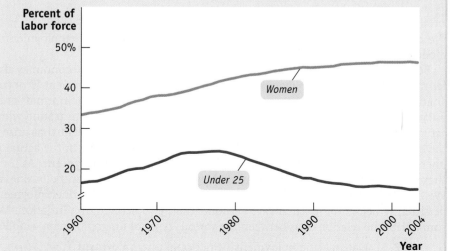

Figure 32-3

The Changing Makeup of the U.S. Labor Force

In the 1970s the percentage of the labor force consisting of women rose rapidly, as did the percentage under age 25. These changes reflected the entry of large numbers of women into the paid labor force for the first time and the fact that baby boomers were reaching working age. The natural rate of unemployment may have risen because many of these workers were relatively inexperienced. Today, the labor force is much more experienced, which is one possible reason the natural rate has fallen since the 1970s.

Source: Bureau of Labor Statistics.

workers under 25 had fallen sharply. This means that the labor force as a whole is more experienced today than it had been in the 1970s, one likely reason that the natural rate of unemployment is lower today than in the 1970s.

Changes in Labor Market Institutions

As we pointed out earlier, unions that negotiate wages above the equilibrium level can be a source of structural unemployment. Some economists believe that strong labor unions are one reason for the high natural rate of unemployment in Europe, discussed below. In the United States, the sharp fall in union membership after 1980 may have been one reason the natural rate of unemployment fell between the 1970s and the 1990s.

Other institutional changes may also be at work. For example, some labor economists believe that temporary employment agencies, which have proliferated in recent years, have reduced frictional unemployment by helping match workers to jobs.

Technological change, coupled with labor market institutions, can also play a role in affecting the natural rate of unemployment. Technological change probably leads to an increase in the demand for skilled workers who are familiar with the technology and a reduction in the demand for unskilled workers. Economic theory predicts that wages should increase for skilled workers and decrease for unskilled workers. But if wages for unskilled workers cannot go down, say due to a binding minimum wage, increased structural unemployment, and hence a higher natural rate of unemployment, will result.

Changes in Government Policies

A high minimum wage can cause structural unemployment. Generous unemployment benefits can increase both structural and frictional unemployment. So government policies intended to help workers can have the undesirable side effect of raising the natural rate of unemployment.

Some government policies, however, may reduce the natural rate. Two examples are job training and employment subsidies. Job-training programs are supposed to provide unemployed workers with skills that widen the range of jobs they can perform. Employment subsidies are payments either to workers or to employers that provide a financial incentive to offer or accept jobs.

Changes in Productivity

Another explanation for changes over time in the natural rate of unemployment involves changes in *labor force productivity*. Productivity changes are an attractive explanation for the changes in the natural rate of unemployment because it's an explanation consistent with the timing of actual events. The rise in the natural rate of unemployment in the 1970s came at the same time as a slowdown in productivity growth, and a fall in the natural rate of unemployment in the 1990s came at the same time as an acceleration in productivity growth.

That said, it is now easy to explain why higher productivity growth should reduce the natural rate of unemployment, as opposed to simply raising real wages. Suppose, for example, there is an acceleration in productivity growth. If workers do not immediately recognize that productivity is rising faster than before, they will be slow to demand wage increases that reflect their productivity gains. Until wages catch up with productivity gains, hiring an additional worker will be profitable for employers. For a while, then, increases in productivity growth can translate into lower unemployment rates.

Alternatively, suppose there is a slowdown in productivity growth. If workers do not immediately recognize that productivity is growing more slowly, they may continue to demand higher wage increases that were consistent with an earlier, higher rate of productivity growth. Until wage demands diminish, an employer will be better off not hiring, and sometimes firing, workers. As a result, a persistent surplus of labor may develop. For a while, then, a productivity slowdown can translate into higher unemployment rates.

In the end, a number of factors can be proposed to explain the patterns in the natural rate of unemployment experienced over the past 30 years. Although each of these explanations seems reasonable, none can be considered solely responsible for the changes over time in the natural rate of unemployment. Different elements have been at work at different times, and there are surely other determinants of the natural rate of unemployment that we have yet to fully understand.

economics in action

Eurosclerosis

Unemployment rates in Western Europe are normally higher than in the United States. Most estimates suggest that the natural rate of unemployment in France and Germany is currently above 8%, compared with somewhere between 5% and 5.5% in the U.S. today.

It wasn't always that way. In fact, in the early 1970s the natural rate of unemployment seemed to be lower in France and Germany than in the United States. As you can see from Figure 32-4, the actual unemployment rate was lower in France than in the United States, but the situation reversed in the 1980s. Why is the natural rate in Europe so high today?

The answer of many (but not all) economists is that high European natural rates of unemployment are an unintended side-effect of government policies. This is often referred to as *Eurosclerosis*.

The Eurosclerosis hypothesis says that persistently high European unemployment is the result of policies intended to help workers. One such set of policies involves the generous benefits to unemployed workers. In many European countries, there is no limit to the amount of time that the unemployed can collect benefits, and the benefits that the unemployed collect at any given point in time tend to be considerably greater than in the United States. For example, benefits replace 48% of the earnings of a typical French worker, compared with only 14% for the typical U.S. worker.

The importance of the European "welfare state" in explaining unemployment differences between Europe and the United States has further increased as the demand for unskilled workers has fallen. If unskilled wages continue to fall, the benefit to these workers of taking a job—as compared to collecting benefits—also falls. Therefore, unskilled workers are increasingly likely to choose unemployment as a long-term option.

In addition, many European countries have high minimum-wage rates. For example, as of 1999 the minimum wage in France was 47% of the average wage rate, compared with only 34% in the United States. Union membership is greater in many European countries than in the United States as well, and unions seem to have strong bargaining power even in European countries such as France that have relatively low union membership. Both of these factors could also contribute to higher unemployment rates in Europe than in the United States.

If the Eurosclerosis explanation of high European unemployment is correct, a European country that moved its policies in an "American" direction—such as by reducing unemployment benefits and limiting the power of unions—should reduce its natural rate of unemployment. In fact, this seems to have happened in the United Kingdom, which had one of the highest unemployment rates in Europe in the early 1980s. Britain undertook a number of economic reforms under Prime Minister Margaret Thatcher and today typically has an unemployment rate of around 5%.

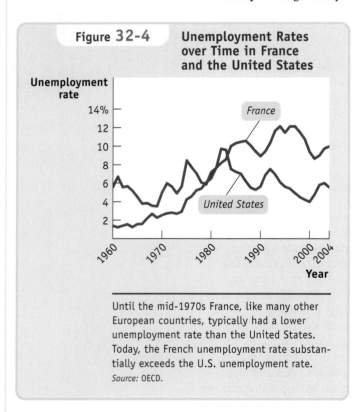

Figure 32-4

Unemployment Rates over Time in France and the United States

Unemployment rate

14%
12
10
8
6
4
2

France

United States

1960   1970   1980   1990   2000 2004

Year

Until the mid-1970s France, like many other European countries, typically had a lower unemployment rate than the United States. Today, the French unemployment rate substantially exceeds the U.S. unemployment rate.
Source: OECD.

It should be noted, however, that an "Americanization" of European policies would come at a cost: reducing welfare benefits would probably reduce unemployment by encouraging individuals to take low-wage jobs. But at the same time it would make many workers worse off, increasing the inequities that were the motivation for the creation of the European social welfare systems. ∎

> >

1. Explain the following:
   a. Why frictional unemployment is inevitable in a modern economy.
   b. Why frictional unemployment accounts for a larger share of total unemployment when the unemployment rate is low.

2. Why does collective bargaining have the same general effect on unemployment as a minimum wage? Illustrate with a diagram.

3. Suppose the United States dramatically increases benefits for unemployed workers. Explain what will happen to the natural rate of unemployment.

Solutions appear at back of book.

Unemployment and the Business Cycle

Although the natural rate of unemployment can change over time, it changes only gradually. The actual rate of unemployment, however, fluctuates around the natural rate, reflecting changes in cyclical unemployment. Panel (a) of Figure 32-5 on page 778 illustrates these fluctuations, showing both the actual unemployment rate and Congressional Budget Office (CBO) estimates of the natural rate of unemployment in the United States from 1959 to 2004. (We'll explain later in the chapter how the CBO arrives at these estimates.)

Fluctuations of the actual unemployment rate around the natural rate reflect fluctuations in aggregate output over the course of the business cycle: the unemployment rate normally rises during recessions and falls during expansions. To understand why, and to understand the exceptions to this rule, we need to look at the links between changes in aggregate output and the unemployment rate.

The Output Gap and the Unemployment Rate

In Chapter 27 we introduced the concept of *potential output*, the level of real GDP that the economy would produce once all prices had adjusted. Potential output typically grows steadily over time, reflecting long-run growth. However, as we learned in the aggregate supply–aggregate demand model, actual aggregate output fluctuates around potential output in the short run: a recessionary gap arises when actual aggregate output falls short of potential output; an inflationary gap arises when actual aggregate output exceeds potential output. In either case, the percentage difference between the actual level of real GDP and potential output is called the **output gap**. A positive or negative output gap occurs when an economy is producing more than or less than what would be "expected" because all prices have not yet adjusted. And wages, as we've learned, are the prices in the labor market.

This realization implies a straightforward relationship between the unemployment rate and the output gap. This relationship consists of two rules:

■ When actual aggregate output is equal to potential output, the actual unemployment rate is equal to the natural rate of unemployment.

■ When the output gap is positive (an inflationary gap), the unemployment rate is *below* the natural rate. When the output gap is negative (a recessionary gap), the unemployment rate is *above* the natural rate.

In other words, fluctuations of aggregate output around the long-run trend of potential output correspond to fluctuations of the unemployment rate around the natural rate.

>>QUICK REVIEW

➤ Due to *job search*, some portion of unemployment—called *frictional unemployment*—is inevitable.

➤ A variety of factors—minimum wages, unions, *efficiency wages*, and the side effects of public policy—lead to *structural unemployment*.

➤ Frictional and structural unemployment result in a *natural rate of unemployment*. In contrast, *cyclical unemployment* changes with the business cycle. Actual unemployment is equal to the sum of natural unemployment (frictional plus structural) plus cyclical unemployment.

➤ The natural rate of unemployment can shift over time, due to changes in labor force characteristics and institutions, and changes in labor productivity. It can also be affected by government policies. In particular, policies designed to help workers are believed to be one reason for high natural rates of unemployment in Europe.

The percentage difference between the actual level of real GDP and potential output is the **output gap**.

Figure 32-5

Cyclical Unemployment and the Output Gap

Panel (a) shows the actual U.S. unemployment rate from 1959 to 2004, together with the Congressional Budget Office estimate of the natural rate of unemployment. The actual rate fluctuates around the natural rate, often for extended periods. Panel (b) shows cyclical unemployment—the difference between the actual unemployment rate and the natural rate—and the output gap, also estimated by the CBO. The output gap is shown with an inverted scale, so that it moves in the same direction as the unemployment rate: when the output gap is positive, the actual unemployment rate is below the natural rate; when the output gap is negative, the actual unemployment rate is above the natural rate. **>web...**

Source: Congressional Budget Office; Bureau of Labor Statistics.

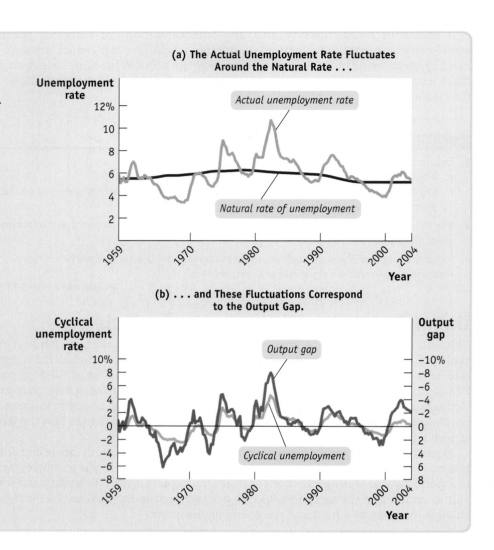

This makes sense. When the economy is producing less than potential output—when the output gap is negative—it is not making full use of its productive resources. Among the resources that are not fully utilized is labor, the economy's most important resource. So we would expect a negative output gap to be associated with unusually high unemployment. Conversely, when the economy is producing more than potential output, it is temporarily using resources at more than normal rates. With this positive output gap, we would expect to see lower-than-normal unemployment.

Figure 32-5 confirms this rule. Panel (a) shows the actual and natural rates of unemployment. Panel (b) shows two series. One is cyclical unemployment: the difference between the actual unemployment rate and the CBO estimate of the natural rate of unemployment, measured on the left. The other is the CBO estimate of the output gap, measured on the right. To make the relationship clearer, the output gap series is "inverted"—shown upside down—so that the line goes down if actual output rises above potential output and up if actual output falls below potential output. As you can see, the two series move together: years of high cyclical unemployment, like 1982 or 1992, were also years of a strongly negative output gap. Years of low cyclical unemployment, like the late 1960s or 2000, were also years of a strongly positive output gap.

You may notice something else, however: although cyclical unemployment and the output gap move together, cyclical unemployment seems to move *less* than the output gap. For example, the output gap reached −8% in 1982, but the cyclical unemployment rate reached only 4%. This observation is the basis of an important relationship known as *Okun's law.*

Okun's Law

In the early 1960s Arthur Okun, who was John F. Kennedy's chief economic adviser, pointed out an important fact about the relationship between aggregate output and the unemployment rate. Although the ups and downs of the unemployment rate correspond closely to fluctuations in real GDP around its long-run trend, fluctuations in the unemployment rate are normally much smaller than the corresponding changes in the output gap. Okun originally estimated that a rise in real GDP of 1 percentage point above potential output would lead to a fall in the unemployment rate of only ⅓ of a percentage point. Today, estimates of **Okun's law**—the negative relationship between the output gap and the unemployment rate—typically find that a rise in the output gap of 1 percentage point reduces the unemployment rate by about ½ of a percentage point. That is, a modern version of Okun's law reads

According to **Okun's law,** each additional percentage point of output gap reduces the unemployment rate by less than 1 percentage point.

(32-3) Unemployment rate = Natural rate of unemployment − (0.5 × Output gap)

For example, suppose that the natural rate of unemployment is 5.2% and that the economy is currently producing only 98% of potential output. In that case, the output gap is −2%, and Okun's law predicts an unemployment rate of 5.2% − (0.5 × (−2%)) = 6.2%.

You should be aware that the "0.5" coefficient in Okun's law is an *estimate*, rather than a physical property, and this relationship can change over time. Indeed, there have been numerous estimates of this coefficient, which vary according to the time period considered and the context in which it is estimated.

Importantly, however, the estimates of the Okun's law coefficient all tend to be considerably less than 1. You might have expected this coefficient to be 1—that is, you might have expected to see a one-to-one relationship between the output gap and unemployment. Doesn't a 1% rise in aggregate output require a 1% increase in employment? And shouldn't that take 1% off the unemployment rate? No.

There are two well-understood reasons for the relationship between changes in the output gap and changes in the unemployment rate to be less than one-to-one. The first is that companies often meet changes in demand in part by changing the number of hours their existing employees work. For example, a company that experiences a sudden increase in demand for its products may cope by asking (or requiring) its workers to put in longer hours, rather than by hiring more workers. Conversely, a company that sees sales drop will often reduce workers' hours rather than lay off employees. This behavior dampens the effect of output fluctuations on the number of workers employed.

The second reason is that the number of workers looking for jobs is affected by the availability of jobs. Suppose that the number of jobs falls by 1 million. Often, measured unemployment will rise by less than 1 million because some unemployed workers become discouraged and give up actively looking for work. (Recall from Chapter 24 that workers aren't counted as unemployed unless they are actively seeking work.) Conversely, if the economy adds 1 million jobs, some people who haven't been actively looking for work will begin doing so; as a result, measured unemployment will fall by less than 1 million. This behavior dampens the effect of output fluctuations on the measured unemployment rate.

In addition to these well-understood factors, the rate of growth of labor productivity generally accelerates during booms (when actual aggregate output is growing faster than potential output) and slows down or even turns negative during busts (when actual aggregate output is growing more slowly than potential output). The reasons for this phenomenon are the subject of some dispute among economists. The consequence, however, is that the effects of booms and busts on the unemployment rate are dampened.

PITFALLS

WHEN IS A "LAW" NOT A LAW?

Economists occasionally refer to a generally observed and accepted pattern of behavior as a "law." The term *law* brings to mind unalterable physical properties or formulaic explanations of the ways in which the world operates. In some cases in economics, such as the law of demand, the economic theory has been so consistent with experience that it approaches the certainty that you may associate with chemical or physical laws.

Economics, however, is a study of human beings, and human behavior is difficult to predict. We may know that the quantity demanded of a given product falls when its price rises, but the law of demand does not tell us *by how much* the quantity demanded will fall.

The same holds true for Okun's law. Okun's law is based on *estimates* that can and do change over time and in different settings. The constant feature of these estimates is not precisely how much the unemployment rate falls when the output gap increases, but that the unemployment rate falls at a ratio of less than 1:1 with increases in the output gap. Okun's law says not that this relationship is, for example, 1:3 or 1:2, but that this relationship is less than 1:1.

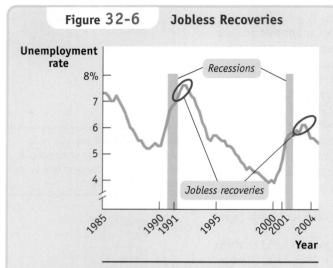

Figure 32-6 **Jobless Recoveries**

The graph shows the unemployment rate in the United States from 1985 to 2004. The shaded areas show official periods of recession. In the recessions of 1990–1991 and 2001, unemployment rose sharply. In both cases, however, unemployment continued to rise for a time after, even though the economy was officially expanding.

Sources: Bureau of Labor Statistics; National Bureau of Economic Research.

>> QUICK REVIEW

> When aggregate output is equal to potential output, the unemployment rate is equal to the natural rate of unemployment.

> When the *output gap* is positive, the unemployment rate is below the natural rate. When the output gap is negative, the unemployment rate is above the natural rate.

> *Okun's law* says that each additional percentage point of output gap reduces the unemployment rate by less than 1 percentage point. Modern estimates indicate that one more percentage point of output gap reduces the unemployment rate by about 1/2 percentage point.

economics in action

Jobless Recoveries

Our explanation of the relationship between the output gap and the unemployment rate is slightly more complex than a statement that the unemployment rate falls when the economy is expanding and rises when the economy is contracting. A good way to see the subtlety is to look at those occasions when the economy expands but unemployment nonetheless rises.

Figure 32-6 shows the U.S. unemployment rate from 1985 to 2004. It also shows, as shaded areas, the periods of recession according to the National Bureau of Economic Research. Officially, the U.S. economy went into recession in July 1990 and began an expansion in March 1991. But tell that to workers: the unemployment rate continued rising and didn't turn downward until July 1992. The same thing happened after the next recession, 11 years later. The recession that began in March 2001 officially ended in November 2001, but the unemployment rate didn't turn downward until July 2003. Both recessions, in other words, were followed by periods of jobless recovery.

Why do jobless recoveries happen? The unemployment rate reflects the output gap: the unemployment rate falls only when the output gap is rising, which happens when real GDP is growing faster than potential output. If real GDP is growing more slowly than potential output—as it did in both 1991–1992 and 2001–2003—the output gap continues to fall even though the economy is officially considered to be expanding. And this falling output gap leads to rising, not falling, unemployment. ∎

< < < < < < < < < < < < < < < < <

>>CHECK YOUR UNDERSTANDING 32-2

1. Examine panel (a) of Figure 32-5. In which years would you expect a large positive output gap? How does your expectation compare with the reality of panel (b)?

2. Suppose the United States imposes strict limits on the number of hours that employees can work in a week. How would this policy affect the relationship between the output gap and the unemployment rate?

Solutions appear at back of book.

Why Doesn't the Labor Market Move Quickly to Equilibrium?

We've now seen that the unemployment rate fluctuates around the natural rate of unemployment. A look back at Figure 32-5 shows that these fluctuations can last for long periods. For example, the actual unemployment rate was above the natural rate from 1980 to 1987.

One way to think about the natural rate of unemployment is that it is an *equilibrium* rate, the rate of unemployment that the labor market achieves when employers and workers have had time to adjust. Deviations from the natural rate, then, are situations in which the labor market is out of equilibrium. Figure 32-5 shows that the labor market often remains out of equilibrium for long stretches of time.

Yet in most economic analyses we assume that markets move quickly to equilibrium. Why is the labor market different?

One compelling answer is that wages behave differently from the prices of many goods and services. Wages do not fall quickly in the face of labor surpluses or rise quickly in the face of shortages. Almost all macroeconomists agree that wages adjust slowly to surpluses or shortages of labor.

There is, however, some dispute about why wages adjust slowly. Broadly speaking, there are two main theories: *misperceptions* and *sticky wages*.

Misperceptions Some macroeconomists believe that an important source of slow wage adjustment is that workers are slow to realize that the equilibrium wage rate has changed. For example, a worker searching for a new job may have expectations based on last year's wage rate. If wage rates have dropped, that worker may spend a long time looking for a job with an unrealistically high wage rate. When workers take longer to find jobs because they are holding out for a wage that may no longer be appropriate, this contributes not only to slow wage adjustment but also to an increased unemployment rate.

Misperceptions by firms can also contribute to slow wage adjustment. Firms, especially those that hire infrequently, may base their wage decisions on old information; this, in turn, causes wages to change slowly. If a firm sets its wages below the market-clearing wage rate, it will have difficulty hiring workers but may be slow to realize this fact and respond to it. If a firm sets its wages above the market-clearing wage rate, it will turn away excess job applicants—and perhaps also contribute to worker misperceptions about the market-clearing wage rate.

You might wonder why firms and workers would not quickly realize when their perceptions about wages are out of line with the reality of market-clearing wages. One reason labor markets may clear more slowly than other markets is that they are so complex. Market-clearing wages are constantly changing as demand conditions change, and firms and workers are collectively responding to ever-changing perceptions about these wages. As a result, when conditions change in the labor market, it may take quite some time before the labor market returns to equilibrium.

Sticky Wages Economists say that **sticky wages** occur when employers are slow to change wages in the face of a surplus or shortage of labor, even when everyone understands that the wage rate isn't at its equilibrium level. Wages may be sticky for several reasons. Some wages are governed by long-term contracts, which set the wage rate a year or more in advance and don't reflect changes in the labor market after the contract has been signed. In other cases there is no formal contract, but there is an implicit agreement between workers and their employers not to change wage rates too often.

> **Sticky wages** occur when employers are slow to change wage rates in the face of a surplus or shortage of labor.

Workers and employers are often concerned about *relative wages*—how the wages of one group of workers compare with those of other workers. Companies believe that the productivity or morale of workers will suffer—or even that they will go on strike—if wages are cut compared with those paid by other companies. As a result, each company is reluctant to reduce wages until other companies do the same, making wages as a whole slow to adjust.

Concerns about relative wages can interact with explicit or implicit contracts to slow down wage adjustment. Even if a worker's contract has just expired, the employer will be cautious about reducing his or her wage rate compared with that of other workers who are still covered by contracts signed in the past. Economists have shown that if employers are concerned about relative wages and contracts are staggered over time, even short contracts—such as contracts that set wages one year ahead—can cause the adjustment of the average wage rate to its equilibrium level to take a number of years.

Wages tend to be stickier when equilibrium wages are falling than when they are rising. When wages are rising, workers may put pressure on firms to renegotiate wages to reflect the new wage reality. This pressure could occur either through negotiation or through worker departure, as competing firms bid up wages. But when wages are falling, firms may be contractually unable to lower wages in response to prevailing market conditions—and even if they are able to lower wages, it may not be in their best interest to do so. Recall the discussion of efficiency wages earlier in this chapter: firms may pay above-market wages to give workers an incentive for better performance.

Although this discussion has focused only on the slow adjustment of wages, prices of some goods and services also seem to adjust slowly. Because it is time-consuming and costly to constantly devise new sets of prices, firms may change prices infrequently even if the market-clearing prices change frequently. An influential economic theory says that these small costs associated with the act of changing prices—known as **menu costs**—can have a surprisingly large effect in postponing price adjustment to surpluses and shortages. (This term derives from the fact that it costs time and money for restaurants to print new menus and that, as a result, restaurants rarely change their prices.) Sticky prices can interact with sticky wages to slow the adjustment of prices and wages in the economy as a whole.

For our purposes, the distinctions between different theories of slow wage and price adjustment don't matter very much. The important point is that wages move toward their equilibrium level, but only slowly.

> **Menu costs** are small costs associated with the act of changing prices.

economics in action

Sticky Wages During the Great Depression

History's most extreme example of disequilibrium in the labor market is the Great Depression, the era of high unemployment between 1929 and World War II. At its peak in 1933, the U.S. unemployment rate exceeded 25%. The Depression also provides the clearest illustration of the sluggish adjustment of wages, which plays a crucial role in our understanding of aggregate supply.

Recent analyses suggest that during the 1930s manufacturing wages in particular were sticky. Nominal hourly wages in manufacturing—wages in dollar amounts—remained almost unchanged during the first two years of the Great Depression. Since prices of almost all goods and services fell during the early years of the Depression, the *real* wages of manufacturing workers—their nominal wages divided by the price level—actually *rose* even though there was a massive surplus of labor. ■

< < < < < < < < < < < < < < < < < < < <

>>CHECK YOUR UNDERSTANDING 32-3

1. The country of Willovia has a tradition of three-year labor contracts, but Malavia has a tradition of one-year labor contracts. In which country would you expect the labor market to move more quickly to equilibrium when demand conditions change? Explain your answer.

2. Why might workers misperceive changes in the market-clearing wage rate? Suppose the market-clearing wage rate is rising but workers are slow to recognize this growth. What does this misperception imply about unemployment in the short run?

Solutions appear at back of book.

Unemployment and Inflation: The Phillips Curve

Earlier in this chapter we saw that in 1978, when the Humphrey–Hawkins bill set a target unemployment rate of 4%, many economists were concerned: they feared an attempt to achieve that target would lead to high and accelerating inflation. What was the basis for these concerns?

We've seen part of the answer: 4% was well below estimates of the natural rate of unemployment. But what's wrong with trying to keep unemployment below the natural rate? To answer that question we need to look at the relationship between unemployment and inflation.

The Short-Run Phillips Curve

In a famous 1958 paper the New Zealand–born economist A. W. H. Phillips found that historical data for the United Kingdom showed that when the unemployment rate is high, the wage rate tends to fall, and when the unemployment rate is low, the wage rate tends to rise. Using data from Britain, the United States, and elsewhere, other economists soon found similar patterns between the unemployment rate and the rate of inflation—that is, the rate of change in the aggregate price level. The negative short-run relationship between the unemployment rate and the inflation rate is called the **short-run Phillips curve,** or *SRPC.* (We'll explain the difference between the short run and the long run in a little while.) Figure 32-7 shows a hypothetical short-run Phillips curve.

The **short-run Phillips curve** is the negative short-run relationship between the unemployment rate and the inflation rate.

Why is there a negative short-run relationship between the unemployment rate and the inflation rate? Recall the short-run aggregate supply curve from earlier chapters. The *SRAS* curve shows that when a rightward shift of the aggregate demand curve leads to an increase in the aggregate price level, real GDP increases as well. In other words, there is a positive relationship between the aggregate price level and real GDP.

But how does this relate to unemployment? Remember that there is a negative relationship between real GDP and the unemployment rate: Okun's law tells us that when real GDP is higher than potential output, the unemployment rate will be lower than when real GDP is below potential output. So increases in the aggregate price level are associated with increases in real GDP, which in turn tend to lead to lower unemployment rates.

The relationship between the short-run Phillips curve and the short-run aggregate supply curve is a bit trickier than presented here. Specifically, the preceding discussion of the short-run aggregate supply curve describes a relationship between *changes* in the unemployment rate and inflation; the short-run Phillips curve, however, describes a relationship between the *level* of the unemployment rate and inflation. For Inquiring Minds on page 784 explains the relationship between the two concepts in more detail.

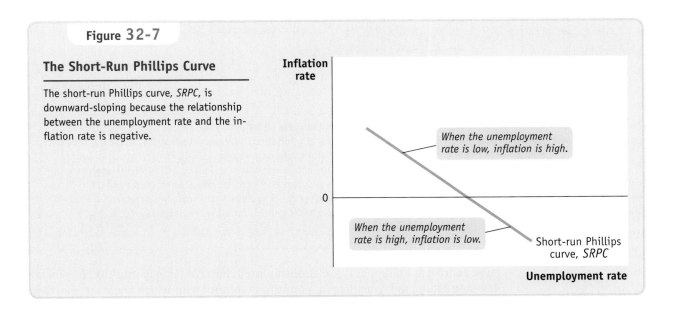

Figure 32-7

The Short-Run Phillips Curve

The short-run Phillips curve, *SRPC,* is downward-sloping because the relationship between the unemployment rate and the inflation rate is negative.

When the unemployment rate is low, inflation is high.

When the unemployment rate is high, inflation is low.

Short-run Phillips curve, *SRPC*

Inflation rate

Unemployment rate

FOR INQUIRING MINDS

THE AGGREGATE SUPPLY CURVE AND THE SHORT-RUN PHILLIPS CURVE

In earlier chapters we made extensive use of the AS–AD model, in which the short-run aggregate supply curve—a relationship between real GDP and the aggregate price level—plays a central role. Now we've introduced the concept of the short-run Phillips curve, a relationship between the unemployment rate and the rate of inflation. How do these two concepts fit together?

We can get a partial answer to this question by looking at panel (a) of Figure 32-8, which shows how changes in the aggregate price level and the output gap depend on changes in aggregate demand. Assume that in year 1 the aggregate demand curve is AD_1, the long-run aggregate supply curve is LRAS, and the short-run aggregate supply curve is SRAS. The initial macroeconomic equilibrium is at E_1, where the price level is 100 and real GDP is $10 trillion. Notice that at E_1 real GDP is equal to potential output, so the output gap is zero.

Now consider two possible paths for the economy over the next year. One is that aggregate demand remains unchanged and the economy stays at E_1. The other is that aggregate demand shifts out to AD_2 and the economy moves to E_2.

At E_2, real GDP is $10.4 trillion, $0.4 trillion more than potential output—a 4% output gap. Meanwhile, at E_2 the aggregate price level is 102—a 2% increase. So panel (a) tells us that in this example a zero output gap is associated with zero inflation and a 4% output gap is associated with 2% inflation.

Panel (b) shows what this implies for the relationship between unemployment and inflation. Assume that the natural rate of unemployment is 6%, and that a rise of 1 percentage point in the output gap causes a fall of $\frac{1}{2}$ percentage point in the unemployment rate by Okun's law. In that case, the two cases shown in panel (a)—aggregate demand either staying put or rising—

correspond to the two points in panel (b). At E_1, the unemployment rate is 6% and the inflation rate is 0%. At E_2, the unemployment rate is 4%, because an output gap of 4% reduces the unemployment rate by 4% × 0.5 = 2%—and the inflation rate is 2%. So there is a negative relationship between unemployment and inflation.

So does the short-run aggregate supply curve say exactly the same thing as the short-run Phillips curve? Not quite. The short-run aggregate supply curve seems to imply a relationship between the *change* in the unemployment rate and the inflation rate, but the short-run Phillips curve shows a relationship between the *level* of the unemployment rate and the inflation rate. Reconciling these views completely would go beyond the scope of this book. The important point is that the short-run Phillips curve is a concept that is closely related, though not identical, to the short-run aggregate supply curve.

Figure 32-8   The AS–AD Model and the Short-Run Phillips Curve

(a) An Increase in Aggregate Demand . . .

(b) . . . Leads to Both Inflation and a Fall in the Unemployment Rate.

The short-run Phillips curve is closely related to the short-run aggregate supply curve. In panel (a), the economy is initially in equilibrium at E_1, with the aggregate price level at 100 and aggregate output at $10 trillion, which we assume is potential output. Now consider two possibilities. If the aggregate demand curve remains at AD_1, there is an output gap of zero and 0% inflation. If the aggregate demand curve shifts out to AD_2, there is an output gap of 4% and 2% inflation, as shown in panel (b). Assuming that the natural rate of unemployment is 6%, the implications for unemployment and inflation are as follows: if aggregate demand does not increase, 6% unemployment and 0% inflation will result; if aggregate demand does increase, 4% unemployment and 2% inflation will result.

The short-run Phillips curve relationship itself, however, is very intuitive. In general, a low rate of unemployment corresponds to an economy in which there are shortages of labor and other resources, leading to rising prices. But when unemployment is high, the economy is far from capacity. When there are surpluses of labor and other resources, prices will fall.

Early estimates of the short-run Phillips curve for the United States were very simple: they showed a relationship between the unemployment rate and the inflation rate, without taking account of any other variables. During the 1960s this simple approach seemed, for a while, to be adequate. Figure 32-9 plots average annual rates of unemployment and inflation from 1961 to 1969. The data look a lot like a simple short-run Phillips curve.

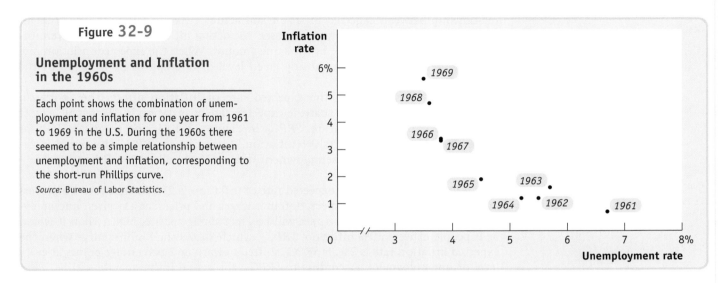

Figure 32-9

Unemployment and Inflation in the 1960s

Each point shows the combination of unemployment and inflation for one year from 1961 to 1969 in the U.S. During the 1960s there seemed to be a simple relationship between unemployment and inflation, corresponding to the short-run Phillips curve.

Source: Bureau of Labor Statistics.

Even at the time, however, some economists argued that a more accurate short-run Phillips curve would include other factors. In Chapter 27 we discussed the effect of *supply shocks,* such as sudden changes in the price of oil, which shift the short-run aggregate supply curve. Such shocks also shift the short-run Phillips curve: surging oil prices were an important factor in the inflation of the 1970s and also played an important role in the acceleration of inflation in early 2004. In general, a negative supply shock shifts *SRPC* up, while a positive supply shock shifts it down.

But supply shocks are not the only factors that could change the inflation rate. In the early 1960s, Americans had little experience with inflation: inflation rates had been low for decades. But by the late 1960s, after inflation had been steadily increasing for a while, they had probably started to expect future inflation. In 1968 two economists—Milton Friedman of the University of Chicago and Edmund Phelps of Columbia University—independently set forth a crucial hypothesis that expectations about future inflation directly affect the present inflation rate. Today most economists accept that the *expected inflation rate*—the rate of inflation that employers and workers expect in the near future—is the most important factor affecting inflation other than the unemployment rate.

Inflation Expectations and the Short-Run Phillips Curve

The **expected rate of inflation** is the rate of inflation that employers and workers expect in the near future. One of the crucial discoveries of modern macroeconomics is that the expected rate of inflation affects the short-run trade-off between unemployment and inflation.

Why does expected inflation affect the short-run Phillips curve? The answer lies in part with the fact that wages are sticky, as discussed earlier in this chapter. Put yourself in the position of a worker or employer about to sign a contract setting the worker's wages over the next year. For a number of reasons, the wage rate they agree to will be higher if everyone expects high inflation (including rising wages) than if

The **expected rate of inflation** is the rate of inflation that employers and workers expect in the near future.

everyone expects prices to be stable. The worker will want a wage rate that takes into account future declines in the purchasing power of earnings. He or she will also want a wage rate that won't fall behind the wages of other workers. And the employer will be more willing to agree to a wage increase now if hiring workers later will be even more expensive. Also, rising prices will make paying a higher wage rate more affordable for the employer because the employer's output will sell for more.

For these reasons, an increase in expected inflation shifts the short-run Phillips curve upward: the actual rate of inflation at any given unemployment rate is higher when the expected inflation rate is higher. In fact, macroeconomists believe that the relationship between expected inflation and actual inflation is one-to-one. That is, when the expected inflation rate increases, the actual inflation rate at any given unemployment rate will increase by the same amount. When the expected inflation rate falls, the actual inflation rate at any given level of unemployment will fall by the same amount.

Figure 32-10 shows how the expected rate of inflation affects the short-run Phillips curve. First, suppose that the expected rate of inflation is 0%: people expect 0% inflation in the near future. $SRPC_0$ in Figure 32-10 is the short-run Phillips curve when the public expects 0% inflation. According to $SRPC_0$, the actual inflation rate will be 0% if the unemployment rate is 6%; it will be 2% if the unemployment rate is 4%.

Alternatively, suppose the expected rate of inflation is 2%. In that case, employers and workers will build this expectation into wages and prices: at any given unemployment rate, the actual inflation rate will be 2 percentage points higher than it would be if people expected 0% inflation. $SRPC_2$, which shows the Phillips curve when the expected inflation rate is 2%, is $SRPC_0$ shifted upward by 2 percentage points at every level of unemployment. According to $SRPC_2$, the actual inflation rate will be 2% if the unemployment rate is 6%; it will be 4% if the unemployment rate is 4%.

What determines the expected rate of inflation? In general, people base their expectations about inflation on experience. If the inflation rate has hovered around 0% in the last few years, people will expect it to be around 0% in the near future. But if the inflation rate has averaged around 5% lately, people will expect inflation to be around 5% in the near future.

Since expected inflation is an important part of the modern short-run Phillips curve discussion, you might wonder why it was not in the original formulation of the Phillips curve. But think back to what we said about the early 1960s: at that point,

Figure 32-10

Expected Inflation and the Short-Run Phillips Curve

Expected inflation shifts the short-run Phillips curve up. $SRPC_0$ is the short-run Phillips curve with an expected inflation rate of 0%; $SRPC_2$ is the short-run Phillips curve with an expected inflation rate of 2%. Each additional percentage point of expected inflation raises the actual inflation rate at any given unemployment rate by 1 percentage point.   **>web...**

people were accustomed to low inflation rates and reasonably expected that future inflation rates would also be modest. It was only after 1965 that persistent inflation became a fact of life as a consequence of the government's attempts to pay for the Vietnam War. So it was only at that point that it became clear that expected inflation would play an important role in price-setting.

The Long-Run Phillips Curve

We can now explain why economists were skeptical of the 4% target for unemployment contained in the Humphrey–Hawkins bill, and believed that an attempt to achieve that target would lead to high and accelerating inflation.

Figure 32-11 reproduces the two short-run Phillips curves from Figure 32-10, $SRPC_0$ and $SRPC_2$. It also adds an additional short-run Phillips curve, $SRPC_4$, representing a 4% expected rate of inflation. We'll explain why these are short-run curves in a moment, and we'll also explain the significance of the vertical long-run Phillips curve, $LRPC$.

Suppose that the economy has, in the past, had a 0% inflation rate. In that case the current short-run Phillips curve will reflect a 0% expected inflation rate, so it will be $SRPC_0$. If the unemployment rate is 6%, the actual inflation rate will be 0%.

Also suppose that policy makers decide to take Humphrey–Hawkins seriously and try to trade off lower unemployment for a higher rate of inflation. They use monetary policy, fiscal policy, or both to drive the unemployment rate down to 4%. This puts the economy at point A on $SRPC_0$, leading to an actual inflation rate of 2%.

Over time, the public will come to expect a 2% inflation rate. *This will shift the short-run Phillips curve upward to $SRPC_2$*. Now, when the unemployment rate is 6%, the actual inflation rate will be 2%. Given this new short-run Phillips curve, keeping the unemployment rate at 4% will lead to a 4% actual inflation rate—point B on $SRPC_2$—rather than 2%.

Eventually, this 4% inflation rate gets built into expectations, and the short-run Phillips curve shifts upward again, to $SRPC_4$. To keep the unemployment rate at 4% would now require accepting a 6% actual inflation rate (point C on $SRPC_4$), and so on. In short, a persistent attempt to trade off lower unemployment for higher inflation leads to *accelerating* inflation over time.

Figure 32-11

The NAIRU and the Long-Run Phillips Curve

$SRPC_0$ is the short-run Phillips curve when the expected inflation rate is 0%. At a 4% unemployment rate, the economy is at point A with an inflation rate of 2%. The higher inflation rate will get built into expectations, and the $SRPC$ will shift upward to $SRPC_2$. If the unemployment rate remains at 4%, the economy will be at B and the inflation rate will rise to 4%. Inflationary expectations will be revised again, and $SRPC$ will shift upward to $SRPC_4$. At a 4% unemployment rate, the economy will be at C, and the inflation rate will rise to 6%.

Here, 6% is the NAIRU, or nonaccelerating inflation rate of unemployment. As long as unemployment is at the NAIRU, the inflation rate will match expectations and remain constant. An unemployment rate below 6% requires ever-accelerating inflation. The long-run Phillips curve, $LRPC$, which passes through E_0, E_2, and E_4, is vertical: no long-run trade-off between unemployment and inflation exists.

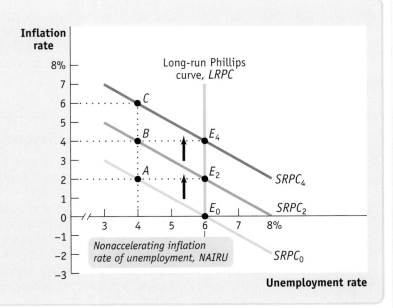

The **nonaccelerating inflation rate of unemployment**, or **NAIRU**, is the unemployment rate at which inflation does not change over time.

The **long-run Phillips curve** shows the relationship between unemployment and inflation after expectations of inflation have had time to adjust to experience.

To avoid accelerating inflation over time, the unemployment rate must be high enough so that the actual rate of inflation matches the expected rate of inflation. This is the situation at E_0 on $SRPC_0$: when the expected inflation rate is 0% and the unemployment rate is 6%, the actual inflation rate is 0%. It is also the situation at E_2 on $SRPC_2$: when the expected inflation rate is 2% and the unemployment rate is 6%, the actual inflation rate is 2%. And it is the situation at E_4 on $SRPC_4$: when the expected inflation rate is 4% and the unemployment rate is 6%, the actual inflation rate is 4%.

The unemployment rate at which inflation does not change over time—6% in Figure 32-11—is known as the **nonaccelerating inflation rate of unemployment, or NAIRU** for short. Unemployment rates below the NAIRU lead to ever-accelerating inflation and cannot be maintained. Most macroeconomists believe that there is a NAIRU and that there is no long-run trade-off between unemployment and inflation.

We can now explain the significance of the vertical line *LRPC*. It is the **long-run Phillips curve,** the relationship between unemployment and inflation in the long run, after expectations of inflation have had time to adjust to experience. It is vertical because any unemployment rate below the NAIRU leads to ever-accelerating inflation (and, a point we have not yet emphasized, any unemployment rate above the NAIRU leads to decelerating inflation). In other words, it shows that an unemployment rate below the NAIRU cannot be maintained in the long run.

The Natural Rate, Revisited

Earlier in this chapter, we introduced the concept of the *natural rate of unemployment,* the normal rate of unemployment around which the actual unemployment rate fluctuates. Now we have introduced the concept of the *NAIRU.* How do these two concepts relate to each other?

The answer is that the NAIRU is another name for the natural rate. The level of unemployment the economy "needs" in order to avoid accelerating inflation is equal to the sum of frictional unemployment plus structural unemployment.

In fact, economists estimate the natural rate of unemployment by looking for evidence about the NAIRU. For example, the way European countries learned, to their dismay, that their natural rates of unemployment were 9% or more was through unpleasant experience: in the late 1980s, and again in the late 1990s, European inflation began to accelerate as the unemployment rates in major economies, which had been above 9%, began to fall, approaching 8%.

Earlier in this chapter we used Congressional Budget Office estimates of the U.S. natural rate of unemployment. The CBO has a model that predicts changes in the inflation rate based on the deviation of the actual unemployment rate from the natural rate. Given data on actual unemployment and inflation, this model can be used to deduce estimates of the natural rate—and that's where the CBO numbers come from.

economics in action

From the Scary Seventies to the Nifty Nineties

Earlier we saw that experience during the 1960s seemed to show the existence of a short-run Phillips curve for the U.S. economy, with a short-run trade-off between unemployment and inflation.

After 1969, however, that apparent relationship fell apart. Figure 32-12 plots the track of the unemployment and inflation rates from 1961 to 1990. The track looks more like a tangled piece of yarn than like a smooth curve.

Through much of the 1970s and early 1980s, the economy suffered from a combination of above-average unemployment rates coupled with inflation rates unprecedented in modern American history. This condition came to be known as "stagflation"—for stagnation combined with inflation. In the late 1990s, by contrast,

Figure 32-12

Unemployment and Inflation, 1961–1990

During the 1970s, the short-run Phillips curve relationship that seemed to work in the 1960s broke down as the economy experienced a combination of high unemployment and high inflation. Economists believe this was the result both of adverse supply shocks and a buildup of expected inflation. Inflation came down during the 1980s, and the 1990s were a time of both low unemployment and low inflation.

Source: Bureau of Labor Statistics.

the economy was experiencing a blissful combination of low unemployment and low inflation. What explains these developments?

Part of the answer lies in the role of supply shocks. During the 1970s the economy suffered a series of adverse supply shocks. The price of oil, in particular, soared as wars and revolutions in the Middle East led to a reduction in oil supplies and as oil-exporting countries deliberately curbed production to drive up prices. There was also a slowdown in labor productivity growth, which may have contributed to the poor economic performance.

During the 1990s, by contrast, supply shocks were positive. Prices of oil and other raw materials were generally falling, and productivity growth accelerated.

Equally important, however, was the role of expected inflation. As mentioned earlier in the chapter, inflation accelerated during the 1960s as the result of an economic boom. During the 1970s the public came to expect high inflation, and this got built into the short-run Phillips curve. It took a sustained and costly effort during the 1980s to get inflation back down. We'll describe that effort in Chapter 33. The result, however, was that expected inflation was very low by the late 1990s, allowing actual inflation to be low even with low rates of unemployment. ∎

> >

>>CHECK YOUR UNDERSTANDING 32-4

1. Explain how the short-run Phillips curve can be thought of as the relationship between cyclical unemployment and the actual inflation rate above and beyond the expected inflation rate.

2. Why is there no long-run trade-off between unemployment and inflation?

Solutions appear at back of book.

● A LOOK AHEAD ●

Few economists now believe that government policy can trade off higher inflation for lower unemployment except in the short run. Nonetheless, the United States and other economies have had periods of substantial inflation; in some times and places, the inflation rate has gone into the thousands of percent. In contrast, in some other countries *deflation*—falling prices—has become a concern.

In Chapter 33 we'll look at why inflation occurs and the harm that it can do if not managed well. We'll also look at why inflation can be hard to eliminate once the public comes to expect it. And we'll explore the flip-side of the coin—the perils of deflation.

SUMMARY

1. There is always a positive amount of unemployment in the economy: **job search** leads to **frictional unemployment.** There may also be **structural unemployment,** which is the result of factors that include minimum wages, unions, **efficiency wages,** and side effects of government policies.

2. Frictional plus structural unemployment make up the **natural rate of unemployment.** It's a rate that can and does shift over time. At any given time, the actual unemployment rate fluctuates around the natural rate because of the business cycle. **Cyclical unemployment** is linked to the **output gap:** when the output gap is positive, cyclical unemployment is negative; when the output gap is negative, cyclical unemployment is positive. Swings in cyclical unemployment are, however, smaller than swings in the output gap, a fact captured by **Okun's law.**

3. Unlike many markets, the labor market doesn't move quickly to equilibrium. This may, in part, reflect misperceptions on the part of workers and employers about the state of the market. **Sticky wages** also appear to play a

role, slowing the adjustment of wages even in the absence of misperceptions. Prices (including the wage rate) are also slow to adjust in some cases, in part reflecting the **menu costs** of changing prices.

4. The **short-run Phillips curve** shows a negative relationship between the unemployment rate and inflation rate. The short-run Phillips curve is related to, but not the same thing as, the short-run aggregate supply curve. Today, macroeconomists believe that the short-run Phillips curve shifts with changes in the **expected rate of inflation.** Because expectations change with experience, attempts to keep the unemployment rate persistently low lead not only to high inflation but also to constantly accelerating inflation. The **nonaccelerating inflation rate of unemployment,** or **NAIRU,** is the rate of unemployment at which inflation is stable. It is equal to the natural rate of unemployment. The **long-run Phillips curve** is vertical because there is no trade-off between the unemployment rate and the inflation rate in the long run.

KEY TERMS

Job search, p. 770
Frictional unemployment, p. 770
Structural unemployment, p. 771
Efficiency wages, p. 773
Natural rate of unemployment, p. 773

Cyclical unemployment, p. 773
Output gap, p. 777
Okun's law, p. 779
Sticky wages, p. 781
Menu costs, p. 782

Short-run Phillips curve, p. 783
Expected rate of inflation, p. 785
Nonaccelerating inflation rate of unemployment, or NAIRU, p. 788
Long-run Phillips curve, p. 788

PROBLEMS

1. In each of the following situations, what type of unemployment is Melanie facing?

   a. After completing a complex programming project, Melanie is laid off. Her prospects for a new job requiring similar skills are good, and she has signed up with a programmer placement service. She has passed up low-paying job offers.

   b. When Melanie and her co-workers refused to accept pay cuts, her employer outsourced their programming tasks to workers in another country. This phenomenon is occurring throughout the programming industry.

   c. Due to the current slump in investment spending, Melanie has been laid off from her programming job. Her employer promises to re-hire her when business picks up.

2. Each month, usually on the first Friday of the month, the Bureau of Labor Statistics releases the Employment Situation Summary for the previous month. Part of the information released concerns how long individuals have been unemployed. Go to www.bls.gov to find the latest report. On the Bureau of

Labor Statistics home page, click on the unemployment rate, in the middle of the page, choose the Employment Situation Summary, and then click on the table titled "Unemployed persons by duration of unemployment." Use the seasonally adjusted numbers to answer the following questions.

   a. How many workers were unemployed less than 5 weeks? What percentage of all unemployed workers do these workers represent? How do these numbers compare to the previous month's data?

   b. How many workers were unemployed 27 or more weeks? What percentage of all unemployed workers do these workers represent? How do these numbers compare to the previous month's data?

   c. How long has the average worker been unemployed (average duration, in weeks)? How does this compare to the average for the previous month's data?

   d. Comparing the latest month for which there is data with the previous month, has the problem of long-term unemployment improved or deteriorated?

3. There is only one labor market in Profunctia. All workers have the same skills and all firms hire workers with these skills. Use the accompanying diagram, which shows the supply of and demand for labor, to answer the following questions.

a. What is the equilibrium wage rate in Profunctia? At this wage rate, what is the level of employment, the size of the labor force, and the unemployment rate?

b. If the government of Profunctia sets a minimum wage equal to $12, what will be the level of employment, the size of the labor force, and the unemployment rate?

c. If unions bargain with the firms in Profunctia and set a wage rate equal to $14, what will be the level of employment, the size of the labor force, and the unemployment rate?

d. If the concern for retaining workers and encouraging high quality work leads firms to set a wage rate equal to $16, what will be the level of employment, the size of the labor force, and the unemployment rate?

4. In Northlandia, there are no labor contracts; that is, wage rates can be renegotiated at any time. But in Southlandia, wage rates are set at the beginning of each odd year and last for two years. Why would equal-sized falls in aggregate output due to a fall in aggregate demand have different effects on the magnitude and duration of unemployment in these two economies?

5. In which of the following cases is it more likely for efficiency wages to exist? Why?

a. Jane and her boss work as a team selling ice cream.

b. Jane sells ice cream without any direct supervision by her boss.

c. Jane speaks Korean and sells ice cream in a neighborhood in which Korean is the primary language. It is difficult to find another worker who speaks Korean.

6. How will the following changes affect the natural rate of unemployment?

a. The government reduces the time during which an unemployed worker can receive benefits.

b. More teenagers focus on their studies and do not look for jobs until after college.

c. Greater access to the Internet leads both potential employers and potential employees to use the Internet to list and find jobs.

d. Union membership declines.

7. With its tradition of a job for life for most citizens, Japan once had a much lower unemployment rate than that of the United States; from 1960 to 1995, the unemployment rate in Japan exceeded 3% only once. However, since the crash of its stock market in 1989 and slow economic growth in the 1990s, the job-for-life system has broken down and unemployment has risen to more than 5% in 2003. Explain the likely effect of these recent changes in Japan on the Japanese natural rate of unemployment.

8. The accompanying scatter diagram shows the relationship between the unemployment rate and the output gap in the United States from 1990 to 2004. Draw a straight line through the scatter of dots in the figure. Assume that this line represents Okun's law:

$$\text{Unemployment rate} = b - (m \times \text{Output gap})$$
where b is the vertical intercept and m is the slope

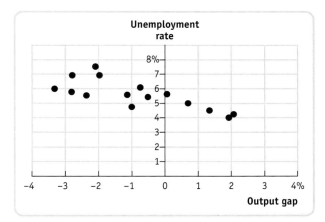

What is the unemployment rate when aggregate output equals potential output? What would the unemployment rate be if the output gap were 2%? What if the output gap were −3%? What do these results tell us about the coefficient m in Okun's law?

9. After experiencing a recession for the past two years, the residents of Albernia were looking forward to a decrease in the unemployment rate. Yet after six months of positive economic growth, the unemployment rate remains the same as it was at the end of the recession. How can you explain why the unemployment rate did not fall although the economy was experiencing economic growth?

10. Due to historical differences, countries often differ in how quickly a change in actual inflation is incorporated into a change in expected inflation. In a country such as Japan that has had very little inflation in recent memory, it will take longer for a change in the actual inflation rate to be reflected in a corresponding change in the expected inflation rate. In contrast, in a country such as Argentina, one that has recently had very high inflation, a change in the actual inflation rate will immediately be reflected in a corresponding change in the expected inflation rate. What does this imply about the short-run and long-run Phillips curves in these two types of countries? What does this imply about the effectiveness of monetary and fiscal policy to reduce the unemployment rate?

11. The accompanying table shows data for the average annual rates of unemployment and inflation for the economy of Britannia from 1995 to 2004. Use it to construct a scatterplot similar to Figure 32-9.

Year	Unemployment rate	Inflation rate
1995	4.0%	2.5%
1996	2.0%	5.0%
1997	10.0%	1.0%
1998	8.0%	1.3%
1999	5.0%	2.0%
2000	2.5%	4.0%
2001	6.0%	1.7%
2002	1.0%	10.0%
2003	3.0%	3.0%
2004	7.0%	1.5%

Are the data consistent with a short-run Phillips curve? If the government pursues expansionary monetary policies in the future to keep the unemployment rate below the natural rate of unemployment, how effective will such a policy be?

>**web**... To continue your study and review of concepts in this chapter, please visit the Krugman/Wells website for quizzes, animated graph tutorials, web links to helpful resources, and more.

www.worthpublishers.com/krugmanwells

>>Inflation, Disinflation, and Deflation

HOURLY WAGES

IN MODERN AMERICA, WE COMPLAIN about inflation when the overall level of prices rises a few percent over the course of a year. But those who lived through the late 1970s scoff—they remember when prices rose as much as 13% in a year. And in other times and places, inflation has gone much, much higher. For example, the accompanying figure shows the inflation rate in Brazil from 1980 to 2004. As you can see, there were many years when the Brazilian inflation rate was in triple digits—and even years when it went into four digits. For a sense of what it felt like to be a Brazilian consumer during this period, consider what happens to the price of a gallon of gas over the course of a year at an inflation rate of 3,000%, equal to Brazil's inflation rate in 1990. At that rate, a gallon of gas that cost $3 at the beginning of the year would cost $90 by the end of the year.

In some months, inflation in Brazil briefly reached the 50%-per-month level

that economists use as a rough dividing line between merely high inflation and *hyperinflation*. Yet Brazil's experience was actually quite mild compared with history's most famous example of hyperinflation, which took place

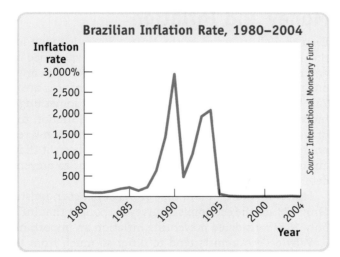

Brazilian Inflation Rate, 1980–2004

Source: International Monetary Fund.

You call what we've seen in the United States inflation? As shown in the graph above, between 1985 and 1995 Brazil demonstrated what really serious inflation—up to almost 3,000% per year—looks like. In 1992, hoping for relief, Brazilians were out on the street demanding new leadership.

What you will learn in this chapter:

➤ Why efforts to collect an **inflation tax** by printing money can lead to high rates of inflation

➤ How high inflation can spiral into hyperinflation as the public tries to avoid paying the inflation tax

➤ The economy-wide costs of inflation and **disinflation,** and the debate over the optimal rate of inflation

➤ Why even moderate levels of inflation can be hard to end

➤ Why deflation is a problem for economic policy and leads policy makers to prefer a low but positive inflation rate in Germany in 1922–1923. Toward the end of the German hyperinflation, prices were rising 16% a *day,* which—through compounding—meant an increase of approximately 500 billion percent over the course of five months. People became so reluctant to hold paper money, which lost value by the hour, that eggs and lumps of coal began to circulate as currency. German firms would pay their workers several times a day so that they could spend their earnings before they lost value (lending new meaning to the term *hourly wage*). Legend has it that men sitting down at a bar would order two beers at a time, out of fear that the price of a beer would rise before they could order a second round!

What causes episodes of high inflation? How do they come to an end? In this chapter, we'll look at the underlying reasons for inflation. We'll also examine the costs of inflation, which aren't as obvious as you might imagine. We'll see that a falling price level, or deflation, has its own special problems. And we'll look at the issues associated with *disinflation,* a reduction in the inflation rate.

Money and Inflation

Even though inflation in the United States is much lower today than it was during the 1970s—and a far cry from the recent experience of Brazil—the American public and media still pay close attention to inflation. Ask any American to name some serious problems that an economy faces and chances are you'll hear the word *inflation.* Yale University economist Robert Shiller did something similar in the mid-1990s, and indeed, he found that Americans consider inflation to be a problem. Three-quarters of those surveyed thought that "inflation hurts my real buying power; it makes me poorer." And over half of the respondents thought that "preventing high inflation is an important national priority, as important as preventing drug abuse or preventing deterioration in the quality of our schools."

However, Shiller found that professional economists rarely shared these concerns. Only 12% of the economists surveyed thought that inflation makes them poorer, and only 18% considered preventing inflation an important national priority.

Why do economists tend to differ so much from the general public in their impressions about inflation, at least at the moderate levels encountered in countries such as the United States? The answer lies in people's perception of how inflation affects them. People often view inflation as reducing the value of their pay raises; however, economists argue that inflation leads to higher nominal pay increases and therefore doesn't automatically reduce households' purchasing power. But even economists who do not consider a moderate level of inflation to be a serious problem still believe there can be costs associated with it.

To understand the true costs of inflation, we first need to analyze its causes. As we'll see later in this chapter, moderate levels of inflation such as those experienced in the United States—even the double-digit inflation of the late 1970s—can have complex causes. But very high inflation is always associated with rapid increases in the money supply.

To understand why, we need to revisit the effect of changes in the money supply on the overall price level. Then we'll turn to the reasons governments sometimes increase the money supply very rapidly.

Money and Prices, Revisited

In Chapter 31 we learned that in the short run an increase in the money supply increases real GDP by lowering the interest rate and stimulating investment spending and consumer spending. However, in the long run, as nominal wages and other sticky prices rise, real GDP falls back to its original level. So in the long run, any given percent increase in the money supply does not change real GDP. Instead, other things equal, it leads to an equal percent rise in the overall price level; that is, the prices of all goods and services in the economy, including nominal wages and the prices of intermediate goods, rise. And when the overall price level rises, the aggregate price level—the prices of all final goods and services—rises as well. As a result, an increase in the *nominal* money supply, *M*, leads in the long run to an increase in the aggregate price level that leaves the *real* quantity of money, *M/P*, at its original level. For example, when Turkey dropped six zeros from its currency, the Turkish lira, in January 2005, Turkish real GDP did not change. The only thing that changed was the number of zeros in prices: instead of something costing 2,000,000 lira, it cost 2 lira.

When analyzing large changes in the aggregate price level, macroeconomists often find it useful to ignore the distinction between the short run and the long run. Instead, they work with a simplified model in which the effect of a change in the money supply on the aggregate price level takes place instantaneously rather than over a long period of time. You might be concerned about this assumption given that in previous chapters we've emphasized the difference between the short run and the long run. However, for reasons we'll explain shortly, this is a reasonable assumption to make in the case of high inflation.

A simplified model in which the real quantity of money, *M/P*, is always at its long-run equilibrium level is known as the **classical model of the price level,** because it was commonly used by "classical" economists who wrote before the work of John Maynard Keynes. To understand the classical model and why it is useful in this context, let's revisit the *AS–AD* model and what it says about the effects of an increase in the money supply. (Unless otherwise noted, we will always be referring to changes in the *nominal* supply of money.)

Figure 33-1 reviews the effects of an increase in the money supply according to the *AS–AD* model. The economy starts at E_1, a point of short-run and long-run macroeconomic equilibrium. It lies at the intersection of the aggregate demand curve AD_1 and the short-run aggregate supply curve $SRAS_1$. It also lies on the long-run aggregate supply curve, *LRAS*. At E_1, the equilibrium aggregate price level is P_1.

Now suppose there is an increase in the money supply. This is an expansionary monetary policy, which shifts the aggregate demand curve to the right, to AD_2, and moves the economy to a new short-run equilibrium at E_2. Over time, however, nominal wages adjust upward in response to the rise in the aggregate price level, and the

According to the **classical model of the price level,** the real quantity of money is always at its long-run equilibrium level.

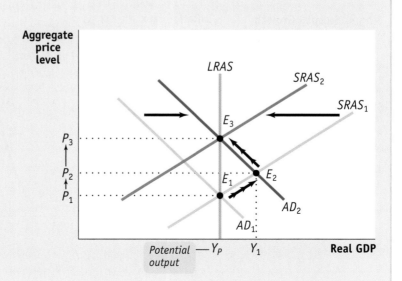

Figure 33-1

The Classical Model of the Price Level

Starting at E_1, an increase in the money supply shifts the aggregate demand curve rightward, as shown by the movement from AD_1 to AD_2. There is a new short-run equilibrium at E_2 and a higher price level at P_2. In the long run, nominal wages adjust upward and push the *SRAS* curve leftward to $SRAS_2$. The total percent increase in the price level from P_1 to P_3 is equal to the percent increase in the money supply. In the *classical model of the price level,* we ignore the transition period and think of the price level as rising to P_3 immediately. This is a good approximation under conditions of high inflation. **>web...**

SRAS curve shifts to the left, to *SRAS*$_2$. The new long-run equilibrium is at E_3, and real GDP returns to its initial level. As we learned in Chapter 31, the long-run increase in the aggregate price level from P_1 to P_3 is proportional to the increase in the money supply. As a result, in the long run changes in the money supply have no effect on the real quantity of money, M/P, or on real GDP. In the long run, money—as we learned—is *neutral*.

The classical model of the price level ignores the short-run movement from E_1 to E_2, assuming that the economy moves directly from one long-run equilibrium to another long-run equilibrium. In other words, it assumes that the economy moves directly from E_1 to E_3 and that real GDP never changes in response to a change in the money supply. In effect, in the classical model the effects of money supply changes are analyzed as if the short-run as well as the long-run aggregate supply curves were vertical.

In reality, this is a poor assumption during periods of low inflation. With a low inflation rate, it may take a while for workers and firms to react to a monetary expansion by raising wages and prices. In this scenario, some nominal wages and the prices of some goods are sticky in the short run. As a result, there is an upward-sloping *SRAS* curve and changes in the money supply can indeed change real GDP in the short run.

But what about periods of high inflation? In the face of high inflation, economists have observed that the short-run stickiness of nominal wages and prices tends to vanish. Workers and businesses, sensitized to inflation, are quick to raise their wages and prices in response to changes in the money supply. This implies that under high inflation there is a quicker adjustment of wages and prices of intermediate goods than occurs in the case of low inflation. So the short-run aggregate supply curve shifts leftward more quickly and there is a more rapid return to long-run equilibrium under high inflation. As a result, the classical model of the price level is much more likely to be a good approximation of reality for economies experiencing persistently high inflation. The following For Inquiring Minds explains this point further.

The consequence of this rapid adjustment of all prices in the economy is that in countries with persistently high inflation, changes in the money supply are quickly translated into changes in the inflation rate. Let's look again at Brazil. Figure 33-2 shows the annual rate of growth in the money supply (as measured by M1) and the annual rate of change of consumer prices from 1980 to 2004. As you can see, surges

---

Figure 33-2

Money Supply Growth and Inflation in Brazil

In the late 1980s and early 1990s, surges in the rate of money supply growth in Brazil were reflected in nearly simultaneous surges in inflation, with no obvious lags.

Source: International Monetary Fund.

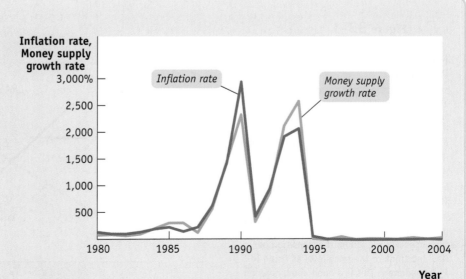

INDEXING TO INFLATION

When an economy experiences high inflation year after year, people take steps to protect themselves from future inflation—and these steps typically have the effect of making prices highly sensitive to changes in the money supply, even in the short run.

The usual response to inflation is *indexation*—contracts of all kinds are written in ways that adjust for inflation. For example, wage contracts typically include a cost-of-living adjustment, or COLA: payments to workers rise automatically with the consumer price index. The best-known COLA in the United States today involves Social Security benefits, which are automatically adjusted upward each year by the previous year's inflation rate: if the consumer price index rose 3% last year, every retiree's benefits are increased by 3%.

Most wage contracts in the United States no longer have COLAs. In the late 1970s, however, when inflation was much higher than it is today, COLAs were widespread. Economist Steven Holland reports that the rate of wage indexation in the American economy increased through the 1970s and then fell during the early 1980s, once inflation began to fall. In high-inflation economies, similar adjustments are regularly written into labor contracts, rental agreements, loan contracts, and so on. For example, during the late 1980s and early 1990s in Brazil, almost every contract that involved delaying payment into the future was indexed for inflation.

Indexation has the effect of speeding up the response of the overall price level to changes in the money supply. Even in an economy without indexation, an increase in the money supply quickly pushes up the prices of some types of goods, such as raw materials. In a highly indexed economy, these higher prices feed into changes in the consumer price index. That, in turn, quickly leads to increases in wages, further leading to increases in other prices, which feed back into wages, and so on. The result is that the long run, the period in which an increase in the money supply raises the overall price level by the same percentage, arrives very quickly—typically in a matter of months.

in the money supply in the late 1980s and early 1990s coincide with roughly equal surges in the inflation rate.

What leads a country to increase its money supply so much that the result is an inflation rate in the hundreds or thousands of percent?

The Inflation Tax

Modern economies use fiat money—pieces of paper that have no intrinsic value but are accepted as a medium of exchange. In the United States and most other wealthy countries, the decision about how many pieces of paper to issue is placed in the hands of a central bank that is somewhat independent of the political process. However, political leaders make the ultimate decision of whether or not to print more money.

So what is to prevent a government from paying for some of its expenses, not by raising taxes or borrowing, but simply by printing money? Nothing. In fact, governments, including the U.S. government, do it all the time. How can the U.S. government do this, given that the Federal Reserve issues money and not the Treasury? The answer is that the Treasury and the Federal Reserve work in concert. The Treasury issues debt to finance the government's purchases of goods and services, and the Fed *monetizes* the debt by creating money and buying the debt back from the public through open-market purchases of Treasury bills. In effect, the U.S. government can and does raise revenue by printing money.

For example, in July 2005 the U.S. monetary base—bank reserves plus currency in circulation—was $26 billion larger than it had been a year earlier. This occurred because, over the course of that year, the Federal Reserve had issued $26 billion in money or its electronic equivalent and put it into circulation through open-market operations. To put it another way, the Fed created money out of thin air and used it to buy valuable government securities from the private sector. Despite the fact that the Fed is officially independent of the U.S. government, its actions enabled the government to pay off $26 billion in outstanding government debt not by raising revenue through taxes but simply by printing money.

An alternative way to look at this is to say that the right to print money is itself a source of revenue. Governments have the exclusive right to print money, and they frequently do so in order to finance government spending. Economists refer to the revenue generated by the government's right to print money as *seigniorage,* an archaic term that goes back to the Middle Ages. It refers to the right to stamp gold and silver into coins, and charge a fee for doing so, that medieval lords—seigneurs, in France—reserved for themselves.

Seigniorage accounts for only a tiny fraction (about 1.5%) of the U.S. government's budget. So the government doesn't rely on the printing press to pay its bills. But there have been many occasions in history when governments turned to their printing presses as a crucial source of revenue. According to the usual scenario, a government finds itself running a large budget deficit—and lacks either the competence or the political will to eliminate this deficit by raising taxes or cutting spending. And the government can't borrow to cover the gap because potential lenders won't extend loans given the fear that the government's weakness will continue and leave it unable to repay its debts.

In such a situation, governments end up printing money to cover the budget deficit. But by printing money to pay its bills, a government increases the quantity of money in circulation. And as we've just seen, increases in the money supply translate into equally large increases in the aggregate price level. So printing money to cover a budget deficit leads to inflation.

Who ends up paying for the goods and services the government purchases with newly printed money? The people who currently hold money pay. They pay because inflation erodes the purchasing power of their money holdings. In other words, a government imposes an **inflation tax,** the reduction in the value of the money held by the public, by printing money to cover its budget deficit and creating inflation.

The **inflation tax** is the reduction in the value of money held by the public caused by inflation.

It's helpful to think about what this tax represents. If the inflation rate is 5%, then a year from now $1 will buy goods and services only worth $0.95 today. This is equivalent to a tax rate of 5% on the value of all money held by the public. So the size of the inflation tax over a given period is equal to the inflation rate over that period multiplied by the money supply:

(33-1)   Inflation tax = Inflation rate × (Nominal) money supply

However, the inflation tax as we've just calculated it may not be a good indicator of the real amount of resources captured by the government from the public because it is a *nominal* measure. If we want to know the *real* burden of the inflation tax on the public, we have to calculate the *real* inflation tax, which is equal to the inflation rate multiplied by the real money supply:

(33-2)   Real inflation tax = Inflation rate × Real money supply

Because it adjusts for changes in the price level, the real inflation tax measures the real value of the goods and services lost by the public through the inflation tax.

As we'll now see, the real inflation tax plays a key role in the process by which high inflation turns into explosive hyperinflation.

The Logic of Hyperinflation

Inflation imposes a tax on individuals who hold money. And, like any tax, it will lead people to change their behavior. In particular, when inflation is high, people will try to avoid holding money and will instead substitute real goods as well as interest-bearing assets for money. In the introduction to this chapter, we described how, during the German hyperinflation, people began using eggs or lumps of coal as a medium of exchange. They did this because lumps of coal maintained their real value over time but money didn't. Indeed, during the peak of German hyperinflation, people often burned paper money, which was less valuable than wood. Moreover, people don't just reduce their nominal money holdings—they reduce their *real* money holdings. Why? Because the more real money holdings they have, the greater the real amount of resources the government captures from them through the inflation tax.

In 1923, Germany's money was worth so little that children used stacks of banknotes as building blocks.

We are now prepared to understand how countries can get themselves into situations of extreme inflation. High inflation arises when the government must collect a large inflation tax to cover a large budget deficit. According to Equation 33-1, the real inflation tax is equal to the inflation rate multiplied by the real money supply.

But as we've just explained, in the face of high inflation the public reduces the real amount of money it holds. In turn, the government must generate a higher rate of inflation to collect the same amount of real inflation tax that it collected before people reduced their money holdings—an amount it needs to raise in order to cover a large budget deficit. And people respond to this new higher rate of inflation by reducing their real money holdings yet again. As the process becomes self-reinforcing, it can easily spiral out of control. Although the amount of real inflation tax that the government must ultimately collect to pay off its deficit does not change, the inflation rate the government needs to impose to collect that amount rises. So the government is forced to increase the money supply more rapidly, leading to an even higher rate of inflation, and so on.

Here's an analogy: imagine a city government that tries to raise a lot of money with a special fee on taxi rides. The fee will raise the cost of taxi rides, and this will cause people to turn to easily available substitutes such as walking or taking the bus. As taxi use declines, the government finds its tax revenue declines and must impose a higher fee to raise the same amount of revenue as before. You can imagine the ensuing vicious circle: the government imposes fees on taxi rides, which leads to less taxi use, which causes the government to raise the fee on taxis, which leads to even less taxi use, and so on.

Substitute the real money supply for taxi rides and the inflation rate for the fee on taxis, and you have the story of hyperinflation. A race develops between the government printing presses and the public: the presses churn out money at a faster and faster rate, to try to compensate for the fact that the public is reducing its real money holdings. At some point the inflation rate explodes into hyperinflation, and people are unwilling to hold any money at all (and resort to trading in eggs and lumps of coal). The government is then forced to abandon its use of the inflation tax and shut down the printing presses.

economics in action

Money and Prices in Brazil, 1985–1995

As we noted in the introduction to this chapter, Brazil offers a relatively recent example of a country experiencing very high inflation. Figure 33-2 showed that surges in Brazil's money supply were matched by almost simultaneous surges in Brazil's inflation rate. But looking at rates of change doesn't give a true feel for just how much prices went up in Brazil.

Figure 33-3 shows Brazil's money supply and aggregate price level from 1985 to 1995. We measure both the money supply and the aggregate price level as index numbers, with their 1985 levels set equal to 1. We also use a logarithmic scale, because equal-size percent changes are drawn as the same size. Over the course of a decade, both the money supply and the aggregate price level increased by approximately 100 billion percent. As you can see, the aggregate price level and the money supply rose in close tandem.

Why did the Brazilian government increase its money supply so excessively over the course of a decade? The reason boils down to political conflict, which made

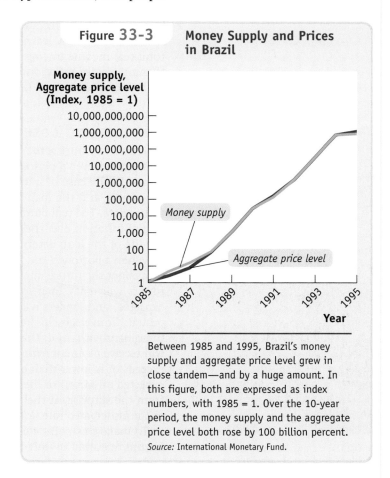

Figure 33-3 **Money Supply and Prices in Brazil**

Between 1985 and 1995, Brazil's money supply and aggregate price level grew in close tandem—and by a huge amount. In this figure, both are expressed as index numbers, with 1985 = 1. Over the 10-year period, the money supply and the aggregate price level both rose by 100 billion percent.
Source: International Monetary Fund.

it impossible for the country's government to balance its budget by either raising taxes or by cutting spending. Financial difficulties during the 1980s left Brazil unable to borrow money in world markets. Like many others before it, Brazil's government turned to the printing press to cover the gap—leading to massive inflation. ∎

< < < < < < < < < < < < < < < < < <

>> CHECK YOUR UNDERSTANDING 33-1

1. Suppose there is a large increase in the money supply in an economy that previously had low inflation. As a consequence, aggregate output expands in the short run. What does this say about situations in which the classical model of the price level applies?

2. Suppose that all wages and prices in an economy are indexed to inflation. Can there still be an inflation tax?

Solutions appear at back of book.

Effects of Inflation

We've seen how the use of the printing press to cover a government deficit leads to inflation. And we've also learned how a government's attempt to collect a large real inflation tax can lead to fiscal disaster. But even in the absence of such a disaster, inflation can have important consequences.

Recall the widespread belief that inflation makes everyone worse off by raising the cost of living. As we discussed earlier, this is a fallacy. It misses the point that inflation raises the prices received by firms—which in turn determine incomes paid in the economy—as well as the prices paid by consumers. In fact, recall from the *AS–AD* model that when an increase in the money supply leads to a rise in the aggregate price level, in the long run real GDP and aggregate real income are unchanged.

Although it is incorrect that inflation makes everyone worse off, inflation does have important effects on the economy that are not fully captured by the *AS–AD* model. We'll soon learn that *unexpected* inflation, although leaving real GDP and total real income unchanged, hurts some people while helping others. Then we'll see that *anticipated* inflation can indeed impose real costs on the economy; if sufficiently high, it can reduce real GDP and real incomes.

Winners and Losers from Unexpected Inflation

Inflation can hurt some people while helping others for one main reason: contracts that extend over a period of time, such as loans, are normally specified in nominal terms. In the case of a loan, the borrower receives a certain amount of funds at the beginning, and the loan contract specifies how much he or she must repay at some future date. The real burden of that repayment to the borrower depends greatly on the rate of inflation over the intervening years of the loan because the inflation rate over the life of the loan determines how large the repayment is in real terms.

When a borrower and a lender enter into a loan contract, each party has an expectation about the future rate of inflation. If the inflation rate is *higher* than expected, borrowers will repay their loans with funds that have a lower real value than they had expected, and lenders will receive payment with a lower real value than they had expected. Conversely, if the inflation rate is *lower* than expected, borrowers will repay their loans with funds that have a higher real value than they had expected, and lenders will receive payment with a higher real value than they had expected. So when inflation exceeds or is lower than expectations, either the borrower (in the case of higher-than-expected inflation) or the lender (in the case of lower-than-expected inflation) benefits from the surprise, at the other party's expense. But if the actual inflation rate is equal to the anticipated rate, inflation does not create winners or losers in loan contracts.

To make this point concrete, we need to recall the distinction between the *nominal interest rate* and the *real interest rate*. The best way to understand the difference between them is with an example. Suppose the owner of a firm borrows $10,000 for one year at a 10% interest rate. At the end of the year, he or she must repay $11,000—the amount borrowed plus interest. But suppose that over the course of the year the average level of prices increases by 10%. Then the $11,000 repayment has the same purchasing power as the original $10,000 loan. In real terms, the borrower has in effect received a zero-interest loan.

In this example, economists would say that the **nominal interest rate** (the interest rate in money terms) is 10%, but the **real interest rate** (the interest rate adjusted for inflation) is 0%. As the example shows, the real interest rate is equal to the nominal interest rate minus the rate of inflation:

> The **nominal interest rate** is the interest rate in money terms.
>
> The **real interest rate** is the interest rate adjusted for inflation, equal to the nominal rate minus the inflation rate.

> **(33-3)** Real interest rate = Nominal interest rate − Inflation rate

You might be tempted to say that inflation necessarily helps borrowers and hurts lenders; but what really matters is how actual inflation compares with the inflation that borrowers and lenders *expected when they entered into the loan contract*. Suppose a borrower and a lender agreed on a one-year loan at a nominal interest rate of 7%, and both expected the inflation rate to be 5% over the next year. Then the expected inflation rate was taken into account when they entered into the contract: the 7% nominal interest rate represented a 2% real interest rate plus 5% for inflation. But suppose people expected a 5% inflation rate and actually experienced a 10% rate. In this case, lenders thought they were lending at a 2% real interest rate, but they actually received a negative real interest rate of *minus* 3%. That is, by lending at a 7% nominal interest rate (2% real interest rate plus 5% expected inflation rate) but experiencing a 10% *actual* inflation rate, lenders received a real interest rate equal to 7% − 10% = −3%. Borrowers won, and lenders lost. Conversely, suppose the actual inflation rate turned out to be 0% rather than 5%. In that case, borrowers who thought they were paying a 2% real interest rate actually ended up paying a real interest rate equal to 7% (7% nominal interest rate minus 0% actual inflation rate). Lenders won, and borrowers lost.

In modern America, home mortgages provide the most important example of how inflation can create winners and losers. A standard mortgage specifies a monthly dollar payment over a period of 15 to 40 years. If the overall price level is rising, the borrower's real payment per month falls over time. How fast the payment falls depends on the rate of inflation. For example, Americans who took out mortgages in the early 1970s quickly found their real payments reduced by higher-than-expected inflation: by 1983 the purchasing power of a dollar was only 45% of what it had been in 1973. Those who took out mortgages in the early 1990s were not so lucky because the inflation rate fell to lower-than-expected levels in the following years: in 2003 the purchasing power of a dollar was 78% of what it had been in 1993.

So borrowers who took out mortgages in the early 1970s gained at the expense of lenders, who found the real value of their loans rapidly eroded by inflation. In fact, one side effect of inflation during the 1970s was to push many savings and loan institutions—a type of bank that traditionally specialized in home loans—into bankruptcy. They failed because the value of the long-term loans they had made were greatly reduced by inflation, but the interest rates they paid on short-term deposits had to keep up with inflation in order to attract depositors.

Expected Inflation and Interest Rates

As the preceding discussion makes clear, people should base the decision of whether or not to borrow on their expectation of the real interest rate, not the nominal rate. It is the real interest rate that measures the quantity of real purchasing power the borrower will have to give up to repay the loan. A loan at 10% interest is very expensive at a time of 0% inflation; it's very cheap if inflation is near 10%; and it's better than free in real terms if the inflation rate is above 10%.

And like borrowers, lenders should be concerned with the real rather than the nominal interest rate. A loan at 10% interest is a very good investment if inflation is at 0% but a poor investment if inflation is running at 15%.

Because inflation affects the real interest rate actually paid by borrowers and received by lenders, *expected* inflation has strong effects on the nominal interest rate. Recall the loanable funds model of the interest rate we developed in Chapter 26, where we described how the equilibrium nominal interest rate equalizes the quantity of loanable funds supplied and the quantity of loanable funds demanded. As with all supply and demand models, this result depends on the "other things equal" assumption. And in this market, one very important thing that must be held equal (that is, unchanged) is the expected inflation rate. So how are the results of the loanable funds model affected by changes in the expected inflation rate?

In Figure 33-4, the curves S_0 and D_0 show the supply and demand for loanable funds given that the expected rate of inflation is 0%. In that case, equilibrium is at E_0 and the equilibrium nominal interest rate is 4%. Because expected inflation is 0%, the equilibrium expected real interest rate, the real interest rate expected by borrowers and lenders when the loan is contracted, is also 4%.

Now suppose that the expected inflation rate rises to 10%. The demand curve for funds shifts upward to D_{10}: borrowers are now willing to borrow as much at a nominal interest rate of 14% as they were previously willing to borrow at 4%. That's because with a 10% inflation rate, a 14% nominal interest rate corresponds to a 4% real interest rate. Similarly, the supply curve of funds shifts upward to S_{10}: lenders require a nominal interest rate of 14% to persuade them to lend as much as they would previously have lent at 4%. The new equilibrium is at E_{10}: the result of an expected inflation rate of 10% is that the equilibrium nominal interest rate rises from 4% to 14%.

This situation can be summarized as a general principle, known as the **Fisher effect** (after the American economist Irving Fisher, who proposed it in 1930): *the expected real interest rate is unaffected by the change in expected inflation.* According to the Fisher effect, expected inflation drives up nominal interest rates, and each additional percentage point of expected inflation drives up the nominal interest rate by 1 percentage point. The central point is that both lenders and borrowers base their decisions on the expected real rate of interest. As long as inflation is expected, it does not affect the equilibrium quantity of loanable funds or the expected real interest rate; all it affects is the equilibrium nominal interest rate.

According to the **Fisher effect**, an increase in expected inflation drives up the nominal interest rate, leaving the expected real interest rate unchanged.

Figure 33-4

The Fisher Effect

D_0 and S_0 are the demand and supply curves for loanable funds when the expected inflation rate is 0%. At an expected inflation rate of 0%, the equilibrium nominal interest rate is 4%. Expected inflation pushes both the demand and supply curves upward by 1 percentage point for every percentage point increase of expected inflation. D_{10} and S_{10} are the demand and supply curves for loanable funds when the expected inflation rate is 10%. Expected inflation raises the equilibrium nominal interest rate to 14%. The expected real interest rate remains at 4%, and the equilibrium quantity of loanable funds also remains unchanged. **>web...**

The Costs of Inflation

We've now seen how unexpected inflation produces winners and losers. The question we want to ask now is whether *anticipated* inflation imposes costs on the economy as a whole and whether, as a result, it changes the overall level of income in the economy. (We are considering the costs that even low or moderate inflation can cause, excluding the costs of a fiscal crisis that high inflation or hyperinflation can impose on an economy.)

The answer to our question is yes; anticipated inflation can impose real costs on the economy. Economists have identified several of these, the most important being *shoe-leather costs*, *menu costs*, and *unit-of-account costs*. We'll discuss each in turn.

Shoe-Leather Costs

People hold money for convenience in making transactions. Inflation, as we've seen, discourages people from holding money. The result is that making transactions becomes more difficult.

One typical response to inflation is that people make more transactions in order to purchase the same amount of goods and services. In 1984–1985, when Israel experienced an episode of very high inflation, Israelis tried to hold as little money as possible, which required visiting a bank or ATM several times a week to move money into or out of interest-bearing accounts. During the German hyperinflation, merchants employed runners to take their cash to the bank many times a day to deposit it into interest-bearing assets or to convert it into a more stable foreign currency. In each case, in an effort to avoid the inflation tax, people devoted valuable resources—the time of Israeli citizens, the labor of those German runners—that could have been used productively elsewhere. During the German hyperinflation, so many banking transactions were taking place that the number of employees at German banks nearly quadrupled—from around 100,000 in 1913 to 375,000 in 1923. Similarly, during the Brazilian hyperinflation, the financial sector of the economy accounted for 15% of GDP, more than twice the size of the financial sector in the United States measured as a share of GDP. The large increase in the banking sector needed to cope with the consequences of inflation represented a loss of real resources to society.

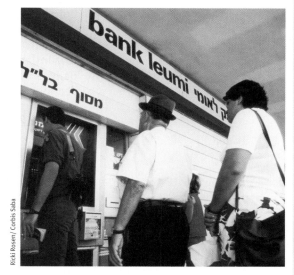

Such are the shoe-leather costs of inflation: when the inflation rate in Israel hit 500% in 1985, people spent a lot of time in line at ATMs.

The increased costs of transactions caused by inflation are known as **shoe-leather costs,** an allusion to the wear and tear of the extra running around that takes place when people are trying to avoid holding money. Shoe-leather costs are substantial in very high-inflation economies, as anyone who has lived through a hyperinflation—or even inflation of, say, 100% per year—can attest. Most estimates suggest, however, that the shoe-leather costs of inflation at the rates seen in the United States—which in peacetime has never had inflation above 13%—are quite small.

> The **shoe-leather costs** of inflation are the increased costs of making transactions that arise from the public's efforts to avoid the inflation tax.

PITFALLS

WHAT INTEREST RATE FOR MONEY DEMAND?

We learned in Chapter 31 that the demand for money depends on the interest rate. But now we've made a distinction between the *nominal* interest rate and the *real* interest rate. Which one affects money demand?

You might be tempted to answer that it's the real interest rate. After all, we know that the demand for money can be viewed as a demand for a *real* quantity of money. So shouldn't it be real values, all the way?

No. Think about the opportunity cost of holding cash: a dollar bill or a *real* (Brazil's currency) offers a 0% interest rate—a 0%

nominal interest rate. The alternative is to hold a bond that yields positive interest—positive *nominal* interest. So the interest rate that matters for money demand is the nominal rate of interest because that is what you forgo by holding money.

In fact, that's why expected inflation leads to reduced holding of money as people substitute money for interest-bearing assets. The real rate of interest doesn't rise, but the nominal rate does. And the nominal rate is the opportunity cost of holding money because it is the rate paid on interest-bearing assets.

Menu Costs We introduced the concept of menu costs—the literal cost of changing listed prices—in Chapter 32 as one reason firms are reluctant to change prices in the face of changes in aggregate demand. In the face of inflation, of course, firms are forced to change prices more often than they would if the aggregate price level was more or less stable. This means higher costs for the economy as a whole.

In times of hyperinflation, menu costs can be very substantial. During the Brazilian hyperinflation, for instance, supermarket workers reportedly spent half of their time replacing old price stickers with new ones. When inflation is high, merchants may decide to stop listing prices in terms of the local currency and use either an artificial unit—in effect, measuring prices relative to one another—or a more stable currency, such as the U.S. dollar. This is exactly what the Israeli real estate market began doing in the mid-1980s: prices were quoted in U.S. dollars, even though payment was made in Israeli shekels.

Menu costs are present in low-inflation economies, but they are not severe. In low-inflation economies, businesses might update their prices only sporadically—not daily or even more frequently, as is the case in high-inflation or hyperinflation economies. Also, with technological advances, menu costs are becoming less and less important, since prices can be changed electronically and fewer merchants attach price stickers to merchandise.

Unit-of-Account Costs Article I, Section 8 of the U.S. Constitution gives Congress the power to "fix the standard of weights and measures" for the nation. The Founding Fathers realized that trade among the states would be greatly facilitated if there were no confusion about units of measurement—a pound in Massachusetts should weigh the same amount as a pound in Virginia; a foot in New York should be the same length as a foot in South Carolina.

As we explained in Chapter 30, one of the roles of money is as a unit of account—a measure individuals use to set prices and make economic calculations. Just as trade among states is facilitated when everyone knows how much a pound weighs, exchange in the economy as a whole is facilitated when everyone knows how much a dollar is worth. Yet inflation causes the real value of a dollar to change over time—a dollar next year is worth less than a dollar this year. The effect, many economists argue, is to reduce the quality of economic decisions: the economy as a whole makes less efficient use of its resources. The **unit-of-account costs** of inflation are the costs arising from the way inflation makes money a less reliable unit of measurement.

Unit-of-account costs may be particularly important in the tax system. The United States has a progressive income tax, meaning that people with higher incomes pay a higher income tax rate on their incomes. In addition, the schedule of income tax rates in the United States is indexed to inflation. That is, the threshold level of income above which a taxpayer must pay a higher tax rate goes up every year with inflation to prevent people from having to pay a higher tax rate on their income if their income is just keeping up with inflation. But in the United States and most other countries, taxable income *itself* is still calculated in nominal terms. For example, taxable profits are calculated as the difference between a company's nominal costs and its nominal revenues. If costs are paid before revenues are received, inflation can distort the calculation of profit in nominal terms, making a case of no profit or loss in real terms appear like a positive profit in nominal terms.

In times of high inflation, this is a serious risk. Imagine a clothing store that buys a coat at a wholesale price of $600 during the summer and sells it at a retail price of $1,000 three months later. By law, the difference between the price at which the store buys the coat and the price at which it sells it is considered a profit—$400 in this case—and is subject to taxes. But under high inflation the store cannot replace coats at the same cost it paid for the coats it just sold. It must pay the prevailing wholesale price of a coat to replace its inventory. If the wholesale price had risen to $800 at the time of the sale, then from the viewpoint of the store's owner, his or her profit on the

---

The **unit-of-account costs** of inflation are the costs arising from the way inflation makes money a less reliable unit of measurement.

sale is only $1,000 − $800 = $200, not $400. But the Internal Revenue Service does not see it this way; it assesses taxes based on the difference between what the firm actually paid in nominal terms and what the firm received in nominal terms.

During the 1970s, when the United States had relatively high inflation, the distorting effects of inflation on the tax system were a serious problem. Some businesses were discouraged from productive investment spending because inflation caused the IRS to exaggerate their true profits. Conversely, inflation encouraged excessive spending on homeownership. The U.S. income tax system allows taxpayers to deduct interest payments on home mortgages, so at a time when nominal—but not real—interest rates were high, owning a home became a very good deal. When inflation (and tax rates) were reduced in the 1980s, these problems became much less important.

The Optimal Rate of Inflation

What is the optimal rate of inflation for an economy? You might be tempted to say 0%—aren't stable prices a good thing? And haven't we just listed several real costs to the economy from inflation? However, some economists argue that there should be a small positive inflation rate, while others suggest that even 0% inflation may be too high!

In a famous analysis, University of Chicago economist Milton Friedman argued that economic policy should aim for steady *deflation* as a way to minimize shoe-leather costs. As explained in For Inquiring Minds, Friedman suggested that the only way to truly eliminate the shoe-leather costs of inflation would be to make people indifferent between holding money and not holding money. This would mean that the nominal interest rate would need to be near 0%. But if the real interest rate is positive, a 0% nominal interest rate requires a negative rate of inflation.

In practice, no central bank has tried to put Friedman's rule into effect. Most central banks aim for **price stability,** usually defined as a low but positive rate of inflation. For example, it is clear from the Federal Reserve's actions that it prefers an inflation rate of 2% to 3%, but it has never made a formal statement to that effect. Other central banks are less cagey. For example, the Bank of England has an explicit inflation rate target of 2.5%.

The main reason most central banks aim for slightly positive inflation is their belief that monetary policy is better able to respond to adverse events when the public expects modest inflation than when the public expects 0% inflation. We'll explain why later in this chapter, when we discuss deflation.

> Most central banks target **price stability,** a low but positive rate of inflation.

FOR INQUIRING MINDS

A CASE FOR DEFLATION?

In 1960, Milton Friedman used the analysis of shoe-leather costs of inflation to arrive at a radical conclusion: the optimal rate of inflation is negative. That is, there should be persistent deflation.

His argument ran as follows. Even at 0% inflation, people incur shoe-leather costs when they economize on the use of money in order to avoid the opportunity cost of interest forgone. Yet it does not cost the economy anything to provide people with fiat money. So Friedman argued that even at 0% inflation, people's efforts to limit their money holdings in favor of holding interest-bearing assets lead to inefficiency.

To eliminate this inefficiency, Friedman concluded that the government should try to push the nominal interest rate close to 0%. But the only way to do this on a sustained basis would be to have a policy dictating a negative inflation rate. A negative expected inflation rate reduces the nominal interest rate through the Fisher effect, leading people to hold a larger real quantity of money.

Although an ingenious analysis, it has never been used as a basis for policy. Negative inflation—deflation—poses risks to economic policy, which most economists believe outweigh any gains from reduced shoe-leather costs.

economics in action

Inflation and Interest Rates in the United States

Does expected inflation really push up interest rates? A quick look at nominal interest rates and inflation in the United States over the past 50 years is strong evidence that it does.

Figure 33-5 shows the nominal interest rate on U.S. Treasury bills and the inflation rate in the United States since 1955. Both peaked around 1980, when inflation rose into double digits—and so did interest rates.

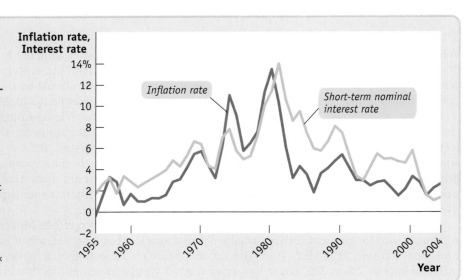

Figure 33-5

Inflation and Nominal Interest Rates

The Fisher effect tells us that each percentage point of expected inflation raises the nominal interest rate by 1 percentage point. These data show the short-term nominal interest rate and the inflation rate in the United States over the past half-century. They moved roughly together, both reaching a double-digit peak around 1980. To the extent that actual inflation eventually represents previously held expectations of inflation, the data are strong evidence for the Fisher effect. **>web...**

Sources: Bureau of Labor Statistics; Federal Reserve Bank of St. Louis.

Movements in inflation and nominal interest rates do not, of course, match exactly. For one thing, other factors besides inflation affect the nominal interest rate. For another, the nominal interest rate reflects *expected* inflation, not actual inflation. To the extent that actual inflation is either higher or lower than expected inflation, the nominal interest rate will not move in tandem with the actual inflation rate. Through much of the 1970s, inflation ran faster than people expected, leading to negative real interest rates. During the 1980s inflation ran below most people's expectations, leading to very high real interest rates.

But, to the extent that the actual inflation rate eventually represents what people had expected the inflation rate to be, the key message from Figure 33-5 is that inflation does push up nominal interest rates. And it does this roughly one-for-one, as the Fisher effect predicts. ■

< < < < < < < < < < < < < < < < <

> **QUICK REVIEW**

➤ An unexpectedly high inflation rate benefits borrowers and hurts lenders by reducing the *real interest rate* paid on loans.

➤ Higher expected inflation raises *nominal interest rates* through the *Fisher effect*.

➤ Even anticipated inflation imposes *shoe-leather costs*, menu costs, and *unit-of-account costs*.

➤ Most central banks target *price stability*.

> **CHECK YOUR UNDERSTANDING 33-2**

1. For each of the following cases, calculate the real interest rate paid on the loans as well as who gained and who lost from unexpected inflation.
   a. The nominal interest rate is 8%, and both borrowers and lenders expect an inflation rate of 5% over the life of their loans. The actual inflation rate is 3%.
   b. The nominal interest rate is 6%, and both borrowers and lenders expect an inflation rate of 4% over the life of their loans. The actual inflation rate is 7%.

2. The widespread use of technology has revolutionized the banking industry, making it much easier for customers to access and manage their assets. Does this mean that the shoe-leather costs of inflation are higher or lower than they used to be?

Solutions appear at back of book.

Moderate Inflation and Disinflation

The governments of wealthy, politically stable countries like the United States and Britain don't find themselves forced to print money to pay their bills. Yet over the past 40 years both countries, along with a number of other nations, have experienced uncomfortable episodes of inflation. In the United States, the inflation rate peaked at 13% at the beginning of the 1980s. In Britain, the inflation rate reached 26% in 1975. Why did policy makers allow this to happen?

To understand inflation rates in such cases, it is helpful to shift our focus away from the link between money and prices and look at the policy trade-offs that governments face.

Causes of Moderate Inflation

In Chapter 32 we learned that most economists believe that in the short run there is a trade-off between unemployment and inflation. If the government makes an effort to keep unemployment below the natural rate of unemployment, the short-run Phillips curve implies that this will lead to a higher inflation rate than people expect. Over time, however, people will come to expect this higher level of inflation, and the short-run Phillips curve will shift upward. If the government insists on keeping unemployment below its natural rate, this will lead to further increases in expected inflation, and so on. So keeping unemployment below its natural rate requires an ever-higher rate of inflation.

This analysis suggests that policy makers should not try to achieve an unemployment rate below the natural rate. However, imagine yourself as a politician facing an election in a year or two, and suppose that inflation is fairly low at the moment. You might well be tempted to create an inflationary gap, pushing the unemployment rate down right now, as a way to please voters. These gains will eventually have to be paid back: low unemployment will lead to gradually rising inflation, and future governments will face an unpleasant choice between raising unemployment or living with inflation. But that's a problem for the future—right now you have an election to win.

This scenario explains why governments might follow expansionary monetary and fiscal policies that lead the economy into inflation. Does this happen in the real world? The evidence is mixed: it's hard to find a systematic pattern of opportunistic behavior, but there are some specific cases in which governments appear to have attempted to stimulate the economy for short-term electoral gain but at long-term economic cost.

A less cynical but similar scenario emphasizes the role of wishful thinking. The natural rate of unemployment changes over time, and estimates of the natural rate are often controversial. A government can easily convince itself that it's safe to target an unemployment rate that is, in fact, well below the natural rate. (It's especially easy to reach that conclusion when it's politically advantageous to do so.) By the time it becomes clear that the target was too ambitious, substantial inflation may be embedded in people's expectations.

Situations like these explain how countries with no need to impose an inflation tax nonetheless developed double-digit inflation rates in the 1970s. And once they found themselves experiencing moderately high inflation, it was difficult to bring inflation back down.

The Problem of Disinflation

Suppose that, for whatever reason, an economy gets into a situation of moderate inflation. Why doesn't it just reverse policy and end the inflation? The answer is that once the public has come to expect continuing inflation, bringing inflation down is painful.

Recall our description in Chapter 32 of how a persistent attempt to keep unemployment below the natural rate leads to accelerating inflation. To reduce inflation that is built into expectations, policy makers need to run the process in reverse, adopting contractionary policies that keep the unemployment rate above the natural rate for an extended period of time. The process of bringing down inflation that has become embedded in expectations is known as **disinflation.**

Disinflation can be very expensive. As the following Economics in Action documents, the U.S. retreat from high inflation at the beginning of the 1980s appears to have cost the equivalent of about 18% of a year's real GDP. The justification for paying these costs is that they lead to a permanent gain. Although the economy does not recover the short-term productivity losses caused by disinflation, it no longer suffers from the other costs associated with the persistently high inflation. In fact, the United States, Britain, and other wealthy countries that experienced inflation in the 1970s eventually decided that the pain of bringing inflation down—the large reduction in real GDP in the short term—was worth the required suffering.

Some economists argue that the costs of disinflation can be reduced if policy makers explicitly state their determination to reduce inflation. A clearly announced, credible policy of disinflation, they contend, can reduce expectations of future inflation and so shift the short-run Phillips curve downward. Some economists believe that the clear determination of the Federal Reserve to combat the inflation of the 1970s was credible enough that the costs of disinflation, huge though they were, were lower than they might otherwise have been.

> **Disinflation** is the process of bringing down inflation that has become embedded in expectations.

Supply Shocks

Another factor that contributed to the rise of U.S. inflation in the 1970s and its decline in the 1980s was a series of *supply shocks,* first negative and then positive.

In Chapter 27 we showed how negative supply shocks can lead both to a fall in aggregate output and to a rise in the aggregate price level. During the 1970s there were major negative supply shocks, driven by political events in the Middle East that drove up the price of oil. These supply shocks led directly to inflation. They also made it hard for the government to pursue an anti-inflationary policy, because high inflation was coupled with relatively high unemployment rates. When it is already high, risking further increases in unemployment is a particularly bitter pill to swallow in order to achieve lower inflation rates.

In the 1980s the same process operated in reverse. A fall in oil prices, especially after 1985, allowed policy makers to preside over declining inflation without the need to impose high unemployment.

economics in action

The Great Disinflation of the 1980s

As we've mentioned several times in this chapter, the United States ended the 1970s with a high rate of inflation, at least by its own peacetime historical standards—13% in 1980. Part of this inflation was the result of one-time events, especially a world oil crisis. But expectations of future inflation at 10% or more per year appeared to be firmly embedded in the economy.

By the mid-1980s, however, inflation was running at about 4% per year. Panel (a) of Figure 33-6 shows the annual rate of change in the "core" consumer price index (CPI)—also called the *core inflation rate*. This index, which excludes energy and food prices, is widely regarded as a better indicator of underlying inflation trends than the

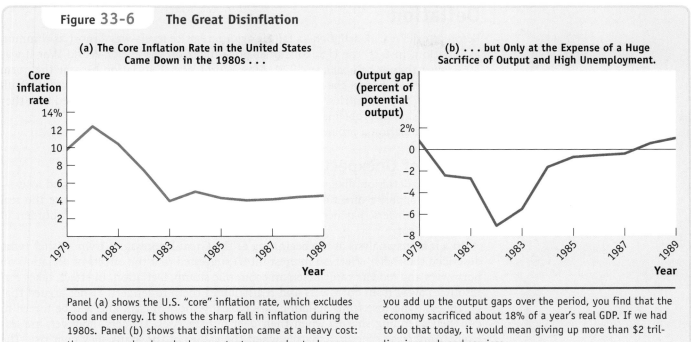

Figure 33-6 The Great Disinflation

(a) The Core Inflation Rate in the United States Came Down in the 1980s . . .

(b) . . . but Only at the Expense of a Huge Sacrifice of Output and High Unemployment.

Panel (a) shows the U.S. "core" inflation rate, which excludes food and energy. It shows the sharp fall in inflation during the 1980s. Panel (b) shows that disinflation came at a heavy cost: the economy developed a huge output gap, and actual aggregate output didn't return to potential output until 1987. If you add up the output gaps over the period, you find that the economy sacrificed about 18% of a year's real GDP. If we had to do that today, it would mean giving up more than $2 trillion in goods and services.

Sources: Bureau of Labor Statistics; Congressional Budget Office.

overall CPI. By this measure, inflation fell from about 12% at the end of the 1970s to about 4%.

How was this disinflation achieved? At great cost. Beginning in late 1979, the Federal Reserve imposed strongly contractionary monetary policies, which pushed the economy into its worst recession since the Great Depression. Panel (b) shows the Congressional Budget Office estimate of the U.S. output gap from 1979 to 1989: by 1982, actual output was 7% below potential output, corresponding to an unemployment rate of more than 9%. Aggregate output didn't get back to potential output until 1987.

Our analysis of the Phillips curve in Chapter 32 tells us that a temporary rise in unemployment, like that of the 1980s, is needed to break the cycle of inflationary expectations. Once expectations of inflation are reduced, the economy can return to the natural rate of unemployment at a lower inflation rate. And that's just what happened.

But the cost was huge. If you add up the output gap over 1980–1987, you find that the economy sacrificed approximately 18% of an average year's output over the period. If we had to do the same thing today, that would mean giving up more than $2 trillion worth of goods and services. ∎

> >

>>CHECK YOUR UNDERSTANDING 33-3

1. British economists believe that the natural rate of unemployment in that country rose sharply during the 1970s, from around 3% to as much as 10%. During that period Britain experienced a sharp acceleration of inflation, which for a time went above 20%. How might these facts be related?

2. Why is disinflation so costly for an economy? Are there ways to reduce these costs?

Solutions appear at back of book.

Deflation

Before World War II, *deflation*—a falling aggregate price level—was almost as common as inflation. In fact, the U.S. consumer price index on the eve of World War II was 30% lower than it had been in 1920. After World War II, inflation became the norm in all countries. But in the 1990s deflation reappeared in Japan and proved difficult to reverse. Other countries, including the United States, became concerned that they might face similar problems.

Why is deflation a problem? And why is it hard to end?

Effects of Unexpected Deflation

Unexpected deflation, like unexpected inflation, produces both winners and losers—but in the opposite direction. Lenders, who are owed money, gain because the real value of borrowers' payments increases. Borrowers lose because the real burden of their debt rises.

In a famous analysis at the beginning of the Great Depression, Irving Fisher (who described the Fisher effect on interest rates) suggested that the effects of deflation on borrowers and lenders can worsen an economic slump. Deflation, in effect, takes real resources away from borrowers and redistributes them to lenders. Fisher argued that borrowers, who lose from deflation, are typically short of cash and will be forced to cut their spending sharply when their debt burden rises. Lenders, however, are less likely to increase spending sharply when the values of the loans they own rise. The overall effect, said Fisher, is that deflation reduces aggregate demand, deepening an economic slump, which, in a vicious circle, may lead to further deflation. The effect of deflation in reducing aggregate demand, known as **debt deflation,** probably played a role in the Great Depression.

> **Debt deflation** is the reduction in aggregate demand arising from the increase in the real burden of outstanding debt caused by deflation.

Effects of Expected Deflation

The effects of expected deflation are, as you might expect, the reverse of the effects of expected inflation: deflation leads to lower nominal interest rates and to increased demand for money. There is, however, a limit to the effect of expected deflation on nominal interest rates. Look back at the example in Figure 33-4, where the equilibrium nominal interest rate is 4% if the expected inflation rate is 0%. Clearly, if the expected inflation rate is −3%—if the public expects deflation at 3% per year—the equilibrium nominal interest rate will be 1%.

But what would happen if the expected rate of inflation is −5%? Would the nominal interest rate fall to −1%? No. Nobody would lend money at a negative nominal rate of interest because they could do better by simply holding cash. Economists say that there is a **zero bound** on the nominal interest rate: it cannot go below zero.

> There is a **zero bound** on the nominal interest rate: it cannot go below zero.

This zero bound can limit the effectiveness of monetary policy. Suppose the economy is depressed, with output below potential output and the unemployment rate above the natural rate. Normally the central bank can respond by cutting interest rates so as to increase aggregate demand. If the nominal interest rate is already zero, however, the central bank cannot push it down any further. Any further increases in the monetary base will either be held in bank vaults or held as cash by individuals and firms, without being spent. (With a negative inflation rate and a 0% nominal interest rate, holding cash yields a positive real interest rate.)

A situation in which monetary policy can't be used because nominal interest rates cannot fall below the zero bound is known as a **liquidity trap.** A liquidity trap can occur whenever there is a sharp reduction in demand for loanable funds. The U.S. economy was up against the zero bound for much of the 1930s. Such situations are, however, more likely to arise when the public expects deflation than when it expects inflation. After World War II, when inflation became the norm around the world, the zero bound largely vanished as a problem—until the 1990s.

> A **liquidity trap** is a situation in which monetary policy can't be used because nominal interest rates cannot fall below zero.

In the 1990s, however, Japan found itself up against the zero bound, and it also experienced persistent deflation. The Japanese experience alarmed other countries, which feared that they might experience similar problems. In 2001 and 2002, deflation concerns increased in the United States as the inflation rate dipped below 2%.

As we first mentioned in Chapter 23, these fears are the main reason most central banks prefer price stability, a low but positive inflation rate—say 2 or 3%—rather than 0% inflation. Studies by economists at the Federal Reserve and elsewhere indicate that inflation at such low rates imposes very small costs on the economy and makes a liquidity trap unlikely.

economics in action

Japan's Trap

After a boom in the late 1980s, Japan experienced a recession in the early 1990s. The recession was not particularly severe, but it proved very persistent. And in the face of a sustained recessionary gap, the inflation rate in Japan steadily declined. By the middle of the 1990s Japan had become the first major economy to experience deflation since the 1930s.

Figure 33-7 shows Japan's inflation rate and the call money rate—the short-term nominal interest rate that corresponds to the Federal funds rate in the United States—from 1990 to 2004. With a brief exception in 1996 and 1997, the inflation rate fell steadily, becoming negative in the late 1990s. The Bank of Japan, the counterpart of the Federal Reserve, steadily reduced interest rates in an effort to fight deflation. By 1998, however, it had reduced the call money rate all the way to 0%—and the economy was still depressed. This experience demonstrated that the liquidity trap is a real problem in the modern world.

Japan's inability to stimulate the economy by reducing interest rates was one reason for its extensive use of expansionary fiscal policy during the 1990s. In Chapter 29 we described the "bridge to nowhere" linking Awaji Island to the Japanese mainland. Such construction projects were, in part, a substitute for monetary expansion. ■

> >

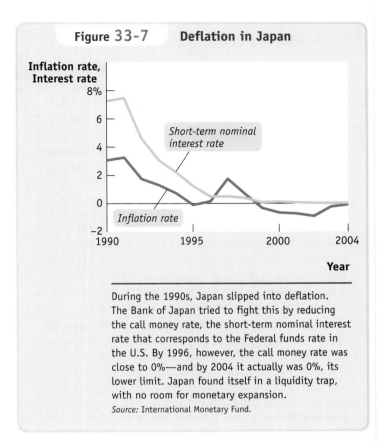

Figure 33-7 **Deflation in Japan**

During the 1990s, Japan slipped into deflation. The Bank of Japan tried to fight this by reducing the call money rate, the short-term nominal interest rate that corresponds to the Federal funds rate in the U.S. By 1996, however, the call money rate was close to 0%—and by 2004 it actually was 0%, its lower limit. Japan found itself in a liquidity trap, with no room for monetary expansion.
Source: International Monetary Fund.

>> QUICK REVIEW

- Unexpected deflation helps lenders and hurts borrowers. This can lead to *debt deflation*, which has a contractionary effect on aggregate demand.
- Deflation makes it more likely that interest rates will end up against the *zero bound*. When this happens, the economy is in a *liquidity trap*, and monetary policy is ineffective.

>> CHECK YOUR UNDERSTANDING 33-4

1. Why won't anyone lend money at a negative nominal rate of interest? How can this pose problems for monetary policy?

Solution appears at back of book.

• A LOOK AHEAD •

In the course of our presentation of macroeconomics, we've referred a number of times to history—both the history of events, such as the Great Depression, and the history of ideas, like those of John Maynard Keynes. Both types of history help us understand why macroeconomics is the way it is.

In the next chapter we'll step back from the details of specific models, and look at the making of modern macroeconomics—at how events and ideas interacted to produce the analysis we now rely on.

SUMMARY

1. In analyzing high inflation, economists use the **classical model of the price level,** which says that changes in the money supply lead to proportional changes in the aggregate price level even in the short run.

2. Governments sometimes print money in order to finance budget deficits. When they do, they impose an **inflation tax,** equal to the inflation rate times the money supply, on those who hold money. The real value of resources captured by the government is reflected by the real inflation tax, the inflation rate times the real money supply. In order to avoid paying the inflation tax, people reduce their real money holdings and force the government to increase inflation to capture the same amount of real inflation tax. In some cases, this leads to a vicious circle of a shrinking real money supply and a rising rate of inflation, leading to hyperinflation and a fiscal crisis.

3. The **real interest rate** is equal to the **nominal interest rate** minus the inflation rate. The expected inflation rate is accounted for in the nominal interest rate on a loan. Inflation that is higher than expected benefits borrowers and hurts lenders; inflation that is lower than expected benefits lenders and hurts borrowers. According to the **Fisher effect,** expected inflation raises the nominal interest rate one-to-one so that the expected real interest rate remains unchanged.

4. Inflation imposes **shoe-leather costs,** costs of making transactions incurred as people try to avoid holding money; menu costs, the costs of changing prices; and **unit-of-account costs,** costs that arise because money ceases to be a reliable measure of value. Although there are arguments for a negative rate of inflation (deflation), in practice policy makers tend to aim for price stability—low but positive rates of inflation.

5. Countries that don't need to print money to cover government deficits can still stumble into moderate inflation, either because of political opportunism or because of wishful thinking. When this happens, getting inflation back down can be difficult because **disinflation** can be very costly, requiring the sacrifice of large amounts of aggregate output and imposing high levels of unemployment. However, policy makers in the United States and other wealthy countries were willing to pay the price of bringing down the high inflation of the 1970s.

6. Deflation poses several problems. It can lead to **debt deflation,** in which a rising real burden of outstanding debt intensifies an economic downturn. Also, interest rates are more likely to run up against the **zero bound** in an economy experiencing deflation. When this happens, the economy enters a **liquidity trap,** rendering monetary policy ineffective. Fears of a liquidity trap are the primary reason policy makers prefer price stability, a low but positive inflation rate.

KEY TERMS

Classical model of the price level, p. 795
Inflation tax, p. 798
Nominal interest rate, p. 801
Real interest rate, p. 801
Fisher effect, p. 802
Shoe-leather costs, p. 803
Unit-of-account costs, p. 804
Price stability, p. 805
Disinflation, p. 808
Debt deflation, p. 810
Zero bound, p. 810
Liquidity trap, p. 810

PROBLEMS

1. In the economy of Scottopia, policy makers want to lower the unemployment rate and raise real GDP by using monetary policy. Using the accompanying diagram, show why this policy will ultimately result in a higher aggregate price level but no change in real GDP.

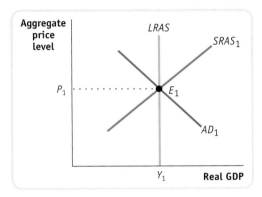

2. In the following examples, would the classical model of the price level be relevant?

a. There is a great deal of unemployment in the economy and no history of inflation.

b. The economy has just experienced five years of hyperinflation.

c. Although the economy experienced inflation in the 10% to 20% range 3 years ago, prices have recently been stable and the unemployment rate has approximated the natural rate of unemployment.

3. The Federal Reserve regularly releases data on the U.S. monetary base. You can access that data at various websites, including the website for the Federal Reserve Bank of St. Louis. Go to http://research.stlouisfed.org/fred2/ and click on "Reserves and Monetary Base" and then on "Board of Governors Monetary Base, Adjusted for Changes in Reserve Requirements, Seasonally Adjusted (SA)" for the latest report.

a. How much did the monetary base grow in the last month?

b. How did this help in the government's efforts to finance its deficit?

c. Why is it important for the central bank to be independent from the part of the government responsible for spending?

4. Answer the following questions about the (real) inflation tax, assuming that the price level starts at 1.

a. Maria Moneybags keeps $1,000 in her sock drawer for a year. Over the year, the inflation rate is 10%. What is the real inflation tax for this year?

b. Maria continues to keep the $1,000 in her drawer for a second year. What is the real value of this $1,000 at the beginning of the second year? Over the year, the inflation rate is again 10%. What is the real inflation tax for the second year?

c. For a third year, Maria keeps the $1,000 in the drawer. What is the real value of this $1,000 at the beginning of

the third year. Over the year, the inflation rate is again 10%. What is the real inflation tax for the third year?

d. After three years, what is the cumulative real inflation tax?

e. Redo parts a through d with an inflation rate of 25%. Why is hyperinflation such a problem?

5. Concerned about the crowding-out effects of government borrowing on private investment spending, a candidate for president argues that the United States should just print money to cover the government's budget deficit. What are the advantages and disadvantages of such a plan?

6. Boris Borrower and Lynn Lender agree that Lynn will lend Boris $10,000 and that Boris will repay the $10,000 with interest in one year. They agree to a nominal interest rate of 8%, reflecting a real interest rate of 3% on the loan and a commonly shared expected inflation rate of 5% over the next year.

a. If the inflation rate is actually 4% over the next year, how does that lower-than-expected inflation rate affect Boris and Lynn? Who is better off?

b. If the actual inflation rate is 7% over the next year, how does that affect Boris and Lynn? Who is better off?

7. Using the accompanying diagram, explain what will happen to the market for loanable funds when there is a fall of 2 percentage points in the expected future inflation rate. How will the change in the expected future inflation rate affect the equilibrium quantity of loanable funds?

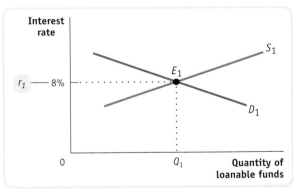

8. In the following examples, is inflation creating winners and losers at no net cost to the economy or is inflation imposing a net cost on the economy? If a net cost is being imposed, which type of cost is involved?

a. When inflation is expected to be high, workers get paid more frequently and make more trips to the bank.

b. Lanwei is reimbursed by her company for her work-related travel expenses. Sometimes, however, the company takes a long time to reimburse her. So when inflation is high, she is less willing to travel for her job.

c. Hector Homeowner has a mortgage with a fixed nominal 6% interest rate that he took out five years ago. Over the years, the inflation rate has crept up unexpectedly to its present level of 7%.

d. In response to unexpectedly high inflation, the manager of Cozy Cottages of Cape Cod must reprint and resend expensive color brochures correcting the price of rentals this season.

9. The accompanying diagram shows mortgage interest rates and inflation during 1990–2005 in the economy of Albernia. When would home mortgages have been especially attractive and why?

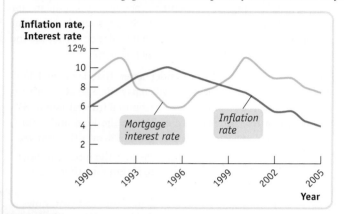

10. The accompanying diagram shows data for the short-term (three-month) nominal interest rate as reported by the European Central Bank and inflation for the euro area for 1996 through mid-2005. How would you describe the relationship between the two? How does the pattern compare to that of the United States in Figure 33-5?

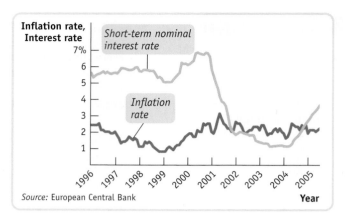

Source: European Central Bank

11. The economy of Brittania has been suffering from high inflation with an unemployment rate equal to its natural rate. Policy makers would like to disinflate the economy with the lowest economic cost possible. Assume that the state of the economy is not the result of a negative supply shock. How can they try to minimize the unemployment cost of disinflation? Is it possible for there to be no cost of disinflation?

12. Who are the winners and losers when a mortgage company lends $100,000 to the Miller family to buy a house worth $105,000 and during the first year prices unexpectedly fall by 10%? What would you expect to happen if the deflation continued over the next few years? How would continuing deflation affect the economy as a whole?

>**web**... To continue your study and review of concepts in this chapter, please visit the Krugman/Wells website for quizzes, animated graph tutorials, web links to helpful resources, and more.

www.worthpublishers.com/krugmanwells

>>The Making of Modern Macroeconomics

PURGE THE ROTTENNESS?

"AGGRESSIVE MONETARY POL-icy," declared the *2004 Economic Report of the President*, "can reduce the depth of a recession." Few modern macroeconomists would disagree. There are many public arguments about macroeconomic policy—arguments that can play a central role in political campaigns. But there is a broad consensus among macro-economists about how the economy works. The view that expansionary monetary policy can be effective in fighting recessions is part of that consensus. And that consensus is reflected in actual policy: as the two panels of the accompanying figure show, monetary policy responded very aggressively to the 2001 recession.

Yet today's consensus about monetary policy didn't always exist. There was a time when many economists opposed any effort to fight recessions. At the beginning of the Great Depression, Herbert Hoover's secretary of the treasury, Andrew Mellon, was firmly opposed to any monetary expansion. Hoover would later claim that Mellon's advice was to let the slump take its course: "It will purge the rottenness out of the system." This advice reflected the views of many eminent economists of the day, who regarded aggressive monetary policy as dangerous and ineffective.

When Franklin Roosevelt, Hoover's successor, took office, there was an intense debate among his advisers about whether to

An Example of Aggressive Monetary Policy

(a) The Money Supply Rose Sharply in Response to the 2001 Recession...

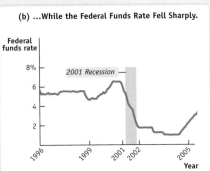

(b) ...While the Federal Funds Rate Fell Sharply.

The Fed responded to the 2001 recession, indicated by the shaded area in both panels, with a rapid expansion of the money supply (panel (a)) and sharp cuts in the federal funds rate (panel (b)).

Source: Federal Reserve Bank of St. Louis; National Bureau of Economic Research.

In 1930, as the U.S. economy plunged into the Great Depression, Herbert Hoover's economic advisers told him to let the economy suffer—it would "purge the rottenness." By contrast, in 2001, George W. Bush's economic advisers supported "aggressive" measures to fight a recession.

pursue expansionary monetary and fiscal policies or to do the opposite. When the expansionists won the debate and the United States went off the gold standard in order to permit monetary expansion, Roosevelt's budget director declared, "This is the end of Western civilization." As far as we can tell, Western civilization is still standing.

How did we get from there to here? How did modern macroeconomics evolve? In preceding chapters we've developed a framework for understanding growth, the business cycle, and inflation. In this chapter, we'll look at how this framework was created—how events and ideas interacted in the making of modern macroeconomics.

Classical Macroeconomics

The term *macroeconomics* appears to have been coined in 1933 by the Norwegian economist Ragnar Frisch; the date, during the worst year of the Great Depression, is no accident. Still, there were economists analyzing what we now consider macroeconomic issues—the behavior of the aggregate price level and aggregate output—before then.

Money and the Price Level

In Chapter 33 we described the *classical model of the price level*. According to the classical model, prices are flexible, making the aggregate supply curve vertical even in the short run. In this model, an increase in the money supply leads, other things equal, to an equal proportional rise in the aggregate price level, with no effect on aggregate output. As a result, increases in the money supply lead to inflation, and that's all. Before the 1930s, the classical model of the price level dominated economic thinking about the effects of monetary policy.

Did classical economists really believe that changes in the money supply affected only aggregate prices, without any effect on aggregate output? Probably not. Historians of economic thought argue that before 1930 most economists were aware that changes in the money supply affect aggregate output as well as aggregate prices in the short run—or, to use modern terms, they were aware that the short-run aggregate supply curve slopes upward. But they regarded such short-run effects as unimportant, stressing the long run instead. It was this attitude that led John Maynard Keynes to scoff at the focus on the long run, in which "we are all dead."

The Business Cycle

Classical economists were, of course, aware that the economy did not grow smoothly. The American economist Wesley Mitchell pioneered the quantitative study of business cycles. In 1920 he founded the National Bureau of Economic Research, an independent, nonprofit organization that to this day has the official role of declaring the beginnings of recessions and expansions. Thanks to Mitchell's work, the *measurement* of business cycles was well advanced by 1930. But there was no widely accepted *theory* of business cycles.

In the absence of any clear theory, views about how policy makers should respond to a recession were conflicting. Some economists favored expansionary monetary and fiscal policies to fight a recession. Others believed that such policies would worsen the slump or merely postpone the inevitable. For example, in 1934 Harvard's Joseph Schumpeter, now famous for his early recognition of the importance of technological change, warned that any attempt to alleviate the Great Depression with expansionary monetary policy "would, in the end, lead to a collapse worse than the one it was called in to remedy." When the Great Depression hit, policy was paralyzed by this lack of consensus. In many cases, economists now believe, policy moved in the wrong direction.

Necessity was, however, the mother of invention. As we'll explain next, the Great Depression provided a strong incentive for economists to develop theories that could serve as a guide to policy—and economists responded.

economics in action

When Did the Business Cycle Begin?

The official chronology of past U.S. business cycles maintained by the National Bureau of Economic Research goes back only to 1854. There are two reasons for this. One is that the farther back in time you go, the less economic data are available. The other is that business cycles, in the modern sense, may have not occurred often in the United States before 1854.

In the first half of the nineteenth century the United States was overwhelmingly a rural, agricultural economy. Figure 34-1 shows estimates of the changing percentages of GDP coming from agriculture and from manufacturing and mining over the period from 1840 to 1900. The figure shows that agriculture dwarfed manufacturing in

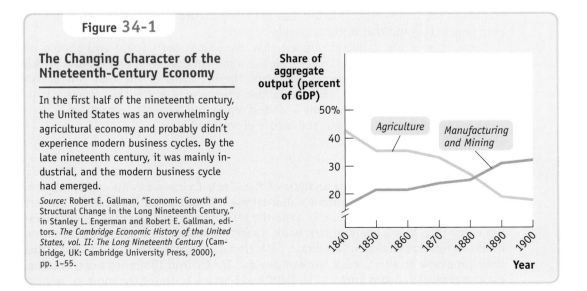

Figure 34-1

The Changing Character of the Nineteenth-Century Economy

In the first half of the nineteenth century, the United States was an overwhelmingly agricultural economy and probably didn't experience modern business cycles. By the late nineteenth century, it was mainly industrial, and the modern business cycle had emerged.

Source: Robert E. Gallman, "Economic Growth and Structural Change in the Long Nineteenth Century," in Stanley L. Engerman and Robert E. Gallman, editors. *The Cambridge Economic History of the United States, vol. II: The Long Nineteenth Century* (Cambridge, UK: Cambridge University Press, 2000), pp. 1–55.

1840 and that manufacturing didn't overtake agriculture in economic importance until the 1880s.

Why does this matter? Fluctuations in aggregate output in agricultural economies are very different from the business cycles we know today. That's because prices of agricultural goods tend to be highly flexible. As a result, the short-run aggregate supply curve of a mainly agricultural economy is probably close to vertical, so demand shocks don't cause output fluctuations. Instead, fluctuations on the farm are driven mainly by weather, making shifts of the short-run aggregate supply curve the primary source of fluctuations. In contrast, modern business cycles are largely the result of shifts in the aggregate demand curve.

The modern business cycle probably originated in Britain—home of the Industrial Revolution—which was already a largely industrial and urban society by 1820. The British recession of 1846–1847 had a particularly modern feel: it followed a bout of "irrational exuberance" in which firms spent heavily on an exciting new technology—railroads—and then realized they had overdone it. ■

< < < < < < < < < < < < < < < < < < <

>> **QUICK REVIEW**

➤ Classical macroeconomists focused on the long-run effects of monetary policy on the aggregate price level, ignoring any short-run effects on aggregate output.
➤ By the time of the Great Depression, the measurement of business cycles was well advanced, but there was no widely accepted theory about why they happened.

>>**CHECK YOUR UNDERSTANDING 34-1**

1. Panel (a) of the figure that opened this chapter, on page 815, shows the behavior of M1 before, during, and after the 2001 recession.
   a. How do these data tie in with the quotation from the *Economic Report of the President* that opens this chapter?
   b. What would a classical economist have said about the Fed's policy?

Solutions appear at back of book.

The Great Depression and the Keynesian Revolution

The Great Depression demonstrated, once and for all, that economists cannot safely ignore the short run. Not only was the economic pain severe; it threatened to destabilize societies and political systems. In particular, the economic plunge helped Adolf Hitler rise to power in Germany.

The whole world wanted to know how this economic disaster could be happening and what should be done about it. But because there was no widely accepted theory of the business cycle, economists gave conflicting and, we now believe, often harmful advice. Some believed that only a huge change in the economic system—such as having the government take over much of private industry and replace markets with a command economy—could end the slump. Others argued that slumps were natural—even beneficial—and that nothing should be done.

Some economists, however, argued that the slump both could and should be cured—without giving up on the basic idea of a market economy. In 1930 the British economist John Maynard Keynes compared the problems of the U.S. and British economies to those of a car with a defective alternator. Getting the economy running, he argued, would require only a modest repair, not a complete overhaul.

Nice metaphor. But what was the nature of the trouble?

Keynes's Theory

In 1936 Keynes presented his analysis of the Great Depression—his explanation of what was wrong with the economy's alternator—in a book titled *The General Theory of Employment, Interest, and Money.* In 1946 the great American economist Paul Samuelson wrote that "it is a badly written book, poorly organized. . . . Flashes of insight and intuition intersperse tedious algebra . . . We find its analysis to be obvious and at the same time new. In short, it is a work of genius." *The General Theory* isn't easy reading, but it stands with Adam Smith's *The Wealth of Nations* as one of the most influential books on economics ever written.

As Samuelson's description suggests, Keynes's book is a vast stew of ideas. The school of thought that came to be known as **Keynesian economics** mainly reflected two innovations.

First, Keynes emphasized the short-run effects of shifts in aggregate demand on aggregate output, rather than the long-run determination of the aggregate price level. As Keynes's famous remark about being dead in the long run suggests, until his book appeared most economists had treated short-run macroeconomics as a minor issue. Keynes focused the attention of economists on situations in which the short-run aggregate supply curve slopes upward and shifts in the aggregate demand curve affect aggregate output and employment as well as aggregate prices.

Figure 34-2 illustrates the difference between Keynesian and classical macroeconomics. Both panels of the figure show the short-run aggregate supply curve, *SRAS*; in both it is assumed that for some reason the aggregate demand curve shifts leftward from AD_1 to AD_2—let's say in response to a fall in stock market values that leads households to reduce consumer spending.

Panel (a) shows the classical view: the short-run aggregate supply curve is vertical. The decline in aggregate demand leads to a fall in the price level, from P_1 to P_2, but no change in real GDP. Panel (b) shows the Keynesian view: the short-run aggregate supply curve slopes upward, so the decline in aggregate demand leads to both a fall in the price level, from P_1 to P_2, and a fall in real GDP, from Y_1 to Y_2. As we've already explained, many classical macroeconomists would have agreed that panel (b) was an accurate story in the short run—but they regarded the short run as unimportant. Keynes disagreed. (Just to be clear, there isn't any diagram that looks like panel (b) of Figure 34-2 in Keynes's *General Theory*. But Keynes's discussion of aggregate supply, translated into modern terminology, clearly implies an upward-sloping *SRAS* curve.)

Second, classical economists emphasized the role of changes in the money supply in shifting the aggregate demand curve, paying little attention to other factors. Keynes, however, argued that other factors, especially changes in "animal spirits"—these days usually referred to with the bland term *business confidence*—are mainly responsible for business cycles. Before Keynes, economists often argued that a decline in business confidence would have no effect on either the aggregate price level or aggregate output, as long as the money supply stayed constant. Keynes offered a very different picture.

The school of thought that emerged out of the works of John Maynard Keynes is known as **Keynesian economics**.

Figure 34-2   Classical Versus Keynesian Macroeconomics

One important difference between classical and Keynesian economics involves the short-run aggregate supply curve. Panel (a) shows the classical view: the *SRAS* curve is vertical, so shifts in aggregate demand affect the aggregate price level but not aggregate output. Panel (b) shows the Keynesian view: in the short run the *SRAS* curve slopes upward, so shifts in aggregate demand affect aggregate output as well as aggregate prices. **>web...**

THE POLITICS OF KEYNES

The term *Keynesian economics* is sometimes used as a synonym for *left-wing economics:* authors seem to believe that because Keynes offered a rationale for some kinds of government activism, he was a leftist of some kind, maybe even a socialist. But the truth is more complicated.

As we explain in the text, Keynesian ideas have actually been accepted across a broad part of the political spectrum. In 2004 the president was a conservative, as was his top economist, N. Gregory Mankiw; but Mankiw is also the editor of a collection of readings titled *New Keynesian Economics*.

And Keynes himself was no socialist—and not much of a leftist. At the time the *General Theory* was published, many intellectuals in Britain believed that the Great Depression was the final crisis of the capitalist economic system and that only a

Some people use *Keynesian economics* as a synonym for *left-wing economics*—but the truth is that the ideas of John Maynard Keynes have been accepted across a broad part of the political spectrum.

government takeover of industry could save the economy. Keynes, in contrast, argued that all the system needed was a narrow technical fix. In that sense, his ideas were pro-capitalist and politically conservative.

What is true is that the rise of Keynesian economics in the 1940s, 1950s, and 1960s went along with a general rise in the role of government in the economy and that those who favored a larger role for government tended to be enthusiastic Keynesians. Conversely, a swing of the pendulum back toward free-market policies in the 1970s and 1980s was accompanied by a series of challenges to Keynesian ideas, which we describe later in this chapter. But it's perfectly possible to have conservative political preferences while respecting Keynes's contribution and equally possible to be very liberal while questioning Keynes's ideas.

Keynes's ideas have penetrated deeply into the public consciousness, to the extent that many people who have never heard of Keynes, or have heard of him but think they disagree with his theory, use Keynesian ideas all the time. For example, suppose that a business commentator says something like this: "Because of a decline in business confidence, investment spending slumped, causing a recession." Whether the commentator knows it or not, that statement is pure Keynesian economics.

Keynes himself more or less predicted that his ideas would become part of what "everyone knows." In another famous passage, this from the end of *The General Theory*, he wrote: "Practical men, who believe themselves to be quite exempt from any intellectual influences, are usually the slaves of some defunct economist."

Policy to Fight Recessions

> **Macroeconomic policy activism** is the use of monetary and fiscal policy to smooth out the business cycle.

The main practical consequence of Keynes's work was that it legitimized **macroeconomic policy activism**—the use of monetary and fiscal policy to smooth out the business cycle.

Macroeconomic policy activism wasn't something completely new. Before Keynes, many economists had argued for using monetary expansion to fight economic downturns—though others were fiercely opposed. Some economists had even argued that temporary budget deficits were a good thing in times of recession—though others disagreed strongly. In practice, during the 1930s many governments followed policies that we would now call Keynesian. In the United States, the administration of Franklin Roosevelt engaged in modest deficit spending in an effort to create jobs.

But these efforts were half-hearted. As we saw in the introduction, Roosevelt's advisers were deeply divided over the appropriate policies to take. In fact, in 1937 Roosevelt gave in to advice from non-Keynesian economists who urged him to balance the budget and raise interest rates, even though the economy was still depressed. The result was a renewed slump.

Today, by contrast, there is broad consensus about the useful role monetary and fiscal policy can play in fighting recessions. The *2004 Economic Report of the President,* quoted at the beginning of this chapter, was issued by a conservative Republican administration that was generally opposed to government intervention in the economy. Yet its view on economic policy in the face of recession was far more like that of Keynes than like that of most economists before 1936.

It would be wrong, however, to suggest that Keynes's ideas have been fully accepted by modern macroeconomists. In the decades that followed the publication of *The General Theory,* Keynesian economics faced a series of challenges, some of which succeeded in modifying the macroeconomic consensus in important ways.

economics in action

The End of the Great Depression

It would make a good story if Keynes's ideas had led to a change in economic policy that brought the Great Depression to an end. Unfortunately, that's not what happened. Still, the way the Depression ended did a lot to convince economists that Keynes was right.

The basic message many of the young economists who adopted Keynes's ideas in the 1930s took from his work was that economic recovery requires aggressive fiscal expansion—deficit spending on a large scale to create jobs. And that is what they eventually got, but it wasn't because politicians were persuaded. Instead, what happened was a very large war.

Figure 34-3 shows the U.S. unemployment rate and the federal budget deficit as a share of GDP from 1930 to 1947. As you can see, deficit spending during the 1930s was on a modest scale. As the risk of war grew larger, the United States began a large military buildup, and the budget moved deep into deficit. After the attack on Pearl Harbor on December 7, 1941, the country began deficit spending on an enormous scale: in fiscal 1943, which began in July 1942, the deficit was 30% of GDP. Today that would be a deficit of $3.5 trillion.

And the economy recovered. World War II wasn't intended as a Keynesian fiscal policy, but it demonstrated that expansionary fiscal policy can, in fact, create jobs in the short run. ■

> >

>>QUICK REVIEW

➤ *Keynesian economics,* based on the ideas of John Maynard Keynes, emerged in the 1930s.
➤ The key ideas of Keynesian economics are an emphasis on the short run, in which the *SRAS* curve slopes upward rather than being vertical, and an emphasis on how factors in addition to the money supply affect the *AD* curve.
➤ Keynesian economics provided a rationale for *macroeconomic policy activism.*
➤ Keynesian ideas are widely used even by people who haven't heard of Keynes or think they disagree with him.

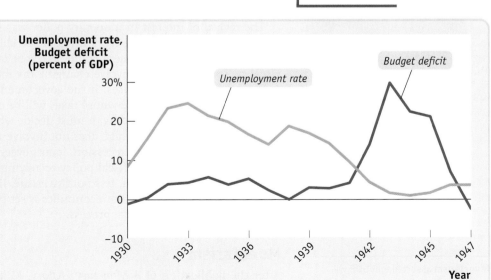

Figure 34-3

Fiscal Policy and the End of the Great Depression

During the 1930s, in an effort to prop up the economy, the U.S. government began deficit spending. The deficits were, however, fairly small as a percentage of GDP. In 1937 the government even tried to balance the budget, only to face a renewed rise in unemployment. The onset of World War II brought on deficit spending on a massive scale and ended the Great Depression.

Source: U.S. Census Bureau.

1. In addition to praising aggressive monetary policy, the *2004 Economic Report of the President* says that "tax cuts can boost economic activity by raising after-tax income and enhancing incentives to work, save, and invest." Is this a Keynesian statement? Why or why not?

Solution appears at back of book.

Challenges to Keynesian Economics

Keynes's ideas fundamentally changed the way economists think about business cycles. They did not, however, go unquestioned. In the decades that followed the publication of *The General Theory*, Keynesian economics faced a series of challenges. As a result, the consensus of macroeconomists retreated somewhat from the strong version of Keynesianism that prevailed in the 1950s. In particular, economists became much more aware of the limits to macroeconomic policy activism.

The Revival of Monetary Policy

Keynes's *General Theory* suggested that monetary policy wouldn't be very effective in depression conditions. Many modern macroeconomists agree: in Chapter 33 we introduced the concept of a *liquidity trap,* a situation in which monetary policy is ineffective because the nominal interest rate is down against the zero bound. In the 1930s, when Keynes wrote, interest rates were, in fact, very close to 0%. (The term *liquidity trap* was first introduced by the British economist John Hicks in a 1937 paper, "Mr. Keynes and The Classics: A Suggested Interpretation," that summarized Keynes's ideas.)

But even when the era of near-0% interest rates came to an end after World War II, many economists continued to emphasize fiscal policy and downplay the usefulness of monetary policy. Eventually, however, macroeconomists reassessed the importance of monetary policy. A key milestone in this reassessment was the 1963 publication of *A Monetary History of the United States, 1867–1960* by Milton Friedman, of the University of Chicago, and Anna Schwartz, of the National Bureau of Economic Research. Friedman and Schwartz showed that business cycles had historically been associated with fluctuations in the money supply. In particular, the money supply fell sharply during the onset of the Great Depression. Friedman and Schwartz persuaded many, though not all, economists that the Great Depression could have been avoided if the Federal Reserve had acted to prevent that monetary contraction. They persuaded most economists that monetary policy should play a key role in economic management.

The revival of interest in monetary policy was significant because it suggested that the burden of managing the economy could be shifted away from fiscal policy—meaning that economic management could largely be taken out of the hands of politicians. Fiscal policy, which must involve changing tax rates or government spending, necessarily involves political choices. If the government tries to stimulate the economy by cutting taxes, it must decide whose taxes will be cut. If it tries to stimulate the economy with government spending, it must decide what to spend the money on.

Monetary policy, in contrast, does not involve such choices: when the central bank cuts interest rates to fight a recession, it cuts everyone's interest rate at the same time. So a shift from relying on fiscal policy to relying on monetary policy makes macroeconomics a more technical, less political issue. In fact, as we learned in Chapter 31, monetary policy in most major economies is set by an independent central bank that is insulated from the political process.

Milton Friedman and his co-author Anna Schwartz played a key role in convincing macroeconomists of the importance of monetary policy.

Roger Ressmeyer / Corbis

Monetarism

After the publication of *A Monetary History,* Milton Friedman led a movement that sought to eliminate macroeconomic policy activism while maintaining the importance of monetary policy. **Monetarism** asserted that GDP will grow steadily if the

Monetarism asserted that GDP will grow steadily if the money supply grows steadily.

money supply grows steadily. The monetarist policy prescription was to have the central bank target a constant rate of growth of the money supply, such as 3% per year, and maintain that target regardless of any fluctuations in the economy.

It's important to realize that monetarism retained many Keynesian ideas. Like Keynes, Friedman asserted that the short run is important and that short-run changes in aggregate demand affect aggregate output as well as aggregate prices. Like Keynes, he argued that policy should have been much more expansionary during the Great Depression.

Monetarists argued, however, that most of the efforts of policy makers to smooth out the economy's ups and downs actually make things worse. In Chapter 29 we discussed the reasons macroeconomists are skeptical about the usefulness of *discretionary fiscal policy*—changes in taxes or spending, or both, in response to the perceived state of the economy. As we explained there, government perceptions about the economy often lag behind reality, and there are further lags both in changing fiscal policy and in the effects of fiscal policy on the economy. As a result, discretionary fiscal policies intended to fight a recession often end up feeding a boom, and vice versa.

Friedman also argued that if the central bank followed his advice and refused to change the money supply in response to fluctuations in the economy, fiscal policy would be much less effective than Keynesians believed. In Chapter 26 we analyzed the phenomenon of *crowding out,* in which government deficits drive up interest rates and lead to reduced investment spending. Friedman and others pointed out that if the money supply is held fixed while the government pursues an expansionary fiscal policy, crowding out will limit the effect of the fiscal expansion on aggregate demand.

Figure 34-4 illustrates this argument. Panel (a) shows aggregate output and the aggregate price level. AD_1 is the initial aggregate demand curve and *SRAS* is the short-run aggregate supply curve. At the initial equilibrium E_1, the level of aggregate output is Y_1 and the aggregate price level is P_1. Panel (b) shows the money market. *MS* is the money supply curve and MD_1 is the initial money demand curve, so the initial interest rate is r_1.

Now suppose the government increases purchases of goods and services. We know that this will shift the *AD* curve rightward, as illustrated by the shift from AD_1 to

Figure 34-4   Fiscal Policy with a Fixed Money Supply

(a) The Increase in Aggregate Demand from an Expansionary Fiscal Policy is Limited When the Money Supply is Fixed...

(b) ...Because the Increase in Money Demand Drives up the Interest Rate, Crowding out Some Investment Spending.

In panel (a) an expansionary fiscal policy shifts the *AD* curve rightward, driving up both the aggregate price level and aggregate output. However, this leads to an increase in the demand for money. If the money supply is held fixed, as in panel (b), the increase in money demand drives up the interest rate, reducing investment spending and offsetting part of the fiscal expansion. So the shift of the *AD* curve is less than it would otherwise be: fiscal policy becomes less effective when the money supply is held fixed.

AD_2, and that aggregate output will rise, from Y_1 to Y_2, and the aggregate price level will rise, from P_1 to P_2. Both the rise in aggregate output and the rise in the aggregate price level will, however, increase the demand for money, shifting the money demand curve rightward from MD_1 to MD_2. This drives up the equilibrium interest rate, to r_2. Friedman's point was that this rise in the interest rate reduces investment spending, partially offsetting the initial rise in government spending. As a result, the rightward shift of the AD curve is smaller than the multiplier analysis in Chapter 29 indicated. And Friedman argued that with a constant money supply, the multiplier is so small that there's not much point in using fiscal policy.

But Friedman didn't favor activist monetary policy either. He argued that the same problems that limit the ability of the government to stabilize the economy using discretionary fiscal policy also apply to **discretionary monetary policy,** in which the central bank changes interest rates or the money supply based on its assessment of the state of the economy.

Friedman's solution was to put monetary policy on "autopilot." The central bank, he argued, should follow a **monetary policy rule,** a formula that determines its actions. During the 1960s and 1970s, most monetarists believed that the best monetary policy rule was to target slow, steady growth in the money supply. They thought this would work because they believed that the *velocity of money,* which we defined in Chapter 31 as the ratio of nominal GDP to the quantity of money, was stable in the short run and changes only gradually. Recall the velocity equation:

$$M \times V = P \times Y$$

In this equation, M is the money supply, V is the velocity of money, P is the aggregate price level, and Y is real GDP (so that $P \times Y$ is nominal GDP.) Monetarists believed that V was stable, so they believed that if the Federal Reserve kept M on a steady growth path, nominal GDP would also grow steadily.

Monetarism strongly influenced actual monetary policy in the late 1970s and early 1980s, as described in the Economics in Action that follows this section. It quickly became clear, however, that steady growth in the money supply didn't ensure steady growth in the economy: the velocity of money wasn't stable enough for such a simple policy rule to work. Figure 34-5 shows both why monetarists of the 1960s and 1970s had reason to believe in their simple monetary policy rule and how later events let them down. The figure shows the velocity of money, as measured by the ratio of nominal GDP to M1, from 1960 to the start of 2005. As you can see, until 1980 velocity followed a fairly smooth, seemingly predictable trend. After 1980, however,

> When the central bank changes interest rates or the money supply based on its assessment of the state of the economy, it is engaging in **discretionary monetary policy.**
>
> A **monetary policy rule** is a formula that determines the central bank's actions.

Figure 34-5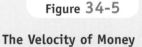

The Velocity of Money

From 1960 to 1980, the velocity of money was stable, leading monetarists to believe that steady growth in the money supply would lead to a stable economy. After 1980, however, velocity began moving erratically, undermining the case for traditional monetarism. **>web...**

Source: Federal Reserve Bank of St. Louis.

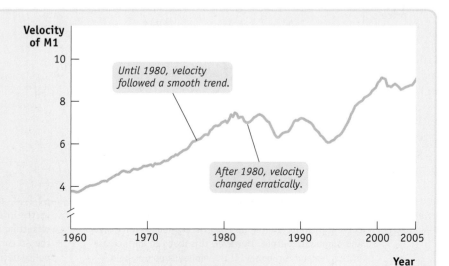

after the Fed began to adopt monetarist ideas, the velocity of money began shifting around erratically—probably due to financial market innovations.

Traditional monetarists are hard to find among today's macroeconomists. As we'll see later in the chapter, however, the monetarist idea that too much discretion in monetary policy is counterproductive has been widely accepted by macroeconomists.

Inflation and the Natural Rate of Unemployment

At the same time that monetarists were challenging Keynesian views about how macroeconomic policy should be conducted, other economists—some but not all of them monetarists—were emphasizing the limits to what activist macroeconomic policy could achieve.

In the 1940s and 1950s, many Keynesian economists believed that expansionary fiscal policy could be used to achieve full employment on a permanent basis. In the 1960s, however, many economists realized that expansionary policies could cause problems with inflation, but they still believed policy makers could choose to trade off low unemployment for higher inflation even in the long run.

In 1968, however, Milton Friedman and Edmund Phelps of Columbia University, working independently, proposed the concept of the natural rate of unemployment, which we discussed in Chapter 32. We showed there that the natural rate of unemployment is also the nonaccelerating inflation rate of unemployment, or NAIRU. According to the hypothesis of the NAIRU, inflation eventually gets built into expectations, so any attempt to keep the unemployment rate below the natural rate will lead to an ever-rising inflation rate.

The natural rate hypothesis gives a more limited role to activist macroeconomic policy than did earlier ideas. Because the government can't keep unemployment below the natural rate, its task is not to keep unemployment low but to keep it *stable*— to prevent large fluctuations in unemployment in either direction.

The important point to notice about the Friedman–Phelps hypothesis is that it made a strong prediction. Friedman and Phelps claimed that the apparent trade-off between unemployment and inflation would not survive an extended period of rising prices: once inflation was embedded in the public's expectations, inflation would continue even in the face of high unemployment. Sure enough, that's exactly what happened in the 1970s. This successful prediction was one of the triumphs of macroeconomic analysis, and it convinced the great majority of economists that the natural rate hypothesis was correct. In contrast to traditional monetarism, which declined in influence as more evidence accumulated, the natural rate hypothesis has become almost universally accepted among macroeconomists, with a few qualifications. (Some macroeconomists believe that at very low or negative rates of inflation the hypothesis doesn't work.)

The Political Business Cycle

One final challenge to Keynesian economics focused not on the validity of the economic analysis but on its political consequences. A number of economists and political scientists pointed out that activist macroeconomic policy lends itself to political manipulation.

Statistical evidence suggests that election results tend to be determined by the state of the economy in the months just before the election. In the United States, if the economy is growing rapidly and the unemployment rate is falling in the six months or so before Election Day, the incumbent party tends to be re-elected even if the economy performed poorly in the preceding three years.

This creates an obvious temptation to abuse activist macroeconomic policy: pump up the economy in an election year, and pay the price in higher inflation and/or higher unemployment later. The result can be unnecessary instability in the economy, a **political business cycle** caused by the use of macroeconomic policy to serve political ends.

An often-cited example is the combination of expansionary fiscal and monetary policy that led to rapid growth in the U.S. economy just before the 1972 election and a sharp acceleration in inflation after the election. Kenneth Rogoff, a respected macroeconomist

A **political business cycle** results when politicians use macroeconomic policy to serve political ends.

who served as chief economist at the International Monetary Fund, has proclaimed Richard Nixon, the president at the time, "the all-time hero of political business cycles."

As we saw in Chapter 31, one way to avoid a political business cycle is to place monetary policy in the hands of an independent central bank, insulated from political pressure. The political business cycle is also a reason to rule out the use of discretionary fiscal policy except in extreme circumstances.

economics in action

The Fed's Flirtation with Monetarism

In the late 1970s and early 1980s the Federal Reserve flirted with monetarism. For most of its prior existence, the Fed had targeted interest rates, adjusting its target based on the state of the economy. In the late 1970s, however, the Fed began announcing target ranges for several measures of the money supply. It also stopped setting targets for interest rates. Most people saw these changes as a strong move toward monetarism.

In 1982, however, the Fed turned its back on monetarism. Since 1982 the Fed has pursued a discretionary monetary policy, which has led to large swings in the money supply. And at the end of the 1980s, the Fed went back to setting target levels for the interest rate.

Why did the Fed flirt with monetarism, then give it up? The turn to monetarism largely reflected the events of the 1970s, when a sharp rise in inflation had the effect of discrediting traditional economic policies. Also, the fact that the natural rate hypothesis had successfully predicted a worsening of the trade-off between unemployment and inflation increased the prestige of Milton Friedman and his intellectual followers. So policy makers were willing to try Friedman's policy proposals.

The turn away from monetarism also reflected events: as we saw in Figure 34-5, the velocity of money, which had followed a smooth trend before 1980, became erratic after 1980. This made monetarism seem like a much less good idea. ∎

< < < < < < < < < < < < < < < < < <

>>CHECK YOUR UNDERSTANDING 34-3

1. Panel (a) of the figure on page 815 shows recent movements in M1. What would that diagram have looked like if the Fed had been following a monetarist policy since 1996?

2. Now look at Figure 34-5 on page 824. What problems do you think the United States would have had since 1996 if the Fed had followed a monetarist policy?

Solutions appear at back of book.

Rational Expectations, Real Business Cycles, and New Classical Macroeconomics

As we have seen, one key difference between classical economics and Keynesian economics is that classical economists believed that the short-run aggregate supply curve is vertical, but Keynes emphasized the idea that the aggregate supply curve slopes upward in the short run. As a result, Keynes argued that demand shocks—shifts in the aggregate demand curve—can cause fluctuations in aggregate output.

The challenges to Keynesian economics that arose in the 1950s and 1960s—the renewed emphasis on monetary policy and the natural rate hypothesis—didn't question the view that an increase in aggregate demand leads to a rise in aggregate output in the short run and that a decrease in aggregate demand leads to a fall in aggregate output in the short run. In the 1970s and 1980s, however, some economists developed an approach to the business cycle known as **new classical macroeconomics,** which returned to the classical view that shifts in the aggregate demand curve affect only the aggregate price level, not aggregate output. The new approach evolved in two steps. First, some economists challenged traditional arguments about the slope of the short-run aggregate supply curve based on the concept

>> QUICK REVIEW

- Early Keynesianism downplayed the effectiveness of monetary as opposed to fiscal policy, but later macroeconomists realized that monetary policy is effective.
- *Monetarism* argued that *discretionary monetary policy* does more harm than good and that a simple *monetary policy rule* is the best way to stabilize the economy. This doctrine was popular for a time but has receded in influence.
- The natural rate hypothesis, now very widely accepted, places sharp limits on what macroeconomic policy can achieve.
- Concerns about a *political business cycle* suggest that the central bank should be independent and that discretionary fiscal policy should be avoided except in dire circumstances.

New classical macroeconomics is an approach to the business cycle that returns to the classical view that shifts in the aggregate demand curve affect only the aggregate price level, not aggregate output.

of *rational expectations*. Second, some economists suggested that changes in productivity cause economic fluctuations, a view known as *real business cycle theory*.

Rational Expectations

In the 1970s a concept known as *rational expectations* had a powerful impact on macroeconomics. **Rational expectations,** a theory originally introduced by John Muth in 1961, is the view that individuals and firms make decisions optimally, using all available information.

> **Rational expectations** is the view that individuals and firms make decisions optimally, using all available information.

For example, workers and employers bargaining over long-term wage contracts need to estimate the inflation rate they expect over the life of that contract. Rational expectations says that in making estimates of future inflation, they won't just look at past rates of inflation; they will also take into account available information about monetary and fiscal policy. Suppose that prices didn't rise last year but that the monetary and fiscal policies announced by policy makers make it clear to economic analysts that there will be substantial inflation over the next few years. According to rational expectations, long-term wage contracts will reflect this future inflation, even though prices didn't rise in the past.

Rational expectations can make a major difference in the effects of government policy. According to the original version of the natural rate hypothesis, a government attempt to trade off higher inflation for lower unemployment would work in the short run but would eventually fail because higher inflation would get built into expectations. According to rational expectations, we should remove the word *eventually*: if it's clear that the government intends to trade off higher inflation for lower unemployment, the public will understand this, and inflation expectations will immediately rise.

In the 1970s Robert Lucas of the University of Chicago, in a series of very influential papers, used this logic to argue that monetary policy can change the level of unemployment only if it comes as a surprise to the public. If his analysis was right, monetary policy isn't useful in stabilizing the economy after all. In 1995, Lucas won the Nobel Prize in economics for this work, which remains widely admired. However, many—perhaps most—macroeconomists, especially those advising policy makers, now believe that his conclusions were overstated. The Federal Reserve certainly thinks that it can play a useful role in economic stabilization, a view seconded by the quote from the *2004 Economic Report of the President* that opened this chapter. Nonetheless, the idea of rational expectations did serve as a useful caution for macroeconomists who had become excessively optimistic about their ability to manage the economy.

Real Business Cycles

In Chapter 25 we introduced the concept of *total factor productivity,* the amount of output that can be generated with a given level of factor inputs. Total factor productivity grows over time, but that growth isn't smooth. In the 1980s a number of economists argued that slowdowns in productivity growth, which they attributed to pauses in technological progress, are the main cause of recessions. **Real business cycle theory** says that fluctuations in the rate of growth of total factor productivity cause the business cycle. In the early days of real business cycle theory, the theory's proponents denied that changes in aggregate demand have any effect on aggregate output.

> According to **real business cycle theory,** fluctuations in the rate of growth of total factor productivity cause the business cycle.

This theory was strongly influential, as shown by the fact that two of the founders of real business cycle theory, Finn Kydland of Carnegie-Mellon University and Edward Prescott of the Federal Reserve Bank of Minneapolis, won the 2004 Nobel Prize in economics. The current status of real business cycle theory, however, is somewhat similar to that of rational expectations. The theory is widely recognized as having made valuable contributions to our understanding of the economy, and it serves as a useful caution against too much emphasis on aggregate demand. But many of the real business cycle theorists themselves now acknowledge that their models need an upward-sloping aggregate supply curve to fit the data—and that this gives aggregate demand a potential role in determining aggregate output. And as we have seen, policy makers believe strongly that aggregate demand policy has an important role to play in fighting recessions.

During the 1970s a group of economic writers began propounding a view of economic policy that came to be known as "supply-side economics." The core of this view was the belief that reducing tax rates, and so increasing the incentives to work and invest, would have a powerful positive effect on the growth rate of potential output. The supply-siders urged the government to cut taxes without worrying about matching spending cuts: economic growth, they argued, would offset any negative effects from budget deficits. Some supply-siders even argued that a cut in tax *rates* would have such a miraculous effect on economic growth that tax *revenues*—the total

amount taxpayers pay to the government—would actually rise.

In the 1970s supply-side economics was enthusiastically supported by the editors of the *Wall Street Journal* and other figures in the media, and it became popular with politicians. In 1980 Ronald Reagan made supply-side economics the basis of his presidential campaign.

Because supply-side economics emphasizes supply rather than demand, and because the supply-siders themselves are harshly critical of Keynesian economics, it might seem as if supply-side theory belongs in our discussion of new classical macroeconomics. But unlike rational expectations and real business cycle

theory, supply-side economics is generally dismissed by economic researchers.

The main reason for this dismissal is lack of evidence. Almost all economists agree that tax cuts increase incentives to work and invest, but attempts to estimate these incentive effects indicate that at current U.S. levels they aren't nearly strong enough to back the strong claims made by supply-siders. In particular, the supply-side doctrine implies that large tax cuts, such as those implemented by Ronald Reagan in the early 1980s, should sharply raise potential output. Yet estimates of potential output by the Congressional Budget Office and others show no sign of an acceleration in growth after the Reagan tax cuts.

economics in action

Total Factor Productivity and the Business Cycle

Real business cycle theory argues that fluctuations in the rate of growth of total factor productivity are the principal cause of business cycles. Although many macroeconomists dispute that claim, the theory did draw attention to the fact that there is a strong correlation between the rate of total factor productivity growth and the business cycle. Figure 34-6 shows the annual rate of total factor productivity growth estimated by the Bureau of Labor Statistics. The shaded areas represent recessions. Clearly, recessions tend also to be periods in which the growth of total factor productivity slows sharply or even turns negative. And real business cycle theorists deserve a lot of credit for drawing economists' attention to this fact.

There are, however, disputes about how to interpret this correlation. In the early days of real business cycle theory, new classical macroeconomists argued that

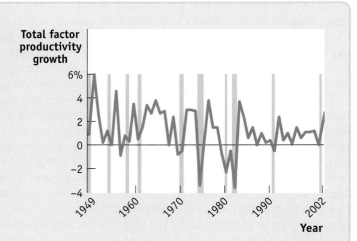

Figure 34-6

Total Factor Productivity and the Business Cycle

There is a clear correlation between declines in the rate of total factor productivity growth and recessions (indicated by the shaded areas). Real business cycle theory says that fluctuations in productivity growth are the main cause of business cycles. Other economists argue, however, that business cycles cause productivity fluctuations, not the other way around.

Source: Bureau of Labor Statistics; National Bureau of Economic Research.

productivity fluctuations are entirely the result of uneven technological progress. Critics pointed out, however, that in really severe recessions, like those of 1974–1975 or the early 1980s, total factor productivity actually declines. And it's hard to believe that technology actually moved backward during those periods.

So what is going on during these periods of declining total factor productivity? Some economists argue that declining productivity during recessions is a result, not a cause, of economic downturns. An example may be helpful. Suppose we measure productivity at the local post office by the number of pieces of mail handled, divided by the number of postal workers. Since the post office doesn't lay off workers whenever there's a slow mail day, days on which not much mail comes in will seem to be days on which the workers are especially unproductive. But the slump in business is causing the apparent decline in productivity, not the other way around.

It's now widely accepted that some of the correlation between total factor productivity and the business cycle is the result of the effect of the business cycle on productivity, rather than the reverse. But the extent to which this is true is a subject of continuing research. ∎   > —

> > ## CHECK YOUR UNDERSTANDING 34-4

1. In early 2001, as it became clear that the United States was experiencing a recession, the Fed stated that it would fight the recession with an aggressive monetary policy. By 2004, most observers concluded that this aggressive monetary expansion should be given credit for ending the recession.

a. What would rational expectations theorists say about this conclusion?

b. What would real business cycle theorists say?

Solutions appear at back of book.

> ## QUICK REVIEW
>
> ➤ *New classical macroeconomics* argues that the short-run aggregate supply curve may be vertical after all.
>
> ➤ *Rational expectations* suggests that because workers and firms take all information into account, only unexpected changes in the money supply affect aggregate output.
>
> ➤ *Real business cycle theory* argues that fluctuations in the rate of productivity growth cause the business cycle.

The Modern Consensus

As we've seen, there were intense debates about macroeconomics in the 1960s, 1970s, and 1980s. More recently, however, things have settled down. The age of macroeconomic controversy is by no means over, but there is now a broad consensus about several crucial macroeconomic issues.

To understand the modern consensus, where it came from, and what still remains in dispute, we'll look at how macroeconomists have changed their answers to five key questions about macroeconomic policy. The five questions, and the answers given by macroeconomists over the past 70 years, are summarized in Table 34-1. Notice that classical macroeconomics said no to each question; basically, classical macroeconomists didn't think macroeconomic policy could accomplish very much. But let's go through the questions one by one.

TABLE **34-1**

Five Key Questions About Macroeconomic Policy

	Classical macroeconomics	Keynesian macroeconomics	Monetarism	Modern consensus
Is expansionary monetary policy helpful in fighting recessions?	No	Not very	Yes	Yes, except in special circumstances
Is fiscal policy effective in fighting recessions?	No	Yes	No	Yes
Can monetary and/or fiscal policy reduce unemployment in the long run?	No	Yes	No	No
Should fiscal policy be used in a discretionary way?	No	Yes	No	No, except in special circumstances
Should monetary policy be used in a discretionary way?	No	Yes	No	Still in dispute

Is Expansionary Monetary Policy Helpful in Fighting Recessions?

As we've seen, classical macroeconomists generally believed that expansionary monetary policy was ineffective or even harmful in fighting recessions. In the early years of Keynesian economics, macroeconomists weren't against monetary expansion during recessions, but they tended to believe that it was of doubtful effectiveness. Milton Friedman and his followers convinced economists that monetary policy is effective after all.

Nearly all macroeconomists now agree that monetary policy can be used to shift the aggregate demand curve and to reduce economic instability. The classical view that changes in the money supply affect only aggregate prices, not aggregate output, has few supporters today. The view once held by some Keynesian economists—that changes in the money supply have little effect—has equally few supporters. The exception to this view is the case of a liquidity trap, in which monetary policy is ineffective.

Is Fiscal Policy Effective in Fighting Recessions?

Classical macroeconomists were, if anything, even more opposed to fiscal expansion than monetary expansion. Keynesian economists, on the other hand, gave fiscal policy a central role in fighting recessions. Monetarists argued that fiscal policy was ineffective as long as the money supply was held constant. But that strong view has become relatively rare.

Most macroeconomists now agree that fiscal policy, like monetary policy, can shift the aggregate demand curve. Most macroeconomists also agree that the government should not seek to balance the budget regardless of the state of the economy: they agree that the role of the budget as an automatic stabilizer, as discussed in Chapter 29, helps keep the economy on an even keel.

Can Monetary and/or Fiscal Policy Reduce Unemployment in the Long Run?

Classical macroeconomists didn't believe the government could do anything about unemployment. Some Keynesian economists moved to the opposite extreme, arguing that expansionary policies could be used to achieve a permanently low unemployment rate, perhaps at the cost of some inflation. Monetarists believed that unemployment could not be kept below the natural rate.

Almost all macroeconomists now accept the natural rate hypothesis. This hypothesis leads them to accept sharp limits to what monetary and fiscal policy can accomplish. Effective monetary and fiscal policy, most macroeconomists believe, can limit the size of fluctuations of the actual unemployment rate around the natural rate, but they can't be used to keep unemployment below the natural rate.

Should Fiscal Policy Be Used in a Discretionary Way?

As we've already seen, views about the effectiveness of fiscal policy have gone back and forth, from rejection by classical macroeconomists, to a positive view by Keynesian economists, to a negative view once again by monetarists. Today most macroeconomists believe that tax cuts and spending increases are at least somewhat effective in increasing aggregate demand.

Many, but not all, macroeconomists, however, believe that *discretionary fiscal policy* is usually counterproductive, for the reasons discussed in Chapter 29: the lags in adjusting fiscal policy mean that all too often, policies intended to fight a slump end up intensifying a boom.

As a result, the macroeconomic consensus gives monetary policy the lead role in economic stabilization. Discretionary fiscal policy plays the leading role only in special circumstances when monetary policy may not be able to do the job, such as those facing Japan in the 1990s.

Should Monetary Policy Be Used in a Discretionary Way?

Classical macroeconomists didn't think that monetary policy should be used to fight recessions; Keynesian economists didn't oppose discretionary policy, but they were skeptical about its effectiveness. Monetarists argued that discretionary monetary policy was doing more harm than good. Where are we today? This remains an area of dispute.

Today there is a broad consensus among macroeconomists on these points:

- Monetary policy should play the main role in stabilization policy.
- The central bank should be independent, insulated from political pressures, in order to avoid a political business cycle.
- Discretionary fiscal policy should be used sparingly, both because of policy lags and because of the risks of a political business cycle.

There are, however, debates over how the central bank should set its policy. Should the central bank be given a simple, clearly defined target for its policies, or should it be given discretion to manage the economy as it sees fit? If the central bank has a target, what should it be? And—a particular concern in recent years—should the central bank consider the management of asset prices, such as stock prices, part of its responsibility?

Central Bank Targets It may sound funny to say this, but it's not clear exactly what the Federal Reserve, the central bank of the United States, is trying to achieve. Clearly it wants a stable economy with price stability, but there isn't any document setting out the Fed's official view about exactly how stable the economy should be or what the inflation rate should be.

This is not necessarily a bad thing. Experienced staff at the Fed generally believe that the absence of specific guidelines gives the central bank flexibility in coping with economic events, and that history proves the Fed uses that flexibility well. In practice, chairmen of the Fed tend to stay in office for a long time—William McChesney Martin was chairman from 1951 to 1970, and Alan Greenspan, appointed in 1987, was still serving as chairman in 2005. These long-serving chairmen acquire personal credibility that reassures the public that the central bank's power will be used well.

But other countries believe that their central banks need formal guidelines, and some American economists—including some members of the Federal Reserve Board of Governors—believe that the United States should follow suit. The best-known example of a central bank using formal guidelines is the Bank of England. Until 1997, the Bank of England was simply an arm of the British Treasury Department, with no independence. When it became an independent organization like the Federal Reserve, it was also given a guideline: it is supposed to keep the inflation rate at 2.1%.

Inflation targeting—requiring the central bank to seek to keep the inflation rate near a predetermined target rate—is now advocated by many macroeconomists. Others, however, believe that such a rule can limit the ability of the central bank to respond to events, such as a stock market crash or a world financial crisis.

In practice, the Fed acts as if it seeks to keep the inflation rate somewhere between 2% and 3%. That is, the Fed's informal policy doesn't look very different from the Bank of England's formal policy. But there is likely to be intense debate over the next few years about whether to give the Fed an explicit inflation target.

Setting a Target Inflation Rate If a central bank has an inflation target, formal or informal, what should that target be? The Bank of England has a 2.1% target; the

Alan Greenspan was appointed chairman of the Federal Reserve Board of Governors in 1987. His long tenure helped give the Fed credibility. In 2006, Ben Bernanke succeeded him.

Inflation targeting requires that the central bank try to keep the inflation rate near a predetermined target rate.

European Central Bank's rules say that it should seek "price stability," which it has defined as 0%–2% inflation. Does it matter, and which target is better?

Some macroeconomists believe that *strict price stability*—an inflation rate close to 0%—helps stabilize the economy because it leads the public to consider money a truly stable measure of value. As we explained in Chapter 33, however, other macroeconomists worry that too low an inflation rate creates a risk that the interest rate will fall to 0% during a recession, making monetary policy ineffective. The rule for the Bank of England reflects that concern. If the Fed ever moves to an explicit inflation target, there will be an intense debate over the issue in the United States.

Asset Prices During the 1990s many economists warned that the stock market was losing touch with reality—that people buying shares in American corporations were paying prices much higher than made sense given realistic forecasts of those companies' future profits. Among these economists was Alan Greenspan, the chairman of the Federal Reserve, who warned about "irrational exuberance" in a famous speech. In 2000 the stock market headed downward. Americans who had invested in the stock market suddenly felt poorer and so cut back on spending, helping push the economy into a recession.

These events brought new emphasis to a long-standing debate over monetary policy. Should the central bank restrict its concerns to inflation and possibly unemployment, or should it also try to prevent extreme movements in asset prices, such as the average value of stocks or the average price of houses?

One view is that the central bank shouldn't try to second-guess the value investors place on assets like stocks or houses, even if it suspects that those prices are getting out of line. That is, the central bank shouldn't raise interest rates to curb stock prices or housing prices if overall consumer price inflation remains low. If an overvalued stock market eventually falls and depresses aggregate demand, the central bank can deal with that by cutting interest rates.

The alternative view warns that after a bubble bursts—after over-valued asset prices fall to earth—it may be difficult to offset the effects on aggregate demand. After having seen the Japanese economy struggle for years with deflation in the aftermath of the collapse of its bubble economy, proponents of this view argue that the central bank should act to rein in irrational exuberance when it is happening, even if consumer price inflation isn't a problem.

As we explain in the Economics in Action that follows, the 2001 recession and its aftermath gave ammunition to both sides in this debate, which shows no sign of ending.

The Clean Little Secret of Macroeconomics

It's important to keep the debates we have just described in perspective. Macroeconomics has always been a contentious field, much more so than microeconomics. There will always be debates about appropriate policies. But the striking thing about current debates is how modest the differences among macroeconomists really are. The clean little secret of modern macroeconomics is how much consensus economists have reached over the past 70 years.

economics in action

After the Bubble

During the 1990s, many economists worried that stock prices were irrationally high, and these worries proved justified. By late 2002 the NASDAQ, an index made up largely of technology stocks, had lost two-thirds of its peak value. And in 2001 the plunge in stock prices helped push the United States into recession.

The Fed responded with large, rapid interest rate cuts. But should it have tried to burst the stock bubble when it was happening?

Many economists expected the aftermath of the 1990s stock market bubble to settle, once and for all, the question of whether central banks should concern themselves about asset prices. But the test results came out ambiguous, failing to settle the issue.

If the Fed had been unable to engineer a recovery—if the U.S. economy had slid into a liquidity trap like that of Japan—critics of the Fed's previous inaction would have had a very strong case. But the recession was, in fact, short: the National Bureau of Economic Research says that the recession began in March 2001 and ended in November 2001.

But if the Fed had been able to produce a quick, strong recovery, its inaction during the 1990s would have been strongly vindicated. Unfortunately, that didn't happen either. Although the economy began recovering in late 2001, the recovery was initially weak—so weak that employment continued to drop until the summer of 2003. Also, the fact that the Fed had to cut the federal funds rate to only 1%—not much above 0%—suggested that the U.S. economy had come dangerously close to a liquidity trap.

In other words, the events of 2001–2003 probably intensified the debate over monetary policy and asset prices, rather than resolving it. ∎

> >—

> > **QUICK REVIEW**
>
> ➤ There is a broad consensus that monetary policy is effective but that it can only stabilize the economy, not reduce unemployment below the natural rate.
> ➤ There is also a broad consensus that discretionary fiscal policy should be avoided except in exceptional cases.
> ➤ There is a broad consensus that central banks should be independent, but there are disagreements about whether they should have formal *inflation targets*, what these targets should be, and how to deal with asset prices.

>>CHECK YOUR UNDERSTANDING 34-5

1. The United States entered the 2001 recession with an inflation rate of about 3%. Suppose that the inflation rate in early 2001 had been much lower, maybe even 0%. How would this have created problems for monetary policy?

2. Why would the Fed's job after 2001 have been easier if it had somehow managed to prevent stock prices from escalating at the end of the 1990s?

Solutions appear at back of book.

• A LOOK AHEAD •

We have now given a comprehensive overview of the state of modern macroeconomics, with one major exception: we haven't looked at the implications of international trade and international movements of capital. These have become increasingly important in the modern world economy. In the next two chapters we will turn to *open-economy macroeconomics,* the issues raised by the fact that modern economies are "open" to the world.

SUMMARY

1. Classical macroeconomics asserted that monetary policy affected only the aggregate price level, not aggregate output, and that the short run was unimportant. By the 1930s, measurement of business cycles was a well-established subject, but there was no widely accepted theory of business cycles.

2. **Keynesian economics** attributed the business cycle to shifts of the aggregate demand curve, often the result of changes in business confidence. Keynesian economics also offered a rationale for **macroeconomic policy activism.**

3. In the decades that followed Keynes's work, economists came to agree that monetary policy as well as fiscal policy is effective under certain conditions. **Monetarism,** a doctrine that called for a **monetary policy rule** as opposed

to **discretionary monetary policy,** and which argued that GDP would grow steadily if the money supply grew steadily, was influential for a time but was eventually rejected by many macroeconomists.

4. The natural rate hypothesis became almost universally accepted, limiting the role of macroeconomic policy to stabilizing the economy rather than seeking a permanently lower unemployment rate. Fears of a **political business cycle** led to a consensus that monetary policy should be insulated from politics.

5. **Rational expectations** suggested that even in the short run there might not be a trade-off between inflation and unemployment because expected inflation would change immediately in the face of expected changes in policy.

Real business cycle theory argued that changes in the rate of growth of total factor productivity are the main cause of business cycles. Both of these versions of **new classical macroeconomics** received wide attention and respect, but policy makers and many economists haven't accepted the conclusion that monetary and fiscal policy are ineffective in changing aggregate output.

6. The modern consensus is that monetary and fiscal policy are both effective in the short run but that neither can re-duce the unemployment rate in the long run. Discretionary fiscal policy is considered generally unadvisable, except in special circumstances.

7. There are continuing debates about the appropriate role of monetary policy. Some economists advocate the explicit use of an **inflation target,** but others oppose it. There's also a debate about whether monetary policy should take steps to manage asset prices.

KEY TERMS

Keynesian economics, p. 819
Macroeconomic policy activism, p. 820
Monetarism, p. 822
Discretionary monetary policy, p. 824

Monetary policy rule, p. 824
Political business cycle, p. 825
New classical macroeconomics, p. 826

Rational expectations, p. 827
Real business cycle theory, p. 827
Inflation targeting, p. 831

PROBLEMS

1. Since the crash of its stock market in 1989, the Japanese economy has seen little economic growth and some deflation. The accompanying table from the Organization for Economic Cooperation and Development (OECD) shows some key macroeconomic data for Japan for 1991 (a "normal" year) and 1995–2003. How did Japan's policy makers try to promote growth in the economy during this time? How does this fit in with the Keynesian and classical models of the macro-economy?

Year	Real GDP annual growth rate	Short-term interest rate	Government debt (percent of GDP)	Government budget deficit (percent of GDP)
1991	3.4%	7.38%	64.8%	−1.81%
1995	1.9	1.23	87.1	4.71
1996	3.4	0.59	93.9	5.07
1997	1.9	0.6	100.3	3.79
1998	−1.1	0.72	112.2	5.51
1999	0.1	0.25	125.7	7.23
2000	2.8	0.25	134.1	7.48
2001	0.4	0.12	142.3	6.13
2002	−0.3	0.06	149.3	7.88
2003	2.5	0.04	157.5	7.67

2. The National Bureau of Economic Research (NBER) maintains the official chronology of past U.S. business cycles. Go to its website at http://www.nber.org/cycles/cyclesmain.html to answer the following questions.

a. How many business cycles have occurred since the end of World War II in 1945?

b. What was the average duration of a business cycle when measured from the end of one expansion (its peak) to the end of the next? That is, what was the average duration of a business cycle in the period from 1945 to the present?

c. When and what was the last announcement by the NBER's Business Cycle Dating Committee?

3. The fall of the Soviet Union in 1989 and the subsequent reduction in U.S. defense spending helped ease some of the inflationary pressure in the United States that could have occurred during the strong economic growth of the late 1990s. Using the data in the accompanying table from the *Economic Report of the President*, replicate Figure 34-3 for the 1990–2000 period. Why would a Keynesian see the decrease in defense spending as fortunate?

Year	Budget deficit (percent of GDP)	Unemployment rate
1990	3.9%	5.6%
1991	4.5	6.8
1992	4.7	7.5
1993	3.9	6.9
1994	2.9	6.1
1995	2.2	5.6
1996	1.4	5.4
1997	0.3	4.9
1998	−0.8	4.5
1999	−1.4	4.2
2000	−2.4	4.0

4. In the modern world, central banks are free to increase or reduce the money supply as they see fit. However, some people harken back to the "good old days" of the gold standard. Under the gold standard, the money supply could only expand when the amount of available gold increased.

   a. Under the gold standard, if the velocity of money was stable when the economy was expanding, what would have had to happen to keep prices stable?

   b. John Maynard Keynes once dismissed the gold standard as a "barbarous relic." Why would he have considered it a bad idea?

5. The chapter explains that Kenneth Rogoff proclaimed Richard Nixon "the all-time hero of political business cycles." Using the accompanying table of data from the *Economic Report of the President*, explain why Nixon may have earned that title. (*Note:* Nixon entered office in January 1969 and was re-elected in November 1972. He resigned in August 1974.)

6. The economy of Albernia is facing a recessionary gap, and the leader of that nation calls together four of its best economists representing the classical, Keynesian, monetarist, and modern consensus views of the macroeconomy. Explain what policies each economist would recommend and why.

7. Which of the following policy recommendations are consistent with the classical, Keynesian, monetarist, and/or modern consensus views of the macroeconomy?

   a. Since the long-run growth of real GDP is 2%, the money supply should grow at 2%.

   b. Decrease government spending in order to decrease inflationary pressure.

   c. Increase the money supply in order to alleviate a recessionary gap.

   d. Always maintain a balanced budget.

   e. Decrease the budget deficit as a percent of GDP when facing a recessionary gap.

Year	Government receipts (billions of dollars)	Government spending (billions of dollars)	Government budget balance (billions of dollars)	M1 growth	M2 growth	3-month Treasury bill rate
1969	$186.9	$183.6	$3.2	3.3%	3.7%	6.68%
1970	192.8	195.6	−2.8	5.1	6.6	6.46
1971	187.1	210.2	−23.0	6.5	13.4	4.35
1972	207.3	230.7	−23.4	9.2	13.0	4.07
1973	230.8	245.7	−14.9	5.5	6.6	7.04

>web... To continue your study and review of concepts in this chapter, please visit the Krugman/Wells website for quizzes, animated graph tutorials, web links to helpful resources, and more.

www.worthpublishers.com/krugmanwells

>> Open-Economy Macroeconomics

EURO DILEMMAS

To JOIN OR NOT TO JOIN, THAT IS the question.

Not long ago, the menu in a French bistro listed prices in francs, the menu in a German Gasthouse listed prices in marks, and the menu in an Italian trattoria listed prices in lire. Today, however, menus in all three countries list prices with a "€" in front—the symbol of the euro.

The euro came into existence on January 1, 1999. France, Germany, and Italy all gave up their national currencies in favor of the euro. So did most, but not all, of their neighbors. The new "eurozone"—the group of countries using the euro—has a combined GDP almost as large as that of the dollar zone, otherwise known as the United States.

But not all of Europe is part of the eurozone. The most conspicuous holdout is Britain, which has decided to keep its national currency, the pound, for the time being. Why hasn't Britain adopted the euro?

Part of the answer is national pride: if Britain gave up the pound, it would also have to give up currency that bears the portrait of the queen. But there are also serious economic concerns about giving up the pound in favor of the euro. British economists who favor adoption of the euro argue that if Britain used the same currency as its neighbors, Britain's international trade would expand and its economy would become more productive. But other economists point out that adopting the euro would take away Britain's ability to have an independent monetary policy and might lead to macroeconomic problems.

For the time being, those who want to keep the pound seem to have the upper hand: Britain doesn't seem likely to adopt the euro anytime soon. But the argument will probably go on for a long time, because both sides have a point. To see why, we need to look at the special issues raised by macroeconomics in the open economy.

What you will learn in this chapter:

➤ The meaning and measurement of the **balance of payments**

➤ The determinants of international capital flows

➤ The role of the **foreign exchange market** and the **exchange rate**

➤ The importance of **real exchange rates** and their role in the **current account**

➤ The considerations that lead countries to choose different **exchange rate regimes,** such as **fixed exchange rates** and **floating exchange rates**

➤ Why open-economy considerations affect macroeconomic policy under floating exchange rates

Most of Europe has given up national currencies in favor of the euro, but for now, at least, the British are sticking with the pound.

Capital Flows and the Balance of Payments

In 2004 people living in the United States sold about $3 trillion worth of stuff to people living in other countries and bought about $3 trillion worth of stuff in return. What kind of stuff? All kinds. Residents of the United States (including firms operating in the United States) sold airplanes, bonds, wheat, and many other items to residents of other countries. Residents of the United States bought cars, stocks, oil, and many other items from residents of other countries.

How can we keep track of these transactions? In Chapter 24 we learned that economists keep track of the domestic economy using the national income and product accounts. Economists keep track of international transactions using a different but related set of numbers, the *balance of payments accounts*.

Balance of Payments Accounts

A country's **balance of payments accounts** are a summary of the country's transactions with other countries. The most important feature of that summary is the distinction between the *balance on current account* and the *balance on financial account*.

Look back at the examples we just gave of U.S. sales to foreigners: airplanes, bonds, wheat. When a U.S. resident sells a good such as wheat to a foreigner, that's the end of the transaction. But a financial asset, such as a bond, is different. Remember, a bond is a promise to pay interest and principal in the future. So when a U.S. resident sells a bond to a foreigner, that sale creates a liability: the U.S. resident will have to pay interest and repay principal in the future. The balance of payments accounts distinguish between transactions that don't create liabilities and those that do.

Most of the transactions that enter the current account consist of international sales and purchases of goods, such as wheat and oil, and services, such as computer consulting and hotel rooms. The **balance of payments on goods and services** is the difference between the value of exports (sales of goods and services to foreigners) and the value of imports (purchases of goods and services from foreigners) during a given period. The difference between a country's exports and imports of goods alone—not including services—is the **merchandise trade balance,** sometimes referred to as the **trade balance** for short. Economists sometimes focus on the merchandise trade balance, even though it's an incomplete measure, because data on international trade in services aren't as accurate as data on trade in physical goods.

The **balance of payments on current account,** often referred to simply as the **current account,** is a slightly broader measure than the balance of payments on goods and services. It consists of the balance of payments on goods and services plus net international transfer payments and net international factor income. Transfer payments are funds sent by residents of one country to residents of another—for example, money that Mexican immigrants to the United States send to their families back home. Factor income consists mainly of the income on assets held abroad—for example, the interest paid on U.S. bonds owned by Japanese pension funds. But it also includes labor payments, such as the fees paid to American oil experts hired as consultants in African nations.

Table 35-1 on page 838 shows the composition of the U.S. balance of payments on current account in 2004. The most important feature of that balance was a huge deficit in the balance of payments on goods and services: $618 billion, or 5.3% of GDP. One way to understand this is to say that in 2004, for every dollar's worth of goods and services the United States sold abroad, Americans spent $1.54 on imports. The United States ran a small surplus on factor income and a larger deficit on transfer payments, for an overall current account deficit of $668 billion.

How did the United States pay for all those imports? By selling a lot of assets to the rest of the world, causing it to run a surplus on its *financial account*. A country's **balance of payments on financial account,** or simply **financial account,** is the difference between the country's sales of assets to foreigners and its purchases of assets from

A country's **balance of payments accounts** are a summary of the country's transactions with other countries.

A country's **balance of payments on goods and services** is the difference between its exports and its imports during a given period.

The **merchandise trade balance,** or **trade balance,** is the difference between a country's exports and imports of goods.

A country's **balance of payments on current account,** or **current account,** is its balance of payments on goods and services plus net international transfer payments and factor income.

A country's **balance of payments on financial account,** or simply its **financial account,** is the difference between its sales of assets to foreigners and its purchases of assets from foreigners during a given period.

TABLE 35-1

The U.S. Balance of Payments on Current Account, 2004

	Payments from foreigners (billions of dollars)	Payments to foreigners (billions of dollars)	Balance (billions of dollars)
Goods and services	Exports of goods and services: $1,151	Imports of goods and services: $1,769	−$618
Factor income	Income receipts: 379	Income payments: 349	30
Transfers	*	*	−81
Total (balance of payments on current account)	*	*	−668

*The U.S. government provides only an estimate of net transfers, without the amounts going in and out.

Note: Numbers do not add due to rounding.

Source: Bureau of Economic Analysis.

foreigners during a given period. (Until a few years ago, economists often referred to the financial account as the *capital account.* We'll use the modern term, but you may run across the older term.) The financial account measures *capital flows,* flows of savings from one country to another.

Like the current account, the financial account can be broken into several sub-accounts. The most important distinction, as we'll see later in the chapter, is between private and official sales and purchases—between, for example, purchases of U.S. government bonds by private investors in Europe and purchases of these bonds by the central banks of Japan and China. Table 35-2 shows this breakdown of the U.S. financial account for 2004. As you can see, official purchases of U.S. assets were $395 billion in 2004. We'll turn to the reasons for these purchases later in the chapter, when we discuss exchange rate policy. As Table 35-2 shows, there was also a net capital flow into the United States from private investors.

The negative balance of payments on current account and the positive balance of payments on financial account for the United States in 2004 were not an accident. They reflect a basic rule of balance of payments accounting for any country:

(35-1)   Balance of payments on current account (*CA*) + Balance of payments on financial account (*FA*) = 0

or,

$$CA = -FA$$

To understand why Equation 35-1 must be true, it helps to look at Figure 35-1, a variant on the circular-flow diagram we have found useful in discussing domestic

TABLE 35-2

The U.S. Balance of Payments on Financial Account, 2004

	Sales of assets to foreigners (billions of dollars)	Purchases of assets from foreigners (billions of dollars)	Balance (billions of dollars)
Official sales and purchases	$395	−$4	$399
Private sales and purchases	1,045	860	185
Total (balance of payments on financial account)	1,440	856	584

Source: Bureau of Economic Analysis.

Figure 35-1

The Balance of Payments

The green arrows represent payments that are counted in the balance of payments on current account. The red arrows represent payments that are counted in the balance of payments on financial account. Because the total flow into the United States must equal the total flow out of the United States, the sum of the balance of payments on current account plus the balance of payments on financial account is zero.

Payments to the rest of the world for assets

Payments to the rest of the world for goods and services, factor income, and transfers

United States

Rest of world

Payments to the United States for goods and services, factor income, and transfers

Payments to the United States for assets

macroeconomics. Instead of showing the flow of money *within* a national economy, Figure 35-1 shows the flow of money *between* national economies. Money flows into the United States from the rest of the world as payment for U.S. exports of goods and services, as payment for the use of U.S.-owned factors of production, and as transfer payments. These flows (indicated by the green arrow) are the positive components of the U.S. balance of payments on current account. Money also flows into the United States from foreigners who purchase U.S. assets (as shown by the red arrow)—the positive component of the U.S. balance of payments on financial account.

At the same time, money flows from the United States to the rest of the world as payment for U.S. imports of goods and services, as payment for the use of foreign-owned factors of production, and as transfer payments. These flows, indicated by another green arrow, are the negative components of the U.S. balance of payments on current account. Money also flows from the United States to purchase foreign assets, as shown by the red arrow—the negative component of the U.S. balance of payments on financial account. As in all circular-flow diagrams, the flow into a box and the flow out of a box are equal. This means that the sum of the red and green arrows going into the United States is equal to the sum of the red and green arrows going out of the United States. That is,

(35-2) Positive entries on current account + Positive entries on financial account = Negative entries on current account + Negative entries on financial account

Equation 35-2 can be rearranged as follows:

(35-3) Positive entries on current account − Negative entries on current account + Positive entries on financial account − Negative entries on financial account = 0

Equation 35-3 is equivalent to Equation 35-1: the balance of payments on current account plus the balance of payments on financial account—both equal to positive entries minus negative entries—is equal to zero.

Even though the balance of payments on current account and the balance of payments on financial account sum to zero by the rules of accounting, you can see by

GDP, GNP, AND THE CURRENT ACCOUNT

When we discussed national income accounting in Chapter 24, we derived the basic equation relating GDP to the components of spending:

$$Y = C + I + G + X - IM$$

where X and IM are exports and imports, respectively, of goods and services. But as we've learned, the balance of payments on goods and services is only one component of the current account balance. Why doesn't the national income equation use the current account as a whole?

The answer is that gross domestic product, which is the value of goods and serv-

ices produced in a country, doesn't include two sources of income that are included in calculating the current account balance: international factor income and international transfers. The profits of Ford Motors U.K. aren't included in America's GDP, and the funds Latin American immigrants send home to their families aren't subtracted from GDP.

Shouldn't we have a broader measure that does include these sources of income? Actually, gross *national* product—GNP—does include international factor income. Estimates of U.S. GNP differ slightly from estimates of GDP because GNP adds in items such as the earnings of U.S. companies abroad and sub-

tracts items such as the interest payments on bonds owned by residents of China and Japan. There isn't, however, any regularly calculated measure that includes transfer payments.

Why do economists use GDP rather than a broader measure? Two reasons. First, the original purpose of the national accounts was to track production rather than income. Second, data on international factor income and transfer payments are generally considered somewhat unreliable. So if you're trying to keep track of movements in the economy, it makes sense to focus on GDP, which doesn't rely on these unreliable data.

comparing Table 35-1 with Table 35-2 that the *measured* balance of payments on current account and the *measured* balance of payments on financial account didn't add up to zero in 2004. The U.S. deficit on current account was offset by a surplus of $584 billion on financial account, but this was $84 billion less than the $668 billion deficit on current account. That difference is known as the *statistical discrepancy*. It tells us that there was an error in the numbers. The reason for such errors is that economic data collection isn't perfect. Economists generally consider current account data more reliable than financial account data, so they often assume that any discrepancy represents unmeasured financial account transactions.

Modeling Private International Capital Flows

In Chapter 17 we described how comparative advantage gives rise to international trade, an exchange of goods and services between countries. Our discussion of the balance of payments already tells us that the picture we gave in Chapter 17 was somewhat simplified, because countries don't exchange just goods and services. They also trade assets—not just for other assets, but for goods and services. In fact, in 2004 inflows of capital paid for about a third of U.S. imports. That is, the United States paid for a large fraction of its imports not by exporting other goods and services but by selling assets to foreigners, creating liabilities that will have to be repaid at some future date. So it's important to understand the determinants of international capital flows.

Part of our explanation will have to wait for a little while, because some international capital flows are carried out by governments and central banks, who sometimes act very differently from private investors. For example, in 2004 non-Chinese individuals and firms were buying Chinese assets, but the Chinese government more than offset this capital inflow by buying assets overseas, especially in the United States. We'll turn later in the chapter to the reasons governments and central banks buy and sell foreign assets. But we can gain insight into the motivations for capital flows that are the result of private decisions by using the *loanable funds model* we developed in Chapter 26. In using this model, we make two important simplifications:

- We simplify the reality of international capital flows by assuming that all flows are in the form of loans. In reality, capital flows take many forms, including purchases of shares of stock in foreign companies and foreign real estate, as well as *direct foreign investment,* in which companies build factories or acquire other productive assets abroad.

- We also ignore the effects of expected changes in *exchange rates,* the relative values of different national currencies. We will analyze the determination of exchange rates later in the chapter.

Figure 35-2 recaps the loanable funds model for a closed economy. Equilibrium corresponds to point E, at an interest rate of 4%, where the supply of loanable funds, curve S, intersects the demand for loanable funds, curve D. But if international capital flows are possible, this diagram changes and E may no longer be the equilibrium. We can analyze the causes and effects of international capital flows using Figure 35-3 on page 842, which places the loanable funds market diagrams for two countries side by side.

Figure 35-3 on page 842 illustrates a world consisting of only two countries, the United States and Britain. Panel (a) shows the loanable funds market in the U.S., where the equilibrium in the absence of international capital flows is at point E_{US} with an interest rate of 6%. Panel (b) shows the loanable funds market in Britain, where the equilibrium in the absence of international capital flows is at point E_B with an interest rate of 2%.

Will the actual interest rate in the United States remain at 6% and that in Britain at 2%? Not if it is easy for British residents to make loans to Americans. In that case, British lenders, attracted by high American interest rates, will send some of their loanable funds to the United States. This capital inflow will increase the quantity of loanable funds supplied to American borrowers, pushing the U.S. interest rate down. At the same time, it will reduce the quantity of loanable funds supplied to British borrowers, pushing the British interest rate up. So, international capital flows will narrow the gap between U.S. and British interest rates.

Let's further suppose that British lenders regard a loan to an American as being just as good as a loan to one of their own compatriots, and American borrowers regard a debt to a British lender as no more costly than a debt to an American lender.

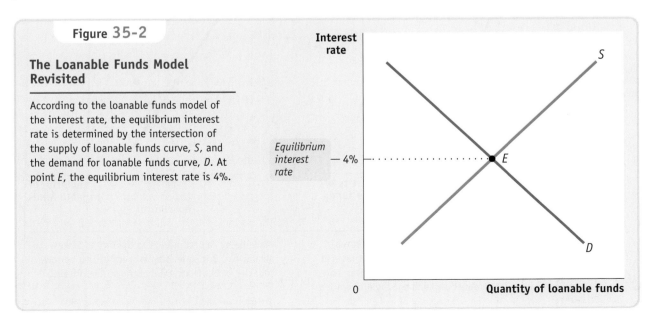

Figure 35-2

The Loanable Funds Model Revisited

According to the loanable funds model of the interest rate, the equilibrium interest rate is determined by the intersection of the supply of loanable funds curve, S, and the demand for loanable funds curve, D. At point E, the equilibrium interest rate is 4%.

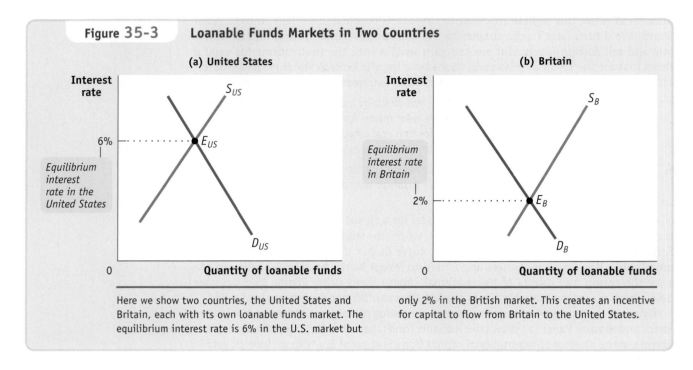

Figure 35-3 **Loanable Funds Markets in Two Countries**

Here we show two countries, the United States and Britain, each with its own loanable funds market. The equilibrium interest rate is 6% in the U.S. market but only 2% in the British market. This creates an incentive for capital to flow from Britain to the United States.

In that case, the flow of funds from Britain to the United States will continue until the gap between their interest rates is eliminated. In other words, when residents of the two countries believe that a foreign asset is as good as a domestic one and that a foreign liability is as good as a domestic one, then international capital flows will equalize the interest rates in the two countries. Figure 35-4 shows an international

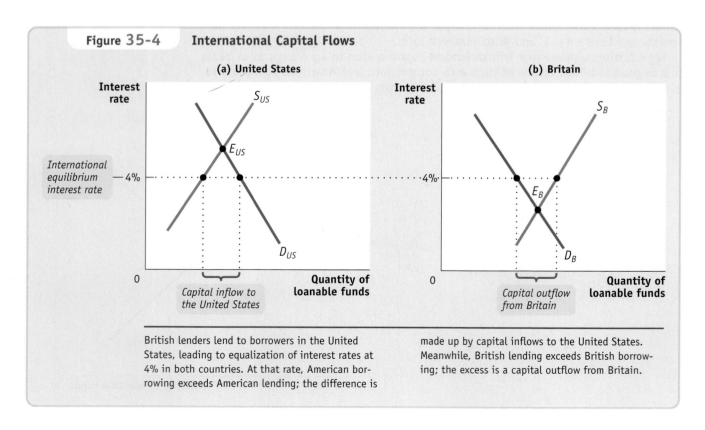

Figure 35-4 **International Capital Flows**

British lenders lend to borrowers in the United States, leading to equalization of interest rates at 4% in both countries. At that rate, American borrowing exceeds American lending; the difference is made up by capital inflows to the United States. Meanwhile, British lending exceeds British borrowing; the excess is a capital outflow from Britain.

equilibrium in the loanable funds markets where the equilibrium interest rate is 4% in both the United States and Britain. At this interest rate, the quantity of loanable funds demanded by American borrowers exceeds the quantity of loanable funds supplied by American lenders. This gap is filled by "imported" funds—a capital inflow from Britain. At the same time, the quantity of loanable funds supplied by British lenders is greater than the quantity of loanable funds demanded by British borrowers. This excess is "exported" in the form of a capital outflow to the United States. And the two markets are in equilibrium at a common interest rate of 4%—at that interest rate, the total quantity of loans demanded by borrowers across the two markets is equal to the total quantity of loans supplied by lenders across the two markets.

In short, international flows of capital are like international flows of goods and services. Capital moves from places where it would be cheap in the absence of international capital flows to places where it would be expensive in the absence of such flows.

Underlying Determinants of International Capital Flows

The open-economy version of the loanable funds model helps us understand international capital flows in terms of the supply and demand for funds. But what underlies differences across countries in the supply and demand for funds? Why, in the absence of international capital flows, would interest rates differ internationally, creating an incentive for international capital flows?

International differences in the demand for funds reflect underlying differences in investment opportunities. In particular, a country with a rapidly growing economy, other things equal, tends to offer more investment opportunities than a country with a slowly growing economy. So rapidly growing economies typically—though not always—offer higher returns to investors than slowly growing economies in the absence of capital flows. As a result, capital tends to flow from slowly growing to rapidly growing economies.

The classic example, described in the Economics in Action that follows on page 844, is the flow of capital from Britain to the United States, among other countries, between 1870 and 1914. During that era, the U.S. economy was growing rapidly as the population increased and spread westward and as the nation industrialized. This

---

FOR INQUIRING MINDS

TWIN DEFICITS?

In the 1980s the United States began to run both large budget deficits and large deficits in its balance of payments on current account; for a time these deficits were roughly the same size. And they soon came to be known as the "twin deficits." But were they linked?

The argument for linkage ran as follows: Budget deficits reduce overall national savings. Capital tends to flow into countries with low savings, other things equal. And capital inflows are always matched by equal-sized deficits in the balance of payments on current account. So there was a chain of economic links from the budget deficit to the current account deficit.

Even at the time, however, economists cautioned that the fact that the budget deficit and the current account deficit were about the same size was largely an accident, because there are many other factors besides budget deficits that affect international capital flows. As a result, there isn't a close relationship between the size of a country's budget deficit and its balance of payments on current account. In fact, sometimes the two numbers have the opposite sign. Japan has large budget deficits but runs large surpluses on its current account. In the late 1990s the United States had a budget surplus but ran a large deficit on its current account.

Still, the concept of the twin deficits did highlight the relationship between savings and international capital flows. And twin deficits reemerged in the United States after 2000.

created a demand for investment spending on railroads, factories, and so on. Meanwhile, Britain had a much more slowly growing population, was already industrialized, and already had a railroad network covering the country. This left Britain with savings to spare, much of which were lent out to the United States and other New World economies.

International differences in the supply of funds reflect differences in savings across countries. These may be the result of differences in private savings rates, which vary widely among countries. For example, in 2002 private savings were 33.6% of Japan's GDP but only 17.6% of U.S. GDP. They may also reflect differences in savings by governments. In particular, as discussed in For Inquiring Minds on page 843, government budget deficits, which reduce overall national savings, can lead to capital inflows.

economics in action

The Golden Age of Capital Flows

Technology, it's often said, shrinks the world. Jet planes have put most of the world's cities within a few hours of one another; modern telecommunications transmit information instantly around the globe. So you might think that international capital flows must now be larger than ever.

But if capital flows are measured as a share of world savings and investment, that belief turns out not to be true. The golden age of capital flows actually preceded World War I—from 1870 to 1914.

These capital flows went mainly from European countries, especially Britain, to what were then known as "zones of recent settlement," countries that were attracting large numbers of European immigrants. Among the big recipients of capital inflows were Australia, Argentina, Canada, and the United States.

The large capital flows reflected differences in investment opportunities. Britain, a mature industrial economy with limited natural resources and a slowly growing population, offered relatively limited opportunities for new investment. The regions of recent settlement, with rapidly growing populations and abundant natural resources, offered investors a higher return and attracted capital inflows. Estimates suggest that over this period Britain sent about 40% of its savings abroad, largely to finance railroads and other large projects. No country has matched that record in modern times.

Why can't we match the capital flows of our great-great-grandfathers? Economists aren't completely sure, but they have pointed to two causes: migration restrictions and political risks.

During the golden age of capital flows, capital movements were complementary to population movements: the big recipients of capital from Europe were also places to which large numbers of Europeans were moving. These large-scale population movements were possible before World War I because there were few legal restrictions on immigration. In today's world, by contrast, migration is limited by extensive legal barriers, as anyone considering a move to the United States or Europe can tell you.

The other factor that has changed is political risk. Modern governments often limit foreign investment because they fear it will diminish their national autonomy. And due to political or security concerns, governments sometimes seize foreign property, a risk that deters investors from sending more than a relatively modest share of their wealth abroad. In the nineteenth century such actions were rare, partly because some major destinations of investment were still European colonies, partly because in those days governments had a habit of sending troops and gunboats to enforce the claims of their investors. ■

‹ ‹ ‹ ‹ ‹ ‹ ‹ ‹ ‹ ‹ ‹ ‹ ‹ ‹ ‹ ‹ ‹ ‹ ‹

1. Which of the balance of payments accounts do the following events affect?
   a. Boeing, a U.S.-based company, sells a newly built airplane to China.
   b. Chinese investors buy stock in Boeing from Americans.
   c. A Chinese company buys a used airplane from American Airlines and ships it to China.
   d. A Chinese investor who owns property in the United States buys a corporate jet, which he will keep in the United States so he can travel around America.

2. In a widely reported speech, a Federal Reserve official declared that there is a "global savings glut": savings are high, and investment returns are low, in the rest of the world. Explain how such a glut would affect the U.S. financial account and interest rates.

Solutions appear at back of book.

The Role of the Exchange Rate

We've just seen how differences in the supply of loanable funds from savings and the demand for loanable funds for investment spending lead to international capital flows. We've also learned that a country's balance of payments on current account plus its balance of payments on financial account add to zero: a country that receives net capital inflows must run a matching current account deficit, and a country that generates net capital outflows must run a matching current account surplus.

The behavior of the financial account—reflecting inflows or outflows of capital—is best described by equilibrium in the international loanable funds market. At the same time, the balance of payments on goods and services, the main component of the current account, is determined by decisions in the international markets for goods and services. So given that the financial account reflects the movement of capital and the current account reflects the movement of goods and services, what ensures that the balance of payments really does balance? That is, what ensures that the two accounts actually offset one another?

The answer lies in the role of the *exchange rate,* which is determined in the *foreign exchange market.*

Understanding Exchange Rates

In general, goods, services, and assets produced in a country must be paid for in that country's currency. American products must be paid for in dollars; European products must be paid for in euros; Japanese products must be paid for in yen. Occasionally, sellers will accept payment in foreign currency, but they will then exchange that currency for domestic money.

International transactions, then, require a market—the **foreign exchange market**— in which currencies can be exchanged for each other. This market determines **exchange rates,** the prices at which currencies trade. (The foreign exchange market is, in fact, not located in any one geographic location. Rather, it is a global electronic market that traders around the world use to buy and sell currencies.)

Table 35-3 shows exchange rates among the world's three most important currencies as of 4:25 P.M., EST, on August 22, 2005. Each entry shows the price of the "row" currency in terms of the "column" currency. For example, at that time US$1 exchanged for €0.8178, so it took €0.8178 to buy US$1. Similarly, it took US$1.2228 to buy one €1. These two numbers reflect the same rate of exchange between the euro and the U.S. dollar: $1/1.2228 = 0.8178$.

There are two ways to write any given exchange rate. In this case, there were €0.8178 to US$1 and US$1.2228 to €1. Which is the correct way to write it? The answer is that there is no fixed rule. In most countries people tend to express the exchange rate as the price of a dollar in domestic currency. However, this rule isn't universal, and the U.S. dollar–euro rate is commonly quoted both ways. The important thing is to be sure you know which one you are using! See Pitfalls on page 846.

Currencies are traded in the **foreign exchange market**.

The prices at which currencies trade are known as **exchange rates**.

TABLE 35-3

Exchange Rates, August 22, 2005, 4:25 P.M.

	U.S. dollars	Yen	Euros
One U.S. dollar exchanged for	1	109.7050	0.8178
One yen exchanged for	0.009115	1	0.007454
One euro exchanged for	1.2228	134.1473	1

When a currency becomes more valuable in terms of other currencies, it **appreciates.**

When a currency becomes less valuable in terms of other currencies, it **depreciates.**

PITFALLS

WHICH WAY IS UP?

Suppose someone says, "The U.S. exchange rate is up." What does that person mean?

It isn't clear. Sometimes the exchange rate is measured as the price of a dollar in terms of foreign currency, sometimes as the price of foreign currency in terms of dollars. So the statement could mean that the dollar either appreciated or that it depreciated!

You have to be particularly careful when using published statistics. Most countries other than the United States state their exchange rates in terms of the price of a dollar in their domestic currency—for example, Mexican officials will say that the exchange rate is 10, meaning 10 pesos per dollar. But Britain, for historical reasons, usually states its exchange rate the other way. At 4:25 P.M. on August 22, 2005, US$1 was worth £0.5553, and £1 was worth US$1.8009. More often than not, this number is reported as an exchange rate of 1.8009. In fact, on occasion, professional economists and consultants embarrass themselves by getting the direction in which the pound is moving wrong!

By the way, Americans generally follow other countries' lead: we usually say that the exchange rate against Mexico is 10 pesos per dollar but the exchange rate against Britain is 1.8 dollars per pound. But this rule isn't reliable; exchange rates against the euro are often stated both ways.

So it's always important to check before using exchange rate data: which way is the exchange rate being measured?

When discussing movements in exchange rates, economists use specialized terms to avoid confusion. When a currency becomes more valuable in terms of other currencies, economists say that the currency **appreciates.** When a currency becomes less valuable in terms of other currencies, it **depreciates.** Suppose, for example, that the value of €1 went from $1 to $1.25, which means that the value of US$1 went from €1 to €0.8 (because 1/1.25 = 0.8). In this case we would say that the euro appreciated and the U.S. dollar depreciated.

Movements in exchange rates, other things equal, affect the relative prices of goods, services, and assets in different countries. Suppose, for example, that the price of an American hotel room is US$100 and the price of a French hotel room is €100. If the exchange rate is €1 = US$1, these hotel rooms have the same price. If the exchange rate is €1.25 = US$1, the French hotel room is 20% cheaper than the American hotel room. If the exchange rate is €0.80 = US$1, the French hotel room is 25% more expensive than the American hotel room.

But what determines exchange rates? Supply and demand in the foreign exchange market.

The Equilibrium Exchange Rate

Imagine, for the sake of simplicity, that there are only two currencies in the world: U.S. dollars and euros. Europeans wanting to purchase American goods, services, and assets come to the foreign exchange market, wanting to exchange euros for U.S. dollars. That is, Europeans demand U.S. dollars from the foreign exchange market and, correspondingly, supply euros to that market. Americans wanting to buy European goods, services, and assets come to the foreign exchange market to exchange U.S. dollars for euros. That is, Americans supply U.S. dollars to the foreign exchange market and, correspondingly, demand euros from that market. (International transfers and payments of factor income also enter into the foreign exchange market, but to make things simple we'll ignore these.)

Figure 35-5 shows how the foreign exchange market works. The quantity of dollars demanded and supplied at any given euro–U.S. dollar exchange rate is shown on the horizontal axis, and the euro–U.S. dollar exchange rate is shown on the vertical axis. The exchange rate plays the same role as the price of a good or service in an ordinary supply and demand diagram.

The figure shows two curves, the demand curve for U.S. dollars and the supply curve for U.S. dollars. The demand curve slopes downward: the more euros it takes to buy a dollar, the fewer dollars Europeans will demand. The key to understanding the slopes of these curves is that the level of the exchange rate affects exports and imports. When a country's currency appreciates (becomes more valuable), exports fall and imports rise. When a country's currency depreciates (becomes less valuable), exports rise and imports fall.

To understand why the demand curve for U.S. dollars slopes downward, recall that the exchange rate, other things equal, determines the prices of American goods, services, and assets relative to those of European goods, services, and assets. If the U.S. dollar rises against the euro (the dollar appreciates), American products will become more expensive to Europeans relative to European goods. So Europeans will buy less from the United States and will acquire fewer dollars in the foreign exchange market: the quantity of U.S. dollars demanded falls as the number of euros needed to buy a U.S. dollar rises. If the U.S. dollar falls against the euro (the dollar depreciates), American products will become cheaper for Europeans. Europeans will respond by buying more from the United States and acquiring more dollars in the foreign exchange market: the quantity of U.S. dollars demanded rises as the number of euros needed to buy a U.S. dollar falls.

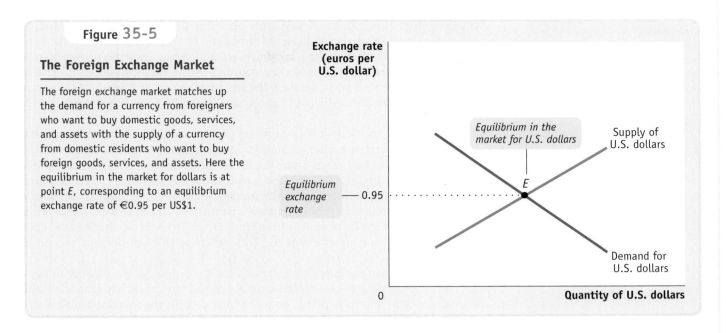

Figure 35-5

The Foreign Exchange Market

The foreign exchange market matches up the demand for a currency from foreigners who want to buy domestic goods, services, and assets with the supply of a currency from domestic residents who want to buy foreign goods, services, and assets. Here the equilibrium in the market for dollars is at point E, corresponding to an equilibrium exchange rate of €0.95 per US$1.

A similar argument explains why the supply curve of U.S. dollars in Figure 35-5 slopes upward: the more euros required to buy a U.S. dollar, the more dollars Americans will supply. Again, the reason is the effect of the exchange rate on relative prices. If the U.S. dollar rises against the euro, European products look cheaper to Americans—who will demand more of them. This will require Americans to convert more dollars into euros.

The **equilibrium exchange rate** is the exchange rate at which the quantity of U.S. dollars demanded in the foreign exchange market is equal to the quantity of U.S. dollars supplied. In Figure 35-5, the equilibrium is at point E, and the equilibrium exchange rate is 0.95. That is, at an exchange rate of €0.95 per US$1, the quantity of U.S. dollars supplied to the foreign exchange market is equal to the quantity of U.S. dollars demanded.

To understand the significance of the equilibrium exchange rate, it's helpful to consider a numerical example of what equilibrium in the foreign exchange market looks like. Such an example is shown in Table 35-4. (This is a hypothetical table that isn't intended to match real numbers.) The first row shows European purchases of U.S. dollars, either to buy U.S. goods and services or to buy U.S. assets. The second row shows U.S. sales of U.S. dollars, either to buy European goods and services or to buy European assets. At the equilibrium exchange rate, the total quantity of U.S. dollars Europeans want to buy is equal to the total quantity of U.S. dollars Americans want to sell.

The **equilibrium exchange rate** is the exchange rate at which the quantity of a currency demanded in the foreign exchange market is equal to the quantity supplied.

TABLE 35-4

Equilibrium in the Foreign Exchange Market: A Hypothetical Example

European purchases of U.S. dollars (trillions of U.S. dollars)	To buy U.S. goods and services: 1.0	To buy U.S. assets: 1.0	**Total purchases of dollars: 2.0**
U.S. sales of U.S. dollars (trillions of U.S. dollars)	To buy European goods and services: 1.5	To buy European assets: 0.5	**Total sales of dollars: 2.0**
	U.S. balance of payments on current account: −0.5	U.S. balance of payments on financial account: +0.5	

Remember that the balance of payments accounts divide international transactions into two types. Purchases and sales of goods and services are counted in the current account. (Again, we're leaving out transfers and factor income to keep things simple.) Purchases and sales of assets are counted in the financial account. At the equilibrium exchange rate, then, we have the situation shown in Table 35-4: the sum of the balance of payments on current account plus the balance of payments on financial account is zero.

Now let's briefly consider how a shift in the demand for U.S. dollars affects equilibrium in the foreign exchange market. Suppose that for some reason capital flows from Europe to the United States increase—say, due to a change in the preferences of European investors. The effects are shown in Figure 35-6. The demand for U.S. dollars in the foreign exchange market increases as European investors convert euros into dollars to fund their new investments in the United States. This is shown by the shift in the demand curve from D_1 to D_2. As a result, the U.S. dollar appreciates: the number of euros per U.S. dollar at the equilibrium exchange rate rises from X_1 to X_2.

What are the consequences of this increased capital inflow for the balance of payments? The total quantity of U.S. dollars supplied to the foreign exchange market still must equal the total quantity of U.S. dollars demanded. So the increased capital inflow to the United States—an increase in the balance of payments on financial account—must be matched by a decline in the balance of payments on current account. What causes the balance of payments on current account to decline? The appreciation of the U.S. dollar. A rise in the number of euros per U.S. dollar leads Americans to buy more European goods and services and Europeans to buy fewer American goods and services.

Table 35-5 shows how this might work. Europeans are buying more U.S. assets, increasing the balance on financial account from 0.5 to 1.0. This is offset by a reduction in European purchases of U.S. goods and services and a rise in U.S. purchases of European goods and services, both the result of the dollar's appreciation. *So any change in the U.S. balance of payments on financial account generates an equal and opposite reaction in the balance of payments on current account.* Movements in the exchange

An Increase in the Demand for U.S. Dollars

An increase in the demand for U.S. dollars might result from a change in the preferences of European investors. The demand curve for U.S. dollars shifts from D_1 to D_2. So the equilibrium number of euros per U.S. dollar rises—the dollar *appreciates*. As a result, the balance of payments on current account falls as the balance of payments on financial account rises.

>web...

Exchange rate (euros per U.S. dollar)

1. An increase in the demand for U.S. dollars...

Supply of U.S. dollars

2. ...leads to an appreciation of the U.S. dollar. XR_2 ... E_2

XR_1 ... E_1

D_2

D_1

Quantity of U.S. dollars

TABLE 35-5

Effects of Increased Capital Inflows

European purchases of U.S. dollars (trillions of U.S. dollars)	To buy U.S. goods and services: 0.75 (down 0.25)	To buy U.S. assets: 1.5 (up 0.5)	**Total purchases of U.S. dollars: 2.25**
U.S. sales of U.S. dollars (trillions of U.S. dollars)	To buy European goods and services: 1.75 (up 0.25)	To buy European assets: 0.5 (no change)	**Total sales of U.S. dollars: 2.25**
	U.S. balance of payments on current account: −1.0 (down 0.5)	**U.S. balance of payments on financial account: +1.0 (up 0.5)**	

rate ensure that changes in the financial account and in the current account offset each other.

Let's briefly run this process in reverse. Suppose there is a reduction in capital flows from Europe to the United States—again due to a change in the preferences of European investors. The demand for U.S. dollars in the foreign exchange market falls, and the dollar depreciates: the number of euros per U.S. dollar at the equilibrium exchange rate falls. This leads Americans to buy fewer European products and Europeans to buy more American products. Ultimately, this generates an increase in the U.S. balance of payments on current account. So a fall in capital flows into the United States leads to a weaker dollar, which in turn generates an increase in U.S. net exports.

Inflation and Real Exchange Rates

In 1992 one U.S. dollar exchanged, on average, for 3.1 Mexican pesos. By 2003, the peso had fallen against the dollar by more than two-thirds, with an average exchange rate in 2003 of 10.8 pesos per dollar. Did Mexican products also become much cheaper relative to U.S. products over that 11-year period? Did the price of Mexican products expressed in terms of U.S. dollars also fall by two-thirds? The answer is no, because Mexico had much higher inflation than the United States over that period. In fact, the relative price of U.S. and Mexican products changed little between 1992 and 2003, although the exchange rate changed a lot.

To take account of the effects of differences in inflation rates, economists calculate **real exchange rates,** exchange rates adjusted for international differences in aggregate price levels. Suppose that the exchange rate we are looking at is the number of Mexican pesos per U.S. dollar. Let P_{US} and P_{Mex} be indexes of the aggregate price levels in the United States and Mexico, respectively. Then the real exchange rate between the Mexican peso and the U.S. dollar is defined as

Real exchange rates are exchange rates adjusted for international differences in aggregate price levels.

$$(35\text{-}4) \quad \text{Real exchange rate} = \text{Mexican pesos per U.S. dollar} \times \frac{P_{US}}{P_{Mex}}$$

To distinguish it from the real exchange rate, the exchange rate unadjusted for aggregate price levels is sometimes called the *nominal* exchange rate.

To understand the significance of the difference between the real and nominal exchange rates, let's consider the following example. Suppose that the Mexican peso depreciates against the U.S. dollar, with the exchange rate going from 10 pesos per U.S. dollar to 15 pesos per U.S. dollar, a 50% change. But suppose that at the same time the price of everything in Mexico, measured in pesos, increases by 50%, so that the Mexican price index rises from 100 to 150. At the same time, suppose that there is no change in U.S. prices, so that the U.S. price index remains at 100. Then the initial real exchange rate is

$$\text{Pesos per dollar} \times \frac{P_{US}}{P_{Mex}} = 10 \times \frac{100}{100} = 10$$

After the peso depreciates and the Mexican price level increases, the real exchange rate is

$$\text{Pesos per dollar} \times \frac{P_{US}}{P_{Mex}} = 15 \times \frac{100}{150} = 10$$

In this example, the peso has depreciated substantially in terms of the U.S. dollar, but the *real* exchange rate between the peso and the U.S. dollar hasn't changed at all. And because the real peso–U.S. dollar exchange rate hasn't changed, the nominal depreciation of the peso against the U.S. dollar will have no effect either on the quantity of goods and services exported by Mexico to the United States or on the quantity of goods and services imported by Mexico from the United States. To see why, consider again the example of a hotel room. Suppose that this room initially costs 1,000 pesos per night, which is $100 at an exchange rate of 10 pesos per dollar. After both Mexican prices and the number of pesos per dollar rise by 50%, the hotel room costs 1,500 pesos per night—but 1,500 pesos divided by 15 pesos per dollar is $100, so the Mexican hotel room still costs $100. As a result, a U.S. tourist considering a trip to Mexico will have no reason to change plans.

The same is true for all goods and services that enter into trade: *the current account responds only to changes in the real exchange rate, not the nominal exchange rate.* A country's products become cheaper to foreigners only when that country's currency depreciates in real terms, and those products become more expensive to foreigners only when the currency appreciates in real terms. As a consequence, economists who analyze movements in exports and imports of goods and services focus on the real exchange rate, not the nominal exchange rate.

Figure 35-7 illustrates just how important it can be to distinguish between nominal and real exchange rates. The line labeled "nominal exchange rate" shows the number of pesos it took to buy a U.S. dollar from 1992 to 2003. As you can see, the peso depreciated massively over that period. But the line labeled "real exchange rate"

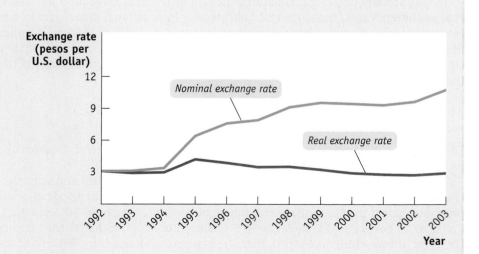

Figure 35-7

Real versus Nominal Exchange Rates, 1992–2003

Between 1992 and 2003, the price of a dollar in Mexican pesos tripled. But because Mexico had higher inflation than the United States, the real exchange rate, which measures the relative price of Mexican goods and services, ended up roughly where it started.

Source: OECD Factbook 2005.

shows the real exchange rate: it was calculated using Equation 35-4, with price indexes for both Mexico and the United States set so that 1992 = 100. In real terms, the peso depreciated between 1992 and 1995, but not by nearly as much as the nominal depreciation. By the end of the period, the real peso–U.S. dollar exchange rate was just about back where it started.

Purchasing Power Parity

A useful tool for analyzing exchange rates, closely connected to the concept of the real exchange rate, is known as *purchasing power parity*. The **purchasing power parity** between two countries' currencies is the nominal exchange rate at which a given basket of goods and services would cost the same amount in each country. Suppose, for example, that a basket of goods and services that costs $100 in the United States costs 1,000 pesos in Mexico. Then the purchasing power parity is 10 pesos per U.S. dollar: at that exchange rate, 1,000 pesos = $100, so the market basket costs the same amount in both countries.

Calculations of purchasing power parities are usually made by estimating the cost of buying broad market baskets containing many goods and services—everything from automobiles and groceries to housing and telephone calls. But as For Inquiring Minds on page 854 explains, once a year the magazine *The Economist* publishes a list of purchasing power parities based on the cost of buying a market basket that contains only one item—a McDonald's Big Mac.

Nominal exchange rates almost always differ from purchasing power parities. Some of these differences are systematic: in general, prices are lower in poor countries than in rich countries because services tend to be cheaper in poor countries. But even among countries at roughly the same level of economic development, nominal exchange rates vary quite a lot from purchasing power parity. Figure 35-8 shows the nominal exchange rate between the Canadian dollar and the U.S. dollar, measured as the number of Canadian dollars per U.S. dollar, from 1990 to 2003, together with an estimate of the purchasing power parity exchange rate between the United States and Canada over the same period. The purchasing power parity didn't change much over the whole period because the United States and Canada had about the same rate of inflation. But at the beginning of the period the nominal exchange rate was below purchasing power parity, so a given market basket was more expensive in Canada than in the United States. By 2002 the nominal exchange rate

> The **purchasing power parity** between two countries' currencies is the nominal exchange rate at which a given basket of goods and services would cost the same amount in each country.

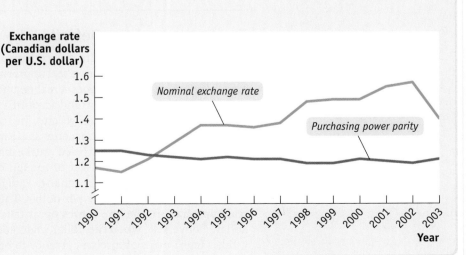

Figure 35-8

Purchasing Power Parity versus the Nominal Exchange Rate, 1990–2003

The purchasing power parity between the United States and Canada—the exchange rate at which a basket of goods and services would have cost the same amount in both countries— changed very little over the period shown, staying near C$1.2 per US$1. But the nominal exchange rate fluctuated widely.

Source: OECD Factbook 2005.

FOR INQUIRING MINDS

BURGERNOMICS

For a number of years the British magazine *The Economist* has produced an annual comparison of the cost in different countries of one particular consumption item that is found around the world—a McDonald's Big Mac. The magazine finds the price of a Big Mac in local currency, then computes two numbers: the price of a Big Mac in U.S. dollars using the prevailing exchange rate, and the exchange rate at which the price of a Big Mac would equal the U.S. price. If purchasing power parity held for Big Macs, the dollar price of a Big Mac would be the same everywhere. If purchasing power parity is a good theory for the long run, the exchange rate at which a Big Mac's price matches the U.S. price should offer some guidance about where the exchange rate will eventually end up.

In the May 2004 version of the Big Mac index, there were some wide variations in the dollar price of a Big Mac. In the U.S.,

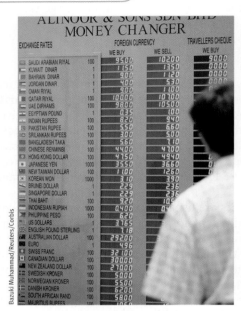

But how much money do I need to exchange if I want to buy lunch?

the price was $2.90. In China, converting at the official exchange rate, a Big Mac cost only $1.26. In Denmark, though, the price was $4.46.

The Big Mac index suggested that the euro would eventually fall against the dollar: the purchasing power parity exchange rate was $1.06 per €1 versus an actual market exchange rate of $1.24. The yen, on the other hand, looked undervalued: at burger purchasing power parity, the yen price of a dollar would be ¥90.3 versus the actual market exchange rate of ¥108.

Serious economic studies of purchasing power parity require data on the prices of many goods and services. It turns out, however, that estimates of purchasing power parity based on the Big Mac index usually aren't that different from more elaborate measures. Fast food seems to make for pretty good fast research.

was far above the purchasing power parity, so a market basket was much cheaper in Canada than in the United States.

Over the long run, however, purchasing power parities are pretty good at predicting actual changes in nominal exchange rates. In particular, nominal exchange rates between countries at similar levels of economic development tend to fluctuate around levels that lead to similar costs for a given market basket. In fact, by July 2005 the nominal exchange rate between the United States and Canada was C$1.22 per US$1—just about the purchasing power parity.

economics in action

The Dollar and the Deficit

As we've seen, the level of the *real* exchange rate affects exports and imports. When a country's currency undergoes a real appreciation, exports fall and imports rise. When a country's currency undergoes a real depreciation, exports rise and imports fall. And as we've just stated, the current account responds to changes in the real exchange rate, not the nominal exchange rate. In fact, the relationship between the real exchange rate and the current account is clear in U.S. data, as shown in Figure 35-9.

In Figure 35-9, the line labeled "real exchange rate" is an index of the value of the U.S. dollar in terms of a basket of foreign currencies, adjusted for differences in aggregate price levels. The real exchange rate is measured on the left axis and expressed in units of foreign currency per dollar. This means that when the dollar undergoes real appreciation, the line moves up: it takes more units of foreign currency to buy a dollar. Conversely, when the dollar undergoes real depreciation, the line moves down: it takes fewer units of foreign currency to buy a dollar.

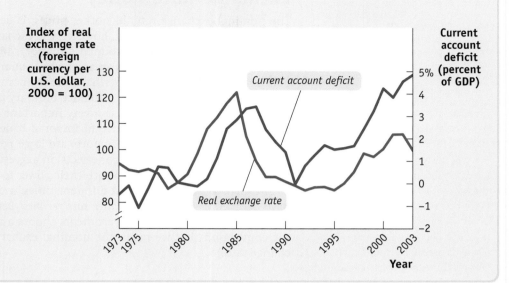

Figure 35-9

The Dollar and the Current Account Deficit, 1973–2003

The U.S. balance of payments on current account has generally followed movements in the real exchange rate. Here we compare the real exchange rate of the U.S. dollar against a basket of foreign currencies with the current account deficit, measured as a percentage of GDP. Notice how the large appreciation and depreciation of the U.S. dollar in the 1980s were followed, with a lag, by a large rise and fall in the current account deficit.

Source: OECD Economic Outlook.

The line labeled "current account deficit" is the U.S. current account deficit as a percentage of GDP, measured on the right axis. Because it shows the *deficit,* it goes up when exports fall or imports rise, and it falls when exports rise or imports fall.

In the 1980s there was a completely clear relationship between the real exchange rate and the current account. On a real basis, the dollar appreciated dramatically in the first half of the 1980s; with a bit of a lag, this caused exports to slump and imports to soar, which in turn caused the current account to move deep into deficit. (We haven't stressed lags in the effect of the exchange rate, but experience shows that it takes time for exporters and importers to respond to exchange rate changes.) When the dollar came down again, so did the current account deficit.

The dollar and the current account deficit both rose again in the late 1990s. The real increase in the dollar wasn't as large as the episode in the 1980s, but the current account deficit grew even larger. This probably reflected other factors, such as the rapid growth of export industries in China. Still, the overall picture strongly confirms the idea that changes in the real exchange rate have a strong effect on the current account balance. ■

> >

>>CHECK YOUR UNDERSTANDING 35-2

1. Mexico discovers huge reserves of oil and starts exporting oil to the United States. Describe how this would affect the following:
   a. The nominal peso–U.S. dollar exchange rate
   b. Mexican exports of other goods and services
   c. Mexican imports of goods and services

2. A basket of goods and services that costs $100 in the United States costs 800 pesos in Mexico, and the current nominal exchange rate is 10 pesos per U.S. dollar. Over the next five years, the cost of that market basket rises to $120 in the United States and to 1,200 pesos in Mexico, although the nominal exchange rate remains at 10 pesos per U.S. dollar. Calculate the following:
   a. The real exchange rate now and five years from now, if today's price index in both countries is 100
   b. Purchasing power parity today and five years from now

Solutions appear at back of book.

Exchange Rate Policy

The nominal exchange rate, like other prices, is determined by supply and demand. Unlike the price of wheat or oil, however, the exchange rate is the price of a country's money (in terms of another country's money). Money isn't a good or service produced by the private sector; it's an asset whose quantity is determined by government policy. As a result, governments have much more power to influence nominal exchange rates than they have to influence ordinary prices.

The nominal exchange rate is a very important price for many countries: the exchange rate determines the price of imports; it determines the price of exports; in economies where exports and imports are large percentages of GDP, movements in the exchange rate can have major effects on aggregate output and the aggregate price level. What do governments do with their power to influence this important price?

The answer is, it depends. At different times and in different places, governments have adopted a variety of *exchange rate regimes*. Let's talk about these regimes, how they are enforced, and how governments choose a regime. (From now on we'll adopt the convention that we mean the nominal exchange rate when we refer to the exchange rate.)

Exchange Rate Regimes

An **exchange rate regime** is a rule governing policy toward the exchange rate. There are two main kinds of exchange rate regime. A country has a **fixed exchange rate** when the government keeps the exchange rate against some other currency at or near a particular target. For example, Hong Kong has an official policy of setting an exchange rate of HK$7.4 per US$1. A country has a **floating exchange rate** when the government lets the exchange rate go wherever the market takes it. This is the policy followed by Britain, Canada, and the United States.

Fixed exchange rates and floating exchange rates aren't the only possibilities. At various times countries have adopted compromise policies that lie somewhere between fixed and floating exchange rates. These include exchange rates that are fixed at any given time but are adjusted frequently, exchange rates that aren't fixed but are "managed" by the government to avoid wide swings, and exchange rates that float within a "target zone" but are prevented from leaving that zone. In this book, however, we'll focus on the two main exchange rate regimes.

The immediate question about a fixed exchange rate is how it is possible for governments to fix the exchange rate when the exchange rate is determined by supply and demand.

How Can an Exchange Rate Be Held Fixed?

To understand how it is possible for a country to fix its exchange rate, let's consider a hypothetical country, Genovia, which for some reason has decided to fix the value of its currency, the geno, at 1.50 U.S. dollars.

The obvious problem is that $1.50 may not be the equilibrium exchange rate in the foreign exchange market: the equilibrium rate may be either higher or lower than the target exchange rate. Figure 35-10 shows the foreign exchange market for genos, with the quantities of genos supplied and demanded on the horizontal axis and the exchange rate of the geno, measured in U.S. dollars per geno, on the vertical axis. Panel (a) shows the case in which the equilibrium value of the geno is *below* the target exchange rate. Panel (b) shows the case in which the equilibrium value of the geno is *above* the target exchange rate.

Consider first the case in which the equilibrium value of the geno is below the target exchange rate. As panel (a) of Figure 35-10 shows, at the target exchange rate there is a surplus of genos in the foreign exchange market, which would normally push the value of the geno down. How can the Genovian government support the

---

An **exchange rate regime** is a rule governing policy toward the exchange rate.

A country has a **fixed exchange rate** when the government keeps the exchange rate against some other currency at or near a particular target.

A country has a **floating exchange rate** when the government lets the exchange rate go wherever the market takes it.

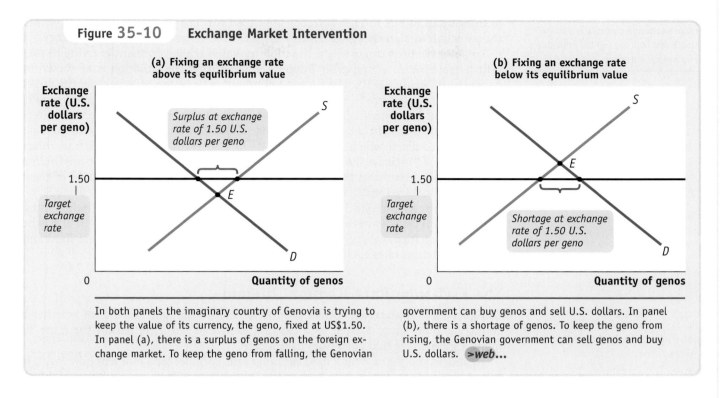

Figure 35-10   Exchange Market Intervention

(a) Fixing an exchange rate above its equilibrium value

(b) Fixing an exchange rate below its equilibrium value

In both panels the imaginary country of Genovia is trying to keep the value of its currency, the geno, fixed at US$1.50. In panel (a), there is a surplus of genos on the foreign exchange market. To keep the geno from falling, the Genovian government can buy genos and sell U.S. dollars. In panel (b), there is a shortage of genos. To keep the geno from rising, the Genovian government can sell genos and buy U.S. dollars. **>web...**

value of the geno to keep the rate where it wants? There are three possible answers, all of which have been used by governments at some point.

One way the Genovian government can support the geno is to "soak up" the surplus of genos by buying its own currency in the foreign exchange market. Government purchases or sales of currency in the foreign exchange market are called **exchange market intervention.** To buy genos in the foreign exchange market, of course, the Genovian government must have U.S. dollars to exchange for genos. In fact, most countries maintain **foreign exchange reserves,** stocks of foreign currency (usually U.S. dollars or euros) that they can use to buy their own currency to support its price.

We mentioned earlier in the chapter that an important part of international capital flows is the result of purchases and sales of foreign assets by governments and central banks. Now we can see why governments sell foreign assets: they are supporting their currency through exchange market intervention. As we'll see in a moment, governments that keep the value of their currency *down* through exchange market intervention must *buy* foreign assets. First, however, let's talk about the other ways governments fix exchange rates.

As an alternative to exchange market intervention, the Genovian government can try to shift the supply and demand curves for the geno in the foreign exchange market. Governments usually do this by changing monetary policy. For example, to support the geno the Genovian central bank can raise the Genovian interest rate. This will increase capital flows into Genovia, increasing the demand for genos, at the same time that it reduces capital flows out of Genovia, reducing the supply of genos. So, other things equal, an increase in a country's interest rate will increase the value of its currency.

Finally, the Genovian government can support the geno by reducing the supply of genos to the foreign exchange market. It can do this by requiring domestic residents who want to buy foreign currency to get a license and giving these licenses only to people engaging in approved transactions (such as the purchase of imported goods the Genovian government thinks are essential). Licensing systems that limit the right

Government purchases or sales of currency in the foreign exchange market are **exchange market intervention.**

Foreign exchange reserves are stocks of foreign currency that governments maintain to buy their own currency on the foreign exchange market.

Foreign exchange controls are licensing systems that limit the right of individuals to buy foreign currency.

of individuals to buy foreign currency are called **foreign exchange controls.** Other things equal, foreign exchange controls increase the value of a country's currency.

So far we've been discussing a situation in which the government is trying to prevent a depreciation of the geno. Suppose, instead, that the situation is as shown in panel (b) of Figure 35-10, where the equilibrium value of the geno is *above* the target exchange rate and there is a shortage of genos. To maintain the target exchange rate, the Genovian government can apply the same three basic options in the reverse direction. It can intervene in the foreign exchange market, in this case *selling* genos and acquiring U.S. dollars, which it can add to its foreign exchange reserves. It can *reduce* interest rates to increase the supply of genos and reduce the demand. Or it can impose foreign exchange controls that limit the ability of foreigners to buy genos. All of these actions, other things equal, will reduce the value of the geno.

As we said, all three techniques have been used to manage fixed exchange rates. But we haven't said whether fixing the exchange rate is a good idea. In fact, the choice of exchange rate regime poses a dilemma for policy makers, because fixed and floating exchange rates each have both advantages and disadvantages.

The Exchange Rate Regime Dilemma

Few questions in macroeconomics produce as many arguments as that of whether a country should adopt a fixed or a floating exchange rate. The reason there are so many arguments is that both sides have a case.

To understand the case for a fixed exchange rate, consider for a moment how easy it is to conduct business across state lines in the United States. There are a number of things that make interstate commerce trouble-free, but one of them is the absence of any uncertainty about the value of money: a dollar is a dollar, in both New York and Los Angeles.

By contrast, a dollar isn't a dollar in transactions between New York and Toronto. The exchange rate between the Canadian dollar and the U.S. dollar fluctuates, sometimes widely. If a U.S. firm promises to pay a Canadian firm a given number of U.S. dollars a year from now, the value of that promise in Canadian currency can vary by 10% or more. This uncertainty has the effect of deterring trade between the two countries. So one benefit of a fixed exchange rate is certainty about the future value of a currency.

There is also, in some cases, an additional benefit to adopting a fixed exchange rate: by committing itself to a fixed rate, a country is also committing itself not to engage in inflationary policies. For example, in 1991 Argentina, which has a long history of irresponsible policies leading to severe inflation, adopted a fixed exchange rate of US$1 per Argentine peso in an attempt to commit itself to noninflationary policies in the future. (Argentina's fixed exchange rate regime collapsed disastrously in late 2001. But that's another story.)

The point is that there is some economic value in having a stable exchange rate. Indeed, as the upcoming For Inquiring Minds explains, the presumed benefits of stable exchange rates motivated the international system of fixed exchange rates created after World War II and was one major reason for creating the euro.

Unfortunately, there are also costs to fixing the exchange rate. To stabilize an exchange rate through intervention, a country must keep large quantities of foreign currency on hand—usually a low-return investment. Furthermore, even large reserves can be quickly exhausted when there are large capital flows out of a country. If a country chooses to stabilize an exchange rate by adjusting monetary policy rather than through intervention, it must divert monetary policy from other goals, notably stabilizing output and the inflation rate. Finally, exchange controls, like import quotas and tariffs, distort incentives for importing and exporting. They can also create substantial costs in terms of red tape and corruption.

So there's a dilemma. Should a country let its currency float, which leaves monetary policy available for macroeconomic stabilization but creates uncertainty for busi-

FOR INQUIRING MINDS

FROM BRETTON WOODS TO THE EURO

In 1944, while World War II was still raging, representatives of Allied nations met in Bretton Woods, New Hampshire, to establish a postwar international monetary system of fixed exchange rates among major currencies. The system was highly successful at first, but it broke down in 1971. After a confusing interval during which policy makers tried unsuccessfully to establish a new fixed exchange rate system, by 1973 most economically advanced countries had moved to floating exchange rates.

In Europe, however, many policy makers were unhappy with floating exchange rates, which they believed created too much uncertainty for business. From the late 1970s onward they tried several times to create a system of more or less fixed exchange rates in Europe, culminating in an arrangement known as the Exchange Rate Mechanism. (The Exchange Rate Mechanism was, strictly speaking, a "target zone" system—exchange rates were free to move within a narrow band, but not outside it.) And in 1991 they agreed to move to the ultimate in fixed exchange rates: a common European currency, the euro. To the surprise of many analysts, they pulled it off: today most of Europe has abandoned national currencies for euros.

Figure 35-11 illustrates the history of European exchange rate arrangements. It shows the exchange rate between the French franc and the German mark, measured as francs per mark, since 1971. The

Figure 35-11

The Road to the Euro

The exchange rate between the French franc and the German mark tells the tale of Europe's long march to a common currency. European nations made several attempts to fix exchange rates in the 1970s and 1980s. The first two attempts failed, but from 1987 on they were mostly successful. The exchange rate was "locked" in the late 1990s, and at the end of 2001 the franc and the mark were replaced by the euro.

Source: Federal Reserve Bank of St. Louis.

exchange rate fluctuated widely at first. The "plateaus" you can see in the data—eras when the exchange rate fluctuated only modestly—are periods when attempts to restore fixed exchange rates were in process. The Exchange Rate Mechanism, after a couple of false starts, became effective in 1987, stabilizing the exchange rate at about 3.4 francs per mark. (The wobbles in 1992–1993 reflect two *currency crises*—episodes in which widespread expectations of imminent devaluations led to large but temporary capital flows.)

In 1999 the exchange rate was "locked"—no further fluctuations were allowed as the countries prepared to switch

from francs and marks to euros. At the end of 2001, the franc and the mark ceased to exist.

The transition to the euro has not been without costs. With most of Europe sharing the same currency, it must also share the same monetary policy. Yet economic conditions in the different countries aren't always the same—there may be a boom in Spain while there's a slump in Germany. In such cases Spain wants to raise interest rates, but Germany wants to cut them. Europeans now complain about a "one size fits all" monetary policy. In fact, a May 2005 poll found that 56% of Germans would prefer a return to their old currency, the mark.

ness? Or should it fix the exchange rate, which eliminates the uncertainty but means giving up monetary policy, adopting exchange controls, or both? Different countries reach different conclusions at different times. Most European countries, except for Britain, have long believed that exchange rates among major European economies, which do most of their international trade with each other, should be fixed. But Canada seems happy with a floating exchange rate with the United States, even though the United States accounts for most of Canada's trade.

Luckily, we don't have to resolve this dilemma. For the rest of the chapter, we'll take exchange rate regimes as given and ask how they affect macroeconomic policy.

economics in action

China Pegs the Yuan

In the early years of the twenty-first century, China provided a striking example of the lengths to which countries sometimes go to maintain a fixed exchange rate. Here's the background: China's spectacular success as an exporter led to a rising surplus on current account. At the same time, private investors became increasingly eager to shift funds into China, to take advantage of its growing domestic economy. These capital flows were somewhat limited by foreign exchange controls—but kept coming in anyway. As a result of the current account surplus and private capital inflows, China found itself in the position described by panel (b) of Figure 35-10: at the target exchange rate the demand for yuan exceeded the supply. Yet the Chinese government was determined to keep the exchange rate fixed at 8.28 yuan per U.S. dollar.

To keep the rate fixed, China had to engage in large-scale exchange market intervention, selling yuan, buying up other countries' currencies (mainly U.S. dollars) on the foreign exchange market, and adding them to its reserves. In 2004, China's foreign currency intervention was $194 billion, bringing total foreign exchange reserves up to $655 billion.

To get a sense of how big these totals are, you have to know that China's nominal GDP, converted into U.S. dollars at the prevailing exchange rate, was $1.65 trillion. So in 2004 China bought U.S. dollars and other currencies equal to almost 12% of its GDP. That's as if the U.S. government had bought $1.3 trillion worth of yen and euros in just a single year—and was continuing to buy yen and euros even though it was already sitting on a $4 trillion pile of foreign currencies. Economists expected China to buy even more foreign currency in 2005.

Will China continue accumulating foreign exchange reserves at this pace? On July 21, 2005, China announced a new scheme under which it would fix the value of the yuan in terms of a basket of currencies, rather than in terms of the U.S. dollar alone. It also suggested that it might gradually increase the value of the yuan in terms of this basket over time. Initially, however, this new scheme led to an appreciation of the yuan by only 2%. ∎

< < < < < < < < < < < < < < < < < < <

>> **CHECK YOUR UNDERSTANDING 35-3**

1. Draw a diagram, similar to Figure 35-10, representing the foreign exchange situation of China in early 2005, before the change in exchange rate policy. (*Hint:* Express the exchange rate as U.S. dollars per yuan.) Then show with a diagram how each of the following policy changes might eliminate the disequilibrium in the market:
   a. An appreciation of the yuan
   b. Placing restrictions on foreigners who want to invest in China
   c. Removing restrictions on Chinese who want to invest abroad
   d. Imposing taxes on Chinese exports, such as shipments of clothing, that are causing a political backlash in the importing countries

Solutions appear at back of book.

Exchange Rates and Macroeconomic Policy

A look at the history of British macroeconomic policy over the past 50 years touches on all the themes we've covered in our study of macroeconomics so far: British policy makers have wrestled with inflation and unemployment and wondered how to get faster long-run growth. But British macroeconomic history also reveals other concerns—notably, whether to fix the exchange rate of the pound, and if so at what level. As we learned in the opening story, the possibility of future changes in the exchange rate regime looms large even when the exchange rate is floating. And the analysis of monetary policy focuses to a large degree on how it affects the exchange rate and the balance of payments. In other words, the fact that modern economies are open to international trade and capital flows adds a new level of complication to our analysis of macroeconomic policy. Let's look at three policy issues raised by open-economy macroeconomics.

Devaluation and Revaluation of Fixed Exchange Rates

Historically, fixed exchange rates haven't been permanent commitments. Sometimes countries with a fixed exchange rate switch to a floating rate, as Argentina did in 2001. In other cases they retain a fixed rate but change the target exchange rate. Such adjustments in the target were common during the Bretton Woods era described in For Inquiring Minds on page 857. For example, in 1967 Britain changed the exchange rate of the pound against the U.S. dollar from US$2.80 per £1 to US$2.40 per £1. A modern example is China: as we explained in Economics in Action on page 858, China maintained a fixed exchange rate against the U.S. dollar from 1994 to 2005 but changed its exchange rate regime in July 2005.

A reduction in the value of a currency that is set under a fixed exchange rate regime is called a **devaluation.** As we've already learned, a *depreciation* is a downward move in a currency. A devaluation is a depreciation that is due to a revision in a fixed exchange rate target. An increase in the value of a currency that is set under a fixed exchange rate regime is called a **revaluation.**

A devaluation, like any depreciation, makes domestic goods cheaper in terms of foreign currency, which leads to higher exports. At the same time, it makes foreign goods more expensive in terms of domestic currency, which reduces imports. The effect is to increase the balance of payments on current account. Similarly, a revaluation makes domestic goods more expensive in terms of foreign currency, which reduces exports, and makes foreign goods cheaper in domestic currency, which increases imports. So a revaluation reduces the balance of payments on current account.

Devaluations and revaluations serve two purposes under fixed exchange rates. First, they can be used to eliminate shortages or surpluses in the foreign exchange market. For example, in early 2005, some economists were urging China to revalue the yuan so that it would not have to buy up so many U.S. dollars on the foreign exchange market.

Second, devaluation and revaluation can be used as tools of macroeconomic policy. A devaluation, by increasing exports and reducing imports, increases aggregate demand. So a devaluation can be used to reduce or eliminate a recessionary gap. A revaluation has the opposite effect, reducing aggregate demand. So a revaluation can be used to reduce or eliminate an inflationary gap.

A **devaluation** is a reduction in the value of a currency that is set under a fixed exchange rate regime.

A **revaluation** is an increase in the value of a currency that is set under a fixed exchange rate regime.

Monetary Policy Under Floating Exchange Rates

Under a floating exchange rate regime, a country's central bank retains its ability to pursue independent monetary policy: it can increase aggregate demand by cutting the interest rate or decrease aggregate demand by raising the interest rate. But the exchange rate adds another dimension to the effects of monetary policy. To see why, let's return to the hypothetical country of Genovia and ask what happens if the central bank cuts the interest rate.

Just as in a closed economy, a lower interest rate leads to higher investment spending and higher consumer spending. But the decline in the interest rate also affects the foreign exchange market. Foreigners have less incentive to move funds into Genovia, because they will receive a lower rate of return on their loans. As a result, they have less need to exchange U.S. dollars for genos, so the demand for genos falls. At the same time, Genovians have *more* incentive to move funds abroad because the rate of return on loans at home has fallen, making investments outside the country more attractive. As a result, they need to exchange more genos for U.S. dollars, so the supply of genos rises.

Figure 35-12

Monetary Policy and the Exchange Rate

Here we show what happens in the foreign exchange market if Genovia cuts its interest rate. Residents of Genovia have a reduced incentive to keep their funds at home, so they invest more abroad. As a result, the supply of genos shifts rightward from S_1 to S_2. Meanwhile, foreigners have less incentive to put funds into Genovia, so the demand for genos shifts leftward from D_1 to D_2. The geno depreciates: the equilibrium exchange rate falls from XR_1 to XR_2. **>web...**

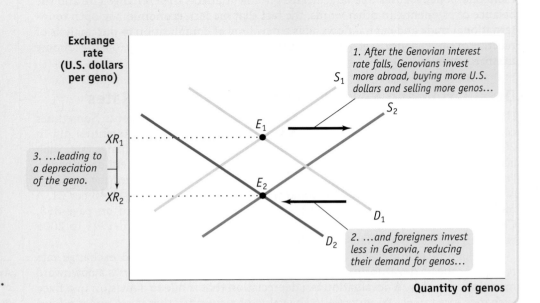

1. After the Genovian interest rate falls, Genovians invest more abroad, buying more U.S. dollars and selling more genos...

3. ...leading to a depreciation of the geno.

2. ...and foreigners invest less in Genovia, reducing their demand for genos...

Figure 35-12 shows the effect of an interest rate reduction on the foreign exchange market. The demand curve for genos shifts leftward, from D_1 to D_2, and the supply curve shifts rightward, from S_1 to S_2. The equilibrium exchange rate, as measured in U.S. dollars per geno, falls from XR_1 to XR_2. That is, a reduction in the Genovian interest rate causes the geno to *depreciate*.

The depreciation of the geno, in turn, affects aggregate demand. We've already seen how a devaluation—a depreciation that is the result of a change in a fixed exchange rate—raises exports and reduces imports, thereby increasing aggregate demand. A depreciation that results from an interest rate cut has the same effect: it increases exports and reduces imports, increasing aggregate demand.

In other words, monetary policy under floating rates has effects beyond those we've described in looking at closed economies. In a closed economy, a reduction in the interest rate leads to a rise in aggregate demand because it leads to more investment spending and consumer spending. In an open economy with a floating exchange rate, the interest rate reduction leads to increased investment spending and consumer spending, but it also increases aggregate demand in another way: it leads to a currency depreciation, which increases exports and reduces imports, increasing aggregate demand.

International Business Cycles

Up to this point we have discussed macroeconomics, even in an open economy, as if all demand shocks originate from the domestic economy. In reality, however, economies sometimes face shocks coming from abroad. For example, recessions in the United States have historically led to recessions in Mexico.

The key point is that changes in aggregate demand affect the demand for goods and services produced abroad as well as at home: other things equal, a recession leads to a fall in imports and an expansion leads to a rise in imports. And one country's imports are another country's exports. This link between aggregate demand in different national economies is one reason business cycles in different countries sometimes—but not always—seem to be synchronized. The prime example is the Great Depression, which affected countries around the world.

The extent of this link depends, however, on the exchange rate regime. To see why, think about what happens if a recession abroad reduces the demand for Genovia's exports. A reduction in foreign demand for Genovian goods and services is also a reduction in demand for genos on the foreign exchange market. If Genovia has a fixed exchange rate, it responds to this decline with exchange market intervention. But if Genovia has a floating exchange rate, the geno depreciates. Because Genovian goods and services become cheaper to foreigners when the demand for exports falls, the quantity of goods and services exported doesn't fall by as much as it would under a fixed rate. At the same time, the fall in the geno makes imports more expensive to Genovians, leading to a fall in imports. Both effects limit the decline in Genovia's aggregate demand.

One of the virtues of a floating exchange rate, according to advocates of such exchange rates, is that they help insulate countries from recessions originating abroad. This theory looked pretty good in the early 2000s: Britain, with a floating exchange rate, managed to stay out of a recession that affected the rest of Europe, and Canada, which also has a floating rate, suffered a less severe recession than the United States.

economics in action

The Joy of a Devalued Pound

In For Inquiring Minds on page 857 we mentioned the Exchange Rate Mechanism, the system of European fixed exchange rates that paved the way for the creation of the euro in 1999. Britain joined that system in 1990 but dropped out in 1992. The story of Britain's exit from the Exchange Rate Mechanism is a classic example of open-economy macroeconomic policy.

Britain originally fixed its exchange rate for both the reasons we described earlier in the chapter: British leaders believed that a fixed exchange rate would help promote international trade, and they also hoped that it would help fight inflation. But by 1992 Britain was suffering from high unemployment: the unemployment rate in September 1992 was over 10%. And as long as the country had a fixed exchange rate, there wasn't much the government could do. In particular, the government wasn't able to cut interest rates because it was using high interest rates to help support the value of the pound.

In the summer of 1992, investors began speculating against the pound—selling pounds in the expectation that the currency would drop in value. This speculation helped force the British government's hand. On September 16, 1992, Britain abandoned its fixed exchange rate. The pound promptly dropped 20% against the German mark, the most important European currency at the time.

At the time, the devaluation of the pound greatly damaged the prestige of the British government. But the chancellor of the exchequer—the equivalent of the U.S. treasury secretary—claimed to be happy about it. "My wife has never before heard me singing in the bath," he told reporters. There were several reasons for his joy. One was that the British government would no longer have to engage in large-scale exchange market intervention to support the pound's value. Another was that devaluation increases aggregate demand, so the pound's fall would help reduce unemployment. Finally, because Britain no longer had a fixed exchange rate, it was free to pursue an expansionary monetary policy.

Indeed, events made it clear that the chancellor's joy was well founded. British unemployment fell over the next two years, even as the unemployment rate rose in France and Germany. One person who did not share in the improving employment picture, however, was the chancellor himself. Soon after his remark about singing in the bath, he was fired. ∎

> > > > > > > > > > > > > > > > > > > >

➤➤QUICK REVIEW

➤ Countries can change fixed exchange rates. *Devaluation* or *revaluation* can help reduce surpluses or shortages in the foreign exchange market and can increase or reduce aggregate demand.

➤ In an open economy with a floating exchange rate, interest rates also affect the exchange rate, and so monetary policy affects aggregate demand through the effects of the exchange rate on imports and exports.

➤ Because one country's imports are another country's exports, business cycles are sometimes synchronized across countries. However, floating exchange rates may reduce this link.

1. Look at the data in Figure 35-11. Where do you see devaluations and revaluations of the franc against the mark?

2. In the late 1980s Canadian economists argued that the high interest rate policies of the Bank of Canada weren't just causing high unemployment—they were also making it hard for Canadian manufacturers to compete with the United States. Explain this complaint, using our analysis of how monetary policy works under floating exchange rates.

Solutions appear at back of book.

● If your interest was sparked by references in this chapter to speculation and currency crises, you can find a supplemental chapter online that explains how expectations can move exchange rates and the balance of payments—sometimes violently. To see the chapter, go to www.worthpublishers.com/krugmanwells.

SUMMARY

1. A country's **balance of payments accounts** summarize its transactions with the rest of the world. The **balance of payments on current account** includes the **balance of payments on goods and services** together with balances on factor income and transfers. The **merchandise trade balance** is a frequently cited component of the balance of payments on goods and services. The **balance of payments on financial account** measures capital flows. By definition, the balance of payments on current account plus the balance of payments on financial account is zero.

2. Capital flows respond to international differences in interest rates and other rates of return; they can be usefully analyzed using an international version of the loanable funds model, which shows how a country where the interest rate would be low in the absence of capital flows sends funds to a country where the interest rate would be high in the absence of capital flows. The underlying determinants of capital flows are international differences in savings and opportunities for investment spending.

3. Currencies are traded in the **foreign exchange market;** the prices at which they are traded are **exchange rates.** When a currency rises against another currency, it **appreciates;** when it falls, it **depreciates.** The **equilibrium exchange rate** matches the quantity of that currency supplied to the foreign exchange market to the quantity demanded.

4. To correct for international differences in inflation rates, economists calculate **real exchange rates,** which multiply the exchange rate between two countries' currencies by the ratio of the countries' price levels. A related concept, **purchasing power parity,** is the exchange rate that makes the cost of a basket of goods and services equal in two countries.

5. Countries adopt different **exchange rate regimes,** rules governing exchange rate policy. The main types are **fixed exchange rates,** where the government takes action to keep the exchange rate at a target level, and **floating exchange rates,** where the exchange rate is free to fluctuate. Countries can fix exchange rates using **exchange market intervention,** which requires them to hold **foreign exchange reserves** that they use to buy any surplus of their currency. Alternatively, they can use **foreign exchange controls.** Finally, they can change domestic policies, especially monetary policy, to shift the demand and supply curves in the foreign exchange market.

6. Exchange rate policy poses a dilemma: there are economic payoffs to stable exchange rates, but the policies used to fix the exchange rate have costs. Exchange market intervention requires large reserves, and exchange controls distort incentives. If monetary policy is used to help fix the exchange rate, it isn't available to use for domestic policy.

7. Fixed exchange rates aren't always permanent commitments: countries with a fixed exchange rate sometimes engage in **devaluations** or **revaluations.** In addition to helping eliminate a surplus of domestic currency on the foreign exchange market, a devaluation increases aggregate demand. Similarly, a revaluation reduces shortages of domestic currency and reduces aggregate demand.

8. Under floating exchange rates, expansionary monetary policy works in part through the exchange rate: cutting domestic interest rates leads to a depreciation, and through that to higher exports and lower imports, which increases aggregate demand. Contractionary monetary policy has the reverse effect.

9. The fact that one country's imports are another country's exports creates a link between the business cycle in different countries. Floating exchange rates, however, may reduce the strength of that link.

KEY TERMS

Balance of payments accounts, p. 837

Balance of payments on goods and services, p. 837

Merchandise trade balance (trade balance), p. 837

Balance of payments on current account (current account), p. 837

Balance of payments on financial account (financial account), p. 837

Foreign exchange market, p. 845

Exchange rates, p. 845

Appreciation, p. 846

Depreciation, p. 846

Equilibrium exchange rate, p. 847

Real exchange rate, p. 849

Purchasing power parity, p. 851

Exchange rate regime, p. 854

Fixed exchange rate, p. 854

Floating exchange rate, p. 854

Exchange market intervention, p. 855

Foreign exchange reserves, p. 855

Foreign exchange controls, p. 856

Devaluation, p. 859

Revaluation, p. 859

PROBLEMS

1. How would the following transactions be categorized in the U.S. balance of payments accounts? Would they be entered in the current account (as a payment to or from a foreigner) or the financial account (as a sale to or purchase of assets from a foreigner)? How will the balance of payments on the current and financial accounts change?

a. A French importer buys a case of California wine for $500.

b. An American who works for a French company deposits her paycheck, drawn on a Paris bank, into her San Francisco bank.

c. An American buys a bond from a Japanese company for $10,000.

d. An American charity sends $100,000 to Africa to help local residents buy food after a harvest shortfall.

2. In the economy of Scottopia in 2005, exports equaled $400 billion of goods and $300 billion of services, imports equaled $500 billion of goods and $350 billion of services, and the rest of the world purchased $250 billion of Scottopia's assets. What was the merchandise trade balance for Scottopia? What was the balance of payments on current account in Scottopia? What was the balance of payments on financial account? What was the value of Scottopia's purchases of assets from the rest of the world?

3. In the economy of Popania in 2005, total Popanian purchases of assets in the rest of the world equaled $300 billion, purchases of Popanian assets by the rest of the world equaled $400 billion, and Popania exported goods and services equal to $350 billion. What was Popania's balance of payments on financial account in 2005? What was its balance of payments on current account? What was the value of its imports?

4. Suppose that Northlandia and Southlandia are the only two trading countries in the world, that each nation runs a balance of payments on both current and financial accounts

equal to zero, and that each nation sees the other's assets as identical to its own. Using the accompanying diagrams, explain how the demand and supply of loanable funds, the interest rate, and the balance of payments on current and financial accounts will change in each country if international capital flows are possible.

(a) Northlandia

(b) Southlandia

5. Based on the exchange rates for the first trading days of 2004 and 2005 shown in the accompanying table, did the U.S. dollar appreciate or depreciate during 2004? Did the movement in the value of the U.S. dollar make American goods and services more or less attractive to foreigners?

January 2, 2004	January 3, 2005
US$1.79 to buy 1 British pound sterling	US$1.91 to buy 1 British pound sterling
33.98 Taiwan dollars to buy US$1	31.71 Taiwan dollars to buy US$1
US$0.78 to buy 1 Canadian dollar	US$0.83 to buy 1 Canadian dollar
104.27 Japanese yen to buy US$1	106.95 Japanese yen to buy US$1
US$1.26 to buy 1 euro	US$1.38 to buy 1 euro
1.24 Swiss francs to buy US$1	1.15 Swiss francs to buy US$1

6. Suppose the United States and Japan are the only two trading countries in the world. What will happen to the value of the U.S. dollar if the following occur, other things equal?

   a. Japan relaxes some of its import restrictions.

   b. The United States imposes some import tariffs on Japanese goods.

   c. Interest rates in the United States rise dramatically.

   d. A report indicates that Japanese cars last much longer than previously thought, especially compared with American cars.

7. In each of the following scenarios, suppose that the two nations are the only trading nations in the world. Given inflation and the change in the nominal exchange rate, which nation's goods become more attractive?

   a. Inflation is 10% in the United States and 5% in Japan; the U.S. dollar–Japanese yen exchange rate remains the same.

   b. Inflation is 3% in the United States and 8% in Mexico; the price of the U.S. dollar falls from 12.50 to 10.25 Mexican pesos.

   c. Inflation is 5% in the United States and 3% in the Euro-area; the price of the euro falls from $1.30 to $1.20.

   d. Inflation is 8% in the United States and 4% in Canada; the price of the Canadian dollar rises from US$0.60 to US$0.75.

8. Starting from a position of equilibrium in the foreign exchange market under a fixed exchange rate system, how must a government react to an increase in the demand for the nation's goods and services by the rest of the world to keep the exchange rate at its fixed value?

9. Suppose that Albernia's central bank has fixed the value of its currency, the bern, to the U.S. dollar (at a rate of US$1.50 to 1 bern) and is committed to that exchange rate. Initially, the foreign exchange market for the bern is also in equilibrium, as shown in the accompanying diagram. However, both Albernians and Americans begin to believe that there are big risks in holding Albernian assets, and as a result, they become unwilling to hold Albernian assets unless they receive a higher rate of return on them than they do on U.S. assets. How would this affect the diagram? If the Albernian central bank tries to keep the exchange rate fixed using monetary policy, how will this affect the Albernian economy?

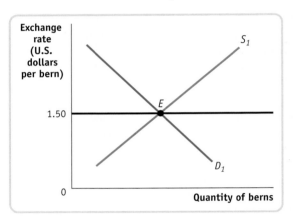

10. Your study partner asks you, "If central banks lose the ability to use discretionary monetary policy under fixed exchange rates, why would nations agree to a fixed exchange rate system?" How do you respond?

>> Solutions to "Check Your Understanding" Questions

This section offers suggested answers to the "Check Your Understanding" questions found within chapters.

Chapter One

1-1

1. **a.** This illustrates the concept of opportunity cost. Given that a person can only eat so much at one sitting, having an additional slice of chocolate cake requires that you forgo eating something else, such as a slice of the coconut cream pie.

   b. This illustrates the concept that resources are scarce. Even if there were more resources in the world, the total amount of those resources would be limited. As a result, scarcity would still arise. For there to be no scarcity, there would have to be unlimited amounts of everything (including unlimited time in a human life), which is clearly impossible.

   c. This illustrates the concept that people usually exploit opportunities to make themselves better off. Students will seek to make themselves better off by signing up for the tutorials of teaching assistants with good reputations and avoiding those teaching assistants with poor reputations. It also illustrates the concept that resources are scarce. If there were unlimited spaces in tutorials with good teaching assistants, they would not fill up.

   d. This illustrates the concept of marginal analysis. Your decision about allocating your time is a "how much" decision: how much time spent exercising versus how much time spent studying. You make your decision by comparing the benefit of an additional hour of exercising to its cost, the effect on your grades of one less hour spent studying.

2. **a.** Yes. The increased time spent commuting is a cost you will incur if you accept the new job. That additional time spent commuting—or equivalently, the benefit you would get from spending that time doing something else—is an opportunity cost of the new job.

   b. Yes. One of the benefits of the new job is that you will be making $50,000. But if you take the new job, you will have to give up your current job; that is, you have to give up your current salary of $45,000. So $45,000 is one of the opportunity costs of taking the new job.

   c. No. A more spacious office is an additional benefit of your new job and does not involve forgoing something else. So, it is not an opportunity cost.

1-2

1. **a.** This illustrates the concept that markets usually lead to efficiency. Any seller who wants to sell a book for at least $X does indeed sell to someone who is willing to buy a book for $X. As a result, there is no way to change how used textbooks are distributed among buyers and sellers in a way that would make one person better off without making someone else worse off.

   b. This illustrates the concept that there are gains from trade. Students trade tutoring services based on their different abilities in academic subjects.

   c. This illustrates the concept that when markets don't achieve efficiency, government intervention can improve society's welfare. In this case the market, left alone, will permit bars and nightclubs to impose costs on their neighbors in the form of loud music, costs that the bars and nightclubs have no incentive to take into account. This is an inefficient outcome because society as a whole can be made better off if bars and nightclubs are induced to reduce their noise.

   d. This illustrates the concept that resources should be used as efficiently as possible to achieve society's goals. By closing neighborhood clinics and shifting funds to the main hospital, better health care can be provided at a lower cost.

   e. This illustrates the concept that markets move toward equilibrium. Here, because books with the same amount of wear and tear sell for about the same price, no buyer or seller can be made better off by engaging in a different trade than he or she undertook. This means that the market for used textbooks has moved to an equilibrium.

2. **a.** This does not describe an equilibrium situation. Many students should want to change their behavior and switch to eating at the restaurants. Therefore, the situation described is not an equilibrium. An equilibrium will be established when students are equally as well off eating at the restaurants as eating at the dining hall—which would happen if, say, prices at the restaurants were higher than at the dining hall.

   b. This does describe an equilibrium situation. By changing your behavior and riding the bus, you would not be made better off. Therefore, you have no incentive to change your behavior.

Chapter Two

Check Your Understanding 2-1

1. a. False. An increase in the resources available to Tom for use in producing coconuts and fish changes his production possibility frontier by shifting it outward. This is because he can now produce more fish and coconuts than before. In the accompanying figure, the line labeled Tom's original *PPF* represents Tom's original production possibility frontier, and the line labeled Tom's new *PPF* represents the new production possibility frontier that results from an increase in resources available to Tom.

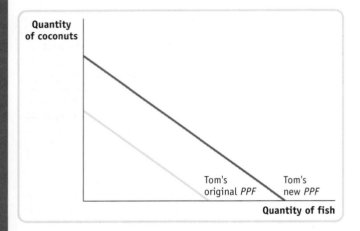

b. True. A technological change that allows Tom to catch more fish for any amount of coconuts gathered results in a change in his production possibility frontier. This is illustrated in the accompanying figure: the new production possibility frontier is represented by the line labeled Tom's new *PPF,* and the original production frontier is represented by the line labeled Tom's original *PPF.* Since the maximum quantity of coconuts that Tom can gather is the same as before, the new production possibility frontier intersects the vertical axis at the same point as the old frontier. But since the maximum possible quantity of fish is now greater than before, the new frontier intersects the horizontal axis to the right of the old frontier.

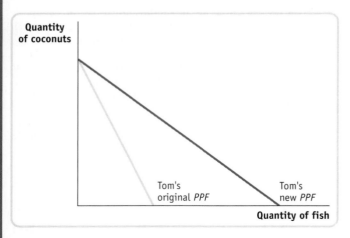

c. False. The production possibility frontier illustrates how much of one good an economy must give up to get more of another good only when resources are used efficiently. If an economy is producing inefficiently—that is, inside the frontier—then it does not have to give up a unit of one good in order to get another unit of the other good. Instead, by becoming more efficient, this economy can have more of both goods.

2. a. The United States has an absolute advantage in automobile production because it takes fewer Americans (6) to produce a car in one day than Italians (8). The United States also has an absolute advantage in washing machine production because it takes fewer Americans (2) to produce a washing machine in one day than Italians (3).

b. In Italy the opportunity cost of a washing machine in terms of an automobile is $3/8$: $3/8$ of a car can be produced with the same number of workers and in the same time it takes to produce 1 washing machine. In the United States the opportunity cost of a washing machine in terms of an automobile is $2/6 = 1/3$: $1/3$ of a car can be produced with the same number of workers and in the same time it takes to produce 1 washing machine. Since $1/3 < 3/8$, the United States has a comparative advantage in the production of washing machines: to produce a washing machine, only $1/3$ of a car must be given up in the United States but $3/8$ of a car must be given up in Italy. This means that Italy has a comparative advantage in automobiles. This can be checked as follows. The opportunity cost of an automobile in terms of a washing machine in Italy is $8/3$, equal to $2\frac{2}{3}$: $2\frac{2}{3}$ washing machines can be produced in the time it takes to produce 1 car in Italy. And the opportunity cost of an automobile in terms of a washing machine in the United States is $6/2$, equal to 3: 3 washing machines can be produced in the time it takes to produce 1 car in the United States.

c. The greatest gains are realized when each country specializes in producing the good for which it has a comparative advantage. Therefore the United States should specialize in washing machines and Italy should specialize in automobiles.

3. An increase in the amount of money spent by households results in an increase in the flow of goods to households. This, in turn, generates an increase in demand for factors of production by firms. Therefore there is an increase in the number of jobs in the economy.

Check Your Understanding 2-2

1. a. This is a normative statement because it stipulates what should be done. In addition, it may have no "right" answer. That is, should people be prevented from all dangerous personal behavior if they enjoy that behavior—like skydiving? Your answer will depend on your point of view.

b. This is a positive statement because it is a description of fact.

2. a. True. Economists often have different value judgments about the desirability of a particular social goal. But despite those differences in value judgments, they will tend to agree that society, once it has decided to pursue a given social goal, should adopt the most efficient policy to achieve that goal. Therefore economists are likely to agree on adopting policy choice B.

b. False. Disagreements between economists are more likely to arise because they base their conclusions on different models or because they have different value judgments about the desirability of the policy.

c. False. Deciding which goals a society should try to achieve is a matter of value judgments, not a question of economic analysis.

Chapter Three

Check Your Understanding 3-1

1. a. The quantity of umbrellas demanded is higher at any given price on a rainy day than on a dry day. This is a rightward *shift of* the demand curve, since at any given price the quantity demanded rises. This implies that any specific quantity can now be sold at a higher price.

b. The quantity of weekend calls demanded rises in response to a price reduction. This is a *movement along* the demand curve for weekend calls.

c. The demand for roses increases the week of Valentine's Day. This is a rightward *shift of* the demand curve.

d. The quantity of gasoline demanded falls in response to a rise in price. This is a *movement along* the demand curve.

Check Your Understanding 3-2

1. a. The quantity of houses supplied rises as a result of an increase in prices. This is a *movement along* the supply curve.

b. The quantity of strawberries supplied is higher at any given price. This is a rightward *shift of* the supply curve.

c. The quantity of labor supplied is lower at any given wage. This is a leftward *shift of* the supply curve compared to the supply curve during the school vacation. So, in order to attract workers, fast-food chains have to offer higher wages.

d. The quantity of labor supplied rises in response to a rise in wages. This is a *movement along* the supply curve.

e. The quantity of cabins supplied is higher at any given price. This is a rightward *shift of* the supply curve.

Check Your Understanding 3-3

1. a. The supply curve shifts rightward. At the original equilibrium price of the year before, the quantity of grapes supplied exceeds the quantity demanded. This is a case of surplus. The price of grapes will fall.

b. The demand curve shifts leftward. At the original equilibrium price, the quantity of hotel rooms supplied exceeds the quantity demanded. This is a case of surplus. The rates for hotel rooms will fall.

c. The demand curve for secondhand snowblowers shifts rightward. At the original equilibrium price, the quantity of secondhand snowblowers demanded exceeds the quantity supplied. This is a case of shortage. The equilibrium price of secondhand snowblowers will rise.

Check Your Understanding 3-4

1. a. The market for large cars: this is a rightward shift in demand caused by a decrease in the price of a complement, gasoline. As a result of the shift, the equilibrium price of large cars will rise and the equilibrium quantity of large cars bought and sold will also rise.

b. The market for fresh paper made from recycled stock: this is a rightward shift in supply due to a technological innovation. As a result of this shift, the equilibrium price of fresh paper made from recycled stock will fall and the equilibrium quantity bought and sold will rise.

c. The market for movies at a local movie theater: this is a leftward shift in demand caused by a fall in the price of a substitute, pay-per-view movies. As a result of this shift, the equilibrium price of movie tickets will fall and the equilibrium number of people who go to the movies will also fall.

2. Upon the announcement of the new chip, the demand curve for computers using the earlier chip shifts leftward, as demand decreases, and the supply curve for these computers shifts rightward, as supply increases.

a. If demand decreases relatively more than supply increases, then the equilibrium quantity falls, as shown here:

b. If supply increases relatively more than demand decreases, then the equilibrium quantity rises, as shown here:

In both cases, the equilibrium price falls.

Chapter Four

1. a. Fewer homeowners are willing to rent out their driveways because the price ceiling has caused a decrease in the payment they receive. This reflects the concept that the quantity supplied decreases as the price decreases. It is shown in the following diagram by the movement from point *E* to point *A* along the supply curve, a reduction in quantity of 400 parking spaces.

b. The quantity demanded increases by 400 spaces as the price decreases. At a lower price, more fans are willing to drive and rent a parking space. It is shown in the diagram by the movement from point *E* to point *B* along the demand curve.

c. Under a price ceiling, the quantity demanded exceeds the quantity supplied; as a result, shortages arise. In this case, there will be a shortage of 800 parking spaces. It is shown by the horizontal distance between points *A* and *B*.

d. Price ceilings result in wasted resources. The additional time fans spend to guarantee a parking space is wasted time.

e. Price ceilings lead to inefficient allocation of a good— here, the parking spaces—to consumers.

f. Price ceilings lead to black markets.

2. a. False. By lowering the price that producers receive, price ceilings lead to a decrease in the quantity supplied.

b. True. Price ceilings lead to a lower quantity supplied than in a free market. As a result, some people who would have been willing to pay the market price, and therefore would have gotten the good in a free market, are unable to obtain it when a price ceiling is imposed.

c. True. Those producers who still sell the product now receive less for it and are therefore worse off. Other producers will no longer find it worthwhile to sell the product at all and therefore will also be made worse off.

1. a. Some gas station owners will benefit from getting a higher price. Point *A* indicates the sales (0.7 million gallons) made by these owners. But some will lose; there are those who made sales at the market price of $2 but do not make sales at the regulated price of $4. These missed sales are indicated on the graph by the fall in the quantity demanded along the demand curve, from point *E* to point *A*. Overall, the effect on station owners is ambiguous.

b. Those who buy gas at the higher price of $4 probably will receive better service; this is an example of *inefficiently high quality* caused by a price floor as gas station owners compete on quality rather than price. But opponents are correct to claim that consumers are generally worse off— those who buy at $4 would have been happy to buy at $2, and many who were willing to buy at a price between $2 and $4 are now unwilling to buy. This is indicated on the graph by the fall in the quantity demanded along the demand curve, from point *E* to point *A*.

c. Proponents are wrong because consumers and some gas station owners are hurt by the price floor, which creates "missed opportunities"—desirable transactions between consumers and station owners that never take place. Moreover, the inefficiency of wasted resources arises as consumers spend time and money driving to other states. The price floor tempts people to engage in black market activity. With the price floor of $4, only 0.7 million gallons are sold. But at prices between $2 and $4, there are drivers who cumulatively want to buy more than 0.7 million gallons and owners who are willing to sell to them, a situation likely to lead to illegal activity.

1. a. The price of a ride is $7 since the quantity demanded at this price is 6 million: $7 is the *demand price* of 6 million rides. This is represented by point *A* in the following figure.

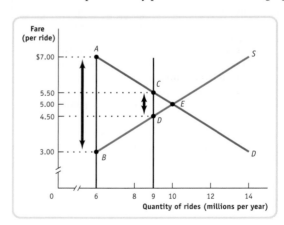

b. At 6 million rides, the supply price is $3, represented by point *B* in the figure. The wedge between the demand price of $7 and the supply price of $3 is the quota rent per ride, $4. This is represented in the figure above by the vertical distance between points *A* and *B*.

c. At 9 million rides, the demand price is $5.50, indicated by point *C* on the figure, and the supply price is $4.50, indicated by point *D*. The quota rent is the difference between the demand price and the supply price: $1.

2. The figure shows how a decrease in demand by 4 million rides, represented by a leftward shift of the demand curve from D_1 to D_2: at any given price, the quantity demanded falls by 4 million rides. This eliminates the effect of a quota limit of 8 million rides. At point E_2, the new market equilibrium, the equilibrium quantity is equal to the quota limit; as a result, the quota has no effect on the market.

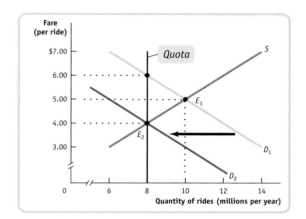

1. a. Under the quota, only 9 million pounds of butter are bought and sold. We can limit the amount of butter that dairies want to sell to 9 million pounds by setting the supply price to $0.90, as indicated by point D in the following figure, which is a replication of Figure 4-3. Similarly, we can limit the amount of butter consumers want to buy to 9 million pounds by setting the demand price to $1.20, as indicated by point C. The difference between these two prices, $0.30, is therefore equal to the tax that reduces sales to only 9 million pounds, indicated by the vertical distance between points C and D. Thus a tax of $0.30 per pound generates the same inefficiency as a quota of 9 million pounds.

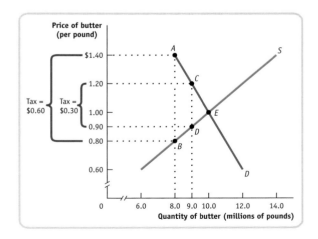

b. To answer this question, we must find a supply price and a demand price that generate the same quantity of butter but differ by $0.60. Examination of the supply and demand schedules shows that the supply price of $0.80 (indicated by point B) and the demand price of $1.40 (indicated by point A) satisfy these conditions: They give rise to the same quantity transacted, 8 million pounds, and they differ by $0.60. Therefore, a quota of 8 million pounds will generate the same level of inefficiency as a tax of $0.60. (Note that a supply price of $1.20 and a demand price of $0.60 also differ by $0.60 and give rise to the same quantity, 12 million pounds. Why is this choice not the right answer here? Because 12 million pounds is more than people want to buy in the free market, so it can't be a valid quota level.)

c. In part a, the unrestricted equilibrium price is $1 per pound. So consumers pay $0.20 ($1.20 − $1.00) of the $0.30 tax and producers pay $0.10 ($1.00 − $0.90).

Chapter Five

1. By the midpoint method, the percent change in the price of strawberries is

$$\frac{\$1.50 - \$1.00}{(\$1.50 + \$1.00)/2} \times 100 = \frac{\$0.50}{\$1.25} \times 100 = 40\%$$

Similarly, the percent change in the quantity of strawberries demanded is

$$\frac{200,000 - 100,000}{(100,000 + 200,000)/2} \times 100 = \frac{100,000}{150,000} \times 100 = 67\%$$

Therefore the price elasticity of demand using the midpoint method is $67\%/40\% = 1.7$.

2. By the midpoint method, the percent change in the quantity of movie tickets demanded in going from 4,000 tickets to 5,000 tickets is

$$\frac{5,000 - 4,000}{(4,000 + 5,000)/2} \times 100 = \frac{1,000}{4,500} \times 100 = 22\%$$

Since the price elasticity of demand is 1 at the current consumption level, it will take a 22% drop in the price of movie tickets to generate a 22% increase in quantity demanded.

3. Since price rises, we know that quantity demanded must fall. Given the current price of $0.50, a $0.05 increase in price represents a 10% change, using the method in Equation 5-2. This implies that

$$\frac{\% \text{ change in quantity demanded}}{10\%} = 1.2$$

so that the percent change in quantity demanded is 12%. A 12% decrease in quantity demanded represents $100,000 \times 0.12$, or 12,000 sandwiches.

Check Your Understanding Question 5-2

1. a. Elastic demand. Consumers are highly responsive to changes in price. For a rise in price, the quantity effect (which tends to reduce total revenue) outweighs the price effect (which tends to increase total revenue). Overall, this leads to a fall in total revenue.

b. Unit-elastic demand. Here the revenue lost to the fall in price is exactly equal to the revenue gained from higher sales. The quantity effect exactly offsets the price effect.

c. Inelastic demand. Consumers are relatively unresponsive to changes in price. For consumers to purchase a given percent increase in output, the price must fall by an even greater percent. The price effect of a fall in price (which tends to reduce total revenue) outweighs the quantity effect (which tends to increase total revenue). As a result, total revenue decreases.

d. Inelastic demand. Consumers are relatively unresponsive to price, so a given percent fall in output is accompanied by an even greater percent rise in price. The price effect of a rise in price (which tends to increase total revenue) outweighs the quantity effect (which tends to reduce total revenue). As a result, total revenue increases.

2. a. Once bitten by a venomous snake, the victim's demand for an antidote is very likely to be perfectly inelastic because there is no substitute and it is necessary for survival. The demand curve will be vertical, at a quantity equal to the needed dose.

b. Students' demand for green erasers is likely to be perfectly elastic because there are easily available substitutes: nongreen erasers. The demand curve will be horizontal, at a price equal to that of nongreen erasers.

Check Your Understanding Question 5-3

1. By the midpoint method, the percent increase in Chelsea's income is

$$\frac{\$18,000 - \$12,000}{(\$12,000 + \$18,000)/2} \times 100 = \frac{\$6,000}{\$15,000} \times 100 = 40\%$$

Similarly, the percent increase in her consumption of CDs is

$$\frac{40 - 10}{(10 + 40)/2} \times 100 = \frac{30}{25} \times 100 = 120\%$$

Chelsea's income elasticity of demand for CDs is therefore 120%/40% = 3.

2. Sanjay's consumption of expensive restaurant meals will fall more than 10% because a given percent change in income (10% here) induces a larger percent change in consumption of an income-elastic good.

3. The cross-price elasticity of demand is 5%/20% = 0.25. Since the cross-price elasticity of demand is positive, the two goods are substitutes.

Check Your Understanding Question 5-4

1. By the midpoint method, the percent change in the number of hours of web-design services contracted is

$$\frac{500,000 - 300,000}{(300,000 + 500,000)/2} \times 100 = \frac{200,000}{400,000} \times 100 = 50\%$$

Similarly, the percent change in the price of web-design services is:

$$\frac{\$150 - \$100}{(\$100 + \$150)/2} \times 100 = \frac{\$50}{\$125} \times 100 = 40\%$$

The price elasticity of supply is 50%/40% = 1.25; hence supply is elastic.

2. True. An increase in demand raises price. If the price elasticity of supply of milk is low, then relatively little additional supply will be forthcoming as the price rises. As a result, the price of milk will rise substantially to satisfy the increased demand for milk. If the price elasticity of supply is high, then a relatively large amount of additional supply will be produced as the price rises. As a result, the price of milk will rise only by a little to satisfy the higher demand for milk.

3. False. It is true that long-run price elasticities of supply are generally larger than short-run elasticities of supply. But this means that the short-run supply curves are generally steeper, not flatter, than the long-run supply curves.

4. True. When supply is perfectly elastic, the supply curve is a horizontal line. A change in demand therefore has no effect on price; it affects only the quantity bought and sold.

Check Your Understanding Question 5-5

1. The fact that demand is very inelastic means that consumers will reduce their demand for textbooks very little in response to an increase in the price caused by the tax. The fact that supply is somewhat elastic means that suppliers will respond to the fall in the price by reducing supply. As a result, the incidence of the tax will fall heavily on consumers of economics textbooks and very little on publishers as shown in the accompanying figure.

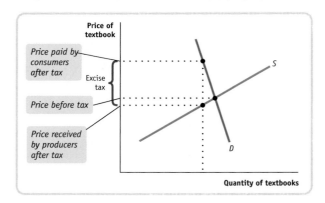

2. True. When a substitute is readily available, demand is elastic. This implies that producers cannot easily pass on the cost of the tax to consumers because consumers will respond to an increased price by switching to the substitute. Furthermore, when producers have difficulty adjusting the amount of the good produced, supply is inelastic. That is, producers cannot easily reduce output in response to a lower price net of the tax. So the tax burden will fall more heavily on producers than consumers.

3. The fact that supply is very inelastic means that producers will reduce their supply of bottled water very little in response to the fall in price caused by the tax. Demand, on the other hand, will fall in response to an increase in price because demand is somewhat elastic. As a result, the incidence of the tax will fall heavily on producers of bottled spring water and very little on consumers as shown in the accompanying figure.

4. True. The lower the elasticity of supply, the more the burden of a tax will fall on producers rather than consumers, other things equal.

Chapter Six

1. A consumer buys each pepper if the price is less than (or just equal to) the consumer's willingness to pay for that pepper. The demand schedule is constructed by asking how many peppers will be demanded at any price. The accompanying table illustrates the demand schedule.

Price of pepper	Quantity of peppers demanded	Quantity of peppers demanded by Casey	Quantity of peppers demanded by Josie
$0.90	1	1	0
0.80	2	1	1
0.70	3	2	1
0.60	4	2	2
0.50	5	3	2
0.40	6	3	3
0.30	8	4	4
0.20	8	4	4
0.10	8	4	4
0.00	8	4	4

When the price is $0.40, Casey's consumer surplus from the first pepper is $0.50, from his second pepper $0.30, from his third pepper $0.10, and he does not buy any more peppers. Casey's individual consumer surplus is therefore $0.90. Josie's consumer surplus from her first pepper is $0.40, from her second pepper $0.20, from her third pepper $0.00 (she is just indifferent between buying it and not buying it, so let's assume she does buy it), and she does not buy any more peppers. Josie's individual consumer surplus is therefore $0.60. Total consumer surplus at a price of $0.40 is therefore $0.90 + $0.60 = $1.50.

1. A producer supplies each pepper if the price is greater than (or just equal to) the producer's cost of producing that pepper. The supply schedule is constructed by asking how many peppers will be supplied at any price. The accompanying table illustrates the supply schedule.

Price of pepper	Quantity of peppers supplied	Quantity of peppers supplied by Cara	Quantity of peppers supplied by Jamie
$0.90	8	4	4
0.80	7	4	3
0.70	7	4	3
0.60	6	4	2
0.50	5	3	2
0.40	4	3	1
0.30	3	2	1
0.20	2	2	0
0.10	2	2	0
0.00	0	0	0

When the price is $0.70, Cara's producer surplus from the first pepper is $0.60, from her second pepper $0.60, from her third pepper $0.30, from her fourth pepper $0.10, and she does not supply any more peppers. Cara's individual producer surplus is therefore $1.60. Jamie's producer surplus from his first pepper is $0.40, from his second pepper $0.20, from his third pepper $0.00 (he is just indifferent between supplying it and not supplying it, so let's assume he does supply it), and he does not supply any more peppers. Jamie's individual producer surplus is therefore $0.60. Total producer surplus at a price of $0.70 is therefore $1.60 + $0.60 = $2.20.

1. The quantity demanded equals the quantity supplied at a price of $0.50, the equilibrium price. At that price, a total quantity of five peppers will be bought and sold. Casey will buy three peppers and receive consumer surplus of $0.40 on his first, $0.20 on his second, and $0.00 on his third pepper. Josie will buy two peppers and receive consumer surplus of $0.30 on her first and $0.10 on her second pepper. Total consumer surplus is therefore $1.00. Cara will supply three peppers and receive producer surplus of $0.40 on her first, $0.40 on her second, and

$0.10 on her third pepper. Jamie will supply two peppers and receive producer surplus of $0.20 on his first and $0.00 on his second pepper. Total producer surplus is therefore $1.10. Total surplus in this market is therefore $1.00 + $1.10 = $2.10.

2. a. If Josie consumes one less pepper, she loses $0.60 (her willingness to pay for her second pepper); if Casey consumes one more pepper, he gains $0.30 (his willingness to pay for his fourth pepper). This results in an overall loss of consumer surplus of $0.60 − $0.30 = $0.30.

b. Cara's cost of the last pepper she supplied (the third pepper) is $0.40, and Jamie's cost of producing one more (his third pepper) is $0.70. Total producer surplus therefore falls by $0.70 − $0.40 = $0.30.

c. Josie's willingness to pay for her second pepper is $0.60; this is what she would lose if she were to consume one less pepper. And Cara's cost of producing her third pepper is $0.40; this is what she would save if she were to produce one less pepper. If we therefore reduced quantity by one pepper, we would lose $0.60 − $0.40 = $0.20 of total surplus.

Check Your Understanding 6-4

1. a. At a price paid by consumers of $0.70, Casey's consumer surplus is $0.20 from his first pepper (he loses $0.20 compared to the market equilibrium), $0.00 from his second pepper (he loses $0.20), and he no longer buys the third pepper. Josie's consumer surplus is $0.10 from her first pepper (she loses $0.20), and she no longer buys the second pepper (she loses $0.10 of consumer surplus that she previously got from that second pepper). So the loss in consumer surplus is $0.70.

b. At a price received by producers of $0.30, Cara's producer surplus is $0.20 from her first pepper (she loses $0.20), $0.20 from her second pepper (she loses $0.20), and she no longer produces the third pepper (she loses $0.10 that she previously got from that third pepper). Jamie's producer surplus is $0.00 from his first pepper (he loses $0.20), and he no longer produces his second pepper. So the loss in producer surplus is $0.70.

c. Since three peppers are now sold and the tax on each is $0.40, the government tax revenue is 3 × $0.40 = $1.20.

d. Introduction of the tax resulted in a loss of total surplus of $0.70 + $0.70 = $1.40. Of that amount, $1.20 went to the government in the form of tax revenue. But $0.20 is lost: that is the amount of deadweight loss from this tax.

2. a. The demand for gasoline is inelastic because there is no close substitute for gasoline itself, and it is difficult for drivers to arrange substitutes for driving, such as taking public transportation. As a result, the deadweight loss from a tax on gasoline would be relatively small, as shown in the accompanying diagram.

b. The demand for milk chocolate bars is elastic because there are close substitutes: dark chocolate bars, milk chocolate kisses, and so on. As a result, the deadweight loss from a tax on milk chocolate bars would be relatively large, as shown in the accompanying diagram.

Chapter Seven

Check Your Understanding Question 7-1

1. a. Supplies are an explicit cost because they require an outlay of money.
   b. If the basement can be used in some other way that generates money, such as renting it to a student, then the implicit cost is that money forgone. Otherwise, the implicit cost is zero.
   c. Wages are an explicit cost.
   d. By using the van for their business, Karma and Don forgo the money they could have gained by selling it. So use of the van is an implicit cost.
   e. Karma's forgone wages from her job are an implicit cost.

Check Your Understanding 7-2

1. a. The marginal cost of doing your laundry is the opportunity cost of your time spent doing laundry today—that is, the value you would place on spending time today on your next best alternative activity, like seeing a movie. The marginal benefit is having more clean clothes today to choose from.
   b. The marginal cost of changing your oil is the opportunity cost of time spent changing your oil now as well as the explicit cost of the oil change. The marginal benefit is the improvement in your car's performance.
   c. The marginal benefit of another jalapeno on your nachos is the pleasant taste that you receive from it. The marginal cost is the unpleasant feeling of a burning mouth that you receive from it plus any explicit cost of the jalapeno.
   d. The marginal benefit of hiring another worker in your company is the value of the output that worker produces. The marginal cost is the wage you must pay that worker.
   e. The marginal benefit of another dose of the drug is the value of the reduction in the patient's disease. The marginal cost is the value of the increased side effects from this additional dose.
   f. The marginal benefit of assigning one more soldier to your invasion force is the increased probability of a successful invasion generated by that extra soldier. The marginal cost is the decreased probability of success in the alternative project for which you could use that soldier, such as defending your borders.

2. a. As can be seen from Table 7-6, the optimal quantity is 6 lawns when marginal cost is constant at $18.50. At the 6th lawn, Felix's marginal benefit is $19.00, exceeding marginal cost by $0.50. At the 7th lawn, however, marginal benefit is $18.00, implying a loss of $0.50 on the 7th lawn if he mows it. His total net gain is equal to ($35.00 − $18.50) + ($30.00 − $18.50) + ($26.00 − $18.50) + ($23.00 − $18.50) + ($21.00 − $18.50) + ($19.00 − $18.50) = $43.00.
   b. The lawn that generates the highest marginal benefit is the 1st lawn; it generates $35.00 in marginal benefit. So the optimal quantity is 0 when marginal cost is always greater than $35.00. In that case, it would never benefit Felix to do even the 1st lawn. In going from the 3rd to the 4th lawn, marginal benefit goes from $26.00 to $23.00. So any marginal cost less than or equal to $26.00 but higher than $23.00 implies an optimal quantity of 3.

Check Your Understanding 7-3

1. a. Your sunk cost is $8,000 because none of the $8,000 you spent on the truck is recoverable.
   b. Your sunk cost is $4,000 because 50 percent of the $8,000 spent on the truck is recoverable.

2. a. This is an invalid argument because the time and money already spent are a sunk cost at this point.
   b. This is also an invalid argument because what you should have done two years ago is irrelevant to what you should do now.
   c. This is a valid argument because it recognizes that sunk costs are irrelevant to what you should do now.
   d. This is a valid argument given that you are concerned about disappointing your parents. But your parents' views are irrational because they do not recognize that the time already spent is a sunk cost.

Check Your Understanding 7-4

1. a. The net present value of project A is unaffected by the interest rate since it is money received today; its present value is still $100. The net present value of project B is now $−10 + $115/1.02 = $102.75. The net present value of project C is now $119 − $20/1.02 = $99.39. Project B is now preferred.
   b. When the interest rate is lower, the cost of waiting for money that arrives in the future is lower. For example, at a 10% interest rate, $1 arriving 1 year from today is worth only 1/$1.10 = $0.91. But when the interest rate is 2%, $1 arriving 1 year from today is worth 1/$1.02 = $0.98, a sizable increase. As a result, project B, which has a benefit one year from today, becomes more attractive. And project C, which has a cost 1 year from today, becomes less attractive.

Chapter Eight

Check Your Understanding 8-1

1. a. The fixed input is the 10-ton machine, and the variable input is electricity.
   b. As you can see from the declining numbers in the third column of the accompanying table, electricity does indeed exhibit diminishing returns: the marginal product of each additional kilowatt of electricity is less than that of the previous kilowatt.

Quantity of electricity (kilowatts)	Quantity of ice (pounds)	Marginal product of electricity (pounds per kilowatt)
0	0	
		1,000
1	1,000	
		800
2	1,800	
		600
3	2,400	
		400
4	2,800	

c. A 50% increase in the size of the fixed input means that Bernie now has a 15-ton machine. So the fixed input is now the 15-ton machine. Since it generates a 100% increase in output for any given amount of electricity, the quantity of output and marginal product are now as shown in the accompanying table.

Quantity of electricity (kilowatts)	Quantity of ice (pounds)	Marginal product of electricity (pounds per kilowatt)
0	0	
		2,000
1	2,000	
		1,600
2	3,600	
		1,200
3	4,800	
		800
4	5,600	

Check Your Understanding 8-2

1. a. As shown in the accompanying table, the marginal cost for each pie is found by multiplying the marginal cost of the previous pie by 1.5. Variable cost for each output level is found by summing the marginal cost for all the pies produced to reach that output level. So, for example, the variable cost of three pies is $1.00 + $1.50 + $2.25 = $4.75. Average fixed cost for Q pies is calculated as $9.00/$Q$ since fixed cost is $9.00. Average variable cost for Q pies is equal to variable cost for the Q pies divided by Q; for example, the average variable cost of five pies is $13.19/5, or approximately $2.64. Finally, average total cost can be calculated in two equivalent ways: as TC/Q or as $AVC + AFC$.

Quantity of pies	Marginal cost of pie	Variable cost	Average fixed cost of pie	Average variable cost of pie	Average total cost of pie
0		$0.00	—	—	—
	$1.00				
1		1.00	$9.00	$1.00	$10.00
	1.50				
2		2.50	4.50	1.25	5.75
	2.25				
3		4.75	3.00	1.58	4.58
	3.38				
4		8.13	2.25	2.03	4.28
	5.06				
5		13.19	1.80	2.64	4.44
	7.59				
6		20.78	1.50	3.46	4.96

b. The spreading effect dominates the diminishing returns effect when average total cost is falling: the fall in AFC dominates the rise in AVC for pies 1 to 4. The diminishing returns effect dominates when average total cost is rising: the rise in AVC dominates the fall in AFC for pies 5 and 6.

c. Alicia's minimum-cost output is 4 pies; this generates the lowest average total cost, $4.28. When output is less than 4, the marginal cost of a pie is less than the average total cost of the pies already produced. So making an additional pie lowers average total cost. For example, the marginal cost of pie 3 is $2.25, whereas the average total cost of pies 1 and 2 is $5.75. So making pie 3 lowers average total cost to $4.58, equal to (2 × $5.75 + $2.25)/3. When output is more than 4, the marginal cost of a pie is greater than the average total cost of the pies already produced. Consequently, making an additional pie raises average total cost. So, although the marginal cost of pie 6 is $7.59, the average total cost of pies 1 through 5 is $4.44. Making pie 6 raises average total cost to $4.96, equal to (5 × $4.44 + $7.59)/6.

Check Your Understanding 8-3

1. a. The accompanying table shows the average total cost of producing 12,000, 22,000, and 30,000 units for each of the three choices of fixed cost. For example, if the firm makes choice 1, the total cost of producing 12,000 units of output is $8,000 + 12,000 × $1.00 = $20,000. The average total cost of producing 12,000 units of output is therefore $20,000/12,000 = $1.67. The other average total costs are calculated similarly.

	12,000 units	22,000 units	30,000 units
Average total cost from choice 1	$1.67	$1.36	$1.27
Average total cost from choice 2	1.75	1.30	1.15
Average total cost from choice 3	2.25	1.34	1.05

Therefore, if the firm wanted to produce 12,000 units, it would make choice 1 because this gives it the lowest average total cost. If it wanted to produce 22,000 units, it would make choice 2. If it wanted to produce 30,000 units, it would make choice 3.

b. Having historically produced 12,000 units, the firm would have adopted choice 1. When producing 12,000 units, the firm would have had an average total cost of $1.67. When output jumps to 22,000 units, the firm cannot alter its choice of fixed cost in the short run, so its average total cost in the short run will be $1.36. In the long run, however, it will adopt choice 2, making its average total cost fall to $1.30.

c. If the firm believes that the increase in demand is temporary, it should not alter its fixed cost from choice 1 because choice 2 generates higher average total cost as soon as output falls back to its original quantity of 12,000 units: $1.75 versus $1.67.

2. a. This firm is likely to experience constant returns to scale. To increase output, the firm must hire more workers, purchase more computers, and pay additional telephone charges. Because these inputs are easily available, their long-run average total cost is unlikely to change as output increases.
   b. This firm is likely to experience diseconomies of scale. As the firm takes on more projects, the costs of communication and coordination required to implement the expertise of the firm's owner are likely to increase.
   c. This firm is likely to experience economies of scale. Because diamond mining requires a large initial set-up cost for excavation equipment, long-run average total cost will fall as output increases.

Chapter Nine

Check Your Understanding
9-1

1. a. With only two producers in the world, each producer will represent a sizable share of the market. So the industry will not be perfectly competitive.
   b. Because each producer of gas from the North Sea has only a small market share of total world supply of natural gas, and since natural gas is a standardized product, the natural gas industry will be perfectly competitive.
   c. Because each designer has a distinctive style, high-fashion clothes are not a standardized product. So the industry will not be perfectly competitive.
   d. The market described here is the market in each city for tickets to baseball games. Since there are only one or two teams in each major city, each team will represent a sizable share of the market. So the industry will not be perfectly competitive.

Check Your Understanding
9-2

1. a. The firm should shut down immediately when price is less than minimum average variable cost, the shut-down price. In the accompanying diagram, this is optimal for prices in the range 0 to P_1.

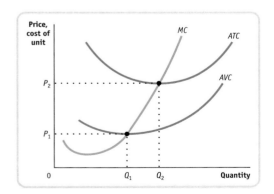

   b. When price is greater than minimum average variable cost (the shut-down price) but less than minimum average total cost (the break-even price), the firm should continue to operate in the short run even though it is making a loss. This is optimal for prices in the range P_1 to P_2 and quantities Q_1 to Q_2.
   c. When price exceeds minimum average total cost (the break-even price), the firm makes a profit. This happens for prices in excess of P_2 and results in quantities greater than Q_2.

2. This is an example of a temporary shut-down by a firm when the market price lies below the shut-down price, the minimum average variable cost. In this case, the market price is the price of a lobster meal and variable cost is the variable cost of serving such a meal, such as the cost of the lobster, employee wages, and so on. In this example, however, it is the average variable cost curve rather than the market price that shifts over time, due to seasonal changes in the cost of lobsters. Maine lobster shacks have relatively low average variable cost during the summer, when cheap Maine lobsters are available; during the rest of the year, their average variable cost is relatively high due to the high cost of imported lobsters. So the lobster shacks are open for business during the summer, when their minimum average variable cost lies below price; but they close during the rest of the year, when price lies below their minimum average variable cost.

Check Your Understanding
9-3

1. a. A fall in the fixed cost of production generates a fall in the average total cost of production and, in the short run, an increase in each firm's profit at the current output level. So in the long run new firms will enter the industry. The increase in supply drives down price and profits. Once profits are driven back to zero, entry will cease.
   b. An increase in wages generates an increase in the average total cost of production at every output level. In the short run, firms incur losses at the current output level, and so in the long run some firms will exit the industry. As firms exit, supply decreases, price rises, and losses are reduced. Exit will cease once losses return to zero.
   c. Price will rise as a result of the increased demand, leading to a short-run increase in profits at the current output level. In the long run, firms will enter the industry, generating an increase in supply, a fall in price, and a fall in profits. Once profits are driven back to zero, entry will cease.
   d. The shortage of a key input causes that input's price to increase, resulting in an increase in average total costs for producers. Firms incur losses in the short run, and some firms will exit the industry in the long run. The fall in supply generates an increase in price and decreased losses. Exit will cease when losses have returned to zero.

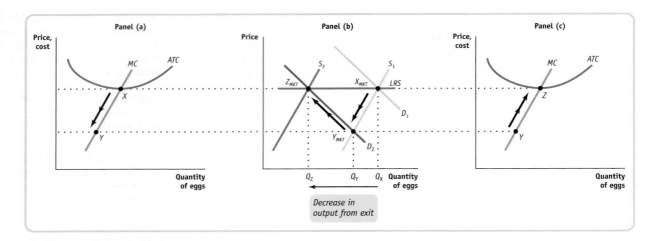

2. In the above diagram, point X_{MKT} in panel (b), the intersection of S_1 and D_1, represents the long-run industry equilibrium before the change in consumer tastes. When tastes change, demand falls and the industry moves in the short run to point Y_{MKT} in panel (b), at the intersection of the new demand curve D_2 and S_1, the short-run supply curve representing the same number of egg producers as in the original equilibrium at point X_{MKT}. As the market price falls, an individual firm reacts by producing less—as shown in panel (a)—as long as the market price remains above the minimum average variable cost. If market price falls below average variable cost, the firm would shut down immediately. At point Y_{MKT} the price of eggs is below minimum average total cost, creating losses for producers. This leads some firms to exit, which shifts the short-run industry supply curve leftward to S_2. A new long-run equilibrium is established at point Z_{MKT}. As this occurs, the market price rises again, and, as shown in panel (c), each remaining producer reacts by increasing output (here, from point Y to point Z). All remaining producers again make zero profits. The decrease in the quantity of eggs supplied in the industry comes entirely from the exit of some producers from the industry. The long-run industry supply curve is the curve labeled LRS in panel (b).

Chapter Ten

10-1

1. Consuming a unit that generates negative marginal utility leaves the consumer with lower total utility than not consuming that unit at all. A rational consumer, a consumer who maximizes utility, would not do that. For example, from Figure 10-1 you can see that Cassie receives 64 utils if she consumes 8 clams; but if she consumes the 9th clam, she loses a util, netting her a total utility of only 63 utils. So whenever consuming a unit generates negative marginal utility, the consumer is made better off by not consuming that unit.

2. Since Marta has diminishing marginal utility of coffee, her first cup of coffee of the day generates the greatest increase in total utility. Her third and last cup of the day generates the least.

3. a. Mabel has increasing marginal utility of exercising since each additional unit consumed brings more additional enjoyment than the previous unit.

b. Mei has constant marginal utility of CDs because each additional unit generates the same additional enjoyment as the previous unit.

c. Dexter has diminishing marginal utility of restaurant meals since the additional utility generated by a good restaurant meal is less when he consumes lots of them than when he consumed few of them.

10-2

1. a. At a price of $5.00 for a movie ticket and income of $10.00, the maximum quantity of tickets that can be purchased is $10/$5 = 2 as shown in the accompanying diagram. This is the vertical intercept. At a price of $2.50 for a bucket of popcorn, the horizontal intercept—the maximum quantity of popcorn that can be purchased given the budget—is $10.00/$2.50 = 4. The slope of the budget line is equal to the rise over run: $-2/4 = -1/2$ (there is a negative sign because the line is downward sloping). The opportunity cost of a bucket of popcorn in terms of movie tickets is equal to minus the slope of the budget line, equal to $1/2$ in this case: 1 bucket of popcorn can be obtained if $1/2$ movie ticket is forgone.

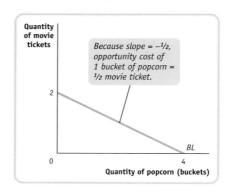

b. At a price of $1.50 for a pair of socks and income of $12.00, the vertical intercept—the maximum quantity of pairs of socks that can be purchased—is $12.00/$1.50 = 8, shown in the accompanying diagram. The horizontal intercept—the maximum quantity of pairs of underwear that can be purchased—is $12.00/$4.00 = 3. The slope of the budget line is $-8/3 = -2^2/3$. The opportunity cost of underwear in terms of socks is equal to minus the slope of the budget line, equal to $2^2/3$ in this case: 1 pair of underwear can be obtained if $2^2/3$ pairs of socks are forgone.

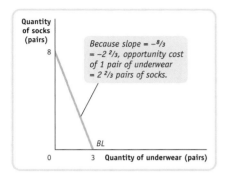

10-3

1. From Figure 10-5 you can see that the marginal utility per dollar at 3 pounds of clams and the marginal utility per dollar at 8 pounds of potatoes are approximately the same, at a value of about 1. But it is not Sammy's optimal consumption bundle because it is not affordable given his income of $20; 3 pounds of clams and 8 pounds of potatoes costs $4 × 3 + $2 × 8 = $28, $8 more than Sammy's income. This can be illustrated with Sammy's budget line from Figure 10-4: a bundle of 3 pounds of clams and 8 pounds of potatoes is represented by point X in the accompanying diagram, a point that lies outside Sammy's budget line.

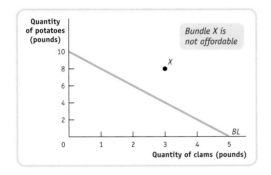

2. If Sammy chose the bundle that maximized his marginal utility per dollar for each good, he would choose to consume 1 pound of potatoes, where $MU_P/P_P = 5.75$, and 1 pound of clams, where $MU_C/P_C = 3.75$. But this bundle generates 26.5 utils for him. Instead, Sammy should choose the consumption bundle that satisfies his budget constraint and for which the marginal utility per dollar for both goods is equal.

10-4

1. Since spending on orange juice is a small share of Clare's spending, the income effect from a rise in the price of orange juice is insignificant. Only the substitution effect, represented by the substitution of lemonade in place of orange juice, is significant.

2. Since rent is a large share of Delia's expenditures, the increase in rent generates an income effect, making Delia feel poorer. Since housing is a normal good for Delia, the income and substitution effects move in the same direction, leading her to reduce her consumption of housing by moving to a smaller apartment.

3. Since a meal ticket is a significant share of the students' living costs, an increase in its price will generate an income effect. Students respond to the price increase by eating more often in the cafeteria. So the substitution effect (which would induce them to eat in the cafeteria less often) and the income effect (which would induce them to eat in the cafeteria more often than at restaurants because they are poorer) move in opposite directions. This happens because cafeteria meals are an inferior good. In fact, since the income effect outweighs the substitution effect (students eat in the cafeteria more as the price of meal tickets increases), cafeteria meals are a Giffen good.

Chapter Eleven

11-1

1. a. As you can see from the accompanying diagram, the four bundles are associated with three indifference curves: B on the 10-util indifference curve, A and C on the 6-util indifference curve, and D on the 4-util indifference curve.

b. From comparing the quantities of chocolate kisses and licorice drops, you can predict that Samantha will prefer *B* to *A* because *B* gives her one more chocolate kiss and the same amount of licorice drops as *A*. Next, you can predict that she will prefer *C* to *D* because *C* gives her one more chocolate kiss and the same amount of licorice drops as *D*. You can also predict that she prefers *B* to *D* because *B* gives her two more licorice drops and the same amount of chocolate kisses as *D*. But without data about utils, you cannot predict how Samantha would rank *A* versus *C* or *D* because *C* and *D* have more chocolate kisses but fewer licorice drops than *A*. Neither can you rank *B* versus *C*, for the same reason.

2. Bundles *A* and *B* each generate 200 utils since they both lie on the 200 util indifference curve. Likewise, bundles *A* and *C* each generate 100 utils since they both lie on the 100 util indifference curve. But this implies that *A* generates 100 utils and also that *A* generates 200 utils, which is a contradiction and so cannot be true. It shows that indifference curves cannot cross.

Check Your Understanding 11-2

1. a. The marginal rate of substitution of books in place of games, MU_B/MU_G, is 2 for Lucinda and 5 for Kyle. This implies that Lucinda is willing to trade 1 more book for 2 fewer games and Kyle is willing to trade 1 more book for 5 fewer games. So starting from a bundle of 3 books and 6 games, Lucinda would be equally content with a bundle of 4 books and 4 games and Kyle would be equally content with a bundle of 4 books and 1 game. Lucinda finds it more difficult to trade games for books: she is willing to give up only 2 games for a book while Kyle is willing to give up 5 games for a book. If books are measured on the horizontal axis and games on the vertical axis, Kyle's indifference curve will be steeper than Lucinda's at the current consumption bundle.

b. Lucinda's current consumption bundle is optimal if P_B/P_G, the relative price of books in terms of games, is 2. Kyle's current consumption bundle is not optimal at this relative price; his bundle would be optimal only if the relative price of books in terms of games is 5. Since, for Kyle, $MU_B/MU_G = 5$ but $P_B/P_G = 2$, Kyle should consume fewer games and more books, thereby lowering his MU_B/MU_G until it is equal to 2.

Check Your Understanding 11-3

1. Since Sanjay cares only about the number of jelly beans, not about whether they are banana- or pineapple-flavored, he is always willing to exchange one for the other at the same rate. This implies that his marginal rate of substitution of one flavor of jelly bean in place of another is constant. So they are perfect substitutes.

2. Cherry pie and vanilla ice cream are complements for Hillary since her marginal utility of cherry pie goes up as she has another scoop of vanilla ice cream. But they are ordinary goods, not perfect complements, because she gains some utility from having cherry pie without any vanilla ice cream.

3. Omnisoft's software programs and its operating system are perfect complements for its customers: they gain no utility from the software programs without the operating system. So their marginal rate of substitution of one good in place of the other is undefined, and their indifference curves have a right-angle shape.

4. Income and leisure are ordinary goods for Darnell: the more income he has made by working more hours, the less willing he is to earn yet more by giving up additional leisure time.

Check Your Understanding 11-4

1. a. Sammy's original budget line is illustrated in the accompanying diagram by BL_1. His original consumption is at point *A*. When the price of clams falls, his budget line rotates outward to BL_2, allowing him to achieve a higher level of utility. The pure substitution effect would involve the same change in the slope of his budget line, but without any increase in utility. So the pure substitution effect is illustrated by the movement from *A* to *B*. In fact, his utility does rise, so his consumption moves from *A* to *C*. The movement from *B* to *C* is the income effect.

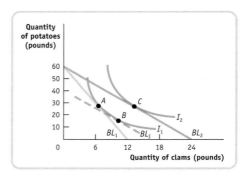

b. Again, in the accompanying diagram Sammy's original budget line is BL_1, and his original consumption is at point *A*. The increase in the price of clams causes his budget line to rotate inward to BL_2. This reduces his total utility. The pure substitution effect is what would happen if the slope of the budget line changed but his total utility did not; it is shown as the movement from *A* to *B*. The full effect of the price change is the movement from *A* to *C*. The movement from *B* to *C* is the income effect.

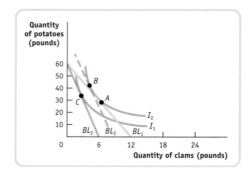

Chapter Twelve

12-1

1. Many college professors will depart for other lines of work if the government imposes a wage that is lower than the market wage. Fewer professors will result in fewer courses taught and therefore fewer college degrees produced. It will adversely affect sectors of the economy that depend directly on colleges, such as the local shopkeepers who sell goods and services to students and faculty, college textbook publishers, and so on. It will also adversely affect firms that use the "output" produced by colleges: new college graduates. Firms that need to hire new employees with college degrees will be hurt as a smaller supply results in a higher market wage for college graduates. Ultimately, the reduced supply of college-educated workers will result in a lower level of human capital in the entire economy relative to what it would have been without the policy. And this will hurt all sectors of the economy that depend on human capital. The sectors of the economy that might benefit are firms that compete with colleges in the hiring of would-be college professors. For example, accounting firms will find it easier to hire people who would otherwise have been professors of accounting, and publishers will find it easier to hire people who would otherwise have been professors of English (easier in the sense that the firms can recruit would-be professors with a lower wage than before). In addition, workers who already have college degrees will benefit; they will command higher wages as the supply of college-educated workers falls.

12-2

1. **a.** As the demand for services increases, the price of services will rise. And as the price of the output produced by the industries increases, this shifts the *VMPL* curve upward—that is, the demand for labor rises. This results in an increase in both the equilibrium wage rate and the quantity of labor employed.
   b. The fall in the catch per day means that the marginal product of labor in the industry declines. The *VMPL* curve shifts downward, generating a fall in the equilibrium wage rate and the equilibrium quantity of labor employed.

2. When firms from different industries compete for the same workers, then each worker in the various industries will be paid the same equilibrium wage, *W*. And since, by the marginal productivity theory of income distribution, $VMPL = P \times MPL = W$ for the last worker hired in equilibrium, the last worker hired in each of these different industries will have the same value of the marginal product of labor.

12-3

1. **a.** False. Income disparities associated with gender, race, or ethnicity can be explained by the marginal productivity theory of income distribution provided that differences in marginal productivity across people are correlated with gender, race, or ethnicity. One possible source for such correlation is past discrimination. Such discrimination can lower individuals' marginal productivity by, for example, preventing them from acquiring the human capital that would raise their productivity. Another possible source of the correlation is differences in work experience that are associated with gender, race, or ethnicity. For example, in jobs where work experience or length of tenure is important, women may earn lower wages because on average more women than men take child-care-related absences from work.
   b. True. Companies that discriminate when their competitors do not are likely to hire less able workers because they discriminate against more able workers who are considered of the wrong gender, race, or ethnicity. And with less able workers, such companies are likely to earn lower profits than their competitors who don't discriminate.
   c. Ambiguous. In general, workers who are paid less because they have less experience may or may not be the victims of discrimination. The answer depends on the reason for the lack of experience. If workers have less experience because they are young or have chosen to do something else rather than gain experience, then they are not victims of discrimination if they are paid less. But if workers lack experience because previous job discrimination prevented them from gaining experience, then they are indeed victims of discrimination when they are paid less.

12-4

1. **a.** Clive is made worse off if, before the new law, he had preferred to work more than 35 hours per week. As a result of the law, he can no longer choose his preferred time allocation; he now consumes fewer goods and more leisure than he would like.
   b. Clive's utility is unaffected by the law if, before the law, he had preferred to work 35 or fewer hours per week. The law has not changed his preferred time allocation.
   c. Clive can never be made better off by a law that restricts the number of hours he can work. He can only be made worse off (case a) or equally as well off (case b).

2. The substitution effect would induce Clive to work fewer hours and consume more leisure after his wage falls—the fall in wage means the price of an hour of leisure falls, leading Clive to consume more leisure. But a fall in his wage also generates a fall in Clive's income. The income effect of this is to induce Clive to consume less leisure and therefore work more hours, since he is now poorer and leisure is a normal good. If the income effect dominates the substitution effect, Clive will in the end work more hours than before.

Chapter Thirteen

Check Your Understanding 13-1

1. **a.** eMarkets! will have to know the willingness to pay of every potential consumer—that is, the demand schedule. It will also have to know the seller's cost for each unit of output of every potential producer—that is, the supply schedule. (Equivalently, it must know the marginal cost curve of every potential producer.)

   b. Some producers who have a seller's cost greater than $199 will produce because they were mistakenly told that the price would be $299; some who have a seller's cost equal to or less than $199 will not produce because they were mistakenly told that the price would be $99. So producer surplus is lower because the market price cannot allocate production efficiently among producers. You cannot tell whether the output will be equal to, less than, or greater than the equilibrium output. Overproduction may occur if a relatively high number of producers think the price will be $299, and underproduction may occur if a relatively high number of producers think the price will be $99.

   c. Consumers with a willingness to pay of $299, who are told that the price is $399, will not purchase the good. For each of these consumers, consumer surplus of $299 − $199 = $100 is lost. Consumers with a willingness to pay of $199, who are allowed to buy the good at a price of $99 each, gain $119 − $99 = $20 in surplus. So this transfer of units from high-willingness-to-pay consumers to low-willingness-to-pay consumers results in a net loss of comsumer surplus of $100 − $20 = $80 per unit.

Check Your Understanding 13-2

1. **a.** Before the change in preferences, the Bountifullian labor market is in equilibrium, defined by the condition $VMPL_C$ = wage rate = $VMPL_S$. After preferences change, a greater demand for breakfast cereal will induce an increase in the price of cereal, P_C. $VMPL_C = P_C \times MPL_C$ will therefore rise, with the result that $VMPL_C$ > wage rate. A lower demand for sausage will induce a decrease in the price of sausage, P_S. $VMPL_S = P_S \times MPL_S$ will fall, with the result that $VMPL_S$ < wage rate. Sausage producers will let some of their workers go; these workers will move to cereal producers, who are hiring additional workers. As labor moves from the sausage to the cereal industry, MPL_C and $VMPL_C$ fall, but MPL_S and $VMPL_S$ rise.

   b. You will know that the economy has fully adjusted when the labor market has reattained equilibrium: when $VMPL_C$ = wage rate = $VMPL_S$ again. Because all consumers face the same price for cereal, P_C, and the same price for sausage, P_S, there will be *efficiency in consumption*: every consumer who consumes a good has a higher willingness to pay for it than someone who does not. Next, because cereal producers and sausage producers compete for workers in a perfectly competitive labor market, there will be no surplus of labor and all labor will be fully employed. So there will be *efficiency in production*: there is no way to produce more of one good without producing less of the other. Finally, there will be *efficiency in output levels*: any other mix of cereal and sausage reduces welfare. Because $VMPL_C$ = wage rate = $VMPL_S$ in equilibrium, the allocation of labor to the two industries, and therefore the mix of outputs of the two goods, fully reflects consumers' valuations of the two goods.

Check Your Understanding 13-3

1. There is an objective way to determine whether an economy is efficient: determine whether there is another allocation of production and/or consumption that makes some people better off without making others worse off. If not, it is efficient; if yes, it is inefficient. It is much harder to determine whether an economy is fair because there is no objective measure of determining this. What a person deems is fair typically depends upon his or her viewpoint.

2. **a.** The problem with this statement is that what one "should contribute" or "should receive" is subject to interpretation. Suppose one person has worked extremely hard to become wealthy but another is born wealthy and has never worked. Should each person be required to contribute the same to society? Some would say yes (those who think the amount of money a person has is the only criterion) but others would say no (those who think that people should be rewarded for working hard relative to those who don't)—it depends upon the person's viewpoint. Similarly, suppose one person needs an operation to be able to see, another person needs an operation to be able to walk, and society doesn't have the resources to perform both operations. Whose need is more important? Again, the answer is unclear because society has no way of measuring whether one person's needs are more compelling than another's.

   b. This statement is also subject to very different interpretations. First, how do we define "work hard"? Do people who spend years working on something they enjoy, such as writing a classical sonata, "work harder" than those who do less intense but very unappealing work? Also, this statement implies that people who cannot work hard for reasons outside their control—say, due to illness—should be rewarded less. Whether or not this is fair is again subject to a person's viewpoint.

Chapter Fourteen

Check Your Understanding 14-1

1. **a.** This does not support the conclusion. Texas Tea has a limited amount of oil, and the price has risen in order to equalize supply and demand.

b. This supports the conclusion because the market for home heating oil has become monopolized, and a monopolist will reduce the quantity supplied and raise price to generate profit.

c. This does not support the conclusion. Texas Tea has raised its price to consumers because the price of its input, home heating oil, has increased.

d. This supports the conclusion. The fact that other firms have begun to supply heating oil at a lower price implies that Texas Tea must have earned profits—profits that attracted the other firms to Frigid.

e. This supports the conclusion. It indicates that Texas Tea enjoys a barrier to entry because it controls access to the only Alaskan heating oil pipeline.

Check Your Understanding 14-2

1. a. The price at each output level is found by dividing the total revenue by the number of emeralds produced; for example, the price when 3 emeralds are produced is $252/3 = $84. The price at the various output levels is then used to construct the demand schedule in the accompanying table.

b. The marginal revenue schedule is found by calculating the change in total revenue as output increases by one unit. For example, the marginal revenue generated by increasing output from 2 to 3 emeralds is ($252 – $186) = $66.

c. The quantity effect component of marginal revenue is the additional revenue generated by selling one more unit of the good at the market price. For example, as shown in the accompanying table, at 3 emeralds, the market price is $84; so, when going from 2 to 3 emeralds the quantity effect is equal to $84.

d. The price effect component of marginal revenue is the decline in total revenue caused by the fall in price when one more unit is sold. For example, as shown in the table, when only 2 emeralds are sold, each emerald sells at a price of $186/2 = $93. However, when Emerald, Inc. sells an additional emerald, the price must fall by $9 to $84. So the price effect component in going from 2 to 3 emeralds is (–$9) × 2 = –$18. That's because 2 emeralds can only be sold at a price of $84 when 3 emeralds in total are sold, although they could have been sold at a price of $93 when only 2 in total were sold.

Quantity of emerald demanded	Price of emerald	Marginal revenue	Quantity effect component	Price effect component
1	$100			
		$86	$93	–$7
2	93			
		66	84	–18
3	84			
		28	70	–42
4	70			
		–30	50	–80
5	50			

e. In order to determine Emerald, Inc.'s profit-maximizing output level, you must know its marginal cost at each output level. Its profit-maximizing output level is the one at which marginal revenue is equal to marginal cost.

2. As the accompanying diagram shows, the marginal cost curve shifts upward to $400. The profit-maximizing quantity falls, and so does profit, from $3,200 to $300 × 6 = $1,800. Competitive industry profits, though, are unchanged at zero.

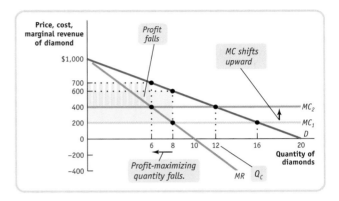

Check Your Understanding 14-3

1. a. Cable Internet service is a natural monopoly. So the government should intervene only if it believes that price exceeds average total cost, where average total cost is based on the cost of laying the cable. In this case it should impose a price ceiling equal to average total cost. Otherwise, it should do nothing.

b. The government should approve the merger only if it fosters competition by transferring some of the company's landing slots to another, competing airline.

2. a. False. As can be see from Figure 14-8, panel (b), the inefficiency arises from the fact that some of the consumer surplus is transformed into deadweight loss (the orange area), not that it is transformed into profit (the green area).

b. True. If a monopolist sold to all customers who have a valuation greater than or equal to marginal cost, all mutually beneficial transactions would occur and there would be no deadweight loss.

3. As shown in the accompanying diagram, a monopolist produces Q_M, the output level at which $MR = MC$. A monopolist who mistakenly believes that $P = MR$ produces the output level at which $P = MC$ (when, in fact, $P > MR$, and at the true profit-maximizing level of output, $P > MR = MC$). This misguided monopolist will produce the output level Q_C, where the demand curve crosses the marginal cost curve—the same output level produced if the industry were perfectly competitive. It will charge the price P_C, which is equal to marginal cost, and make zero profit. The entire shaded area is equal to the consumer surplus, which is also equal to total surplus in this case (since the monopolist receives zero producer surplus). There is no deadweight loss since every consumer who is willing to pay as much as or more than marginal cost gets the good. A smart monopolist, however, will produce the output level Q_M, and charge the price P_M. Profit equals the green area, consumer surplus corresponds to the blue area, and total surplus is equal to the sum of the green and blue areas. The orange area is the deadweight loss generated by the monopolist.

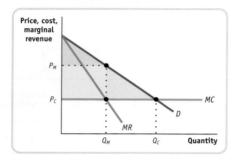

1. **a.** False. A price-discriminating monopolist will sell to some customers that a single-price monopolist will refuse to—namely, customers with a high price elasticity of demand who are willing to pay only a relatively low price for the good.
   b. False. Although a price-discriminating monopolist does indeed capture more of the consumer surplus, inefficiency is lower: more mutually beneficial transactions occur because the monopolist makes more sales to customers with a low willingness to pay for the good.
   c. True. Under price discrimination consumers are charged prices that depend on their price elasticity of demand. A consumer with highly elastic demand will pay a lower price than a consumer with inelastic demand.

2. **a.** This is not a case of price discrimination because all consumers, regardless of their price elasticities of demand, value the damaged merchandise less than undamaged merchandise. So the price must be lowered to sell the merchandise.
   b. This is a case of price discrimination. Senior citizens have a higher price elasticity of demand for restaurant meals (their demand for restaurant meals is more responsive to price changes) than other patrons. Restaurants lower the price to high-elasticity consumers (senior citizens). Consumers with low price elasticity of demand will pay the full price.

   c. This is a case of price discrimination. Consumers with a high price elasticity of demand will pay a lower price by collecting and using discount coupons. Consumers with a low price elasticity of demand will not use coupons.
   d. This is not a case of price discrimination; it is simply a case of supply and demand.

Chapter Fifteen

1. **a.** The world oil industry is an oligopoly because a few countries control a necessary resource for production, oil reserves.
   b. The microprocessor industry is an oligopoly because two firms possess superior technology and so dominate industry production.
   c. The wide-bodied passenger jet industry is an oligopoly because there are economies of scale in production.

1. **a.** The firm is likely to act noncooperatively and raise output, which will generate a negative price effect. But because the firm's current market share is small, the negative price effect will fall much more heavily on its rivals' revenues than on its own. At the same time the firm benefits from a positive quantity effect.
   b. The firm is likely to act noncooperatively and raise output, which will generate a fall in price. Because its rivals have higher costs, they will lose money at the lower price while the firm continues to make profits. So the firm may be able to drive its rivals out of business by increasing its output.
   c. The firm is likely to collude. Because it is costly for consumers to switch products, the firm would have to lower its price quite substantially (by increasing quantity a lot) to induce consumers to switch to its product. So increasing output is likely to be unprofitable given the large negative price effect.
   d. The firm is likely to collude. It cannot increase sales because it is currently at maximum production capacity.

1. When Margaret builds a missile, Nikita's payoff from building a missile as well is −10; it is −20 if he does not. The same set of payoffs holds for Margaret when Nikita builds a missile: her payoff is −10 if she builds one as well, −20 if she does not. So it is a Nash (or noncooperative) equilibrium for both Margaret and Nikita to build missiles, and their total payoff is (−10) + (−10) = −20. But their total payoff is greatest when neither builds a missile: their total payoff is 0 + 0 = 0. But this outcome—the cooperative outcome—is unlikely. If Margaret builds a missile but Nikita does not, Margaret gets a payoff of +8,

rather than the 0 she gets if she doesn't build a missile. So Margaret is better off if she builds a missile but Nikita doesn't. Similarly, Nikita is better off if he builds a missile but Margaret does not: he gets a payoff of +8, rather than the 0 he gets if he doesn't build a missile. So both players have an incentive to build a missile. Both will build a missile, and each gets a payoff of −10. So unless Nikita and Margaret are able to communicate in some way to enforce cooperation, they will act in their own individual interests and each will build a missile.

2. a. Future entry by several new firms will increase competition and drive down industry profits. As a result, there is less future profit to protect by behaving cooperatively today. So each oligopolist is more likely to behave noncooperatively today.

b. When it is very difficult for a firm to detect if another firm has raised output, then it is very difficult to enforce cooperation by playing "tit for tat." So it is more likely that a firm will behave noncooperatively.

c. When firms have coexisted while maintaining high prices for a long time, each expects cooperation to continue. So the value of behaving cooperatively today is high and it is likely that firms will engage in tacit collusion.

Check Your Understanding
15-4

1. a. This is likely to be interpreted as evidence of tacit collusion. Firms in the industry are able to tacitly collude by setting their prices according to the published "suggested" price of the largest firm in the industry. This is a form of price leadership.

b. This is not likely to be interpreted as evidence of tacit collusion. Considerable variation in market share indicates that firms have been competing to capture each others' business.

c. This is not likely to be interpreted as evidence of tacit collusion. These features make it more unlikely that consumers will switch products in response to lower prices. So this is a way for firms to avoid any temptation to gain market share by lowering price. This is a form of product differentiation used to avoid direct competition.

d. This is likely to be interpreted as evidence of tacit collusion. In the guise of discussing sales targets, firms can create a cartel by designating quantities to be produced by each firm.

e. This is likely to be interpreted as evidence of tacit collusion. By raising prices together, each firm in the industry is refusing to undercut its rivals by leaving its price unchanged or lowering it. Because it could gain market share by doing so, refusing to do it is evidence of tacit collusion.

Chapter Sixteen
Check Your Understanding
16-1

1. a. Ladders are not differentiated as a result of monopolistic competition. A ladder producer makes different ladders (tall ladders versus short ladders) to satisfy different consumer needs, not to avoid competition with rivals. So two tall ladders made by two different producers will be indistinguishable by consumers.

b. Soft drinks are an example of product differentiation as a result of monopolistic competition. For example, several producers make colas; each is differentiated in terms of taste, which fast-food chains sell it, and so on.

c. Department stores are an example of product differentiation as a result of monopolistic competition. They serve different clienteles that have different price sensitivities and different tastes. They also offer different levels of customer service and are situated in different locations.

d. Steel is not differentiated as a result of monopolistic competition. Different types of steel (beams versus sheets) are made for different purposes, not to distinguish one steel manufacturer's products from another's.

2. a. Perfectly competitive industries and monopolistically competitive industries both have many sellers. So it may be hard to distinguish between them solely in terms of number of firms. And in both market structures, there is free entry into and exit from the industry in the long run. But in a perfectly competitive industry, one standardized product is sold, while in a monopolistically competitive industry, products are differentiated. So you should ask whether products are differentiated in the industry.

b. In a monopoly there is only one firm, but a monopolistically competitive industry contains many firms. So you should ask whether or not there is a single firm in the industry.

Check Your Understanding
16-2

1. a. An increase in fixed cost raises average total cost and shifts the average total cost curve upward. In the short run firms incur losses, and some will exit the industry. In the long run, this results in a rightward shift of the demand curves for those firms that remain in the industry, since each one now serves a larger share of the market. Long-run equilibrium is reestablished when the demand curve for each remaining firm has shifted rightward to the point where it is tangent to the firm's new, higher average total cost curve. At this point each firm's price just equals its average total cost, and each firm makes zero profit.

b. A decrease in marginal cost lowers average total cost and shifts the average total cost curve and the marginal cost curve downward. Because firms make profits, in the long run new entrants are attracted into the industry. In the long run, this results in a leftward shift of each firm's demand curve since each firm now has a smaller share of the market. Long-run equilibrium is reestablished when each firm's demand curve has shifted leftward to the point where it is tangent to the new, lower average total cost curve. At this point each firm's price just equals average total cost, and each firm makes zero profit.

2. If all the existing firms in the industry joined together to create a monopoly, they would achieve monopoly profits. But this would induce new firms to create new, differentiated products and then enter the industry and capture some of the monopoly profits. So in the long run it would be impossible to maintain a monopoly. The problem arises from the fact that because new firms can create new products, there is no barrier to entry that can maintain a monopoly.

Check Your Understanding 16-3

1. a. False. As can be seen from panel (b) of Figure 16-4, a monopolistically competitive firm produces at a point where price exceeds marginal cost—unlike a perfectly competitive firm, which produces where price equals marginal cost (at the point of minimum average total cost). A monopolistically competitive firm will refuse to sell at marginal cost. This would be below average total cost and the firm would incur a loss.
   b. True. Firms in a monopolistically competitive industry could achieve higher profits (monopoly profits) if they all joined together. In addition, since the industry possesses economies of scale, producing a larger quantity of output would lower the firm's average total cost. The effect on consumers, however, is ambiguous. They would experience less choice. But if consolidation substantially reduces industry-wide average total cost and therefore substantially increases industry-wide output, consumers may experience lower prices under monopoly.
   c. True. Fads and fashions are created and promulgated by advertising, which is found in oligopolies and monopolistically competitive industries but not in monopolies or perfectly competitive industries.

Check Your Understanding 16-4

1. a. This is economically useful because such advertisements are likely to focus on the medical benefits of aspirin.
   b. This is economically wasteful because such advertisements are likely to focus on promoting Bayer aspirin versus a rival's aspirin product. The two products are medically indistinguishable.
   c. This is economically useful because such advertisements are likely to focus on the health and enjoyment benefits of orange juice.
   d. This is economically wasteful because such advertisements are likely to focus on promoting Tropicana orange juice versus a rival's product. The two are likely to be indistinguishable by consumers.
   e. This is economically useful because the longevity of a business gives a potential customer information about its quality.

2. A successful brand name indicates a desirable attribute, such as quality, to a potential buyer. So, other things

equal—such as price—a firm with a successful brand name will achieve higher sales than a rival with a comparable product but without a successful brand name. This is likely to deter new firms from entering an industry in which an existing firm has a successful brand name.

Chapter Seventeen

Check Your Understanding 17-1

1. a. To determine comparative advantage, we must compare the two countries' opportunity costs for a given good. Take the opportunity cost of 1 ton of corn in terms of bicycles. In China, the opportunity cost of 1 bicycle is 0.01 ton of corn; so the opportunity cost of 1 ton of corn is 1/0.01 bicycles = 100 bicycles. The United States has the comparative advantage in corn since its opportunity cost in terms of bicycles is 50, a smaller number. Similarly, the opportunity cost in the United States of 1 bicycle in terms of corn is 1/50 ton of corn = 0.02 ton of corn. This is greater than 0.01, the Chinese opportunity cost of 1 bicycle in terms of corn, implying that China has a comparative advantage in bicycles.
   b. Given that the United States can produce 200,000 bicycles if no corn is produced, it can produce 200,000 bicycles × 0.02 ton of corn/bicycle = 4,000 tons of corn when no bicycles are produced. Likewise, if China can produce 3,000 tons of corn if no bicycles are produced, it can produce 3,000 tons of corn × 100 bicycles/ton of corn = 300,000 bicycles if no corn is produced. These points determine the vertical and horizontal intercepts of the U.S. and Chinese production possibility frontiers as shown in the accompanying diagram.

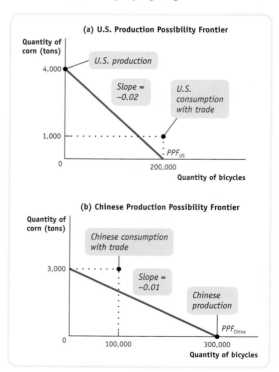

(a) U.S. Production Possibility Frontier

(b) Chinese Production Possibility Frontier

c. The figure shows the production and consumption points of the two countries. Each country is clearly better off with international trade because each now consumes a bundle of the two goods that lies outside its own production possibility frontier, indicating that these bundles were unattainable when each country was in autarky.

2. **a.** According to the Heckscher–Ohlin model, this pattern of trade occurs because the United States has a relatively larger endowment of factors of production, such as human capital and physical capital, that are suited to the production of movies, but France has a relatively larger endowment of factors of production suited to wine-making, such as vineyards and the human capital of vintners.

b. According to the Heckscher–Ohlin model, this pattern of trade occurs because the United States has a relatively larger endowment of factors of production, such as human and physical capital, that are suited to making machinery, but Brazil has a relatively larger endowment of factors of production suited to shoe-making, such as labor and leather.

Check Your Understanding 17-2

1. In the accompanying diagram, P_A is the price of U.S. grapes in autarky and P_W is the world price of grapes under international trade. With trade, U.S. consumers pay a price of P_W for grapes and consume quantity C_T, U.S. grape producers produce quantity Q_T, and the difference, $C_T - Q_T$, represents imports of Mexican grapes. As a consequence of the strike by truckers, imports are halted, the price paid by American consumers rises to the autarky price, P_A, and U.S. consumption falls to the autarky quantity Q_A.

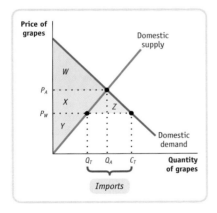

a. Before the strike, U.S. consumers enjoy consumer surplus equal to the area $W + X + Z$. After the strike, their consumer surplus shrinks to the area W. So consumers are worse off, losing consumer surplus represented by the area $X + Z$.

b. Before the strike, U.S. producers have producer surplus equal to the area Y. After the strike, their producer surplus increases to the area $Y + X$. So U.S. producers are better off, gaining producer surplus represented by the area X.

c. U.S. total surplus falls as a result of the strike by an amount represented by the area Z, the loss in consumer surplus that does not accrue to producers.

2. Mexican grape producers are worse off because they lose sales in the amount of $C_T - Q_T$, and Mexican grape pickers are worse off because they lose the wages that were associated with the lost sales. The lower demand for Mexican grapes caused by the strike implies that the price that Mexican consumers pay for grapes falls, making them better off. American grape pickers are better off because their wages increase as a result of the increase of $Q_A - Q_T$ in U.S. sales.

Check Your Understanding 17-3

1. **a.** If the tariff is $0.50, the price paid by domestic consumers for a pound of imported butter is $0.50 + $0.50 = $1.00, the same price as a pound of domestic butter. Imported butter will no longer have a price advantage over domestic butter, imports will cease, and domestic producers will capture all the feasible sales to domestic consumers, selling amount Q_A in the accompanying figure. But if the tariff is less than $0.50—say only $0.25—the price paid by domestic consumers for a pound of imported butter is $0.50 + $0.25 = $0.75, $0.25 cheaper than a pound of domestic butter. American butter producers will gain sales in the amount of $Q_2 - Q_1$ as a result of the $0.25 tariff. But this is smaller than the amount they would have gained under the $0.50 tariff, the amount $Q_A - Q_1$.

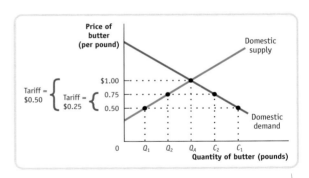

b. As long as the tariff is at least $0.50, increasing it more has no effect. At a tariff of $0.50, all imports are effectively blocked.

2. All imports are effectively blocked at a tariff of $0.50. So such a tariff corresponds to an import quota of 0.

Check Your Understanding 17-4

1. There are many fewer businesses that use steel as an input than there are consumers who buy sugar or clothing. So it will be easier for such businesses to communicate and coordinate among themselves to lobby against tariffs than it will be for consumers. In addition, each business will perceive that the cost of a steel tariff is quite costly to its profits, but an individual consumer is either unaware of or perceives little loss from tariffs on sugar or clothing.

2. Countries are often tempted to protect domestic industries by claiming that an import poses a quality, health, or environmental danger to domestic consumers. A WTO official should examine whether domestic producers are subject to the same stringency in the application of quality, health, or environmental regulations as foreign producers. If they are, then it is more likely that the regulations are for legitimate, non–trade protection purposes; if they are not, then it is more likely that the regulations are intended as trade protection measures.

Chapter Eighteen

Check Your Understanding 18-1

1. a. This will make it more likely that you will buy car insurance. Suppose you were uninsured. If a bad state of the world occurs and your car is damaged, you can no longer get to work. That is, in a bad state of the world, your income for consumption is reduced not only because you have to pay for car repairs but also because you no longer have income from work. This increases the risk to your income from damage to your car. If you are risk-averse, you are more likely to buy insurance.

b. This will make it less likely that you will buy car insurance. Suppose you were uninsured. If a bad state of the world occurs and your car is damaged, your parents can easily buy you another car. That is in a bad state of the world, your income is not reduced by as much as if you did not have wealthy parents. So the risk to your income from damage to your car is lower, making you less likely to buy insurance.

2. a. Karma's expected income is the weighted average of all possible values of her income, weighted by the probabilities with which she earns each possible value of her income. Since she makes $22,000 with a probability of 0.6 and $35,000 with a probability of 0.4, her expected income is $(0.6 \times \$22,000) + (0.4 \times \$35,000) = \$13,200 + \$14,000 = \$27,200$. Her expected utility is simply the expected value of the total utilities she will experience.

Since with a probability of 0.6 she will experience a total utility of 850 utils (the utility to her from making $22,000), and with a probability of 0.4 she will experience a total utility of 1,260 utils (the utility to her from making $35,000), her expected utility is $(0.6 \times 850 \text{ utils}) + (0.4 \times 1,260 \text{ utils}) = 510 \text{ utils} + 504 \text{ utils} = 1,014$ utils.

b. If Karma makes $25,000 for certain, she experiences a utility level of 1,014 utils. From the answer to part a, we know that this leaves her equally as well off as when she has a risky expected income of $27,200. Since Karma is indifferent between a risky expected income of $27,200 and a certain income of $25,000, you can conclude that she would prefer a certain income of $27,200 to a risky expected income of $27,200. That is, she would definitely be willing to reduce the risk she faces when this reduction in risk leaves her expected income unchanged. In other words, Karma is risk-averse.

c. Yes. Karma experiences a utility level of 1,056 utils when she has a certain income of $26,000. This is higher than the expected utility level of 1,014 utils generated by a risky expected income of $27,200. So Karma is willing to pay a premium to guarantee a certain income of $26,000.

Check Your Understanding 18-2

1. a. An increase in the number of ships implies an increase in the quantity of insurance demanded at any given premium. This is a rightward shift of the demand curve, resulting in a rise in both the equilibrium premium and the equilibrium quantity of insurance bought and sold.

b. An increase in the number of trading routes means that investors can diversify more. In other words, they can reduce risk further. At any given premium, there are now more investors willing to supply insurance. This is a rightward shift of the supply curve for insurance, leading to a fall in the equilibrium premium and a rise in the equilibrium quantity of insurance bought and sold.

c. If ship-owners in the market become even more risk-averse, they will be willing to pay even higher premiums for insurance. That is, at any given premium, there are now more people willing to buy insurance. This is a rightward shift of the demand curve for insurance, leading to a rise in both the equilibrium premium and the equilibrium quantity of insurance bought and sold.

d. If investors in the market become more risk-averse, they will be less willing to accept risk at any given premium. This is a leftward shift of the supply curve for insurance, leading to a rise in the equilibrium premium and a fall in the equilibrium quantity of insurance bought and sold.

e. As the overall level of risk increases, those willing to buy insurance will be more willing to buy insurance at any given premium; the demand curve for insurance shifts to the right. But since overall risk cannot be diversified away, those ordinarily willing to take on risk will be less willing to do so, leading to a leftward shift in the supply curve for insurance. As a result, the equilibrium premium will rise; the effect on the equilibrium quantity of insurance is uncertain.

f. If the wealth levels of investors fall, investors will become more risk-averse and so less willing to supply insurance at any given premium. This is a leftward shift of the supply curve for insurance, leading to a rise in the equilibrium premium and a fall in the equilibrium quantity of insurance bought and sold.

Check Your Understanding
18-3

1. The inefficiency caused by adverse selection is that an insurance policy with a premium based on the average risk of all drivers will attract only an adverse selection of bad drivers. Good (that is, safe) drivers will find this insurance premium too expensive and so will remain uninsured. This is inefficient. However, safe drivers are also those drivers who have had fewer moving violations for several years. Lowering premiums for only those drivers allows the insurance company to screen its customers and sell insurance to safe drivers, too. This means that at least some of the good drivers now are also insured, which decreases the inefficiency that arises from adverse selection. In a way, having no moving violations for several years is building a reputation for being a safe driver.

2. The moral hazard problem in home construction arises from private information about what the contractor does: whether she takes care to reduce the cost of construction or allows costs to increase. The homeowner cannot, or can only imperfectly, observe the cost-reduction effort of the contractor. If the contractor were fully reimbursed for all costs incurred during construction, she would have no incentive to reduce costs. Making the contractor responsible for any additional costs above the original estimate means that she now has an incentive to keep costs low. However, this imposes risk on the contractor. For instance, if the weather is bad, home construction will take longer, and will be more costly, than if the weather had been good. Since the contractor pays for any additional costs (such as weather-induced delays) above the original estimate, she now faces risk that she cannot control.

3. a. True. Drivers with higher deductibles have more incentive to take care in their driving, to avoid paying the deductible. This is a moral hazard phenomenon.
  b. True. Suppose you know that you are a safe driver. You have a choice of a policy with a high premium but a low deductible or one with a lower premium but a higher deductible. In this case, you would be more likely to choose the cheap policy with the high deductible because you know that you will be unlikely to have to pay the deductible. When there is adverse selection, insurance companies use screening devices such as this to make inferences about people's private information about how skillful they are as drivers.

  c. True. The wealthier you are, the less risk-averse you are. If you are less risk-averse, you are more willing to bear risk yourself. Having an insurance policy with a high deductible means that you are exposed to more risk: you have to pay more of any insurance claim yourself. This is an implication of how risk aversion changes with a person's income or wealth.

Chapter Nineteen
Check Your Understanding
19-1

1. a. The external cost is the pollution caused by the wastewater runoff, an uncompensated cost imposed by the poultry farms on their neighbors.
  b. Since poultry farmers do not take the external cost of their actions into account when making decisions about how much wastewater to generate, they will create more runoff than is socially optimal in the absence of government intervention or a private deal. They will produce runoff up to the point at which the marginal social benefit of an additional unit of runoff is zero; however, their neighbors experience a high, positive level of marginal social cost of runoff from this output level. So the quantity of wastewater runoff is inefficient: reducing runoff by one unit would reduce total social benefit by less than it would reduce total social cost.
  c. At the socially optimal quantity of wastewater runoff, the marginal social benefit is equal to the marginal social cost. This quantity is lower than the quantity of wastewater runoff that would be created in the absence of government intervention or a private deal.

2. Yasmin's reasoning is not correct: allowing some late returns of books is likely to be socially optimal. Although you impose a marginal social cost on others every day that you are late in returning a book, there is some positive marginal social benefit to you of returning a book late—for example, you get a longer period to use it in working on a term paper.

The socially optimal number of days that a book is returned late is the number at which the marginal social benefit equals the marginal social cost. A fine so stiff that it prevents any late returns is likely to result in a situation in which people return books although the marginal social benefit of keeping them another day is greater than the marginal social cost—an inefficient outcome. In that case, allowing an overdue patron another day would increase total social benefit more than it would increase total social cost. So charging a moderate fine that reduces the number of days that books are returned late to the socially optimal number of days is appropriate.

Check Your Understanding 19-2

1. This is a misguided argument. Allowing polluters to sell emissions permits makes polluters face a cost of polluting: the opportunity cost of the permit. If a polluter chooses not to reduce its emissions, it cannot sell its emissions permits. As a result, it forgoes the opportunity of making money from the sale of the permits. So despite the fact that the polluter receives a monetary benefit from selling the permits, the scheme has the desired effect: to make polluters internalize the externality of their actions.

2. **a.** If the emissions tax is smaller than the marginal social cost at Q_{OPT}, a polluter will face a marginal cost of polluting (equal to the amount of the tax) that is less than the marginal social cost at the socially optimal quantity of pollution. Since a polluter will produce emissions up to the point where the marginal social benefit is equal to its marginal cost, the resulting amount of pollution will be larger than the socially optimal quantity. As a result, there is inefficiency: if the amount of pollution is larger than the socially optimal quantity, the marginal social cost exceeds the marginal social benefit, and society could gain from a reduction in emissions levels.

   If the emissions tax is greater than the marginal social cost at Q_{OPT}, a polluter will face a marginal cost of polluting (equal to the amount of the tax) that is greater than the marginal social cost at the socially optimal quantity of pollution. This will lead the polluter to reduce emissions below the socially optimal quantity. This also is inefficient: whenever the marginal social benefit is greater than the marginal social cost, society could benefit from an increase in emissions levels.

   b. If the total amount of allowable pollution is set too high, the supply of emissions permits will be high and so the equilibrium price at which permits trade will be low. That is, polluters will face a marginal cost of polluting (the price of a permit) that is "too low"—lower than the marginal social cost at the socially optimal quantity of pollution. As a result, pollution will be greater than the socially optimal quantity. This is inefficient.

   If the total level of allowable pollution is set too low, the supply of emissions permits will be low and so the equilibrium price at which permits trade will be high. That is, polluters will face a marginal cost of polluting (the price of a permit) that is "too high"—higher than the marginal social cost at the socially optimal quantity of pollution. As a result, pollution will be lower than the socially optimal quantity. This also is inefficient.

Check Your Understanding 19-3

1. The London congestion charge acts like a Pigouvian tax on driving in central London. If the marginal external cost in terms of pollution and congestion of an additional car driven in central London is indeed £5, then the scheme is an optimal policy.

2. **a.** Planting trees imposes an external benefit: the marginal social benefit of planting trees is higher than the marginal benefit to individual tree planters, since many people (not just those who plant the trees) can benefit from the increased air quality and lower summer temperatures. The difference between the marginal social benefit and the marginal benefit to individual tree planters is the marginal external benefit. A Pigouvian subsidy could be placed on each tree planted in urban areas in order to increase the marginal benefit to individual tree planters to the same level as the marginal social benefit.

   b. Water-saving toilets impose an external benefit: the marginal benefit to individual homeowners from replacing a traditional toilet with a water-saving toilet is zero, since water is virtually costless. But the marginal social benefit is large, since fewer rivers and aquifers need to be pumped. The difference between the marginal social benefit and the marginal benefit to individual homeowners is the marginal external benefit. A Pigouvian subsidy on installing water-saving toilets could bring the marginal benefit to individual homeowners in line with the marginal social benefit.

   c. Disposing of old computer monitors imposes an external cost: the marginal cost to those disposing of old computer monitors is lower than the marginal social cost, since environmental pollution is borne by people other than the person disposing of the monitor. The difference between the marginal social cost and the marginal cost to those disposing of old computer monitors is the marginal external cost. A Pigouvian tax on disposing of computer monitors, or a system of tradable permits for their disposal, could raise the marginal cost to those disposing of old computer monitors sufficiently to make it equal to the marginal social cost.

Chapter Twenty

Check Your Understanding 20-1

1. **a.** Use of a public park is nonexcludable, but it may or may not be rival in consumption, depending on the circumstances. For example, if both you and I use the park for jogging, then your use will not prevent my use—use of the park is nonrival in consumption. In this case the public park is a public good. But use of the park is rival in consumption if there are many people trying to use the jogging path at the same time or when my use of the public tennis court prevents your use of the same court. In this case the public park is a common resource.

   b. A cheese burrito is both excludable and rival in consumption. Hence it is a private good.

   c. Information from a password-protected website is excludable but nonrival in consumption. So it is an artificially scarce good.

   d. Publicly announced information on the path of an incoming hurricane is nonexcludable and nonrival in consumption. So it is a public good.

2. A private producer will supply only a good that is excludable; otherwise, the producer won't be able to charge a price for it that covers the costs of production. So a private producer would be willing to supply a cheese burrito and information from a password-protected website but unwilling to supply a public park or publicly announced information about an incoming hurricane.

Check Your Understanding
20-2

1. a. With 10 Homebodies and 6 Revelers, the marginal social benefit schedule of money spent on the party is as shown in the accompanying table.

Money spent on party	Marginal social benefit
$0	
1	(10 × $0.05) + (6 × $0.13) = $1.28
2	(10 × $0.04) + (6 × $0.11) = $1.06
3	(10 × $0.03) + (6 × $0.09) = $0.84
4	(10 × $0.02) + (6 × $0.07) = $0.62

The efficient spending level is $2, the highest level for which the marginal social benefit is greater than the marginal cost ($1).

b. With 6 Homebodies and 10 Revelers, the marginal social benefit schedule of money spent on the party is as shown in the accompanying table.

Money spent on party	Marginal social benefit
$0	
1	(6 × $0.05) + (10 × $0.13) = $1.60
2	(6 × $0.04) + (10 × $0.11) = $1.34
3	(6 × $0.03) + (10 × $0.09) = $1.08
4	(6 × $0.02) + (10 × $0.07) = $0.82

The efficient spending level is now $3, the highest level for which the marginal social benefit is greater than the marginal cost ($1). The efficient level of spending has increased from that in part a because with relatively more Revelers than Homebodies, an additional dollar spent on the party generates a higher level of social benefit compared to when there are relatively more Homebodies than Revelers.

c. When the numbers of Homebodies and Revelers are unknown but residents are asked their preferences, then Homebodies will pretend to be Revelers to induce a higher level of spending on the public party. That's because a Homebody still receives a positive individual marginal benefit from an additional $1 spent, despite the fact that his or her individual marginal benefit is lower than that of a Reveler for every additional $1. In this case the "reported" marginal social benefit schedule of money spent on the party will be as shown in the accompanying table.

Money spent on party	Marginal social benefit
$0	
1	16 × $0.13 = $2.08
2	16 × $0.11 = $1.76
3	16 × $0.09 = $1.44
4	16 × $0.07 = $1.12

As a result, $4 will be spent on the party, the highest level for which the "reported" marginal social benefit is greater than the marginal cost ($1). Regardless of whether there are 10 Homebodies and 6 Revelers (part a) or 6 Homebodies and 10 Revelers (part b), spending $4 in total on the party is clearly inefficient because marginal cost exceeds marginal social benefit at this spending level.

As a further exercise, consider how much Homebodies gain by this misrepresentation. In part a, the efficient level of spending is $2. So by misrepresenting their preferences, the 10 Homebodies gain, in total, 10 × ($0.03 + $0.02) = $0.50—that is, they gain the marginal individual benefit in going from a spending level of $2 to $4. The 6 Revelers also gain from the misrepresentations of the Homebodies; they gain 6 × ($0.09 + $0.07) = $0.96 in total. This outcome is clearly inefficient—when $4 in total is spent, the marginal cost is $1 but the marginal social benefit is only $0.62, indicating that too much money is being spent on the party.

In part b, the efficient level of spending is actually $3. The misrepresentation by the 6 Homebodies gains them, in total, 6 × $0.02 = $0.12, but the 10 Revelers gain 10 × $0.07 = $0.70 in total. This outcome is also clearly inefficient—when $4 is spent, marginal social benefit is only $0.12 + $0.70 = $0.82 but marginal cost is $1.

Check Your Understanding
20-3

1. When individuals are allowed to harvest freely, the government-owned forest becomes a common resource, and individuals will overuse it—they will harvest an inefficiently excessive number of trees. In economic terms, the marginal social cost of harvesting a tree is greater than a private logger's individual marginal cost.

2. The three methods consistent with economic theory are (a) Pigouvian taxes, (b) a system of tradable licenses, and (c) allocation of property rights.

a. *Pigouvian taxes.* You would enforce a tax on loggers that equals the difference between the marginal social cost and the individual marginal cost of logging a tree at the socially efficient harvest amount. In order to do this, you must know the marginal social cost schedule and the individual marginal cost schedule.

b. *System of tradable licenses.* You would issue tradable licenses, setting the total number of trees harvested equal to the socially efficient harvest number. The market that arises in these licenses will allocate the right to log efficiently when loggers differ in their costs of logging: licenses will be purchased by those who have a relatively lower cost of logging. The market price of a license will be equal to the difference between the marginal social cost and the individual marginal cost of logging a tree at the socially efficient harvest amount. In order to implement this level, you need to know the socially efficient harvest amount.

c. *Allocation of property rights.* Here you would sell or give the forest to a private party. This party will have the right to exclude others from harvesting trees. Harvesting is now a private good—it is excludable and rival in consumption. As a result, there is no longer any divergence between social and private costs, and the private party will harvest the efficient level of trees. You need no additional information to use this method.

Check Your Understanding 20-4

1. a. The efficient price to a consumer is $0, since the marginal cost of allowing a consumer to download it is $0.

b. Xenoid will not produce the software unless it can charge a price that allows it at least to make back the $300,000 cost of producing it. So the lowest price at which Xenoid is willing to produce it is $150. At this price, it makes a total revenue of $150 \times 2,000 = $300,000$; at any lower price, Xenoid will not cover its cost. The shaded area in the accompanying diagram shows the deadweight loss when Xenoid charges a price of $150.

Chapter Twenty-one

Check Your Understanding 21-1

1. a. Since drivers are the beneficiaries of highway safety programs, this tax performs well according to the benefits principle. But since the level of the tax does not depend on ability to pay, it does not perform well according to the ability-to-pay principle. Since higher-income car purchasers are likely to spend more on a new car, a tax assessed as a percentage of the purchase price of the car would perform better on the ability-to-pay principle. This tax will distort the action of car-buying: people will purchase fewer cars or less expensive cars as a result of the tax.

b. This tax does not perform well according to the benefits principle because the payers are nonresidents of the local area, but the beneficiaries are local residents who will enjoy greater government services. But to the extent that people who stay in more expensive hotels have higher income compared to those who don't, the tax performs well according to the ability-to-pay principle. It will distort the action of staying in an expensive hotel room in this area, resulting in fewer nights of expensive hotel room stays.

c. This tax performs well according to the benefits principle because local homeowners are the users of local schools. It also performs well according to the ability-to-pay principle because it is assessed as a percentage of home value: higher-income residents, who own more expensive homes, will pay higher taxes. It will distort the action of buying a house in this area versus another area with a lower property rate or the action of making changes to a house that increase its assessed value.

d. This tax performs well according to the benefits principle because food consumers are the beneficiaries of government food safety programs. It does not perform well according to the ability-to-pay principle because food is a necessity, and lower-income people will pay approximately as much as higher-income people. This tax will distort the action of buying food, leading people to purchase cheaper varieties of food.

Check Your Understanding 21-2

1. A taxpayer who has $20,000 of wealth will pay a tax of $(1\% \times $10,000) + (2\% \times $10,000) = $100 + $200 = 300. This is equivalent to an average tax rate of 1.5%; that is, $($300/$20,000) \times 100 = 1.5\%$. But the marginal tax rate, the rate paid on an additional dollar of wealth accrued, is higher at 2%.

2. A 1% tax on consumption spending means that a family earning $15,000 and spending $10,000 will pay a tax of $1\% \times $10,000 = 100, equivalent to 0.67% of its income; $($100/$15,000) \times 100 = 0.67\%$. But a family earning $10,000 and spending $8,000 will pay a tax of $1\% \times $8,000 = 80, equivalent to 0.80% of its income; $($80/$10,000) \times 100 = 0.80\%)$. So the tax is regressive, since the lower-income family pays a higher percentage of its income in tax than the higher-income family.

3. a. False. Recall from Chapter 5 that a seller always bears some burden of a tax as long as his or her supply of the good is not perfectly inelastic—that is, as long as quantity supplied is not completely insensitive to the price offered. Since the supply of labor a worker offers is not perfectly inelastic (he or she will always respond to some degree to a change in the wage offered), the worker will bear some burden of a payroll tax, and therefore the tax will affect the person's incentive to take a job.

b. False. Under a proportional tax, the percentage of the tax base is the same for everyone. Under a lump-sum tax, the total tax paid is the same for everyone, regardless of their income. A lump sum tax is regressive.

Check Your Understanding 21-3

1. With an unemployment insurance program that covers the two states, workers in one state who are employed in a given year contribute tax payments that are then used to pay benefits to unemployed workers in the other state during that year. So in even-numbered years employed workers in Florida will help unemployed workers in Alaska, and in odd-numbered years employed workers in Alaska will help unemployed workers in Florida. Workers in the two states are better off with this program because they are assured of having benefits when unemployed.

2. a. Natural disaster emergency relief provides social insurance because it is not means-tested.

b. Heating cost assistance for low-income families is redistributive because it is means-tested.

c. Health care for people over 65 provides social insurance because it is not means-tested.

d. Aid grants to low-income students are redistributive because they are means-tested.

Check Your Understanding 21-4

1. Government spending programs that benefit Americans over 65 have increased in generosity over time. Meanwhile, aid payments that benefit families with children have not kept up with inflation, making them less generous over time. As a consequence, the poverty rate has risen for Americans under 18 but fallen for those over 65.

2. Under a negative income tax, low-income adults are more likely to seek work because the negative income tax payments supplement the income of low-income employed people, effectively offering them a higher wage rate if they become employed.

3. The gap in living standards has grown over time.

Check Your Understanding 21-5

1. a. A family will experience a very high marginal tax rate on the dollar it earns in going from an income of $14,999 to $15,000 because earning this additional dollar will cause it to lose all its health benefits. As a result, the marginal tax rate on that dollar may be several hundred or several thousand percent (depending on the family's health care costs). This will severely discourage a family from earning more than $14,999 per year.

b. A decrease in benefits as an additional dollar is earned is experienced by the family as a marginal tax rate on that dollar. As a result, a large decrease in benefits as an additional dollar is earned translates into a large disincentive to the family to earn that dollar. The program should be restructured so that benefits are reduced gradually as income increases in an effort to reduce the disincentive effects on work.

2. a. This program improves equity by aiding farmers in years when their income is low. However, it can generate inefficiency in farmers' incentives—for example, taking insufficient precautions against crop failures, farming in overly risky ways (such as on flood-prone land), and so on.

b. This program improves equity because rent is often a sizable expense for low-income families. It can generate inefficiency in their incentives, however, such as reducing the incentive to earn more income.

Chapter Twenty-two

Check Your Understanding 22-1

1. a. This is an information good because the value to a consumer, the viewer, is the information conveyed in the program. It also satisfies the cost conditions of an information good: there are high fixed costs associated with creating the show and installing cables to homes; there is low marginal cost associated with delivering the show over cable lines to homes.

b. This is not an information good. Although the coat embodies a lot of information through its high-tech fabric, the value to the consumer comes from its use as a garment.

c. This is an information good because the value to the consumer is in the information conveyed in the newspaper. It also satisfies the cost conditions of an information good: it has high fixed cost (the cost of gathering and reporting the news) and low marginal cost (the cost of printing and distributing the paper).

d. This is not an information good. Despite the fact that the car engine embodies a lot of information in its engineering, the value to a consumer comes from its use as a vehicle.

2. The fact that fixed cost is high but marginal cost is low for an information good explains the statement that "bigger is better." A bigger market for the good means more sales over which to defray the fixed cost of production; low marginal cost means that the cost of making an additional sale is low. So the larger the market, the better off the firm because its average total cost falls as it produces more output.

Check Your Understanding 22-2

1. a. The voltage of an appliance must be consistent with the voltage of the electrical outlet it is plugged into. So consumers will wish to have 110-volt appliances when houses are wired for 110-volt outlets, and builders will want to install 110-volt outlets when most prospective homeowners use 110-volt appliances. Therefore a network externality arises because a consumer will want to use appliances that operate with the same voltage as the appliances used by most other consumers.

b. Printers, copy machines, fax machines, and so on are designed for specific paper sizes. Consumers will want to purchase paper of a size that can be used in these machines, and machine manufacturers will want to manufacture their machines for the size of paper that most consumers use. So a network externality arises because a consumer will want to use the size of paper used by most other consumers—namely 8½-by-11-inch paper rather than 8-by-12½-inch paper.

2. Of the two competing companies, the company that can achieve the higher number of sales is likely to see the market tip in its favor, as more new consumers want to use its standard because more existing consumers have already adopted it. So it is important for a company to make a large number of sales early on. It can do this by pricing its good cheaply—by taking a loss on each unit sold. So the company that can best afford to subsidize a large number of sales early on is likely to be the winner of this competition.

Check Your Understanding 22-3

1. **Pro:** It can be argued that AOL attempted to create a monopoly by creating artificial barriers to other Internet service providers. Because it is the largest Internet service provider, a potential customer would be more likely to use AOL than a rival company if AOL restricted its pop-up message service to its own customers. If you wanted to reach the largest number of people possible with pop-up messages, and most people were AOL users, and AOL restricted its pop-up messaging to its own customers, then you would have had to become an AOL user. So by pursuing this policy, AOL believed it could eventually achieve a monopoly position in the Internet service provider industry.

Con: It can be argued that AOL was simply offering a superior product to its customers and that it has no obligation to offer it without charge to customers of competing firms. To put it another way, if AOL had been required to provide customers of other companies with the superior products it developed and provided to its own customers, then it could never charge its own customers a price large enough to recoup its investment in developing the product. So it had to restrict this product to its own customers in order to make it worthwhile to offer it. Using a term from Chapter 20, AOL must make the good "excludable" in order to earn revenue from it.

Chapter Twenty-Three

Check Your Understanding 23-1

1. a. This is a microeconomic question because it considers the economic circumstances facing an individual firm.

b. This is a macroeconomic question because it considers how the overall level of an activity changes as the whole economy changes.

c. This is a macroeconomic question because it addresses the causes of long-run growth.

d. This is a microeconomic question because it addresses the economic decision-making of a single individual.

2. There is typically less scope for government intervention in microeconomics because government intervention in markets reduces society's welfare except in certain well-defined cases. There is more scope for government intervention in macroeconomics because society's welfare is enhanced when the government can reduce the severity of economic fluctuations or promote factors that increase a country's long-run growth.

Check Your Understanding 23-2

1. When fewer people are employed, the unemployment rate rises. Because fewer people are employed in production, the amount of aggregate output produced falls. As a result, the unemployment rate rises when aggregate output falls. When more people are employed, the unemployment rate falls. The amount of aggregate output produced rises because more people are employed in production. So the unemployment rate falls when aggregate output rises. Putting all these facts together means that the unemployment rate and aggregate output move in opposite directions over the business cycle.

2. A high unemployment rate results in lost wages for people who would like to be employed but aren't. It results in lost output for firms, output of goods and services that consumers could have enjoyed. It can also result in political instability.

3. An economy with a successful stabilization policy experiences relatively few and shallow recessions. Equivalently, the economy experiences a low unemployment rate over time. It also experiences few overly robust expansions and therefore fewer inflationary pressures.

Check Your Understanding 23-3

1. The 1950s and 1960s were characterized by a high growth rate of real GDP, which significantly improved Americans' living standards over that period. In contrast, the 1970s and 1980s were characterized by a much lower growth rate of real GDP, which made Americans feel poorer, particularly when viewed in comparison to the gains that had been achieved in the 1950 and 1960s.

2. Countries with high rates of population growth will have to maintain higher growth rates of aggregate output than countries with low rates of population growth in order to achieve an increased standard of living per person because aggregate output will have to be divided among a larger number of people.

Check Your Understanding 23-4

1. a. You are better off because your wages have risen 5 percentage points more than prices (10% increase in wages − 5% increase in prices = 5%).

b. You are worse off because your wages have risen 5 percentage points less than prices (10% increase in wages − 15% increase in prices = − 5%).

c. You are better off because your wages have risen 12 percentage points more than prices (10% increase in wages + 2% fall in prices = 12%).

Check Your Understanding 23-5

1. a. The fall in the euro from $1.15 in 1999 to $0.85 in 2001 made European goods less expensive for Americans because a euro cost less to buy with a dollar. Conversely, American goods became more expensive for Europeans because a dollar cost more to buy with a euro.

b. The total value of European goods bought by Americans would have risen, and the total value of American goods bought by Europeans, would have fallen.

Chapter Twenty-Four

Check Your Understanding 24-1

1. Let's start by considering the relationship between the total value added of all domestically produced final goods and services and aggregate spending on domestically produced final goods and services. These two quantities are equal because every final good and service produced in the economy is either purchased by someone or added to inventories. And additions to inventories are counted as spending by firms. Next, consider the relationship between aggregate spending on domestically produced final goods and services and total factor income. These two quantities are equal because all spending that is channeled to firms to pay for purchases of domestically produced final goods and services is revenue for firms. Those revenues must be paid out by firms to their factors of production in the form of wages, profit, interest, and rent. Taken together, this means that all three methods of calculating GDP are equivalent.

2. Firms make sales to other firms, households, the government, and the rest of the world. Households are linked to firms through the sale of factors of production to firms, through purchases from firms of final goods and services, and through lending funds to firms in the financial markets. Households are linked to the government through their payment of taxes, their receipt of transfers, and their lending of funds to the government to finance government borrowing via the financial markets. Finally, households are linked to the rest of the world through their purchases of imports and transactions with foreigners in financial markets.

3. You would be counting the value of the steel twice—once as it was sold by American Steel to American Motors and once as part of the car sold by American Motors.

Check Your Understanding 24-2

1. a. In 2004 nominal GDP was $(1,000,000 \times \$0.40) + (800,000 \times \$0.60) = \$400,000 + \$480,000 = \$880,000$. A 25% rise in the price of french fries from 2004 to 2005 means that the 2005 price of french fries was $1.25 \times \$0.40 = \$0.50$. A 10% fall in servings means that $1,000,000 \times 0.9 = 900,000$ servings were sold in 2005. As a result, the total value of sales of french fries in 2005 was $900,000 \times \$0.50 = \$450,000$. A 15% fall in the price of onion rings from 2004 to 2005 means that the 2005 price of onion rings was $0.85 \times \$0.60 = \$0.51$. A 5% rise in servings sold means that $800,000 \times 1.05 = 840,000$ servings were sold in 2005. As a result, the total value of sales of onion rings in 2005 was $840,000 \times \$0.51 = \$428,400$. Nominal GDP in 2005 was $\$450,000 + \$428,400 = \$878,400$. To find real GDP in 2005, we must calculate the value of sales in 2005 using 2004 prices: $(900,000 \text{ french fries} \times \$0.40) + (840,000 \text{ onion rings} \times \$0.60) = \$360,000 + \$504,000 = \$864,000$.

b. A comparison of nominal GDP in 2004 to nominal GDP in 2005 shows a decline of $((\$880,000 − \$878,400) / \$880,000) \times 100 = 0.18\%$. But a comparison using real GDP shows a decline of $((\$880,000 − \$864,000) / \$880,000) \times 100 = 1.8\%$. That is, a calculation based on real GDP shows a drop 10 times larger (1.8%) than a calculation based on nominal GDP (0.18%): in this case, the calculation based on nominal GDP underestimates the true magnitude of the change.

2. A price index based on 1990 prices will contain a relatively high price of electronics and a relatively low price of housing compared to a price index based on 2000 prices. This means that a 1990 price index used to calculate real GDP in 2005 will magnify the value of electronics production in the economy, but a 2000 price index will magnify the value of housing production in the economy.

Check Your Understanding 24-3

1. The advent of websites that enable job-seekers to find jobs more quickly will reduce the unemployment rate over time. However, websites that induce discouraged workers to begin actively looking for work again will lead to an increase in the unemployment rate over time.

2. Both parts a and b are consistent with the relationship between growth in real GDP and changes in the unemployment rate that is illustrated in Figure 24-6: during years of above-average growth, the unemployment rate fell, and vice versa. They are consistent with this relationship because they both entail either a fall in the unemployment rate during a recovery or a rise in the unemployment rate during a recession. However, part c is not consistent: it implies that a recession is associated with a fall in the unemployment rate.

Check Your Understanding 24-4

1. This market basket costs, pre-frost, $(100 \times \$0.20) + (50 \times \$0.60) + (200 \times \$0.25) = \$20 + \$30 + \$50 = \$100$. The same market basket, post-frost, costs $(100 \times \$0.40) + (50 \times \$1.00) + (200 \times \$0.45) = \$40 + \$50 + \$90 = \$180$. So the price index is $(\$100/\$100) \times 100 = 100$ before the frost and $(\$180/\$100) \times 100 = 180$ after the frost, implying a rise in the price index of 80%. This increase in the price index is less than the 84.2% increase calculated in the text. The reason for this difference is that the new market basket of 100 oranges, 50 grapefruit, and 200 lemons contains proportionately more of the items that have experienced relatively lower price increases (the lemons, whose price has increased by 80%) and proportionately fewer of the items that have experienced relatively large price increases (the oranges, whose price has increased by 100%). This shows that the price index can be very sensitive to the composition of the market basket. If the market basket contains a large proportion of goods whose prices have risen faster than the prices of other goods, it will lead to a higher estimate of the increase in the price level. If it contains a large proportion of goods whose prices have risen more slowly than the prices of other goods, it will lead to a lower estimate of the increase in the price level.

2. a. A market basket determined 10 years ago will contain fewer cars than at present. Given that the average price of a car has grown faster than the average prices of other goods, this basket will underestimate the true increase in the price level because it contains relatively too few cars.

 b. A market basket determined 10 years ago will not contain broadband Internet access. So, it cannot track the fall in prices of Internet access over the past few years. As a result, it will overestimate the true increase in the price level.

3. Using Equation 24-3, the inflation rate from 2003 to 2004 is $(188.9 - 184.0)/184.0 \times 100 = 2.7\%$.

Chapter Twenty-Five

Check Your Understanding 25-1

1. Economic progress raises the living standards of the average resident of a country. An increase in overall real GDP does not accurately reflect an increase in an average resident's living standard because it does not account for growth in the number of residents. If, for example, real GDP rises by 10% but population grows by 20%, the living standard of the average resident falls: after the change, the average resident has only $(110/120) \times 100 = 91.6\%$ as much real income as before the change. Similarly, an increase in nominal GDP does not accurately reflect an increase in living standards because it does not account for any change in prices. For example, a 5% increase in nominal GDP generated by a 5% increase in prices implies that there has been no change in living standards. Real GDP per capita is the only measure that accounts for both changes in the population and changes in prices.

2. Using the rule of 70, the amount of time it will take for China to double its real GDP per capita is $(70/7.6) = 9.2$ years; Ireland, $(70/5.2) = 13.5$ years; the United States, $(70/2.0) = 35$ years; France, $(70/1.8) = 38.9$ years; and Argentina $(70/0.1) = 700$ years. If Ireland continues to have a higher growth rate of real GDP per capita than the United States, then Irish real GDP per capita will eventually surpass that of the United States.

Check Your Understanding 25-2

1. a. Significant technological progress will result in an increase in the growth rate of productivity even though physical capital per worker and human capital per worker are unchanged.

 b. The growth rate of productivity will fall but remain positive due to diminishing returns to physical capital.

2. It will take a period of time for workers to learn how to use the new computer system and to adjust their routines. And because there are often setbacks in learning a new system, such as accidentally erasing your computer files, productivity at Multinomics may decrease for a period of time.

Check Your Understanding 25-3

1. Funds borrowed from abroad must eventually be paid back to foreigners, meaning that in the future there will be fewer funds available to the country for investment spending. In contrast, funds that are paid back to domestic savers stay in the country and are available for future investment spending. This is why some economists believe that foreign investment may result in a lower growth rate than if the same amount of funds were generated by domestic savings. Other economists disagree because they believe that foreign investment brings with it new technology, which leads to an increase in a country's growth rate that more than offsets the reduction in funds that occurs when funds from abroad must be paid back to foreigners.

2. It is likely that the United States will experience a greater pace of creation and development of new drugs because closer links between private companies and academic research centers will lead to work more directly focused on producing new drugs than on pure research.

3. It is likely that these events resulted in a fall in the country's growth rate because the lack of property rights would have dissuaded people from making investments in productive capacity.

4. Countries have found that foreign investment usually brings new technology that increases the country's growth rate and living standards.

Check Your Understanding 25-4

1. The conditional version of the convergence hypothesis says that countries grow faster, other things equal, when they start from relatively low GDP per capita and grow more slowly, other things equal, when their GDP per capita is relatively higher; this points to lower future Asian growth. However, other things might not be equal: if Asian economies continue investing in human capital, if savings rates continue to be high, if governments invest in infrastructure, and so on, growth might continue at an accelerated pace.

2. As you can see from panel (b) of Figure 25-8, although it is important in determining the growth rate for some countries (such as those of Western Europe), the initial level of GDP per capita isn't the only factor. High rates of savings and investment appear to be better predictors of future growth than today's standard of living.

3. The evidence suggests that both sets of factors matter: better infrastructure is important for growth, but so is political stability. Policies should try to address both areas.

Chapter Twenty-Six

Check Your Understanding 26-1

1. As the budget deficit becomes a budget surplus, the government needs to borrow less money; as a result, the demand for loanable funds decreases. In the accompanying diagram, the demand curve, D_1, represents the demand for government borrowing plus private demand. The elimination of government borrowing shifts D_1 leftward to D_2, where D_2 represents only the private demand for loanable funds. The equilibrium interest rate falls from r_1 to r_2. As a result—although the *total* quantity of lending falls—the *private* quantity of loanable funds demanded rises from Q_1 to Q_2.

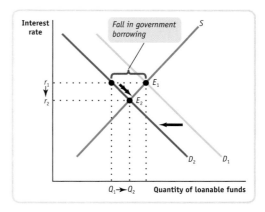

2. **a.** As capital flows into the economy, the supply of loanable funds increases. This is illustrated by the shift of the supply curve from S_1 to S_2 in the accompanying diagram. As the equilibrium moves from E_1 to E_2, the equilibrium interest rate falls from r_1 to r_2, and the equilibrium quantity of loanable funds increases from Q_1 to Q_2.

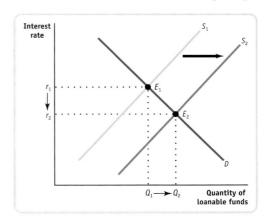

b. Savings fall due to the higher proportion of retired people, and the supply of loanable funds decreases. This is illustrated by the leftward shift of the supply curve from S_1 to S_2 in the accompanying diagram. The equilibrium moves from E_1 to E_2, the equilibrium interest rate rises from r_1 to r_2, and the equilibrium quantity of loanable funds falls from Q_1 to Q_2.

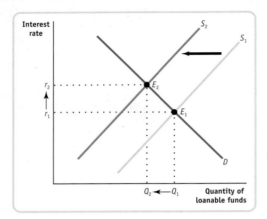

3. We know from the loanable funds market that as the interest rate rises, households want to save more and consume less. But at the same time, an increase in the interest rate lowers the number of investment spending projects with returns at least as high as the interest rate. The statement "households will want to save more money than businesses will want to invest" cannot represent an equilibrium in the loanable funds market because it says that the quantity of loanable funds offered exceeds the quantity of loanable funds demanded. If that were to occur, the interest rate must fall to make the quantity of loanable funds offered equal to the quantity of loanable funds demanded.

Check Your Understanding 26-2

1. The transaction costs for (a) a bank deposit and (b) a share of a mutual fund are approximately equivalent because each can typically be accomplished by making a phone call, going online, or visiting a branch office. Transaction costs are highest for (c) a share of the family business, since finding a buyer for the share consumes time and resources. The level of risk is probably lowest for (a) a bank deposit, since these deposits are insured by the Federal Deposit Insurance Corporation (FDIC) up to $100,000; somewhat higher for (b) a share of a mutual fund, since despite diversification, there is still risk associated with holding stocks; and highest for (c) a share of the family business, since this investment is not diversified. The level of liquidity is highest for (a) a bank deposit, since withdrawals can usually be made immedi-

ately; somewhat lower for (b) a share of a mutual fund, since it may take a few days between selling your shares and the payment being processed; and lowest for (c) a share of the family business, since it can only be sold with the unanimous agreement of other members and it will take some time to find a buyer.

2. Economic development and growth are the result of, among other factors, investment spending on physical capital. Since investment spending is equal to savings, the greater the amount saved, the higher investment spending will be, and so the higher growth and economic development will be. So the existence of institutions that facilitate savings will help a country's growth and economic development. As a result, a country with a financial system that provides low transaction costs, simple opportunities for diversification of risk, and high liquidity to its savers will experience faster growth and economic development than a country that doesn't.

Check Your Understanding 26-3

1. a. Today's stock prices reflect the market's expectation of future stock prices, and according to the efficient markets hypothesis, stock prices always take account of all available information. The fact that this year's profits are low is not new information, so it is already built into the share price. However, when it becomes known that the company's profit will be high next year, the price of a share of its stock will rise today, reflecting this new information.

b. The expectations of investors about high profits were already built into the stock price. Since profits are lower than expected, the market's expectations about the company's future stock price will be revised downward. This new information will lower the stock price.

c. These announcements will lower investors' expectations about the company's future stock price. This new information will lower the stock price.

d. This announcement will either have no effect on the company's stock price or will increase it only slightly. It does not add any new information, beyond removing some uncertainty about whether the profit forecast was correct. It should therefore result in either no increase, or only a small increase in the stock price.

2. The efficient markets hypothesis states that all available information is immediately taken account in stock prices. So if investors consistently bought stocks the day after the Dow rose by 1%, a smart investor would *sell* on that day because demand—and therefore stock prices—would be high. If a profit can be made that way, eventually many investors would be selling, and it would no longer be true that investors always bought stocks the day after the Dow rose by 1%.

Chapter Twenty-Seven

Check Your Understanding
27-1

1. **a.** This represents a movement along the *SRAS* curve because the CPI—like the GDP deflator—is a measure of the aggregate price level, the overall price level of final goods and services in the economy.

   b. This represents a shift of the *SRAS* curve because oil is a commodity. The *SRAS* will shift to the right because production costs are now lower, leading to a higher quantity of aggregate output supplied at any given aggregate price level.

   c. This represents a shift of the *SRAS* curve because it involves a change in nominal wages. An increase in legally mandated benefits to workers is equivalent to an increase in nominal wages. As a result, the *SRAS* curve will shift leftward because production costs are now higher, leading to a lower quantity of aggregate output supplied at any given aggregate price level.

2. You would need to know what happened to the aggregate price level. If the increase in the quantity of aggregate output supplied was due to a movement along the *SRAS* curve, the aggregate price level would increase at the same time as the quantity of aggregate output supplied increases. If the increase in the quantity of aggregate output supplied was due to a rightward shift of the *LRAS* curve, the aggregate price level might not rise. Alternatively, you could make the determination by observing what happened to aggregate output in the long run. If it falls back to its initial level in the long run, then the temporary increase in aggregate output was due to a movement along the *SRAS* curve. If it stays at the higher level in the long run, the increase in aggregate output was due to a rightward shift of the *LRAS* curve.

Check Your Understanding
27-2

1. **a.** This is a shift of the aggregate demand curve. A decrease in the quantity of money raises the interest rate, since people now want to borrow more and lend less. A higher interest rate reduces investment and consumer spending at any given aggregate price level, so the aggregate demand curve shifts to the left.

   b. This is a movement up along the aggregate demand curve. As the aggregate price level rises, the real value of money holdings falls. This is the interest rate effect of a change in the aggregate price level: as the value of money falls, people want to hold more money. They do so by borrowing more and lending less. This leads to a rise in the interest rate and a reduction in consumer and investment spending. So it is a movement along the aggregate demand curve.

   c. This is a shift of the aggregate demand curve. Expectations of a poor job market, and so lower average disposable incomes, will reduce people's consumer spending today at any given aggregate price level. So the aggregate demand curve shifts to the left.

   d. This is a shift of the aggregate demand curve. A fall in tax rates raises people's disposable income. At any given aggregate price level, consumer spending is now higher, so the aggregate demand curve shifts to the right.

   e. This is a movement down along the aggregate demand curve. As the aggregate price level falls, the real value of assets rises. This is the wealth effect of a change in the aggregate price level: as the value of assets rises, people will increase their consumption plans. This leads to higher consumer spending, so it is a movement along the aggregate demand curve.

   f. This is a shift of the aggregate demand curve. A rise in the real value of assets in the economy due to a surge in real estate values raises consumer spending at any given aggregate price level. So the aggregate demand curve shifts to the right.

Check Your Understanding
27-3

1. A decline in investment spending, like a rise in investment spending, has a multiplier effect on real GDP—the only difference in this case is that real GDP falls instead of rises. The fall in *I* leads to an initial fall in real GDP, which leads to a fall in disposable income, which leads to lower consumer spending, which leads to another fall in real GDP, and so on. So consumer spending falls as an indirect result of the fall in investment spending.

Check Your Understanding
27-4

1. **a.** An increase in the minimum wage raises the nominal wage and, as a result, shifts the short-run aggregate supply curve to the left. As a result of this negative supply shock, the aggregate price level rises, and aggregate output falls.

   b. Increased investment spending shifts the aggregate demand curve to the right. As a result of this positive demand shock, both the aggregate price level and aggregate output rise.

   c. An increase in taxes and a reduction in government spending both result in negative demand shocks, shifting the aggregate demand curve to the left. As a result, both the aggregate price level and aggregate output fall.

   d. This is a negative supply shock, shifting the short-run aggregate supply curve to the left. As a result, the aggregate price level rises and aggregate output falls.

2. As long-run growth increases potential output, the long-run aggregate supply curve shifts to the right. If, in the short run, there is now a recessionary gap (aggregate output is less than potential output), nominal wages will fall, shifting the short-run aggregate supply curve to the right. This results in a falling aggregate price level and a rise in aggregate output. As prices fall, we move along the aggregate demand curve due to the wealth and interest rate effects of a change in the aggregate price level. Eventually, as long-run macroeconomic equilibrium is reestablished, aggregate output will rise to be equal to potential output.

Check Your Understanding
27-5

1. a. An economy is overstimulated when an inflationary gap is present. This will arise if an expansionary monetary or fiscal policy is implemented when the economy is currently in long-run macroeconomic equilibrium. This shifts the aggregate demand curve to the right, in the short run raising the aggregate price level and aggregate output and creating an inflationary gap. Eventually nominal wages will rise and shift the short-run aggregate supply curve to the left, and aggregate output will fall back to potential output. This is the scenario envisaged by the speaker.

b. No, this is not a valid argument. When the economy is not currently in long-run macroeconomic equilibrium, an expansionary monetary or fiscal policy does not lead to the outcome described above. Suppose a negative demand shock has shifted the aggregate demand curve to the left, resulting in a recessionary gap. An expansionary monetary or fiscal policy can shift the aggregate demand curve back to its original position in long-run macroeconomic equilibrium. In this way, the short-run fall in aggregate output and deflation caused by the original negative demand shock can be avoided. So, if used in response to demand shocks, fiscal or monetary policy is a an effective policy tool.

Chapter Twenty-Eight

Check Your Understanding
28-1

1. a. Angelina's autonomous consumer spending is $8,000. When her current disposable income rises by $10,000, her consumer spending rises by $4,000 ($12,000 − $8,000). So her MPC is $4,000/$10,000 = 0.4 and her consumption function is $c = \$8,000 + 0.4 \times yd$.

Felicia's autonomous consumer spending is $6,500. When her current disposable income rises by $10,000, her consumer spending rises by $8,000 ($14,500 − $6,500). So her MPC is $8,000/$10,000 = 0.8 and her consumption function is $c = \$6,500 + 0.8 \times yd$.

Marina's autonomous consumer spending is $7,250. When her current disposable income rises by $10,000, her consumer spending rises by $7,000 ($14,250 − $7,250). So her MPC is $7,000/$10,000 = 0.7 and her consumption function is $c = \$7,250 + 0.7 \times yd$.

b. The aggregate autonomous consumer spending in this economy is $8,000 + $6,500 + $7,250 = $21,750. A $30,000 increase in disposable income (3 × $10,000) leads to a $4,000 + $8,000 + $7,000 = $19,000 increase in consumer spending. So the economy-wide MPC is $19,000/$30,000 = 0.63 and the aggregate consumption function is $C = \$21,750 + 0.63 \times YD$.

2. If you expect your future disposable income to fall, you would like to save some of today's disposable income to tide you over in the future. But you cannot do this if you cannot save. If you expect your future disposable income to rise, you would like to spend some of tomorrow's higher income today. But you cannot do this if you cannot borrow. If you cannot save or borrow, your expected future disposable income will have no effect on your consumer spending today. In fact, your MPC must always equal 1: you must consume all your current disposable income today, and you will be unable to smooth your consumption over time.

Check Your Understanding
28-2

1. a. This unexpected increase in consumer spending will result in a reduction in inventories as producers sell items from their inventories to satisfy this short-term increase in demand. This is negative unplanned inventory investment: it reduces the value of producers' inventories.

b. A rise in the cost of borrowing is equivalent to a rise in the interest rate: fewer investment spending projects are now profitable to producers, whether they are financed through borrowing or retained earnings. As a result, producers will reduce the amount of planned investment spending.

c. A sharp increase in the rate of real GDP growth leads to a higher level of planned investment spending by producers, according to the accelerator principle, as they increase production capacity to meet higher demand.

d. As sales fall, producers sell less, and their inventories grow. This leads to positive unplanned inventory investment.

2. Since the marginal propensity to consume is less than 1, consumer spending does not fully respond to fluctuations in current disposable income. This behavior is explained by the life-cycle hypothesis: households engage in "consumption smoothing" by borrowing against future income if current disposable income falls or by saving if current disposable income rises. This behavior diminishes the effect of fluctuations in the economy on consumer spending. In contrast, by the accelerator principle, fluctuations in the economy have magnified effects on investment spending.

3. When consumer demand is sluggish, firms with excess production capacity will cut back on planned investment spending because they think their existing capacities are sufficient for expected future sales. Similarly, when consumer demand is sluggish and firms have a large amount of unplanned inventory investment, they are likely to cut back their production of output because they think their existing inventories are sufficient for expected future sales. So an inventory overhang is likely to depress economic activity as firms cut back their output.

Check Your Understanding 28-3

1. A slump in planned investment spending will lead to a fall in real GDP in response to an unanticipated increase in inventories. The fall in real GDP will translate into a fall in households' disposable income, and households will respond by reducing consumer spending. The decrease in consumer spending leads producers to further decrease output, further lowering disposable income and leading to further reductions in consumer spending. So although the slump originated in investment spending, it will cause a reduction in consumer spending.

2. a. After an autonomous fall in planned aggregate spending, the economy is no longer in equilibrium: real GDP is greater than planned aggregate spending. Panel (a) of the accompanying figure shows this autonomous fall in planned aggregate spending by the shift of the aggregate spending curve from AE_1 to AE_2. The difference between the two results in positive unplanned inventory investment: there is an unanticipated increase in inventories. Firms will respond by reducing production. This will eventually move the economy to a new equilibrium. In the accompanying figure, this is illustrated by the movement from the initial income–expenditure equilibrium at E_1 to the new income–expenditure equilibrium at E_2. As the economy moves to its new equilibrium, real GDP falls from its initial income–expenditure equilibrium level at Y_1^* to its new lower level, Y_2^*. As panel (b) shows, at the fixed aggregate price

level P^*, aggregate output falls from Y_1^* to Y_2^*, and therefore the aggregate demand curve shifts leftward from AD_1 to AD_2.

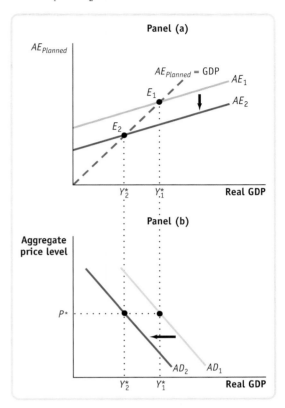

b. We know from Equation 28-12 that the change in income–expenditure equilibrium GDP is given by: $\Delta Y^* =$ Multiplier $\times \Delta AAE_{Planned}$. Here, the multiplier $= 1/(1 - 0.5) = 1/0.5 = 2$. So a $300 million autonomous fall in planned aggregate spending will lead to a 2×300 million $= 600$ million ($0.6 billion) fall in income–expenditure equilibrium GDP. The new Y^* will be $500 billion $- 0.6$ billion $= 499.4$ billion.

Chapter Twenty-Nine

Check Your Understanding 29-1

1. a. This is a contractionary fiscal policy because it is a reduction in government purchases of goods and services.
   b. This is an expansionary fiscal policy because it is an increase in government transfers that will increase disposable income.
   c. This is a contractionary fiscal policy because it is an increase in taxes that will reduce disposable income.

2. Federal disaster relief that is quickly disbursed is more effective than legislated aid because there is very little time lag between the time of the disaster and the time it is received by victims. Hence, it will stabilize the economy after a disaster. In contrast, legislated aid is likely to entail a time lag in its disbursment, leading to potential destabilization of the economy.

29-2

1. A $500 million increase in government purchases of goods and services directly increases aggregate spending by $500 million, which then starts the multiplier in motion. It will increase real GDP by $500 million × $1/(1 - MPC)$. A $500 million increase in government transfers increases aggregate spending only to the extent that it leads to an increase in consumer spending. Consumer spending rises by $$MPC$ for every $1 increase in disposable income, where MPC is less than 1. Thus, a $500 million increase in government transfers shifts the aggregate demand curve only MPC times as much as a $500 million increase in government purchases of goods and services. It will increase real GDP by $500 million × $MPC/(1 - MPC)$.

2. This is the same issue as in problem 1, but in reverse. If government purchases of goods and services fall by $500 million, the initial fall in aggregate spending is $500 million. If there is a $500 million reduction in government transfers, the initial fall in aggregate spending is $MPC \times$ $500 million, which is less than $500 million.

29-3

1. When your work–study earnings are low, your parents help softens the impact on your disposable income: your disposable income (and so your consumer spending) does not fall by as much as it otherwise would. But when your earnings are high, the requirement that you contribute to your tuition bill dampens the increase in your disposable income: your disposable income (and so your consumer spending) does not rise by as much as it otherwise would. As a result, the arrangement reduces the size of the fluctuations of your disposable income: it acts like the automatic stabilizing effect of the government's budget.

2. In recessions, real GDP falls. This implies that consumers' incomes, consumer spending, and producers' profits also fall. So in recessions, states' tax revenue (which depends in large part on consumers' incomes, consumer spending, and producers' profits) falls. In order to balance the state budget, states have to cut spending or raise taxes. But that implies deepening the recession. Without a balanced-budget requirement, states could use expansionary fiscal policy during a recession to lessen the fall in real GDP. The same is true during an expansion but with contractionary fiscal policy instead of expansionary fiscal policy. As real GDP rises, government rev-

enue also rises. To balance the budget, states have to increase spending or cut taxes, further boosting real GDP and leading to an even greater expansion. Without a balanced-budget requirement, states could use contractionary fiscal policy during expansions to dampen the rise in real GDP.

29-4

1. a. A higher growth rate of real GDP implies that tax revenue will increase. If government spending remains constant and the government runs a budget surplus, the size of the public debt will be less than it would otherwise have been.
   b. If retirees live longer, the average age of the population increases. As a result, the implicit liabilities of the government increase because spending on programs for older Americans, such as Social Security and Medicare, will rise.
   c. A decrease in tax revenue without offsetting reductions in government spending will cause the public debt to increase.
   d. Public debt will increase as a result of government borrowing to pay interest on its current public debt.

2. In order to stimulate the economy in the short run, the government can use fiscal policy to increase real GDP. This entails borrowing, increasing the size of the public debt further and leading to undesirable consequences: in extreme cases, governments can be forced to default on their debts. Even in less extreme cases, a large public debt is undesirable because government borrowing "crowds out" borrowing for private investment spending. This reduces the amount of investment spending, reducing the long-run potential of the economy to grow.

Chapter Thirty

30-1

1. The defining characteristic of money is its liquidity: how easily it can be used to purchase goods and services. Although a gift certificate can easily be used to purchase a very defined set of goods or services (the goods or services available at the store issuing the gift certificate), it cannot be used to purchase any other goods and services. A gift certificate is therefore not money, since it cannot easily be used to purchase all goods or services.

2. Again, the important characteristic of money is its liquidity: how easily it can be used to purchase goods and services. M1, the narrowest definition of the money supply, contains only currency in circulation, traveler's checks, and checkable bank deposits. CDs aren't checkable—and they can't be made checkable without incurring a cost because there's a penalty for early withdrawal. This makes them less liquid than the assets counted in M1.

Check Your Understanding 30-2

1. Even though you know that the rumor about the bank is not true, you are concerned about other depositors pulling their money out of the bank. And you know that if enough other depositors pull their money out, the bank will fail. In that case, it is rational for you to pull your money out before the bank fails. All depositors will think like this, so even if they all know that the rumor is false, they may still rationally pull their money out, leading to a bank run. Deposit insurance leads depositors to worry less about the possibility of a bank run. Even if a bank fails, the FDIC will pay each depositor up to $100,000 per account. This will make you much less likely to pull your money out in response to a rumor. Since other depositors will think the same, there will be no bank run.

2. The aspects of modern bank regulation that would frustrate this scheme are *capital requirements* and *reserve requirements*. Capital requirements mean that a bank has to have a certain amount of capital—the difference between its assets (loans plus reserves) and its liabilities (deposits). So the con man could not open a bank without putting any of his own wealth in because the bank needs a certain amount of capital—that is, it needs to hold more assets (loans plus reserves) than deposits. So the con man would be at risk of losing his own wealth if his loans turn out badly.

Check Your Understanding 30-3

1. Since they only have to hold $100 in reserves, instead of $200, banks now lend out $100 of their reserves. Whoever borrows the $100 will deposit it in a bank, which will lend out $100 × (1 − rr) = $100 × 0.9 = $90. Whoever borrows the $90 will put it into a bank, which will lend out $90 × 0.9 = $81, and so on. Overall, deposits will increase by $100/0.1 = $1,000.

2. Silas puts $1,000 in the bank, of which the bank lends out $1,000 × (1 − rr) = $1,000 × 0.9 = $900. Whoever borrows the $900 will keep $450 in cash and deposit $450 in a bank. The bank will lend out $450 × 0.9 = $405. Whoever borrows the $405 will keep $202.50 in cash and deposit $202.50 in a bank. The bank will lend out $202.50 × 0.9 = $182.25, and so on. Overall, this leads to an increase in deposits of $1,000 + $450 + $202.50 + . . . But it decreases the amount of currency in circulation: the amount of cash is reduced by the $1,000 Silas puts into the bank. This is offset, but not fully, by the amount of cash held by each borrower. The amount of currency in circulation therefore changes by −$1,000 + $450 + $202.50 + . . . The money supply therefore increases by the sum of the increase in deposits and the change in currency in circulation, which is $1,000 − $1,000 + $450 + $450 + $202.50 + $202.50 + . . . and so on.

Check Your Understanding 30-4

1. An open-market purchase of $100 million by the Fed increases banks' reserves by $100 million as the Fed credits their accounts with additional reserves. In other words, this open-market purchase increases the monetary base (currency in circulation plus bank reserves) by $100 million. Banks lend out the additional $100 million. Whoever borrows the money puts it back into the banking system in the form of deposits. Of these deposits, banks lend out $100 million × (1 − rr) = $100 million × 0.9 = $90 million. Whoever borrows the money deposits it back into the banking system. And banks lend out $90 million × 0.9 = $81 million, and so on. As a result, bank deposits increase by $100 million + $90 million + $81 million + . . . = $100 million/rr = $100 million/0.1 = $1,000 million = $1 billion. Since in this simplified example all money lent out is deposited back in the banking system, there is no increase of currency in circulation, so the increase in bank deposits is equal to the increase in the money supply. In other words, the money supply increases by $1 billion. This is greater than the increase in the monetary base by a factor of 10: in this simplified model in which deposits are the only component of the money supply and in which banks hold no excess reserves, the money multiplier is 1/rr = 10.

Chapter Thirty-One

Check Your Understanding 31-1

1. a. By increasing the opportunity cost of holding money, a high interest rate reduces the nominal and the real quantity of money demanded. This is a movement along the (nominal and real) money demand curve.

b. A 10% fall in prices, other things equal, reduces the nominal quantity of money demanded by exactly 10% at any given interest rate, shifting the nominal money demand curve leftward. Because the real quantity of money demanded is unchanged, the real money demand curve does not shift.

c. This technological change, which is widely expected in the fairly near future, would make currency unnecessary for many purchases, reducing the nominal and real quantity of money demanded at any given interest rate. That is, it would shift the nominal and real money demand curves leftward.

d. Payment in cash would require firms to hold more money, increasing the nominal and real quantity of money demanded at any given interest rate. That is, it would shift the nominal and real money demand curves rightward.

Check Your Understanding 31-2

1. In the accompanying diagram, the increase in the demand for money is shown as a rightward shift of the money demand curve, from MD_1 to MD_2. This raises the equilibrium interest rate from r_1 to r_2.

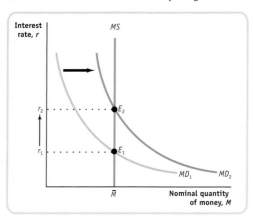

2. In order to prevent the interest rate from rising, the Federal Reserve must make an open-market purchase of Treasury bills, shifting the money supply curve rightward. This is shown in the accompanying diagram as the move from MS_1 to MS_2.

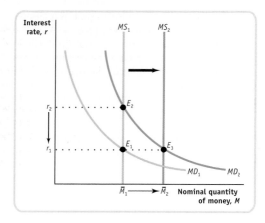

Check Your Understanding 31-3

1. a. The money supply curve shifts to the right.
b. The equilibrium interest rate falls.
c. Investment spending rises, due to the fall in the interest rate.
d. Consumer spending rises, due to the multiplier process.
e. Aggregate output rises because of the rightward shift in the aggregate demand curve.
f. The aggregate price level rises because the economy moves up the short-run aggregate supply curve.
g. Savings rise because disposable income rises; part of the increase in disposable income is saved.
h. The supply curve of loanable funds shifts rightward because savings rise.

Check Your Understanding 31-4

1. a. Aggregate output rises in the short run, then falls back to equal potential output in the long run.
b. The aggregate price level rises in the short run, but by less than 25%. It rises further in the long run, for a total increase of 25%.
c. The real quantity of money rises in the short run, but by less than 25% because the aggregate price level also rises. In the long run, the real quantity of money returns to its original level.
d. The interest rate falls in the short run, then rises back to its original level in the long run.

Chapter Thirty-Two

Check Your Understanding 32-1

1. a. Frictional unemployment is unemployment due to the time workers spend searching for jobs. It is inevitable because workers may leave one job in search of another for a variety of reasons. Furthermore, there will always be new entrants in the labor force who are seeking a first job. During the search process, these individuals will be counted as part of the frictionally unemployed.
b. When the unemployment rate is low, frictional unemployment will account for a larger share of total unemployment because other sources of unemployment will be diminished. So the share of total unemployment composed of the frictionally unemployed will rise.

2. A binding minimum wage represents a price floor below which wages cannot fall. As a result, actual wages cannot move toward equilibrium. So a minimum wage causes the quantity of labor supplied to exceed the quantity of labor demanded. Because this surplus of labor reflects unemployed workers, it affects the unemployment rate. Collective bargaining has a similar effect—unions are able to raise the wage above the equilibrium level. This will act like a minimum wage by causing the number of job seekers to be larger than the number of workers firms are willing to hire. Collective bargaining causes the unemployment rate to be higher than it otherwise would be, as shown in in the accompanying figure.

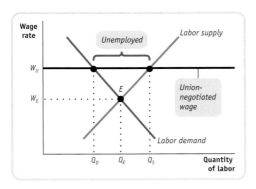

3. An increase in unemployment benefits reduces the cost to individuals of being unemployed, causing them to spend more time searching for a new job. So the natural rate of unemployment would increase.

Check Your Understanding 32-2

1. **a.** A positive output gap implies that actual output is above potential output. Given the relationship between output and unemployment, we would expect the output gap to be most positive when the difference between the natural unemployment rate and actual unemployment rate is greatest. Specifically, the output gap will be positive when the actual unemployment rate is below the natural rate of unemployment. This occurs from 1964 to 1972 and again from 1996 to 2001. There were several other brief periods when actual unemployment was below the natural rate of unemployment (the mid-1970s and again in the mid- to late 1980s). Although the relationship is not perfect, these periods are similar to those predicted by an examination of the actual and natural rates of unemployment.

2. Such a policy would increase the magnitude of the relationship between the output gap and the unemployment rate. An increase in output generally causes firms to increase first the number of hours they employ their workforce. This is one of the reasons there is not a one-for-one relationship between the percent change in output and the unemployment rate. However, if there is a limit on the number of hours a worker can be employed, firms will not have the same flexibility to change output without changing the number of workers employed. With such a policy, firms will be more likely to respond to an increase in output by increasing employment. This would result in a greater reduction in the unemployment rate for a given increase in output.

Check Your Understanding 32-3

1. The more rapidly labor contracts can adjust to changing macroeconomic conditions, the more rapidly the economy will return to potential output. Since contracts of shorter duration often will be renegotiated more than those of longer duration, the country that has contracts of shorter duration (Malavia) will move more quickly to equilibrium when demand changes.

2. Workers may misperceive changes in the market-clearing wage rate because they are using old information to assess current equilibrium wage rates. More generally, workers may not be aware of rapidly changing supply and demand conditions in particular segments of the labor market. Until information about changes in labor supply or labor demand becomes more widespread, workers may misperceive the market-clearing wage. If the market-clearing wage is rising but workers are slow to recognize this, the extent to which the wage will rise in the short run will be diminished. With less upward pressure on the actual wage paid to workers, employment will be higher than it otherwise would be. This implies that the unemployment rate will be lower than it otherwise would be.

Check Your Understanding 32-4

1. The short-run Phillips curve illustrates the negative relationship between the unemployment rate and the inflation rate for a given expected inflation rate (and natural rate of unemployment). The economy will operate at the NAIRU only if the actual inflation rate and the expected inflation rate are equal. Now suppose that demand increases, causing an increase in employment, a reduction in the unemployment rate, and an increase in economic activity. As output rises above the potential output, the actual inflation rate will rise above the expected inflation rate. The subsequent reduction in the unemployment rate reflects a reduction in cyclical unemployment. So we will observe an increase in the inflation rate above the expected rate and a reduction in cyclical unemployment.

2. There is no long-run trade-off between inflation and unemployment because once expectations of inflation adjust, wages will also adjust, returning employment and the unemployment rate to their equilibrium (natural) levels. This implies that once expectations of inflation fully adjust to any change in actual inflation, the unemployment rate will return to the natural rate of unemployment, or NAIRU. This also implies that the long-run Phillips curve is vertical.

Chapter Thirty-Three

Check Your Understanding
33-1

1. The inflation rate is more likely to quickly reflect changes in the money supply when the economy has had an extended period of high inflation. That's because an extended period of high inflation sensitizes workers and firms to raise nominal wages and prices of intermediate goods when the aggregate price level rises. As a result, there will be little or no increase in real output in the short run after an increase in the money supply, and the increase in the money supply will simply be reflected in an equal-size percent increase in prices. In an economy where people are not sensitized to high inflation because of low inflation in the past, an increase in the money supply will lead to an increase in real output in the short run. This illustrates the fact that the classical model of the price level best applies to economies with *persistently* high inflation and not those with little or no history of high inflation while currently having high inflation.

2. Yes, there can still be an inflation tax because the tax is levied on people who hold money. As long as people hold money, regardless of whether prices are indexed or not, the government is able to use seigniorage to capture real resources from the public.

Check Your Understanding
33-2

1. a. With a nominal interest rate of 8% and an actual inflation rate of 3%, the real interest rate paid on the loan is 8% − 3% = 5%. Borrowers and lenders, however, expected the loan to have a real interest rate of 8% − 5% = 3%. Since this is lower than the actual real interest rate of 5%, lenders benefited and borrowers lost from the unexpected change in inflation.

b. With a nominal interest rate of 6% and an actual inflation rate of 7%, the real interest rate paid on the loan is 6% − 7% = −1%. Borrowers and lenders, however, expected the loan to have a real interest rate of 6% − 4% = 2%. Since this is higher than the actual real interest rate of −1%, borrowers benefited and lenders lost from the unexpected change in inflation.

2. Shoe-leather costs as a result of inflation will be lower because it is now less costly for individuals to manage their assets in order to economize on their money holdings. This reduction in the costs associated with converting non-money assets into money translates into the lower shoe-leather costs.

Check Your Understanding
33-3

1. There are two possible explanations for this. First, negative supply shocks (for example, increases in the price of oil) will cause an increase in unemployment and an increase in inflation. Second, it is possible that British policy makers attempted to peg the unemployment rate below the natural rate of unemployment. Any attempt to peg unemployment below the natural rate will result in an increase in inflation.

2. Disinflation is costly because to reduce the inflation rate, aggregate output in the short run must typically fall below potential output. This, in turn, results in an increase in the unemployment rate above the natural rate. In general, we would observe a reduction in real GDP. The costs of disinflation can be reduced by not allowing inflation to increase in the first place. Second, the costs of any disinflation will be lower if the central bank is credible and it announces in advance its policy to reduce inflation. In this situation, the adjustment to the disinflationary policy will be more rapid, resulting in a smaller loss of aggregate output.

Check Your Understanding
33-4

1. If the nominal interest rate is negative, an individual is better off simply holding cash, which has a 0% nominal rate of return. If the options facing an individual are to lend and receive a negative nominal interest rate or to hold cash and receive a 0% nominal interest rate, the individual will hold cash. Such a scenario creates the possibility of a liquidity trap, in which monetary policy is ineffective because the nominal interest rate cannot fall below zero. Once the nominal interest rate falls to zero, further increases in the money supply will lead firms and individuals to simply hold the additional cash.

Chapter Thirty-Four

Check Your Understanding
34-1

1. a. The figure on page 815 shows that the Fed pursued a policy that led to a rapid rise in the money supply during and after the 2001 recession. So the data support the first part of the quotation—that there was an "aggressive monetary policy." Whether this did in fact "reduce the depth" of that particular recession is a different question, one that cannot be answered just by looking at the data in the figure. To address the latter part of the quotation, we would have to ask what the size and depth of the 2001 recession would have been had the Fed not aggressively pursued an expansionary monetary policy.

b. A classical economist would have said that the aggressive monetary expansion would have had no short-run effect on aggregate output and would simply have resulted in a proportionate increase in the aggregate price level.

Check Your Understanding
34-2

1. This is partly a Keynesian statement. Tax cuts will increase after-tax income and, from a Keynesian perspective, increase economic activity. A Keynesian would typically argue that a tax cut will increase disposable income, causing households to increase consumer spending. This increase in consumer spending will cause an increase in aggregate demand and, given an upward-sloping aggregate supply curve, will cause an increase in aggregate output. The Keynesian explanation of the way in which tax cuts affect economic activity, however, is not based on the latter part of the quotation. The latter part of the quotation suggests that the tax cuts will increase economic activity by increasing "incentives to work, save, and invest." That part doesn't seem to have much to do with Keynesian ideas.

Check Your Understanding
34-3

1. Monetarists argue that central banks should implement policy so that the money supply grows at some constant rate. Had the Fed pursued a monetarist policy during this period, we would have observed movements in M1 that would have shown a fixed rate of growth during this period. We would not, therefore, have observed any of the reductions in M1 that are observed in the figure nor would we have observed the acceleration in the rate of growth of M1 that occured in 2001.

2. As in Question 1, a monetarist policy would have resulted in a constant rate of growth in M1. Between 1960 and approximately 1981, the velocity of M1 rose smoothly. After 1981, the velocity of money experienced a number of shocks, where we observe increases and reductions in velocity. Given a constant rate of money growth, these changes in the velocity of M1 would have caused changes in aggregate demand and in economic activity, other things equal. In this situation, a monetarist policy would have allowed these shocks to the velocity of money to cause fluctuations in economic activity.

Check Your Understanding
34-4

1. a. Rational expectations theorists would argue that only unexpected changes in the money supply would have any short-run effect on economic activity. They would also argue that expected changes in the money supply would

affect only the aggregate price level, with no short-run effect on aggregate output. So such theorists would give credit to the Fed for limiting the severity of the 2001 recession only if the Fed's monetary policy had been more aggressive than individuals expected during this period.

b. Real business cycle theorists would argue that the Fed's policy had no effect on ending the 2001 recession because they believe that fluctuations in aggregate output are caused largely by changes in total factor productivity.

Check Your Understanding
34-5

1. Had inflation been much lower in early 2001, we would also expect that nominal interest rates would have been lower. In a situation like this, where inflation is near 0% and nominal interest rates are already low as well, a liquidity trap could occur. In a liquidity trap, the nominal interest rate is already low and close to 0%. In such a situation, it would be difficult for the Fed to further reduce the interest rate. This would have limited the Fed's ability to increase aggregate demand and, by doing so, attempt to limit the severity of any recession.

2. The large drop in stock prices is believed to have had at least two negative effects on the macroeconomy. First, the drop in stock prices reduced individuals' wealth, causing them to reduce consumer spending and so causing aggregate demand to fall. Second, the drop in stock prices may also have caused a reduction in consumer confidence that would also have resulted in a reduction in consumer spending and a fall in aggregate demand. Any reduction in aggregate demand caused by lower stock prices would have meant that the Fed had to be even more aggressive in implementing expansionary monetary policy in order to reduce the length and severity of the recession.

Chapter Thirty-Five

Check Your Understanding
35-1

1. a. The sale of the new airplane to China represents an export of a good to China, and so affects the current account.

b. The sale of Boeing stock to Chinese investors is a sale of a U.S. asset and so enters into the financial account.

c. Even though the plane already exists, when it is shipped to China it is an export of a good from the United States. So the sale of the plane enters the current account.

d. Because the plane stays in the United States, the Chinese investor is buying a U.S. asset. So this is identical to the answer to part b: the sale of the jet enters the financial account.

2. The high savings combined with the low returns in the rest of the world will cause an increase in the capital inflow into the United States—an increase in the U.S. balance of payments on financial account. This will cause an increase in the quantity of loanable funds supplied in the United States, which will cause the U.S. interest rate to fall.

1. a. The increased purchase of Mexican oil will cause U.S. individuals (and firms) to increase their demand for the peso. To purchase pesos, individuals will increase their supply of U.S. dollars to the foreign exchange market, causing a rightward shift in the supply curve of U.S. dollars. This will cause the peso price of the dollar to fall (the amount of pesos per dollar will fall). The peso has appreciated and the U.S. dollar has depreciated as a result.

b. This appreciation of the peso means it will take more U.S. dollars to obtain the same quantity of Mexican pesos. If we assume that the price level (measured in Mexican pesos) of other Mexican goods and services does not change, other Mexican goods and services become more expensive to U.S. households and firms. The dollar cost of other Mexican goods and services will rise as the peso appreciates. So Mexican exports of goods and services other than oil will fall.

c. U.S. goods and services become cheaper in terms of pesos, so Mexican imports of goods and services will rise.

2. a. The real exchange rate equals

$$\text{Pesos per U.S. dollar} \times \frac{\text{Aggregate price level in the U.S.}}{\text{Aggregate price level in Mexico}}$$

Today, the aggregate price levels in both countries are both equal to 100. The real exchange rate today is: $10 \times (100/100) = 10$. The aggregate price level in five years in the U.S. is $100 \times (120/100) = 120$ and in Mexico it will be $100 \times (1,200/800) = 150$. The real exchange rate in five years, assuming the nominal exchange rate does not change, will be $10 \times (120/150) = 8$.

b. Today, a basket of goods and services that costs $100 costs 800 pesos; so the purchasing power parity is 8 pesos per U.S. dollar. In five years, a basket that costs $120 will cost 1,200 pesos, so the purchasing power parity will be 10 pesos per U.S. dollar.

1. The accompanying diagram shows the supply of and demand for the yuan with the U.S. dollar price of the yuan on the vertical axis. In 2005, prior to the revaluation, the exchange rate was pegged at 8.28 yuan per U.S. dollar or, equivalently, 0.121 U.S. dollars per yuan ($0.121). At the target exchange rate of $0.121, the quantity of yuan demanded exceeded the quantity of yuan supplied, creating the shortage depicted in the diagram. Without any intervention by the Chinese government, the U.S. dollar price of the yuan would be bid up, causing an appreciation of the yuan. The Chinese government, however, intervened to prevent this appreciation.

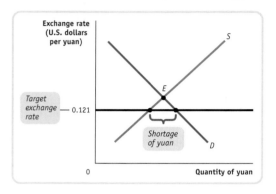

a. If the exchange rate were allowed to move freely, the U.S. dollar price of the exchange rate would move toward the equilibrium exchange rate (labeled XR^* in the accompanying diagram). This would occur as a result of the shortage, when buyers of the yuan would bid up its U.S. dollar price. As the exchange rate increases, the quantity of yuan demanded would fall and the quantity of yuan supplied would increase. If the exchange rate were to increase to XR^*, the disequilibrium would be entirely eliminated.

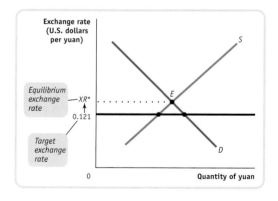

b. Placing restrictions on foreigners who want to invest in China would reduce the demand for the yuan, causing the demand curve to shift in the accompanying diagram from D_1 to something like D_2. This would cause a reduction in the shortage of the yuan. If demand fell to D_3, the disequilibrium would be completely eliminated.

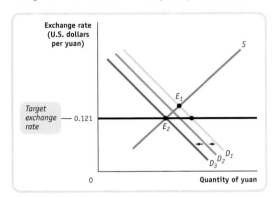

c. Removing restrictions on Chinese who wish to invest abroad would cause an increase in the supply of the yuan and a rightward shift in the supply curve. This increase in supply would also cause a reduction in the size of the shortage. If, for example, supply increased from S_1 to S_2, the disequilibrium would be eliminated completely in the accompanying diagram.

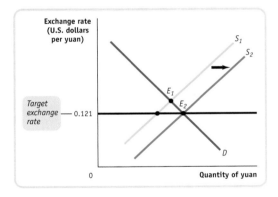

d. Imposing a tax on exports (Chinese goods sold to foreigners) would raise the price of these goods and decrease the amount of Chinese goods purchased. This would also decrease the demand for the yuan. The graphical analysis here is virtually identical to that found in the figure accompanying part b.

Check Your Understanding 35-4

1. The devaluations and revaluations most likely occurred in those periods when there was a sudden change in the franc–mark exchange rate: 1974, 1976, the early 1980s, 1986, and 1993–1994.

2. The high Canadian interest rates would likely have caused an increase in capital inflows to Canada. To obtain these assets (which yielded a relatively higher interest rate) in Canada, investors would first have had to obtain Canadian dollars. The increase in the demand for the Canadian dollar would have caused the Canadian dollar to appreciate. This appreciation of the Canadian currency would have raised the price of Canadian goods to foreigners (measured in terms of the foreign currency). This would have made it more difficult for Canadian firms to compete in other markets.

MACROECONOMIC DATA 1929–2004

The following section presents macroeconomic data for the United States. The data include selected early years that illustrate the behavior of the economy during the Great Depression and the postwar boom. The series also include data for each from 1970 to 2004 for full coverage of recent years.

MACROECONOMIC DATA 1929–2004[1]

	1929	1933	1939	1945	1950	1955	1960	1965	1966
Nominal GDP and Its Components									
1. + Consumer spending (C)	77.4	45.9	67.2	120.0	192.2	258.8	331.7	443.8	480.9
2. + Investment spending (I)	16.5	1.7	9.3	10.8	54.1	69.0	78.9	118.2	131.3
3. + Government purchases of goods and services (G)	9.4	8.7	14.8	93.0	46.8	86.5	111.6	151.5	171.8
4. + Exports (X)	5.9	2.0	4.0	6.8	12.4	17.7	27.0	37.1	40.9
5. − Imports (IM)	5.6	1.9	3.1	7.5	11.6	17.2	22.8	31.5	37.1
6. = Gross domestic product (GDP)	103.6	56.4	92.2	223.1	293.8	414.8	526.4	719.1	787.8
7. + Income from abroad earned by Americans	1.1	0.4	0.7	0.8	2.2	3.5	4.9	7.9	8.1
8. − Income paid to foreigners	0.4	0.1	0.3	0.5	0.7	1.1	1.8	2.6	3.0
9. = Gross national product	104.4	56.7	92.5	223.4	295.2	417.2	529.5	724.4	792.9
10. National income	94.2	48.9	82.2	198.4	264.4	372.7	474.9	653.4	711.0
11. Government transfers	1.2	1.7	2.5	5.6	14.0	15.7	25.7	36.2	39.6
12. Taxes	1.7	0.8	1.5	19.4	18.9	32.9	46.1	57.7	66.4
13. Disposable income (YD)	83.4	46.1	71.4	152.2	210.1	283.3	365.4	498.1	537.5
14. Private savings ($S_{private}$)	3.8	−0.7	3.2	31.1	15.1	19.7	26.7	43.0	44.4
Real GDP and Growth Measures									
15. Real GDP (billions of 2000 dollars)	865.2	635.5	950.7	1,786.3	1,777.3	2,212.8	2,501.8	3,191.1	3,399.1
16. Real GDP growth (percent change from previous year)	-	−1.3%	8.1%	−1.1%	8.7%	7.1%	2.5%	6.4%	6.5%
17. Real GDP per capita (2000 dollars)	7,099	5,056	7,256	12,766	11,717	13,389	13,840	16,420	17,290
18. Real GDP per capita growth (percent change from previous year)	-	−1.9%	7.2%	−2.2%	6.9%	5.3%	0.4%	5.1%	5.3%
Prices and Inflation									
19. Consumer Price Index (1982 − 1984 = 100)	17.1	13.0	13.9	18.0	24.1	26.8	29.6	31.5	32.4
20. CPI Inflation rate	-	−5.1%	−1.4%	2.3%	1.3%	−0.4%	1.7%	1.6%	2.9%
21. Producer Price Index (all commodities, 1982 = 100)	16.4	11.4	13.3	18.2	27.3	29.3	31.7	32.3	33.3
22. PPI Inflation rate	-	1.8%	−1.5%	1.7%	3.8%	0.0%	0.0%	2.2%	3.1%
23. GDP deflator (2000 = 100)	11.9	8.9	9.7	12.5	16.5	18.7	21.0	22.5	23.2
24. GDP deflator inflation rate	-	−2.6%	−1.2%	2.6%	0.8%	1.5%	1.4%	1.8%	2.8%
Population and Employment									
25. Population (thousands)	121,878	125,690	131,028	139,928	151,684	165,275	180,760	194,347	196,599
26. Labor force (thousands)[2]	49,180	51,590	55,230	53,860	62,208	65,023	69,628	74,455	75,770
27. Unemployed (thousands)[2]	1,550	12,830	9,480	1,040	3,288	2,852	3,852	3,366	2,875
28. Unemployment rate	3.2%	24.9%	17.2%	1.9%	5.3%	4.4%	5.5%	4.5%	3.8%
Government Finance and Money									
29. Government (federal, state and local) budget balance	2.6	−0.5	−0.1	−27.4	6.8	9.2	11.5	9.9	10
30. Budget balance (percent of GDP)	2.5%	−0.9%	−0.1%	−12.3%	2.3%	2.2%	2.2%	1.4%	1.3%
31. M1	-	-	-	-	-	-	140	163	171
32. M2	-	-	-	-	-	-	304	443	471
33. Federal funds rate (yearly average)	-	-	-	-	-	1.8%	3.2%	4.1%	5.1%
International Trade									
34. Current account balance	-	-	-	-	-	-	2.8	5.4	3.0

Sources: Bureau of Economic Analysis, Bureau of Labor Statistics, Federal Reserve Bank of St. Louis.

1. Data in billions of current dollars unless otherwise stated.
2. Until 1947, includes workers 14 years and older; 1948 and after, includes workers 16 years and older.

1967	1968	1969	1970	1971	1972	1973	1974	1975	1976	1977	1978	1979	1980
507.8	558.0	605.2	648.5	701.9	770.6	852.4	933.4	1,034.4	1,151.9	1,278.6	1,428.5	1,592.2	1,757.1
128.6	141.2	156.4	152.4	178.2	207.6	244.5	249.4	230.2	292.0	361.3	438.0	492.9	479.3
192.7	209.4	221.5	233.8	246.5	263.5	281.7	317.9	357.7	383.0	414.1	453.6	500.8	566.2
43.5	47.9	51.9	59.7	63.0	70.8	95.3	126.7	138.7	149.5	159.4	186.9	230.1	280.8
39.9	46.6	50.5	55.8	62.3	74.2	91.2	127.5	122.7	151.1	182.4	212.3	252.7	293.8
832.6	**910.0**	**984.6**	**1,038.5**	**1,127.1**	**1,238.3**	**1,382.7**	**1,500.0**	**1,638.3**	**1,825.3**	**2,030.9**	**2,294.7**	**2,563.3**	**2,789.5**
8.7	10.1	11.8	12.8	14.0	16.3	23.5	29.8	28.0	32.4	37.2	46.3	68.3	79.1
3.3	4.0	5.7	6.4	6.4	7.7	10.9	14.3	15.0	15.5	16.9	24.7	36.4	44.9
838.0	**916.1**	**990.7**	**1,044.9**	**1,134.7**	**1,246.8**	**1,395.3**	**1,515.5**	**1,651.3**	**1,842.1**	**2,051.2**	**2,316.3**	**2,595.3**	**283.7**
751.9	823.2	889.7	930.9	1,008.1	1,111.2	1,247.4	1,342.1	1,445.9	1,611.8	1,798.9	2,027.4	2,249.1	2,439.3
48.0	56.1	62.3	74.7	88.1	97.9	112.6	133.3	170.0	184.0	194.2	209.6	235.3	279.5
73.0	87.0	104.5	103.1	101.7	123.6	132.4	151.0	147.6	172.3	197.5	229.4	268.7	298.8
575.3	625.0	674.0	735.7	801.8	869.1	978.3	1,071.6	1,187.4	1,302.5	1,435.7	1,608.3	1,793.5	2,009.0
54.4	52.8	52.5	69.5	80.6	77.2	102.7	113.6	125.6	122.3	125.3	142.5	159.1	201.4
3,484.6	3,652.7	3,765.4	3,771.9	3,898.6	4,105.0	4,341.5	4,319.6	4,311.2	4,540.9	4,750.5	5,015.0	5,173.4	5,161.7
2.5%	4.8%	3.1%	0.2%	3.4%	5.3%	5.8%	−0.5%	−0.2%	5.3%	4.6%	5.6%	3.2%	−0.2%
17,533	18,196	18,573	18,391	18,771	19,555	20,484	20,195	19,961	20,822	21,565	22,526	22,982	22,666
1.4%	3.8%	2.1%	−1.0%	2.1%	4.2%	4.8%	−1.4%	−1.2%	4.3%	3.6%	4.5%	2.0%	−1.4%
33.4	34.8	36.7	38.8	40.5	41.8	44.4	49.3	53.8	56.9	60.6	65.2	72.6	82.4
3.1%	4.2%	5.5%	5.7%	4.4%	3.2%	6.2%	11.0%	9.1%	5.8%	6.5%	7.6%	11.3%	13.5%
33.4	34.2	35.6	36.9	38.1	39.8	45	53.5	58.4	61.1	64.9	69.9	78.7	89.8
0.3%	2.4%	4.1%	3.7%	3.3%	4.5%	13.1%	18.9%	9.2%	4.6%	6.2%	7.7%	12.6%	14.1%
23.9	24.9	26.2	27.5	28.9	30.2	31.9	34.7	38.0	40.2	42.8	45.8	49.6	54.1
3.1%	4.3%	5.0%	5.3%	5.0%	4.3%	5.6%	9.0%	9.5%	5.8%	6.4%	7.0%	8.3%	9.1%
198,752	200,745	202,736	205,089	207,692	209,924	211,939	213,898	215,981	218,086	220,289	222,629	225,106	227,726
77,347	78,737	80,734	82,771	84,382	87,034	89,429	91,949	93,775	96,158	99,009	102,251	104,962	106,940
2,975	2,817	2,832	4,093	5,016	4,882	4,365	5,156	7,929	7,406	6,991	6,202	6,137	7,637
3.8%	3.6%	3.5%	4.9%	5.9%	5.6%	4.9%	5.6%	8.5%	7.7%	7.1%	6.1%	5.8%	7.1%
−2.4	5.2	16.7	−8.1	−21.9	−8.8	4.4	−4.4	−66.6	−44.4	−31	−7.8	1.7	−44.8
−0.3%	0.6%	1.7%	−0.8%	−1.9%	−0.7%	0.3%	−0.3%	−4.1%	−2.4%	−1.5%	−0.3%	0.1%	−1.6%
178	190	201	209	223	239	256	269	281	297	320	346	373	396
504	545	579	601	674	758	832	881	964	1,087	1,221	1,322	1,426	1,540
4.2%	5.7%	8.2%	7.2%	4.7%	4.4%	8.7%	10.5%	5.8%	5.0%	5.5%	7.9%	11.2%	13.4%
2.6	0.6	0.4	2.3	−1.4	−5.8	7.1	2.0	18.1	4.3	−14.3	−15.1	−0.3	2.3

MACROECONOMIC DATA 1929–2004[1]

	1981	1982	1983	1984	1985	1986	1987	1988	1989	1990
Nominal GDP and Its Components										
1. + Consumer spending (C)	1,941.1	2,077.3	2,290.6	2,503.3	2,720.3	2,899.7	3,100.2	3,353.6	3,598.5	3,839.9
2. + Investment spending (I)	572.4	517.2	564.3	735.6	736.2	746.5	785.0	821.6	874.9	861.0
3. + Government purchases of goods and services (G)	627.5	680.5	733.5	797.0	879.0	949.3	999.5	1,039.0	1,099.1	1,180.2
4. + Exports (X)	305.2	283.2	277.0	302.4	302.0	320.5	363.9	444.1	503.3	552.4
5. – Imports (IM)	317.8	303.2	328.6	405.1	417.2	453.3	509.1	554.5	591.5	630.3
6. = Gross domestic product (GDP)	**3,128.4**	**3,255.0**	**3,536.7**	**3,933.2**	**4,220.3**	**4,462.8**	**4,739.5**	**5,103.8**	**5,484.4**	**5,803.1**
7. + Income from abroad earned by Americans	92.0	101.0	101.9	121.9	112.4	111.4	123.2	152.1	177.7	189.1
8. – Income paid to foreigners	59.1	64.5	64.8	85.6	85.9	93.6	105.3	128.5	151.5	154.3
9. = Gross national product	**3,161.4**	**3,291.5**	**3,573.8**	**3,969.5**	**4,246.8**	**4,480.6**	**4,757.4**	**5,127.4**	**5,510.6**	**5,837.9**
10. National income	2,742.4	2,864.3	3,084.2	3,482.3	3,723.4	3,902.3	4,173.7	4,549.4	4,826.6	5,089.1
11. Government transfers	318.4	354.8	383.7	400.1	424.9	451.0	467.6	496.6	543.4	595.2
12. Taxes	345.2	354.1	352.3	377.4	417.4	437.3	489.1	505.0	566.1	592.8
13. Disposable income (YD)	2,246.1	2,421.2	2,608.4	2,912.0	3,109.3	3,285.1	3,458.3	3,748.7	4,021.7	4,285.8
14. Private savings ($S_{private}$)	244.3	270.8	233.6	314.8	280.0	268.4	241.4	272.9	287.1	299.4
Real GDP and Growth Measures										
15. Real GDP (billions of 2000 dollars)	5,291.7	5,189.3	5,423.8	5,813.6	6,053.7	6,263.6	6,475.1	6,742.7	6,981.4	7,112.5
16. Real GDP growth (percent change from previous year)	2.5%	–1.9%	4.5%	7.2%	4.1%	3.5%	3.4%	4.1%	3.5%	1.9%
17. Real GDP per capita (2000 dollars)	23,007	22,346	23,146	24,593	25,382	26,024	26,664	27,514	28,221	28,429
18. Real GDP per capita growth (percent change from previous year)	1.5%	–2.9%	3.6%	6.3%	3.2%	2.5%	2.5%	3.2%	2.6%	0.7%
Prices and Inflation										
19. Consumer Price Index (1982 – 1984 = 100)	90.9	96.5	99.6	103.9	107.6	109.6	113.6	118.3	124.0	130.7
20. CPI Inflation rate	10.3%	6.2%	3.2%	4.3%	3.6%	1.9%	3.6%	4.1%	4.8%	5.4%
21. Producer Price Index (all commodities, 1982 = 100)	98	100	101.3	103.7	103.2	100.2	102.8	106.9	112.2	116.3
22. PPI Inflation rate	9.1%	2.0%	1.3%	2.4%	–0.5%	–2.9%	2.6%	4.0%	5.0%	3.7%
23. GDP deflator (2000 = 100)	59.1	62.7	65.2	67.7	69.7	71.3	73.2	75.7	78.6	81.6
24. GDP deflator inflation rate	9.4%	6.1%	3.9%	3.8%	3.0%	2.2%	2.7%	3.4%	3.8%	3.9%
Population and Employment										
25. Population (thousands)	230,008	232,218	234,333	236,394	238,506	240,683	242,843	245,061	247,387	250,181
26. Labor force (thousands)[2]	108,670	110,204	111,550	113,544	115,461	117,834	119,865	121,669	123,869	125,840
27. Unemployed (thousands)[2]	8,273	10,678	10,717	8,539	8,312	8,237	7,425	6,701	6,528	7,047
28. Unemployment rate	7.6%	9.7%	9.6%	7.5%	7.2%	7.0%	6.2%	5.5%	5.3%	5.6%
Government Finance and Money										
29. Government (federal, state and local) budget balance	–45.7	–134.1	–168.1	–144.1	–152.6	–169.9	–132.6	–116.6	–109.3	–164.8
30. Budget balance (percent of GDP)	–1.5%	–4.1%	–4.8%	–3.7%	–3.6%	–3.8%	–2.8%	–2.3%	–2.0%	–2.8%
31. M1	425	453	503	539	587	666	743	775	782	811
32. M2	1,680	1,833	2,058	2,222	2,420	2,616	2,787	2,937	3,060	3,228
33. Federal funds rate (yearly average)	16.4%	12.3%	9.1%	10.2%	8.1%	6.8%	6.7%	7.6%	9.2%	8.1%
International Trade										
34. Current account balance	5.0	–5.5	–38.7	–94.3	–118.2	–147.2	–160.7	–121.2	–99.5	–79.0

Sources: Bureau of Economic Analysis, Bureau of Labor Statistics, Federal Reserve Bank of St. Louis.

1. Data in billions of current dollars unless otherwise stated.
2. Until 1947, includes workers 14 years and older; 1948 and after, includes workers 16 years and older.

1991	1992	1993	1994	1995	1996	1997	1998	1999	2000	2001	2002	2003	2004
3,986.1	4,235.3	4,477.9	4,743.3	4,975.8	5,256.8	5,547.4	5,879.5	6,282.5	6,739.4	7,055.0	7,376.1	7,760.9	8,229.9
802.9	864.8	953.4	1,097.1	1,144.0	1,240.3	1,389.8	1,509.1	1,625.7	1,735.5	1,614.3	1,579.2	1,665.8	1,927.3
1,234.4	1,271.0	1,291.2	1,325.5	1,369.2	1,416.0	1,468.7	1,518.3	1,620.8	1,721.6	1,825.6	1,956.6	2,075.5	2,183.9
596.8	635.3	655.8	720.9	812.2	868.6	955.3	955.9	991.2	1,096.3	1,032.8	1,005.0	1,046.2	1,175.5
624.3	668.6	720.9	814.5	903.6	964.8	1,056.9	1,115.9	1,251.7	1,475.8	1,399.8	1,429.9	1,544.3	1,781.6
5,995.9	**6,337.7**	**6,657.4**	**7,072.2**	**7,397.7**	**7,816.9**	**8,304.3**	**8,747.0**	**9,268.4**	**9,817.0**	**10,128.0**	**10,487.0**	**11,004.0**	**11,735.0**
168.9	152.7	156.2	186.4	233.9	248.7	286.7	287.1	320.8	382.7	322.4	301.8	329.0	405.8
138.5	123.0	124.3	160.2	198.1	213.7	253.7	265.8	287.0	343.7	278.8	274.7	273.9	361.9
6,026.3	**6,367.4**	**6,689.3**	**7,098.4**	**7,433.4**	**7,851.9**	**8,337.3**	**8,768.3**	**9,302.2**	**9,855.9**	**10,171.6**	**10,514.1**	**11,059.2**	**11,778.9**
5,227.9	5,512.8	5,773.4	6,122.3	6,453.9	6,840.1	7,292.2	7,752.8	8,236.7	8,795.2	8,979.8	9,225.4	9,679.6	10,339.6
666.4	749.4	790.1	827.3	877.4	925.0	951.2	978.6	1,022.1	1,084.0	1,193.9	1,282.7	1,335.4	1,405.9
586.7	610.6	646.6	690.7	744.1	832.1	926.3	1,027.0	1,107.5	1,235.7	1,237.3	1,051.2	1,001.9	1,042.6
4,464.3	4,751.4	4,911.9	5,151.8	5,408.2	5,688.5	5,988.8	6,395.9	6,695.0	7,194.0	7,486.8	7,827.7	8,159.9	8,646.9
324.2	366.0	284.0	249.5	250.9	228.4	218.3	276.8	158.6	168.5	132.3	159.2	110.6	115.0
7,100.5	7,336.6	7,532.7	7,835.5	8,031.7	8,328.9	8,703.5	9,066.9	9,470.3	9,817.0	9,890.7	10,074.8	10,381.3	10,841.9
−0.2%	3.3%	2.7%	4.0%	2.5%	3.7%	4.5%	4.2%	4.5%	3.7%	0.8%	1.9%	3.0%	4.4%
28,007	28,556	28,940	29,741	30,128	30,881	31,886	32,833	33,904	34,759	34,660	34,955	35,666	36,883
−1.5%	2.0%	1.3%	2.8%	1.3%	2.5%	3.3%	3.0%	3.3%	2.5%	−0.3%	0.9%	2.0%	3.4%
136.2	140.3	144.5	148.2	152.4	156.9	160.5	163.0	166.6	172.2	177.1	179.9	184.0	188.9
4.2%	3.0%	3.0%	2.6%	2.8%	3.0%	2.3%	1.6%	2.2%	3.4%	2.8%	1.6%	2.3%	2.7%
116.5	117.2	118.9	120.4	124.7	127.7	127.6	124.4	125.5	132.7	134.2	131.1	138.1	146.7
0.2%	0.6%	1.5%	1.3%	3.6%	2.4%	−0.1%	−2.5%	0.9%	5.7%	1.1%	−2.3%	5.3%	6.2%
84.5	86.4	88.4	90.3	92.1	93.9	95.4	96.5	97.9	100.0	102.4	104.1	106.0	108.3
3.5%	2.3%	2.3%	2.1%	2.0%	1.9%	1.7%	1.1%	1.4%	2.2%	2.4%	1.7%	1.8%	2.2%
253,530	256,922	260,282	263,455	266,588	269,714	272,958	276,154	279,328	282,429	285,366	288,217	291,073	293,951
126,346	128,105	129,200	131,056	132,304	133,943	136,297	137,673	139,368	142,583	143,734	144,863	146,510	147,401
8,628	9,613	8,940	7,996	7,404	7,236	6,739	6,210	5,880	5,692	6,801	8,378	8,774	8,149
6.8%	7.5%	6.9%	6.1%	5.6%	5.4%	4.9%	4.5%	4.2%	4.0%	4.7%	5.8%	6.0%	5.5%
−217.9	−296.7	−272.6	−201.9	−184.9	−116	−16.7	90.8	154	239.4	51.5	−279.5	−367.8	−351.9
−3.6%	−4.7%	−4.1%	−2.9%	−2.5%	−1.5%	−0.2%	1.0%	1.7%	2.4%	0.5%	−2.7%	−3.3%	−3.0%
859	966	1,079	1,145	1,143	1,106	1,069	1,080	1,101	1,104	1,136	1,191	1,267	1,337
3,349	3,412	3,449	3,495	3,566	3,737	3,920	4,206	4,523	4,799	5,216	5,610	5,998	6,270
5.7%	3.5%	3.0%	4.2%	5.8%	5.3%	5.5%	5.4%	5.0%	6.2%	3.9%	1.7%	1.1%	1.3%
2.9	−50.1	−84.8	−121.6	−113.7	−124.9	−140.9	−214.1	−300.1	−416.0	−389.5	−475.2	−519.7	−668.1

Glossary

Italicized terms within definitions are key terms that are defined elsewhere in this glossary.

ability-to-pay principle: the principle of *tax fairness* by which those with greater ability to pay a tax should pay more tax.

absolute advantage: the advantage conferred by the ability to produce a good more efficiently—at lower cost of *resources*—than other producers.

absolute value: the value of a number without regard to a plus or minus sign.

accelerator principle: the proposition that a higher rate of growth in real GDP leads to higher planned investment spending, because high growth in real GDP is indicative of high growth in sales, which encourages firms to invest.

accounting profit: revenue minus *explicit costs* and depreciation.

actual investment spending: the sum of *planned investment spending* and *unplanned inventory investment*.

administrative costs (of a tax): the *resources* used (which is a cost) both to collect the tax and to pay it.

adverse selection: occurs when an individual knows more about the way things are than other people do. Adverse selection problems can lead to market problems: private information leads buyers to expect hidden problems in items offered for sale, which leads to low prices, which leads to the best items being kept off the market.

aggregate consumption function: an equation relating aggregate current disposable income and aggregate consumer spending for the economy as a whole. A common form for the aggregate consumption function is $C = A + MPC \times YD$.

aggregate demand curve: a graphical representation of the relationship between the aggregate price level and the quantity of aggregate output demanded by households, businesses, the government, and the rest of the world. The aggregate demand curve has a negative slope due to the *wealth effect of a change in the aggregate price level* and the *interest rate effect of a change in the aggregate price level*.

aggregate output: the economy's total production of final goods and services for a given time period, usual-

ly a year. Real GDP is the numerical measure of aggregate output typically used by economists.

aggregate price level: the overall price level for final goods and services in the economy.

aggregate production function: a hypothetical function that describes how productivity (real GDP per worker) depends on the quantities of physical capital per worker and human capital per worker as well as the state of technology. It has the general form $Y/L = f(K/L, H/L, T)$.

aggregate spending: the sum of consumer spending, investment spending, government purchases, and exports minus imports. It is the total spending on domestically produced final goods and services in the economy.

aggregate supply curve: a graphical representation of the relationship between the aggregate price level and the quantity of aggregate output supplied.

antitrust policy: legislative and regulatory efforts of the government to prevent industries from becoming or behaving like *monopolies*.

appreciation: a rise in the value of one currency in terms of other currencies.

artificially scarce good: a good that is *excludable* but *nonrival in consumption*.

AS–AD model: the basic model used to understand fluctuations in aggregate output and the aggregate price level. It uses the *aggregate supply curve* and the *aggregate demand curve* together to analyze the behavior of the economy in response to shocks or government policy.

autarky: occurs when a country cannot trade with other countries.

automatic stabilizers: government spending and taxation rules that cause fiscal policy to be expansionary when the economy contracts and contractionary when the economy expands. Taxes that depend on disposable income are the most important example of automatic stabilizers.

autonomous change in aggregate spending: a change in the desired level of spending by firms, house-

holds, or government at a constant level of GDP.

average cost: an alternative term for *average total cost*; the *total cost* divided by the total quantity of output.

average fixed cost: the *fixed cost* per unit of output.

average tax rate on income: the ratio of income taxes paid to income.

average total cost: *total cost* divided by the total quantity of output.

average variable cost: the *variable cost* per unit of output.

backward-bending individual labor supply curve: an *individual labor supply curve* that is upward sloping when the *substitution effect* predominates (usually at low to moderate wage rates) and downward sloping when the *income effect* predominates (at very high wage rates).

balance of payments accounts: a summary of a country's transactions with other countries, including two main elements: the *balance of payments on current account* and the *balance of payments on financial account*.

balance of payments on current account (**current account**): a country's *balance of payments on goods and services* plus net international transfer payments and factor income.

balance of payments on financial account (**financial account**): the difference between a country's sales of assets to foreigners and its purchases of assets from foreigners during a given period.

balance of payments on goods and services: the difference between a country's exports of goods and services and its imports of goods and services during a given period.

bank: a *financial intermediary* that provides *liquid* assets in the form of *bank deposits* to lenders and uses those funds to finance the *illiquid* investments or investment spending needs of borrowers.

bank deposit: a claim on a *bank* that obliges the bank to give the depositor his or her cash when demanded.

bank reserves: currency held by banks in their vaults plus their deposits at the Federal Reserve.

bank run: a phenomenon in which many of a bank's depositors try to withdraw their funds due to fears of a bank failure.

bar graph: a graph that uses bars of varying height or length to show the comparative sizes of different observations of a variable.

barrier to entry: something that prevents other firms from entering an industry. Crucial in protecting the profits of a *monopolist*. There are four types of barriers to entry: control over scarce resources or inputs, *economies of scale*, technological superiority, and government-created barriers such as *licenses*.

barter: the direct exchange of goods or services without the use of money.

benefits principle: the principle of *tax fairness* by which those who benefit from public spending should bear the burden of the tax that pays for that spending.

black market: a market in which goods or services are bought and sold illegally, either because it is illegal to sell them at all or because the prices charged are legally prohibited by a *price ceiling*.

bond: a legal document issued by a corporation or government promising the repayment of a loan, usually with interest.

brand name: a name owned by a particular firm that distinguishes its products from those of other firms.

break-even price: the market price at which a firm earns zero profits.

budget balance: the difference between net tax revenue and government spending. A positive budget balance is referred to as a *budget surplus*; a negative budget balance is referred to as a *budget deficit*.

budget constraint: the cost of a consumer's *consumption bundle* cannot exceed the consumer's total income.

budget deficit: the difference between net tax revenue and government spending when government spending exceeds tax revenue; dissaving by the government in the form of a budget deficit is a negative contribution to national savings.

budget line: all the *consumption bundles* available to a consumer, assuming all income is spent.

budget surplus: the difference between net tax revenue and government spending when tax revenue exceeds government spending; saving by the government in the form of a budget surplus is a positive contribution to national savings.

business cycle: the short-run alternation between economic downturns, known as *recessions*, and economic upturns, known as *expansions*.

capital: the combined value of assets; includes equipment, buildings, tools, inventory, and financial assets.

capital at risk: funds that an insurer places at risk when agreeing to provide insurance.

capital flows: international movements of *financial assets*.

capital inflow: the net inflow of funds into a country; the difference between the total inflow of foreign funds to the home country and the total outflow of domestic funds to other countries. A positive net capital inflow represents funds borrowed from foreigners to finance domestic investment; a negative net capital inflow represents funds lent to foreigners to finance foreign investment.

cartel: an agreement among several producers setting production quotas for each, thereby leading to oligopoly profits.

causal relationship: the relationship between two variables in which the value taken by one variable directly influences or determines the value taken by the other variable.

central bank: an institution that oversees and regulates the banking system and controls the *monetary base*.

checkable bank deposits: bank accounts on which people can write checks.

circular-flow diagram: a model that represents the transactions in an *economy* by two kinds of flows around a circle: a flow of physical things such as goods or labor and the flow of money to pay for these physical things.

classical model of the price level: a model of the price level in which the real quantity of money is always at its long-run equilibrium level. This model ignores the distinction between the short run and the long run but is useful for analyzing the case of high inflation.

closed economy: an economy that does not trade goods, services, or assets with other countries.

Coase theorem: the proposition that even in the presence of *externalities* an *economy* can always reach an *efficient* solution as long as *transaction costs* are sufficiently low.

collusion: cooperation among producers to limit production and raise prices so as to raise one another's profits.

commodity: output of different producers regarded by consumers as all the same good; also referred to as a *standardized product*.

commodity money: a good that is used as a medium of exchange but also has intrinsic worth because it has other uses. Gold or silver coins are commodity money.

commodity-backed money: a medium of exchange that has no intrinsic value but is guaranteed by a promise that it can be converted into valuable goods. Paper money that can be exchanged freely for gold or silver coins is commodity-backed money.

common resource: a *resource* that is *nonexcludable* and *rival in consumption*.

comparative advantage: the advantage conferred on an individual or nation if it can produce a good at a lower *opportunity cost* than another producer.

compensating differentials: wage differences across jobs that reflect the fact that some jobs are less pleasant or more dangerous than others.

competitive market economy: an *economy* in which all markets, for goods and for factors, are perfectly competitive. All market participants are price-takers.

competitive market: a market in which all market participants are price-takers.

complements: pairs of goods for which a fall in the price of one good results in greater demand for the other.

constant returns to scale: a range of production in which *long-run average total cost* is constant as output increases.

consumer price index (CPI): a measure of the cost of a market basket intended to represent the consumption of a typical urban American family of four. It is the most commonly used measure of prices in the United States.

consumer spending: household spending on goods and services produced by domestic and foreign firms.

consumer surplus: a term often used to refer both to *individual consumer surplus* and to *total consumer surplus.*

consumption bundle (of an individual)**:** the collection of all the goods and services consumed by a given individual.

consumption function: an equation showing how an individual household's consumer spending varies with current disposable income. Generally, consumption is positively related to disposable income. A common and simple version of a consumption function that captures this relationship is linear: $c = a + MPC \times yd$.

consumption possibilities: the set of all *consumption bundles* available to a consumer, given that consumer's income and prevailing prices.

contractionary fiscal policy: *fiscal policy* that reduces aggregate demand by increasing taxes, decreasing transfers, or decreasing government purchases.

contractionary monetary policy: monetary policy that, through the raising of the interest rate, reduces aggregate demand and therefore output.

convergence hypothesis: a theory of economic growth that holds that international differences in real GDP per capita tend to narrow over time because countries with low GDP per capita generally have higher growth rates.

copyright: the exclusive legal right of the creator of a literary or artistic work to profit from that work; like a *patent,* it is a temporary monopoly.

cost (of potential seller)**:** the lowest price at which a seller is willing to sell a good.

cost-benefit analysis: an estimate of the costs and benefits of providing a good. When governments use cost-benefit analysis, they estimate the social costs and social benefits of providing a public good.

critical mass: the size at which a network suddenly begins to grow rapidly.

cross-price elasticity of demand: the ratio of the percent change in the *quantity demanded* of one good to the percent change in the price of another good; a measure of the effect of the change in the price of one good on the quantity demanded of the other.

crowding out: the negative effect of budget deficits on private investment, which occurs because government borrowing drives up interest rates.

currency in circulation: cash, in either paper or coin form, held by the public.

curve: a line on a graph, which may be curved or straight, that depicts a relationship between two variables.

cyclical unemployment: unemployment resulting from the business cycle; equivalently, the difference between the actual rate of unemployment and the *natural rate of unemployment.*

cyclically adjusted budget balance: an estimate of what the *budget balance* would be if real GDP were exactly equal to potential output.

deadweight loss (from a tax)**:** the extra cost in the form of inefficiency that results because a tax discourages mutually beneficial transactions; also referred to as *excess burden.*

debt deflation: the reduction in aggregate demand arising from the increase in the real burden of outstanding debt caused by deflation; occurs because borrowers, whose real debt rises as a result of deflation, are likely to cut spending sharply, and lenders, whose real assets are now more valuable, are less likely to increase spending.

debt–GDP ratio: government debt as a percentage of GDP, frequently used as a measure of a government's ability to pay its debts.

decreasing marginal benefit: *marginal benefit* that decreases with each additional unit of the activity.

deductible: a sum specified in an insurance policy that the insured must pay before being compensated for a loss; deductibles reduce *moral hazard.*

deflation: a falling *aggregate price level.*

demand curve: a graphical representation of the *demand schedule,* showing how much of a good or service consumers would buy at a given price.

demand price: the price of a given quantity at which consumers will demand that quantity.

demand schedule: a list or table showing the relationship between price and the quantity of a good consumers would buy.

demand shock: any event that shifts the *aggregate demand curve.* A positive demand shock is associated with higher demand for aggregate output at any price level and shifts the curve to the right. A negative demand shock is associated with lower demand for aggregate output at any price level and shifts the curve to the left.

dependent variable: the determined variable in a causal relationship.

deposit insurance: a guarantee that a bank's depositors will be paid even if the bank can't come up with the funds, up to a maximum amount per account.

depreciation: a fall in the value of one currency in terms of other currencies.

depression: a very deep and prolonged downturn.

devaluation: a reduction in the value of a currency that is set under a fixed *exchange rate* regime.

diminishing marginal rate of substitution: the principle that the more of one good that is consumed in proportion to another, the less of the second good the consumer is willing to substitute for another unit of the first good.

diminishing returns to an input: the effect observed when an increase in the quantity of an *input,* while holding the levels of all other inputs fixed, leads to a decline in the *marginal product* of that input.

diminishing returns to physical capital: property of an *aggregate production function* whereby each successive increase in the amount of physical capital, holding the amount of human capital and the state of technology fixed, leads to a smaller increase in productivity.

discount rate: the rate of interest the Federal Reserve charges on loans to banks that fall short of *reserve requirements.*

discouraged workers: nonworking people who are capable of working but have given up looking for a job because they believe no jobs are available.

discretionary fiscal policy: *fiscal policy* that is the result of deliberate actions by policy makers rather than rules.

discretionary monetary policy: policy actions, either changes in interest rates or changes in the money supply, undertaken by the central bank based on its assessment of the state of the economy.

diseconomies of scale: a range of production in which *long-run average total cost* increases as output increases.

disinflation: the process of lowering inflation that has become embedded in expectations by keeping the unemployment rate above the natural rate for an extended period of time.

disposable income: income plus *government transfers* minus taxes; the total amount of household income available to use for consumption and saving.

diversification: investment in several different assets with unrelated risks, so that the possible losses are independent events.

domestic demand curve: a *demand curve* for domestic consumers.

domestic supply curve: a *supply curve* for domestic producers.

dominant strategy: in *game theory,* an action that is a player's best action regardless of the action taken by the other player.

duopolist: one of the two firms in a *duopoly.*

duopoly: an *oligopoly* consisting of only two firms.

economic aggregate: an economic measure that summarizes data across different markets for goods, services, workers, and assets.

economic growth: a *long-run* trend toward the production of more goods and services.

economic profit: revenue minus the *opportunity cost* of *resources;* often less than *accounting profit.*

economic signal: any piece of information that helps people make better economic decisions.

economics: the study of *economies,* at the level of individuals and of society as a whole.

economies of scale: a range of production in which *long-run average total cost* declines as output increases.

economy: a system for coordinating a society's productive activities.

efficiency wages: wages that employers set above the equilibrium wage rate as an incentive for better performance.

efficiency-wage model: a model in which some employers pay an above-equilibrium wage as an *incentive* to better performance.

efficient allocation of resources: the case in which there is no way for an economy to reallocate *factors of production* among producers to produce more of some goods without producing less of others.

efficient allocation of risk: the case in which those most willing to bear *risk* are those who bear it.

efficient in consumption: description of an *economy* in which there is no way to redistribute goods that makes some consumers better off without making others worse off.

efficient in output levels: description of an *economy* in which no different mix of output would make some consumers better off without making others worse off.

efficient in production: description of an *economy* in which there is no way to produce more of some goods without producing less of others.

efficient markets hypothesis: a theory of asset price determination that holds that asset prices embody all publicly available information. The theory implies that stock prices should be unpredictable, or follow a *random walk,* since changes should occur only in response to new information about fundamentals.

efficient: description of a market or *economy* that uses its resources in such a way as to exploit all opportunities to make some individuals better off without making others worse off.

elastic demand: when the *price elasticity of demand* is greater than 1. A percentage increase in price will cause a correspondingly greater percentage decrease in quantity demanded, and vice versa.

emissions tax: a tax that depends on the amount of pollution a firm produces.

employment: the number of people currently employed for pay in the economy.

environmental standards: rules established by a government to protect the environment by specifying actions to be taken by producers and consumers.

equilibrium: an economic balance in which no individual would be better off doing something different; an equality of supply and demand.

equilibrium exchange rate: the *exchange rate* at which the quantity of a currency demanded in the *foreign exchange market* is equal to the quantity supplied.

equilibrium price: the price at which the market is in *equilibrium,* that is, the quantity of a good demanded equals the quantity supplied; also referred to as the *market-clearing price.*

equilibrium quantity: the quantity of a good bought and sold at the *equilibrium* (or *market-clearing) price.*

equilibrium value of the marginal product: the additional value produced by the last unit of a factor employed in the *factor market* as a whole.

equity: fairness; because individuals can disagree about what is "fair," equity is not as well defined a concept as efficiency.

excess burden (from a tax): the extra cost in the form of inefficiency that results because a tax discourages mutually beneficial transactions; also referred to as *deadweight loss.*

excess capacity: when firms produce less than the output at which *average total cost* is minimized; characteristic of *monopolistically competitive* firms.

excess reserves: a bank's *reserves* over and above the reserves required by law or regulation.

exchange market intervention: government purchases or sales of currency in the *foreign exchange market.*

exchange rate: the price of one currency in terms of another, determined by the *foreign exchange market.* The nominal exchange rate is unadjusted for international differences in price levels; the *real exchange rate* is adjusted for those differences.

exchange rate regime: a rule governing a country's policy toward the *exchange rate.*

excise tax: a tax on the consumption of a given good or service.

excludable: referring to a good, describes the case in which the supplier can prevent those who do not pay from consuming the good.

expansion: a period when output and employment are rising; also referred to as a *recovery.*

expansionary fiscal policy: *fiscal policy* that increases aggregate demand by decreasing taxes, increasing transfers, or increasing government purchases.

expansionary monetary policy: monetary policy that, through the lowering of the interest rate, increases aggregate demand and therefore output.

expected rate of inflation: the rate of inflation that employers and workers expect in the near future.

expected utility: the expected value of total *utility,* given uncertainty about outcomes.

expected value: in reference to a *random variable,* the weighted average of all possible variables; the weights on each possible value correspond to the probability of that value.

explicit cost: a cost that requires an outlay of money.

exporting industries: industries that produce goods or services for sale abroad.

exports: goods and services sold to residents of other countries.

external benefit: an uncompensated benefit that an individual or firm confers on others; also known as *positive externalities.*

external cost: an uncompensated cost that an individual or firm imposes on others; also known as *negative externalities.*

externalities: *external benefits* and *external costs.*

factor distribution of income: the division of total income among labor, land, and *capital.*

factor intensity: the difference in the ratio of *factors* used to produce a good

in various industries. For example, oil refining is capital-intensive compared to clothing manufacture because oil refiners use a higher ratio of capital to labor than do clothing producers.

factor markets: markets in which *firms* buy *factors of production.*

factors of production: the *resources* needed to produce goods or services. Labor and capital are examples of factors.

fair insurance policy: an insurance policy for which the *premium* is equal to the expected value of the claims.

federal funds market: the market in which banks that fall short of *reserve requirements* can borrow funds from banks with *excess reserves.*

federal funds rate: the interest rate at which banks short of reserves can borrow from other banks with *excess reserves.* It is determined in the *federal funds market.*

fiat money: a medium of exchange that derives its value entirely from its official status as a means of payment. The U.S. dollar is fiat money.

final goods and services: goods and services sold to the final, or end, user.

financial asset: a paper claim that entitles the buyer to future income from the seller. Loans, stocks, bonds, and bank deposits are types of financial assets.

financial intermediary: an institution, such as a *mutual fund, pension fund, life insurance company,* or *bank,* that transforms the funds it gathers from many individuals into financial assets.

financial markets: the banking, stock, and bond markets, which channel private savings and foreign lending into investment spending, government borrowing, and foreign borrowing.

financial risk: uncertainty about future outcomes that involve financial losses and gains.

financial risk: uncertainty about monetary outcomes.

firm: an organization that produces goods or services for sale.

fiscal policy: a type of stabilization policy that involves the use of changes in taxation, government transfers, or government purchases of goods and services.

fiscal year: the time period used for much of government accounting, running from October 1 to September 30. Fiscal years are named by the calendar year in which they end.

Fisher effect: the principle by which an increase in expected inflation drives up the nominal interest rate, leaving the expected real interest rate unchanged.

fixed cost: a cost that does not depend on the quantity of output produced; the cost of a *fixed input.*

fixed exchange rate: an *exchange rate regime* in which the government keeps the exchange rate against some other currency at or near a particular target.

fixed input: an *input* whose quantity is fixed and cannot be varied (for example, land).

floating exchange rate: an *exchange rate regime* in which the government lets the exchange rate go wherever the market takes it.

forecast: a simple prediction of the future under current assumptions.

foreign exchange controls: licensing systems that limit the right of individuals to buy foreign currency.

foreign exchange market: the market in which currencies are traded.

foreign exchange reserves: stocks of foreign currency that governments maintain in order to buy their own currency on the *foreign exchange market.*

free entry and exit: describes an industry that potential producers can easily enter or current producers can leave.

free trade: *trade* that is unregulated by government *tariffs* or other artificial barriers; the levels of *exports* and *imports* occur naturally, as a result of supply and demand.

free-rider problem: when individuals have no *incentive* to pay for their own consumption of a good, they will take a "free ride" on anyone who does pay; a problem with goods that are *nonexcludable.*

frictional unemployment: unemployment due to time spent searching for a job. Because this type of unemployment can occur even when jobs exist for all of the unemployed, it does not necessarily signal a labor surplus.

gains from trade: the benefit that each party receives from a trade, which, because of *specialization,* is greater than if each attempted to be self-sufficient.

game theory: the study of behavior in situations of *interdependence.* Used to explain the behavior of an *oligopoly*.

GDP deflator: for a given year, 100 times the ratio of *nominal GDP* to *real GDP* in that year.

GDP per capita: GDP divided by the size of the population; equivalent to the average GDP per person.

general equilibrium: an economic balance in which the *quantity supplied* is equal to the *quantity demanded* in all markets in an economy.

government borrowing: funds borrowed by the government in financial markets.

government purchases of goods and services: government expenditures on goods and services.

government transfers: payments by the government to individuals for which no good or service is provided in return.

gross domestic product (GDP): the total value of all final goods and services produced in the economy during a given year.

growth accounting: an estimation of the contribution to economic growth of each of the major factors (physical and human capital, labor, and technology) in the aggregate production function. Most growth accounting finds that increases in *total factor productivity* are central to a country's economic growth.

Hecksher–Olin model: a *model* of international trade that shows how a country's *comparative advantage* can be determined by its supply of *factors of production.*

horizontal axis: the horizontal number line of a graph along which values of the *x*-variable are measured; also referred to as the *x-axis.*

horizontal intercept: the point at which a curve intersects the horizontal axis, showing the value of the *x*-variable when the value of the *y*-variable is zero.

household: a group of people that share a dwelling and their income (a household may also consist of one person).

human capital: the improvement in labor created by the education and knowledge embodied in the workforce.

illiquid: refers to an asset that cannot be quickly converted into cash without much loss of value.

imperfect competition: a market structure in which no firm is a *monopolist,* but producers nonetheless have *market power* they can use to affect market prices.

implicit cost: a cost that does not require the outlay of money; it is measured by the value, in dollar terms, of forgone benefits.

implicit cost of capital: the *opportunity cost* of the capital used; that is, the income that could have been realized had the capital been used in the next best alternative way.

implicit liabilities: spending promises made by governments that are like a debt although they are not included in the usual debt statistics. In the United States, the largest implicit liabilities arise from Social Security and Medicare, which promise transfer payments to current and future retirees (Social Security) and to the elderly (Medicare).

import quota: a legal limit on the quantity of a good that can be imported.

import-competing industries: industries that produce goods or services that are also imported.

imports: goods and services purchased from residents of other countries.

in-kind transfers: specific goods and services (such as food stamps) provided to poor families by government.

incentive: a reward offered to people who change their behavior.

incidence (of a tax): a measure of who actually bears the burden of a tax.

income effect: the change in the quantity of a good consumed that results from the change in a consumer's purchasing power due to the change in the price of the good.

income elasticity of demand: the ratio of the percentage change in *quantity demanded* of a good or service to the percentage change in a consumer's income.

income tax: a tax on the income of an individual or family.

income-elastic demand: when the *income elasticity of demand* is greater than 1. Occurs when the demand for certain goods (such as luxury goods) rises faster than the increase in income.

income-inelastic demand: when the *income elasticity of demand* is positive but less than 1. Occurs when the demand for certain goods (such as food and clothing) rises but more slowly than the increase in income.

income–expenditure equilibrium: a situation in which aggregate output, measured by real GDP, is equal to planned aggregate spending and firms have no incentive to change output.

income–expenditure equilibrium GDP: the level of real GDP at which real GDP equals *planned aggregate spending.*

increasing marginal cost: *marginal cost* that becomes greater with each additional unit of the activity.

independent events: events for which the occurrence of one does not affect the likelihood of occurrence of any of the others.

independent variable: the determining variable in a causal relationship.

indifference curve: a contour line showing all *consumption bundles* that yield the same amount of total *utility* for an individual.

indifference curve map: a collection of *indifference curves* for a given individual that represents the individual's total *utility function;* each curve corresponds to a different level of total utility.

individual choice: the decision by an individual of what to do, which necessarily involves a decision of what not to do.

individual consumer surplus: the net gain to an individual buyer from the purchase of a good; equal to the difference between the buyer's *willingness to pay* and the price paid.

individual demand curve: a graphical representation of the relationship between *quantity demanded* and price for an individual consumer.

individual labor supply curve: a graphical representation of the relationship between the wage rate and the number of hours supplied by an individual worker.

individual producer surplus: the net gain to an individual seller from selling a good; equal to the difference between the price received and the seller's *cost*.

industrial policy: a policy that supports industries believed to yield *positive externalities*.

industry supply curve: a graphical representation that shows the relationship between the price of a good and the total output of the industry for that good.

inefficient allocation of sales among sellers: a form of inefficiency in which sellers who are willing to sell a good at a lower price are not always those who actually manage to sell it; often the result of a *price floor*.

inefficient allocation to consumers: a form of inefficiency in which consumers who are willing to pay a high price for a good do not get it, and those willing to pay only a low price do; often a result of a *price ceiling*.

inefficient: describes a market or *economy* in which there are missed opportunities for making some individuals better off without making others worse off.

inefficiently high quality: a form of inefficiency in which sellers offer high-quality goods at a high price even though buyers would prefer a lower quality at a lower price; often the result of a *price floor*.

inefficiently low quality: a form of inefficiency in which sellers offer low-quality goods at a low price even though buyers would prefer a higher quality at a higher price; often a result of a *price ceiling*.

inelastic demand: when the *price elasticity of demand* is less than 1. A percentage increase in price will cause a correspondingly lesser percentage decrease in quantity demanded, and vice versa.

inferior good: a good for which a rise in income decreases the demand for the good.

inflation: a rising *aggregate price level*.

inflation rate: the percent change per year in a price index—typically the *consumer price index*. The inflation rate is positive when the aggregate price level is rising (*inflation*) and negative when the aggregate price level is falling (*deflation*).

inflation targeting: an approach to *monetary policy* that requires that the central bank try to keep the inflation rate near a predetermined target rate.

inflation tax: the reduction in the value of money held by the public caused by inflation.

inflationary gap: occurs when aggregate output is above *potential output*.

information good: a good whose value derives from the information it contains.

infrastructure: physical capital, such as roads, power lines, ports, and information networks, that provides the foundation for economic activity.

input: a good used to produce another good.

interaction (of choices): the mutual influence of the choices of various parties (the results are often quite different from what was intended).

interdependence: the relationship among firms when their decisions significantly affect one another's profits; characteristic of oligopolies.

interest rate: the price, calculated as a percentage of the amount borrowed, charged by lenders to borrowers for the use of their savings for one year.

interest rate effect of a change in the aggregate price level: the effect on consumer and investment spending caused by a change in the purchasing power of consumers' money holdings when the aggregate price level changes. A rise (fall) in the aggregate price level decreases (increases) the purchasing power of consumers' money holdings. In response, consumers try to increase (decrease) their money holdings, which drives up (down) interest rates, thereby decreasing (increasing) consumption and investment.

intermediate goods and services: goods and services, bought from one firm by another firm, that are inputs for production of final goods and services.

internalize the externality: take into account *external costs* and *external benefits*.

international trade agreements: treaties by which countries agree to lower *trade protections* against one another.

inventories: stocks of goods held to satisfy future sales.

inventory investment: the value of the change in total inventories held in the economy during a given period. Unlike other types of investment spending, inventory investment can be negative, if inventories fall.

investment spending: spending on productive physical capital, such as machinery and construction of structures, and on changes to inventories.

invisible hand: a phrase used by Adam Smith to describe the way in which an individual's pursuit of self-interest can lead, without the individual intending it, to good results for society as a whole.

job search: the act of looking for employment.

Keynesian cross: a diagram that identifies income–expenditure equilibrium as the point where the planned aggregate spending line crosses the 45-degree line.

Keynesian economics: the school of thought emerging out of the works of John Maynard Keynes and emphasizing two important concepts: the short run effects of shifts in *aggregate demand* on output and the ability of factors other than the money supply to create *business cycles*.

kinked demand curve: a model used to explain the stability of oligopoly pricing; a *demand curve* that kinks (bends) because the *oligopolist* will lose sales if price is increased but gain only momentarily if price is lowered (because the lower price will be matched at once by other oligopolists).

labor force: the number of people who are either actively employed for pay or unemployed and actively looking for work; the sum of *employment* and *unemployment*.

labor productivity: output per worker; also referred to as simply *productivity*. Increases in labor productivity are the only source of long-run economic growth.

law of demand: a higher price charged for a good, other things equal, leads to a smaller quantity of the good demanded.

leisure: the time available for purposes other than earning money to buy marketed goods.

liability: a requirement to pay income in the future.

license: the right, conferred by the government or an owner, to supply some good or perform some activity, often in exchange for a fee.

life insurance company: a *financial intermediary* that sells policies guaranteeing a payment to a policyholder's beneficiaries when the policyholder dies.

linear relationship: the relationship between two variables in which the *slope* is constant and therefore is depicted on a graph by a *curve* that is a straight line.

liquid: refers to an asset that can be quickly converted into cash without much loss of value.

liquidity preference model of the interest rate: a model of the market for money, in which the interest rate is determined by the supply and demand for money.

liquidity trap: a situation in which the nominal interest rate has hit its lower bound of zero; as a result, expansionary monetary policy can no longer be used.

loan: a lending agreement between a particular lender and a particular borrower. Loans are usually tailored to the individual borrower's needs and ability to pay but carry relatively high transaction costs.

loanable funds market: a hypothetical market in which the demand for funds is generated by borrowers and the supply of funds is provided by lenders. The market equilibrium determines the quantity and price, or *interest rate*, of loanable funds.

long run: the time period in which all *inputs* can be varied.

long-run aggregate supply curve: a graphical representation of the relationship between the aggregate price level and the quantity of aggregate output supplied if all prices, including nominal wages, were fully flexible. The long-run aggregate supply curve is vertical because the aggregate price level has no effect on aggregate output in the long run; in the long run, aggregate output is determined by the economy's *potential output.*

long-run average total cost curve: a graphical representation showing the relationship between output and *average total cost* when *fixed cost* has been chosen to minimize *total cost* for each level of output.

long-run growth: see *secular long-run growth.*

long-run industry supply curve: a graphical representation that shows how *quantity supplied* responds to price once producers have had time to enter or exit the industry.

long-run macroeconomic equilibrium: a situation in which *short-run macroeconomic equilibrium* is also on the *long-run aggregate supply curve;* so *short-run equilibrium aggregate output* is equal to *potential output.*

long-run market equilibrium: an economic balance in which, given sufficient time for producers to enter or exit an industry, the *quantity supplied* equals the *quantity demanded.*

long-run Phillips curve: a graphical representation of the relationship between unemployment and inflation after expectations of inflation have had time to adjust to experience. It is vertical at the *natural rate of unemployment.*

long-term interest rate: the interest rate on financial assets that mature a number of years in the future.

lump-sum tax: a tax that is the same for everyone, regardless of any actions individuals take.

macroeconomic policy activism: the use of monetary and fiscal policy to smooth out the *business cycle.*

macroeconomics: the branch of *economics* concerned with the overall ups and downs in the *economy.*

marginal analysis: the study of *marginal decisions,* those resulting from small changes in an activity.

marginal benefit curve: a graphical representation showing how the benefit from undertaking one more unit of an activity depends on the quantity of that activity that has already been done.

marginal benefit: the additional benefit derived by performing one more unit of an activity.

marginal cost: the additional cost incurred by performing one more unit of an activity.

marginal cost curve: a graphical representation showing how the cost of undertaking one more unit of an activity depends on the quantity of that activity that has already been done.

marginal decision: a decision made at the "margin" of an activity to do a little more or a little less.

marginal product: the additional quantity of output produced by using one more unit of a given *input.*

marginal productivity theory of income distribution: the proposition that every *factor of production* is paid its *equilibrium value of the marginal product.*

marginal propensity to consume, or MPC: the increase in consumer spending when income rises by $1. Because consumers normally spend part but not all of an additional dollar of disposable income, *MPC* is between zero and one.

marginal propensity to save, or MPS: the increase in household savings when disposable income rises by $1.

marginal rate of substitution (MRS): the ratio of the *marginal utility* of one good to the marginal utility of another.

marginal revenue: the change in *total revenue* generated by an additional unit of output.

marginal revenue curve: a graphical representation showing how *marginal revenue* varies as output varies.

marginal social benefit of a good or activity: the *marginal benefit* that accrues to consumers plus the marginal *external benefit.*

marginal social benefit of pollution: the additional gain to society from an additional unit of pollution.

marginal social cost of a good or activity: the *marginal cost* of production plus the marginal *external cost* to society of that production.

marginal social cost of pollution: the additional cost imposed on society by an additional unit of pollution.

marginal tax rate on income: the additional income tax paid if income increases by $1.

marginal utility: the change in total *utility* generated by consuming one additional unit of a good or service.

marginal utility curve: a graphical representation showing how *marginal utility* depends on the quantity of the good or service consumed.

marginal utility per dollar: the additional *utility* gained from spending an additional dollar on a good or service.

market basket: a hypothetical set of consumer purchases of goods and services, used to measure changes in the overall price level.

market economy: an *economy* in which decisions about production and consumption are made by individual producers and consumers.

market failure: occurs when a market fails to be efficient.

market power: the ability of a producer to raise prices.

market share: the fraction of the total industry output represented by a given producer's output.

market-clearing price: the price at which the market is in *equilibrium,* that is, the quantity of a good demanded equals the quantity supplied; also referred to as the *equilibrium price.*

markets for goods and services: markets in which households buy goods and services from *firms.*

maximum: the highest point on a *nonlinear curve,* where the *slope* changes from positive to negative.

means-tested: having an income qualification, as certain government social programs.

median voter theorem: the proposition that in a majority-rule election concerning the extent of a given policy action, the actual policies will reflect the preference of the median voter—the one in the center of the left–right spectrum.

medium of exchange: an asset that individuals acquire for the purpose of trading rather than for their own consumption. One of *money*'s main roles in the economy is to serve as the primary medium of exchange.

menu costs: small costs associated with the act of changing prices.

merchandise trade balance: the difference between a country's exports of goods and its imports of goods.

microeconomics: the branch of *economics* that studies how individuals make decisions and how those decisions interact.

midpoint method: a technique for calculating the percent change in which changes in a variable are compared with the average, or midpoint, of the starting and final values.

minimum: the lowest point on a *nonlinear curve,* where the *slope* changes from negative to positive.

minimum wage: a legal floor on the wage rate. The wage rate is the market price of labor.

minimum-cost output: the quantity of output at which the *average total cost* is lowest—the bottom of the *U-shaped average total cost curve.*

model: a simplified representation of a real-life situation that uses data and assumptions to make predictions about that situation and understand it better.

monetarism: a theory of *business cycles,* associated primarily with Milton Friedman, that asserts that GDP will grow steadily if the money supply grows steadily; implies that policy makers' attempts to smooth business cycles are often counterproductive.

monetary aggregate: an overall measure of the money supply. The most common monetary aggregates in the United States are M1, which includes *currency in circulation*, traveler's checks, and *checkable bank deposits*, and M2, which includes M1 as well as *near-moneys.*

monetary base: the sum of currency in circulation and *bank reserves;* controlled by the monetary authority.

monetary neutrality: the principle by which changes in the money supply have no real effects on the economy in the long run and only result in a proportional change in the price level.

monetary policy: a type of *stabilization policy* that involves changes in the quantity of money in circulation or in the interest rate, or both.

monetary policy rule: a formula that determines the central bank's actions.

money: any asset that can easily be used to purchase goods and services.

money demand curve: a graphical representation of the negative relationship between the quantity of money demanded and the interest rate. The money demand curve slopes downward because, other things equal, a higher interest rate increases the opportunity cost of holding money.

money multiplier: the ratio of the *money supply* to the *monetary base.*

money supply: the total value of financial assets in the economy that are considered money. There are several different measures of the money supply, called *monetary aggregates.*

money supply curve: a graphical representation of the relationship between the nominal quantity of money supplied by the Federal Reserve and the interest rate. The money supply curve is vertical at the money supply chosen by the Fed.

monopolist: a firm that is the only producer of a good that has no close substitutes.

monopolistic competition: a market structure in which there are many competing producers in an industry, each producer sells a differentiated product, and there is *free entry and exit* into and from the industry in the *long run.*

monopoly: an industry controlled by a *monopolist.*

moral hazard: the situation that can exist when an individual knows more about his or her own actions than other people do. This leads to a distortion of incentives to take care or to expend effort, especially when someone else bears the costs of the lack of care or effort.

movement along the demand curve: a change in the *quantity demanded* of a good that results from a change in the price of that good.

movement along the supply curve: a change in the *quantity supplied* of a good that results from a change in the price of that good.

multiplier: the ratio of the eventual change in GDP caused by an autonomous change in aggregate spending to the size of that autonomous change.

mutual fund: a *financial intermediary* that creates a stock portfolio and then resells shares of this portfolio to individual investors.

Nash equilibrium: in *game theory,* the *equilibrium* that results when all players choose their optimal action given the actions of other players, ignoring the effect of that action on the *payoffs* of other players; also known as *noncooperative equilibrium.*

national income and product accounts: an accounting of *consumer spending,* sales of producers, business *investment spending,* and other flows of money between different sectors of the economy; also referred to as *national accounts.* Calculated by the Bureau of Economic Analysis.

national savings: the total amount of savings generated within the economy, which equals the sum of private savings and the government's *budget balance.*

natural monopoly: a *monopoly* that arises because *economies of scale* over the range of output of an industry provide a large cost advantage to having all output produced by a single firm.

natural rate of unemployment: the normal unemployment rate arising from *frictional* and *structural unemployment.* The actual unemployment rate fluctuates around the natural rate.

near-money: a financial asset that can't be directly used as a medium of exchange but can be readily converted into cash or checkable bank deposits.

negative externalities: *external costs.*

negative income tax: a government program that supplements the earnings of low-income families.

negative relationship: a relationship between two variables in which an increase in the value of one variable is associated with a decrease in the value of the other variable. It is described by a *curve* that slopes downward from left to right.

net exports: the difference between the value of *exports* and the value of *imports.* A positive value for net exports indicates that a country is a net exporter of goods and services; a negative value indicates that a country is a net importer of goods and services.

net present value: the *present value* of current and future benefits minus the present value of current and future costs.

network externality: the increase in the value of a good to an individual is greater when a large number of others own or use the same good.

new classical macroeconomics: an approach to the *business cycle* that returns to the classical view that, even in the short run, shifts in the *aggregate demand* curve affect only the aggregate price level, not aggregate output.

nominal: refers to a measure or quantity that has not been adjusted for changes in prices over time.

nominal GDP: the value of all final goods and services produced in the economy during the year, calculated using the prices current in the year in which the output is produced.

nominal interest rate: the interest rate unadjusted for inflation.

nominal wage: the dollar amount of the wage paid.

nonaccelerating inflation rate of unemployment (NAIRU): the unemployment rate at which, other things equal, inflation does not change over time.

noncooperative behavior: actions by firms that ignore the effects of those actions on the profits of other firms.

noncooperative equilibrium: in *game theory,* the *equilibrium* that results when all players choose their optimal action given the actions of other players, ignoring the effect of that action on the *payoffs* of other players; also known as *Nash equilibrium.*

nonexcludable: referring to a good, describes the case in which the supplier cannot prevent those who do not pay from consuming the good.

nonlinear curve: a curve whose *slope* is not constant.

nonlinear relationship: the relationship between two variables in which the *slope* is not constant and therefore is depicted on a graph by a *curve* that is not a straight line.

nonprice competition: competition in areas other than price to increase sales, such as new product features and advertising; especially engaged in

by firms that have a tacit understanding not to compete on price.

nonrival in consumption: referring to a good, describes the case in which the same unit can be consumed by more than one person at the same time.

normal good: a good for which a rise in income increases the demand for that good—the "normal" case.

normative economics: the branch of economic analysis that makes prescriptive statements about how the *economy* should work.

Okun's law: the generally observed relationship between the output gap and the unemployment rate, whereby each additional percentage point of output gap reduces the unemployment rate by less than 1 percentage point.

oligopolist: a firm in an industry with only a small number of producers.

oligopoly: an industry with only a small number of producers.

omitted variable: an unobserved *variable* that, through its influence on other variables, creates the erroneous appearance of a direct *causal relationship* among those variables.

open economy: an economy that trades goods, services, and assets with other countries.

open-economy macroeconomics: the study of those aspects of macroeconomics that are affected by movements of goods, services, and assets across national boundaries.

open-market operation: a purchase or sale of U.S. Treasury bills by the Federal Reserve, undertaken to change the *monetary base,* which in turn changes the *money supply.*

opportunity cost: the real cost of an item, including what must be given up to obtain it.

optimal consumption bundle: the *consumption bundle* that maximizes a consumer's total *utility,* given that consumer's *budget constraint.*

optimal consumption rule: when a consumer maximizes *utility,* the *marginal utility per dollar* spent is the same for all goods and services in the *consumption bundle.*

optimal output rule: profit is maximized by producing the quantity of output at which the *marginal cost* of the last unit produced is equal to its *marginal revenue.*

optimal quantity: the level of activity that generates the maximum possible total net gain.

optimal time allocation rule: an individual should allocate time in such a way that the *marginal utility* of an hour spent working is equal to the marginal utility of an additional hour of *leisure.*

ordinary goods: in a consumer's *utility function,* those for which additional units of one good are required to compensate for fewer units of another, and for which the consumer experiences a *diminishing marginal rate of substitution* in substituting one good for another.

origin: the point where the axes of a two-variable graph meet.

other things equal assumption: in the development of a model, the assumption that all relevant factors except the one under study remain unchanged.

output gap: the percentage difference between the actual level of real GDP and potential output.

overuse: the depletion of a *common resource* that occurs when individuals ignore the effect their use has on the amount of the resource remaining for others.

patent: a temporary monopoly given by the government to an inventor for the use or sale of an invention.

payoff: in *game theory,* the reward received by a player (for example, the profit earned by an *oligopolist*).

payoff matrix: in *game theory,* a diagram that shows how the *payoffs* to each of the participants in a two-player game depend on the actions of both; a tool in analyzing *interdependence.*

payroll tax: a tax on the amount an employer pays to an employee.

pension fund: a type of *mutual fund* that holds assets in order to provide retirement income to its members.

perfect complements: goods a consumer wants to consume in a given ratio, regardless of their *relative price.*

perfect price discrimination: charging each consumer the maximum that consumer is willing to pay.

perfect substitutes: goods for which the *indifference curves* are straight lines; the *marginal rate of substitution* is constant, no matter how much of each is consumed.

perfectly competitive industry: an industry in which all producers are price-takers.

perfectly competitive market: a market in which all participants are price-takers.

perfectly elastic demand: the case in which any price increase causes the *quantity demanded* to fall to zero; the *demand curve* is a horizontal line.

perfectly elastic supply: the case in which even small changes in price lead to large changes in the *quantity supplied,* so the *price elasticity of supply* is infinite; the *supply curve* is a horizontal line.

perfectly inelastic demand: the case in which the *quantity demanded* does not respond to price; the *demand curve* is a vertical line.

perfectly inelastic supply: the case in which the *price elasticity of supply* is zero, so changes in price have no effect on the *quantity supplied;* the *supply curve* is a vertical line.

physical asset: a claim on a tangible object that gives the owner the right to dispose of the object as he or she wishes.

physical capital: human-made physical resources, such as buildings and machines, that are used in production.

pie chart: a circular graph that shows how some total is divided among its components; the proportions are indicated by the sizes of the "wedges."

Pigouvian subsidy: a payment designed to encourage activities that yield *external benefits.*

Pigouvian taxes: taxes designed to reduce *external costs.*

planned aggregate spending: the total amount of planned spending in the economy, which includes consumer spending, planned investment spending, government spending, and net export spending.

planned investment spending: the investment spending that businesses intend to undertake during a given period. Planned investment spending may differ from actual investment

spending due to *unplanned inventory investment.*

political business cycle: a *business cycle* that results from politicians using macroeconomic policy to serve political ends.

pooling: a strong form of *diversification;* the individual investor takes a small share in many *independent events,* so the *payoff* has very little uncertainty.

positive economics: the branch of economic analysis that describes the way the *economy* actually works.

positive externalities: *external benefits.*

positive feedback: put simply, success breeds success, failure breeds failure; the effect is seen with goods that are subject to *network externalities.*

positive relationship: a relationship between two variables in which an increase in the value of one variable is associated with an increase in the value of the other variable. It is described by a *curve* that slopes upward from left to right.

positively correlated: a relationship between events such that each event is more likely to occur if the other also occurs.

potential output: the level of real GDP the economy would produce if all prices, including nominal wages, were fully flexible. Although an economy's actual output is rarely exactly at potential output, potential output defines the trend around which actual output fluctuates from year to year.

poverty line: a minimum income defined by the government as adequate; families whose income falls below the poverty line are considered poor.

poverty rate: the percentage of the population living below the *poverty line.*

premium: a payment to an insurance company in return for the promise to pay in certain circumstances.

present value: the amount of money needed at the present time to produce, at the prevailing *interest rate,* a given amount of money at a specified future time.

price ceiling: a government-set maximum price that sellers are allowed to charge for a good; a form of *price control.*

price controls: legal restrictions on how high or low a market price may go.

price discrimination: charging different prices to different consumers for the same good.

price elasticity of demand: the ratio of the percent change in the *quantity demanded* to the percent change in price at a given point on the *demand curve.*

price elasticity of supply: the ratio of the percent change in the *quantity supplied* to the percent change in price at a given point on the *supply curve.*

price floor: a government-set minimum price that buyers are required to pay for a good; a form of price control.

price index: a measure of the overall price level; it measures the cost of purchasing a given market basket in a given year, where that cost is normalized so that it is equal to 100 in the selected base year.

price leadership: a pattern of behavior in which one firm sets its price and other firms in the industry follow.

price regulation: a limitation by the government on the price a *monopolist* is allowed to charge.

price stability: a low but positive rate of inflation targeted by most central banks.

price war: a collapse of prices when *tacit collusion* breaks down.

price-taking consumer: a consumer whose actions have no effect on the market price of the good bought.

price-taking firm's optimal output rule: the profit of a price-taking firm is maximized by producing the quantity of output at which the *marginal cost* of the last unit produced is equal to the market price.

price-taking producer: a producer whose actions have no effect on the market price of the good sold.

principle of diminishing marginal utility: the proposition that each successive unit of a good or service consumed adds less to total *utility* than did the previous unit.

principle of marginal analysis: the proposition that the *optimal* quantity of an activity is that at which *marginal benefit* is equal to *marginal cost.*

prisoner's dilemma: a game for two players in which the pursuit of self-interest rather than cooperation, if followed by both players, makes both worse off.

private good: a good that is both *excludable* and *rival in consumption.*

private information: information affecting all parties to a transaction or decision that only some parties have.

private savings: *disposable income* minus *consumer spending;* disposable income that is not spent on consumption.

producer price index (PPI): a measure of the cost of a typical basket of goods and services purchased by producers. Because these commodity prices respond quickly to changes in demand, the PPI is often regarded as a leading indicator of changes in the inflation rate.

producer surplus: a term often used to refer both to *individual producer surplus* and to *total producer surplus.*

product differentiation: the effort by firms to convince buyers that their products are different from those of other firms in the industry. If firms can so convince buyers, they can charge a higher price.

production function: the relationship between the quantity of *inputs* used and the quantity of output produced.

production possibility frontier: illustrates the trade-offs facing an economy that produces only two goods. It shows the maximum quantity of one good that can be produced for any given production of the other.

profits tax: a tax on the profits of a firm.

progressive tax: a tax that takes a larger share of the income of high-income taxpayers than of low-income taxpayers.

property rights: the rights of owners of *resources* or goods to dispose of them as they choose.

property tax: a tax on the value of property, such as a home.

proportional tax: a tax that is the same percentage of the *tax base* regardless of the taxpayer's income or wealth.

protection: an alternative term for *trade protection;* policies that limit *imports.*

public debt: government debt held by individuals and institutions outside the government.

public good: a good that is both *nonexcludable* and *nonrival in consumption.*

public ownership: control of an industry by a public agency of the government to provide a good and protect the interests of the consumer; a response to *natural monopoly.*

purchasing power parity (between two countries' currencies): the nominal *exchange rate* at which a given basket of goods and services would cost the same amount in each country.

quantity control: an upper limit, set by the government, on the quantity of some good that can be bought or sold; also referred to as a *quota.*

quantity demanded: the actual amount of a good or service consumers are willing to buy at some specific price.

quantity equation: an equation that states that the nominal quantity of money multiplied by the velocity of money is equal to nominal GDP.

quantity supplied: the actual amount of a good or service sellers are willing to sell at some specific price.

quota: an upper limit, set by the government, on the quantity of some good that can be bought or sold; also referred to as a *quantity control.*

quota limit: the total amount of a good under a *quota* or *quantity control* that can be legally transacted.

quota rent: the difference between the *demand price* and the *supply price* at the *quota limit;* this difference, the earnings that accrue to the license-holder, is equal to the market price of the *license* when the license is traded.

QWERTY problem: an inferior industry standard that has prevailed, possibly because of historical accident. Refers to the first six letters of a typewriter keyboard.

random variable: a *variable* with an uncertain future value.

random walk: the movement over time of an unpredictable variable.

rate of return (of an investment project): the profit earned on an investment project expressed as a percentage of its cost.

rational expectations: a theory of expectation formation that holds that individuals and firms make decisions optimally, using all available information.

real: refers to a measure or quantity that has been adjusted for changes in prices over time.

real business cycle theory: a theory of *business cycles* that asserts that fluctuations in the growth rate of *total factor productivity* cause the business cycle.

real exchange rate: the *exchange rate* adjusted for international differences in aggregate price levels.

real GDP: the value of all final goods and services produced in the economy during the year, calculated using the prices of a selected base year.

real interest rate: the interest rate adjusted for inflation, equal to the nominal interest rate minus the inflation rate.

real money demand curve: a graphical representation of the negative relationship between the real quantity of money demanded and the interest rate. The real money demand curve slopes downward because, other things equal, a higher interest rate increases the opportunity cost of holding money.

real quantity of money: the nominal quantity of money divided by the aggregate price level; equivalently, the quantity of money adjusted for the purchasing power of a dollar.

recession: a period when output and employment are falling.

recessionary gap: occurs when aggregate output is below *potential output.*

redistribution of income: a movement of income, such as revenue from taxes on the well-off, that is used to support those less well off.

regressive tax: a tax that takes a smaller share of the income of high-income taxpayers than of low-income taxpayers.

relative price rule: at the *optimal consumption bundle,* the *marginal rate of substitution* of one good in place of another is equal to the *relative price.*

relative price: the ratio of the price of one good to the price of another.

rental rate: the cost, implicit or explicit, of using a unit of land or capital for a given period of time.

reputation: a long-term standing in the public regard that serves to reassure others that *private information* is not being concealed; a valuable asset in the face of *adverse selection.*

research and development: spending to create and implement new technologies.

reserve ratio: the fraction of deposits that a bank holds as reserves. In the United States, the minimum required reserve ratio is set by the Federal Reserve.

reserve requirements: rules set by the Federal Reserve that determine the minimum reserve ratio for a bank. For checkable bank deposits in the United States, the minimum reserve ratio is set at 10%.

resource: anything, such as land, labor, and capital, that can be used to produce something else; includes natural resources (from the physical environment) and human resources (labor, skill, intelligence).

revaluation: an increase in the value of a currency that is set under a fixed *exchange rate* regime.

reverse causality: the error committed when the true direction between *variables* is reversed, and the *independent variable* and the *dependent variable* are incorrectly identified.

Ricardian model of international trade: a model that analyzes international *trade* under the assumption that *production possibility frontiers* are straight lines.

risk: uncertainty about outcomes.

risk-averse: describes individuals who choose to reduce *risk* when that reduction leaves the expected value of income or wealth unchanged.

rival in consumption: referring to a good, describes the case in which one unit cannot be consumed by more than one person at the same time.

Rule of 70: a formula that states that the time it takes a variable growing at some annual rate to double is approximately 70 divided by that variable's annual growth rate.

sales tax: a tax on the value of goods sold.

savings–investment spending identity: an accounting fact that states that savings and investment spending are always equal for the economy as a whole. For a closed economy, savings are composed of *national savings*, so that national savings is equal to investment. For an open economy, savings are composed of national savings plus foreign savings (also called *capital inflow*), so that investment is equal to national savings plus capital inflow.

scarce: in short supply; a *resource* is scarce when the quantity available is insufficient to satisfy all productive uses.

scatter diagram: a graph that displays points that correspond to actual observations of the *x-* and *y-*variables; a curve is usually fitted to the scatter of points to indicate the trend in the data.

screening: using observable information to make inferences about *private information;* a way to reduce *adverse selection.*

secular long-run growth: the sustained upward trend in aggregate output over several decades; also referred to as *long-run growth.*

self-correcting: refers to the fact that in the long run, shocks to aggregate demand affect aggregate output in the short run, but not the long run.

share: a partial ownership of a company.

shift of the demand curve: a change in the *quantity demanded* at any given price, represented graphically by the movement of the original *demand curve* to a new position.

shift of the supply curve: a change in the *quantity supplied* at any given price, represented graphically by the movement of the original *supply curve* to a new position.

shoe-leather costs (of inflation): the increased costs associated with making transactions that arise from the public's efforts to avoid the inflation tax.

short run: the time period in which at least one *input* is fixed.

short-run aggregate supply curve: a graphical representation of the relationship between the aggregate price level and the quantity of aggregate output supplied that exists in the short run, the time period when many production costs can be taken as fixed. The short-run aggregate supply curve has a positive slope because a rise in the aggregate price level leads to a rise in profits, and therefore output, when production costs are fixed

short-run equilibrium aggregate output: the quantity of aggregate output produced in *short-run macroeconomic equilibrium.*

short-run equilibrium aggregate price level: the aggregate price level in *short-run macroeconomic equilibrium.*

short-run individual supply curve: a graphical representation showing how an individual producer's optimal output quantity depends on the market price, taking *fixed cost* as given.

short-run industry supply curve: a graphical representation that shows how the quantity supplied by an industry depends on the market price, given a fixed number of producers.

short-run macroeconomic equilibrium: a situation in which the quantity of aggregate output supplied is equal to the quantity demanded.

short-run market equilibrium: an economic balance that results when the *quantity supplied* equals the *quantity demanded,* taking the number of producers as given.

short-run Phillips curve: a graphical representation of the negative short-run relationship between the unemployment rate and the inflation rate.

short-term interest rate: the interest rate on financial assets that mature within six months or less.

shortage: the insufficiency of a good when the quantity supplied is less than the quantity demanded; shortages occur when the price is below the *equilibrium price.*

shut-down price: the price at which a firm ceases production in the short run because the market price has fallen below the minimum *average variable cost.*

signaling: taking some action to establish credibility despite possessing *private information;* a way to reduce *adverse selection.*

single-price monopolist: a *monopolist* that charges all consumers the same price.

slope: the ratio of the "rise" (the change between two points on the *y*-axis) to the "run" (the difference between the same two points on the *x*-axis); a measure of the steepness of a curve.

social insurance: government programs intended to protect individuals against financial risk.

social insurance: government programs—like Social Security, Medicare, unemployment insurance, and food stamps—intended to protect families against economic hardship.

socially optimal quantity of pollution: the quantity of pollution that society would choose if all the costs and benefits of pollution were fully accounted for.

specialization: occurs when each person concentrates on the task that he or she is good at performing; generally leads to improved quality or to increase in output.

stabilization policy: policy efforts undertaken to reduce the severity of recessions and to rein in excessively strong expansions. There are two main tools of stabilization policy: *monetary policy* and *fiscal policy.*

stagflation: the combination of rising inflation and falling aggregate output.

standard: a set of rules for operation that allows competing goods to operate as a single network.

standardized product: output of different producers regarded by consumers as all the same good; also referred to as a *commodity.*

state of the world: a possible future event.

sticky wages: refers to a situation in which employers are slow to change wage rates in the face of a surplus or shortage of labor.

stock: a share in the ownership of a company held by a shareholder.

store of value: an asset that is a means of holding purchasing power over time. In a well-functioning economy, *money* is one of the assets that plays this role.

strategic behavior: actions taken by a firm that attempt to influence the behavior of other firms.

structural unemployment: unemployment that results when there are more people seeking jobs in a labor market than there are jobs available at the current wage rate.

substitutes: pairs of goods for which a fall in the price of one results in less demand for the other.

substitution effect: the change in the quantity consumed when a consumer substitutes a good that has become relatively cheaper in place of one that has become relatively more expensive.

sunk cost: a cost that has already been incurred and is not recoverable.

supply and demand model: a model that describes how a *competitive market* works.

supply curve: a graphical representation of the *supply schedule,* showing how much of a good or service would be supplied at a given price.

supply price: the price of a given quantity at which producers will supply that quantity.

supply schedule: a list or table showing the relationship between price and the quantity of a good or service that would be supplied to consumers.

supply shock: any event that shifts the *short-run aggregate supply curve.* A negative supply shock raises production costs and reduces the quantity supplied at any aggregate price level, shifting the curve leftward. A positive supply shock decreases production costs and increases the quantity supplied at any aggregate price level, shifting the curve rightward.

surplus: the excess of a good that occurs when the quantity supplied is greater than the quantity demanded; surpluses occur when the price is above the *equilibrium price.*

tacit collusion: cooperation among producers, without a formal agreement, to limit production and raise prices so as to raise one anothers' profits.

tangency condition: on a graph of a consumer's *budget line* and available *indifference curves* of available *consumption bundles,* the point at which an indifference curve and the budget line touch. When the indifference curves have the typical convex shape, this point determines the *optimal consumption bundle.*

tangent line: a straight line that touches a *nonlinear curve* at a given point; the *slope* of the tangent line equals the *slope* of the nonlinear curve at that point.

target federal funds rate: the Federal Reserve's desired *federal funds rate.* The Federal Reserve adjusts the money supply through the purchase and sale of Treasury bills until the actual rate equals the desired rate.

tariff: a tax levied on *imports.*

tax base: the measure or value, such as income or property value, that determines how much tax an individual pays.

tax efficiency: the degree to which a tax system minimizes the cost to the *economy* of tax collection.

tax equity: the degree to which the "right" people bear the burden of taxes; also referred to as *tax fairness.*

tax fairness: the degree to which the "right" people bear the burden of taxes; also referred to as *tax equity.*

tax structure: specifies how a tax depends on the *tax base;* usually expressed in percentage terms.

technology: the technical means for the production of goods and services.

technology spillover: an *external benefit* that is conferred when knowledge spreads among individuals and firms.

threshold network size: in a market subject to *network externalities,* the smallest number of current members of the network that leads a given individual to join.

time allocation: the decision about how many hours to expend on different activities, which leads to a decision about how much labor to supply.

time allocation budget line: an individual's possible trade-offs between consumption of *leisure* and the income that allows consumption of marketed goods.

time-series graph: a two-variable graph in which the values on the *horizontal axis* are dates and those on the

vertical *axis* are values of a variable that occurred on those dates.

tipping: a sudden rapid increase in the network size that occurs when *positive feedback* due to *network externalities* causes consumers to swing to one of two competing goods or technologies.

tit for tat: in *game theory,* a strategy in which players begin cooperatively, then each repeats the other player's action in the previous round.

total consumer surplus: the sum of the *individual consumer surpluses* of all the buyers of a good.

total cost: the sum of the *fixed cost* and the *variable cost* of producing a given quantity of output.

total cost curve: a graphical representation of the *total cost,* showing how total cost depends on the quantity of output.

total factor productivity: the total amount of output that can be achieved with a given amount of the factor inputs physical capital, human capital, and labor. Increases in total factor productivity are central to economic growth.

total producer surplus: the sum of the *individual producer surpluses* of all the sellers of a good.

total product curve: a graphical representation of the *production function,* showing how the quantity of output depends on the quantity of the *variable input* for a given amount of *fixed input.*

total revenue: the total value of sales of a good (the price of the good multiplied by the quantity sold).

total surplus: the total net gain to consumers and producers from trading in a market; the sum of the *consumer surplus* and the *producer surplus.*

tradable emissions permits: *licenses* to emit limited quantities of pollutants that can be bought and sold by polluters.

trade: the exchange of goods or services for other goods or services.

trade balance: the difference between the value of the goods and services a country sells to other countries and the value of the goods and services it buys from other countries.

trade protection: policies that limit *imports.*

trade-off: a comparison of costs and benefits; the amount of a good that must be sacrificed to obtain another good.

trade-off between equity and efficiency: the dynamic whereby a well-designed tax system can be made more efficient only by making it less fair, and vice versa.

transaction costs: the expenses of negotiating and executing a deal.

transfer payment: money received by an individual from the government for which no good or service is returned to the government.

truncated: cut; in a truncated axis, some of the range of values are omitted, usually to save space.

U-shaped average total cost curve: a distinctive graphical representation of the relationship between output and *average total cost;* the average total cost curve at first falls when output is low and then rises as output increases.

underemployment: the number of people who work during a *recession* but receive lower wages than they would during an *expansion* due to fewer number of hours worked, lower-paying jobs, or both.

unemployment: the number of people who are actively looking for work but aren't currently employed.

unemployment rate: the percentage of the total number of people in the *labor force* who are unemployed. It is calculated as: unemployment rate = *unemployment* / (*unemployment* + *employment*).

unions: organizations of workers that engage in collective bargaining to raise wages and improve working conditions for their members.

unit of account: a measure used to set prices and make economic calculations.

unit-elastic demand: the case in which the *price elasticity of demand* is 1. A specific percentage increase in price leads to an equal percentage decrease in quantity demanded, and vice versa.

unit-of-account costs (of inflation): the costs arising from the way inflation makes money a less reliable unit of measurement.

unplanned inventory investment: unplanned changes in inventories, which occur when actual sales are more or less than businesses expected.

util: a unit of *utility*.

utility (of a consumer)**:** a measure of the satisfaction derived from consumption of goods and services.

utility function (of an individual)**:** the relationship between an individual's *consumption bundle* and the total amount of *utility* it generates.

utility possibility frontier: on a graph plotting the total *utility* of two individuals or groups, the curve that shows how well off one individual or group could be for each given total utility level of the other.

value added (of a producer)**:** the value of sales minus the value of input purchases.

value of the marginal product curve: a graphical representation showing how the *value of the marginal product* of a factor depends on the quantity of the factor employed.

value of the marginal product: the value of the additional output generated by employing one more unit of a given factor, such as labor.

variable: a quantity that can take on more than one value.

variable cost: a cost that depends on the quantity of output produced; the cost of a *variable input*.

variable input: an *input* whose quantity can be varied (for example, labor).

velocity of money: nominal GDP divided by the nominal quantity of money; a measure of how many times a unit of money is spent over the course of a year.

vertical axis: the vertical number line of a graph along which values of the *y*-variable are measured; also referred to as the *y-axis*.

vertical intercept: the point at which a curve intersects the vertical axis, showing the value of the *y*-variable when the value of the *x*-variable is zero.

wasted resources: a form of inefficiency; consumers waste resources when they must spend money and expend effort to deal with shortages caused by a *price ceiling*.

wealth (of a household)**:** the value of accumulated savings.

wealth effect of a change in the aggregate price level: the effect on consumer spending caused by the change in the purchasing power of consumers' assets when the aggregate price level changes. A rise in the aggregate price level decreases the purchasing power of consumers' assets, so they decrease their consumption; a fall in the aggregate price level increases the purchasing power of

consumers' assets, so they increase their consumption.

wealth tax: a tax on the wealth of an individual.

wedge: the difference between the *demand price* of the quantity transacted and the *supply price* of the quantity transacted for a good when the supply of the good is legally restricted. Often created by a quota or a tax.

welfare: government monetary aid to poor families.

willingness to pay: the maximum price a consumer is prepared to pay for a good.

World Trade Organization: an international organization of member countries that oversees *international trade agreements* and rules on *trade* disputes.

world price: the price at which a good can be bought or sold abroad.

x-axis: the horizontal number line of a graph along which values of the *x*-variable are measured; also referred to as the *horizontal axis*.

y-axis: the vertical number line of a graph along which values of the *y*-variable are measured; also referred to as the *vertical axis*.

zero bound: the lower bound of zero on the nominal interest rate.

zero-profit equilibrium: an economic balance in which each firm makes zero profit at its profit-maximizing output level.

Index

Key terms and the pages on which they are defined appear in **boldface** in this index.

Continued from the
inside front cover

APPLICATIONS IN ECONOMICS